THE CONTINENTAL EDITION

OF

World Masterpieces

VOLUME 2

THIRD EDITION

Uniform with this volume,
and also under the General Editorship of
Maynard Mack

THE TWO-VOLUME EDITION OF
World Masterpieces, Third Edition

VOLUME 1
Literature of Western Culture through the Renaissance

VOLUME 2
Literature of Western Culture since the Renaissance

THE CONTINENTAL EDITION OF
World Masterpieces, Third Edition

IN ONE VOLUME

Masterpieces of the Orient
Edited by G. L. Anderson
UNIVERSITY OF HAWAII

THE CONTINENTAL EDITION
OF
World Masterpieces
THIRD EDITION

Maynard Mack, *General Editor*
YALE UNIVERSITY

Bernard M. W. Knox
CENTER FOR HELLENIC STUDIES

John C. McGalliard
THE UNIVERSITY OF IOWA

P. M. Pasinetti
UNIVERSITY OF CALIFORNIA, LOS ANGELES

Howard E. Hugo
UNIVERSITY OF CALIFORNIA, BERKELEY

René Wellek
YALE UNIVERSITY

Kenneth Douglas
FORMERLY OF YALE UNIVERSITY

VOLUME 2
Continental Literature since the Renaissance

W · W · NORTON & COMPANY · INC · *New York*

Library of Congress Cataloging in Publication Data

Mack, Maynard, 1909–   ed.
    The continental edition of World masterpieces.

    Includes bibliographical references.
    CONTENTS: v.1. Continental literature through the Renaissance.—
v.2. Continental literature since the Renaissance.
    1. Literature—Translations into English.
    2. English literature—Translations from foreign literature. I. Title.
PN6019.M2   1974   808.8   73-16390
ISBN 0-393-09313-1 (v.2)

Book design by John Woodlock

PRINTED IN THE UNITED STATES OF AMERICA

3 4 5 6 7 8 9 0

Contents

Masterpieces of Nineteenth-Century Realism and Naturalism

Masterpieces of the Modern World

Preface to the Third Edition

The Continental Edition of *World Masterpieces* is an anthology of Western literature containing only writings from the ancient and the modern foreign languages.

It reaches in time from Homer and the Old Testament writers to Isaac Singer and Alexander Solzhenitsyn, and the literatures represented in it include French, German, Gaelic, Greek, Hebrew, Italian, Latin, Norwegian, Russian, Spanish, Swedish, and Yiddish.

In modes and genres, its range is similarly comprehensive. Epic poetry appears liberally in large selections from works as different as *The Iliad*, *The Odyssey*, *The Aeneid*, *The Song of Roland*, *The Divine Comedy* (the *Inferno* is given complete in the sensitive new translation by Mark Musa), and *Faust* (Part I is given complete in the spirited English of Louis MacNeice. Prose fiction also appears in a dazzling variety of styles and moods. Selections are drawn from Petronius, Boccaccio, Rabelais, Cervantes, Voltaire, Flaubert, Dostoevsky, Tolstoy, Proust, Mann, Gide, Kafka, Camus, Sartre, and Solzhenitsyn. Four novels or seminovels are represented complete—*Candide*, *Madame Bovary*, *Notes from Underground*, and *Felix Krull*—along with a number of the finest "long-stories" of modern times: *The Death of Iván Ilyich*, *The Return of the Prodigal Son*, *The Metamorphosis*, *The Renegade*, and *Matryona's House*. In addition, the anthology contains fifteen full-length plays. Seven of these come from the ancient world (*Agamemnon*, *Prometheus Bound*, *Oedipus Tyrannus*, *Antigone*, *Medea*, *The Trojan Women*, *Lysistrata*); one is from Golden-Age Spain (*Life Is a Dream*); two are from the French Classical Theater (*Tartuffe* and *Phaedra*); and the remainder exemplify currents in the main stream of modern drama (*The Wild Duck*, *The Ghost Sonata*, *The Cherry Orchard*, Pirandello's *Henry IV*, and *The Caucasian Chalk Circle*).

All this, thanks to the generosity of our publisher, we have been able to bring together in the Continental Edition without scanting either the lyric vein in poetry (represented by Archilochus, Tyrtaeus, Mimnermus, Sappho, Alcaeus, Solon, Anacreon, Xeno-

phanes, Theognis, Catullus, Ovid, Petrarch, La Fontaine, Hölderlin,
Novalis, Heine, Pushkin, Lamartine, Hugo, Nerval, Leopardi,
Baudelaire, Rimbaud, Rilke) or the philosophic discursive vein in
prose (Thucydides, Plato, Cicero, St. Augustine, Erasmus, Casti-
glione, Machiavelli, Cellini, Aretino, Montaigne, La Rochefoucauld,
Diderot, Rousseau, Chateaubriand). Those who have already used
the Continental Edition of *World Masterpieces* in either of its two
forms, one-volume or two-volume, will rejoice with us, we feel
sure, at the many hundreds of pages of new selections now added
to both formats. Though the one-volume version is necessarily more
compact, its survey of some twenty-eight hundred years of human
experience as expressed in literature remains remarkably full. It
affords, in fact—as Dryden said of Chaucer's poetry—"God's
plenty."

Teachers and students making the acquaintance of this anthology
for the first time in the new edition will perhaps find it helpful
to know the principles by which its editors have been guided:

(1) Like all versions of *World Masterpieces*, the Continental
Edition is an anthology of *Western* literature. Eastern literatures
(apart from the Old Testament) have been excluded, on the
ground that the principal aim of a course in world literature is to
bring American students into live contact with their own tradition,
and that this aim cannot be adequately realized in a single course if
they must also be introduced to a very different tradition, one requiring extended treatment to be correctly understood.

(2) The emphasis of all editions of *World Masterpieces* is
decidedly on imaginative literature. We have not tried to cover
the entire history of the West in print, and have avoided filling
our pages with philosophy, political theory, theology, historiog-
raphy, and the like. This principle was adopted not because we disapprove of coming at the history of an epoch by way of literature,
but because imaginative literature, in our view, itself best defines
the character of its epoch: Great monuments of art, we would be
inclined to say, furnish the best documents for history. They lead
us deeper into the meaning of a past age than other modes of
writing do, because they convey its unformulated aspirations and
intuitions as well as its conscious theorems and ideals; and yet,
being timeless, they have also an unmatched appeal to our own
age. For this reason, we have admitted into *World Masterpieces*
only works which have something important to say to modern
readers, and we have made it a point to interpret them with reference not only to their time but to ours.

(3) We believe that effective understanding of any author depends upon studying an autonomous and substantial piece of his

work: a whole drama, a whole story, at least a whole canto or book
of a long poem. Our anthology therefore contains no snippets.
Where it has been necessary to represent a long work by extracts,
they are large extracts, forming a coherent whole. These considerations have also affected our treatment of lyric poems. Our conviction that the value of reading poems in translation diminishes
in proportion as the poetry assumes the intensive iconic character
of lyric is set forth clearly and, we hope, persuasively, in the Note
on Translation with which all volumes of *World Masterpieces*
close. We are aware, nevertheless, that there are readers from whom
lyric poetry, even when seriously impaired by translation, offers a
more satisfying glimpse of the self-hood of an age than any other
genre. We have consequently sought to meet this problem by
selecting (upon the whole) longer rather than shorter lyrics and
by choosing them from periods in which, as in the Romantic period
notably, they are a dominant form of expression; or, as in the Greek
sixth and seventh centuries B.C., the chief surviving form; or, as
with, say, Ovid, Petrarch, and La Fontaine, indicative of attitudes
and values not found elsewhere in our selections from that period.

(4) Since nothing has so deterred students from enjoying the
great masterpieces of the classical and modern foreign languages as
translations in an English idiom that is no longer alive, we have
taken special pains in all editions of *World Masterpieces* to use
translations that show a powerful feeling for the English language
as it is written and spoken today. In the current editions, we believe we have fulfilled our obligation in this matter with some distinction. Fresh renderings of *Oedipus Tyrannus* (Theodore Brun-
ner and Luci Berkowitz), "Dinner with Trimalchio" (J. P. Sulli-
van), *The Song of Roland* (Dorothy Sayers), *The Inferno* (Mark
Musa), and *Candide* (R. M. Adams), now join forces with works
translated by Roy Campbell, Robert Fitzgerald, Richmond Lattimore, C. Day Lewis, Robert Lowell, Louis MacNeice, Edwin
Muir, Charles Murphy, Samuel Putnam, Rex Warner, and Richard
Wilbur, among the selections held over from the last edition, and
with work by Thomas Chubb, Wallace Fowlie, Horace Gregory,
Guy Lee, Elizabeth Sprigge, Marianne Moore, Vernon Watkins,
and Avraham Yarmolinsky, among those now presented for the
first time. A more dignified company of translators we are sure this
world has not, and we indicate here with pleasure our gratitude
to them and to their publishers for permission to reprint their work.

(5) Our introductions—in consonance with the scheme of the
book—emphasize criticism rather than history. While providing
all that seems to us necessary in the way of historical background
(and supplying biographical summaries in the appendix following

each introduction), we aim to give the student primarily a critical and analytical discussion of the works themselves. We try to suggest what these works have to say to us in our own time and generation, and why they should be valued now. With the same ends in view, we give exceptional space to seminal writers of our own century, feeling that this is the best way to help students grasp the continuity of literature and realize that all of it, however remote at first glance, is in one way or other about us.

> Though grave diggers' toil is long,
> Sharp their spades, their muscles strong,
> They but thrust their buried men
> Back in the human mind again.

The Editors

THE CONTINENTAL EDITION

OF

World Masterpieces

VOLUME 2

THIRD EDITION

Masterpieces of Neoclassicism

EDITED BY
HOWARD E. HUGO
Professor of English, University of California, Berkeley

FROM MOLIÈRE TO DIDEROT

Words such as "Reformation" and "Renaissance" are rich in connotations of drastic alteration, rebirth, and revolt—the new arising from the old and the old interpreted with sudden vigor and apparent heterodoxy. Not so are the names given at the time or by posterity to the last half of the seventeenth century and the first half of the eighteenth: the "neoclassical" period, the "Age of Reason," the "Enlightenment," the "Century of Light." Here are terms indicative of relative quiescence, the triumph of consolidation and harmony over innovation and disorder. There is some truth in these phrases, but not the whole truth.

While men have never ceased to invigorate their thought by returning to the masterpieces of Greece and Rome, the special task of the Renaissance—to bring back to life a world bypassed or partly forgotten—seemed finished by the end of the seventeenth century. The "Quarrel of the Ancients and the Moderns" (to be referred to again later on) was fought with an acerbity that happily cost nobody's blood. Was modern man inferior, equal, or possibly superior to his glorious classical ancestors? Whatever their answer, the participants in the "Quarrel" recognized continuity with the great minds of classical antiquity. Similarly the religious strife occasioned by Protestant attacks on the institution of the Roman Catholic Church lost its acrimony. Conflicts henceforward were likely to be between nations, not sects, and to concern politics and the balance of

1

power instead of the individual's private relation to God. True, Louis XIV's revocation of the Edict of Nantes in 1685 upsets any easy picture of the gradual emergence of religious toleration, for the "Sun King" thereby denied to Protestants the right to practice their own variety of Christianity. Yet the French Regency repented that monarch's action some thirty years later, and in 1689 the English Toleration Acts set a broad pattern slowly emulated by most European commonwealths.

Political and economic wars, on the other hand, abounded: struggles about Spanish, Austrian, Polish, and Bavarian successions; various Silesian engagements; the war between Peter the Great and Charles XII of Sweden; ancillary combats in the New World and in the recently colonized East. Nationalistic marches and countermarches fill the years we now consider. The punctilio and formal splendor portrayed in Chapter 3 of Voltaire's *Candide* (in this volume) is that author's ironical commentary on his own best of all possible worlds from the point of view of man's organized inhumanity to man. Certainly it cannot be said that peace elected the Enlightenment as the moment to proclaim "olives of endless age." Yet fortunately the horrible slaughter of the Thirty Years' War (1618-1648) was not soon repeated. Europe had almost two hundred years from the start of that catastrophe before undergoing devastation on a similar scale. Then the battles of Napoleon's *Grande Armée* and his opponents involved hundreds, not merely tens, of thousands.

Classical Greece viewed its gods as residing serenely on Mount Olympus. Neoclassicism produced a pantheon of monarchs who enacted comparable roles within a more human, but also more elegant, environment. The modern state had arisen from its feudal antecedents; and kings, both absolute and enlightened, tended more and more to symbolize the aspirations of the countries they headed. At first glance the age seems to be dominated by the lengthening shadows of its rulers. What other epoch, for instance, could boast three political personalities of the order of Peter and Catherine of Russia, and Frederick II of Prussia—all called "the Great"? Add to them Maria Theresa of Austria and the Holy Roman Empire, with her forty-year reign; the radiant figure of Louis XIV; and the less spectacular but equally important English monarchs—Anne and her Hanoverian descendants, the first three Georges.

Nevertheless, the growth of certain theories about kingship made the condition of royalty less secure. Simpler medieval and Renaissance assumptions had invested earthly rulers with divine rights (even if the problem of Church and State, pope and emperor, persisted). When for example the English under Cromwell executed Charles I—to the horror of many contemporary Europeans—John Milton, in his *Tenure of Kings and Magistrates* (1649), attempted to justify the regicide by invoking precedents, history, common sense, and Holy Scripture. A true king, said Milton, enjoys his office by "the eminence of his wisdom and integrity." A tyrant, in contradistinction, "reigns only for himself and his faction." But his arguments for and against monarchy were slowly superseded by the notion that men live together by virtue of a social contract—the theme of such disparate thinkers as Hobbes, Locke, Rousseau, and many of the French *philosophes*. At the start of the eighteenth century a monarch, acting *in loco parentis*, was still generally considered necessary for the state, particularly if the royal prerogatives were circumscribed by custom or constitution. The age of neoclassicism and the Enlightenment accepted its rulers, but in good rationalist fashion attempted to define their station and duties within an orderly civil society. Future generations were to find more radical and violent solutions. Chapter 26 of *Candide* is strangely prophetic of the shape of things to come. Here the six indigent and dispossessed kings convening at the Carnival of Venice are portrayed as ultimately inferior to the commoner, Candide, who joins them: "Who is this fellow who is able to give a hundred times as much as any of us, and who gives it?"

These are broad cultural and political characteristics of the age. When we turn from them to the contributions of the philosophers of the period, generalization becomes more difficult: Descartes, Spinoza, Locke, Leibnitz, Berkeley, Hume, La Mettrie, D'Alembert, Holbach—what common denominator will reconcile such differing minds? Yet most thinkers manifested two tendencies. First, they challenged traditional Christianity and classical philosophy by posing questions of a complex and problematic nature and thus helped to bring about what Paul Hazard has called a crisis in European thought. And second, they stressed that man's mind alone is the sole judge of the readings we make of the universe, of God, and of man; they assumed, as almost no earlier philosophers had done, that the cosmos conforms to what human experience and our judgments and abstractions seem to prove. They were, in short, *rationalists*, although many of them would be surprised at being so labeled.

In England, Sir Francis Bacon had earlier laid down a program for new scientific studies, although for him these were but dimly ascertained. Induction was to be the tool whereby we would derive "axioms from the senses and particulars, rising by a gradual and unbroken ascent, so that it [i.e., the inductive method] arrives at the most general axioms last of all. This is the true way, but as yet untried." (*Novum organum*, 1620). His comment may seem relevant chiefly to the growth of the physical sciences, as indeed it was. Nevertheless, it also helped to determine the cast of thought in the subsequent century.

Descartes' *Discourse of Method* (*Discours de la méthode*, 1637) indicated that he was no Baconian worshiper of induction; yet he insisted on starting from one certain "truth" of observation—"I think, therefore I am"—in building up a philosophical system. Perhaps most important,

Descartes sharpened the distinction between mind and matter, spirit and body. After him philosophers tended to fall into one camp or the other: either 'asserting, as "idealists" (like Berkeley), that all reality is ultimately mind and spirit; or, as materialists (like Hobbes and many of the more extreme French *philosophes*), that reality is finally reduced to the world of matter. But whatever their beliefs, they all held one belief in common. To these thinkers the universe made *rational* sense; it possessed a discernible pattern; it moved according to fixed scientific and mathematical laws. And here the early scientists came to the aid of their more abstract-minded colleagues, with Newton making the greatest contribution; for it was he who synthesized the scientific work done from Copernicus to his own day, to produce a plausible and orderly picture of the material universe, the "Newtonian world-machine." At least one writer included in this portion of the anthology — Voltaire —wrote with full conviction of its existence.

TYPES OF NEOCLASSICISM— MOLIÉRE AND RACINE

Seventeenth-century religious conflicts created a strongly centralized Catholic France, particularly after the revocation of the Edict of Nantes in 1685, which effectively ended French Protestantism. The emergence of a strongly centralized Catholic France may be viewed in one aspect as a triumph of the Counter Reformation—the various efforts taken by the Roman Catholic Church, in the face of the Protestant Reformation, to strengthen doctrine and dogma. Yet this monolithic new commonwealth had secular antecedents. Under Louis XIV Versailles and Paris were soon felt to be what Rome had been under Augustus Caesar, and the line from Greece and Rome to France was asserted to be direct and unbroken. Racine and Molière wrote in a milieu that united Renaissance and Counter Reformation. Whatever the precise ingredients may have been, seventeenth-century French neoclassicism emerges as a combination of these cultural forces, one religious and the other secular. Stated in other terms, two conceptions of the human condition were in opposition—man in a state of grace and man in a state of nature.

Even the famous "Quarrel of the Ancients and the Moderns," mentioned earlier, was symptomatic of the tension between these antithetical outlooks. The Renaissance had extolled classical, pagan antiquity and made it the model for human conduct and aspiration. But now the possibility gained credence that modern man might *excel* the Greeks and Romans and not merely emulate them in an effort to regain a lost golden age. Hence the birth of the idea of progress in history—a concept relatively new to mankind, and one hard to reconcile with the Christian notion of man's fall from his pristine felicity. The "Moderns" were those who insisted that modern culture could equal or surpass that of the classical period; the "Ancients," those who joined literary modesty to something very like a Christian sense of imperfection. Yet while one side felt itself to be an inglorious heir and the other a superior son, *all* were convinced that they were neoclassic, a happy synthesis of the ancient and modern.

MOLIÈRE

Within this cultural environment of neoclassicism, France's two greatest dramatists, one in the comic and one in the tragic vein, wrote their plays. Molière, the comic dramatist, leaned heavily toward the pole of the natural, rational, and humanistic. His concern is not with metaphysics or with an eventual state of eternal salvation. He portrays man as a product of the social order. As Sainte-Beuve long ago pointed out, Molière's characters are untouched by any thought of Christian grace. Only one of his plays, the famous *Tartuffe* (1664), is concerned with a near-religious theme, and even this work is preoccupied more with an analysis of mundane hypocrisy than with the assessment of true belief. Each of Molière's plays is actually an *exemplum* and a critical study of the failure to conform to an ideal of urbanity, solid pragmatism, worldly common sense, good taste, and moderation—all the secular virtues of antiquity and Louis XIV's new state. Both Tartuffe and Orgon are ludicrous, for each fails to meet these criteria of behavior. Tartuffe is a rogue and a scoundrel, a hypocrite whose apparent religiosity and asceticism are eventually unmasked. Orgon is a dupe, in whom Molière satirizes

the solid, middle-class citizen. Orgon's false values impel him to give his daughter a "good" marriage against her wishes, disinherit his son, sign over his property to Tartuffe, and himself be tricked by a fashionable rascal who uses pretended piety as an excuse for financial gain and amatory satisfaction.

Voltaire's description of true comedy as "the speaking picture of the follies and foibles of a nation" can readily be applied to Molière's plays. Actually Voltaire had the Greek comic playwright Aristophanes in mind; to compare Molière with Aristophanes is to see once more how close was the bond between neoclassicism and classical antiquity. Aristophanes' panorama of Athenian citizens displays the same infinite variety as Molière's collection taken from the Parisian scene. Stock characters were easily drawn from two societies where social stratification was menaced by a rising commercialism, and the resulting *parvenu* became material for the satirist's pen. Finally the problems of the day—political, religious, educational, ethical—served as subject matter for both Aristophanes and Molière. From the Greek playwright through the Latin authors Plautus and Terence and later the creators of the Italian Renaissance *commedia dell' arte*, the tradition of classical comedy moves to Molière. The topical issues may no longer interest us— arranged marriages, the excessive refinement of precious fops, and so on—but the classical vision of man in society rather than man the individual, the ideals of universality and rationality, these transcend the local and the temporary.

RACINE

When we move from the racy, realistic prose of comedy to Racine's lofty language of tragedy, more comprehension of the age and its conventions is required. It has always been difficult for the English reader, accustomed to the apparent looseness and gusto of Shakespearean drama, to savor the French playwright's decorous elegance. We are puzzled by the careful control and compression insisted on through adherence to the unities of time, place, and action; by the intrusion of long, distracted monologues, the alternating debatelike interchange between characters, and the operalike duets, and by the circumlocution of the vocabulary.

Racine's model for *Phaedra* (*Phèdre*, 1677) was the *Hippolytus* of Euripides. Racine assures us in his preface that he has retained all that is suitable from the Greek tragedy—and added to it ingredients which make it more pertinent to the audience of his own time. In Euripides' drama the protagonist is not Phaedra but Hippolytus, depicted as a follower of Artemis (Diana) and thus bound by vows of rigid chastity. This condition leads him into *hubris* (overweening human pride) toward Aphrodite (Venus) and thus brings Nemesis (judgment) upon him —all according to the conventional Greek view of life. Phaedra appears in only two scenes, never face to face with Hippolytus; and her death occurs halfway through the play. No doubt the more

thoughtful, discerning members of Euripides' audience caught a note of his own skepticism about the dubious ethics of the gods; but the action of the drama is satisfying on a human level alone, since the cause of Hippolytus' downfall is the pride implicit in his excessive, vehement denial of Phaedra. For the story of Theseus, Racine was indebted also to Plutarch's life of Theseus; and possibly, although he denied it, to the *Phaedra* (alternatively entitled *Hippolytus*) of the Roman Stoic Seneca. In Seneca's play Hippolytus is portrayed as a Stoic philosopher; Phaedra, not Hippolytus, suffers the wrath of Venus; and while he remains technically the protagonist, Phaedra is the focal figure, with her shameless love mixed with guilt. No divinities enter Seneca's declamatory, rhetorical drama, and Venus is the mere personification of passion.

Like his Greek predecessor and like Milton in *Samson Agonistes*, Racine deals with one terrible day—the culmination of previous events and states of feeling—and his technique is in keeping also with the tenets of French classical drama. He concentrates not on the pale Hippolytus, who even in Euripides' drama seems more a passive instrument of two rival goddesses than an active protagonist, but rather on the tormented, passion-racked Phaedra. She becomes a Greek woman with a Christian conscience, for the peculiar remorse Racine has his heroine exhibit when once she is aware of her illicit love is an emotion that was unknown to the ancient world.[1] Within her soul the fundamental conflict is between one overwhelming passion and the restraining power of reason. Her tragic flaw, to use the Aristotelian phrase, is her abnegation of rational responsibility for her moral conduct. The entire play is a slow unfolding, rather than a record of the development, of this fatal weakness. Only the most insensitive reader could be unaffected by Racine's skillfully conveyed, intricate psychological analysis—the cognizance of forces deep within the well of the unconscious that imperil the tenuously held supremacy of the intellect—and by the tone of majestic, dignified sadness.

TYPES OF NEOCLASSICISM— LA ROCHEFOUCAULD, LA FONTAINE

The word *moraliste* which describes these two authors is difficult to translate into English. Naturally "moralist" is the cognate, but for us the word has overtones of someone preaching a definite moral code and employing didactic persuasion. This description does not quite fit the *moraliste*. From Montaigne and Pascal to Gide, Camus, and Sartre, French literature has abounded with writers employing all the traditional literary forms—as well as diaries, notebooks, fables, essays, and aphorisms—to present a total "morality" and outlook on life, a commentary based on observations about the given elements, the *données*, of human nature. Generally the *moraliste* says, "This is the way human nature is"—not, "This is the way human nature should be." Satire is occasionally the mode of expression, but seldom evoked with any burning desire to correct man's vices and foibles. The animal universe of La Fontaine is emblematic of our own, where silly geese, clever foxes, pretentious frogs, and lazy grasshoppers sketch the rich varieties of human foolishness. But even here the human comedy seems more to be observed and savored than censured. To exercise the intellect in an acute dissection of motives and conduct is an end in itself.

LA ROCHEFOUCAULD

La Rochefoucauld's *Maxims* (from which we have excerpted nearly sixty from more than three hundred) shocked his contemporaries when first they appeared in 1665. The modern reader, insulated against shock by his post-Freudian worldliness, may do well to ponder *Maxim* 384: "We ought never to be

---

1. So intense is her self-recrimination that some critics have attributed it to Racine's Jansenist background. The Jansenist order was a group within the Catholic Church concerned chiefly with the Augustinian concept of predistination and Divine Election. This preoccupation, as well as their general austerity and asceticism, links the Jansenists to Calvinism and the Puritan movement in England. The order was bitterly opposed by the Jesuits, and the Jansenist center at Port-Royal was destroyed in 1709-1710. Like the heroine of Euripides' tragedy, Racine's Phaedra implies that the gods have brought about her destruction. It is also possible to interpret her assertion in Jansenist-Christian terms as referring to a fall from grace.

surprised, save that we can still be surprised." The social milieu and the course of La Rochefoucauld's career offer some explanation for the mood of acerbity and bitter reflectiveness, even downright cynicism, in these pithy statements. When he was a young man, La Rochefoucauld's family and the class to which he belonged still enjoyed real power and prestige. But the age of Richelieu and later the reign of Louis XIV witnessed a steady decline of both these factors. What privileges the nobility entertained were increasingly the gift of monarchs and ministers whose concern was the consolidation of royal prerogatives. Moreover, failure and defeat marked La Rochefoucauld's active life, both politically and militarily. His castle was burned in the wars of the *Fronde*, a natural son was killed in battle, near-blindness for himself came as the result of a wound. Poverty and the infidelity of several mistresses scarcely contributed to produce in him a vision of life as bliss, and in his *Memoirs* (1662) can be traced a pattern of deepening disillusionment. Yet such data only partially explain the cast of La Rochefoucauld's mind, which had a genius like Newton's for reducing complex phenomena to a single simple (and also over-simple) principle.

La Rochefoucauld, indeed, accomplished for the domain of human nature what Machiavelli had achieved for statecraft some centuries earlier, and accomplished it with such apparent stark simplicity of phrasing that we are often dazzled. *Maxim* 218

is a good example. "Hypocrisy is the tribute that vice pays to virtue" ("L'hypocrisie est un hommage que le vice rend à la vertu"). Here four abstractions, carefully balanced in pairs, occur within barely twice as many words. Vice and virtue we are accustomed to consider in opposition, but hypocrisy coupled with homage or tribute startles the mind, so that the relation between vice and virtue takes on new dimensions.

One other characteristic of La Rochefoucauld's commentaries is the generality of his expression. A major tenet of neoclassical criticism, Continental and English, was the asserted superiority of the universal statement over the particular, the generic class over the individual. Hence the *Maxims*, delivered in a tone of assurance that twentieth-century man with his dubieties might well covet, deliberately aim at the typical rather than at the unique. Sainte-Beuve aptly described La Rochefoucauld as "the polished misanthrope, insinuating and smiling," and while the tender-minded may be appalled at the aphorist's ruthless dissection of love, honor, friendship, and the like, they will be hard pressed to phrase a rebuttal with such precision combined with such grandeur of generality.

LA FONTAINE

La Fontaine's *Fables* describe a more genial world than that of his cynical contemporary. They too, especially in the abstract statements that conclude most of the little tales in verse, have all of mankind as their concern, and their association with children's literature is more apparent than real. Though La Fontaine shrewdly dedicated the first six books of *Fables* to France's most important child, the six-year-old son of Louis XIV, obviously his talking animals are far removed from the inanities of Donald Duck and his friends, and from those conversing beasts in today's comic strips ostensibly created to delight the juvenile reader. His pungent tags—e.g., "Every flatterer lives at the expense of the person who listens to him" ("Chaque flatteur vit au dépens de celui qui l'écoute") —are not the sort of observations that bring chortles to the nursery. The timeless appeal of his tales, full of anecdotal skill and psychological subtlety, is better summed up in Alexander Pope's neoclassical dictum: "True wit is Nature to advantage dressed,/ What oft was thought, but ne'er so well expressed:/ Something whose truth convinced at sight we find. . . ." La Fontaine's borrowings from Aesop, Phaedrus, and other minor Greek and Latin fabulists may also be thus explained. They are in keeping with the aesthetics of an age that felt its chief artistic merit to lie in perpetuating and renewing the classical tradition. Perhaps the highest compliment paid to these *Fables* is the remark of the critic who submitted that if the world were suddenly shattered, the next day (if man were permitted to reconstruct its animalian content) the birds and beasts would behave precisely as they are made to do by La Fontaine.

As modern readers and hence heirs willy-nilly to romanticism and the cultural tradition of the last one hundred and fifty years, we may feel that these two seventeenth-century writers are excessively objective and impersonal. We are accustomed to veiled autobiography in literature, where the "I" of the artist is never far from his creation. Romantic affinities for the peculiarities of each individual have blunted our appreciation of the grandeur of generality, where human nature is viewed as a totality, permanent and unchanging, and the task of the man of letters is to treat mankind in its public rather than its private context. La Rochefoucauld's and La Fontaine's minds, critical and decorous, chary of enthusiasm and aristocratically scornful of democratic friendliness (today's "togetherness"), may strike us as chilly. They speak with a *courage de tête* (literally, "courage of the head") and a surety we often attribute to intellectual arrogance. Finally, they lack the solemnity that our own Age of Anxiety too often confuses with profundity. They are witty and seemingly casual. Their grace, ease, and apparent simplicity deceive us. It is good to remember Horace Walpole's remark, "The world is a comedy to those that think, a tragedy to those who feel." With them, as with Voltaire, the rapid play of mind over human experience should not obscure an underlying seriousness of intention.

TOWARD THE EN-
LIGHTENMENT

In our day, or within the last twenty-five years, we have become accustomed to seeing our own cultural milieu, and that of our immediate predecessors, defined only in terms which are deprecatory, negative, or cynical —for example, "the Jazz Age," "the Lost Generation," "the Age of Anxiety," or "the Age of Longing." Hence, we are not well equipped to appreciate the eighteenth century, when for the first time in history men announced to each other and to posterity that theirs was an Age of Reason, an *Enlightenment*. Voltaire, in his *Last Remarks on the "Pensées of M. Pascal*, exclaimed with joy, "What a light has burst over Europe within the last few years! It first illuminated all the princes of the North; it has even come into the universities. It is the light of common sense!" Crane Brinton epitomizes the movement in *Ideas and Men* (1950) when he speaks of "the belief that all human beings can attain here on this earth a state of perfection hitherto in the West thought to be possible only for Christians in a state of grace, and for them only after death."

Traditional Christianity had been securely moored by a pair of anchors: *faith* ("the substance of things hoped for, and the evidence of things not seen") and *reason*. The two elements were always linked in an unstable combination. To watch the progress of thought in the seventeenth century is to see the latter gradually usurp the position of the former. Biblical exegesis had succeeded in weakening the concept of the biblical God of miracles. Of what practical use were the records of an obscure Hebrew tribe for the "modern" man who trusted in his subjective rational capabilities, and for whom the wonders of the orderly universe were disclosed daily by contemporary scientists and philosophers? Reason, rapidly assuming a state of near-deification, could show men how to control themselves and their environment. Furthermore this same environment—nature —began to seem increasingly benign as man explored its previously concealed workings.

Deism became the most satisfying metaphysical position for most intellectuals. Taking their departure from the traditional arguments of "first cause" and "design" which were used to demonstrate the existence of God, they could conceive of a Supreme Being—*Monsieur l'Être*, a French wit said—who was an impersonal cosmic clockmaker, the prime mover of Newton's vast mechanical machine, remote and abstract. In short, one now invented a God to whom one could not pray and from whom one could not expect forgiveness. (Voltaire once wrote an article describing the fallacy of prayer, finding the act impious, superfluous, and ineffective.) The doctrinal handbook of the Middle Ages had been the *Summa theologica* of St. Thomas Aquinas; the Century of Light was to produce its *Encyclopedia* (*Encyclopédie*), a joint effort published from 1751 to 1776 by the leading French *philosophes*, edited by Diderot, and designed to popularize and disseminate the new doctrines.

Deism attempted to reconcile Christianity with "modern" rationalism. In one sense this was nothing new. We must remember that from the very start, Christian thinkers—St. Paul and the early Church fathers—faced the task of amalgamating Hebraic ideas about a revealed Messiah, the Son of God, with Greek rationalist philosophy. Many centuries later it was inevitable that for intellectuals imbued with scientific attitudes, the revelatory aspects of Christianity—invoking that same God who spoke to Pascal—would retreat before more analytical approaches. The period when modern philosophy was formed can be placed between Galileo (1564–1642) and Leibnitz (1646–1716). While differences between interim thinkers such as Hobbes, Spinoza, and Descartes may seem to be more paramount than similarities, these men were unanimous in their rejection of medieval logic and in their insistence that the axioms of the new mathematical physics were consonant with the authentic workings of the universe. The omniscience and activity of God has to conform with the same laws He had established, and there could be no room for divine caprice and arbitrary conduct. The critical climate of the age is succinctly revealed in Alexander Pope's epitaph intended for Sir Isaac Newton's tomb in Westminster Abbey. "Nature and Nature's Laws lay hid in Night:/ God said, *Let Newton be!* and all was Light."

Hence Deistic thinkers constructed or adumbrated complicated philosophic abstractions such as the Great Chain of Being, plenitude, and the principle of sufficient reason. Gott-

fried Wilhelm Leibnitz, himself a respectable figure in the history of philosophy, was responsible for much of the dissemination of the new doctrine, mostly through the writings of his more superficial disciples. Leibnitz's hypothesis of "many possible worlds"—which in less capable hands became a theory of "the best of all possible worlds"—ran somewhat as follows. God considered an infinite number of possible worlds before the Creation; but His final decision was to make a world where good predominates over evil. A cosmos *without* evil would actually not have been as "good" as one where evil is a minor ingredient, since many "goods" are related to certain evils. (For example, by definition the existence of free will implies the possibility of sin, for there must be an alternative upon which to exercise the power of free choice. God therefore invented the forbidden apple, and Adam's fall ensued.) According to this view, the world contains a preponderance of good over evil in the long run, and the evil it does possess is no argument against God's benevolence. Reduced to finite, human terms, this philosophical outlook became known as *Optimism*. The student must be careful not to confuse it with our everyday use of the word.

VOLTAIRE AND THE ENLIGHTENMENT

The younger Voltaire began as an Optimist and embraced these ideas in his early *Discourse in Verse on Mankind* (*Discours en vers sur l'homme*, 1738). For a time it may have appeared to him, particularly since he participated in the writing of the *Encyclopédie*, that he and his fellow philosophers were leading the rest of humanity toward a revival of the golden age on earth by dint of unaided "reason." But the course of Voltaire's own life and the pattern of his intellectual development brought about inevitable disillusion.

Tragedy has been described as a pattern in which theory is destroyed by a fact. For Voltaire and many of his contemporaries, the stubborn fact that threatened to destroy the theories of the Century of Light was the Lisbon earthquake of November 1, 1755, when an estimated thirty to fifty thousand persons perished—ironically on All Saints' Day, when the churches were crowded. It was the greatest natural catastrophe in Western Europe since Pompeii disappeared under Vesuvius' lava. In 1756 Voltaire wrote his first bitter rebuttal of the Optimists, the *Poem on the Disaster of Lisbon* (*Poème sur le désastre de Lisbonne*). He revaluated the self-satisfied cosmic acceptance of these philosophers as complacent, negative fatalism. For him it was "an insult to the sadness of our existence"—we who are "Tormented atoms on this pile of mud/ Swallowed up by death, the mere playthings of Fate." Voltaire's concluding line in the poem expresses his *respect* for God and his *love* for humanity.

The major work that grew out of Voltaire's disgust with Optimistic metaphysics was *Candide*. Written with incredible speed in 1758 (he claimed in three days) and out of white-hot indignation, it was published in 1759 and ran to some forty editions within twenty years. Like Dante, Voltaire immortalized his enemies. Pangloss, Candide's mentor, is a caricature of the Optimistic philosophers Christian Wolf(f) and Leibnitz. Jean-Jacques Rousseau, Voltaire's intellectual enemy (he once remarked, "If Rousseau is dead, it's one scoundrel the less"), flattered himself into believing that the portrait was of him. But Voltaire's satiric concern with individual thinkers was peripheral, and the truth is that his main target was a system, a way of looking at the world. Here he joins the company of great French *moralistes* we have earlier discussed. The framework for *Candide* is one that was popular with seventeenth- and eighteenth-century writers—the exotic romance, the travel story. The romancer could use such a story to satisfy the age's desire for vicarious voyaging and knowledge of distant, strange lands. The satirist could use it to indulge in contemporary and often dangerous criticism without fear of persecution. The philosopher could use it to reinforce the rationalists' conviction that all men are basically alike—children of "reason."

But we must not ignore the subtle ingredient added by Voltaire, the element that gives the book its distinctive flavor. This is Voltaire's *parody* of his literary models. The tale is a satire, almost a burlesque, of the romance, the adventure story, and the pedagogical novel. Did a novel ever contain more ridiculous improbabilities? Within a rigid formal structure (ten chapters in the Old World, ten in the New World, and the last ten back in Europe and Asia Minor) we are presented with dozens of recognition scenes, most of them accompanied by appropriate flashbacks as the once-lost character tells his tale to the wondering Candide. "I am consoled by one thing," says the ingenuous young man. "We see that we often meet people we thought we should never meet again." The recognition device is an excellent way to impose a design upon what otherwise would be a series of loosely linked adventures. It is also Voltaire's ironical commentary on storybook life in comparison with our own sorry existence, where the lost stay lost and the dead remain dead. Several of the major "deaths" in the story fortunately turn out to be not permanent; but half of Lisbon, two entire armies, the inhabitants of one ship and two castles, and miscellaneous llamas, monkeys, and sheep are summarily dispatched. A dim view of this best of all possible worlds!

In a later tale, *The Simple Fellow* (*L'Ingénu*, 1767), Voltaire has a priest tell the wandering Huron hero that God must have great designs for him, since He moves the young man about so freely. To this the Indian retorts that more likely the devil plans his itinerary. Candide never descends to such pessimism, even when at last he recovers his beloved Cunégonde, now a haggard washerwoman on the shores of the Bosphorus. Perhaps it is the vision of Eldorado that saves Candide (and Voltaire) from complete despair. For a brief time the hero is allowed to dwell in a never-never land, a composite of all the utopian dreams of the Enlightenment.

The nineteenth-century writer Flaubert said that *Candide* was a book that made you want to gnash your teeth. Flaubert also commented that the conclusion of *Candide*, with its admonition to work, may be "serene and stupid, like life itself." Yet the garden must be cultivated. In a letter written in 1759, Voltaire remarked, "I have read a great deal; I have found nothing but uncertainties, lies, fanaticisms, and I am just about in the same certainty concerning our existence as I was when I was a suckling babe; I much prefer to plant, to sow, to build, and above all to be free." Voltaire seems to say that the answer is neither a complacent acceptance of existence —Optimism—nor an equally fatuous condemnation—pessimism —but rather an intermediate path which may be called *meliorism*.

DIDEROT AND THE END OF NEOCLASSICISM

Naturally no single author, even less a single work, can merit the fame of "ending" a cultural epoch. Yet so far as a single work may mark finis to an age, Diderot's *Rameau's Nephew* (*Le Neveu de Rameau*, written sometime during the 1760's and early 1770's) marks finis to at least those attitudes associated with the eighteenth century in popular thought: restraint, reasonableness, and *bon goût* (good taste) as personal ideals; formal order in the arts and a high sense of measure and proportion; respect for the past and the classical tradition; concern for man in society and general human nature rather than for the individual with his unique personality. Add to these the general sentiment shared by the writers we have been considering: that man may be merely *rationis capax*—a creature *capable* of reason—rather than rational; yet this is the primary attribute of the human condition.

Through his impertinent, parasitic, nay-saying musician, Diderot brings all such criteria into question; and the critical response to this erosion of classical values demonstrates the efficacy of his book. Carlyle praised what he held to be Diderot's exaltation of the superior man over the average. Baudelaire singled out the writer's "Satanism." Karl Voss discovered a proto-Nietzsche. Maurice Barrès took the *Nephew* to be proof that the Enlightenment had died well before the end of the eighteenth century. John Morley called Rameau's dissolute nephew a "squalid and tattered Satan," "a Mephistopheles out at elbow, a Lucifer in low waters; yet always diabolic, with the bright fire of the pit in his eyes." For Karl Marx the young beggar showed Diderot's awareness of a disintegrating socio-economic situation and the eternal class struggle. Hegel found in him the embodiment of a dialectical turning point in world history. Shaw and Freud read into him

their own interpretations of the human personality. This formidable barrage of names may intimidate the reader rather than encourage him, and in many cases the critics have found more in the little work than may legitimately be located there. Let us consider a few points which, however, justify their variant responses.

The dialogue form—popular with Greek and Roman satirists and taken over by neoclassic writers—enabled Diderot to convey shocking sentiments through the mouth of the impudent nephew. Yet the presence of the conservative "Myself"—who acts as "straight man"—also freed Diderot from any imputation that Rameau's attitudes were necessarily his. Indeed, as in many of the Socratic dialogues, it is difficult to say what the author's position *is*. We know from Diderot's life that his volatile and tempestuous personality carried him from idea to idea, and consistency of outlook was alien to his temperament. He also once stated that to make a convincing literary character, the counterpoint most needed was that of "extreme and opposite feelings in his soul." Thus "He" and "Myself," ostensibly protagonist and antagonist, perhaps form one composite figure—namely Diderot. At the same time the dichotomies are real: moralist-amoralist, bourgeois-bohemian, abstract philosopher-creative artist, idealist-cynic, social man–anarchist, teacher-buffoon.

The *Nephew* belongs to an old literary tradition of parasitical vagabondage and self-proclaimed roguery. But his antecedents and predecessors—which include the "vice" or "ruffler" in late medieval plays, the Arlecchino (Harlequin) of Italian *commedia dell' arte*, the picaresque hero in seventeenth- and eighteenth-century novels, and even Diogenes, the father of all cynics, for whom Diderot had a professed admiration—practiced their vagrant lives within certain social frameworks and conventions to which they implicitly adhered. Not so the musician. His negativism seems to admit no values. For him even egotism dissolves in self-denigration, as we see from the pantomiming and play-acting. In the course of an apparently random conversation, this itinerant artist genially touches on a range of topics of whose scope the casual reader may remain unaware, so deft is Diderot's artistry. Indeed, the haphazard progression of ideas and sentiments within the piece

is as unclassical as the ideas adopted. Both in spirit and in method we seem closer to the Romantic revolt than to the world extending in time from Molière to Diderot. Society, he tells us, is a fraud, and so he can cynically enjoy being a "happy brigand" among "wealthy brigands." Human nature resembles animal nature, where each species devours the other. If the Nephew plays the hypocrite, at least he is forthright and no mean dissembler like his fellows. His vices are "natural," and he derides any attempt to suppress them by rational means: reason's standards are unobtainable. The late Albert Camus, who singled out *Rameau's Nephew* as an eighteenth-century literary landmark, might aptly have applied to it one of his favorite *bons mots*: not the Cartesian "Cogito, ergo sum" ("I think, therefore I am"), but "Je me révolte, donc nous sommes" ("I rebel, therefore we are").

LIVES, WRITINGS, AND CRITICISM
Biographical and critical works are listed only if they are available in English.

JEAN-BAPTISTE POQUELIN MOLIÈRE

LIFE. Born in Paris in 1622 as Jean-Baptiste Poquelin. His father was upholsterer to the king. Molière attended the Jesuit school at Clermont and later studied under the famous "libertine" and Epicurean philosopher Gassendi. At about the age of twenty-five he joined the Illustrious Theater (*Illustre Théâtre*), a company of traveling players formed by the Béjart family. From 1646 to 1658 Molière and his troupe toured the provinces, playing mostly short pieces after the fashion of the Italian *commedia dell' arte*. In 1658 the players were ordered to perform before Louis XIV in Paris, and soon after their initial success they became the Troupe de Monsieur, enjoying royal patronage. Despite the intrigues of rival companies, particularly that of the

Hôtel de Bourgogne, Molière's prestige increased; and when his theater of the Petit Bourbon was demolished, the king gave him the Palais-Royal theater in 1661. Molière married Armande Béjart in 1662—an unfortunate match, since his enemies spread the scandal that she was his daughter by a former mistress, Madeleine Béjart, although in reality the women were sisters. *Tartuffe*, a study in religious hypocrisy, first produced in 1664, embroiled the playwright with certain groups in the Church. The king was forced to ban it, but Molière succeeded in having the play published and reperformed by 1669. In 1673, although ailing, the author-actor insisted on playing the lead role in his *Imaginary Invalid*, and he died a few hours after a performance on February 17, 1673. The

Church refused him burial; but Louis XIV interceded at the pleas of his widow, and a compromise was effected.

CHIEF WRITINGS. Molière's first great success was *The High-Brow Ladies* (*Les Précieuses ridicules*, 1659), a satire on the intellectual pretensions of Parisian fashionable society. Approximately two dozen comedies can be definitely identified as his own. Among these are *The School for Husbands* (*L'École des maris*, 1661); *Don Juan* (1665)—a treatment of the legendary hero; *The Misanthrope* (*Le Misanthrope*, 1666); *Tartuffe*(1664-1669); *The Miser* (*L'Avare*, 1668); *The Bourgeois Gentleman* (*Le Bourgeois Gentilhomme*, 1670); *The Wise Ladies* (*Les Femmes savantes*, 1672); and his last play, *The Imaginary Invalid* (*Le Malade imaginaire*, 1673). *The Bourgeois Gentleman* was first performed at Chambord on November 14, 1670, and in Paris on November 29. Molière played the part of M. Jourdain. It is actually entitled a "comedy-ballet"; the court composer Lully (Lulli) wrote the incidental music for the play and sang the role of the Mufti. The part of Lucile was taken by Molière's wife.

BIOGRAPHY AND CRITICISM. Karl Mantzius, *Molière* (1908), is a good factual account of the author's life. C. H. C. Wright, *French Classicism* (1920), offers a brief survey of the period; Martin Turnell. *The Classical Moment* (1947), includes studies of Molière, Racine, and Corneille; W. G. Moore, *Molière: A New Criticism* (1950), is a recent study in English, as are J. D. Hubert, *Molière and the Comedy of Intellect* (1962) and D. B. Wyndham Lewis, *Molière: The Comic Mask* (1959). Recommended also are the chapter on Molière in E. Auerbach, *Mimesis* (1953), and L. Gossman, *Men and Masks: A Study of Molière* (1963).

JEAN RACINE

LIFE. Born in 1639 in the Valois district, eighty miles from Paris. His father was a 'government official. Racine attended the College de Beauvais, and from 1655 to 1659 studied at the Jansenist center of Port-Royal, when that institution was at its peak. (Pascal wrote his *Provincial Letters*, the *Provinciales*, dealing with Port-Royal, in 1656 and 1657.) Racine came to Paris in 1660, encouraged by a friend, the poet La Fontaine. His early plays were failures, and he went into seclusion at Uzès, in Provence—for an interval of retirement similar to Milton's Horton period. He returned to Paris early in 1663, received the patronage of the court and the nobility, and soon came to be one of the leading playwrights, along with Molière and Corneille. He left Paris in 1677, officially to write history; married Catherine de Romanet (after earlier liaisons with two of his actresses); and returned to Port-Royal—a move indicative of his increasing piety and interest in religious speculation. (Most of his seven children became nuns or priests.) He led the life of the affluent country gentleman, interrupted by occasional trips to Paris and by missions as historiographer on Louis XIV's campaigns during the period from 1678 to 1693. Racine died in 1699 and was buried at Port-Royal. His body was exhumed when the place was destroyed in 1711, and he was placed next to Pascal at the church of St. Étienne-du-Mont in Paris.

CHIEF WRITINGS. Racine's plays, twelve in all, consist of an early comedy, *The Suitors* (*Les Plaideurs*, 1668), based on Aristophanes; two tragedies, *The Thebaid* (*La Thébaïde*, 1664), and *Alexander the Great* (*Alexandre le Grand*, 1665), both imitative of Corneille; seven "profane" or secular tragedies; and two biblical dramas. His first major writing was *Andromache* (*Andromaque*, 1667), and this play enjoyed a success almost as great as that of the famous *Cid* of Corneille. *Britannicus* followed in 1669, *Bérénice* in 1670, *Mithridates* (*Mithridate*) in 1673—three tragedies whose sources were classical historians: Tacitus, Suetonius, and Plutarch. *Bajazet* (1672), marked an excursion into oriental *decor*; it is perhaps the most contemporary of Racine's plays, since despite the exotic locale, the plot—according to Racine—came from an adventure that had taken place only thirty years before. Both *Iphegenia* (*Iphigénie*, 1674), and *Phaedra* (*Phèdre*, 1677), were modeled on plays by Euripides. The latter was performed at the Hôtel de Bourgogne, the theater used by Molière's rivals; and it was after the play's success that Racine went into semiretirement. Twelve years later, at the request of Mme. de Maintenon, Racine wrote his first biblical drama, *Esther* (1689); this, like *Athalia* (*Athalie*, 1691), dealt with Old Testament material, and both plays were designed for performance at Mme. de Maintenon's school for girls at Saint-Cyr.

BIOGRAPHY AND CRITICISM. An excellent biography of the playwright, A. F. B. Clark, *Racine* (1939), may be supplemented by M. Duclaux, *The Life of Racine* (1925); K. Vossler, *Racine* (1926). C. H. C. Wright, *French Classicism* (1920), and Martin Turnell, *The Classical Moment* (1947), are recommended for background material. A recent and interesting study of Racine's plays is V. Orgel, *A New View of the Plays of Racine* (1948); a valuable edition of *Phèdre* has been prepared by R. C. Knight (1943); and translations by Lacy Lockert of several of Racine's plays—including *Phèdre*—in rhymed alexandrine couplets were published in

1936. E. Auerbach's chapter on Racine in *Mimesis* (1953) is excellent; and there is also G. Brereton, *Jean Racine: A Critical Biography* (1951); K. Wheatley, *Racine and English Classicism* (1956); M. Bowra, *The Simplicity of Racine* (1956); and the chapters on Racine in W. Sypher, *Four Stages of Renaissance Style* (1955) and in F. Fergusson, *The Idea of a Theater* (1949). More recently, there is B. Weinberg, *The Art of Jean Racine* (1963); P. France, *Racine's Rhetoric* (1965); O. de Mourgues, *Racine: Or, The Triumph of Relevance* (1967); a series of essays about Racine edited by R. C. Knight (1969); and P. H. Nurse, *Classical Voices* (1971), with a chapter on Racine.

FRANÇOIS, DUC DE LA ROCHEFOUCAULD

LIFE. Born on September 15, 1613, in Paris as Prince de Marcillac, La Rochefoucauld later received the title of Duke. He had an early army career. At 16 (in 1629), the year he married, he came to court. Through Mme. de Chevreuse he became attached to Anne of Austria, Louis XIII's wife, whose escape to Brussels he once tried to effect. He spent eight days in the Bastille, and was then exiled to his family estates after eight years of intriguing at Court. When Anne became regent, La Rochefoucauld opposed her advisor, Mazarin. La Rochefoucauld fought on the side of the Prince de Condé in the two outbreaks during Louis XIV's minority: the *Fronde of the Parlement* (1648–1649), and the *Fronde of the Princes* (1650–1653), and was wounded in 1652. He spent the remainder of his life as close friend to Mme. de Sablé, Mme. de La Fayette, and Mme. de Sevigné, whose salons were intellectual centers in Paris. He died March 17, 1680 —legend has it in the arms of the theologian Bossuet.

CHIEF WRITINGS. His *Maxims* were first published anonymously in 1665; the last augmented edition appeared in 1678. La Rochefoucauld's *Memoirs* (1662) are chiefly concerned with his experiences as a *Frondeur*.

BIOGRAPHY AND CRITICISM: E. Gosse, *Three French Moralists* (1918); H. A. Grubbs, *The Originality of La Rochefoucauld's Maxims* (1929); M. Bishop, *The Life and Adventures of La Rochefoucauld* (1951); Sister M. F. Zeller, *New Aspects of La Rochefoucauld's Style* (1954); and W. G. Moore, *La Rochefoucauld* (1969).

JEAN DE LA FONTAINE

LIFE. Born July 8, 1621, at Château-Thierry in Compiègne, where his father was chief huntsman and forester on the royal preserves. At one time La Fontaine briefly considered entering holy orders; he studied law, was admitted to the bar, but never practised. He married Marie Héricart when he was 26 (in 1647); they were separated in 1649. An indolent life in the provinces was succeeded after 1656 by an equally pleasant existence in Paris, where he was the favorite of various elegant ladies: the dowager Duchesse d'Orléans, Mme. de la Sablière (at whose residence he lived for many years), Mme. d'Hervart. Nicolas Fouquet, Superintendent of Finance (1653-1661) under Louis XIV, became his patron. When Fouquet fell, denounced by Colbert and others for his dubious financial operations, La Fontaine readily found other benefactors to guarantee him a life devoid of monetary worries. Molière, Racine, and Boileau were his close friends. He became a member of the French Academy in 1684; La Fontaine was on the side of the "Ancients" in the famous literary quarrel between the Ancients and the Moderns. Epicurean and skeptic, by temperament inclined toward neither philosophy nor religion, he increased his Christian devotions after a serious illness in 1692. He died April 13, 1695.

CHIEF WRITINGS. The *Fables*, published in twelve books (1668, 1678–1679, 1694) were his masterpiece. Other works included *Stories and Tales in Verse* (1664), mainly imitations from Ariosto and Boccaccio.

BIOGRAPHY AND CRITICISM. F. Hamel, *La Fontaine* (1912); P. A. Wadsworth, *Young La Fontaine* (1952); M. Sutherland, *La Fontaine* (1953); M. Guiton, *La Fontaine: Poet and Counterpoet* (1961).

FRANCOIS-MARIE AROUET DE VOLTAIRE

LIFE. Born on November 21, 1694, in Paris, as François-Marie Arouet. His father was a minor treasury official, originally from Poitou. Voltaire attended a Jesuit school and later undertook and abandoned the study of law. He spent eleven months in the Bastille (1717–1718), imprisoned by *lettre de cachet*, for writing satiric verses about the aristocracy. By 1718 he was using the name Voltaire. Literary and social success soon followed; speculations in the Compagnie des Indes made him wealthy by 1726. That same year the Chevalier de Rohan had him beaten and again sent to the Bastille, and 1726–1729 saw him in exile, mostly in England. From 1734 to 1749 he pursued philosophical, historical, and scientific studies, and became the companion of Mme. du Châtelet on her estate at Cirey. His election to the French Academy took place in 1746. From 1750 to 1753 he stayed with Frederick the Great of Prussia, at Potsdam, after Louis XV had failed to give him sufficient patronage. That unstable alliance broke in 1753. Soon after, Voltaire bought adjacent property in France and Switzerland, and settled first at his château, Les Délices, just outside Geneva, and then at nearby Ferney, on French soil. It was from there that he, as the foremost representative of the Enlightenment, directed his campaigns against intolerance and injustice. He made a triumphant return to Paris in 1778, and died there on May 30.

CHIEF WRITINGS. Voltaire's first serious work was a tragedy on Greek lines, *Oedipus* (*Oedipe*, 1715). His epic, *The*

Henriad (*La Henriade*)—in praise of the tolerance of Henry IV—was published in 1728. His stay in England produced the *Letters on the English* (*Lettres sur les Anglais*, 1733); but before that, in 1731, appeared the *History of Charles XII* (*Histoire de Charles XII*) of Sweden—perhaps the first "modern" history. *Zadig* (1748), was his first famous philosophical tale, and *Candide* (1759), marked the summit of his achievement in this genre. Another major historical enterprice was *The Century of Louis XIV* (*Le Siècle de Louis XIV*, 1751). His *Philosophical Dictionary* (*Dictionnaire philosophique*, 1764) may be considered most typical both of Voltaire and of the Encyclopedists. In quantity, Voltaire's correspondence is almost unequaled, since he wrote to virtually every important intellectual, social, and political figure of his age.

BIOGRAPHY AND CRITICISM. Good biographies and studies of Voltaire are H. N. Brailsford, *Voltaire* (1935); R. Aldington, *Voltaire* (1934); G. Brandes, *The Life of Voltaire* (undated); and N. Torrey, *The Spirit of Voltaire* (1938). The best edition of *Candide*—to which this editor is greatly indebted—is by A. Morize, 1913. Also recommended are more recent studies: I. O. Wade, *Voltaire and "Candide"* (1959); P. Gay, *Voltaire's Politics: The Poet as Realist* (1961); two articles by W. Bottiglia in *Publications of the Modern Language Association*, "Candide's Garden," LXVI (September, 1951), and "The Eldorado Episode in *Candide*," LXXIII (September, 1958). T. Besterman, *Voltaire* (1969).

DENIS DIDEROT

LIFE. Born on October 5, 1713, in Langres, the eldest son of a mastercutler. He attended a Jesuit school, was tonsured at twelve, and almost entered that order. Diderot went to college in Paris, and gradually shifted toward secularism. In 1743 he married his former mistress, Antoinette Champion, against his father's wishes. He met Rousseau in 1743. He frequented the salons and cafés attended by the intellectuals, and made a

living by translating and similar literary hack-work. He was appointed chief editor (January 21, 1746) of the projected *Encyclopedia*. Volume I appeared on July 1, 1751, and the same year Diderot was elected to the Berlin Academy. From 1751 to 1757 the seven volumes of the *Encyclopedia* were published, but increasing opposition made each volume successively more difficult to print. The Attorney General banned the work in 1759; Rome condemned it the same year. Ten more volumes were secretly published in 1765, and a four-volume supplement in 1776. Diderot's friendship with Sophie Volland commenced in 1756. Catherine II of Russia bought his library in 1767 (with the author acting as custodian until his death). He went to Russia as her guest in 1773, returning to Paris in 1774. He met Voltaire in 1778, when that writer made his triumphant return to Paris to die there. Diderot died July 30, 1784.

CHIEF WRITINGS. His first important work was *The Indiscreet Jewels* (1748), a bawdy satire. A short novel, *The Nun* (1770)—anticlerical and pornographic—was published posthumously in 1796. Two plays were performed in 1757 and 1758: *The Natural Son* and *The Father of the Family*. *Rameau's Nephew* (written in the 1760's, possibly concluded in the early 1770's) appeared first in Goethe's German translation (1805). Not until 1891 was there any edition based on the original manuscript. *Discussion Between D'Alembert and Diderot, D'Alembert's Dream, Continuation of the Discussion, etc.* (all written 1769, published in 1830), are dialogues like the *Nephew*. *The Paradox about the Comedian* (1773, published 1830) concerns the art of acting. *A Treatise on Beauty* (1750) and the *Essay on Painting* (1765), along with the posthumously printed *Salons*, establish Diderot as one of the first modern critics of the fine arts.

BIOGRAPHY AND CRITICISM. J. Morley, *Diderot and the Encyclopedists* (1897); E. M. Steel, *Diderot's Imagery* (1941); A. Vartanian, *Diderot and Descartes* (1953); R. Wellek, *A History of Modern Criticism* (*1750–1950*) (1955); L. G. Crocker, *The Embattled Philosopher* (1954); A. M. Wilson, *Diderot* (1957); J. Lough, *Essays on the Encyclopédie of Diderot and D'Alembert* (1968).

JEAN-BAPTISTE POQUELIN MOLIÈRE
(1622–1673)

Tartuffe or The Imposter (Le Tartuffe ou L'Imposteur) *

Preface

Here is a comedy that has excited a good deal of discussion and that has been under attack for a long time; and the persons who are mocked by it have made it plain that they are more powerful in France than all whom my plays have satirized up to this time. Noblemen, ladies of fashion, cuckolds, and doctors all kindly consented to their presentation,[1] which they themselves seemed to enjoy along with everyone else; but hypocrites do not understand banter: they became angry at once, and found it strange that I was bold enough to represent their actions and to care to describe a profession shared by so many good men. This is a crime for which they cannot forgive me, and they have taken up arms against my comedy in a terrible rage. They were careful not to attack it at the point that had wounded them: they are too crafty for that and too clever to reveal their true character. In keeping with their lofty custom, they have used the cause of God to mask their private interests; and *Tartuffe*, they say, is a play that offends piety: it is filled with abominations from beginning to end, and nowhere is there a line that does not deserve to be burned. Every syllable is wicked, the very gestures are criminal, and the slightest glance, turn of the head, or step from right to left conceals mysteries that they are able to explain to my disadvantage. In vain did I submit the play to the criticism of my friends and the scrutiny of the public: all the corrections I could make, the judgment of the king and queen who saw the play,[2] the approval of great princes and ministers of state who honored it with their presence, the opinion of good men who found it worthwhile, all this did not help. They will not let go of their prey, and every day of the week they have pious zealots abusing me in public and damning me out of charity.

I would care very little about all they might say except that their devices make enemies of men whom I respect and gain the support of genuinely good men, whose faith they know and who, because of

* Molière's *Tartuffe* translated by Richard Wilbur. © 1961, 1962, 1963, by Richard Wilbur. Reprinted by permission of Harcourt, Brace & World, Inc. The preface and the three petitions are from Molière's *Tartuffe*, translated and edited by Haskell M. Block. Copyright © 1958, Appleton-Century-Crofts, Inc. Reprinted by permission of Appleton-Century-Crofts.

The first version of *Tartuffe* was performed in 1664 and the second in 1667.

The third and final version was published in March, 1669, accompanied by this preface. When a second edition of the third version was printed in June, 1669, Molière added his three petitions to Louis XIV; they follow the preface.

1. a reference to some of Molière's earlier plays, such as *Les Précieuses ridicules* and *L'Ecole des femmes*.

2. Louis XIV was married to Marie Thérèse of Austria.

the warmth of their piety, readily accept the impressions that others present to them. And it is this which forces me to defend myself. Especially to the truly devout do I wish to vindicate my play, and I beg of them with all my heart not to condemn it before seeing it, to rid themselves of preconceptions, and not aid the cause of men dishonored by their actions.

If one takes the trouble to examine my comedy in good faith, he will surely see that my intentions are innocent throughout, and tend in no way to make fun of what men revere; that I have presented the subject with all the precautions that its delicacy imposes; and that I have used all the art and skill that I could to distinguish clearly the character of the hypocrite from that of the truly devout man. For that purpose I used two whole acts to prepare the appearance of my scoundrel. Never is there a moment's doubt about his character; he is known at once from the qualities I have given him; and from one end of the play to the other, he does not say a word, he does not perform an action which does not depict to the audience the character of a wicked man, and which does not bring out in sharp relief the character of the truly good man which I oppose to it.

I know full well that by way of reply, these gentlemen try to insinuate that it is not the role of the theater to speak of these matters; but with their permission, I ask them on what do they base this fine doctrine. It is a proposition they advance as no more than a supposition, for which they offer not a shred of proof; and surely it would not be difficult to show them that comedy, for the ancients, had its origin in religion and constituted a part of its ceremonies; that our neighbors, the Spaniards, have hardly a single holiday celebration in which a comedy is not a part; and that even here in France, it owes its birth to the efforts of a religious brotherhood who still own the Hôtel de Bourgogne, where the most important mystery plays of our faith were presented[3]; that you can still find comedies printed in gothic letters under the name of a·learned doctor of the Sorbonne[4]; and without going so far, in our own day the religious dramas of Pierre Corneille[5] have been performed to the admiration of all France.

If the function of comedy is to correct men's vices, I do not see why any should be exempt. Such a condition in our society would be much more dangerous than the thing itself; and we have seen that the theater is admirably suited to provide correction. The most forceful lines of a serious moral statement are usually less powerful than

3. a reference to the *Confrérie de la Passion et Résurrection de Notre-Seigneur* (the Fraternity of the Passion and Resurrection of Our Saviour), founded in 1402. The Hôtel de Bourgogne was a rival theater of Molière.
4. probably Maitre Jehan Michel, a

medical doctor who wrote mystery plays.
5. Pierre Corneille (1606–1684) and Racine were France's two greatest writers of classic tragedy. The two dramas Molière doubtlessly had in mind were *Polyeucte* (1643) and *Théodore, vierge et martyre* (1645).

those of satire; and nothing will reform most men better than the depiction of their faults. It is a vigorous blow to vices to expose them to public laughter. Criticism is taken lightly, but men will not tolerate satire. They are quite willing to be mean, but they never like to be ridiculed.

I have been attacked for having placed words of piety in the mouth of my impostor. Could I avoid doing so in order to represent properly the character of a hypocrite? It seemed to me sufficient to reveal the criminal motives which make him speak as he does, and I have eliminated all ceremonial phrases, which nonetheless he would not have been found using incorrectly. Yet some say that in the fourth act he sets forth a vicious morality; but is not this a morality which everyone has heard again and again? Does my comedy say anything new here? And is there any fear that ideas so thoroughly detested by everyone can make an impression on men's minds; that I make them dangerous by presenting them in the theater; that they acquire authority from the lips of a scoundrel? There is not the slightest suggestion of any of this; and one must either approve the comedy of *Tartuffe* or condemn all comedies in general.

This has indeed been done in a furious way for some time now, and never was the theater so much abused.[6] I cannot deny that there were Church Fathers who condemned comedy; but neither will it be denied me that there were some who looked on it somewhat more favorably. Thus authority, on which censure is supposed to depend, is destroyed by this disagreement; and the only conclusion that can be drawn from this difference of opinion among men enlightened by the same wisdom is that they viewed comedy in different ways, and that some considered it in its purity, while others regarded it in its corruption and confused it with all those wretched performances which have been rightly called performances of filth.

And in fact, since we should talk about things rather than words, and since most misunderstanding comes from including contrary notions in the same word, we need only to remove the veil of ambiguity and look at comedy in itself to see if it warrants condemnation. It will surely be recognized that as it is nothing more than a clever poem which corrects men's faults by means of agreeable lessons, it cannot be condemned without injustice. And if we listened to the voice of ancient times on this matter, it would tell us that its most famous philosophers have praised comedy—they who professed so austere a wisdom and who ceaselessly denounced the vices of their times. It would tell us that Aristotle spent his evenings at the theater[7] and took the trouble to reduce the art of making comedies to

6. Molière had in mind Nicole's two attacks on the theater: *Visionnaires* (1666) and *Traité de Comédie,* the Prince de Conti's *Traité de Comédie*

(1666).
7. a reference to Aristotle's *Poetics* (composed between 335 and 322 B.C., the year of his death).

rules. It would tell us that some of its greatest and most honored men took pride in writing comedies themselves[8]; and that others did not disdain to recite them in public; that Greece expressed its admiration for this art by means of handsome prizes and magnificent theaters to honor it; and finally, that in Rome this same art also received extraordinary honors; I do not speak of Rome run riot under the license of the emperors, but of disciplined Rome, governed by the wisdom of the consuls, and in the age of the full vigor of Roman dignity.

I admit that there have been times when comedy became corrupt. And what do men not corrupt every day? There is nothing so innocent that men cannot turn it to crime; nothing so beneficial that its values cannot be reversed; nothing so good in itself that it cannot be put to bad uses. Medical knowledge benefits mankind and is revered as one of our most wonderful possessions; and yet there was a time when it fell into discredit, and was often used to poison men. Philosophy is a gift of Heaven; it has been given to us to bring us to the knowledge of a God by contemplating the wonders of nature; and yet we know that often it has been turned away from its function and has been used openly in support of impiety. Even the holiest of things are not immune from human corruption, and every day we see scoundrels who use and abuse piety, and wickedly make it serve the greatest of crimes. But this does not prevent one from making the necessary distinctions. We do not confuse in the same false inference the goodness of things that are corrupted with the wickedness of the corrupt. The function of an art is always distinguished from its misuse; and as medicine is not forbidden because it was banned in Rome,[9] nor philosophy because it was publicly condemned in Athens,[10] we should not suppress comedy simply because it has been condemned at certain times. This censure was justified then for reasons which no longer apply today; it was limited to what was then seen; and we should not seize on these limits, apply them more rigidly than is necessary, and include in our condemnation the innocent along with the guilty. The comedy that this censure attacked is in no way the comedy that we want to defend. We must be careful not to confuse the one with the other. There may be two persons whose morals may be completely different. They may have no resemblance to one another except in their names, and it would be a terrible injustice to want to condemn Olympia, who is a good woman, because there is also an Olympia who is lewd. Such procedures would make for great confusion everywhere. Everything under the sun

---

8. The Roman consul and general responsible for the final destruction of Carthage in 146 B.C., Scipio Africanus Minor (*ca.* 185-129 B.C.), collaborated with the writer of comedies, Terence (Publius Terentius Afer, *ca.* 195 or 185 *-ca.* 159 B.C.).

9. Pliny the Elder says that the Romans expelled their doctors at the same time that the Greeks did theirs.

10. an allusion to Socrates' condemnation to death.

would be condemned; now since this rigor is not applied to the count-less instances of abuse we see every day, the same should hold for comedy, and those plays should be approved in which instruction and virtue reign supreme.

I know there are some so delicate that they cannot tolerate a com-edy, who say that the most decent are the most dangerous, that the passions they present are all the more moving because they are vir-tuous, and that men's feelings are stirred by these presentations. I do not see what great crime it is to be affected by the sight of a generous passion; and this utter insensitivity to which they would lead us is indeed a high degree of virtue! I wonder if so great a perfection resides within the strength of human nature, and I wonder if it is not better to try to correct and moderate men's passions than to try to suppress them altogether. I grant that there are places better to visit than the theater; and if we want to condemn every single thing that does not bear directly on God and our salvation, it is right that comedy be included, and I should willingly grant that it be condemned along with everything else. But if we admit, as is in fact true, that the exercise of piety will permit interruptions, and that men need amusement, I maintain that there is none more innocent than comedy. I have dwelled too long on this matter. Let me finish with the words of a great prince on the comedy, *Tartuffe*.[11]

Eight days after it had been banned, a play called *Scaramouche the Hermit*[12] was performed before the court; and the king, on his way out, said to this great prince: "I should really like to know why the persons who make so much noise about Molière's comedy do not say a word about *Scaramouche*." To which the prince replied, "It is because the comedy of *Scaramouche* makes fun of Heaven and religion, which these gentlemen do not care about at all, but that of Molière makes fun of *them*, and that is what they cannot bear."

THE AUTHOR

First Petition[13]

(*presented to the King on the comedy of Tartuffe*)

Sire,

As the duty of comedy is to correct men by amusing them, I be-

11. One of Molière's benefactors who liked the play was the Prince de Condé; de Condé had *Tartuffe* read to him and also privately performed for him.
12. A troupe of Italian comedians had just performed the licentious farce, where a hermit dressed as a monk makes love to a married woman, announcing that *questo e per mortificar la carne* ("this is to mortify the flesh").
13. The first of the three *petitions* or *placets* to Louis XIV concerning the play. On May 12, 1664, *Tartuffe*—or at least the first three acts roughly as they now stand—was performed at Versailles. A cabal unfavorable to Molière, includ-ing the Archbishop of Paris, Hardouin de Péréfixe, Queen-Mother Anne of Austria, certain influential courtiers, and the Brotherhood or Company of the Holy Sacrament (formed in 1627 to enforce morality), arranged that the play be banned and Molière censured.

lieved that in my occupation I could do nothing better than attack the vices of my age by making them ridiculous; and as hypocrisy is undoubtedly one of the most common, most improper, and most dangerous, I thought, Sire, that I would perform a service for all good men of your kingdom if I wrote a comedy which denounced hypocrites and placed in proper view all of the contrived poses of these incredibly virtuous men, all of the concealed villainies of these counterfeit believers who would trap others with a fraudulent piety and a pretended virtue.

I have written this comedy, Sire, with all the care and caution that the delicacy of the subject demands; and so as to maintain all the more properly the admiration and respect due to truly devout men, I have delineated my character as sharply as I could; I have left no room for doubt; I have removed all that might confuse good with evil, and have used for this painting only the specific colors and essential lines that make one instantly recognize a true and brazen hypocrite.

Nevertheless, all my precautions have been to no avail. Others have taken advantage of the delicacy of your feelings on religious matters, and they have been able to deceive you on the only side of your character which lies open to deception: your respect for holy things. By underhanded means, the Tartuffes have skillfully gained Your Majesty's favor, and the models have succeeded in eliminating the copy, no matter how innocent it may have been and no matter what resemblance was found between them.

Although the suppression of this work was a serious blow for me, my misfortune was nonetheless softened by the way in which Your Majesty explained his attitude on the matter; and I believed, Sire, that Your Majesty removed any cause I had for complaint, as you were kind enough to declare that you found nothing in this comedy that you would forbid me to present in public.

Yet, despite this glorious declaration of the greatest and most enlightened king in the world, despite the approval of the Papal Legate[14] and of most of our churchmen, all of whom, at private readings of my work, agreed with the views of Your Majesty, despite all this, a book has appeared by a certain priest[15] which boldly contradicts all of these noble judgments. Your Majesty expressed himself in vain, and the Papal Legate and churchmen gave their opinion to no avail: sight unseen, my comedy is diabolical, and so is my brain; I am a devil garbed in flesh and disguised as a man,[16] a libertine, a disbeliever who deserves a punishment that will set an example. It is not

14. Cardinal Legate Chigi, nephew to Pope Alexander VII, heard a reading of *Tartuffe* at Fontainebleau on August 4, 1664.

15. Pierre Roullé, the curate of St.

Barthélémy, who wrote a scathing attack on the play and sent his book to the king.

16. Molière took some of these phrases from Roullé.

enough that fire expiate my crime in public, for that would be letting me off too easily: the generous piety of this good man will not stop there; he will not allow me to find any mercy in the sight of God; he demands that I be damned, and that will settle the matter.

This book, Sire, was presented to Your Majesty; and I am sure that you see for yourself how unpleasant it is for me to be exposed daily to the insults of these gentlemen, what harm these abuses will do my reputation if they must be tolerated, and finally, how important it is for me to clear myself of these false charges and let the public know that my comedy is nothing more than what they want it to be. I will not ask, Sire, for what I need for the sake of my reputation and the innocence of my work: enlightened kings such as you do not need to be told what is wished of them; like God, they see what we need and know better than we what they should give us. It is enough for me to place my interests in Your Majesty's hands, and I respectfully await whatever you may care to command.

(August, 1664)

Second Petition[17]

(presented to the King in his camp before the city of Lille, in Flanders)

Sire,

It is bold indeed for me to ask a favor of a great monarch in the midst of his glorious victories; but in my present situation, Sire, where will I find protection anywhere but where I seek it, and to whom can I appeal against the authority of the power that crushes me,[18] if not to the source of power and authority, the just dispenser of absolute law, the sovereign judge and master of all?

My comedy, Sire, has not enjoyed the kindnesses of Your Majesty. All to no avail, I produced it under the title of *The Hypocrite* and disguised the principal character as a man of the world; in vain I gave him a little hat, long hair, a wide collar, a sword, and lace clothing,[19] softened the action and carefully eliminated all that I thought might provide even the shadow of grounds for discontent on the part of the famous models of the portrait I wished to present; nothing did any good. The conspiracy of opposition revived even at mere conjecture of what the play would be like. They found a way

17. On August 5, 1667, *Tartuffe* was performed at the Palais-Royal. The opposition—headed by the First President of Parliament—brought in the police, and the play was stopped. Since Louis was campaigning in Flanders, friends of Molière brought the second *placet* to Lille. Louis had always been favorable toward the playwright; in August, 1665, Molière's company, the *Troupe de Monsieur* (nominally sponsored by Louis's brother Philippe, Duc d'Orléans) had become the *Troupe du Roi.*

18. President de Lanvignon, in charge of the Paris police.

19. There is evidence that in 1664 Tartuffe played his role dressed in a cassock, thus allying him more directly to the clergy.

of persuading those who in all other matters plainly insist that they are not to be deceived. No sooner did my comedy appear than it was struck down by the very power which should impose respect; and all that I could do to save myself from the fury of this tempest was to say that Your Majesty had given me permission to present the play and I did not think it was necessary to ask this permission of others, since only Your Majesty could have refused it.

I have no doubt, Sire, that the men whom I depict in my comedy will employ every means possible to influence Your Majesty, and will use, as they have used already, those truly good men who are all the more easily deceived because they judge of others by themselves.[20] They know how to display all of their aims in the most favorable light; yet, no matter how pious they may seem, it is surely not the interests of God which stir them; they have proven this often enough in the comedies they have allowed to be performed hundreds of times without making the least objection. Those plays attacked only piety and religion, for which they care very little; but this play attacks and makes fun of them, and that is what they cannot bear. They will never forgive me for unmasking their hypocrisy in the eyes of everyone. And I am sure that they will not neglect to tell Your Majesty that people are shocked by my comedy. But the simple truth, Sire, is that all Paris is shocked only by its ban, that the most scrupulous persons have found its presentation worthwhile, and men are astounded that individuals of such known integrity should show so great a deference to people whom everyone should abominate and who are so clearly opposed to the true piety which they profess.

I respectfully await the judgment that Your Majesty will deign to pronounce; but it is certain, Sire, that I need not think of writing comedies if the Tartuffes are triumphant, if they thereby seize the right to persecute me more than ever, and find fault with even the most innocent lines that flow from my pen.

Let your goodness, Sire, give me protection against their envenomed rage, and allow me, at your return from so glorious a campaign, to relieve Your Majesty from the fatigue of his conquests, give him innocent pleasures after such noble accomplishments, and make the monarch laugh who makes all Europe tremble!

(*August, 1667*)

---

20. Molière apparently did not know that de Lanvignon had been affiliated with the Company of the Holy Sacrament for the previous ten years.

Third Petition

(*presented to the King*)

Sire,

A very honest doctor[21] whose patient I have the honor to be, promises and will legally contract to make me live another thirty years if I can obtain a favor for him from Your Majesty. I told him of his promise that I do not deserve so much, and that I should be glad to help him if he will merely agree not to kill me. This favor, Sire, is a post of canon at your royal chapel of Vincennes, made vacant by death.

May I dare to ask for this favor from Your Majesty on the very day of the glorious resurrection of *Tartuffe*, brought back to life by your goodness? By this first favor I have been reconciled with the devout, and the second will reconcile me with the doctors.[22] Undoubtedly this would be too much grace for me at one time, but perhaps it would not be too much for Your Majesty, and I await your answer to my petition with respectful hope.

(*February*, 1669)

21. a physician friend, M. de Mauvillain, who helped Molière with some of the medical details of *Le Malade imaginaire*.

22. Doctors are ridiculed to varying degrees in earlier plays of Molière: *Dom Juan, L'Amour médecin*, and *Le Médecin malgré lui*.

Characters†

MME PERNELLE, *Orgon's mother*
ORGON, *Elmire's husband*
ELMIRE, *Orgon's wife*
DAMIS, *Orgon's son, Elmire's stepson*
MARIANE, *Orgon's daughter, Elmire's stepdaughter, in love with Valère*

† The name Tartuffe has been traced back to an older word associated with liar or charlatan: *truffer*, "to deceive" or "to cheat". Then there was also the Italian actor, Tartufo, physically deformed and truffle-shaped. Most of the other names are typical of this genre of court-comedy and possess rather elegant connotations of pastoral and *bergerie*.

Dorine would be a *demoiselle de compagne* and not a mere maid; that is, a female companion to Mariane of roughly the same social status. This in part accounts for the liberties she takes in conversation with Orgon, Madame Pernelle, and others. Her name is short for Théodorine.

VALERE, *in love with Mariane*
CLEANTE, *Orgon's brother-in-law*
TARTUFFE, *a hypocrite*
DORINE, *Mariane's lady's-maid*
M. LOYAL, *a bailiff*
A POLICE OFFICER
FLIPOTE, *Mme Pernelle's maid*
The SCENE *throughout: Orgon's house in Paris*

Act I

SCENE 1. *Madame Pernelle and Flipote, her maid, Elmire,
Mariane, Dorine, Damis, Cleante*

MADAME PERNELLE. Come, come, Flipote; it's time I left this place.
ELMIRE. I can't keep up, you walk at such a pace.
MADAME PERNELLE. Don't trouble, child; no need to show me out.
It's not your manners I'm concerned about.
ELMIRE. We merely pay you the respect we owe.   5
But, Mother, why this hurry? Must you go?
MADAME PERNELLE. I must. This house appals me. No one in it
Will pay attention for a single minute.
I offer good advice, but you won't hear it.
Children, I take my leave much vexed in spirit.   10
You all break in and chatter on and on.
It's like a madhouse with the keeper gone.
DORINE. If . . .
MADAME PERNELLE. Girl, you talk too much, and I'm afraid
You're far too saucy for a lady's-maid.
You push in everywhere and have your say.   15
DAMIS. But . . .
MADAME PERNELLE. You, boy, grow more foolish every day.
To think my grandson should be such a dunce!
I've said a hundred times, if I've said it once,
That if you keep the course on which you've started,
You'll leave your worthy father broken-hearted.   20
MARIANE. I think . . .
MADAME PERNELLE.   And you, his sister, seem so pure,
So shy, so innocent, and so demure.
But you know what they say about still waters.
I pity parents with secretive daughters.
ELMIRE. Now, Mother . . .

---

12. *Madhouse:* in the original, *la cour
du roi Pétaud*, the Court of King Pétaud   where all are masters; a house of mis-
rule.

MADAME PERNELLE.   And as for you, child, let me add   25
  That your behavior is extremely bad,
  And a poor example for these children, too.
  Their dear, dead mother did far better than you.
  You're much too free with money, and I'm distressed
  To see you so elaborately dressed.   30
  When it's one's husband that one aims to please,
  One has no need of costly fripperies.
CLEANTE. Oh, Madam, really . . .
MADAME PERNELLE.   You are her Brother, Sir,
  And I respect and love you; yet if I were
  My son, this lady's good and pious spouse,   35
  I wouldn't make you welcome in my house.
  You're full of worldly counsels which, I fear,
  Aren't suitable for decent folk to hear.
  I've spoken bluntly, Sir; but it behooves us
  Not to mince words when righteous fervor moves us.   40
DAMIS. Your man Tartuffe is full of holy speeches . . .
MADAME PERNELLE. And practises precisely what he preaches.
  He's a fine man, and should be listened to.
  I will not hear him mocked by fools like you.
DAMIS. Good God! Do you expect me to submit   45
  To the tyranny of that carping hypocrite?
  Must we forgo all joys and satisfactions
  Because that bigot censures all our actions?
DORINE. To hear him talk—and he talks all the time—
  There's nothing one can do that's not a crime.   50
  He rails at everything, your dear Tartuffe.
MADAME PERNELLE. Whatever he reproves deserves reproof.
  He's out to save your souls, and all of you
  Must love him, as my son would have you do.
DAMIS. Ah no, Grandmother, I could never take   55
  To such a rascal, even for my father's sake.
  That's how I feel, and I shall not dissemble.
  His every action makes me seethe and tremble,
  With helpless anger, and I have no doubt
  That he and I will shortly have it out.   60
DORINE. Surely it is a shame and a disgrace
  To see this man usurp the master's place—
  To see this beggar who, when first he came,
  Had not a shoe or shoestring to his name
  So far forget himself that he behaves   65
  As if the house were his, and we his slaves.
MADAME PERNELLE. Well, mark my words, your souls would fare
    far better

If you obeyed his precepts to the letter.

DORINE. You see him as a saint. I'm far less awed;
  In fact, I see right through him. He's a fraud.   70

MADAME PERNELLE. Nonsense!

DORINE.   His man Laurent's the same, or
      worse;
  I'd not trust either with a penny purse.

MADAME PERNELLE. I can't say what his servant's morals may be;
  His own great goodness I can guarantee.
  You all regard him with distaste and fear   75
  Because he tells you what you're loath to hear,
  Condemns your sins, points out your moral flaws,
  And humbly strives to further Heaven's cause.

DORINE. If sin is all that bothers him, why is it
  He's so upset when folk drop in to visit?   80
  Is Heaven so outraged by a social call
  That he must prophesy against us all?
  I'll tell you what I think: if you ask me,
  He's jealous of my mistress' company.

MADAME PERNELLE. Rubbish! [*To* ELMIRE] He's not alone, child,
      in complaining   85
  Of all of your promiscuous entertaining.
  Why, the whole neighborhood's upset, I know,
  By all these carriages that come and go,
  With crowds of guests parading in and out
  And noisy servants loitering about.   90
  In all of this, I'm sure there's nothing vicious;
  But why give people cause to be suspicious?

CLEANTE. They need no cause; they'll talk in any case.
  Madam, this world would be a joyless place
  If, fearing what malicious tongues might say,   95
  We locked our doors and turned our friends away.
  And even if one did so dreary a thing,
  D' you think those tongues would cease their chattering?
  One can't fight slander; it's a losing battle;
  Let us instead ignore their tittle-tattle.   100
  Let's strive to live by conscience' clear decrees,
  And let the gossips gossip as they please.

DORINE. If there is talk against us, I know the source:
  It's Daphne and her little husband, of course.
  Those who have greatest cause for guilt and shame   105
  Are quickest to besmirch a neighbor's name.
  When there's a chance for libel, they never miss it;
  When something can be made to seem illicit
  They're off at once to spread the joyous news,

Adding to fact what fantasies they choose.   110
By talking up their neighbor's indiscretions
They seek to camouflage their own transgressions,
Hoping that others' innocent affairs
Will lend a hue of innocence to theirs,
Or that their own black guilt will come to seem   115
Part of a general shady color-scheme.

MADAME PERNELLE. All that is quite irrelevant. I doubt
That anyone's more virtuous and devout
Than dear Orante; and I'm informed that she
Condemns your mode of life most vehemently.   120

DORINE. Oh, yes, she's strict, devout, and has no taint
Of worldliness; in short, she seems a saint.
But it was time which taught her that disguise;
She's thus because she can't be otherwise.
So long as her attractions could enthrall,   125
She flounced and flirted and enjoyed it all,
But now that they're no longer what they were
She quits a world which fast is quitting her,
And wears a veil of virtue to conceal
Her bankrupt beauty and her lost appeal.   130
That's what becomes of old coquettes today:
Distressed when all their lovers fall away,
They see no recourse but to play the prude,
And so confer a style on solitude.
Thereafter, they're severe with everyone,   135
Condemning all our actions, pardoning none,
And claiming to be pure, austere, and zealous
When, if the truth were known, they're merely jealous,
And cannot bear to see another know
The pleasures time has forced them to forgo.   140

MADAME PERNELLE. [*Initially to* ELMIRE] That sort of talk
is what you like to hear;
Therefore you'd have us all keep still, my dear,
While Madam rattles on the livelong day.
Nevertheless, I mean to have my say.
I tell you that you're blest to have Tartuffe   145
Dwelling, as my son's guest, beneath this roof;
That Heaven has sent him to forestall its wrath
By leading you, once more, to the true path;
That all he reprehends is reprehensible,
And that you'd better heed him, and be sensible.   150
These visits, balls, and parties in which you revel

141. *That sort of talk:* in the original, a reference to a collection of novels about chivalry found in *La Bibliothèque bleue* (*The Blue Library*), written for children.

Are nothing but inventions of the Devil.
One never hears a word that's edifying:
Nothing but chaff and foolishness and lying,
As well as vicious gossip in which one's neighbor   155
Is cut to bits with épée, foil, and saber.
People of sense are driven half-insane
At such affairs, where noise and folly reign
And reputations perish thick and fast.
As a wise preacher said on Sunday last,   160
Parties are Towers of Babylon, because
The guests all babble on with never a pause;
And then he told a story which, I think . . .
    [*To* CLEANTE] I heard that laugh, Sir, and I saw that wink!
Go find your silly friends and laugh some more!   165
Enough; I'm going; don't show me to the door.
I leave this household much dismayed and vexed;
I cannot say when I shall see you next.
    [*Slapping* FLIPOTE]Wake up, don't stand there gaping into
    space!
I'll slap some sense into that stupid face.   170
Move, move, you slut.

SCENE 2. *Cléante, Dorine*

CLEANTE.   I think I'll stay behind;
I want no further pieces of her mind.
How that old lady . . .
DORINE.   Oh, what wouldn't she say
If she could hear you speak of her that way!
She'd thank you for the *lady*, but I'm sure   5
She'd find the *old* a little premature.
CLEANTE. My, what a scene she made, and what a din!
And how this man Tartuffe has taken her in!
DORINE. Yes, but her son is even worse deceived;
His folly must be seen to be believed.   10
In the late troubles, he played an able part
And served his king with wise and loyal heart,
But he's quite lost his senses since he fell
Beneath Tartuffe's infatuating spell.
He calls him brother, and loves him as his life,   15
Preferring him to mother, child, or wife.
In him and him alone will he confide;
He's made him his confessor and his guide;

161. *Towers of Babylon:* i.e. Tower of Babel. Mme. Pernelle's malapropism is the cause of Cléante's laughter.
11. *the late troubles:* a series of political disturbances during the minority of Louis XIV. Specifically these consisted of the *Fronde* ("opposition") of the Parlement (1648-1649) and the *Fronde* of the Princes (1650-1653). Orgon is depicted as supporting Louis XIV in these outbreaks and their resolution.

He pets and pampers him with love more tender
Than any pretty maiden could engender,   20
Gives him the place of honor when they dine,
Delights to see him gorging like a swine,
Stuffs him with dainties till his guts distend,
And when he belches, cries "God bless you, friend!"
In short, he's mad; he worships him; he dotes;   25
His deeds he marvels at, his words, he quotes,
Thinking each act a miracle, each word
Oracular as those that Moses heard.
Tartuffe, much pleased to find so easy a victim,
Has in a hundred ways beguiled and tricked him,   30
Milked him of money, and with his permission
Established here a sort of Inquisition.
Even Laurent, his lackey, dares to give
Us arrogant advice on how to live;
He sermonizes us in thundering tones   35
And confiscates our ribbons and colognes.
Last week he tore a kerchief into pieces
Because he found it pressed in a *Life of Jesus:*
He said it was a sin to juxtapose
Unholy vanities and holy prose.   40

SCENE 3. *Elmire, Mariane, Damis, Cléante, Dorine*

ELMIRE. [To CLEANTE] You did well not to follow; she stood in
the door
And said *verbatim* all she'd said before.
I saw my husband coming. I think I'd best
Go upstairs now, and take a little rest.
CLEANTE. I'll wait and greet him here; then I must go.   5
I've really only time to say hello.
DAMIS. Sound him about my sister's wedding, please.
I think Tartuffe's against it, and that he's
Been urging Father to withdraw his blessing.
As you well know, I'd find that most distressing.   10
Unless my sister and Valère can marry,
My hopes to wed *his* sister will miscarry.
And I'm determined . . .
DORINE.   He's coming.

SCENE 4. *Orgon, Cléante, Dorine*

ORGON.   Ah, Brother, good-day.
CLEANTE. Well, welcome back. I'm sorry I can't stay.

37. Laurent's act is more salacious than the translation might suggest.

How was the country? Blooming, I trust, and green?
ORGON. Excuse me, Brother; just one moment.
    [*To* DORINE]   Dorine ...
    [*To* CLEANTE] To put my mind at rest, I always learn   5
The household news the moment I return.
    [*To* DORINE] Has all been well, these two days I've been gone?
How are the family? What's been going on?
DORINE. Your wife, two days ago, had a bad fever,
    And a fierce headache which refused to leave her.   10
ORGON. Ah. And Tartuffe?
DORINE.   Tartuffe? Why, he's round and red,
    Bursting with health, and excellently fed.
ORGON. Poor fellow!
DORINE.   That night, the mistress was unable
    To take a single bite at the dinner-table.
    Her headache-pains, she said, were simply hellish.   15
ORGON. Ah. And Tartuffe?
DORINE.   He ate his meal with relish,
    And zealously devoured in her presence
    A leg of mutton and a brace of pheasants.
ORGON. Poor fellow!
DORINE.   Well, the pains continued strong,
    And so she tossed and tossed the whole night long,   20
    Now icy-cold, now burning like a flame.
    We sat beside her bed till morning came.
ORGON. Ah. And Tartuffe?
DORINE.   Why, having eaten, he rose
    And sought his room, already in a doze,
    Got into his warm bed, and snored away   25
    In perfect peace until the break of day.
ORGON. Poor fellow!
DORINE.   After much ado, we talked her
    Into dispatching someone for the doctor.
    He bled her, and the fever quickly fell.
ORGON. Ah. And Tartuffe?
DORINE.   He bore it very well.   30
    To keep his cheerfulness at any cost,
    And make up for the blood *Madame* had lost,
    He drank, at lunch, four beakers full of port.
ORGON. Poor fellow!
DORINE.   Both are doing well, in short.
    I'll go and tell *Madame* that you've expressed   35
    Keen sympathy and anxious interest.

SCENE 5. Orgon, Cléante

CLEANTE. That girl was laughing in your face, and though
    I've no wish to offend you, even so

I'm bound to say that she had some excuse.
How can you possibly be such a goose?
Are you so dazed by this man's hocus-pocus   5
That all the world, save him, is out of focus?
You've given him clothing, shelter, food, and care;
Why must you also . . .
ORGON.   Brother, stop right there.
You do not know the man of whom you speak.
CLEANTE. I grant you that. But my judgment's not so weak   10
That I can't tell, by his effect on others . . .
ORGON. Ah, when you meet him, you two will be like brothers!
There's been no loftier soul since time began.
He is a man who . . . a man who . . . an excellent man.
To keep his precepts is to be reborn,   15
And view this dunghill of a world with scorn.
Yes, thanks to him I'm a changed man indeed.
Under his tutelage my soul's been freed
From earthly loves, and every human tie:
My mother, children, brother, and wife could die,   20
And I'd not feel a single moment's pain.
CLEANTE. That's a fine sentiment, Brother; most humane.
ORGON. Oh, had you seen Tartuffe as I first knew him,
Your heart, like mine, would have surrendered to him.
He used to come into our church each day   25
And humbly kneel nearby, and start to pray.
He'd draw the eyes of everybody there
By the deep fervor of his heartfelt prayer;
He'd sigh and weep, and sometimes with a sound
Of rapture he would bend and kiss the ground;   30
And when I rose to go, he'd run before
To offer me holy-water at the door.
His serving-man, no less devout than he,
Informed me of his master's poverty;
I gave him gifts, but in his humbleness   35
He'd beg me every time to give him less.
"Oh, that's too much," he'd cry, "too much by twice!
I don't deserve it. The half, Sir, would suffice."
And when I wouldn't take it back, he'd share
Half of it with the poor, right then and there.   40
At length, Heaven prompted me to take him in
To dwell with us, and free our souls from sin.
He guides our lives, and to protect my honor
Stays by my wife, and keeps an eye upon her;
He tells me whom she sees, and all she does,   45
And seems more jealous than I ever was!
And how austere he is! Why, he can detect
A moral sin where you would least suspect;

In smallest trifles, he's extremely strict.
Last week, his conscience was severely pricked   50
Because, while praying, he had caught a flea
And killed it, so he felt, too wrathfully.
CLEANTE. Good God, man! Have you lost your common sense—
Or is this all some joke at my expense?
How can you stand there and in all sobriety . . .   55
ORGON. Brother, your language savors of impiety.
Too much free-thinking's made your faith unsteady,
And as I've warned you many times already,
'Twill get you into trouble before you're through.
CLEANTE. So I've been told before by dupes like you: 60
Being blind, you'd have all others blind as well;
The clear-eyed man you call an infidel,
And he who sees through humbug and pretense
Is charged, by you, with want of reverence.
Spare me your warnings, Brother; I have no fear   65
Of speaking out, for you and Heaven to hear,
Against affected zeal and pious knavery.
There's true and false in piety, as in bravery,
And just as those whose courage shines the most
In battle, are the least inclined to boast,   70
So those whose hearts are truly pure and lowly
Don't make a flashy show of being holy.
There's a vast difference, so it seems to me,
Between true piety and hypocrisy:
How do you fail to see it, may I ask?   75
Is not a face quite different from a mask?
Cannot sincerity and cunning art,
Realty and semblance, be told apart?
Are scarecrows just like men, and do you hold
That a false coin is just as good as gold?   80
Ah, Brother, man's a strangely fashioned creature
Who seldom is content to follow Nature,
But recklessly pursues his inclination
Beyond the narrow bounds of moderation,
And often, by transgressing Reason's laws,   85
Perverts, a lofty aim or noble cause.
A passing observation, but it applies.
ORGON. I see, dear Brother, that you're profoundly wise;
You harbor all the insight of the age.
You are our one clear mind, our only sage,   90

50-52. *Last week* . . . *wrathfully:* In
the *Golden Legend* (*Legenda santorum*),
a popular collection of the lives of the
saints written in the thirteenth century,
it is said of St. Marcarius the Elder (d.
390) that he dwelt naked in the desert
for six months, a penance he felt appropriate for having killed a flea.

The era's oracle, its Cato too,
And all mankind are fools compared to you.
CLEANTE. Brother, I don't pretend to be a sage,
Nor have I all the wisdom of the age.
There's just one insight I would dare to claim: 95
I know that true and false are not the same;
And just as there is nothing I more revere
Than a soul whose faith is steadfast and sincere,
Nothing that I more cherish and admire
Than honest zeal and true religious fire,   100
So there is nothing that I find more base
Than specious piety's dishonest face—
Than these bold mountebanks, these histrios
Whose impious mummeries and hollow shows
Exploit our love of Heaven, and make a jest   105
Of all that men think holiest and best;
These calculating souls who offer prayers
Not to their Maker, but as public wares,
And seek to buy respect and reputation
With lifted eyes and sighs of exaltation;   110
These charlatans, I say, whose pilgrim souls
Proceed, by way of Heaven, toward earthly goals,
Who weep and pray and swindle and extort,
Who preach the monkish life, but haunt the court,
Who make their zeal the partner of their vice—   115
Such men are vengeful, sly, and cold as ice,
And when there is an enemy to defame
They cloak their spite in fair religion's name,
Their private spleen and malice being made
To seem a high and virtuous crusade,   120
Until, to mankind's reverent applause,
They crucify their foe in Heaven's cause.
Such knaves are all too common; yet, for the wise,
True piety isn't hard to recognize,
And, happily, these present times provide us   125
With bright examples to instruct and guide us.
Consider Ariston and Périandre;
Look at Oronte, Alcidamas, Clitandre;
Their virtue is acknowledged; who could doubt it?
But you won't hear them beat the drum about it.   130
They're never ostentatious, never vain,
And their religion's moderate and humane;
It's not their way to criticize and chide:

127-128. *Ariston . . . Clitandre:* vaguely Greek and Roman names derived
from the elegant literature of the day;
not names of actual persons.

They think censoriousness a mark of pride,
And therefore, letting others preach and rave,   135
They show, by deeds, how Christians should behave.
They think no evil of their fellow man,
But judge of him as kindly as they can.
They don't intrigue and wangle and conspire;
To lead a good life is their one desire;   140
The sinner wakes no rancorous hate in them;
It is the sin alone which they condemn;
Nor do they try to show a fiercer zeal
For Heaven's cause than Heaven itself could feel.
These men I honor, these men I advocate   145
As models for us all to emulate.
Your man is not their sort at all, I fear:
And, while your praise of him is quite sincere,
I think that you've been dreadfully deluded.
ORGON. Now then, dear Brother, is your speech concluded?   150
CLEANTE. Why, yes.
ORGON.   Your servant, Sir.   [*He turns to go.*]
CLEANTE.   No, Brother; wait.
   There's one more matter. You agreed of late
   That young Valère might have your daughter's hand.
ORGON. I did.
CLEANTE.   And set the date, I understand.
ORGON. Quite so.
CLEANTE.   You've now postponed it; is that true?   155
ORGON. No doubt.
CLEANTE.   The match no longer pleases you?
ORGON. Who knows?
CLEANTE.   D'you mean to go back on your word?
ORGON. I won't say that.
CLEANTE.   Has anything occurred
   Which might entitle you to break your pledge?
ORGON. Perhaps.
CLEANTE.   Why must you hem, and haw, and hedge?
   The boy asked me to sound you in this affair . . .   160
ORGON. It's been a pleasure.
CLEANTE.   But what shall I tell Valère?
ORGON. Whatever you like.
CLEANTE.   But what have you decided?
   What are your plans?
ORGON.   I plan, Sir, to be guided
   By Heaven's will.
CLEANTE.   Come, Brother, don't talk rot.   165
   You've given Valère your word; will you keep it, or not?

ORGON. Good day.
CLEANTE.   This looks like poor Valère's undoing;
    I'll go and warn him that there's trouble brewing.

Act II

SCENE 1. *Orgon, Mariane*

ORGON. Mariane.
MARIANE.   Yes, Father?
ORGON.   A word with you; come here.
MARIANE. What are you looking for?
ORGON. [*Peering into a small closet*] Eavesdroppers, dear.
    I'm making sure we shan't be overheard.
    Someone in there could catch our every word.
    Ah, good, we're safe. Now, Mariane, my child,   5
    You're a sweet girl who's tractable and mild,
    Whom I hold dear, and think most highly of.
MARIANE. I'm deeply grateful, Father, for your love.
ORGON. That's well said, Daughter; and you can repay me
    If, in all things, you'll cheerfully obey me.   10
MARIANE. To please you, Sir, is what delights me best.
ORGON. Good, good. Now, what d'you think of Tartuffe, our guest?
MARIANE. I, Sir?
ORGON.   Yes. Weigh your answer; think it through.
MARIANE. Oh, dear. I'll say whatever you wish me to.
ORGON. That's wisely said, my Daughter. Say of him, then,   15
    That he's the very worthiest of men,
    And that you're fond of him, and would rejoice
    In being his wife, if that should be my choice.
    Well?
MARIANE. What
ORGON.   What's that?
MARIANE.   I . . .
ORGON.   Well?
MARIANE.   Forgive me, pray.
ORGON. Did you not hear me?
MARIANE.   Of *whom*, Sir, must I say   20
    That I am fond of him, and would rejoice
    In being his wife, if that should be your choice?
ORGON. Why, of Tartuffe.
MARIANE.   But, Father, that's false, you know.
    Why would you have me say what isn't so?
ORGON. Because I am resolved it shall be true.   25
    That it's my wish should be enough for you.
MARIANE. You can't mean, Father . . .

ORGON.   Yes, Tartuffe shall be
Allied by marriage to this family,
And he's to be your husband, is that clear?
It's a father's privilege . . .

SCENE 2. *Dorine, Orgon, Mariane*

ORGON. [*To* DORINE]   What are you doing in here?
Is curiosity so fierce a passion
With you, that you must eavesdrop in this fashion?
DORINE. There's lately been a rumor going about—
Based on some hunch or chance remark, no doubt—   5
That you mean Mariane to wed Tartuffe.
I've laughed it off, of course, as just a spoof.
ORGON. You find it so incredible?
DORINE.   Yes, I do.
I won't accept that story, even from you.
ORGON. Well, you'll believe it when the thing is done.   10
DORINE. Yes, yes, of course. Go on and have your fun.
ORGON. I've never been more serious in my life.
DORINE. Ha!
ORGON.   Daughter, I mean it; you're to be his wife.
DORINE. No, don't believe your father; it's all a hoax.
ORGON. See here, young woman . . .
DORINE.   Come, Sir, no more jokes;   15
You can't fool us.
ORGON.   How dare you talk that way?
DORINE. All right, then: we believe you, sad to say.
But how a man like you, who looks so wise
And wears a moustache of such splendid size,
Can be so foolish as to . . .
ORGON.   Silence, please!   20
My girl, you take too many liberties.
I'm master here, as you must not forget.
DORINE. Do let's discuss this calmly; don't be upset.
You can't be serious, Sir, about this plan.
What should that bigot want with Mariane?   25
Praying and fasting ought to keep him busy.
And then, in terms of wealth and rank, what is he?
Why should a man of property like you
Pick out a beggar son-in-law?
ORGON.   That will do.
Speak of his poverty with reverence.   30

29. *Allied by marriage:* This assertion
is important and more than a mere device in the plot of the play. The second
placet or petition insists that Tartuffe be
costumed as a layman, and Orgon's plan
for him to marry again asserts Tartuffe's
position in the laity. In the 1664 version
of the play Tartuffe had been dressed in
a cassock suggestive of the priesthood,
and Molière was now anxious to avoid
any suggestion of this kind.

His is a pure and saintly indigence
Which far transcends all worldly pride and pelf.
He lost his fortune, as he says himself,
Because he cared for Heaven alone, and so
Was careless of his interests here below.   35
I mean to get him out of his present straits
And help him to recover his estates—
Which, in his part of the world, have no small fame.
Poor though he is, he's a gentleman just the same.
DORINE. Yes, so he tells us; and, Sir, it seems to me   40
Such pride goes very ill with piety.
A man whose spirit spurns this dungy earth
Ought not to brag of lands and noble birth;
Such worldly arrogance will hardly square
With meek devotion and the life of prayer.   45
. . . But this approach, I see, has drawn a blank;
Let's speak, then, of his person, not his rank.
Doesn't it seem to you a trifle grim
To give a girl like her to a man like him?
When two are so ill-suited, can't you see   50
What the sad consequence is bound to be?
A young girl's virtue is imperilled, Sir,
When such a marriage is imposed on her;
For if one's bridegroom isn't to one's taste,
It's hardly an inducement to be chaste,   55
And many a man with horns upon his brow
Has made his wife the thing that she is now.
It's hard to be a faithful wife, in short,
To certain husbands of a certain sort,
And he who gives his daughter to a man she hates   60
Must answer for her sins at Heaven's gates.
Think, Sir, before you play so risky a role.
ORGON. This servant-girl presumes to save my soul!
DORINE. You would do well to ponder what I've said.
ORGON. Daughter, we'll disregard this dunderhead.   65
Just trust your father's judgment. Oh, I'm aware
That I once promised you to young Valère;
But now I hear he gambles, which greatly shocks me;
What's more, I've doubts about his orthodoxy.
His visits to church, I note, are very few.   70
DORINE. Would you have him go at the same hours as you,
And kneel nearby, to be sure of being seen?
ORGON. I can dispense with such remarks, Dorine.
[*To* MARIANE] Tartuffe, however, is sure of Heaven's blessing.
And that's the only treasure worth possessing.   75
This match will bring you joys beyond all measure;
Your cup will overflow with every pleasure;

You two will interchange your faithful loves
Like two sweet cherubs, or two turtle-doves.
No harsh word shall be heard, no frown be seen,   80
And he shall make you happy as a queen.
DORINE. And she'll make him a cuckold, just wait and see.
ORGON. What language!
DORINE.   Oh, he's a man of destiny;
He's *made* for horns, and what the stars demand
Your daughter's virtue surely can't withstand.   85
ORGON. Don't interrupt me further. Why can't you learn
That certain things are none of your concern?
DORINE. It's for your own sake that I interfere.
     [*She repeatedly interrupts* ORGON *just as he is turning to speak
     to his daughter.*]
ORGON. Most kind of you. Now, hold your tongue, d'you hear?
DORINE. If I didn't love you . . .
ORGON.   Spare me your affection.   90
DORINE. I'll love you, Sir, in spite of your objection.
ORGON. Blast!
DORINE.   I can't bear, Sir, for your honor's sake,
To let you make this ludicrous mistake.
ORGON. You mean to go on talking?
DORINE.   If I didn't protest
This sinful marriage, my conscience couldn't rest.   95
ORGON. If you don't hold your tongue, you little shrew . . .
DORINE. What, lost your temper? A pious man like you?
ORGON. Yes! Yes! You talk and talk. I'm maddened by it.
Once and for all, I tell you to be quiet.
DORINE. Well, I'll be quiet. But I'll be thinking hard.   100
ORGON. Think all you like, but you had better guard
That saucy tongue of yours, or I'll . . .
     [*Turning back to* MARIANE]   Now, child,
I've weighed this matter fully.
DORINE. [*Aside*]   It drives me wild
That I can't speak.
     [ORGON *turns his head, and she is silent.*]
ORGON.   Tartuffe is no young dandy,
But, still, his person . . .
DORINE. [*Aside*]   Is as sweet as candy.   105
ORGON. Is such that, even if you shouldn't care
For his other merits . . .
     [*He turns and stands facing* DORINE, *arms crossed.*]
DORINE. [*Aside*]   They'll make a lovely pair.
If I were she, no man would marry me
Against my inclination, and go scot-free.

He'd learn, before the wedding-day was over,   110
How readily a wife can find a lover.
ORGON. [*To* DORINE] It seems you treat my orders as a joke.
DORINE. Why, what's the matter? 'Twas not to you I spoke.
ORGON. What *were* you doing?
DORINE.   Talking to myself, that's all
ORGON. Ah! [*Aside*] One more bit of impudence and gall,   115
And I shall give her a good slap in the face.
    [*He puts himself in position to slap her;* DORINE, *whenever
    he glances at her, stands immobile and silent.*]
Daughter, you shall accept, and with good grace,
The husband I've selected . . . Your wedding-day . . .
[*To* DORINE] Why don't you talk to yourself?
DORINE.   I've nothing to say.
ORGON. Come, just one word.
DORINE.   No thank you, Sir. I pass.   120
ORGON. Come, speak; I'm waiting.
DORINE.   I'd not be such an ass.
ORGON. [*Turning to* MARIANE] In short, dear Daughter, I mean
    to be obeyed,
And you must bow to the sound choice I've made.
DORINE. [*Moving away*] I'd not wed such a monster, even in jest.
    [ORGON *attempts to slap her, but misses.*]
ORGON. Daughter, that maid of yours is a thorough pest;   125
She makes me sinfully annoyed and nettled.
I can't speak further; my nerves are too unsettled.
She's so upset me by her insolent talk,
I'll calm myself by going for a walk.

SCENE 3. *Dorine, Mariane*

DORINE. [*Returning*] Well, have you lost your tongue, girl? Must
    I play
Your part, and say the lines you ought to say?
Faced with a fate so hideous and absurd,
Can you not utter one dissenting word?
MARIANE. What good would it do? A father's power is great.   5
DORINE. Resist him now, or it will be too late.
MARIANE. But . . .
DORINE.   Tell him one cannot love at a father's whim;
That you shall marry for yourself, not him;
That since it's you who are to be the bride,
It's you, not he, who must be satisfied;   10
And that if his Tartuffe is so sublime,
He's free to marry him at any time.
MARIANE. I've bowed so long to Father's strict control,

I couldn't oppose him now, to save my soul.   14
DORINE. Come, come, Mariane. Do listen to reason, won't you?
   Valère has asked your hand. Do you love him, or don't you?
MARIANE. Oh, how unjust of you! What can you mean
   By asking such a question, dear Dorine?
   You know the depth of my affection for him;
   I've told you a hundred times how I adore him.   20
DORINE. I don't believe in everything I hear;
   Who knows if your professions were sincere?
MARIANE. They were, Dorine, and you do me wrong to doubt it,
   Heaven knows that I've been all too frank about it.
DORINE. You love him, then?
MARIANE.   Oh, more than I can express.   25
DORINE. And he, I take it, cares for you no less?
MARIANE. I think so.
DORINE.   And you both, with equal fire,
   Burn to be married?
MARIANE.   That is our one desire.
DORINE. What of Tartuffe, then? What of your father's plan?
MARIANE. I'll kill myself, if I'm forced to wed that man.   30
DORINE. I hadn't thought of that recourse. How splendid!
   Just die, and all your troubles will be ended!
   A fine solution. Oh, it maddens me
   To hear you talk in that self-pitying key.
MARIANE. Dorine, how harsh you are! It's most unfair.   35
   You have no sympathy for my despair.
DORINE. I've none at all for people who talk drivel
   And, faced with difficulties, whine and snivel.
MARIANE. No doubt I'm timid, but it would be wrong . . .
DORINE. True love requires a heart that's firm and strong.   40
MARIANE. I'm strong in my affection for Valère,
   But coping with my father is his affair.
DORINE. But if your father's brain has grown so cracked
   Over his dear Tartuffe that he can retract
   His blessing, though your wedding-day was named,   45
   It's surely not Valère who's to be blamed.
MARIANE. If I defied my father, as you suggest,
   Would it not seem unmaidenly, at best?
   Shall I defend my love at the expense
   Of brazenness and disobedience?   50
   Shall I parade my heart's desires, and flaunt . . .
DORINE. No. I ask nothing of you. Clearly you want
   To be Madame Tartuffe, and I feel bound
   Not to oppose a wish so very sound.
   What right have I to criticize the match?   55

Indeed, my dear, the man's a brilliant catch.
Monsieur Tartuffe! Now, there's a man of weight!
Yes, yes, Monsieur Tartuffe, I'm bound to state,
Is quite a person; that's not to be denied;
'Twill be no little thing to be his bride.   60
The world already rings with his renown;
He's a great noble—in his native town;
His ears are red, he has a pink complexion,
And all in all, he'll suit you to perfection.

MARIANE. Dear God!

DORINE.   Oh, how triumphant you will feel   65
At having caught a husband so ideal!

MARIANE. Oh, do stop teasing, and use your cleverness
To get me out of this appalling mess.
Advise me, and I'll do whatever you say.

DORINE. Ah, no, a dutiful daughter must obey   70
Her father, even if he weds her to an ape.
You've a bright future; why struggle to escape?
Tartuffe will take you back where his family lives,
To a small town aswarm with relatives—
Uncles and cousins whom you'll be charmed to meet.   75
You'll be received at once by the elite,
Calling upon the bailiff's wife, no less—
Even, perhaps, upon the mayoress,
Who'll sit you down in the *best* kitchen chair.
Then, once a year, you'll dance at the village fair   80
To the drone of bagpipes—two of them, in fact—
And see a puppet-show, or an animal act.
Your husband . . .

MARIANE.   Oh, you turn my blood to ice!
Stop torturing me, and give me your advice.

DORINE. [*Threatening to go*] Your servant, Madam.

MARIANE.   Dorine, I
beg of you . . .   85

DORINE. No, you deserve it; this marriage must go through.

MARIANE. Dorine!

DORINE.   No.

MARIANE.   Not Tartuffe! You know I think him . . .

---

77. *bailiff:* a high-ranking official in the judiciary, not simply a sheriff's deputy as today.

78. *mayoress:* the wife of a tax collector (*élu*), an important official controlling imports, elected by the Estates General.

79. *the best chair:* In elegant society of Molière's day, there was a hierarchy of seats and the use of each was determined by rank. The seats descended from *fauteuils, chaises, perroquets, tabourets,* to *pliants.* Thus Mariane would get the lowest seat in the room.

82. *puppet-show . . . act:* in the original, *fagotin,* literally a monkey dressed up in a man's clothing.

DORINE. Tartuffe's your cup of tea, and you shall drink him.

MARIANE. I've always told you everything, and relied . . .

DORINE. No. You deserve to be tartuffified.   90

MARIANE. Well, since you mock me and refuse to care,
    I'll henceforth seek my solace in despair:
    Despair shall be my counsellor and friend,
    And help me bring my sorrows to an end. [*She starts to leave.*]

DORINE. There now, come back; my anger has subsided.   95
    You do deserve some pity, I've decided.

MARIANE. Dorine, if Father makes me undergo
    This dreadful martyrdom, I'll die, I know.

DORINE. Don't fret; it won't be difficult to discover
    Some plan of action . . . But here's Valère, your lover.   100

SCENE 4. *Valère, Mariane, Dorine*

VALERE. Madam, I've just received some wondrous news
    Regarding which I'd like to hear your views.

MARIANE. What news?

VALERE.   You're marrying Tartuffe.

MARIANE.   I find
    That Father does have such a match in mind.

VALERE. Your father, Madam . . .

MARIANE.   . . . has just this minute said
    That it's Tartuffe he wishes me to wed.   5

VALERE. Can he be serious?

MARIANE.   Oh, indeed he can;
    He's clearly set his heart upon the plan.

VALERE. And what position do you propose to take,
    Madam?

MARIANE.   Why—I don't know.

VALERE.   For heaven's sake—   10
    You don't know?

MARIANE.   No.

VALERE.   Well, well!

MARIANE.   Advise me, do.

VALERE. Marry the man. That's my advice to you.

MARIANE. That's your advice?

VALERE.   Yes.

MARIANE.   Truly?

VALERE.   Oh, absolutely.
    You couldn't choose more wisely, more astutely.

MARIANE. Thanks for this counsel; I'll follow it, of course.   15

VALERE. Do, do; I'm sure 'twill cost you no remorse.

MARIANE. To give it didn't cause your heart to break.

VALERE. I gave it, Madam, only for your sake.

MARIANE. And it's for your sake that I take it, Sir.

DORINE. [*Withdrawing to the rear of the stage*]
  Let's see which fool will prove the stubborner. 20

VALERE. So! I am nothing to you, and it was flat
  Deception when you . . .

MARIANE.   Please, enough of that.
  You've told me plainly that I should agree
  To wed the man my father's chosen for me,
  And since you've deigned to counsel me so wisely, 25
  I promise, Sir, to do as you advise me.

VALERE. Ah, no, 'twas not by me that you were swayed.
  No, your decision was already made;
  Though now, to save appearances, you protest
  That you're betraying me at my behest. 30

MARIANE. Just as you say.

VALERE.   Quite so. And I now see
  That you were never truly in love with me.

MARIANE. Alas, you're free to think so if you choose.

VALERE. I choose to think so, and here's a bit of news:
  You've spurned my hand, but I know where to turn 35
  For kinder treatment, as you shall quickly learn.

MARIANE. I'm sure you do. Your noble qualities
  Inspire affection . . .

VALERE.   Forget my qualities, please.
  They don't inspire you overmuch, I find.
  But there's another lady I have in mind 40
  Whose sweet and generous nature will not scorn
  To compensate me for the loss I've borne.

MARIANE. I'm no great loss, and I'm sure that you'll transfer
  Your heart quite painlessly from me to her.

VALERE. I'll do my best to take it in my stride. 45
  The pain I feel at being cast aside
  Time and forgetfulness may put an end to.
  Or if I can't forget, I shall pretend to.
  No self-respecting person is expected
  To go on loving once he's been rejected. 50

MARIANE. Now, that's a fine, high-minded sentiment.

VALERE. One to which any sane man would assent.
  Would you prefer it if I pined away
  In hopeless passion till my dying day?
  Am I to yield you to a rival's arms 55
  And not console myself with other charms?

MARIANE. Go then; console yourself; don't hesitate.
  I wish you to; indeed, I cannot wait.

VALERE. You wish me to?

MARIANE.   Yes.

VALERE.   That's the final straw.

Madam, farewell. Your wish shall be my law.   60

[*He starts to leave, and then returns: this repeatedly.*]

MARIANE. Splendid.

VALERE. [*Coming back again*]

       This breach, remember, is of your
making; It's you who've driven me to the step I'm taking.

MARIANE. Of course.

VALERE. [*Coming back again*] Remember, too, that I am merely
Following your example.

MARIANE.   I see that clearly.

VALERE. Enough. I'll go and do your bidding, then.   65

MARIANE. Good.

VALERE. [*Coming back again*] You shall never see my face again.

MARIANE. Excellent.

VALERE. [*Walking to the door, then turning about*]
     Yes?

MARIANE.   What?

VALERE.   What's that? What did you
say?

MARIANE. Nothing. You're dreaming.

VALERE.   Ah. Well, I'm on my way.
 Farewell, *Madame.*   [*He moves slowly away.*]

MARIANE.   Farewell.

DORINE. [*To* MARIANE] If you ask me,
Both of you are as mad as mad can be.   70
Do stop this nonsense, now. I've only let you
Squabble so long to see where it would get you.
Whoa there, Monsieur Valère!

[*She goes and seizes* VALERE *by the arm; he makes a great
show of resistance.*]

VALERE.   What's this, Dorine?

DORINE. Come here.

VALERE.   No, no, my heart's too full of spleen.
Don't hold me back; her wish must be obeyed.   75

DORINE. Stop!

VALERE.   It's too late now; my decision's made.

DORINE. Oh, pooh!

MARIANE. [*Aside*] He hates the sight of me, that's plain.
I'll go, and so deliver him from pain.

DORINE. [*Leaving* VALERE, *running after* MARIANE]
And now *you* run away! Come back.

MARIANE.   No, no.
Nothing you say will keep me here. Let go!   80

VALERE. [*Aside*] She cannot bear my presence, I perceive.
To spare her further torment, I shall leave.

DORINE. [*Leaving* MARIANE, *running after* VALERE]
Again! You'll not escape, Sir; don't you try it.
Come here, you two. Stop fussing and be quiet.
   [*She takes* VALERE *by the hand, then* MARIANE, *and draws
   them together.*]

VALERE. [*To* DORINE] What do you want of me?   85

MARIANE. [*To* DORINE] What is the point of this?

DORINE. We're going to have a little armistice.
   [*To* VALERE] Now, weren't you silly to get so overheated?

VALERE. Didn't you see how badly I was treated?

DORINE. [*To* MARIANE] Aren't you a simpleton, to have lost your head?

MARIANE. Didn't you hear the hateful things he said?   90

DORINE. [*To* VALERE] You're both great fools. Her sole desire, Valère,
Is to be yours in marriage. To that I'll swear.
   [*To* MARIANE] He loves you only, and he wants no wife
But you, Mariane. On that I'll stake my life.   95

MARIANE. [*To* VALERE] Then why you advised me so, I cannot see.

VALERE. [*To* MARIANE] On such a question, why ask advice of *me?*

DORINE. Oh, you're impossible. Give me your hands, you two.
   [*To* VALERE] Yours first.

VALERE. [*Giving* DORINE *his hand*] But why?

DORINE. [*To* MARIANE]   And now a hand from you.

MARIANE. [*Also giving* DORINE *her hand*]
What are you doing?

DORINE.   There: a perfect fit.   100
You suit each other better than you'll admit.
   [VALERE *and* MARIANE *hold hands for some time without
   looking at each other.*]

VALERE. [*Turning toward* MARIANE]
Ah, come, don't be so haughty. Give a man
A look of kindness, won't you, Mariane?
   [MARIANE *turns toward* VALERE *and smiles.*]

DORINE. I tell you, lovers are completely mad!

VALERE. [*To* MARIANE] Now come, confess that you were very bad
To hurt my feelings as you did just now.   105
I have a just complaint, you must allow.

MARIANE. *You* must allow that you were most unpleasant . . .

DORINE. Let's table that discussion for the present;
Your father has a plan which must be stopped.   110

MARIANE. Advise us, then; what means must we adopt?

DORINE. We'll use all manner of means, and all at once.
   [*To* MARIANE] Your father's addled; he's acting like a dunce.
Therefore you'd better humor the old fossil.
Pretend to yield to him, be sweet and docile,   115
And then postpone, as often as necessary,

The day on which you have agreed to marry.
You'll thus gain time, and time will turn the trick.
Sometimes, for instance, you'll be taken sick,
And that will seem good reason for delay;   120
Or some bad omen will make you change the day—
You'll dream of muddy water, or you'll pass
A dead man's hearse, or break a looking-glass.
If all else fails, no man can marry you
Unless you take his ring and say "I do."   125
But now, let's separate. If they should find
Us talking here, our plot might be divined.
[*To* VALERE] Go to your friends, and tell them what's occurred,
And have them urge her father to keep his word.
Meanwhile, we'll stir her brother into action,   130
And get Elmire, as well, to join our faction.
Good-bye.

VALERE. [*To* MARIANE] Though each of us will do his best,
  It's your true heart on which my hopes shall rest.

MARIANE. [*To* VALERE] Regardless of what Father may decide,
  None but Valère shall claim me as his bride.   135

VALERE. Oh, how those words content me! Come what will . . .

DORINE. Oh, lovers, lovers! Their tongues are never still.
 ·Be off, now.

VALERE. [*Turning to go, then turning back.*]
            One last word . . .

DORINE.   No time to chat:
  You leave by this door; and *you* leave by that.
  [DORINE *pushes them, by the shoulders, toward opposing doors.*]

Act III

SCENE 1. *Damis, Dorine*

DAMIS. May lightning strike me even as I speak,
  May all men call me cowardly and weak,
  If any fear or scruple holds me back
  From settling things, at once, with that great quack!

DORINE. Now, don't give way to violent emotion.   5
  Your father's merely talked about this notion,
  And words and deeds are far from being one.
  Much that is talked about is never done.

DAMIS. No, I must stop that scoundrel's machinations;
  I'll go and tell him off; I'm out of patience.   10

---

130. *Elmire:* Orgon's second wife.

DORINE. Do calm down and be practical. I had rather
  My mistress dealt with him—and with your father.
  She has some influence with Tartuffe, I've noted.
  He hangs upon her words, seems most devoted,
  And may, indeed, be smitten by her charm.   15
  Pray Heaven it's true! 'Twould do our cause no harm.
  She sent for him, just now, to sound him out
  On this affair you're so incensed about;
  She'll find out where he stands, and tell him, too,
  What dreadful strife and trouble will ensue   20
  If he lends countenance to your father's plan.
  I couldn't get in to see him, but his man
  Says that he's almost finished with his prayers.
  Go, now. I'll catch him when he comes downstairs.
DAMIS. I want to hear this conference, and I will.   25
DORINE. No, they must be alone.
DAMIS.   Oh, I'll keep still.
DORINE. Not you. I know your temper. You'd start a brawl,
  And shout and stamp your foot and spoil it all.
  Go on.
DAMIS.   I won't; I have a perfect right . . .   30
DORINE. Lord, you're a nuisance! He's coming; get out of sight.
  [DAMIS *conceals himself in a closet at the rear of the stage.*]

SCENE 2. *Tartuffe, Dorine*

TARTUFFE. [*Observing* DORINE, *and calling to his manservant off-stage*] Hang up my hair-shirt, put my scourge in place,
  And pray, Laurent, for Heaven's perpetual grace.
  I'm going to the prison now, to share
  My last few coins with the poor wretches there.
DORINE. [*Aside*] Dear God, what affectation! What a fake!   5
TARTUFFE. You wished to see me?
DORINE.   Yes . . .
TARTUFFE. [*Taking a handkerchief from his pocket*]
                                        For mercy's sake,
  Please take this handkerchief, before you speak.
DORINE. What?
TARTUFFE.   Cover that bosom, girl. The flesh is weak,
  And unclean thoughts are difficult to control.
  Such sights as that can undermine the soul.   10
DORINE. Your soul, it seems, has very poor defenses,

---

8. *Cover that bosom:* The Brotherhood of the Holy Sacrament (*cf.* note 13, p. 23) practiced almsgiving to prisoners and kept a careful, censorious check on female wearing apparel if they deemed it lascivious. Thus, Molière's audience would have identified Tartuffe as sympathetic—hypocritically—to the aims of the organization.

And flesh makes quite an impact on your senses.
It's strange that you're so easily excited;
My own desires are not so soon ignited,
And if I saw you naked as a beast,   15
Not all your hide would tempt me in the least.
TARTUFFE. Girl, speak more modestly; unless you do,
   I shall be forced to take my leave of you.
DORINE. Oh, no, it's I who must be on my way;
   I've just one little message to convey.   20
   Madame is coming down, and begs you, Sir,
   To wait and have a word or two with her.
TARTUFFE. Gladly.
DORINE. [*Aside*]   *That* had a softening effect!
   I think my guess about him was correct.
TARTUFFE. Will she be long?
DORINE.   No: that's her step I hear.   25
   Ah, here she is, and I shall disappear.

SCENE 3. Elmire, Tartuffe

TARTUFFE. May Heaven, whose infinite goodness we adore,
   Preserve your body and soul forevermore,
   And bless your days, and answer thus the plea
   Of one who is its humblest votary.
ELMIRE. I thank you for that pious wish. But please,   5
   Do take a chair and let's be more at ease.
      [*They sit down.*]
TARTUFFE. I trust that you are once more well and strong?
ELMIRE. Oh, yes: the fever didn't last for long.
TARTUFFE. My prayers are too unworthy, I am sure,
   To have gained from Heaven this most gracious cure;   10
   But lately, Madam, my every supplication
   Has had for object your recuperation.
ELMIRE. You shouldn't have troubled so. I don't deserve it.
TARTUFFE. Your health is priceless, Madam, and to preserve it
   I'd gladly give my own, in all sincerity.   15
ELMIRE. Sir, you outdo us all in Christian charity.
   You've been most kind. I count myself your debtor.
TARTUFFE. 'Twas nothing, Madam. I long to serve you better.
ELMIRE. There's a private matter I'm anxious to discuss.
   I'm glad there's no one here to hinder us.   20
TARTUFFE. I too am glad; it floods my heart with bliss
   To find myself alone with you like this.
   For just this chance I've prayed with all my power—
   But prayed in vain, until this happy hour.
ELMIRE. This won't take long, Sir, and I hope you'll be   25

Entirely frank and unconstrained with me.
TARTUFFE. Indeed, there's nothing I had rather do
Than bare my inmost heart and soul to you.
First, let me say that what remarks I've made
About the constant visits you are paid   30
Were prompted not by any mean emotion,
But rather by a pure and deep devotion,
A fervent zeal . . .
ELMIRE.   No need for explanation.
Your sole concern, I'm sure, was my salvation.
TARTUFFE. [*Taking* ELMIRE'S *hand and pressing her fingertips*]
Quite so; and such great fervor do I feel . . .   35
ELMIRE. Ooh! Please! You're pinching!
TARTUFFE.   'Twas from excess of zeal.
I never meant to cause you pain, I swear.
I'd rather . . .   [*He places his hand on* ELMIRE'S *knee.*]
ELMIRE.   What can your hand be doing there?
TARTUFFE. Feeling your gown: what soft, fine-woven stuff!
ELMIRE. Please, I'm extremely ticklish. That's enough.   40
[*She draws her chair away;* TARTUFFE *pulls his after her.*]
TARTUFFE. [*Fondling the lace collar of her gown*]
My, my, what lovely lacework on your dress!
The workmanship's miraculous, no less.
I've not seen anything to equal it.
ELMIRE. Yes, quite. But let's talk business for a bit.
They say my husband means to break his word   45
And give his daughter to you, Sir. Had you heard?
TARTUFFE. He did once mention it. But I confess
I dream of quite a different happiness.
It's elsewhere, Madam, that my eyes discern
The promise of that bliss for which I yearn.   50
ELMIRE. I see: you care for nothing here below.
TARTUFFE. Ah, well—my heart's not made of stone, you know.
ELMIRE. All your desires mount heavenward, I'm sure,
In scorn of all that's earthly and impure.
TARTUFFE. A love of heavenly beauty does not preclude   55
A proper love for earthly pulchritude;
Our senses are quite rightly captivated
By perfect works our Maker has created.
Some glory clings to all that Heaven has made;
In you, all Heaven's marvels are displayed.   60
On that fair face, such beauties have been lavished,
The eyes are dazzled and the heart is ravished;
How could I look on you, O flawless creature,
And not adore the Author of all Nature,

Feeling a love both passionate and pure   65
For you, his triumph of self-portraiture?
At first, I trembled lest that love should be
A subtle snare that Hell had laid for me;
I vowed to flee the sight of you, eschewing
A rapture that might prove my soul's undoing;   70
But soon, fair being, I became aware
That my deep passion could be made to square
With rectitude, and with my bounden duty,
I thereupon surrendered to your beauty.
It is, I know, presumptuous on my part   75
To bring you this poor offering of my heart,
And it is not my merit, Heaven knows,
But your compassion on which my hopes repose.
You are my peace, my solace, my salvation;
On you depends my bliss—or desolation;   80
I bide your judgment and, as you think best,
I shall be either miserable or blest.
ELMIRE. Your declaration is most gallant, Sir,
But don't you think it's out of character?
You'd have done better to restrain your passion   85
And think before you spoke in such a fashion.
It ill becomes a pious man like you . . .
TARTUFFE. I may be pious, but I'm human too:
With your celestial charms before his eyes,
A man has not the power to be wise.   90
I know such words sound strangely, coming from me,
But I'm no angel, nor was meant to be,
And if you blame my passion, you must needs
Reproach as well the charms on which it feeds.
Your loveliness I had no sooner seen   95
Than you became my soul's unrivalled queen;
Before your seraph glance, divinely sweet,
My heart's defenses crumbled in defeat,
And nothing fasting, prayer, or tears might do
Could stay my spirit from adoring you.   100
My eyes, my sighs have told you in the past
What now my lips make bold to say at last,
And if, in your great goodness, you will deign
To look upon your slave, and ease his pain,—
If, in compassion for my soul's distress,   105
You'll stoop to comfort my unworthiness,
I'll raise to you, in thanks for that sweet manna,
An endless hymn, an infinite hosanna.
With me, of course, there need be no anxiety,

No fear of scandal or of notoriety. 110
These young court gallants, whom all the ladies fancy,
Are vain in speech, in action rash and chancy;
When they succeed in love, the world soon knows it;
No favor's granted them but they disclose it
And by the looseness of their tongues profane 115
The very altar where their hearts have lain.
Men of my sort, however, love discreetly,
And one may trust our reticence completely.
My keen concern for my good name insures
The absolute security of yours; 120
In short, I offer you, my dear Elmire,
Love without scandal, pleasure without fear.

ELMIRE. I've heard your well-turned speeches to the end,
And what you urge I clearly apprehend.
Aren't you afraid that I may take a notion 125
To tell my husband of your warm devotion,
And that, supposing he were duly told,
His feelings toward you might grow rather cold?

TARTUFFE. I know, dear lady, that your exceeding charity
Will lead your heart to pardon my temerity; 130
That you'll excuse my violent affection
As human weakness, human imperfection;
And that—O fairest!—you will bear in mind
That I'm but flesh and blood, and am not blind.

ELMIRE. Some women might do otherwise, perhaps, 135
But I shall be discreet about your lapse;
I'll tell my husband nothing of what's occurred
If, in return, you'll give your solemn word
To advocate as forcefully as you can
The marriage of Valère and Mariane, 140
Renouncing all desire to dispossess
Another of his rightful happiness,
And . . .

SCENE 4. *Damis, Elmire, Tartuffe*

DAMIS. [*Emerging from the closet where he has been hiding*]
        No! We'll not hush up this vile affair;
I heard it all inside that closet there,
Where Heaven, in order to confound the pride
Of this great rascal, prompted me to hide.
Ah, now I have my long-awaited chance 5
To punish his deceit and arrogance,
And give my father clear and shocking proof
Of the black character of his dear Tartuffe.

ELMIRE. Ah no, Damis; I'll be content if he
    Will study to deserve my leniency.   10
    I've promised silence—don't make me break my word;
    To make a scandal would be too absurd.
    Good wives laugh off such trifles, and forget them;
    Why should they tell their husbands, and upset them?
DAMIS. You have your reasons for taking such a course,   15
    And I have reasons, too, of equal force.
    To spare him now would be insanely wrong.
    I've swallowed my just wrath for far too long
    And watched this insolent bigot bringing strife
    And bitterness into our family life.   20
    Too long he's meddled in my father's affairs,
    Thwarting my marriage-hopes, and poor Valère's.
    It's high time that my father was undeceived,
    And now I've proof that can't be disbelieved—
    Proof that was furnished me by Heaven above.   25
    It's too good not to take advantage of.
    This is my chance, and I deserve to lose it
    If, for one moment, I hesitate to use it.
ELMIRE. Damis . . .
DAMIS.   No, I must do what I think right.
    Madam, my heart is bursting with delight,   30
    And, say whatever you will, I'll not consent
    To lose the sweet revenge on which I'm bent.
    I'll settle matters without more ado;
    And here, most opportunely, is my cue.

      SCENE 5. *Orgon, Damis, Tartuffe, Elmire*

DAMIS. Father, I'm glad you've joined us. Let us advise you
    Of some fresh news which doubtless will surprise you.
    You've just now been repaid with interest
    For all your loving-kindness to our guest.
    He's proved his warm and grateful feelings toward you;   5
    It's with a pair of horns he would reward you.
    Yes, I surprised him with your wife, and heard
    His whole adulterous offer, every word.
    She, with her all too gentle disposition,
    Would not have told you of his proposition;   10
    But I shall not make terms with brazen lechery,
    And feel that not to tell you would be treachery.

---

34. *My cue:* In the original stage directions, Tartuffe now reads silently from his breviary—in the Roman Catholic Church, the book containing the Divine Office for each day, which those in holy orders are required to recite.

ELMIRE. And I hold that one's husband's peace of mind
Should not be spoilt by tattle of this kind.
One's honor doesn't require it: to be proficient   15
In keeping men at bay is quite sufficient.
These are my sentiments, and I wish, Damis,
That you had heeded me and held your peace.

SCENE 6. *Orgon, Damis, Tartuffe*

ORGON. Can it be true, this dreadful thing I hear?
TARTUFFE. Yes, Brother, I'm a wicked man, I fear:
A wretched sinner, all depraved and twisted,
The greatest villain that has ever existed.
My life's one heap of crimes, which grows each minute;   5
There's naught but foulness and corruption in it;
And I perceive that Heaven, outraged by me,
Has chosen this occasion to mortify me.
Charge me with any deed you wish to name;
I'll not defend myself, but take the blame.   10
Believe what you are told, and drive Tartuffe
Like some base criminal from beneath your roof;
Yes, drive me hence, and with a parting curse:
I shan't protest, for I deserve far worse.
ORGON. [*To* DAMIS] Ah, you deceitful boy, how dare you try 15
To stain his purity with so foul a lie?
DAMIS. What! Are you taken in by such a bluff?
Did you not hear . . . ?
ORGON.   Enough, you rogue, enough!
TARTUFFE. Ah, Brother, let him speak: you're being unjust.
Believe his story; the boy deserves your trust.   20
Why, after all, should you have faith in me?
How can you know what I might do, or be?
Is it on my good actions that you base
Your favor? Do you trust my pious face?
Ah, no, don't be deceived by hollow shows;   25
I'm far, alas, from being what men suppose;
Though the world takes me for a man of worth,
I'm truly the most worthless man on earth.
     [*To* DAMIS]
Yes, my dear son, speak out now: call me the chief
Of sinners, a wretch, a murderer, a thief;   30
Load me with all the names men most abhor;
I'll not complain; I've earned them all, and more;
I'll kneel here while you pour them on my head
As a just punishment for the life I've led.

ORGON. [*To* TARTUFFE] This is too much, dear Brother.
    [*To* DAMIS]   Have you no heart?
DAMIS. Are you so hoodwinked by this rascal's art . . . ?   35
ORGON. Be still, you monster.
    [*To* TARTUFFE]   Brother, I pray you, rise.
    [*To* DAMIS] Villain!
DAMIS.   But . . .
ORGON.   Silence!
DAMIS.   Can't you realize . . . ?
ORGON. Just one word more, and I'll tear you limb from limb.
TARTUFFE. In God's name, Brother, don't be harsh with him.   40
    I'd rather far be tortured at the stake
    Than see him bear one scratch for my poor sake.
ORGON. [*To* DAMIS] Ingrate!
TARTUFFE   If I must beg you, on bended knee,
    To pardon him . . .
ORGON. [*Falling to his knees, addressing Tartuffe*]
             Such goodness cannot be!
    [*To* DAMIS] Now, *there's* true charity!
DAMIS.   What, you . . . ?
ORGON. Villain, be still!   45
    I know your motives; I know you wish him ill:
    Yes, all of you—wife, children, servants, all—
    Conspire against him and desire his fall,
    Employing every shameful trick you can
    To alienate me from this saintly man.   50
    Ah, but the more you seek to drive him away,
    The more I'll do to keep him. Without delay,
    I'll spite this household and confound its pride
    By giving him my daughter as his bride.
DAMIS. You're going to force her to accept his hand?   55
ORGON. Yes, and this very night, d'you understand?
    I shall defy you all, and make it clear
    That I'm the one who gives the orders here.
    Come, wretch, kneel down and clasp his blessed feet,
    And ask his pardon for your black deceit.   60
DAMIS. I ask that swindler's pardon? Why, I'd rather . . .
ORGON. So! You insult him, and defy your father!
    A stick! A stick! [*To* TARTUFFE] No, no—release me, do.
    [*To* DAMIS.] Out of my house this minute! Be off with you,
    And never dare set foot in it again.   65
DAMIS. Well, I shall go, but . . .
ORGON.   Well, go quickly, then.
    I disinherit you; an empty purse
    Is all you'll get from me—except my curse!

SCENE 7. *Orgon, Tartuffe*

ORGON. How he blasphemed your goodness! What a son!
TARTUFFE. Forgive him, Lord, as I've already done.
  [*To* ORGON] You can't know how it hurts when someone tries
  To blacken me in my dear Brother's eyes.
ORGON. Ahh!
TARTUFFE.   The mere thought of such ingratitude   5
  Plunges my soul into so dark a mood . . .
  Such horror grips my heart . . . I gasp for breath,
  And cannot speak, and feel myself near death.
ORGON. [*He runs, in tears, to the door through which he has just
      driven his son.*]
  You blackguard! Why did I spare you? Why did I not
  Break you in little pieces on the spot?   10
  Compose yourself, and don't be hurt, dear friend.
TARTUFFE. These scenes, these dreadful quarrels, have got to end.
  I've much upset your household, and I perceive
  That the best thing will be for me to leave.
ORGON. What are you saying!
TARTUFFE.   They're all against me here;
  They'd have you think me false and insincere.   15
ORGON. Ah, what of that? Have I ceased believing in you?
TARTUFFE. Their adverse talk will certainly continue,
  And charges which you now repudiate
  You may find credible at a later date.   20
ORGON. No, Brother, never.
TARTUFFE.   Brother, a wife can sway
  Her husband's mind in many a subtle way.
ORGON. No, no.
TARTUFFE.   To leave at once is the solution;
  Thus only can I end their persecution.
ORGON. No, no, I'll not allow it; you shall remain.   25
TARTUFFE. Ah, well; 'twill mean much martyrdom and pain,
  But if you wish it . . .
ORGON.   Ah!
TARTUFFE.   Enough; so be it.
  But one thing must be settled, as I see it.
  For your dear honor, and for our friendship's sake,
  There's one precaution I feel bound to take.   30
  I shall avoid your wife, and keep away . . . .
ORGON. No, you shall not, whatever they may say.
  It pleases me to vex them, and for spite
  I'd have them see you with her day and night.
  What's more, I'm going to drive them to despair   35

By making you my only son and heir;
This very day, I'll give to you alone
Clear deed and title to everything I own.
A dear, good friend and son-in-law-to-be
Is more than wife, or child, or kin to me.   40
Will you accept my offer, dearest son?
TARTUFFE. In all things, let the will of Heaven be done.
ORGON. Poor fellow! Come, we'll go draw up the deed.
Then let them burst with disappointed greed!

Act IV

SCENE 1. *Cleante, Tartuffe*

CLEANTE. Yes, all the town's discussing it, and truly,
Their comments do not flatter you unduly.
I'm glad we've met, Sir, and I'll give my view
Of this sad matter in a word or two.
As for who's guilty, that I shan't discuss;   5
Let's say it was Damis who caused the fuss;
Assuming, then, that you have been ill-used
By young Damis, and groundlessly accused,
Ought not a Christian to forgive, and ought
He not to stifle every vengeful thought?   10
Should you stand by and watch a father make
His only son an exile for your sake?
Again I tell you frankly, be advised:
The whole town, high and low, is scandalized;
This quarrel must be mended, and my advice is   15
Not to push matters to a further crisis.
No, sacrifice your wrath to God above,
And help Damis regain his father's love.
TARTUFFE. Alas, for my part I should take great joy
In doing so. I've nothing against the boy.   20
I pardon all, I harbor no resentment;
To serve him would afford me much contentment.
But Heaven's interest will not have it so:
If he comes back, then I shall have to go.
After his conduct—so extreme, so vicious—   25
Our further intercourse would look suspicious.
God knows what people would think! Why, they'd describe
My goodness to him as a sort of bribe;
They'd say that out of guilt I made pretense
Of loving-kindness and benevolence—   30
That, fearing my accuser's tongue, I strove

To buy his silence with a show of love.
CLEANTE. Your reasoning is badly warped and stretched,
   And these excuses, Sir, are most far-fetched.
   Why put yourself in charge of Heaven's cause?   35
   Does Heaven need our help to enforce its laws?
   Leave vengeance to the Lord Sir; while we live,
   Our duty's not to punish, but forgive;
   And what the Lord commands, we should obey
   Without regard to what the world may say.   40
   What! Shall the fear of being misunderstood
   Prevent our doing what is right and good?
   No, no: let's simply do what Heaven ordains,
   And let no other thoughts perplex our brains.
TARTUFFE. Again, Sir, let me say that I've forgiven   45
   Damis, and thus obeyed the laws of Heaven;
   But I am not commanded by the Bible
   To live with one who smears my name with libel.
CLEANTE. Were you commanded, Sir, to indulge the whim
   Of poor Orgon, and to encourage him   50
   In suddenly transferring to your name
   A large estate to which you have no claim?
TARTUFFE. 'Twould never occur to those who know me best
   To think I acted from self-interest.
   The treasures of this world I quite despise;   55
   Their specious glitter does not charm my eyes;
   And if I have resigned myself to taking
   The gift which my dear Brother insists on making,
   I do so only, as he well understands,
   Lest so much wealth fall into wicked hands,   60
   Lest those to whom it might descend in time
   Turn it to purposes of sin and crime,
   And not, as I shall do, make use of it
   For Heaven's glory and mankind's benefit.
CLEANTE. Forget these trumped-up fears. Your argument   65
   Is one the rightful heir might well resent;
   It *is* a moral burden to inherit
   Such wealth, but give Damis a chance to bear it.
   And would it not be worse to be accused
   Of swindling, than to see that wealth misused?   70
   I'm shocked that you allowed Orgon to broach
   This matter, and that you feel no self-reproach;
   Does true religion teach that lawful heirs
   May freely be deprived of what is theirs?
   And if the Lord has told you in your heart   75
   That you and young Damis must dwell apart,

Would it not be the decent thing to beat
A generous and honorable retreat,
Rather than let the son of the house be sent,
For your convenience, into banishment?   80
Sir, if you wish to prove the honesty
Of your intentions . . .
TARTUFFE.   Sir, it is a half past three.
I've certain pious duties to attend to,
And hope my prompt departure won't offend you.
CLEANTE. [*Alone*] Damn.

SCENE 2. *Elmire, Mariane, Cleante, Dorine*

DORINE. Stay, Sir, and help Mariane, for Heaven's sake!
She's suffering so, I fear her heart will break.
Her father's plan to marry her off tonight
Has put the poor child in a desperate plight.
I hear him coming. Let's stand together, now,   5
And see if we can't change his mind, somehow,
About this match we all deplore and fear.

SCENE 3. *Orgon, Elmire, Mariane, Cleante, Dorine*

ORGON. Hah! Glad to find you all assembled here.
[*To* MARIANE] This contract, child, contains your happiness,
And what it says I think your heart can guess.
MARIANE. [*Falling to her knees*]
Sir, by that Heaven which sees me here distressed,
And by whatever else can move your breast,   5
Do not employ a father's power, I pray you,
To crush my heart and force it to obey you,
Nor by your harsh commands oppress me so
That I'll begrudge the duty which I owe—
And do not so embitter and enslave me   10
That I shall hate the very life you gave me.
If my sweet hopes must perish, if you refuse
To give me to the one I've dared to choose,
Spare me at least—I beg you, I implore—
The pain of wedding one whom I abhor;   15
And do not, by a heartless use of force,
Drive me to contemplate some desperate course.
ORGON. [*Feeling himself touched by her*]
Be firm, my soul. No human weakness, now.
MARIANE. I don't resent your love for him. Allow
Your heart free rein, Sir; give him your property,   20
And if that's not enough, take mine from me;
He's welcome to my money; take it, do,

But don't, I pray, include my person too.
Spare me, I beg you; and let me end the tale
Of my sad days behind a convent veil.   25
ORGON. A convent! Hah! When crossed in their amours,
All lovesick girls have the same thought as yours.
Get up! The more you loathe the man, and dread him,
The more ennobling it will be to wed him.
Marry Tartuffe, and mortify your flesh!   30
Enough; don't start that whimpering afresh.
DORINE. But why . . . ?
ORGON.   Be still, there. Speak when you're spoken to.
Not one more bit of impudence out of you.
CLEANTE. If I may offer a word of counsel here . . .
ORGON. Brother, in counselling you have no peer;   35
All your advice is forceful, sound, and clever;
I don't propose to follow it, however.
ELMIRE. [*To* ORGON] I am amazed, and don't know what to say;
Your blindness simply takes my breath away.
You are indeed bewitched, to take no warning   40
From our account of what occurred this morning.
ORGON. Madam, I know a few plain facts, and one
Is that you're partial to my rascal son;
Hence, when he sought to make Tartuffe the victim
Of a base lie, you dared not contradict him.   45
Ah, but you underplayed your part, my pet;
You should have looked more angry, more upset.
ELMIRE. When men make overtures, must we reply
With righteous anger and a battle-cry?
Must we turn back their amorous advances   50
With sharp reproaches and with fiery glances?
Myself, I find such offers merely amusing,
And make no scenes and fusses in refusing;
My taste is for good-natured rectitude,
And I dislike the savage sort of prude   55
Who guards her virtue with her teeth and claws,
And tears men's eyes out for the slightest cause:
The Lord preserve me from such honor as that,
Which bites and scratches like an alley-cat!
I've found that a polite and cool rebuff   60
Discourages a lover quite enough.
ORGON. I know the facts, and I shall not be shaken.
ELMIRE. I marvel at your power to be mistaken.
Would it, I wonder, carry weight with you
If I could *show* you that our tale was true?   65
ORGON. Show me?

ELMIRE.   Yes.

ORGON.   Rot.

ELMIRE.   Come, what if I found a way
To make you see the facts as plain as day?

ORGON. Nonsense.

ELMIRE.   Do answer me; don't be absurd.
I'm not now asking you to trust our word.
Suppose that from some hiding-place in here   70
You learned the whole sad truth by eye and ear—
What would you say of your good friend, after that?

ORGON. Why, I'd say . . . nothing, by Jehoshaphat!
It can't be true.

ELMIRE.   You've been too long deceived,
And I'm quite tired of being disbelieved.   75
Come now: let's put my statements to the test,
And you shall see the truth made manifest.

ORGON. I'll take that challenge. Now do your uttermost.
We'll see how you make good your empty boast.

ELMIRE. [*To* DORINE] Send him to me.

DORINE.   He's crafty; it may be hard
To catch the cunning scoundrel off his guard.   80

ELMIRE. No, amorous men are gullible. Their conceit
So blinds them that they're never hard to cheat.
Have him come down. [*To* CLEANTE *&* MARIANE] Please leave us,
for a bit.

SCENE 4. *Elmire, Orgon*

ELMIRE. Pull up this table, and get under it.

ORGON. What?

ELMIRE.   It's essential that you be well-hidden.

ORGON. Why there?

ELMIRE.   Oh, Heavens! Just do as you are bidden.
I have my plans; we'll soon see how they fare.
Under the table, now; and once you're there,   5
Take care that you are neither seen nor heard.

ORGON. Well, I'll indulge you, since I gave my word
To see you through this infantile charade.

ELMIRE. Once it is over, you'll be glad we played.
[*To her husband, who is now under the table*]
I'm going to act quite strangely, now, and you   10
Must not be shocked at anything I do.
Whatever I may say, you must excuse
As part of that deceit I'm forced to use.
I shall employ sweet speeches in the task
Of making that impostor drop his mask;   15

I'll give encouragement to his bold desires,
And furnish fuel to his amorous fires.
Since it's for your sake, and for his destruction,
That I shall seem to yield to his seduction,
I'll gladly stop whenever you decide   20
That all your doubts are fully satisfied.
I'll count on you, as soon as you have seen
What sort of man he is, to intervene,
And not expose me to his odious lust
One moment longer than you feel you must.   25
Remember: you're to save me from my plight
Whenever . . . He's coming! Hush! Keep out of sight!

SCENE 5. *Tartuffe, Elmire, Orgon*

TARTUFFE. You wish to have a word with me, I'm told.
ELMIRE. Yes, I've a little secret to unfold.
Before I speak, however, it would be wise
To close that door, and look about for spies.
    [TARTUFFE *goes to the door, closes it, and returns.*]
The very last thing that must happen now   5
Is a repetition of this morning's row.
I've never been so badly caught off guard.
Oh, how I feared for you! You saw how hard
I tried to make that troublesome Damis
Control his dreadful temper, and hold his peace.   10
In my confusion, I didn't have the sense
Simply to contradict his evidence;
But as it happened, that was for the best,
And all has worked out in our interest.
This storm has only bettered your position;   15
My husband doesn't have the least suspicion,
And now, in mockery of those who do,
He bids me be continually with you.
And that is why, quite fearless of reproof,
I now can be alone with my Tartuffe,   20
And why my heart—perhaps too quick to yield—
Feels free to let its passion be revealed.
TARTUFFE. Madam, your words confuse me. Not long ago,
You spoke in quite a different style, you know.
ELMIRE. Ah, Sir, if that refusal made you smart,   25
It's little that you know of woman's heart,
Or what that heart is trying to convey
When it resists in such a feeble way!
Always, at first, our modesty prevents
The frank avowal of tender sentiments: 30

However high the passion which inflames us,
Still, to confess its power somehow shames us.
Thus we reluct, at first, yet in a tone
Which tells you that our heart is overthrown,
That what our lips deny, our pulse confesses,   35
And that, in time, all noes will turn to yesses.
I fear my words are all too frank and free,
And a poor proof of woman's modesty;
But since I'm started, tell me, if you will——
Would I have tried to make Damis be still,   40
Would I have listened, calm and unoffended,
Until your lengthy offer of love was ended,
And been so very mild in my reaction,
Had your sweet words not given me satisfaction?
And when I tried to force you to undo   45
The marriage-plans my husband has in view,
What did my urgent pleading signify
If not that I admired you, and that I
Deplored the thought that someone else might own
Part of a heart I wished for mine alone?   50
TARTUFFE. Madam, no happiness is so complete
As when, from lips we love, come words so sweet;
Their nectar floods my every sense, and drains
In honeyed rivulets through all my veins.
To please you is my joy, my only goal;   55
Your love is the restorer of my soul;
And yet I must beg leave, now, to confess
Some lingering doubts as to my happiness.
Might this not be a trick? Might not the catch
Be that you wish me to break off the match   60
With Mariane, and so have feigned to love me?
I shan't quite trust your fond opinion of me
Until the feelings you've expressed so sweetly
Are demonstrated somewhat more concretely,
And you have shown, by certain kind concessions,   65
That I may put my faith in your professions.
ELMIRE. [*She coughs, to warn her husband.*] Why be in such a
     hurry? Must my heart
Exhaust its bounty at the very start?
To make that sweet admission cost me dear,
But you'll not be content, it would appear,   70
Unless my store of favors is disbursed
To the last farthing, and at the very first.
TARTUFFE. The less we merit, the less we dare to hope,
And with our doubts, mere words can never cope.

We trust no promised bliss till we receive it;   75
  Not till a joy is ours can we believe it.
  I, who so little merit your esteem,
  Can't credit this fulfillment of my dream,
  And shan't believe it, Madam, until I savor
  Some palpable assurance of your favor.   80
ELMIRE. My, how tyrannical your love can be,
  And how it flusters and perplexes me!
  How furiously you take one's heart in hand,
  And make your every wish a fierce command!
  Come, must you hound and harry me to death?   85
  Will you not give me time to catch my breath?
  Can it be right to press me with such force,
  Give me no quarter, show me no remorse,
  And take advantage, by your stern insistence,
  Of the fond feelings which weaken my resistance?   90
TARTUFFE. Well, if you look with favor upon my love,
  Why, then, begrudge me some clear proof thereof?
ELMIRE. But how can I consent without offense
  To Heaven, toward which you feel such reverence?
TARTUFFE. If Heaven is all that holds you back, don't worry.   95
  I can remove that hindrance in a hurry.
  Nothing of that sort need obstruct our path.
ELMIRE. Must one not be afraid of Heaven's wrath?
TARTUFFE. Madam, forget such fears, and be my pupil,
  And I shall teach you how to conquer scruple.   100
  Some joys, it's true, are wrong in Heaven's eyes;
  Yet Heaven is not averse to compromise;
  There is a science, lately formulated,
  Whereby one's conscience may be liberated,
  And any wrongful act you care to mention   105
  May be redeemed by purity of intention.
  I'll teach you, Madam, the secrets of that science;
  Meanwhile, just place on me your full reliance.
  Assuage my keen desires, and feel no dread:
  The sin, if any, shall be on my head.   110
        [ELMIRE *coughs, this time more loudly.*]
  You've a bad cough.
ELMIRE.   Yes, yes. It's bad indeed.
TARTUFFE. [*Producing a little paper bag*]
  A bit of licorice may be what you need.
ELMIRE. No, I've a stubborn cold, it seems. I'm sure it
  Will take much more than licorice to cure it.

---

104. *Whereby ... liberated:* Molière appended his own footnote to this line: "It
is a scoundrel who speaks."

TARTUFFE. How aggravating.

ELMIRE.   Oh, more than I can say.   115

TARTUFFE. If you're still troubled, think of things this way:
  No one shall know our joys, save us alone,
  And there's no evil till the act is known;
  It's scandal, Madam, which makes it an offense,
  And it's no sin to sin in confidence.   120

ELMIRE. [*Having coughed once more*]
  Well, clearly I must do as you require,
  And yield to your importunate desire.
  It is apparent, now, that nothing less
  Will satisfy you, and so I acquiesce.
  To go so far is much against my will;   125
  I'm vexed that it should come to this; but still,
  Since you are so determined on it, since you
  Will not allow mere language to convince you,
  And since you ask for concrete evidence, I
  See nothing for it, now, but to comply.   130
  If this is sinful, if I'm wrong to do it,
  So much the worse for him who drove me to it.
  The fault can surely not be charged to me.

TARTUFFE. Madam, the fault is mine, if fault there be,
  And . . .

ELMIRE.   Open the door a little, and peek out;   135
  I wouldn't want my husband poking about.

TARTUFFE. Why worry about the man? Each day he grows
  More gullible; one can lead him by the nose.
  To find us here would fill him with delight,
  And if he saw the worst, he'd doubt his sight.   140

ELMIRE. Nevertheless, do step out for a minute
  Into the hall, and see that no one's in it.

SCENE 6. *Orgon, Elmire*

ORGON. [*Coming out from under the table*]
  That man's a perfect monster, I must admit!
  I'm simply stunned. I can't get over it.

ELMIRE. What, coming out so soon? How premature!
  Get back in hiding, and wait until you're sure.
  Stay till the end, and be convinced completely;   5
  We mustn't stop till things are proved concretely.

ORGON. Hell never harbored anything so vicious!

ELMIRE. Tut, don't be hasty. Try to be judicious.
  Wait, and be certain that there's no mistake.
  No jumping to conclusions, for Heaven's sake!   10
    [*She places* ORGON *behind her, as* TARTUFFE *re-enters.*]

SCENE 7. *Tartuffe, Elmire, Orgon*

TARTUFFE. [*Not seeing* ORGON]
  Madam, all things have worked out to perfection;
  I've given the neighboring rooms a full inspection;
  No one's about; and now I may at last . . .
ORGON. [*Intercepting him*] Hold on, my passionate fellow, **not so**
  fast!
  I should advise a little more restraint.   5
  Well, so you thought you'd fool me, my dear saint!
  How soon you wearied of the saintly life—
  Wedding my daughter, and coveting my wife!
  I've long suspected you, and had a feeling
  That soon I'd catch you at your double-dealing.   10
  Just now, you've given me evidence galore;
  It's quite enough; I have no wish for more.
ELMIRE. [*To* TARTUFFE] I'm sorry to have treated you so slyly,
  But circumstances forced me to be wily.
TARTUFFE. Brother, you can't think . . .
ORGON.   No more talk from you;
  Just leave this household, without more ado.   15
TARTUFFE. What I intended . . .
ORGON.   That seems fairly clear.
  Spare me your falsehoods and get out of here.
TARTUFFE. No, I'm the master, and you're the one to go!
  This house belongs to me, I'll have you know,   20
  And I shall show you that you can't hurt *me*
  By this contemptible conspiracy,
  That those who cross me know not what they do,
  And that I've means to expose and punish you,
  Avenge offended Heaven, and make you grieve   25
  That ever you dared order me to leave.

SCENE 8. *Elmire, Orgon*

ELMIRE. What was the point of all that angry chatter?
ORGON. Dear God, I'm worried. This is no laughing matter.
ELMIRE. How so?
ORGON.   I fear I understood his drift.
  I'm much disturbed about that deed of gift.
ELMIRE. You gave him . . . ?
ORGON.   Yes, it's all been drawn and signed.
  But one thing more is weighing on my mind.   6
ELMIRE. What's that?
ORGON.   I'll tell you; but first let's see if there's
  A certain strong-box in his room upstairs.

Act V

CLEANTE. Where are you going so fast?
ORGON.   God knows!
CLEANTE.   Then wait;
   Let's have a conference, and deliberate
   On how this situation's to be met.
ORGON. That strong-box has me utterly upset;
   This is the worst of many, many shocks.   5
CLEANTE. Is there some fearful mystery in that box?
ORGON. My poor friend Argas brought that box to me
   With his own hands, in utmost secrecy;
   'Twas on the very morning of his flight.
   It's full of papers which, if they came to light,   10
   Would ruin him—or such is my impression.
CLEANTE. Then why did you let it out of your possession?
ORGON. Those papers vexed my conscience, and it seemed best
   To ask the counsel of my pious guest.
   The cunning scoundrel got me to agree   15
   To leave the strong-box in his custody,
   So that, in case of an investigation,
   I could employ a slight equivocation
   And swear I didn't have it, and thereby,
   At no expense to conscience, tell a lie.   20
CLEANTE. It looks to me as if you're out on a limb.
   Trusting him with that box, and offering him
   That deed of gift, were actions of a kind
   Which scarcely indicate a prudent mind.
   With two such weapons, he has the upper hand,   25
   And since you're vulnerable, as matters stand,
   You erred once more in bringing him to bay.
   You should have acted in some subtler way.
ORGON. Just think of it: behind that fervent face,
   A heart so wicked, and a soul so base!   30
   I took him in, a hungry beggar, and then . . .
   Enough, by God! I'm through with pious men:
   Henceforth I'll hate the whole false brotherhood,
   And persecute them worse than Satan could.
CLEANTE. Ah, there you go—extravagant as ever!   35
   Why can you not be rational? You never
   Manage to take the middle course, it seems,
   But jump, instead, between absurd extremes.
   You've recognized your recent grave mistake

In falling victim to a pious fake;   40
Now, to correct that error, must you embrace
An even greater error in its place,
And judge our worthy neighbors as a whole
By what you've learned of one corrupted soul?
Come, just because one rascal made you swallow   45
A show of zeal which turned out to be hollow,
Shall you conclude that all men are deceivers,
And that, today, there are no true believers?
Let atheists make that foolish inference;
Learn to distinguish virtue from pretense,   50
Be cautious in bestowing admiration,
And cultivate a sober moderation.
Don't humor fraud, but also don't asperse
True piety; the latter fault is worse,
And it is best to err, if err one must,   55
As you have done, upon the side of trust.

SCENE 2. *Damis, Orgon, Cléante*

DAMIS. Father, I hear that scoundrel's uttered threats
Against you; that he pridefully forgets
How, in his need, he was befriended by you,
And means to use your gifts to crucify you.
ORGON. It's true, my boy. I'm too distressed for tears.   5
DAMIS. Leave it to me, Sir; let me trim his ears.
Faced with such insolence, we must not waver.
I shall rejoice in doing you the favor
Of cutting short his life, and your distress.
CLEANTE. What a display of young hotheadedness!   10
Do learn to moderate your fits of rage.
In this just kingdom, this enlightened age,
One does not settle things by violence.

SCENE 3. *Madame Pernelle, Mariane, Elmire, Dorine, Damis,*
Orgon, Cléante

MADAME PERNELLE. I hear strange tales of very strange events.
ORGON. Yes, strange events which these two eyes beheld.
The man's ingratitude is unparalleled.
I save a wretched pauper from starvation,
House him, and treat him like a blood relation,   5
Shower him every day with my largesse,
Give him my daughter, and all that I possess;
And meanwhile the unconscionable knave
Tries to induce my wife to misbehave;
And not content with such extreme rascality,   10

Now threatens me with my own liberality,
And aims, by taking base advantage of
The gifts I gave him out of Christian love,
To drive me from my house, a ruined man,
And make me end a pauper, as he began.   15
DORINE. Poor fellow!
MADAME PERNELLE.   No, my son, I'll never bring
Myself to think him guilty of such a thing.
ORGON. How's that?
MADAME PERNELLE.   The righteous always were maligned.
ORGON. Speak clearly, Mother. Say what's on your mind.
MADAME PERNELLE. I mean that I can smell a rat, my dear.
You know how everybody hates him, here.   20
ORGON. That has no bearing on the case at all.
MADAME PERNELLE. I told you a hundred times, when you were
    small,
That virtue in this world is hated ever;
Malicious men may die, but malice never.   25
ORGON. No doubt that's true, but how does it apply?
MADAME PERNELLE. They've turned you against him by a clever lie.
ORGON. I've told you, I was there and saw it done.
MADAME PERNELLE. Ah, slanderers will stop at nothing, Son.
ORGON. Mother, I'll lose my temper . . . For the last time,   30
I tell you I was witness to the crime.
MADAME PERNELLE. The tongues of spite are busy night and noon,
And to their venom no man is immune.
ORGON. You're talking nonsense. Can't you realize
I saw it; saw it; saw it with my eyes?   35
Saw, do you understand me? Must I shout it
Into your ears before you'll cease to doubt it?
MADAME PERNELLE. Appearances can deceive, my son. Dear me,
We cannot always judge by what we see.
ORGON. Drat! Drat!
MADAME PERNELLE.   One often interprets things awry;   40
Good can seem evil to a suspicious eye.
ORGON. Was I to see his pawing at Elmire
As an act of charity?
MADAME PERNELLE.   Till his guilt is clear,
A man deserves the benefit of the doubt.
You should have waited, to see how things turned out.   45
ORGON. Great God in Heaven, what more proof did I need?
Was I to sit there, watching, until he'd . . .
You drive me to the brink of impropriety.
MADAME PERNELLE. No, no, a man of such surpassing piety

Could not do such a thing. You cannot shake me. 50
I don't believe it, and you shall not make me.
ORGON. You vex me so that, if you weren't my mother,
I'd say to you . . . some dreadful thing or other.
DORINE. It's your turn now, Sir, not to be listened to;
You'd not trust us, and now she won't trust you. 55
CLEANTE. My friends, we're wasting time which should be spent
In facing up to our predicament.
I fear that scoundrel's threats weren't made in sport.
DAMIS. Do you think he'd have the nerve to go to court?
ELMIRE. I'm sure he won't: they'd find it all too crude 60
A case of swindling and ingratitude.
CLEANTE. Don't be too sure. He won't be at a loss
To give his claims a high and righteous gloss;
And clever rogues with far less valid cause
Have trapped their victims in a web of laws. 65
I say again that to antagonize
A man so strongly armed was most unwise.
ORGON. I know it; but the man's appalling cheek
Outraged me so, I couldn't control my pique.
CLEANTE. I wish to Heaven that we could devise 70
Some truce between you, or some compromise.
ELMIRE. If I had known what cards he held, I'd not
Have roused his anger by my little plot.
ORGON. [*To* DORINE, *as* M. LOYAL *enters*] What is that fellow
looking for? Who is he?
Go talk to him—and tell him that I'm busy. 75

SCENE 4. *Monsieur Loyal, Madame Pernelle, Orgon, Damis,*
Mariane, Dorine, Elmire, Cléante

MONSIEUR LOYAL. Good day, dear sister. Kindly let me see
Your master.
DORINE.   He's involved with company,
And cannot be disturbed just now, I fear.
MONSIEUR LOYAL. I hate to intrude; but what has brought me here
Will not disturb your master, in any event. 5
Indeed, my news will make him most content.
DORINE. Your name?
MONSIEUR LOYAL.   Just say that I bring greetings from
Monsieur Tartuffe, on whose behalf I've come.
DORINE. [*To* ORGON] Sir, he's a very gracious man, and bears
A message from Tartuffe, which, he declares, 10
Will make you most content.

CLEANTE.   Upon my word,
  I think this man had best be seen, and heard.
ORGON. Perhaps he has some settlement to suggest.
  How shall I treat him? What manner would be best?
CLEANTE. Control your anger, and if he should mention   15
  Some fair adjustment, give him your full attention.
MONSIEUR LOYAL. Good health to you, good Sir. May Heaven con-
    found
  Your enemies, and may your joys abound.
ORGON. [*Aside, to* CLEANTE] A gentle salutation: it confirms
  My guess that he is here to offer terms.   20
MONSIEUR LOYAL. I've always held your family most dear;
  I served your father, Sir, for many a year.
ORGON. Sir, I must ask your pardon; to my shame,
  I cannot now recall your face or name.
MONSIEUR LOYAL. Loyal's my name; I come from Normandy,   25
  And I'm a bailiff, in all modesty.
  For forty years, praise God, it's been my boast
  To serve with honor in that vital post,
  And I am here, Sir, if you will permit
  The liberty, to serve you with this writ . . .   30
ORGON. To—*what?*
MONSIEUR LOYAL.   Now, please, Sir, let us have no friction:
  It's nothing but an order of eviction.
  You are to move your goods and family out
  And make way for new occupants, without
  Deferment or delay, and give the keys . . .   35
ORGON. I? Leave this house?
MONSIEUR LOYAL.   Why yes, Sir, if you please.
  This house, Sir, from the cellar to the roof,
  Belongs now to the good Monsieur Tartuffe,
  And he is lord and master of your estate
  By virtue of a deed of present date,   40
  Drawn in due form, with clearest legal phrasing . . .
DAMIS. Your insolence is utterly amazing!
MONSIEUR LOYAL. Young man, my business here is not with you,
  But with your wise and temperate father, who,
  Like every worthy citizen, stands in awe   45
  Of justice, and would never obstruct the law.
ORGON. But . . .
MONSIEUR LOYAL. Not for a million, Sir, would you rebel
  Against authority; I know that well.
  You'll not make trouble, Sir, or interfere
  With the execution of my duties here.   50
DAMIS. Someone may execute a smart tattoo

On that black jacket of yours, before you're through.

MONSIEUR LOYAL. Sir, bid your son be silent. I'd much regret
Having to mention such a nasty threat
Of violence, in writing my report.   55

DORINE. [*Aside*] This man Loyal's a most disloyal sort!

MONSIEUR LOYAL. I love all men of upright character,
And when I agreed to serve these papers, Sir,
It was your feelings that I had in mind.
I couldn't bear to see the case assigned   60
To someone else, who might esteem you less
And so subject you to unpleasantness.

ORGON. What's more unpleasant than telling a man to leave
His house and home?

MONSIEUR LOYAL.   You'd like a short reprieve?
If you desire it, Sir, I shall not press you,   65
But wait until tomorrow to dispossess you.
Splendid. I'll come and spend the night here, then,
Most quietly, with half a score of men.
For form's sake, you might bring me, just before
You go to bed, the keys to the front door.   70
My men, I promise, will be on their best
Behavior, and will not disturb your rest.
But bright and early, Sir, you must be quick
And move out all your furniture, every stick:
The men I've chosen are both young and strong,   75
And with their help it shouldn't take you long.
In short, I'll make things pleasant and convenient,
And since I'm being so extremely lenient,
Please show me, Sir, a like consideration,
And give me your entire cooperation.   80

ORGON. [*Aside*] I may be all but bankrupt, but I vow
I'd give a hundred louis, here and now,
Just for the pleasure of landing one good clout
Right on the end of that complacent snout.

CLEANTE. Careful; don't make things worse.

DAMIS.   My bootsole itches
To give that beggar a good kick in the breeches.   85

DORINE. Monsieur Loyal, I'd love to hear the whack
Of a stout stick across your fine broad back.

MONSIEUR LOYAL. Take care: a woman too may go to jail if
She uses threatening language to a bailiff.   90

CLEANTE. Enough, enough, Sir. This must not go on.
Give me that paper, please, and then begone.

---

52. *black jacket:* in the original, *just-*
aucorps à longues basques, a close-fitting,
long black coat with skirts, the customary dress of a bailiff.

MONSIEUR LOYAL. Well, *au revoir*. God give you all good cheer!
ORGON. May God confound you, and him who sent you here!

SCENE 5. *Orgon, Cléante, Mariane, Elmire, Madame Pernelle,*
Dorine, Damis

ORGON. Now, Mother, was I right or not? This writ
  Should change your notion of Tartuffe a bit.
  Do you perceive his villainy at last?
MADAME PERNELLE. I'm thunderstruck. I'm utterly aghast.
DORINE. Oh, come, be fair. You mustn't take offense   5
  At this new proof of his benevolence.
  He's acting out of selfless love, I know.
  Material things enslave the soul, and so
  He kindly has arranged your liberation
  From all that might endanger your salvation.   10
ORGON. Will you not ever hold your tongue, you dunce?
CLEANTE. Come, you must take some action, and at once.
ELMIRE. Go tell the world of the low trick he's tried.
  The deed of gift is surely nullified
  By such behavior, and public rage will not   15
  Permit the wretch to carry out his plot.

SCENE 6. *Valère, Orgon, Cléante, Elmire, Mariane, Madame*
Pernelle, Damis, Dorine

VALERE. Sir, though I hate to bring you more bad news,
  Such is the danger that I cannot choose.
  A friend who is extremely close to me
  And knows my interest in your family
  Has, for my sake, presumed to violate   5
  The secrecy that's due to things of state,
  And sends me word that you are in a plight
  From which your one salvation lies in flight.
  That scoundrel who's imposed upon you so
  Denounced you to the King an hour ago   10
  And, as supporting evidence, displayed
  The strong-box of a certain renegade
  Whose secret papers, so he testified,
  You had disloyally agreed to hide.
  I don't know just what charges may be pressed,   15
  But there's a warrant out for your arrest;
  Tartuffe has been instructed, furthermore,
  To guide the arresting officer to your door.
CLEANTE. He's clearly done this to facilitate
  His seizure of your house and your estate.   20

ORGON. That man, I must say, is a vicious beast!
VALERE. You can't afford to delay, Sir, in the least.
  My carriage is outside, to take you hence;
  This thousand louis should cover all expense.
  Let's lose no time, or you shall be undone;   25
  The sole defense, in this case, is to run.
  I shall go with you all the way, and place you
  In a safe refuge to which they'll never trace you.
ORGON. Alas, dear boy, I wish that I could show you
  My gratitude for everything I owe you.   30
  But now is not the time; I pray the Lord
  That I may live to give you your reward.
  Farewell, my dears; be careful . . .
CLEANTE.   Brother, hurry.
  We shall take care of things; you needn't worry.

SCENE 7. *The Officer, Tartuffe, Valère, Orgon, Elmire, Mariane,*
    Madame Pernelle, Dorine, Cléante, Damis

TARTUFFE. Gently, Sir, Gently; stay right where you are.
  No need for haste; your lodging isn't far.
  You're off to prison, by order of the Prince.
ORGON. This is the crowning blow, you wretch; and since
  It means my total ruin and defeat,   5
  Your villainy is now at last complete.
TARTUFFE. You needn't try to provoke me; it's no use.
  Those who serve Heaven must expect abuse.
CLEANTE. You are indeed most patient, sweet, and blameless.
DORINE. How he exploits the name of Heaven! It's shameless.   10
TARTUFFE. Your taunts and mockeries are all for naught;
  To do my duty is my only thought.
MARIANE. Your love of duty is most meritorious,
  And what you've done is little short of glorious.
TARTUFFE. All deeds are glorious, Madam, which obey   15
  The sovereign prince who sent me here today.
ORGON. I rescued you when you were destitute;
  Have you forgotten that, you thankless brute?
TARTUFFE. No, no, I well remember everything;
  But my first duty is to serve my King.   20
  That obligation is so paramount
  That other claims, beside it, do not count;
  And for it I would sacrifice my wife,
  My family, my friend, or my own life.
ELMIRE. Hypocrite!
DORINE.   All that we most revere, he uses   25
  To cloak his plots and camouflage his ruses.

CLEANTE. If it is true that you are animated
  By pure and loyal zeal, as you have stated,
  Why was this zeal not roused until you'd sought
  To make Orgon a cuckold, and been caught?   30
  Why weren't you moved to give your evidence
  Until your outraged host had driven you hence?
  I shan't say that the gift of all his treasure
  Ought to have damped your zeal in any measure;
  But if he is a traitor, as you declare,   35
  How could you condescend to be his heir?
TARTUFFE. [*To the* OFFICER] Sir, spare me all this clamor; it's growing shrill.
  Please carry out your orders, if you will.
OFFICER. Yes, I've delayed too long, Sir. Thank you kindly.
  You're just the proper person to remind me.   40
  Come, you are off to join the other boarders
  In the King's prison, according to his orders.
TARTUFFE. Who? I, Sir?
OFFICER.   Yes.
TARTUFFE.   To prison? This can't be true!
OFFICER. I owe an explanation, but not to you.
  [*To* ORGON] Sir, all is well; rest easy, and be grateful.   45
  We serve a Prince to whom all sham is hateful,
  A Prince who sees into our inmost hearts,
  And can't be fooled by any trickster's arts.
  His royal soul, though generous and human,
  Views all things with discernment and acumen;   50
  His sovereign reason is not lightly swayed,
  And all his judgments are discreetly weighed.
  He honors righteous men of every kind,
  And yet his zeal for virtue is not blind,
  Nor does his love of piety numb his wits   55
  And make him tolerant of hypocrites.
  'Twas hardly likely that this man could cozen
  A King who's foiled such liars by the dozen.
  With one keen glance, the King perceived the whole
  Perverseness and corruption of his soul,   60
  And thus high Heaven's justice was displayed:
  Betraying you, the rogue stood self-betrayed.
  The King soon recognized Tartuffe as one
  Notorious by another name, who'd done
  So many vicious crimes that one could fill   65

---

39. *police officer:* in the original, *un exempt.* He would actually have been a gentleman from the king's personal body- guard with the rank of lieutenant-colonel or "master of the camp."

Ten volumes with them, and be writing still.
But to be brief: our sovereign was appalled
By this man's treachery toward you, which he called
The last, worst villainy of a vile career,
And bade me follow the impostor here   70
To see how gross his impudence could be,
And force him to restore your property.
Your private papers, by the King's command,
I hereby seize and give into your hand.
The King, by royal order, invalidates   75
The deed which gave this rascal your estates,
And pardons, furthermore, your grave offense
In harboring an exile's documents.
By these decrees, our Prince rewards you for
Your loyal deeds in the late civil war,   80
And shows how heartfelt is his satisfaction
In recompensing any worthy action,
How much he prizes merit, and how he makes
More of men's virtues than of their mistakes.
DORINE. Heaven be praised!
MADAME PERNELLE.   I breathe again, at last.   85
ELMIRE. We're safe.
MARIANE.   I can't believe the danger's past.
ORGON. [*To* TARTUFFE]. Well, traitor, now you see ...
CLEANTE. Ah, brother, please,
    Let's not descend to such indignities.
    Leave the poor wretch to his unhappy fate,
    And don't say anything to aggravate   90
    His present woes; but rather hope that he
    Will soon embrace an honest piety,
    And mend his ways, and by a true repentance
    Move our just King to moderate his sentence.
    Meanwhile, go kneel before your sovereign's throne   95
    And thank him for the mercies he has shown.
ORGON. Well said: let's go at once and, gladly kneeling,
    Express the gratitude which all are feeling.
    Then, when that first great duty has been done,
    We'll turn with pleasure to a second one,   100
    And give Valère, whose love has proven so true,
    The wedded happiness which is his due.

---

80. *late civil war:* a reference to Orgon's role in supporting the king during the
Fronde (see note 11, p. 32).

JEAN RACINE
(1639–1699)
Phaedra (Phèdre) *

Preface †

Behold another tragedy whose theme is borrowed from Euripides! Although I have followed a rather different path than did this author for the course of the action, I have not failed to embellish my play with everything that seemed to me to be striking in his. While I took from him only the simple idea of the character of Phaedra, I might say that I owe to him perhaps the most logical elements of his stagecraft. I am not at all surprised that this character has had such a happy success since the days of Euripides, and that moreover it has been so successful in our own century, since the character has all the qualities required by Aristotle for the tragic hero that are proper for the raising of pity and terror. In all truth, Phaedra is neither completely guilty nor completely innocent. She is plunged by her fate, and by the anger of the gods, into an illegitimate passion for which she feels horror from the very start. She makes every attempt to surmount it. . . .

I have even taken care to make her a little less repellent than she is in classical tragedy, where she herself resolves to accuse Hippolytus. I believed that calumny was too low and too black to put in the mouth of a princess who otherwise showed such noble and virtuous feelings. This baseness seemed to me more fitting for a nurse, who could possess more servile inclinations, and who nevertheless only delivered this false accusation to save the life and honor of her mistress. . . .

Hippolytus, in Euripides and in Seneca, is accused of having in effect seduced his stepmother. . . . But here he is merely accused of planning to do it. I wished to spare Theseus a confusion in his character which might have made him less appealing to the audience.

Concerning the character of Hippolytus, I have noticed that among the Ancients Euripides was blamed for representing him as a philosopher free from any imperfection. The result was that the

* First produced in 1677; the original title, *Phèdre et Hippolyte*, was later shortened to *Phèdre*. Reprinted from *Phaedra & Figaro* by Robert Lowell, by permission of Farrar, Straus & Company, Inc. Copyright © 1960, 1961 by Robert Lowell, copyright © 1961 by Farrar, Straus & Cudahy, Inc. The original play was written in rhymed Alexandrine couplets. Mr. Lowell says the following about his own version: "My meter, with important differences, is based on Dryden and Pope. In his heroic plays, Dryden uses an end-stopped couplet, loaded with inversions, heavily alliterated, and varied by short unrhymed lines. My couplet is run on, avoids inversions and alliteration, and loosens its rhythm with shifted accents and occasional extra syllables. . . ."

† From the Preface published with the first edition in March, 1677. Translated by Howard E. Hugo.

death of the young prince caused more indignation than pity. I thought I should give him some weakness which would make him slightly culpable in his relations with his father, without however, robbing him of the magnanimity with which he spares Phaedra's honor, and let himself be charged without implicating her. I term "weakness" that passion that he bears for Aricia, in spite of himself: she who is the daughter and the sister of his father's mortal enemies. . . .

To conclude, I do not yet dare state that this play is my best tragedy. . . . What I can affirm is that I have never written one where virtue is brought more to light than in this. The slightest errors are severely punished here. The mere idea of crime is regarded with as much horror as the crime itself. . . . Passions are only revealed to the eyes to show all the disorder that they cause; and vice here is painted in colors so that one may recognize it and hate its hideousness. . . . This is what the first tragic poets always maintained. Their theater was a school where virtue was no less well taught than in the schools of philosophy. . . .

Characters

THESEUS (THÉSÉE), *son of Ægeus and king of Athens*

PHAEDRA (PHÈDRE), *wife of Theseus and daughter of Minos and Pasiphaë*

HIPPOLYTUS (HIPPOLYTE), *son of Theseus and Antiope, queen of the Amazons*

THERAMENES (THÉRAMÈNE), *tu-*

tor of Theseus

ARICIA (ARICIE), *princess of the blood royal of Athens*

OENONE, *Phaedra's nurse and confidante*

ISMENE (ISMENE), *Aricia's confidante*

PANOPE, *Phaedra's lady in waiting*

GUARDS

The SCENE *is laid at Troezen, a town in the Peloponnesus, on the south shore of the Saronic Gulf, opposite Athens.*

Act 1

SCENE I. *Hippolytus, Theramenes*

HIPPOLYTUS. No, no, my friend, we're off! Six months have passed since Father heard the ocean howl and cast
his galley on the Aegean's skull-white froth.
Listen! The blank sea calls us—off, off, off!
I'll follow Father to the fountainhead   5
and marsh of hell. We're off. Alive or dead,
I'll find him.

THERAMENES.   Where, my lord? I've sent a host of veteran seamen up and down the coast:

each village, creek and cove from here to Crete
has been ransacked and questioned by my fleet;   10
my flagship skirted Hades' rapids, furled
sail there a day, and scoured the underworld.
Have you fresh news? New hopes? One even doubts
if noble Theseus wants his whereabouts
discovered. Does he need helpers to share   15
the plunder of his latest love affair;
a shipload of spectators and his son
to watch him ruin his last Amazon—
some creature, taller than a man, whose tanned
and single bosom slithers from his hand,   20
when he leaps to crush her like a waterfall
of honeysuckle?

HIPPOLYTUS.   You are cynical,
my friend. Your insinuations wrong a king,
sick as myself of his philandering.
His heart is Phaedra's and no rivals dare   25
to challenge Phaedra's sole possession there.
I sail to find my father. The command
of duty calls me from this stifling land.

THERAMENES. This stifling land? Is that how you deride
this gentle province where you used to ride   30
the bridle-paths, pursuing happiness?
You cured your orphaned childhood's loneliness
and found a peace here you preferred to all
the blaze of Athens' brawling protocol.
A rage for exploits blinds you. Your disease is boredom.   35

HIPPOLYTUS. Friend, this kingdom lost its peace,
when Father left my mother for defiled
bull-serviced Pasiphaë's child. The child
of homicidal Minos is our queen!

THERAMENES. Yes, Phaedra reigns and rules here. I have seen   40
you crouch before her outbursts like a cur.
When she first met you, she refused to stir
until your father drove you out of court.
The news is better now; our friends report
the queen is dying. Will you cross the seas,   45
desert your party and abandon Greece?

11. *Hades' rapids:* The river Acheron
in Epirus was thought to flow into the
Underworld.
18. *Amazon:* that tribe of Greek
women who spent their time in warfare
and hunting.
20. *single bosom:* a reference to the
legend that the Amazons cut off the
right breast in order to draw their bows
further.
45. *queen:* i.e., Phaedra, daughter of
Minos of Crete and of Pasiphaë, sister to
Circe. Enamored of a white bull sent by
Poseidon, Pasiphaë consequently gave
birth to the Minotaur, the Cretan monster later slain by Theseus. Thus Phaedra
was half-sister to the Minotaur.

Why flee from Phaedra? Phaedra fears the night
less than she fears the day that strives to light.
the universal ennui of her eye—
this dying woman, who desires to die!   50
HIPPOLYTUS. No, I despise her Cretan vanity,
hysteria and idle cruelty.
I fear Aricia; she alone survives
the blood-feud that destroyed her brothers' lives.
THERAMENES. Prince, Prince, forgive my laughter. Must you fly 55
beyond the limits of the world and die,
floating in flotsam, friendless, far from help,
and clubbed to death by Tartars in the kelp?
Why arm the shrinking violet with a knife?
Do you hate Aricia, and fear for your life,   60
Prince?
HIPPOLYTUS. If I hated her, I'd trust myself and stay.
THERAMENES. Shall I explain you to yourself?
Prince, you have ceased to be that hard-mouthed, proud
and pure Hippolytus, who scorned the crowd
of common lovers once and rose above   65
your wayward father by despising love.
Now you justify your father, and you feel
love's poison running through you, now you kneel
and breathe the heavy incense, and a god
possesses you and revels in your blood!   70
Are you in love?
HIPPOLYTUS.   Theramenes, when I call
and cry for help, you push me to the wall.
Why do you plague me, and try to make me fear
the qualities you taught me to revere?
I sucked in prudence with my mother's milk.   75
Antiope, no harlot draped in silk,
first hardened me. I was my mother's son
and not my father's. When the Amazon,
my mother, was dethroned, my mind approved
her lessons more than ever. I still loved   80
her bristling chastity. Later, you told
stories about my father's deeds that made me hold

53-54. *survives . . . lives:* According to one legend, Aegeus, father of Theseus, was the adopted son of Pandion. Pallas, Pandion's second son, had in turn fifty sons. These were the Pallantids and all brothers to Aricia; Theseus killed them because they threatened his own kingship of Athens.

76. *Antiope:* an Amazon, and sister to Hippolyta, the queen of the Amazons.

Antiope was beloved by Theseus, who carried her off to Athens. The Amazons then invaded Attica (Athens) in an effort to recover Antiope, but they were defeated in battle and Hippolyta lost her life. Antiope's son by Theseus was Hippolytus.

81. *chastity:* The Amazons were traditionally scornful of love.

back judgment—how he stood for Hercules,
a second Hercules who cleared the Cretan seas
of pirates, throttled Scirron, Cercyon,   85
Procrustes, Sinnis, and the giant man
of Epidaurus writhing in his gore.
He pierced the maze and killed the Minotaur.
Other things turned my stomach: that long list
of women, all refusing to resist.   90
Helen, caught up with all her honeyed flesh
from Sparta; Periboea, young and fresh,
already tired of Salinis. A hundred more,
their names forgotten by my father—whore
and virgin, child and mother, all deceived,   95
if their protestations can be believed!
Ariadne declaiming to the rocks,
her sister, Phaedra, kidnapped. Phaedra locks
the gate at last! You know how often I
would weary, fall to nodding and deny   100
the possiblity of hearing the whole
ignoble, dull, insipid boast unroll.
And now I too must fall. The gods have made me creep.
How can I be in love? I have no specious heap
of honors, friend. No mastered monsters drape   105
my shoulders—Theseus' excuse to rape
at will. Suppose I chose a woman. Why
choose an orphan? Aricia is eternally
cut off from marriage, lest she breed
successors to her fierce brothers, and seed   110
the land with treason. Father only grants
her life on one condition. This—he wants
no bridal torch to burn for her. Unwooed
and childless, she must answer for the blood
her brothers shed. How can I marry her,   115
gaily subvert our kingdom's character,
and sail on the high seas of love?

THERAMENES.   You'll prove
nothing by reason, for you are in love.
Theseus' injustice to Aricia throws
her in the light; your eyes he wished to close   120

---

91. *Helen:* famed as the most beautiful of women, daughter of Zeus and
Leda, sister of Castor and Pollux, later
the wife of Menelaus of Sparta. When
still a young girl, she was abducted by
Theseus and Pirithoüs (king of the La-
piths in Thessaly). Her brothers rescued
her and brought her back home to Leda
and Leda's husband, Tyndareus.

92. *Periboea:* mother of Ajax.
93. *Salinis:* Salamis, island in the
Gulf of Aegina on the eastern shore of
Greece, off which the Greeks later defeated the Persians in a naval battle, 480
B.C.
97. *Ariadne:* Phaedra's sister, deserted by Theseus after she rescued him
from the Minotaur.

are open. She dazzles you. Her pitiful
seclusion makes her doubly terrible.
Does this innocent passion freeze your blood?
There's sweetness in it. Is your only good
the dismal famine of your chastity?   125
You shun your father's path? Where would you be,
Prince, if Antiope had never burned
chastely for Theseus? Love, my lord, has turned
the head of Hercules, and thousands—fired
the forge of Vulcan! All your uninspired,   130
cold moralizing is nothing, Prince. You have changed!
Now no one sees you riding, half-deranged
along the sand-bars, where you drove your horse
and foaming chariot with all your force,
tilting and staggering upright through the surf—   135
far from their usual course across the turf.
The woods are quiet . . . How your eyes hang down!
You often murmur and forget to frown.
All's out, Prince. You're in love; you burn. Flames, flames,
Prince! A dissimulated sickness maims   140
The youthful quickness of your daring. Does
lovely Aricia haunt you?

HIPPOLYTUS.   Friend, spare us.
I sail to find my father.

THERAMENES.   Will you see.
Phaedra before you go?

HIPPOLYTUS.   I mean to be
here when she comes. Go, tell her. I will do   145
my duty. Wait, I see her nurse. What new
troubles torment her?

SCENE II. *Hippolytus, Theramenes, Oenone*

OENONE.   Who has griefs like mine,
my lord? I cannot help the queen in her decline.
Although I sit beside her day and night,
she shuts her eyes and withers in my sight.   150
An eternal tumult roisters through her head,
panics her sleep, and drags her from her bed.
Just now she fled me at the prime
of day to see the sun for the last time.
She's coming.

HIPPOLYTUS.   So! I'll steal away. My flight   155
removes a hateful object from her sight.

127. *Antiope:* Hippolytus' mother.

SCENE III. *Phaedra, Oenone*

PHAEDRA. Dearest, we'll go no further. I must rest.
I'll sit here. My emotions shake my breast,
the sunlight throws black bars across my eyes.
My knees give. If I fall, why should I rise,   160
Nurse?

OENONE.   Heaven help us! Let me comfort you.

PHAEDRA. Tear off these gross, official rings, undo
these royal veils. They drag me to the ground.
Why have you frilled me, laced me, crowned me, and wound
my hair in turrets? All your skill torments   165
and chokes me. I am crushed by ornaments.
Everything hurts me, and drags me to my knees!

OENONE. Now this, now that, Madam. You never cease
commanding us, then cancelling your commands.
You feel your strength return, summon all hands   170
to dress you like a bride, then say you choke!
We open all the windows, fetch a cloak,
rush you outdoors. It's no use, you decide
that sunlight kills you, and only want to hide.

PHAEDRA. I feel the heavens' royal radiance cool   175
and fail, as if it feared my terrible
shame has destroyed its right to shine on men.
I'll never look upon the sun again.

OENONE. Renunciation or renunciation!
Now you slander the source of your creation.   180
Why do you run to death and tear your hair?

PHAEDRA. Oh God, take me to some sunless forest lair . . .
There hoof-beats raise a dust-cloud, and my eye
follows a horseman outlined on the sky!

OENONE. What's this, my lady?

PHAEDRA.   I have lost my mind.   185
Where am I? Oh forget my words! I find
I've lost the habit now of talking sense.
My face is red and guilty—evidence
of treason! I've betrayed my darkest fears,
Nurse, and my eyes, despite me, fill with tears.   190

OENONE. Lady, if you must weep, weep for your silence
that filled your days and mine with violence.
Ah deaf to argument and numb to care,
you have no mercy. Spare me, spare
yourself. Your blood is like polluted water,   195

---

178. *sun:* i.e., Helios, the sun-god,   184. *horseman:* Phaedra is thinking of
father of Pasiphaë, Phaedra's mother.   Hippolytus.

fouling a mind desiring its own slaughter.
The sun has died and shadows filled the skies
thrice now, since you have closed your eyes;
the day has broken through the night's content
thrice now, since you have tasted nourishment. 200
Is your salvation from your terrified
conscience this passive, servile suicide?
Lady, your madness harms the gods who gave
you life, betrays your husband. Who will save
your children? Your downfall will orphan them, 205
deprive them of their kingdom, and condemn
their lives and future to the discipline
of one who abhors you and all your kin,
a tyrant suckled by an amazon,
Hippolytus . . .

PHAEDRA.　　　　　Oh God!

OENONE.　　　　　　　　　You still hate someone; 210
thank heaven for that, Madam!

PHAEDRA.　　　　　　　　　You spoke his name!

OENONE. Hippolytus, Hippolytus! There's hope
in hatred, Lady. Give your anger rope.
I love your anger. If the winds of love
and fury stir you, you will live. Above 215
your children towers this foreigner, this child
of Scythian cannibals, now wild
to ruin the kingdom, master Greece, and choke
the children of the gods beneath his yoke.
Why dawdle? Why deliberate at length? 220
Oh, gather up your dissipated strength.

PHAEDRA. I've lived too long.

OENONE.　　　　　　　Always, always agonized!
Is your conscience still stunned and paralyzed?
Do you think you have washed your hands in blood?

PHAEDRA. Thank God, my hands are clean still. Would to God 225
my heart were innocent!

OENONE.　　　　　　　Your heart, your heart!
What have you done that tears your soul apart?

PHAEDRA. I've said too much. Oenone, let me die;
by dying I shall escape blasphemy.

OENONE. Search for another hand to close your eyes. 230
Oh cruel Queen, I see that you despise
my sorrow and devotion. I'll die first,

---

205. *children:* Phaedra's sons, Acamas
and Demophöon.
217. *Scythian cannibals:* Scythia, the
home of the Amazons, was for the ancient Greeks associated with barbarians.

and end the anguish of this service cursed
by your perversity. A thousand roads
always lie open to the killing gods.   235
I'll choose the nearest. Lady, tell me how
Oenone's love has failed you. Will you allow
your nurse to die, your nurse, who gave up all—
nation, parents, children, to serve in thrall.
I saved you from your mother, King Minos' wife!   240
Will your death pay me for giving up my life?
PHAEDRA. What I could tell you, I have told you. Nurse,
only my silence saves me from the curse
of heaven.
OENONE.   How could you tell me anything
worse than watching you dying?
PHAEDRA.   I would bring   245
my life and rank dishonor. What can I say
to save myself, or put off death a day.
OENONE. Ah Lady, I implore you by my tears
and by your suffering body. Heaven hears,
and knows the truth already. Let me see.   250
PHAEDRA. Stand up.
OENONE.   Your hesitation's killing me!
PHAEDRA. What can I tell you? How the gods reprove me!
OENONE. Speak!
PHAEDRA.   On Venus, murdering Venus! love
gored Pasiphaë with the bull.
OENONE.   Forget
your mother! When she died, she paid her debt.   255
PHAEDRA. Oh Ariadne, oh my Sister, lost
for love of Theseus on that rocky coast.
OENONE. Lady, what nervous languor makes you rave
against your family; they are in the grave.
PHAEDRA. Remorseless Aphrodite drives me. I,   260
my race's last and worst love-victim, die.
OENONE. Are you in love?
PHAEDRA.   I am insane with love!
OENONE.   Who is he?
PHAEDRA. I'll tell you. Nothing love can do could
equal . . . Nurse, I am in love. The shame
kills me. I love the . . . Do not ask his name.   265
OENONE. Who?
PHAEDRA.   Nurse, you know my old loathing for the son
of Theseus and the barbarous amazon?

257. *rocky coast:* Theseus abandoned   southern coast of Greece in the Aegean
Ariadne on the island of Naxos, off the   Sea.

OENONE. Hippolytus! My God, oh my God!

PHAEDRA.   You,
  not I, have named him.

OENONE.   What can you do,
  but die? Your words have turned my blood to ice.   270
  Oh righteous heavens, must the blasphemies
  of Pasiphaë fall upon her daughter?
  Her Furies strike us down across the water.
  Why did we come here?

PHAEDRA. My evil comes from farther off. In May,   275
  in brilliant Athens, on my marriage day,
  I turned aside for shelter from the smile
  of Theseus. Death was frowning in an aisle—
  Hippolytus! I saw his face, turned white!
  My lost and dazzled eyes saw only night,   280
  capricious burnings flickered through my bleak
  abandoned flesh. I could not breathe or speak
  I faced my flaming executioner,
  Aphrodite, my mother's murderer!
  I tried to calm her wrath by flowers and praise,   285
  I built her a temple, fretted months and days
  on decoration. I even hoped to find
  symbols and stays for my distracted mind,
  searching the guts of sacrificial steers.
  Yet when my erring passions, mutineers   290
  to virtue, offered incense at the shrine
  of love, I failed to silence the malign
  Goddess, Alas, my hungry open mouth,
  thirsting with adoration, tasted drouth—
  Venus resigned her altar to my new lord—   295
  and even while I was praying, I adored
  Hippolytus above the sacred flame,
  now offered to his name I could not name.
  I fled him, yet he stormed me in disguise,
  and seemed to watch me from his father's eyes.   300
  I even turned against myself, screwed up
  my slack courage to fury, and would not stop
  shrieking and raging, till half-dead with love
  and the hatred of a stepmother, I drove
  Hippolytus in exile from the rest   305
  and strenuous wardship of his father's breast.
  Then I could breathe, Oenone; he was gone;
  my lazy, nerveless days meandered on
  through dreams and daydreams, like a stately carriage
  touring the level landscape of my marriage.   310

Yet nothing worked. My husband sent me here
to Troezen, far from Athens; once again the dear
face shattered me; I saw Hippolytus
each day, and felt my ancient, venomous
passion tear my body limb from limb;   315
naked Venus was clawing down her victim.
What could I do? Each moment, terrified
by loose diseased emotions, now I cried
for death to save my glory and expel
my gloomy frenzy from this world, my hell.   320
And yet your tears and words bewildered me,
and so endangered my tranquillity,
at last I spoke. Nurse, I shall not repent,
if you will leave me the passive content
of dry silence and solitude.   325

SCENE IV. *Phaedra, Oenone, Panope*

PANOPE. My heart breaks. Would to God, I could refuse
to tell your majesty my evil news.
The King is dead! Listen, the heavens ring
with shouts and lamentations for the King.
PHAEDRA. The King is dead? What's this?
PANOPE.   In vain   330
you beg the gods to send him back again.
Hippolytus has heard the true report,
he is already heading for the port.
PHAEDRA. Oh God!
PANOPE.   They've heard in Athens. Everyone
is joining factions—some salute your son,   335
others are calling for Hippolytus;
they want him to reform and harden us—
even Aricia claims the loyalty
of a fanatical minority.
The Prince's captains have recalled their men.   340
His flag is up and now he sails again
for Athens. Queen, if he appear there now,
he'll drag the people with him!
OENONE.   Stop, allow
the Queen a little respite for her grief.
She hears you, and will act for our relief.   345

SCENE V. *Phaedra, Oenone*

OENONE. I'd given up persuading you to live;
death was your refuge, only death could give

What sights I've seen, Ismene! "Heads will roll,"
my brothers told me, "we will rule." I, the sole
survivor of those fabulous kings, who tilled
the soil of Greece, have seen my brothers killed, 55
six brothers murdered! In a single hour,
the tyrant, Theseus, lopped them in their flower.
The monster spared my life, and yet decreed
the torments of this childless life I lead
in exile, where no Greek can look on me; 60
my forced, perpetual virginity
preserves his crown; no son shall bear my name
or blow my brothers' ashes into flame.
Ismene, you know how well his tyranny
favors my temperament and strengthens me 65
to guard the honor of my reputation;
his rigor fortified my inclination.
How could I test his son's civilities?
I'd never even seen him with my eyes!
I'd never seen him. I'd restrained my eye, 70
that giddy nerve, from dwelling thoughtlessly
upon his outward grace and beauty—on mere
embellishments of nature, a veneer
the Prince himself despises and ignores.
My heart loves nobler virtues, and adores 75
in him his father's hard intelligence.
He has his father's daring and a sense
of honor his father lacks. Let me confess,
I love him for his lofty haughtiness
never submitted to a woman's yoke. 80
How could Phaedra's splendid marriage provoke
my jealousy? Have I so little pride,
I'd snatch at a rake's heart, a heart denied
to none—all riddled, opened up to let
thousands pass in like water through a net? 85
To carry sorrows to a heart, alone
untouched by passion, inflexible as stone,
to fasten my dominion on a force
as nervous as a never-harnessed horse—
this stirs me, this enflames me. Devilish Zeus 90
is easier mastered than Hippolytus;
heaven's love-infatuated emperor
confers less glory on his conqueror!
Ismene, I'm afraid. Why should I boast?
His very virtues I admire most 95
threaten to rise and throw me from the brink

of hope. What girlish folly made me think
Hippolytus could love Aricia?

ISMENE.   Here
    he is. He loves you, Princess. Have no fear.

SCENE II. *Aricia, Ismene, Hippolytus*

HIPPOLYTUS. Princess, before   100
    I leave here, I must tell you what's in store
    for you in Greece. Alas, my father's dead.
    The fierce forebodings that disquieted
    my peace are true. Death, only death, could hide
    his valor from this world he pacified.   105
    The homicidal Fates will not release
    the comrade, friend and peer of Hercules.
    Princess, I trust your hate will not resent
    honors whose justice is self-evident.
    A single hope alleviates my grief,   110
    Princess, I hope to offer you relief.
    I now revoke a law whose cruelty
    has pained my conscience. Princess, you are **free**
    to marry. Oh enjoy this province, whose
    honest, unhesitating subjects choose   115
    Hippolytus for king. Live free as air,
    here, free as I am, much more free!

ARICIA.   I dare
    not hope. You are too gracious. Can you free
    Aricia from your father's stern decree?

HIPPOLYTUS. Princess, the Athenian people, torn in two   120
    between myself and Phaedra's son, want you.

ARICIA. Want me, my Lord!

HIPPOLYTUS.   I've no illusions. Lame
    Athenian precedents condemn my claim,
    because my mother was a foreigner.
    But what is that? If my only rival were   125
    my younger brother, his minority
    would clear my legal disability.
    However, a better claim than his or mine
    now favors you, ennobled by the line
    of great Erectheus. Your direct descent   130
    sets you before my father; he was only lent

---

124. *foreigner:* In Euripides' time, Athenian law made the son of an Athenian and a non-Greek woman illegitimate. Hippolytus' mother was Antiope the Amazon. Yet in Racine, and in Euripides, it is not made clear why Phaedra's childen do not suffer from the same liability.

130. *Erectheus:* son of Hephaestus and Gaea, brought up secretly by Athene in her temple. He subsequently became king of Athens, where he introduced her cult.

this kingdom by adoption. Once the common
Athenian, dazed by Theseus' superhuman
energies, had no longing to exhume
the rights that rushed your brothers to their doom.   135
Now Athens calls you home; the ancient feud
too long has stained the sacred olive wood;
blood festers in the furrows of our soil
to blight its fruits and scorch the farmer's toil.
This province suits me; let the vines of Crete   140
offer my brother a secure retreat.
The rest is yours. All Attica is yours;
I go to win you what your right assures.

ARICIA. Am I awake, my lord? Your sayings seem
like weird phantasmagoria in a dream.   145
How can your sparkling promises be true?
Some god, my lord, some god, has entered you!
How justly you are worshiped in this town;
oh how the truth surpasses your renown!
You wish to endow me with your heritage!   150
I only hoped you would not hate me. This rage
your father felt, how can you put it by
and treat me kindly?

HIPPOLYTUS.   Princess, is my eye
blind to beauty? Am I a bear, a bull, a boar,
some abortion fathered by the Minotaur?   155
Some one-eyed Cyclops, able to resist
Aricia's loveliness and still exist?
How can a man stand up against your grace?

ARICIA. My lord, my lord!

HIPPOLYTUS.   I cannot hide my face,
Princess! I'm driven. Why does my violence   160
so silence reason and intelligence?
Must I be still, and let my adoration
simmer away in silent resignation?
Princess, I've lost all power to restrain
myself. You see a madman, whose insane   165
pride hated love, and hoped to sit ashore,
watching the galleys founder in the war;
I was Diana's liegeman, dressed in steel.
I hoped to trample love beneath my heel—

---

156. *Cyclops:* one-eyed giants possessing vast strength, generally thought by
the Greeks to dwell in Sicily, where they
lived in a lawless and cannibalistic
fashion.

168-170. *Diana's liegeman ... flaming*

Venus: In the original play by Euripides,
even more is made of Hippolytus worshipping Artemis (Diana), to the exclusion of Aphrodite (Venus), and the
latter goddess' jealousy brings about his
destruction.

alas, the flaming Venus burns me down,   170
I am the last dependent on her crown.
What left me charred and writhing in her clutch?
A single moment and a single touch.
Six months now, bounding like a wounded stag,
I've tried to shake this poisoned dart, and drag   175
myself to safety from your eyes that blind
when present, and when absent leave behind
volleys of burning arrows in my mind.
Ah Princess, shall I dive into the sea,
or steal the wings of Icarus to flee   180
love's Midas' touch that turns my world to gold?
Your image drives me stumbling through the cold,
floods my deserted forest caves with light,
darkens the day and dazzles through my night.
I'm grafted to your side by all I see;   185
all things unite us and imprison me.
I have no courage for the Spartan exercise
that trained my hand and steeled my energies.
Where are my horses? I forget their names.
My triumphs with my chariot at the games   190
no longer give me strength to mount a horse.
The ocean drives me shuddering from its shores.
Does such a savage conquest make you blush?
My boorish gestures, headlong cries that rush
at you like formless monsters from the sea?   195
Ah, Princess, hear me! Your serenity
must pardon the distortions of a weak
and new-born lover, forced by you to speak
love's foreign language, words that snarl and yelp . . .
I never could have spoken without your help.   200

SCENE III. *Aricia, Ismene, Hippolytus, Theramenes*

THERAMENES. I announce the Queen. She comes hurriedly,
     looking for you.
HIPPOLYTUS.   For me!
THERAMENES. Don't ask me why;
     she insisted. I promised I'd prevail
     on you to speak with her before you sail.   205
HIPPOLYTUS. What can she want to hear? What can I say?

---

180. *Icarus:* son of Daedalus. With his
father he escaped from Minos of Crete
by means of wings made from feathers
and wax. Despite Daedalus' warnings,
Icarus flew too high; the sun melted the
wax, and he fell into the sea.
     181. *Midas:* King of Phrygia, to whom
the god Dionysus granted the wish that
all he touched might be changed to gold.

ARICIA. Wait for her, here! You cannot turn away.
Forget her malice. Hating her will serve
no purpose. Wait for her! Her tears deserve
your pity.
HIPPOLYTUS.   You're going, Princess? And I must go   210
to Athens, far from you. How shall I know
if you accept my love.
ARICIA.   My lord, pursue
your gracious promise. Do what you must do,
make Athens tributary to my rule.
Nothing you offer is unacceptable;   215
yet this empire, so great, so glorious,
is the least precious of your gifts to us.

SCENE IV. *Hippolytus, Theramenes*

HIPPOLYTUS. We're ready. Wait, the Queen's here. I need you.
You must interrupt this tedious interview.
Hurry down to the ship, then rush back, pale   220
And breathless. Say the wind's up and we must sail.

SCENE V. *Hippolytus, Oenone, Phaedra*

PHAEDRA. He's here! Why does he scowl and look away
from me? What shall I do? What shall I say?
OENONE. Speak for your son, he has no other patron.
PHAEDRA. Why are you so impatient to be gone   225
from us, my lord? Stay! we will weep together.
Pity my son; he too has lost his father.
My own death's near. Rebellion, sick with wrongs,
now like a sea-beast, lifts its slimey prongs,
its muck, its jelly. You alone now stand   230
to save the state. Who else can understand
a mother? I forget. You will not hear
me! An enemy deserves no pity. I fear
your anger. Must my son, your brother, Prince,
be punished for his cruel mother's sins?   235
HIPPOLYTUS. I've no such thoughts.
PHAEDRA.   I persecuted you
blindly, and now you have good reason to
return my impudence. How could you find
the motivation of this heart and mind
that scourged and tortured you, till you began   240
to lose the calm composure of a man,
and dwindle to a harsh and sullen boy,
a thing of ice, unable to enjoy
the charms of any civilized resource

except the heavy friendship of your horse, 245
that whirled you far from women, court and throne,
to course the savage woods for wolves alone?
You have good reason, yet if pain's a measure,
no one has less deserved your stern displeasure.
My lord, no one has more deserved compassion. 250

HIPPOLYTUS. Lady, I understand a mother's passion,
a mother jealous for her children's rights.
How can she spare a first wife's son? Long nights
of plotting, devious ways of quarrelling—
a madhouse! What else can remarriage bring? 255
Another would have shown equal hostility,
pushed her advantage more outrageously.

PHAEDRA. My lord, if you had known how far my love
and yearning have exalted me above
this usual weakness . . . Our afflicting kinship 260
is ending . . .

HIPPOLYTUS.   Madame, the precious minutes slip
by, I fatigue you. Fight against your fears.
Perhaps Poseidon has listened to our tears,
perhaps your husband's still alive. He hears
us, he is surging home—only a short 265
day's cruise conceals him, as he scuds for port.

PHAEDRA. That's folly, my lord. Who has twice visited
black Hades and the river of the dead
and returned? No, the poisonous Acheron
never lets go. Theseus drifts on and on, 270
a gutted galley on that clotted waste—
he woos, he wins Persephone, the chaste . . .
What am I saying? Theseus is not dead.
He lives in you. He speaks, he's taller by a head,
I see him, touch him, and my heart—a reef . . . 275
Ah Prince, I wander. Love betrays my grief . . .

HIPPOLYTUS. No, no, my father lives. Lady, the blind
furies release him; in your loyal mind,
love's fullness holds him, and he cannot die.

PHAEDRA. I hunger for Theseus. Always in my eye 280
he wanders, not as he appeared in hell,
lascivious eulogist of any belle
he found there, from the lowest to the Queen;
no, faithful, airy, just a little mean
through virtue, charming all, yet young and new, 285
as we would paint a god—as I now see you!
Your valiant shyness would have graced his speech,

---

263. *Poseidon:* Neptune, god of the sea, son of Cronus and Rhea.

he would have had your stature, eyes, and reach,
Prince, when he flashed across our Cretan waters,
the loved enslaver of King Minos' daughters.   290
Where were you? How could he conscript the flower
of Athens' youth against my father's power,
and ignore you? You were too young, they say;
you should have voyaged as a stowaway.
No dawdling bypath would have saved our bull,   295
when your just vengeance thundered through its skull.
There, light of foot, and certain of your goal,
you would have struck my brother's monstrous soul,
and pierced our maze's slow meanders, led
by Ariadne and her subtle thread.   300
By Ariadne? Prince I would have fought
for precedence; my every flaming thought,
love-quickened, would have shot you through the dark,
straight as an arrow to your quaking mark.
Could I have waited, panting, perishing,   305
entrusting your survival to a string,
like Ariadne, when she skulked behind,
there at the portal, to bemuse her mind
among the solemn cloisters of the porch?
No, Phaedra would have snatched your burning torch,   310
and lunged before you, reeling like a priest
of Dionysus to distract the beast.
I would have reached the final corridor
a lap before you, and killed the Minotaur!
Lost in the labyrinth, and at your side,   315
would it have mattered, if I lived or died?
HIPPOLYTUS. What are you saying, Madam? You forget
my father is your husband!
PHAEDRA.   I have let
you see my grief for Theseus! How could I
forget my honor and my majesty,
Prince?
HIPPOLYTUS. Madame, forgive me! My foolish youth   320
conjectured hideous untruths from your truth.
I cannot face my insolence. Farewell . . .
PHAEDRA. You monster! You understood me too well!
Why do you hang there, speechless, petrified,
polite! My mind whirls. What have I to hide?   325
Phaedra in all her madness stands before you.
I love you! Fool, I love you, I adore you!
Do not imagine that my mind approved
my first defection, Prince, or that I loved

your youth light-heartedly, and fed my treason 330
with cowardly compliance, till I lost my reason.
I wished to hate you, but the gods corrupt
us; though I never suffered their abrupt
seductions, shattering advances, I
too bear their sensual lightnings in my thigh. 335
I too am dying. I have felt the heat
that drove my mother through the fields of Crete,
the bride of Minos, dying for the full
magnetic April thunders of the bull.
I struggled with my sickness, but I found 340
no grace or magic to preserve my sound
intelligence and honor from this lust,
plowing my body with its horny thrust.
At first I fled you, and when this fell short
of safety, Prince, I exiled you from court. 345
Alas, my violence to resist you made
my face inhuman, hateful. I was afraid
to kiss my husband lest I love his son.
I made you fear me (this was easily done);
you loathed me more, I ached for you no less. 350
Misfortune magnified your loveliness.
I grew so wrung and wasted, men mistook
me for the Sibyl. If you could bear to look
your eyes would tell you. Do you believe my passion
is voluntary? That my obscene confession 355
is some dark trick, some oily artifice?
I came to beg you not to sacrifice
my son, already uncertain of his life.
Ridiculous, mad embassy, for a wife
who loves her stepson! Prince, I only spoke 360
about myself! Avenge yourself, invoke
your father; a worse monster threatens you
than any Theseus ever fought and slew.
The wife of Theseus loves Hippolytus!
See, Prince! Look, this monster, ravenous 365
for her execution, will not flinch.
I want your sword's spasmodic final inch.
OENONE. Madam, put down this weapon. Your distress
attracts the people. Fly these witnesses.
Hurry! Stop kneeling! What a time to pray! 370

---

353. *Sibyl*: originally the daughter of Dardanus and Neso, who had prophetic powers. Later the name was used about many old women who could foretell the future. Apollo granted the Cumaean Sibyl a lifetime of a thousand years, but not lasting youth.

SCENE VI. *Theramenes, Hippolytus*

THERAMENES. Is this Phaedra, fleeing, or rather dragged away
　　sobbing? Where is your sword? Who tore
　　this empty scabbard from your belt?
HIPPOLYTUS.　　　　　　　　　　　No more!
　　Oh let me get away! I face disaster.
　　Horrors unnerve me. Help! I cannot master　　　　375
　　my terror. Phaedra . . . No, I won't expose
　　her. No! Something I do not dare disclose . . .
THERAMENES. Our ship is ready, but before you leave,
　　listen! Prince, what we never would believe
　　has happened: Athens has voted for your brother.　　380
　　The citizens have made him king. His mother
　　is regent.
HIPPOLYTUS. Phaedra is in power!
THERAMENES. An envoy sent from Athens came this hour
　　to place the scepter in her hands. Her son
　　is king.
HIPPOLYTUS. Almighty gods, you know this woman!　　385
　　Is it her spotless virtue you reward?
THERAMENES. I've heard a rumor. Someone swam aboard
　　a ship off Epirus. He claims the King
　　is still alive. I've searched. I know the thing
　　is nonsense.
HIPPOLYTUS.　　Search! Nothing must be neglected.　　390
　　If the king's dead, I'll rouse the disaffected
　　people, crown Aricia, and place our lands,
　　our people, and our lives in worthy hands.

Act 3

SCENE I. *Phaedra, Oenone*

PHAEDRA. Why do my people rush to crown me queen?
　　Who can even want to see me? They have seen
　　my downfall. Will their praise deliver me?
　　Oh bury me at the bottom of the sea!
　　Nurse, I have said too much! Led on by you,　　　5
　　I've said what no one should have listened to.
　　He listened. How could he pretend my drift
　　was hidden? Something held him, and made him shift
　　his ground . . . He only wanted to depart
　　and hide, while I was pouring out my heart.　　　10
　　Oh how his blushing multiplied my shame!
　　Why did you hold me back! You are to blame,

Oenone. But for you, I would have killed
myself. Would he have stood there, iron-willed
and merciless, while I fell upon his sword?   15
He would have snatched it, held me, and restored
my life. No! No!

OENONE.   Control yourself! No peace
comes from surrendering to your disease,
Madam. Oh daughter of the kings of Crete,
why are you weeping and fawning at the feet   20
of this barbarian, less afraid of fate
than of a woman? You must rule the state.

PHAEDRA. Can I, who have no courage to restrain
the insurrection of my passions, reign?
Will the Athenians trust their sovereignty   25
to me? Love's despotism is crushing me,
I am ruined.

OENONE.   Fly!

PHAEDRA.   How can I leave him?

OENONE. Lady, you have already banished him.
Can't you take flight?

PHAEDRA.   The time for flight has passed.
He knows me now. I rushed beyond the last   30
limits of modesty, when I confessed.
Hope was no longer blasting through my breast;
I was resigned to hopelessness and death,
and gasping out my last innocent breath,
Oenone, when you forced me back to life.   35
You thought I was no longer Theseus' wife,
and let me feel that I was free to love.

OENONE. I would have done anything to remove
your danger. Whether I'm guilty or innocent
is all the same to me. Your punishment   40
should fall on one who tried to kill you, not
on poor Oenone. Lady, you must plot
and sacrifice this monster, whose unjust
abhorence left you dying in the dust.
Oh humble him, undo him, oh despise   45
him! Lady, you must see him with my eyes.

PHAEDRA. Oenone, he was nourished in the woods;
he is all shyness and ungracious moods
because the forests left him half-inhuman.
He's never heard love spoken by a woman!   50
We've gone too far. Oenone, we're unwise;
perhaps the young man's silence was surprise.

OENONE. His mother, the amazon, was never moved
by men.

PHAEDRA.   The boy exists. She must have loved!
OENONE. He has a sullen hatred for our sex.   55
PHAEDRA. Oh, all the better; rivals will not vex
  my chances. Your advice is out of season;
  now you must serve my frenzy, not my reason!
  You tell me love has never touched his heart;
  we'll look, we'll find an undefended part.   60
  He's turned his bronze prows seaward; look, the wind
  already blows like a trumpeter behind
  his bulging canvas! The Acropolis
  of Athens and its empire shall be his!
  Hurry, Oenone, hunt the young man down,   65
  blind him with dazzling visions of the crown.
  Go tell him I relinquish my command,
  I only want the guidance of his hand.
  Let him assume these powers that weary me,
  he will instruct my son in sovereignty.   70
  Perhaps he will adopt my son, and be
  the son and mother's one divinity!
  Oenone, rush to him, use every means
  to bend and win him; if he fears the Queen's
  too proud, he'll listen to her slave. Plead, groan,   75
  insist, say I am giving him my throne . . .
  No, say I'm dying!

SCENE II. *Phaedra*

PHAEDRA.   Implacable Aphrodite, now you see
  the depths to which your tireless cruelty
  has driven Phaedra—here is my bosom;
  every thrust and arrow has struck home!   80
  Oh Goddess, if you hunger for renown,
  rise now, and shoot a worthier victim down!
  Conquer the barbarous Hippolytus,
  who mocks the graces and the power of Venus,
  and gazes on your godhead with disgust.   85
  Avenge me, Venus! See, my cause is just,
  my cause is yours. Oh bend him to my will! . . .
  You're back, Oenone? Does he hate me still?

SCENE III. *Phaedra, Oenone*

OENONE. Your love is folly, dash it from your soul,
  gather your scattered pride and self-control,   90
  Madam! I've seen the royal ship arrive.
  Theseus is back, Theseus is still alive!
  Thousands of voices thunder from the docks.
  People are waving flags and climbing rocks.

While I was looking for Hippolytus . . .   95
PHAEDRA. My husband's living! Must you trouble us
   by talking? What am I living for?
   He lives, Oenone, let me hear no more
   about it.
OENONE.   Why?
PHAEDRA.   I told you, but my fears
   were stilled, alas, and smothered by your tears.   100
   Had I died this morning, I might have faced
   the gods. I heeded you and die disgraced!
OENONE. You are disgraced!
PHAEDRA.   Oh Gods of wrath,
   how far I've travelled on my dangerous path!
   I go to meet my husband; at his side   105
   will stand Hippolytus. How shall I hide
   my thick adulterous passion for this youth,
   who has rejected me, and knows the truth?
   Will the stern Prince stand smiling and approve
   the labored histrionics of my love   110
   for Theseus, see my lips, still languishing
   for his, betray his father and his King?
   Will he not draw his sword and strike me dead?
   Suppose he spares me? What if nothing's said?
   Am I a gorgon, or Circe, or the infidel   115
   Medea, stifled by the flames of hell,
   yet rising like Aphrodite from the sea,
   refreshed and radiant with indecency?
   Can I kiss Theseus with dissembled poise?
   I think each stone and pillar has a voice.   120
   The very dust rises to disabuse
   my husband—to defame me and accuse!
   Oenone, I want to die. Death will give
   me freedom; oh it's nothing not to live;
   death to the unhappy's no catastrophe!   125
   I fear the name that must live after me,
   and crush my son until the end of time.
   Is his inheritance his mother's crime,
   his right to curse me, when my pollution stains

115-116. *gorgon* . . . *Medea:* The Gorgons were three sisters, the most famed being Medusa; they were frightful in appearance, with snakes in their hair, large mouths and irregular teeth, and flaming eyes; they were winged, and had claws. Circe, Pasiphaë's sister, was a magician who lived on the island of Aeaea. Her chief feat was changing Odysseus' men into swine. Medea, at one time beloved by Jason when he was questing for the Golden Fleece, had a notably bloodthirsty career: she strewed her brother's limbs on the sea, killed Jason's uncle by persuading his daughters to cut him up in small pieces and boil them in a cauldron, killed Jason's second wife with a poisoned bridal robe, and murdered the two children she had had by Jason.

the blood of heaven bubbling in his veins?   130
The day will come, alas, the day will come,
when nothing will be left to save him from
the voices of despair. If he should live
he'll flee his subjects like a fugitive.
OENONE. He has my pity. Who has ever built   135
firmer foundations to expose her guilt?
But why expose your son? Is your contribution
for his defense to serve the prosecution?
Suppose you kill yourself? The world will say
you fled your outraged husband in dismay.   140
Could there be stronger evidence and proof
than Phaedra crushed beneath the horse's hoof
of blasphemous self-destruction to convince
the crowds who'll dance attendance on the Prince?
The crowds will mob your children when they hear   145
their defamation by a foreigner!
Wouldn't you rather see earth bury us?
Tell me, do you still love Hippolytus?
PHAEDRA. I see him as a beast, who'd murder us.
OENONE. Madam, let the positions be reversed!   150
You fear the Prince; you must accuse him first.
Who'll dare assert your story is untrue,
if all the evidence shall speak for you:
your present grief, your past despair of mind,
the Prince's sword so luckily left behind?   155
Do you think Theseus will oppose his son's
second exile? He has consented once!
PHAEDRA. How dare I take this murderous, plunging course?
OENONE. I tremble, Lady, I too feel remorse.
If death could rescue you from infamy,   160
Madam, I too would follow you and die.
Help me by being silent. I will speak
in such a way the King will only seek
a bloodless exile to assert his rights.
A father is still a father when he smites,   165
You shudder at this evil sacrifice,
but nothing's evil or too high a price
to save your menaced honor from defeat.
Ah Minos, Minos, you defended Crete
by killing young men? Help us! If the cost   170
for saving Phaedra is a holocaust
of virtue, Minos, you must sanctify
our undertaking, or watch your daughter die.
I see the King.

PHAEDRA.   I see Hippolytus!

SCENE IV. *Phaedra, Theseus, Hippolytus, Oenone*

THESEUS. Fate's heard me, Phaedra, and removed the bar   175
   that kept me from your arms.
PHAEDRA.   Theseus, stop where you are!
   Your raptures and endearments are profane.
   Your arm must never comfort me again.
   You have been wronged, the gods who spared your life   180
   have used your absence to disgrace your wife,
   unworthy now to please you or come near.
   My only refuge is to disappear.

SCENE V. *Theseus, Hippolytus*

THESEUS. What a strange welcome! This bewilders me.
   My son, what's happened?
HIPPOLYTUS.   Phaedra holds the key.   185
   Ask Phaedra. If you love me, let me leave
   this kingdom. I'm determined to achieve
   some action that will show my strength. I fear
   Phaedra. I am afraid of living here,
THESEUS. My son, you want to leave me?
HIPPOLYTUS.   I never sought   190
   her grace or favor. Your decision brought
   her here from Athens. Your desires prevailed
   against my judgment, Father, when you sailed
   leaving Phaedra and Aricia in my care.
   I've done my duty, now I must prepare   195
   for sterner actions, I must test my skill
   on monsters far more dangerous to kill
   than any wolf or eagle in this wood.
   Release me, I too must prove my manhood.
   Oh Father, you were hardly half my age,   200
   when herds of giants writhed before your rage—
   you were already famous as the scourge
   of insolence. Our people saw you purge
   the pirates from the shores of Greece and Thrace,
   the harmless merchantman was free to race   205
   the winds, and weary Hercules could pause
   from slaughter, knowing you upheld his cause.
   The world revered you. I am still unknown;
   even my mother's deeds surpass my own.
   Some tyrants have escaped you; let me meet   210
   with them and throw their bodies at your feet.

I'll drag them from their wolf-holes; if I die,
my death will show I struggled worthily.
Oh, Father, raise me from oblivion;
my deeds shall tell the universe I am your son.   215
THESEUS. What do I see? Oh gods, what horror drives
my queen and children fleeing for their lives
before me? If so little warmth remains,
oh why did you release me from my chains?
Why am I hated, and so little loved?   220
I had a friend, just one. His folly moved
me till I aided his conspiracy
to ravish Queen Persephone.
The gods, tormented by our blasphemous
designs, befogged our minds and blinded us—   225
we invaded Epirus instead of hell.
There a diseased and subtle tyrant fell
upon us as we slept, and while I stood
by, helpless, monsters crazed for human blood
consumed Pirithoüs. I myself was chained   230
fast in a death-deep dungeon. I remained
six months there, then the gods had pity,
and put me in possession of the city.
I killed the tyrant; now his body feasts
the famished, pampered bellies of his beasts.   235
At last, I voyaged home, cast anchor, furled
my sails. When I was rushing to my world—
what am I saying? When my heart and soul
were mine again, unable to control
themselves for longing—who receives me? All run   240
and shun me, as if I were a skeleton.
Now I myself begin to feel the fear
I inspire. I wish I were a prisoner
again or dead. Speak! Phaedra says my home
was outraged. Who betrayed me? Someone come   245
and tell me. I have fought for Greece. Will Greece,
sustained by Theseus, give my enemies
asylum in my household? Tell me why
I've no avenger? Is my son a spy?
You will not answer. I must know my fate.   250
Suspicion chokes me, while I hesitate
and stand here pleading. Wait, let no one stir.
Phaedra shall tell me what has troubled her.

221. *a friend:* Pirithoüs.
226. *Epirus:* a district in western Greece, on the Ionian Sea.

SCENE VI. *Hippolytus*

HIPPOLYTUS. What now? His anger turns my blood to ice.
Will Phaedra, always uncertain, sacrifice   255
herself? What will she tell the King? How hot
the air's becoming here! I feel the rot
of love seeping like poison through this house.
I feel the pollution. I cannot rouse
my former loyalties. When I try to gather   260
the necessary strength to face my father,
my mind spins with some dark presentiment . . .
How can such terror touch the innocent?
I LOVE ARICIA! Father, I confess
my treason to you is my happiness!   265
I LOVE ARICIA! Will this bring you joy,
our love you have no power to destroy?

Act 4

SCENE I. *Theseus, Oenone*

THESEUS. What's this, you tell me he dishonors me,
and has assaulted Phaedra's chastity?
Oh heavy fortune, I no longer know
who loves me, who I am, or where I go.
Who has ever seen such disloyalty   5
after such love? Such sly audacity!
His youth made no impression on her soul,
so he fell back on force to reach his goal!
I recognize this perjured sword; I gave
him this myself to teach him to be brave!   10
Oh Zeus, are blood-ties no impediment?
Phaedra tried to save him from punishment!
Why did her silence spare this parricide?
OENONE. She hoped to spare a trusting father's pride.
She felt so sickened by your son's attempt,   15
his hot eyes leering at her with contempt,
she had no wish to live. She read out her will
to me, then lifted up her arm to kill
herself. I struck the sword out of her hand.
Fainting, she babbled the secret she had planned   20
to bury with her in the grave. My ears
unwillingly interpreted her tears.
THESEUS. Oh traitor! I know why he seemed to blanch
and toss with terror like an aspen branch
when Phaedra saw him. Now I know why he stood   25
back, then embraced me so coldly he froze my blood.

Was Athens the first stage for his obscene
attentions? Did he dare attack the Queen
before our marriage?

OENONE.   Remember her disgust
and hate then? She already feared his lust.   30

THESEUS. And when I sailed, this started up again?

OENONE. I've hidden nothing. Do you want your pain
redoubled? Phaedra calls me. Let me go,
and save her. I have told you what I know.

SCENE II. *Theseus, Hippolytus*

THESEUS. My son returns! Oh God, reserved and cool,   35
dressed in a casual freedom that could fool
the sharpest. Is it right his brows should blaze
and dazzle me with virtue's sacred rays?
Are there not signs? Should not ADULTERER
in looping scarlet script be branded there?   40

HIPPOLYTUS. What cares becloud your kingly countenance,
Father! What is this irritated glance?
Tell me! Are you afraid to trust your son?

THESEUS. How dare you stand here? May the great Zeus stone
me, if I let my fondness and your birth   45
protect you! Is my strength which rid the earth
of brigands paralysed? Am I so sick
and senile, any coward with a stick
can strike me? Am I a schoolboy's target? Oh God,
am I food for vultures? Some carrion you must prod   50
and poke to see if it's alive or dead?
Your hands are moist and itching for my bed,
Coward! Wasn't begetting you enough
dishonor to destroy me? Must I snuff
your perjured life, my own son's life, and stain   55
a thousand glories? Let the gods restrain
my fury! Fly! live hated and alone—
there are places where my name may be unknown.
Go, find them, follow your disastrous star
through filth; if I discover where you are,   60
I'll add another body to the hill
of vermin I've extinguished by my skill.
Fly from me, let the grieving storm-winds bear
your contagion from me. You corrupt the air.
I call upon Poseidon. Help me, Lord   65
of Ocean, help your servant! Once my sword
heaped crucified assassins on your shore
and let them burn like beacons. God, you swore

my first request would be fulfilled. My first!
I never made it. Even through the worst   70
torments of Epirus I held my peace;
no threat or torture brought me to my knees
beseeching favors; even then I knew
some greater project was reserved for you!
Poseidon, now I kneel. Avenge me, dash   75
my incestuous son against your rocks, and wash
his dishonor from my household; wave on wave
of roaring nothingness shall be his grave.

HIPPOLYTUS. Phaedra accuses me of lawless love!
Phaedra! My heart stops, I can hardly move   80
my lips and answer. I have no defense,
if you condemn me without evidence.

THESEUS. Oh coward, you were counting on the Queen
to hide your brutal insolence and screen
your outrage with her weakness! You forgot   85
something. You dropped your sword and spoiled your plot.
You should have kept it. Surely you had time
to kill the only witness to your crime!

HIPPOLYTUS. Why do I stand this, and forbear to clear
away these lies, and let the truth appear?   90
I could so easily. Where would you be,
if I spoke out? Respect my loyalty,
Father, respect your own intelligence.
Examine me. What am I? My defense
is my whole life. When have I wavered, when   95
have I pursued the vices of young men?
Father, you have no scaffolding to rig
your charges on. Small crimes precede the big.
Phaedra accused me of attempting rape!
Am I some Proteus, who can change his shape?   100
Nature despises such disparities.
Vice, like virtue, advances by degrees.
Bred by Antiope to manly arms,
I hate the fever of this lust that warms
the loins and rots the spirit. I was taught   105
uprightness by Theramenes. I fought
with wolves, tamed horses, gave my soul to sport,
and shunned the joys of women and the court.
I dislike praise, but those who know me best
grant me one virtue—it's that I detest   110
the very crimes of which I am accused.

100 *Proteus:* an old man of the ocean, keeper of Poseidon's seals, capable of assuming any form he wished.

How often you yourself have been amused
and puzzled by my love of purity,
pushed to the point of crudeness. By the sea
and in the forest, I have filled my heart   115
with freedom, far from women.
THESEUS.   When this part
was dropped, could only Phaedra violate
the cold abyss of your immaculate
reptilian soul. How could this funeral urn
contain a heart, a living heart, or burn   120
for any woman but my wife?
HIPPOLYTUS.   Ah no!
Father, I too have seen my passions blow
into a tempest. Why should I conceal
my true offense? I feel, Father, I feel
what other young men feel. I love, I love   125
Aricia. Father, I love the sister of
your worst enemies. I worship her!
I only feel and breathe and live for her!
THESEUS. You love Aricia? God! No, this is meant
to blind my eyes and throw me off the scent.   130
HIPPOLYTUS. Father, for six months I have done my worst
to kill this passion. You shall be the first
to know . . . You frown still. Nothing can remove
your dark obsession. Father, what will prove
my innocence? I swear by earth and sky,   135
and nature's solemn, shining majesty . . .
THESEUS. Oaths and religion are the common cant
of all betrayers. If you wish to taunt
me, find a better prop than blasphemy.
HIPPOLYTUS. All's blasphemy to eyes that cannot see.   140
Could even Phaedra bear me such ill will?
THESEUS. Phaedra, Phaedra! Name her again, I'll kill
you! My hand's already on my sword.
HIPPOLYTUS.   Explain
my terms of exile. What do you ordain?
THESEUS. Sail out across the ocean. Everywhere   145
on earth and under heaven is too near.
HIPPOLYTUS. Who'll take me in? Oh who will pity me,
and give me bread, if you abandon me?
THESEUS. You'll find fitting companions. Look for friends
who honor everything that most offends.   150
Pimps and jackals who praise adultery

---

116. *women:* In Euripides' play, much
is made of Hippolytus' allegiance to Artemis (Diana), the "queen and huntress,
chaste and fair."

and incest will protect your purity!

HIPPOLYTUS. Adultery! Is it your privilege
to fling this word in my teeth? I've reached the edge
of madness . . . No, I'll say no more. Compare   155
my breeding with Phaedra's. Think and beware . . .
She had a mother . . . No, I must not speak.

THESEUS. You devil, you'll attack the queen still weak
from your assault. How can you stand and face
your father? Must I drive you from this place   160
with my own hand. Run off, or I will flog
you with the flat of my sword like a dog!

SCENE III. *Theseus*

THESEUS. You go to your inevitable fate,
Child—by the river immortals venerate.
Poseidon gave his word. You cannot fly: 165
death and the gods march on invisibly.
I loved you once; despite your perfidy,
my bowels writhe inside me. Must you die?
Yes; I am in too deep now to draw back.
What son has placed his father on such a rack?   170
What father groans for such a monstrous birth?
Oh gods, your thunder throws me to the earth.

SCENE IV. *Theseus, Phaedra*

PHAEDRA. Theseus, I heard the deluge of your voice,
and stand here trembling. If there's time for choice,
hold back your hand, still bloodless; spare your race!   175
I supplicate you, I kneel here for grace.
Oh, Theseus, Theseus, will you drench the earth
with your own blood? His virtue, youth and birth
cry out for him. Is he already slain
by you for me—spare me this incestuous pain!   180

THESEUS. Phaedra, my son's blood has not touched my hand;
and yet I'll be avenged. On sea and land,
spirits, the swift of foot, shall track him down
Poseidon owes me this. Why do you frown?

PHAEDRA. Poseidon owes you this? What have you done   185
in anger?

THESEUS.   What! You wish to help my son?
No, stir my anger, back me to the hilt,
call for blacker colors to paint his guilt.
Lash, strike and drive me on! You cannot guess

---

164. *river:* the Styx, the chief river in   the Styx. If such an oath were broken,
Hades and sacred to the gods themselves,   the god would lie as one dead for a year.
so that their most binding oath was by

the nerve and fury of his wickedness.   190
Phaedra, he slandered your sincerity,
he told me your accusation was a lie.
He swore he loved Aricia, he wants to wed
Aricia. . . .

PHAEDRA.   What, my lord!

THESEUS.   That's what he said.
Of course, I scorn his shallow artifice.   195
Help me, Poseidon, hear me, sacrifice
my son. I seek the altar. Come! Let us both
kneel down and beg the gods to keep their oath.

SCENE V. *Phaedra*

PHAEDRA. My husband's gone, still rumbling his own name
and fame. He has no inkling of the flame   200
his words have started. If he hadn't spoken,
I might have . . . I was on my feet, I'd broken
loose from Oenone, and had just begun
to say I know not what to save his son.
Who knows how far I would have gone? Remorse,   205
longing and anguish shook me with such force,
I might have told the truth and suffered death,
before this revelation stopped my breath:
Hippolytus is not insensible,
only insensible to me! His dull   210
heart chases shadows. He is glad to rest
upon Aricia's adolescent breast!
Oh thin abstraction! When I saw his firm
repugnance spurn my passion like a worm,
I thought he had some magic to withstand   215
the lure of any woman in the land,
and now I see a schoolgirl leads the boy,
as simply as her puppy or a toy.
Was I about to perish for this sham,
this panting hypocrite? Perhaps I am   220
the only woman that he could refuse!

SCENE VI. *Phaedra, Oenone*

PHAEDRA. Oenone, dearest, have you heard the news?

OENONE. No, I know nothing, but I am afraid.
How can I follow you? You have betrayed
your life and children. What have you revealed,   225
Madam?

PHAEDRA.   I have a rival in the field,
Oenone.

OENONE.   What?

PHAEDRA.   Oenone, he's in love—
this howling monster, able to disprove
my beauty, mock my passion, scorn each prayer,
and face me like a tiger in its lair—   230
he's tamed, the beast is harnessed to a cart;
Aricia's found an entrance to his heart.
OENONE. Aricia?
PHAEDRA.   Nurse, my last calamity
has come. This is the bottom of the sea,
All that preceded this had little force—   235
the flames of lust, the horrors of remorse,
the prim refusal by my grim young master,
were only feeble hints of this disaster.
They love each other! Passion blinded me.
I let them blind me, let them meet and see   240
each other freely! Was such bounty wrong?
Oenone, you have known this all along,
you must have seen their meetings, watched them sneak
off to their forest, playing hide-and-seek!
Alas, such rendezvous are no offence: 245
innocent nature smiles of innocence,
for them each natural impulse was allowed,
each day was summer and without a cloud.
Oenone, nature hated me. I fled
its light, as if a price were on my head.   250
I shut my eyes and hungered for my end.
Death was the only God my vows could bend.
And even while my desolation served
me gall and tears, I knew I was observed;
I never had security or leisure   255
for honest weeping, but must steal this pleasure.
Oh hideous pomp; a monarch only wears
the robes of majesty to hide her tears!
OENONE. How can their folly help them? They will never
enjoy its fruit.   260
PHAEDRA.   Ugh, they will love forever—
even while I am talking, they embrace,
they scorn me, they are laughing in my face!
In the teeth of exile, I hear them swear
they will be true forever, everywhere.
Oenone, have pity on my jealous rage;   265
I'll kill this happiness that jeers at age.
I'll summon Theseus; hate shall answer hate!
I'll drive my husband to annihilate
Aricia—let no trivial punishment,

her instant death, or bloodless banishment . . . 270
What am I saying? Have I lost my mind?
I am jealous, and call my husband! Bind
me, gag me; I am frothing with desire.
My husband is alive, and I'm on fire!
For whom? Hippolytus. When I have said 275
his name, blood fills my eyes, my heart stops dead.
Imposture, incest, murder! I have passed
the limits of damnation; now at last,
my lover's lifeblood is my single good.
Nothing else cools my murderous thirst for blood. 280
Yet I live on! I live, looked down upon
by my progenitor, the sacred sun,
by Zeus, by Europa, by the universe
of gods and stars, my ancestors. They curse
their daughter. Let me die. In the great night 285
of Hades, I'll find shelter from their sight.
What am I saying? I've no place to turn:
Minos, my father, holds the judge's urn.
The gods have placed damnation in his hands,
the shades in Hades follow his commands. 290
Will he not shake and curse his fatal star
that brings his daughter trembling to his bar?
His child by Pasiphaë forced to tell
a thousand sins unclassified in hell?
Father, when you interpret what I speak, 295
I fear your fortitude will be too weak
to hold the urn. I see you fumbling for
new punishments for crimes unknown before.
You'll be your own child's executioner!
You cannot kill me; look, my murderer 300
is Venus, who destroyed our family;
Father, she has already murdered me.
I killed myself—and what is worse I wasted
my life for pleasures I have never tasted.
My lover flees me still, and my last gasp 305
is for the fleeting flesh I failed to clasp.
OENONE. Madam, Madam, cast off this groundless terror!
Is love now an unprecedented error?
You love! What then! You love! Accept your fate.
You're not the first to sail into this strait. 310

---

283. *Europa:* Carried off by Zeus in
the form of a bull, Europa conceived
three children by him, of whom one was
Minos, Phaedra's father.

288. *judge's urn:* After his death,
Minos of Crete became, along with his
brother Rhadamanthus, one of the judges
of souls in the Underworld. The urn held
the lots which determined to what abode
in the Underworld the souls of the dead
were to be sent.

Will chaos overturn the earth and Jove,
because a mortal woman is in love?
Such accidents are easy, all too common.
A woman must submit to being woman.
You curse a failure in the source of things.   315
Venus has feasted on the hearts of kings;
even the gods, man's judges, feel desire,
Zeus learned to live with his adulterous fire.

PHAEDRA. Must I still listen and drink your poisoned breath?
My death's redoubled on the edge of death.   320
I'd fled Hippolytus and I was free
till your entreaties stabbed and blinded me,
and dragged me howling to the pit of lust.
Oenone, I was learning to be just.
You fed my malice. Attacking the young Prince   325
was not enough; you clothed him with my sins.
You wished to kill him; he is dying now,
because of you, and Theseus' brutal vow.
You watch my torture; I'm the last ungorged
scrap rooting in this trap your plots have forged.   330
What binds you to me? Leave me, go, and die,
may your punishment be to terrify
all those who ruin princes by their lies,
hints, acquiescence, filth, and blasphemies—
panders who grease the grooves of inclination,   335
and lure our willing bodies from salvation.
Go die, go frighten false flatterers, the worst
friends the gods can give to kings they've cursed!

OENONE. I have given all and left all for her service,
almighty gods! I have been paid my price!   340

Act 5

SCENE I. *Hippolytus, Aricia*

ARICIA. Take a stand, speak the truth, if you respect
your father's glory and your life. Protect
yourself! I'm nothing to you. You consent
without a struggle to your banishment.
If you are weary of Aricia, go;   5
at least do something to prevent the blow
that dooms your honor and existence—both
at a stroke! Your father must recall his oath;
there is time still, but if the truth's concealed,
you offer your accuser a free field.   10
Speak to your father!

HIPPOLYTUS.   I've already said

what's lawful. Shall I point to his soiled bed,
tell Athens how his marriage was foresworn,
make Theseus curse the day that he was born?
My aching heart recoils. I only want   15
God and Aricia for my confidants.
See how I love you; love makes me confide
in you this horror I have tried to hide
from my own heart. My faith must not be broken;
forget, if possible, what I have spoken.   20
Ah Princess, if even a whisper slips
past you, it will perjure your pure lips
God's justice is committed to the cause
of those who love him, and uphold his laws;
sooner or later, heaven itself will rise   25
in wrath and punish Phaedra's blasphemies.
I must not. If I rip away her mask,
I'll kill my father. Give me what I ask.
Do this! Then throw away your chains; it's right
for you to follow me, and share my flight.   30
Fly from this prison; here the vices seethe
and simmer, virtue has no air to breathe.
In the confusion of my exile, none
will even notice that Aricia's gone.
Banished and broken, Princess, I am still   35
a force in Greece. Your guards obey my will,
powerful intercessors wish us well:
our neighbors, Argos' citadel
is armed, and in Mycenae our allies
will shelter us, if lying Phaedra tries   40
to hurry us from our paternal throne,
and steal our sacred titles for her son.
The gods are ours, they urge us to attack.
Why do you tremble, falter and hold back?
Your interests drive me to this sacrifice.   45
While I'm on fire, your blood has changed to ice.
Princess, is exile more than you can face?
ARICIA. Exile with you, my lord? What sweeter place
is under heaven? Standing at your side,
I'd let the universe and heaven slide.   50
You're my one love, my king, but can I hope
for peace and honor, Prince, if I elope
unmarried? This . . . I wasn't questioning
the decency of flying from the King.
Is he my father? Only an abject   55

38. *Argos:* chief city in Argolis, in   center of the Mycenaean civilization,
the northeastern Peloponnesus.   with close Cretan connections.
39. *Mycenae:* also in Argolis, and

spirit honors tyrants with respect.
You say you love me. Prince, I am afraid.
HIPPOLYTUS. Aricia, you shall never be betrayed;
   accept me! Let our love be sanctified,
   then flee from your oppressor as my bride.   60
   Bear witness, oh you gods, our love released
   by danger, needs no temple or a priest.
   It's faith, not ceremonial, that saves.
   Here at the city gates, among these graves
   the resting places of my ancient line,   65
   there stands a sacred temple and a shrine.
   Here, where no mortal ever swore in vain,
   here in these shadows, where eternal pain
   is ready to engulf the perjurer;
   here heaven's scepter quivers to confer   70
   its final sanction; here, my Love, we'll kneel,
   and pray the gods to consecrate and seal
   our love. Zeus, the father of the world will stand
   here as your father and bestow your hand.
   Only the pure shall be our witnesses: 75
   Hera, the guarantor of marriages,
   Demeter and the virgin Artemis.
ARICIA. The King is coming. Fly. I'll stay and meet
   his anger here and cover your retreat.
   Hurry. Be off, send me some friend to guide   80
   my timid footsteps, husband, to your side.

SCENE II. Theseus, Ismene, Aricia

THESEUS. Oh God, illuminate my troubled mind.
   Show me the answer I have failed to find.
ARICIA. Go, Ismene, be ready to escape.

SCENE III. Theseus, Aricia

THESEUS. Princess, you are disturbed. You twist your cape   85
   and blush. The Prince was talking to you. Why
   is he running?
ARICIA.   We've said our last goodbye,
   my lord.
THESEUS.   I see the beauty of your eyes
   moves even my son, and you have gained a prize
   no woman hoped for.
ARICIA.   He hasn't taken on   90
   your hatred for me, though he is your son.

---

76. *Hera . . . Demeter:* Hera was Zeus's wife, hence queen of the gods. She was closely associated with marriage. Demeter, the daughter of Cronus and Rhea, mother of Persephone, was also associated with marriage and fertility.

THESEUS. I follow. I can hear the oaths he swore.
  He knelt, he wept. He has done this before
  and worse. You are deceived.
ARICIA.   Deceived, my lord?
THESEUS. Princess, are you so rich? Can you afford   95
  to hunger for this lover that my queen
  rejected? Your betrayer loves my wife.
ARICIA. How can you bear to blacken his pure life?
  Is kingship only for the blind and strong,
  unable to distinguish right from wrong?   100
  What insolent prerogative obscures
  a light that shines in every eye but yours?
  You have betrayed him to his enemies.
  What more, my lord? Repent your blasphemies.
  Are you not fearful lest the gods so loathe   105
  and hate you they will gratify your oath?
  Fear God, my lord, fear God. How many times
  he grants men's wishes to expose their crimes.
THESEUS. Love blinds you, Princess, and beclouds your reason.
  Your outburst cannot cover up his treason.   110
  My trust's in witnesses that cannot lie.
  I have seen Phaedra's tears. She tried to die.
ARICIA. Take care, your Highness. When your killing hand
  drove all the thieves and reptiles from the land,
  you missed one monster, one was left alive,   115
  one. . . . No, I must not name her, Sire, or strive
  to save your helpless son; he wants to spare
  your reputation. Let me go. I dare
  not stay here. If I stayed I'd be too weak
  to keep my promise. I'd be forced to speak.   120

SCENE V. *Theseus*

THESEUS. What was she saying? I must try to reach
  the meaning of her interrupted speech.
  Is it a pitfall? A conspiracy?
  Are they plotting together to torture me?
  Why did I let the rash, wild girl depart?   125
  What is this whisper crying in my heart?
  A secret pity fills my soul with pain.
  I must question Oenone once again.
  My guards summon Oenone to the throne.
  Quick, bring her. I must talk with her alone.   130

SCENE V. *Theseus, Panope*

PANOPE. The Queen's deranged, your Highness. Some accursed
  madness is driving her; some fury stalks

behind her back, possesses her, and talks
its evil through her, and blasphemes the world.
She cursed Oenone. Now Oenone's hurled   135
herself into the ocean Sire, and drowned.
Why did she do it? No reason can be found.
THESEUS. Oenone's drowned?
PANOPE.   Her death has brought no peace.
The cries of Phaedra's troubled soul increase.
Now driven by some sinister unrest,   140
she snatches up her children to her breast,
pets them and weeps, till something makes her scoff
at her affection and she drives them off.
Her glance is drunken and irregular,
she looks through us and wonders who we are;   145
thrice she has started letters to you, Sire,
thrice tossed the shredded fragments in the fire.
Oh call her to you. Help her!
THESEUS. The nurse is drowned? Phaedra wishes to die?
Oh gods! Summon my son. Let him defend   150
himself, tell him I'm ready to attend.
I want him!
     [*Exit* PANOPE.]
                    Neptune, hear me, spare my son!
My vengeance was too hastily begun.
Oh why was I so eager to believe
Oenone's accusation? The gods deceive   155
the victims they are ready to destroy!

SCENE VI. *Theseus, Theramenes*

THESEUS. Here is Theramenes. Where is my boy,
my first-born? He was yours to guard and keep.
Where is he? Answer me. What's this? You weep?
THERAMENES. Oh, tardy, futile grief, his blood is shed.   160
My lord, your son, Hippolytus, is dead.
THESEUS. Oh gods, have mercy!
THERAMENES.   I saw him die. The most
lovely and innocent of men is lost.
THESEUS. He's dead? The gods have hurried him away
and killed him? . . . just as I began to pray . . .   165
What sudden thunderbolt has struck him down?
THERAMENES. We'd started out, and hardly left the town.
He held the reins; a few feet to his rear,
a single, silent guard held up a spear.
He followed the Mycenae highroad, deep   170
in thought, reins dangling, as if half asleep;
his famous horses, only he could hold,

trudged on with lowered heads, and sometimes rolled
their dull eyes slowly—they seemed to have caught
their master's melancholy, and aped his thought.   175
Then all at once winds struck us like a fist,
we heard a sudden roaring through the mist;
from underground a voice in agony
answered the prolonged groaning of the sea.
We shook, the horses' manes rose on their heads,   180
and now against a sky of blacks and reds,
we saw the flat waves hump into a mountain
of green-white water rising like a fountain,
as it reached land and crashed with a last roar
to shatter like a galley on the shore.   185
Out of its fragments rose a monster, half
dragon, half bull; a mouth that seemed to laugh
drooled venom on its dirty yellow scales
and python belly forking to three tails.
The shore was shaken like a tuning fork,   190
ships bounced on the stung sea like bits of cork,
the earth moved, and the sun spun round and round,
a sulphur-colored venom swept the ground.
We fled; each felt his useless courage falter,
and sought asylum at a nearby altar.   195
Only the Prince remained; he wheeled about,
and hurled a javelin through the monster's snout.
Each kept advancing. Flung from the Prince's arm,
dart after dart struck where the blood was warm.
The monster in its death-throes felt defeat,   200
and bounded howling to the horses' feet.
There its stretched gullet and its armor broke,
and drenched the chariot with blood and smoke,
and then the horses, terror-struck, stampeded.
Their master's whip and shouting went unheeded,   205
they dragged his breathless body to the spray.
Their red mouths bit the bloody surf, men say
Poseidon stood beside them, that the god
was stabbing at their bellies with a goad.
Their terror drove them crashing on a cliff,   210
the chariot crashed in two, they ran as if
the Furies screamed and crackled in their manes,
their fallen hero tangled in the reins,
jounced on the rocks behind them. The sweet light
of heaven never will expunge this sight: 215
the horses that Hippolytus had tamed,

212. *Furies:* Roman name *(Furiae)* for the Greek Erinyes—the three winged goddesses of vengeance, with snakes for hair, named Alecto, Tisiphone, and Megaera.

now dragged him headlong, and their mad hooves maimed
his face past recognition. When he tried
to call them, calling only terrified;
faster and ever faster moved their feet,   220
his body was a piece of bloody meat.
The cliffs and ocean trembled to our shout,
at last their panic failed, they turned about,
and stopped not far from where those hallowed graves,
the Prince's fathers, overlook the waves.   225
I ran on breathless, guards were at my back,
my master's blood had left a generous track.
The stones were red, each thistle in the mud
was stuck with bits of hair and skin and blood.
I came upon him, called; he stretched his right   230
hand to me, blinked his eyes, then closed them tight.
"I die," he whispered, "it's the gods' desire.
Friend, stand between Aricia and my sire—
some day enlightened, softened, disabused,
he will lament his son, falsely accused;   235
then when at last he wishes to appease
my soul, he'll treat my lover well, release
and honor Aricia. . . ." On this word, he died.
Only a broken body testified
he'd lived and loved once. On the sand now lies   240
something his father will not recognize.
THESEUS. My son, my son! Alas, I stand alone
before the gods. I never can atone.
THERAMENES. Meanwhile, Aricia, rushing down the path,
approached us. She was fleeing from your wrath,   245
my lord, and wished to make Hippolytus
her husband in God's eyes. Then nearing us,
she saw the signs of struggle in the waste,
she saw (oh what a sight) her love defaced,
her young love lying lifeless on the sand.   250
At first she hardly seemed to understand;
while staring at the body in the grass,
she kept on asking where her lover was.
At last the black and fearful truth broke through
her desolation! She seemed to curse the blue   255
and murdering ocean as she caught his head
up in her lap; then fainting lay half dead,
until Ismene somehow summoned back her breath,
restored the child to life—or rather death.
I come, great King, to urge my final task,   260
your dying son's last outcry was to ask
mercy for poor Aricia, for his bride.
Now Phaedra comes. She killed him. She has lied.

SCENE VII. *Theseus, Phaedra, Panope*

THESEUS. Ah Phaedra, you have won. He's dead. A man
   was killed. Were you watching? His horses ran   265
   him down, and tore his body limb from limb.
   Poseidon struck him, Theseus murdered him.
   I served you! Tell me why Oenone died?
   Was it to save you? Is her suicide
   A proof of your truth? No, since he's dead, I must   270
   accept your evidence, just or unjust.
   I must believe my faith has been abused;
   you have accused him; he shall stand accused.
   He's friendless even in the world below.
   There the shades fear him! Am I forced to know   275
   the truth? Truth cannot bring my son to life.
   If fathers murder, shall I kill my wife
   too? Leave me, Phaedra. Far from you, exiled
   from Greece, I will lament my murdered child.
   I am a murdered gladiator, whirled   280
   in black circles. I want to leave the world;
   my whole life rises to increase my guilt—
   all those dazzled, dazzling eyes, my glory built
   on killing killers. Less known, less magnified,
   I might escape, and find a place to hide.   285
   Stand back, Poseidon. I know the gods are hard
   to please. I pleased you. This is my reward:
   I killed my son. I killed him! Only a god
   spares enemies, and wants his servants' blood!
PHAEDRA. No, Theseus, I must disobey your prayer.   290
   Listen to me. I'm dying. I declare
   Hippolytus was innocent.
THESEUS. Ah Phaedra, on your evidence, I sent
   him to his death. Do you ask me to forgive
   my son's assassin? Can I let you live?   295
PHAEDRA. My time's too short, your highness. It was I,
   who lusted for your son with my hot eye.
   The flames of Aphrodite maddened me;
   I loathed myself, and yearned outrageously
   like a starved wolf to fall upon the sheep.   300
   I wished to hold him to me in my sleep
   and dreamt I had him. Then Oenone's tears,
   troubled my mind; she played upon my fears,
   until her pleading forced me to declare
   I loved your son. He scorned me. In despair,   305
   I plotted with my nurse, and our conspiracy
   made you believe your son assaulted me.
   Oenone's punished; fleeing from my wrath,
   she drowned herself, and found a too easy path

to death and hell. Perhaps you wonder why   310
I still survive her, and refuse to die?
Theseus, I stand before you to absolve
your noble son. Sire, only this resolve
upheld me, and made me throw down my knife.
I've chosen a slower way to end my life—   315
Medea's poison; chills already dart
along my boiling veins and squeeze my heart.
A cold composure I have never known
gives me a moment's poise. I stand alone
and seem to see my outraged husband fade   320
and waver into death's dissolving shade.
My eyes at last give up their light, and see
the day they've soiled resume its purity.

PANOPE. She's dead, my lord.

THESEUS.   Would God, all memory
of her and me had died with her! Now I   325
must live. This knowledge that has come too late
must give me strength and help me expiate
my sacrilegious vow. Let's go, I'll pay
my son the honors he has earned today.
His father's tears shall mingle with his blood.   330
My love that did my son so little good
asks mercy from his spirit. I declare
Aricia is my daughter and my heir.

324-325. *Would . . . her:* The performances of the *Comédie Française* traditionally end with this line, the remainder being regarded as anticlimactic.

FRANÇOIS, DUC DE LA ROCHEFOUCAULD
(1613–1680)
Maxims*

5. The continuance of our passions no more depends on us than
does the continuance of our lives.

6. Passion often makes a fool out of the ablest of men, and renders ability to the silliest.

9. The passions show an unfair and personal bias, which makes
them dangerous to follow; and one should beware of them, even
when they seem the most reasonable.

---

* First published 1665; last augmented
edition 1678. Translated by Howard E.
Hugo. La Rochefoucauld published five
editions during his lifetime (1665, 1666,
1671, 1675, 1678), in the process of
which he added new maxims and rewrote
some of the earlier ones.

14. Men are apt not only to forget kindness and injuries; they even hate those who have benefited them, and cease to hate those who have wronged them. Diligence in rewarding good and punishing evil seems to them a bondage to which they will scarcely submit.

17. The modesty of happy persons comes from the peace of mind which good fortune lends to their spirits.

19. We all have strength enough to bear the misfortunes of others.

22. Philosophy easily triumphs over past and future evils; but present evils triumph over philosophy.

25. It requires greater virtue to bear good fortune than bad.

26. Neither the sun nor death can be looked at steadily.

38. We make our promises according to our hopes, and keep them according to our fears.

43. Man often believes he leads, when indeed he is being led; and while his mind directs him toward one goal, his heart drags him unconsciously toward another.

49. We are never as happy or as unhappy as we imagine ourselves to be.

64. Truth does not accomplish as much good in the world, as its counterfeits work evil.

72. If you judge love by most of its results, it seems more akin to hate than to friendship.

76. With true loves as with ghosts: everyone speaks of them, but few have seen them.

78. For most of mankind, love of justice is nothing more than the fear of suffering injustice.

93. The old love to give good advice, to console themselves for no longer being in a condition to give bad examples.

98. Each speaks well of his heart, and no one dares speak so well about his mind.

102. The head is forever fooled by the heart.

119. We are so accustomed to disguising ourselves from others, that we end by disguising ourselves from ourselves.

123. We would scarcely ever enjoy ourselves, if we never flattered ourselves.

132. It is easier to be wise for others than to be wise about oneself.

136. There are those who would never have been in love, had they never heard about love.

149. To refuse praise means that you want to be praised twice.

155. Some disgusting persons possess virtue, and others also exist who are pleasing with all their blemishes.

169. Although sloth and timidity impel us toward our duty, often our virtue gets all the credit.

174. We would do better to employ our intelligence in coping with present misfortunes, than in foreseeing those which might happen to us.

185. Evil, like good, has its own heroes.

190. Only great men can possess great faults.

195. What often prohibits us from abandonment to a single vice is that we own many more.

210. As we grow old, we become sillier and wiser.

218. Hypocrisy is a tribute that vice pays to virtue.

235. We easily console ourselves when our friends suffer disgrace, if the occasion serves to bring out our affection for them.

259. The pleasure of love is in loving; and we are happier in our own passion than in the passion we inspire.

298. For most of mankind, gratitude is no more than a secret wish to receive even greater benefits.

303. No matter how many nice things they say about us, we never learn anything new.

304. We often pardon those who bore us; we can never forgive those whom we bore.

308. Moderation has been made a virtue in order to curb the ambition of the great, and also to console those who are mediocre in either fortune or merit.

310. Sometimes occasions occur in life from whence you have to be slightly mad in order to extricate yourself.

326. Ridicule hurts our honor more than does dishonor itself.

327. We admit our small failings only in order to persuade others that we have no greater ones.

354. Certain defects, when placed in a good setting, shine more brilliantly than virtue itself.

384. We ought never to be surprised, save that we can still be surprised.

391. Fate never seems so blind as she does to those she has not favored.

392. One should cope with luck as one does with health: enjoy it when things go well, be patient when things go badly, and never take recourse to extreme remedies except in the last resort.

409. We would often be ashamed of our finest acts, if the world were aware of the motives behind them.

417. In love, first cured is best cured.

422. All the passions cause us to make mistakes, but love causes us to make the most ridiculous ones.

428. We easily forgive our friends those faults that personally do not touch us.

429. Women in love forgive major indiscretions more easily than they do small infidelities.

439. We would scarcely wish zealously for things, if we really understood the things we wanted.

442. We try to ennoble those faults which we do not wish to correct.

445. Weakness, rather than virtue, is vice's adversary.

453. In major affairs, we should strive less to create situations than to profit from those already present.

458. Our enemies come closer in their judgments about us than we ever do about ourselves.

464. There exist extremes of well-being and misery that go beyond our sensibility and imagination.

496. Quarrels would not last long, if the wrong were only on one side.

499. Ordinarily one pays no attention to a woman's first love-affair until she has had a second.

15. In the misfortunes of our best friends, we always find something not displeasing.[1]

1. *In . . . displeasing:* from Barbin's *Supplementary Maxims* (1693).

JEAN DE LA FONTAINE
(1621–1695)
Fables*

The Grasshopper and the Ant[a]

Until fall, a grasshopper
    Chose to chirr;
With starvation as foe
When northeasters would blow,
And not even a gnat's residue   5
Or caterpillar's to chew,
She chirred a recurrent chant
Of want beside an ant,
Begging it to rescue her
With some seeds it could spare   10
Till the following year's fell.
"By August you shall have them all,
Interest and principal."
Share one's seeds? Now what is worse
For any ant to do?   15
Ours asked, "When fair, what brought you through?"
—"I sang for those who might pass by chance—
Night and day, an't you please."
—"Sang, you say? You have put me at ease.
A singer! Excellent. Now dance."   20

* From *The Fables of La Fontaine* translated by Marianne Moore. Copyright 1954, "The Fox and the Crow" copyright 1952, by Marianne Moore. Reprinted by permission of The Viking Press, Inc. Original title: *Aesop's Fables Rendered into Verse by M. de La Fontaine.* In twelve books: the first six were published in 1668; the seventh through the eleventh in 1678-1679; the twelfth in 1694.
a. Book I, No. 1; Aesop No. 134. (Aesop, a slave of Samos, reputedly lived in the 6th century B.C., although his actual existence is doubtful. But fables were early collected under his name.)

The Fox and the Crow[b]

On his airy perch among the branches
    Master Crow was holding cheese in his beak.
Master Fox, whose pose suggested fragrances,
    Said in language which of course I cannot speak,
        "Aha, superb Sir Ebony, well met.   5
How black! who else boasts your metallic jet!
    If your warbling were unique,
    Rest assured, as you are sleek,
One would say that our wood had hatched nightingales."
All aglow, Master Crow tried to run a few scales,   10
    Risking trills and intervals,

b. Book I, No. 2; Aesop, No. 204. Cf. also Phaedrus (Latin fabulist, first century A.D.), I, 13.

Dropping the prize as his huge beak sang false.
The fox pounced on the cheese and remarked, "My dear sir,
    Learn that every flatterer
  Lives at the flattered listener's cost: 15
A lesson worth more than the cheese that you lost."
    The tardy learner, smarting under ridicule,
Swore he'd learned his last lesson as somebody's fool.

The Frog Who Would Be an Ox[c]

    That great ox, built just right!
    Eying the beast, although at best
A mere egg's height or less, the frog mustered might
And spread out and swelled and expanded his chest
    To approximate the ox, his despair;   5
    Then said to another frog, "Compare:
I'm his size. See, now I need not defer."
"Still small."—"Now?"—"By no means."—"Now I am
                  not outclassed."
"Not nearly large enough." The poor envier
    Burst; overtested at last.   10
Our world is full of mentalities quite as crude:
The man of trade must house himself so kings would stare;
    Each small prince's deputies are everywhere.
    Each marquis has pages—a multitude.

c. Book I, No. 3; Aesop No. 420; Phaedrus, I, 24.

The Town Rat and the Country Rat[d]

    In this ancient parable,
    Town rat proffered country rat
    A fashionable meal
    As a change from this and that,

    Where on a rug from Turkey,   5
    A feast for two was ready.
    Fond fancy alone could see
    The pair's joint ecstasy.

    Fine food made each's plate replete—
    More dainties there than greed could paint,   10
    But as they were about to eat,
    Noises were heard; the pair felt faint.

d. Book I, No. 9; Aesop, No. 301; Horace, *Satires*, II, 6.

At the door, sniff and smell.
What was scratching steadily?
Both frightened ill, half fell,   15
Then fled confusedly.

When they had dared to reappear,
In seclusion with relief,
The city rat resumed, "My dear,
Come now, divide the beef."   20

—"I have dined," the field rat said;
"Be my guest, pray, a day hence,
Though you'll not find, I am afraid,
Similar magnificence.

Yet I'm never in danger: I've supped,   25
Carefree from year to year;
And so farewell. What is good cheer
Which death threats can disrupt?"

The Wolf and the Lamb*

Force has the best of any argument:
        Soon proved by the story which I present.

        A thirsty lamb was drinking where
        A brook ran crystal clear.
Up came a wolf who had been lured there   5
        By hunger, since it was a spot where prey might be.
"Soiling it, intrepid transgressor?" the wolf growled,
        "Leaving me to drink what you fouled?
Such impropriety involves a penalty."
—"Bear with me," the lamb said, "your Majesty.   10
        I've not trespassed anywhere.
        I'm twenty feet from where you were;
        Am here, where what you can't drink went
                In its descent;
        And to be mathematical,   15
How have I possibly by what I have done
        Polluted water of your own?"
—"You stirred the mud." Bloodthirsty minds are small.
"And the past year as well, I know you slandered me."
—"How?" the lamb asked. "I, unweaned, born recently—   20
        This very year? I still require home care."
        —"Your brother then, you've one somewhere."
        —"But I have none."—"It was some relative then;

e. Book I, No. 10; Phaedrus. I, 1.

All of you sheep are unfair;
You, your shepherds, and the dogs they train.   25
I have a debt to myself to discharge."
Dragged down a wooded gully,
The small was eaten by the large
Unconditionally.

The Oak and the Reed[f]

The oak said to the reed, "You grow
Too unprotectedly. Nature has been unfair;
A tiny wren alights, and you are bending low;
If a fitful breath of air
Should freshen till ripples show,   5
You heed her and lower your head;
Whereas my parasol makes welcome shade each day
And like the Caucasus need never sway,
However it is buffeted.
Your so-called hurricanes are too faint to fear.   10
Would that you'd been born beneath this towering tent I've made,
Which could afford you ample shade;
Your hazards would not be severe:
I'd shield you when the lightning played;
But grow you will, time and again,   15
On the misty fringe of the wind's domain.
I perceive that you are grievously oppressed."
The rush said, "Bless you for fearing that I might be distressed;
It is you alone whom the winds should alarm.
I bend and do not break. You've seemed consistently   20
Impervious to harm—
Erect when blasts rushed to and fro;
As for the end, who can foresee how things will go?"
Relentless wind was on them instantly—
A fury of destruction   25
Which the North had nursed in some haunt known to none.
The bulrush bent, but not the tree.
Confusion rose to a roar,
Until the hurricane threw prone
That thing of kingly height whose head had all but touched
God's throne—   30
Who had shot his root to the threshold of Death's door.

The Dairymaid and Her Milk-Pot[g]

Perrette's milk-pot fitted her head-mat just right—
Neatly quilted to grip the pot tight.

---

f. Book I, No. 22; Aesop, Nos. 143 and 180.

g. Book VII, No. 10. Source is Bonaventure des Périers, *Novella* 14.

Then she set off to market and surely walked well,
In her short muslin dress that encouraged long strides,
Since to make better time she wore shoes with low heel   5
      And had tucked up her skirt at the sides.
      Like summer attire her head had grown light,
      Thinking of what she'd have bought by night.
In exchange for the milk, since supposing it gone,
She'd buy ten times ten eggs and three hens could be set.   10
Taking care all hatched out, she'd not lose more than one
      And said, "Then there'll be pullets to sell.
I'll raise them at home; it is quite within reason,
      Since shrewd Master Fox will be doing well
If I can't shortly buy a young pig and grow bacon.   15
The one I had bought would be almost half grown;
He'd need next to no feed—almost nothing at all;
When he's sold I'll have funds—good hard cash to count on.
Then with room at the barn for some stock in the stall,
I could buy cow and calf if the pig had sold high;   20
If I'd not had a loss, I'd add sheep by and by."
Perrette skipped for joy as she dreamt of what she'd bought.
The crock crashed. Farewell, cow, calf, fat pig, eggs not
                    hatched out.
The mistress of wealth grieved to forfeit forever
      The profits that were mounting.   25
      How ask her husband to forgive her
      Lest he beat her as was fitting?
      And thus ended the farce we have watched:
      Don't count your chickens before they are hatched.

      Whom does a daydream not entrance?   30
      Have castles in air no romance?
Picrochole, Pyrrhus, Perrette—a fool's or wisdom's mirth—
      Every hearth can give them birth.
Each of us loves a daydream—the fondest think on earth,
Illusion has a charm to which our minds succumb;   35
      Since it captures whatever has worth.
      All hearts are ours, we pluck each plum.
When alone, I tower so tall that the bravest shiver.
I crush and see Persian emperors suffer.
      I am a king, an idol.   40
My head is diademed with gems that rain:
Then the king's deep problems by some unjust reversal,
      Are Jean de La Fontaine's again.

---

32. *Picrochole . . . Perrette:* names
that belong to the seventeenth-century
tradition of the pastoral (*bergerie*),
where elegant aristocrats played at being shepherds and shepherdesses.

FRANÇOIS-MARIE AROUET DE VOLTAIRE

(1694–1778)

Candide, or Optimism*

translated from the German of Doctor Ralph with the additions which were found in the Doctor's pocket when he died at Minden in the Year of Our Lord 1759

CHAPTER 1

How Candide Was Brought up in a Fine Castle and How He Was Driven Therefrom

There lived in Westphalia,[1] in the castle of the Baron of Thunder-Ten-Tronckh, a young man on whom nature had bestowed the perfection of gentle manners. His features admirably expressed his soul; he combined an honest mind with great simplicity of heart; and I think it was for this reason that they called him Candide. The old servants of the house suspected that he was the son of the Baron's sister by a respectable, honest gentleman of the neighborhood, whom she had refused to marry because he could prove only seventy-one quarterings,[2] the rest of his family tree having been lost in the passage of time.

The Baron was one of the most mighty lords of Westphalia, for his castle had a door and windows. His great hall was even hung with a tapestry. The dogs of his courtyard made up a hunting pack on occasion, with the stableboys as huntsmen; the village priest was his grand almoner. They all called him "My Lord," and laughed at his stories.

The Baroness, who weighed in the neighborhood of three hundred and fifty pounds, was greatly respected for that reason, and did the honors of the house with a dignity which rendered her even more imposing. Her daughter Cunégonde,[3] aged seventeen, was a ruddy-cheeked girl, fresh, plump, and desirable. The Baron's son seemed in every way worthy of his father. The tutor Pangloss was the oracle of the household, and little Candide listened to his lectures with all the good faith of his age and character.

Pangloss gave instruction in metaphysico-theologico-cosmoloonigology.[4] He proved admirably that there cannot possibly be an effect

---

* Translated with notes by Robert M. Adams. Reprinted by permission of Robert M. Adams.

1. Westphalia is a province of western Germany, near Holland and the lower Rhineland. Flat, boggy, and drab, it is noted chiefly for its excellent ham. In a letter to his niece, written during his German expedition of 1750, Voltaire described the "vast, sad, sterile, detestable countryside of Westphalia."
2. Quarterings are genealogical divisions of one's family tree. Seventy-one of them is a grotesque number to have, representing something over 2,000 years of uninterrupted nobility.
3. Cunégonde gets her odd name from Kunigunda, wife to Emperor Henry II, who walked barefoot and blindfolded on red-hot irons to prove her chastity; Pangloss gets his name from Greek words meaning all-tongue.
4. The "looney" I have buried in this burlesque word corresponds to a buried *nigaud*—"booby" in the French. Christian Wolff, disciple of Leibniz, invented and popularized the word "cosmology."

without a cause and that in this best of all possible worlds[5] the Baron's castle was the best of all castles and his wife the best of all possible Baronesses.

—It is clear, said he, that things cannot be otherwise than they are, for since everything is made to serve an end, everything necessarily serves the best end. Observe: noses were made to support spectacles, hence we have spectacles. Legs, as anyone can plainly see, were made to be breeched, and so we have breeches. Stones were made to be shaped and to build castles with; thus My Lord has a fine castle, for the greatest Baron in the province should have the finest house; and since pigs were made to be eaten, we eat pork all year round.[6] Consequently, those who say everything is well are uttering mere stupidities; they should say everything is for the best.

Candide listened attentively and believed implicitly; for he found Miss Cunégonde exceedingly pretty, though he never had the courage to tell her so. He decided that after the happiness of being born Baron of Thunder-Ten-Tronckh, the second order of happiness was to be Miss Cunégonde; the third was seeing her every day, and the fourth was listening to Master Pangloss, the greatest philosopher in the province and consequently in the entire world.

One day, while Cunégonde was walking near the castle in the little woods that they called a park, she saw Dr. Pangloss in the underbrush; he was giving a lesson in experimental physics to her mother's maid, a very attractive and obedient brunette. As Miss Cunégonde had a natural bent for the sciences, she watched breathlessly the repeated experiments which were going on; she saw clearly the doctor's sufficient reason, observed both cause and effect, and returned to the house in a distracted and pensive frame of mind, yearning for knowledge and dreaming that she might be the sufficient reason of young Candide—who might also be hers.

As she was returning to the castle, she met Candide, and blushed; Candide blushed too. She greeted him in a faltering tone of voice; and Candide talked to her without knowing what he was saying. Next day, as everyone was rising from the dinner table, Cunégonde and Candide found themselves behind a screen; Cunégonde dropped her handkerchief, Candide picked it up; she held his hand quite innocently, he kissed her hand quite innocently

5. These catch phrases, echoed by popularizers of Leibniz, make reference to the determinism of his system, its linking of cause with effect, and its optimism. As his correspondence indicates, Voltaire habitually thought of Leibniz's philosophy (which, having been published in definitive form as early as 1710, had been in the air for a long time) in terms of these catch phrases.
6. The argument from design supposes that everything in this world exists for a specific reason; Voltaire objects not to the argument as a whole, but to the abuse of it. He grants, for example, that noses were made to smell and stomachs to digest but denies that feet were made to put shoes on or stones to be cut up into building blocks. His full view finds expression in the article on "causes finales" in the *Philosophical Dictionary*

with remarkable vivacity and emotion; their lips met, their eyes lit up, their knees trembled, their hands wandered. The Baron of Thunder-Ten-Tronckh passed by the screen and, taking note of this cause and this effect, drove Candide out of the castle by kicking him vigorously on the backside. Cunégonde fainted; as soon as she recovered, the Baroness slapped her face; and everything was confusion in the most beautiful and agreeable of all possible castles.

CHAPTER 2

What Happened to Candide Among the Bulgars[7]

Candide, ejected from the earthly paradise, wandered for a long time without knowing where he was going, weeping, raising his eyes to heaven, and gazing back frequently on the most beautiful of castles which contained the most beautiful of Baron's daughters. He slept without eating, in a furrow of a plowed field, while the snow drifted over him; next morning, numb with cold, he dragged himself into the neighboring village, which was called Waldberghoff-trarbk-dikdorff; he was penniless, famished, and exhausted. At the door of a tavern he paused forlornly. Two men dressed in blue[8] took note of him:

—Look, chum, said one of them, there's a likely young fellow of just about the right size.

They approached Candide and invited him very politely to dine with them.

—Gentlemen, Candide replied with charming modesty, I'm honored by your invitation, but I really don't have enough money to pay my share.

—My dear sir, said one of the blues, people of your appearance and your merit don't have to pay; aren't you five feet five inches tall?

—Yes, gentlemen, that is indeed my stature, said he, making a bow.

—Then, sir, you must be seated at once; not only will we pay your bill this time, we will never allow a man like you to be short of money; for men were made only to render one another mutual aid.

—You are quite right, said Candide; it is just as Dr. Pangloss always told me, and I see clearly that everything is for the best.

They beg him to accept a couple of crowns, he takes them, and offers an I.O.U.; they won't hear of it, and all sit down at table

7. Voltaire chose this name to represent the Prussian troops of Frederick the Great because he wanted to make an insinuation of pederasty against both the soldiers and their master. *Cf.* French *bougre,* English "bugger."

8. The recruiting officers of Frederick the Great, much feared in eighteenth-century Europe, wore blue uniforms. Frederick had a passion for sorting out his soldiers by size; several of his regiments would accept only six-footers.

together.

—Don't you love dearly . . . ?

—I do indeed, says he, I dearly love Miss Cunégonde.

—No, no, says one of the gentlemen, we are asking if you don't love dearly the King of the Bulgars.

—Not in the least, says he, I never laid eyes on him.

—What's that you say? He's the most charming of kings, and we must drink his health.

—Oh, gladly, gentlemen; and he drinks.

—That will do, they tell him; you are now the bulwark, the support, the defender, the hero of the Bulgars; your fortune is made and your future assured.

Promptly they slip irons on his legs and lead him to the regiment. There they cause him to right face, left face, present arms, order arms, aim, fire, doubletime, and they give him thirty strokes of the rod. Next day he does the drill a little less awkwardly and gets only twenty strokes; the third day, they give him only ten, and he is regarded by his comrades as a prodigy.

Candide, quite thunderstruck, did not yet understand very clearly how he was a hero. One fine spring morning he took it into his head to go for a walk, stepping straight out as if it were a privilege of the human race, as of animals in general, to use his legs as he chose.[9] He had scarcely covered two leagues when four other heroes, each six feet tall, overtook him, bound him, and threw him into a dungeon. At the court-martial they asked which he preferred, to be flogged thirty-six times by the entire regiment or to receive summarily a dozen bullets in the brain. In vain did he argue that the human will is free and insist that he preferred neither alternative; he had to choose; by virtue of the divine gift called "liberty" he decided to run the gauntlet thirty-six times, and actually endured two floggings. The regiment was composed of two thousand men. That made four thousand strokes, which laid open every muscle and nerve from his nape to his butt. As they were preparing for the third beating, Candide, who could endure no more, begged as a special favor that they would have the goodness to smash his head. His plea was granted; they bandaged his eyes and made him kneel down. The King of the Bulgars, passing by at this moment, was told of the culprit's crime; and as this king had a rare genius, he understood, from everything they told him of Candide, that this was a

---

9. This episode was suggested by the experience of a Frenchman named Courtilz, who had deserted from the Prussian army and been bastionadoed for it. Voltaire intervened with Frederick to gain his release. But it also reflects the story that Wolff, Leibniz's disciple, got into trouble with Frederick's father when someone reported that his doctrine denying free will had encouraged several soldiers to desert. "The argument of the grenadier," who was said to have pleaded pre-established harmony to justify his desertion, so infuriated the king that he had Wolff expelled from the country.

young metaphysician, extremely ignorant of the ways of the world, so he granted his royal pardon, with a generosity which will be praised in every newspaper in every age. A worthy surgeon cured Candide in three weeks with the ointments described by Dioscorides.[1] He already had a bit of skin back and was able to walk when the King of the Bulgars went to war with the King of the Abares.[2]

CHAPTER 3
How Candide Escaped from the Bulgars, and What Became of Him

Nothing could have been so fine, so brisk, so brilliant, so well-drilled as the two armies. The trumpets, the fifes, the oboes, the drums, and the cannon produced such a harmony as was never heard in hell. First the cannons battered down about six thousand men on each side; then volleys of musket fire removed from the best of worlds about nine or ten thousand rascals who were cluttering up its surface. The bayonet was a sufficient reason for the demise of several thousand others. Total casualties might well amount to thirty thousand men or so. Candide, who was trembling like a philosopher, hid himself as best he could while this heroic butchery was going on.

Finally, while the two kings in their respective camps celebrated the victory by having *Te Deums* sung, Candide undertook to do his reasoning of cause and effect somewhere else. Passing by mounds of the dead and dying, he came to a nearby village which had been burnt to the ground. It was an Abare village, which the Bulgars had burned, in strict accordance with the laws of war. Here old men, stunned from beatings, watched the last agonies of their butchered wives, who still clutched their infants to their bleeding breasts; there, disemboweled girls, who had first satisfied the natural needs of various heroes, breathed their last; others, half-scorched in the flames, begged for their death stroke. Scattered brains and severed limbs littered the ground.

Candide fled as fast as he could to another village; this one belonged to the Bulgars, and the heroes of the Abare cause had given it the same treatment. Climbing over ruins and stumbling over corpses, Candide finally made his way out of the war area, carrying

1. Dioscorides' treatise on *materia medica*, dating from the first century A.D., was not the most up to date.

2. The name "Abares" actually designates a tribe of semicivilized Scythians, who might be supposed at war with the Bulgars; allegorically, the Abares are the French, who opposed the Prussians in the conflict known to hindsight history as the Seven Years' War (1756–1763). For Voltaire, at the moment of writing *Candide*, it was simply the current war. One notes that according to the title page of 1761, "Doctor Ralph," the dummy author of *Candide*, himself perished at the battle of Minden (Westphalia) in 1759.

a little food in his knapsack and never ceasing to dream of Miss Cunégonde. His supplies gave out when he reached Holland; but having heard that everyone in that country was rich and a Christian, he felt confident of being treated as well as he had been in the castle of the Baron before he was kicked out for the love of Miss Cunégonde.

He asked alms of several grave personages, who all told him that if he continued to beg, he would be shut up in a house of correction and set to hard labor.

Finally he approached a man who had just been talking to a large crowd for an hour on end; the topic was charity. Looking doubtfully at him, the orator demanded:

—What are you doing here? Are you here to serve the good cause?

—There is no effect without a cause, said Candide modestly; all events are linked by the chain of necessity and arranged for the best. I had to be driven away from Miss Cunégonde, I had to run the gauntlet, I have to beg my bread until I can earn it; none of this could have happened otherwise.

—Look here, friend, said the orator, do you think the Pope is Antichrist?[3]

—I haven't considered the matter, said Candide; but whether he is or not, I'm in need of bread.

—You don't deserve any, said the other; away with you, you rascal, you rogue, never come near me as long as you live.

Meanwhile, the orator's wife had put her head out of the window, and, seeing a man who was not sure the Pope was Antichrist, emptied over his head a pot full of ———— Scandalous! The excesses into which women are led by religious zeal!

A man who had never been baptized, a good Anabaptist[4] named Jacques, saw this cruel and heartless treatment being inflicted on one of his fellow creatures, a featherless biped possessing a soul[5]; he took Candide home with him, washed him off, gave him bread and beer, presented him with two florins, and even undertook to give him a job in his Persian-rug factory—for these items are widely manufactured in Holland. Candide, in an ecstasy of gratitude, cried out:

—Master Pangloss was right indeed when he told me everything

3. Voltaire is satirizing extreme Protestant sects that have sometimes seemed to make hatred of Rome the sum and substance of their creed.
4. Holland, as the home of religious liberty, had offered asylum to the Anabaptists, whose radical views on property and religious discipline had made them unpopular during the sixteenth century. Granted tolerance, they settled down into respectable burghers. Since this behavior confirmed some of Voltaire's major theses, he had a high opinion of contemporary Anabaptists.
5. Plato's famous minimal definition of a man, which he corrected by the addition of a soul to distinguish man from a plucked chicken. The point is that the Anabaptist sympathizes with men simply because they are human.

is for the best in this world; for I am touched by your kindness far more than by the harshness of that black-coated gentleman and his wife.

Next day, while taking a stroll about town, he met a beggar who was covered with pustules, his eyes were sunken, the end of his nose rotted off, his mouth twisted, his teeth black, he had a croaking voice and a hacking cough, and spat a tooth every time he tried to speak.

CHAPTER 4

How Candide Met His Old Philosophy Tutor, Doctor Pangloss, and What Came of It

Candide, more touched by compassion even than by horror, gave this ghastly beggar the two florins that he himself had received from his honest Anabaptist friend Jacques. The phantom stared at him, burst into tears, and fell on his neck. Candide drew back in terror.

—Alas, said one wretch to the other, don't you recognize your dear Pangloss any more?

—What are you saying? You, my dear master! you, in this horrible condition? What misfortune has befallen you? Why are you no longer in the most beautiful of castles? What has happened to Miss Cunégonde, that pearl among young ladies, that masterpiece of Nature?

—I am perishing, said Pangloss.

—Candide promptly led him into the Anabaptist's stable, where he gave him a crust of bread, and when he had recovered: —Well, said he, Cunégonde?

—Dead, said the other.

Candide fainted. His friend brought him around with a bit of sour vinegar which happened to be in the stable. Candide opened his eyes.

—Cunégonde, dead! Ah, best of worlds, what's become of you now? But how did she die? It wasn't of grief at seeing me kicked out of her noble father's elegant castle?

—Not at all, said Pangloss; she was disemboweled by the Bulgar soldiers, after having been raped to the absolute limit of human endurance; they smashed the Baron's head when he tried to defend her, cut the Baroness to bits, and treated my poor pupil exactly like his sister.[6] As for the castle, not one stone was left on another, not a shed, not a sheep, not a duck, not a tree; but we had the satisfaction of revenge, for the Abares did exactly the same thing to a

---

6. The theme of homosexuality which attaches to Cunégonde's brother seems to have no general satiric point, but its presence is unmistakable. See Chapters 14, 15, and 28.

nearby barony belonging to a Bulgar nobleman.

At this tale Candide fainted again; but having returned to his senses and said everything appropriate to the occasion, he asked about the cause and effect, the sufficient reason, which had reduced Pangloss to his present pitiful state.

—Alas, said he, it was love; love, the consolation of the human race, the preservative of the universe, the soul of all sensitive beings, love, gentle love.

—Unhappy man, said Candide, I too have had some experience of this love, the sovereign of hearts, the soul of our souls; and it never got me anything but a single kiss and twenty kicks in the rear. How could this lovely cause produce in you such a disgusting effect?

Pangloss replied as follows: —My dear Candide! you knew Paquette, that pretty maidservant to our august Baroness. In her arms I tasted the delights of paradise, which directly caused these torments of hell, from which I am now suffering. She was infected with the disease, and has perhaps died of it. Paquette received this present from an erudite Franciscan, who took the pains to trace it back to its source; for he had it from an elderly countess, who picked it up from a captain of cavalry, who acquired it from a marquise, who caught it from a page, who had received it from a Jesuit, who during his novitiate got it directly from one of the companions of Christopher Columbus.[7] As for me, I shall not give it to anyone, for I am a dying man.

—Oh, Pangloss, cried Candide, that's a very strange genealogy. Isn't the devil at the root of the whole thing?

—Not at all, replied that great man; it's an indispensable part of the best of worlds, a necessary ingredient; if Columbus had not caught, on an American island, this sickness which attacks the source of generation and sometimes prevents generation entirely— which thus strikes at and defeats the greatest end of Nature herself —we should have neither chocolate nor cochineal. It must also be noted that until the present time this malady, like religious controversy, has been wholly confined to the continent of Europe. Turks, Indians, Persians, Chinese, Siamese, and Japanese know nothing of it as yet; but there is a sufficient reason for which they in turn will make its acquaintance in a couple of centuries. Meanwhile, it has made splendid progress among us, especially among those big armies of honest, well-trained mercenaries who decide the destinies of nations. You can be sure that when thirty thousand men fight a pitched battle against the same number of the enemy, there will be about twenty thousand with the pox on either side.

7. Syphilis was the first contribution of the New World to the happiness of the Old. Voltaire's information comes from Astruc, *Traité des maladies vénériennes* (1734).

—Remarkable indeed, said Candide, but we must see about curing you.

—And how can I do that, said Pangloss, seeing I don't have a cent to my name? There's not a doctor in the whole world who will let your blood or give you an enema without demanding a fee. If you can't pay yourself, you must find someone to pay for you.

These last words decided Candide; he hastened to implore the help of his charitable Anabaptist, Jacques, and painted such a moving picture of his friend's wretched state that the good man did not hesitate to take in Pangloss and have him cured at his own expense. In the course of the cure, Pangloss lost only an eye and an ear. Since he wrote a fine hand and knew arithmetic, the Anabaptist made him his bookkeeper. At the end of two months, being obliged to go to Lisbon on business, he took his two philosophers on the boat with him. Pangloss still maintained that everything was for the best, but Jacques didn't agree with him.

—It must be, said he, that men have corrupted Nature, for they are not born wolves, yet that is what they become. God gave them neither twenty-four-pound cannon nor bayonets, yet they have manufactured both in order to destroy themselves. Bankruptcies have the same effect, and so does the justice which seizes the goods of bankrupts in order to prevent the creditors from getting them.[8]

—It was all indispensable, replied the one-eyed doctor, since private misfortunes make for public welfare, and therefore the more private misfortunes there are, the better everything is.

While he was reasoning, the air grew dark, the winds blew from all directions, and the vessel was attacked by a horrible tempest within sight of Lisbon harbor.

CHAPTER 5

Tempest, Shipwreck, Earthquake, and What Happened to Doctor Pangloss, Candide, and the Anabaptist, Jacques

Half of the passengers, weakened by the frightful anguish of sea-sickness and the distress of tossing about on stormy waters, were incapable of noticing their danger. The other half shrieked aloud and fell to their prayers, the sails were ripped to shreds, the masts snapped, the vessel opened at the seams. Everyone worked who could stir, nobody listened for orders or issued them. The Anabaptist was lending a hand in the after part of the ship when a frantic sailor struck him and knocked him to the deck; but just at that moment, the sailor lurched so violently that he fell head first over the side, where he hung, clutching a fragment of the broken mast.

8. Voltaire had suffered losses from various bankruptcy proceedings, which lend a personal edge to his satire here, besides diverting its point a bit.

The good Jacques ran to his aid, and helped him to climb back on board, but in the process was himself thrown into the sea under the very eyes of the sailor, who allowed him to drown without even glancing at him. Candide rushed to the rail, and saw his benefactor rise for a moment to the surface, then sink forever. He wanted to dive to his rescue; but the philosopher Pangloss prevented him by proving that the bay of Lisbon had been formed expressly for this Anabaptist to drown in. While he was proving the point *a priori*, the vessel opened up and everyone perished except for Pangloss, Candide, and the brutal sailor who had caused the virtuous Anabaptist to drown; this rascal swam easily to shore, while Pangloss and Candide drifted there on a plank.

When they had recovered a bit of energy, they set out for Lisbon; they still had a little money with which they hoped to stave off hunger after escaping the storm.

Scarcely had they set foot in the town, still bewailing the loss of their benefactor, when they felt the earth quake underfoot; the sea was lashed to a froth, burst into the port, and smashed all the vessels lying at anchor there. Whirlwinds of fire and ash swirled through the streets and public squares; houses crumbled, roofs came crashing down on foundations, foundations split; thirty thousand inhabitants of every age and either sex were crushed in the ruins.[9] The sailor whistled through his teeth, and said with an oath:
—There'll be something to pick up here.

—What can be the sufficient reason of this phenomenon? asked Pangloss.

—The Last Judgment is here, cried Candide.

But the sailor ran directly into the middle of the ruins, heedless of danger in his eagerness for gain; he found some money, laid violent hands on it, got drunk, and, having slept off his wine, bought the favors of the first streetwalker he could find amid the ruins of smashed houses, amid corpses and suffering victims on every hand. Pangloss however tugged at his sleeve.

—My friend, said he, this is not good form at all; your behavior falls short of that required by the universal reason; it's untimely, to say the least.

—Bloody hell, said the other, I'm a sailor, born in Batavia; I've been four times to Japan and stamped four times on the crucifix[1]; get out of here with your universal reason.

---

9. The great Lisbon earthquake and fire occurred on November 1, 1755; between thirty and forty thousand deaths resulted.
1. The Japanese, originally receptive to foreign visitors, grew fearful that priests and proselytizers were merely advance agents of empire, and expelled both the Portuguese and Spanish early in the seventeenth century. Only the Dutch were allowed to retain a small foothold, under humiliating conditions, of which the notion of stamping on the crucifix is symbolic. It was never what Voltaire suggests here, an actual requirement for entering the country.

Some falling stonework had struck Candide; he lay prostrate in the street, covered with rubble, and calling to Pangloss: —For pity's sake bring me a little wine and oil; I'm dying.

—This earthquake is nothing novel, Pangloss replied; the city of Lima, in South America, underwent much the same sort of tremor, last year; same causes, same effects; there is surely a vein of sulphur under the earth's surface reaching from Lima to Lisbon.

—Nothing is more probable, said Candide; but, for God's sake, a little oil and wine.

—What do you mean, probable? replied the philosopher; I regard the case as proved.

Candide fainted and Pangloss brought him some water from a nearby fountain.

Next day, as they wandered amid the ruins, they found a little food which restored some of their strength. Then they fell to work like the others, bringing relief to those of the inhabitants who had escaped death. Some of the citizens whom they rescued gave them a dinner as good as was possible under the circumstances; it is true that the meal was a melancholy one, and the guests watered their bread with tears; but Pangloss consoled them by proving that things could not possibly be otherwise.

—For, said he, all this is for the best, since if there is a volcano at Lisbon, it cannot be somewhere else, since it is unthinkable that things should not be where they are, since everything is well.

A little man in black, an officer of the Inquisition,[2] who was sitting beside him, politely took up the question, and said: —It would seem that the gentleman does not believe in original sin, since if everything is for the best, man has not fallen and is not liable to eternal punishment.

—I most humbly beg pardon of your excellency, Pangloss answered, even more politely, but the fall of man and the curse of original sin entered necessarily into the best of all possible worlds.

—Then you do not believe in free will? said the officer.

—Your excellency must excuse me, said Pangloss; free will agrees very well with absolute necessity, for it was necessary that we should be free, since a will which is determined . . .

Pangloss was in the middle of his sentence, when the officer nodded significantly to the attendant who was pouring him a glass of port, or Oporto, wine.

2. Specifically, a *familier* or *poursuivant*, an undercover agent with powers of arrest.

CHAPTER 6

How They Made a Fine Auto-da-Fé to Prevent Earthquakes, and How Candide Was Whipped

After the earthquake had wiped out three quarters of Lisbon, the learned men of the land could find no more effective way of averting total destruction than to give the people a fine auto-da-fé[3]; the University of Coimbra had established that the spectacle of several persons being roasted over a slow fire with full ceremonial rites is an infallible specific against earthquakes.

In consequence, the authorities had rounded up a Biscayan convicted of marrying a woman who had stood godmother to his child, and two Portuguese who while eating a chicken had set aside a bit of bacon used for seasoning.[4] After dinner, men came with ropes to tie up Doctor Pangloss and his disciple Candide, one for talking and the other for listening with an air of approval; both were taken separately to a set of remarkably cool apartments, where the glare of the sun is never bothersome; eight days later they were both dressed in *san-benitos* and crowned with paper mitres[5]; Candide's mitre and *san-benito* were decorated with inverted flames and with devils who had neither tails nor claws; but Pangloss's devils had both tails and claws, and his flames stood upright. Wearing these costumes, they marched in a procession, and listened to a very touching sermon, followed by a beautiful concert of plainsong. Candide was flogged in cadence to the music; the Biscayan and the two men who had avoided bacon were burned, and Pangloss was hanged, though hanging is not customary. On the same day there was another earthquake, causing frightful damage.[6]

Candide, stunned, stupefied, despairing, bleeding, trembling, said to himself: —If this is the best of all possible worlds, what are the others like? The flogging is not so bad, I was flogged by the Bulgars. But oh my dear Pangloss, greatest of philosophers, was it necessary for me to watch you being hanged, for no reason that I can see? Oh my dear Anabaptist, best of men, was it necessary that you should be drowned in the port? Oh Miss Cunégonde, pearl of young ladies, was it necessary that you should have your belly slit open?

He was being led away, barely able to stand, lectured, lashed, ab-

3. Literally, "act of faith," a public ceremony of repentance and humiliation. Such an auto-da-fé was actually held in Lisbon, June 20, 1756.
4. The Biscayan's fault lay in marrying someone within the forbidden bounds of relationship, an act of spiritual incest. The men who declined pork or bacon were understood to be crypto-Jews.
5. The cone-shaped paper cap (intended to resemble a bishop's mitre) and flowing yellow cape were customary garb for those pleading before the Inquisition.
6. In fact, the second quake occurred December 21, 1755.

solved, and blessed, when an old woman approached and said, —My son, be of good cheer and follow me.

CHAPTER 7
How an Old Woman Took Care of Candide, and How He Regained What He Loved

Candide was of very bad cheer, but he followed the old woman to a shanty; she gave him a jar of ointment to rub himself, left him food and drink; she showed him a tidy little bed; next to it was a suit of clothing.

—Eat, drink, sleep, she said; and may Our Lady of Atocha, Our Lord St. Anthony of Padua, and Our Lord St. James of Compostela watch over you. I will be back tomorrow.

Candide, still completely astonished by everything he had seen and suffered, and even more by the old woman's kindness, offered to kiss her hand.

—It's not *my* hand you should be kissing, said she. I'll be back tomorrow; rub yourself with the ointment, eat and sleep.

In spite of his many sufferings, Candide ate and slept. Next day the old woman returned bringing breakfast; she looked at his back and rubbed it herself with another ointment; she came back with lunch; and then she returned in the evening, bringing supper. Next day she repeated the same routine.

—Who are you? Candide asked continually. Who told you to be so kind to me? How can I ever repay you?

The good woman answered not a word; she returned in the evening, and without food.

—Come with me, says she, and don't speak a word.

Taking him by the hand, she walks out into the countryside with him for about a quarter of a mile; they reach an isolated house, quite surrounded by gardens and ditches. The old woman knocks at a little gate, it opens. She takes Candide up a secret stairway to a gilded room furnished with a fine brocaded sofa; there she leaves him, closes the door, disappears. Candide stood as if entranced; his life, which had seemed like a nightmare so far, was now starting to look like a delightful dream.

Soon the old woman returned; on her feeble shoulder leaned a trembling woman, of a splendid figure, glittering in diamonds, and veiled.

—Remove the veil, said the old woman to Candide.

The young man stepped timidly forward, and lifted the veil. What an event! What a surprise! Could it be Miss Cunégonde? Yes, it really was! She herself! His knees give way, speech fails him, he falls at her feet, Cunégonde collapses on the sofa. The old woman plies them with brandy, they return to their senses, they exchange words. At first they could utter only broken phrases, questions and answers at cross purposes, sighs, tears, exclamations. The old woman warned them not to make too much noise, and left them alone.

—Then it's really you, said Candide, you're alive, I've found you again in Portugal. Then you never were raped? You never had your belly ripped open, as the philosopher Pangloss assured me?

—Oh yes, said the lovely Cunégonde, but one doesn't always die of these two accidents.

—But your father and mother were murdered then?

—All too true, said Cunégonde, in tears.

—And your brother?

—Killed too.

—And why are you in Portugal? and how did you know I was here? and by what device did you have me brought to this house?

—I shall tell you everything, the lady replied; but first you must tell me what has happened to you since that first innocent kiss we exchanged and the kicking you got because of it.

Candide obeyed her with profound respect; and though he was overcome, though his voice was weak and hesitant, though he still had twinges of pain from his beating, he described as simply as possible everything that had happened to him since the time of their separation. Cunégonde lifted her eyes to heaven; she wept at the death of the good Anabaptist and at that of Pangloss; after which she told the following story to Candide, who listened to every word while he gazed on her with hungry eyes.

CHAPTER 8
Cunégonde's Story

—I was in my bed and fast asleep when heaven chose to send the Bulgars into our castle of Thunder-Ten-Tronckh. They butchered my father and brother, and hacked my mother to bits. An enormous Bulgar, six feet tall, seeing that I had swooned from horror at the scene, set about raping me; at that I recovered my senses, I screamed and scratched, bit and fought, I tried to tear the eyes out of that big Bulgar—not realizing that everything which had happened in my father's castle was a mere matter of routine. The brute then stabbed me with a knife on my left thigh, where I still bear the scar.

—What a pity! I should very much like to see it, said the simple Candide.

—You shall, said Cunégonde; but shall I go on?

—Please do, said Candide.

So she took up the thread of her tale: —A Bulgar captain appeared, he saw me covered with blood and the soldier too intent to get up. Shocked by the monster's failure to come to attention, the captain killed him on my body. He then had my wound dressed, and took me off to his quarters, as a prisoner of war. I laundered his few shirts and did his cooking; he found me attractive, I confess it, and I won't deny that he was a handsome fellow, with a smooth, white skin; apart from that, however, little wit, little philosophical training; it was evident that he had not been brought up by Doctor Pangloss. After three months, he had lost all his money and grown sick of me; so he sold me to a jew named Don Issachar, who traded in Holland and Portugal, and who was mad after women. This jew developed a mighty passion for my person, but he got nowhere with it; I held him off better than I had done with the Bulgar soldier; for though a person of honor may be raped once, her virtue is only strengthened by the experience. In order to keep me hidden, the jew brought me to his country house, which you see here. Till then I had thought there was nothing on earth so beautiful as the castle of Thunder-Ten-Tronckh; I was now undeceived.

—One day the Grand Inquisitor took notice of me at mass; he ogled me a good deal, and made known that he must talk to me on a matter of secret business. I was taken to his palace; I told him of my rank; he pointed out that it was beneath my dignity to belong to an Israelite. A suggestion was then conveyed to Don Issachar that he should turn me over to My Lord the Inquisitor. Don Issachar, who is court banker and a man of standing, refused out of hand. The inquisitor threatened him with an auto-da-fé. Finally my jew, fearing for his life, struck a bargain by which the house and I would belong to both of them as joint tenants; the jew would get Mondays, Wednesdays, and the Sabbath, the inquisitor would get the other days of the week. That has been the arrangement for six months now. There have been quarrels; sometimes it has not been clear whether the night from Saturday to Sunday belonged to the old or the new dispensation. For my part, I have so far been able to hold both of them off; and that, I think, is why they are both still in love with me.

—Finally, in order to avert further divine punishment by earthquake, and to terrify Don Issachar, My Lord the Inquisitor chose to celebrate an auto-da-fé. He did me the honor of inviting me to attend. I had an excellent seat; the ladies were served with refreshments between the mass and the execution. To tell you the truth, I was horrified to see them burn alive those two jews and that decent Biscayan who had married his child's godmother; but what was my surprise, my terror, my grief, when I saw, huddled in a *san-benito* and wearing a mitre, someone who looked like Pangloss! I rubbed my eyes, I watched his every move, I saw him hanged; and I fell back in a swoon. Scarcely had I come to my senses again, when I saw you stripped for the lash; that was the peak of my horror, consternation, grief, and despair. I may tell you, by the way, that your skin is even whiter and more delicate than that of my Bulgar captain. Seeing you, then, redoubled the torments which were already overwhelming me. I shrieked aloud, I wanted to call out, 'Let him go, you brutes!' but my voice died within me, and my cries would have been useless. When you had been thoroughly thrashed: 'How can it be,' I asked myself, 'that agreeable Candide and wise Pangloss have come to Lisbon, one to receive a hundred whiplashes, the other to be hanged by order of My Lord the Inquisitor, whose mistress I am? Pangloss must have deceived me cruelly when he told me that all is for the best in this world.'

—Frantic, exhausted, half out of my senses, and ready to die of weakness, I felt as if my mind were choked with the massacre of my father, my mother, my brother, with the arrogance of that ugly Bulgar soldier, with the knife slash he inflicted on me, my slavery, my cookery, my Bulgar captain, my nasty Don Issachar, my abominable inquisitor, with the hanging of Doctor Pangloss, with that great plainsong *miserere* which they sang while they flogged you—and above all, my mind was full of the kiss which I gave you behind the screen, on the day I saw you for the last time. I praised God, who had brought you back to me after so many trials. I asked my old woman to look out for you, and to bring you here as soon as she could. She did just as I asked; I have had the indescribable joy of seeing you again, hearing you and talking with you once more. But you must be frightfully hungry; I am, myself; let us begin with a dinner.

So then and there they sat down to table; and after dinner, they adjourned to that fine brocaded sofa, which has already been mentioned; and there they were when the eminent Don Issachar, one of the masters of the house, appeared. It was the day of the Sabbath; he was arriving to assert his rights and express his tender passion.

CHAPTER 9
What Happened to Cunégonde, Candide, the Grand Inquisitor, and a Jew

This Issachar was the most choleric Hebrew seen in Israel since the Babylonian captivity.

—What's this, says he, you bitch of a Christian, you're not satisfied with the Grand Inquisitor? Do I have to share you with this rascal, too?

So saying, he drew a long dagger, with which he always went

armed, and, supposing his opponent defenceless, flung himself on Candide. But our good Westphalian had received from the old woman, along with his suit of clothes, a fine sword. Out it came, and though his manners were of the gentlest, in short order he laid the Israelite stiff and cold on the floor, at the feet of the lovely Cunégonde.

—Holy Virgin! she cried. What will become of me now? A man killed in my house! If the police find out, we're done for.

—If Pangloss had not been hanged, said Candide, he would give us good advice in this hour of need, for he was a great philosopher. Lacking him, let's ask the old woman.

She was a sensible body, and was just starting to give her opinion of the situation, when another little door opened. It was just one o'clock in the morning, Sunday morning. This day belonged to the inquisitor. In he came, and found the whipped Candide with a sword in his hand, a corpse at his feet, Cunégonde in terror, and an old woman giving them both good advice.

Here now is what passed through Candide's mind in this instant of time; this is how he reasoned: —If this holy man calls for help, he will certainly have me burned, and perhaps Cunégonde as well; he has already had me whipped without mercy; he is my rival; I have already killed once; why hesitate?

It was a quick, clear chain of reasoning; without giving the inquisitor time to recover from his surprise, he ran him through, and laid him beside the jew.

—Here you've done it again, said Cunégonde; there's no hope for us now. We'll be excommunicated, our last hour has come. How is it that you, who were born so gentle, could kill in two minutes a jew and a prelate?

—My dear girl, replied Candide, when a man is in love, jealous, and just whipped by the Inquisition, he is no longer himself.

The old woman now spoke up and said:—There are three Andalusian steeds in the stable, with their saddles and bridles; our brave Candide must get them ready: my lady has some gold coin and diamonds; let's take to horse at once, though I can only ride on one buttock; we will go to Cadiz. The weather is as fine as can be, and it is pleasant to travel in the cool of the evening.

Promptly, Candide saddled the three horses. Cunégonde, the old woman, and he covered thirty miles without a stop. While they were fleeing, the Holy Brotherhood[7] came to investigate the house; they buried the inquisitor in a fine church, and threw Issachar on the dunghill.

Candide, Cunégonde, and the old woman were already in the lit-

---

7. A semireligious order with police powers, very active in eighteenth-century Spain.

tle town of Avacena, in the middle of the Sierra Morena; and there, as they sat in a country inn, they had this conversation.

CHAPTER 10

In Deep Distress, Candide, Cunégonde, and the Old Woman Reach Cadiz; They Put to Sea

—Who then could have robbed me of my gold and diamonds? said Cunégonde, in tears. How shall we live? what shall we do? where shall I find other inquisitors and jews to give me some more?

—Ah, said the old woman, I strongly suspect that reverend Franciscan friar who shared the inn with us yesterday at Badajoz. God save me from judging him unfairly! But he came into our room twice, and he left long before us.

—Alas, said Candide, the good Pangloss often proved to me that the fruits of the earth are a common heritage of all, to which each man has equal right. On these principles, the Franciscan should at least have left us enough to finish our journey. You have nothing at all, my dear Cunégonde?

—Not a maravedi, said she.

—What to do? said Candide.

—We'll sell one of the horses, said the old woman; I'll ride on the croup behind my mistress, though only on one buttock, and so we will get to Cadiz.

There was in the same inn a Benedictine prior; he bought the horse cheap. Candide, Cunégonde, and the old woman passed through Lucena, Chillas, and Lebrixa, and finally reached Cadiz. There a fleet was being fitted out and an army assembled, to reason with the Jesuit fathers in Paraguay, who were accused of fomenting among their flock a revolt against the kings of Spain and Portugal near the town of St. Sacrement.[8] Candide, having served in the Bulgar army, performed the Bulgar manual of arms before the general of the little army with such grace, swiftness, dexterity, fire, and agility, that they gave him a company of infantry to command. So here he is, a captain; and off he sails with Miss Cunégonde, the old woman, two valets, and the two Andalusian steeds which had belonged to My Lord the Grand Inquisitor of Portugal.

Throughout the crossing, they spent a great deal of time reasoning about the philosophy of poor Pangloss.

—We are destined, in the end, for another universe, said Candide; no doubt that is the one where everything is well. For in

8. Actually, Colonia del Sacramento. Voltaire took great interest in the Jesuit role in Paraguay, which he has much oversimplified and largely misrepresented here in the interests of his satire. In 1750 they did, however, offer armed resistance to an agreement made between Spain and Portugal. They were subdued and expelled in 1769.

this one, it must be admitted, there is some reason to grieve over our physical and moral state.

—I love you with all my heart, said Cunégonde; but my soul is still harrowed by thoughts of what I have seen and suffered.

—All will be well, replied Candide; the sea of this new world is already better than those of Europe, calmer and with steadier winds. Surely it is the New World which is the best of all possible worlds.

—God grant it, said Cunégonde; but I have been so horribly unhappy in the world so far, that my heart is almost dead to hope.

—You pity yourselves, the old woman told them; but you have had no such misfortunes as mine.

Cunégonde nearly broke out laughing; she found the old woman comic in pretending to be more unhappy than she.

—Ah, you poor old thing, said she, unless you've been raped by two Bulgars, been stabbed twice in the belly, seen two of your castles destroyed, witnessed the murder of two of your mothers and two of your fathers, and watched two of your lovers being whipped in an auto-da-fé, I do not see how you can have had it worse than me. Besides, I was born a baroness, with seventy-two quarterings, and I have worked in a scullery.

—My lady, replied the old woman, you do not know my birth and rank; and if I showed you my rear end, you would not talk as you do, you might even speak with less assurance.

These words inspired great curiosity in Candide and Cunégonde, which the old woman satisfied with this story.

CHAPTER 11
The Old Woman's Story

—My eyes were not always bloodshot and red-rimmed, my nose did not always touch my chin, and I was not born a servant. I am in fact the daughter of Pope Urban the Tenth and the Princess of Palestrina.[9] Till the age of fourteen, I lived in a palace so splendid that all the castles of all your German barons would not have served it as a stable; a single one of my dresses was worth more than all the assembled magnificence of Westphalia. I grew in beauty, in charm, in talent, surrounded by pleasures, dignities, and glowing visions of the future. Already I was inspiring the young men to love; my breast was formed—and what a breast! white, firm, with the shape of the Venus de Medici; and what eyes! what lashes, what black brows! What fire flashed from my glances and outshone the glitter

9. Voltaire left behind a comment on this passage, a note first published in 1829: "Note the extreme discretion of the author; hitherto there has never been a pope named Urban X; he avoided attributing a bastard to a known pope. What circumspection! what an exquisite conscience!"

of the stars, as the local poets used to tell me! The women who helped me dress and undress fell into ecstasies, whether they looked at me from in front or behind; and all the men wanted to be in their place.

—I was engaged to the ruling prince of Massa-Carrara; and what a prince he was! as handsome as I, softness and charm compounded, brilliantly witty, and madly in love with me. I loved him in return as one loves for the first time, with a devotion approaching idolatry. The wedding preparations had been made, with a splendor and magnificence never heard of before; nothing but celebrations, masks, and comic operas, uninterruptedly; and all Italy composed in my honor sonnets of which not one was even passable. I had almost attained the very peak of bliss, when an old marquise who had been the mistress of my prince invited him to her house for a cup of chocolate. He died in less than two hours, amid horrifying convulsions. But that was only a trifle. My mother, in complete despair (though less afflicted than I), wished to escape for a while the oppressive atmosphere of grief. She owned a handsome property near Gaeta.[1] We embarked on a papal galley gilded like the altar of St. Peter's in Rome. Suddenly a pirate ship from Salé swept down and boarded us. Our soldiers defended themselves as papal troops usually do; falling on their knees and throwing down their arms, they begged of the corsair absolution *in articulo mortis*.[2]

—They were promptly stripped as naked as monkeys, and so was my mother, and so were our maids of honor, and so was I too. It's a very remarkable thing, the energy these gentlemen put into stripping people. But what surprised me even more was that they stuck their fingers in a place where we women usually admit only a syringe. This ceremony seemed a bit odd to me, as foreign usages always do when one hasn't traveled. They only wanted to see if we didn't have some diamonds hidden there; and I soon learned that it's a custom of long standing among the genteel folk who swarm the seas. I learned that my lords the very religious knights of Malta never overlook this ceremony when they capture Turks, whether male or female; it's one of those international laws which have never been questioned.

—I won't try to explain how painful it is for a young princess to be carried off into slavery in Morocco with her mother. You can imagine everything we had to suffer on the pirate ship. My mother was still very beautiful; our maids of honor, our mere chambermaids, were more charming than anything one could find in all Africa. As for myself, I was ravishing, I was loveliness and grace su-

1. About halfway between Rome and Naples.
2. Literally, when at the point of death.

Absolution from a corsair in the act of murdering one is of very dubious validity.

preme, and I was a virgin. I did not remain so for long; the flower which had been kept for the handsome prince of Massa-Carrara was plucked by the corsair captain; he was an abominable negro, who thought he was doing me a great favor. My Lady the Princess of Palestrina and I must have been strong indeed to bear what we did during our journey to Morocco. But on with my story; these are such common matters that they are not worth describing.

—Morocco was knee deep in blood when we arrived. Of the fifty sons of the emperor Muley-Ismael,[3] each had his faction, which produced in effect fifty civil wars, of blacks against blacks, of blacks against browns, halfbreeds against halfbreeds; throughout the length and breadth of the empire, nothing but one continual carnage.

—Scarcely had we stepped ashore, when some negroes of a faction hostile to my captor arrived to take charge of his plunder. After the diamonds and gold, we women were the most prized possessions. I was now witness of a struggle such as you never see in the temperate climate of Europe. Northern people don't have hot blood; they don't feel the absolute fury for women which is common in Africa. Europeans seem to have milk in their veins; it is vitriol or liquid fire which pulses through these people around Mount Atlas. The fight for possession of us raged with the fury of the lions, tigers, and poisonous vipers of that land. A Moor snatched my mother by the right arm, the first mate held her by the left; a Moorish soldier grabbed one leg, one of our pirates the other. In a moment's time almost all our girls were being dragged four different ways. My captain held me behind him while with his scimitar he killed everyone who braved his fury. At last I saw all our Italian women, including my mother, torn to pieces, cut to bits, murdered by the monsters who were fighting over them. My captive companions, their captors, soldiers, sailors, blacks, browns, whites, mulattoes, and at last my captain, all were killed, and I remained half dead on a mountain of corpses. Similar scenes were occurring, as is well known, for more than three hundred leagues around, without anyone skimping on the five prayers a day decreed by Mohammed.

—With great pain, I untangled myself from this vast heap of bleeding bodies, and dragged myself under a great orange tree by a neighboring brook, where I collapsed, from terror, exhaustion, horror, despair, and hunger. Shortly, my weary mind surrendered to a sleep which was more of a swoon than a rest. I was in this state of weakness and languor, between life and death, when I felt myself

3. Having reigned for more than fifty years, a potent and ruthless sultan of Morocco, he died in 1727 and left his kingdom in much the condition described.

touched by something which moved over my body. Opening my eyes, I saw a white man, rather attractive, who was groaning and saying under his breath: '*O che sciagura d'essere senza coglioni!*'[4]

CHAPTER 12
The Old Woman's Story Continued

—Amazed and delighted to hear my native tongue, and no less surprised by what this man was saying, I told him that there were worse evils than those he was complaining of. In a few words, I described to him the horrors I had undergone, and then fainted again. He carried me to a nearby house, put me to bed, gave me something to eat, served me, flattered me, comforted me, told me he had never seen anyone so lovely, and added that he had never before regretted so much the loss of what nobody could give him back.

'I was born at Naples, he told me, where they caponize two or three thousand children every year; some die of it, others acquire a voice more beautiful than any woman's, still others go on to become governors of kingdoms.[5] The operation was a great success with me, and I became court musician to the Princess of Palestrina . . .'

'Of my mother,' I exclaimed.

'Of your mother,' cried he, bursting into tears; 'then you must be the princess whom I raised till she was six, and who already gave promise of becoming as beautiful as you are now!'

'I am that very princess; my mother lies dead, not a hundred yards from here, buried under a pile of corpses.'

—I told him my adventures, he told me his: that he had been sent by a Christian power to the King of Morocco, to conclude a treaty granting him gunpowder, cannon, and ships with which to liquidate the traders of the other Christian powers.

'My mission is concluded,' said this honest eunuch; 'I shall take ship at Ceuta and bring you back to Italy. *Ma che sciagura d'essere senza coglioni!*'

—I thanked him with tears of gratitude, and instead of returning me to Italy, he took me to Algiers and sold me to the dey of that country. Hardly had the sale taken place, when that plague which has made the rounds of Africa, Asia, and Europe broke out in full fury at Algiers. You have seen earthquakes; but tell me, young lady, have you ever had the plague?

—Never, replied the baroness.

—If you had had it, said the old woman, you would agree that it is far worse than an earthquake. It is very frequent in Africa, and I

4. "Oh what a misfortune to have no testicles!"
5. The castrate Farinelli (1705–1782), originally a singer, came to exercise considerable political influence on the Kings of Spain, Philip V and Ferdinand VI.

had it. Imagine, if you will, the situation of a pope's daughter, fifteen years old, who in three months' time had experienced poverty, slavery, had been raped almost every day, had seen her mother quartered, had suffered from famine and war, and who now was dying of pestilence in Algiers. As a matter of fact, I did not die; but the eunuch and the dey and nearly the entire seraglio of Algiers perished.

—When the first horrors of this ghastly plague had passed, the slaves of the dey were sold. A merchant bought me and took me to Tunis; there he sold me to another merchant, who resold me at Tripoli; from Tripoli I was sold to Alexandria, from Alexandria resold to Smyrna, from Smyrna to Constantinople. I ended by belonging to an aga of janizaries, who was shortly ordered to defend Azov against the besieging Russians.[6]

—The aga, who was a gallant soldier, took his whole seraglio with him, and established us in a little fort amid the Maeotian marshes,[7] guarded by two black eunuchs and twenty soldiers. Our side killed a prodigious number of Russians, but they paid us back nicely. Azov was put to fire and sword without respect for age or sex; only our little fort continued to resist, and the enemy determined to starve us out. The twenty janizaries had sworn never to surrender. Reduced to the last extremities of hunger, they were forced to eat our two eunuchs, lest they violate their oaths. After several more days, they decided to eat the women too.

—We had an imam,[8] very pious and sympathetic, who delivered an excellent sermon, persuading them not to kill us altogether.

'Just cut off a single rumpsteak from each of these ladies,' he said, 'and you'll have a fine meal. Then if you should need another, you can come back in a few days and have as much again; heaven will bless your charitable action, and you will be saved.'

—His eloquence was splendid, and he persuaded them. We underwent this horrible operation. The imam treated us all with the ointment that they use on newly circumcised children. We were at the point of death.

—Scarcely had the janizaries finished the meal for which we furnished the materials, when the Russians appeared in flat-bottomed boats; not a janizary escaped. The Russians paid no attention to the state we were in; but there are French physicians everywhere, and one of them, who knew his trade, took care of us. He cured us, and I shall remember all my life that when my wounds were healed, he made me a proposition. For the rest, he counselled us simply to

---

6. Azov, near the mouth of the Don, was besieged by the Russians under Peter the Great in 1695–1696. The janizaries were an élite corps of the Ottoman armies.

7. The Roman name of the so-called Sea of Azov, a shallow swampy lake near the town.

8. In effect, a chaplain.

have patience, assuring us that the same thing had happened in several other sieges, and that it was according to the laws of war.

—As soon as my companions could walk, we were herded off to Moscow. In the division of booty, I fell to a boyar who made me work in his garden, and gave me twenty whiplashes a day; but when he was broken on the wheel after about two years, with thirty other boyars, over some little court intrigue,[9] I seized the occasion; I ran away; I crossed all Russia; I was for a long time a chambermaid in Riga, then at Rostock, Vismara, Leipzig, Cassel, Utrecht, Leyden, The Hague, Rotterdam; I grew old in misery and shame, having only half a backside and remembering always that I was the daughter of a Pope; a hundred times I wanted to kill myself, but always I loved life more. This ridiculous weakness is perhaps one of our worst instincts; is anything more stupid than choosing to carry a burden that really one wants to cast on the ground? to hold existence in horror, and yet to cling to it? to fondle the serpent which devours us till it has eaten out our heart?

—In the countries through which I have been forced to wander, in the taverns where I have had to work, I have seen a vast number of people who hated their existence; but I never saw more than a dozen who deliberately put an end to their own misery: three negroes, four Englishmen, four Genevans, and a German professor named Robeck.[1] My last post was as servant to the jew Don Issachar; he attached me to your service, my lovely one; and I attached myself to your destiny, till I have become more concerned with your fate than with my own. I would not even have mentioned my own misfortunes, if you had not irked me a bit, and if it weren't the custom, on shipboard, to pass the time with stories. In a word, my lady, I have had some experience of the world, I know it; why not try this diversion? Ask every passenger on this ship to tell you his story, and if you find a single one who has not often cursed the day of his birth, who has not often told himself that he is the most miserable of men, then you may throw me overboard head first.

9. Voltaire had in mind an ineffectual conspiracy against Peter the Great known as the "revolt of the strelitz" or musketeers, which took place in 1698. Though easily put down, it provoked from the emperor a massive and atrocious program of reprisals.

1. Johann Robeck (1672–1739) published a treatise advocating suicide and showed his conviction by drowning himself. But he waited till he was 67 before putting his theory to the test. For a larger view of the issue, see L. G. Crocker, "The Discussion of Suicide in the 18th Century," *Journal of the History of Ideas*, XIII, 47–72 (1952).

CHAPTER 13

How Candide Was Forced to Leave the Lovely
Cunégonde and the Old Woman

Having heard out the old woman's story, the lovely Cunégonde paid her the respects which were appropriate to a person of her rank and merit. She took up the wager as well, and got all the passengers, one after another, to tell her their adventures. She and Candide had to agree that the old woman had been right.

—It's certainly too bad, said Candide, that the wise Pangloss was hanged, contrary to the custom of autos-da-fé; he would have admirable things to say of the physical evil and moral evil which cover land and sea, and I might feel within me the impulse to dare to raise several polite objections.

As the passengers recited their stories, the boat made steady progress, and presently landed at Buenos Aires. Cunégonde, Captain Candide, and the old woman went to call on the governor, Don Fernando d'Ibaraa y Figueroa y Mascarenes y Lampourdos y Souza. This nobleman had the pride appropriate to a man with so many names. He addressed everyone with the most aristocratic disdain, pointing his nose so loftily, raising his voice so mercilessly, lording it so splendidly, and assuming so arrogant a pose, that everyone who met him wanted to kick him. He loved women to the point of fury; and Cunégonde seemed to him the most beautiful creature he had ever seen. The first thing he did was to ask directly if she were the captain's wife. His manner of asking this question disturbed Candide; he did not dare say she was his wife, because in fact she was not; he did not dare say she was his sister, because she wasn't that either; and though this polite lie was once common enough among the ancients,[2] and sometimes serves moderns very well, he was too pure of heart to tell a lie.

—Miss Cunégonde, said he, is betrothed to me, and we humbly beg your excellency to perform the ceremony for us.

Don Fernando d'Ibaraa y Figueroa y Mascarenes y Lampourdos y Souza twirled his moustache, smiled sardonically, and ordered Captain Candide to go drill his company. Candide obeyed. Left alone with My Lady Cunégonde, the governor declared his passion, and protested that he would marry her tomorrow, in church or in any other manner, as it pleased her charming self. Cunégonde asked for a quarter-hour to collect herself, consult the old woman, and make up her mind.

The old woman said to Cunégonde: —My lady, you have

2. Voltaire has in mind Abraham's adventures with Sarah (Genesis xii) and Isaac's with Rebecca (Genesis xxvi).

seventy-two quarterings and not one penny; if you wish, you may be the wife of the greatest lord in South America, who has a really handsome moustache; are you going to insist on your absolute fidelity? You have already been raped by the Bulgars; a jew and an inquisitor have enjoyed your favors; miseries entitle one to privileges. I assure you that in your position I would make no scruple of marrying My Lord the Governor, and making the fortune of Captain Candide.

While the old woman was talking with all the prudence of age and experience, there came into the harbor a small ship bearing an alcalde and some alguazils.[3] This is what had happened.

As the old woman had very shrewdly guessed, it was a long-sleeved Franciscan who stole Cunégonde's gold and jewels in the town of Badajoz, when she and Candide were in flight. The monk tried to sell some of the gems to a jeweler, who recognized them as belonging to the Grand Inquisitor. Before he was hanged, the Franciscan confessed that he had stolen them, indicating who his victims were and where they were going. The flight of Cunégonde and Candide was already known. They were traced to Cadiz, and a vessel was hastily dispatched in pursuit of them. This vessel was now in the port of Buenos Aires. The rumor spread that an alcalde was aboard, in pursuit of the murderers of My Lord the Grand Inquisitor. The shrewd old woman saw at once what was to be done.

—You cannot escape, she told Cunégonde, and you have nothing to fear. You are not the one who killed my lord, and, besides, the governor, who is in love with you, won't let you be mistreated. Sit tight.

And then she ran straight to Candide: —Get out of town, she said, or you'll be burned within the hour.

There was not a moment to lose; but how to leave Cunégonde, and where to go?

CHAPTER 14

How Candide and Cacambo Were Received by the Jesuits of Paraguay

Candide had brought from Cadiz a valet of the type one often finds in the provinces of Spain and in the colonies. He was one quarter Spanish, son of a halfbreed in the Tucuman[4]; he had been choirboy, sacristan, sailor, monk, merchant, soldier, and lackey. His name was Cacambo, and he was very fond of his master because his

---

3. Police officers.
4. A city and province of Argentina, to the northwest of Buenos Aires, just

at the juncture of the Andes and the Grand Chaco.

master was a very good man. In hot haste he saddled the two Andalusian steeds.

—Hurry, master, do as the old woman says; let's get going and leave this town without a backward look.

Candide wept: —O my beloved Cunégonde! must I leave you now, just when the governor is about to marry us! Cunégonde, brought from so far, what will ever become of you?

—She'll become what she can, said Cacambo; women can always find something to do with themselves; God sees to it; let's get going.

—Where are you taking me? where are we going? what will we do without Cunégonde? said Candide.

—By Saint James of Compostela, said Cacambo, you were going to make war against the Jesuits, now we'll go make war for them. I know the roads pretty well, I'll bring you to their country, they will be delighted to have a captain who knows the Bulgar drill; you'll make a prodigious fortune. If you don't get your rights in one world, you will find them in another. And isn't it pleasant to see new things and do new things?

—Then you've already been in Paraguay? said Candide.

—Indeed I have, replied Cacambo; I was cook in the College of the Assumption, and I know the government of Los Padres[5] as I know the streets of Cadiz. It's an admirable thing, this government. The kingdom is more than three hundred leagues across; it is divided into thirty provinces. Los Padres own everything in it, and the people nothing; it's a masterpiece of reason and justice. I myself know nothing so wonderful as Los Padres, who in this hemisphere make war on the kings of Spain and Portugal, but in Europe hear their confessions; who kill Spaniards here, and in Madrid send them to heaven; that really tickles me; let's get moving, you're going to be the happiest of men. Won't Los Padres be delighted when they learn they have a captain who knows the Bulgar drill!

As soon as they reached the first barricade, Cacambo told the frontier guard that a captain wished to speak with My Lord the Commander. A Paraguayan officer ran to inform headquarters by laying the news at the feet of the commander. Candide and Cacambo were first disarmed and deprived of their Andalusian horses. They were then placed between two files of soldiers; the commander was at the end, his three-cornered hat on his head, his cassock drawn up, a sword at his side, and a pike in his hand. He nods, and twenty-four soldiers surround the newcomers. A sergeant then informs them that they must wait, that the commander cannot talk to them, since the reverend father provincial has forbidden all

5. The Jesuit fathers. R. B. Cunningham-Grahame has written an account of the Jesuits in Paraguay 1607–1767, under the title *A Vanished Arcadia.*

Spaniards from speaking, except in his presence, and from remaining more than three hours in the country.[6]

—And where is the reverend father provincial? says Cacambo.

—He is reviewing his troops after having said mass, the sergeant replies, and you'll only be able to kiss his spurs in three hours.

—But, says Cacambo, my master the captain, who, like me, is dying from hunger, is not Spanish at all, he is German; can't we have some breakfast while waiting for his reverence?

The sergeant promptly went off to report this speech to the commander.

—God be praised, said this worthy; since he is German, I can talk to him; bring him into my bower.

Candide was immediately led into a leafy nook surrounded by a handsome colonnade of green and gold marble and trellises amid which sported parrots, birds of paradise,[7] humming birds, guinea fowl, and all the rarest species of birds. An excellent breakfast was prepared in golden vessels; and while the Paraguayans ate corn out of wooden bowls in the open fields under the glare of the sun, the reverend father commander entered into his bower.

He was a very handsome young man, with an open face, rather blonde in coloring, with ruddy complexion, arched eyebrows, liquid eyes, pink ears, bright red lips, and an air of pride, but a pride somehow different from that of a Spaniard or a Jesuit. Their confiscated weapons were restored to Candide and Cacambo, as well as their Andalusian horses; Cacambo fed them oats alongside the bower, always keeping an eye on them for fear of an ambush.

First Candide kissed the hem of the commander's cassock, then they sat down at the table.

—So you are German? said the Jesuit, speaking in that language.

—Yes, your reverence, said Candide.

As they spoke these words, both men looked at one another with great surprise, and another emotion which they could not control.

—From what part of Germany do you come? said the Jesuit.

—From the nasty province of Westphalia, said Candide; I was born in the castle of Thunder-Ten-Tronckh.

—Merciful heavens! cries the commander. Is it possible?

—What a miracle! exclaims Candide.

---

6. In fact, the Jesuits, who had organized their Indian parishes into villages under a system of tribal communism, did their best to discourage contact with the outside world.

7. In this passage and several later ones, Voltaire uses in conjunction two words, both of which mean humming bird. The French system of classifying humming birds, based on the work of the celebrated Buffon, distinguishes *oiseaux-mouches* with straight bills from *colibris* with curved bills. This distinction is wholly fallacious. Humming birds have all manner of shaped bills, and the division of species must be made on other grounds entirely. At the expense of ornithological accuracy, I have therefore introduced birds of paradise to get the requisite sense of glitter and sheen.

—Can it be you? asks the commander.

—It's impossible, says Candide.

They both fall back in their chairs, they embrace they shed streams of tears.

—What, can it be you, reverend father! you, the brother of the lovely Cunégonde! you, who were killed by the Bulgars! you, the son of My Lord the Baron! you, a Jesuit in Paraguay! It's a mad world, indeed it is. Oh, Pangloss! Pangloss! how happy you would be, if you hadn't been hanged.

The commander dismissed his negro slaves and the Paraguayans who served his drink in crystal goblets. He thanked God and Saint Ignatius a thousand times, he clasped Candide in his arms, their faces were bathed in tears.

—You would be even more astonished, even more delighted, even more beside yourself, said Candide, if I told you that My Lady Cunégonde, your sister, who you thought was disemboweled, is enjoying good health.

—Where?

—Not far from here, in the house of the governor of Buenos Aires; and to think that I came to make war on you!

Each word they spoke in this long conversation added another miracle. Their souls danced on their tongues, hung eagerly at their ears, glittered in their eyes. As they were Germans, they sat a long time at table, waiting for the reverend father provincial; and the commander spoke in these terms to his dear Candide.

CHAPTER 15

How Candide Killed the Brother of His Dear Cunégonde

—All my life long I shall remember the horrible day when I saw my father and mother murdered and my sister raped. When the Bulgars left, that adorable sister of mine was nowhere to be found; so they loaded a cart with my mother, my father, myself, two serving girls, and three little murdered boys, to carry us all off for burial in a Jesuit chapel some two leagues from our ancestral castle. A Jesuit sprinkled us with holy water; it was horribly salty, and a few drops got into my eyes; the father noticed that my lid made a little tremor; putting his hand on my heart, he felt it beat; I was rescued, and at the end of three weeks was as good as new. You know, my dear Candide, that I was a very pretty boy; I became even more so; the reverend father Croust,[8] superior of the abbey, conceived a most tender friendship for me; he accepted me as a novice, and shortly after, I was sent to Rome. The Father General had need of

8. It is the name of a Jesuit rector at Colmar with whom Voltaire had quarreled in 1754.

a resupply of young German Jesuits. The rulers of Paraguay accept as few Spanish Jesuits as they can; they prefer foreigners, whom they think they can control better. I was judged fit, by the Father General, to labor in this vineyard. So we set off, a Pole, a Tyrolean, and myself. Upon our arrival, I was honored with the posts of sub-deacon and lieutenant; today I am a colonel and a priest. We are giving a vigorous reception to the King of Spain's men; I assure you they will be excommunicated as well as trounced on the battlefield. Providence has sent you to help us. But is it really true that my dear sister, Cunégonde, is in the neighborhood, with the governor of Buenos Aires?

Candide reassured him with a solemn oath that nothing could be more true. Their tears began to flow again.

The baron could not weary of embracing Candide; he called him his brother, his savior.

—Ah, my dear Candide, said he, maybe together we will be able to enter the town as conquerors, and be united with my sister Cunégonde.

—That is all I desire, said Candide; I was expecting to marry her, and I still hope to.

—You insolent dog, replied the baron, you would have the effrontery to marry my sister, who has seventy-two quarterings! It's a piece of presumption for you even to mention such a crazy project in my presence.

Candide, terrified by this speech, answered: —Most reverend father, all the quarterings in the world don't affect this case; I have rescued your sister out of the arms of a jew and an inquisitor; she has many obligations to me, she wants to marry me. Master Pangloss always taught me that men are equal; and I shall certainly marry her.

—We'll see about that, you scoundrel, said the Jesuit baron of Thunder-Ten-Tronckh; and so saying, he gave him a blow across the face with the flat of his sword. Candide immediately drew his own sword and thrust it up to the hilt in the baron's belly; but as he drew it forth all dripping, he began to weep.

—Alas, dear God! said he, I have killed my old master, my friend, my brother-in-law; I am the best man in the world, and here are three men I've killed already, and two of the three were priests.

Cacambo, who was standing guard at the entry of the bower, came running.

—We can do nothing but sell our lives dearly, said his master; someone will certainly come; we must die fighting.

Cacambo, who had been in similar scrapes before, did not lose his head; he took the Jesuit's cassock, which the commander had been wearing, and put it on Candide; he stuck the dead man's square hat on Candide's head, and forced him onto horseback. Everything was done in the wink of an eye.

—Let's ride, master; everyone will take you for a Jesuit on his way to deliver orders; and we will have passed the frontier before anyone can come after us.

Even as he was pronouncing these words, he charged off, crying in Spanish: —Way, make way for the reverend father colonel!

CHAPTER 16

What Happened to the Two Travelers with Two Girls, Two Monkeys, and the Savages Named Biglugs

Candide and his valet were over the frontier before anyone in the camp knew of the death of the German Jesuit. Foresighted Cacambo had taken care to fill his satchel with bread, chocolate, ham, fruit, and several bottles of wine. They pushed their Andalusian horses forward into unknown country, where there were no roads. Finally a broad prairie divided by several streams opened before them. Our two travelers turned their horses loose to graze; Cacambo suggested that they eat too, and promptly set the example. But Candide said: —How can you expect me to eat ham when I have killed the son of My Lord the Baron, and am now condemned never to see the lovely Cunégonde for the rest of my life? Why should I drag out my miserable days, since I must exist far from her in in the depths of despair and remorse? And what will the *Journal de Trévoux* say of all this?[9]

Though he talked this way, he did not neglect the food. Night fell. The two wanderers heard a few weak cries which seemed to be voiced by women. They could not tell whether the cries expressed grief or joy; but they leaped at once to their feet, with that uneasy suspicion which one always feels in an unknown country. The outcry arose from two girls, completely naked, who were running swiftly along the edge of the meadow, pursued by two monkeys who snapped at their buttocks. Candide was moved to pity; he had learned marksmanship with the Bulgars, and could have knocked a nut off a bush without touching the leaves. He raised his Spanish rifle, fired twice, and killed the two monkeys.

—God be praised, my dear Cacambo! I've saved these two poor creatures from great danger. Though I committed a sin in killing an inquisitor and a Jesuit, I've redeemed myself by saving the lives of two girls. Perhaps they are two ladies of rank, and this good deed may gain us special advantages in the country.

He had more to say, but his mouth shut suddenly when he

9. A journal published by the Jesuit order, founded in 1701 and consistently hostile to Voltaire.

saw the girls embracing the monkeys tenderly, weeping over their bodies, and filling the air with lamentations.

—I wasn't looking for quite so much generosity of spirit, said he to Cacambo; the latter replied: —You've really fixed things this time, master; you've killed the two lovers of these young ladies.

—Their lovers! Impossible! You must be joking, Cacambo; how can I believe you?

—My dear master, Cacambo replied, you're always astonished by everything. Why do you think it so strange that in some countries monkeys succeed in obtaining the good graces of women? They are one quarter human, just as I am one quarter Spanish.

—Alas, Candide replied, I do remember now hearing Master Pangloss say that such things used to happen, and that from these mixtures there arose pans, fauns, and satyrs, and that these creatures had appeared to various grand figures of antiquity; but I took all that for fables.

—You should be convinced now, said Cacambo; it's true, and you see how people make mistakes who haven't received a measure of education. But what I fear is that these girls may get us into real trouble.

These sensible reflections led Candide to leave the field and to hide in a wood. There he dined with Cacambo; and there both of them, having duly cursed the inquisitor of Portugal, the governor of Buenos Aires, and the baron, went to sleep on a bed of moss. When they woke up, they found themselves unable to move; the reason was that during the night the Biglugs,[1] natives of the country, to whom the girls had complained of them, had tied them down with cords of bark. They were surrounded by fifty naked Biglugs, armed with arrows, clubs, and stone axes. Some were boiling a caldron of water, others were preparing spits, and all cried out: —It's a Jesuit, a Jesuit! We'll be revenged and have a good meal; let's eat some Jesuit, eat some Jesuit!

—I told you, my dear master, said Cacambo sadly, I said those two girls would play us a dirty trick.

Candide, noting the caldron and spits, cried out: —We are surely going to be roasted or boiled. Ah, what would Master Pangloss say if he could see these men in a state of nature? All is for the best, I agree; but I must say it seems hard to have lost Miss Cunégonde and to be stuck on a spit by the Biglugs.

Cacambo did not lose his head.

—Don't give up hope, said he to the disconsolate Candide; I

---

1. Voltaire's name is "Oreillons" from Spanish "Orejones," a name mentioned in Garcilaso de Vega's *Historia General del Perú* (1609), on which Voltaire drew for many of the details in his picture of South America. See Richard A. Brooks, "Voltaire and Garcilaso de Vega" in *Studies in Voltaire and the 18th Century*, XXX, 189-204.

understand a little of the jargon these people speak, and I'm going to talk to them.

—Don't forget to remind them, said Candide, of the frightful inhumanity of eating their fellow men, and that Christian ethics forbid it.

—Gentlemen, said Cacambo, you have a mind to eat a Jesuit today? An excellent idea; nothing is more proper than to treat one's enemies so. Indeed, the law of nature teaches us to kill our neighbor, and that's how men behave the whole world over. Though we Europeans don't exercise our right to eat our neighbors, the reason is simply that we find it easy to get a good meal elsewhere; but you don't have our resources, and we certainly agree that it's better to eat your enemies than to let the crows and vultures have the fruit of your victory. But, gentlemen, you wouldn't want to eat your friends. You think you will be spitting a Jesuit, and it's your defender, the enemy of your enemies, whom you will be roasting. For my part, I was born in your country; the gentleman whom you see is my master, and far from being a Jesuit, he has just killed a Jesuit, the robe he is wearing was stripped from him; that's why you have taken a dislike to him. To prove that I am telling the truth, take his robe and bring it to the nearest frontier of the kingdom of Los Padres; find out for yourselves if my master didn't kill a Jesuit officer. It won't take long; if you find that I have lied, you can still eat us. But if I've told the truth, you know too well the principles of public justice, customs, and laws, not to spare our lives.

The Biglugs found this discourse perfectly reasonable; they appointed chiefs to go posthaste and find out the truth; the two messengers performed their task like men of sense, and quickly returned bringing good news. The Biglugs untied their two prisoners, treated them with great politeness, offered them girls, gave them refreshments, and led them back to the border of their state, crying joyously: —He isn't a Jesuit, he isn't a Jesuit!

Candide could not weary of exclaiming over his preservation.

—What a people! he said. What men! what customs! If I had not had the good luck to run a sword through the body of Miss Cunégonde's brother, I would have been eaten on the spot! But, after all, it seems that uncorrupted nature is good, since these folk, instead of eating me, showed me a thousand kindnesses as soon as they knew I was not a Jesuit.

CHAPTER 17
*Arrival of Candide and His Servant at the
Country of Eldorado,[2] and What They Saw There*

When they were out of the land of the Biglugs, Cacambo said to
Candide: —You see that this hemisphere is no better than the
other; take my advice, and let's get back to Europe as soon as possible.

—How to get back, asked Candide, and where to go? If I go to
my own land, the Bulgars and Abares are murdering everyone in
sight; if I go to Portugal, they'll burn me alive; if we stay here, we
risk being skewered any day. But how can I ever leave that part of
the world where Miss Cunégonde lives?

—Let's go toward Cayenne, said Cacambo, we shall find some
Frenchmen there, for they go all over the world; they can help us;
perhaps God will take pity on us.

To get to Cayenne was not easy; they knew more or less which
way to go, but mountains, rivers, cliffs, robbers, and savages ob-
structed the way everywhere. Their horses died of weariness; their
food was eaten; they subsisted for one whole month on wild fruits,
and at last they found themselves by a little river fringed with coco-
nut trees, which gave them both life and hope.

Cacambo, who was as full of good advice as the old woman, said
to Candide: —We can go no further, we've walked ourselves out; I
see an abandoned canoe on the bank, let's fill it with coconuts, get
into the boat, and float with the current; a river always leads to
some inhabited spot or other. If we don't find anything pleasant, at
least we may find something new.

—Let's go, said Candide, and let Providence be our guide.

They floated some leagues between banks sometimes flowery,
sometimes sandy, now steep, now level. The river widened steadily;
finally it disappeared into a chasm of frightful rocks that rose high
into the heavens.[3] The two travelers had the audacity to float with
the current into this chasm. The river, narrowly confined, drove
them onward with horrible speed and a fearful roar. After twenty-
four hours, they saw daylight once more; but their canoe was
smashed on the snags. They had to drag themselves from rock to
rock for an entire league; at last they emerged to an immense horizon, ringed with remote mountains. The countryside was tended for
pleasure as well as profit; everywhere the useful was joined to the
agreeable. The roads were covered, or rather decorated, with ele-

2. The myth of this land of gold somewhere in Central or South America had
been widespread since the sixteenth
century.

3. This journey down an underground
river is probably adapted from a similar episode in the story of Sinbad the
Sailor.

gantly shaped carriages made of a glittering material, carrying men and women of singular beauty, and drawn by great red sheep which were faster than the finest horses of Andalusia, Tetuan, and Mequinez.

—Here now, said Candide, is a country that's better than Westphalia.

Along with Cacambo, he climbed out of the river at the first village he could see. Some children of the town, dressed in rags of gold brocade, were playing quoits at the village gate; our two men from the other world paused to watch them; their quoits were rather large, yellow, red, and green, and they glittered with a singular luster. On a whim, the travelers picked up several; they were of gold, emeralds, and rubies, and the least of them would have been the greatest ornament of the Great Mogul's throne.

—Surely, said Cacambo, these quoit players are the children of the king of the country.

The village schoolmaster appeared at that moment, to call them back to school.

—And there, said Candide, is the tutor of the royal household.

The little rascals quickly gave up their game, leaving on the ground their quoits and playthings. Candide picked them up, ran to the schoolmaster, and presented them to him humbly, giving him to understand by sign language that their royal highnesses had forgotten their gold and jewels. With a smile, the schoolmaster tossed them to the ground, glanced quickly but with great surprise at Candide's face, and went his way.

The travelers did not fail to pick up the gold, rubies, and emeralds.

—Where in the world are we? cried Candide. The children of this land must be well trained, since they are taught contempt for gold and jewels.

Cacambo was as much surprised as Candide. At last they came to the finest house of the village; it was built like a European palace. A crowd of people surrounded the door, and even more were in the entry; delightful music was heard, and a delicious aroma of cooking filled the air. Cacambo went up to the door, listened, and reported that they were talking Peruvian; that was his native language, for every reader must know that Cacambo was born in Tucuman, in a village where they talk that language exclusively.

—I'll act as interpreter, he told Candide; it's an hotel, let's go in.

Promptly two boys and two girls of the staff, dressed in cloth of gold, and wearing ribbons in their hair, invited them to sit at the host's table. The meal consisted of four soups, each one garnished with a brace of parakeets, a boiled condor which weighed two hundred pounds, two roast monkeys of an excellent flavor, three hundred birds of paradise in one dish and six hundred humming birds in another, exquisite stews, delicious pastries, the whole thing served up in plates of what looked like rock crystal. The boys and girls of the staff poured them various beverages made from sugar cane.

The diners were for the most part merchants and travelers, all extremely polite, who questioned Cacambo with the most discreet circumspection, and answered his questions very directly.

When the meal was over, Cacambo as well as Candide supposed he could settle his bill handsomely by tossing onto the table two of those big pieces of gold which they had picked up; but the host and hostess burst out laughing, and for a long time nearly split their sides. Finally they subsided.

—Gentlemen, said the host, we see clearly that you're foreigners; we don't meet many of you here. Please excuse our laughing when you offered us in payment a couple of pebbles from the roadside. No doubt you don't have any of our local currency, but you don't need it to eat here. All the hotels established for the promotion of commerce are maintained by the state. You have had meager entertainment here, for we are only a poor town; but everywhere else you will be given the sort of welcome you deserve.

Cacambo translated for Candide all the host's explanations, and Candide listened to them with the same admiration and astonishment that his friend Cacambo showed in reporting them.

—What is this country, then, said they to one another, unknown to the rest of the world, and where nature itself is so different from our own? This probably is the country where everything is for the best; for it's absolutely necessary that such a country should exist somewhere. And whatever Master Pangloss said of the matter, I have often had occasion to notice that things went badly in Westphalia.

CHAPTER 18

What They Saw in the Land of Eldorado

Cacambo revealed his curiosity to the host, and the host told him: —I am an ignorant man and content to remain so; but we have here an old man, retired from the court, who is the most knowing person in the kingdom, and the most talkative.

Thereupon he brought Cacambo to the old man's house. Candide now played second fiddle, and acted as servant to his own valet. They entered an austere little house, for the door was merely of silver and the paneling of the rooms was only gold, though so tastefully wrought that the finest paneling would not surpass it. If the truth must be told, the lobby was only decorated with rubies and emeralds; but the patterns in which they were arranged atoned for the extreme simplicity.

The old man received the two strangers on a sofa stuffed with bird-of-paradise feathers, and offered them several drinks in diamond carafes; then he satisfied their curiosity in these terms.

—I am a hundred and seventy-two years old, and I heard from my late father, who was liveryman to the king, about the astonishing revolutions in Peru which he had seen. Our land here was formerly part of the kingdom of the Incas, who rashly left it in order to conquer another part of the world, and who were ultimately destroyed by the Spaniards. The wisest princes of their house were those who had never left their native valley; they decreed, with the consent of the nation, that henceforth no inhabitant of our little kingdom should ever leave it; and this rule is what has preserved our innocence and our happiness. The Spaniards heard vague rumors about this land, they called it El Dorado; and an English knight named Raleigh[4] even came somewhere close to it about a hundred years ago; but as we are surrounded by unscalable mountains and precipices, we have managed so far to remain hidden from the rapacity of the European nations, who have an inconceivable rage for the pebbles and mud of our land, and who, in order to get some, would butcher us all to the last man.

The conversation was a long one; it turned on the form of the government, the national customs, on women, public shows, the arts. At last Candide, whose taste always ran to metaphysics, told Cacambo to ask if the country had any religion.

The old man grew a bit red.

—How's that? he said. Can you have any doubt of it? Do you suppose we are altogether thankless scoundrels?

Cacambo asked meekly what was the religion of Eldorado. The old man flushed again.

—Can there be two religions? he asked. I suppose our religion is the same as everyone's, we worship God from morning to evening.

—Then you worship a single deity? said Cacambo, who acted throughout as interpreter of the questions of Candide.

—It's obvious, said the old man, that there aren't two or three or four of them. I must say the people of your world ask very remarkable questions.

Candide could not weary of putting questions to this good old man; he wanted to know how the people of Eldorado prayed to God.

—We don't pray to him at all, said the good and respectable

4. *The Discovery of Guiana,* published in 1595, described Sir Walter Raleigh's infatuation with the myth of Eldorado and served to spread the story still further.

sage; we have nothing to ask him for, since everything we need has already been granted; we thank God continually.

Candide was interested in seeing the priests; he had Cacambo ask where they were. The old gentleman smiled.

—My friends, said he, we are all priests; the king and all the heads of household sing formal psalms of thanksgiving every morning, and five or six thousand voices accompany them.

—What! you have no monks to teach, argue, govern, intrigue, and burn at the stake everyone who disagrees with them?

—We should have to be mad, said the old man; here we are all of the same mind, and we don't understand what you're up to with your monks.

Candide was overjoyed at all these speeches, and said to himself: —This is very different from Westphalia and the castle of My Lord the Baron; if our friend Pangloss had seen Eldorado, he wouldn't have called the castle of Thunder-Ten-Tronckh the finest thing on earth; to know the world one must travel.

After this long conversation, the old gentleman ordered a carriage with six sheep made ready, and gave the two travelers twelve of his servants for their journey to the court.

—Excuse me, said he, if old age deprives me of the honor of accompanying you. The king will receive you after a style which will not altogether displease you, and you will doubtless make allowance for the customs of the country if there are any you do not like.

Candide and Cacambo climbed into the coach; the six sheep flew like the wind, and in less than four hours they reached the king's palace at the edge of the capital. The entryway was two hundred and twenty feet high and a hundred wide; it is impossible to describe all the materials of which it was made. But you can imagine how much finer it was than those pebbles and sand which we call gold and jewels.

Twenty beautiful girls of the guard detail welcomed Candide and Cacambo as they stepped from the carriage, took them to the baths, and dressed them in robes woven of humming-bird feathers; then the high officials of the crown, both male and female, led them to the royal chamber between two long lines, each of a thousand musicians, as is customary. As they approached the throne room, Cacambo asked an officer what was the proper method of greeting his majesty: if one fell to one's knees or on one's belly; if one put one's hands on one's head or on one's rear; if one licked up the dust of the earth—in a word, what was the proper form?[5]

—The ceremony, said the officer, is to embrace the king and kiss him on both cheeks.

5. Candide's questions are probably derived from those of Gulliver on a similar occasion; see *Gulliver's Travels*, Book IV.

Candide and Cacambo fell on the neck of his majesty, who received them with all the dignity imaginable, and asked them politely to dine.

In the interim, they were taken about to see the city, the public buildings rising to the clouds, the public markets and arcades, the fountains of pure water and of rose water, those of sugar cane liquors which flowed perpetually in the great plazas paved with a sort of stone which gave off odors of gillyflower and rose petals. Candide asked to see the supreme court and the hall of parliament; they told him there was no such thing, that lawsuits were unknown. He asked if there were prisons, and was told there were not. What surprised him more, and gave him most pleasure, was the palace of sciences, in which he saw a gallery two thousand paces long, entirely filled with mathematical and physical instruments.

Having passed the whole afternoon seeing only a thousandth part of the city, they returned to the king's palace. Candide sat down to dinner with his majesty, his own valet Cacambo, and several ladies. Never was better food served, and never did a host preside more jovially than his majesty. Cacambo explained the king's witty sayings to Candide, and even when translated they still seemed witty. Of all the things which astonished Candide, this was not, in his eyes, the least astonishing.

They passed a month in this refuge. Candide never tired of saying to Cacambo: —It's true, my friend, I'll say it again, the castle where I was born does not compare with the land where we now are; but Miss Cunégonde is not here, and you doubtless have a mistress somewhere in Europe. If we stay here, we shall be just like everybody else, whereas if we go back to our own world, taking with us just a dozen sheep loaded with Eldorado pebbles, we shall be richer than all the kings put together, we shall have no more inquisitors to fear, and we shall easily be able to retake Miss Cunégonde.

This harangue pleased Cacambo; wandering is such pleasure, it gives a man such prestige at home to be able to talk of what he has seen abroad, that the two happy men resolved to be so no longer, but to take their leave of his majesty.

—You are making a foolish mistake, the king told them; I know very well that my kingdom is nothing much; but when you are pretty comfortable somewhere, you had better stay there. Of course I have no right to keep strangers against their will, that sort of tyranny is not in keeping with our laws or our customs; all men are free; depart when you will, but the way out is very difficult. You cannot possibly go up the river by which you miraculously came; it runs too swiftly through its underground caves. The mountains which surround my land are ten thousand feet high, and steep as walls; each one is more than ten leagues across; the only way down is over precipices. But since you really must go, I shall order my engineers to make a machine which can carry you conveniently. When we take you over the mountains, nobody will be able to go with you, for my subjects have sworn never to leave their refuge, and they are too sensible to break their vows. Other than that, ask of me what you please.

—We only request of your majesty, Cacambo said, a few sheep loaded with provisions, some pebbles, and some of the mud of your country.

The king laughed.

—I simply can't understand, said he, the passion you Europeans have for our yellow mud; but take all you want, and much good may it do you.

He promptly gave orders to his technicians to make a machine for lifting these two extraordinary men out of his kingdom. Three thousand good physicists worked at the problem; the machine was ready in two weeks' time, and cost no more than twenty million pounds sterling, in the money of the country. Cacambo and Candide were placed in the machine; there were two great sheep, saddled and bridled to serve them as steeds when they had cleared the mountains, twenty pack sheep with provisions, thirty which carried presents consisting of the rarities of the country, and fifty loaded with gold, jewels, and diamonds. The king bade tender farewell to the two vagabonds.

It made a fine spectacle, their departure, and the ingenious way in which they were hoisted with their sheep up to the top of the mountains. The technicians bade them good-bye after bringing them to safety, and Candide had now no other desire and no other object than to go and present his sheep to Miss Cunégonde.

—We have, said he, enough to pay off the governor of Buenos Aires—if, indeed, a price can be placed on Miss Cunégonde. Let us go to Cayenne, take ship there, and then see what kingdom we can find to buy up.

CHAPTER 19

*What Happened to Them at Surinam, and
How Candide Got to Know Martin*

The first day was pleasant enough for our travelers. They were encouraged by the idea of possessing more treasures than Asia, Europe, and Africa could bring together. Candide, in transports, carved the name of Cunégonde on the trees. On the second day two of their sheep bogged down in a swamp and were lost with their loads; two other sheep died of fatigue a few days later; seven or

eight others starved to death in a desert; still others fell, a little after, from precipices. Finally, after a hundred days' march, they had
only two sheep left. Candide told Cacambo: —My friend, you see
how the riches of this world are fleeting; the only solid things are
virtue and the joy of seeing Miss Cunégonde again.

—I agree, said Cacambo, but we still have two sheep, laden with
more treasure than the king of Spain will ever have; and I see in
the distance a town which I suspect is Surinam; it belongs to the
Dutch. We are at the end of our trials and on the threshold of our
happiness.

As they drew near the town, they discovered a negro stretched on
the ground with only half his clothes left, that is, a pair of blue
drawers; the poor fellow was also missing his left leg and his right
hand.

—Good Lord, said Candide in Dutch, what are you doing in that
horrible condition, my friend?

—I am waiting for my master, Mr. Vanderdendur,[6] the famous
merchant, answered the negro.

—Is Mr. Vanderdendur, Candide asked, the man who treated
you this way?

—Yes, sir, said the negro, that's how things are around here.
Twice a year we get a pair of linen drawers to wear. If we catch a
finger in the sugar mill where we work, they cut off our hand; if we
try to run away, they cut off our leg: I have undergone both these
experiences. This is the price of the sugar you eat in Europe. And
yet, when my mother sold me for ten Patagonian crowns on the
coast of Guinea, she said to me: 'My dear child, bless our witch
doctors, reverence them always, they will make your life happy; you
have the honor of being a slave to our white masters, and in this
way you are making the fortune of your father and mother.' Alas! I
don't know if I made their fortunes, but they certainly did not
make mine. The dogs, monkeys, and parrots are a thousand times
less unhappy than we are. The Dutch witch doctors who converted
me tell me every Sunday that we are all sons of Adam, black and
white alike. I am no genealogist; but if these preachers are right,
we must all be remote cousins; and you must admit no one could
treat his own flesh and blood in a more horrible fashion.

—Oh Pangloss! cried Candide, you had no notion of these
abominations! I'm through, I must give up your optimism after all.

—What's optimism? said Cacambo.

—Alas, said Candide, it is a mania for saying things are well

6. A name perhaps intended to suggest
VanDuren, a Dutch bookseller with
whom Voltaire had quarreled. In particular, the incident of gradually raising
one's price recalls VanDuren, to whom
Voltaire had successively offered 1,000,
1,500, 2,000, and 3,000 florins for the
return of the manuscript of Frederick
the Great's *Anti-Machiavel*.

when one is in hell.

And he shed bitter tears as he looked at his negro, and he was still weeping as he entered Surinam.

The first thing they asked was if there was not some vessel in port which could be sent to Buenos Aires. The man they asked was a Spanish merchant who undertook to make an honest bargain with them. They arranged to meet in a cafe; Candide and the faithful Cacambo, with their two sheep, went there to meet with him.

Candide, who always said exactly what was in his heart, told the Spaniard of his adventures, and confessed that he wanted to recapture Miss Cunégonde.

—I shall take good care *not* to send you to Buenos Aires, said the merchant; I should be hanged, and so would you. The lovely Cunégonde is his lordship's favorite mistress.

This was a thunderstroke for Candide; he wept for a long time; finally he drew Cacambo aside.

—Here, my friend, said he, is what you must do. Each one of us has in his pockets five or six millions' worth of diamonds; you are cleverer than I; go get Miss Cunégonde in Buenos Aires. If the governor makes a fuss, give him a million; if that doesn't convince him, give him two millions; you never killed an inquisitor, nobody will suspect you. I'll fit out another boat and go wait for you in Venice. That is a free country, where one need have no fear either of Bulgars or Abares or jews or inquisitors.

Cacambo approved of this wise decision. He was in despair at leaving a good master who had become a bosom friend; but the pleasure of serving him overcame the grief of leaving him. They embraced, and shed a few tears; Candide urged him not to forget the good old woman. Cacambo departed that very same day; he was a very good fellow, that Cacambo.

Candide remained for some time in Surinam, waiting for another merchant to take him to Italy, along with the two sheep which were left him. He hired servants and bought everything necessary for the long voyage; finally Mr. Vanderdendur, master of a big ship, came calling.

—How much will you charge, Candide asked this man, to take me to Venice—myself, my servants, my luggage, and those two sheep over there?

The merchant set a price of ten thousand piastres; Candide did not blink an eye.

—Oh ho, said the prudent Vanderdendur to himself, this stranger pays out ten thousand piastres at once, he must be pretty well fixed.

Then, returning a moment later, he made known that he could not set sail under twenty thousand.

—All right, you shall have them, said Candide.

—Whew, said the merchant softly to himself, this man gives twenty thousand piastres as easily as ten.

He came back again to say he could not go to Venice for less than thirty thousand piastres.

—All right, thirty then, said Candide.

—Ah ha, said the Dutch merchant, again speaking to himself; so thirty thousand piastres mean nothing to this man; no doubt the two sheep are loaded with immense treasures; let's say no more; we'll pick up the thirty thousand piastres first, and then we'll see.

Candide sold two little diamonds, the least of which was worth more than all the money demanded by the merchant. He paid him in advance. The two sheep were taken aboard. Candide followed in a little boat, to board the vessel at its anchorage. The merchant bides his time, sets sail, and makes his escape with a favoring wind. Candide, aghast and stupefied, soon loses him from view.

—Alas, he cries, now there is a trick worthy of the old world!

He returns to shore sunk in misery; for he had lost riches enough to make the fortunes of twenty monarchs.

Now he rushes to the house of the Dutch magistrate, and, being a bit disturbed, he knocks loudly at the door; goes in, tells the story of what happened, and shouts a bit louder than is customary. The judge begins by fining him ten thousand piastres for making such a racket; then he listens patiently to the story, promises to look into the matter as soon as the merchant comes back, and charges another ten thousand piastres as the costs of the hearing.

This legal proceeding completed the despair of Candide. In fact he had experienced miseries a thousand times more painful, but the coldness of the judge, and that of the merchant who had robbed him, roused his bile and plunged him into a black melancholy. The malice of men rose up before his spirit in all its ugliness, and his mind dwelt only on gloomy thoughts. Finally, when a French vessel was ready to leave for Bordeaux, since he had no more diamond-laden sheep to transport, he took a cabin at a fair price, and made it known in the town that he would pay passage and keep, plus two thousand piastres, to any honest man who wanted to make the journey with him, on condition that this man must be the most disgusted with his own condition and the most unhappy man in the province.

This drew such a crowd of applicants as a fleet could not have held. Candide wanted to choose among the leading candidates, so he picked out about twenty who seemed companionable enough, and of whom each pretended to be more miserable than all the others. He brought them together at his inn and gave them a dinner, on condition that each would swear to tell truthfully his entire history. He would select as his companion the most truly miserable and rightly discontented man, and among the others he would distribute various gifts.

The meeting lasted till four in the morning. Candide, as he listened to all the stories, remembered what the old woman had told him on the trip to Buenos Aires, and of the wager she had made, that there was nobody on the boat who had not undergone great misfortunes. At every story that was told him, he thought of Pangloss.

—That Pangloss, he said, would be hard put to prove his system. I wish he was here. Certainly if everything goes well, it is in Eldorado and not in the rest of the world.

At last he decided in favor of a poor scholar who had worked ten years for the booksellers of Amsterdam. He decided that there was no trade in the world with which one should be more disgusted.

This scholar, who was in fact a good man, had been robbed by his wife, beaten by his son, and deserted by his daughter, who had got herself abducted by a Portuguese. He had just been fired from the little job on which he existed; and the preachers of Surinam were persecuting him because they took him for a Socinian.[7] The others, it is true, were at least as unhappy as he, but Candide hoped the scholar would prove more amusing on the voyage. All his rivals declared that Candide was doing them a great injustice, but he pacified them with a hundred piastres apiece.

CHAPTER 20
What Happened to Candide and Martin at Sea

The old scholar, whose name was Martin, now set sail with Candide for Bordeaux. Both men had seen and suffered much; and even if the vessel had been sailing from Surinam to Japan via the Cape of Good Hope, they would have been able to keep themselves amused with instances of moral evil and physical evil during the entire trip.

However, Candide had one great advantage over Martin, that he still hoped to see Miss Cunégonde again, and Martin had nothing to hope for; besides, he had gold and diamonds, and though he had lost a hundred big red sheep loaded with the greatest treasures of the earth, though he had always at his heart a memory of the Dutch merchant's villainy, yet, when he thought of the wealth that remained in his hands, and when he talked of Cunégonde, especially just after a good dinner, he still inclined to the system of Pangloss.

7. A follower of Faustus and Laelius Socinus, sixteenth-century Polish theologians, who proposed a form of "rational" Christianity which exalted the rational conscience and minimized such mysteries as the trinity. The Socinians, by a special irony, were vigorous optimists.

—But what about you, Monsieur Martin, he asked the scholar, what do you think of all that? What is your idea of moral evil and physical evil?

—Sir, answered Martin, those priests accused me of being a Socinian, but the truth is that I am a Manichee.[8]

—You're joking, said Candide; there aren't any more Manichees in the world.

—There's me, said Martin; I don't know what to do about it, but I can't think otherwise.

—You must be possessed of the devil, said Candide.

—He's mixed up with so many things of this world, said Martin, that he may be in me as well as elsewhere; but I assure you, as I survey this globe, or globule, I think that God has abandoned it to some evil spirit—all of it except Eldorado. I have scarcely seen one town which did not wish to destroy its neighboring town, no family which did not wish to exterminate some other family. Everywhere the weak loathe the powerful, before whom they cringe, and the powerful treat them like brute cattle, to be sold for their meat and fleece. A million regimented assassins roam Europe from one end to the other, plying the trades of murder and robbery in an organized way for a living, because there is no more honest form of work for them; and in the cities which seem to enjoy peace and where the arts are flourishing, men are devoured by more envy, cares, and anxieties than a whole town experiences when it's under siege. Private griefs are worse even than public trials. In a word, I have seen so much and suffered so much, that I am a Manichee.

—Still there is some good, said Candide.

—That may be, said Martin, but I don't know it.

In the middle of this discussion, the rumble of cannon was heard. From minute to minute the noise grew louder. Everyone reached for his spyglass. At a distance of some three miles they saw two vessels fighting; the wind brought both of them so close to the French vessel that they had a pleasantly comfortable seat to watch the fight. Presently one of the vessels caught the other with a broadside so low and so square as to send it to the bottom. Candide and Martin saw clearly a hundred men on the deck of the sinking ship; they all raised their hands to heaven, uttering fearful shrieks; and in a moment everything was swallowed up.

—Well, said Martin, that is how men treat one another.

8. Mani, a Persian mage and philosopher of the third century A.D., taught (probably under the influence of traditions stemming from Zoroaster and the worshippers of the sun god Mithra) that the earth is a field of dispute between two almost equal powers, one of light and one of darkness, both of which must be propitiated. Saint Augustine was much exercised by the heresy, to which he was at one time himself addicted, and Voltaire came to some knowledge of it through the encyclopedic learning of the seventeenth century scholar Pierre Bayle.

—It is true, said Candide, there's something devilish in this business.

As they chatted, he noticed something of a striking red color floating near the sunken vessel. They sent out a boat to investigate; it was one of his sheep. Candide was more joyful to recover this one sheep than he had been afflicted to lose a hundred of them, all loaded with big Eldorado diamonds.

The French captain soon learned that the captain of the victorious vessel was Spanish and that of the sunken vessel was a Dutch pirate. It was the same man who had robbed Candide. The enormous riches which this rascal had stolen were sunk beside him in the sea, and nothing was saved but a single sheep.

—You see, said Candide to Martin, crime is punished sometimes; this scoundrel of a Dutch merchant has met the fate he deserved.

—Yes, said Martin; but did the passengers aboard his ship have to perish too? God punished the scoundrel, and the devil drowned the others.

Meanwhile the French and Spanish vessels continued on their journey, and Candide continued his talks with Martin. They disputed for fifteen days in a row, and at the end of that time were just as much in agreement as at the beginning. But at least they were talking, they exchanged their ideas, they consoled one another. Candide caressed his sheep.

—Since I have found you again, said he, I may well rediscover Miss Cunégonde.

CHAPTER 21

*Candide and Martin Approach the Coast of France:
They Reason Together*

At last the coast of France came in view.

—Have you ever been in France, Monsieur Martin? asked Candide.

—Yes, said Martin, I have visited several provinces. There are some where half the inhabitants are crazy, others where they are too sly, still others where they are quite gentle and stupid, some where they venture on wit; in all of them the principal occupation is love-making, the second is slander, and the third stupid talk.

—But, Monsieur Martin, were you ever in Paris?

—Yes, I've been in Paris; it contains specimens of all these types, it is a chaos, a mob, in which everyone is seeking pleasure and where hardly anyone finds it, at least from what I have seen. I did not live there for long; as I arrived, I was robbed of everything I possessed by thieves at the fair of St. Germain; I myself was taken for a thief, and spent eight days in jail, after which I took a proofreader's job to earn enough money to return on foot to Holland. I knew the writing gang, the intriguing gang, the gang with fits and convulsions.[9] They say there are some very civilized people in that town; I'd like to think so.

—I myself have no desire to visit France, said Candide; you no doubt realize that when one has spent a month in Eldorado, there is nothing else on earth one wants to see, except Miss Cunégonde. I am going to wait for her at Venice; we will cross France simply to get to Italy; wouldn't you like to come with me?

—Gladly, said Martin; they say Venice is good only for the Venetian nobles, but that on the other hand they treat foreigners very well when they have plenty of money. I don't have any; you do, so I'll follow you anywhere.

—By the way, said Candide, do you believe the earth was originally all ocean, as they assure us in that big book belonging to the ship's captain?[1]

—I don't believe that stuff, said Martin, nor any of the dreams which people have been peddling for some time now.

—But why, then, was this world formed at all? asked Candide.

—To drive us mad, answered Martin.

—Aren't you astonished, Candide went on, at the love which those two girls showed for the monkeys in the land of the Biglugs that I told you about?

—Not at all, said Martin, I see nothing strange in these sentiments; I have seen so many extraordinary things that nothing seems extraordinary any more.

—Do you believe, asked Candide, that men have always massacred one another as they do today? That they have always been liars, traitors, ingrates, thieves, weaklings, sneaks, cowards, backbiters, gluttons, drunkards, misers, climbers, killers, calumniators, sensualists, fanatics, hypocrites, and fools?

—Do you believe, said Martin, that hawks have always eaten pigeons when they could get them?

—Of course, said Candide.

—Well, said Martin, if hawks have always had the same character, why do you suppose that men have changed?

—Oh, said Candide, there's a great deal of difference, because freedom of the will . . .

As they were disputing in this manner, they reached Bordeaux.

---

9. The Jansenists, a sect of strict Catholics, became notorious for spiritual ecstasies. Their public displays reached a height during the 1720's, and Voltaire described them in *Le Siècle de* *Louis XIV* (chap. 37), as well as in the article on "Convulsions" in the *Philosophical Dictionary*.

1. The Bible. Voltaire is straining at a dark passage in Genesis 1.

CHAPTER 22
What Happened in France to Candide and Martin

Candide paused in Bordeaux only long enough to sell a couple of Dorado pebbles and to fit himself out with a fine two-seater carriage, for he could no longer do without his philosopher Martin; only he was very unhappy to part with his sheep, which he left to the academy of science in Bordeaux. They proposed, as the theme of that year's prize contest, the discovery of why the wool of the sheep was red; and the prize was awarded to a northern scholar who demonstrated[2] by A plus B minus C divided by Z that the sheep ought to be red and die of sheep rot.

But all the travelers with whom Candide talked in the roadside inns told him: —We are going to Paris.

This general consensus finally inspired in him too a desire to see the capital; it was not much out of his road to Venice.

He entered through the Faubourg Saint-Marceau,[3] and thought he was in the meanest village of Westphalia.

Scarcely was Candide in his hotel, when he came down with a mild illness caused by exhaustion. As he was wearing an enormous diamond ring, and people had noticed among his luggage a tremendously heavy safe, he soon found at his bedside two doctors whom he had not called, several intimate friends who never left him alone, and two pious ladies who helped to warm his broth. Martin said: —I remember that I too was ill on my first trip to Paris; I was very poor; and as I had neither friends, pious ladies, nor doctors, I got well.

However, as a result of medicines and bleedings, Candide's illness became serious. A resident of the neighborhood came to ask him politely to fill out a ticket, to be delivered to the porter of the other world.[4] Candide wanted nothing to do with it. The pious ladies assured him it was a new fashion; Candide replied that he wasn't a man of fashion. Martin wanted to throw the resident out the window. The cleric swore that without the ticket they wouldn't bury Candide. Martin swore that he would bury the cleric if he continued to be a nuisance. The quarrel grew heated; Martin took him by the shoulders and threw him bodily out the door; all of which caused a great scandal, from which developed a legal case.

2. The satire is pointed at Maupertuis Le Lapon, philosopher and mathematician, whom Voltaire had accused of trying to adduce mathematical proofs of the existence of God and whose algebraic formulae were easily ridiculed.
3. A district on the left bank, notably grubby in the eighteenth century. " 'As I entered [Paris] through the Faubourg Saint-Marceau, I saw nothing but dirty stinking little streets, ugly black houses, a general air of squalor and poverty, beggars, carters, menders of clothes, sellers of herb-drinks and old hats,' J.-J. Rousseau, *Confessions*, Book IV."
4. In the middle of the eighteenth century, it became customary to require persons who were grievously ill to sign *billets de confession*, without which they could not be given absolution, admitted to the last sacraments, or buried in consecrated ground.

Candide got better; and during his convalescence he had very good company in to dine. They played cards for money; and Candide was quite surprised that none of the aces were ever dealt to him, and Martin was not surprised at all.

Among those who did the honors of the town for Candide there was a little abbé from Perigord, one of those busy fellows, always bright, always useful, assured, obsequious, and obliging, who waylay passing strangers, tell them the scandal of the town, and offer them pleasures at any price they want to pay. This fellow first took Candide and Martin to the theatre. A new tragedy was being played. Candide found himself seated next to a group of wits. That did not keep him from shedding a few tears in the course of some perfectly played scenes. One of the commentators beside him remarked during the intermission: —You are quite mistaken to weep, this actress is very bad indeed; the actor who plays with her is even worse; and the play is even worse than the actors in it. The author knows not a word of Arabic, though the action takes place in Arabia; and besides, he is a man who doesn't believe in innate ideas.[5] Tomorrow I will show you twenty pamphlets written against him.[6]

—Tell me, sir, said Candide to the abbé, how many plays are there for performance in France?

—Five or six thousand, replied the other.

—That's a lot, said Candide; how many of them are any good?

—Fifteen or sixteen, was the answer.

—That's a lot, said Martin.

Candide was very pleased with an actress who took the part of Queen Elizabeth in a rather dull tragedy[7] that still gets played from time to time.

—I like this actress very much, he said to Martin, she bears a slight resemblance to Miss Cunégonde; I should like to meet her.

The abbé from Perigord offered to introduce him. Candide, raised in Germany, asked what was the protocol, how one behaved in France with queens of England.

—You must distinguish, said the abbé; in the provinces, you take them to an inn; at Paris they are respected while still attractive, and thrown on the dunghill when they are dead.[8]

—Queens on the dunghill! said Candide.

—Yes indeed, said Martin, the abbé is right; I was in Paris when

5. Descartes proposed certain ideas as innate, Voltaire followed Locke in categorically denying innate ideas. The point is simply that in faction fights all the issues get muddled together.
6. Here begins a long passage interpolated by Voltaire in 1761; it ends on p. 186.
7. *Le Comte d'Essex* by Thomas Corneille.
8. Voltaire engaged in a long and vigorous campaign against the rule that actors and actresses could not be buried in consecrated ground. The superstition probably arose from a feeling that by assuming false identities they denied their own souls.

Miss Monime herself[9] passed, as they say, from this life to the other; she was refused what these folk call 'the honors of burial,' that is, the right to rot with all the beggars of the district in a dirty cemetery; she was buried all alone by her troupe at the corner of the Rue de Bourgogne; this must have been very disagreeable to her, for she had a noble character.

—That was extremely rude, said Candide.

—What do you expect? said Martin; that is how these folk are. Imagine all the contradictions, all the incompatibilities you can, and you will see them in the government, the courts, the churches, and the plays of this crazy nation.

—Is it true that they are always laughing in Paris? asked Candide.

—Yes, said the abbé, but with a kind of rage too; when people complain of things, they do so amid explosions of laughter; they even laugh as they perform the most detestable actions.

—Who was that fat swine, said Candide, who spoke so nastily about the play over which I was weeping, and the actors who gave me so much pleasure?

—He is a living illness, answered the abbé, who makes a business of slandering all the plays and books; he hates the successful ones, as eunuchs hate successful lovers; he's one of those literary snakes who live on filth and venom; he's a folliculator . . .

—What's this word *folliculator?* asked Candide.

—It's a folio filler, said the abbé, a Fréron.[1]

It was after this fashion that Candide, Martin, and the abbé from Perigord chatted on the stairway as they watched the crowd leaving the theatre.

—Although I'm in a great hurry to see Miss Cunégonde again, said Candide, I would very much like to dine with Miss Clairon,[2] for she seemed to me admirable.

The abbé was not the man to approach Miss Clairon, who saw only good company.

—She has an engagement tonight, he said; but I shall have the honor of introducing you to a lady of quality, and there you will get to know Paris as if you had lived here four years.

Candide, who was curious by nature, allowed himself to be brought to the lady's house, in the depths of the Faubourg St.-

9. Adrienne Lecouvreur (1690–1730), so called because she made her debut as Monime in Racine's *Mithridate.* Voltaire had assisted at her secret midnight funeral and wrote an indignant poem about it.

1. A successful and popular journalist, who had attacked several of Voltaire's plays, including *Tancrède.* Voltaire had a fine story that the devil attended the first night of *Tancrède* disguised as Fréron: when a lady in the balcony wept at the play's pathos, her tear dropped on the devil's nose; he thought it was holy water and shook it off—psha! psha! G. Desnoiresterres, *Voltaire et Jean-Jacques Rousseau,* pp. 3–4.

2. Actually Claire Leris (1723–1803). She had played the lead role in *Tancrède* and was for many years a leading figure on the Paris stage.

Honoré; they were playing faro[3]; twelve melancholy punters held in their hands a little sheaf of cards, blank summaries of their bad luck. Silence reigned supreme, the punters were pallid, the banker uneasy; and the lady of the house, seated beside the pitiless banker, watched with the eyes of a lynx for the various illegal redoublings and bets at long odds which the players tried to signal by folding the corners of their cards; she had them unfolded with a determination which was severe but polite, and concealed her anger lest she lose her customers. The lady caused herself to be known as the Marquise of Parolignac.[4] Her daughter, fifteen years old, sat among the punters and tipped off her mother with a wink to the sharp practices of these unhappy players when they tried to recoup their losses. The abbé from Perigord, Candide, and Martin came in; nobody arose or greeted them or looked at them; all were lost in the study of their cards.

—My Lady the Baroness of Thunder-Ten-Tronckh was more civil, thought Candide.

However, the abbé whispered in the ear of the marquise, who, half rising, honored Candide with a gracious smile and Martin with a truly noble nod; she gave a seat and dealt a hand of cards to Candide, who lost fifty thousand francs in two turns; after which they had a very merry supper. Everyone was amazed that Candide was not upset over his losses; the lackeys, talking together in their usual lackey language, said: —He must be some English milord.

The supper was like most Parisian suppers: first silence, then an indistinguishable rush of words; then jokes, mostly insipid, false news, bad logic, a little politics, a great deal of malice. They even talked of new books.

—Have you seen the new novel by Dr. Gauchat, the theologian?[5] asked the abbé from Perigord.

—Oh yes, answered one of the guests; but I couldn't finish it. We have a horde of impudent scribblers nowadays, but all of them put together don't match the impudence of this Gauchat, this doctor of theology. I have been so struck by the enormous number of detestable books which are swamping us that I have taken up punting at faro.

—And the *Collected Essays* of Archdeacon T——[6] asked the abbé, what do you think of them?

3. A game of cards, about which it is necessary to know only that a number of punters play against a banker or dealer. The pack is dealt out two cards at a time, and each player may bet on any card as much as he pleases. The sharp practices of the punters consist essentially of tricks for increasing their winnings without corresponding risks.
4. A *paroli* is an illegal redoubling of one's bet; her name therefore implies a title grounded in cardsharping.
5. He had written against Voltaire, and Voltaire suspected him (wrongly) of having committed a novel, *L'Oracle des nouveaux philosophes*.
6. His name was Trublet, and he had said, among other disagreeable things, that Voltaire's epic poem, the *Henriade*, made him yawn and that Voltaire's genius was "the perfection of mediocrity."

—Ah, said Madame de Parolignac, what a frightful bore he is! He takes such pains to tell you what everyone knows; he discourses so learnedly on matters which aren't worth a casual remark! He plunders, and not even wittily, the wit of other people! He spoils what he plunders, he's disgusting! But he'll never disgust me again; a couple of pages of the archdeacon have been enough for me.

There was at table a man of learning and taste, who supported the marquise on this point. They talked next of tragedies; the lady asked why there were tragedies which played well enough but which were wholly unreadable. The man of taste explained very clearly how a play could have a certain interest and yet little merit otherwise; he showed succinctly that it was not enough to conduct a couple of intrigues, such as one can find in any novel, and which never fail to excite the spectator's interest; but that one must be new without being grotesque, frequently touch the sublime but never depart from the natural; that one must know the human heart and give it words; that one must be a great poet without allowing any character in the play to sound like a poet; and that one must know the language perfectly, speak it purely, and maintain a continual harmony without ever sacrificing sense to mere sound.

—Whoever, he added, does not observe all these rules may write one or two tragedies which succeed in the theatre, but he will never be ranked among the good writers; there are very few good tragedies; some are idylls in well-written, well-rhymed dialogue, others are political arguments which put the audience to sleep, or revolting pomposities; still others are the fantasies of enthusiasts, barbarous in style, incoherent in logic, full of long speeches to the gods because the author does not know how to address men, full of false maxims and emphatic commonplaces.

Candide listened attentively to this speech and conceived a high opinion of the speaker; and as the marquise had placed him by her side, he turned to ask her who was this man who spoke so well.

—He is a scholar, said the lady, who never plays cards and whom the abbé sometimes brings to my house for supper; he knows all about tragedies and books, and has himself written a tragedy that was hissed from the stage and a book, the only copy of which ever seen outside his publisher's office was dedicated to me.

—What a great man, said Candide, he's Pangloss all over.

Then, turning to him, he said: —Sir, you doubtless think everything is for the best in the physical as well as the moral universe, and that nothing could be otherwise than as it is?

—Not at all, sir, replied the scholar, I believe nothing of the sort. I find that everything goes wrong in our world; that nobody knows his place in society or his duty, what he's doing or what he ought to be doing, and that outside of mealtimes, which are cheerful and congenial enough, all the rest of the day is spent in useless quarrels, as of Jansenists against Molinists,[7] parliament-men against churchmen, literary men against literary men, courtiers against courtiers, financiers against the plebs, wives against husbands, relatives against relatives—it's one unending warfare.

Candide answered: —I have seen worse; but a wise man, who has since had the misfortune to be hanged, taught me that everything was marvelously well arranged. Troubles are just the shadows in a beautiful picture.

—Your hanged philosopher was joking, said Martin; the shadows are horrible ugly blots.

—It is human beings who make the blots, said Candide, and they can't do otherwise.

—Then it isn't their fault, said Martin.

Most of the faro players, who understood this sort of talk not at all, kept on drinking; Martin disputed with the scholar, and Candide told part of his story to the lady of the house.

After supper, the marquise brought Candide into her room and sat him down on a divan.

—Well, she said to him, are you still madly in love with Miss Cunégonde of Thunder-Ten-Tronckh?

—Yes, ma'am, replied Candide. The marquise turned upon him a tender smile.

—You answer like a young man of Westphalia, said she; a Frenchman would have told me: 'It is true that I have been in love with Miss Cunégonde; but since seeing you, madame, I fear that I love her no longer.'

—Alas, ma'am, said Candide, I will answer any way you want.

—Your passion for her, said the marquise, began when you picked up her handkerchief; I prefer that you should pick up my garter.

—Gladly, said Candide, and picked it up.

—But I also want you to put it back on, said the lady; and Candide put it on again.

—Look you now, said the lady, you are a foreigner; my Paris lovers I sometimes cause to languish for two weeks or so, but to you I surrender the very first night, because we must render the honors of the country to a young man from Westphalia.

The beauty, who had seen two enormous diamonds on the two hands of her young friend, praised them so sincerely that from the fingers of Candide they passed over to the fingers of the marquise.

As he returned home with his Perigord abbé, Candide felt

---

7. .The Jansenists (from Corneille Jansen, 1585–1638) were a relatively strict party of religious reform; the Molinists (from Luis Molina) were the party of the Jesuits. Their central issue of controversy was the relative importance of divine grace and human will to the salvation of man.

some remorse at having been unfaithful to Miss Cunégonde; the abbé sympathized with his grief; he had only a small share in the fifty thousand francs which Candide lost at cards, and in the proceeds of the two diamonds which had been half-given, half-extorted. His scheme was to profit, as much as he could, from the advantage of knowing Candide. He spoke at length of Cunégonde, and Candide told him that he would beg forgiveness for his beloved for his infidelity when he met her at Venice.

The Perigordian overflowed with politeness and unction, taking a tender interest in everything Candide said, everything he did, and everything he wanted to do.[8]

—Well, sir, said he, so you have an assignation at Venice?

—Yes indeed, sir, I do, said Candide; it is absolutely imperative that I go there to find Miss Cunégonde.

And then, carried away by the pleasure of talking about his love, he recounted, as he often did, a part of his adventures with that illustrious lady of Westphalia.

—I suppose, said the abbé, that Miss Cunégonde has a fine wit and writes charming letters.

—I never received a single letter from her, said Candide; for, as you can imagine, after being driven out of the castle for love of her, I couldn't write; shortly I learned that she was dead; then I rediscovered her; then I lost her again, and I have now sent, to a place more than twentyfive hundred leagues from here, a special agent whose return I am expecting.

The abbé listened carefully, and looked a bit dreamy. He soon took his leave of the two strangers, after embracing them tenderly. Next day Candide, when he woke up, received a letter, to the following effect:

—Dear sir, my very dear lover, I have been lying sick in this town for a week, I have just learned that you are here. I would fly to your arms if I could move. I heard that you had passed through Bordeaux; that was where I left the faithful Cacambo and the old woman, who are soon to follow me here. The governor of Buenos Aires took everything, but left me your heart. Come; your presence will either return me to life or cause me to die of joy.

8. Here ends the long passage interpolated by Voltaire in 1761, which began on p. 181. In the original version the transition was managed as follows. After the "commentator's" speech, ending: —Tomorrow I will show you twenty pamphlets written against him.
    —Sir, said the abbé from Perigord, do you notice that young person over there with the attractive face and the delicate figure? She would only cost you ten thousand francs a month, and for fifty thousand crowns of diamonds . . .
    —I could spare her only a day or or two, replied Candide, because I have an urgent appointment at Venice.
    Next night after supper, the sly Perigordian overflowed with politeness and assiduity.
    —Well, sir, said he, so you have an assignation at Venice?

This charming letter, coming so unexpectedly, filled Candide with inexpressible delight, while the illness of his dear Cunégonde covered him with grief. Torn between these two feelings, he took gold and diamonds, and had himself brought, with Martin, to the hotel where Miss Cunégonde was lodging. Trembling with emotion, he enters the room; his heart thumps, his voice breaks. He tries to open the curtains of the bed, he asks to have some lights.

—Absolutely forbidden, says the serving girl; light will be the death of her.

And abruptly she pulls shut the curtain.

—My dear Cunégonde, says Candide in tears, how are you feeling? If you can't see me, won't you at least speak to me?

—She can't talk, says the servant.

But then she draws forth from the bed a plump hand, over which Candide weeps a long time, and which he fills with diamonds, meanwhile leaving a bag of gold on the chair.

Amid his transports, there arrives a bailiff followed by the abbé from Perigord and a strong-arm squad.

—These here are the suspicious foreigners? says the officer; and he has them seized and orders his bullies to drag them off to jail.

—They don't treat visitors like this in Eldorado, says Candide.

—I am more a Manichee than ever, says Martin.

—But, please sir, where are you taking us? says Candide.

—To the lowest hole in the dungeons, says the bailiff.

Martin, having regained his self-possession, decided that the lady who pretended to be Cunégonde was a cheat, the abbé from Perigord was another cheat who had imposed on Candide's innocence, and the bailiff still another cheat, of whom it would be easy to get rid.

Rather than submit to the forms of justice, Candide, enlightened by Martin's advice and eager for his own part to see the real Cunégonde again, offered the bailiff three little diamonds worth about three thousand pistoles apiece.

—Ah, my dear sir! cried the man with the ivory staff, even if you have committed every crime imaginable, you are the most honest man in the world. Three diamonds! each one worth three thousand pistoles! My dear sir! I would gladly die for you, rather than take you to jail. All foreigners get arrested here; but let me manage it; I have a brother at Dieppe in Normandy; I'll take you to him; and if you have a bit of a diamond to give him, he'll take care of you, just like me.

—And why do they arrest all foreigners? asked Candide.

The abbé from Perigord spoke up and said: —It's because a beggar from Atrebatum[9] listened to some stupidities; that made him commit a parricide, not like the one of May, 1610, but like the one of December, 1594, much on the order of several other crimes committed in other years and other months by other beggars who had listened to stupidities.

The bailiff then explained what it was all about.[1]

—Foh! what beasts! cried Candide. What! monstrous behavior of this sort from a people who sing and dance? As soon as I can, let me get out of this country, where the monkeys provoke the tigers. In my own country I've lived with bears; only in Eldorado are there proper men. In the name of God, sir bailiff, get me to Venice where I can wait for Miss Cunégonde.

—I can only get you to Lower Normandy, said the guardsman.

He had the irons removed at once, said there had been a mistake, dismissed his gang, and took Candide and Martin to Dieppe, where he left them with his brother. There was a little Dutch ship at anchor. The Norman, changed by three more diamonds into the most helpful of men, put Candide and his people aboard the vessel, which was bound for Portsmouth in England. It wasn't on the way to Venice, but Candide felt like a man just let out of hell; and he hoped to get back on the road to Venice at the first possible occasion.

CHAPTER 23

Candide and Martin Pass the Shores of England; What They See There

—Ah, Pangloss! Pangloss! Ah, Martin! Martin! Ah, my darling Cunégonde! What is this world of ours? sighed Candide on the Dutch vessel.

—Something crazy, something abominable, Martin replied.

—You have been in England; are people as crazy there as in France?

—It's a different sort of crazy, said Martin. You know that these two nations have been at war over a few acres of snow near Canada, and that they are spending on this fine struggle more than Canada itself is worth.[2] As for telling you if there are more people

9. The Latin name for the district of Artois, from which came Robert-François Damiens, who tried to stab Louis XV in 1757. The assassination failed, like that of Châtel, who tried to kill Henri Quatre in 1594, but unlike that of Ravaillac, who succeeded in killing him in 1610.
1. The point, in fact, is not too clear since arresting foreigners is an indirect way at best to guard against home-grown fanatics, and the position of the

abbé from Perigord in the whole transaction remains confused. Has he called in the officer just to get rid of Candide? If so, why is he sardonic about the very suspicions he is trying to foster? Candide's reaction is to the notion that Frenchmen should be capable of political assassination at all; it seems excessive.
2. The wars of the French and English over Canada dragged intermittently through the eighteenth century till the

in one country or the other who need a strait jacket, that is a judgment too fine for my understanding; I know only that the people we are going to visit are eaten up with melancholy.

As they chatted thus, the vessel touched at Portsmouth. A multitude of people covered the shore, watching closely a rather bulky man who was kneeling, his eyes blindfolded, on the deck of a man-of-war. Four soldiers, stationed directly in front of this man, fired three bullets apiece into his brain, as peaceably as you would want; and the whole assemblage went home, in great satisfaction.[3]

—What's all this about? asked Candide. What devil is everywhere at work?

He asked who was that big man who had just been killed with so much ceremony.

—It was an admiral, they told him.

—And why kill this admiral?

—The reason, they told him, is that he didn't kill enough people; he gave battle to a French admiral, and it was found that he didn't get close enough to him.

—But, said Candide, the French admiral was just as far from the English admiral as the English admiral was from the French admiral.

—That's perfectly true, came the answer; but in this country it is useful from time to time to kill one admiral in order to encourage the others.

Candide was so stunned and shocked at what he saw and heard, that he would not even set foot ashore; he arranged with the Dutch merchant (without even caring if he was robbed, as at Surinam) to be taken forthwith to Venice.

The merchant was ready in two days; they coasted along France, they passed within sight of Lisbon, and Candide quivered. They entered the straits, crossed the Mediterranean, and finally landed at Venice.

—God be praised, said Candide, embracing Martin; here I shall recover the lovely Cunégonde. I trust Cacambo as I would myself. All is well, all goes well, all goes as well as possible.

CHAPTER 24
About Paquette and Brother Giroflée

As soon as he was in Venice, he had a search made for Cacambo in all the inns, all the cafés, all the stews—and found no trace of

peace of Paris sealed England's conquest (1763). Voltaire thought the French should concentrate on developing Louisiana where the Jesuit influence was less marked.
3. Candide has witnessed the execution of Admiral John Byng, defeated off Minorca by the French fleet under Galisonnière and executed by firing squad on March 14, 1757. Voltaire had intervened to avert the execution.

him. Every day he sent to investigate the vessels and coastal traders; no news of Cacambo.

—How's this? said he to Martin. I have had time to go from Surinam to Bordeaux, from Bordeaux to Paris, from Paris to Dieppe, from Dieppe to Portsmouth, to skirt Portugal and Spain, cross the Mediterranean, and spend several months at Venice—and the lovely Cunégonde has not come yet! In her place, I have met only that impersonator and that abbé from Perigord. Cunégonde is dead, without a doubt; and nothing remains for me too but death. Oh, it would have been better to stay in the earthly paradise of Eldorado than to return to this accursed Europe. How right you are, my dear Martin; all is but illusion and disaster.

He fell into a black melancholy, and refused to attend the fashionable operas or take part in the other diversions of the carnival season; not a single lady tempted him in the slightest. Martin told him: —You're a real simpleton if you think a half-breed valet with five or six millions in his pockets will go to the end of the world to get your mistress and bring her to Venice for you. If he finds her, he'll take her for himself; if he doesn't, he'll take another. I advise you to forget about your servant Cacambo and your mistress Cunégonde.

Martin was not very comforting. Candide's melancholy increased, and Martin never wearied of showing him that there is little virtue and little happiness on this earth, except perhaps in Eldorado, where nobody can go.

While they were discussing this important matter and still waiting for Cunégonde, Candide noticed in St. Mark's Square a young Theatine [4] monk who had given his arm to a girl. The Theatine seemed fresh, plump, and flourishing; his eyes were bright, his manner cocky, his glance brilliant, his step proud. The girl was very pretty, and singing aloud; she glanced lovingly at her Theatine, and from time to time pinched his plump cheeks.

—At least you must admit, said Candide to Martin, that these people are happy. Until now I have not found in the whole inhabited earth, except Eldorado, anything but miserable people. But this girl and this monk, I'd be willing to bet, are very happy creatures.

—I'll bet they aren't, said Martin.

—We have only to ask them to dinner, said Candide, and we'll find out if I'm wrong.

Promptly he approached them, made his compliments, and invited them to his inn for a meal of macaroni, Lombardy partridges, and caviar, washed down with wine from Montepulciano, Cyprus,

4. A Catholic order founded in 1524 by Cardinal Cajetan and G. P. Caraffa, later Pope Paul IV.

and Samos, and some Lacrima Christi. The girl blushed but the Theatine accepted gladly, and the girl followed him, watching Candide with an expression of surprise and confusion, darkened by several tears. Scarcely had she entered the room when she said to Candide: —What, can it be that Master Candide no longer knows Paquette?

At these words Candide, who had not yet looked carefully at her because he was preoccupied with Cunégonde, said to her: —Ah, my poor child! so you are the one who put Doctor Pangloss in the fine fix where I last saw him.

—Alas, sir, I was the one, said Paquette; I see you know all about it. I heard of the horrible misfortunes which befell the whole household of My Lady the Baroness and the lovely Cunégonde. I swear to you that my own fate has been just as unhappy. I was perfectly innocent when you knew me. A Franciscan, who was my confessor, easily seduced me. The consequences were frightful; shortly after My Lord the Baron had driven you out with great kicks on the backside, I too was forced to leave the castle. If a famous doctor had not taken pity on me, I would have died. Out of gratitude, I became for some time the mistress of this doctor. His wife, who was jealous to the point of frenzy, beat me mercilessly every day; she was a gorgon. The doctor was the ugliest of men, and I the most miserable creature on earth, being continually beaten for a man I did not love. You will understand, sir, how dangerous it is for a nagging woman to be married to a doctor. This man, enraged by his wife's ways, one day gave her as a cold cure a medicine so potent that in two hours' time she died amid horrible convulsions. Her relatives brought suit against the bereaved husband; he fled the country, and I was put in prison. My innocence would never have saved me if I had not been rather pretty. The judge set me free on condition that he should become the doctor's successor. I was shortly replaced in this post by another girl, dismissed without any payment, and obliged to continue this abominable trade which you men find so pleasant and which for us is nothing but a bottomless pit of misery. I went to ply the trade in Venice. Ah, my dear sir, if you could imagine what it is like to have to caress indiscriminately an old merchant, a lawyer, a monk, a gondolier, an abbé; to be subjected to every sort of insult and outrage; to be reduced, time and again, to borrowing a skirt in order to go have it lifted by some disgusting man; to be robbed by this fellow of what one has gained from that; to be shaken down by the police, and to have before one only the prospect of a hideous old age, a hospital, and a dunghill, you will conclude that I am one of the most miserable creatures in the world.

Thus Paquette poured forth her heart to the good Candide in a hotel room, while Martin sat listening nearby. At last he said to Candide: —You see, I've already won half my bet.

Brother Giroflée[5] had remained in the dining room, and was having a drink before dinner.

—But how's this? said Candide to Paquette. You looked so happy, so joyous, when I met you; you were singing, you caressed the Theatine with such a natural air of delight; you seemed to me just as happy as you now say you are miserable.

—Ah, sir, replied Paquette, that's another one of the miseries of this business; yesterday I was robbed and beaten by an officer, and today I have to seem in good humor in order to please a monk.

Candide wanted no more; he conceded that Martin was right. They sat down to table with Paquette and the Theatine; the meal was amusing enough, and when it was over, the company spoke out among themselves with some frankness.

—Father, said Candide to the monk, you seem to me a man whom all the world might envy; the flower of health glows in your cheek, your features radiate pleasure; you have a pretty girl for your diversion, and you seem very happy with your life as a Theatine.

—Upon my word, sir, said Brother Giroflée, I wish that all the Theatines were at the bottom of the sea. A hundred times I have been tempted to set fire to my convent, and go turn Turk. My parents forced me, when I was fifteen years old, to put on this detestable robe, so they could leave more money to a cursed older brother of mine, may God confound him! Jealousy, faction, and fury spring up, by natural law, within the walls of convents. It is true, I have preached a few bad sermons which earned me a little money, half of which the prior stole from me; the remainder serves to keep me in girls. But when I have to go back to the monastery at night, I'm ready to smash my head against the walls of my cell; and all my fellow monks are in the same fix.

Martin turned to Candide and said with his customary coolness: —Well, haven't I won the whole bet?

Candide gave two thousand piastres to Paquette and a thousand to Brother Giroflée.

—I assure you, said he, that with that they will be happy.

—I don't believe so, said Martin; your piastres may make them even more unhappy than they were before.

—That may be, said Candide; but one thing comforts me, I note that people often turn up whom one never expected to see again; it may well be that, having rediscovered my red sheep and Paquette, I will also rediscover Cunégonde.

5. His name means "gillyflower," and Paquette means "daisy." They are lilies of the field who spin not, neither do they reap.

—I hope, said Martin, that she will some day make you happy; but I very much doubt it.

—You're a hard man, said Candide.

—I've lived, said Martin.

—But look at these gondoliers, said Candide; aren't they always singing?

—You don't see them at home, said Martin, with their wives and squalling children. The doge has his troubles, the gondoliers theirs. It's true that on the whole one is better off as a gondolier than as a doge; but the difference is so slight, I don't suppose it's worth the trouble of discussing.

—There's a lot of talk here, said Candide, of this Senator Pococurante,[6] who has a fine palace on the Brenta and is hospitable to foreigners. They say he is a man who has never known a moment's grief.

—I'd like to see such a rare specimen, said Martin.

Candide promptly sent to Lord Pococurante, asking permission to call on him tomorrow.

CHAPTER 25

Visit to Lord Pococurante, Venetian Nobleman

Candide and Martin took a gondola on the Brenta, and soon reached the palace of the noble Pococurante. The gardens were large and filled with beautiful marble statues; the palace was handsomely designed. The master of the house, sixty years old and very rich, received his two inquisitive visitors perfectly politely, but with very little warmth; Candide was disconcerted and Martin not at all displeased.

First two pretty and neatly dressed girls served chocolate, which they whipped to a froth. Candide could not forbear praising their beauty, their grace, their skill.

—They are pretty good creatures, said Pococurante; I sometimes have them into my bed, for I'm tired of the ladies of the town, with their stupid tricks, quarrels, jealousies, fits of ill humor and petty pride, and all the sonnets one has to make or order for them; but, after all, these two girls are starting to bore me too.

After lunch, Candide strolled through a long gallery, and was amazed at the beauty of the pictures. He asked who was the painter of the two finest.

—They are by Raphael, said the senator; I bought them for a lot of money, out of vanity, some years ago; people say they're the finest in Italy, but they don't please me at all; the colors have all turned brown, the figures aren't well modeled and don't stand out

6. His name means "small care."

enough, the draperies bear no resemblance to real cloth. In a word, whatever people may say, I don't find in them a real imitation of nature. I like a picture only when I can see in it a touch of nature itself, and there are none of this sort. I have many paintings, but I no longer look at them.

As they waited for dinner, Pococurante ordered a concerto performed. Candide found the music delightful.

—That noise? said Pococurante. It may amuse you for half an hour, but if it goes on any longer, it tires everybody though no one dares to admit it. Music today is only the art of performing difficult pieces, and what is merely difficult cannot please for long. Perhaps I should prefer the opera, if they had not found ways to make it revolting and monstrous. Anyone who likes bad tragedies set to music is welcome to them; in these performances the scenes serve only to introduce, inappropriately, two or three ridiculous songs designed to show off the actress's sound box. Anyone who wants to, or who can, is welcome to swoon with pleasure at the sight of a castrate wriggling through the role of Caesar or Cato, and strutting awkwardly about the stage. For my part, I have long since given up these paltry trifles which are called the glory of modern Italy, and for which monarchs pay such ruinous prices.

Candide argued a bit, but timidly; Martin was entirely of a mind with the senator.

They sat down to dinner, and after an excellent meal adjourned to the library. Candide, seeing a copy of Homer [7] in a splendid binding, complimented the noble lord on his good taste.

—That is an author, said he, who was the special delight of great Pangloss, the best philosopher in all Germany.

—He's no special delight of mine, said Pococurante coldly. I was once made to believe that I took pleasure in reading him; but that constant recital of fights which are all alike, those gods who are always interfering but never decisively, that Helen who is the cause of the war and then scarcely takes any part in the story, that Troy which is always under siege and never taken—all that bores me to tears. I have sometimes asked scholars if reading it bored them as much as it bores me; everyone who answered frankly told me the book dropped from his hands like lead, but that they had to have it in their libraries as a monument of antiquity, like those old rusty coins which can't be used in real trade.

—Your Excellence doesn't hold the same opinion of Virgil? said Candide.

7. Since the mid-sixteenth century, when Julius Caesar Scaliger established the dogma, it had been customary to prefer Virgil to Homer. Voltaire's youthful judgments, as delivered in the *Essai sur la poésie épique* (1728), are here summarized with minor revisions—upward for Ariosto, downward for Milton.

—I concede, said Pococurante, that the second, fourth, and sixth books of his *Aeneid* are fine; but as for his pious Aeneas, and strong Cloanthes, and faithful Achates, and little Ascanius, and that imbecile King Latinus, and middle-class Amata, and insipid Lavinia, I don't suppose there was ever anything so cold and unpleasant. I prefer Tasso and those sleepwalkers' stories of Ariosto.

—Dare I ask, sir, said Candide, if you don't get great enjoyment from reading Horace?

—There are some maxims there, said Pococurante, from which a man of the world can profit, and which, because they are formed into vigorous couplets, are more easily remembered; but I care very little for his trip to Brindisi, his description of a bad dinner, or his account of a quibblers' squabble between some fellow Pupilus, whose words he says *were full of pus*, and another whose words *were full of vinegar*.[8] I feel nothing but extreme disgust at his verses against old women and witches; and I can't see what's so great in his telling his friend Maecenas that if he is raised by him to the ranks of lyric poets, he will strike the stars with his lofty forehead. Fools admire everything in a well-known author. I read only for my own pleasure; I like only what is in my style.

Candide, who had been trained never to judge for himself, was much astonished by what he heard; and Martin found Pococurante's way of thinking quite rational.

—Oh, here is a copy of Cicero, said Candide. Now this great man I suppose you're never tired of reading.

—I never read him at all, replied the Venetian. What do I care whether he pleaded for Rabirius or Cluentius? As a judge, I have my hands full of lawsuits. I might like his philosophical works better, but when I saw that he had doubts about everything, I concluded that I knew as much as he did, and that I needed no help to be ignorant.

—Ah, here are eighty volumes of collected papers from a scientific academy, cried Martin; maybe there is something good in them.

—There would be indeed, said Pococurante, if one of these silly authors had merely discovered a new way of making pins; but in all those volumes there is nothing but empty systems, not a single useful discovery.

—What a lot of stage plays I see over there, said Candide, some in Italian, some in Spanish and French.

—Yes, said the senator, three thousand of them, and not three dozen good ones. As for those collections of sermons, which all to-

8. The reference is to Horace, *Satires* I. vii; Pococurante, with gentlemanly negligence, has corrupted Rupilius to Pupilus. Horace's poems against witches are *Epodes* V, VIII, XII; the one about striking the stars with his lofty forehead is *Odes* I.i.

gether are not worth a page of Seneca, and all these heavy volumes of theology, you may be sure I never open them, nor does anybody else.

Martin noticed some shelves full of English books.

—I suppose, said he, that a republican must delight in most of these books written in the land of liberty.

—Yes, replied Pococurante, it's a fine thing to write as you think; it is mankind's privilege. In all our Italy, people write only what they do not think; men who inhabit the land of the Caesars and Antonines dare not have an idea without the permission of a Dominican. I would rejoice in the freedom that breathes through English genius, if partisan passions did not corrupt all that is good in that precious freedom.

Candide, noting a Milton, asked if he did not consider this author a great man.

—Who? said Pococurante. That barbarian who made a long commentary on the first chapter of Genesis in ten books of crabbed verse? That clumsy imitator of the Greeks, who disfigures creation itself, and while Moses represents the eternal being as creating the world with a word, has the messiah take a big compass out of a heavenly cupboard in order to design his work? You expect me to admire the man who spoiled Tasso's hell and devil? who disguises Lucifer now as a toad, now as a pigmy? who makes him rehash the same arguments a hundred times over? who makes him argue theology? and who, taking seriously Ariosto's comic story of the invention of firearms, has the devils shooting off cannon in heaven? Neither I nor anyone else in Italy has been able to enjoy these gloomy extravagances. The marriage of Sin and Death, and the monster that Sin gives birth to, will nauseate any man whose taste is at all refined; and his long description of a hospital is good only for a gravedigger. This obscure, extravagant, and disgusting poem was despised at its birth; I treat it today as it was treated in its own country by its contemporaries. Anyhow, I say what I think, and care very little whether other people agree with me.

Candide was a little cast down by this speech; he respected Homer, and had a little affection for Milton.

—Alas, he said under his breath to Martin, I'm afraid this man will have a supreme contempt for our German poets.

—No harm in that, said Martin.

—Oh what a superior man, said Candide, still speaking softly, what a great genius this Pococurante must be! Nothing can please him.

Having thus looked over all the books, they went down into the garden. Candide praised its many beauties.

—I know nothing in such bad taste, said the master of the house;

we have nothing but trifles here; tomorrow I am going to have one set out on a nobler design.

When the two visitors had taken leave of his excellency: —Well now, said Candide to Martin, you must agree that this was the happiest of all men, for he is superior to everything he possesses.

—Don't you see, said Martin, that he is disgusted with everything he possesses? Plato said, a long time ago, that the best stomachs are not those which refuse all food.

—But, said Candide, isn't there pleasure in criticizing everything, in seeing faults where other people think they see beauties?

—That is to say, Martin replied, that there's pleasure in having no pleasure?

—Oh well, said Candide, then I am the only happy man . . . or will be, when I see Miss Cunégonde again.

—It's always a good thing to have hope, said Martin.

But the days and the weeks slipped past; Cacambo did not come back, and Candide was so buried in his grief, that he did not even notice that Paquette and Brother Giroflée had neglected to come and thank him.

CHAPTER 26

About a Supper that Candide and Martin Had with Six Strangers, and Who They Were

One evening when Candide, accompanied by Martin, was about to sit down for dinner with the strangers staying in his hotel, a man with a soot-colored face came up behind him, took him by the arm, and said: —Be ready to leave with us, don't miss out.

He turned and saw Cacambo. Only the sight of Cunégonde could have astonished and pleased him more. He nearly went mad with joy. He embraced his dear friend.

—Cunégonde is here, no doubt? Where is she? Bring me to her, let me die of joy in her presence.

—Cunégonde is not here at all, said Cacambo, she is at Constantinople.

—Good Heavens, at Constantinople! but if she were in China, I must fly there, let's go.

—We will leave after supper, said Cacambo; I can tell you no more; I am a slave, my owner is looking for me, I must go wait on him at table; mum's the word; eat your supper and be prepared.

Candide, torn between joy and grief, delighted to have seen his faithful agent again, astonished to find him a slave, full of the idea of recovering his mistress, his heart in a turmoil, his mind in a whirl, sat down to eat with Martin, who was watching all these events coolly, and with six strangers who had come to pass the carnival season at Venice.

Cacambo, who was pouring wine for one of the strangers, leaned respectfully over his master at the end of the meal, and said to him: —Sire, Your Majesty may leave when he pleases, the vessel is ready.

Having said these words, he exited. The diners looked at one another in silent amazement, when another servant, approaching his master, said to him: —Sire, Your Majesty's litter is at Padua, and the bark awaits you.

The master nodded, and the servant vanished. All the diners looked at one another again, and the general amazement redoubled. A third servant, approaching a third stranger, said to him: —Sire, take my word for it, Your Majesty must stay here no longer; I shall get everything ready.

Then he too disappeared.

Candide and Martin had no doubt, now, that it was a carnival masquerade. A fourth servant spoke to a fourth master: —Your majesty will leave when he pleases—and went out like the others. A fifth followed suit. But the sixth servant spoke differently to the sixth stranger, who sat next to Candide. He said: —My word, sire, they'll give no more credit to Your Majesty, nor to me either; we could very well spend the night in the lockup, you and I. I've got to look out for myself, so good-bye to you.

When all the servants had left, the six strangers, Candide, and Martin remained under a pall of silence. Finally Candide broke it.

—Gentlemen, said he, here's a funny kind of joke. Why are you all royalty? I assure you that Martin and I aren't.

Cacambo's master spoke up gravely then, and said in Italian: —This is no joke, my name is Achmet the Third.[9] I was grand sultan for several years; then, as I had dethroned my brother, my nephew dethroned me. My viziers had their throats cut; I was allowed to end my days in the old seraglio. My nephew, the Grand Sultan Mahmoud, sometimes lets me travel for my health; and I have come to spend the carnival season at Venice.

A young man who sat next to Achmet spoke after him, and said: —My name is Ivan; I was once emperor of all the Russias.[1] I was dethroned while still in my cradle; my father and mother were locked up, and I was raised in prison; I sometimes have permission to travel, though always under guard, and I have come to spend the carnival season at Venice.

The third said: —I am Charles Edward, king of England[2]; my

9. His dates are 1673–1736; he was deposed in 1730.
1. Ivan VI reigned from his birth in 1740 till 1756, then was confined in the Schlusselberg, and executed in 1764.

2. This is the Young Pretender (1720–1788), known to his supporters as Bonnie Prince Charlie. The defeat so theatrically described took place at Culloden, April 16, 1746.

father yielded me his rights to the kingdom, and I fought to uphold them; but they tore out the hearts of eight hundred of my partisans, and flung them in their faces. I have been in prison; now I am going to Rome, to visit the king, my father, dethroned like me and my grandfather; and I have come to pass the carnival season at Venice.

The fourth king then spoke up, and said: —I am a king of the Poles[3]; the luck of war has deprived me of my hereditary estates; my father suffered the same losses; I submit to Providence like Sultan Achmet, Emperor Ivan, and King Charles Edward, to whom I hope heaven grants long lives; and I have come to pass the carnival season at Venice.

The fifth said: —I too am a king of the Poles[4]; I lost my kingdom twice, but Providence gave me another state, in which I have been able to do more good than all the Sarmatian kings ever managed to do on the banks of the Vistula. I too have submitted to Providence, and I have come to pass the carnival season at Venice.

It remained for the sixth monarch to speak.

—Gentlemen, said he, I am no such great lord as you, but I have in fact been a king like any other. I am Theodore; I was elected king of Corsica.[5] People used to call me *Your Majesty,* and now they barely call me *Sir*; I used to coin currency, and now I don't have a cent; I used to have two secretaries of state, and now I scarcely have a valet; I have sat on a throne, and for a long time in London I was in jail, on the straw; and I may well be treated the same way here, though I have come, like your majesties, to pass the carnival season at Venice.

The five other kings listened to his story with noble compassion. Each one of them gave twenty sequins to King Theodore, so that he might buy a suit and some shirts; Candide gave him a diamond worth two thousand sequins.

—Who in the world, said the five kings, is this private citizen who is in a position to give a hundred times as much as any of us, and who actually gives it?[6]

3. Augustus III (1696–1763), Elector of Saxony and King of Poland, dethroned by Frederick the Great in 1756.
4. Stanislas Leczinski (1677–1766), father-in-law of Louis XV, who abdicated the throne of Poland in 1736, was made Duke of Lorraine and in that capacity befriended Voltaire.
5. Theodore von Neuhof (1690–1756), an authentic Westphalian, an adventurer and a soldier of fortune, who in 1736 was (for about eight months) the elected king of Corsica. He spent time in an Amsterdam as well as a London debtor's prison.
6. A late correction of Voltaire's makes this passage read: —Who is this man who is in a position to give a hundred times as much as any of us, and who actually gives it? Are you a king too, sir?
—No, gentlemen, and I have no desire to be.
But this reading, though Voltaire's on good authority, produces a conflict with Candide's previous remark: —Why are you all royalty? I assure you that Martin and I aren't.
Thus, it has seemed better for literary reasons to follow an earlier reading. Voltaire was very conscious of his situation as a man richer than many princes; in 1758 he had money

Just as they were rising from dinner, there arrived at the same establishment four most serene highnesses, who had also lost their kingdoms through the luck of war, and who came to spend the rest of the carnival season at Venice. But Candide never bothered even to look at these newcomers because he was only concerned to go find his dear Cunégonde at Constantinople.

CHAPTER 27
Candide's Trip to Constantinople

Faithful Cacambo had already arranged with the Turkish captain who was returning Sultan Achmet to Constantinople to make room for Candide and Martin on board. Both men boarded ship after prostrating themselves before his miserable highness. On the way, Candide said to Martin: —Six dethroned kings that we had dinner with! and yet among those six there was one on whom I had to bestow charity! Perhaps there are other princes even more unfortunate. I myself have only lost a hundred sheep, and now I am flying to the arms of Cunégonde. My dear Martin, once again Pangloss is proved right, all is for the best.

—I hope so, said Martin.

—But, said Candide, that was a most unlikely experience we had at Venice. Nobody ever saw, or heard tell of, six dethroned kings eating together at an inn.

—It is no more extraordinary, said Martin, than most of the things that have happened to us. Kings are frequently dethroned; and as for the honor we had from dining with them, that's a trifle which doesn't deserve our notice.[7]

Scarcely was Candide on board than he fell on the neck of his former servant, his friend Cacambo.

—Well! said he, what is Cunégonde doing? Is she still a marvel of beauty? Does she still love me? How is her health? No doubt you have bought her a palace at Constantinople.

—My dear master, answered Cacambo, Cunégonde is washing dishes on the shores of the Propontis, in the house of a prince who has very few dishes to wash; she is a slave in the house of a onetime king named Ragotski,[8] to whom the Great Turk allows three crowns a day in his exile; but, what is worse than all this, she has lost all her beauty and become horribly ugly.

on loan to no fewer than three highnesses, Charles Eugene, Duke of Wurtemburg; Charles Theodore, Elector Palatine; and the Duke of Saxe-Gotha.
7. Another late change adds the following question: —What does it matter whom you dine with as long as you fare well at table?
I have omitted it, again on literary grounds (the observation is too heavy and commonplace), despite its superior claim to a position in the text.
8. Francis Leopold Rakoczy (1676–1735) who was briefly king of Transylvania in the early eighteenth century. After 1720 he was interned in Turkey.

—Ah, beautiful or ugly, said Candide, I am an honest man, and my duty is to love her forever. But how can she be reduced to this wretched state with the five or six millions that you had?

—All right, said Cacambo, didn't I have to give two millions to Señor don Fernando d'Ibaraa y Figueroa y Mascarenes y Lampourdos y Souza, governor of Buenos Aires, for his permission to carry off Miss Cunégonde? And didn't a pirate cleverly strip us of the rest? And didn't this pirate carry us off to Cape Matapan, to Melos, Nicaria, Samos, Petra, to the Dardanelles, Marmora, Scutari? Cunégonde and the old woman are working for the prince I told you about, and I am the slave of the dethroned sultan.

—What a lot of fearful calamities linked one to the other, said Candide. But after all, I still have a few diamonds, I shall easily deliver Cunégonde. What a pity that she's become so ugly!

Then, turning toward Martin, he asked: —Who in your opinion is more to be pitied, the Emperor Achmet, the Emperor Ivan, King Charles Edward, or myself?

—I have no idea, said Martin; I would have to enter your hearts in order to tell.

—Ah, said Candide, if Pangloss were here, he would know and he would tell us.

—I can't imagine, said Martin, what scales your Pangloss would use to weigh out the miseries of men and value their griefs. All I will venture is that the earth holds millions of men who deserve our pity a hundred times more than King Charles Edward, Emperor Ivan, or Sultan Achmet.

—You may well be right, said Candide.

In a few days they arrived at the Black Sea canal. Candide began by repurchasing Cacambo at an exorbitant price; then, without losing an instant, he flung himself and his companions into a galley to go search out Cunégonde on the shores of Propontis, however ugly she might be.

There were in the chain gang two convicts who bent clumsily to the oar, and on whose bare shoulders the Levantine[9] captain delivered from time to time a few lashes with a bullwhip. Candide naturally noticed them more than the other galley slaves, and out of pity came closer to them. Certain features of their disfigured faces seemed to him to bear a slight resemblance to Pangloss and to that wretched Jesuit, that baron, that brother of Miss Cunégonde. The notion stirred and saddened him. He looked at them more closely.

—To tell you the truth, he said to Cacambo, if I hadn't seen Master Pangloss hanged, and if I hadn't been so miserable as to murder the baron, I should think they were rowing in this very galley.

9. From the eastern Mediterranean.

At the names of 'baron' and 'Pangloss' the two convicts gave a great cry, sat still on their bench, and dropped their oars. The Levantine captain came running, and the bullwhip lashes redoubled.

—Stop, stop, captain, cried Candide. I'll give you as much money as you want.

—What, can it be Candide? cried one of the convicts.

—What, can it be Candide? cried the other.

—Is this a dream? said Candide. Am I awake or asleep? Am I in this galley? Is that My Lord the Baron, whom I killed? Is that Master Pangloss, whom I saw hanged?

—It is indeed, they replied.

—What, is that the great philosopher? said Martin.

—Now, sir, Mr. Levantine Captain, said Candide, how much money do you want for the ransom of My Lord Thunder-Ten-Tronckh, one of the first barons of the empire, and Master Pangloss, the deepest metaphysician in all Germany?

—Dog of a Christian, replied the Levantine captain, since these two dogs of Christian convicts are barons and metaphysicians, which is no doubt a great honor in their country, you will give me fifty thousand sequins for them.

—You shall have them, sir, take me back to Constantinople and you shall be paid on the spot. Or no, take me to Miss Cunégonde.

The Levantine captain, at Candide's first word, had turned his bow toward the town, and he had them rowed there as swiftly as a bird cleaves the air.

A hundred times Candide embraced the baron and Pangloss.

—And how does it happen I didn't kill you, my dear baron? and my dear Pangloss, how can you be alive after being hanged? and why are you both rowing in the galleys of Turkey?

—Is it really true that my dear sister is in this country? asked the baron.

—Yes, answered Cacambo.

—And do I really see again my dear Candide? cried Pangloss.

Candide introduced Martin and Cacambo. They all embraced; they all talked at once. The galley flew, already they were back in port. A jew was called, and Candide sold him for fifty thousand sequins a diamond worth a hundred thousand, while he protested by Abraham that he could not possibly give more for it. Candide immediately ransomed the baron and Pangloss. The latter threw himself at the feet of his liberator, and bathed them with tears; the former thanked him with a nod, and promised to repay this bit of money at the first opportunity.

—But is it really possible that my sister is in Turkey? said he.

—Nothing is more possible, replied Cacambo, since she is a dish-washer in the house of a prince of Transylvania.

At once two more jews were called; Candide sold some more dia-monds; and they all departed in another galley to the rescue of Cunégonde.

CHAPTER 28
What Happened to Candide, Cunégonde, Pangloss, Martin, &c.

—Let me beg your pardon once more, said Candide to the baron, pardon me, reverend father, for having run you through the body with my sword.

—Don't mention it, replied the baron. I was a little too hasty myself, I confess it; but since you want to know the misfortune which brought me to the galleys, I'll tell you. After being cured of my wound by the brother who was apothecary to the college, I was attacked and abducted by a Spanish raiding party; they jailed me in Buenos Aires at the time when my sister had just left. I asked to be sent to Rome, to the father general. Instead, I was named to serve as almoner in Constantinople, under the French ambassador. I had not been a week on this job when I chanced one evening on a very handsome young ichoglan.[1] The evening was hot; the young man wanted to take a swim; I seized the occasion, and went with him. I did not know that it is a capital offense for a Christian to be found naked with a young Moslem. A cadi sentenced me to receive a hun-dred blows with a cane on the soles of my feet, and then to be sent to the galleys. I don't suppose there was ever such a horrible miscar-riage of justice. But I would like to know why my sister is in the kitchen of a Transylvanian king exiled among Turks.

—But how about you, my dear Pangloss, said Candide; how is it possible that we have met again?

—It is true, said Pangloss, that you saw me hanged; in the normal course of things, I should have been burned, but you recall that a cloudburst occurred just as they were about to roast me. So much rain fell that they despaired of lighting the fire; thus I was hanged, for lack of anything better to do with me. A surgeon bought my body, carried me off to his house, and dissected me. First he made a cross-shaped incision in me, from the navel to the clavicle. No one could have been worse hanged than I was. In fact, the executioner of the high ceremonials of the Holy Inquisition, who was a subdeacon, burned people marvelously well, but he was not in the way of hanging them. The rope was wet, and tightened badly; it caught on a knot; in short, I was still breathing. The cross-

1. A page to the sultan.

shaped incision made me scream so loudly that the surgeon fell over backwards; he thought he was dissecting the devil, fled in an agony of fear, and fell downstairs in his flight. His wife ran in, at the noise, from a nearby room; she found me stretched out on the table with my cross-shaped incision, was even more frightened than her husband, fled, and fell over him. When they had recovered a little, I heard her say to him: 'My dear, what were you thinking of, trying to dissect a heretic? Don't you know those people are always possessed of the devil? I'm going to get the priest and have him exorcised.' At these words, I shuddered, and collected my last remaining energies to cry: 'Have mercy on me!' At last the Portuguese barber[2] took courage; he sewed me up again; his wife even nursed me; in two weeks I was up and about. The barber found me a job and made me lackey to a Knight of Malta who was going to Venice; and when this master could no longer pay me, I took service under a Venetian merchant, whom I followed to Constantinople.

—One day it occurred to me to enter a mosque; no one was there but an old imam and a very attractive young worshipper who was saying her prayers. Her bosom was completely bare; and between her two breasts she had a lovely bouquet of tulips, roses, anemones, buttercups, hyacinths, and primroses. She dropped her bouquet, I picked it up, and returned it to her with the most respectful attentions. I was so long getting it back in place that the imam grew angry, and, seeing that I was a Christian, he called the guard. They took me before the cadi, who sentenced me to receive a hundred blows with a cane on the soles of my feet, and then to be sent to the galleys. I was chained to the same galley and precisely the same bench as My Lord the Baron. There were in this galley four young fellows from Marseilles, five Neapolitan priests, and two Corfu monks, who assured us that these things happen every day. My Lord the Baron asserted that he had suffered a greater injustice than I; I, on the other hand, proposed that it was much more permissible to replace a bouquet in a bosom than to be found naked with an ichoglan. We were arguing the point continually, and getting twenty lashes a day with the bullwhip, when the chain of events within this universe brought you to our galley, and you ransomed us.

—Well, my dear Pangloss, Candide said to him, now that you have been hanged, dissected, beaten to a pulp, and sentenced to the galleys, do you still think everything is for the best in this world?

—I am still of my first opinion, replied Pangloss; for after all I am a philosopher, and it would not be right for me to recant since Leibniz could not possibly be wrong, and besides pre-established harmony is the finest notion in the world, like the plenum and subtle matter.[3]

2. The two callings of barber and surgeon, since they both involved sharp instruments, were interchangeable in the early days of medicine.

CHAPTER 29

How Candide Found Cunégonde and the Old Woman Again

While Candide, the baron, Pangloss, Martin, and Cacambo were telling one another their stories, while they were disputing over the contingent or non-contingent events of this universe, while they were arguing over effects and causes, over moral evil and physical evil, over liberty and necessity, and over the consolations available to one in a Turkish galley, they arrived at the shores of Propontis and the house of the prince of Transylvania. The first sight to meet their eyes was Cunégonde and the old woman, who were hanging out towels on lines to dry.

The baron paled at what he saw. The tender lover Candide, seeing his lovely Cunégonde with her skin weathered, her eyes bloodshot, her breasts fallen, her cheeks seamed, her arms red and scaly, recoiled three steps in horror, and then advanced only out of politeness. She embraced Candide and her brother; everyone embraced the old woman; Candide ransomed them both.

There was a little farm in the neighborhood; the old woman suggested that Candide occupy it until some better fate should befall the group. Cunégonde did not know she was ugly, no one had told her; she reminded Candide of his promises in so firm a tone that the good Candide did not dare to refuse her. So he went to tell the baron that he was going to marry his sister.

—Never will I endure, said the baron, such baseness on her part, such insolence on yours; this shame at least I will not put up with; why, my sister's children would not be able to enter the Chapters in Germany.[4] No, my sister will never marry anyone but a baron of the empire.

Cunégonde threw herself at his feet, and bathed them with her tears; he was inflexible.

—You absolute idiot, Candide told him, I rescued you from the galleys, I paid your ransom, I paid your sister's; she was washing dishes, she is ugly, I am good enough to make her my wife, and you still presume to oppose it! If I followed my impulses, I would kill you all over again.

—You may kill me again, said the baron, but you will not marry my sister while I am alive.

3. Rigorous determinism requires that there be no empty spaces in the universe, so wherever it seems empty, one posits the existence of the "plenum." "Subtle matter" describes the soul, the mind, and all spiritual agencies—which can, therefore, be supposed subject to the influence and control of the great world machine, which is, of course, visibly material. Both are concepts needed to round out the system of optimistic determinism.

4. Knightly assemblies.

CHAPTER 30
Conclusion

At heart, Candide had no real wish to marry Cunégonde; but the baron's extreme impertinence decided him in favor of the marriage, and Cunégonde was so eager for it that he could not back out. He consulted Pangloss, Martin, and the faithful Cacambo. Pangloss drew up a fine treatise, in which he proved that the baron had no right over his sister and that she could, according to all the laws of the empire, marry Candide morganatically.[5] Martin said they should throw the baron into the sea. Cacambo thought they should send him back to the Levantine captain to finish his time in the galleys, and then send him to the father general in Rome by the first vessel. This seemed the best idea; the old woman approved, and nothing was said to his sister; the plan was executed, at modest expense, and they had the double pleasure of snaring a Jesuit and punishing the pride of a German baron.

It is quite natural to suppose that after so many misfortunes, Candide, married to his mistress, and living with the philosopher Pangloss, the philosopher Martin, the prudent Cacambo, and the old woman—having, besides, brought back so many diamonds from the land of the ancient Incas—must have led the most agreeable life in the world. But he was so cheated by the jews[6] that nothing was left but his little farm; his wife, growing every day more ugly, became sour-tempered and insupportable; the old woman was ailing and even more ill-humored than Cunégonde. Cacambo, who worked in the garden and went into Constantinople to sell vegetables, was worn out with toil, and cursed his fate. Pangloss was in despair at being unable to shine in some German university. As for Martin, he was firmly persuaded that things are just as bad wherever you are; he endured in patience. Candide, Martin, and Pangloss sometimes argued over metaphysics and morals. Before the windows of the farmhouse they often watched the passage of boats bearing effendis, pashas, and cadis into exile on Lemnos, Mytilene, and Erzeroum; they saw other cadis, other pashas, other effendis coming, to take the place of the exiles and to be exiled in their turn. They saw various heads, neatly impaled, to be set up at the Sublime Porte.[7] These sights gave fresh impetus to their discussions; and

5. A morganatic marriage confers no rights on the partner of lower rank or on the offspring. Pangloss always uses more language than anyone else to achieve fewer results.

6. Voltaire's anti-Semitism, derived from various unhappy experiences with Jewish financiers, is not the most at-

tractive aspect of his personality.

7. The gate of the sultan's palace is often used by extension to describe his government as a whole. But it was in fact a real gate where the heads of traitors and public enemies were gruesomely exposed.

when they were not arguing, the boredom was so fierce that one day the old woman ventured to say: —I should like to know which is worse, being raped a hundred times by negro pirates, having a buttock cut off, running the gauntlet in the Bulgar army, being flogged and hanged in an auto-da-fé, being dissected and rowing in the galleys—experiencing, in a word, all the miseries through which we have passed—or else just sitting here and doing nothing?

—It's a hard question, said Candide.

These words gave rise to new reflections, and Martin in particular concluded that man was bound to live either in convulsions of misery or in the lethargy of boredom. Candide did not agree, but expressed no positive opinion. Pangloss asserted that he had always suffered horribly; but having once declared that everything was marvelously well, he continued to repeat the opinion and didn't believe a word of it.

One thing served to confirm Martin in his detestable opinions, to make Candide hesitate more than ever, and to embarrass Pangloss. It was the arrival one day at their farm of Paquette and Brother Giroflée, who were in the last stages of misery. They had quickly run through their three thousand piastres, had split up, made up, quarreled, been jailed, escaped, and finally Brother Giroflée had turned Turk. Paquette continued to ply her trade everywhere, and no longer made any money at it.

—I told you, said Martin to Candide, that your gifts would soon be squandered and would only render them more unhappy. You have spent millions of piastres, you and Cacambo, and you are no more happy than Brother Giroflée and Paquette.

—Ah ha, said Pangloss to Paquette, so destiny has brought you back in our midst, my poor girl! Do you realize you cost me the end of my nose, one eye, and an ear? And look at you now! eh! what a world it is, after all!

This new adventure caused them to philosophize more than ever.

There was in the neighborhood a very famous dervish, who was said to be the best philosopher in Turkey; they went to ask his advice. Pangloss was spokesman, and he said: —Master, we have come to ask you to tell us why such a strange animal as man was created.

—What are you getting into? answered the dervish. Is it any of your business?

—But, reverend father, said Candide, there's a horrible lot of evil on the face of the earth.

—What does it matter, said the dervish, whether there's good or evil? When his highness sends a ship to Egypt, does he worry whether the mice on board are comfortable or not?

—What shall we do then? asked Pangloss.

—Hold your tongue, said the dervish.

—I had hoped, said Pangloss, to reason a while with you concerning effects and causes, the best of possible worlds, the origin of evil, the nature of the soul, and pre-established harmony.

At these words, the dervish slammed the door in their faces.

During this interview, word was spreading that at Constantinople they had just strangled two viziers of the divan,[8] as well as the mufti, and impaled several of their friends. This catastrophe made a great and general sensation for several hours. Pangloss, Candide, and Martin, as they returned to their little farm, passed a good old man who was enjoying the cool of the day at his doorstep under a grove of orange trees. Pangloss, who was as inquisitive as he was explanatory, asked the name of the mufti who had been strangled.

—I know nothing of it, said the good man, and I have never cared to know the name of a single mufti or vizier. I am completely ignorant of the episode you are discussing. I presume that in general those who meddle in public business sometimes perish miserably, and that they deserve their fate; but I never listen to the news from Constantinople; I am satisfied with sending the fruits of my garden to be sold there.

Having spoken these words, he asked the strangers into his house; his two daughters and two sons offered them various sherbets which they had made themselves, Turkish cream flavored with candied citron, orange, lemon, lime, pineapple, pistachio, and mocha coffee uncontaminated by the inferior coffee of Batavia and the East Indies. After which the two daughters of this good Moslem perfumed the beards of Candide, Pangloss, and Martin.

—You must possess, Candide said to the Turk, an enormous and splendid property?

I have only twenty acres, replied the Turk; I cultivate them with my children, and the work keeps us from three great evils, boredom, vice, and poverty.

Candide, as he walked back to his farm, meditated deeply over the words of the Turk. He said to Pangloss and Martin: —This good old man seems to have found himself a fate preferable to that of the six kings with whom we had the honor of dining.

—Great place, said Pangloss, is very perilous in the judgment of all the philosophers; for, after all, Eglon, king of the Moabites, was murdered by Ehud; Absalom was hung up by the hair and pierced with three darts; King Nadab, son of Jeroboam, was killed by Baasha; King Elah by Zimri; Ahaziah by Jehu; Athaliah by Jehoiada; and Kings Jehoiakim, Jeconiah, and Zedekiah were enslaved. You know how death came to Croesus, Astyages, Darius, Dionysius of Syracuse, Pyrrhus, Perseus, Hannibal, Jugurtha, Ariovistus, Caesar, Pompey, Nero, Otho, Vitellius, Domitian, Rich-

---

8. Intimate advisers of the sultan.

ard II of England, Edward II, Henry VI, Richard III, Mary Stuart, Charles I, the three Henrys of France, and the Emperor Henry IV? You know . . .

—I know also, said Candide, that we must cultivate our garden.

—You are perfectly right, said Pangloss; for when man was put into the garden of Eden, he was put there *ut operaretur eum*, so that he should work it; this proves that man was not born to take his ease.

—Let's work without speculating, said Martin; it's the only way of rendering life bearable.

The whole little group entered into this laudable scheme; each one began to exercise his talents. The little plot yielded fine crops. Cunégonde was, to tell the truth, remarkably ugly; but she became an excellent pastry cook. Paquette took up embroidery; the old woman did the laundry. Everyone, down even to Brother Giroflée, did something useful; he became a very adequate carpenter, and even an honest man; and Pangloss sometimes used to say to Candide: —All events are linked together in the best of possible worlds; for, after all, if you had not been driven from a fine castle by being kicked in the backside for love of Miss Cunégonde, if you hadn't been sent before the Inquisition, if you hadn't traveled across America on foot, if you hadn't given a good sword thrust to the baron, if you hadn't lost all your sheep from the good land of Eldorado, you wouldn't be sitting here eating candied citron and pistachios.

—That is very well put, said Candide, but we must cultivate our garden.

DENIS DIDEROT
(1713–1784)
Rameau's Nephew (Le Neveu de Rameau)*

Vertumnis, quotquot sunt, natus iniquis.—Horace[1]

Rain or shine, it is my regular habit every day about five to go and take a walk around the Palais-Royal.[2] I can be seen, all by myself, dreaming on D'Argenson's bench.[3] I discuss with myself questions of politics, love, taste, or philosophy. I let my mind rove wantonly, give it free rein to follow any idea, wise or mad, that may come uppermost; I chase it as do our young libertines along Foy's Walk,[4] when they are on the track of a courtesan whose mien is giddy and face smiling, whose nose turns up. The youth drops one and picks up another, pursuing all and clinging to none: my ideas are my trollops.

If the weather is too cold or rainy, I take shelter in the Regency Café,[5] where I entertain myself by watching chess being played. Paris is the world center, and this café is the Paris center, for the finest skill at this game. It is there that one sees the clash of the profound Legal, the subtle Philidor, the staunch Mayot;[6] that one sees the most surprising strokes and that one hears the stupidest remarks. For although one may be a wit and a great chess player, like Legal, one may also be a great chess player and a fool, like Foubert[7] and Mayot.

One day I was there after dinner, looking hard, saying little, and listening the least amount possible, when I was accosted by one of the oddest characters in this country, where God has not stinted us. The fellow[8] is a compound of elevation and abjectness, of good

* From *Rameau's Nephew and Other Works* by Denis Diderot, translated by Jacques Barzun & Ralph Bowen. Copyright 1956 by Jacques Barzun and Ralph Bowen. Reprinted by permission of Doubleday & Company, Inc. Unpublished during his life, Diderot's work has a strange history. After his death in 1784, Catherine the Great bought his books and some of his manuscripts, including *Rameau's Nephew*. A second manuscript copy somehow reached Germany around 1800; Schiller read it, and Goethe translated it in 1805. This and other versions reached nineteenth-century readers, but imperfectly; and 1950 saw the first complete critical edition. Diderot probably wrote the dialogue during the 1760's and early 1770's. The editor has abridged the present version.

1. *Vertumnis . . . iniquis:* "Born beneath all the changeful stars there are."
2. *Palais-Royal:* palace north of the Louvre.
3. *D'Argenson's bench:* René-Louis, Marquis D'Argenson (1694–1757), one-

time Minister of Foreign Affairs who devoted his old age to philosophy. His "bench" was a favorite spot for Diderot.
4. *Foy's Walk:* This, and Argenson's Walk, marked the east-west boundaries of the gardens surrounding the *Palais*. *Foy's Café* was in the Palais-Royal, *galérie Montpensier*, and existed until 1863. Foy's Walk was noted for its attractive perambulating courtesans.
5. *Regency Café:* on the square of the *Palais-Royal*.
6. *Legal . . . Philidor . . . Mayot:* friends of Diderot, the first two noted chess-players.
7. *Foubert:* a surgeon.
8. *fellow:* Jean-Philipe Rameau (1683–1764), leading French composer and musical theorist, had a nephew, Jean-François Rameau: baptized 1716, married 1757, mentioned in police archives (1748) as having "a scarcely sociable character . . . insulted the directors of the Opera." Since he was a beggar, his death was unrecorded.

sense and lunacy. The ideas of decency and depravity must be strangely scrambled in his head, for he shows without ostentation the good qualities that nature has bestowed upon him, just as he does the bad ones without shame. Apart from this, he is endowed with a strong constitution, a special warmth of imagination, and an unusual power of lung. If you ever meet him and are not put off by his originality, you will either stuff your fingers into your ears or run away. Lord, what lungs!

He has no greater opposite than himself. Sometimes he is thin and wan like a patient in the last stages of consumption; you could count his teeth through his skin; he looks as if he had been days without food or had just come out of a Trappist monastery.[9] The next month, he is sleek and fat as if he ate regularly at a banker's or had shut himself up in a Bernardine convent.[10] Today his linen is filthy, his clothes torn to rags, he is virtually barefoot, and he hangs his head furtively; one is tempted to hail him and toss him a coin. Tomorrow he is powdered, curled, well dressed; he holds his head high, shows himself off—you would almost take him for a man of quality. He lives from day to day, sad or cheerful according to luck. His first care on arising in the morning is to ascertain where he will dine; after dinner he ponders supper. Night brings its own worries—whether to return on foot to the garret where he sleeps (unless the landlady has taken back the key from impatience at receiving no rent); or whether to repair to a suburban tavern and await the dawn over a crust of bread and a mug of beer. When he hasn't as much as sixpence in his pocket, as sometimes happens, he falls back on a cab-driving friend of his, or the coachman of a noble lord, who gives him a shakedown in a stable, alongside the horses. The next morning he still has bits of his mattress in his hair. If the weather is mild, he perambulates all night up and down the Cours-la-reine[11] or the Champs-Elysées.[12] Daybreak sees him back in town, all dressed from yesterday for today and from today perhaps for the remainder of the week.

I have no great esteem for such eccentrics. Some people take them on as regular acquaintances or even friends. But for my part it is only once a year that I stop and fall in with them, largely because their character stands out from the rest and breaks that tedious uniformity which our education, our social conventions, and our customary good manners have brought about. If such a character makes his appearance in some circle, he is like a grain of yeast that ferments and restores to each of us a part of his native individuality.

---

9. *Trappist monastery:* order of monks famed for their austerity.
10. *Bernardine convent:* Cistercian monks, reformed by St. Bernard of Clairvaux. In eighteenth-century France, their order was associated with good living.
11. *Cours-la-reine:* a popular eighteenth-century promenade along the Seine.
12. *Champs-Elysées:* By 1770, this now-famous boulevard was just starting to become popular.

He shakes and stirs us up, makes us praise or blame, smokes out the truth, discloses the worthy and unmasks the rascals. It is then that the sensible man keeps his ears open and sorts out his company.

I knew my man from quite a while back. He used to frequent a house to which his talent had given him entrée. There was an only daughter; he swore to the father and mother that he would marry her. They shrugged it off, laughed in his face, told him he was crazy. But I lived to see it happen. He asked me for a little money, which I gave him. He had somehow made his way into a few good families, where he could always dine provided he would not speak without asking permission first. He kept quiet and ate with fury. He was remarkable to see under that restraint. If he had the inclination to break the treaty and open his mouth, at the first word all the guests would shout "Why Rameau!" Then rage would blaze in his eyes and he fell to eating with greater fury still. You wanted to know his name and now you know it. He is the nephew of the famous musician who delivered us from the plainsong of Lully[13] that we had intoned for over a century, and who wrote so much visionary gibberish and apocalyptic truth about the theory of music —writings that neither he nor anyone else ever understood. We have from him a number of operas in which one finds harmony, snatches of song, disconnected ideas, clatter, flights, triumphal processions, spears, apotheoses, murmurings, endless victories, and dance tunes that will last for all time. Having eliminated "the Florentine"[14] in public favor, he will be eliminated by the Italian virtuosos—as he himself foresaw with grief, rancor, and depression of spirits. For no one, not even a pretty woman who wakes up to find a pimple on her nose, feels so vexed as an author who threatens to survive his own reputation—witness Marivaux[15] and the younger Crébillon.[16]

He accosts me: Ha ha! So there you are, master Philosopher! And what are you up to among all these idlers? Do you waste your time, too, pushing wood? (That is the contemptuous way of describing chess and checkers.)

MYSELF. No, but when I have nothing better to do, I enjoy watching those who push well.

HE. In that case you don't enjoy yourself very often. Apart from Legal and Philidor, the others don't know what they're doing.

13. *Lully:* Jean-Baptiste Lully (1632–1687), appointed chamber composer and conductor to Louis XIV in 1653. Lully wrote ballet scores for many of Molière's plays, including *The Bourgeois Gentleman;* he is best known for his operas and instrumental and keyboard suites.
14. *"the Florentine":* i.e., Lully, born in Italy.

15. *Marivaux:* Pierre de Marivaux (1688–1763), dramatist whose comedies are famous for their light wit and badinage.
16. *Crébillon:* Prosper Crébillon (1674–1762), dramatist—although "the younger" suggests his son Claude (1707–77), author of suggestive tales.

MYSELF. What of M. de Bissy?[17]

HE. Oh that one is to chess what Mlle. Clairon[18] is to acting: they know about their respective playing all that can be *learned*.

MYSELF. I see you're hard to please. You forgive nothing but sublime genius.

HE. True: in chess, checkers, poetry, eloquence, music and other nonsense of that kind, what's the use of mediocrity?

MYSELF. Not much use, I admit. But it takes a crowd to cultivate the game before one man of genius emerges. He is one out of many. But let it go. It's an age since I've seen you. I don't think about you very much when I don't see you but I'm always glad when I do. What have you been doing?

HE. What you and I and the rest do, namely, good and evil, and also nothing. And then I was hungry and I ate when I had the chance. After eating I was thirsty and I have occasionally drunk. Meanwhile my beard grew and when grown I had it shaved.

MYSELF. There you did wrong. A beard is all you lack to be a sage.

HE. Right you are. My forehead is broad and wrinkled; I have a glowing eye, a beaky nose, spacious cheeks, thick black brows, a clean-cut mouth, curved-out lips and a square jaw. Cover this ample chin with a flowing beard and I assure you it would look splendid in bronze or marble.

MYSELF. Side by side with Caesar, Marcus Aurelius, and Socrates.

HE. No. I should like it better between Diogenes[19] and Phryne.[20] I am as cheeky as the one and often visit the sisters of the other.

MYSELF. And you are still in good health?

HE. Usually, yes, but not so well today.

MYSELF. How is that? You have a paunch like Silenus[21] and a face like——

HE. A face like its counterpart. That's because the spleen which is wasting my dear uncle seems to fatten his dear nephew.

MYSELF. Speaking of the uncle, do you ever see him?

HE. I see him pass in the street.

MYSELF. Doesn't he do anything for you?

HE. If he ever has done anything for anybody, it must be without knowing it. He is a philosopher after a fashion: he thinks of no one but himself; the rest of the universe doesn't matter a tinker's dam to him. His wife, his daughter, may die as soon as they please. Provided the parish bells that toll for them continue to sound the intervals of the twelfth and the seventeenth, all will be well. It's lucky for him and that's what I envy especially in men of genius.

17. *Bissy:* Claude Henri de Bissy (1721–1810), playwright, member of the French Academy; admired by Diderot.
18. *Mlle. Clairon:* an actress who, like Bissy, was noted for her restraint and control.

19. *Diogenes:* blunt-spoken Cynic philosopher of Athens (ca. 412–323 B.C.).
20. *Phryne:* Athenian courtesan.
21. *Silenus:* fat god of wine and fertility.

They are good for only one thing—apart from that, zero. They don't know what it is to be citizens, fathers, mothers, cousins, friends. Between you and me, one should try to be like them in every way, but without multiplying the breed. The world needs men, but men of genius, no; I say, no! No need of them. They are the ones who change the face of the earth. Even in small things stupidity is so common and powerful that it is not changed without fracas. What results is partly the reformer's vision, partly the old status quo —whence two gospels, a parti-colored world. The wisdom of the monk Rabelais[22] is the true wisdom for his own peace of mind and other people's too: to do one's duty, more or less, always speak well of the father superior, and let the world wag. It must be all right since the majority is content with it. If I knew history, I could prove to you that evil has always come here below through a few men of genius; but I don't know any history because I don't know anything at all. The devil take me if I've ever learnt a single thing and if, having learnt nothing, I am worse off. One day I was at table with one of the King's Ministers who has brains enough for ten. Well, he showed us as plain as two and two make four that nothing is more useful to the nations of the earth than lies, nothing more harmful than the truth. I don't quite recall his proof but it followed very clearly that men of genius are poisonous and that if at birth a child bore the mark of this dangerous gift of nature, he should be either smothered or thrown to the dogs.

MYSELF. And yet those people who are so down on genius all pretend to have some.

HE. I'm sure they think so inside, but they don't dare admit it.

MYSELF. From modesty! So you developed from then on an undying hatred of genius?

HE. Which I'll never get over.

MYSELF. But I remember the time when you were in despair at the thought of being a common man. You'll never be happy if the pros and cons weigh with you equally. You should make up your mind and stick to it. I agree with you that men of genius are usually odd, or—as the saying goes, "great wits are sure to madness near allied";[23] but that doesn't change the truth that ages without genius are despised. Men will continue to honor the nations where genius thrived. Sooner or later they put up statues to them and call them benefactors of the race. With all due respect to the sublime minister you were quoting. I believe that although a lie may serve for a while, it is harmful in the long run; and, contrariwise, truth necessarily is best in the long run, even though it may do harm at the

---

22. *Rabelais:* François Rabelais (ca. 1490–1553), author of *Gargantua and Pantagruel.* The sentiments are those of Friar John, who accompanies first the father, then the son, in their exploits.

23. *"great wits . . . allied"*: Cf. Dryden, *Absalom and Achitophel,* line 163.

moment. From which I incline to think that the man of genius who denounces a common error or who establishes a general truth always deserves our veneration. Such a man may fall a victim to prejudice or existing law; but there are two kinds of laws—those based on equity, which are universally true, and those based on whim, which owe their force only to blindness or local necessity. These last cast odium on their violator for only a brief moment, an odium which time casts back upon the judges and the peoples who carried out the law. Which of the two, Socrates or the judge who made him drink hemlock, is today the dishonored man?

HE. A great comfort to Socrates! Was he any the less convicted? any the less put to death? Was he less of an agitator? In violating a bad law, did he not encourage fools to despise the good ones? Wasn't he in any case a queer and troublesome citizen? A while ago you yourself were not far from marking down the man of genius too!

MYSELF. Listen, my dear fellow. A society should not tolerate any bad laws, and if it had only good ones it would never find itself persecuting men of genius. I never said that genius went with evil nor evil with genius. A fool is more often a knave than a genius is. And even if the latter is difficult to get on with, irritating and irritable—add wicked, if you like—what do you infer from it?

HE. That he should be drowned.

MYSELF. Gently, dear fellow. Look and tell me—I shan't take your uncle as an example. He is a hard man, brutal, inhuman, miserly, a bad father, bad husband, and bad uncle. And it is by no means sure that he is a genius who has advanced his art to such a point that ten years from now we shall still discuss his works. Take Racine instead—there was a genius, and his reputation as a man was none too good. Take Voltaire——

HE. Don't press the point too far: I am a man to argue with you.

MYSELF. Well, which would you prefer—that he should have been a good soul, at one with his ledger, like Briasson,[24] or with his yardstick, like Barbier;[25] legitimately getting his wife with child annually—a good husband, good father, good uncle, good neighbor, fair trader and nothing more; or that he should have been deceitful, disloyal, ambitious, envious, and mean, but also the creator of *Andromaque, Britannicus, Iphigénie, Phèdre,* and *Athalie?*[26]

HE. For himself I daresay it would have been better to be the former.

MYSELF. That is infinitely truer than you think.

HE. There you go, you fellows! If we say anything good, it's like lunatics or people possessed—by accident. It's only people like you

24. *Briasson:* Antoine-Claude Briasson, printer and publisher, associated with Diderot in the *Encyclopedia.*

25. *Barbier:* a shopkeeper who sold silk, gold, and silver.

26. *Andromaque . . . Athalie:* plays by Racine.

who really know what they're saying. I tell you, Master Philosopher, I know what I say and know it as well as you know what you say.

MYSELF. Let's find out: why better for Racine?

HE. Because all those mighty works of his did not bring him in twenty thousand francs, and if he had been a good silk merchant of rue St. Denis or St. Honoré, a good grocer or apothecary in a large way of business, he would have amassed a huge fortune, in the course of doing which there is no pleasure he would have failed to enjoy. From time to time he would have given a dollar to a poor buffoon like me and I would have made him laugh, besides procuring for him an occasional young girl to distract him a little from eternally living with his wife. We would have eaten excellent meals at his table, played high, drunk excellent wines, coffee, liqueurs; we would have had delightful picnics—you can see I knew perfectly well what I was saying—you laugh, but let me finish—it would have been better for those around him.

MYSELF. Unquestionably. Provided he hadn't used unworthily the riches acquired in legitimate trade, and had kept from his house all the gamblers, parasites, sycophants, idlers, and debauchees, as well as ordered his shopboys to beat up the officious gentlemen who would help husbands to a little distraction from habitually living with their wives.

HE. Beat up, my good sir, beat up! No one is beaten up in a well-ordered city. The profession is respectable; many people, even persons of title, are in it. And what in hell do you think money is for, if not to have good board, good company, pretty women, every kind of pleasure and every sort of amusement? I'd rather be a beggar than own a fortune without these enjoyments. But to come back to Racine. The fellow was of use only to people he didn't know, at a time when he had ceased to live.

MYSELF. Granted. But compare the good and the evil. A thousand years from now he will draw tears, will be admired by men all over the earth, will inspire compassion, human kindness, love. People will wonder who he was, from what country, and France will be envied. As against this, he brought suffering on a few persons who are dead and in whom we take no interest. We have nothing more to fear from his vices or his errors. It would no doubt have been preferable if nature had bestowed upon him the virtues of a good man as well as the talents of a great one. He is a tree which has stunted a few trees in his vicinage and blighted the plants growing at his feet; but his topmost branch reached the sky and his boughs spread afar. He has afforded shade to those past, present, and future who come to rest close to his majestic trunk. He bore fruit of exquisite savor and that will not perish. Again, it would be desirable if Voltaire had the sweetness of Duclos,[27] the ingenuousness of Abbé Trublet,[28] the rectitude of Abbé d'Olivet;[29] but as that cannot be, consider the really interesting side of the problem; forget for a moment the point we occupy in time and space, and project your vision into centuries to come, into the most remote places, and nations yet unborn. Think of the welfare of our species and, supposing that we ourselves are not generous enough, let us thank nature for knowing her business better than we. If you throw cold water on Greuze's[30] head, you will extinguish his talent together with his vanity. If you make Voltaire less restive under criticism, he will not delve into the soul of Merope[31] and will no longer move you.

HE. But if nature is as powerful as she is wise, why not make them as good as they are great?

MYSELF. Don't you see that if you argue this way you upset the general order of things? If everything here below were excellent, nothing would be excellent.

HE. You are right. The important point is that you and I should exist, and that we should be you and I. Outside of that, let everything carry on as it may. The best order, for me, is that in which I had to exist—and a fig for the most perfect world if I am not of it. I'd rather *be*—and be even a silly logic-chopper—than not be at all.

MYSELF. There is nobody who thinks otherwise and yet who fails to attack the scheme of things, blind to the fact that in doing so he repudiates his own existence.

HE. True enough.

MYSELF. So let's accept things as they are, find out their worth and their cost, and forget whatever we do not know well enough to assess it. It perhaps is neither good nor bad, but only necessary, as so many good people think.

HE. I don't follow all that you're preaching to me. Apparently it's philosophy and I tell you I will have no truck with it. All I know is that I'd be quite well pleased to be somebody else, on the chance of being a genius, a great man. I have to admit it. Something tells me I'd like it. I have never heard any genius praised without its making me secretly furious. I am full of envy. When I hear something discreditable about their private lives, I listen with pleasure: it brings me closer to them; makes me bear my mediocrity more easily. I say to myself: to be sure, you would never have been

27. *Duclos:* Charles Duclos (1704–1772), noted for his elegant language and vulgar behavior.

28. *Trublet:* Nicolas-Joseph-Charles Trublet (1697–1770), satirized by both Voltaire and Diderot for the subtlety beneath his apparent friendliness. Elsewhere Diderot described Trublet as "an animal with much wit."

29. *Olivet:* Pierre Jean Thoulier Olivet (1682–1768), whom Diderot and his friends attacked for his hypocrisy.

30. *Greuze's:* Jean Baptiste Greuze (1725–1805), portrait painter who painted according to Diderot's esthetic theories, known for his excessive vanity.

31. *Merope:* tragedy (1743) by Voltaire.

able to write *Mohammed*,[32] but then neither would you have praised Maupeou.[33] So I have been and I still am vexed at being mediocre. Yes, it's true, I am both mediocre and vexed. I have never heard the overture to *Les Indes Galantes*,[34] nor the singing of "*Profonds abîmes du Ténare, Nuit, éternelle nuit*,"[35] without thinking painfully: these are things I shall never be author of. I was obviously jealous of my uncle, and if at his death were found some grand pieces for harpsichord, I would not hesitate to remain myself and be him too.

MYSELF. If that's all that's troubling you, it isn't worth it.

HE. It's nothing, just a passing shadow.

[Then he started to sing the overture of *Les Indes Galantes* and the air "*Profonds abîmes*," adding:]

The whatever-it-is inside me speaks and says to me: "Rameau; you'd give a great deal to have composed those two pieces; if you had done two, you would surely have done two more; and after a certain number you would be played and sung everywhere. You would walk about with head erect, your mind would bear witness to your own merit. Other people would point you out and say— 'That's the man who wrote those lovely gavottes.' "[36] [And he sang the gavottes. Then with the appearance of a man deeply moved by a rush of happiness, he added with a moist eye, while rubbing his hands together:] "You would have a comfortable house" [measuring its breadth with his arms], "a good bed" [he made as if to recline carelessly on it], "good wine" [tasting it with a smack of tongue against palate], "a good carriage and pair" [raising his foot to climb in], "pretty women" [whom he seized by the breast and gazed at voluptuously]. "A hundred loungers would come and flatter you daily." [He thought he saw them around him—Palissot,[37] Poinsinet,[38] the Frérons father and son,[39] La Porte.[40] He heard them, preened himself, agreed with what they said, smiled at them, ignored them, despised them, sent them off, recalled them—then continued:] "Thus you would be told at breakfast that you are a

32. *Mohammed*: play by Voltaire (1742), a strong attack on religious fanaticism.

33. *Maupeou*: René Nicolas de Maupeou (1714–1792), chancellor of France from 1768–1774, dissolved the *parlements* in 1771. The popularity of Voltaire's satirical *History of the Parlement of Paris*, written just previous to this event, helped prepare public opinion for Maupeou's *coup d'état*, which Voltaire favored. Obviously the nephew did not.

34. *Les Indes Galantes*: ballet by Rameau, 1735.

35. "*Profonds . . . nuit*": "Deep abysses of Tenares, Night, eternal night." Song from Rameau's opera, *Castor and Pollux* (1737).

36. *gavottes*: The gavotte was originally a peasant dance, later introduced into the court of Louis XIV.

37. *Palissot*: Charles Palissot de Montenoi (1730–1814), bad writer and plagiarist, ridiculed by Diderot.

38. *Poinsinet*: Antoine-Henri Poinsinet (1734–1769), another fraudulent writer.

39. *Frérons father and son*: Elie-Catherine Fréron (1719–1776) and his son Stanislaus-Louis-Marie (born 1754), literary enemies of Diderot. The elder Fréron was also strongly disliked by Voltaire.

40. *La Porte*: Abbé Joseph Delaporte (1718–1779), who attempted to mediate in the Diderot-Fréron quarrel.

great man, you would read in *Three Centuries of French Literature*[41] that you are a great man, by nightfall you would be convinced that you are a great man, and that great man, Rameau the Nephew, would fall asleep to the soft hum of praise buzzing in his ears. Even while asleep, he would look sated, his chest would rise and fall with bliss, he would snore like a great man."

[In saying this, he collapsed softly on the bench, closed his eyes and imitated the blissful sleep he was imagining. Having enjoyed this felicity of restfulness for a few moments, he awoke, stretched, yawned, rubbed his eyes and looked about him for the dull flatterers who might linger.]

MYSELF. You think, then, that a happy mortal snores in his sleep?

HE. Think so! When I, poor wretch, am back in my garret for the night and I have stuck myself within covers, I am shriveled up, my chest is tight and my breath uneasy—it is a sort of feeble plaint that can hardly be heard; whereas a financier makes the whole house resound and astonishes the entire street. But what grieves me today is not that I sleep meanly and snore wretchedly.

MYSELF. That's sad enough.

HE. What's happened to me is far worse.

MYSELF. What is it?

HE. You've always taken an interest in me because I'm a good fellow whom you despise at bottom but who amuses you——

MYSELF. I don't deny it.

HE. —so I'm going to tell you.

[Before he begins he gives a mighty sigh and puts both his hands to his head; then he recovers his composure and says:] "You know that I am an ignoramus, a fool, a lunatic, a lazy, impudent, greedy good-for-nothing—what we Burgundians call a ne'er-do-well—a blackguard, in short."

MYSELF. What a eulogy!

HE. Gospel truth from beginning to end, not a word out of place. Let's not argue about it, please; no one knows me better than I and I haven't said all I know.

MYSELF. I don't mean to annoy you: I accept everything you say.

HE. Well, I used to live with people who had taken a liking to me precisely because I had all these qualities to a rare degree.

MYSELF. Strange! Until now I had thought that one hid them from oneself, or that one forgave oneself while condemning them in others.

HE. Hide them from oneself! Who can? You may be sure that when Palissot is alone and reflects upon himself he tells himself different. In tête-à-tête with his colleague he and the other confess

41. *Three Centuries of French Litera-* Sabatier de Castres, wherein Diderot was
ture: pretentious work (1772) edited by   treated in negative terms.

that they're a pair of prize scoundrels. Despise defects in others! My people were fairer than to do that and my character was a pleasure to them. I was treated like a king. They missed every moment I was away from them. I was their dear Rameau, pretty Rameau, *their* Rameau—the jester, the buffoon, the lazy dog, the saucy rogue, the great greedy boob. Not one of these epithets went without a smile, a chuck under the chin, a pat on the back, a cuff, a kick. At table it was a choice morsel tossed to me; elsewhere a liberty I could take with no consequence—for I am truly a person of no consequence. Anyone can do what he pleases with me, about me, in front of me. I never get on my high horse. Ah, the little gratuities that came my way! What a consummate ass I am to have lost all that! I have lost it all because once, once in my life, I showed common sense. I promise you, never again!

MYSELF. What was it all about?

HE. A piece of incredible folly, unimaginable, unforgivable.

MYSELF. But what kind of folly was it?

HE. Rameau, Rameau, you weren't taken on for your folly, the folly of possessing a little good taste, a little wit, a little sense. Rameau, my friend, this will teach you to stay the way God made you, the way your patrons wanted you. Failing which, they seized you by the shoulder and showed you the door. They said: "Faker, beat it and don't come back. It wants to be sensible, does it? Beat it! Good sense, we have more of that than we know what to do with." You went, biting your fingernails: it's your tongue you should have bitten off first. You thought of that too late and here you are, in the gutter, penniless, and nowhere to go. You were being fed like a fatted calf, and now you're back at the slop shop; well-housed, and now you'll be lucky to have your garret back. You had a bed; now the loose straw awaits you between the coachman of M. de Soubise[42] and Robbé[43] the grubstreet hack. Instead of sweet silent sleep, as you had it, one ear will be filled with the neighing and stamping of horses, the other with the far worse noise of a thousand harsh verses. Wretch, idiot, lunatic at the mercy of a million damnable fiends!

MYSELF. But is there no way to regain your passport? Did you commit so unpardonable a crime? Were I in your place, I'd go back to my patrons: you must be more indispensable than you think.

HE. Oh, I'm convinced that without me around to make them laugh, they're bored stiff.

MYSELF. That's why I'd go back. I wouldn't give them time to

42. *Soubise:* owner of the largest stables in Paris, which were favored by vagabonds for shelter.

43. *Robbé:* Pierre-Honoré Robbé de Beauveset (1712–1792), author of a poem about smallpox.

get used to my absence, or to take up some decent amusement. Who knows what might come of it!

HE. That's not what I'm afraid of: it couldn't happen.

MYSELF. Well then, some other genius may take your place.

HE. With difficulty.

MYSELF. Granted. Just the same, I'd go back as you are—my face fallen, my eyes wandering, unbuttoned and unkempt—in the really tragic attire in which you are. I'd throw myself at the feet of the goddess, glue my face to the ground, and without once getting up, I'd say in a weak sobbing voice: "Forgive, my lady, forgive! I am a wretch, a monster, the victim of a momentary lapse, for you know very well I am not subject to suffering from common sense. I promise it will never happen again."

[What is amusing is that while I was saying this, he was acting it out in pantomime. He was prostrate at my feet, his face on the ground, and seemed to be clutching in both his hands the tip of a slipper. He was crying and sobbing out words: "I swear it, my dear Queen, I promise, never will I do it again, never, never, never." Then, suddenly jumping up, he said in a perfectly sober, serious way:]

HE. You're right, of course. I can see it's the better way. She is kind. M. Vieillard[44] says she is very kind, and I know somewhat that she is. But still, to go and humiliate myself before the little bitch, to cry mercy at the feet of a second-rate actress who is invariably hissed off the stage! I, Rameau, son of M. Rameau, apothecary of Dijon, a man of substance who has never crooked the knee to anyone, I, Rameau, the nephew of him who is called the great Rameau, him who can be seen pacing the Palais-Royal upright and with arms akimbo ever since M. Carmontelle[45] depicted him bent and with his hands behind his back! I who have composed keyboard works that no one plays but which may be the only works of today posterity will like, I (in short) would go and—no, my dear sir, impossible! [And putting his right hand on his heart he added:] I feel something here which swells in pride and says to me: "Rameau, you will do no such thing. A certain dignity attaches to the nature of man that nothing must destroy. It stirs in protest at the most unexpected times, yes, unexpected, for there are days when I could be as vile as required without its costing me anything. On those days, for a penny I'd kiss the arse of the little Hus."

MYSELF. But see here, she's pretty, kind, plump, and white-skinned, and that's an act of humility that even a prouder man than you could condescend to.

---

44. *She . . . Vieillard:* Rameau refers to an actress, Adelaide Hus, mistress of a banker named Bertin. Vieillard also became her lover, replacing Bertin; and the story became a comic scandal in Paris.

45. *Carmontelle:* His sketch of Rameau was then famous.

HE. Let's be clear about this—there's kissing and kissing, literal and metaphorical. Consult that old Bergier[46] who kisses the arse of the Duchess de La Marck,[47] both literally and metaphorically—a case in which the two species disgust me equally.

MYSELF. If my suggestion does not seem expedient to you, then at least be courageous enough to be poor.

HE. It's very hard to be poor while there are so many wealthy fools to sponge on. And then contempt for oneself—that's unbearable! . . .*

MYSELF. Why resort to these vile little tricks?

HE. Why vile, if I may ask? They are part of my profession. There's nothing degrading in acting like everybody else. I did not invent these tricks. And I should be a clumsy oaf not to make use of them. I know well enough that if you apply to my case certain general principles of morals which they all talk about and never put into practice, it will turn out that white is black and black is white. But, Master Philosopher, it is with universal morality just as with universal grammar: there are exceptions in each language that you learned people call—what is it you call them?

MYSELF. Idioms?

HE. That's what I mean. Well, each profession makes exceptions to universal morality and those I'd like to call *trade idioms*.

MYSELF. I follow you. Fontenelle[48] speaks and writes well even though his style is full of French idioms.

HE. Likewise the sovereign, the minister, the financier, the judge, the soldier, the writer, the lawyer, the public prosecutor, the merchant, the banker, the workman, the singing teacher, the dancing master, are very respectable people even though their conduct deviates in several ways from absolute good behavior and is full of moral idioms. The older the profession the more the idioms; the worse the times become, the more the idioms multiply. A man is worth what his trade is worth; in the end they're equal; hence people make the trade go for as much as they can.

MYSELF. What appears clearest in all this tangle is that there are no honest trades and no honest men in them.

HE. Have it your own way. But as a compensation there are but few gougers outside their own shops. The world would get on pretty well if it weren't for a number of people who are called industrious, reliable, conscientious followers of duty, strict. Or what amounts to

---

46. *Bergier:* Nicolas-Sylvestre Bergier (1718–1790), theologian disliked by Diderot.
47. *Duchess de La Marck:* Marie de Noailles (born 1719), strongly devotional and opposed to Diderot and the *philosophes.*
* In the passage deleted by the editor, Rameau satirizes the young daughter of

a middle-class family. He also pantomimes a violinist and a keyboard performer—the "vile little tricks" referred to in the following passage.
48. *Fontenelle:* Bernard le Bouvier de Fontenelle (1657–1757), author of *The Plurality of the Worlds* (1686)—an elegant piece of scientific popularization.

the same thing: ever in their shops practicing their trades from morn till night and doing nothing else. Result is: they're the only ones to get rich and full of reputation.

MYSELF. By sheer strength of idiom!

HE. Exactly. I see you understand. Now an idiom that is common to all trades—as there are some common to all nations and no less common than folly—is to try to get as many customers as possible. The common folly is to think that the largest tradesman is the best. Those are two exceptions to universal ethics one can do nothing about. Call it credit or "good will," it is nothing in itself but it's worth a great deal in public opinion. Don't they say: "A good name is worth a money belt?" Yet plenty of people have a good name who have no money belt, and I notice that nowadays the money insures the name. The great thing is to have both and that is precisely what I am after when I employ what you call my vile tricks. I give lessons and give them the right way—that's the absolute rule. I make people believe that I have more-pupils than there are hours in the day—that's my idiom.

MYSELF. And you really give good lessons?

HE. Yes, or not bad, passable. The ground bass theory of the dear uncle has simplified everything. Formerly I swindled my pupil, yes, undoubtedly swindled. Nowadays I earn my feet at least as much as my colleagues.

MYSELF. Did you formerly swindle without qualms?

HE. Without qualms. They say, when one thief robs another the Devil laughs. My pupils' parents were fat with ill-gotten gains. They were courtiers, tax collectors, wholesalers, bankers, stockbrokers. I merely helped them—I and some others in their employ —to make restitution. In Nature all species live off one another; in society all classes do the same. We square things up with one another without benefit of the law. La Deschamps[49] some time since, and now la Guimard,[50] avenges the King upon his tax collector; after which the dressmaker, the jeweler, the upholsterer, the lace-maker, the confidence man, the lady's maid, the cook, and the saddler avenge the tax collector upon la Deschamps. Amid all this no one but the idiot or the loafer is taken advantage of without levying tribute on anybody else—and it serves him right. You can infer from this that the exceptions to universal ethics, or moral idioms, about which people make so much fuss under the name of mutual depredations, don't amount to anything, really. When all is said and done the only thing that matters is to see straight.

MYSELF. I admire you for that.

---

49. *La Deschamps:* Anne Marie Pagès (1730–1775?), famous courtesan who sold her town house in Paris to pay off huge debts, and entered the money-lending business.

50. *la Guimard:* another prostitute or courtesan whose career was similar.

HE. And think of poverty! The voice of conscience and honor is pretty feeble when the guts cry out. Isn't it enough that if I ever get rich I shall be bound to make restitution? I am prepared to do this in every conceivable way—through gorging, through gambling, through guzzling, and through wenching.

MYSELF. But I'm afraid you will never get rich.

HE. I suspect it too.

MYSELF. Suppose it did work out, what then?

HE. I would act like all beggars on horseback. I'd be the most insolent ruffian ever seen. I'd remember every last thing they made me go through and pay them back with slings and arrows. I love bossing people and I will boss them. I love being praised and they will praise me. I'll have the whole troop of Villemorien's[51] boot-lickers on salary, and I'll say to them what's been said to me: "Come on, dogs, entertain me." And they will. "I want decent people pulled to pieces." And they will be—if any can be found. Then too, we'll have women, and when drunk we'll thee-and-thou one another. We will drink and make up tales and develop all sorts of whims and vices. It will be delightful. We'll prove that Voltaire has no genius; that Buffon[52] is always up on stilts like the turgid declaimer he is; that Montesquieu[53] was only a wit. We'll tell D'Alembert[54] to stick to his ciphering and we'll kick behind and before all the little stoics like you who despise us from sour grapes, whose modesty is the prop of pride, and whose good conduct springs from lack of means. Ah, what music you'll hear from us!

MYSELF. Knowing what worthy use you would make of wealth, I see how deplorable it is that you are poor. You would certainly be doing honor to human nature, good to your compatriots and credit to yourself.

HE. I almost think you're making fun of me, Master Philosopher. But you don't even suspect with whom you're tangling; you don't seem to know that at this very moment I represent the most important part of Town and Court. The well-to-do of every description have either said or not said to themselves the words I've just confided to you; the fact remains that the life I would lead in their position is precisely theirs. That's where you fellows are behind the times. You think everybody aims at the same happiness. What an idea! Your conception presupposes a sentimental turn of mind which is not ours, an unusual spirit, a special taste. You call your quirks virtue, or philosophy. But virtue and philosophy are not made

---

51. *Villemorien's:* Philippe-Charles Legendre de Villemorien, wealthy landowner.

52. *Buffon:* Georges Louis Leclerc Buffon (1707–1788), naturalist and author of a famous *Natural History*.

53. *Montesquieu:* Charles de Secondat, Baron de Montesquieu (1689–1755), political philosopher; author of the satirical *Persian Letters* (1721) and *The Spirit of the Laws* (1748), a study of comparative government.

54. *D'Alembert:* Jean le Rond D'Alembert (1717–1783); philosopher, mathematician, and co-editor of the *Encyclopedia* with Diderot.

for everybody. The few who can, have it; the few who can, keep it. Just imagine the universe philosophical and wise, and tell me if it would not be devilishly dull. Listen! I say hurrah for wisdom and philosophy—the wisdom of Solomon: to drink good wines, gorge on choice food, tumble pretty women, sleep in downy beds—outside of that, all is vanity.

MYSELF. What! And fighting for your country?

HE. Vanity! There are no countries left. All I see from pole to pole is tyrants and slaves.

MYSELF. What of helping your friends?

HE. Vanity! No one has any friends. And even if one had, should one risk making them ungrateful? Look close and you'll see that's all you get for being helpful. Gratitude is a burden and burdens are to be shuffled off.

MYSELF. To hold a position in society and discharge its duties?

HE. Vanity! What difference whether you hold a position or not, provided you have means, since you only seek a position in order to get wealth. Discharge one's duties—what does that bring you?— jealousy, worries, persecution. Is that the way to get on? Nonsense! Pay court, pay court, know the right people, flatter their tastes and fall in with their whims, serve their vices and second their misdeeds—there's the secret.

MYSELF. Watch over the education of one's children?

HE. Vanity! That's a tutor's business.

MYSELF. But if a tutor, imbued with your principles, neglects his duty, who will pay the penalty?

HE. Not I anyhow. Possibly, some day, my daughter's husband or my son's wife.

MYSELF. But suppose that either or both plunge into vice and debauchery?

HE. Then that is part of their social position.

MYSELF. If they disgrace themselves?

HE. It's impossible to disgrace yourself, no matter what you do, if you are rich.

MYSELF. Ruin themselves, then?

HE. Too bad for them.

MYSELF. It seems to me that if you overlook the conduct of your wife, your children and your servants, you might easily overlook your own affairs.

HE. Not so, if you will permit me: it is sometimes difficult to procure money, hence one uses a prudent foresight.

MYSELF. You will pay little attention to your wife?

HE. None, an it please you. The best behavior toward one's dearer half, I think, is to do what suits her. Do you suppose company would be tolerable if everyone minded his own business?

MYSELF. Why not? I'm never so happy in the evening as when I'm pleased with my forenoon.

HE. Me too.

MYSELF. What makes society people so choosey about their entertainment is that they are utterly idle.

HE. Don't you believe it: they are always on the go.

MYSELF. They never tire themselves and so can never feel refreshed.

HE. Don't you believe it: they are constantly weary.

MYSELF. Pleasure is always their business, never a desire.

HE. All the better: desires are ever nagging.

MYSELF. They wear everything out. Their soul gets dull, boredom masters them. Whoever should take their life at the height of their load of plenty would be doing them a good turn. For they know of pleasure only that portion which soonest loses its zest. I am far from despising sensual pleasures. I have a palate too and it is tickled by a delicate wine or dish; I have eyes and a heart and I like to look at a pretty woman, like to feel the curve of her breast under my hand, press her lips to mine, drink bliss from her eyes and die of ecstasy in her arms. Sometimes a gay party with my friends, even if it becomes a little rowdy, is not displeasing to me. But I must confess that I find it infinitely sweeter to succor the unfortunate, to disentangle a bad business, to give helpful advice, to read some pleasant book, to take a walk with a man or woman who is dear to me, to spend a few instructive hours with my children, to write a page of good prose, to carry out my duties, or to tell her whom I love something tender and true which brings her arms about my neck.

I know of certain deeds which I would give all I possess to have done. Voltaire's *Mohammed* is a sublime work, but I would rather have rehabilitated the Calas family.[55] A man I know left home for Cartagena;[56] he was a younger son in a country where primogeniture is the law. While abroad he learns that his elder brother, a spoiled child, has ruined his father and mother, driven them out of the castle, and left them to languish in some provincial town. What does the younger son do, who after the harsh treatment meted out by his parents had gone to seek his fortune far away? He sends them help. He winds up his affairs, comes back rich, restores his parents to their home, marries off his sisters. Ah, my dear Rameau, that man looked upon this period as the happiest in his life. He had

---

55. *Calas family:* In 1762, Jean Calas —a Protestant living in Toulouse—was accused of hanging his son, who wished to leave the Protestant faith. The senior Calas was tortured on the wheel; the trial was a judiciary sham, and Voltaire tried to get the trial reviewed. Jean Calas was officially exonerated on March 9, 1765.

56. *Cartagena:* Spanish port on the Mediterranean.

tears in his eyes as he spoke of it and as I tell you this, I feel my heart dilate with gladness and my tongue falter with emotion.

HE. Queer people, you are!

MYSELF. And you are people to be pitied, unless you can see that one can rise above one's fate and make oneself independent of misfortune by actions such as I have described.

HE. That's a kind of happiness I would find it hard to become familiar with, it is so rarely found. Then according to you, people should be decent?

MYSELF. To be happy?—Certainly.

HE. Yet I see a quantity of decent people unhappy and a quantity of people happy without being decent.

MYSELF. So it seems to you.

HE. Wasn't it because I acted sensibly and frankly for one instant that tonight I don't know where to find a meal?

MYSELF. Not at all: it's because you have not always been sensible and frank; because you did not learn soon enough that the first step is to secure the means of life apart from servitude.

HE. Apart or not, my way is surely the easiest.

MYSELF. And the least assured and the least decent.

HE. But the most consistent with my nature, which is idle, stupid, and crooked.

MYSELF. Granted.

HE. Since I can secure my well-being with the aid of vices natural to me, that I have acquired without labor and that I retain without effort, vices congenial to the habits of my countrymen, agreeable to the tastes of my protectors, and closer to their little needs than any virtues could be—for virtues would annoy them all day long like so many accusations—in view of all this, it would be strange indeed for me to bedevil myself like a damned soul and turn myself into what I am not; to acquire a character alien to mine, with laudable traits, no doubt (I won't argue), but difficult to maintain and make use of. It would do me no good, perhaps worse than no good, by implying a satire of the rich people in whose company paupers like me must find their livelihood.

Virtue is praised, but hated. People run away from it, for it is ice-cold and in this world you must keep your feet warm. Besides, I would grow bad-humored, infallibly. For note how often devout people are harsh, touchy, unsociable. The reason is that they have compelled themselves to do an unnatural thing. They're in pain, and people in pain make others suffer. That's not the life for me, nor for my patrons. I must be gay, easy, jolly, droll, entertaining. Virtue earns respect and respect is inconvenient; virtue is bound to be admired, and admiration is no fun. I deal with people who are bored and I have to make them laugh. Now what is laughable is absurdity and folly. I must consequently be absurd and a fool. Even had nature not made me such, the quickest way would be to put on the appearance. Fortunately, I don't need to be a hypocrite; there are enough of them around, not counting those who deceive themselves. The Chevalier Morlière[57] who snaps his hatbrim on his ear, sniffs the air and looks at every passer-by over his shoulder; who drags the longest sword next to his thigh and has an insult ready for anyone unarmed; in short, who defies every man on principle, what is he really up to? He does what he can to persuade himself that he is a man of spirit, though he's a coward. Tweak his nose and he will take it mildly. If you want to make him pipe down, just raise your voice, lift your cane, or let your foot contact his buttocks. Full of surprise at finding himself a coward, he will ask you who told you of it, how you knew. Himself did not suspect it the moment before. His long and habitual aping of bravery had fooled him; so much mimicry had ended by seeming real.

And what of that woman who mortifies her flesh, who visits prisons, who attends all meetings organized for charity, who walks with lowered lids and would not dare look a man in the eye; who is continually on guard against the temptations of the senses—does any of this keep her heart from burning, her breast from sighing, her flaming desires from obsessing her? Her imagination at night rehearses the scenes of the *Portier des Chartrains* and the postures of Aretino.[58] What then happens to her? What does her maid think when she has to get up in her shift and fly to the aid of her mistress who is suffocating? Justine, you can go back to bed, it isn't you your mistress is calling for in her fever.

And if friend Rameau himself should ever show indifference to wealth, women, good cheer, and idleness, if he should begin to stoicize, what would he be? A hypocrite. Rameau must stay what he is—a scoundrel in luck among well-heeled scoundrels; not a holier-than-thou character nor even a virtuous man eating his dry crust alone or near some other beggar. To cut it short, I want none of your kind of happiness, none of the satisfactions of a few visionaries like yourself.

MYSELF. I can see, my dear fellow, that you don't know what I refer to and that you are apparently not made to find out.

HE. Thank God for that! It would only make me starve to death, die of boredom, and croak with remorse.

---

57. *Morlière:* Jacques Rochette de la Morlière (1719–1785), elegant gentleman whose scandalous life forced him to resign from the *Musketeers,* and who at one point was chief *claqueur* (leader of applause) at the theater, served several jail sentences.

58. *Portier . . . Aretino:* referring to one of Diderot's own books, published first at Rome, then at Frankfurt (1748) —anonymously, due to its pornographic content; and to Pietro Aretino (1492–1556?), sixteen of whose sonnets, illustrated by Julio Romano, became pornographic classics.

MYSELF. That being so, the one piece of advice I can give you is to hurry back into the place whence you so carelessly got kicked out.

HE. You want me to do that which you do not object to when it's literal, but which is a little repugnant to you when metaphorical?

MYSELF. That's my advice.

HE. Well—apart from the metaphor, which repels me now and may not repel me later——

MYSELF. How odd you are!

HE. Not in the least. I'm perfectly ready to be abject, but not under duress. I'm willing to lower my dignity—you're laughing!

MYSELF. Certainly. Your dignity makes me laugh.

HE. To each man his own kind. I'm willing to forget mine, but at my pleasure, not on somebody else's order. Shall it be said that at the word "Crawl!" I am to crawl? That's the worm's natural gait and it is mine too, when we are left alone, but we turn and rear, both of us, when stepped on. I was stepped on and mean to rear off. And then you have no idea what a shambles that house is. Imagine a melancholy crotchety individual, a prey to vapors, wrapped up in two or three layers of dressing gown, who likes himself but dislikes everything else; who can hardly be made to smile by one's utmost contortions of body and mind, who looks with a lackluster eye on the lively twistings of my face and the even livelier ones of my intellect. For between ourselves, compared to me the ugly Benedictine so famous at court for his grimacing is, all boasting aside, nothing but a wooden Indian. I badger myself in vain to reach the sublimest lunacy—it's no use. Will he laugh or won't he? That's what I have to keep asking myself in the midst of my exertions. You can guess what harm so much uncertainty does to talent. My hypochondriac with his head swallowed up in a nightcap down to his eyes looks like an immovable idol with a string tied to its chin and running down beneath his chair. You wait for the string to be pulled but it is never pulled; or if the jaw drops it is only to let out some chilling word, from which you learn that you have not been understood and that your apish tricks have been wasted. That word is the answer to a question you put four days ago. The word spoken, the mastoid muscle contracts and the jaw clamps. . . .*

MYSELF. What have you read?

HE. I keep rereading Theophrastus,[59] La Bruyère and Molière.

MYSELF. Excellent books.

HE. They're even better than people think, but who knows how to read them?

---

* At this point the Nephew describes how to flatter a stupid, obese, and wealthy girl.

59. *Theophrastus:* Greek author (ca. 372–287 B.C.), whose *Characters* were imitated by La Bruyère.

MYSELF. Everybody according to his capacity.

HE. I should say almost no one. Can you tell me what they look for in them?

MYSELF. Instruction mixed with entertainment.

HE. But what kind of instruction: that's the point!

MYSELF. The knowledge of one's duty, the love of virtue and the hatred of vice.

HE. Now what I find there is a compendium of what to do and what not to say. When I read *The Miser*, I say to myself: "Be as miserly as you like, but don't talk like the miser." When I read *Tartuffe*,[60] I say: "Be a hypocrite if you choose, but don't talk like one. Keep any useful vices, but don't acquire the tone and air which would make you ridiculous. Now to avoid these one must know what they are, and the authors mentioned have give us excellent portraits. I am myself and I remain such, but I act and speak just as I ought to. Far from despising the moralists, I find profit in them, particularly those who depict morals in action. Vice offends men only from time to time; but the symptoms of vice offend day and night. It is surely better to be arrogant than to look it. The arrogant character insults you only now and then; the arrogant look insults you continually. And by the way, don't suppose that I am the only reader of my kind. My sole merit is to have accomplished systematically, through good judgment and right reason, what most other people do by instinct. Hence their reading does not make them better than I, and they remain ridiculous despite their efforts; whereas I am such only when I choose, and so surpass them by far. The same skill which saves me from ridicule on certain occasions, enables me at other times to incur it with high art. I recall whatever others have said, whatever I have read, and I add to all this my original contribution, which is surprisingly abundant.

MYSELF. It was wise of you to impart these mysteries to me, else I would have thought you self-contradictory.

HE. I'm nothing of the kind, for if it is necessary to avoid ridicule once, it is fortunately just as necessary to incur it a hundred times. There is no fitter role in high society than that of fool. For a long time the King had an appointed fool. At no time was there an appointed sage. I am Bertin's[61] fool and that of many others— yours, possibly, this minute; or maybe you are mine. A real sage would want no fool; hence he who has a fool is no sage; and if no sage, must be a fool. And were he the King himself; he may be his own fool's fool. In any event, remember that in a subject as variable as manners and morals nothing is absolutely, essentially, universally true or false—unless it be that one must be whatever self-interest

---

60. *Miser . . . Tartuffe:* plays by Molière, 1668 and 1664–1669.

61. *Bertin's:* Louis-Auguste Bertin de Blagny, a pedant disliked by Diderot.

requires, good or bad, wise or foolish, decent or ridiculous, honest or vicious. If virtue by chance led to fortune, I should have been as virtuous—or virtuous-seeming—as the next man. I was bidden to be ridiculous and I made myself so. As to vice, nature alone took care of that; though when I say vicious I am merely using your language. For if we really thrashed things out, we might find ourselves each calling virtue what the other calls vice and t'other way round. . . .*

MYSELF. Enough of your naughtiness, will you! Let's talk of something else. I've had a question on the tip of my tongue since we started chatting.

HE. Why have you held it back so long?

MYSELF. I was afraid to be inquisitive.

HE. After what I've told you, I can't imagine what secret I could withhold from you.

MYSELF. You are in no doubt about the opinion I have of you?

HE. No doubt at all. You think me most abject and contemptible. And so I am in my own eyes—sometimes. Not often. I congratulate myself on my vices more often than blame myself. But your contempt does not vary.

MYSELF. Just so. But then why show yourself to me in all your turpitude?

HE. First, because you know a good deal of it to start with, and I stand to gain more than I lose by confessing the rest.

MYSELF. How is that, tell me?

HE. If there's one realm in which it is essential to be sublime, it is in wickedness. You spit on ordinary scum, but you can't deny a kind of respect to a great criminal: his courage amazes, his ferocity overawes. People especially admire integrity of character.

MYSELF. But this admirable integrity, you haven't reached it yet. I find you now and again weak in principle. You don't seem to know if your wickedness comes from nature or from study, nor whether you have pursued your studies far enough. . . .†

HE. . . . Gold, gold is everything; and everything, without gold, is nothing. Therefore, instead of having my son's head stuffed with grand maxims which he would have to forget under pain of being a pauper, this is what I do whenever I have a gold piece—not often, to be sure: I plant myself in front of him, draw the piece from my pocket, show it to him with admiring looks, raise my eyes to heaven, kiss the gold in front of him, and to show him still more forcibly the importance of the sacred coin, I stammer out the names and point out with the finger all the things one can buy with it—a beau-

---

* Here the Nephew describes a dinner party and other occasions where he excels in the role of a parasite.
† Here a technical discussion about contemporary music is deleted, as well as a scene where the Nephew parodies certain popular singers of the day. Through *Rameau's Nephew,* Diderot is able to criticize musical tendencies which he deplored.

tiful gown, a beautiful hat, a good cake; next I put the coin in my pocket, parade before him proudly, pull up my coat tails and strike my waistcoat where the money lies. Thus do I make him understand that it is from that coin I draw the self-assurance he beholds.

MYSELF. Nothing could be better. But what if some day, being deeply persuaded of the value of money, he should . . .

HE. I follow you! One must shut one's eyes to that. There is no principle of conduct wholly without drawbacks. At the worst, one goes through a bad half hour, then all is over.

MYSELF. Yet in spite of your wise and courageous views, I continue to think it would be a good thing to make him a musician. I know of no better way to approach the rich, to serve their vices, and to turn one's own to advantage.

HE. True. But I have projects for even quicker and surer success. Ah, if I only had a daughter! But no man can do as he likes, he must take what he gets and do the best he can with it. For which purpose one must not, like most fathers, stupidly give children who are destined to live in Paris the education of ancient Sparta. One might as well plot their ruin. If the native training is bad, the fault lies with the manners and customs of my country, and not with me. No matter who is responsible, I want my child happy, or what amounts to the same thing, honored, rich, powerful. I know the easiest ways to accomplish this, and I mean to teach them to my son early in life. If you wise men blame me, the majority (and success itself) will absolve me. He will have gold—it's I who tell you so, I guarantee it—and if he has a great deal, he will lack nothing, not even your admiration and respect.

MYSELF. You might be wrong about those.

HE. If so, he can do without, like many other people.

[There was in all he said much that one thinks to oneself, and acts on, but that one never says. This was in fact the chief difference between my man and the rest of us. He admitted his vices, which are also ours: he was no hypocrite. Neither more nor less destestable than other men, he was franker than they, more logical, and thus often profound in his depravity. I was appalled to think of what his child would become under such a tutor. It was clear that if he was brought up on a system so exactly framed on our actual behavior, he would go far—unless he was prematurely cut off on the way.]

HE. Never you fear! The important thing that a good father must do is not so much to give his child vices that will bring him wealth and foolish traits that will make him a favorite of the great—everybody does as much: not systematically like me, but by casual precept and example. No, what is more difficult is to teach him the golden art by which he can avert disgrace, shame, and the penalties of the law. These last are dissonances in the harmony of society, which one must know how to use, prepare, and resolve. Nothing is duller than a progression of common chords. One wants some contrast, which breaks up the clear white light and makes it iridescent.

MYSELF. Very good. Your comparison brings me back from morals to music. I digressed in spite of myself, for to speak frankly, I prefer you as musician rather than as moralist.

HE. And yet I am only second-rate in music, whereas I am a superior moralist.

MYSELF. I doubt this; but even if it were so, I am an honest man and your principles do not suit me.

HE. So much the worse for you. Oh, if I only had your talent!

MYSELF. Leave my talent alone; let's go back to yours.

HE. If I could express myself as you do! But my vocabulary is a damned mongrel—half literary and well-bred, half guttersnipe.

MYSELF. Don't think I speak well. I can only tell the truth and, as you know, that doesn't always go down.

HE. It's not for telling the truth that I envy you your gifts. Just the opposite—it's to tell lies. If I only knew how to throw together a book, how to turn a dedication, intoxicate some fool with praises and make my way among women!

MYSELF. As for all that, you know much more about it than I do; I am not even fit to be your pupil.

HE. Oh, what abilities you are letting go to waste, not even suspecting what they're worth!

MYSELF. I reap whatever I sow, no more, no less.

HE. If that were true, you wouldn't be wearing these coarse clothes —linen coat, woollen stockings, thick-soled shoes and superannuated wig.

MYSELF. Granted. One must be terribly clumsy if one isn't rich after sticking at nothing to acquire wealth. But there are people like me, you see, who don't consider wealth the most important thing in the world—queer people.

HE. Very queer. No one is born that way. It's an acquired idea; it's unnatural.

MYSELF. For man?

HE. For man. Everything that lives, man included, seeks its well-being at the expense of whoever withholds it. I'm sure that if I let my little savage grow up without saying a word to him, he would of his own accord want to be richly dressed, magnificently fed, liked by men and loved by women, and concentrate on himself all the goods of life.

MYSELF. If your little savage were left to himself and to his native blindness, he would in time join the infant's reasoning to the grown man's passions—he would strangle his father and sleep with his mother.

HE. Which only proves the need of a good education. There's no argument. But what is a good education if it is not one that leads to all the enjoyments without trouble or danger?

MYSELF. I am almost with you there, but let's not go into it.

HE. Why not?

MYSELF. Because I think we are only superficially in agreement, and if we look into the question of troubles and dangers, we shall no longer be at one.

HE. And what's the harm of that?

MYSELF. Let it go, I say. What I know on the subject I shan't be able to teach you. You will have an easier time teaching me what you know about music, of which I am ignorant. Dear Rameau, let us talk music; and tell me how it is that with your remarkable power for understanding, remembering and rendering the most beautiful works of the great masters, with your contagious enthusiasm for them and for conveying them, you have never done anything that amounts to anything. . . .*

HE. From tumble to tumble I had fallen you know where. I lived there like a rat in a cheese. I left, and now we'll have to squeeze the guts again, go back to the gesture of the finger and the gaping mouth. Nothing is stable in this world. Today at the top of the heap, tomorrow at the bottom. Accursed circumstance guides us and does it very badly.

[Then drinking what was left in one of the bottles and addressing his neighbor, he said: "Sir, a pinch of snuff, for kindness' sake. You have a mighty handsome snuffbox. You are not a musician? No? So much the better for you, for they're all poor buggers, a pitiable lot. Fate has decreed that I should be one, while in Montmartre[62] there may be in a windmill, a miller or a miller's helper who has never heard anything but the click of the ratchet but who would have found the most enchanting melodies. To the mill, Rameau! To the mill, that's the place for you!"]

MYSELF. Whatever a man tries, Nature destined him for that.

HE. Then she makes some very odd blunders. I can't for myself see from those heights where everything comes to the same thing— the man who prunes a tree with his shears and the slug that eats off the leaves being just two insects each doing his duty. You go and perch on the epicycle of Mercury,[63] and like Réaumur,[64] who classifies the flies into seamstresses, surveyors, and reapers, you classify mankind into carpenters, builders, roofers, dancers, and singers: that's your affair, I shan't meddle with it. I am in this

---

* Here several pages are deleted, where the Nephew deplores his own lack of genius, his own artistic mediocrity—"to be called Rameau is extremely embarrassing"—and describes his life as an itinerant musician.

62. *Montmartre:* in Diderot's time, still a rural area on the right bank of the Seine, later to be famous as a center of Bohemian life.

63. *perch . . . Mercury:* image used by Montaigne to criticize those who pretend to superior knowledge. The idea of the epicycle, which attempted to explain the discrepancies between observed planetary motion and Ptolemaic astronomical theory, was derided by eighteenth-century *philosophes*.

64. *Réaumur:* R.-A. F. de Réaumur, celebrated physicist and naturalist.

world and here I stay. But if it is natural to be hungry—I always come back to hunger, for it's with me an ever-present sensation—I find that it is no part of good order to be sometimes without food. What a hell of an economy! Some men replete with everything while others, whose stomachs are not less importunate, whose hunger is just as recurrent, have nothing to bite on. The worst of it is the constrained posture in which need holds you. The needy man doesn't walk like the rest, he skips, twists, cringes, crawls. He spends his life choosing and performing positions.

MYSELF. What kind of "positions"?

HE. Go ask Noverre the choreographer.[65] The world numbers more positions than his art can reproduce.

MYSELF. So you too, if I may use your expression—or rather that of Montaigne—are perched on the epicycle of Mercury and considering the different pantomimes of humankind.

HE. No, I tell you, no. I am far too clumsy to rise so high. I yield to the cranes their foggy realms. I crawl on the earth, look about me, and take my positions. Or else I entertain myself watching others take theirs. I am good at pantomime, as you shall see.

[Thereupon he begins to smile, to ape a man admiring, a man imploring, a man complying. His right foot forward, the left behind, his back arched, head erect, his glance riveted as if on another's, openmouthed, his arms are stretched out toward some object. He waits for a command, receives it, flies like an arrow, returns. The order has been carried out; he is giving a report. Attentive, nothing escapes him. He picks up what is dropped, places pillow or stool under feet, holds a salver, brings a chair, opens a door, shuts a window, draws curtains, gazes at master and mistress. He is motionless, arm hanging, legs parallel; he listens and tries to read faces.] Then he says: "There you have my pantomime; it's about the same as the flatterer's, the courtier's, the footman's, and the beggar's."

This man's vagaries, like the tales of Abbé Galiani[66] and the extravaganzas of Rabelais, have often plunged me in deep reverie. Those are three storehouses from which I have drawn some absurd masks that I have then projected on the faces of the gravest figures. I seem to see Pantaloon[67] in a prelate, a satyr in a presiding judge, a porker in a friar, an ostrich in a king's minister, and a goose in his under secretary.

MYSELF. According to you [I went on], there are innumerable beggars in this world, for I hardly know anyone who doesn't use at least a few of your dance steps.

65. *choreographer:* Jean-George Noverre (1727–1810), ballet-master at the *Opéra-Comique* from 1753 to 1756.
66. *Galiani:* Abbé Ferdinand Galiani (1728–1787), statesman, man-of-letters, economist; one of Diderot's best friends;

part of the circle of *philosophes* that included Diderot, Grimm, D'Holbach, Helvétius, etc.
67. *Pantaloon:* stock figure of the aged pedant, selfish and libidinous.

HE. You are right. In the whole country only one man walks—the King. Everybody else takes a position.

MYSELF. The King? Even about him there might be something more to say. Don't you suppose that from time to time he finds near him a little foot, a little nose, a little curl that makes him perform a bit of pantomime? Whoever stands in need of another is needy and takes a position. The King takes a position before his mistress and before God: he dances his pantomime steps. The minister trips it too, as courtier, flatterer, footman and beggar before his king. The crowd of self-seekers dance all your positions in a hundred ways, each viler than the next, in front of the minister. The noble Abbé, in furred cape and cloak, dances attendance once a week at least before the official who appoints to benefices. Really, what you call the beggar's pantomime is what makes the world go round. Every man has his Bertin and his little Hus.

HE. It's very consoling to me.

[While I spoke he mimicked in killing fashion the positions of the figures I enumerated. For the little Abbé, for example, he held his hat under his arm and his breviary in the left hand. With the right he lifted the train of his cloak, stepping forward with his head a little to one side, eyes lowered, and giving the very image of the hypocrite. I thought I was seeing the author of *The Refutation*[68] petitioning the Bishop of Orleans. When he came to the courtiers and self-seekers, he crawled like a worm—the image of Bouret[69] before the Auditor-General.]

MYSELF. Your performance is unsurpassable [said I]. But there is one human being who is exempted from the pantomime. That is the philosopher who has nothing and asks for nothing.

HE. And where does the creature hide? If he has nothing, he must be suffering; if he asks for nothing, he will get nothing—and so will always suffer.

MYSELF. No. Diogenes made fun of his wants.

HE. But a man needs clothes.

MYSELF. He went naked.

HE. Wasn't it ever cold in Athens?

MYSELF. Not so often as here.

HE. But people had to eat.

MYSELF. No doubt.

HE. At whose expense?

MYSELF. At Nature's. Whom does the savage beg from? The earth, the animals and fishes, the trees and plants and roots and streams.

HE. An inferior menu.

---

68. *The Refutation:* Abbé Gabriel Gauchat (1709–1774) attacked the doctrines of Diderot and the *philosophes* in nineteen volumes.

69. *Bouret:* possibly alluding to a role played by the celebrated comedian, Claude-Antoine Bouret (d. 1783), whom Diderot admired.

MYSELF. But abundant.

HE. And badly served.

MYSELF. Yet it's the one whose leavings appear on all our tables.

HE. You have to admit that our cooks, pastrymen, confectioners, and caterers add a little of their own. If your Diogenes stuck to his austere diet, his organs must have been exceedingly docile.

MYSELF. You are wrong. The Cynic's costume was that of our monks and equally virtuous. The Cynics were the Carmelites and Cordeliers[70] of Athens.

HE. I've caught you then! Diogenes must have danced a pantomime, if not in front of Pericles,[71] at least in front of Lais and Phryne?[72]

MYSELF. Wrong again. The others paid dear the same courtesan who gave herself to him for pleasure.

HE. What if the courtesan was busy and the Cynic in haste?

MYSELF. He went back to his tub and did without.

HE. Do you advise me to do the same?

MYSELF. I'll stake my life it is better than to crawl, eat dirt and prostitute yourself.

HE. But I want a good bed, good food, warm clothes in winter, cool in summer, plenty of rest, money, and other things that I would rather owe to kindness than earn by toil.

MYSELF. That is because you are a lazy, greedy lout, a coward and a rotting soul.

HE. I believe I told you so myself.

MYSELF. The good things of life have their worth, no doubt, but you overlook the price of what you give up for them. You dance, you have danced, and you will keep on dancing the vilest pantomime.

HE. True enough. But it's cost me little and it won't cost me anything more. For which reason I should be quite wrong to take up another position, which would cause me trouble and which I could not hold. But from what you tell me I see that my poor dear little wife was a kind of philosopher. She had the courage of a lion. Sometimes we had no bread and no money and had already sold all our clothes. I would throw myself across the foot of the bed and rack my wits to find someone who would lend us a fiver that I'd never repay. She, gay as a lark, would sing and accompany herself at the clavier. She had the throat of a nightingale; I'm sorry you never heard her. When I took part in some musical evening I took her with me and on the way I would say: "Come, my lady, get yourself admired, display your talents and your charms, overwhelm, captivate." She would sing, overwhelm, captivate. Alas! I lost her, the

---

70. *Carmelites and Cordeliers:* Roman Catholic mendicant orders.
71. *Pericles:* Athenian statesman (495?–429 B.C.).
72. *Lais and Phryne:* courtesans.

poor thing. Besides her talents, she had a tiny mouth the width of a finger, a row of pearls for teeth, and then eyes, feet, a skin, cheeks, breasts, legs like a doe, thighs and buttocks for a sculptor. Sooner or later she would have had a chief tax collector at least. Her walk, her rump, ye gods, what a rump!"

[At once he imitated his wife's walk, taking little steps, perking his nose up in the air, flirting with a fan, swinging his hips. It was the caricature of our little coquettes, laughable and true. Then resuming his speech, he said: "I used to take her everywhere—to the Tuileries, the Palais-Royal, the Boulevards. She could not possibly have stayed with me. When she went across the street in the morning, hatless and in her smock, you would have stopped just to look at her and you could have held her waist with both thumbs and forefingers without squeezing her. Those who followed her and watched her trot along on her little feet or who gauged that rich rump outlined in her thin petticoats would hasten their pace. She let them come up then turned on them two big dark and glowing eyes that stopped them in their tracks. For the right side of the medal fully matched the reverse. But alas! I lost her and all my hopes of fortune went with her. I had taken her for no other reason, I had told her my plans. She was too intelligent not to see that they were assured of success and too sound of judgment not to agree with their aim."

[At which he began to sob and choke as he said: "No, no, I never shall get over it. Ever since, I've taken minor orders and wear a skullcap."]

MYSELF. From grief?

HE. If you like. But really in order to carry my soup plate upon my head. . . . But let's see what time it is, because I am going to the Opera.

MYSELF. What's on the program?

HE. Dauvergne's *Les Troqueurs*.[73] The music has some fine things in it. Too bad he wasn't the first to write them. Among the dead there are always a few to annoy the living. Can't be helped. *Quisque suos patimur manes*.[74] But it's half past five; I hear the bell ringing vespers for me and Abbé Canaye.[75] Farewell, Master Philosopher, isn't it true that I am ever the same?

MYSELF. Alas! Yes, unfortunately.

HE. Here's hoping this ill fortune lasts me another forty years. He laughs best who laughs last.

---

73. *Dauvergne's "Les Troqueurs"*: *The Barterers*, opera by Antoine Dauvergne (1713–1797), mediocre operatic composer who tried to unite the French and Italian styles.
74. *Quisque . . . manes*: from Virgil (*Aeneid*, VI, 743): "Each of us has to endure his own misdeeds"—i.e., live down the past.
75. *Canaye*: Abbé Canaye (1694–1782), lover of the opera. Diderot points out that the bell at the *Palais-Royal* rings at 5:30 to announce the opening of the theater, at the same time that the vesper chimes are rung.

Masterpieces of Romanticism

EDITED BY
HOWARD E. HUGO

Professor of English, University of California, Berkeley

FROM ROUSSEAU
TO **PUSHKIN**

Only a little less than a hundred years separate Rousseau's completion of his *Confessions* (1770) from Pushkin's *Eugene Onegin* (1830). Though there are broader chronological stretches in other sections of this anthology, one may venture to say that few periods offer more radical shifts in man's entire outlook than do these years. In fact one measure of the works we have selected is the awareness their authors show (often more implicit than explicit) of such mutations.

"Everything goes to the people and deserts the kings, even literary themes, which descend from royal misfortunes to private misfortunes, from Priam to Birotteau"—so lamented the Goncourt brothers in 1866. From Homer's great monarch of Troy to Balzac's perfume manufacturer in Paris in the 1830's there is a vast movement, not only in time but also in the human spirit—a movement from the heroic hero that still interested Shakespeare and Racine to the unheroic hero of the nineteenth-century bourgeoisie. The dates 1775, 1789, 1830, and 1848 (all falling within the confines of this portion of the anthology) mark years of revolution when middle-class protests against the *status quo* emerged with various degrees of violence. Only one major monarch—Charles I of England—was deposed in the seventeenth century. By contrast, the reader will recall having met six kings in Chapter 26 of *Candide*, all impoverished and in exile. The nineteenth century was to see political alterations unanticipated by political theorists, as "the divinity [that] doth hedge a king" was examined with rational suspicion, and monarchical and aristocratic powers were curtailed or abolished. The firing of "the shot heard round the world" at Concord (1775) and the fall of the Bastille (1789) mark dramatic moments which made actual the abstract political thought of eighteenth-century philosophers (with their paper constitutions, social contracts, declarations of the rights of man, and plans for perpetual peace). By 1850, it seemed to many political liberals that the bourgeoisie was politically and socially canonized. Continental revolutions in 1830 and 1848 and legislative reforms in England (chiefly in 1832) may have disappointed a few radicals by their compromises; but on the whole, the ascendancy of the middle class was guaranteed.

The change just outlined was "horizontal," cutting across national boundaries. The Enlightenment had set the goal, for the rational man, of being a "citizen of the world"; later eighteenth-century thought and nineteenth-century Romanticism moved from such universality toward the phenomenon known as nationalism. Rousseau's claim for personal uniqueness was expanded to apply to the individuality of the *Volk*, the nation, or the race. Nationalism was curiously intertwined with political liberalism from the French Revolution on. At times "vertical" national interests even superseded more generous ideas of man's brotherhood and the abolition of world-wide tyranny. The Year One, announced in Paris in September, 1792, was intended to inaugurate a new egalitarian millenium for the *entire* human race; yet twelve years later Napoleon was crowned Emperor of the French. The amalgam of political liberalism and nationalism was not rare: many thinkers, the Italian liberal Mazzini, for example, regarded nationalism as a necessary stage before man reached true awareness of humanity as a whole. From 1815 to 1853 the comparative absence of all warfare save colonial engagements seemed to display the relative harmlessness of nationalism. We have had the dubious advantage of another hundred years of history, to watch it flourishing in its full horror.

Political upheavals in this period had their counterpart in the Industrial Revolution, which indeed accentuated notions of "class" and "nation" and began the transformation of most of Western Europe from an agrarian to a primarily industrial culture. The Reformation had earlier underscored the dignity and necessity of individual labor, and had indicated a connection between spiritual and material prudence and enterprise. With the growth of wealth, industry, manufacturing, and colonies came a need for more comprehensive theories. Adam Smith's *Wealth of Nations* (1776) set the pattern for subsequent economic speculation and practice: the laissez-faire state, permitting free trade, free markets, and free competition, in keeping with what Smith termed the "obvious and simple system of natural liberty." The advocacy of economic liberalism places Smith and his followers squarely within the tradition of middle-class liberalism, broadly defined. The modern reader should note Smith's assumption that economic individualism, without any form of government regulation, will result in public benefit and ultimate harmony. This difference in viewpoint distinguishes the early liberal from his spiritual descendants, who enlarged, rather than circumscribed, the scope of governmental function.

The Industrial Revolution was made possible by the technological innovations of applied science. One thinks of the steam engine perfected by James Watt toward the end of the eighteenth century; George Stephenson's locomotive, built in 1814; the telegraph, in 1844, and so on. What theology had been to the Middle Ages, science was to become to the nineteenth century. To the already established abstract field of mathematics were slowly added the more empirical studies of astronomy, physics, geology, and chemistry. Shortly after 1800, biology became a recognized area of study, as scientists dealt more and more systematically with the organic as well as the inorganic. When Auguste Comte expounded his "Positive philosophy" in the 1820's, and spoke of the need of an additional "life science" (sociology), the definition of the scientific disciplines seemed complete. Comte divided human history into "religious-superstitious," philosoph-

ical," and "scientific-positivistic" periods, and announced that the world was now enjoying the last of the three.

The trends we have just discussed inevitably gave rise to countertrends. The rise of the bourgeoisie and of democratic egalitarianism had opponents— not only defenders of privilege, and those who could say with Talleyrand, "No man not alive before 1789 knows the sweetness of life," but also those who anticipated the horrible potentialities implicit in "the revolt of the masses," later described by Ortega y Gasset. The "liberating" impulses of early nineteenth-century nationalism too frequently evolved into aggressive national pride or, worse, into rampant racism. The exponents of a free mercantile economy, assuming without justification that man's individual actions will naturally produce economic harmony, inspired economists like Karl Marx to correct the balance by elaborating theories according to which the independent capitalist would disappear altogether in the inexorable class struggle that (in Marx's view) he was helping to create. Finally, the faith in progress and the future which science apparently underwrote—the belief that man was destined to be biologically, materially, and morally better—was from its inception queried by those who feared the sin of pride, whether defined in Christian or in classical terms, and by those who resented the displacement of absolute truth by the relative, pragmatic truths which science asserted.

If some common direction is sought beneath these manifold tendencies, it may be found in the rise of secularity and in what the historian Lecky called "a declining sense of the miraculous." Medieval man knew that he lived in God's world, and Christianity had permeated every aspect of daily living. Whether the Reformation came as a symptom or a cause of weakened faith, the existence in the West of several hundred churches in 1700, in comparison with one Church in 1300, indicated doubts and questionings where once had been absolute doctrinal certainty. Politics and economics were increasingly shorn of theocratic presuppositions; and by the time of the Age of Reason, religious truth itself had to pass the tests of empirical and rational inquiry. Naturally there were individual thinkers, and even mass movements, who protested the departure from Christian orthodoxy; but, in general, during the first half of the nineteenth century, Christianity for the intellectual was absorbed into what Comte called vaguely "a religion of humanity." (Christianity for the average man often was summed up in a remark attributed to Lord Melbourne: "No man has more respect for the Christian religion than I have, but really, when it comes to intruding it into private life. . . .")

In 1859, Darwin published his *Origin of Species*. At first hailed with delight by many critics—for did not evolution make progress as *real* as the law of gravitation, and even coincide with ideas of Christian teleology?—Darwin's book was soon attacked by churchmen for destroying certain fundamentalist theses, and the fight between religion and science began in earnest. More important, as the century moved on, certain deeper minds were disturbed by the new conceptions of a universe from which mind and spirit seemed excluded, where chance determined change, where "survival of the fittest" and "natural selection" suggested that might and force won over right, and where moral laws were illusory fictions. Herbert Spencer's remark—"Nature's discipline is a little cruel that it may be very kind"—was then regarded either as small comfort or as downright erroneous. It is within this climate of opinion that romanticism ends and realism begins.

ROMANTICISM—SENTIMENT AND NATURE

The preceding remarks range far ahead of the first works in this section. Let us return briefly to the mid-eighteenth century, when, in the period of transition from the Enlightenment to romanticism, certain philosophical, political, and cultural presuppositions at one time thought to be eternally true were discussed, then criticized, then finally abandoned. Once again we are faced with the fact that men very radically change their opinions within a relatively short span of history. Out of the mass of attitudes and ideas, we abstract two which seem particularly significant: the change in the concept of nature and the growing importance attributed to the sentiments, feelings, emotions, passions.

Frederick the Great, onetime patron of Voltaire, described *Candide* as "Job in modern dress," and it is good to remember that the Book of Job ends in mystery. In *Candide* the same mystery is posed en route, although the work itself ends with acceptance. Why does evil exist in the universe? Why does the good man suffer? What is the relation of God to mankind? Does the cosmos run according to some rational scheme comprehensible to the human mind? Eighteenth-century science and mathematics had seemed to confirm the mechanistic view that all parts of nature were intelligible. Yet an increasing number of dark spots on the once illuminated intellectual horizon puzzled and confused later thinkers. Nature was to remain the comforting talisman for romanticism that it had been for the Age of Reason, but we shall see that "nature" came to be redefined. The romantics were as anxious as their classical and neoclassical forbears to fathom the riddle of man in his world, but henceforth it was felt that perhaps the heart—the emotions—and not the head held the key to ultimate comprehension of the universe. To understand this change, we must examine the growing cult of sentiment in the eighteenth century.

It would be foolish to imagine that at a certain moment people stopped thinking and began feeling. The Enlightenment had made much of the "moral sense," and the early decades of the eighteenth century had enjoyed an honest tear with innumerable sentimental novels and plays. But on the whole the deliberate exploitation of the emotions had been held suspect; and if ultimate values—laws about the cosmos, the arts, society, and so on—were at stake, those areas of the psyche which related to the feelings were conceived to be irrelevant. Spinoza, in *Of Human Bondage, or The Power of the Affections* (1667) said, "In so far as men are subject to passions, they cannot be said to agree in nature." The idiosyncrasy resulting from adherence to personal emotion rather than to the generally accepted principles of reason was not considered ideal material for literature in a period unusually dedicated to ideas of universality, social man, communication between minds, and conformity to classical norms. Then, for reasons that are still not clear, philosophical introspection, reverie, the melancholy heart became fashionable. The brooding, solitary daydreamer came into his own, with varieties of "spleen," "the blue devils," *Weltschmerz* ("world sorrow"), *le mal du siècle* ("the sickness of the century"). Rousseau's *Confessions* (1781-1788), filled with this kind of passionate unrest, were hailed by a reading public already assured of the primacy of the emotions.

I am commencing [said Rousseau] an undertaking, hitherto without precedent, and which will never find an imitator. I desire to set before my fellow-men the likeness of a man in all the truth of nature, and that man is myself. Myself alone! I know the feelings of my heart, and I know men. I am not made like any of those I have seen; I venture to believe that I am not made like any of those who are in existence.

From the objective norms that were the delight of the Age of Reason, we turn to the subjective, innate, indefinable, and *unique* core of each individual. The "man of feeling" (the phrase forms the title of a popular novel by the Scottish writer, Henry MacKenzie, published in 1771) replaced the elegant conversationalist of the salon, coffee house, and boudoir. And his feelings were mostly mournful. Earlier eighteenth-century sentimental literature had displayed *both* pleasurable and painful experiences, enriched by laughter and tears. The romantics endeavored to show that sensibility was not equated with happiness, and romantic literature in general is rarely comical or amusing. Pushkin does occasionally smile wryly, but after the manner of Byron, whom he so admired: "And if I laugh at any mortal thing, 'Tis that I may not weep." In Rousseau's novel, *Julie ou La Nouvelle Héloïse* (*Julia, or The New Héloïse*, 1761), the young hero Saint-Preux exclaims poignantly, "For me there is only a single way to be happy, but there are millions of ways to be miserable."

For the romantics, the so-called "tender passion"—love—gained pre-eminence among all the feelings. The modern colloquial usage of "romantic" with connotations of moon-June-spoon is in part a legacy from

that period. With the exception of Racine's *Phèdre*, the preceding section of this anthology contains, significantly, no literature dealing with love. Candide voyages from continent to continent to find his elusive Cunégonde, but her chief virtue—physical indestructibility—scarcely qualifies her for the role of a *romantic* heroine. The eighteenth century —despite its finesse, social decorum, and elegance—abounds with works displaying the relations between the sexes as surprisingly lusty and earthy, or as a kind of psychological game with possession the assumed goal of the male partner. Against such amorous franchise the romantics rebelled. We shall watch Faust and Margaret, among other heroes and heroines, asserting that love is a genuine spiritual entity and a condition eagerly to be coveted—not for purposes of physical satisfaction but because unhappy as the condition may be, life is meaningless unless we exist in that state of morose delight.

Even as the age brought a revaluation of the less ratiocinative, more intuitive processes of the psyche, it also brought new colorings to the concept of nature. From classical antiquity through most of the eighteenth century, the word *nature* had meant the totality of existence, the entire cosmos—animate and inanimate—with its laws and activity, and when it meant anything less than this, it had usually meant the whole nature of man—common human nature. But in the cult of nature inspired by the romantic movement, the term came to mean something much more limited: the physical world apart from man's achievements—that is, the landscape and countryside, the sea and mountains. In a sense this idealization of nature was no innovation. The Hebraic-Christian tradition had begun with a garden. Pagan antiquity in Greece and Rome had produced pastorals and bucolics, in which the vision of the simple life in close proximity to animals and the land was portrayed. But the cleavage that Rousseau and his heirs now felt to exist between the individual and his environment led to a redefinition of "nature." Neoclassical society, polished and polite, had been essentially urban, although the philosopher-gentleman could enjoy the country as a respite from strenuous city life with its Court and Parliament, salons and coffee houses, wit and conversation. The formal garden—like Voltaire's at Ferney, with two head gardeners and twenty laborers—may be taken as a symbol of what was held to be a happy compromise between the country's annoying miscellaneousness and civilized mankind's love of order. As Dr. Johnson, Voltaire's contemporary, put it: "Sir, they who are content to live in the country are fit for it."

In the passage above from Rousseau, he stated that he is psychologically unique and like no other man past or present. From this sense of acute individuality, it is only a short step to a feeling of being alien and misunderstood. If our insensitive contemporaries reject us, we can always find comfort in the great sympathetic soul of nature —nature who "never did betray/The heart that loved her."

The heroes of later eighteenth-century literature move out from the confines of city and drawing room to the seas and forests. By the early nineteenth century the new hero has become stereotyped and hostility to organized society a cliché. If any member of society gained the romantic's approbation, it was generally the simple rustic who—like the innocent child— was close to nature and therefore morally purer than his sophisticated fellows. Primitivism long had interested the rationalist thinkers, and the untutored mind afforded the *philosophes* fascinating material for their studies of general mankind, although for this purpose distant, exotic savages (Voltaire's *Oreillons*, for instance) were more pleasing and more conveniently remote than the local peasantry. Later eighteenth-century expansions of this concept marked a shift from mere interest in the Noble Savage to positive approval. Serious doubts were raised as to the validity of urbanity and cultivation and about the notion of progress itself. Perhaps the unspoiled savage partook of a Golden Age where hearts rather than purses were gold, where there was no *mine* or *thine*, no artificial legislation, no social hierarchy. Though Rousseau's "natural man" drew a shout of derision from Voltaire, who saw men once more getting down on all fours in abdication of their rational-human capabilities, Voltaire was fighting a rearguard action, and the success of a work he ridiculed proved it. Few literary productions have attained the popularity of the Ossian poems (1760-1763), ostensibly translated by James Macpherson. *Fingal* and *Temora*, two "epics" in the group, depicted early Scottish-Celtic-"Erse" days in an elegiac, melancholy tone. What critics seemed most to admire was the *goodness* of all the characters. The poems of Ossian, for example, were among the favorite reading of a most unprimitive figure—Napoleon. That Macpherson's work was later proved a forgery in no way diminished his incredible influence. Twenty-five years afterward, Bernardin de Saint-Pierre published *Paul and Virginia* (*Paul et Virginie*, 1788), in which the life of decadent Europe was contrasted unfavorably with life on an unspoiled, Eden-like island. "Here there is merely wooden furniture, but there you find serene faces and hearts of gold."

France had been the Continental fortress of the Age of Reason, as our selection of readings in the preceding section of the anthology indicates. The headquarters of the new ideology moved to the "misty" north and Germany. That country demonstrated conscious romantic symptoms during the 1770's with its "Storm and Stress" (*Sturm und Drang*) movement in literature —led by a coterie of young writers fired by naturalistic, anti-French, anticlassical feeling. In their twenties, they were impregnated with notions about "genius" that should transcend any fettering rules and standards, convinced of the primacy of the passions over the meddling intellect, desirous of writing simple folk poetry stemming directly from the heart of the race, anxious to identify the spirit of man with the spirit of the new "nature," and, finally, eager to use literature as a vehicle in the search for philosophic truth— the pursuit of the Absolute, the underlying reality of existence. This was one of the first *avantgarde* groups. Among those who contributed to the "Storm and Stress" movement was Johann Wolfgang von Goethe. His *Faust*, Part I, begun during these years, is an illustration of the fully developed romantic mood.

ROMANTICISM AND THE METAPHYSICAL QUEST— GOETHE'S *FAUST*

Goethe, speaking of *Faust* to his friend and amanuensis Eckermann, once commented, "I think that I have given them a bone to pick." Seldom in Western literature has a work been so provocative to its audience; yet many a critic has sunk deep in the morass of intellectualism when attempting to explicate the play. The average reader will find *Faust* difficult going. He will be aware that there is more to it than meets the eye, although perhaps his feeling of disquietude will overbalance any pleasure the reading has afforded. If he is honest with himself, however, he will be forced to one conclusion upon completing *Faust*: he has been in the presence of one of the greatest of the world's masterpieces. Such an experience *should* lead to healthy confusion, since the reader—with the artist—has just taken a plunge into the unknown.

The first part of *Faust* was published by Goethe in 1808. Many years had gone into its creation. His so-called *Ur-Faust* ("early" or "primitive" *Faust*) was written between 1770 and 1775, and *Faust, a Fragment,* appeared in 1790. Behind Goethe's extensive labors lay the whole legend of the Renaissance scholar, Dr. Faustus, who quested after universal knowledge by means of white magic— that is, orthodox science—and the more terrible instrument of black magic. A real Johannes Faustus lived from 1480 to 1540. His adventures, much embroidered, were related by Johannes Spies twenty-seven years later, and these became the subject for innumerable puppet shows and popular folk-dramas throughout the seventeenth and eighteenth centuries in Germany. Hence from childhood on, the Faust myth was familiar to Goethe; and from the time he was twenty until he died at eighty-two, the theme never left his imagination. To trace the slow genesis of *Faust*, Part I, and later *Faust*, Part II (the sequel published posthumously in 1833), is fascinating to the scholar, but dull for the student. The important fact to be grasped is simple. Once again, as in Greek tragedy and Racine's *Phèdre*, we have the playwright using traditional, legendary, even mythical material.

The "Prologue in Heaven" Benedetto Croce has called "the jest of a great artist . . . deliberately archaic, and slightly in the style of Voltaire." We should not be misled by its cosmic humor and high irony. It must be read with care, for the key to subsequent events is found in the dialogue between God and Mephistopheles. The paean of the Archangels in praise of the wonderful universe is succeeded by the nay-sayer's insouciant remarks. Like Satan in the Book of Job (the opening scene is obviously modeled on Job 1:6-12 and 2:1-6) Goethe's devil has just returned "from going to and fro in the earth, and from walking up and down on it." What he has seen has only increased his contempt for that silly grasshopper, man. The angels may place man a little lower than themselves. Mephistopheles finds restless mankind scarcely an improvement over primordial chaos. Already we note that Mephistopheles' quarrel is not with man or with Faust; his challenge is leveled at God and His fitness as a creator!

Then follows the *first* wager, which is between God and a fallen divinity. Faust is discontented, says Mephistopheles. That beautiful gift of reason has induced nothing but fatal curiosity. His bewilderment, answers God, is temporary; and He turns Faust over to this most cynical of devils for the rest of his life. No holds are barred for Mephistopheles. He is given *carte blanche* to lure Faust in any fashion. The cryptic language may obscure the real issue for the reader. Here is no simple temptation to be naughty. Mephistopheles' aim is to undermine Faust's whole *moral* sense, the awareness that values of good and evil do exist despite man's difficulties in defining them. A being of searchings and questionings, living a life of constant aspiration toward goals but dimly seen—this, as described by God, is the being He has created in His own image. We shall see shortly how the terms of the *second* pact between man and devil are an attempt on Mephistopheles' part to stop this vital activity, thus implicitly defeating God's description of life as an eternal Becoming.

Such a vitalistic and dynamic interpretation of the human condition is the essence of romantic philosophy. Christianity had posited a state of grace, and Christian thought is the history of attempts to determine how erring man might finally enjoy eternal bliss. The Enlightenment, ignoring the mystery of faith implicit in Christian doctrine, had expanded the element of reason to be an end in itself. Romanticism, suddenly aware of dynamic (even irrational) principles underlying both man and nature, took striving—tentative progression and development, and pure endeavor—and made it the defining quality of mankind. In the second part of *Faust* (about which we shall speak briefly later on), Goethe has a chorus of angels proclaim, "Should a man strive with all his heart/ Heaven can foil the devil." The paradox of *Faust*

is that of a man finally redeemed by a God whose reality Faust doubts. Goethe has written a modern *Divine Comedy* paralleling Dante's, but it is "divine comedy" of the profoundest irony.

Following the prologue we move from heaven to earth—a shift in background reminiscent of the epic. The setting of the opening of the play is traditional: "a high-vaulted narrow *Gothic* room." It reminds us of Goethe's role in the "Storm and Stress" group, the young writers of Germany who were anxious to rescue the native scene, and also the Middle Ages, and also Shakespeare (their idol), from the undervaluations of the Enlightenment—by which they meant France and French neoclassicism. The late C. S. Lewis, in *The Screwtape Letters* (1942), pointed out how "the long, dull, monstrous years of middle-aged prosperity or middle-aged adversity are excellent campaigning weapons" for the devil, and Goethe's Heinrich Faust is in the full maturity of worldly success. He owns everything—and nothing. He as polymath has investigated the entire field of human knowledge to find a chaos of relativism. A simple three-meal-a-day life is impossible for him. He cherishes a passion for the Absolute which his pedantic assistant Wagner cannot comprehend. Black magic yields little save despair. Death is one road to possession of final truth, but a childhood memory of naïve faith averts suicide. At this critical stage Mephistopheles enters (first in the guise of a poodle, and we remember that the Greek root of the word *cynic* means "dog"). The real action of the play begins.

The Prince of Darkness is a gentleman, and the devil soon abandons his earlier disguises for the elegant costume of the polished gallant and wit. He had minced no words when he said previously, "I am the Spirit which always denies" (*"Ich bin der Geist der stets verneint"*). Now he offers *his* wager to Faust. Their pact is a corollary of the one we witnessed in Heaven. An interesting point, however, is that Faust frames the terms. We have already indicated that God's picture of Mephistopheles does not coincide with the devil's view of himself. The relation of the tempter to Faust presents us with an additional facet to his character, for Mephistopheles never really understands the nature of his companion's problem. *If* Mephistopheles can destroy Faust's sense of aspiration, *if* Faust can say of any single moment in time that *this* is complete fulfillment of desire—then the devil wins, and God and man are defeated. Such repose and satiety would represent an end to striving. It would also—and here is the subtle touch—mean a cessation of Faust's moral awareness. By the achievement of a final "good" on earth, the whole conception of good and evil as being in a state of development would be denied. Faust examines existence in terms of a question that only modern man could conceive; certainly it was unknown to the Greeks with their feeling for

limitation. Is a life of tireless movement toward an undefined goal worth living? And the devil (orthodox conservative and traditionalist that he is) can hardly be expected to grasp such a radical query.

The varieties of pleasure that the devil parades before the hero are proffered in an effort to supply *the* moment of complete satisfaction, and thus obfuscate Faust's values. Mephistopheles almost wins with Margaret (Gretchen). But love is more complicated than mere sex, and Faust's love comes to mean the acme of human aspiration. From love he learns to break through the bonds of his individual ego and to see his state in humanity. Margaret's tragedy enhances rather than diminishes Faust's moral sensibility, and Mephistopheles is a puzzled, disappointed sensualist when he takes Faust back to Gretchen's dungeon for the last poignant scene in the play. It is essential that the reader comprehend how much the author stresses the nature of Faust's affection, how love is raised to the level of a high philosophical concept. Stendhal showed only his lack of perception when he remarked: "Goethe gives Faust the Devil for a friend; and with this powerful ally, Faust does what we have all done at the age of twenty—he seduces a seamstress."

Even before the first part of *Faust* was published, Goethe thought of writing a second drama where the hero would turn from individual to social concerns. From approximately 1800 to 1831 Goethe worked on

Faust, Part II, a play designed principally to be read. To read it is, in the words of one critic, "a pilgrimage from which few have returned safe and sound." Few works in modern times present us with such a conglomeration of shifting symbols, and we move from mystery to mystery, carried forward by Goethe's incomparable verse and brilliant ideas. A "Classical Walpurgis Night" synthesizes ancient Greece and the Gothic north. Goethe returns to the older Faust legend to have his aging protagonist marry Helen of Troy, now a widow after the death of Menelaus. Their union begets Euphorion (the spirit of new humanity; it is said that Goethe had Byron in mind as his model). Faust also undertakes a military career to save a shaky kingdom from falling. The ultimate activity pursued by Faust consists in reclaiming land from the sea, and he sees the vision of a new, happy community composed of industrious mankind. This is at last the consummate moment for him, and Mephistopheles—a nearly exhausted tempter—wins the wager in a dubious victory. But Faust's satisfaction is potential rather than actual: the vision lies in the indeterminate future for which he strives. The angels rescue Faust's soul from the forces of evil and bear him in triumph to heaven. Goethe's God seems to say that Faust's errors are necessary imperfections of man's growth. Imperfections in time are perfections in eternity. Faust's has been a "good" life. The final lines of the great drama, declaimed by the *Chorus Mysticus*

in heaven, sum up the author's profound affirmation of existence.

> All that is past of us
> Was but reflected;
> All that was lost in us
> Here is corrected;
> All indescribables
> Here we descry;
> Eternal Womanhead
> Leads us on high.
> [*Das Ewig-Weibliche/*
> *Zieht uns hinan*]

GERMAN ROMANTIC POETRY: HÖLDERLIN AND NOVALIS

While posterity has labelled Goethe's *Faust* as *the* incarnation of certain romantic tendencies, the student is cautioned to remember the author's own Enlightenment (*Aufklärung*) heritage, and indeed Goethe's strictures about "modern" romantic literary trends when he became older. There is Goethe's often-quoted remark to his friend and amanuensis Eckermann: "I call the classic *healthy*, the romantic *sickly* . . . Most modern productions are romantic—not because they are new; but because they are weak, morbid, and sickly. And the antique is classic—not because it is old; but because it is strong, fresh, joyous, and healthy."

The generation of German writers and philosophers born twenty-five years after Goethe did not, on the whole, meet with the Olympian's approval. Yet it was they who displayed what might be termed true romantic self - consciousness: Fichte, Hegel, Wackenroder, Tieck, Kleist, Schelling, August and Friedrich Schlegel, and the two poets chosen for this anthology—Hölderlin and Novalis. All shared the sentiment that they were spearheading a new civilization and a new way of looking at the world: the historical past, the engaging present, the visionary future. "The world must be made romantic. Then once more we shall discover its original meaning." Thus speaks Novalis in one of his hermetic *Fragments*, neatly stating the sense of cultural urgency he and his contemporaries shared. Neither he nor Hölderin was widely known in his own day, and it was the task of twentieth-century critics to rescue them from literary oblivion. Yet each in his short career—Hölderlin's terminated by madness, Novalis's by an early tubercular death—contributed to a richer formulation of romanticism.

Hölderlin ranks foremost among German romantic Hellenists, and is rightly placed alongside Keats and Shelley. Hölderlin's epistolary novel *Hyperion* (1799) portrays a young, melancholy hero who determines to invigorate modern Germany with the spirit of ancient Greece. In effect this was Hölderlin's own artistic mission, a goal he hoped to achieve through his verse. He adopted the complex metrical patterns of the classic Greek poets, chiefly Pindar, by engrafting Greek "quantities"—long and short syllables—onto essentially qualitative structures—stressed and unstressed syllables. Like his model Pindar, Hölderlin aspired to be the poet-seer-prophet, and formal affiliations with his glorious predecessor took on more than mere metrical allegiance. The modern world for Hölderlin was moribund, decadent, and spiritually empty. Ancient Hellas represented canonical perfection: an age of complete moral, aesthetic, political and social unity such as the most ardent neoclassicist never dreamed. Reviewing the past, he found as did the Schlegel brothers that neoclassicism had been a distortion of true Greek ideals, where formal and rational elements had been exaggerated at the expense of the darker side of Greek culture. Neoclassic critics had made much of the plastic serenity of Hellenic art, the harmony and repose of white marble columns against a tranquil blue Mediterranean sky —what the eighteenth-century aesthetician Winckelmann described as "a quiet grandeur and a noble simplicity." Romantic Hellenists found this observation only partially true, as they revaluated what they read and saw. Nietzsche's *Birth of Tragedy from the Spirit of Music* (1872) is but the culmination of earlier romantic insights. Apollo (the god of light) and Dionysus (the deity whose activity was associated with the libidinous orgy and the wine barrel) were now conceived as polar opposites, with the less "respectable" and rational god as possibly the more effective force. Hence part of Hölderlin's greatness, evident in these few poems, was his awareness of the balance in Greek thought between the eternal desire to stake out rational claims over inchoate experience, and the simultaneous perception that fate, the Gods, the given elements in human existence, were all mysterious and even terrible in their implications.

Patmos—which like *The Rhine, Mother Asia, Bread and Wine* and Hölderlin's other last long poems in free verse—shows the poet to belong to a myth-making tradition shared by his English contemporary William Blake. In *Patmos* the blend of Greek mythology with orthodox Christian symbolism perplexes the most sophisticated modern reader, schooled as he may be in the intricacies of Yeats, Joyce, and T. S. Eliot. Christ for Hölderlin was the last of the Greek gods; and like Novalis, Hölderlin rewrote cultural and theological history to suit his own arcane purpose. The diverse contributions in our own day of C. G. Jung and his followers, with their notions of recurrent myths and the archetypal unconscious, seem less radical after we follow the strange voyages of the mind undertaken by these speculative poets writing a century and a half ago.

Novalis (Friedrich von Hardenberg) received praise from Goethe, disparate as were their temperaments, who said of the short-lived genius that he might have been an "Imperator des Geistes" ("Emperor of the Spirit"). Novalis wrote most of his major poems in four years, all centering about his dead fiancée Sophie von Kühn, who died when she was fifteen. "Sehnsucht nach dem Tod" ("longing for death") became paramount for him; and this death wish—whether genuine or assumed—was one of many morbid romantic themes. The blue flower sought by the hero of Novalis's unfinished novel *Heinrich von Ofterdingen*, as the youth wandered through medieval Germany, Atlantis, and the fabulous world of the *Märchen* (fairy tale), came to be emblematic of romantic longing for some infinite and unobtainable goal, for both Novalis and the small coterie of readers familiar with his writings. The *Hymns to the Night* have antecedents in the eighteenth century, with graveyard poetry and "night thoughts." Dante too transmuted his love for Beatrice into a mystic vision of the afterlife and "the love that moves the sun and the other stars." Yet Novalis's amalgam of the mystic and the erotic, the sacred and the profane, goes far beyond the author of the *Divine Comedy* in the Middle Ages.

Novalis's plea for a spiritual and religious revaluation reminds us of Hölderlin's similar exhortations. While the poetry of Novalis overlays traditional Christian symbols with myths drawn from his reading in Eastern theology, and he was attracted by private mystics and theosophists of preceding centuries, his essay *Christendom or Europe* (1799) was more in keeping with general intellectual currents at the turn of the century. Deism and philosophical skepticism were congenial to most of the leading proponents of the Age of Reason. (Naturally there had always been practicing Protestants and Catholics, but we speak of the extremes.) A definite Christian revival took place in various quarters around 1800, spurred on when the excesses of the French Revolution and its aftermath were regarded by many intellectuals as the logical, horrifying outcome of secular and "enlightened" thought. Novalis, Bonald, De Maistre, Burke, Coleridge, and Chateaubriand comprise a curious, yet surprisingly cohesive, group. Whether they talked of conserving cathedrals—as did the younger Victor Hugo in the 1820's—or abstract conservatism for Church and State (Count Joseph de Maistre set his slogan "throne and altar" against the motto of the French Revolution, "liberty, equality, fraternity"), or revered tradition, loyalty and duty, they all were demanding a return to Christian principles they felt had been abandoned. The next work we consider, Chateaubriand's *René* (1802), ostensibly aimed to prove in "modern" terms the validity of Christianity. "In *René* I exposed the weakness of my century," the author later announced in his *Memoirs from Beyond the Grave* (posthumously published in 1849–1850). That the readers of *René* discovered in that hero the avatar of their own spiritual malaise and tended to ignore Chateaubriand's theological *apologia*, demonstrates that an author may aim at one target but his contemporaries observe that he hits another. Another statement from the *Memoirs*, equally flamboyant, places the little work in a larger cultural context.

"With me began the so-called romantic school, a revolution in French literature."

CHATEAUBRIAND AND THE ROMANTIC HERO

While a royalist exile in England, Chateaubriand conceived of a plan to write an apology for Christianity, wherein certain fictional tales would serve as *exempla* to illustrate the efficacy of true belief. He had flirted with philosophical skepticism in his youth. The statement he made about his conversion is interesting: "My conviction came from the heart; I wept and I believed." Anxious to return to France, he was unsure about the reception such an ambitious work, *The Genius of Christianity* (*Le Génie du Christianisme*), would obtain. He produced *Atala* (1801) as a trial balloon, and the results were highly gratifying. A rapid sequence of events in 1802 displays the changing temper of the times. On April 8 Napoleon signed a Concordat with the pope, restoring the Church to France after ten years of enforced secularism. On April 14 *The Genius of Christianity* was published, including both *Atala* and *René*. On April 18 a *Te Deum* was sung in Notre Dame Cathedral in Paris, with all the ancient splendor of the *ancien régime*, to celebrate peace between Church and State. That fantastic creation of the Revolution, the Goddess of Reason, was dethroned; and the Madonna returned to supplant her. Thus a changing religious mood contributed to ensure the triumph of Chateaubriand's book. His decision in 1805 to reprint *Atala* and *René* apart from the larger work shows that his impressive arguments in the *Genius* had been brushed aside by the common reader who preferred imaginative enjoyment to moral edification. This is the impression one receives from three contemporaries. "I read *René*, and I shuddered," said Sainte-Beuve. George Sand, leading female novelist who preferred a male *nom de plume*, behaved true-to-form when she commented, "It seemed that René was myself." Maurice de Guérin confided to his *Journal*, "This reading [of *René*] soaked my soul like rain from a storm." *René* came to be for the youth of France in the 1810's and 1820's what Goethe's *Werther* (1774) had been for readers across the Rhine a generation earlier. In each case social and philosophical dislocations had produced a state of mind such that a single book articulated sentiments dimly felt. With *René* the eternal theme of moral man in immoral society received a new local habitation and a name.

Behind the creation of this *novella* lay Chateaubriand's grander plan, and *René* is best comprehended if the author's ideas—sometimes barely implicit in the story—are sketched. *The Genius of Christianity* starts with an attack on the *Encyclopédie*—"that tower of Babel of science and reason." Chateaubriand then takes recourse to history. Christianity is *better* because it represents an emotional increase over all prior faiths, and even Adam's fall was caused by his sterile intellectualism before

he succumbed to the temptation. Chateaubriand's digressions deal less with the intelligent design of the circumambient universe often celebrated by the Deists than with its aesthetic charms and beauty. "The Christian God is poetically superior to ancient Jupiter," he declares—a declaration that must have been surprising to theologians in Rome, Geneva, and Canterbury; and also both Testaments are more moving *qua* literature than the classics of Greece and Rome. Theologians had always emphasized that man's sojourn on earth was but a temporary phase. Chateaubriand reverts to their idea and reaffirms the role of the Christian pilgrim-voyager, faced with salvation or damnation, whose emotional intensity is an improvement on pagan intellect. Gothic architecture, ecclesiastical ruins and tombs, remind the Christian of his dim mortality; the aspiration of the church spire pointing toward heaven displays a yearning for divinity that the more "horizontal" dimensions of Greek temples can never possess. Finally, in a chapter entitled *About the Vagueness of the Passions* ("Du Vague des Passions"), he cites the contribution that Christianity has made in canonizing the emotion of love, and lists famous lovers, all postdating the birth of Christ. For him progress meant not mere intellectual aggrandizement, the progress of the *philosophes*. "The more that people advance in civilization, the more increases this condition of the *vagueness* of the passions." Christian love, an aspect of such "vagueness," meant a salutary synthesis of *eros* and *agape*, profane and sacred love, in Chateaubriand's mind. Thus *René* is in part an *exemplum*, in which the incestuous feelings of brother and sister clash with Amelia's Christian decision to enter a convent, and René is made to feel the full horror of his illicit passion. Yet the resulting unalleviated melancholy exalts him as a hero of sensibility above crasser fellow men. Here lay René's appeal to the readers who discovered in him a paradigm for their own conditions.

Romantic themes abound in the novel: the hero's childhood is unhappy in that he is misunderstood by others; nature responds like a violin to his fluctuating moods; incestuous love tragically distinguishes him from his happier but duller contemporaries. Most romantic of all, perhaps, are his voyages. Candide, that epitome of the rationalist in search of a better world, travels extensively, and the eighteenth century fairly swarms with accounts of young men who take the Grand Tour to fill out their education and acquaint themselves with the ways of polite society. But the romantic voyage which frames René's lugubrious narrative adds a new element. Here the hero moves from civilization and the company of insensitive fellow beings toward an unknown, exotic, mysterious terrain, where there is always the promise—though rarely the fulfillment—that the jaded soul will discover peace. Thus we gradually arrive at those curious romantic voyages of the imagination, quests we normally associate with the world of dreams: Hoffmann's *Tales*, Coleridge's *Ancient Mariner*, Melville's *Moby Dick*—works that look ahead to Rimbaud's *Drunken Ship* (*Bateau ivre*) and the bizarre universe of Franz Kafka with that castle forever out of reach. "Anywhere out of this world," cried Baudelaire in a dialogue he undertook with his soul (from *The Spleen of Paris*, 1869). "Life is a hospital where every invalid wants to exchange his bed for someone else's."

HEINE AND LATER GERMAN ROMANTIC POETRY

The complex metrical structures employed by Novalis and Hölderlin places them outside one major tradition in German romanticism: the interest in folk-poetry, and the aspiration of most German poets during the first half of the nineteenth century to write with the *Volkston* ("sound of the people"). From 1778 to 1789 Gottfried Herder, Goethe's friend, collected folk songs whose publication had an incalculable influence on the course of German verse. A second major collection was *The Child's Horn of Plenty* (*Des Knaben Wunderhorn*, 1806–1808) by Achim von Arnim and Clemens Brentano, dedicated to Goethe—who responded courteously to their gift by saying that the book should be on every table and read by every German. The blend of folkish diction, apparent artlessness and simple emotionalism soon created a poetic idiom as stereotyped as the Elizabethan sonnet. The storehouse of folk imagery—girls at wells, talking birds, linden and oak trees, roses and nightingales, faithless lovers —became, alas, conveniently accessible to even the smallest talent. Only Brentano, Eichendorff, Chamisso, and Heine were able to rise above the resultant *clichés*, and then not always.

Perhaps one clue to Heine's achievement is a remark he once made to Wilhelm Müller, a minor poet whom Heine praised. Yours, he said, are pure folk songs. As for me, I borrow the form alone. "The contents belong to conventional, sophisticated society." He had neither antiquarian interest nor a conception of any mission to remind the German public of its national and folk heritage. A self-styled "good soldier in the wars of human liberation," German nationalism filled him with dismay, and primitivism had similar scant appeal for this latter-day Voltairean skeptic. Yet the folk song afforded him a vehicle where sentiment and wit might be combined: brief moments of pathos, light and lucidity coupled with strength, ease of communication, flexibility of rhyme and meter, and a heavy use of assonance and alliteration. The broad humor contained in much folk poetry Heine replaced by his epigrammatic endings and occasional acerbic final cadences, the "cold shower" of which critics have frequently spoken.

His love poems, particularly those we have included from *The Lyrical Intermezzo* (1822–1823), at first glance seem to belong to the romantic tradition where love was apostrophized as the spiritual condition eagerly to be coveted. Romanticism, as we said earlier, *is* so very romantic. But Heine along with another later-romantic, Stendhal—whose book *Concerning Love* is an acute, quasi-serious, dissection of that passion—seems often to display a skeptical ambivalence. Stendhal's fictional heroes seek to be in love as much as did their creator, and often with as little success. Both Heine and his French contemporary ("romantics" who nevertheless were realistically critical of the literary attitudes of their own age), agree on the one hand that love is primary, then suggest on the other that perhaps love is a chimerical ideal concocted by poetic souls. They return in effect to the toughness of mind exhibited by certain eighteenth-century writers, while they simultaneously enjoy the life of high romantic emotionalism.

FRENCH ROMANTIC POETRY

Chateaubriand said that he started the Romantic school in France with *René*. At about the same time, Mme. de Staël introduced German literature to French readers, and the "new" romantic mood received further implementation. Yet not until the 1820's and 1830's did certain configurations we associate with full-blown romanticism emerge in the generation that included Hugo, Lamartine, and Nerval—all born around 1800. Both this cultural lag (when contrasted with Germany and England) and the relative orthodoxy of subject and style—save for Nerval, whose strange verse is reminiscent of Novalis's puzzling incantations—may have several explanations. Romanticism thrived on revolt against the immediate past. This, we shall see, is partly true for these writers. But French intellectuals have always prided themselves as being the true heirs to classicism. Their golden age was the period of Molière and Racine, unlike ours and Shakespeare, a most "unclassical" author. Hugo's occasional attacks on eighteenth-century sterility are tepid compared with the fulminations of the German "Storm and Stress" group in the 1770's and the young German intellectuals around 1800. Then, too, arms rather than the gentler arts, political rather than cultural revolution, occupied France between 1789 and 1815. Primitivism and the authentic voice of the people, another romantic concern, has never enjoyed much currency in France; and folk poetry is difficult to reconcile with the whole centripetal tendency of the French artists toward Paris and away from the provinces and the country. Finally, the entire metaphysical passion of the German romantics with their eternal search for the Absolute seems less pressing for the "logical" French.

Hence what revolt is apparent in these poets is chiefly stylistic rather than thematic. Preceding French verse had been unusually ornate. "Noble style" governed the choice of vocabulary, and the form of the alexandrine became increasingly circumscribed, guarded by elaborate rules concerning the position of the *caesura*, masculine and feminine endings to lines, and rhymes which could be neither "rich" nor "weak" but "sufficient." Long descriptive and didactic poems had featured elegant periphrasis, shorter lyrics a tone of rococo *badinage* and sophisticated playfulness. The medium of translation makes the extent of romantic modifications difficult to apprehend, since they were so subtle. To the English reader the intensity of the battle to replace the customary single *caesura* in the alexandrine with two pauses seems trivial. Hugo sang proudly, "J'ai disloqué ce grand niais d'alexandrin" ("I put out of action that silly fool of an alexandrine"); and his play *Hernani* (1830), where this metrical action is occasionally repeated, took on the contours of a major revolution with political overtones—the young rebels versus the old conservatives.

Lamartine was convinced some ten years earlier that he was inaugurating a new movement in poetry. "I am he who made poetry come down from Parnassus; he who has given the so-called Muse the very fibres from the heart of mankind—touched and moved by the countless tremblings of the soul of nature—in place of the lyre with its customary seven strings." His protest was mainly against the insistence that a poet work within certain classical verse-forms: elegy, idyll, pastoral, lyric, each with its appropriate and special formal technique. The French romantics sought for more fluidity. Hence they varied the inflexible alexandrine by employing irregular lines and stanzas, or else they worked in the ode, ballad, and sonnet—structures for the most part abandoned since the sixteenth century.

New verse for a new age also included transformations in mood and subject. A few phrases from Hugo's preface to *Twilight Songs* (*Chants du Crépuscule*, 1835) are illuminating. "Everything today, ideas as well as things, society as well as the individual, is in a state of twilight. What is the condition of this twilight? What will follow it? . . . Hence these cries of hope mixed with hesitation, these love-songs interrupted by groans, this serenity penetrated by sadness . . ." Many of Hugo's poems and those of his contemporaries attempt to forge a bond between man and nature, to assert that an unbroken continuum exists if only the melancholy heart of modern man is sensitive enough to discover such harmonious affinity. While nature can be all things to all men, still it is never neutral (the lake is asked to remember the once-happy lovers in Lamartine's poem). Nature's seeming indifference is personified, and cruelty or kindness are qualities a scientific universe is incapable of manifesting. To us, such a personalized vision of nature may be unacceptable, but we must recall that for many romantic writers nature was more than a refuge from urban society or

from the wounds inflicted by others. It was "the living garment of God," as Faust says— the origin of truth and knowledge, and the certainty that the universe is interfused with mind and spirit. Pantheism, in short, infects much of their verse; although as individuals with a Roman Catholic background, toward which they reacted variously, one can speculate that pantheism was less of a force for them than for their English and German fellow-romantics, most of whom were of the Protestant persuasion.

The mood of "mal du siècle" ("sickness of the century") for the generation born around 1800 has still another cause. The social disruption after 1789 created a new class of young men released from ancient and restricting social hierarchies, each one of them anxious to find the career open to his talents. The phrase reminds us of the meteoric rise of the man who seemed to prove that heroism was not dead in the modern world: Napoleon. His success, even his ultimate defeat, became a paradigm for those whose aspirations were non-military. Balzac constructed the *Human Comedy*, stating that he was completing with the pen what Napoleon had begun with the sword. Alfred de Vigny defined himself as belonging "to that generation born when the century began; which, nourished with the Emperor's bulletins, always had an unsheathed sword before its eyes." The eagles and the trumpets, alas, disappeared after Waterloo; and Hugo's poem about the battle—memorized by every French schoolboy today—incarnates all the high hopes as well as the disappointments of the age. Through Napoleon, romanticism discovered a quality—greatness and genius; or contrariwise, he proved an hypothesis already current. After his demise, the "twilight state" described by Victor Hugo a few paragraphs back—the hateful, bourgeois, unheroic present—meant two alternatives for French romantic poets. Either they could write visionary hymns to some Utopian future, or more often they could sing in an elegiac strain, where the echo, the dying fall, the suggestive horn call, the agonic moment of twilight and the setting sun all served to remind them of the past that was no more. Hence the pervading mood of melancholy.

If Hugo and Lamartine are representative of the main tradition, Nerval stands on the periphery. His translation of Goethe's *Faust* links him with German letters, and the cast of his mind—we earlier mentioned him with Novalis—seems to resemble certain German romantics, with their quests for the absolute and the infinite. Some of his writing is curious dream literature prefiguring Surrealism; his poems have long been regarded as a link between romanticism and the symbolist poets who followed—Baudelaire, Rimbaud, Mallarmé. A visionary and private mystic who tried to create a mythology capable of expressing his mysterious ideas and emotions, certain modern poets have found him a spirit akin to their own.

ITALIAN ROMANTIC VERSE: LEOPARDI

This editor has no intention of entering the critical dispute as to whether there *was* an Italian romanticism or whether such a movement was more "classical" than in other Western nations. Names like Foscolo (1778–1827), Berchet (1783–1851), Manzoni (1785–1873), and Leopardi (1798–1837) represent both partisans and detractors for certain romantic tendencies already discussed. Furthermore, the first four decades in Italy were years when intellectuals crossed party lines with baffling rapidity. Threads of nationalism, liberalism, secularism, Christian poetry, modernism, and "true" classicism were unusually entangled. But a reading of the few poems included here will reveal romantic themes of varying familiarity. For the English reader, there is a sense of a near-Wordsworthian attitude toward nature, where often emotion recollected in tranquillity, and the landscape suggestive of pains or pleasures past, provides the framework for inspiration. With Leopardi there is also a partiality for sunsets—that agonic moment, when each day seems to approach its miniature death in the oncoming night; and if not sunset, then the equally suggestive and mild illumination of the moon is evoked. Lost loves and lost illusions render Leopardi's poems pessimistic, and again we are exposed to a Mediterranean—

and perhaps more classically restrained—version of romantic melancholy, *taedium vitae* and *noia*. Leopardi also ranks as one of the greatest romantic Hellenists, and saw—as did Hölderlin before him—ancient Greece to be the model for modern aspirations.

RUSSIAN ROMANTICISM: PUSHKIN'S *EUGENE ONEGIN*

It has long been a critical commonplace to say that all the currents of the eighteenth century meet in Pushkin, and all the rivers of the nineteenth flow from him. *Eugene Onegin* is acknowledged his masterpiece, the novel in verse that took him eight years to complete (1823–1830), with a few minor touches added in 1831). The initial idea came from Byron's immensely popular *Beppo*, his *Childe Harold*, and chiefly his *Don Juan* (1819–1824). From the latter Pushkin derived the notion of a long narrative poem in regular stanzaic patterns—fourteen lines of iambic tetrameter, with carefully alternating masculine and feminine endings; a subject taken from contemporary life in society—a departure from some of Pushkin's earlier works, with their exotic historical or geographical milieus; and a tone mixing wit with seriousness, irony with lyricism. Byronic too is the hero: handsome, debonair, elegant, a "child of his century" in his frequent fits of melancholy and ennui, and his overriding contempt for the feelings of others, which then fill him—as satanic dandy and fallen angel—

with remorse and self-recrimination. The poem abounds in the same sort of digressions of which Byron was so fond—humorous, serious, lyrical, occasionally polemical. Even certain epic machinery is burlesqued and parodied (just as Byron opens Canto III of *Don Juan* with the invocation "Hail, Muse! *et caetera*"). But Pushkin's plot is far tighter, despite his admission that when he began he had no definite plan for the poem's conclusion, and there is a definite deepening of the emotions through the eight cantos. The young St. Petersburg dandy, rake, and cynic comes to know the meaning of tragedy when we arrive at what Prince D. S. Mirsky has called "the unhappy, suggestively muffled ending." The moral stature attained by Tatyana in her final rejection of Onegin (she remains the virtuous wife despite the realization of her love for him) molds her into a most un-Byronic heroine. Yet, as noted earlier, both Don Juan and Onegin share a quality of mind caught up in two of Byron's lines: "And if I laugh at any mortal thing,/ 'Tis that I may not weep." This is *Romantic irony*, or at least one aspect of that attitude: not verbal irony, where a statement means something different from what it seems to say, but the irony resulting from the individual's compartmentalizing his personality, so that the "thinking ego" watches the "feeling ego" with objectivity; and the human being, split between actor and spectator, experiences a desire to plunge into life coupled with an equally strong urge to stand apart from it. We have mentioned Horace Walpole's aphorism in another context: "The world is a comedy to those that think, a tragedy to those who feel." It is almost as if certain Romantics had discovered that the same person could do both, and would consequently be doomed to remain in a state of unstable equilibrium.

Eugene Onegin is best understood if the reader is also cognizant of a larger cultural trend in Russian literature, the dichotomy between Slavophiles and Westerners. Onegin is a Europeanized aristocrat—typically from St. Petersburg, a "French" city, and not from Moscow—infected by Western intellectualism and skepticism, and a prototype for the "useless hero" who appears in so many Russian novels in the nineteenth century. Tatyana, on the other hand, was acclaimed by Dostoevsky, in a famous *Address on Pushkin* (1880), to be the embodiment of all the Russian and Slavophile virtues, untainted by Western decadence and spiritual corruption, existing in harmonious rapport with her environment. This pattern of East versus West was to be repeated with variations by most of the major Russian writers until the Revolution in 1917, and it is testimony to Pushkin's genius that he was one of the first to seize upon its larger implications.

LIVES, WRITINGS, AND CRITICISM
Biographical and critical works are listed only if they are available in English.

JEAN-JACQUES ROUSSEAU

LIFE. Born on June 28, 1712, in Geneva, son of a watchmaker. Unhappy as an engraver's apprentice, he left home while still in his teens, and for a time lived with Mme. de Warens—the first of many female protectors. He led a peripatetic existence and held many positions: as music teacher, secretary, footman, government official under the king of Sardinia, clerk in the Bureau of Taxes in Paris (where he settled in 1745). There he lived with Thérèse le Vasseur, with whom he had five children (all deposited at an orphanage). In 1756 Mme. d'Épinay invited him to live on her estate at Montmorency. Official criticism of his books several times forced Rousseau, like Voltaire, to leave France for Switzerland; in 1766 he traveled to England as guest of the philosopher David Hume. He was permitted to return to Paris in 1770 on condition that he write nothing against government or religion. Rousseau died on July 3, 1778, at Ermenonville. His body was brought to the Pantheon in Paris in 1794, during the Revolution.

CHIEF WRITINGS. His writings fall into four categories: Works involving music: *On Modern Music* (*Dissertation sur la musique moderne*, 1743); *Letter on French Music* (*Lettre sur la musique française*, 1752); *Musical Dictionary* (*Dictionnaire de musique*, 1767); and an opera, *The Village Soothsayer* (*Le Devin du village*, 1752). Political writings: *Concerning the Origin of Inequality among Men* (*Discours sur l'origine et les fondements de l'inégalité parmi les hommes*, 1754) and *The Social Contract* (*Le Contrat social*, 1762). A book, nominally a novel, on education: *Emile* (1762). Autobiographical productions: a novel, *Julie, or the New Heloise* (*Julie, ou La Nouvelle Héloïse*, 1761); the *Confessions*, composed between 1765 and 1770, published in 1781–1788; and *Musings of a Solitary Stroller* (*Les Rêveries du promeneur solitaire*), composed between 1776 and 1778, published in 1782.

BIOGRAPHY AND CRITICISM. J. Morley, *Rousseau* (1873, revised 1886); F. Macdonald, *Rousseau* (1906); I. Babbitt, *Rousseau and Romanticism* (1919); M. B. Ellis, *Julie: A Synthesis of Rousseau's Thought* (1949); E. Cassirer, "Rousseau," in *Rousseau, Kant, Goethe* (1945): H. Höffding, *Rousseau and His*

Philosophy (1930); Frances Winwar, Jean-Jacques Rousseau: Conscience of a Era (1961); F. C. Green, Jean-Jacques Rousseau: A Critical Study of His Life and Writings (1955). Excellent is the series of essays about the author in Yale French Studies, No. 28 (1962). There are also J. Guéhenno, Jean-Jacques Rousseau (1966); W. and A. Durant, Rousseau and Revolution (1968); J. McManners, The Social Contract and Rousseau's Revolt against Society (1968); W. Blanchard, Rousseau and the Spirit of Revolt (1968); M. Einaudi, The Early Rousseau (1968).

JOHANN WOLFGANG VON GOETHE

LIFE. Born on August 28, 1749, in Frankfurt-am-Main, Germany. From 1765 to 1768 Goethe attended Leipzig University, then the center of French culture in Germany. It was at the end of that time that he met Suzanna von Klettenberg, eminent Pietist and mystic, who interested him in the theosophy of the period. At the University of Strassburg, in 1770–1771, he made the acquaintance of Gottfried Herder, leader of the new German literary movement later called the "Storm and Stress" (Sturm und Drang) movement. Herder showed the young writer the importance of Shakespeare (as opposed to the French neoclassic authors) and interested him in folk songs and in the need for an indigenous German literature. On a series of trips to Switzerland he began his scientific and philosophical studies. In 1775 Goethe moved to Weimar, and there his long friendship with the reigning duke, Karl August, began. He also received the first of several government appointments which guaranteed him financial independence. From 1786 to 1788 he took his famous Italian trip. He met the author Schiller in 1794, and their fruitful relationship was terminated only by the latter's death in 1805. Goethe married Christiane Vulpius in 1806 and subsequently legitimitized the son they had had some twelve years earlier. In 1808 occurred his meeting with Napoleon, an encounter mutually impressive; and four years later he met Beethoven. From 1823 to 1832 he was in the daily company of Johann Peter Eckermann, who was thus able to record, in his Conversations with Goethe (Gespräche mit Goethe, 1836–1848), all the commentary and criticism that Goethe's long life had accumulated. Goethe's presence made Weimar a cultural mecca for twenty years, and during that period there was scarcely a prominent European intellectual who did not come there to pay his respects. He died on March 22, 1832.

CHIEF WRITINGS. Goethe's earliest verse is in the rococo tradition of French and German eighteenth-century poetry. It was not until he was influenced by Herder—and until his many love affairs took on a more serious cast—that he achieved writing of high stature. His first great play, Götz von Berlichingen,1773), was a product of his Shakespeare studies and his enthusiasm for the preromantic "Storm and Stress" movement. About the same time, he started the first of many sketches for Faust, Part I. The Sorrows of Young Werther (Die Leiden des jungen Werthers), the short novel that inflamed the youth of Europe as did no other book before or after, was published in 1774. Goethe's increasing interest in classical literature led to the creation of such plays as Iphigenia (Iphigenie auf Tauris, 1787), and Torquato Tasso (1790) and the epic-idyll Hermann and Dorothea (Hermann und Dorothea, 1798). His two largest novels were Wilhelm Meister's Apprenticeship (Wilhelm Meisters Lehrjahre, 1795–1796), and Wilhelm Meister's Travels (Wilhelm Meisters Wanderjahre, 1821). Faust, Part I, appeared in 1808; Faust, Part II, completed in 1831, was published in 1833. Goethe's fame as a lyric poet rests on the many volumes of verse he wrote, from his first Poems (Gedichte, 1771) through the Roman Elegies (Römische Elegien, 1795); Ballads (Balladen, 1798); the enigmatic West-East Divan (Westöstlicher Diwan, 1819); and the last great Marienbad Elegies (Marienbad Elegien, 1823). His scientific writings fill several volumes. Most of Goethe's critical commentary is found in the penetrating Truth and Poetry (Dichtung und Wahrheit, 1811–1833).

BIOGRAPHY AND CRITICISM. Biographies and general studies of Goethe include A. Bielschowsky, Life of Goethe (1905–1908); K. Viëtor, Goethe the Poet(1949); E. Ludwig, Goethe(1928); B. Fairley, A Study of Goethe (1948); T. Mann, Essays of Three Decades (1947), and introduction to The Permanent Goethe (1948); A. Schweitzer, Goethe (1949); E. M. Wilkinson and L. A. Willoughby, Goethe, Poet and Thinker (1962); H. Hatfield, Goethe (1963); B. Croce, Goethe (1923); W. H. Bruford, Culture and Society in Classical Weimar (1962). For Faust, consult D. J. Enright, Commentary on Goethe's Faust (1949); F. M. Stawell and G. L. Dickinson, Goethe and Faust (1928); E. M. Butler, The Myth of the Magus (1948) and The Fortunes of Faust (1952); S. Atkins, Goethe's Faust: A Literary Analysis (1958); P. M. Palmer and R. P. More, Sources of the Faust Tradition (1910); G. Santayana, "Goethe," in Three Philosophical Poets (1910); A. Gillies, Goethe's Faust: An Interpretation (1957); R. Peacock, Goethe's Major Plays (1959); E. Mason, Goethe's Faust (1967); G. Lukacs, Goethe and His Age (1969).

FRIEDRICH HÖLDERLIN

LIFE. Born March 20, 1770, at Lauffen am Neckar. After an early Lutheran seminary education, he attended the university at Tübingen (he was a classmate of Hegel and Schelling). His studies in Greek, seventeenth- and eighteenth-century philosophy (Leibniz, Spinoza, Kant, Rousseau) and the French Revolution were strong shaping influences. His friend Schiller obtained for Hölderlin a tutor's position in 1794, in the Von Kalb family near Jena. In 1796 he became tutor for the Gontards in Frankfurt: Herr Gontard was a banker, with a much younger wife and four children. A love affair with Frau Gontard (mainly literary) resulted in the poet's departure for Homburg, where he stayed with his friend Sinclair (1798). Suzette Gontard became "Diotima," the ideal woman to whom he wrote many of his poems. His chief writing took place in the year 1799–1801. Frau Gontard died in 1802; Hölderlin subsequently spent brief periods in France and Switzerland. With Schiller's aid, he tried in vain to obtain a lectureship at Jena. In 1802 (he was then thirty-two) he returned home to his mother with definite marks of insanity. His mental health improved enough for him to become librarian for the Landgraf von Hesse-Homburg (in 1804). By 1806 his madness (probably schizophrenia) became complete, save for brief moments of sanity. For the rest of his life (thirty-seven years) he lived principally under a carpenter's care. Hölderlin died June 7, 1843.

CHIEF WRITINGS. *Hyperion, or The Hermit of Greece* (1798), a novel in poetic prose; *The Death of Empedocles* (1797–1799), an unfinished tragedy about the legendary Greek poet-prophet; miscellaneous youthful poems; then the *Odes and Hymns*—*Patmos, The Rhine, The Mother of Asia, Bread and Wine*, etc. (1799–1804). Hölderlin also translated Pindar.

BIOGRAPHY AND CRITICISM. M. Montgomery, *Hölderlin* (1923); R. Peacock, *Hölderlin* (1938); L. S. Salzourger, *Hölderlin*; M. Hamburger, *Hölderlin's Poems* (1952: translated, with a critical study); R. D. Miller, *Hölderlin* (1958); A. Stansfield, *Hölderlin* (1944); M. B. Benn, *Hölderlin and Pindar* (1962); W. Bennett, *German Verse in Classical Metres* (1963).

NOVALIS
(FRIEDRICH VON HARDENBERG)

LIFE. Born May 2, 1772, in Oberwiederstedt, Prussian Saxony, of pious Moravian parents. In 1790, Novalis (the name he used: Latin for "fallow land" or "ploughed anew") went to Jena, became interested in the German mystics (Jakob Böhme, Meister Eckhardt) and in philosophy (Kant, Schiller, Fichte, etc.). He also studied law at Leipzig and Wittenberg. In November, 1794, he met Sophie von Kühn. They became secretly engaged, but she died March 19, 1797, at the age of fifteen—to become the subject of his mystical experiences, and an ideal of eternal womanhood. A short career as a salt-mine inspector at Weisenfels marked his one venture into the

practical world, although the scientists of the day—Galvani, Mesmer, Priestley, A. G. Werner—increasingly interested him. By 1799 he belonged to the group of young intellectuals at Jena—including the Schlegel brothers, Tieck, Schelling, Fichte—associated with early German romanticism. He died of tuberculosis on March 25, 1801.

CHIEF WRITINGS. *The Apprentices of Sais* (1798) and *Heinrich von Ofterdingen* (1799–1800) were *Märchen* or philosophical fairy-tales; and the blue flower sought by the latter hero became for many romantics the symbol of infinite striving for some absolute. *Christianity or Europe* (1799) was a long essay preaching a Christian and Catholic revival. *The Hymns to the Night* (1800), inspired by Sophie von Kühn, were an effort to describe his own mystical revelations. Most of his writing was virtually unknown during his short life.

BIOGRAPHY AND CRITICISM. T. Carlyle, "Novalis" in *Essays* (1829); L. E. Wagner, *The Scientific Interest of Friedrich von Hardenberg* (1937); H. P. Spring, *Novalis* (1937); F. Hiebel, *Novalis* (1954); B. Haywood, *Novalis* (1959).

FRANÇOIS RENÉ DE CHATEAUBRIAND

LIFE. Born September 4, 1768, at Combourg, St. Malo, Brittany, to a noble family allied to both the Spanish and English ruling houses. Chateaubriand obtained a lieutenant's commission in the army, just before the Revolution in 1789. In 1791 he spent five months in North America, returning in January, 1792. He married Céleste Buisson de la Vigne. He joined the royalist, counter-Revolutionary forces, and was wounded at the battle of Valmy (1792). Chateaubriand left (May, 1793) for exile in England, where he lived as a teacher and translator. His mother died in 1798; Chateaubriand, hitherto mildly skeptical, became an ardent Catholic ("I wept and I believed"). He returned to France in 1800. The success of *The Genius of Christianity* (1802) was in part responsible for Napoleon's appointing him to two diplomatic posts, one to the Vatican. He resigned after the execution of the Duc D'Enghien, traveled extensively in Italy, Greece, and the Holy Land (1806–1807), then retired to his country estate at Aulnay. He was appointed by Louis XVIII as Minister of the Interior (1815). In 1818 he became the lover of Mme. de Recamier, who was but one of his many mistresses. He was appointed ambassador to Berlin in 1821, to London in 1822 and Foreign Minister in 1823; Charles X made him ambassador to Rome in 1828. He retired from politics when the Bourbons fell in 1830. His last years were spent writing and traveling. Chateaubriand died July 4, 1848.

CHIEF WRITINGS. *The Essay on Revolutions* was his first work: it was politically ambiguous, and at times anticlerical. *Atala* (1801) was a pilot study intended to test the future reception of *The Genius of Christianity* (1802), into which it was incorporated—the book that included *René* and *The Martyrs*. (The latter was an epic treating the early persecution of the Christians under Domitian). *An Itinerary from Paris to Jerusalem* (1811) described his travels; *Memoirs from Beyond the Grave* (published 1849–1850) was his autobiography.

BIOGRAPHY AND CRITICISM. A. Maurois, *Chateaubriand* (1938); J. Evans, *Chateaubriand* (1939); T. C. Walker, *Chateaubriand's Nature Scenery* (1946).

HEINRICH HEINE

LIFE. Born December 13, 1797, in Düsseldorf, then occupied by the French. Heine was an early admirer of Napoleon in his youth. He was brought up by his dandified father and "Rousseauian" mother; later he lived with his wealthy uncle Salomon (a banker) in Hamburg, where Heine fell in love with his cousin Amalie, the subject of *The Lyrical Intermezzo*. He went to Bonn (in 1819) to study law; he attended A. W. Schlegel's lectures, and was stimulated to write poetry. He transferred to Göttingen, from whence he was expelled for challenging an anti-Semite to a duel. In Berlin in 1821, Heine heard Hegel's lectures at the University, and became a member of the literary salon of Rahel and Varnhagen von Ense. Heine received a law degree from Göttingen in 1825, and then was "converted" to Lutheranism in order to obtain a government appointment. A brief trip to England (1827) impressed him with that nation's political freedom and "Philistinism;" he subsequently spent two years in Italy. Heine worked for a short time at his uncle's banking firm, and at about the same time became engaged in a celebrated literary quarrel with the poet, August von Platen. Disgusted by German nationalism and the increasing Jewish pogroms, he left (1831) for exile in Paris, where he undertook a career of journalism. Political affiliations with the Young German group (Börne, Herwegh, Gutzkow, Grabbe) placed Heine on the Prussian proscription list. A nostalgic trip to Germany (1843–1844) heightened his disillusionment. By 1847 Heine was an invalid, suffering from syphilitic paralysis. He married Mathilde Mirat (in 1841), who with Camille Selden ("La Mouche") cared for him during those last years spent on his "mattress grave." He died February 17, 1856.

CHIEF WRITINGS. Heine's first poems appeared in 1821, but *The Book of Songs* (1827) brought him fame as a lyric poet. Heine experimented with two Byronic dramas: *Almansor* and *Ratcliff* (1823); one unfinished novel, *The Rabbi of Bacherach*. *Travel Sketches* (1826–1831) included *The Trip Through the Harz*. His best critical writings are to be found in his *Salons* (1834–1840) and *The Romantic School* (1833). *New Poems* (1844), *Atta Troll*, a long narrative tale in verse (1847); *Romanzero* (1851) and the posthumous *Last Poems* constitute the remainder of his writing.

BIOGRAPHY AND CRITICISM. M. Arnold, "Heine," in *Essays in Criticism* (1865); W. Sharp, *Heine* (1888); H. G. Atkins, *Heine* (1929); A. Vallentin, *Poet in Exile* (1934); L. Untermeyer, *Heine* (1937); M. Brod, *Heine* (1956); E. M. Butler, *Heine* (1956); W. Rose, *Heine* (1956); B. Fairley, *Heine* (1956); S. S. Prawler,

Heine (1960); C. Brinitzer, *Heinrich Heine* (1960); S. S. Prawer, *Heine the Tragic Satirist* (1961); L. Hofrichter, *Heinrich Heine*, translated by B. Fairley (1965).

ALPHONSE DE LAMARTINE

LIFE. Born October 21, 1790, at Mâcon, Burgundy; his father was a member of the lesser nobility, imprisoned and later released during the Terror. Lamartine was schooled at Lyons, then spent four year at the Jesuit *Collège* at Belley. He served briefly (during 1814) in Louis XVIII's Royal Guard. In 1816 he met Mme. Julie Charles, with whom he had a brief, passionate love affair. During the period 1820–1830, Lamartine occupied various diplomatic posts in Italy. He married an English girl, Eliza Marianne Birch, in 1820. He was elected to the Academy in 1830, and supported the July Revolution in the same year; after an unsuccessful candidacy for the Chamber of Deputies, he traveled in the Near East, 1832–1833. He was elected to the Chamber upon his return. During the years 1839–1849, increasingly liberal in politics, he opposed both Thiers and Guizot. Lamartine was one of the leaders in the provisional government after 1848, and briefly Minister of Foreign Affairs. Increasing financial difficulties led him to sell his estate at Milly (1861); Napoleon III granted him an annuity of 25,000 francs in 1867. He died February 28, 1869.

CHIEF WRITINGS. *Poetic Meditations* (1820), *New Poetic Meditations* (1823), and *Poetic and Religious Harmonies* (1830) gave Lamartine status as a leading poet of the new Romantic school. *Jocelyn* (1836) and *The Fall of an Angel* (1838) were two attempts at creating modern epics. His other principal works are a novel, *Graziella* (1852); other volumes of poetry (1839, 1873 posthumous); travel books about the Near East (1835, 1852); histories of the Girondins, the 1848 Revolution, and the Restoration.

BIOGRAPHY AND CRITICISM. Sainte-Beuve, *Contemporary Portraits* (1870); H. R. Whitehouse, *Life of Lamartine* (1918); J. S. Schapiro, *The Poetic Temperament in Politics* (1919); A. Pirazzini, *Influence of Italy on Lamartine* (1917); A. J. George, *Lamartine and Romantic Unanimism* (1940).

VICTOR HUGO

LIFE. Born February 26, 1802, at Besançon. His mother was an ardent Royalist; his father was an officer under Napoleon, and during the period 1811–1812 became General, Count of the Empire, and Governor of Madrid. Hugo had a sporadic education in Paris after the collapse of Napoleon. He edited two journals, *The Literary Conservative* (1819) and *The French Muse* (1823–1824). He married Adèle Foucher in 1822. His poems, novels, and dramas soon made him the acknowledged leader of French romanticism. (Gautier described the opening night of *Hernani*, February 25, 1830, as "the evening which determined our whole life".) A Legitimist after the Restoration, and a supporter of Louis-

Philippe after 1830, he became a democrat after 1848, and was elected to the Constitutional Assembly. He was elected to the Academy after several defeats, in 1841. He became a Peer of France in 1845. Hugo's early admiration for "Prince-President" Louis Napoleon turned to dislike after the *coup d'état* (1851). From 1852 to 1870 Hugo went into exile in the Channel Islands (Jersey, later Guernsey), from whence he bitterly attacked "Napoleon the Little." Hugo was in Paris during the Prussian siege; he was elected deputy in the provisional government established after France fell, and was made a lifetime senator in 1876. His mistress from 1833 for over fifty years was Juliette Drouet. Hugo died May 22, 1885, and received one of Paris's greatest funerals. He was buried in the Pantheon May 31, 1885.

CHIEF WRITINGS. Hugo's *Odes* (1822), *Odes and Ballads* (1826), *Oriental Poems* (1828), *Autumn Leaves* (1831), *Twilight Songs* (1835), *Interior Voices* (1837), *Lights and Shadows* (1840) established his reputation as poet. The literary creed voiced in the *Preface to Cromwell* (1827) and his plays (*Hernani*, 1830; *Ruy Blas*, 1838) give him an important position in the history of the French stage. His most famous novels are *Notre Dame de Paris* (1831), *Les Misérables* (1862), *Toilers of the Sea* (1866), *Ninety-Three* (1879). Many more volumes of verse appeared in his later life, including two long poems composed during exile: *The Punishments* (1852), and *The Legend of the Centuries* (1856–1867).

BIOGRAPHY AND CRITICISM. A. C. Swinburne, *A Study of Victor Hugo* (1886); W. H. Hudson, *Victor Hugo and His Poetry* (1918); W. F. Giese, *Hugo* (1926); M. Josephson, *Victor Hugo* (1942); E. M. Grant, *The Career of Victor Hugo* (1945); A. Maurois, *Olympio* (1956); M. Easton, *Artists and Writers in Paris: The Bohemian Idea, 1803–1867* (1965); A. Maurois, *Victor Hugo and His World* (1966).

GÉRARD DE NERVAL

LIFE. Born May 22, 1808; he took the name "Nerval" from the *Clos de Nerval*, property belonging to his uncle's family in the Valois. His early childhood was spent in the Valois; in 1814 he went to Paris with his father, a surgeon in Napoleon's army, and was educated at the *Lycée Charlemagne*. Nerval frequented the salons where the romantics gathered, was a friend of Pétrus Borel, Philothée O'Neddy, Gautier, and Hugo; he was present at the famous opening night of Hugo's *Hernani*. He inherited a small legacy in 1834; during the same year he made his first trip to Italy, and met the English girl referred to as "Octavie." ("Sylvie" was a composite figure of women he knew during his youth in the country.) In 1835 Nerval met the actress-singer Jenny Colon ("Aurélie"), who died in 1842. His first attacks of insanity began in 1840; he was forced (in 1841) to enter a sanatorium. In 1842 he traveled in Byzantium, Egypt, Italy; in 1844 he went to Holland and Germany. He was again confined in a lunatic asylum in 1851 and 1852. Heine became a close friend after 1853. He hanged himself January 25, 1855, with an apron string he claimed to be either (a) the Queen of Sheba's garter or (b) the corset string of Mme. de Maintenon or of Marie de Valois. The final pages of *Aurélie* were in his pocket.

CHIEF WRITINGS. Nerval translated Goethe's *Faust*, Part I, in 1828. His poetry and prose were published in "little" magazines over a twenty-year period. *The Trip to the Orient* appeared in 1851; *Little Castles in Bohemia*, 1853; *Daughters of Fire*—including a series of sonnets, *Les Chimères* (*The Chimerae*)—1854; *La Bohème galante*, 1855. His two most famous tales are *Sylvie* (in *Daughters of Fire*) and *Aurélie, or The Dream and Life* (1855).

BIOGRAPHY AND CRITICISM. G. Wagner, *Selected Writings of Gérard de Nerval* (1958); B. Hill, *Gérard de Nerval, Fortune's Fool* (1959); S. A. Rhodes, *Gérard de Nerval* (1957).

COUNT GIACOMO LEOPARDI

LIFE. Born June 29, 1798, in Recanati, in Ancona—of a noble, somewhat financially impoverished family. Leopardi, who suffered from curvature of the spine and delicate health, displayed youthful precocity: he wrote a Latin treatise at sixteen, at seventeen a work citing more than four hundred classical authors; he was fluent in Latin, Greek, and Hebrew. In 1817 he experienced his first love affair: a passion for his married cousin, Countess Cassi. A long correspondence with the scholar and patriot, Abbate Pietro Giordani, increased his feeling for Italian nationalism. He went to Rome in 1822, then returned to Recanati for three unhappy years. Sojourns in Milan, Pisa, and Florence followed. By 1830 he was deaf, half-blind, and in constant pain; in that year friends subscribed enough money for him to live in Florence. They also underwrote publication of the *Canti* in 1831 (all his previously printed poems, with additions), and with this volume he soon became relatively famous throughout Europe. An unhappy attachment to a professor's wife (Fanny Tozzetti-Targioni) caused him to leave Florence for Rome and Naples, where he spent the rest of his sick life. A friend, Antonio Ranieri, and Ranieri's sister took care of the poet, who lived in a villa on the slope of Vesuvius. He died of dropsy June 15, 1837.

CHIEF WRITINGS. His major poems date in composition from 1819: chief volumes were the *Versi* (1826) and *Canti* (1831). The *Operette Morali* (1827) consisted of satirical dialogues modeled on Lucian, and a biography of an imaginary philosopher, Filippo Ottonieri. A selection of his philosophical writings appeared in 1834. *The Sequel to the Battle of Frogs and Mice* (1837) satirized the abortive Neapolitan revolution of 1820, was composed in *ottava rima*.

BIOGRAPHY AND CRITICISM. G. L. Bickersteth, *Leopardi* (1923); Sainte-Beuve, *Contemporary Portraits* (1870); I. Origo, *Leopardi* (1935; revised 1953);

J. N. Whitfield, *Leopardi* (1954) ; N. A. Robb, *Four in Exile* (1948).

ALEXANDER PUSHKIN

LIFE. Born at Moscow, June 6, 1799 (May 26, Old Style). Pushkin was a member of an old boyar family; his maternal great-grandfather was an Abyssinian general ennobled by Peter the Great. He entered the *Lyceum* (at Tzarkoe Selo, near St. Petersburg) in 1811. Upon finishing his schooling (in 1817) he was attached to the Ministry of Foreign Affairs, in a nominal position enabling him to lead the life of a dandy and man of fashion. Suspected of political liberalism, he was exiled (in 1820) to southern Russia to aid in the administration of newly founded colonies. He made his first trip to the Caucasus; in 1823 he was transferred to Odessa. Suspected of atheistic tendencies and dismissed from the service (1824), Pushkin was ordered to stay on the family estate at Mikhailovskoye, near Pskov—an exile which fortunately saved him from a more active involvement in the ill-fated Decembrist Revolution (1825). Pardoned by the new Tsar, Nicholas I, he was allowed to return to Moscow. He married Natalie Goncharov (1831), and was reappointed to the Foreign Service in 1832. Pushkin was fatally wounded in a duel with Baron George Heckeren d'Anthès. He died February 10, 1837 (January 29, Old Style).

CHIEF WRITINGS. Pushkin was an avid reader of Byron, whose work many of his pieces resemble. Early tales include *The Captive of the Caucasus* and *The Fountain of Bakhchisarai* (1822); a long poem, *The Gypsies* (1824). He wrote a Shakespearean drama, *Boris Godunov* (1825, published 1831), and the narrative poem *Poltava* (1829); he began his *History of Pugachev's Revolt in 1773* in 1834; he completed his one long novel, *The Captain's Daughter,* in 1836. His most famous short story is *The Queen of Spades* (1833). Pushkin completed *Eugene Onegin* in 1830 (it was published in 1833). This and *The Queen of Spades* were made into operas by Tchaikovsky, *Boris Godunov* by Moussorgsky, *Ruslan and Ludmilla* by Glinka, *The Golden Cockerel* by Rimsky-Korsakov.

BIOGRAPHY AND CRITICISM. Walter Arndt, *Pushkin Threefold: Narrative, Lyric, Polemic and Ribold Verse* (1972); John Bayley, *Pushkin: A Comparative Commentary* (1971); B. L. Brasol, *The Mighty Three* (1934); J. Lavrin, *Pushkin and Russian Literature* (1947); David Magarshack, *Pushkin;* D. S. Mirsky, *Pushkin* (1926); Vladimir Nabakov, *Eugene Onegin in Verse,* 4 *vols.* (1964), this is the most complete and reliable explication of *Eugene Onegin;* Henri Troyat, *Pushkin* (1970); S. H. Cross and E. J. Simmons, *Pushkin* (1937).

JEAN-JACQUES ROUSSEAU
(1712–1778)
Confessions*

Part I

BOOK I

[The Years 1712–1719.] I am commencing an undertaking, hitherto without precedent, and which will never find an imitator. I desire to set before my fellows the likeness of a man in all the truth of nature, and that man myself.

Myself alone! I know the feelings of my heart, and I know men. I am not made like any of those I have seen; I venture to believe that I am not made like any of those who are in existence. If I am not better, at least I am different. Whether Nature has acted rightly or wrongly in destroying the mould in which she cast me, can only be decided after I have been read.

Let the trumpet of the Day of Judgment sound when it will, I will present myself before the Sovereign Judge with this book in my hand. I will say boldly: "This is what I have done, what I have thought, what I was. I have told the good and the bad with equal frankness. I have neither omitted anything bad, nor interpolated anything good. If I have occasionally made use of some immaterial embellishments, this has only been in order to fill a gap caused by lack of memory. I may have assumed the truth of that which I knew might have been true, never of that which I knew to be false. I have shown myself as I was: mean and contemptible, good, high-minded and sublime, according as I was one or the other. I have unveiled my inmost self even as Thou hast seen it, O Eternal Being. Gather round me the countless host of my fellow-men; let them hear my confessions, lament for my unworthiness, and blush for my imperfections. Then let each of them in turn reveal, with the same frankness, the secrets of his heart at the foot of the Throne, and say, if he dare, '*I was better than that man!*' " . . .

I felt before I thought: this is the common lot of humanity. I experienced it more than others. I do not know what I did until I was five or six years old. I do not know how I learned to read; I only remember my earliest reading, and the effect it had upon me; from that time I date my uninterrupted self-consciousness. My mother had left some romances behind her, which my father and I began to read after supper. At first it was only a question of practising me

* Completed in 1770; published in 1781–1788. The selections reprinted here are from *The Confessions of Jean-* *Jacques Rousseau*, Everyman's Library, E. P. Dutton and Co., Inc., New York.

in reading by the aid of amusing books; but soon the interest became so lively, that we used to read in turns without stopping, and spent whole nights in this occupation. We were unable to leave off until the volume was finished. Sometimes, my father, hearing the swallows begin to twitter in the early morning, would say, quite ashamed, "Let us go to bed; I am more of a child than yourself."

In a short time I acquired, by this dangerous method, not only extreme facility in reading and understanding what I read, but a knowledge of the passions that was unique in a child of my age. I had no idea of things in themselves, although all the feelings of actual life were already known to me. I had conceived nothing, but felt everything. These confused emotions which I felt one after the other, certainly did not warp the reasoning powers which I did not as yet possess; but they shaped them in me of a peculiar stamp, and gave me odd and romantic notions of human life, of which experience and reflection have never been able wholly to cure me. . . .

How could I become wicked, when I had nothing but examples of gentleness before my eyes, and none around me but the best people in the world? My father, my aunt, my nurse, my relations, our friends, our neighbours, all who surrounded me, did not, it is true, obey me, but they loved me; and I loved them in return. My wishes were so little excited and so little opposed, that it did not occur to me to have any. I can swear that, until I served under a master, I never knew what a fancy was. Except during the time I spent in reading or writing in my father's company, or when my nurse took me for a walk, I was always with my aunt, sitting or standing by her side, watching her at her embroidery or listening to her singing; and I was content. Her cheerfulness, her gentleness and her pleasant face have stamped so deep and lively an impression on my mind that I can still see her manner, look, and attitude; I remember her affectionate language: I could describe what clothes she wore and how her head was dressed, not forgetting the two little curls of black hair on her temples, which she wore in accordance with the fashion of the time.

I am convinced that it is to her I owe the taste, or rather passion, for music, which only became fully developed in me a long time afterwards. She knew a prodigious number of tunes and songs which she used to sing in a very thin, gentle voice. This excellent woman's cheerfulness of soul banished dreaminess and melancholy from herself and all around her. The attraction which her singing possessed for me was so great, that not only have several of her songs always remained in my memory, but even now, when I have lost her, and as I grew older, many of them, totally forgotten since the days of my childhood, return to my mind with inexpressible charm. Would anyone believe that I, an old dotard, eaten up by cares and troubles, sometime find myself weeping like a child, when I mumble one of those little airs in a voice already broken and trembling?

. . . I have spent my life in idle longing, without saying a word, in the presence of those whom I loved most. Too bashful to declare my taste, I at least satisfied it in situations which had reference to it and kept up the idea of it. To lie at the feet of an imperious mistress, to obey her commands, to ask her forgiveness—this was for me a sweet enjoyment; and, the more my lively imagination heated my blood, the more I presented the appearance of a bashful lover. It may be easily imagined that this manner of making love does not lead to very speedy results, and is not very dangerous to the virtue of those who are its object. For this reason I have rarely possessed, but have none the less enjoyed myself in my own way —that is to say, in imagination. Thus it has happened that my senses, in harmony with my timid disposition and my romantic spirit, have kept my sentiments pure and my morals blameless, owing to the very tastes which, combined with a little more impudence, might have plunged me into the most brutal sensuality. . . .

I am a man of very strong passions, and, while I am stirred by them, nothing can equal my impetuosity; I forget all discretion, all feelings of respect, fear and decency; I am cynical, impudent, violent and fearless; no feeling of shame keeps me back, no danger frightens me; with the exception of the single object which occupies my thoughts, the universe is nothing to me. But all this lasts only for a moment, and the following moment plunges me into complete annihilation. In my calmer moments I am indolence and timidity itself; everything frightens and discourages me; a fly, buzzing past, alarms me; a word which I have to say, a gesture which I have to make, terrifies my idleness; fear and shame overpower me to such an extent that I would gladly hide myself from the sight of my fellow-creatures. If I have to act, I do not know what to do; if I have to speak, I do not know what to say; if anyone looks at me, I am put out of countenance. When I am strongly moved I sometimes know how to find the right words, but in ordinary conversation I can find absolutely nothing, and my condition is unbearable for the simple reason that I am obliged to speak.

Add to this, that none of my prevailing tastes centre in things that can be bought. I want nothing but unadulterated pleasures, and money poisons all. For instance, I am fond of the pleasures of the table; but, as I cannot endure either the constraint of good society or the drunkenness of the tavern, I can only enjoy them with a friend; alone, I cannot do so, for my imagination then occupies itself with other things, and eating affords me no pleasure. If my heated blood longs for women, my excited heart longs still more for affection. Women who could be bought for money would lose for me all their charms; I even doubt whether it would be in me to make use of them. I find it the same with all pleasures within my reach; unless they cost me nothing, I find them insipid. I only love those enjoyments which belong to no one but the first man who knows how to enjoy them.

. . . I worship freedom; I abhor restraint, trouble, dependence. As long as the money in my purse lasts, it assures my independence; it relieves me of the trouble of finding expedients to replenish it, a necessity which always inspired me with dread; but the fear of seeing it exhausted makes me hoard it carefully. The money which a man possesses is the instrument of freedom; that which we eagerly pursue is the instrument of slavery. Therefore I hold fast to that which I have, and desire nothing.

My disinterestedness is, therefore, nothing but idleness; the pleasure of possession is not worth the trouble of acquisition. In like manner, my extravagance is nothing but idleness; when the opportunity of spending agreeably presents itself, it cannot be too profitably employed. Money tempts me less than things, because between money and the possession of the desired object there is always an intermediary, whereas between the thing itself and the enjoyment of it there is none. If I see the thing, it tempts me; if I only see the means of gaining possession of it, it does not. For this reason I have committed thefts, and even now I sometimes pilfer trifles which tempt me, and which I prefer to take rather than to ask for; but neither when a child nor a grown-up man do I ever remember to have robbed anyone of a farthing, except on one occasion, fifteen years ago, when I stole seven *livres* ten *sous*. . . .

BOOK II

[The Years 1728–1731.] . . . I have drawn the great moral lesson, perhaps the only one of any practical value, to avoid those situations of life which bring our duties into conflict with our interests, and which show us our own advantage in the misfortunes of others; for it is certain that, in such situations, however sincere our love of virtue, we must, sooner or later, inevitably grow weak without perceiving it, and become unjust and wicked in act, without having ceased to be just and good in our hearts.

This principle, deeply imprinted on the bottom of my heart, which, although somewhat late, in practice guided my whole conduct, is one of those which have caused me to appear a very strange and foolish creature in the eyes of the world, and, above all, amongst my acquaintances. I have been reproached with wanting to pose as an original, and different from others. In reality, I have never troubled about acting like other people or differently from them. I sincerely desired to do what was right. I withdrew, as far as it lay in my power, from situations which opposed my interests to those of others, and might, consequently, inspire me with a secret, though involuntary, desire of injuring them.

. . . I loved too sincerely, too completely, I venture to say, to be able to be happy easily. Never have passions been at once more lively and purer than mine; never has love been tenderer, truer, more disinterested. I would have sacrificed my happiness a thousand times for that of the person whom I loved; her reputation was dearer to me than my life, and I would never have wished to endanger her repose for a single moment for all the pleasures of enjoyment. This feeling has made me employ such carefulness, such secrecy, and such precaution in my undertakings, that none of them have ever been successful. My want of success with women has always been caused by my excessive love for them. . . .

BOOK III

[The Years 1731–1732.] . . . I only felt the full strength of my attachment when I no longer saw her.[1] When I saw her, I was only content; but, during her absence, my restlessness became painful. The need of living with her caused me outbreaks of tenderness which often ended in tears. I shall never forget how, on the day of a great festival, while she was at vespers, I went for a walk outside the town, my heart full of her image and a burning desire to spend my life with her. I had sense enough to see that at present this was impossible, and that the happiness which I enjoyed so deeply could only be short. This gave to my reflections a tinge of melancholy, about which, however, there was nothing gloomy, and which was tempered by flattering hopes. The sound of the bells, which always singularly affects me, the song of the birds, the beauty of the daylight, the enchanting landscape, the scattered country dwellings in which my fancy placed our common home—all these produced upon me an impression so vivid, tender, melancholy and touching, that I saw myself transported, as it were, in ecstasy, into that happy time and place, wherein my heart, possessing all the happiness it could desire, tasted it with inexpressible rapture, without even a thought of sensual pleasure. I never remember to have plunged into the future with greater force and illusion than on that occasion; and what has struck me most in the recollection of this dream after it had been realised, is that I have found things again exactly as I had imagined them. If ever the dream of a man awake resembled a prophetic vision, it was assuredly that dream of mine. I was only deceived in the imaginary duration; for the days, the years, and our whole life were spent in serene and undisturbed tranquillity, whereas in reality it lasted only for a moment. Alas! my most lasting happiness belongs

1. Rousseau refers here to Mme. de Warens, whom he also calls "mamma."

to a dream, the fulfilment of which was almost immediately followed by the awakening. . . .

Two things, almost incompatible, are united in me in a manner which I am unable to understand: a very ardent temperament, lively and tumultuous passions, and, at the same time, slowly developed and confused ideas, which never present themselves until it is too late. One might say that my heart and my mind do not belong to the same person. Feeling takes possession of my soul more rapidly than a flash of lightning; but, instead of illuminating, inflames and dazzles me. I feel everything and see nothing. I am carried away by my passions, but stupid; in order to think, I must be cool. The astonishing thing is that, notwithstanding, I exhibit tolerably sound judgment, penetration, even finesse, if I am not hurried; with sufficient leisure I can compose excellent impromptus; but I have never said or done anything worthy of notice on the spur of the moment. I could carry on a very clever conversation through the post, as the Spaniards are said to carry on a game of chess. When I read of that Duke of Savoy, who turned round on his journey, in order to cry, "At your throat, Parisian huckster," I said, "There you have myself!"

This sluggishness of thought, combined with such liveliness of feeling, not only enters into my conversation, but I feel it even when alone and at work. My ideas arrange themselves in my head with almost incredible difficulty; they circulate in it with uncertain sound, and ferment till they excite and heat me, and make my heart beat fast; and, in the midst of this excitement, I see nothing clearly and am unable to write a single word—I am obliged to wait. Imperceptibly this great agitation subsides, the confusion clears up, everything takes its proper place, but slowly, and only after a period of long and confused agitation. . . .

BOOK IV

[The Years 1731–1732.] . . . I returned, not to Nyon, but to Lausanne. I wanted to sate myself with the sight of this beautiful lake, which is there seen in its greatest extent. Few of the secret motives which have determined me to act have been more rational. Things seen at a distance are rarely powerful enough to make me act. The uncertainty of the future has always made me look upon plans, which need considerable time to carry them out, as decoys for fools. I indulge in hopes like others, provided it costs me nothing to support them; but if they require continued attention, I have done with it. The least trifling pleasure which is within my reach tempts me more than the joys of Paradise. However, I make an exception of the pleasure which is followed by pain; this has no temptation for me, because I love only pure enjoyments, and these a man never has when he knows that he is preparing for himself repentance and regret. . . .

Why is it that, having found so many good people in my youth, I find so few in my later years? Is their race extinct? No; but the class in which I am obliged to look for them now, is no longer the same as that in which I found them. Among the people, where great passions only speak at intervals, the sentiments of nature make themselves more frequently heard; in the higher ranks they are absolutely stifled, and, under the mask of sentiment, it is only interest or vanity that speaks.

. . . Whenever I approach the Canton of Vaud, I am conscious of an impression in which the remembrance of Madame de Warens, who was born there, of my father who lived there, of Mademoiselle de Vulson who enjoyed the first fruits of my youthful love, of several pleasure trips which I made there when a child and, I believe, some other exciting cause, more mysterious and more powerful than all this, is combined. When the burning desire of this happy and peaceful life, which flees from me and for which I was born, inflames my imagination, it is always the Canton of Vaud, near the lake, in the midst of enchanting scenery, to which it draws me. I feel that I must have an orchard on the shore of this lake and no other, that I must have a loyal friend, a loving wife, a cow, and a little boat. I shall never enjoy perfect happiness on earth until I have all that. I laugh at the simplicity with which I have several times visited this country merely in search of this imaginary happiness. I was always surprised to find its inhabitants, especially the women, of quite a different character from that which I expected. How contradictory it appeared to me! The country and its inhabitants have never seemed to me made for each other.

During this journey to Vévay, walking along the beautiful shore, I abandoned myself to the sweetest melancholy. My heart eagerly flung itself into a thousand innocent raptures; I was filled with emotion, I sighed and wept like a child. How often have I stopped to weep to my heart's content, and, sitting on a large stone, amused myself with looking at my tears falling into the water! . . .

How greatly did the entrance into Paris belie the idea I had formed of it! The external decorations of Turin, the beauty of its streets, the symmetry and regularity of the houses, had made me look for something quite different in Paris. I had imagined to myself a city of most imposing aspect, as beautiful as it was large, where nothing was to be seen but splendid streets and palaces of gold and marble. Entering by the suburb of St. Marceau, I saw nothing but dirty and stinking little streets, ugly black houses, a general air of slovenliness and poverty, beggars, carters, menders of old clothes, criers of decoctions and old hats. All this, from the outset, struck me so forcibly, that all the real magnificence I have since seen in Paris has been unable to destroy this first impression, and I have always retained a secret dislike against residence in this capital. I may say that the whole time, during which I afterwards lived there, was employed solely in trying to find means to enable me to live away from it.

Such is the fruit of a too lively imagination, which exaggerates beyond human exaggeration, and is always ready to see more than it has been told to expect. I had heard Paris so much praised, that I had represented it to myself as the ancient Babylon, where, if I had ever visited it, I should, perhaps, have found as much to take off from the picture which I had drawn of it. The same thing happened to me at the Opera, whither I hastened to go the day after my arrival. The same thing happened to me later at Versailles; and again, when I saw the sea for the first time; and the same thing will always happen to me, when I see anything which has been too loudly announced; for it is impossible for men, and difficult for Nature herself, to surpass the exuberance of my imagination.

. . . The sight of the country, a succession of pleasant views, the open air, a good appetite, the sound health which walking gives me, the free life of the inns, the absence of all that makes me conscious of my dependent position, of all that reminds me of my condition— all this sets my soul free, gives me greater boldness of thought, throws me, so to speak, into the immensity of things, so that I can combine, select, and appropriate them at pleasure, without fear or restraint. I dispose of Nature in its entirety as its lord and master; my heart, roaming from object to object, mingles and identifies itself with those which soothe it, wraps itself up in charming fancies, and is intoxicated with delicious sensations. If, in order to render them permanent, I amuse myself by describing them by myself, what vigorous outlines, what fresh colouring, what power of expression I give them!

. . . At night I lay in the open air, and, stretched on the ground or on a bench, slept as calmly as upon a bed of roses. I remember, especially, that I spent a delightful night outside the city, on a road which ran by the side of the Rhône or Saône, I do not remember which. Raised gardens, with terraces, bordered the other side of the road. It had been very hot during the day; the evening was delightful; the dew moistened the parched grass; the night was calm, without a breath of wind; the air was fresh, without being cold; the sun, having gone down, had left in the sky red vapours, the reflection of which cast a rose-red tint upon the water; the trees on the terraces were full of nightingales answering one another. I walked on in a kind of ecstasy, abandoning my heart and senses to the enjoyment of all, only regretting, with a sigh, that I was obliged to enjoy it alone. Absorbed in my delightful reverie, I continued my walk late into the night, without noticing that I was tired. At last, I noticed it. I threw myself with a feeling of delight upon the shelf of a sort of niche or false door let into a terrace wall; the canopy of my bed was formed by the tops of trees; a nightingale was perched just over my head, and lulled me to sleep with his song; my slumbers were sweet, my awaking was still sweeter. . . .

In relating my journeys, as in making them, I do not know how to stop. My heart beat with joy when I drew near to my dear mamma, but I walked no faster. I like to walk at my ease, and to stop when I like. A wandering life is what I want. To walk through a beautiful country in fine weather, without being obliged to hurry, and with a pleasant prospect at the end, is of all kinds of life the one most suited to my taste. My idea of a beautiful country is already known. No flat country, however beautiful, has ever seemed so to my eyes. I must have mountain torrents, rocks, firs, dark forests, mountains, steep roads to climb or descend, precipices at my side to frighten me. . . .

BOOK V

[The Years 1732–1736.] . . . It is sometimes said that the sword wears out the scabbard. That is my history. My passions have made me live, and my passions have killed me. What passions? will be asked. Trifles, the most childish things in the world, which, however, excited me as much as if the possession of Helen or the throne of the universe had been at stake. In the first place—women. When I possessed one, my senses were calm; my heart, never. The needs of love devoured me in the midst of enjoyment; I had a tender mother, a dear friend; but I needed a mistress. I imagined one in her place; I represented her to myself in a thousand forms, in order to deceive myself. If I had thought that I held mamma in my arms when I embraced her, these embraces would have been no less lively, but all my desires would have been extinguished; I should have sobbed from affection, but I should never have felt any enjoyment. Enjoyment! Does this ever fall to the lot of man? If I had ever, a single time in my life, tasted all the delights of love in their fulness, I do not believe that my frail existence could have endured it; I should have died on the spot.

Thus I was burning with love, without an object; and it is this state, perhaps, that is most exhausting. I was restless, tormented by the hopeless condition of poor mamma's affairs, and her imprudent conduct, which were bound to ruin her completely at no distant date. My cruel imagination, which always anticipates misfortunes, exhibited this particular one to me continually, in all its extent and in all its results. I already saw myself compelled by want to separate from her to whom I had devoted my life, and without whom I could not enjoy it. Thus my soul was ever in a state of agitation; I was devoured alternately by desires and fears. . . .

BOOK VI

[The Year 1736.] . . . At this period commences the brief happiness of my life; here approach the peaceful, but rapid moments which have given me the right to say, *I have lived*. Precious and regretted moments! begin again for me your delightful course; and, if it be possible, pass more slowly in succession through my memory, than you did in your fugitive reality. What can I do, to prolong, as I should like, this touching and simple narrative, to repeat the same things over and over again, without wearying my readers by such repetition, any more than I was wearied of them myself, when I recommenced the life again and again? If all this consisted of facts, actions, and words, I could describe, and in a manner, give an idea of them; but how is it possible to describe what was neither said nor done, nor even thought, but enjoyed and felt, without being able to assign any other reason for my happiness than this simple feeling? I got up at sunrise, and was happy; I walked, and was happy; I saw mamma, and was happy; I left her, and was happy; I roamed the forests and hills, I wandered in the valleys, I read, I did nothing, I worked in the garden, I picked the fruit, I helped in the work of the house, and happiness followed me everywhere— happiness, which could not be referred to any definite object, but dwelt entirely within myself, and which never left me for a single instant. . . .

I should much like to know, whether the same childish ideas ever enter the hearts of other men as sometimes enter mine. In the midst of my studies, in the course of a life as blameless as a man could have led, the fear of hell still frequently troubled me. I asked myself: "In what state am I? If I were to die this moment, should I be damned?" According to my Jansenists, there was no doubt about the matter; but, according to my conscience, I thought differently. Always fearful, and a prey to cruel uncertainty, I had recourse to the most laughable expedients to escape from it, for which I would unhesitatingly have anyone locked up as a madman if I saw him doing as I did. One day, while musing upon this melancholy subject, I mechanically amused myself by throwing stones against the trunks of trees with my usual good aim, that is to say, without hardly hitting one. While engaged in this useful exercise, it occurred to me to draw a prognostic from it to calm my anxiety. I said to myself: "I will throw this stone at the tree opposite; if I hit it, I am saved; if I miss it, I am damned." While speaking, I threw my stone with a trembling hand and a terrible palpitation of the heart, but with so successful an aim that it hit the tree right in the middle, which, to tell the truth, was no very difficult feat, for I had been careful to choose a tree with a thick trunk close at hand. From that time I have never had any doubt about my salvation! When I recall this characteristic incident, I do not know whether to laugh or cry at myself. You great men, who are most certainly laughing, may congratulate yourselves; but do not mock my wretchedness, for I swear to you that I feel it deeply. . . .

Musings of a Solitary Stroller (Les Rêveries du promeneur solitaire) *

Fifth Promenade

. . . I found my existence so charming, and led a life so agreeable to my humor, that I resolved here to end my days. My only source of disquiet was whether I should be allowed to carry my project out. . . . In the midst of the presentiments that disturbed me, I would fain have had people make a perpetual prison of my refuge, to confine me in it for all the rest of my life. I longed for them to cut off all chance and all hope of leaving it; to forbid my holding any communication with the mainland, so that knowing nothing of what was going on in the world, I might have forgotten the world's existence, and people might have forgotten mine too.

They suffered me to pass only two months in the island,[1] but I could have passed two years, two centuries, and all eternity, without a moment's weariness; though I had not, with my companion,[2] any other society than that of the steward, his wife, and their servants. They were in truth honest souls and nothing more, but that was just what I wanted. . . .

Carried thither in a violent hurry, alone and without a thing, I afterwards sent for my housekeeper, my books, and my scanty possessions,—of which I had the delight of unpacking nothing,—leaving my boxes and chests just as they had come, and dwelling in the house where I counted on ending my days exactly as if it were an inn whence I must set forth on the morrow. All things went so well, just as they were, that to think of ordering them better were to spoil them. One of my greatest joys was to leave my books fastened up in their boxes, and to be without even a case for writing. When any luckless letter forced me to take up a pen for an answer,

* Written in 1776–1778; published in 1782. The passages reprinted here were written in 1777.

1. Rousseau had taken refuge in Switzerland in 1762, when the French government ordered his arrest for the publication of *Émile*. He lived on the Île de Saint-Pierre (St. Peter's Island), in the Lake of Bienne, Bern, from September through October, 1765.

2. Thérèse le Vasseur, with whom Rousseau had five children. All were raised in an orphanage.

I grumblingly borrowed the steward's inkstand, and hurried to give it back to him with all the haste I could, in the vain hope that I should never have need of the loan any more. Instead of meddling with those weary quires and reams and piles of old books, I filled my chamber with flowers and grasses; for I was then in my first fervor for botany. . . . Having given up employment that would be a task to me, I needed one that would be an amusement, nor cause me more pains than a sluggard might choose to take. I undertook to make the 'Flora Petrinsularis';[3] and to describe every single plant on the island, in detail enough to occupy me for the rest of my days. . . . In consequence of this fine scheme, every morning after breakfast, which we all took in company, I used to go with a magnifying-glass in my hand, and my 'Systema Naturae'[4] under my arm, to visit some district of the island. I had divided it for that purpose into small squares, meaning to go through them one after another in each season of the year. . . . At the end of two or three hours I used to return laden with an ample harvest,—a provision for amusing myself after dinner indoors, in case of rain. I spent the rest of the morning in going with the steward, his wife, and Thérèse, to see the laborers and the harvesting, and I generally set to work along with them: many a time when people from Berne came to see me, they found me perched on a high tree, with a bag fastened round my waist; I kept filling it with fruit, and then let it down to the ground with a rope. The exercise I had taken in the morning, and the good-humor that always comes from exercise, made the repose of dinner vastly pleasant to me. But if dinner was kept up too long, and fine weather invited me forth, I could not wait; but was speedily off to throw myself all alone into a boat, which, when the water was smooth enough, I used to pull out to the middle of the lake. There, stretched at full length in the boat's bottom, with my eyes turned up to the sky, I let myself float slowly hither and thither as the water listed, sometimes for hours together; plunged in a thousand confused delicious musings, which, though they had no fixed nor constant object, were not the less on that account a hundred times dearer to me than all that I had found sweetest in what they call the pleasures of life. Often warned by the going down of the sun that it was time to return, I found myself so far from the island that I was forced to row with all my might to get in before it was pitch dark. At other times, instead of losing myself in the midst of the waters, I had a fancy to coast along the green shores of the island, where the clear waters and cool shadows tempted me to bathe. But one of my most frequent expeditions was from the larger island to the smaller: there I disembarked and spent

3. i.e., a botanical guide to St. Peter's Island.

4. a work, published in 1735, by Linnaeus (Carl von Linné), 1708–1778, the great Swedish botanist.

my afternoon,—sometimes in limited rambles among wild elders,
persicaries,[5] willows, and shrubs of every species; sometimes settling myself on the top of a sandy knoll, covered with turf, wild
thyme, flowers, even sainfoin and trefoil that had most likely been
sown there in old days, making excellent quarters for rabbits. They
might multiply in peace without either fearing anything or harming
anything. I spoke of this to the steward. He at once had male and
female rabbits brought from Neuchâtel,[6] and we went in high state
—his wife, one of his sisters, Thérèse, and I—to settle them in the
little islet. . . . The foundation of our colony was a feast-day. The
pilot of the Argonauts[7] was not prouder than I, as I bore my company and the rabbits in triumph from our island to the smaller
one. . . .

When the lake was too rough for me to sail, I spent my afternoon in going up and down the island, gathering plants to right
and left; seating myself now in smiling lonely nooks to dream at
my ease, now on little terraces and knolls, to follow with my eyes
the superb and ravishing prospect of the lake and its shores, crowned
on one side by the neighboring hills, and on the other melting into
rich and fertile plains up to the feet of the pale-blue mountains on
their far-off edge.

As evening drew on, I used to come down from the high ground,
and sit on the beach at the water's brink in some hidden sheltering-
place. There the murmur of the waves and their agitation charmed
all my senses, and drove every other movement away from my soul:
they plunged it into delicious dreamings, in which I was often surprised by night. The flux and reflux of the water, its ceaseless stir,
swelling and falling at intervals, striking on ear and sight, made up
for the internal movements which my musings extinguished; they
were enough to give me delight in mere existence, without taking
any trouble of thinking. From time to time arose some passing
thought of the instability of the things of this world, of which the
face of the waters offered an image: but such light impressions were
swiftly effaced in the uniformity of the ceaseless motion, which
rocked me as in a cradle; it held me with such fascination that
even when called at the hour and by the signal appointed, I could
not tear myself away without summoning all my force.

After supper, when the evening was fine, we used to go all together for a saunter on the terrace, to breathe the freshness of the
air from the lake. We sat down in the arbor,—laughing, chatting, or
singing some old song,—and then we went home to bed, well pleased

5. of the genus *Persicaria;* a flower-
ing shrub.
6. in Motiers-Travers, where Rousseau lived before coming to the Lake
of Bienne. His neighbors—who looked
at him as highly suspect—broke his
windows, and he fled in fear of being
stoned.
7. those accompanying Jason on the
ship *Argo,* when that mythical Greek
hero sought the Golden Fleece.

with the day, and only craving another that should be exactly like it on the morrow. . . .

All is a continual flux upon the earth. Nothing in it keeps a form constant and determinate; our affections—fastening on external things—necessarily change and pass just as they do. Ever in front of us or behind us, they recall the past that is gone, or anticipate a future that in many a case is destined never to be. There is nothing solid to which the heart can fix itself. Here we have little more than a pleasure that comes and passes away; as for the happiness that endures, I cannot tell if it be so much as known among men. There is hardly in the midst of our liveliest delights a single instant when the heart could tell us with real truth, "*I would this instant might last forever.*"[8] And how can we give the name of happiness to a fleeting state that all the time leaves the heart unquiet and void,—that makes us regret something gone, or still long for something to come?

But if there is a state in which the soul finds a situation solid enough to comport with perfect repose, and with the expansion of its whole faculty, without need of calling back the past or pressing on towards the future; where time is nothing for it, and the present has no ending; with no mark for its own duration, and without a trace of succession; without a single other sense of privation or delight, of pleasure or pain, of desire or apprehension, than this single sense of existence,—so long as such a state endures, he who finds himself in it may talk of bliss, not with a poor, relative, and imperfect happiness such as people find in the pleasures of life, but with a happiness full, perfect, and sufficing, that leaves in the soul no conscious unfilled void. Such a state was many a day mine in my solitary musings in the isle of St. Peter, either lying in my boat as it floated on the water, or seated on the banks of the broad lake, or in other places than the little isle,—on the brink of some broad stream, or a rivulet murmuring over a gravel bed.

What is it that one enjoys in a situation like this? Nothing outside of one's self, nothing except one's self and one's own existence. . . . But most men, tossed as they are by unceasing passion, have little knowledge of such a state: they taste it imperfectly for a few moments, and then retain no more than an obscure confused idea of it, that is too weak to let them feel its charm. It would not even be good, in the present constitution of things, that in their eagerness for these gentle ecstasies, they should fall into a disgust for the active life in which their duty is prescribed to them by needs that are ever on the increase. But a wretch cut off from human society, who can do nothing here below that is useful and good

---

8. Rousseau's words foreshadow Faust's pact with Mephistopheles, in Goethe's *Faust,* Part I.

either for himself or for other people, may in such a state find for all lost human felicities many recompenses, of which neither fortune nor men can ever rob him.

It is true that these recompenses cannot be felt by all souls, nor in all situations. The heart must be in peace, nor any passion come to trouble its calm. There must be in the surrounding objects neither absolute repose nor excess of agitation; but a uniform and moderated movement, without shock, without interval. With no movement, life is only a lethargy. If the movement be unequal or too strong, it awakes us; by recalling us to the objects around, it destroys the charm of our musing, and plucks us from within ourselves, instantly to throw us back under the yoke of fortune and man, in a moment to restore us to all the consciousness of misery. Absolute stillness inclines one to gloom. It offers an image of death: then the help of a cheerful imagination is necessary, and presents itself naturally enough to those whom Heaven has endowed with such a gift. The movement which does not come from without then stirs within us. The repose is less complete, it is true; but it is also more agreeable when light and gentle ideas, without agitating the depths of the soul, only softly skim the surface. This sort of musing we may taste whenever there is tranquillity about us; and I have thought that in the Bastille,[9] and even in a dungeon where no object struck my sight, I could have dreamed away many a thrice pleasurable day.

But it must be said that all this came better and more happily in a fruitful and lonely island, where nothing presented itself to me save smiling pictures, where nothing recalled saddening memories, where the fellowship of the few dwellers there was gentle and obliging, without being exciting enough to busy me incessantly; where, in short, I was free to surrender myself all day long to the promptings of my taste or to the most luxurious indolence. . . . As I came out from a long and most sweet musing fit, seeing myself surrounded by verdure and flowers and birds, and letting my eyes wander far over romantic shores that fringed a wide expanse of water bright as crystal, I fitted all these attractive objects into my dreams; and when at last I slowly recovered myself, and recognized what was about me, I could not mark the point that cut off dream from reality, so equally did all things unite to endear to me the lonely retired life I led in this happy spot! Why can that life not come back to me again? Why can I not go finish my days in the beloved island, never to quit it, never again to see in it one dweller from the mainland, to bring back to me the memory of all the woes of every sort that they have delighted in heaping on my head for all these long years? . . . Freed from the earthly passions engen-

9. the famous prison in Paris, destroyed on July 14, 1789, which stood as a symbol of the tyranny of the *ancien régime*.

dered by the tumult of social life, my soul would many a time lift itself above this atmosphere, and commune beforehand with the heavenly intelligences, into whose number it trusts to be ere long taken. . . .

JOHANN WOLFGANG VON GOETHE
(1749–1832)
Faust*

Prologue in Heaven[a]

The LORD. The HEAVENLY HOSTS. MEPHISTOPHELES[b] *following.*

[*The* THREE ARCHANGELS *step forward.*]

RAPHAEL. The chanting sun, as ever, rivals
    The chanting of his brother spheres
    And marches round his destined circuit—
    A march that thunders in our ears.
    His aspect cheers the Hosts of Heaven   5
    Though what his essence none can say;
    These inconceivable creations
    Keep the high state of their first day.
GABRIEL. And swift, with inconceivable swiftness,
    The earth's full splendour rolls around,   10
    Celestial radiance alternating
    With a dread night too deep to sound;
    The sea against the rocks' deep bases
    Comes foaming up in far-flung force,
    And rock and sea go whirling onward   15
    In the swift spheres' eternal course.
MICHAEL. And storms in rivalry are raging
    From sea to land, from land to sea,
    In frenzy forge the world a girdle
    From which no inmost part is free.   20
    The blight of lightning flaming yonder
    Marks where the thunder-bolt will play;
    And yet Thine envoys, Lord, revere

* From *Goethe's Faust*, translated by Louis MacNeice. Copyright 1951 by Louis MacNeice. Reprinted by permission of Oxford University Press, Inc. Part I was first published in 1808. Goethe's Dedication and the Prologue at the Theater have not been included, since neither is part of the play itself. All of Part I, except for a few minor omissions made by the translator (in-dicated in the footnotes), is reprinted here.

a. probably written in 1798. The scene is patterned on Job 1:6–12 and 2:1–6.

b. The origin of the name is still debatable. It may come from Hebrew, Persian, or Greek, with such meanings as "destroyer-liar," "no friend of Faust," "no friend of light."

The gentle movement of Thy day.

CHOIR OF ANGELS. Thine aspect cheers the Hosts of Heaven   25
   Though what Thine essence none can say,
         And all Thy loftiest creations
         Keep the high state of their first day.
   [*Enter* MEPHISTOPHELES.]

MEPHISTOPHELES. Since you, O Lord, once more approach and ask
   If business down with us be light or heavy—   30
   And in the past you've usually welcomed me—
   That's why you see me also at your levee.
   Excuse me, I can't manage lofty words—
   Not though your whole court jeer and find me low;
   My pathos certainly would make you laugh   35
   Had you not left off laughing long ago.
   Your suns and worlds mean nothing much to me;
   How men torment themselves, that's all I see.
   The little god of the world, one can't reshape, reshade him;
   He is as strange to-day as that first day you made him.   40
   His life would be not so bad, not quite,
   Had you not granted him a gleam of Heaven's light;
   He calls it Reason, uses it not the least
   Except to be more beastly than any beast.
   He seems to me—if your Honour does not mind—   45
   Like a grasshopper—the long-legged kind—
   That's always in flight and leaps as it flies along
   And then in the grass strikes up its same old song.
   I could only wish he confined himself to the grass!
   He thrusts his nose into every filth, alas.   50

LORD. Mephistopheles, have you no other news?
   Do you always come here to accuse?
   Is nothing ever right in your eyes on earth?

MEPHISTOPHELES. No, Lord! I find things there as downright bad
      as ever.
   I am sorry for men's days of dread and dearth;   55
   Poor things, *my* wish to plague 'em isn't fervent.

LORD. Do you know Faust?

MEPHISTOPHELES.   The Doctor?

LORD.   Aye, my servant.

MEPHISTOPHELES. Indeed! He serves you oddly enough, I think.   60
   The fool has no earthly habits in meat and drink.
   The ferment in him drives him wide and far,
   That he is mad he too has almost guessed;
   He demands of heaven each fairest star

---

58. *Doctor:* i.e., doctor of philosophy.
60. *you:* In the German text, Mephistopheles shifts from *du* to *ihr*, indicating his lack of respect for God.

And of earth each highest joy and best,   65
And all that is new and all that is far
Can bring no calm to the deep-sea swell of his breast.

LORD. Now he may serve me only gropingly,
Soon I shall lead him into the light.
The gardener knows when the sapling first turns green   70
That flowers and fruit will make the future bright.

MEPHISTOPHELES. What do you wager? You will lose him yet,
Provided *you* give *me* permission
To steer him gently the course I set.

LORD. So long as he walks the earth alive,   75
So long you may try what enters your head;
Men make mistakes as long as they strive.

MEPHISTOPHELES. I thank you for that; as regards the dead,
The dead have never taken my fancy.
I favour cheeks that are full and rosy-red;   80
No corpse is welcome to my house;
I work as the cat does with the mouse.

LORD. Very well; you have my permission.
Divert this soul from its primal source
And carry it, if you can seize it,   85
Down with you upon your course—
And stand ashamed when you must needs admit:
A good man with his groping intuitions
Still knows the path that is true and fit.

MEPHISTOPHELES. All right—but it won't last for long.   90
I'm not afraid my bet will turn out wrong.
And, if my aim prove true and strong,
Allow me to triumph wholeheartedly.
Dust shall he eat—and greedily—
Like my cousin the Snake renowned in tale and song.   95

LORD. That too you are free to give a trial;
I have never hated the likes of you.
Of all the spirits of denial
The joker is the last that I eschew.
Man finds relaxation too attractive—   100
Too fond too soon of unconditional rest;
Which is why I am pleased to give him a companion
Who lures and thrusts and must, as devil, be active.
But ye, true sons of Heaven, it is your duty
To take your joy in the living wealth of beauty.   105
The changing Essence which ever works and lives
Wall you around with love, serene, secure!
And that which floats in flickering appearance

95. *Snake:* the serpent in Genesis, who tempted Adam and Eve.

Fix ye it firm in thoughts that must endure.
CHOIR OF ANGELS. Thine aspect cheers the Hosts of Heaven   110
    Though what Thine essence none can say,
    And all Thy loftiest creations
    Keep the high state of their first day.
    [*Heaven closes.*]
MEPHISTOPHELES. [*Alone*] I like to see the Old One now and then
    And try to keep relations on the level.   115
    It's really decent of so great a person
    To talk so humanely even to the Devil.

The First Part of the Tragedy

NIGHT

In a high-vaulted narrow Gothic room FAUST, *restless, in a chair
at his desk.*

FAUST. Here stand I, ach, Philosophy
    Behind me and Law and Medicine too
    And, to my cost, Theology—
    All these I have sweated through and through
    And now you see me a poor fool   5
    As wise as when I entered school!
    They call me Master, they call me Doctor,
    Ten years now I have dragged my college
    Along by the nose through zig and zag
    Through up and down and round and round   10
    And this is all that I have found—
    The impossibility of knowledge!
    It is this that burns away my heart;
    Of course I am cleverer than the quacks,
    Than master and doctor, than clerk and priest,   15
    I suffer no scruple or doubt in the least,
    I have no qualms about devil or burning,
    Which is just why all joy is torn from me,
    I cannot presume to make use of my learning,
    I cannot presume I could open my mind   20
    To proselytize and improve mankind.

    Besides, I have neither goods nor gold,
    Neither reputation nor rank in the world;
    No dog would choose to continue so!
    Which is why I have given myself to Magic   25
    To see if the Spirit may grant me to know
    Through its force and its voice full many a secret,

May spare the sour sweat that I used to pour out
In talking of what I know nothing about,
May grant me to learn what it is that girds   30
The world together in its inmost being,
That the seeing its whole germination, the seeing
Its workings, may end my traffic in words.

O couldst thou, light of the full moon,
Look now thy last upon my pain,   35
Thou for whom I have sat belated
So many midnights here and waited
Till, over books and papers, thou
Didst shine, sad friend, upon my brow!
O could I but walk to and fro   40
On mountain heights in thy dear glow
Or float with spirits round mountain eyries
Or weave through fields thy glances glean
And freed from all miasmal theories
Bathe in thy dew and wash me clean!   45

Oh! Am I still stuck in this jail?
This God-damned dreary hole in the wall
Where even the lovely light of heaven
Breaks wanly through the painted panes!
Cooped up among these heaps of books   50
Gnawed by worms, coated with dust,
Round which to the top of the Gothic vault
A smoke-stained paper forms a crust.
Retorts and canisters lie pell-mell
And pyramids of instruments,   55
The junk of centuries, dense and mat—
Your world, man! World? They call it that!

And yet you ask why your poor heart
Cramped in your breast should feel such fear,
Why an unspecified misery   60
Should throw your life so out of gear?
Instead of the living natural world
For which God made all men his sons
You hold a reeking mouldering court
Among assorted skeletons.   65

Away! There is a world outside!
And this one book of mystic art
Which Nostradamus wrote himself,

---

68. *Nostradamus:* Latin name of the   lection of rhymed prophecies, *The Cen-*
French astrologer and physician Michel   *turies,* appeared in 1555.
de Notredame, born in 1503. His col-

Is this not adequate guard and guide?
By this you can tell the course of the stars,   70
By this, once Nature gives the word,
The soul begins to stir and dawn,
A spirit by a spirit heard.
In vain your barren studies here
Construe the signs of sanctity.   75
You Spirits, you are hovering near;
If you can hear me, answer me!
    [*He opens the book and perceives the sign of the Macrocosm.*[a]]

Ha! What a river of wonder at this vision
Bursts upon all my senses in one flood!
And I feel young, the holy joy of life   80
Glows new, flows fresh, through nerve and blood!
Was it a god designed this hieroglyph to calm
The storm which but now raged inside me,
To pour upon my heart such balm,
And by some secret urge to guide me   85
Where all the powers of Nature stand unveiled around me?
Am I a God? It grows so light!
And through the clear-cut symbol on this page
My soul comes face to face with all creating Nature.
At last I understand the dictum of the sage: 90
'The spiritual world is always open,
Your mind is closed, your heart is dead;
Rise, young man, and plunge undaunted
Your earthly breast in the morning red.'
    [*He contemplates the sign.*]

Into one Whole how all things blend,   95
Function and live within each other!
Passing gold buckets to each other
How heavenly powers ascend, descend!
The odour of grace upon their wings,
They thrust from heaven through earthly things   100
And as all sing so *the* All sings!

What a fine show! Aye, but only a show!
Infinite Nature, where can I tap thy veins?
Where are thy breasts, those well-springs of all life
On which hang heaven and earth,   105
Towards which my dry breast strains?
They well up, they give drink, but I feel drought and dearth.

a. literally, "the great world"; the universe as a whole.

[*He turns the pages and perceives the sign of the* EARTH
SPIRIT.]

How differently this new sign works upon me!
Thy sign, thou Spirit of the Earth, 'tis thine
And thou art nearer to me.   110
At once I feel my powers unfurled,
At once I glow as from new wine
And feel inspired to venture into the world,
To cope with the fortunes of earth benign or malign,
To enter the ring with the storm, to grapple and clinch,   115
To enter the jaws of the shipwreck and never flinch.
Over me comes a mist,
The moon muffles her light,
The lamp goes dark.
The air goes damp. Red beams flash   120
Around my head. There blows
A kind of a shudder down from the vault
And seizes on me.
It is thou must be hovering round me, come at my prayers!
Spirit, unveil thyself!   125
My heart, oh my heart, how it tears!
And how each and all of my senses
Seem burrowing upwards towards new light, new breath!
I feel my heart has surrendered, I have no more defences.
Come then! Come! Even if it prove my death!   130
    [*He seizes the book and solemnly pronounces the sign of the*
    EARTH SPIRIT. *There is a flash of red flame and the* SPIRIT
    appears in it.]
SPIRIT. Who calls upon me?
FAUST. Appalling vision!
SPIRIT. You have long been sucking at my sphere,
    Now by main force you have drawn me here
    And now—   135
FAUST. No! Not to be endured!
SPIRIT. With prayers and with pantings you have procured
    The sight of my face and the sound of my voice—
    Now I am here. What a pitiable shivering
    Seizes the Superman. Where is the call of your soul?   140
    Where the breast which created a world in itself
    And carried and fostered it, swelling up, joyfully quivering,
    Raising itself to a level with Us, the Spirits?
    Where are you, Faust, whose voice rang out to me,

109. *Spirit of the Earth:* The Mac-
rocosm represented the ordered, harmonious universe in its totality; this
figure seems to be a symbol for the
energy of terrestrial nature—neither
good nor bad, merely powerful.

Who with every nerve so thrust yourself upon me?   145
Are you the thing that at a whiff of my breath
Trembles throughout its living frame,
A poor worm crawling off, askance, askew?
FAUST. Shall I yield to Thee, Thou shape of flame?
I am Faust, I can hold my own with Thee.   150
SPIRIT. In the floods of life, in the storm of work,
   In ebb and flow,
   In warp and weft,
   Cradle and grave,
   An eternal sea,   155
   A changing patchwork,
   A glowing life,
   At the whirring loom of Time I weave
   The living clothes of the Deity.
FAUST. Thou who dost rove the wide world round,   160
   Busy Spirit, how near I feel to Thee!
SPIRIT. You are like that Spirit which you can grasp,
   Not me!
      [*The* SPIRIT *vanishes.*]
FAUST. Not Thee!
   Whom then?   165
   I who am Godhead's image,
   Am I not even like Thee!
      [*A knocking on the door.*]
   Death! I know who that is. My assistant!
   So ends my happiest, fairest hour.
   The crawling pedant must interrupt   170
   My visions at their fullest flower!
      [WAGNER *enters in dressing-gown and nightcap, a lamp in his hand.*]
WAGNER. Excuse me but I heard your voice declaiming—
   A passage doubtless from those old Greek plays.
   That is an art from which I would gladly profit,
   It has its advantages nowadays.   175
   And I've often heard folks say it's true
   A preacher can learn something from an actor.
FAUST. Yes, when the preacher is an actor too;
   Which is a not uncommon factor.
WAGNER. Ah, when your study binds up your whole existence 180
   And you scarcely can see the world on a holiday
   Or through a spyglass—and always from a distance—
   How can your rhetoric make it walk your way?
FAUST. Unless you feel it, you cannot gallop it down,
   Unless it thrust up from your soul   185

Forcing the hearts of all your audience
With a primal joy beyond control.
Sit there for ever with scissors and paste!
Gather men's leavings for a rehash
And blow up a little paltry flicker   190
Out of your own little heap of ash!
It will win you claps from apes and toddlers—
Supposing your palate welcome such—
But heart can never awaken a spark in heart
Unless your own heart keep in touch.   195

WAGNER. However, it is the delivery wins all ears
And I know that I am still far, too far, in arrears.

FAUST. Win your effects by honest means,
Eschew the cap and bells of the fool!
True insight and true sense will make   200
Their point without the rhetoric school
And, given a thought that must be heard,
Is there such need to chase a word?
Yes, your so glittering purple patches
In which you make cat's cradles of humanity   205
Are like the foggy wind which whispers in the autumn
Through barren leaves—a fruitless vanity.

WAGNER. Ah God, we know that art
Is long and short our life!
Often enough my analytical labours   210
Pester both brain and heart.
How hard it is to attain the means
By which one climbs to the fountain head;
Before a poor devil can reach the halfway house,
Like as not he is dead.   215

FAUST. Your manuscript, is that your holy well
A draught of which for ever quenches thirst?
You have achieved no true refreshment
Unless you can tap your own soul first.

WAGNER. Excuse me—it is considerable gratification   220
To transport oneself into the spirit of times past,
To observe what a wise man thought before our days
And how we now have brought his ideas to consummation.

FAUST. Oh yes, consummated in heaven!
There is a book, my friend, and its seals are seven—   225
The times that have been put on the shelf.
Your so-called spirit of such times
Is at bottom merely the spirit of the gentry

225. *its seals are seven:* See Revelation 5:1.

In whom each time reflects itself,
And at that it often makes one weep 230
And at the first glance run away,
A lumber-room and a rubbish heap,
At best an heroic puppet play
With excellent pragmatical Buts and Yets
Such as are suitable to marionettes. 235
WAGNER. And yet the world! The heart and spirit of men!
We all would wish to understand the same.
FAUST. Yes, what is known as understanding—
But who dare call the child by his real name?
The few who have known anything about it, 240
Whose hearts unwisely overbrimmed and spake,
Who showed the mob their feelings and their visions,
Have ended on the cross or at the stake.
My friend, I beg you, the night is now far gone;
We must break off for this occasion. 245
WAGNER. I'd have been happy sitting on and on
To continue such a learned conversation.
To-morrow however, as it is Easter Day,
I shall put you some further questions if I may.
Having given myself to knowledge heart and soul 250
I have a good share of it, now I would like the whole.
        [*Exit* WAGNER.]
FAUST. [*Alone*] To think this head should still bring hope to
        birth
Sticking like glue to hackneyed rags and tags,
Delving with greedy hand for treasure
And glad when it finds an earthworm in the earth! 255

That such a human voice should here intrude
Where spiritual fulness only now enclosed me!
And yet, my God, you poorest of all the sons
Of earth, this time you have earned my gratitude.
For you have snatched me away from that despair 260
Which was ripe and ready to destroy my mind;
Beside that gigantic vision I could not find
My normal self; only a dwarf was there.

I, image of the Godhead, who deemed myself but now
On the brink of the mirror of eternal truth and seeing 265
My rapturous fill of the blaze of clearest Heaven,
Having stripped off my earthly being;
I, more than an angel, I whose boundless urge
To flow through Nature's veins and in the act of creation

To revel it like the gods—what a divination,   270
What an act of daring—and what an expiation!
One thundering word has swept me over the verge.

To boast myself thine equal I do not dare.
Granted I owned the power to draw thee down,
I lacked the power to hold thee there.   275
In that blest moment I felt myself,
Felt myself so small, so great;
Cruelly thou didst thrust me back
Into man's uncertain fate.
Who will teach me? What must I shun?   280
Or must I go where that impulse drives?
Alas, our very actions like our sufferings
Put a brake upon our lives.
Upon the highest concepts of the mind
There grows an alien and more alien mould;   285
When we have reached what in this world is good
That which is better is labelled a fraud, a blind.
What gave us life, feelings of highest worth,
Go dead amidst the madding crowds of earth.

Where once Imagination on daring wing   290
Reached out to the Eternal, full of hope,
Now, that the eddies of time have shipwrecked chance on chance,
She is contented with a narrow scope.
Care makes her nest forthwith in the heart's deep places,
And there contrives her secret sorrows,   295
Rocks herself restlessly, destroying rest and joy;
And always she is putting on new faces,
Will appear as your home, as those that you love within it,
As fire or water, poison or steel;
You tremble at every blow that you do not feel   300
And what you never lose you must weep for every minute.

I am not like the gods—that I too deeply feel—
No, I am like the worm that burrows through the dust
Which, as it keeps itself alive in the dust,
Is annulled and buried by some casual heel.   305

Is it not dust that on a thousand shelves
Narrows this high wall round me so?
The junk that with its thousandfold tawdriness
In this moth world keeps me so low?
Shall I find here what I require?   310
Read maybe in a thousand books how men
Have in the general run tortured themselves,

With but a lucky one now and then?
Why do you grin at me, you hollow skull?
To point out that your brain was once, like mine, confused   315
And looked for the easy day but in the difficult dusk,
Lusting for truth was led astray and abused?
You instruments, I know you are mocking me
With cog and crank and cylinder.
I stood at the door, you were to be the key;   320
A key with intricate wards—but the bolt declines to stir.
Mysterious in the light of day
Nature lets none unveil her; if she refuse
To make some revelation to your spirit
You cannot force her with levers and with screws.   325
You ancient gear I have never used, it is only
Because my father used you that I retain you.
You ancient scroll, you have been turning black
Since first the dim lamp smoked upon this desk to stain you.
Far better to have squandered the little I have   330
Than loaded with that little to stay sweating here.
Whatever legacy your fathers left you,
To own it you must earn it dear.
The thing that you fail to use is a load of lead;
The moment can only use what the moment itself has bred.   335

But why do my eyes fasten upon that spot?
Is that little bottle a magnet to my sight?
Why do I feel of a sudden this lovely illumination
As when the moon flows round us in a dark wood at night?

Bottle, unique little bottle, I salute you   340
As now I devoutly lift you down. In you
I honour human invention and human skill.
You, the quintessence of all sweet narcotics,
The extract of all rare and deadly powers,
I am your master—show me your good will!   345
I look on you, my sorrow is mitigated,
I hold you and my struggles are abated,
The flood-tide of my spirit ebbs away, away.
The mirroring waters glitter at my feet,
I am escorted forth on the high seas,   350
Allured towards new shores by a new day.
A fiery chariot floats on nimble wings
Down to me and I feel myself upbuoyed
To blaze a new trail through the upper air

326–327. *gear . . . father:* Later we find that Faust's father was a doctor of medicine.

Into new spheres of energy unalloyed.   355
Oh this high life, this heavenly rapture! Do *you*
Merit this, you, a moment ago a worm?
Merit it? Aye—only turn your back on the sun
Which enchants the earth, turn your back and be firm!
And brace yourself to tear asunder the gates   360
Which everyone longs to shuffle past if he can;
Now is the time to act and acting prove
That God's height need not lower the merit of Man;
Nor tremble at that dark pit in which our fancy
Condemns itself to torments of its own framing,   365
But struggle on and upwards to that passage
At the narrow mouth of which all hell is flaming.
Be calm and take this step, though you should fall
Beyond it into nothing—nothing at all.

And you, you loving-cup of shining crystal—   370
I have not given a thought to you for years—
Down you come now out of your ancient chest!
You glittered at my ancestors' junketings
Enlivening the serious guest
When with you in his hand he proceeded to toast his neigh-
    bour—   375
But to-day no neighbour will take you from my hand.
Here is a juice that makes one drunk in a wink;
It fills you full, you cup, with its brown flood.
It was I who made this, I who had it drawn;
So let my whole soul now make my last drink   380
A high and gala greeting, a toast to the dawn!
    [*He raises the cup to his mouth. There is an outburst of*
    bells and choirs.]
CHORUS OF ANGELS. Christ is arisen!
                  Joy to mortality
                  Whom its own fatally
                  Earth-bound mortality   385
                  Bound in a prison.
FAUST. What a deep booming, what a ringing tone
Pulls back the cup from my lips—and with such power!
So soon are you announcing, you deep bells,
Easter Day's first festive hour?   390
You choirs, do you raise so soon the solacing hymn
That once round the night of the grave rang out from the
    seraphim

---

381. *dawn:* See l. 248.   an old medieval Easter hymn, freely
382. *Christ is arisen!:* first line of adapted by Goethe.

As man's new covenant and dower?

CHORUS OF WOMEN. With balm and with spices
'Twas we laid him out,   395
We who tended him,
Faithful, devout;
We wound him in linen,
Made all clean where he lay,
Alas—to discover   400
Christ gone away.

CHORUS OF ANGELS. Christ is arisen!
The loving one! Blest
After enduring the
Grievous, the curing, the   405
Chastening test.

FAUST. You heavenly music, strong as you are kind,
Why do you search me out in the dust?
Better ring forth where men have open hearts!
I hear your message, my faith it is that lags behind;   410
And miracle is the favourite child of faith.
Those spheres whence peals the gospel of forgiving,
Those are beyond what I can dare,
And yet, so used am I from childhood to this sound,
It even now summons me back to living.   415
Once I could feel the kiss of heavenly love
Rain down through the calm and solemn Sabbath air,
Could find a prophecy in the full-toned bell,
A spasm of happiness in a prayer.
An ineffably sweet longing bound me   420
To quest at random through field and wood
Where among countless burning tears
I felt a world rise up around me.
This hymn announced the lively games of youth, the lovely
Freedom of Spring's own festival;   425
Now with its childlike feelings memory holds me back
From the last and gravest step of all.
But you, sweet songs of heaven, keep sounding forth!
My tears well up, I belong once more to earth.

CHORUS OF DISCIPLES. Now has the Buried One,   430
Lowliness ended,
Living in lordliness,
Lordly ascended;
He in the zest of birth

394–401. *With balm . . . away:* Goethe makes free use of the New Testament here. None of the Evangelists says that Christ was laid in the tomb by women. According to Mark and Luke, they came on the third day *intending* to anoint the body, but He was gone from the tomb.

Near to creating light; 435
We on the breast of earth
Still in frustrating night!
He left us, his own ones,
Pining upon this spot,
Ah, and lamenting, 440
Master, thy lot.

CHORUS OF ANGELS. Christ is arisen
From the womb of decay!
Burst from your prison,
Rejoice in the day! 445
Praising him actively,
Practising charity,
Giving alms brotherly,
Preaching him wanderingly,
Promising sanctity, 450
You have your Master near,
You have him here!

EASTER HOLIDAY

Holidaymakers of all kinds come out through the city gate.[a]

FIRST STUDENT. Lord, these strapping wenches they go a lick!
Hurry up, brother, we must give 'em an escort.
My programme for to-day is a strong ale,
A pipe of shag and a girl who's got up chic.
FIRST GIRL. Look! Will you look at the handsome boys! 5
Really and truly its degrading;
They could walk out with the best of us
And they have to run round scullery-maiding!
SECOND STUDENT. Hold on, hold on! There are two coming up
behind
With a very pretty taste in dress; 10
One of those girls is a neighbour of mine,
She appeals to me, I must confess.
You see how quietly they go
And yet in the end they'll be taking *us* in tow.
BEGGAR. [*Singing*] Good gentlemen and lovely ladies, 15
Rosy of cheek and neat of dress,
Be kind enough to look upon me
And see and comfort my distress.
Leave me not here a hopeless busker!

a. It has been shown that Goethe had Frankfurt-am-Main in mind for this scene, and the "gate" referred to is the Sachsenhausen Tor, or Affenthor. The translator omits a few lines here which include other local references—to a hunting lodge, or *Forsthaus*, two miles southwest of the gate; to an inn called the Gerbermühle on the Main River; and to a village, probably Oberrad.

Only the giver can be gay.   20
A day when all the town rejoices,
Make it for me a harvest day.

FIRST BURGHER. I know nothing better on Sundays or on holidays
Than to have a chat about war and warlike pother
When far away, in Turkey say,   25
The peoples are socking one another.
One stands at the window, drinks one's half of mild,
And sees the painted ships glide down the waterways;
Then in the evening one goes happily home
And blesses peace and peaceful days.   30

SECOND BURGHER. Yes indeed, neighbour! That is all right with me.
They can break heads if they like it so
And churn up everything topsyturvy.
But at home let us keep the status quo.

OLD WOMAN. Eh, but how smart they look! Pretty young things!   35
Whoever saw you should adore you!
But not so haughty! It's all right—
Tell me your wish and I can get it for you.

FIRST GIRL. Come, Agatha! Such witches I avoid
In public places—it's much wiser really;   40
It's true, she helped me on St. Andrew's night
To see my future sweetheart clearly.

SECOND GIRL. Yes, mine she showed me in a crystal,
A soldier type with dashing chaps behind him;
I look around, I seek him everywhere   45
And yet—and yet I never find him.

SOLDIERS. [*Singing*] Castles with towering
                      Walls to maintain them,
                      Girls who have suitors
                      But to disdain them,
                      Would I could gain them!   50
                      Bold is the venture,
                      Lordly the pay.

                      Hark to the trumpets!
                      They may be crying   55
                      Summons to gladness,
                      Summons to dying.
                      Life is a storming!
                      Life is a splendour!
                      Maidens and castles   60
                      Have to surrender.

---

41. *St. Andrew's night:* Actually, St. Andrew's eve, November 29. This was the traditional time for young girls to consult fortunetellers about their future lovers or husbands.

Bold is the venture,
Lordly the pay;
Later the soldiers
Go marching away.   65

[FAUST *and* WAGNER *are now walking off on the road to the
village.*]

FAUST. River and brook are freed from ice
By the lovely enlivening glance of spring
And hope grows green throughout the dale;
Ancient winter, weakening,
Has fallen back on the rugged mountains   70
And launches thence his Parthian shafts
Which are merely impotent showers of hail
Streaking over the greening mead;
But the sun who tolerates nothing white
Amidst all this shaping and stirring of seed,   75
Wants to enliven the world with colour
And, flowers being lacking, in their lieu
Takes colourful crowds to mend the view.
Turn round and look back from this rise
Towards the town. From the gloomy gate   80
Look, can you see them surging forth—
A harlequin-coloured crowd in fête!
Sunning themselves with one accord
In homage to the risen Lord
For they themselves to-day have risen: 85
Out of the dismal room in the slum,
Out of each shop and factory prison,
Out of the stuffiness of the garret,
Out of the squash of the narrow streets,
Out of the churches' reverend night—   90
One and all have been raised to light.
Look, only look, how quickly the gardens
And fields are sprinkled with the throng,
How the river all its length and breadth
Bears so many pleasure-boats along,   95
And almost sinking from its load
How this last dinghy moves away.
Even on the furthest mountain tracks
Gay rags continue to look gay.
Already I hear the hum of the village,   100
Here is the plain man's real heaven—
Great and small in a riot of fun;
Here I'm a man—and dare be one.

WAGNER. Doctor, to take a walk with you
    Is a profit and a privilege for me   105
    But I wouldn't lose my way alone round here,
    Sworn foe that I am of all vulgarity.
    This fiddling, screaming, skittle-playing,
    Are sounds I loathe beyond all measure;
    They run amuck as if the devil were in them   110
    And call it music, call it pleasure.
        [*They have now reached the village.*]
OLD PEASANT. Doctor, it is most good of you
    Not to look down on us to-day
    And, pillar of learning that you are,
    To mill around with folk at play.   115
    So take this most particular jug
    Which we have filled for you at the tap,
    This is a pledge and I pray aloud
    That it quench your thirst and more mayhap:
    As many drops as this can give,   120
    So many days extra may you live.
FAUST. Thank you for such a reviving beer
    And now—good health to all men here.
        [*The people collect round him.*]
OLD PEASANT. Of a truth, Doctor, you have done rightly
    To appear on this day when all are glad,   125
    Seeing how in times past you proved
    Our own good friend when days were bad.
    Many a man stands here alive
    Whom your father found in the grip
    Of a raging fever and tore him thence   130
    When he put paid to the pestilence.
    You too—you were a youngster then—
    Where any was ill you went your round,
    Right many a corpse left home feet first
    But you came out of it safe and sound,   135
    From many a gruelling trial—Aye,
    The helper got help from the Helper on high.
CROWD. Health to the trusty man. We pray
    He may live to help us many a day.
FAUST. Kneel to the One on high, our friend   140
    Who teaches us helpers, who help can send.
        [FAUST *and* WAGNER *leave the* CROWD *and move on.*]

---

129. *your father:* See l. 327 in the preceding scene. The old German Faust legend made Faust's father a peasant; but Nostradamus (see note to l. 68 in the preceding scene) and Paracelsus (1493–1541), two physician-astrologers closely linked to the Faust myth, were famous for their plague-curing remedies.

WAGNER. You great man, how your heart must leap
　To be so honoured by the masses!
　How happy is he who has such talents
　And from them such a crop can reap!　　　　145
　The father points you out to his boy,
　They all ask questions, run and jostle,
　The fiddles and the dancers pause
　And, as you pass, they stand in rows
　And caps go hurtling in the sky;　　　　150
　They almost kneel to you as though
　The eucharist were passing by.
FAUST. Only a few steps more up to that stone!
　Here, after our walk, we will take a rest.
　Here I have often sat, thoughtful, alone,　　　　155
　Torturing myself with prayer and fast.
　Rich in hope and firm in faith,
　With tears and sighs to seven times seven
　I thought I could end that epidemic
　And force the hand of the Lord of Heaven.　　　　160
　But now the crowd's applause sounds to me like derision.
　O could you only read in my inmost heart
　How little father and son
　Merited their great reputation!
　My father was a worthy man who worked in the dark,　　　165
　Who in good faith but on his own wise
　Brooded on Nature and her holy circles
　With laborious whimsicalities;
　Who used to collect the connoisseurs
　Into the kitchen and locked inside　　　　170
　Its black walls pour together divers
　Ingredients of countless recipes;
　Such was our medicine, the patients died
　And no one counted the survivors.
　And thus we with our hellish powders　　　　175
　Raged more perniciously than the plague
　Throughout this district—valley and town.
　Myself I have given the poison to thousands;
　They drooped away, *I* must live on to sample
　The brazen murderers' renown.　　　　180
WAGNER. How can you let that weigh so heavily?
　Does not a good man do enough
　If he works at the art that he has received
　Conscientiously and scrupulously?
　As a young man you honour your father,　　　　185
　What he can teach, you take with a will;

As a man you widen the range of knowledge
And your son's range may be wider still.

FAUST. Happy the man who swamped in this sea of Error   190
Still hopes to struggle up through the watery wall;
What we don't know is exactly what we need
And what we know fulfils no need at all.
But let us not with such sad thoughts
Make this good hour an hour undone!
Look how the cottages on the green   195
Shine in the glow of the evening sun!
He backs away, gives way, the day is overspent,
He hurries off to foster life elsewhere.
Would I could press on his trail, on his trail for ever—
Alas that I have no wings to raise me into the air!   200
Then I should see in an everlasting sunset
The quiet world before my feet unfold,
All of its peaks on fire, all of its vales becalmed,
And the silver brook dispersed in streams of gold.
Not the wild peaks with all their chasms   205
Could interrupt my godlike flight;
Already the bays of the sea that the sun has warmed
Unfurl upon my marvelling sight.
But in the end the sungod seems to sink away,
Yet the new impulse sets me again in motion,   210
I hasten on to drink his eternal light,
With night behind me and before me day,
Above me heaven and below me ocean.
A beautiful dream—yet the sun leaves me behind.
Alas, it is not so easy for earthly wing   215
To fly on level terms with the wings of the mind.
Yet born with each of us is the instinct
That struggles upwards and away
When over our heads, lost in the blue,
The lark pours out her vibrant lay;   220
When over rugged pine-clad ranges
The eagle hangs on outspread wings
And over lake and over plain
We see the homeward-struggling crane.

WAGNER. I myself have often had moments of fancifulness   225
But I never experienced yet an urge like this.
Woods and fields need only a quick look
And *I* shall never envy the bird its pinions.
How differently the joys of the mind's dominions
Draw us from page to page, from book to book.   230
That's what makes winter nights lovely and snug—

The blissful life that warms you through your body—
And, ah, should you unroll a worthwhile manuscript,
You bring all heaven down into your study.

FAUST. You are only conscious of one impulse. Never   235
Seek an acquaintance with the other.
Two souls, alas, cohabit in my breast,
A contract one of them desires to sever.
The one like a rough lover clings
To the world with the tentacles of its senses;   240
The other lifts itself to Elysian Fields
Out of the mist on powerful wings.
Oh, if there be spirits in the air,
Princes that weave their way between heaven and earth,
Come down to me from the golden atmosphere   245
And carry me off to a new and colourful life.
Aye, if I only had a magic mantle
On which I could fly abroad, a-voyaging,
I would not barter it for the costliest raiment,
Not even for the mantle of a king.   250

WAGNER. Do not invoke the notorious host
Deployed in streams upon the wind,
Preparing danger in a thousand forms
From every quarter for mankind.
Thrusting upon you from the North   255
Come fanged spirits with arrow tongues;
From the lands of morning they come parching
To feed themselves upon your lungs;
The South despatches from the desert
Incendiary hordes against your brain   260
And the West a swarm which first refreshes,
Then drowns both you and field and plain.
They are glad to listen, adepts at doing harm,
Glad to obey and so throw dust in our eyes;
They make believe that they are sent from heaven   265
And lisp like angels, telling lies.
But let us move! The world has already gone grey,
The air is beginning to cool and the mist to fall.
It's in the evening one really values home—
But why do you look so astonished, standing there, staring that
      way?   270
What's there to see in the dusk that's worth the trouble?

FAUST. The black dog, do you mark him ranging through corn and
      stubble?

WAGNER. I noticed him long ago; he struck me as nothing much.

FAUST. Have a good look at the brute. What do you take him for?

WAGNER. For a poodle who, as is the way of such,   275
  Is trailing his master, worrying out the scent.

FAUST. But don't you perceive how in wide spirals around us
  He is getting nearer and nearer of set intent?
  And, unless I'm wrong, a running fire
  Eddies behind him in his wake.   280

WAGNER. I can see nothing but a black poodle;
  It must be your eyes have caused this mistake.

FAUST. He is casting, it seems to me, fine nooses of magic
  About our feet as a snare.

WAGNER. *I* see him leaping round us uncertainly, timidly,   285
  Finding instead of his master two strangers there.

FAUST. The circle narrows; now he is near.

WAGNER. Just a dog, you see; no phantoms here.
  He growls and hesitates, grovels on the green
  And wags his tail. Pure dog routine.   290

FAUST. Heel, sir, heel! Come, fellow, come!

WAGNER. He is a real poodle noodle.
  Stand still and he'll sit up and beg;
  Speak to him and he's all over you;
  Lose something and he'll fetch it quick,   295
  He'll jump in the water after your stick.

FAUST. I think you're right, I cannot find a trace
  Of a spirit here; it is all a matter of training.

WAGNER. If a dog is well brought up, a wise man even
  Can come to be fond of him in such a case.   300
  Yes, he fully deserves your name upon his collar,
  He whom the students have found so apt a scholar.

FAUST'S STUDY

He enters with the poodle.

FAUST. I have forsaken field and meadow
    Which night has laid in a deep bed,
    Night that wakes our better soul
    With a holy and foreboding dread.
    Now wild desires are wrapped in sleep   5
    And all the deeds that burn and break,
    The love of Man is waking now,
    The love of God begins to wake.

Poodle! Quiet! Don't run hither and thither!
Leave my threshold! Why are you snuffling there?   10
Lie down behind the stove and rest.
Here's a cushion; it's my best.
Out of doors on the mountain paths

You kept us amused by running riot;
But as my protégé at home   15
You'll only be welcome if you're quiet.

    Ah, when in our narrow cell
    The lamp once more imparts good cheer,
    Then in our bosom—in the heart
    That knows itself—then things grow clear.   20
    Reason once more begins to speak
    And the blooms of hope once more to spread;
    One hankers for the brooks of life,
    Ah, and for life's fountain head.

Don't growl, you poodle! That animal sound   25
Is not in tune with the holy music
By which my soul is girdled round.
We are used to human beings who jeer
At what they do not understand,
Who grouse at the good and the beautiful   30
Which often causes them much ado;
But must a dog snarl at it too?

But, ah, already, for all my good intentions
I feel contentment ebbing away in my breast.
Why must the stream so soon run dry   35
And we be left once more athirst?
I have experienced this so often;
Yet this defect has its compensation,
We learn to prize the supernatural
And hanker after revelation,   40
Which burns most bright and wins assent
Most in the New Testament.
I feel impelled to open the master text
And this once, with true dedication,
Take the sacred original   45
And make in my mother tongue my own translation.
    [*He opens a Bible.*]
It is written: In the beginning was the Word.
Here I am stuck at once. Who will help me on?
I am unable to grant the Word such merit,
I must translate it differently   50
If I am truly illumined by the spirit.
It is written: In the beginning was the Mind.
But why should my pen scour

---

43. *master text:* i.e., the Greek.   47. *In the beginning . . . Word:*
John 1:1.

So quickly ahead? Consider that first line well.
Is it the Mind that effects and creates all things?   55
It *should* read: In the beginning was the Power.
Yet, even as I am changing what I have writ,
Something warns me not to abide by it.
The spirit prompts me, I see in a flash what I need,
And write: In the beginning was the Deed!   60

Dog! If we two are to share this room,
Leave off your baying,
Leave off your barking!
I can't have such a fellow staying
Around me causing all this bother.   65
One of us or the other
Will have to leave the cell.
Well?
I don't really like to eject you so
But the door is open, you may go.   70

But what? What do I see?
Can this really happen naturally?
Is it a fact or is it a fraud?
My dog is growing so long and broad!
He raises himself mightily,   75
That is not a dog's anatomy!
What a phantom have I brought to my house!
He already looks like a river horse
With fiery eyes and frightful jaws—
Aha! But I can give you pause!   80
For such a hybrid out of hell
Solomon's Key is a good spell.
        [SPIRITS *are heard in the passage.*]
SPIRITS. Captured within there is one of us!
Wait without, follow him none of us!
Like a fox in a snare   85
An old hell-cat's trembling there.
But on the alert!
Fly against and athwart,
To starboard and port,
And he's out with a spurt!   90
If help you can take him,
Do not forsake him!
For often, to earn it, he

---

82. *Solomon's Key:* the *Clavicula*
Salomonis, a standard work used by
magicians for conjuring; in many medieval legends, Solomon was noted as a
great magician.

Helped our fraternity.

FAUST. First, to confront the beast,   95
     Be the Spell of the Four released:
          Salamander shall glow,
          Undine shall coil,
          Sylph shall vanish
          And gnome shall toil.   100
    One without sense
    Of the elements,
    Of their force
    And proper course,
    The spirits would never   105
    Own him for master.
          Vanish in flames,
          Salamander!
          Commingle in babble of streams,
          Undine!   110
          Shine meteor-like and majestic,
          Sylph!
          Bring help domestic,
          Lubber-fiend! Lubber-fiend!
          Step out of him and make an end!   115
    None of the Four
    Is the creature's core.
    He lies quite quiet and grins at me,
    I have not yet worked him injury.
    To exercise you   120
    I'll have to chastise you.
          Are you, rapscallion,
          A displaced devil?
          This sign can level
          Each dark battalion;   125
          Look at this sign!
    He swells up already with bristling spine.
          You outcast! Heed it—
          This name! Can you read it?
          The unbegotten one,   130
          Unpronounceable,
          Poured throughout Paradise,
          Heinously wounded one?
    Behind the stove, bound by my spells,
    Look, like an elephant it swells,   135
    Filling up all the space and more,

---

96. *Spell of the Four:* Salamanders were spirits of fire; undines, of water; sylphs, of air; and gnomes, of earth.

It threatens to melt away in mist.
Down from the ceiling! Down before—!
Down at your master's feet! Desist!
You see, I have not proved a liar;
I can burn you up with holy fire!
Do not await
The triply glowing light!
Do not await
My strongest brand of necromancy!   145
[*The mist subsides and* MEPHISTOPHELES *comes forward from
behind the stove, dressed like a travelling scholar.*]

MEPHISTOPHELES. What is the noise about? What might the gentleman fancy?

FAUST. So that is what the poodle had inside him!
A travelling scholar? That *casus* makes me laugh.

MEPHISTOPHELES. My compliments to the learned gentleman.
You have put me a sweat—not half!   150

FAUST. What is your name?

MEPHISTOPHELES. The question strikes me as petty
For one who holds the Word in such low repute,
Who, far withdrawn from all mere surface,
Aims only at the Essential Root.   155

FAUST. With you, you gentry, what is essential
The name more often than not supplies,
As is indeed only too patent
When they call you Fly-God, Corrupter, Father of Lies.
All right, who are you then?   160

MEPHISTOPHELES. A part of that Power
Which always wills evil, always procures good.

FAUST. What do you mean by this conundrum?

MEPHISTOPHELES. I am the Spirit which always denies.
And quite rightly; whatever has a beginning   165
Deserves to have an undoing;
It would be better if nothing began at all.
Thus everything that you call
Sin, destruction, Evil in short,
Is my own element, my resort.   170

FAUST. You call yourself a part, yet you stand before me whole?

MEPHISTOPHELES. This is the unassuming truth.
Whereas mankind, that little world of fools,
Commonly takes itself for a whole—
I am a part of the Part which in the beginning was all, 175

140

---

143. *triply glowing light:* perhaps
the Trinity, or a triangle with divergent rays.
153. *Word:* See l. 47 in this scene.

159. *Fly-God:* an almost literal translation of the name of the Philistine
deity Beelzebub.

A part of the darkness which gave birth to light,
To that haughty light which is struggling now to usurp
The ancient rank and realm of its mother Night,
And yet has no success, try as it will,
Being bound and clamped by bodies still.   180
It streams from bodies, bodies it beautifies,
A body clogs it when it would run,
And so, I hope, it won't be long
Till, bodies and all, it is undone.

FAUST. Ah, now I know your honourable profession!   185
You cannot destroy on a large scale,
So you are trying it on a small.

MEPHISTOPHELES. And, candidly, not getting far at all.
That which stands over against the Nothing,
The Something, I mean this awkward world,   190
For all my endeavours up to date
I have failed to get it under foot
With waves, with storms, with earthquakes, fire—
Sea and land after all stay put.
And this damned stuff, the brood of beasts and men,   195
There is no coming to grips with them;
I've already buried heaps of them!
And always new blood, fresh blood, circulates again.
So it goes on, it's enough to drive one crazy.
A thousand embryos extricate themselves   200
From air, from water and from earth
In wet and dry and hot and cold.
Had I not made a corner in fire
I should find myself without a berth.

FAUST. So you when faced with the ever stirring,   205
The creative force, the beneficent,
Counter with your cold devil's fist
Spitefully clenched but impotent.
You curious son of Chaos, why
Not turn your hand to something else?   210

MEPHISTOPHELES. We will give it our serious attention—
But more on that subject by and by.
Might I for this time take my leave?

FAUST. Why you ask I cannot see.
I have already made your acquaintance;   215
When you feel like it, call on me.
Here is the window, here is the door—
And a chimney too—if it comes to that.

176. *darkness:* Mephistopheles here
speaks as the Prince of Darkness, the
rôle in Christianity acquired by the
devil from the Persian Manichaean deity
Ahriman.

MEPHISTOPHELES. I must confess; there's a slight impediment
   That stops me making my exit pat,   220
   The pentagram upon your threshold—
FAUST. So the witch's foot is giving you trouble?
   Then tell me, since you're worried by that spell,
   How did you ever enter, child of Hell?
   How was a spirit like you betrayed?   225
MEPHISTOPHELES. You study that sign! It's not well made;
   One of its corners, do you see,
   The outside one's not quite intact.
FAUST. A happy accident in fact!
   Which means you're in my custody?   230
   I did not intend to set a gin.
MEPHISTOPHELES. The dog—he noticed nothing, jumping in;
   The case has now turned round about
   And I, the devil, can't get out.
FAUST. Then why not leave there by the window?   235
MEPHISTOPHELES. It is a law for devils and phantoms all:
   By the way that we slip in by the same we must take our
      leave.
   One's free in the first, in the second one's a thrall.
FAUST. So Hell itself has its regulations?
   That's excellent; a contract in that case   240
   Could be made with you, you gentry—and definite?
MEPHISTOPHELES. What we promise, you will enjoy with no reserva-
      tions,
   Nothing will be nipped off from it.
   But all this needs a little explaining
   And will keep till our next heart-to-heart;   245
   But now I beg and doubly beg you:
   Let me, just for now, depart.
FAUST. But wait yet a minute and consent
   To tell me first some news of moment.
MEPHISTOPHELES. Let me go now! I'll soon be back   250
   To be questioned to your heart's content.
FAUST. It was not I laid a trap for you,
   You thrust your own head in the noose.
   A devil in the hand's worth two in hell!
   The second time he'll be longer loose.   255
MEPHISTOPHELES. If you so wish it, I'm prepared
   To keep you company and stay;
   Provided that by my arts the time
   Be to your betterment whiled away.

---

221. *pentagram:* a magic five-pointed star designed to keep away evil spirits, principally the female incubus or witch. 222. *witch's foot:* the pentagram.

FAUST. I am in favour, carry on—   260
   But let your art be a pleasing one.
MEPHISTOPHELES. My friend, your senses will have more
   Gratification in this hour
   Than in a year's monotony.
   What the delicate spirits sing to you   265
   And the beauties that they bring to you
   Are no empty, idle wizardry.
   You'll have your sense of smell delighted,
   Your palate in due course excited,
   Your feelings rapt enchantingly.   270
   Preparation? There's no need,
   We are all here. Strike up! Proceed!
      [*The* SPIRITS *sing.*]
SPIRITS. Vanish, you darkling
      Arches above him,
      That a more witching   275
      Blue and enriching
      Sky may look in!
      If only the darkling
      Clouds were unravelled!
      Small stars are sparkling,   280
      Suns are more gently
      Shining within!
      Spiritual beauty
      Of the children of Heaven
      Swaying and bowing   285
      Floats in the air,
      Leanings and longings
      Follow them there;
      And ribbons of raiment
      The breezes have caught   290
      Cover the country,
      Cover the arbour
      Where, drowning in thought,
      Lovers exchange their
      Pledges for life.   295
      Arbour on arbour!
      Creepers run rife!
      Grapes in great wreathing
      Clusters are poured into
      Vats that are seething,   300
      Wines that are foaming
      Pour out in rivulets
      Rippling and roaming

Through crystalline stones,
Leaving the sight of   305
The highlands behind them,
Widening to lakes
Amid the delight of
Green-growing foothills.
And the winged creatures   310
Sipping their ecstasy,
Sunwards they fly,
Fly to discover
The glittering islands
Which bob on the wave-tops   315
Deceiving the eye.
There we can hear
Huzzaing in chorus,
A landscape of dancers
Extending before us,   320
All in the open,
Free as the air.
Some of them climbing
Over the peaks,
Some of them swimming   325
Over the lakes,
Or floating in space—
All towards existence,
All towards the distance
Of stars that will love them,   330
The blessing of grace.

MEPHISTOPHELES. He is asleep. That's fine, you airy, dainty young-
    sters
You have sung him a real cradle song.
For this performance I am in your debt.
You are not yet the man to hold the devil for long.   335
Play round him with your sweet dream trickeries
And sink him in a sea of untruth!
But to break the spell upon this threshold
What I need now is a rat's tooth.
And I needn't bother to wave a wand,   340
I can hear one rustling already, he'll soon respond.
The lord of rats, the lord of mice,
Of flies, frogs, bugs and lice,
Commands you to come out of that
And gnaw away this threshold, rat,   345
While he takes oil and gives it a few—
So there you come hopping? Quick on your cue!

Now get on the job! The obstructing point
Is on the edge and right in front.
One bite more and the work's done.   350
Now, Faust, till we meet again, dream on!
FAUST. [*Waking*] Am I defrauded then once more?
Does the throng of spirits vanish away like fog
To prove that the devil appeared to me in a dream
But what escaped was only a dog?   355

FAUST'S STUDY

The same room. Later.

FAUST. Who's knocking? Come in! *Now* who wants to annoy me?
MEPHISTOPHELES. [*Outside door*] It's I.
FAUST.   Come in!
MEPHISTOPHELES. [*Outside door*]
                    You must say 'Come in' three times.
FAUST. Come in then!   5
MEPHISTOPHELES. [*Entering*] Thank you; you overjoy me.
We two, I hope, we shall be good friends;
To chase those megrims of yours away
I am here like a fine young squire to-day,
In a suit of scarlet trimmed with gold   10
And a little cape of stiff brocade,
With a cock's feather in my hat
And at my side a long sharp blade,
And the most succinct advice I can give
Is that you dress up just like me,   15
So that uninhibited and free
You may find out what it means to live.
FAUST. The pain of earth's constricted life, I fancy,
Will pierce me still, whatever my attire;
I am too old for mere amusement,   20
Too young to be without desire.
How can the world dispel my doubt?
You must do without, you must do without!
That is the everlasting song
Which rings in every ear, which rings,   25
And which to us our whole life long
Every hour hoarsely sings.
I wake in the morning only to feel appalled,
My eyes with bitter tears could run
To see the day which in its course   30
Will not fulfil a wish for me, not one;

9. *a fine young squire:* In the popular plays based on the Faust legend, the devil often appeared as a monk when the play catered to a Protestant audience, and as a cavalier when the audience was predominantly Catholic.

The day which whittles away with obstinate carping
All pleasures—even those of anticipation,
Which makes a thousand grimaces to obstruct
My heart when it is stirring in creation.   35
And again, when night comes down, in anguish
I must stretch out upon my bed
And again no rest is granted me,
For wild dreams fill my mind with dread.
The God who dwells within my bosom   40
Can make my inmost soul react;
The God who sways my every power
Is powerless with external fact.
And so existence weighs upon my breast
And I long for death and life—life I detest.   45
MEPHISTOPHELES. Yet death is never a wholly welcome guest.
FAUST. O happy is he whom death in the dazzle of victory
Crowns with the bloody laurel in the battling swirl!
Or he whom after the mad and breakneck dance
He comes upon in the arms of a girl!   50
O to have sunk away, delighted, deleted,
Before the Spirit of the Earth, before his might!
MEPHISTOPHELES. Yet I know someone who failed to drink
A brown juice on a certain night.
FAUST. Your hobby is espionage—is it not?   55
MEPHISTOPHELES. Oh I'm not omniscient—but I know a lot.
FAUST. Whereas that tumult in my soul
Was stilled by sweet familiar chimes
Which cozened the child that yet was in me
With echoes of more happy times,   60
I now curse all things that encompass
The soul with lures and jugglery
And bind it in this dungeon of grief
With trickery and flattery.
Cursed in advance be the high opinion   65
That serves our spirit for a cloak!
Cursed be the dazzle of appearance
Which bows our senses to its yoke!
Cursed be the lying dreams of glory,
The illusion that our name survives!   70
Cursed be the flattering things we own,
Servants and ploughs, children and wives!
Cursed be Mammon when with his treasures
He makes us play the adventurous man

73. *Mammon:* the Aramaic word for
"riches," used in the New Testament;
medieval writers interpreted the word
as a proper noun, the name of the
devil, as representing covetousness or
avarice.

Or when for our luxurious pleasures   75
He duly spreads the soft divan!
A curse on the balsam of the grape!
A curse on the love that rides for a fall!
A curse on hope! A curse on faith!
And a curse on patience most of all!   80
    [*The invisible* SPIRITS *sing again.*]

SPIRITS.   Woe! Woe!
You have destroyed it,
The beautiful world;
By your violent hand
'Tis downward hurled!   85
A half-god has dashed it asunder!
From under
We bear off the rubble to nowhere
And ponder
Sadly the beauty departed.   90
Magnipotent
One among men,
Magnificent
Build it again,
Build it again in your breast!   95
Let a new course of life
Begin
With vision abounding
And new songs resounding
To welcome it in!   100

MEPHISTOPHELES. These are the juniors
Of my faction.
Hear how precociously they counsel
Pleasure and action.
Out and away   105
From your lonely day
Which dries your senses and your juices
Their melody seduces.

Stop playing with your grief which battens
Like a vulture on your life, your mind!   110
The worst of company would make you feel
That you are a man among mankind.
Not that it's really my proposition
To shove you among the common men:
Though I'm not one of the Upper Ten,   115
If you would like a coalition
With me for your career through life,

I am quite ready to fit in,
I'm yours before you can say knife.
I am your comrade;   120
If you so crave,
I am your servant, I am your slave.
FAUST. And what have I to undertake in return?
MEPHISTOPHELES. Oh it's early days to discuss what that is.
FAUST. No, no, the devil is an egoist   125
And ready to do nothing gratis
Which is to benefit a stranger.
Tell me your terms and don't prevaricate!
A servant like you in the house is a danger.
MEPHISTOPHELES. I will bind myself to your service in this
world,
To be at your beck and never rest nor slack;
When we meet again on the other side,
In the same coin you shall pay me back.
FAUST. The other side gives me little trouble;
First batter this present world to rubble,   135
Then the other may rise—if that's the plan.
This earth is where my springs of joy have started,
And this sun shines on me when broken-hearted;
If I can first from them be parted,
Then let happen what will and can!   140
I wish to hear no more about it—
Whether there too men hate and love
Or whether in those spheres too, in the future,
There is a Below or an Above.
MEPHISTOPHELES. With such an outlook you can risk it.   145
Sign on the line! In these next days you will get
Ravishing samples of my arts;
I am giving you what never man saw yet.
FAUST. Poor devil, can *you* give anything ever?
Was a human spirit in its high endeavour   150
Even once understood by one of your breed?
Have you got food which fails to feed?
Or red gold which, never at rest,
Like mercury runs away through the hand?
A game at which one never wins?   155
A girl who, even when on my breast,
Pledges herself to my neighbour with her eyes?
The divine and lovely delight of honour
Which falls like a falling star and dies?
Show me the fruits which, before they are plucked, decay 160
And the trees which day after day renew their green!

MEPHISTOPHELES. Such a commission doesn't alarm me,
  I have such treasures to purvey.
  But, my good friend, the time draws on when we
  Should be glad to feast at our ease on something good.   165
FAUST. If ever I stretch myself on a bed of ease,
  Then I am finished! Is that understood?
  If ever your flatteries can coax me
  To be pleased with myself, if ever you cast
  A spell of pleasure that can hoax me—   170
  Then let *that* day be my last!
  That's my wager!
MEPHISTOPHELES. Done!
FAUST.   Let's shake!
  If ever I say to the passing moment   175
  'Linger a while! Thou art so fair!'
  Then you may cast me into fetters,
  I will gladly perish then and there!
  Then you may set the death-bell tolling,
  Then from my service you are free,   180
  The clock may stop, its hand may fall,
  And that be the end of time for me!
MEPHISTOPHELES. Think what you're saying, we shall not forget it.
FAUST. And you are fully within your rights;
  I have made no mad or outrageous claim.   185
  If I stay as I am, I am a slave—
  Whether yours or another's, it's all the same.
MEPHISTOPHELES. I shall this very day at the College Banquet
  Enter your service with no more ado,
  But just one point—As a life-and-death insurance   190
  I must trouble you for a line or two.
FAUST. So you, you pedant, you too like things in writing?
  Have you never known a man? Or a man's word? Never?
  Is it not enough that my word of mouth
  Puts all my days in bond for ever?   195
  Does not the world rage on in all its streams
  And shall a promise hamper *me?*
  Yet this illusion reigns within our hearts
  And from it who would be gladly free?
  Happy the man who can inwardly keep his word;   200
  Whatever the cost, he will not be loath to pay!
  But a parchment, duly inscribed and sealed,
  Is a bogey from which all wince away.
  The word dies on the tip of the pen
  And wax and leather lord it then.   205

188. *College Banquet:* actually the *Doctorschmaus*, or dinner given by a successful candidate for a Ph.D. degree.

What do you, evil spirit, require?
Bronze, marble, parchment, paper?
Quill or chisel or pencil of slate?
You may choose whichever you desire.
MEPHISTOPHELES. How can you so exaggerate   210
With such a hectic rhetoric?
Any little snippet is quite good—
And you sign it with one little drop of blood.
FAUST. If that is enough and is some use,
One may as well pander to your fad.   215
MEPHISTOPHELES. Blood is a very special juice.
FAUST. Only do not fear that I shall break this contract.
What I promise is nothing more
Than what all my powers are striving for.
I have puffed myself up too much, it is only   220
Your sort that really fits my case.
The great Earth Spirit has despised me
And Nature shuts the door in my face.
The thread of thoughts is snapped asunder,
I have long loathed knowledge in all its fashions.   225
In the depths of sensuality
Let us now quench our glowing passions!
And at once make ready every wonder
Of unpenetrated sorcery!
Let us cast ourselves into the torrent of time,   230
Into the whirl of eventfulness,
Where disappointment and success,
Pleasure and pain may chop and change
As chop and change they will and can;
It is restless action makes the man.   235
MEPHISTOPHELES. No limit is fixed for you, no bound;
If you'd like to nibble at everything
Or to seize upon something flying round—
Well, may you have a run for your money!
But seize your chance and don't be funny!   240
FAUST. I've told you, it is no question of happiness.
The most painful joy, enamoured hate, enlivening
Disgust—I devote myself to all excess.
My breast, now cured of its appetite for knowledge,
From now is open to all and every smart,   245
And what is allotted to the whole of mankind
That will I sample in my inmost heart,
Grasping the highest and lowest with my spirit,

213. *blood:* This method of con- it always appears—and is partly a
firming an agreement with the devil is parody of the rôle of blood in the Chris-
older than the Faust legend—in which tian Sacrament.

Piling men's weal and woe upon my neck,
To extend myself to embrace all human selves   250
And to founder in the end, like them, a wreck.

MEPHISTOPHELES. O believe *me*, who have been chewing
These iron rations many a thousand year,
No human being can digest
This stuff, from the cradle to the bier.   255
This universe—believe a devil—
Was made for no one but a god!
He exists in eternal light
But *us* he has brought into the darkness
While *your* sole portion is day and night.   260

FAUST. I will all the same!

MEPHISTOPHELES.   That's very nice.
There's only one thing I find wrong;
Time is short, art is long.
You could do with a little artistic advice.   265
Confederate with one of the poets
And let him flog his imagination
To heap all virtues on your head,
A head with such a reputation:
Lion's bravery,   270
Stag's velocity,
Fire of Italy,
Northern tenacity.
Let *him* find out the secret art
Of combining craft with a noble heart   275
And of being in love like a young man,
Hotly, but working to a plan.
Such a person—*I'd* like to meet him;
'Mr. Microcosm' is how I'd greet him.

FAUST. What am I then if fate must bar   280
My efforts to reach that crown of humanity
After which all my senses strive?

MEPHISTOPHELES. You are in the end . . . what you are.
You can put on full-bottomed wigs with a million locks,
You can put on stilts instead of your socks,   285
You remain for ever what you are.

FAUST. I feel my endeavours have not been worth a pin
When I raked together the treasures of the human mind,
If at the end I but sit down to find
No new force welling up within.   290
I have not a hair's breadth more of height,

---

279. *Mr. Microcosm:* i.e., man viewed as the epitome of the universe.

I am no nearer the Infinite.

MEPHISTOPHELES. My very good sir, you look at things
    Just in the way that people do;
    We must be cleverer than that   295
    Or the joys of life will escape from you.
    Hell! You have surely hands and feet,
    Also a head and you-know-what;
    The pleasures I gather on the wing,
    Are they less mine? Of course they're not!   300
    Suppose I can afford six stallions,
    I can add that horse-power to my score
    And dash along and be a proper man
    As if my legs were twenty-four.
    So good-bye to thinking! On your toes!   305
    The world's before us. Quick! Here goes!
    I tell you, a chap who's intellectual
    Is like a beast on a blasted heath
    Driven in circles by a demon
    While a fine green meadow lies round beneath.   310

FAUST. How do we start?

MEPHISTOPHELES.   We just say go—and skip.
    But please get ready for this pleasure trip.
    [*Exit* FAUST.]
    Only look down on knowledge and reason,
    The highest gifts that men can prize,   315
    Only allow the spirit of lies
    To confirm you in magic and illusion,
    And then I have you body and soul.
    Fate has given this man a spirit
    Which is always pressing onwards, beyond control,   320
    And whose mad striving overleaps
    All joys of the earth between pole and pole.
    Him shall I drag through the wilds of life
    And through the flats of meaninglessness,
    I shall make him flounder and gape and stick   325
    And to tease his insatiableness
    Hang meat and drink in the air before his watering lips;
    In vain he will pray to slake his inner thirst,
    And even had he not sold himself to the devil
    He would be equally accursed.[a]   330
    [*Re-enter* FAUST.]

FAUST. And now, where are we going?

---

a. Between Faust's exit and entrance, the translator omits a scene in which Mephistopheles cynically interviews one of Faust's students.

MEPHISTOPHELES.   Wherever you please.
The small world, then the great for us.
With what pleasure and what profit
You will roister through the syllabus!   335
FAUST. But I, with this long beard of mine,
I lack the easy social touch,
I know the experiment is doomed;
Out in the world I never could fit in much.
I feel so small in company   340
I'll be embarrassed constantly.
MEPHISTOPHELES. My friend, it will solve itself, any such mis
    giving;
Just trust yourself and you'll learn the art of living.
FAUST. Well, then, how do we leave home?
Where are your grooms? Your coach and horses?   345
MEPHISTOPHELES. We merely spread this mantle wide,
It will bear us off on airy courses.
But do not on this noble voyage
Cumber yourself with heavy baggage.
A little inflammable gas which I'll prepare   350
Will lift us quickly into the air.
If we travel light we shall cleave the sky like a knife.
Congratulations on your new course of life![a]

THE WITCH'S KITCHEN[b]

Every sort of witch prop. A large cauldron hangs over the fire.
MONKEYS *sit around it, seen through the fumes.*

MEPHISTOPHELES. Look, what a pretty species of monkey!
She is the kitchen-maid, he is the flunkey.
It seems your mistress isn't at home?
MONKEYS. Out at a rout!
            Out and about!   5
            By the chimney spout!
MEPHISTOPHELES. How long does she keep it up at night?
MONKEYS. As long as we warm our paws at this fire.
MEPHISTOPHELES. How do you like these delicate animals?
FAUST. I never saw such an outré sight.   10
    I find it nauseating, this crazy witchcraft!

350. *gas:* indicative of Goethe's
scientific interests. The first hydrogen
balloon was sent aloft in Paris in
1783, and several letters by Goethe refer
to this new experiment.
    a. The translator omits the next
scene, in Auerbach's Cellar, where Faust
and Mephistopheles join a group of
genial drinking companions and Mephistopheles performs the trick—traditional
in early Faust stories—of making wine
flow from the table.
    b. Certain transpositions have been
made in this scene. [Translator's note.]
    11. *crazy witchcraft:* In composing
this scene, Goethe may have had in
mind certain paintings by the Flemish
artists David Teniers the Younger
(1610–1690) and Pieter Breughel the
Younger (1564?–1638).

Do you promise me that I shall improve
In this cesspit of insanity?
Do I need advice from an old hag?
And can this filthy brew remove   15
Thirty years from my age? O vanity,
If you know nothing better than this!
My hope has already vanished away.
Surely Nature, surely a noble spirit
Has brought some better balm to the light of day?   20

MEPHISTOPHELES. My friend, you once more talk to the point.
There is also a natural means of rejuvenation;
But that is written in another book
And is a chapter that needs some explanation.

FAUST. I want to know it.   25

MEPHISTOPHELES.   Right. There is a means requires
No money, no physician, and no witch:
Away with you this moment back to the land,
And there begin to dig and ditch,
Confine yourself, confine your mind,   30
In a narrow round, ever repeating,
Let your diet be of the simplest kind,
Live with the beasts like a beast and do not think it cheating
To use your own manure to insure your crops are weighty!
Believe me, that is the best means   35
To keep you young till you are eighty.

FAUST. I am not used to it, I cannot change
My nature and take the spade in hand.
The narrow life is not my style at all.

MEPHISTOPHELES. Then it's a job for the witch to arrange.   40

FAUST. The hag—but why do we need just her?
Can you yourself not brew the drink?

MEPHISTOPHELES. A pretty pastime! I'd prefer
To build a thousand bridges in that time.
It is not only art and science   45
That this work needs but patience too.
A quiet spirit is busy at it for years
And time but fortifies the subtle brew.
And the most wonderful ingredients
Go into it—you couldn't fake it!   50
The devil taught it her, I admit;
The devil, however, cannot make it.
Tell me, you monkeys, you damned puppets,
What are you doing with that great globe?

44. *bridges:* The folk legend existed
that the devil built bridges at the request of men. As a reward, he caught
either the first or the thirteenth soul to
cross each new bridge.

HE-MONKEY. This is the world: 55
    It rises and falls
    And rolls every minute;
    It rings like glass—
    But how soon it breaks!
    And there's nothing in it.   60
    It glitters here
    And here still more:
    I am alive!
    O my son, my dear,
    Keep away, keep away!   65
    You are bound to die!
    The shards are sharp,
    It was made of clay.
  [FAUST *has meanwhile been gazing in a mirror.*]
FAUST. What do I see in this magic mirror?
 What a heavenly image to appear!   70
 O Love, lend me the swiftest of your wings
 And waft me away into her sphere!
 But, alas, when I do not keep this distance,
 If to go nearer I but dare
 I can see her only as if there were mist in the air—   75
 The fairest image of a woman!
 But can Woman be so fair?
 In that shape in the mirror must I see the quintessence
 Of all the heavens—reclining there?
 Can such a thing be found on earth?   80
MEPHISTOPHELES. Naturally, when a God works six days like a black
 And at the end of it slaps himself on the back,
 Something should come of it of some worth.
 For this occasion look your fill.
 I can smell you out a sweetheart as good as this,   85
 And happy the man who has the luck
 To bear her home to wedded bliss.
  [*The* WITCH *enters down the chimney—violently.*]
WITCH. What goes on here?
    Who are you two?
    What d'you want here?
    Who has sneaked through?   90
    May the fever of fire
    Harrow your marrow!
MEPHISTOPHELES. Don't you know me, you bag of bones? You
 monster, you!
 Don't you know your lord and master?   95
 What prevents me striking you

And your monkey spirits, smashing you up like plaster?
Has my red doublet no more claim to fame?
Can you not recognize the cock's feather?
Have I concealed my countenance?
Must I myself announce my name?   100

WITCH. My lord, excuse this rude reception.
It is only I miss your cloven foot.
And where is your usual brace of ravens?

MEPHISTOPHELES. I'll forgive you this once, as an exception;   105
Admittedly some time has pass't
Since we two saw each other last.
Culture too, which is licking the whole world level,
Has latterly even reached the devil.
The Nordic spook no longer commands a sale;   110
Where can you see horns, claws or tail?
And as regards the foot, which is my *sine qua non,*
It would prejudice me in the social sphere;
Accordingly, as many young men have done,
I have worn false calves this many a year.   115

WITCH. Really and truly I'm knocked flat
To see Lord Satan here again!

MEPHISTOPHELES. Woman, you must not call me that!

WITCH. Why! What harm is there in the name?

MEPHISTOPHELES. Satan has long been a myth without sense or
sinew;   120
Not that it helps humanity all the same,
They are quit of the Evil One but the evil ones continue.
You may call me the Noble Baron, that should do;
I am a cavalier among other cavaliers,
You needn't doubt my blood is blue—   125
[*He makes an indecent gesture.*]

WITCH. Ha! Ha! Always true to type!
You still have the humour of a guttersnipe!

MEPHISTOPHELES. Observe my technique, my friend—not a single
hitch;
This is the way to get round a witch.

WITCH. Now tell me, gentlemen, what do you want?   130

MEPHISTOPHELES. A good glass of your well-known juice.
And please let us have your oldest vintage;
When it's been kept it's twice the use.

WITCH. Delighted! Why, there's some here on the shelf—
I now and then take a nip myself—   135
And, besides, this bottle no longer stinks;

104. *brace of ravens:* Perhaps Goethe was thinking of the Norse god Odin, who owned two such birds: Hugin (Thought) and Munin (Memory).

You're welcome while I've a drop to give.
[*Aside*] But, if this man is unprepared when he drinks,
You very well know he has not an hour to live.
MEPHISTOPHELES. He's a good friend and it should set him up;   140
I'd gladly grant him the best of your kitchen,
So draw your circle and do your witching
And give the man a decent cup.
        [*The* WITCH *begins her conjuration.*]
FAUST. But, tell me, how will this mend my status?
These lunatic gestures, this absurd apparatus,   145
This most distasteful conjuring trick—
I've known it all, it makes me sick.
MEPHISTOPHELES. Pooh, that's just fooling, get it in focus,
And don't be such a prig for goodness' sake!
As a doctor she must do her hocus-pocus   150
So that when you have drunk your medicine it will take.
WITCH. The lofty power
        That is wisdom's dower,
        Concealed from great and clever,
        Don't use your brain   155
        And that's your gain—
        No trouble whatsoever.
FAUST. What nonsense is she saying to us?
My head is splitting; I've the sensation
Of listening to a hundred thousand   160
Idiots giving a mass recitation.
MEPHISTOPHELES. Enough, enough, you excellent Sibyl!
Give us your drink and fill the cup
Full to the brim and don't delay!
This draught will do my friend no injury;   165
He is a man of more than one degree
And has drunk plenty in his day.
        [*The* WITCH *gives* FAUST *the cup.*]
Now lower it quickly. Bottoms up!
And your heart will begin to glow and perk.
Now out of the circle! You mustn't rest.   170
WITCH. I hope the little drink will work.
MEPHISTOPHELES. [*To* WITCH] And you, if there's anything you
        want, all right;
Just mention it to me on Walpurgis Night.
[*To* FAUST] Come now, follow me instantly!
You've got to perspire, it's necessary,   175
That the drug may pervade you inside and out.

---

173. *Walpurgis Night:* the eve of   supposed to assemble on the Brocken,
May Day (May 1), when witches are   a peak in the Harz Mountains.

I can teach you later to value lordly leisure
And you soon will learn with intensest pleasure
How Cupid stirs within and bounds about.

FAUST. Just one more look, one quick look, in the mirror!   180
That woman was too fair to be true.

MEPHISTOPHELES. No, no! The paragon of womanhood
Will soon be revealed in the flesh to you.
[*Aside*] With a drink like this in you, take care—
You'll soon see Helens everywhere.   185

IN THE STREET

FAUST *accosts* GRETCHEN *as she passes.*

FAUST. My pretty young lady, might I venture
To offer you my arm and my escort too?

GRETCHEN. I'm not a young lady nor am I pretty
And I can get home without help from you.
[*She releases herself and goes off.*]

FAUST. By Heaven, she's beautiful, this child!   5
I have never seen her parallel.
So decorous, so virtuous,
And just a little pert as well.
The light of her cheek, her lip so red,
I shall remember till I'm dead!   10
The way that she cast down her eye
Is stamped on my heart as with a die;
And the way that she got rid of me
Was a most ravishing thing to see!
[*Enter* MEPHISTOPHELES.]
Listen to me! Get me that girl!   15

MEPHISTOPHELES. Which one?

FAUST.   The one that just went past.

MEPHISTOPHELES. She? She was coming from her priest,
Absolved from her sins one and all;
I'd crept up near the confessional.   20
An innocent thing. Innocent? Yes!
At church with nothing to confess!
Over that girl I have no power.

FAUST. Yet she's fourteen if she's an hour.

MEPHISTOPHELES. Why, you're talking like Randy Dick   25
Who covets every lovely flower
And all the favours, all the laurels,
He fancies are for him to pick;

---

185. *Helens:* Faust marries Helen
of Troy in the second part of *Faust.*
25. *Randy Dick:* in the original

German, "Hans Liederlich"—i.e., a
profligate, since *liederlich* means "careless" or "dissolute."

But it doesn't always work out like that.

FAUST. My dear Professor of Ancient Morals, 30
    Spare me your trite morality!
    I tell you straight—and hear me right—
    Unless this object of delight
    Lies in my arms this very night,
    At midnight we part company. 35

MEPHISTOPHELES. Haven't you heard: more haste less speed?
    A fortnight is the least I need
    Even to work up an occasion.

FAUST. If I had only seven hours clear,
    I should not need the devil here 40
    To bring *this* quest to consummation.

MEPHISTOPHELES. It's almost French, your line of talk;
    I only ask you not to worry.
    Why make your conquest in a hurry?
    The pleasure is less by a long chalk 45
    Than when you first by hook and by crook
    Have squeezed your doll and moulded her,
    Using all manner of poppycock
    That foreign novels keep in stock.

FAUST. I am keen enough without all that. 50

MEPHISTOPHELES. Now, joking apart and without aspersion,
    You cannot expect, I tell you flat,
    This beautiful child in quick reversion.
    Immune to all direct attack—
    We must lay our plots behind her back. 55

FAUST. Get me something of my angel's!
    Carry me to her place of rest!
    Get me a garter of my love's!
    Get me a kerchief from her breast!

MEPHISTOPHELES. That you may see the diligent fashion 60
    In which I shall abet your passion,
    We won't let a moment waste away,
    I will take you to her room to-day.

FAUST. And shall I see her? Have her?

MEPHISTOPHELES.   No! 65
    She will be visiting a neighbour.
    But you in the meanwhile, quite alone,
    Can stay in her aura in her room
    And feast your fill on joys to come.

FAUST. Can we go now? 70

MEPHISTOPHELES.   It is still too soon.

---

30. *Professor:* in the original German, Herr Magister Lobesan ("Master Worshipful")—stuffed shirt, or academic prig.

FAUST Then a present for her! Get me one!
    [*Exit* FAUST.]
MEPHISTOPHELES. Presents already? Fine. A certain hit!
  I know plenty of pretty places
  And of long-buried jewel-cases;   75
  I must take stock of them a bit.

GRETCHEN'S ROOM

GRETCHEN. [*Alone, doing her hair*] I'd give a lot to be able to say
  Who the gentleman was to-day.
  He cut a fine figure certainly
  And is sprung from nobility;
  His face showed that—Besides, you see,   5
  He'd otherwise not have behaved so forwardly.
    [*She goes out; then* MEPHISTOPHELES *and* FAUST *enter.*]
MEPHISTOPHELES. Come in—very quietly—Only come in!
FAUST. [*After a silence*] I ask you: please leave me alone!
MEPHISTOPHELES. Not all girls keep their room so clean.
FAUST. [*Looking around*] Welcome, sweet gleaming of the
    gloaming   10
  That through this sanctuary falls aslope!
  Seize on my heart, sweet fever of love
  That lives and languishes on the dews of hope!
  What a feeling of quiet breathes around me,
  Of order, of contentedness!   15
  What fulness in this poverty,
  And in this cell what blessedness!

  Here I could while away hour after hour.
  It was here, O Nature, that your fleeting dreams
  Brought this born angel to full flower.   20
  Here lay the child and the warm life
  Filled and grew in her gentle breast,
  And here the pure and holy threads
  Wove a shape of the heavenliest.

  And you! What brought you here to-day?   25
  Why do I feel this deep dismay?
  What do you want here? Why is your heart so sore?
  Unhappy Faust! You are Faust no more.

  Is this an enchanted atmosphere?
  To have her at once was all my aim,   30
  Yet I feel my will dissolve in a lovesick dream.
  Are we the sport of every current of air?

And were she this moment to walk in,
You would pay for this outrage, how you would pay!
The big man, now, alas, so small,   35
Would lie at her feet melted away.

MEPHISTOPHELES. Quick! I can see her coming below.

FAUST. Out, yes out! I'll never come back!

MEPHISTOPHELES. Here is a casket, it's middling heavy,
I picked it up in a place I know.   40
Only put it at once here in the cupboard,
I swear she won't believe her eyes;
I put some nice little trinkets in it
In order to win a different prize.
Still child is child and a game's a game.   45

FAUST. I don't know; shall I?

MEPHISTOPHELES.   You ask? For shame!
Do you perhaps intend to keep the spoil?
Then I advise Your Lustfulness
To save these hours that are so precious   50
And save me any further toil.
I hope you aren't avaricious.
After scratching my head so much and twisting my hands—
     [*He puts the casket in the cupboard.*]
Now quick! We depart!
In order to sway the dear young thing   55
To meet the dearest wish of your heart;
And *you* assume
A look that belongs to the lecture room,
As if Physics and Metaphysics too
Stood grey as life in front of you!   60
Come on!
     [*They go out; then* GRETCHEN *reappears.*]

GRETCHEN. It is so sultry, so fusty here,
And it's not even so warm outside.
I feel as if I don't know what—
I wish my mother would appear.   65
I'm trembling all over from top to toe—
I'm a silly girl to get frightened so.
     [*She sings as she undresses.*]
     There was a king in Thule
     Was faithful to the grave,

68. *Thule:* the fabled *ultima Thule* of Latin literature—those distant lands just beyond the reach of every explorer. In Roman times, the phrase probably denoted the Shetland Islands. Goethe wrote this ballad in 1774; it was published and set to music in 1782. The poem also served as the inspiration for the slow movement of Mendelssohn's *Italian Symphony*.

To whom his dying lady
A golden winecup gave. 70

He drained it at every banquet—
A treasure none could buy;
Whenever he filled and drank it
The tears o'erflowed his eye. 75

And when his days were numbered
He numbered land and pelf;
He left his heir his kingdom,
The cup he kept himself.

He sat at the royal table 80
With his knights of high degree
In the lofty hall of his fathers
In the castle on the sea.

There stood the old man drinking
The last of the living glow, 85
Then threw the sacred winecup
Into the waves below.

He saw it fall and falter
And founder in the main;
His eyelids fell, thereafter 90
He never drank again.

[*She opens the cupboard to put away her clothes and sees the casket.*]

How did this lovely casket get in here?
I locked the cupboard, I'm quite sure.
But what can be in it? It's very queer.
Perhaps someone left it here in pawn 95
And my mother gave him a loan on it.
Here's a little key tied on with tape—
I've a good mind to open it.
What is all this? My God! But see!
I have never come across such things. 100
Jewels—that would suit a countess
At a really grand festivity.
To whom can these splendid things belong?

[*She tries on the jewels and looks in the looking-glass.*]

If only the ear-rings belonged to me!
They make one look quite differently. 105
What is the use of looks and youth?
That's all very well and fine in truth

But people leave it all alone,
They praise you and pity you in one;
Gold is their sole   110
Concern and goal.
Alas for us who have none!

A WALK

Elsewhere and later. MEPHISTOPHELES *joins* FAUST.

MEPHISTOPHELES. By every despised love! By the elements of hell!
    I wish I knew something worse to provide a curse as well!
FAUST. What's the trouble? What's biting you?
    I never saw such a face in my life.
MEPHISTOPHELES. I would sell myself to the devil this minute   5
    If only I weren't a devil too.
FAUST. What is it? Are you mad? Or sick?
    It suits you to rage like a lunatic!
MEPHISTOPHELES. Imagine! The jewels that Gretchen got,
    A priest has gone and scooped the lot!   10
    Her mother got wind of it and she
    At once had the horrors secretly.
    That woman has a nose beyond compare,
    She's always snuffling in the Book of Prayer,
    And can tell by how each object smells   15
    If it is sacred or something else;
    So the scent of the jewels tells her clear
    There's nothing very blessed here.
    'My child,' she cries, 'unrighteous wealth
    Invests the soul, infects the health.   20
    We'll dedicate it to the Virgin
    And *she'll* make heavenly manna burgeon!'
    Gretchen's face, you could see it fall;
    She thought: 'It's a gift-horse after all,
    And he *can't* be lacking in sanctity   25
    Who brought it here so handsomely!'
    The mother had a priest along
    And had hardly started up her song
    Before he thought things looked all right
    And said: 'Very proper and above board!   30
    Self-control is its own reward.
    The Church has an excellent appetite,
    She has swallowed whole countries and the question
    Has never arisen of indigestion.
    Only the Church, my dears, can take   35
    Ill-gotten goods without stomach-ache!'

FAUST. That is a custom the world through,
  A Jew and a king observe it too.
MEPHISTOPHELES. So brooch, ring, chain he swipes at speed
  As if they were merely chicken-feed,   40
  Thanks them no more and no less for the casket
  Than for a pound of nuts in a basket,
  Promises Heaven will provide
  And leaves them extremely edified.
FAUST. And Gretchen?   45
MEPHISTOPHELES.   Sits and worries there,
  Doesn't know what to do and doesn't care,
  Thinks day and night on gold and gem,
  Still more on the man who presented them.
FAUST. My sweetheart's grief distresses me.   50
  Get her more jewels instantly!
  The first lot barely deserved the name.
MEPHISTOPHELES. So the gentleman thinks it all a nursery game!
FAUST. Do what I tell you and get it right;
  Don't let her neighbour out of your sight.   55
  And don't be a sloppy devil; contrive
  A new set of jewels. Look alive!
      [*Exit* FAUST.]
MEPHISTOPHELES. Yes, my dear sir, with all my heart.
  This is the way that a fool in love
  Puffs away to amuse his lady   60
  Sun and moon and the stars above.

MARTHA'S HOUSE

MARTHA. [*Alone*] My dear husband, God forgive him,
  His behaviour has *not* been without a flaw!
  Careers away out into the world
  And leaves me alone to sleep on straw.
  And yet I never trod on his toes,   5
  I loved him with all my heart, God knows.   [*Sobs.*]
  Perhaps he is even dead——O fate!
  If I'd only a death certificate!
      [GRETCHEN *enters.*]
GRETCHEN. Frau Martha!
MARTHA.   Gretelchen! What's up?   10
GRETCHEN. My legs are sinking under me,
  I've just discovered in my cupboard
  Another casket—of ebony,
  And things inside it, such a store,
  Far richer than the lot before.   15
MARTHA. You mustn't mention it to your mother;

She'd take it straight to the priest—like the other.

GRETCHEN. But only look! Just look at this!

MARTHA. O you lucky little Miss!

GRETCHEN. I daren't appear in the street, I'm afraid,   20
Or in church either, thus arrayed.

MARTHA. Just you visit me often here
And put on the jewels secretly!
Walk up and down for an hour in front of my glass
And that will be fun for you and me;   25
And then an occasion may offer, a holiday,
Where one can let them be seen in a gradual way;
A necklace to start with, then a pearl ear-ring; your mother
Most likely won't see; if she does one can think up something
   or other.

GRETCHEN. But who brought these two cases, who could it be?   30
It doesn't seem quite right to me.
   [*Knocking.*]
My God! My mother? Is that her?

MARTHA. It is a stranger. Come in, sir!
   [*Enter* MEPHISTOPHELES.]

MEPHISTOPHELES. I have made so free as to walk straight in;
The ladies will pardon me? May I begin   35
By inquiring for a Frau Martha Schwerdtlein?

MARTHA. That's me. What might the gentleman want?

MEPHISTOPHELES. [*Aside to* MARTHA] Now I know who you are,
      that's enough for me;
You have very distinguished company.
Forgive my bursting in so soon;   40
I will call again in the afternoon.

MARTHA. Imagine, child, in the name of Piety!
The gentleman takes you for society.

GRETCHEN. I'm a poor young thing, not at all refined;
My God, the gentleman is too kind.   45
These jewels and ornaments aren't my own.

MEPHISTOPHELES. Oh, it's not the jewellery alone;
She has a presence, a look so keen—
How delighted I am that I may remain.

MARTHA. What is your news? I cannot wait—   50

MEPHISTOPHELES. I wish I'd a better tale to relate.
I trust this will not earn me a beating:
Your husband is dead and sends his greeting.

MARTHA. Dead? The good soul? Oh why! Oh why!
My husband is dead! Oh I shall die!   55

GRETCHEN. Oh don't, dear woman, despair so.

36. *Schwerdtlein:* literally. "little sword." Her husband is a soldier.

MEPHISTOPHELES. Listen to my tale of woe!
GRETCHEN. Now, while I live, may I never love;
  Such a loss would bring me to my grave.
MEPHISTOPHELES. Joy must have grief, grief must have joy.   60
MARTHA. How was his end? Oh tell it me.
MEPHISTOPHELES. He lies buried in Padua
  At the church of Holy Anthony,
  In properly consecrated ground
  Where he sleeps for ever cool and sound.   65
MARTHA. Have you nothing else for me? Is that all?
MEPHISTOPHELES. Yes, a request; it's heavy and fat.
  You must have three hundred masses said for his soul.
  My pockets are empty apart from that.
MARTHA. What! Not a trinket? Not a token?   70
  What every prentice keeps at the bottom of his bag
  And saves it up as a souvenir
  And would sooner starve and sooner beg—
MEPHISTOPHELES. Madam, you make me quite heart-broken.
  But, really and truly, he didn't squander his money.   75
  And, besides, he repented his mistakes,
  Yes, and lamented still more his unlucky breaks.
GRETCHEN. Alas that men should be so unlucky!
  Be assured I shall often pray that he may find rest above.
MEPHISTOPHELES. *You* deserve to be taken straight to the altar;   80
  You are a child a man could love.
GRETCHEN. No, no, it's not yet time for that.
MEPHISTOPHELES. Then, if not a husband, a lover will do.
  It's one of the greatest gifts of Heaven
  To hold in one's arms a thing like you.   85
GRETCHEN. That is not the custom of our race.
MEPHISTOPHELES. Custom or not, it's what takes place.
MARTHA. But tell me!
MEPHISTOPHELES.   His deathbed, where I stood,
  Was something better than a dungheap—   90
  Half-rotten straw; however, he died like a Christian
  And found he had still a great many debts to make good.
  How thoroughly, he cried, I must hate myself
  To leave my job and my wife like that on the shelf!
  When I remember it, I die!   95
  If only she would forgive me here below!
MARTHA. Good man! I have forgiven him long ago.
MEPHISTOPHELES. All the same, God knows, she was more at fault
    than I.

63. *Anthony:* Mephistopheles' lie acquires added irony from the fact that this is one of Padua's most famous churches, its basilica holding the bones of St. Anthony.

MARTHA. That's a lie! To think he lied at the point of death!

MEPHISTOPHELES. He certainly fibbed a bit with his last breath, 100
If I'm half a judge of the situation.
I' had no need, said he, to gape for recreation;
First getting children, then getting bread to feed 'em—
And bread in the widest sense, you know—
And I couldn't even eat my share in peace. 105

MARTHA. So all my love, my loyalty, went for naught,
My toiling and moiling without cease!

MEPHISTOPHELES. Not at all; he gave it profoundest thought.
When I left Malta—that was how he began—
I prayed for my wife and children like one demented 110
And Heaven heard me and consented
To let us capture a Turkish merchantman,
With a treasure for the Sultan himself on board.
Well, bravery got its due reward
And I myself, as was only fit, 115
I got a decent cut of it.

MARTHA. Eh! Eh! How? Where? Has he perhaps buried it?

MEPHISTOPHELES. Who knows where the four winds now have
carried it?
As he lounged round Naples, quite unknown,
A pretty lady made him her friend, 120
She was so fond of him, so devoted,
He wore her colours at his blessed end.

MARTHA. The crook! The robber of his children!
Could no misery, no poverty,
Check the scandalous life he led! 125

MEPHISTOPHELES. You see! That is just why he's dead.
However, if I were placed like you,
I would mourn him modestly for a year
While looking round for someone new.

MARTHA. Ah God! My first one was so dear, 130
His like in this world will be hard to discover.
There could hardly be a more sweet little fool than mine.
It was only he was too fond of playing the rover,
And of foreign women and foreign wine,
And of the God-damned gaming-table. 135

MEPHISTOPHELES. Now, now, he might have still got by
If he on his part had been able
To follow your suit and wink an eye.
With that proviso, I swear, I too
Would give an engagement ring to you. 140

MARTHA. The gentleman is pleased to be witty.

MEPHISTOPHELES. [*Aside*] I had better go while the going's good;

She'd hold the devil to his word, she would!
And how is it with *your* heart, my pretty?
GRETCHEN. What does the gentleman mean?　　　　145
MEPHISTOPHELES. [*Aside*]　　Good, innocent child!
Farewell, ladies!
GRETCHEN.　　　Farewell!
MARTHA.　　　　　O quickly! Tell me;
I'd like to have the evidence filed　　　　150
Where, how and when my treasure died and was buried.
I have always liked things orderly and decent
And to read of his death in the weeklies would be pleasant.
MEPHISTOPHELES. Yes, Madam, when two witnesses are agreed,
The truth, as we all know, is guaranteed;　　　　155
And I have a friend, an excellent sort,
I'll get him to swear you this in court.
I'll bring him here.
MARTHA.　　　O yes! Please do!
MEPHISTOPHELES. And the young lady will be here too?　　　160
He's an honest lad. He's been around,
His politeness to ladies is profound.
GRETCHEN. I'll be all blushes in his presence.
MEPHISTOPHELES. No king on earth should so affect you.
MARTHA. Behind the house there—in my garden—　　　165
This evening—both of you—we'll expect you.

IN THE STREET

FAUST. How is it? Going ahead? Will it soon come right?
MEPHISTOPHELES. Excellent! Do I find you all on fire?
Gretchen is yours before many days expire.
You will see her at Martha's, her neighbour's house to-night
And that's a woman with a special vocation,　　　5
As it were, for the bawd-cum-gipsy occupation.
FAUST. Good!
MEPHISTOPHELES. But there is something *we* must do.
FAUST. One good turn deserves another. True.
MEPHISTOPHELES. It only means the legal attesting　　　10
That her husband's played-out limbs are resting
At Padua in consecrated ground.
FAUST. Very smart! I suppose we begin by going to Padua!
MEPHISTOPHELES. There's no need for that. What a simple lad
you are!
Only bear witness and don't ask questions.　　　15
FAUST. The scheme's at an end if you have no better suggestions.
MEPHISTOPHELES. Oh there you go! What sanctity!
Is this the first time in your life

You have committed perjury?
God and the world and all that moves therein,   20
Man and the way his emotions and thoughts take place,
Have you not given downright definitions
Of these with an iron breast and a brazen face?
And if you will only look below the surface,
You must confess you knew as much of these   25
As you know to-day of Herr Schwerdtlein's late decease.

FAUST. You are and remain a sophist and a liar.

MEPHISTOPHELES. Quite so—if that is as deep as you'll inquire.
Won't you to-morrow on your honour
Befool poor Gretchen and swear before her   30
That all your soul is set upon her?

FAUST. And from my heart.

MEPHISTOPHELES.   That's nice of you!
And your talk of eternal faith and love,
Of one single passion enthroned above   35
All others—will that be heartfelt too?

FAUST. Stop! It will! If I have feeling, if I
Feel this emotion, this commotion,
And can find no name to call it by;
If then I sweep the world with all my senses casting   40
Around for words and all the highest titles
And call this flame which burns my vitals
Endless, everlasting, everlasting,
Is that a devilish game of lies?

MEPHISTOPHELES. I'm right all the same.   45

FAUST.   Listen! Mark this well,
I beg you, and spare me talking till I'm hoarse:
The man who *will* be right, provided he has a tongue,
Why, he'll be right of course.
But come, I'm tired of listening to your voice;   50
You're right, the more so since I have no choice.

MARTHA'S GARDEN

They are walking in pairs: MARTHA *with* MEPHISTOPHELES,
GRETCHEN *on* FAUST'S *arm.*

GRETCHEN. The gentleman's only indulging me, I feel,
And condescending, to put me to shame.
You travellers are all the same,
You put up with things out of sheer good will.
I know too well that my poor conversation   5
Can't entertain a person of your station.

FAUST. One glance from you, one word, entertains me more

Than all this world's wisdom and lore.
> [*He kisses her hand.*]

GRETCHEN. Don't go to such inconvenience! How could you kiss
> my hand?
> It is so ugly, it is so rough.   10
> I have had to work at Heaven knows what!
> My mother's exacting, true enough.
> > [*They pass on.*]

MARTHA. And you, sir, do you always move round like this?

MEPHISTOPHELES. Oh, business and duty keep us up to the min-
> ute!
> With what regret one often leaves a place   15
> And yet one cannot ever linger in it.

MARTHA. That may go in one's salad days—
> To rush all over the world at random;
> But the evil time comes on apace
> And to drag oneself to the grave a lonely bachelor   20
> Is never much good in any case.

MEPHISTOPHELES. The prospect alarms me at a distant glance.

MARTHA. Then, worthy sir, be wise while you have the chance.
> > [*They pass on.*]

GRETCHEN. Yes, out of sight, out of mind!
> You are polite to your finger-ends   25
> But you have lots of clever friends
> Who must leave *me* so far behind.

FAUST. Believe me, dearest, what the world calls clever
> More often is vanity and narrowness.

GRETCHEN.   What?   30

FAUST. Alas that simplicity, that innocence,
> Cannot assess itself and its sacred value ever!
> That humility, lowliness, the highest gifts
> That living Nature has shared out to men—

GRETCHEN. Only think of *me* one little minute,   35
> I shall have time enough to think of you again.

FAUST. You are much alone, I suppose?

GRETCHEN. Yes, our household's only small
> But it needs running after all.
> We have no maid; I must cook and sweep and knit   40
> And sew and be always on the run,
> And my mother looks into every detail—
> Each single one.
> Not that she has such need to keep expenses down;
> We could spread ourselves more than some others do;   45
> My father left us a decent property,

14. *business:* Mephistopheles speaks as a traveling salesman.

A little house with a garden outside town.
However, my days at the present are pretty quiet;
My brother's in the army,
My little sister is dead.   50
The child indeed had worn me to a thread;
Still, all that trouble, I'd have it again, I'd try it,
I loved her so.

FAUST.   An angel, if she was like you!

GRETCHEN. I brought her up, she was very fond of me.   55
She was born after my father died,
We gave my mother up for lost,
Her life was at such a low, low tide,
And she only got better slowly, bit by bit;
The poor little creature, she could not even   60
Think for a minute of suckling it;
And so I brought her up quite alone
On milk and water; so she became my own.
On my own arm, on my own knee,
She smiled and kicked, grew fair to see.   65

FAUST. You felt, I am sure, the purest happiness.

GRETCHEN. Yes; and—be sure—many an hour of distress.
The little one's cradle stood at night
Beside my bed; she could hardly stir
But I was awake,   70
Now having to give her milk, now into my bed with her,
Now, if she went on crying, try to stop her
By getting up and dandling her up and down the room,
And then first thing in the morning stand at the copper;
Then off to the market and attend to the range,   75
And so on day after day, never a change.
Living like that, one can't always feel one's best;
But food tastes better for it, so does rest.
        [*They pass on.*]

MARTHA. No, the poor women don't come out of it well,
A *vieux garçon* is a hard nut to crack.   80

MEPHISTOPHELES. It only rests with you and your like
To put me on a better tack.

MARTHA. Tell me, sir: have you never met someone you fancy?
Has your heart been nowhere involved among the girls?

MEPHISTOPHELES. The proverb says: A man's own fireside   85
And a good wife are gold and pearls.

MARTHA. I mean, have you never felt any inclination?

MEPHISTOPHELES. I've generally been received with all consideration.

MARTHA. What I wanted to say: has your heart never been serious?

MEPHISTOPHELES. To make a joke to a woman is always precarious.

MARTHA. Oh you don't understand me!

MEPHISTOPHELES. Now *that* I really mind!
But I do understand—that you are very kind.
    [*They pass on.*]

FAUST. You knew me again, you little angel,
As soon as you saw me enter the garden?   95

GRETCHEN. Didn't you see me cast down my eyes?

FAUST. And the liberty that I took you pardon?
The impudence that reared its head
When you lately left the cathedral door.

GRETCHEN. I was upset; it had never happened before;   100
No one could ever say anything bad of me—
Oh can he, I thought, have seen in my behaviour
Any cheekiness, any impropriety?
The idea, it seemed, had come to you pat:
'I can treat this woman just like that'.   105
I must admit I did not know what it was
In my heart that began to make me change my view,
But indeed I was angry with myself because
I could not be angrier with you.

FAUST. Sweet love!   110

GRETCHEN. Wait a moment!
    [*She plucks a flower and starts picking off the petals.*]

FAUST. What is that? A bouquet?

GRETCHEN. No, only a game.

FAUST. A what?

GRETCHEN. You will laugh at me. Go away!   115
    [GRETCHEN *murmurs.*]

FAUST. What are you murmuring?

GRETCHEN. Loves me—Loves me not—

FAUST. You flower from Heaven's garden plot!

GRETCHEN. Loves me—Not—Loves me—Not—
Loves me!   120

FAUST. Yes, child. What this flower has told you
Regard it as God's oracle. He loves you!
Do you know the meaning of that? He loves you!
    [*He takes her hands.*]

GRETCHEN. Oh I feel so strange.

FAUST. Don't shudder. Let this look,   125
Let this clasp of the hand tell you
What mouth can never express:
To give oneself up utterly and feel
A rapture which must be everlasting.

Everlasting! Its end would be despair.   130
No; no end! No end!
    [*She breaks away from him and runs off. After a moment's
    thought he follows her.*]
MARTHA. [*Approaching*] The night's coming on.
MEPHISTOPHELES.   Yes—and we must go.
MARTHA. I would ask you to remain here longer
But this is a terrible place, you know.   135
It's as if no one were able to shape at
Any vocation or recreation
But must have his neighbour's comings and goings to gape at
And, whatever one does, the talk is unleashed, unfurled.
And our little couple?   140
MEPHISTOPHELES.   Carefree birds of summer!
Flown to the summerhouse.
MARTHA.   He seems to like her.
MEPHISTOPHELES. And vice versa. That is the way of the world.

A SUMMERHOUSE

GRETCHEN *runs in and hides behind the door.*

GRETCHEN. He comes!
FAUST. [*Entering*]   You rogue! Teasing me so!
I've caught you!
    [*He kisses her.*]
GRETCHEN.   Dearest! I love you so!
    [MEPHISTOPHELES *knocks.*]
FAUST. Who's there?   5
MEPHISTOPHELES.   A friend.
FAUST.   A brute!
MEPHISTOPHELES.   It is time to part, you know.
MARTHA. [*Joining them*] Yes, it is late, sir.
FAUST.   May I not see you home?   10
GRETCHEN. My mother would—Farewell!
FAUST.   I must go then?
    Farewell!
MARTHA.   Adieu!
GRETCHEN.   Let us soon meet again!   15
    [FAUST *and* MEPHISTOPHELES *leave.*]
Dear God! A man of such a kind,
What things must go on in his mind!
I can only blush when he talks to me;
Whatever he says, I must agree.
Poor silly child, I cannot see   20
What it is he finds in me.

FAUST. [*Alone*] Exalted Spirit, you gave me, gave me all
  I prayed for. Aye, and it is not in vain
  That you have turned your face in fire upon me.
  You gave me glorious Nature for my kingdom
  With power to feel her and enjoy her. Nor   5
  Is it a mere cold wondering glance you grant me
  But you allow me to gaze into her depths
  Even as into the bosom of a friend.
  Aye, you parade the ranks of living things
  Before me and you teach me to know my brothers   10
  In the quiet copse, in the water, in the air.
  And when the storm growls and snarls in the forest
  And the giant pine falls headlong, bearing away
  And crushing its neighbours, bough and bole and all,
  With whose dull fall the hollow hill resounds,   15
  Then do you carry me off to a sheltered cave
  And show me myself, and wonders of my own breast
  Unveil themselves in their deep mystery.
  And now that the clear moon rises on my eyes
  To soften things, now floating up before me   20
  From walls of rocks and from the dripping covert
  Come silver forms of the past which soothe and temper
  The dour delight I find in contemplation.

  That nothing perfect falls to men, oh now
  I feel that true. In addition to the rapture   25
  Which brings me near and nearer to the gods
  You gave me that companion whom already
  I cannot do without, though cold and brazen
  He lowers me in my own eyes and with
  One whispered word can turn your gifts to nothing.   30
  He is always busily fanning in my breast
  A fire of longing for that lovely image.
  So do I stagger from desire to enjoyment
  And in enjoyment languish for desire.
    [MEPHISTOPHELES *enters.*]
MEPHISTOPHELES. Haven't you yet had enough of this kind of
    life?   35
  How can it still appeal to you?
  It is all very well to try it once,
  Then one should switch to something new.
FAUST. I wish you had something else to do
  On my better days than come plaguing me.   40
MEPHISTOPHELES. Now, now! I'd gladly leave you alone;

You needn't suggest it seriously.
So rude and farouche and mad a friend
Would certainly be little loss.
One has one's hands full without end!   45
One can never read in the gentleman's face
What he likes or what should be left alone.

FAUST. That is exactly the right tone!
He must be thanked for causing me ennui.

MEPHISTOPHELES. Poor son of earth, what sort of life   50
Would you have led were it not for me?
The flim-flams of imagination,
I have cured you of those for many a day.
But for me, this terrestrial ball
Would already have seen you flounce away.   55
Why behave as an owl behaves
Moping in rocky clefts and caves?
Why do you nourish yourself like a toad that sips
From moss that oozes, stone that drips?
A pretty pastime to contrive!   60
The doctor in you is still alive.

FAUST. Do you comprehend what a new and vital power
This wandering in the wilderness has given me?
Aye, with even an inkling of such joy,
You would be devil enough to grudge it me.   65

MEPHISTOPHELES. A supernatural gratification!
To lie on the mountain tops in the dark and dew
Rapturously embracing earth and heaven,
Swelling yourself to a godhead, ferreting through
The marrow of the earth with divination,   70
To feel in your breast the whole six days of creation,
To enjoy I know not what in arrogant might
And then, with the Old Adam discarded quite,
To overflow into all things in ecstasy;
After all which your lofty intuition   75
      [*He makes a gesture.*]
Will end—hm—unmentionably.

FAUST. Shame on you!

MEPHISTOPHELES.   Am I to blame?
You have the right to be moral and cry shame!
One must not mention to the modest ear   80
What the modest heart is ever agog to hear.
And, in a word, you are welcome to the pleasure
Of lying to yourself in measure;
But this deception will not last.

61. *doctor:* i.e., the doctor of philosophy.

Already overdriven again,   85
If this goes on you must collapse,
Mad or tormented or aghast.
Enough of this! Back there your love is sitting
And all her world seems sad and small;
You are never absent from her mind,   90
Her love for you is more than all.
At first your passion came overflowing
Like a brook that the melted snows have bolstered high;
You have poured your passion into her heart
And now your brook once more is dry.   95
I think, instead of lording it here above
In the woods, the great man might think fit
In view of that poor ninny's love
To make her some return for it.
She finds the time wretchedly long;   100
She stands at the window, watches the clouds
As over the old town walls they roll away.
'If I had the wings of a dove'—so runs her song
Half the night and all the day.
Now she is cheerful, mostly low,   105
Now has spent all her tears,
Now calm again, it appears,
But always loves you so.

FAUST. You snake! You snake!

MEPHISTOPHELES. [*Aside*] Ha! It begins to take!   110

FAUST. You outcast! Take yourself away
And do not name that lovely woman.
Do not bring back the desire for her sweet body
Upon my senses that are half astray.

MEPHISTOPHELES. Where's this to end? She thinks you have run
off,   115
And so you have—about half and half.

FAUST. I am still near her, though far removed,
Her image must be always in my head;
I already envy the body of the Lord
When her lips rest upon the holy bread.   120

MEPHISTOPHELES. Very well, my friend. I have often envied you
Those two young roes that are twins, I mean her two—

FAUST. Pimp! Get away!

MEPHISTOPHELES.   Fine! So you scold? I must laugh.
The God who created girl and boy   125
Knew very well the high vocation
Which facilitates their joy.
But come, this is a fine excuse for gloom!

You should take the road to your sweetheart's room,
Rather than that to death, you know.   130
FAUST. What is the joy of heaven in her arms?
Even when I catch fire upon her breast
Do I not always sense her woe?
Am I not the runaway? The man without a home?
The monster restless and purposeless   135
Who roared like a waterfall from rock to rock in foam
Greedily raging towards the precipice?
And she on the bank in childlike innocence
In a little hut on the little alpine plot
And all her little household world   140
Concentrated in that spot.
And I, the loathed of God,
I was not satisfied
To seize and crush to powder
The rocks on the river side!   145
Her too, her peace, I must undermine as well!
This was the sacrifice I owed to Hell!
Help, Devil, to shorten my time of torment!
What must be, must be; hasten it!
Let her fate hurtle down with mine,   150
Let us go together to the pit!
MEPHISTOPHELES. How it glows again, how it boils again!
Go in and comfort her, my foolish friend!
When such a blockhead sees no outlet
He thinks at once it is the end.   155
Long live the man who does not flinch!
But you've a devil in you, somewhere there.
I know of nothing on earth more unattractive
Than your devil who feels despair.

GRETCHEN'S ROOM

GRETCHEN *is alone, singing at the spinning-wheel.*

GRETCHEN. My peace is gone,
     My heart is sore,
     I shall find it never
     And never more.

     He has left my room   5
     An empty tomb,
     He has gone and all
     My world is gall.

     My poor head

Is all astray,
My poor mind   10
Fallen away.

My peace is gone,
My heart is sore,
I shall find it never   15
And never more.

'Tis he that I look through
The window to see,
He that I open
The door for—he!   20

His gait, his figure,
So grand, so high!
The smile of his mouth,
The power of his eye,

And the magic stream   25
Of his words—what bliss!
The clasp of his hand
And, ah, his kiss!

My peace is gone,
My heart is sore,   30
I shall find it never
And never more.

My heart's desire
Is so strong, so vast;
Ah, could I seize him   35
And hold him fast

And kiss him for ever
Night and day—
And on his kisses
Pass away!   40

MARTHA'S GARDEN

GRETCHEN. Promise me, Heinrich!
FAUST.   If I can!
GRETCHEN. Tell me: how do you stand in regard to religion?
     You are indeed a good, good man
     But I think you give it scant attention.   5
FAUST. Leave that, my child! You feel what I feel for you;

---

1. *Heinrich:* i.e., Faust. In the   Johann (John). Goethe changed it to
legend, Faust's first name was generally   Heinrich (Henry).

For those I love I would give my life and none
Will I deprive of his sentiments and his church.

GRETCHEN. That is not right; one must believe thereon.

FAUST. Must one? 10

GRETCHEN.   If only I had some influence!
Nor do you honour the holy sacraments.

FAUST. I honour them.

GRETCHEN.   Yes, but not with any zest.
When were you last at mass, when were you last confessed? 15
Do you believe in God?

FAUST.   My darling, who dare say:
I believe in God?
Ask professor or priest,
Their answers will make an odd 20
Mockery of you.

GRETCHEN.   You don't believe, you mean?

FAUST. Do not misunderstand me, my love, my queen!
Who can name him?
Admit on the spot: 25
I believe in him?
And who can dare
To perceive and declare:
I believe in him not?
The All-Embracing One, 30
All-Upholding One,
Does he not embrace, uphold,
You, me, Himself?
Does not the Heaven vault itself above us?
Is not the earth established fast below? 35
And with their friendly glances do not
Eternal stars rise over us?
Do not my eyes look into yours,
And all things thrust
Into your head, into your heart, 40
And weave in everlasting mystery
Invisibly, visibly, around you?
Fill your heart with *this*, great as it is,
And when this feeling grants you perfect bliss,
Then call it what you will— 45
Happiness! Heart! Love! God!
I have no name for it!
Feeling is all;
Name is mere sound and reek
Clouding Heaven's light. 50

GRETCHEN. That sounds quite good and right;

And much as the priest might speak,
Only not word for word.
FAUST. It is what all hearts have heard
In all the places heavenly day can reach,   55
Each in his own speech;
Why not I in mine?
GRETCHEN. I could almost accept it, you make it sound so fine,
Still there is something in it that shouldn't be;
For you have no Christianity.   60
FAUST. Dear child!
GRETCHEN.   It has long been a grief to me
To see you in such company.
FAUST. You mean?
GRETCHEN.   The man who goes about with you,   65
I hate him in my soul, right through and through.
And nothing has given my heart
In my whole life so keen a smart
As that man's face, so dire, so grim.
FAUST. Dear poppet, don't be afraid of him!   70
GRETCHEN. My blood is troubled by his presence.
All other people, I wish them well;
But much as I may long to see you,
He gives me a horror I cannot tell,
And I think he's a man too none can trust.   75
God forgive me if I'm unjust.
FAUST. Such queer fish too must have room to swim.
GRETCHEN. I wouldn't live with the like of him!
Whenever that man comes to the door,
He looks in so sarcastically,   80
Half angrily,
One can see he feels no sympathy;
It is written on his face so clear
There is not a soul he can hold dear.
I feel so cosy in your arms,   85
So warm and free from all restraint,
And his presence ties me up inside.
FAUST. You angel, with your wild alarms!
GRETCHEN. It makes me feel so ill, so faint,
That, if he merely happens to join us,   90
I even think I have no more love for you.
Besides, when he's there, I could never pray,
And that is eating my heart away;
You, Heinrich, you must feel it too.
FAUST. You suffer from an antipathy.   95
GRETCHEN. Now I must go.

FAUST.   Oh, can I never rest
  One little hour hanging upon your breast,
  Pressing both breast on breast and soul on soul?
GRETCHEN. Ah, if I only slept alone!   100
  I'd gladly leave the door unlatched for you to-night;
  My mother, however, sleeps so light
  And if she found us there, I own
  I should fall dead upon the spot.
FAUST. You angel, there is no fear of that.   105
  Here's a little flask. Three drops are all
  It needs—in her drink—to cover nature
  In a deep sleep, a gentle pall.
GRETCHEN. What would I not do for your sake!
  I hope it will do her no injury.   110
FAUST. My love, do you think that of me?
GRETCHEN. Dearest, I've only to look at you
  And I do not know what drives me to meet your will
  I have already done so much for you
  That little more is left me to fulfil.   115
      [*She goes out—and* MEPHISTOPHELES *enters.*]
MEPHISTOPHELES. The monkey! Is she gone?
FAUST.   Have you been spying again?
MEPHISTOPHELES. I have taken pretty good note of it,
  The doctor has been catechised—
  And much, I hope, to his benefit;   120
  The girls are really keen to be advised
  If a man belongs to the old simple-and-pious school.
  'If he stand that', they think, 'he'll stand *our* rule.'
FAUST. You, you monster, cannot see
  How this true and loving soul   125
  For whom faith is her whole
  Being and the only road
  To beatitude, must feel a holy horror
  Having to count her beloved lost for good.
MEPHISTOPHELES. You supersensual, sensual buck,   130
  Led by the nose by the girl you court!
FAUST. O you abortion of fire and muck!
MEPHISTOPHELES. And she also has skill in physiognomy;
  In my presence she feels she doesn't know what,
  She reads some hidden sense behind my little mask,   135
  She feels that I am assuredly a genius—
  Maybe the devil if she dared to ask.
  Now: to-night—
FAUST.   What is to-night to you?
MEPHISTOPHELES. I have my pleasure in it too.   140

AT THE WELL

GRETCHEN *and* LIESCHEN *with pitchers.*

LIESCHEN. Haven't you heard about Barbara? Not what's passed?
GRETCHEN. Not a word. I go out very little.
LIESCHEN. It's true, Sibylla told me to-day:
    She has made a fool of herself at last.
    So much for her fine airs!   5
GRETCHEN.   Why?
LIESCHEN.   It stinks!
    Now she feeds two when she eats and drinks.
GRETCHEN. Ah!
LIESCHEN. Yes; she has got her deserts in the end.   10
    What a time she's been hanging on her friend!
    Going the rounds
    To the dances and the amusement grounds,
    She had to be always the first in the line,
    He was always standing her cakes and wine;   15
    She thought her looks so mighty fine,
    She was so brazen she didn't waver
    To take the presents that he gave her.
    Such cuddlings and such carryings on—
    But now the pretty flower is gone.   20
GRETCHEN. Poor thing!
LIESCHEN.   Is that the way you feel?
    When we were at the spinning-wheel
    And mother kept us upstairs at night,
    She was below with her heart's delight;
    On the bench or in the shady alley   25
    They never had long enough to dally.
    But now she must grovel in the dirt,
    Do penance in church in a hair shirt.
GRETCHEN. But surely he will marry her.
LIESCHEN. He'd be a fool! A smart young chap   30
    Has plenty of other casks to tap.
    Besides he's gone.
GRETCHEN.   That's not right.
LIESCHEN. If she hooks him she won't get off light!   35
    The boys will tear her wreath in half
    And we shall strew her door with chaff.
    [LIESCHEN *goes off.*]

3. *Sibylla:* a friend of Gretchen's; not to be confused with the "Sibyl" named in l. 162 of the scene in the witch's kitchen.

37. *chaff:* in contrast to the bridal bouquet. In Germany this treatment was reserved for girls who had "fallen."

GRETCHEN. [*Going home*] What scorn I used to pour upon her
    When a poor maiden lost her honour!
    My tongue could never find a name   40
    Bad enough for another's shame!
    I thought it black and I blackened it,
    It was never black enough to fit,
    And I blessed myself and acted proud—
    And now I too am under a cloud.   45
    Yet, God! What drove me to this pass,
    It was all so good, so dear, alas!

RAMPARTS

*In a niche in the wall is an image of the Mater Dolorosa.[a] In
front of it* GRETCHEN *is putting fresh flowers in the pots.*

GRETCHEN. Mary, bow down,
        Beneath thy woeful crown,
        Thy gracious face on me undone!

        The sword in thy heart,
        Smart upon smart,   5
        Thou lookest up to thy dear son;

        Sending up sighs
        To the Father which rise
        For his grief and for thine own.

        Who can gauge   10
        What torments rage
        Through the whole of me and how—
        How my poor heart is troubled in me,
        How fears and longings undermine me?
        Only thou knowest, only thou!   15

        Wherever I may go,
        What woe, what woe, what woe
        Is growing beneath my heart!
        Alas, I am hardly alone,
        I moan, I moan, I moan   20
        And my heart falls apart.

        The flower-pots in my window
        I watered with tears, ah me,
        When in the early morning
        I picked these flowers for thee.   25

a. literally, "sorrowful mother"; i.e., the Virgin Mary.

Not sooner in my bedroom
The sun's first rays were shed
Than I in deepest sorrow
Sat waking on my bed.

Save me from shame and death in one!   30
Ah, bow down
Thou of the woeful crown,
Thy gracious face on me undone.

NIGHT SCENE AT GRETCHEN'S DOOR

VALENTINE. When I was at some drinking bout
  Where big talk tends to blossom out,
  And my companions raised their voice
  To praise the maidens of their choice
  And drowned their praises in their drink,   5
  Then I would sit and never blink,
  Propped on my elbow listening
  To all their brags and blustering.
  Then smiling I would stroke my beard
  And raise the bumper in my hand   10
  And say: 'Each fellow to his taste!
  But is there one in all the land
  To hold a candle to my own
  Dear sister, Gretchen? No, there's none!'
  Hear! Hear! Kling! Kling! It went around;   15
  Some cried: 'His judgment is quite sound,
  She is the pearl of womanhood!'
  That shut those boasters up for good.
  And now! It would make one tear one's hair
  And run up walls in one's despair!   20
  Each filthy fellow in the place
  Can sneer and jeer at my disgrace!
  And I, like a man who's deep in debt,
  Every chance word must make me sweat.
  I could smash their heads for them if I tried—   25
  I could not tell them that they lied.
    [FAUST *and* MEPHISTOPHELES *enter.*]
VALENTINE. Who comes there, slinking? Who comes there?
  If I mistake not, they're a pair.
  If it's he, I'll scrag him on the spot;
  He'll be dead before he knows what's what!   30
FAUST. How from the window of the sacristy there
  The undying lamp sends up its little flicker

Which glimmers sideways weak and weaker
And round it presses the dark air.
My heart too feels its night, its noose.   35
MEPHISTOPHELES. And I feel like a tom-cat on the loose,
Brushing along the fire escape
And round the walls, a stealthy shape;
Moreover I feel quite virtuous,
Just a bit burglarious, a bit lecherous.   40
You see, I'm already haunted to the marrow
By the glorious Walpurgis Night.
It returns to us the day after to-morrow,
Then one knows why one's awake all right.
FAUST. I'd like some ornament, some ring,   45
For my dear mistress. I feel sad
To visit her without anything.
MEPHISTOPHELES. It's really nothing to regret—
That you needn't pay for what you get.
Now that the stars are gems on heaven's brocade,   50
You shall hear a real masterpiece.
I will sing her a moral serenade
That her folly may increase.
        [*He sings to the guitar.*]
MEPHISTOPHELES. Catherine, my dear,
                What? Waiting here   55
            At your lover's door
        When the stars of the night are fading?
            Oh don't begin!
            When he lifts the pin,
            A maid goes in—   60
        But she won't come out a maiden.

            So think aright!
            Grant him delight
            And it's good night,
        You poor, poor things—Don't linger!   65
            A girl who's wise
            Will hide her prize
            From robber's eyes—
        Unless she's a ring on her finger.
        [VALENTINE *comes forward.*]
VALENTINE. Damn you! Who're you seducing here?   70
    You damned pied piper! You magician!
    First to the devil with your guitar!

54-69. *Catherine . . . finger:* adapted by Goethe from Shakespeare's *Hamlet*, Act IV, Scene 5.

Then to the devil with the musician!

MEPHISTOPHELES. The guitar is finished. Look, it's broken in two.

VALENTINE. Now then, to break your heads for you!   75

MEPHISTOPHELES. Doctor! Courage! All you can muster!

Stick by me and do as I say!

Quick now, draw your feather duster!

I'll parry his blows, so thrust away!

VALENTINE. Then parry that!   80

MEPHISTOPHELES.   Why not, why not?

VALENTINE. And that!

MEPHISTOPHELES.   Of course.

VALENTINE.   Is he the devil or what?

What's this? My hand's already lamed.   85

MEPHISTOPHELES. Strike, you!

VALENTINE.   Oh!

          [VALENTINE *falls.*]

MEPHISTOPHELES.   Now the lout is tamed!

But we must go! Vanish in the wink of an eye!

They're already raising a murderous hue and cry.   90

MARTHA. [*At the window*] Come out! Come out!

GRETCHEN. [*At the window*]   Bring a light!

MARTHA. [*As before*] There's a row and a scuffle, they're having a
     fight.

MAN. Here's one on the ground; he's dead.

MARTHA. [*Coming out*] The murderers, have they gone?   95

GRETCHEN. [*Coming out*] Who's here?

MAN.   Your mother's son.

GRETCHEN. O God! What pain! O God!

VALENTINE. I am dying—that's soon said

And sooner done, no doubt.

Why do you women stand howling and wailing?   100

Come round and hear me out.

          [*They all gather round him.*]

Look, my Gretchen, you're young still,

You have not yet sufficient skill,

You bungle things a bit.

Here is a tip—you need no more—   105

Since you are once for all a whore,

Then make a job of it!

GRETCHEN. My brother? O God! Is it I you blame!

VALENTINE. Leave our Lord God out of the game!

What is done I'm afraid is done,   110

As one starts one must carry on.

You began with one man on the sly,

There will be more of them by and by,
And when a dozen have done with you
The whole town will have you too.   115

When Shame is born, she first appears
In this world in secrecy,
And the veil of night is drawn so tight
Over her head and ears;
Yes, people would kill her and forget her.   120
But she grows still more and more
And brazenly roams from door to door
And yet her appearance grows no better.
The more her face creates dismay,
The more she seeks the light of day.   125

Indeed I see the time draw on
When all good people in this town
Will turn aside from you, you tart,
As from a corpse in the plague cart.
Then your heart will sink within you,   130
When they look you in the eye!
It's good-bye to your golden chains!
And church-going and mass—good-bye!
No nice lace collars any more
To make you proud on the dancing floor!   135
No, in some dark and filthy nook
You'll hide with beggars and crippled folk
And, if God pardon you, he may;
You are cursed on earth till your dying day.
MARTHA. Commend your soul to the mercy of God!   140
   Will you add slander to your load?
VALENTINE. If I could get at your withered body,
   You bawd, you sinner born and hardened!
   Then I should hope that all my sins
   And in full measure might be pardoned.   145
GRETCHEN. My brother! O hell's misery!
VALENTINE. I tell you: let your weeping be.
   When you and your honour came to part,
   It was you that stabbed me to the heart.
   I go to God through the sleep of death,   150
   A soldier—brave to his last breath.
      [*He dies.*]

CATHEDRAL

Organ and anthem. GRETCHEN *in the congregation. An* EVIL
SPIRIT *whispers to her over her shoulder.*

EVIL SPIRIT. How different it all was
Gretchen, when you came here
All innocent to the altar,
Out of the worn-out little book
Lisping your prayers,   5
Half a child's game,
Half God in the heart!
Gretchen!
How is your head?
And your heart—   10
What are its crimes?
Do you pray for your mother's soul, who thanks to you
And your sleeping draught overslept into a long, long
    pain?
And whose blood stains your threshold?
Yes, and already under your heart   15
Does it not grow and quicken
And torture itself and you
With its foreboding presence?

GRETCHEN. Alas! Alas!
If I could get rid of the thoughts   20
Which course through my head hither and thither
Despite me!

CHOIR.   Dies irae, dies illa
              Solvet saeclum in favilla.

[*The organ plays.*]

EVIL SPIRIT. Agony seizes you!   25
The trumpet sounds!
The graves tremble
And your heart
From its ashen rest
To fiery torment   30
Comes up recreated
Trembling too!

GRETCHEN. Oh to escape from here!
I feel as if the organ
Were stifling me,   35
And the music dissolving
My heart in its depths.

CHOIR.   Judex ergo cum sedebit,
              Quidquid latet adparebit,

23–24. *Dies . . . favilla:* Day of
wrath, that day that dissolves the world
into ashes. (The choir is singing the
famous thirteenth-century hymn by
Thomas Celano.)

38–40. *Judex . . . remanebit:* When
the judge shall be seated, what is hidden
shall appear, nothing shall remain un-
avenged.

Nil inultum remanebit.   40

GRETCHEN.   I cannot breathe!
            The pillars of the walls
            Are round my throat!
            The vaulted roof
            Chokes me!—Air!   45

EVIL SPIRIT. Hide yourself! Nor sin nor shame
             Remains hidden.
             Air? Light?
             Woe to you!

CHOIR.   Quid sum miser tunc dicturus?   50
                    Quem patronum rogaturus?
                    Cum vix justus sit securus.

EVIL SPIRIT. The blessed turn
             Their faces from you.
             The pure shudder   55
             To reach out their hands to you.
             Woe!

CHOIR.   Quid sum miser tunc dicturus?

GRETCHEN.   Neighbour! Help! Your smelling bottle!
            [*She faints.*]

WALPURGIS NIGHT

FAUST *and* MEPHISTOPHELES *making their way through the Hartz
Mountains.*

MEPHISTOPHELES. A broomstick—don't you long for such a con-
               veyance?
   I'd find the coarsest he-goat some assistance.
   Taking this road, our goal is still in the distance.
FAUST. No, so long as my legs are not in abeyance,
   I can make do with this knotted stick.   5
   What is the use of going too quick?
   To creep along each labyrinthine valley,
   Then climb this scarp, downwards from which
   The bubbling spring makes its eternal sally,
   This is the spice that makes such journeys rich.   10
   Already the spring is weaving through the birches,
   Even the pine already feels the spring;
   Should not our bodies too give it some purchase?
MEPHISTOPHELES. Candidly—I don't feel a thing.
   In my body all is winter,   15
   I would prefer a route through frost and snow.
   How sadly the imperfect disc

50–52. *Quid . . . securus:* What   whom shall I appeal when scarcely the
shall I say in my wretchedness? To   righteous man is safe?

Of the red moon rises with belated glow
And the light it gives is bad, at every step
One runs into some rock or tree!   20
Permit me to ask a will o' the wisp.
I see one there, he's burning heartily.
Ahoy, my friend! Might I call on you to help us?
Why do you blaze away there to no purpose?
Be so good as to light us along our road.   25
WILL O' THE WISP. I only hope my sense of your mightiness
Will control my natural flightiness;
A zigzag course is our accustomed mode.
MEPHISTOPHELES. Ha! Ha! So it's men you want to imitate.
In the name of the Devil you go straight   30
Or I'll blow out your flickering, dickering light!
WILL O' THE WISP. You're the head of the house, I can see that all
    right,
You are welcome to use me at your convenience.
But remember, the mountain is magic-mad to-day
And, if a will o' the wisp is to show you the way,   35
You too must show a little lenience.
FAUST, MEPHISTOPHELES, WILL O' THE WISP. [*Singing successively*]
Into realms of dreams and witchcraft
We, it seems, have found an ingress.
Lead us well and show your woodcraft,
That we may make rapid progress   40
Through these wide and desert spaces.

Trees on trees—how each one races,
Pushing past—how each one hastens!
And the crags that make obeisance!
And the rocks with long-nosed faces—   45
Hear them snorting, hear them blowing!

Through the stones and lawns are flowing
Brook and brooklet, downward hustling.
Is that song—or is it rustling?
Sweet, sad notes of love—a relic—   50
Voices from those days angelic?
Thus we hope, we love—how vainly!
Echo like an ancient rumour
Calls again, yes, calls back plainly.

Now—Tu-whit!—we near the purlieu   55
Of—Tu-whoo!—owl, jay and curlew;
Are they all in waking humour?

21. *will o' the wisp:* the Jack o'   folklore, this was thought of as leading
lantern, or ignis fatuus. In German   travelers to their destruction.

In the bushes are those lizards—
Straggling legs and bloated gizzards?
And the roots like snakes around us   60
Coil from crag and sandy cranny,
Stretch their mad and strange antennae
Grasping at us to confound us;
Stretch from gnarled and living timber
Towards the passer-by their limber   65
Polyp-suckers!
      And in legions
Through these mossy, heathy regions
Mice, all colours, come cavorting!
And above, a serried cohort,   70
Fly the glow-worms as our escort—
More confusing than escorting.

Tell me what our real case is!
Are we stuck or are we going?
Rocks and trees, they all seem flying   75
Round and round and making faces,
And the will o' the wisps are blowing
Up so big and multiplying.

MEPHISTOPHELES. Hold my coat-tails, hold on tight!
Standing on this central height   80
Marvelling see how far and wide
Mammon lights the peaks inside.

FAUST. How strangely through the mountain hollows
A sad light gleams as of morning-red
And like a hound upon the scent   85
Probes the gorges' deepest bed!
Here fumes arise, there vapours float,
Here veils of mist catch sudden fire
Which creeps along, a flimsy thread,
Then fountains up, a towering spire.   90
Here a whole stretch it winds its way
With a hundred veins throughout the glen,
And here in the narrow neck of the pass
Is suddenly one strand again.
There, near by, are dancing sparks   95
Sprinkled around like golden sand.
But look! The conflagration climbs
The crags' full height, hand over hand.

MEPHISTOPHELES. Does not Sir Mammon light his palace

---

82. *Mammon:* See the note to l. 73
in the second scene titled FAUST'S STUDY.
Mammon is portrayed as the architect
of Satan's palace in Milton's *Paradise
Lost,* Book I, ll. 678 ff.

In splendid style for this occasion?　　　　　　100
You are lucky to have seen it;
Already I sense the noisy guests' invasion.
FAUST. How the Wind Hag rages through the air!
What blows she rains upon the nape of my neck!
MEPHISTOPHELES. You must clamp yourself to the ancient ribs of
　　the rock　　　　　　　　　　　　　　　105
Or she'll hurl you into this gorge, to find your grave down there.
A mist is thickening the night.
Hark to the crashing of the trees!
The owls are flying off in fright.
And the ever-green palaces—　　　　　　　110
Hark to their pillars sundering!
Branches moaning and breaking!
Tree-trunks mightily thundering!
Roots creaking and yawning!
Tree upon tree in appalling　　　　　　　115
Confusion crashing and falling,
And through the wreckage on the scarps
The winds are hissing and howling.
Do you hear those voices in the air?
Far-off voices? Voices near?　　　　　　　120
Aye, the whole length of the mountain side
The witch-song streams in a crazy tide.
WITCHES. [*In chorus*]. The witches enter the Brocken scene,
　　The stubble is yellow, the corn is green.
　　There assembles the mighty horde,　　　125
　　Urian sits aloft as lord.
　　So we go—over stock and stone—
　　Farting witch on stinking goat.
A VOICE. But ancient Baubo comes alone,
　　She rides on a mother sow—take note.　　130
CHORUS. So honour to whom honour is due!
　　Let Mother Baubo head the queue!
　　A strapping sow and Mother on top
　　And we'll come after, neck and crop.

　　The way is broad, the way is long,　　　135
　　How is this for a crazy throng?
　　The pitchfork pricks, the broomstick pokes,
　　The mother bursts and the child chokes.
VOICE FROM ABOVE. Come along, come along, from Felsensee!
VOICES FROM BELOW. We'd like to mount with you straight away.
　　We wash ourselves clean behind and before　　141

126. *Urian:* a name for the devil.　　nurse of Demeter, noted for her ob-
129. *Baubo:* In Greek mythology, the　scenity and bestiality.

But we are barren for evermore.

CHORUS. The wind is silent, the star's in flight,
    The sad moon hides herself from sight.
    The soughing of the magic choir   145
    Scatters a thousand sparks of fire.

VOICE FROM BELOW. Wait! Wait!

VOICE FROM ABOVE. Who calls there from the cleft in the rock?

VOICE FROM BELOW. Don't leave me behind! Don't leave me
    behind!
    Three hundred years I've been struggling up   150
    And I can never reach the top;
    I want to be with my own kind.

CHORUS. Ride on a broom or ride on a stick,
    Ride on a fork or a goat—but quick!
    Who cannot to-night achieve the climb   155
    Is lost and damned till the end of time.

HALF-WITCH. So long, so long, I've been on the trot;
    How far ahead the rest have got!
    At home I have neither peace nor cheer
    And yet I do not find it here.   160

CHORUS. Their ointment makes the witches hale,
    A rag will make a decent sail
    And any trough a ship for flight;
    You'll never fly, if not to-night.
    Once at the peak, you circle round   165
    And then you sweep along the ground
    And cover the heath far and wide—
    Witchhood in swarms on every side.
    [*The* WITCHES *land.*]

MEPHISTOPHELES. What a push and a crush and a rush and a
    clatter!
    How they sizzle and whisk, how they babble and batter!   170
    Kindle and sparkle and blaze and stink!
    A true witch-element, I think.
    Only stick to me or we shall be swept apart!
    Where are you?

FAUST.   Here!   175

MEPHISTOPHELES.   What! Carried so far already!
    I must show myself the master on this ground.
    Room! Here comes Voland! Room, sweet rabble! Steady!
    Here, Doctor, catch hold of me. Let's make one bound
    Out of this milling crowd and so get clear.   180
    Even for the likes of me it's *too* mad here.

---

178. *Voland:* one of Mephistopheles' names for himself. *Voland,* or *Valand,* is an old German word for "evil fiend."

There's something yonder casting a peculiar glare,
Something attracts me towards those bushes.
Come with me! We will slip in there.

FAUST. You spirit of contradiction! Go on though! I'll follow.   185
You have shown yourself a clever fellow. Quite!
We visit the Brocken on Walpurgis Night
To shut ourselves away in this lonely hollow!

MEPHISTOPHELES. Only look—what motley flames!
It's a little club for fun and games   190
One's not alone with a few, you know.

FAUST. I'd rather be above there though.
Already there's fire and whorls of smoke.
The Prince of Evil is drawing the folk;
Many a riddle must there be solved.   195

MEPHISTOPHELES. And many a new one too evolved.
Let the great world, if it likes, run riot;
We will set up here in quiet.
It is a custom of old date
To make one's own small worlds within the great.   200
I see young witches here, bare to the buff,
And old ones dressed—wisely enough.
If only for my sake, do come on;
It's little trouble and great fun.
I hear some music being let loose too.   205
What a damned clack! It's what one must get used to.
Come along! Come along! You have no choice.
I'll lead the way and sponsor you
And you'll be obliged to me anew.
What do you say? This milieu isn't small.   210
Just look! You can see no end to it at all.
A hundred fires are blazing in a row;
They dance and gossip and cook and drink and court—
Tell me where there is better sport!

FAUST. Do you intend, to introduce us here,   215
To play the devil or the sorcerer?

MEPHISTOPHELES. I am quite accustomed to go incognito
But one wears one's orders on gala days, you know.
I have no garter for identification
But my cloven foot has here some reputation.   220
See that snail? Creeping up slow and steady?
Her sensitive feelers have already
Sensed out something odd in me.
Here I could *not* hide my identity.

187. *Walpurgis Night:* the eve of
May Day (May 1).

219. *garter:* i.e., he has no decoration
of nobility, such as the Order of the
Garter.

But come! Let us go the round of the fires 225
And I'll play go-between to your desires.

COSTER-WITCH. Gentlemen, don't pass me by!
Don't miss your opportunity!
Inspect my wares with careful eye;
I have a great variety. 230
And yet there is nothing on my stall
Whose like on earth you could not find,
That in its time has done no small
Harm to the world and to mankind.
No dagger which has not drunk of blood, 235
No goblet which has not poured its hot and searing
Poison into some healthy frame,
No gewgaw which has not ruined some endearing
Woman, no sword which has not been used to hack
A bond in two and stab a partner in the back. 240

MEPHISTOPHELES. Auntie! You are behind the times.
Past and done with! Past and done!
You must go in for novelties!
You'll lose our custom if you've none.

FAUST. I mustn't go crazy unawares! 245
This is a fair to end all fairs.

MEPHISTOPHELES. The whole crowd's forcing its way above;
You find you're shoved though you may think you shove.

FAUST. Who then is that?

MEPHISTOPHELES.   Look well at Madam; 250
That's Lilith.

FAUST.   Who?

MEPHISTOPHELES.   First wife of Adam.
Be on your guard against her lovely hair,
That shining ornament which has no match; 255
Any young man whom those fair toils can catch,
She will not quickly loose him from her snare.

FAUST. Look, an old and a young one, there they sit.
They have already frisked a bit.

MEPHISTOPHELES. No rest to-night for 'em, not a chance. 260
They're starting again. Come on! Let's join the dance.

[FAUST *dances with a* YOUNG WITCH.]

FAUST.   A lovely dream once came to me
          In which I saw an apple tree,

---

227. *Coster-Witch:* The original, *Trödelhexe,* literally means "a witch (dealing in) old rags and clothes."

251. *Lilith:* According to an old rabbinical legend, Adam's first wife

(the "female" mentioned in Genesis 1:27) was Lilith. After Eve was created, Lilith became a ghost who seduced men and inflicted evil upon children.

On which two lovely apples shine,
They beckon me, I start to climb.   265

YOUNG WITCH. Those little fruit you long for so
     Just as in Eden long ago.
     Joy runs through me, through and through;
     My garden bears its apples too.

[FAUST *breaks away from the dance.*]

MEPHISTOPHELES. Why did you let that lovely maiden go   270
Who danced with you and so sweetly sang?

FAUST. Ugh, in the middle of it there sprang
  Out of her mouth a little red mouse.

MEPHISTOPHELES. Why complain? That's nothing out of the way;
  You should be thankful it wasn't grey.   275
  In an hour of love! What a senseless grouse!

FAUST. And then I saw—

MEPHISTOPHELES.   What?

FAUST.   Mephisto, look over there!
  Do you see a girl in the distance, pale and fair?   280
  Who drags herself, only slowly, from the place?
  And seems to walk with fetters on her feet?
  I must tell you that I think I see
  Something of dear Gretchen in her face.

MEPHISTOPHELES. That can do no good! Let it alone! Beware!   285
  It is a lifeless phantom, an image of air.
  It is a bad thing to behold;
  Its cold look makes the blood of man run cold,
  One turns to stone almost upon the spot;
  You have heard of Medusa, have you not?   290

FAUST. Indeed, they are the eyes of one who is dead,
  Unclosed by loving hands, left open, void.
  That is the breast which Gretchen offered me,
  And that is the sweet body I enjoyed.

MEPHISTOPHELES. That is mere magic, you gullible fool! She can   295
  Appear in the shape of his love to every man.

FAUST. What ravishment! What pain! Oh stay!
  That look! I cannot turn away!
  How strange that that adorable neck
  In one red thread should be arrayed   300
  As thin as the back of a knife-blade.

MEPHISTOPHELES. You are quite correct! I see it too.
  She can also carry her head under her arm,

290. *Medusa:* the Gorgon, with hair made of serpents, whose glance turned men to stone. She was finally killed by Perseus, and her head was given to Athene.

Perseus has cut it off for her.
Always this love of things untrue![a]   305

[A CHOIR *is heard, pianissimo.*]

CHOIR. Drifting cloud and gauzy mist
Brighten and dissever.
Breeze on the leaf and wind in the reeds
And all is gone for ever.

DREARY DAY—OPEN COUNTRY

FAUST. In misery! In despair! Long on the earth a wretched wanderer, now a prisoner! A criminal cooped in a dungeon for horrible torments, that dear and luckless creature! To end so! So! Perfidious, worthless spirit—and this you have kept from me!
Stand, Just stand there! Roll your devilish eyes spitefully round in your head! Stand and brave me with your unbearable presence! A prisoner! In irremediable misery! Abandoned to evil spirits, to judging, unfeeling man! And I in the meantime—you lull me with stale diversions, you hide her worsening plight from me, you abandon her to perdition!

MEPHISTOPHELES. She is not the first.

FAUST. Dog! Loathsome monster! Change him, Thou eternal Spirit! Change this serpent back to his shape of a dog, in which he often delighted to trot before me at night—to roll about at the feet of the harmless wanderer and, as he tripped, to sink his teeth in his shoulders. Change him back to his fancy-shape that he may crouch in the sand on his belly before me, that I may trample over his vileness!

Not the first, you say! O the pity of it! What human soul can grasp that more than one creature has sunk to the depth of this misery, that the first did not pay off the guilt of all the rest, writhing and racked in death before the eyes of the Ever-Pardoning! It pierces me to my marrow and core, the torment of this one girl—and you grin calmly at the fate of thousands!

MEPHISTOPHELES. Now we're already back at our wits' end—the point where your human intelligence snaps. Why do you enter our company, if you can't carry it through? So you want to fly—and have no head for heights? Did we force ourselves on you—or you on us?

FAUST. Do not bare at me so those greedy fangs of yours! You sicken me! O great and glorious Spirit, Thou who didst deign to appear to me, Thou who knowest my heart and my soul, why fetter me to this odious partner who grazes on mischief and laps up destruction?

---

a. The Walpurgis Night's Dream, which is always cut from performances of *Faust*, is omitted. It occurs between l. 305 and l. 306 of our text.

MEPHISTOPHELES. Have you finished?

FAUST. Save her! Or woe to you! The most withering curse upon you for thousands of years!

MEPHISTOPHELES. I cannot undo the avenger's bonds, his bolts I cannot open. Save her! Who was it plunged her into ruin? I or you?

[FAUST *looks wildly around.*]

MEPHISTOPHELES. Are you snatching at the thunder? Luckily, that is forbidden you wretched mortals. To smash to pieces his innocent critic, that is the way the tyrant relieves himself when in difficulties.

FAUST. Bring me to her! She shall be free!

MEPHISTOPHELES. And what of the risk you will run? Let me tell you; the town is still tainted with blood-guilt from your hand. Over the site of the murder there float avenging spirits who await the returning murderer.

FAUST. That too from *you?* Murder and death of a world on your monstrous head! Take me to her, I tell you; set her free!

MEPHISTOPHELES. I will take you, and what I *can* do—listen! Am I omnipotent in heaven and earth? I will cast a cloud on the gaoler's senses; do you get hold of the keys and carry her out with your own human hands. I meanwhile wait, my magic horses are ready, I carry you off. That much I can manage.

FAUST. Away! Away!

NIGHT

FAUST *and* MEPHISTOPHELES *fly past on black horses.*

FAUST. What do they weave round the Gallows Rock?

MEPHISTOPHELES. Can't tell what they're cooking and hatching.

FAUST. Floating up, floating down, bending, descending.

MEPHISTOPHELES. A witch corporation.

FAUST. Black mass, black water.   5

MEPHISTOPHELES. Come on! Come on!

DUNGEON

FAUST *with a bunch of keys and a lamp, in front of an iron door.*

FAUST. A long unwonted trembling seizes me,
The woe of all mankind seizes me fast.
It is here she lives, behind these dripping walls,
Her crime was but a dream too good to last!
And *you*, Faust, waver at the door?   5
You fear to see your love once more?
Go in at once—or her hope of life is past.

1. *Gallows Rock:* the masonry supporting a gallows.

[*He tries the key.* GRETCHEN *starts singing inside.*]

GRETCHEN. My mother, the whore,
     Who took my life!
     My father, the rogue,   10
     Who ate my flesh!
     My little sister
     My bones did lay
     In a cool, cool glen;
     And there I turned to a pretty little wren;   15
     Fly away! Fly away!
     [FAUST *opens the lock.*]

FAUST. She does not suspect that her lover is listening—
To the chains clanking, the straw rustling.
     [*He enters.*]

GRETCHEN. Oh! They come! O death! It's hard! Hard!

FAUST. Quiet! I come to set you free.   20
     [*She throws herself at his feet.*]

GRETCHEN. If you are human, feel my misery.

FAUST. Do not cry out—you will wake the guard.
     [*He takes hold of the chains to unlock them.*]

GRETCHEN. [*On her knees*] Who has given you this power,
     Hangman, so to grieve me?
     To fetch me at this midnight hour!   25
     Have pity! O reprieve me!
     Will to-morrow not serve when the bells are rung?
          [*She gets up.*]
     I am still so young, I am still so young!
     Is my death so near?
     I was pretty too, that was what brought me here.   30
     My lover was by, he's far to-day;
     My wreath lies torn, my flowers have been thrown away.
     Don't seize on me so violently!
     What have I done to you? Let me be!
     Let me not vainly beg and implore;   35
     You know I have never seen you before.

FAUST. Can I survive this misery?

GRETCHEN. I am now completely in your power.
     Only let me first suckle my child.
     This night I cherished it, hour by hour;   40
     To torture me they took it away
     And now I murdered it, so they say.
     And I shall never be happy again.
     People make ballads about me—the heartless crew!
     An old story ends like this—   45
     Must mine too?

[FAUST *throws himself on the ground.*]

FAUST. Look! At your feet a lover lies
  To loose you from your miseries.

  [GRETCHEN *throws herself beside him.*]

GRETCHEN. O, let us call on the saints on bended knee!
  Beneath these steps—but see—   50
  Beneath this sill
  The cauldron of Hell!
  And within,
  The Evil One in his fury
  Raising a din!   55

FAUST. Gretchen! Gretchen!

GRETCHEN. That was my lover's voice!

  [*She springs up: the chains fall off.*]

  I heard him calling. Where can he be?
  No one shall stop me. I am free!
  Quick! My arms round his neck!   60
  And lie upon his bosom! Quick!
  He called 'Gretchen!' He stood at the door.
  Through the whole of Hell's racket and roar,
  Through the threats and jeers and from far beyond
  I heard that voice so sweet, so fond.   65

FAUST. It is I!

GRETCHEN.   It's you? Oh say so once again!

  [*She clasps him.*]

  It is! It is! Where now is all my pain?
  And where the anguish of my captivity?
  It's you; you have come to rescue me!   70
  I am saved!
  The street is back with me straight away
  Where I saw you that first day,
  And the happy garden too
  Where Martha and I awaited you.   75

FAUST. Come! Come!

GRETCHEN.   Oh stay with me, oh do!
  Where *you* stay, I would like to, too.

FAUST. Hurry!
  If you don't,   80
  The penalty will be sore.

GRETCHEN. What! Can you kiss no more?
  So short an absence, dear, as this
  And you've forgotten how to kiss!
  Why do I feel so afraid, clasping your neck?   85
  In the old days your words, your looks,
  Were a heavenly flood I could not check

And you kissed me as if you would smother me—
Kiss me now!
Or I'll kiss you!   90
　　[*She kisses him.*]
Oh your lips are cold as stone!
And dumb!
What has become
Of your love?
Who has robbed me of my own?   95
　　[*She turns away from him.*]
FAUST. Come! Follow me, my love! Be bold!
I will cherish you after a thousandfold.
Only follow me now! That is all I ask of you.
GRETCHEN. And is it you then? Really? Is it true?
FAUST. It is! But come!   100
GRETCHEN. 　　　　　　　You are undoing each chain,
You take me to your arms again.
How comes it you are not afraid of me?
Do you know, my love, *whom* you are setting free?
FAUST. Come! The deep night is passing by and beyond.   105
GRETCHEN. My mother, I have murdered her;
I drowned my child in the pond.
Was it not a gift to you and me?
To you too—You! Are you what you seem?
Give me your hand! It is not a dream!   110
Your dear hand—but, oh, it's wet!
Wipe it off! I think
There is blood on it.
Oh God! What have you done?
Put up your sword,   115
I beg you to.
FAUST. Let what is gone be gone!
You are killing me.
GRETCHEN. No! *You* must live on!
I will tell you about the graves—   120
You must get them put right
At morning light;
Give the best place to my mother,
The one next door to my brother,
Me a shade to the side—   125
A gap, but not too wide.
And the little one on my right breast.
No one else shall share my rest.
When it was you, when I could clasp you,
That was a sweet, a lovely day!   130

But I no longer can attain it,
I feel I must use force to grasp you,
As if you were thrusting me away.
And yet it's you and you look so kind, so just.

FAUST. If you feel it's I, then come with me! You must!   135
GRETCHEN. Outside there?
FAUST. Into the air!
GRETCHEN.   If the grave is there
And death on the watch, then come!
Hence to the final rest of the tomb   140
And not a step beyond—
You are going now? O Heinrich, if I could too!
FAUST. You can! The door is open. Only respond!
GRETCHEN. I dare not go out; for me there is no more hope.
They are lying in wait for me; what use is flight?   145
To have to beg, it is so pitiable
And that with a conscience black as night!
So pitiable to tramp through foreign lands—
And in the end I must fall into their hands!
FAUST. I shall stay by you.   150
GRETCHEN. Be quick! Be quick!
Save your poor child!
Go! Straight up the path—
Along by the brook—
Over the bridge—   155
Into the wood—
Left where the plank is—
In the pond!
Catch hold of it quickly!
It's trying to rise,   160
It's kicking still!
Save it! Save it!
FAUST. Collect yourself!
One step—just one—and you are free.
GRETCHEN. If only we were past the hill!   165
There sits my mother on a stone—
My brain goes cold and dead—
There sits my mother on a stone—
And wags and wags her head.
No sign, no nod, her head is such a weight   170
She'll wake no more, she slept so late.
She slept that we might sport and play.
What a time that was of holiday!
FAUST. If prayer and argument are no resource,
I will risk saving you by force.   175

GRETCHEN. No! I will have no violence! Let me go!
  Don't seize me in that murderous grip!
  I have done everything else for you, you know.
FAUST. My love! My love! The day is dawning!
GRETCHEN. Day! Yes, it's growing day! The last day breaks on
    me!   180
  My wedding day it was to be!
  Tell no one you had been before with Gretchen.
  Alas for my garland!
  There's no more chance!
  We shall meet again—   185
  But not at the dance.
  The people are thronging—but silently;
  Street and square
  Cannot hold them there.
  The bell tolls—it tolls for *me*.   190
  How they seize me, bind me, like a slave!
  Already I'm swept away to the block.
  Already there jabs at every neck,
  The sharp blade which jabs at mine.
  The world lies mute as the grave.   195
FAUST. I wish I had never been born!
      [MEPHISTOPHELES *appears outside*.]
MEPHISTOPHELES. Away! Or you are lost.
  Futile wavering! Waiting and prating!
  My horses are shivering,
  The dawn's at the door.   200
GRETCHEN. What rises up from the floor?
  It's he! Send him away! It's he!
  What does he want in the holy place?
  It is I he wants!
FAUST.   You shall live!   205
GRETCHEN. Judgment of God! I have given myself to Thee!
MEPHISTOPHELES. [*To* FAUST] Come! Or I'll leave you both in the
    lurch.
GRETCHEN. O Father, save me! I am Thine!
  You angels! Hosts of the Heavenly Church,
  Guard me, stand round in serried line!   210
  Heinrich! I shudder to look at you.
MEPHISTOPHELES. She is condemned!
VOICE FROM ABOVE.   Redeemed!
MEPHISTOPHELES. Follow me!
      [*He vanishes with* FAUST.]
VOICE [*From within, dying away*] Heinrich! Heinrich!   215

FRIEDRICH HÖLDERLIN
(1770–1843)
Hyperion's Song of Fate (Hyperions Schicksalslied)*

You wander above in the holy light
  On tender ground, O holiest of spirits!
    Glittering god-given breezes
      Lightly move you,
        As her fingers, the artist's,   5
          Pluck holy strings.

Fateless, sleeping like a
  Nurseling, breathe those heavenly ones;
    Chastely kept
      In modest buds,   10
        Their souls
          Are ever-blooming,
            And their blessed eyes
              Gaze out quietly
                In eternal clarity.   15

But we have the fortune
  Never to stay in one place,
    We vanish, we topple,
      We, suffering mankind,
        Blindly from one   20
          Hour to the next,
            Tossed like water from one cliff
              To yet another cliff,
                Yearlong down to depths deep in doubt.

To the Fates (An die Parzen)ᵃ

Grant me only one summer, ye mighty ones!
  And one autumn for ripe song,

---

* Translated by Howard E. Hugo from *The Portable Romantic Reader*, copyright © 1957. Reprinted by permission of the Viking Press, Inc. The song is sung by the hero of Hölderlin's novel *Hyperion, or The Hermit in Greece* (1798), who fights for that country's independence against the Turks in 1770. He is named after Hyperion, one of the mythical Titans, son of Heaven and Earth (Uranus and Ge).

a. Translated by Howard E. Hugo. The *Parcae* ("Fates") were three female goddesses in Greek mythology—Clotho, Lachesis, Atropos. They respectively wove, measured, and then cut the thread of each man's life. The original poem, which was written in 1798, follows the Greek Alcaic strophe: a complicated arrangement of long and short syllables:

```
* _ * _ * _ ** _ * _
* _ * _ * _ ** _ * _
* _ * _ * _ * _ *
* _ * _ * _ * _ *
```

So that my heart more willingly, with sweet
   Lyre-playing sated, then may die.

The soul, not given her divinely appointed right   5
   In life, neither rests below in Orcus;
      But once I achieve the sacred thing, that
        Lies in my heart, the poem,

Welcome then, O peace of the world of shadows!
   Content I shall be, though my lyre   10
      Accompanies me not; Once
        I shall have lived like the Gods, and I need no more.

Sunset (Sonnenuntergang)[b]

Where are you? my soul is in twilight, drunk
   With all your rapture; for even now
      I heard how, full of golden sounds
        The entrancing young Sun God

Played his evening song on a divine lyre;   5
   It echoed from the woods and hills.
      But he has gone far, far away
        To pious people who still do him honor.

Brevity (Die Kürze)[c]

"Why are you so brief? Do you no longer love song
   As you did? Yet as a youth when you sang
      In those days of hope,
        You never found the end!"

Like my joy is my song.—In sunset glow   5
   Would you bathe joyfully? All is gone, the earth is cold,
      And the night-bird whirrs
        Uncomfortably before your eyes.

5-6. *The soul . . . Orcus.*: I.e., if the poet cannot achieve artistic fulfillment in this world, he will not repose easily in the next. The theme is vaguely similar to that of John Keats—who resembles Hölderlin in his Romantic Hellenism—in the sonnet, "When I have fears that I may cease to be / Before my pen has glean'd my teeming brain . . ."
6. *Orcus:* the Underworld.
b. Translated by Howard E. Hugo. Probably written 1799–1800. As in "To the Fates," the original adheres to the Alcaic strophe.
4. *Sun God:* Apollo.
8. *pious people:* possibly the modern Greeks. Hölderlin's hope was that the spirit of ancient Greece might invigorate the modern, moribund world. But in his novel *Hyperion* he comes, *via* his hero, to acknowledge the gap betwen past ideals and present actualities.
c. Translated by Howard E. Hugo. Written in 1798. The original adheres to another Greek form, the third Ascepiadean strophe.

  – * – * * – / – * * – * *
  – * – * – / – * * – * *
  * * – * * – *
  – * – * * – * –

7. *night-bird:* the owl, symbol of Athene, goddess of wisdom—also a bird of ill omen, associated with death.

NOVALIS

(FRIEDRICH VON HARDENBERG)

(1772–1801)

Hymns to the Night (Hymnen an die Nacht)^a

I

What living being,
Sense-endowed,
Loves not most of all
Wonderful appearances
Of circumambient space about him?   5
That all-joyous Light—
With its beams and rays
Its colors,
Its mild all-presence
In the Day?   10
As life's
Inmost soul
The giant world breathes it,
Those restless stars
That bathe in its blue sea,   15
The sparkling stones breathe it,
The peaceful plants
And the beasts
Manifold,
Eternally-moving strength—   20
Multi-colored clouds and breezes
Breathe it
And foremost
The glorious strangers
With their sensitive eyes   25
Their gliding gait

a. The six *Hymns* were composed between 1798 and 1800, published in the *Athenäum* in 1800. The translations of the first two hymns are based on Novalis's manuscript copy, written in free verse; the *Athenäum* printed these and other free-verse sections as prose. "Now upward comes the stone" is the last portion of the fifth *Hymn*. Translated by Howard E. Hugo. The selection from the fifth *Hymn* is reprinted from *Wake Magazine* by permission of the editors.

24. *glorious strangers:* i.e., mankind.

And their sonorous mouths.
Like a king
Of nature and earth
It calls forth every power   30
To numberless metamorphoses
And its mere presence
Unseals the wonderful majesty
Of the kingdom of earth.
Downward turn I   35
To the holy, inexpressible
Secret-filled Night.
Far off lies the world,
As if sunk in some deep tomb
How wild and lonely   40
Her abode!
Deepest sadness
Stirs the heart-strings.
Distant memories
Wishes of youth   45
Childhood's dreams
Brief joys
And vain, idle hopes
Of one's whole long life
Come in gray garments   50
Like evening mists
After the sun
Has gone down.
Far off lies the world
With its gay-colored pleasures.   55
The Light has pitched
Its merry tents
In other places.
Shall it never return
To its own true children,   60
To its gardens,
Back to its glorious house?
But what flows
So cool and refreshing
So full of portents   65
Beneath our hearts
And swallows
The soft breeze of sadness?

Have you also
A human heart,   70
O dark Night?
What do you keep
Under your mantle
That steals unseen and powerful
Into my soul?   75
You only seem frightening—
Precious balsam
Drips from your hand,
From the bunch of poppies
You unfold the soul's weighty wings   80
In sweet drunkenness
And give us joys
Dark and inexpressible
Secret, as you yourself are,
Joys, that allow us   85
Promise of heaven.
How poor and childish
Light seems to me,
With its gay-colored objects
How joyful and blessed   90
Is the Day's departure.
Because Night seduces
Your servants away
Only then
Do you sow   95
Shining globes
In wide reaches of space
To proclaim your omnipotence
And your return
During times of your absence.   100
More heavenly than those flashing stars
In those wide reaches
Seem to us the infinite eyes
That the Night
Opens in us.   105
They see further
Than the palest
From that numberless host
Needing no light
They look through the depths   110

Of a loving soul,
Which fills a loftier space
With unspeakable bliss.
Praise to the World's Queen!
To the exalted proclaimer   115
Of a holy world,
To the fosterer
Of holy love.
You come, Beloved—
The Night is here—   120
My soul is enraptured—
The earthly day is done
And again you are mine.
I gaze into your deep dark eye,
I see nothing but love and bliss.   125
We sink upon Night's altar
On the soft couch—
The veil drops
And kindled by the warming pressure
The pure flame of the sweet sacrifice   130
Glows.

                              II

Must morning always return?
Will earthly power never end?
Wretched activity consumes
The heavenly advent of Night.
Will the secret offering of love   5
Never burn eternally?
To Light was appointed
Its allotted moment
And its watching—
But the majesty of Night is timeless,   10
Sleep's duration is eternal.
Holy sleep!
Bless not too seldom
Those consecrated to Night—
Only the fools misunderstand you   15
And know of no sleep

---

114. *World's Queen*: i.e., the Virgin
Mary.
119. *Beloved*: i.e., Christ the Bridegroom; although in Novalis's private
mythology, the image partakes of his
mystical adoration for his dead fiancée,
Sophie von Kühn.

Save shadows,
Which you compassionately cast over us
As that twilight
Of the true night.   20
They do not glimpse you
In the golden liquid of the grape
In the almond-tree's
Marvelous oil
And in the brown juice of the poppy.   25
They do not know
That it is you
Who hovers over
The breast of the tender maiden
And makes a heaven out of her breast—   30
They do not guess
You come to meet us to reveal heaven
You come from the ancient tales
And you carry the key
To the dwellings of the blessed,   35
Silent messenger
Of infinite secrets.

V

Now upward comes the stone—
Mankind makes its ascent—
With Thee we now are one
And all our bonds are rent.
Our harshest woes retreat   5
Before Thy Holy Grail,
Both earth and life are sweet
At this last Holy Meal.

Death calls us to the wedding—
Where all the lamps burn fair—   10
The virgins here are speeding—
For oil we have no care.
Now see we from afar
The image of Thy face,
Triumphant shouts each star   15
With human-sounding voice.

---

30. *breast: Schoss* in German also means "womb."
3. *Thee:* i.e., Christ.

9-12. *wedding . . . oil:* a reference to the parable of the five wise and five foolish virgins (Matthew 25:1-13).

For Thee, divine Maria,
A thousand bosoms burn.
In this pale, shadowy sphere
For Thee alone they yearn.   20
With Thee they would recover,
Already they feel at rest—
Embrace them, Holy Mother,
To thy compassionate breast.

So many are there, smarting,   25
Consumed by bitter pain,
From this earth a parting
Would bring them home again;
Thou, lovely benefactress,
For us who have no rest—   30
Let us join those poor hapless
To be forever blessed.

No grave is washed by weeping,
Those who believe have no grief.
Those who hold love in keeping   35
Need fear no mortal thief—
In longing they find consolation
The night brings them new faith—
With celestial guards for protection
They know their hearts will be safe.   40

Convinced our lives move forward
Toward life eternal, complete,
An inner glow makes us stalwart,
We feel our souls replete.
The constellations shall perish   45
Distilled in golden wine,
Transfigured, we shall flourish
And like those same stars shine.

A freer love will engage us,
No segregation shall be.   50
One single life shall embrace us
Like waves in an endless sea.
One single, blissful night—
One never-ending ode—·
And then the sun, so bright,   55
Shall be the face of God.

FRANÇOIS RENÉ DE CHATEAUBRIAND
(1768–1848)
René*

On arriving among the Natchez René[1] was obliged to take a wife in order to conform to the Indian customs; but he did not live with her. His melancholy nature drew him constantly away into the depths of the woods. There he would spend entire days in solitude, a savage among the savages. Aside from Chactas, his foster father, and Father Souël, a missionary at Fort Rosalie, he had given up all fellowship with men. These two elders had acquired a powerful influence over his heart, Chactas, through his kindly indulgence, and Father Souël, on the contrary, through his extreme severity. Since the beaver hunt, when the blind sachem[2] had told his adventures to René, the young man had consistently refused to talk about his own. And yet both Chactas and the missionary keenly desired to know what sorrow had driven this well-born European to the strange decision of retiring into the wildernesses of Louisiana. René had always claimed that he would not tell his story because it was too insignificant, limited as it was to his thoughts and feelings. "As for the circumstance which induced me to leave for America," he added, "that must forever be buried in oblivion."

Thus several years[3] went by, and the two elders were unable to draw his secret from him. One day, however, he received a letter from Europe, through the Office of Foreign Missions, which so increased his sadness that he felt he had to flee even from his old friends. Now more than ever they exhorted him to open his heart to them. And so great was their tact, so gentle their manner, and so deep the respect they commanded, that he finally felt obliged to yield. He therefore set a day to tell them, not the adventures of his life, for he had never had any, but the innermost feelings of his soul.

On the twenty-first day of the month the Indians call the "moon of flowers," René went to the cabin of Chactas. Giving his arm to the sachem, he led him to a spot under a sassafras tree on the bank of the Meschacebe.[4] Soon afterwards Father Souël arrived at the meeting place. Day was breaking. Off on the plain, some distance

---

* Translated by Irving Putter (University of California Press, 1957) and reprinted with the permission of the publishers. *René* was included in Chateaubriand's *Genius of Christianity* (1802), a long work designed to illustrate its subtitle: *The Poetic and Moral Beauties of Christianity*. Atala, also in the volume, had appeared a year earlier, partly to test the public's reception.

1. *René:* He appears in *Atala* as the melancholy youth who has fled Europe for Louisiana in 1725, and to whom the Indian sage tells the sad tale of his love for Atala.
2. *sachem:* chief.
3. *several years:* René, killed in 1730, tells his story sometime between 1728 and 1730.
4. *Meschacebe:* Mississippi.

away, the Natchez village could be seen with its grove of mulberry trees and its cabins which looked like beehives. The French colony and Fort Rosalie were visible on the river bank at the right. Tents, half-built houses, fortresses just begun, hosts of negroes clearing tracts of land, groups of white men and Indians, all offered a striking contrast of social and primitive ways in this limited space. Towards the east, in the background of this setting, the sun was just beginning to show behind the jagged peaks of the Appalachians, which stood forth like azure symbols against the golden reaches of the sky. In the west, the Meschacebe rolled its waves in majestic stillness, forming for the picture a border of indescribable grandeur.

For some time the young man and the missionary stood marveling at this splendid scene and pitying the sachem who could no longer enjoy it. Then Father Souël and Chactas sat down on the grass at the foot of the tree. René took his place between them, hesitated a moment, and then began speaking in the following manner.

As I open my story, I cannot stifle a feeling of shame. The peace in your hearts, respected elders, and the calm of nature all about me make me blush for the disorder and turmoil of my soul.

How you will pity me! How wretched my perpetual anxieties will seem to you! You who have passed through all the hardships of life, what will you think of a young man with neither strength nor moral courage, who finds the source of his torments within himself, and can hardly lament any misfortunes save those he has brought on himself? Alas! Do not condemn him too severely; he has already been harshly punished!

I cost my mother[5] her life as I came into this world and had to be drawn from her womb with an instrument. My father gave his blessing to my brother because he saw in him his elder son; as for me, I was soon abandoned to strange hands and brought up far from my father's roof.

I was spirited in temper and erratic by nature. As I alternated turbulence and joy with silence and sadness, I would gather my young friends around me, then leave them suddenly and go off to sit by myself watching the swift clouds or listening to the rain falling among the leaves.

Each autumn I would return to the family château,[6] off in the midst of the forests, near a lake in a remote province.

I was timid and inhibited in my father's presence, and found freedom and contentment only with my sister Amelia.[7] We were

5. *mother:* Actually Chateaubriand's mother died in 1798, when he was thirty.
6. *château:* The author's home was a castle at Combourg, on the sea near St. Malo in Brittany.
7. *Amelia:* closely modeled on Chateaubriand's sister Lucile, born in 1764.

closely bound together by our tender affinities in mood and taste;
my sister was only slightly older than I. We loved to climb the hillside together or go sailing on the lake or wander through the woods
under the falling leaves, and even now memories of those rambles
fill my soul with delight. O illusions of childhood and homeland,
can your sweetness ever fade away?

Sometimes we strolled in silence hearkening to the muffled
rumbling of the autumn or the crackling of the dry leaves trailing
sadly under our feet. In our innocent games we ran after the
swallow in the meadows or the rainbow on the storm-swept hills.
At other times we would whisper poetry inspired in us by the
spectacle of nature. In my youth I courted the Muses. Nothing is
more poetic than a heart of sixteen in all the pristine freshness of
its passions. The morning of life is like the morning of the day,
pure, picturesque, and harmonious.

On Sundays and holidays I often stood in the deep woods as the
sound of the distant bell drifted through the trees, calling from the
temple to the man of the fields. Leaning against the trunk of an
elm, I would listen in rapt silence to the devout tolling. Each tremor
of the resounding bronze would waft into my guileless soul the
innocence of country ways, the calm of solitude, the beauty of religion, and the cherished melancholy of memories out of my early
childhood! Oh! What churlish heart has never started at the sound
of the bells in his birthplace, those bells which trembled with joy
over his cradle, which rang out the dawn of his life, which signaled
his first heartbeat, announcing to all surrounding places the reverent
gladness of his father, the ineffable anguish and supreme joy of his
mother! All is embraced in that magical revery which engulfs us at
the sound of our native bell—faith, family, homeland, the cradle
and the grave, the past and the future.

True enough, Amelia and I enjoyed these solemn, tender thoughts
far more than did others, for in the depths of our heart we both had
a strain of sadness, given us by God or our mother.

Meanwhile my father was attacked by a disease which brought
him to his grave in a short time. He passed away in my arms, and I
learned to know death from the lips of the very person who had
given me life. The impression was profound; it is vivid still. It was
the first time that the immortality of the soul was clearly present
before my eyes. I could not believe that this lifeless body was the
creator of my thought; I felt it had to come from some other source,
and, in my religious sorrow, close akin to joy, I hoped one day to
join the spirit of my father.

Another circumstance fixed this lofty idea even more firmly in
my mind. My father's features had taken on a sublime quality in
his coffin. Why should this astonishing mystery not be an indica-

tion of our immortality? Could not all-knowing death have stamped the secrets of another universe on the brow of its victim? And why could the tomb not have some great vision of eternity?

Overcome with grief Amelia had withdrawn to the seclusion of a tower from which she could hear the chanting of the priests in the funeral procession and the death knell reverberating under the vaults of the Gothic château.

I accompanied my father to his last abode, and the earth closed over his remains. Eternity and oblivion pressed down on him with all their weight, and that very evening the indifferent passer-by trod over his grave. Aside from his daughter and son, it was already as though he had never existed.

Then I had to leave the family shelter, which my brother had inherited. Amelia and I went to live with some aged relatives.

Pausing before the deceptive paths of life, I considered them one by one, but dared not set out along any of them. Amelia would frequently speak of the joy of the religious life, adding that I was the only bond still holding her to the outside world; and her eyes would fix themselves upon me sadly.

With my heart stirred by these devout talks, I would often make by way toward a monastery close by my new dwelling. Once I was even tempted to retire within its walls forever. Happy are they who reach the end of their travels without ever leaving the harbor and have never, as have I, dragged their barren days out over the face of the earth!

In our endless agitation we Europeans are obliged to erect lonely retreats for ourselves. The greater the turmoil and din in our hearts, the more we are drawn to calmness and silence. These shelters in my country are always open to the sad and weak. Often they are hidden in little valleys, which seem to harbor in their bosom a vague feeling of sorrow and a hope for a future refuge. Sometimes, too, they are found in high places where the religious soul, like some mountain plant, seems to rise toward heaven, offering up its perfumes.

I can still see the majestic mingling of waters and forests around that ancient abbey, where I hoped to shelter my life from the whims of fate; I still wander at eventide in those reverberating, solitary cloisters. When the moon cast its wan light on the pillars of the arcades and outlined their shadow on the opposite wall, I would stop to contemplate the cross marking the burial ground and the tall grass growing among the tombstones. O men who once lived far removed from the world and have passed from the silence of life to the silence of death, how your tombs filled my soul with disgust for this earth!

Whether it was my natural instability or a dislike of the monastic life, I do not know, but I changed my plans and decided to go abroad. As I bade my sister farewell, she clasped me in her arms in an almost joyful gesture, as though she were happy to see me leave, and I could not repress a bitter thought about the inconstancy of human affections.

Nevertheless, I set forth all alone and full of spirit on the stormy ocean of the world, though I knew neither its safe ports nor its perilous reefs. First I visited peoples[8] who exist no more. I went and sat among the ruins of Rome and Greece, those countries of virile and brilliant memory, where palaces are buried in the dust and royal mausoleums hidden beneath the brambles. O power of nature and weakness of man! A blade of grass will pierce through the hardest marble of these tombs, while their weight can never be lifted by all these mighty dead!

Sometimes a tall column rose up solitary in a waste land, as a great thought may spring from a soul ravaged by time and sorrow.

I meditated on these monuments at every hour and through all the incidents of the day. Sometimes, I watched the same sun which had shone down on the foundation of these cities now setting majestically over their ruins; soon afterwards, the moon rose between crumbling funeral urns into a cloudless sky, bathing the tombs in pallid light. Often in the faint, dream-wafting rays of that planet, I thought I saw the Spirit of Memory sitting pensive by my side.

But I grew weary of searching through graveyards, where too often I stirred up only the dust of a crime-ridden past.

I was anxious to see if living races had more virtue and less suffering to offer than those which had vanished. One day, as I was walking in a large city, I passed through a secluded and deserted courtyard behind a palace. There I noticed a statue pointing to a spot made famous by a certain sacrifice. I was struck by the stillness of the surroundings; only the wind moaned weakly around the tragic marble. Workmen were lying about indifferently at the foot of the statue or whistled as they hewed out stones. I asked them what the monument meant; some knew little indeed, while the others were totally oblivious of the catastrophe it commemorated. Nothing could indicate so vividly the true import of human events and the vanity of our existence. What has become of those figures whose fame was so widespread? Time has taken a step and the face of the earth has been made over.

In my travels I especially sought out artists and those inspired poets whose lyres glorify the gods and the joy of peoples who honor their laws, their religion, and their dead. These singers come of a

---

8. *I visited peoples:* Chateaubriand's own romantic voyaging came after the publication of *René.*

divine race and possess the only sure power which heaven has granted earth. Their life is at once innocent and sublime. They speak like immortals or little children. They explain the laws of the universe and cannot themselves understand the most elementary concerns of life. They have marvelous intuitions of death and die with no consciousness of it, like new-born infants.

On the mountain peaks of Caledonia, the last bard[9] ever heard in those wildernesses sang me poems which had once consoled a hero in his old age. We were sitting on four stones overgrown with moss; at our feet ran a brook, and in the distance the roebuck strayed among the ruins of a tower, while from the seas the wind whistled in over the waste land of Cona. The Christian faith, itself a daughter of the lofty mountains, has now placed crosses over the monuments of Morven heroes and plucked the harp of David on the banks of the very stream where once the harp of Ossian sighed. Loving peace even as the divinities of Selma loved war, it now shepherds flocks where Fingal once joined battle and has strewn angels of peace amongst clouds once occupied by murderous phantoms.

Ancient, lovely Italy offered me its host of masterworks. With what reverent and poetic awe I wandered through those vast edifices consecrated to religion by the arts! What a labyrinth of columns! What a sequence of arches and vaults! How beautiful are the echoes circling round those domes like the rolling of waves in the ocean, like the murmur of winds in the forest or the voice of God in his temple! The architect seems to build the poet's thoughts and make them accessible to the senses.

And yet with all my effort what had I learned until then? I had discovered nothing stable among the ancients and nothing beautiful among the moderns. The past and present are imperfect statues —one, quite disfigured, drawn from the ruins of the ages, and the other still devoid of its future perfection.

But, my old friends, you who have lived so long in the wilderness, you especially will be surprised that I have not once spoken of the glories of nature in this story of my travels.

One day I climbed to the summit of Etna, that great volcano burning in the middle of an island. Above me, I saw the sun rising in the vast reaches of the horizon, while at my feet Sicily shrank to a point and the sea retreated into the distant spaces. In this vertical view of the picture the rivers seemed little more than lines traced on a map. But while on one side I observed this sight, on the

9. *last bard:* All references in this paragraph are to MacPherson's *Poems of Ossian* (1760–1763), which Chateaubriand knew in the Letourneur translation. MacPherson claimed to have discovered Gaelic (Erse) poems, including an epic *Fingal*, by a third-century blind bard Ossian, which MacPherson published in English translation. Though spurious, their popularity was immense throughout Europe. Caledonia here is Scotland; Cona and Morven are in that country; Selma is northern Ireland (near modern Belfast), where the fighting in *Fingal* takes place.

other my eye plunged into the depths of Etna's crater, whose bowels I saw blazing between billows of black smoke.

A young man full of passion, sitting at the mouth of a volcano and weeping over mortal men whose dwellings he could barely distinguish far off below him—O revered elders! Such a creature is doubtless worthy only of your pity! But think what you may, such a picture reveals my character and my whole being. Just so, throughout my life, I have had before my eyes an immense creation which I could barely discern, while a chasm yawned at my side.

As he uttered these last words René grew silent and soon sank into revery. Father Souël looked at him in surprise, while the blind and aged sachem, not hearing the young man's voice any more, did not know what to make of this silence.

René had fixed his eyes on a group of Indians gaily passing through the plain. Suddenly his countenance softened, and tears fell from his eyes.

"Happy Indians," he exclaimed, "oh, why can I not enjoy the peace which always goes with you! While my fruitless wanderings led me through so many lands, you, sitting quietly under your oaks, let the days slip by without counting them. Your needs were your only guide, and, far better than I, you have reached wisdom's goal through your play and your sleep—like children. Your soul may sometimes have been touched by the melancholy of extreme happiness, but you emerged soon enough from this fleeting sadness, and your eyes rose toward heaven, tenderly seeking the mysterious presence which takes pity on the poor Indian."

Here René's voice broke again, and the young man bowed his head. Chactas held his hands out in the shadows, and, touching his son's arm, he exclaimed, deeply moved, "My son! My dear son!" The ring of his voice drew René from his revery, and, blushing at his weakness, he begged his father to forgive him.

Then the aged Indian spoke thus: "My young friend, a heart such as yours cannot be placid; but you must try to temper your character, which has already brought you so much grief. Do not be surprised that you suffer more than others from the experiences of life; a great soul necessarily holds more sorrow than a little one. Go on with your story. You have taken us through part of Europe; now tell us about your own country. As you know, I have seen France and am deeply attached to it. I would like to hear of the great chief who has now passed on, and whose magnificent cabin[10] I once visited. My child, I live only for the past. An old man with his memories is like a decrepit oak in our woods; no longer able to

10. *great chief . . . cabin:* Louis XIV and Versailles.

adorn itself with its own foliage, it is obliged to cover its nakedness with foreign plants which have taken root on its ancient boughs."

Calmed by these words, René once more took up the story of his heart.

Alas, father, I cannot tell you about that great century, for I saw only the end of it as a child; it had already drawn to a close when I returned to my land. Never has a more astonishing, nor a more sudden change taken place in a people. From the loftiness of genius, from respect for religion and dignity in manners everything suddenly degenerated to cleverness and godlessness and corruption.

So it had been useless indeed to try to find something in my own country to calm this anxiety, this burning desire which pursues me everywhere. Studying the world had taught me nothing, and yet I had lost the freshness of innocence.

By her strange behavior, my sister seemed bent on increasing my gloom. She had left Paris a few days before my arrival, and when I wrote that I expected to join her, she hastened to dissuade me, claiming she did not know where her business might take her. How sadly I reflected on human affection. It cools in our presence and vanishes in our absence; in adversity it grows weak and in good fortune weaker still.

Soon I found myself lonelier in my native land than I had been on foreign soil. I was tempted to plunge for a time into a totally new environment which I could not understand and which did not understand me. My heart was not yet wasted by any kind of passion, and I sought to find someone to whom I could become attached. But I soon discovered that I was giving more of myself than I was receiving of others. It was neither lofty language nor deep feeling which the world asked of me. I was simply reducing my being to the level of society. Everywhere I was taken for an impractical dreamer. Ashamed of the role I was playing and increasingly repulsed by men and things, I finally decided to retire to some smaller community where I could live completely by myself.

At first I was happy enough in this secluded, independent life. Unknown by everyone, I could mingle with the crowd—that vast desert of men! Often I would sit in some lonely church, where I could spend hour after hour in meditation. I saw poor women prostrating themselves before the Almighty or sinners kneeling at the seat of penitence. None emerged from this retreat without a more serene expression, and the muffled noises drifting in from outside seemed like waves of passion or storms of the world subsiding at the foot of the Lord's temple. Mighty God, who from Thy solitude couldst see my tears falling in that holy shelter, Thou knowest how many times I threw myself at Thy feet, imploring Thee to relieve me of the weight of my existence or make over the old man within me! Ah, who has never felt a need of regeneration, of growing young in the waters of the spring and refreshing his soul in the fountain of life? Who does not sometimes feel himself crushed by the burden of his own corruption and incapable of anything great or noble or just!

When night had closed in I would start back to my retreat, pausing on the bridges to watch the sunset. As the great star kindled the mists of the city, it seemed to swing slowly in a golden fluid like the pendulum of some clock of the ages. Then I retired with the night through a labyrinth of solitary streets. As I passed lights shining in the dwellings of men, I imagined myself among the scenes of sorrow and joy which they revealed, and I reflected that under all those roofs sheltering so many people, I had not a single friend. In the midst of these thoughts, the hour began tolling in measured cadence from the tower of the Gothic cathedral, and its message was taken up from church to church in a wide range of tones and distances. Alas!! Every hour in society lays open a grave and draws fresh tears.

But this life, which at first was so delightful, soon became intolerable. I grew weary of constantly repeating the same scenes and the same thoughts, and I began to search my soul to discover what I really sought. I did not know; but suddenly it occurred to me that I might be happy in the woods. Immediately I resolved to adopt a country exile where I could spend the rest of my days, for, though scarcely begun, my life had already consumed centuries.

I adopted this plan with the ardor typical of all my projects and left at once to retire into seclusion in some rustic cabin, just as previously I had left to travel around the world.

People accuse me of being unpredictable in my tastes, of being unable for long to cherish any single illusion. They consider me the victim of an imagination which plunges toward the end of all pleasures as though it suffered from their duration. They accuse me of forever overreaching the goal I can achieve. Alas! I am only in search of some unknown good, whose intuition pursues me relentlessly. Am I to blame if everywhere I find limitations, if all that is finite I consider worthless? And yet, I feel that I love the monotony in the feelings of life, and, if I were still foolish enough to believe in happiness, I would seek it in an orderly existence.

Total solitude and the spectacle of nature soon brought me to a state almost impossible to describe. Practically bereft of relatives and friends on earth, and never having been in love, I was furiously driven by an excess of life. Sometimes I blushed suddenly and felt torrents of burning lava surging through my heart. Sometimes I would cry out involuntarily, and the night was disturbed both by my dreams and by sleepless cares. I felt I needed something to fill the vast emptiness of my existence. I went down into the valley and up on the mountain, calling, with all the strength of my desire, for the ideal creature of some future passion. I embraced her in the winds and thought I heard her in the river's moaning. Everything became this vision of my imagination—the stars in the skies and the very principle of life in the universe.

Nevertheless, this state of calm and anxiety, of poverty and wealth was not wholly without charm. One day I amused myself by stripping the leaves from a willow branch, one by one, and throwing them into the stream, attaching a thought to each leaf as the current carried it off. A king in fear of losing his crown in a sudden revolution does not feel sharper pangs of anguish than did I, as I watched each peril threatening the remains of my bough. O frailty of mortal man! O childishness of the human heart, which never grows old! How infantile our haughty reason can become! And yet how many men attach their existence to such petty things as my willow leaves!

How can I describe the host of fleeting sensations I felt in my rambles? The echoes of passion in the emptiness of a lonely heart are like the murmurings of wind and water in the silence of the wilderness—they offer their joy, but cannot be portrayed.

Autumn came upon me in the midst of this uncertainty, and I welcomed the stormy months with exhilaration. Sometimes I wished I were one of those warriors who wander amongst winds, clouds, and phantoms, while at other times I was envious even of the shepherd's lot, as I watched him warming his hands by the humble brushwood fire he had built in a corner of the woods. I listened to his melancholy airs and remembered that in every land the natural song of man is sad, even when it renders happiness. Our heart is a defective instrument, a lyre with several chords missing, which forces us to express our joyful moods in notes meant for lamentation.

During the day I roamed the great heath with its forests in the distance. How little I needed to wander off in revery—a dry leaf blown before me by the wind, a cabin with smoke drifting up through the bare tree tops, the moss trembling in the north wind on the trunk of an oak, an isolated rock, or a lonely pond where the withered reed whispered . . . The solitary steeple far off in the valley often drew my attention. Many times, too, my eyes followed birds of passage as they flew overhead. I imagined the unknown shores and distant climes for which they were bound—and how I would have loved to be on their wings! A deep intuition tormented me; I felt that I was no more than a traveler myself, but a voice from heaven seemed to be telling me, "Man, the season for thy migration is not yet come; wait for the wind of death to spring up, then wilt thou spread thy wings and fly toward those unexplored realms for which thy heart longs."

Rise swiftly, coveted storms, coming to bear me off to the spaces of another life! This was my plea, as I plunged ahead with great strides, my face all aflame and the wind whistling through my hair, feeling neither rain nor frost, bewitched, tormented, and virtually possessed by the demon of my heart.

At night, when the fierce wind shook my hut and the rain fell in torrents on my roof, as I looked out through my window and saw the moon furrowing the thick clouds like a pallid vessel plough-ing through the waves, it seemed to me that life grew so strong in the depths of my heart that I had the power to create worlds. Ah, if only I could have shared with someone else the delight I felt! O Lord, if only Thou hadst given me a woman after my heart's desire, if Thou hadst drawn from my side an Eve, as Thou didst once for our first father, and brought her to me by the hand . . . Heavenly beauty! I would have knelt down before you, and then, clasping you in my arms, I would have begged the Eternal Being to grant you the rest of my life!

Alas! I was alone, alone in the world! A mysterious apathy gradu-ally took hold of my body. My aversion for life, which I had felt as a child, was returning with renewed intensity. Soon my heart sup-plied no more nourishment for my thought, and I was aware of my existence only in a deep sense of weariness.

For some time I struggled against my malady, but only half-heartedly, with no firm will to conquer it. Finally, unable to find any cure for this strange wound of my heart, which was nowhere and everywhere, I resolved to give up my life.[11]

Priest of the Almighty, now listening to my story, forgive this poor creature whom Heaven had almost stripped of his reason. I was imbued with faith, and I reasoned like a sinner; my heart loved God, and my mind knew Him not. My actions, my words, my feel-ings, my thoughts were nothing but contradictions, enigmas, and lies. But does man always know what he wishes, and is he always sure of what he thinks?

Affection, society, and seclusion, everything was slipping away from me at once. I had tried everything, and everything had proved disastrous. Rejected by the world and abandoned by Amelia, what had I left now that solitude had failed me? It was the last support which I had hoped could save me, and now I felt it too giving way and dropping into the abyss!

Having decided to rid myself of life's burden, I now resolved to use the full consciousness of my mind in committing this desperate

11. *resolved . . . life:* In his *Memories from Beyond the Grave,* Chateaubriand mentions he once tried suicide as a youth, but the gun failed to fire.

act. Nothing made it necessary to take action quickly. I did not set a definite time for my death, so that I might savor the final moments of my existence in long, full draughts and gather all my strength, like the men of antiquity, to feel my soul escaping.

I felt obliged, however, to make arrangements about my worldly goods and had to write to Amelia. A few complaints escaped me concerning her neglect, and doubtless I let her sense the tenderness which overcome my heart as I wrote. Nevertheless, I thought I had succeeded in concealing my secret; but my sister was accustomed to reading into the recesses of my heart, and she guessed it at once. She was alarmed at the restrained tone of my letter and at my questions about business matters, which had never before concerned me. Instead of answering she came to see me at once with no advance warning.

To realize how bitter my sorrow was later to be and how delighted I was now to see Amelia again, you must understand that she was the only person in the world I had ever loved, and all my feelings converged in her with the sweetness of my childhood memories. And so I welcomed Amelia with a kind of ecstasy in my heart. It had been so long since I had found someone who could understand me and to whom I could reveal my soul!

Throwing herself in my arms, Amelia said to me: "How ungrateful! You want to die and your sister is still alive! You doubt her heart! Don't explain and don't apologize, I know everything; I guessed your intention as though I had been with you. Do you suppose I can be misled, I who watched the first stirrings of your heart? So this is your unhappy character, your dislikes and injustices! Swear to me, while I press you to my heart, swear that this is the last time you will give in to your foolishness; make an oath never to try to take your life again."

As she uttered these words, Amelia looked at me compassionately, tenderly, covering my brow with kisses; she was almost a mother, she was something more tender. Alas! Once again my heart opened out to life's every joy. Like a child, I had only to be consoled, and I quickly surrendered to Amelia's influence. She insisted on a solemn oath, and I readily swore it, not suspecting that I could ever again be unhappy.

Thus we spent more than a month getting used to the delight of being together again. When, instead of finding myself alone in the morning, I heard my sister's voice, I felt a thrill of joy and contentment. Amelia had received some divine attribute from nature. Her soul had the same innocent grace as her body; her feelings were surpassingly gentle, and in her manner there was nothing but softness and a certain dreamy quality. It seemed as though her heart, her thought, and her voice were all sighing in harmony. From her womanly side came her shyness and love, while her purity and melody were angelic.

But the time had come when I was to atone for all my erratic ways. In my madness I had gone so far as to hope some calamity would strike me, so that I might at least have some real reason for suffering—it was a terrible wish, which God in His anger has granted all too well!

O my friends, what am I about to reveal to you! See how these tears flow from my eyes. Can I even . . . Only a few days ago nothing could have torn this secret from me . . . But now, it is all over!

Still, O revered elders, let this story be buried in silence forever; remember that it was meant to be told only under this tree in the wilderness.

Winter was drawing to a close, when I became aware that Amelia was losing her health and repose, even as she was beginning to restore them to me. She was growing thin, her eyes became hollow, her manner listless, and her voice unsteady. People or solitude, my absence or presence, night or day—everything frightened her. Involuntary sighs would die on her lips. Sometimes long distances would not tire her out, and at other times she could barely move about. She would take up her work and set it down, open a book and find it impossible to read, begin a sentence and not finish it, and then she would suddenly burst into tears and go off to pray.

I tried vainly to discover her secret. When I pressed her in my arms and questioned her, she smilingly answered that she was like myself—she did not know what was wrong with her.

Thus three months went by, and each day her state grew worse. The source of her tears seemed to be a mysterious correspondence she was having, for she appeared calmer or more disturbed according to the letters she received. Finally one morning as the time for breakfast had passed, I went up to her rooms. I knocked, but received no answer. I pushed the door ajar; no one was in the room. On the mantel there was an envelope addressed to me. Snatching it up with trembling fingers, I tore it open and read this letter, which will remain with me forever to discourage any possible feeling of joy.

To René:

"My brother, Heaven bears me witness that I would give up my life a thousand times to spare you one moment's grief. But miserable as I am, I can do nothing to make you happy. Forgive me, then, for stealing away from you as though I were guilty. I could never have resisted your pleas, and yet I had to leave. . . . Lord, have pity on me!

"You know, René, that the religious life has always attracted me. Now the time has come to heed Heaven's call. Only why have I waited so long? God is punishing me for it. It was for you alone that I remained in the world . . . But forgive me; I am upset by the sadness of having to leave you.

"Dear brother, it is only now that I feel the full need of those retreats which I have heard you condemn so often. There are certain sorrows which separate us from men forever; were it not for such shelters, what would become of some unfortunate women! . . . I am convinced that you, too, would find rest in these religious havens, for the world has nothing to offer which is worthy of you.

"I shall not remind you of your oath; I know how reliable your word is. You have sworn it, and you will go on living for my sake. Is there anything more pitiful than thinking constantly of suicide? For a man of your character it is easy to die. Believe me, it is far more difficult to live.

"But, my brother, you must give up this solitude at once; it is not good for you. Try to find some kind of occupation. I realize that you bitterly despise the usual necessity of 'becoming established' in France. But you must not scorn all the experience and wisdom of our fathers. Dear René, it is better to resemble ordinary men a little more and be a little less miserable.

"Perhaps you will find relief from your cares in marriage. A wife and children would take up your days. And what woman would not try to make you happy! The ardor of your soul, the beauty of your thought, your noble, passionate air, that proud and tender expression in your eyes, everything would assure you of her love and loyalty. Ah, how joyfully she would clasp you in her arms and press you to her heart! How her eyes and her thoughts would always be fixed on you to shield you from the slightest pain! In your presence she would become all love and innocence; you would feel that you had found a sister again.

"I am leaving for the convent of B——. It is a cloister built by the edge of the sea and wholly suited to the state of my soul. At night, from within my cell, I shall hear the murmur of the waves as they lap against the convent walls. I shall dream of those walks we once took through the woods, when we fancied we heard the sound of the sea in the tops of the waving pines. Beloved childhood friend, will I ever see you again? Though hardly older than you, I once rocked you in your cradle. Many times we used to sleep together. Ah, if we might one day be together again in the same tomb! But no, I must sleep alone beneath the icy marble of that sanctuary where girls who have never known love rest in eternal peace.

"I do not know whether you will succeed in reading these lines, blurred as they are by my tears. After all, sweet friend, a little sooner or a little later, would we not have had to part? Need I speak of the uncertainty and emptiness of life? You remember young M——whose ship was lost off the island of Mauritius.[12] When you received his last letter a few months after his death, his earthly remains did not even exist any more, and just when you began to mourn for him in Europe, others in the Indies were ending their mourning. What can man be, then, when his memory perishes so quickly! When some of his friends learn of his death, others are already consoled! Tell me, dear, beloved René, will my memory, too, vanish so quickly from your heart? O my brother, I tear myself away from you in earthly time only that we may not be parted in eternity.

AMELIA

"P.S. I am enclosing the deed of my worldly goods. I hope you will not reject this token of my affection."

Had lightning struck at my feet I could not have been seized by greater panic. What secret was Amelia hiding from me? Who was forcing her into the religious life so suddenly? And had she reconciled me to life through her tender affection only to abandon me now so abruptly? Oh, why had she come back to turn me aside from my plan? A feeling of pity had brought her back to me, but now, tired of her disagreeable duty, she was impatiently leaving me to my misery, though I had no one but her in all the world. People imagine they have done something wonderful when they have kept a man from death! Such were my sad reflections. Then, examining my own feelings, I said, "Ungrateful Amelia, if you were in my place, if, like myself, you were lost in the void of your existence, ah, you would not be forsaken by your bother!"

And yet, as I reread the letter, I felt in its tone something so sad, so tender, that my heart melted completely. Suddenly I had a thought which gave me hope. It occurred to me that Amelia might have fallen in love with a man, and dared not admit it. This suspicion seemed to explain her melancholy, her mysterious correspondence, and the passionate tone pervading her letter. I wrote to her at once, begging her to open her heart to me. Her answer was not long in coming, but revealed nothing about her secret. She wrote only that she had obtained dispensation from the novitiate and was about to pronounce her vows.

I was exasperated by Amelia's stubbornness, by the enigma of her words, and her lack of confidence in my affection. After hesitating a little about what I would do next, I decided to go to B——to attempt one last effort to win back my sister. On my way I had to pass through the region where I was brought up. When I caught sight of the woods where I had spent the only happy moments of

12. *Mauritius:* in the Indian Ocean.

my life I could not hold back my tears, and I found it impossible to resist the temptation of bidding them a last farewell.[13]

My elder brother had sold the family heritage, and the new owner did not live on the estate. I went up to the château through a long lane of pines. Walking across the deserted courtyard I stopped to gaze at the closed or partly broken windows, the thistle growing at the foot of the walls, the leaves strewn over the threshold of the doors, and that lonely stone stairway where so often I had seen my father and his faithful servants. The steps were already covered with moss, and yellow stock grew between the loose, shaky stones. A new caretaker brusquely opened the doors for me. When I hesitated in crossing the threshold, the fellow exclaimed: "Well, are you going to do what that strange woman did who was here a few days ago? She fainted as she was about to come in, and I had to carry her back to her carriage." It was easy enough for me to recognize the "strange woman" who, like myself, had come back to this spot to find memories and tears!

Drying my eyes with a handkerchief I entered the dwelling of my ancestors. I paced through the resounding halls where nothing could be heard but the beat of my footsteps. The chambers were barely lit by a faint glimmer filtering in through the closed shutters. First I went to see the room where my mother had given her life to bring me into the world, then the room to which my father used to retire, after that the one where I had slept in my cradle, and finally the one where my sister had received my first confessions into the bosom of her love. Everywhere the rooms were neglected, and spiders spun their webs in the abandoned beds. I left the château abruptly and strode quickly away, never daring to turn my head. How sweet, but how fleeting, are those moments spent together by brothers and sisters in their younger years under the wing of their aged parents! The family of man endures but a day, and then God's breath scatters it away like smoke. The son barely knows the father or the father the son, the brother the sister or the sister the brother! The oak sees its acorns take root all around it; it is not so with the children of men!

Arriving at B—— I was taken to the convent, where I asked for an opportunity to speak with my sister. I was told she could not see anybody. I wrote to her, and she replied that, as she was about to be consecrated to God,[14] she was not permitted to turn her thought to the world, and if I loved her, I would avoid burdening her with my sorrow. To this she added: "However, if you plan to appear at

---

13. *farewell:* Chateaubriand saw the old château at Combourg in 1791, just before he left for America, and revisited it once more in 1801.

14. *consecrated to God:* Chateau-

briand's sister Lucile never entered a convent, but was briefly married when she was 32 to a man over twice her age. She died at the age of 40.

the altar on the day of my profession, be pleased to serve as my father. It is the only role worthy of your courage, and the only fitting one for our affection and my peace of mind."

This cold determination resisting my burning affection threw me into a violent rage. There were times when I was about to return where I had come from; then, again, I wanted to stay for the sole purpose of disturbing the sacrifice. Hell even goaded me on with the thought of stabbing myself in the church and mingling my last sighs with the vows tearing my sister away from me. The mother superior of the convent sent word that a bench had been prepared for me in the sanctuary and invited me to attend the ceremony, which was to take place the very next day.

At daybreak I heard the first sound of the bells . . . About ten o'clock I dragged myself to the convent in a deathlike stupor. Nothing can ever again be tragic to a man who has witnessed such a spectacle, nor can anything ever again be painful for one who has lived through it. The church was filled with a huge throng. I was led to the bench in the sanctuary, and immediately I fell on my knees, practically unconscious of where I was or what I intended to do. The priest was already at the altar. Suddenly the mysterious grille swung open and Amelia came forward resplendent in all the finery of the world. So beautiful was she, so divinely radiant her countenance, that she brought a gasp of surprise and admiration from the onlookers. Overcome by the glorious sorrow of her saintly figure and crushed by the grandeur of religion, I saw all my plans of violence crumbling. My strength left me. I felt myself bound by an all-powerful hand, and, instead of blasphemy and threats, I could find in my heart only profound adoration and sighs of humility.

Amelia took her place beneath a canopy, and the sacrifice began by the light of torches amid flowers and aromas which lent their charm to this great renunciation. At the offertory the priest put off all his ornaments, keeping only a linen tunic; then, mounting the pulpit, he described in a simple, moving discourse the joy of the virgin who is consecrated to the Lord. As he pronounced the words, "She appeared like the incense consumed in the fire," deep calm and heavenly fragrances seemed to spread through the audience. It was as if the mystic dove had spread its wings to offer its shelter, while angels seemed to hover over the altar and fly back toward heaven with crowns and perfumes.

Ending his discourse, the priest donned his vestments once more and went on with the sacrifice. Sustained by two young sisters, Amelia knelt down on the bottom step of the altar. Then someone came to get me in order that I might fulfill my role as a father. At the sound of my faltering steps in the sanctuary Amelia was about to collapse. I was placed beside the priest for I was to offer him the scissors. At that moment once again I suddenly felt my passion flame up within me. I was about to burst out in fury, when Amelia recovered her courage and darted such a sad and reproachful glance at me that I was transfixed. Religion was triumphant. Taking advantage of my confusion, Amelia boldly brought her head forward; under the holy blades her magnificent tresses fell in every direction. Her worldly ornaments were replaced by a long muslin robe, which sacrificed none of her appeal. The cares of her brow vanished under a linen headband, and the mysterious veil, that two-fold symbol of virginity and religion, was placed on her shorn head. Never had she appeared so beautiful. The penitent's eye was fixed on the dust of the world, while her soul was already in heaven.

However, Amelia had not yet pronounced her vows, and in order to die for the world she had to pass through the tomb. She therefore lay down on the marble slab, and over her. was spread a pall, while a torch burned at each of the four corners. With his stole round his neck and his book in his hand, the priest began the service for the dead. The young virgins took it up. O joys of religion, you are powerful indeed, but oh, how terrible! I was obliged to kneel beside this mournful sight. Suddenly a confused murmur emerged from under the shroud, and as I leaned over, my ears were struck by these dreadful words, audible only to myself: "Merciful God, let me never again rise from this deathbed, and may Thy blessings be lavished on my brother, who has never shared my forbidden passion!"[15]

With these words escaping from the bier the horrible truth suddenly grew clear, and I lost control of my senses. Falling across the death sheet I pressed my sister in my arms and cried out: "Chaste spouse of Christ, receive this last embrace through the chill of death and the depths of eternity which already have parted you from your brother!"

This impulse, this cry, and these tears disturbed the ceremony. The priest interrupted himself, the sisters shut the grille, the crowd pushed forward toward the altar, and I was carried away unconscious. Surely I was not grateful to those who revived me! Opening my eyes, I learned that the sacrifice had been consummated, and my sister had been taken with a violent fever. She sent word begging me not to try to see her again. O misery of my life—a sister fearing to talk to her brother, and a brother afraid of having his sister hear his voice! I left the convent as though it were the place of atonement which prepares us in flames for the blessed life, and where all has been lost, as it is in hell—save hope.

15. *forbidden passion:* Some scholars have tried to demonstrate that Amelia's incestuous love had a basis in Chateaubriand's reciprocated affection for his sister Lucile. It is perhaps safest to recall that incest became a popular romantic theme: in Gothic novels, Goethe's *Wilhelm Meister*, Shelley's *Cenci*, Byron's *Manfred*, etc.

There is strength in our soul to sustain us in our own misfortunes, but to become the involuntary cause of someone else's misfortune is completely unbearable. Now that I understood my sister's grief, I imagined how she must have suffered. Several things which I had been unable to understand now became clear—the joy tinged with sadness which my sister had felt when I was leaving on my travels, the efforts she made to avoid me when I had returned, and at the same time, the weakness which kept her from entering a convent for so long. In her sorrow she must have tried to convince herself that she could yet be cured! As for the secret correspondence which had so deceived me—that was apparently made up of her plans to retire from the world and her arrangements for dispensation from the novitiate, as well as the transfer of her property to me.

O my friends, now I knew what it meant to shed tears for grief which was far from imaginary! My emotions, which had been vague for so long, now seized avidly upon this, its first prey. I even felt a kind of unexpected satisfaction in the fullness of my anguish, and I became aware, with a sense of hidden joy, that sorrow is not a feeling which consumes itself like pleasure.

I had wanted to withdraw from the world before receiving the Almighty's command—that was a great crime. God had sent me Amelia both to save and to punish me. Thus does every guilty thought and forbidden act bring on disorder and sorrow. Amelia had begged me to continue living, and I owed it to her not to aggravate her woes. Besides—how strange it seems!—now that my sorrows were real, I no longer wished to die. My grief had become an immediate concern occupying my every moment, so thoroughly is my heart molded of weariness and misery!

And so I suddenly settled on another plan of action; I determined to leave Europe and go to America.[16] At that very time, in the port of B——, they were fitting out a fleet of ships bound for Louisiana. I made arrangements with one of the captains, wrote to Amelia about my plan, and prepared to leave.

My sister had been at the gates of death, but God had reserved for her the supreme crown of virgins and chose not to call her to Him so soon. Her trials on earth were prolonged. Coming down once again into life's painful path she went courageously forward as a heroine in the face of affliction; bent under the cross she saw in her struggles the certainty of triumph and overwhelming glory in her overwhelming woe.

The sale to my brother of what little property I still had, the long preparations of the convoy, and unfavorable winds, all held me in

16. *America:* Chateaubriand spent some five months in America (1791– 1792), though it is doubtful whether he saw the "Meschacebe."

port a long time. Each morning I would go for news of Amelia, and always I returned with new reasons for weeping and admiring.

I wandered endlessly about the convent at the edge of the sea. Often I would notice, in a little grilled window overlooking the deserted beach, a nun sitting in a pensive attitude. She was meditating as she gazed out over the broad ocean, where some vessel could be seen sailing toward the ends of the earth. Several times, in the moonlight, I again saw the nun at the bars of the same window. With the star of night shining down upon her, she was contemplating the sea, listening, it seemed, to the sound of the waves breaking sadly on the lonely shores.

I can still hear the bell in the silence of the night calling the sisters to vigils and prayer. As it tolled in slow rhythm and the virgins moved silently toward the altar of the Almighty, I hastened to the convent. There, alone at the foot of the walls, I would listen in reverent rapture to the last strains of the hymns, as they blended beneath the temple vaults with the gentle murmur of the waves.

I do not know why all these things, which should have intensified my anguish, served instead to soften its sting. My tears were less bitter when I shed them out there on those rocks in the wind. My very grief, which was so rare, bore within itself some remedy; for there is joy in the uncommon, even if it is an uncommon calamity. This almost gave me hope that my sister too might become less miserable.

A letter I received from her before my departure seemed to confirm this feeling. Amelia pitied me tenderly for my sorrow, and assured me that time was healing her wound. "I have not given up hoping for happiness," she wrote. "The very immensity of my sacrifice calms me somewhat, now that it is all over. The simplicity of my companions, the purity of their vows, the regularity of their life, everything spreads its healing balm over my days. When I hear the storms raging and the sea bird beating its wings at my window, I, poor dove of heaven, reflect on my joy in finding a shelter from the tempest. Here is the holy mountain, the lofty summit where we hear the last faint murmurs of the earth and the opening harmonies of heaven. It is here that religion gently beguiles a tender soul. For the most violent passion it substitutes a kind of burning chastity in which lover and virgin are at one. It purifies every sigh, it makes the ephemeral flame inviolate, and it blends its divine calm and innocence with the remains of confusion and worldly joy in a heart seeking rest and a life seeking solitude."

I do not know what heaven still holds in store for me, or whether it meant to warn me that everywhere my steps would be harried by storms. The order was given for our fleet to set sail; as the sun began sinking, several vessels had already weighed anchor. I made

arrangements to spend the last night on shore writing my farewell
letter to Amelia. Around midnight, as my attention was absorbed
in my thoughts and tears moistened my paper, my ear was suddenly drawn to the wailing of the winds. As I listened, cannon shots
of alarm could be heard through the storm, together with the knell
tolling in the convent. I plunged out to the shore where all was
deserted and nothing could be heard but the roar of the surf. I sat
down on a rock. On one side I could see the vast expanse of shimmering waves, and on the other the somber walls of the convent
vaguely reaching up and fading away in the skies. A dim light shone
out from the grilled window. O my Amelia! Was it you, on your
knees at the foot of the cross, praying to the God of Tempests to
spare your unhappy brother? Storm on the waves, and calm in your
retreat; men shattered on the reefs before an unshakeable haven;
infinity on the other side of a cell wall; the tossing lights of ships,
and the motionless beacon of the convent; the uncertain lot of the
seaman, and the vestal's vision in a single day of all the days of her
life; and yet, O Amelia, a soul such as yours, stormy as the ocean;
a catastrophe more dreadful than the mariner's—this whole picture
is still deeply engraved in my memory.

Sun of this new sky, now witness to my tears, echoes of American shores repeating these accents, it was on the morrow of that
terrible night that I leaned over the ship's stern and watched my
native land disappearing forever! Long I stood there and gazed for
the last time at the trees of my country swaying on the shore and
the height of the convent sinking over the horizon.

As René came to the end of his story he drew a sheet of paper
from his breast and gave it to Father Souël; then, throwing himself
into the arms of Chactas and stifling his sobs, he waited as the missionary read through the letter.

It came from the mother superior of B——, and described the
last hours in the life of Sister Amelia of Mercy, who had died a
victim of her zeal and charity, while caring for companions stricken
by a contagious disease. The entire community was inconsolable,
and Amelia was regarded as a saint. The mother superior added that
in her thirty years as head of the house she had never seen a sister
so gentle and calm in disposition and none so happy to be relieved
of the world's tribulations.

Chactas clasped René in his arms; the old man was weeping.
"My child," he said to his son, "how I wish Father Aubry[17] were
here. He could draw from the depths of his heart a strange calm
which could pacify storms and yet seemed akin to them. He was

17. *Father Aubry:* the missionary in *Atala,* who shelters the two Indian lov-ers. It is Aubry who with Chactas buries Atala, after she commits suicide.

the moon on a stormy night. The moving clouds are powerless to carry it along in their flight; pure and unperturbed, it advances serenely above them. Alas, as for me, everything disturbs me and carries me away!"

Until now Father Souël had listened to René's story with a severe countenance and without uttering a word. Although inwardly warm-hearted, he presented to the world an inflexible character. It was the sachem's tenderness which made him break his silence.

"Nothing," he began, "nothing in your story deserves the pity you are now being shown. I see a young man infatuated with illusions, satisfied with nothing, withdrawn from the burdens of society, and wrapped up in idle dreams. A man is not superior, sir, because he sees the world in a dismal light. Only those of limited vision can hate men and life. Look a little farther and you will soon be convinced that all those griefs about which you complain are absolutely nothing. Why, what a shame not to be able to think of the only real misfortune in your life without having to blush! All the purity, all the virtue and faith, and all the crowns of a saint can scarcely make the very idea of your troubles tolerable. Your sister has atoned for her sin, but if I must speak frankly, I fear that through some terrible justice, that confession, emerging from the depths of the tomb, has in turn stirred up your own soul. What do you do all alone in the woods using up your days and neglecting all your duties? You will tell me that saints have retired to the wilderness. Yes, but they were there weeping and subduing their passions, while you seem to be wasting your time inflaming your own. Presumptuous youth, you thought man sufficient unto himself. Know now that solitude is bad for the man who does not live with God. It increases the soul's power while robbing it at the same time of every opportunity to find expression. Whoever has been endowed with talent must devote it to serving his fellow men, for if he does not make use of it, he is first punished by an inner misery, and sooner or later Heaven visits on him a fearful retribution."

Disturbed and humiliated by these words, René raised his head from the bosom of Chactas. The blind sachem began to smile, and this smile of the lips, unrelated as it was to the expression in his eyes, seemed to possess some mysterious, heavenly quality. "My son," said the old man who had once loved Atala, "he speaks severely to both of us; he is reprimanding the old man and the young, and he is right. Yes, you must give up this strange life, which holds nothing but care. Happiness can be found only in the common paths.

"One day the Meschacebe, while yet rather close to its source, grew weary of being only a limpid stream. It called for snows from the mountains, waters from the rivers, and rains from the tempests, and it overran its banks and laid waste its lovely forests. At first the haughty stream applauded its own power. But soon, seeing how everything grew barren along its path and how it now flowed abandoned in its solitude with its waters always troubled, it longed once again for the humble bed which nature had prepared for it, and it pined for the birds and the flowers, the trees and the streams which were once its modest companions along its peaceful course."

Chactas grew silent, and off in the reeds of the Meschacebe the flamingo's call could be heard announcing a storm for the middle of the day. The three friends started back toward their cabins. René walked silently between the missionary, who was praying, and the blind sachem, who kept feeling his way. It is said that, encouraged by the two elders, René returned to his wife, but still found no happiness. Soon afterwards, along with Chactas and Father Souël, he perished in the massacres of the French and Natchez in Louisiana. They still point out a rock where he would go off and sit in the setting sun.

HEINRICH HEINE
(1797–1856)
Poems from The Lyrical Intermezzo
(Das lyrische Intermezzo)*

1

In May-month, wonderfully fair,[a]
When buds burst forth in glee,
Then deep within my heart,
Love too awoke for me.

In May-month, wonderfully fair,   5
When birds' songs filled the air,
To her I then confessed
My longing and despair.

2

All of my tears engender[b]
Flowers that bloom in throngs,
And nightingales render
My sighs in lovely songs.

* *Das lyrische Intermezzo:* a cycle of sixty-five short poems with a verse prologue, composed 1822–1823, and included in *The Book of Songs,* published in 1827. Translated by Howard E. Hugo. Numbers 1, 2, 18, 59, and 65 are from *The Portable Romantic Reader,* copyright © 1957. Reprinted by permission of the Viking Press, Inc.; number 3 is reprinted by permission of Angel Flores, Doubleday & Company (1960).

    a. "Im wunderschönen Monat Mai."
    b. "Aus meinen Thränen spriessen."

And sweetheart, if you love me,   5
Yours are the buds below
That window, whence lovely
Nightingales' songs shall flow.

3

The rose, the fair lily, the dove, and the sunlight,[c]
Time was when I loved them with love's own delight.
I love them no longer, I love with exclusion,
The small one, the fine one, the pure one, the true one;
She who is fountain from whence pours out love,   5
The rose and fair lily, and sunlight, and dove.

18

Rage I'll yet scorn, although my heart is torn,[d]
Oh love now gone for good! Rage I'll yet scorn.
Despite the way you shine, so diamond-bright,
No single beam falls in your heart's black night.

I've known it long. I saw you while you slept,   5
And saw your heart so black by darkness kept,
And saw the snake, while at your heart it ate,
I saw how miserable you are, my sweet.

59

A single star drops swiftly[e]
Down through the sparkling sky!
This is the star of lovers
That drops before my eye.

An apple-tree drops blossoms   5
And leaves to the waiting ground!
The playful breezes gaily
Whirl the leaves around.

A dying swan in the fish-pond
Sings as it glides on the wave,
And finally, weakly singing,   10
It sinks to its watery grave.

It is so still in the darkness!
The blossoms have blown from the tree,
The star has sputtered and vanished,   15
And faded the swan's melody.

---

c. "Die Rose, die Lilie, die Taube, die   Herz auch bricht."
Sonne."   e. "Es fällt ein Stern herunter."
d. "Ich grolle nicht, und wenn das

Where? (Wo?)'

Where will at last the wander-weary
On his final bed recline?
Under palm-trees in the Southland?
Under lindens by the Rhine?

Will I, in some distant desert,   5
Buried be by stranger's hand?
Or will my last abode be rather
On some sea-shore, in the sand?

Ever onward! God's own Heaven
Will surround me, then as now;   10
And at night, like death-watch lanterns,
Stars will sway above my brow.

f. **Posthumous, from Heine's literary**   Translated by Howard E. Hugo. "Wo
remains. Probably written before 1840.   wird einst des Wandermüden."

Heine Dying in Paris*

I

Death and Morphine

Yes, in the end they are much of a pair,
my twin gladiator beauties—thinner than a hair,
their bronze bell-heads hum with the void; one's more austere,
however, and much whiter; none dares cry down his character.
How confidingly the corrupt twin rocked me in his arms;   5
his poppy garland, nearing, hushed death's alarms
at sword-point for a moment.
Soon a pinpoint of infinite regression! And now that incident
is closed. There's no way out,
unless the other turn about   10
and, pale, distinguished, perfect, drop his torch.
He and I stand alerted for life's Doric, drilled, withdrawing march:
sleep is lovely, death is better still,
not to have been born is of course the miracle.

II

Every idle desire has died in my breast;   15
even hatred of evil things, even my feeling
for my own and other men's distress.
What lives in me is death.

* Translated by Robert Lowell. Re-   & Giroux and Faber & Faber Ltd.
printed by permission of Farrar, Straus

The curtain falls, the play is done;
my dear German public is goosestepping home, yawning.   20
They are no fools, these good people:
they are slurping their dinners quite happily,
bear-hugging beer-mugs—singing and laughing.

That fellow in Homer's book was quite right:
he said: the meanest little Philistine living   25
in Stukkert-am-Neckar is luckier
than I, the golden-haired Achilles, the dead lion,
glorious shadow-king of the underworld.

III

My zenith was luckily happier than my night:
whenever I touched the lyre of inspiration, I smote   30
the Chosen People. Often—all sex and thunder—
I pierced those overblown and summer clouds . . .
But my summer has flowered. My sword is scabbarded
in the marrow of my spinal discs.
Soon I must lose all these half-gods   35
that made my world so agonizingly half-joyful.

Sea-Sickness*

The grey afternoon clouds
Droop, descending upon the sea
Which rises darkly to meet them,
And between them races the ship.

Sea-sick I sit, still, at the mast   5
And make meditations about myself.
Very old, ashen-grey meditations,
Which already Father Lot made
When he had enjoyed too much bounty
And found himself so ill afterwards.   10
Then, now and again, I think of old stories,
How cross-carrying pilgrims of earlier time
Believing, kissed, on the storm-tossed voyage,
the Virgin's image, rich in comfort,
How knights brought low in this sea-emergency   15
Pressed the dear glove of their cherished lady
Against their lips and were likewise comforted—
I, however, sit and chew disagreeably
An old herring, the salty comforter
In cat-crises and dog's distemper.   20

* Translated by **Vernon Watkins**. Reprinted by permission of **Faber & Faber Ltd.**

Meanwhile the ship contends
With the wild, upheaving tide;
It lands back now like a rearing war-horse
On the stern, so that the rudder cracks,
Now plunges down again headlong,   25
Into the chasm of moaning water,
Then again, as if carelessly love-weary,
It hovers, thinking to rest
On the black bosom of the giant wave
Which mightily rages on,   30
And suddenly, a confused sea-cataract,
Crashes into white water-curls
And covers my self with foam.

This rolling and hovering and pitching
Is unendurable!   35
Vainly my eye peers out, seeking
The German coast. But ah! only water,
And once again water, stirred-up water!

As the traveller in Winter longs at evening
For a hot cup of tea inside him,   40
So my heart now longs for you,
My German Fatherland.
Though your precious earth may always be covered
With insanity, hussars, bad verses,
And tepidly thin little treatises;   45
Although your zebras may always
Feed on roses instead of thistles,
Though your aristocratic apes may always
Swagger in grand, idle clothes refinedly,
And think themselves better than all the other   50
Heavily plodding low-browed cattle;
Though your council of snails may always
Consider itself immortal
Because it crawls on so slowly,
And though it may daily collect its votes   55
On whether the cheese belongs to the maggots,
And deliberate a long time
On how to perfect Egyptian sheep
So that their wool would grow better
And the shepherd could shear them like others   60
Without distinction—
Though folly and injustice may always
Cover you whole, O Germany;
Nevertheless I long for you,
For you are at least **firm** land.   65

ALPHONSE DE LAMARTINE
(1790–1869)
The Lake (Le Lac)*

Thus forever driven toward new shores,
Borne in eternal night without return,
Why is it that we never on time's sea
    Cast anchor for one day?

O lake! Scarce had the year run through its course,   5
See! All alone I sit upon this stone
Near those loved waves she was to see again,
    Where once you saw her sit.

Thus did you moan beneath these craggy rocks,
Thus did you break beneath their clefted flanks,   10
Thus threw the wind the spray from off your waves
    Upon her cherished feet.

Do you recall that night? We rowed all still,
From far, upon the water, beneath the sky,
We only heard the rowers' cadenced oars   15
    Against harmonious waves.

When suddenly in sounds unheard on land
The echoes struck from out the charming bank:
Waves listened, and the voice so dear to me
    Sang with these words: 20

"O time! delay your flight; you happy hours!
    Delay your course:
Let us partake of all the fleet delights
    This loveliest of days!

"On earth enough sad souls call out to you,   25
    Flow, flow for them!
Take them along with their devouring days;
    Forget we˜happy few.

---

* From *Poetic Meditations*, 1820. Translated by Howard E. Hugo.
5. *O lake!*: Lake Bourget at Aix-les-Bains, Savoy, France.
7. *she*: Lamartine's mistress, Julie Charles, whom he met at Aix-les-Bains in 1816. He revisited the lake in August–September, 1817; she was to have met him there, but was too ill to attempt the journey. Lamartine wrote the poem in September, and Mme. Charles died December 18, 1817.

"Yet these few moments I beg all in vain,
    Time runs away from me and flees;   30
I tell the night: 'Go slowly'; and the dawn
    Appears to chase away the night.

"So love and let us love! Rejoice with speed
    In this short, passing hour!
Man has no port, and time too has no shores;   35
    It flows, and we pass on."

Could it be these mad moments, jealous time,
When love's long waves fill us with happiness,
Fly far away from us, and just as fast
    As any mournful day?   40

Alas! Can't we at least retain some trace?
Is everything forever gone, all lost?
Time gives all to us, then time rubs all out,
    Will he give nothing back?

Eternity, the void, the past, deep depths,   45
Where are those days that you have swallowed up?
Speak! Will you give us back those sublime joys
    You robbed from us?

O lake! mute crags! grottoes! Gloomy woods!
All spared by time, or by time youth-renewed,   50
At least, guard lovely nature, from this night,
    Some recollection, memory!

May it be in your peace, be in your storms,
Fair lake, or in the view from laughing hills,
And in your sable firs, your savage rocks   55
    That hang above your waves!

Be in the trembling zephyr which then fades,
Be in the sounds repeated shore to shore,
The star with silver brow, who makes your waves
    White with soft light!   60

May moaning wind, and may the sighing reed,
May those light odors perfumed by your breeze,
May all that we can hear, can see, can breathe,
    All say: "They loved!"

VICTOR HUGO
(1802–1885)
The Child (L'Enfant)*

O horror! horror! horror!—SHAKESPEARE, Macbeth[a]

The Turks passed through. All is ruin and grief.
Chios, isle of wines, now gloomy shoal,
　　Chios, bower-shadowed,
Chios, whose waves reflected her great woods,
Her hills and palaces, and where each night   5
　　The maiden-chorus danced.

Deserted. No: alone by blackened walls,
A blue-eyed infant sits, a small Greek boy,
　　His humbled head hung low.
He had for shelter, he had for his support   10
A single hawthorn, a white bloom like him
　　Forgotten amid havoc.

O! poor child, barefoot on the jagged rocks!
Alas! To wipe the tears from your eyes,
　　Blue as the sky and sea,   15
That in their azure, from the tearful storm,
Once more may shine the light of joy and play,
　　To lift up your blond head,

What do you want? Sweet child, what must I give
To bind again with joy, to rearrange   20
　　Those locks on shoulders white,
Which have not felt insulting steel shears,
Which weep disheveled on your lovely brow,
　　Like weeping-willow leaves?

What is there might dispel your gloomy grief?   25
You wish that lily, blue like your blue eyes,
　　That grows near Persian wells?
You want that tuba-fruit, colossal tree,

* Translated by Howard E. Hugo.
From Oriental Poems, published in 1829.
This poem was composed June 8–10,
1828; the original is rhymed a-a-b-c-c-b,
with alexandrine couplets separated by
eight-syllable lines—a form associated
with Remi Belleau, sixteenth-century
French poet.
　　a. From Macbeth II, iii, 68: MacDuff's
exclamation when he reports the death
of the murdered King Duncan.
　　1. Turks: The poem refers to the
Greek War of Independence, which broke
out in 1821.
　　2. Chios: island in the Greek archi-
pelago.
　　28. tuba: an Oriental tree. Hugo, in a
note, said: "Consult the Koran for the
tuba tree . . . the Turkish Paradise, like
their Hell, has its tree."

So large an ever-racing horse must take
 One hundred years to leave its shade?   30

You wish a forest bird to make you smile,
Whose voice is sweeter than an oboe sounds,
 Shriller than cymbal-clash?
What is it? flower, fruit, or wonderful bird?
"My friend," the Greek child spoke, the blue-eyed child,   35
 "I want powder and shot."

Tomorrow, at Dawn . . . (Demain, dès l'aube . . .)[b]

Tomorrow, dawn, the hour when fields are white,
I'll leave. You see, I know you wait for me.
I'll cross the woods, I'll climb the mountain height.
I can no longer live with you away.

I'll walk, my eyes affixed upon my thoughts,   5
No sound I'll hear, nor gaze on any sight,
Alone, unknown, back bent, with folded hands,
Sad, and the day for me shall be like night.

I shall not see the evening gold descend,
Nor far-off sails making for Harfleur,   10
When I arrive, upon your tomb I'll place
A green spray of heather and holly in flower.

b. From Book IV of *The Contempla-
tions* (1856), composed September 3,
1847. Translated by Howard E. Hugo.
The original poem is written in alexan-
drines, its rhyme scheme is followed here.
 2. *you:* The poem is addressed to
Hugo's daughter Léopoldine, drowned in
a boating accident in 1843, buried at
Harfleur.
 12. *heather and holly:* evergreens sym-
bolizing eternal life.

GÉRARD DE NERVAL

(GÉRARD LABRUNIE)

(1808–1855)

El Desdichado*

I am the shadowy—the widowed—sadly mute,
At ruined tower still the Prince of Aquitaine:

* *El Desdichado:* "The Unhappy One."
From *Les Chimères* (1854). Translated
by Howard E. Hugo.
 2. *tower . . . Aquitaine:* Aquitaine is
that part of France between the Loire
and the Garonne; it was united with the
crown of France in 1137, when Louis
VII married Eleanor of Aquitaine. Most
critics feel Nerval had no special
"Prince" in mind. Nerval claimed descent from the Chevalier d'Othon, whose
ruined château with *three* "towers" is
still extant in the Dordogne. Many of
Nerval's symbols are also taken from the
Tarot Arcana—playing cards with occult
meanings. A "ruined tower," Card 16 in
the *Major Arcana* (also called "The
House of God") means "destruction
through antagonism: breaking material
equilibrium."

My single *star* is dead—my constellated lute
Now bears the sable *sun* of melancholy pain.

In darkness in my grave, you who once could cheer,   5
Return me Posilipo and the Italian sea,
The flower which was to my tormented heart so dear,
The trellis where the rose and vine entwined could be.

Am I Amor or Phoebus? . . . Lusignan or Biron?
My forehead is still red from that kiss by the queen;   10
That grotto where the siren swims, I've had my dream . . .

Two times the conquerer I've crossed the Acheron,
And on the lyre of Orpheus, changing from key to key,
I've sung both saintly sighs and sung the fairy's lay.

Myrto[a]

It is of you, divine enchantress, I am thinking, Myrto,
Burning with a thousand fires at haughty Posilipo,
Of your forehead flowing with an Oriental glare,
Of the black grapes mixed with the gold of your hair.

From your cup also I drank to intoxication,   5
And from the furtive lightning of your smiling eyes,
While I was seen praying at the feet of Iacchus,
For the Muse has made me one of Greece's sons.

Over there the volcano has re-opened, and I know
It is because yesterday you touched it with your nimble toe,   10
And suddenly the horizon was covered with ashes.

3. *star:* possibly Adrienne (Sophie Dawes), Sylvie (a village girl Nerval knew as a young boy), or Aurelia (the actress Jenny Colon, who died in 1842): all women he had loved. Card 17 in the *Tarot* pack—"the star"—shows a naked woman kneeling beneath eight stars.
4. *sun:* Card 19 is "the sun."
6. *Posilipo . . . sea:* Posilipo is a suburb of Naples, on the Bay. Nerval traveled in Italy in 1834 and 1843, and had a love affair with an English girl on his second visit.
9. *Amor . . . Biron:* Amor, the god of love; Phoebus, Apollo the sun-god; Lusignan probably refers to the château of Lusignan in the department of Vienne. "Biron" may be an allusion to an old folksong, "Quand Biron voulut danser" ("When Biron wanted to dance"), or to Armand-Louis de Gontaut (1747–1793), Duc de Lauzun.
11. *grotto:* possibly the Sirens' Grotto at Tivoli.
12. *Acheron:* river in Hades over which the dead had to pass. Some critics have suggested that Nerval was referring to

his two previous incarcerations in the lunatic asylum.
13. *Orpheus:* Thracian musician who invented the lyre, or received it from Apollo. He visited Hades to recover his dead wife Eurydice, disobeyed the injunction not to look back at her, and she returned to the Underworld. Another legend tells how he was torn to pieces by wild Thracian women, when grief for Eurydice made him reject their advances.
  a. From *Selected Writings of Gérard de Nerval* translated with a critical introduction and notes by Geoffrey Wagner. Copyright © 1957 by Geoffrey Wagner. Reprinted by permission of Grove Press, Inc. Published in *Les Chimères* (1854). Myrto, a Greek name, probably alludes to the English girl Nerval met in 1834, with whom he visited Pompeii, Portici, and Herculaneum—the heroine of his tale *Octavie.*
2. *Posilipo:* suburb of Naples, on the Bay.
7. *Iacchus:* Bacchus, god of wine.
9. *volcano:* i.e., Vesuvius.

Since a Norman Duke shattered your gods of clay,
Evermore, beneath the branches of Virgil's laurel,
The pale hydrangea mingles with the green myrtle!

12. *Norman Duke . . . gods of clay:*
Duke Roger besieged and captured Naples
in 1130; the "gods" are statues of Roman
divinities.
13. *Virgil's laurel:* Virgil lived for a
while at Naples, and his tomb is in
Posilipo. Petrarch is said to have planted

laurel by Virgil's grave.
14. *hydrangea . . . myrtle:* It has been
suggested that, within the context of
Nerval's flower symbolism, the image
represents the blending of modern times
with pagan antiquity.

GIACOMO LEOPARDI

(1798–1837)

The Infinite (L'infinito)*

This lonely hill was always dear to me,
And this hedgerow, that hides so large a part
Of the far sky-line from my view. Sitting and gazing
I fashion in my mind what lie beyond—
Unearthly silences, and endless space,   5
And very deepest quiet; until almost
My heart becomes afraid. And when I hear
The wind come blustering among the trees
I set that voice against this infinite silence:
And then I call to mind Eternity,   10
The ages that are dead, and the living present
And all the noise of it. And thus it is
In that immensity my thought is drowned:
And sweet to me the foundering in that sea.

The Evening after the Holy Day
(La sera del dì di festa)ª

The night is soft and clear, and no wind blows;
The quiet moon stands over roofs and orchards
Revealing from afar each peaceful hill.
Sweetheart, now every field-path is silent;
At intervals along the balconies   5
The night-long lantern gleams: you are asleep,
And gentle slumber now gathers about
Your quiet chamber, and no single care
Gnaws at your heart; you do not know at all,
Nor think that you have opened in my breast   10

* Written September, 1819, the first of
the six *Idylls;* published December, 1825,
and included in *Verses,* 1826. The Leopardi selections have been translated by
John Heath-Stubbs (New Directions,
1946). Reprinted by permission of New

Directions. All rights reserved.
a. Written probably in 1820, first published December, 1825. Reprinted by permission of New Directions. All rights
reserved.

A very grievous wound. You are asleep:
And I have come abroad to reverence
This sky whose aspect seems to be so gentle,
And ancient Nature powerful over all,
Who has fashioned me for trouble. "I deny   15
All hope to you," she has said, "Yea, even hope;
Your eyes shall not be bright for any cause,
Except with weeping." This was a festal day:
And you are resting after its amusements;
And maybe in your dreams you still remember   20
How many eyes took pleasure in your beauty,
How many, too, pleased you: I find no place—
Not that I hoped it now—among your thoughts.
Meantime I ask how many years of life
Remain to me, and then it is I cast   25
Myself upon the ground, and cry, and rage.
Oh terrible days, even of our green youth!
Alas, I hear not far along the road
The lonely singing of a workman, coming
Back to his poor home so late at night,   30
After the sports; and fiercely my heart aches
Thinking how all this world passes away
And leaves no trace. For look, the festival
Is over now, an ordinary day
Succeeds tomorrow; all things our race has known   35
Time likewise bears away. Where now is the voice
Of the ancient peoples, the clamour of our ancestors
Who were renowned, and that great Empire of Rome,
The arms, and the clash they made by land and sea?
All is silence and peace; the world is still;   40
There are no tidings now remain of them.
Once in my boyhood, when so eagerly
We would look forward to the holiday,
Finding it over, I lay upon my bed,
Wakeful and very unhappy; late that night   45
A singing heard along the field-paths
Little by little dying into the distance,
Even as this does now, pierced through my heart.

To the Moon (Alla luna)[b]

O gracious Moon, I call to mind again
It was a year ago I climbed this hill

b. Written 1819; first published 1825, the third of the six *Idylls*. The original title was "The Memory": the present title is that found in the *Canti* (1813). Reprinted by permission of New Directions. All rights reserved.

To gaze upon you in my agony;
And you were hanging then above the woods,
Filling them all with light, as you do now.   5
But dim and tremulous your face appeared,
Seen through the tears that rose beneath my eyelids,
My life being full of travail; as it is still—
It does not change, O my sweet Moon. And now
I would remember it, and reckon up   10
The cycles of my sorrow. How sweet the thought
That brings to mind things past, when we are young—
When long's the road for Hope, for Memory brief—
Though they were sad, and though our pain endures.

ALEXANDER PUSHKIN

(1799–1837)

Eugene Onegin*

And he is in haste to live, and in a wild hurry to feel.—PRINCE VYAZEMSKY†

Canto I

1

"My uncle's life was always upright
And now that he has fallen ill
In earnest he makes one respect him:
He is a pattern for us still.
One really could not ask for more—   5
But heavens, what a fearful bore
To play the sick-nurse day and night
And never stir beyond his sight!
What petty, mean dissimulation
To entertain a man half dead   10
To poke his pillows up in bed,
And carry in some vile potation,
While all the time one's thinking, 'Why
The devil take so long to die?' "

2

So mused a youthful scapegrace flying   15
Along the post road thick in dust,
The only heir of all his kindred,
By the decree of Jove the Just.

---

* Cantos I and II, translated by Dorothea Prall Radin and George Z. Patrick, reprinted by permission of the University of California Press (Berkeley). Pushkin completed his verse-novel in 1830, made subsequent revisions until its publication in 1833.
† *Vyazemsky:* Pushkin's friend: poet, critic, satirist.
18. *Jove the Just:* i.e. Jupiter—Pushkin is being facetious about fate and chance.

Friends of Lyudmila and Ruslan,
Let me bring forward this young man   20
As hero of my tale without
More preamble or roundabout.
My friend Eugene Onegin, then,
Was born beside the Neva; you
May have been born there, reader, too,   25
Or lived as glittering denizen.
I also used to sojourn there,
But now I dread the northern air.

3
His father served with great distinction
And lived along on credit. He   30
Would give his three balls every season
And so went bankrupt finally.
The fates were gentle with Eugene:
At first a French *Madame* had been
His guardian—then *Monsieur*. The child   35
Was lovable though somewhat wild.
Monsieur l'Abbé, the needy tutor,
Taught him his lessons half in jest
And treated morals lightly, lest
He should appear the persecutor.   40
The Summer Garden saw the pair
Come frequently to take the air.

4
Now when Eugene had reached the season
Of ardent youth when passion soars
Or tender longing fills the bosom,   45
Monsieur was driven out of doors.
Behold our hero!—not a flaw;
Modeled on fashion's latest law;
A London dandy, combed and curled,
Prepared at last to see the world.   50
His French was perfect; he could write
And speak without a foreign taint;
His bow was free of all constraint,
His step in the mazurka light.

---

19. *Lyudmila and Ruslan:* characters in Pushkin's first narrative poem, published 1830.
24. *Neva:* river at Leningrad (formerly St. Petersburg) connecting Lake Ladoga with the Gulf of Finland.
34-7. *Madame . . . l'Abbé:* Eugene is raised first by a French governess, then a male tutor, then a priest.
41. *Summer Garden:* Summer Palace of Peter the Great, later a public garden.
54. *mazurka:* lively Polish dance resembling a polka.

The verdict was no more than truth: 55
A charming, cultivated youth.

5

We all achieve a little learning
Somehow, somewhere, with the result
That dazzling by one's erudition
With us is never difficult. 60
And so Eugene, by those who grudged
Their praises often, was adjudged
Well read—almost to pedantry.
He could discourse most happily
Like an inspired amateur 65
On anything in Christendom,
And when the talk grew grave, become
The wise and silent connoisseur,
Then suddenly let fly a shaft
Of wit, till all the ladies laughed. 70

6

Latin of late is out of fashion,
And so our scholar, if I am
To tell the truth, could muster barely
Enough to read an epigram,
To mention Juvenal, and, better, 75
To add a *Vale* to his letter,
Or quote from Virgil without break
Two lines, though not without mistake.
He had no love for history's pages
Nor any antiquarian lust 80
For digging into ancient dust,
But anecdotes of other ages
From Romulus to us he'd find
And store away within his mind.

7

Of poetry, that lofty mistress, 85
He was no votary devout
Nor knew an iamb from a trochee
However one might count them out.

---

75. *Juvenal:* Decimus Junius Juvenalis (ca. A.D. 60–130), Roman satirical poet.
76. *Vale:* Latin, "farewell."
83. *Romulus:* legendary founder of Rome, eighth century B.C.

87. *iamb . . . trochee:* metrical feet consisting respectively of an unaccented syllable and an accented one (˘ ¯), and an accented syllable and an unaccented one (¯ ˘).

Theocritus and Homer with
Their kind be damned, but Adam Smith   90
He read till he was a profound
Economist. He could expound
Wherein the wealth of nations lies
And what it lives on and how all   95
It needs is raw material,
Not gold. His father was less wise,
It seems, and could not understand
His son: he mortgaged all his land.

8

All the things Eugene had studied
I could not possibly impart,   100
But that wherein he was a genius,
Which was his own peculiar art,
That which from youth had been his pleasure
The toil and torment of his leisure,
Which filled his days of idleness   105
With melancholy, vague distress—
That was the art which Ovid sung,
The art of love, to which he died
A martyr in Moldavia's wide
And barren wilderness, among   110
Barbarian tribes, no more to see
His own far-distant Italy.

9

The fire of love torments us early,
Chateaubriand has said. Indeed,
Nature is not our guide, but rather   115
The first salacious book we read.
Beholding love in some romance
We seek to know it in advance
Of our own season, and meanwhile
All other joys seem puerile.   120
Intent on this foretaste of bliss
We spoil it by our very haste,
Our youthful fervor goes to waste
And all our lives are lived amiss.

89. *Theocritus:* Greek pastoral poet in the third century B.C., author of the *Idylls.*
90. *Adam Smith:* Scottish philosopher and economist (1723–1790), author of *The Wealth of Nations* (1776).

107. *Ovid:* Publius Ovidius Naso (43 B.C.–A.D. 18), author of *The Art of Love, Metamorphoses,* and much amatory verse; he spent his last years in exile in Moldavia on the Black Sea.

Such realizations came to vex   125
Eugene. But how he knew the sex!

10

How soon he learned to cloak his feelings,
To force his quarry to believe
Him true, to languish, dark and jealous,
To hide his hope—then undeceive;   130
To seem by turns subservient,
Proud, thoughtful, or indifferent,
With flaming eloquence to burn,
Or sit profoundly taciturn.
How in his notes of love unbounded   135
He threw discretion to the breeze,
Careless of all but how to please,
And how his glance, at once compounded
Of soft and keen, would then appear
To start with the obedient tear.   140

11

How skillfully he played the novice!
How well he knew the smiling ways
That startle an unpracticed maiden
And capture her with pleasant praise.
How he could seize the moment where,   145
Relenting at his feigned despair,
She yielded some half-meant caress
To his impassioned, shrewd address!
How ardently he then would sue
For an avowal! And at last,   150
When he perceived her heart beat fast,
Demand a secret rendezvous!
And then alone with her how he
Would tutor her in privacy!

12

How early he had learned to trouble   155
The heart of many a tried coquette;
And when he chose to crush his rivals,
What cunning pitfalls he could set!
With what malevolence he stung
Them with the poison of his tongue!   160
But you, you happy husbands, stayed
His friends: the married rake who made
A special point to pay him court,

Well versed in Faublas's strategy,
The old man prone to jealousy,   165
The cuckhold with the pompous port,
Completely satisfied with life,
Himself, his dinner, and his wife.

13–14[b]

How from some meek and modest widow
He could attract a pious glance   170
And enter into conversation
With bashful, blushing countenance!
How, trifling with some ladylove,
He could discourse upon the worth
Of Plato's doctrines and could move   175
A pretty simpleton to mirth!
So from the forest's inmost heart
The savage starving wolf will creep
Upon the fold—all are asleep
And helpless; swifter than a dart   180
The cruel thief has snatched his prey
And in a flash is far away.

15

They bring his letters in the morning
Before he's thought of getting dressed;
Three houses ask him for the evening,   185
Requesting him to be their guest.
A children's name-day feast, a ball,
Which shall he start with of them all?
No matter, he will manage it!
Meantime, in raiment exquisite,   190
And hatted à la Bolivar,
The picture of a youthful spark,
Eugene is driven to the Park
To saunter in the open air
Until his watch with pleasant chime   195
Announces it is dinnertime.

16

Then to a sledge. The dark has fallen,
And to the driver's loud "Make way!"

---

164. *Faublas's strategy:* Faublas was the hero of the novel *The Adventures of Faublas* (1798), by Jean Baptiste Louvet de Couvray (1760–1797). His "adventures" are mainly amatory.
    b. Stanzas with two numbers occur because either Pushkin or the Russian censor made deletions. Missing lines are also to be thus explained.
    191. *hatted à la Bolivar:* the reference is to Simon Bolivar (1783–1830), leader of the revolution of Venezuela against Spain, later dictator of Chile. Bolivar's portraits indicate he favored broad-brimmed headgear.

He's whirled along; his beaver collar
Grows white beneath the frosty spray.   200
So to Talon's, for he's aware
His friend Kaverin waits him there.
He enters, and the pleasant pop
Of corks arises, and the plop
Of gurgling wine. The roast beef vies   205
With truffles, youth's delight,—the queen
And flower of the French cuisine,—
And the far-famed Strassburg pies.
Then Limburg cheese, mature and old,
And pineapple, all yellow gold.   210

17

The thirst that comes from eating cutlets
Still calls for wine, but the ballet,
His watch announces to Onegin,
Already must be under way.
And so the caustic arbiter   215
Of greenrooms and the theater,
The somewhat fickle appanage
Of lovely ladies of the stage,
Is driven off to view the play.
The stormy audience huzza,   220
Ready to clap the *entrechat*
And hiss Racine and boo Corneille,
Or call Moïna back because
They love to hear their own applause.

18

O magic country! There Fonvizin,   225
The friend of freedom, satire's bold
Old master, and the imitative
Knyazhnin shone forth in days of old.
There young Semyonova bore off

---

201. *Talon's:* famous restaurant in St. Petersburg.
202. *Kaverin:* dandy, sport, man-about-town, and friend of Pushkin, to whom the poet wrote several affectionate poems.
208. *Strassburg pies:* possibly made of goose-liver, for which Strasbourg—the capital of Alsace—is famous.
209. *Limburg cheese:* known for its odor; a product of the Belgian and Dutch provinces bearing the same name.
216. *greenrooms:* reception rooms in theaters and concert halls.
221. *entrechat:* a ballet step, where the feet are struck or crossed while the dancer is in the air.
222. *Corneille:* Pierre Corneille (1606–1684), elder contemporary of Racine; author of *Le Cid* (1637), *Cinna* and *Horace* (1640), *Polyeucte* (1643).
223. *Moïna:* heroine in the play *Fingal* by Ozerov, based on James MacPherson's spurious epic of that name (cf. the notes to *René*).
225. *Fonvizin:* writer of comedies during the reign of Catherine the Great.
228. *Knyazhnin:* minor dramatist of the same period.
229. *Semyonova:* popular actress (1786–1849).

The palm of praise with Ozerov,   230
The idols of their countrymen.
Katenin brought to life again
The stately genius of Corneille;
And Shakhovskoy's tumultuous rout
Of biting farces were brought out   235
And Didelot was crowned with bay.
And in the shadow of the wings
I dreamed youth's sweet imaginings.

19

Dear goddesses of mine! Where are you?
Hear my unhappy voice and say,   240
Have other maidens filled your places
To triumph where you once held sway?
And shall I hear you sing once more?
Shall I behold you sweep and soar,
The spirits of the Russian dance?   245
Or shall my melancholy glance
View faces in a world unknown,
Turning upon them as they pass
My disenchanted opera glass,
Gazing at mirth I have outgrown!   250
Then shall I yawn and silently
Regret my past felicity?

20

The house is full, the boxes glitter,
The pit is like a seething cup,
The gallery claps with loud impatience,   255
The curtain rustles—and goes up.
There, half of air and all aglow,
Obedient to the magic bow,
Circled by nymphs in lovely bands,
Istomina, resplendent, stands.   260
Balanced on one toe, tremulous,
She slowly whirls the other round,
Then with a sudden leap and bound
Flies as if blown by Aeolus.
She winds, unwinds and, light as feather,   265
In mid-air beats her feet together.

---

230. *Ozerov:* Cf. note, line 223.
232. *Katenin:* translator of plays by
Corneille and Racine.
234. *Shakhovskoy's:* a prince, and patron of the theater.

236. *Didelot:* French ballet-master in
St. Petersburg.
261. *Istomina:* a dancer who died in
1848.
264. *Aeolus:* Greek god of the winds.

21

The house applauds. Onegin enters,
And, having trod on many a toe,
He studies through his opera glasses
The ladies whom he does not know.   270
His eye runs over every tier,
But gowns and faces all appear
To leave him far from satisfied.
He bows to men on every side,
Then carelessly begins to view   275
The stage and what is going on,
Averts his face and starts to yawn,
And mutters, "Time for something new!
The ballet pleased me once, but how
Didelot himself does bore me now!"   280

22

But still the cupids, snakes, and devils
Career about and scream and roar;
The tired lackeys in their sheepskins
Still doze before the entrance door;
And still they stamp and hiss and rap,   285
Or blow their noses, cough, and clap,
And still, outside and in, the night
Is all ablaze with lantern light.
The coach horse paws the ground or stands
Half frozen by the tedious wait,   290
And round the fires the cabbies rate
Their masters as they warm their hands;
But our Eugene, as you may guess,
Has long since left to change his dress.

23

Shall I depict in faithful colors   295
The private room where the mundane
Disciple of exacting fashion
Was dressed, undressed, and dressed again?
Everything London's nicest taste
Exports across the Baltic waste   300
To get, for gewgaws smart or strange,
Timber and tallow in exchange,
All that the workshop and the loom
Of greedy Paris could produce
Of luxuries as an excuse   305
For useful barter, in the room

Of our philosopher were seen—
The seer and sage just turned eighteen.

24

Pipes from Stamboul with stems of amber,
Bronzes and porcelain *en masse*,   310
And, that enjoyment of the pampered,
Perfumes in flagons of cut glass.
Steel files and combs elaborate
And scissors curved and scissors straight,
Brushes with thirty-odd details,   315
Some for the teeth, some for the nails.
(Rousseau could never understand,
They tell us, how the worthy Grimm
Could clean his nails in front of him,
The visionary firebrand: 320
The champion of natural rights
Here hardly followed his own lights.)

25

A man may see his nails are polished,
Yet be a useful citizen;
Why quarrel with one's generation?   325
Custom's a despot among men.
At any rate in our Eugene
A new Kaverin now was seen,
A dandy envied, watched, and thus
Forced to be most meticulous.   330
So when at last he sallied forth
After three hours before the glass,—
For so three hours at least would pass,—
'Twas like a Venus come to earth
Who thus in flighty mood essayed   335
The rôle of man in masquerade.

26

Now that I've drawn your kind attention
To fashion and the mode, you may
Expect me to describe more fully
My hero's elegant array;   340
A somewhat trying task, I fear,
Although description is my sphere,

---

309. *Stamboul:* Istanbul, Constantinople.
310. *en masse:* in a bulk.
318. *Grimm:* Friedrich Melchior,
Baron Grimm (1723–1807), friend of
Rousseau, Diderot, D'Alembert, etc.
321. *champion:* i.e., Rousseau.

For *pantaloons, frock coat,* and *vest*
No Russian wording can suggest,
And even now you must behold   345
How I have patched my halting style
With words of foreign domicile
Too lavishly. And yet of old,
To freshen my vocabulary,
I searched the Academy Dictionary.   350

27

But that is not the point at present:
Let's rather hurry to the ball
Where headlong in his cab Onegin
Has dashed already. On past tall
Dim houses where the horses' feet   355
Make echoes in the sleeping street
The carriage lamps, a double row,
Cast rainbow shadows on the snow.
Sown all around with firepots
A great house gleams; across the glass   360
Of lighted windows shadows pass,
Profiles of heads, and groups and knots
Of ladies with their cavaliers—
One moment, then each disappears.

28

Up drives our hero. Past the doorman   365
He darts and up the marble stair
Swift as an arrow; with one gesture
He brushes back a lock of hair—
And enters. Everywhere a crowd:
The orchestra is playing loud   370
And a mazurka fills the floor
While all about is crush and roar.
The spurs of many a guardsman clash
And tiny feet go flying by
And many a captivated eye   375
Flies after them. Then while the crash
Of violins drowns out the sound
A jealous whispering goes round.

29

In my gay days of youthful passion
Balls were my mad delight. Then, too,   380

350. *Academy Dictionary:* the French Academy's conservative guide to correct French vocabulary, begun in the seventeenth century and not yet finished.

No better spot for an avowal
Or for delivering *billets-doux*.
You married folk, discreet and nice,
I offer you some sound advice:
(I beg you, note my words with care)   385
For I would caution you, Beware!
And you, Mammas, had better bend
A stricter glance on those coquettes
Your daughters. Up with your lorgnettes!
For otherwise—Ah, Heaven forfend!   390
These secrets I instruct you in,
Since I myself long ceased to sin.

30

Alas! In my pursuit of pleasure
How many years have slipped away!
Yet were my morals not to suffer   395
I still should dote on balls today.
I love mad youth; I love the crowd,
Glitter and joy without a cloud,
The dresses, exquisite, complete,
And I adore the ladies' feet!   400
But you will hardly find, all told,
Six pretty feet in Russia. Yet
Two tiny feet I can't forget,
Although I've grown so sad and cold.
Their memory will not depart   405
And still in dreams they stir my heart.

31

Ah, little feet! To me, the madman,
What desert land will fail to bring
A vision of you! In what country
Do you now tread the flowers of spring?   410
Bred in the softness of the East,
Our sullen northern snow long ceased
To hold your imprint. You were such
As loved the soft luxurious touch
Of silky rugs—And are they past,   415
Those days when in you I forgot
Glory and country and my lot
As exile? Yes, they could not last,
And no more trace of them is seen
Than of your footfalls on the green.   420

382. *billets-doux:* little love-notes.

32

Diana's breast, the cheeks of Flora,
Are no doubt charming. But to me
Far lovelier and more enthralling
The fair feet of Terpsichore!
They promise us they will afford   425
An incomputable reward
And with their beauty light the fire
Of uncontrollable desire.
Elvina! I commemorate
Your feet! at all times: half concealed   430
Beneath the table; on the field
Of spring; in winter by the grate;
Upon the polished parquet floor;
Or granite rocks along the shore!

33

I can recall a stormy seashore: 435
The waves came rushing one above
Another in a fury, only
To lie before her feet in love.
I would have found it ah! how sweet,
As did the waves, to kiss her feet.   440
For never in my maddest days
When all my youth was yet ablaze
Did I so wildly long to press
The lips of Armida, or burn
To kiss her rosy cheeks or yearn   445
To touch her breast with a caress.
No, such a transport as then tore
My heart I never felt before.

34

And I remember one more picture—
In secret dreams again I stand   450
Holding for her the happy stirrup,
Her little foot within my hand.
Once more my fancy burns, once more
Her touch seems suddenly to pour
New streams of lifeblood through my heart,   455

421. *Diana's . . . Flora:* Latin goddess of the hunt; Latin goddess of flowers.
424. *Terpsichore:* Muse of dancing.
429. *Elvina:* Certain critics have suggested that Pushkin used the name as a conventional device; and in his lyrics, "Elvina" may represent three different females. Here she may be Maria Rajevsky, whom the poet knew when he was exiled to the Caucasus in 1820.
444. *Armida:* name of the enchantress in *Jerusalem Delivered,* epic by *Torquato Tasso* (1544–1595), perhaps used here to represent a love of Pushkin's youth.

Once more with love and pain I smart.
But sing no more, my noisy lyre,
These haughty damsels of the earth,
Enchantresses who are not worth
The love and songs that they inspire.   460
Their speeches and their glances cheat
As often as their little feet.

35

And our Onegin? He abandons
The ball for bed, half overcome
With sleep, as Petersburg the tireless   465
Is wakened by the noisy drum.
The cabman trudges to his stand,
Merchant and peddler are at hand,
An Ochta milkgirl hurries by,
The hard snow crunching frostily.   470
It is the pleasant morning stir:
The shutters open, in blue curls
The smoke from many a chimney whirls,
And, careful German manager,
The baker in his paper cap   475
Has answered many an early rap.

36

But wearied of the evening's turmoil,
Turning the morning into night,
The child of luxury and pleasure
Sleeps softly in the shaded light.   480
Then well past midday he awakes
To lead again, till morning breaks,
His life monotonous though gay,
Tomorrow like its yesterday.
But in this round of daily bliss   485
Was my Eugene quite satisfied?
To the proud victor in the pride
Of youth did nothing seem amiss?
In spite of all did he remain
At feasts and fêtes unspoiled and sane?   490

37

No, he had lost his freshness early
And wearied of society.
Beauties and belles no longer caused him

469. *Ochta:* a district in St. Petersburg.

A stronger passion than ennui.
He took no pleasure in intrigue,   495
His friendships only brought fatigue;
He could not sit the livelong day
Drinking champagne to wash away
The rare beefsteak and Strassburg pie;
Nor could he be prepared to make   500
Bright sallies with a bad headache;
And though a hothead, finally
He found his interest weakening
In pistols, swords, and dueling.

38

A sickness,—for its cure and treatment   505
We ought to find the formula,—
The thing they call the spleen in England,
Our Russian hypochondria,
Had mastered him by slow degrees;
And though, thank God, it did not please   510
The youth to blow his brains out, still
Life was a desert, dark and chill.
So, like Childe Harold, steeped in gloom,
Oblivious to the allure
Of gossip, Boston, sighs demure,   515
He would pass through a drawing room
Observing nothing that was there,
Nor altering his cheerless air.

42c

Fine ladies of the world of fashion,
You he abandoned first of all,   520
For at our age your upper circles
Undoubtedly begin to pall.
And though perhaps some lady may
Discourse on Bentham and on Say,
Their conversation as a rule   525
Is innocent but tedious drool.
Besides, they are so virtuous,
So lofty-minded and so clever,
So full of pious, pure endeavor,

---

513. *Childe Harold:* Byron's disenchanted hero in the poem by the same name (1812–1818).

515. *Boston:* a game of cards resembling whist, in which the technical terms refer to the British siege of Boston at the start of the American Revolution.

c. Stanzas 39 through 41 are missing from the original Russian text.

524. *Bentham . . . Say:* Jeremy Bentham (1748–1832), founder of the Utilitarian philosophy; Jean-Baptiste Say (1767–1832), French economist who popularized the ideas of Adam Smith.

So circumspect, so scrupulous,   530
So inaccessible of mien,
Their very sight brings on the spleen.

43

And you, young beauties of the evening,
Whom the wild droshkies dash along
The streets of Petersburg at midnight,   535
Eugene has left your boisterous throng.
Refusing all his visitors,
He had immured himself indoors
And shunned all riotous delight.
Yawning, he seized his pen to write—   540
But any stubborn work instilled
Disgust in him; no line would flow
From off his wavering pen, and so
He did not join that vexing guild
Of scribblers on whom I may pass   545
No judgment, being of their class.

44

Once more a prey to doing nothing,
His spirit sick with futile rage,
He sat down with the worthy purpose
Of mastering wisdom's heritage.   550
He filled a shelf with books and read—
But all to no avail. Instead,
One was a bore, one, mad pretense,
No conscience here, and there no sense;
Stale judgments everywhere he looks,   555
The old too old, the new all cast
In the old forms, and so at last,
Like women, he abandoned books,
And covered with a mourning-veil
The shelf of wisdom dead and stale.   560

45

Now I had likewise left the turmoil
And thrown convention's yoke aside,
And at this time we formed our friendship.
His traits and temper satisfied
My liking, the unique degree   565
To which he raised his oddity,
His dreams, his wit, that struck so close.

534. *droshkies:* low four-wheeled Russian carriages.

I was malicious, he morose.
We both had suffered passion's play
And we were weary of our parts,   570
The fire had died out in our hearts,
Though barely started on life's way,
And from blind fortune or from men
We hoped for nothing good again.

46

He who has lived and thought can hardly   575
Do otherwise than scorn his race;
He who has ever felt is troubled
With dreams of that which once took place,
No magic moments now will cause
Delight, the worm of memory gnaws   580
His heart and brings him vain regret;
But still it often does beget
A certain charm in conversation.
At first Onegin's sharp retorts
Put me a little out of sorts,   585
But later I felt no vexation
At his half-bilious sallies and
The sarcasm at his command.

47

How often in the summer evenings
When the night sky hung clear and bright   590
Above the waters of the Neva
Where yet there shone no mirrored light
From fair Diana's countenance,
We dreamed again of young romance
And thought of early love, again   595
Carefree and fond as we were then.
And the night air, so pure and good,
Without a word we breathed in deep;
Till like the prisoner whom sleep
Bears from his cell to some green wood.   600
Our reveries and musings bore
Us back to days of youth once more.

48

Eugene would stand in silence, leaning
Against the granite parapet,
Just as the poet did, he tells us,   605
Lost in old longing and regret.

No sound except a distant shout
When watchmen called the hours out
Or suddenly the rush and beat
Of cabs along a far-off street.   610
A lonely boat swept down the stream
And with the splash of oars were borne
A wild song and a fainter horn,
And we were spellbound in a dream.
But sweeter still than this delight   615
Are Tasso's octaves on the night.

49

O blue waves of the Adriatic,
O Brenta, river of my choice,
I yet shall look on you in rapture,
I yet shall hear your magic voice,   620
Sacred to all Apollo's sons
And known to me through Albion's
Proud lyre and ever dear to me.
The nights of golden Italy
I shall delight in to my fill!   625
Then in a dark mysterious boat
Some Venice maid with me will float
And now speak softly, now be still.
And she shall teach to me the tongue
Of Petrarch in which love is sung.   630

50

Oh, will it come, my hour of freedom?
For it is time to hear my cry.
I wait fair winds upon the seashore
And hail the vessels sailing by.
When shall I start my own free course?   635
When, under storm clouds, shall I force
My way across the battling sea
And leave a land so harsh to me?
And when at last I leave it, then
By the warm seas beneath the sky   640
Of sunny Africa I'll sigh

---

616. *Tasso's octaves:* the eight-line
stanza (*ottava rima*) of Tasso's poetry.
618. *Brenta:* river near Venice, emptying into the Adriatic.
621. *Apollo's sons:* i.e., poets.
622–3. *Albion's proud lyre:* e.g., Byron's *Childe Harold.*
629–30. *tongue of Petrarch:* i.e., Italian, the language in which Francesco
Petrarca (1304–1374), first and greatest
of the Italian humanists, wrote his

poems to Laura.
641. *Africa:* Pushkin's maternal great-
grandfather may have been Hannibal, son
of an Ethiopian king, brought to Constantinople as a hostage and taken by
the Russian envoy to Russia; there he
became a favorite of Peter the Great,
who stood godfather to him, ennobled
him, and married him off to one of the
Court ladies.

For gloomy Russia once again,
Where I had learned to love and weep
And where my heart lies buried deep.

51

Onegin was about to travel   645
With me in foreign countries when
Fate cut the tie that bound our fortunes;
For years we did not meet again.
His father died. The creditors
Gathered before Onegin's doors   650
In greedy crowds, and each one came
Prepared to justify his claim.
Eugene, who hated legal traps
And law courts, took what came from chance,
Renouncing his inheritance   655
As no great forfeit. Or perhaps
Some vague presentiment, some breath
Spoke of his uncle's coming death.

52

And then a letter from the bailiff
Came suddenly, to notify   660
Him that his uncle now lay dying
And wished to bid his heir goodbye.
Eugene no sooner read the news
Than he was off, prepared to use
What speed he could along the way,   665
But yawning as he thought what lay
Ahead—what tedious hours he'd spend
Before he was a moneyed man.
(And at this point my tale began.)
But when he reached his journey's end   670
He found the body laid in state
And finished with its earthly fate.

53

The courtyard swarmed with neighbors' servants:
From north and south, from west and east,
The dead man's friends and foes had gathered,   675
All lovers of a funeral feast.
They buried him, and priest and guest
Refreshed themselves. Then, as if pressed
By weighty business matters, they
Took solemn leave and went away.   680

Behold Eugene, a country squire,
Owner of factory and river,
Of wood and field! The spendthrift liver
Of yesterday was all afire
To lead a life of order here   685
And end his former free career.

54

Two days the new enchantment lasted:
The fields with their deserted look,
The coolness of the shady forest,
The quiet murmuring of the brook.   690
But on the third, field, wood, and hill
No longer caused his heart to thrill
And later sent him fast asleep,
So that he could no longer keep
The knowledge from himself: he knew   695
That though here were no palace halls,
No cards, no verses, and no balls,
The spleen dwelt in the country, too,
And would attend him all his life
Like one's own shadow or one's wife.   700

55

Now, I was born for country quiet,
To be some peaceful villager,
For there my lyre's note grows louder,
My dreams and fancies livelier.
There, consecrated to the sway   705
Of *far niente*, every day
I wander round the lonely lake
And every morning I awake
To leisure, sweet and innocent.
I seldom read, but sleep, nor aim   710
To capture swiftly flying fame.
Was it not so my past was spent?
And then, obscure, unknown to praise,
Did I not live my happiest days?

56

A country house upon its acres,   715
Love, flowers, and utter idleness—
I love them all, unlike Onegin.
Indeed, I'm always glad to stress

706. *far niente:* "doing nothing."

The great dissimilarity
Between my friend Eugene and me,   720
So that no mocking reader nor
Malicious-tongued inquisitor,
Searching a likeness out, may sniff
And shamelessly asseverate
I've drawn myself upon the slate,   725
Like Byron in his pride. As if
No artist ever had been known
To paint a portrait not his own!

57

All poets, let me say, are dreamers,
The friends of love. And so of old   730
Sweet phantoms visited me sleeping
Whose images my heart would hold
Long after, till the Muse had brought
Life to these secret forms of thought.
Indifferently I have sung   735
An ideal mountain maid or young
Girl slave upon the Salhir's shore.
But you, my friends, keep asking me:
"Which of these jealous maids is she
Whom in your verses you adore?   740
Who is the loved one to inspire
The song that rises from your lyre?

58

"Whose glance has fired your inspiration?
Whose sweet caress was adequate
Reward for all your pensive music?   745
Whom do your verses celebrate?"
No one, my friends, no one, God knows.
The pangs of love, its senseless throes,
I suffered without recompense.
Happy the man who can condense   750
The heat of love to poetry!
So, following in Petrarch's ways,
His heart's hot torment he allays
And yet augments his ecstasy.
He tastes of glory and its fruit—   755
But love has always made me mute.

---

736. *mountain maid:* heroine of Pushkin's narrative, Byronic poem, *The Caucasian Prisoner,* written with similar
works (*The Gypsies, The Brother Robbers*) between 1820 and 1824.

737. *girl slave:* character in *The Fountain of Bakhchisirai* (1824), which takes
place in the Crimea.
Salhir: river in the Crimea.

59

Only when stormy love was over
Did my Muse enter. Then I found
My mind made free to seek the union
Between my dreams and magic sound.   760
I write, and my sad heart is eased,
My wandering pen no longer pleased
At each unfinished line to trace
Some tiny foot, some charming face.
The fire that was is burned to coal;   765
Now I, though sad, no longer weep,
And soon the storm will go to sleep
Forever in my quiet soul.
Then I may well begin a song
Some five-and-twenty cantos long.   770

60

Already I have planned my story
And named the hero, and meantime
I see that of my present novel
One chapter has been turned to rhyme.
I've looked it over carefully.   775
The contradictions that I see
I shall not alter now, but let
The censorship collect its debt.
And to the critics with my thanks
I send you, to be torn apart,   780
Newborn creation of my heart!
There on the Neva's well-known banks
To earn the tribute paid to fame:
Envy, abuse, and noisy blame.

Canto II

O Rus. O Rus!—Horace*

1

The place in which Onegin languished
Was a delightful country spot
Where lovers made for simpler pleasures
Would have been grateful for their lot.
The manor house itself was set   5
Apart beside a rivulet,
Cut off by hills from every storm.
Before it, flowery, golden-warm,
Meadows and cornfields stretched away,

* "O Russia!" Also a pun on *Horace*.

And cattle cropped the grassy land,　　　　　10
And hamlets shone; while near at hand
The great neglected gardens lay
Where wistful dryads came and made
Their refuge in the deep green shade.

2

The ancient and time-honored mansion　　　15
Was built, as mansions ought to be,
According to the bygone liking
For sober, wise solidity.
High-ceilinged chambers everywhere,
Silk tapestry on couch and chair,　　　　20
Ancestral portraits in a style
Outworn, and stoves of colored tile.
To us all this seems antiquated,—
I can't say why,—but then, our friend
Most probably did not descend　　　　　25
To notice that they were outdated;
For fashion or antiquity
Produced in him the same ennui.

3

So in the room where the old landlord
Had forty years of exercise　　　　　30
In bickering with his woman servant
Or staring out and catching flies
Eugene took up his domicile.
No inkstain there that might defile
The plainness of the oaken floor:　　　35
Two cupboards, sofa, desk—no more.
Behind one cupboard door a great
Account book lay and close at hand
Bottles and jugs of cider and
A calendar of 1808.　　　　　40
Onegin's uncle would not look
At any other kind of book.

4

Alone on his ancestral acres,
Hard put to it for any scheme
To pass the time, Eugene decided　　　45
To introduce a new régime.
Here in the wilds the sage recluse
Declared forced labor an abuse

And changed it for a light quitrent.
His serfs thanked fate and were content.   50
Not so the neighboring landlords; some
Smiled mockingly, while others found
These innovations going round
Unsafe, and looked extremely glum.
But on one point they all were clear: 55
Eugene was dangerous and queer.

5

At first, indeed, they came to visit,
But presently, when they had found
He usually had his stallion
Led out and saddled and brought round   60
To the back porch, when he should hear
Their family coaches drawing near—
Affronted by such insolence,
They one and all took deep offense.
"Our neighbor's just a firebrand,   65
A freemason, a boor. They say
He sits and drinks red wine all day.
He will not kiss a lady's hand.
He won't say 'Sir,' just 'Yes' and 'No.' "
Their view of him was very low.   70

6

Just then another country squire
Had come to live on his estate
Who caused the same amount of gossip
And called forth censure just as great.
Vladimir Lensky was his name.   75
Direct from Göttingen he came,
A poet and a devotee
Of Kant. From misty Germany
He brought complete enlightenment:
High dreams of freedom democratic,   80
A spirit ardent if erratic,
A tongue forever eloquent.
A handsome youth, with fire and grace,
And black curls falling round his face.

---

49. *quitrent*: rent paid by a freeholder
in lieu of services which he might otherwise be bound to perform.

67. *red wine*: i.e., a man of foreign
tastes. A "good" Russian would drink
vodka.

75. *Lensky*: He becomes Onegin's
closest friend; they duel (Canto VI)
over Lensky's misconceived jealousy—he

thinks Onegin is flirting with Lensky's
beloved Olga—and Lensky is killed.

76. *Göttingen*: university (founded
1737) popular with "Westernized" Russians in the early nineteenth century.

78. *Kant*: Immanuel Kant (1724–
1804), professor at Königsberg, one of
the most influential philosophers of the
late eighteenth century.

7

Unblighted by the world's corruption   85
And by its cold perfidiousness,
His soul was set on fire by friendship
Or by a maiden's soft caress.
He was a charming innocent
In matters of the heart, intent   90
Upon the glamour and the noise
Of this new world of untried joys
Which hope held up to view. He lulled
His doubts with dreams. But still for him
The aim of life was strange and dim,   95
A riddle over which he mulled
And struggled, eager to divine
The miracle of its design.

8

He thought somewhere some kindred spirit
Was born for union with his own,   100
Some maiden waiting for him hourly
And longing to be his alone.
He thought the men he loved would spend
Their lives in prison to defend
His honor, and would not demur   105
To crush his venomous slanderer.
He thought there were some men appointed
By fate whose lot it was to be
A sort of friendly hierarchy,
A deathless band of the anointed,   110
Whose light would pierce our dark abyss
Some day and lead the world to bliss.

9

Pity and generous indignation,
A passion for the common good,
The torment caused by love of glory,   115
All worked together in his blood.
And so he wandered, lyre in hand,
His heart exalted, through the land
Where Goethe and where Schiller sung,
In air where still their genius clung.   120
Nor did he shame the lofty arts
Protected by the sacred Nine;

119. *Schiller:* Friedrich Schiller (1759–1805), close friend of Goethe in Weimar: dramatist, poet, historian, philosopher.   122. *sacred Nine:* the Muses, godesses presiding over the arts and the sciences.

His songs endeavored to enshrine
The noblest feelings of our hearts:
A maiden's dream of ecstasy,   125
The charm of grave simplicity.

10

The slave of love, he sang its praises
In stanzas like a limpid stream,
As simple as a maiden's fancies,
As artless as a childhood dream,   130
Clear as the moon in desert skies
That listens to a lover's sighs.
He sang of parting and of sorrow,
Of what-not and the misty morrow
And of the roses of romance.   135
He sang of countries far away
Where, weeping hotly, once he lay
Pillowed on silence' broad expanse.
He sang life's flowers dead and sere:
He then was in his eighteenth year.   140

11

Eugene alone could rightly value
Such talents in this arid waste,
And Lensky found the neighbors' dinners
Completely foreign to his taste.
He shunned their noisy conversations   145
About their dogs and their relations.
Indeed their sober talk of wine
And crops, though shrewd and genuine,
Did not exactly blaze with wit;
Nor was there any poet's fire   150
Nor brilliancy nor keen desire
Nor art nor social grace in it.
And certainly the ladies' words
Were quite as dull as were their lords'.

12

Both rich and personable, Lensky   155
Was thought an enviable match
And everyone who had a daughter—
Such was the custom—planned a match
With this half-Russian neighbor. They
Would manage, when he called, to say   160
How sad a single life must be

And ask the bachelor to tea
With Dunya at the samovar
To do the honors for their guest.
They'd whisper, "Dunya, do your best,"   165
And then they'd bring her her guitar,
And she would pipe as she was told,
Poor child, "Come to my halls of gold."

13

But Lensky had no inclination
For dalliance, it must be confessed;   170
While on the other hand Onegin
Aroused his deepest interest.
They met; and prose and poetry,
Cold ice and flame, firm rock and sea,
Were not so wholly different.   175
Quite bored at first, they underwent
A change of feeling to a state
Of liking in a certain way.
They met on horseback every day
And finally grew intimate.   180
So idleness achieved its end:
Each was the other's bosom friend.

14

But even such friendships are discarded
As prejudices of the past.
We rate ourselves alone as digits,   185
All others ciphers, to be classed
As vile by us, Napoleons
Among a million lesser ones
Created only for our tools,
And men of feeling we think fools.   190
Eugene was more forbearing. Though
Of course he knew and scorned mankind
As something very dull and blind,
All rules have their exceptions, so
Though alien to his intellect   195
He treated feeling with respect.

15

He listened with a smile to Lensky;
His bright and ardent conversation,

---

163. *samovar:* Russian tea-urn.

His unripe reasoning, and always
The poet's glance of inspiration,— 200
All this was novel to Eugene.
He struggled not to intervene
And chill such youthful ecstasy,
Thinking: "It is too bad of me
When bliss endures so short a space 205
To cloud this moment with regret.
His time will come; but meanwhile let
Him think the world a perfect place.
We must set down to youth's extremes
His youthful fire, his youthful dreams." 210

16

Between them everything was subject
For controversy and debate.
The treaty rights of ancient tribesmen,
Prejudices of antique date,
The fruits of learning, good and ill, 215
And life and fortune versatile,
And death, the mystery of ages,
Hung on the utterance of these sages.
Then, in the heat of argument,
Would Lensky eagerly rehearse 220
Fragments of northern poets' verse,
And our Eugene, the lenient,
Though missing an enormous deal
Would listen to his youthful zeal.

17

But oftener the tender passions 225
Engaged our youthful hermits' minds.
Onegin, freed from their dominion,
Discoursed of them as one who finds
Himself regretting quietly
The former tumult. Happy he 230
Who has outlived it. Happier still
The man who never felt that thrill,
Who conquered love by separation,
Hatred by lies—and yawned through life,
Bored by his friends and by his wife, 235
Untouched by jealous perturbation,
And never risked the ancestral hoard
Upon the treacherous gaming board.

18

When we enroll beneath the standard
Of safe and wise tranquillity,   240
And when love's passions are extinguished
And our wild whims and ecstasy
With their belated echoes seem
A foolish and outgrown extreme—
Then we, delivered from our spell,   245
May like to hear a stranger tell
His passionate and frenzied story
And feel our pulses stir again.
Just so some ancient veteran
Alone and shorn of former glory   250
Still loves to hear the young hussars
Recount their exploits in the wars.

19

And ardent youth is not secretive,
But always ready to impart
The love and hate, the joy and sorrow   255
Which animate its inmost heart.
Eugene, whose pride it was to be
The veteran lover, solemnly
Attended while his friend laid bare
His simple, fervent love affair,   260
Delighting in the utterance
Which artlessly disclosed his heart.
Thus without effort on his part
Onegin learned the youth's romance,
A tale of feeling it is true,   265
But long since anything but new.

20

He was indeed the sort of lover
Whose like we do not find today;
Only the mad soul of a poet
Is born to love in such a way.   270
At every time, in every place,
One single dream, one single face,
And one familiar sorrow still.
And neither distance bleak and chill,
Nor all the years of separation   275
Nor hours devoted to the arts
Nor lovely girls of foreign parts
Nor books nor scenes of animation

Could moderate his heart's desire
Still burning with its virgin fire.   280

21

Bewitched when still a boy by Olga,
Before he knew love's burning flames,
He used to watch the little maiden
With gentle pleasure at her games,
And in the shady wood he played   285
Alone with her. Their fathers made
Betrothal plans without demur,
Old friends and neighbors as they were.
Here in her peaceful country home
Beneath her parents' eyes she grew   290
As lilies of the valley do
That come at last to hidden bloom
Unnoticed in the clustering grass
By bees and butterflies that pass.

22

She gave the poet that first rapture   295
So poignant and so absolute.
Her image was the inspiration
Which first aroused his silent flute.
Farewell, you golden games of childhood,
For now he loved the deep-grown wildwood,   300
Silence and solitude and night,
The stars in heaven, the pale moon's light.
O Moon, the lamp of heaven! How
We used to walk in lonely grief
Until our tears would bring relief,   305
And vow the night to you—and now
You're but a makeshift, none too good,
For street-lamps in the neighborhood.

23

Olga was always good and modest,
Gay as the morning sun above,   310
As simple-hearted as the poet,
Sweet as the kiss of one's true love.
Her smile, her flaxen curls, her eyes
As blue as are the summer skies,
Her voice, her slimness, and her quick   315
And graceful movements—all.—But pick
Up any novel, you will see

Her portrait; it is charming, too,
And once it thrilled me through and through
But now it bores me utterly.   320
Her elder sister, in her turn,
Is now, dear reader, our concern.

24

Her sister had been called Tatyana—
We are the earliest to proclaim
Deliberately in a novel   325
A heroine by such a name.
Why not? It has a pleasant ring
Although, I know, around it cling
The odors of the servants' hall
Or of antiquity. We all   330
Must grant the names in poorest taste
With us have greatest currency
(I am not counting poetry):
Our education is a waste
From which we learn to set great store   335
On affectation—nothing more.

25

Her sister, then, was named Tatyana,
We've said, and she did not possess
The charm of Olga's rosy freshness
Nor of her winning prettiness.   340
Somber and silent and withdrawn,
As timid as a woodland fawn,
Even in her own family
She seemed some stranger child. For she
Had never learned the childish art   345
Of blandishment, so sure a way
To please one's parents. And for play
She never seemed to have the heart;
But often sat alone and still
All day beside the window sill.   350

26

She was a friend to meditation
And always had been so; the stream
Of quiet country days she colored
With the bright fancies of her dream.
Her tender fingers never held   355
A needle while the blossoms swelled

In silken fullness and became
A pattern on the embroidery frame.
It is a sign of love of power
Which little girls who like to play   360
With an obedient doll betray
When decorously by the hour
They solemnly repeat to it
Their mother's lessons, bit by bit.

27

But from her very little-girlhood   365
Tatyana never had been known
To touch a doll or tell it gossip
Or what the fashion was in town.
And childish naughtiness was quite
As strange to her; but when at night   370
In winter darkness they would start
Old grisly tales, it thrilled her heart.
And when the nursemaid would collect
All Olga's friends from round about
Upon the grass to run and shout   375
With laughter hearty and unchecked,
Tatyana never joined their game—
It seemed so boisterous yet so tame.

28

She loved to stand before the sunrise
Upon the balcony and watch   380
The galaxy of stars departing
From the pale sky, and the first blotch
Of faintest light where earth met sky,
And feel the little winds that sigh
In greeting to the risen dawn.   385
And long before the dark had gone
In winter or the shadows ceased
To lie on half the world, while still
The quiet moon, remote and chill,
Shone dimly on the lazy east,   390
This hour was still her favorite
And she got up by candlelight.

29

She took to novel-reading early,
And all her days became a glow
Of rapturous love for the creations   395

Of Richardson and of Rousseau.
Her father, who was good and kind,
Had long ago been left behind
By modern ways, but in the main,
Although he thought books light and vain,   400
He did not think them any harm.
And when a man has never read,
The books his daughter takes to bed
With her will cause him no alarm.
As for his wife, there was no one   405
So much in love with Richardson.

30

She worshiped Richardson not only
Because she read so much of him;
Nor because Lovelace suited better
Than Grandison her girlish whim.   410
But in old days Princess Aline,
Her Moscow cousin there, had been
His satellite. Then she was still
A girl, engaged against her will.
To him she later married, though   415
She sighed for one—unseen, unheard—
Whose mind and heart she much preferred.
Her Grandison was quite a beau,
A zealous devotee of cards,
And a young sergeant in the Guards.   420

31

Like his, her dress was always modish
And always most appropriate;
But, without asking her opinion,
They named the maiden's wedding date.
Her husband, in the wise belief   425
That he might thus divert her grief,
Moved to his country place where she
With God knows whom for company
Gave way to grief and was quite bent
On a divorce—then seemed to find   430
Her household duties claim her mind,

---

396. *Richardson . . . Rousseau:* for
the latter, cf. notes in this volume;
Samuel Richardson (1689–1761) was an
English author of epistolary novels:
Pamela (1740–1741), *Clarissa Harlowe*
(1747–1748).

409. *Lovelace:* seducer of Clarissa.
410. *Grandison:* priggish hero of Richardson's *The History of Sir Charles
Grandison.*
420. *Guards:* élite regiment attached
to the ruling monarch.

Grew used to things, and then content.
For heaven-sent habit soothes distress
And takes the place of happiness.

32

So habit quieted a sorrow   435
Which nothing else could have allayed,
And soon her cure was quite completed
By a discovery she made.
In days now empty and now full
She learned the trick of how to rule   440
Her husband like an autocrat,
And all went smoothly after that.
She watched the field-work under way,
She salted mushrooms for the next
Long winter, beat her maids when vexed,   445
And took the baths on Saturday,
Kept books, sent off the new recruits—
All without marital disputes.

33

She had been wont to write in albums
Or girlish friends in blood, and call   450
Praskovya her Pauline, and lengthen
Each sentence to a genteel drawl.
She laced her corsets very tight
And said her Russian *n*'s in quite
The best French manner, through her nose.   455
But by degrees she dropped her pose:
Corsets and album and Pauline,
The notebook full of tender rhyme—
All were forgotten, and in time
Akulka had replaced Céline;   460
Till finally she went about
In cap and wrapper wadded out.

34

Her husband loved his wife sincerely
And never gave her cause to frown,
But spent his days, serene and trustful,   465
Attired in a dressing gown.
So life rolled placidly along:

---

451. *Praskovya . . . Pauline:* She preferred French to Russian names.

460. *Akulka . . . Céline:* She reverts
back to Russian.

Sometimes at night a little throng
Of friendly neighbors would arrive,
All intimates, and all alive   470
With gossip or with sympathy;
And they would laugh and chat and smile
And time would pass unnoticed, while
Olga was bid to make the tea.
Supper, the end of one more day—   475
And then the guests would drive away.

35

In this calm life, the good old customs
Were laws from which they never swerved;
When Shrovetide came and merrymaking,
Then Russian pancakes must be served.   480
They made confession twice a year;
They held a carrousel as dear
As bowl-songs and the circle-dance.
And when with yawning countenance
The peasants listened to the mass   485
On Trinity, they'd drop a tear
Upon a sprig of lovage; air
Was not more needful than was kvass;
And guests at dinner ate and drank
In strict accordance with their rank.   490

36

And so they lived for years together
Till for the husband, old and hoary,
Death drew aside the final curtain
And he received his crown of glory.
One afternoon he left this life,   495
Mourned by his children and his wife,
The neighborhood, and all his clan,
More truly than is many a man.
A simple squire without caprice,
Kindly to all—and on the stone   500
That marks his grave these verses run.

A HUMBLE SINNER, NOW AT PEACE,
GOD'S SERVANT AND A BRIGADIER,
'TIS DMITRI LARIN SLEEPETH HERE.

479. *Shrovetide:* Sunday through Tuesday preceding Ash Wednesday. Shrove Tuesday was once called "pancake day."
486. *Trinity:* Trinity Sunday, next after Whit Sunday: i.e., the eighth Sunday after Easter.
487. *lovage:* a medicinal herb.
488. *kvass:* a sour Russian beer, brewed from rye.

37

When he returned to his Penates,   505
Vladimir Lensky visited
His neighbor's unpretentious gravestone
And breathed a sigh above the dead.
He mourned him with sincerity.
"Poor Yorick!" he said mournfully,   510
"He used to hold me, as a child,
And many a moment I beguiled
With his Ochakov decoration.
He gave me Olga, and he'd say,
'Shall I be here to see the day?' "   515
And thereupon, his inspiration
Wakened by grief, Vladimir penned
An elegy upon his friend.

38

Then with another sad inscription
He paid the patriarchal dust   520
Of his own parents tearful tribute.
Alas! that generations must
By laws inscrutable and sealed
Like some brief harvest in the field
Rise up, mature, and die again,   525
Surrendering to other men!
So our ephemeral human race
Will wax and stew and seethe and boil
And finally, in great turmoil,
Themselves fill up their fathers' place.   530
And our own children, even so,
Will crowd us out, and we must go.

39

But meanwhile drink your fill of living,
Abortive as it is, my friends!
I know its emptiness and folly   535
And care but little how it ends.
I closed my eyes long since to dreams,
And yet one hope far distant seems
At times to agitate my heart:
I should be sorry to depart   540
And be entirely forgot.
I do not covet great renown,

505. *Penates:* household (from the Roman gods associated with the welfare of
one's house).
510. *"Poor Yorick!":* Hamlet's address
to the skull of the clown who once carried him about (V, i, 172 ff).
513. *Ochakov decoration:* medal awarded
by Catherine the Great, after the capture of Ochakov (on the Black Sea) from
the Turks in 1788.

Yet I am not averse, I own,
To singing of my mournful lot
So that one line of poetry,   545
Like a true friend, may speak of me.

40

Somewhere some heart may be affected,
And so the verses I create
May not be drowned at last in Lethe
But be preserved by fickle fate.   550
Perhaps—oh, flattering hope—some day
A future ignoramus may
Point to my picture and declare,
"You see a genuine poet there!"

Receive my grateful salutations,   555
You lover of the Grecian Nine,
Whose memory may yet enshrine
My brief and fugitive creations,
Whose reverent hands may yet caress
An old man's bays with tenderness!*   560

549. *Lethe:* i.e., oblivion (from the river in Hades of which the dead must drink).

560. *bays:* figuratively, the poet's laurel wreath.

* Six more cantos complete *Eugene Onegin*. Tatyana falls in love with Onegin, and writes him a letter stating her affection. The gloomy hero informs her of his fraternal love for her, but says that he could only make her miserable. Meanwhile Lensky courts Olga, Tatyana's younger sister. At her name-day ball, Onegin dances with Olga and arouses the jealousy of Lensky (Canto V), who is unaware of Tatyana's love for Onegin. Lensky challenges Onegin to a pistol duel, and is killed (Canto VI). Onegin leaves the village; Olga marries an Uhlan and departs. Tatyana visits Onegin's empty house, reads his volumes of Byron, and at last understands his melancholy. She and her mother move to Moscow, to enjoy the social life (Canto VII).

Several years later, Onegin (now twenty-six) attends a ball in Moscow; he inquires of a prince about a beautiful woman, to discover it is the prince's wife. Onegin calls upon her, and now realizes he loves Tatyana. On his last visit to her —when he finds her reading the last of his several unanswered letters—he falls before her feet, but she rejects him. They once might have been happy, she tells him, but now she will remain faithful to her husband.

Masterpieces of Nineteenth-Century Realism and Naturalism

EDITED BY
RENÉ WELLEK
Sterling Professor of Comparative Literature, Yale University

As was indicated in the preceding introduction, the nineteenth century is the century of greatest change in the history of Western civilization. The upheavals following the French Revolution broke up the old order of Europe. The Holy Roman Empire and the Papal States were dissolved. Nationalism, nourished by the political and social aspirations of the middle classes, grew by leaps and bounds. "Liberty" became the main political slogan of the century. In different countries and different decades it meant different things: here liberation from the rule of the foreigner, there the emancipation of the serf; here the removal of economic restrictions on trade and manufacturing, there the introduction of a constitution, free speech, parliamentary institutions. Almost all over Europe, the middle classes established their effective rule, though monarchs often remained in more or less nominal power. Two large European countries, Germany and Italy, achieved their centuries-old dreams of political unification. The predominance of France, still marked at the beginning of the century, was broken, and England—or rather Great Britain—ruled the sea throughout the century. The smaller European nations, especially in the Balkans, began to emancipate themselves from foreign rule.

These major political changes were caused by, and in their turn caused, great social and economic changes. The Industrial Revolution which had begun in England in the eighteenth century spread over the Continent and transformed living conditions radically. The enormous increase in the speed and availability of transportation due to the development of railroads and steamships, the greatly increased urbanization following from the establishment of industries, changed the whole pattern of human life in most countries, and made possible, within a century, an unprecedented increase in the population (as much as threefold in most European countries), which was also fostered by the advances of medicine and hygiene. The increase of widespread wealth and prosperity is, in spite of the wretched living conditions and other hardships of the early factory workers, an undeniable fact. The barriers between the social classes diminished appreciably almost everywhere: both the social and the political power of the aristocracy declined. The industrial laborer began to be felt as a political force.

These social and economic changes were closely bound up with shifts in the prevailing outlooks and philosophies. Technological innovation is impossible without the discoveries of science. The scientific outlook, hitherto dominant only in a comparatively limited area, spread widely and permeated almost all fields of human thought and endeavor. It raised enormous hopes for the future betterment of man's condition on earth, especially when Darwin's evolutionary theories fortified the earlier, vaguer faith in unlimited progress. "Liberty," "science," "progress," "evolution" are the concepts which define the mental atmosphere of the nineteenth century.

But tendencies hostile to these were by no means absent. Feu-

dal or Catholic conservatism succeeded, especially in Austria-Hungary, in Russia, and in much of the south of Europe, in preserving old regimes, and the philosophies of a conservative and religious society were reformulated in modern terms. At the same time, in England the very assumptions of the new industrial middle-class society were powerfully attacked by writers such as Carlyle and Ruskin who recommended a return to medieval forms of social co-operation and handicraft. The industrial civilization of the nineteenth century was also opposed by the fierce individualism of many artists and thinkers who were unhappy in the ugly commercial "Philistine" society of the age. The writings of Nietzsche, toward the end of the century, and the whole movement of "art for art's sake," which asserted the independence of the artist from society, are the most obvious symptoms of this revolt. The free-enterprise system and the liberalism of the ruling middle classes also early clashed with the rising proletariat, which was won over to diverse forms of socialism, preaching a new collectivism with the stress on equality. Socialism could have Christian or romantic motivations, or it could become "scientific" and revolutionary, as Marx's brand of socialism (a certain stage of which he called "communism") claimed to be.

While up through the eighteenth century religion was, at least in name, a major force in European civilization, in the nineteenth century there was a marked decrease in its influence on both the intellectual leaders and the masses. Local intense revivals of religious consciousness, such as the Oxford Movement in England, did occur, and the traditional religious institutions were preserved everywhere, but the impact of science on religion was such that many tenets of the old faiths crumbled. The discoveries of astronomy, geology, evolutionary biology, archaeology, and biblical criticism forced, almost everywhere, a restatement of the old creeds. Religion, especially in the Protestant countries, was frequently confined to an inner feeling of religiosity or to a system of morality which preserved the ancient Christian virtues. During the early nineteenth century, in Germany, Hegel and his predecessors and followers tried to interpret the world in spiritual terms outside the bounds of traditional religion. There were many attempts even late in the century to restate this view, but the methods and discoveries of science seemed to invalidate it, and various formulas which took science as their base in building new lay religions of hope in humanity gained popularity. French Positivism, English utilitarianism, the evolutionism of Herbert Spencer, are some of the best-known examples. Meanwhile, for the first time in history, at least in Europe, profoundly pessimistic and atheistic philosophies arose, of which Schopenhauer's was the most subtle, while a purely physical materialism was the most widespread. Thus the whole gamut of views of the universe was represented during the century in new and impressive formulations.

The plastic arts did not show a similar vitality. For a long time, in most countries, painting and architecture floundered in a sterile eclecticism, in a bewildering variety of historical masquerades in which the neo-Gothic style was replaced by the neo-Renaissance and that by the neo-Baroque and other decorative revivals of past forms. Only in France, painting, with the impressionists, found a new style which was genuinely original. In music the highly romantic art of Richard Wagner attracted most attention, but the individual national schools either continued in their tradition, like Italian opera (Verdi) or founded an idiom of their own, often based on a revival of folklore, as in Russia (Tchaikovsky), Poland (Chopin), Bohemia (Dvořák), and Norway (Grieg).

But literature was the most representative and the most widely influential art of the nineteenth century. It found new forms and methods and expressed the social and intellectual situation of the time most fully and memorably.

After the great wave of the international romantic movement had spent its force in the fourth decade of the nineteenth century, European literature moved in the direction of what is usually called *realism*. Realism was not a coherent general movement which established itself unchallenged for a long period of time, as classicism had succeeded in doing during the eighteenth century. There were many authors in the nineteenth century who continued to practice a substantially romantic art (Tennyson and Hugo, for example); there were even movements which upheld a definitely romantic "escapist," antirealist program, such as that of the Pre-Raphaelites in England or the Parnassians in France. But, with whatever exceptions and reservations, in retrospect the nineteenth century appears as the period of the great realistic writers: Flaubert in France, Dostoevsky and Tolstoy in Russia, Dickens in England, James in America, Ibsen in Norway.

What is meant by realism? The term, in literary use (there is a much older philosophical use), apparently dates back to the Germans at the turn of the century—to Schiller and the Schlegels. It cropped up in France as early as 1826 but became a commonly accepted literary and artistic slogan only in the 1850's. (A review called *Réalisme* began publication in 1856, and a critic, Champfleury, published a volume of critical articles with the title *Le Réalisme* in the following year.) Since then the word has been bandied about, discussed, analyzed, and abused as all slogans are. It is frequently confused with naturalism, an ancient philosophical term for materialism, epicureanism, or any secularism. As a specifically literary term, it crystallized only in France. In French, as in English, naturalist means, of course, simply student of nature, and the analogy between the writer and the naturalist, specifically the botanist and the

zoologist, was ready at hand. Emile Zola, in the Preface to a new edition of his early novel, *Thérèse Raquin* (1866), proclaimed the naturalist creed most boldly. His book, he claims, is "an analytical labor on two living bodies like that of a surgeon on corpses." He proudly counts himself among the group of "naturalist writers."

The program of the groups of writers and critics who used these terms can be easily summarized. The realists wanted a truthful representation in literature of reality—that is, of contemporary life and manners. They thought of their method as inductive, observational, and hence "objective." The personality of the author was to be suppressed, or was at least to recede into the background, since reality was to be seen "as it is." The naturalistic program, as formulated by Zola, was substantially the same except that Zola put greater stress on the analogies to science, considering the procedure of the novelist as identical with that of the experimenting scientist. He also more definitely and exclusively embraced the philosophy of scientific materialism, with its deterministic implications, its stress on heredity and environment, while the older realists were not always so clear in drawing the philosophical consequences. These French theories were anticipated, paralleled, or imitated all over the world of Western literature. In Germany, the movement called Young Germany, with which Heine was associated, had propounded a substantially antiromantic realistic program as early as the thirties, but versions of the French theories definitely triumphed there only in the 1880's. In Russia, as early as the forties, the most prominent critic of the time, Vissarion Belinsky, praised the "natural" school of Russian fiction, which described contemporary Russia with fidelity. Italy also, from the late seventies on, produced an analogous movement, which called itself *verismo*. The English-speaking countries were the last to adopt the critical programs and slogans of the Continent: George Moore and George Gissing brought the French theories to England in the late eighties, and in the United States William Dean Howells began his campaign for realism in 1886, when he became editor of *Harper's Magazine*. Realistic and naturalistic theories of literature have since been widely accepted in spite of many twentieth-century criticisms and the whole general trend of twentieth-century literature. Especially in the United States, the contemporary novel is usually considered naturalistic and judged by standards of nature and truth. The officially promoted doctrine in Russia is called "socialist Realism."

The slogans "realism" and "naturalism" were thus new in the nineteenth century. They served as effective formulas directed against the romantic creed. Truth, contemporaneity, and objectivity were the obvious counterparts of romantic imagination, of romantic historicism and its glorification of the past, and of romantic subjectivity, the exaltation of the ego and the individual. But, of course, the emphasis on truth and objectiv-

ity was not really new: these qualities had been demanded by many older, classical theories of imitation, and in the eighteenth century there were great writers such as Diderot who wanted a literal "imitation of life" even on the stage.

The practice of realism, it could be argued, is very old indeed. There are realistic scenes in the *Odyssey*, and there is plenty of realism in ancient comedy and satire, in medieval stories (fabliaux) like some of Chaucer's and Boccaccio's, in many Elizabethan plays, in the Spanish rogue novels, in the English eighteenth-century novel beginning with Defoe, and so on almost ad infinitum. But while it would be easy to find in early literature anticipations of almost every single element of modern realism, still the systematic description of contemporary society, with a serious purpose, often even with a tragic tone as well, and with sympathy for heroes drawn from the middle and lower classes, was a real innovation of the nineteenth century.

It is usually rash to explain a literary movement in social and political terms. But the new realistic art surely has something to do with the triumph of the middle classes in France after the July revolution in 1830, and in England after the passage of the Reform Bill in 1832, and with the increasing influence of the middle classes in almost every country. Russia is somewhat of an exception as no large middle class could develop there during the nineteenth century. An absolute feudal regime continued in power and the special character of most of Russian literature must be due to this distinction, but even in Russia there emerged an "intelligentsia" (the term comes from Russia) which was open to Western ideas and was highly critical of the czarist regime and its official "ideology." But while much nineteenth-century literature reflects the triumph of the middle classes, it would be an error to think of the great realistic writers as spokesmen or mouthpieces of the society they described. Balzac was politically a Catholic monarchist who applauded the Bourbon restoration after the fall of Napoleon, but he had an extraordinary imaginative insight into the processes leading to the victory of the middle classes. Flaubert despised the middle-class society of the Third Empire with an intense hatred and the pride of a self-conscious artist. Dickens became increasingly critical of the middle classes and the assumptions of industrial civilization. Dostoevsky, though he took part in a conspiracy against the Russian government early in his life and spent ten years in exile in Siberia, became the propounder of an extremely conservative nationalistic and religious creed which was definitely directed against the revolutionary forces in Russia. Tolstoy, himself a count and a landowner, was violent in his criticism of the czarist regime, especially later in his life, but he cannot be described as friendly to the middle classes, to the aims of the democratic movements in Western Europe, or to the science of the time. Ibsen's political attitude is that of a proud individualist who condemns the "compact majority"

and its tyranny. Possibly all art is critical of its society, but in the nineteenth century this criticism became much more explicit, as social and political issues became much more urgent or, at least, were regarded as more urgent by the writing groups. To a far greater degree than in earlier centuries, writers felt their isolation from society, viewed the structure and problems of the prevailing order as debatable and reformable, and in spite of all demands for objectivity became, in many cases, social propagandists and reformers in their own right.

The program of realism, while defensible enough as a reaction against romanticism, raises critical questions which were not answered theoretically by its defenders. What is meant by "truth" of representation? Photographic copying? This seems the implication of many famous pronouncements. "A novel is a mirror walking along the road," said Stendhal as early as 1830. But such statements can hardly be taken literally. All art must select and represent; it cannot be and has never been a simple transcript of reality. What such analogies are intended to convey is rather a claim for an all-inclusiveness of subject matter, a protest against the exclusion of themes which before were considered "low," "sordid," or "trivial" (like the puddles along the road the mirror walks). Chekhov formulated this protest with the usual parallel between the scientist and the writer: "To a chemist nothing on earth is unclean. A writer must be as objective as a chemist; he must abandon the subjective line: he must know that dungheaps play a very respectable part in a landscape, and that evil passions are as inherent in life as good ones." Thus the "truth" of realistic art includes the sordid, the low, the disgusting, and the evil; and, the implication is, the subject is treated objectively, without interference and falsification by the artist's personality and his own desires. But in practice, while the realistic artist succeeded in expanding the themes of art, he could not fulfill the demand for total objectivity. Works of art are written by human beings and inevitably express their personalities and their points of view. As Conrad admitted, "even the most artful of writers will give himself (and his morality) away in about every third sentence." Objectivity, in the sense which Zola had in mind when he proposed a scientific method in the writing of novels and conceived of the novelist as a sociologist collecting human documents, is impossible in practice. When it has been attempted, it has led only to bad art, to dullness and the display of inert materials, to the confusion between the art of the novel and reporting, "documentation." The demand for "objectivity" can be understood only as a demand for a specific method of narration, in which the author does not interfere explicitly, in his own name, and as a rejection of personal themes of introspection and reverie.

The realistic program, while it has made innumerable new subjects available to art, also implies a narrowing of its themes and methods—a condemnation of the fantastic, the historical, the remote, the idealized, the "unsullied," the idyllic. Realism professes to present us with a "slice of life." But one should recognize that it is an artistic method and convention like any other. Romantic art could, without offending its readers, use coincidences, improbabilities, and even impossibilities, which were not, theoretically at least, tolerated in realistic art. Ibsen, for instance, avoided many older conventions of the stage: asides, soliloquies, eavesdropping, sudden unmotivated appearances of new characters, and so on; but his dramas have their own marked conventions, which seem today almost as "unnatural" as those of the romantics. Realistic theories of literature cannot be upheld in their literal sense; objective and impersonal truth is unobtainable, at least in art, since all art is a "making," a creating of a world of symbols which differs radically from the world which we call reality. The value of realism lies in its negation of the conventions of romanticism, its expansion of the themes of art, and its new demonstration (never forgotten by artists) that literature has to deal also with its time and society and has, at its best, an insight into reality (not only social reality) which is not necessarily identical with that of science. Many of the great writers make us "realize" the world of their time, evoke an imaginative picture of it which seems truer and will last longer than that of historians and sociologists. But this achievement is due to their imagination and their art, or craft, two requisites which realistic theory tended to forget or minimize.

When we observe the actual practice of the great realistic

writers of the nineteenth century, we notice a sharp contradiction between theory and practice, and an independent evolution of the art of the novel which is obscured for us if we pay too much attention to the theories and slogans of the time, even those that the authors themselves propounded. Flaubert, the high priest of a cult of "art for art's sake," the most consistent advocate of absolute objectivity, was actually, at least in a good half of his work, a writer of romantic fantasies of blood and gold, flesh and jewels. There is some truth in his saying that Madame Bovary is himself, for in the drab story of a provincial adulteress he castigated his own romanticism and romantic dreams.

So too with Dostoevsky. Although some of his settings resemble those of the "grime novel," he is actually a writer of high tragedy, of a drama of ideas in which ordinary reality is transformed into a symbol of the spiritual world. His technique is closely associated with Balzac's (it is significant that his first publication was a translation of Balzac's *Eugénie Grandet*) and thus with many devices of the sensational melodramatic novel of French romanticism. Tolstoy's art is more concretely real than that of any of the other great masters mentioned, yet he is, at the same time, the most personal and even literally autobiographical author in the history of the novel—a writer, besides, who knows nothing of detachment toward social and religious problems, but frankly preaches his own very peculiar religion. And if we turn to Ibsen,

we find essentially the same situation. Ibsen began as a writer of historical and fantastic dramas and slowly returned to a style which is fundamentally symbolist. All his later plays are organized by symbols, from the duck of *The Wild Duck* (1884) to the white horses in *Rosmersholm* (1886) and the tower in *The Master Builder* (1892). Even Zola, the propounder of the most scientific theory, was in practice a novelist who used the most extreme devices of melodrama and symbolism. In *Germinal* (1885), his novel of mining, the mine is the central symbol, alive as an animal, heaving, breathing. It would be an odd reader who could find literal truth in the final catastrophe of the cave-in or even in such "naturalistic" scenes as a dance where the beer oozes from the nostrils of the drinkers.

One could assert, in short, that all the great realists were at bottom romanticists, but it is probably wiser to conclude that they were simply artists who created worlds of imagination and knew (at least instinctively) that in art one can say something about reality only through symbols. The attempts at documentary art, at mere reporting and transcribing, are today forgotten.

FLAUBERT, MADAME BOVARY

Flaubert's novel, *Madame Bovary* (1856), is deservedly considered the showpiece of French realism. It would be impossible to find a novel, certainly before Flaubert, in which humble persons in a humble setting are treated with such seriousness, restraint, verisimilitude, and imaginative clarity. At first sight, *Madame Bovary* is a solidly documented and clearly visualized account of life in a village of the French province of Normandy sometime in the forties of the last century. We meet a whole spectrum of social types found in such a time and place: the doctor (actually a "health officer" with a lower degree), a pharmacist, a storekeeper, a notary and his clerk, a tax collector, a woman innkeeper and her stableboy, the priest and his sacristan, a neighboring landowner, and a farmer. We are told the story of a young peasant woman brought up in a convent, who marries a dull man and commits adultery first with a ruthless philanderer and then with a spineless younger man. Overwhelmed by debts concealed from her unsuspecting husband, faced by sudden demands for repayment, disillusioned in love, rebuffed by everybody who might help her, she commits suicide by poisoning herself with arsenic. Nothing seems simpler and more ordinary, and the manner of telling seems completely objective, detached, impersonal. A case is presented which is observed with almost scientific curiosity. The descriptions are obviously accurate, sometimes based on expert knowledge; the clubfoot operation and the effects of arsenic poisoning agree with medical evidence. The setting—the topography of the two villages, the interior of the houses, the inn, the pharmacy, the city of Rouen, the cathedral there, the river landscape, and the particular things and sounds—imprints itself vividly on our memory. Every detail serves its purpose

of characterization—from the absurd cap of the schoolboy Charles to the mirror and the crucifix in the deathbed scene; from the sound of Binet's lathe turning out napkin rings to the tap of the stableboy's wooden leg. "The technique of *Madame Bovary* has become the model of all novels" (Albert Thibaudet).

But surely the book could not have kept its grip on modern readers if it were only a superbly accurate description of provincial life in France (as the added subtitle, *Mœurs de province*, suggests). The book transcends its time and place if one thinks of Emma Bovary as the type of the unfulfilled dreamer, as the failed and foiled romanticist, as a female Don Quixote, corrupted by sentimental reading, caught in a trap of circumstance, pitiful and to be pitied in her horrible self-inflicted death.

This central theme has, however, remained ambiguous. What attracted and shocked readers was the uncertainty about the author's attitude toward Emma, particularly at the time of publication when readers were accustomed to being told clearly by addresses and comments what they were to think of the actions and morals of the characters of a novel. *Madame Bovary*, at publication, caused a scandal. The review (*Revue de Paris*) in which it was published serially and the author were hauled into court for immorality and blasphemy and the prosecutor described the book as an incitement to adultery and atheism. In his rebuttal, the defense counsel argued that the novel is rather a highly moral work in which adultery is punished even excessively. Flaubert was acquitted but neither the prosecutor nor the defending attorney interpreted the book correctly. It is neither a salacious novel nor a didactic tract. Some parts of the book are frankly satirical (and thus far from purely objective): The gross village priest who cannot even understand the distress of Emma is flanked by the fussy, shallow, pseudoscientific, enlightened, "progressive" pharmacist Homais. Though they argue and quarrel they are finally reduced to a common level when they eat and snore at the wake next to Emma's corpse. The rightly famous scene of the country fair satirizes and parodies the pompous rhetoric of the officials extolling the glories of agriculture, counterpointing it to the equally platitudinous love talk of Rodolphe and the lowing of the cattle in an amalgam which reduces men and women to a common level of animality. Even Emma is not spared: Her sentimental religiosity, her taste for luxury, her financial improvidence are diagnosed as disguised eroticism. She would not have minded if Rodolphe had drawn a pistol against her husband. In her desperate search for escape she asks Léon to steal for her. In the last attempt to get money she is ready to sell herself. She is indifferent to her child, deceitful even in small matters. Her longing for sensual satisfaction becomes, in the scenes with Léon in the hotel at Rouen, frantic and corrupt. The author weighed the scales against her: She married an excessively stupid and insensitive man; she met two callous lovers; she is tricked by a merciless usurer; she is utterly alone at last. When Charles meeting Rodolphe after her death and after he had discovered her infidelities tells him, ineptly, awkwardly: "It was the fault of destiny," the author expressly approves of this saying. The novel conveys a sense of inexorable determinism, of the vanity of dreaming, of the impossibility of escape from one's nature and station. It conveys a sense of despair, of man's and woman's alienation in an incomprehensible universe but also a hatred for all the stupidity, mediocrity and baseness of people there and everywhere. (Flaubert called them "bourgeois," but included the proletarian masses in his contempt). Emma is pitied because she has, at least, a spark of discontent, the yearning to escape the cage of her existence. But baseness triumphs and the book ends with a sudden change to the present tense: "Homais has just received the cross of the Legion of Honor."

This sense of the inexorable, the fatal, the inescapable is secured also by the precision and firmness of Flaubert's style and the carefully planned architectonics of his composition. If we mean by style the systematic exploitation of the syntactical and lexical possibilities of a language we must class Flaubert with the great stylists: the exact descriptive epithet, the one right word (*le mot juste*) even when he uses the most trivial cliché or the most recondite scientific term coheres with the skillful modulations and rhythms of the sentences, the organization of the paragraphs and the divisions of the sections which are grouped around a series of pictorial scenes: the schoolroom, the rustic wedding, the ball, the visit to the priest, the country fair, the ride in the woods, the clubfoot operation, the opera, the cathedral, the cab ride, the deathbed, to mention only the most memorable.

Madame Bovary is constantly cited as an example for the handling of narrative perspective. The story begins in the schoolroom ostensibly told by a schoolfellow (the word "we" is used in the first pages); it shifts then to the narration of an omniscient author and, off and on, narrows to the point of view of Emma. Much is seen only through her eyes, but one cannot say that the author identifies with her or enters her mind sympathetically. He keeps his distance and on occasion conveys his own opinion. He is not averse even to moral judgments: He speaks of Emma's hardhearted and tightfisted peasant nature (p. 529), he refers to her corruption (p. 622), and Rodolphe is several times condemned for his brutality and cynicism (pp. 575, 620, 708). In the description of extreme unction (p. 719) the author pronounces solemnly his forgiveness (which he suggests would be also God's) for her coveting all worldly goods, her greediness "for the warm breeze and scents of love," and even her sensuality and lust. But mostly Flaubert depicts the scenes by simple description or reproduction of speech or imagined silent reflections. Things and people become at times symbolic even in

an obtrusive way: the wedding bouquet, the plate of boiled beef, and the apparition of the blind beggar who turns up conveniently at the hour of Emma's death. Much is said about her which she could not have observed herself. The famous saying "Madame Bovary c'est moi" cannot be traced back to an earlier date than 1909 when it is reported on distant hearsay in René Descharmes, *Flaubert avant 1857* (p. 103). There are dozens of passages in the letters during the composition of *Madame Bovary* which express Flaubert's distaste for the "vulgarity of his subject," "the fetid smell of the milieu," and his opinion of Emma Bovary as "a woman of false poetry and false sentiments." Usually he defends his choice of theme as a "prodigious *tour de force*," as "an act of crude will power," as "a deliberate made-up thing" though we suspect him sometimes of exaggerating his efforts in order to impress his correspondent in Paris, a facile and prolific novelist and poetess, Louise Colet.

Still, the saying "Madame Bovary c'est moi" has been widely quoted and accepted because it contains a kernel of truth. In Emma, Flaubert combats his own vices of daydreaming, romanticism, exoticism, of which he thought he could cure himself by writing this antiromantic book. But the identification with Emma distracts us from noticing Flaubert's deepseated sympathies with the slowwitted, abused, but honest and loving Charles who rightly opens and closes the book and for the other good people: Emma's father, the farmer Rouault, kind and distressed by all he could not foresee; Justin, the pharmacist's apprentice adoring Emma from afar, praying on her grave; the clubfoot stableboy tortured and exploited for a dream of medical reputation; poor neglected Berthe sent to the cotton mill; the old peasant woman at the fair who for fifty-four years of service got a medal worth twenty-five francs; and even the blind beggar with his horrible skin disease. Moreover, there is the admirable Dr. Lavrière who appears fleetingly like an apparition from a saner, loftier world of good sense and professional devotion. Thus it seems unjust of Martin Turnell to say that the novel is "an onslaught on the whole basis of human feeling and on all spiritual and moral values."

In Flaubert's mind, the novel was also an assertion of the redeeming power of art. His long struggle with its composition, which took him more than five years of grinding drudgery: five days in which he had written a single page, five or six pages in a week, twenty-five pages in six weeks, thirteen pages in seven weeks, a whole night spent in hunting for the right adjective; the ruthless pruning to which he subjected his enormous manuscript, eliminating many fine touches, similes, metaphors, and descriptions of elusive mental states (as a study of the manuscripts has shown) were to him a victory of art over reality, a passionate search for Beauty, which he knew to be an illusion. But one wonders whether the conflict of Flaubert's scientific detachment and cruel observation with the intense adoration of beauty, the thirst for calcu-

lated purity and structure, for "style" as perfection, can be resolved. He tried to achieve this synthesis in *Madame Bovary*. Watching this struggle between heterogeneous elements, and even opposites, should explain some of the fascination of the book.

An explanation of the plot and the stage business is needed to understand properly the performance in *Madame Bovary* of the opera *Lucia di Lammermoor*, which occurs on pages 642–48 of this text. The French libretto by Alp. Royer and Gust. Vaez[1] (published in Brussels in 1839) must be consulted, as it differs greatly from the original Italian libretto by Salvatore Cammarano and resembles only distantly the novel by Walter Scott. The story is one of family hatred: Edgar, the owner of the castle of Ravenswood in the Scottish Highlands, has been expelled by Lord Henry Ashton who had killed his father. He is in hiding as an outlaw. He loves and is loved clandestinely by Lucy, Lord Henry's sister. The opera opens with a hunting scene on the grounds of Ravenswood castle where Henry, his forester called Gilbert (Normanno in the Italian), and other followers comb the grounds for traces of a mysterious stranger whom they suspect to be the outcast Edgar. They are joined by Lord Arthur who is a suitor for Lucy's hand and is favored by her brother as he can save him from financial ruin. Arthur declares his love for Lucy (no such scene is in the Italian). Lucy in the next scene prepares to meet Edgar in a secluded spot; she gives a purse to Gilbert whom she believes to be

---

1. A pseudonym of J. N. G. Van Niewenhuysen.

her friend though Gilbert is actually scheming with Lord Henry against her. (The scene is not in the Italian original.) Then Lucy is left alone and sings a cavatina beginning: "Que n'avons-nous des ailes." Edgar appears then, played by Lagardy, a fictional tenor. He tells of his hatred for Lucy's brother because of the death of his father. He had sworn vengeance but is ready to forget it in his love for her. Edgar has to leave on a mission to France but in parting the lovers pledge their troth and exchange rings. The stretto contains the words, "Une fleur pour ma tombe," "donne une larme à l'exilé," phrases alluded to in Flaubert's account.

Charles is so obtuse that he thinks that Edgar is torturing Lucy, and Emma has to tell him that he is her lover. Charles protests that he heard him vowing vengeance on her family. He had heard him saying: "J'ai juré vengeance et guerre." Charles has also heard Lord Arthur say, "J'aime Lucie et m'en crois aimé," and has seen Lord Arthur going off with her father arm in arm. But Charles obviously takes her brother Henry for her father.

The second act begins with Gilbert telling his master Henry that he slipped Lucy's ring from the sleeping Edgar, had made a copy and will produce it in order to convince Lucy of Edgar's faithlessness. Charles mistakes the false ring which is shown Lucy for a love gift sent by Edgar. The business with the ring replaced an analogous deception with forged letters in the Italian libretto. Lucy appears dressed for

the wedding with Lord Arthur, unhappily, resisting and imploring, reminding Emma of her own wedding day and the contrast with her false joy soon turned to bitterness. Brandishing a sword Edgar suddenly returns voicing his indignation. There follows a sextet (Lucy, Henry, Edgar, Raimondo the minister, Arthur, Gilbert) which suggests to Emma her desire to flee and to be carried off as Edgar wants to carry off Lucy. But the marriage contract has been signed and Edgar curses her. The third act does not interest Emma any more as Léon has appeared in the interval. She does not care for the scene between Lord Henry and his retainer (called here "servant") Gilbert who introduces a disguised stranger, Edgar of course. The duet between Henry Lord Ashton and Edgar reaffirms their mutual hatred. The mad scene follows. Lucy flees the marriage chamber; she has stabbed her husband and gone mad. She dreams of Edgar and dies. The great aria which was considered the climax of coloratura singing was lost on Emma absorbed in Léon.

One must assume that Flaubert had the French libretto in front of him or remembered its wordings and stage business accurately.[2] A modern reader who knows the Italian libretto from recordings may be puzzled by the discrepancies, and ascribe to Flaubert's imagination or confused memory what is actually an accurate description of the French version.

DOSTOEVSKY, *NOTES FROM UNDERGROUND*

Dostoevsky, like every great writer, can be approached in dif-

---

2. Flaubert had seen the opera first in Rouen in 1840 and again in Constantinople in November 1850.

ferent ways and read on different levels. We can try to understand him as a religious philosopher, a political commentator, a psychologist, and a novelist, and if we know much about his fascinating and varied life, we can interpret his works as biographical.

The biographical interpretation is the one that has been pushed furthest. The lurid crimes of Dostoevsky's characters (such as the rape of a young girl) have been ascribed to him, and all his novels have been studied as if they constituted a great personal confession. Dostoevsky certainly did use many of his experiences in his books (as every writer does): he several times described the feelings of a man facing a firing squad as he himself faced it on December 22, 1849, only to be reprieved at the last moment. His writings also reflect his years in Siberia: four years working in a loghouse, in chains, as he describes it in an oddly impersonal book, *Memoirs from the House of the Dead* (1862), and six more years as a common soldier on the borders of Mongolia, in a small, remote provincial town. Similarly, he used the experience of his disease (epilepsy), ascribing great spiritual significance to the ecstatic rapture preceding the actual seizure. He assigned his disease to both his most angelic "good" man, the "Idiot," Prince Myshkin, and his most diabolical, inhuman figure, the cold-blooded unsexed murderer of the old Karamazov, the flunky Smerdyakov. Dostoevsky also used something of his experiences in Germany, where in the 1860's he succumbed to a passion for gambling which he overcame only much later, during his second marriage. The short novel *The Gambler* (1866) gives an especially vivid account of this life and its moods.

There are other autobiographical elements in Dostoevsky's works, but it seems a gross misunderstanding of his methods and the procedures of art in general to conclude from his writings (as Thomas Mann has done) that he was a "saint and criminal" in one. Dostoevsky, after all, was an extremely hard worker who wrote and rewrote some twenty volumes. He was a novelist who employed the methods of the French sensational novel; he was constantly on the lookout for the most striking occurrences —the most shocking crimes and the most horrible disasters and scandals—because only in such fictional situations could he exalt his characters to their highest pitch, bringing out the clash of ideas and temperaments, revealing the deepest layers of their souls. But these fictions cannot be taken as literal transcripts of reality and actual experience.

Whole books have been written to explain Dostoevsky's religious philosophy and conception of man. The Russian philosopher Berdayev concludes his excellent study by saying, "So great is the value of Dostoevsky that to have produced him is by itself sufficient justification for the existence of the Russian people in the world." But there is no need for such extravagance. Dostoevsky's philosophy of religion is rather a personal version of extreme mystical Christianity, and assumes flesh and blood only in the context of the novels. Reduced to the bare bones of abstract propositions, it amounts to saying that man is fallen but is free to choose between evil and Christ. And choosing Christ means taking upon oneself the burden of humanity in love and pity, since "everybody is guilty for all and before all." Hence in Dostoevsky there is tremendous stress on personal freedom of choice, and his affirmation of the worth of every individual is combined, paradoxically, with an equal insistence on the substantial identity of all men, their equality before God, the bond of love which unites them.

Dostoevsky also develops a philosophy of history, with practical political implications, based upon this point of view. According to him, the West is in complete decay; only Russia has preserved Christianity in its original form. The West is either Catholic—and Catholicism is condemned by Dostoevsky as an attempt to force salvation by magic and authority—or bourgeois, and hence materialistic and fallen away from Christ; or socialist, and socialism is to Dostoevsky identical with atheism, as it dreams of a utopia in which man would not be free to choose even at the expense of suffering. Dostoevsky—who himself had belonged to a revolutionary group and come into contact with Russian revolutionaries abroad—had an extraordinary insight into the mentality of the Russian underground. In *The Possessed* (1871-1872) he gave a lurid satiric picture of these would-be saviors of Russia and mankind. But while he was afraid of the revolution, Dostoevsky himself hoped and prophesied that Russia would save Europe from the dangers of commu-

nism, as Russia alone was the uncorrupted Christian land. Put in terms of political propositions (as Dostoevsky himself preached them in his journal, *The Diary of a Writer*, 1876-1881), what he propounds is a conservative Russian nationalism with messianic hopes for Russian Christianity. It is hard to imagine a political creed more remote from present-day realities.

When translated into abstractions, Dostoevsky's psychology is as unimpressive as his political theory. It is merely a derivative of theories propounded by German writers about the unconscious, the role of dreams, the ambivalence of human feelings. What makes it electric in the novels is his ability to dramatize it in scenes of sudden revulsions, in characters who in today's terminology would be called split personalities, in people twisted by isolation, lust, humiliation, and resentment. The dreams of Raskolnikov may be interpreted according to Freudian psychology, but to the reader without any knowledge of science they are comprehensible in their place in the novel and function as warnings and anticipations.

Dostoevsky is first of all an artist—a novelist who succeeded in using his ideas (many old and venerable, many new and fantastic) and psychological insights for the writing of stories of absorbing interest. As an artist, Dostoevsky treated the novel like a drama, constructing it in large, vivid scenes which end with a scandal or a crime or some act of violence, filling it with unforgettable "stagelike" figures torn by great passions and swayed by great ideas. Then he set this world in an environment of St. Petersburg slums, or of towns, monasteries, and country houses, all so vividly realized that we forget how the setting, the figures, and the ideas melt together into one cosmos of the imagination only remotely and obliquely related to any reality of nineteenth-century Russia. We take part in a great drama of pride and humility, good and evil, in a huge allegory of man's search for God and himself. We understand and share in this world because it is not merely Russia in the nineteenth century, where people could hardly have talked and behaved as Dostoevsky's people do, but a myth of humanity, universalized as all art is.

Notes from Underground (1864) precedes the four great novels, *Crime and Punishment* (1866), *The Idiot* (1868), *The Possessed*, and *The Brothers Karamazov* (1880). The *Notes* can be viewed as a prologue, an introduction to the cycle of the four great novels, an anticipation of the mature Dostoevsky's method and thought. Though it cannot compare in dramatic power and scope with these, the story has its own peculiar and original artistry. It is made up of two parts, at first glance seemingly independent: the monologue of the Underground man and the confession which he makes about himself, called "À Propos of the Wet Snow." The monologue, though it includes no action, is dramatic—a long address to an imaginary hostile reader, whom the Underground man ridicules, defies, jeers at, but also flatters. The confession is an autobiographical reminiscence of the Underground man. It de-

scribes events which occurred long before the delivery of the monologue, but it functions as a confirmation in concrete terms of the self-portrait drawn in the monologue and as an explanation of the isolation of the hero.

The narrative of the confession is a comic variation on the old theme of the rescue of a fallen woman from vice, a seesaw series of humiliations permitting Dostoevsky to display all the cruelty of his probing psychology. The hero, out of spite and craving for human company, forces himself into the company of former schoolfellows and is shamefully humiliated by them. He reasserts his ego (as he cannot revenge himself on them) in the company of a humble prostitute by impressing her with florid and moving speeches, which he knows to be insincere, about her horrible future. Ironically, he converts her, but when she comes to him and surprises him in a degrading scene with his servant, he humiliates her again. When, even then, she understands and forgives and thus shows her moral superiority, he crowns his spite by deliberately misunderstanding her and forcing money on her. She is the moral victor and the Underground man returns to his hideout to jeer at humanity. It is hard not to feel that we are shown a tortured and twisted soul almost too despicable to elicit our compassion.

Still it would be a complete misunderstanding of Dostoevsky's story to take the philosophy expounded jeeringly in the long monologue of the first part merely as the irrational railings of a sick soul. The Underground man, though abject and spiteful, represents not only a specific Russian type of the time —the intellectual divorced from the soil and his nation—but also modern humanity, even Everyman, and, strangely enough, even the author, who through the mouth of this despicable character, as through a mask, expresses his boldest and most intimate convictions. In spite of all the exaggerated pathos, wild paradox, and jeering irony used by the speaker, his self-criticism and his criticism of society and history must be taken seriously and interpreted patiently if we are to extract the meaning accepted by Dostoevsky.

The Underground man is the hyperconscious man who examines himself as if in a mirror, and sees himself with pitiless candor. His very self-consciousness cripples his will and poisons his feelings. He cannot escape from his ego; he knows that he has acted badly toward the girl but at the same time he cannot help acting as he does. He knows that he is alone, that there is no bridge from him to humanity, that the world is hostile to him, and that he is being humiliated by everybody he meets. But though he resents the humiliation, he cannot help courting it, provoking it, and liking it in his perverse manner. He understands (and knows from his own experience) that man is not good but enjoys evil and destruction.

His self-criticism widens, then, into a criticism of the assumptions of modern civilization, of nineteenth-century optimism about human nature and progress, of utilitarianism, and of all kinds of utopias. It is possible to identify definite allusions to a contemporary novel by a radical socialist and revolutionary, Chernyshevsky, entitled *What Shall We Do?* (1863), but we do not need to know the exact target of Dostoevsky's satire to recognize what he attacks: the view that man is good, that he always seeks his enlightened self-interest, that science propounds immutable truths, and that a paradise on earth will be just around the corner once society is reformed along scientific lines. In a series of vivid symbols these assumptions are represented, parodied, exposed. Science says that "twice two makes four" but the Underground man laughs that "twice two makes five is sometimes a very charming thing too." Science means to him (and to Dostoevsky) the victory of the doctrine of fatality, of iron necessity, of determinism, and thus finally of death. Man would become an "organ-stop," a "piano-key," if deterministic science were valid.

Equally disastrous are the implications of the social philosophy of liberalism and of socialism (which Dostoevsky considers its necessary consequence). Man, in this view, need only follow his enlightened self-interest, need only be rational, and he will become noble and good and the earth will be a place of prosperity and peace. But the Underground man knows that this conception of man is entirely false. What if mankind does not follow, and never will follow, its own enlightened self-interest, is consciously and purposely irrational, even bloodthirsty and evil? History seems to the Underground man to speak a clear language: ". . . civilization has made mankind if not more bloodthirsty, at least more vilely, more loathsomely bloodthirsty." Man wills the irrational and evil because he does not want to become an organ-stop, a piano key, because he wants to be left with the freedom to choose between good and evil. This freedom of choice, even at the expense of chaos and destruction, is what makes him man.

Actually, man loves something other than his well-being and happiness, loves even suffering and pain, because he is a man and not an animal inhabiting some great organized rational "ant-heap." The ant-heap, the hen house, the block of tenements, and finally the Crystal Palace (then the newest wonder of architecture, a great hall of iron and glass erected for the Universal Exhibition in London) are the images used by the Underground man to represent his hated utopia. The heroine of *What Shall We Do?* had dreamed of a building, made of cast iron and glass and placed in the middle of a beautiful garden where there would be eternal spring and summer, eternal joy. Dostoevsky had recognized there the utopian dream of Fourier, the French socialist whom he had admired in his youth and whose ideals he had come to hate with a fierce revulsion. But we must realize that the Underground man, and Dostoevsky, despises this "ant heap," this perfectly organized society of robots, in the name of something higher, in the name of freedom. Dostoevsky does not believe that man can achieve

freedom and happiness at the same time; he thinks that man can buy happiness only at the expense of freedom, and all utopian schemes seem to him devices to lure man into the yoke of slavery. This freedom is, of course, not political freedom but freedom of choice, indeterminism, even caprice and willfulness, in the paradoxical formulation of the Underground man.

There are hints at a positive solution only in the one section (Section X), which was mutilated by the censor. A letter by Dostoevsky to his brother about the "swine of a censor who let through the passages where I jeered at everything and blasphemed ostensibly" refers to the fact that he "suppressed everything where I drew the conclusion that faith in Christ is needed." In Section XI of the present text (and Dostoevsky never restored the suppressed passages) the Underground man says merely, "I am lying because I know myself that it is not underground that is better, but something different, quite different, for which I am thirsting, but which I cannot find!" This "something . . . quite different" all the other writings of Dostoevsky show to be the voluntary following of Christ even at the expense of suffering and pain.

In a paradoxical form, through the mouth of one of his vilest characters, Dostoevsky reveals in the story his view of man and history—of the evil in man's nature and of the blood and tragedy in history—and his criticism of the optimistic, utilitarian, utopian, progressive view of man which was spreading to Russia from the West during the nineteenth century and which found its most devoted adherents in the Russian revolutionaries. Preoccupied with criticism, Dostoevsky does not here suggest any positive remedy. But if we understand the *Notes* we can understand how Raskolnikov, the murderer out of intellect in *Crime and Punishment*, can find salvation at last, and how Dmitri, the guilty-guiltless parricide of *The Brothers Karamazov*, can sing his hymn to joy in the Siberian mines. We can even understand the legend of the Great Inquisitor told by Ivan Karamazov, in which we meet the same criticism of a utopia (this time that of Catholicism) and the same exaltation of human freedom even at the price of suffering.

TOLSTOY, *THE DEATH OF IVÁN ILYICH*

Tolstoy excited the interest of the West mainly as a public figure: a count owning large estates who decided to give up his wealth and live like a simple Russian peasant—to dress in a blouse, to eat peasant food, and even to plow the fields and make shoes with his own hands. Tragically, this renunciation involved him in a conflict with his wife and family; at the age of eighty-two he left his home and died in a stationmaster's house (at Astápovo, in 1910). By then he had become the leader of a religious cult, the propounder of a new religion. It was, in substance, a highly simplified primitive Christianity which he put into a few moral commands (such as, "Do not resist evil") and from which he drew, with radical consistency, a complete condemnation of modern civilization: the state, courts and law, war, patriotism, marriage, modern art and literature, science and medicine. In debating this Christian anarchism people have tended to forget that Tolstoy established his command of the public ear as a novelist, or they have exaggerated the contrast between the early worldly novelist and the later prophet.

In his youth, Tolstoy served as a Russian artillery officer in the little wars against the mountain tribes of the Caucasus and in the Crimean War against the English and French. His reputation in Russia was at first based on his war stories. In 1862 he married and settled down on his estate, Yásnaya Polyána, where he wrote his enormous novel *War and Peace* (1865-1869). The book made him famous in Russia but was not translated into English until long afterward. Superficially, *War and Peace* is a historical novel about the Napoleonic invasion of Russia in 1812, a huge swarming epic of a nation's resistance to the foreigner. Tolstoy himself interprets history in general as a struggle of anonymous collective forces which are moved by unknown irrational impulses, waves of communal feeling. Heroes, great men, are actually not heroes but merely insignificant puppets; the best general is the one who does nothing to prevent the unknown course of Providence. But *War and Peace* is not only an impressive and vivid panorama of historical events but also the profound story—centered in two main characters, Pierre Bezúkhov and Prince Andrey Bolkónsky—of a search for the meaning of life. Andrey finds the meaning of life in love and forgiveness of his enemies. Pierre, at the end of a long groping struggle, an education by suffering, finds it in an acceptance of ordinary existence, its duties and pleasures, the family, the continuity of the race.

Tolstoy's next long novel, *Anna Karénina* (1875-1877), resumes this second thread of *War and Peace*. It is a novel of contemporary manners, a narrative of adultery and suicide. But this vivid story, told with incomparable concrete imagination, is counterpointed and framed by a second story, that of Levin, another seeker after the meaning of life, a figure who represents the author as Pierre did in the earlier book; the work ends with a promise of solution, with the ideal of a life in which we should "remember God." Thus *Anna Karénina* also anticipates the approaching crisis in Tolstoy's life. When it came, with the sudden revulsion he describes in *A Confession* (1879), he condemned his earlier books and spent the next years in writing pamphlets and tracts expounding his religion. Later, he returned to the writing of fiction, now regarded entirely as a means of presenting his creed. The earlier novels seemed to him unclear in their message, overdetailed in their method. Hence Tolstoy tried to simplify his art; he wrote plays with a thesis, stories which are like fables or parables, and one long, rather inferior novel, *The Resurrection* (1899), his most savage satire on Russian and modern institutions.

But surely if we look back on all of Tolstoy's work, we must recognize its complete continuity. From the very beginning Tolstoy was a Rousseauist. As early as 1851, when he was in the Caucasus, his diary announced his intention of founding a new, simplified religion. Even as a young man on his estate he had lived quite simply, like a peasant, except for occasional sprees and debauches. He had been horrified by war from the very beginning, though he admired the heroism of the individual soldier and had remnants of patriotic feeling. All his books concern the same theme, the good life, and they all say that the good life lies outside of civilization, near to the soil, in simplicity and humility, in love of one's neighbor. Power, the lust for power, luxury, are always evil.

As a novelist Tolstoy is rooted in the tradition of the older realism. He read and knew the English writers of the eighteenth century, and also Thackeray and Trollope. He did not care for the recent French writers (he was strong in his disapproval of Flaubert) except for Maupassant, who struck him as truthful and useful in his struggle against hypocrisy. Tolstoy's long novels are loosely plotted, though they have large over-all designs. They work by little scenes vividly visualized, by an accumulation of exact detail. Each character is drawn by means of repeated emphasis on certain physical traits, like Pierre's shortsightedness and his hairy, clumsy hands, or Princess Marya's luminous eyes, the red patches on her face, and her shuffling gait. This concretely realized surface, however, everywhere recedes into depths: to the depiction of disease, delirium, and death and to glimpses into eternity. In *War and Peace* the blue sky is the recurrent symbol for the metaphysical relationships of man. Tolstoy is so robust, has his feet so firmly on the ground, presents what he sees with such clarity and objectivity, that one can be easily deluded into considering his dominating quality to be physical, sensual, antithetical to Dostoevsky's spirituality. The contrasts between the two greatest Russian novelists are indeed obvious. While Tolstoy's method can be called epic, Dostoevsky's is dramatic; while Tolstoy's view of man is Rousseauistic, Dostoevsky stresses the fall of man; while Tolstoy rejects history and status, Dostoevsky appeals to the past and wants a hierarchical society, and so on. But these profound differences should not obscure one basic similarity: the deep spirituality of both, their rejection of the basic materialism and the conception of truth propounded by modern science and theorists of realism.

The Death of Iván Ilyich (1886) belongs to the period after Tolstoy's religious conversion when he slowly returned to fiction writing. It represents a happy medium between the early and late manner of Tolstoy. Its story and moral are simple and obvious, as always with Tolstoy (in contrast to Dostoevsky). And it says what almost all of his works are intended to convey—that man is leading the wrong kind of life, that he should return to essentials, to "nature." In *The Death of Iván Ilyich* Tolstoy combines a savage satire on the futility and hypocrisy of conventional life with a powerful symbolic presentation of man's isolation in the struggle with death and of man's hope for a final resurrection. Iván Ilyich is a Russian judge, an official, but he is also the average man of the prosperous middle classes of his time and ours, and he is also Everyman confronted with disease and dying and death. He is an ordinary person, neither virtuous nor particularly vicious, a "go-getter" in his profession, a "family man," as marriages go, who has children but has drifted apart from his wife. Through his disease, which comes about by a trivial accident in the trivial business of fixing a curtain, Iván Ilyich is slowly awakened to self-consciousness and a realization of the falsity of his life and ambitions. The isolation which disease imposes upon him, the wall of hypocrisy erected around him by his family and his doctors, his suffering and pain, drive him slowly to the recognition of *It*, to a knowledge, not merely theoretical but proved on his pulses, of his own mortality. At first he would like simply to return to his former pleasant and normal life—even in the last days of his illness, knowing he must die, he screams in his agony, "I won't!"—but at the end, struggling in the black sack into which he is being pushed, he sees the light at the bottom. " 'Death is finished,' he said to himself. 'It is no more!' "

All the people around him are egotists and hypocrites: his wife, who can remember only how she suffered during his agony; his daughter, who thinks only of the delay in her marriage; his colleagues, who speculate only about the room his death will make for promotions in the court; the doctors, who think only of the name of the disease and not of the patient; all except his shy and frightened son, Vásya, and the servant Gerásim. Gerásim is a healthy peasant lad, assistant to the butler, but because he is near to nature, he is free from hypocrisy, helps his master to be comfortable, and even mentions death, while all the others conceal the truth from him. The doctors, especially, are shown as mere specialists, inhuman and selfish. The first doctor is like a judge, like Iván himself when he sat in court, summing up and cutting off further questions of the patient (or is it the prisoner?). The satire at points appears ineffectively harsh in its violence, but it will not seem exceptional to those who know the older Tolstoy's general attitude toward courts, medicine, marriage, and even modern literature. The cult of art is jeered at, in small touches, only incidentally; it belongs, according to Tolstoy, to the falsities of modern civilization, alongside marriage (which merely hides bestial sensuality), and science (which merely hides rapacity and ignorance).

The story is deliberately deprived of any element of suspense, not only by the announcement contained in the title but by the technique of the cutback. We first hear of Iván Ilyich's death and see the reaction of the widow and friends, and only then listen to the story of his life. The detail, as always in Tolstoy, is superbly concrete and realistic: he does not shy away from the smell of disease, the physical necessity of using a commode, or the sound of screaming. He can employ the creaking of a hassock as a recur-

rent motif to point up the comedy of hypocrisy played by the widow and her visitor. He can seriously and tragically use the humble image of a black sack or the illusion of the movement of a train.

But all this naturalistic detail serves the one purpose of making us realize, as Iván Ilyich realizes, that not only Caius is mortal but you and I also, and that the life of most of us civilized people is a great lie because it disguises and ignores its dark background, the metaphysical abyss, the reality of Death. While the presentation of *The Death of Iván Ilyich* approaches, at moments, the tone of a legend or fable ("Iván Ilyich's life had been most simple and most ordinary and therefore most terrible"), Tolstoy in this story manages to stay within the concrete situation of our society and to combine the aesthetic method of realism with the universalizing power of symbolic art.

IBSEN, *THE WILD DUCK*

Ibsen's plays can be viewed as the culmination point of the *bourgeois* drama which has flourished fitfully, in France and Germany particularly, since the eighteenth century, when Diderot advocated and wrote plays about the middle classes, their "conditions" and problems. But his works can also be seen as the fountainhead of much modern drama—of the plays of Shaw and Galsworthy, who discuss social problems, and of Maeterlinck and Chekhov, who have learned from the later "symbolist" Ibsen. After a long period of incubation and experimentation with romantic and historical themes, Ibsen wrote a series of "problem" plays, beginning with *The Pillars of Society* (1877), which in their time created a furor by their fearless criticism of the nineteenth-century social scene: the subjection of women, hypocrisy, hereditary disease, seamy politics, and corrupt journalism. He wrote these plays using naturalistic modes of presentation: ordinary colloquial speech, a simple setting in a drawing room or study, a natural way of introducing or dismissing characters. Ibsen had learned from the "well-made" Parisian play (typified by those of Scribe) how to confine his action to one climactic situation and how gradually to uncover the past by retrogressive exposition. But he went far beyond it in technical skill and intellectual honesty.

The success of Ibsen's problem plays was international. But we must not forget that he was a Norwegian, the first writer of his small nation (its population at that time was less than two million) to win a reputation outside of Norway. Ibsen more than anyone else widened the scope of world literature beyond the confines of the great modern nations, which had entered its community roughly in this order: Italy, Spain, France, England, Germany, Russia. Since the time of Ibsen, the other small nations have begun to play their part in the concert of European literature. Paradoxically, however, Ibsen rejected his own land. He had dreamed of becoming a great national poet, but in 1864 he left his country for voluntary exile in Italy, Germany, and Austria. In exile, he wrote the plays depicting Norwegian society—a stuffy, provincial middle class, redeemed, in Ibsen's eyes, by single upright, even fiery, individuals of initiative and courage.

Ibsen could hardly have survived his time if he had been merely a painter of society, a dialectician of social issues, and a magnificent technician of the theater. Many of his discussions are now dated. We smile at some of the doings in *A Doll's House* (1879) and *Ghosts* (1881). His stagecraft is not unusual, even on Broadway. But Ibsen stays with us because he has more to offer—because he was an artist who managed to create, at his best, works of poetry which, under their mask of sardonic humor, express his dream of humanity reborn by intelligence and self-sacrifice.

The Wild Duck (1884) surprised the "Ibsenites." The prophet and reformer who had torn the masks of hypocrisy from marriage, respectability, the rule of the "compact majority," seemed here to turn against his own teachings. Through the mouth of Dr. Relling, the *raisonneur* of the play, Ibsen recommends the "life-lie," an illusion which, however unfounded, keeps up the spirit and supports the morale. The meddling "idealist," Gregers Werle, destroys the happiness of a family and causes, indirectly at least, the death of a young and innocent girl. The moral of the play seems to be: better happiness based on a lie than unhappiness based on truth. The ancient adage *Fiat justitia, pereat mundus,*[3]

---

3. "Justice must take its course even if the world should perish," supposedly the motto of Emperor Ferdinand I (1556-1564).

seems to be refuted and even savagely ridiculed here.

While there is this element of self-criticism in the play, the work does not, actually, constitute a break with the preceding "reformist" Ibsen. Gregers Werle, the "idealist," is too insensitive, too doctrinaire, even too stupid, to be a serious self-portrait of the mistaken reformer. At most, he is a caricature of the "idealist." Poor Hialmar Ekdal, whose life-illusion is destroyed, is no suffering hero. At the end, Dr. Relling predicts that even Hedvig's death will be nothing to him but a "pretty theme for declamation." He will, we are sure, recover his life-illusion, and he may even flourish on the tragedy of the girl. Idealism is really not abandoned in the play. Ibsen only criticizes wrongheaded, stubborn "idealism," the lack of human comprehension and insight in Werle, who makes a mess of everything, including his lodgings. Ibsen smiles with a new tolerance at people enmeshed in illusions, fancies, and even escapist vices. The one person of common sense in the play is Gina, who has her feet on the ground but is vulgar and narrow-minded. She, at least, knows that things bygone should be left bygone and that sins can be atoned by a life of love and sacrifice.

The tragedy in *The Wild Duck* (one cannot call the play as a whole a tragedy) is that of Hedvig, who, puzzled and grieved by her father's rejection, shoots herself in a gesture of self-sacrifice. Though hardly fully prepared for, the act is made psychologically comprehensible: she is a girl in her teens, in puberty, clinging in adoration to her charming father. She is prodded to shoot the duck by Gregers, who wants to destroy the symbol of escape and ineffectiveness. She thus conceives the whole idea of the need of sacrifice in order to conciliate her father. She is profoundly shocked by his histrionic aversion for her —her expulsion from a loving intimacy—for which she cannot conceive any proper reason. She overhears Hialmar's doubts about her love and readiness for sacrifice. But still her suicide comes as a shock, as a *coup de théâtre*, more surprising than the double suicide at the end of *Rosmersholm* (1886), the suicide of Hedda Gabler, or the accidental death (or suicide) of the Master Builder. Hedvig's tragedy is an episode, not quite central to the main theme of the play, which is carried by Hialmar and the older Ekdal.

Hialmar Ekdal is a charming but also absurd and hypocritical dreamer. He is supposed to be thinking out an invention, though he does not even cut the pages of his technical magazines. He pretends to be magnanimous and sturdily independent, but he carefully pastes together the pieces of the letter offering an income to his father, which he had torn into bits. He is supposed to be idealistic, unselfish, and unmaterialistic, but he loves his food and drink, his comfort, and, above all, his grandiose talk. He is a sham, but somehow an amusing and likeable sham. Old Ekdal is also comic, but pathos is the prevailing tone in his characterization. He lives in the past, in the illusion of former grandeur as an officer and a great hunter, though now he can only go shooting rabbits in his loft and put on his lieutenant's cap when no stranger is present. His gruff, pathetic senility sounds only a grim superstitious note when he comments on Hedvig's death that the "woods avenge themselves."

Gregers Werle is also made psychologically comprehensible. In modern terms, we would describe him as a victim of "mother fixation": he hates his overbearing father mainly for the sake of the memory of his injured mother. He adores Hialmar uncritically, refusing to see the shoddy reality behind the charming surface of his lackadaisical friend. He senses the failure of his own life, the position of being always "the thirteenth" at the table. But at times we feel that the author has ridiculed him too savagely. His scheme of putting the marriage of the Ekdals on a foundation of truth and honesty is too absurdly and improbably quixotic. Molvik, the drunken clergyman possessed by his "daemon," also verges at times, like Werle, on becoming a figure of farce; whereas Dr. Relling, in spite of his own drunkenness, is actually an impressive man of haughty disillusionment but fundamental kindness. The doctor voices the author's anger at the "idealism" of Werle, his compassion for the Ekdals, his insight into their characters, and he speaks the words about the "life-lie," which have become the most famous bit of the play.

In its first act, *The Wild Duck* seems simply a social comedy with tragic undertones;

there is little hint of what is to come. The exposition slowly reveals the past, which is not fully explained till the last act. The basic realism of the first two acts is later modified by hints of symbolism, by the queer poetic world of the old lumber room, with its withered Christmas trees, its pigeons and rabbits, and the wild duck. It is still a real garret behind a studio, a little implausible in its size but not impossible. The duck is a real duck shot by old Werle. But it is also a symbol of the general defeat of these people, of old Ekdal's fate, of Hialmar's enmeshment in the "seaweed," and it belongs, by right, to Hedvig. As a true symbol it has many meanings and relationships. Old Werle, referring to Ekdal in the first act, long before we have heard of the wild duck, speaks of "people . . . who dive to the bottom the moment they get a couple of slugs in their body and never come to the surface again." Later, Ekdal takes up almost the same phrases: "They shoot to the bottom as deep as they can . . . and bite themselves fast in the tangle and seaweed. . . . And they never come up again." Hialmar—Gregers tells him twice—has something of the wild duck in him. Sacrificing herself instead of her wild duck, Hedvig identifies herself with the wounded and lame bird.

The many-sided symbol of the wild duck hovers over the play, always on the hither side of reality but lending a tone of unreality and poetry. Other such motifs seem less successfully carried out—the idea of "thirteen" at a table, which recurs in the last words of Gregers, appears trivial, and the motif of Hedvig's approaching blindness is somewhat overworked. It is used to make Hialmar's suspicion of his fatherhood plausible, but apparently on purpose the truth of the matter is left unclear. Hialmar's insinuations about Hedvig's plotting with Mrs. Sörby seem out of character with his easygoing nature.

Even if we feel that some details of the play are too farcical or too contrived in their tragic irony—like Hialmar's speech, presumably overheard by Hedvig just before her gun goes off backstage—*The Wild Duck* still represents Ibsen at his best and richest. It is a wonderful gallery of portraits. It allows actors even in the minor roles (such as that of the earthy Gina) a wide scope. It has action and excitement, provided by Ibsen's sense of theater. It brings into a successful blend humor and pathos, comedy and tragedy, realism and symbolism, prose and poetry. It fulfills the demand—made implicitly of all art—for richness and complexity, a demand which on today's stage is all too frequently disappointed.

CHEKHOV, THE CHERRY ORCHARD

Chekhov differs sharply from the two giants of Russian literature. His work is of smaller scope. With the exception of an immature, forgotten novel and a travel book, he never wrote anything but short stories and plays. He belongs, furthermore, to a very different moral and spiritual atmosphere. Chekhov had studied medicine, and practiced it for a time. He shared the scientific outlook of his age and had too skeptical a mind to believe in Christianity or in any metaphysical system. He confessed that an intelligent believer was a puzzle to him. His attitude toward his materials and characters is detached, "objective." He is thus much more in the stream of Western realism than either Tolstoy or Dostoevsky, and his affinities with Maupassant (to whom he is related also in technical matters) are obvious. But extended reading of Chekhov does convey an impression of his view of life. There is implied in his stories a philosophy of kindness and humanity, a sense of the unexplainable mystery of life, a sense, especially, of man's utter loneliness in this universe and among his fellow men. Chekhov's pessimism has nothing of the defiance of the universe or the horror at it which we meet in other writers with similar attitudes; it is somehow merely sad, pathetic, and yet also comforting and comfortable.

The Russia depicted in Chekhov's stories and plays is of a later period than that presented by Tolstoy and Dostoevsky. It seems to be nearing its end; there is a sense of decadence and frustration which heralds the approach of the catastrophe. The aristocracy still keeps up a beautiful front, but is losing its fight without much resistance, resignedly. Officialdom is stupid and venal. The Church is backward and narrow-minded. The intelligentsia are hopelessly ineffectual, futile, lost in the provinces or absorbed in their egos. The peasants live subject to the lowest degradations of poverty and drink, apparently rather aggravated than improved since the much-heralded emancipation of the serfs in 1861. There seems no hope for society except in a gradual spread of enlightenment, good sense, and hygiene, for Chekhov is skeptical of the revolution and revolutionaries as well as of Tolstoy's followers.

The plays of Chekhov seem to go furthest in the direction of naturalism, the depiction of a "slice of life" on stage. Compared to Ibsen's plays they seem plotless; they could be described as a succession of little scenes, composed like a mosaic or like the dots on an impressionist painting. The characters often do not engage in the usual dialogue; they speak often in little soliloquies, hardly justified by the situation and they often do not listen to the words of their ostensible partners. They seem alone even in a crowd. Human communication seems difficult and even impossible. There is no clear message, no zeal for social reform; life seems to flow quietly, even sluggishly, until interrupted by some desperate outbreak or even a pistol shot.

Chekhov's last play, *The Cherry Orchard* (composed in 1903, first performed at the Moscow Art Theatre on January 17, 1904) differs, however, from this pattern in several respects. It has a strongly articulated central theme: the loss of the orchard, and it has a composition which roughly follows the traditional scheme of a well-made play. Arrival and departure from the very same room, the nursery, frame the two other acts: the outdoor idyll of Act II and the dance in Act III. Act III is the turning point of the

action: Lopahin appears and announces, somewhat shamefacedly, that he has bought the estate. The orchard was lost from the very beginning—there is no real struggle to prevent its sale—but still the news of Lopahin's purchase is a surprise as he had no intention of buying it but did so only when during the auction sale a rival seemed to have a chance of acquiring it. A leading action runs its course, and one may even argue, many— too many—subplots crisscross each other: the shy and awkward love affair of the student Trofimov and the gay daughter Anya; the love triangle among the three dependents, Yepihodov, the unlucky clerk, Dunyasha, the silly chambermaid, and Yasha, the conceited and insolent footman. Varya, the practical, spinsterish stepdaughter, has her troubles with Lopahin, and Simeonov-Pishchik is beset by the same financial problems as the owners of the orchard and is rescued by the discovery of some white clay on his estate. The German governess Charlotta drifts around alluding to her obscure origins and past. There are undeveloped references to events preceding the action on stage: the lover in Paris, the drowned boy Grisha, but there is no revelation of the past as in Ibsen, no mystery, no intrigue.

While the events on the stage follow each other naturally, though hardly always in a logical, causal order, a symbolic device is used conspicuously: In Act II after a pause, "suddenly a distant sound is heard, coming from the sky as it were, the sound of a snapping string, mournfully dying away." It occurs again at the very end of the play followed by "the stroke of an ax felling a tree far away in the orchard." An attempt is made to explain this sound at its first occurrence as a bucket's fall in a far away pit, or as the cries of a heron or an owl, but the effect is weird and even supernatural; it establishes an ominous mood. Even the orchard carries more than its obvious meaning: It is white, drowned in blossoms when the party arrives in the spring; it is bare and desolate in the autumn when the axes are heard cutting it down. "The old bark on the trees gleams faintly, and the cherry trees seem to be dreaming of things that happened a hundred, two hundred years ago and to be tormented by painful visions," declaims Trofimov, defining his feeling for the orchard as a symbol of repression and serfdom. For Lubov Ranevskaya it is an image of her lost innocence and of the happier past, while Lopahin sees it only as an investment. It seems to draw together the meaning of the play.

But what is this meaning? Can we even decide whether it is a tragedy or a comedy? It has been commonly seen as the tragedy of the downfall of the Russian aristocracy (or more correctly, the landed gentry) victimized by the newly rich, upstart peasantry. One could see the play as depicting the defeat of a group of feckless people at the hand of a ruthless "developer" who destroys nature and natural beauty for profit. Or one can see it as prophesying,

through the mouth of the student Trofimov, the approaching end of feudal Russia and the coming happier future. Soviet interpretations and performances lean that way.

Surely none of these interpretations can withstand inspection of the actual text of the play. They all run counter to Chekhov's professed intentions. He called the play a comedy. In a letter of September 15, 1903, he declared expressly that the play "has not turned out as drama but as comedy, in places even a farce" and a few days later (September 21, 1903) he wrote that "the whole play is gay and frivolous." Chekhov did not like the staging of the play at the Moscow Art Theatre and complained of its tearful tone and its slow pace. He objected that "they obstinately call my play a drama in playbill and newspaper advertisements" while he had called it a comedy (April 10, 1904).

No doubt, there are many comical and even farcical characters and scenes in the play. Charlotta with her dog eating nuts, her card tricks, her ventriloquism, her disappearing acts, is a clownish figure. Gayev, the landowner, though "suave and elegant," is a windbag obsessed by his passion for billiards, constantly popping candy into his mouth, telling the waiters in a restaurant about the "decadents" in Paris. Yepihodov, the clerk, carries a revolver and, threatening suicide, asks foolishly whether you have read Buckle (the English historian) and complains of his ill-luck: a spider on his chest, a cockroach in his drink. Simeonov-Pishchik empties a whole bottle of pills, eats a gallon and a half of cucumbers, quotes Nietzsche supposedly recommending the forging of banknotes and, fat as he is, puffs and prances at the dance ordering the "cavaliers aux genoux." Even the serious characters are put into ludicrous predicaments: Trofimov falls down the stairs; Lopahin, coming to announce the purchase of the estate, is almost hit with a stick by Varya (and was hit in the original version). Lopahin, teasing his intended Varya, "moos like a cow." The ball with the Jewish orchestra, the hunting for the galoshes, and the champagne drinking by Yasha in the last act have all a touch of absurdity. The grand speeches, Gayev's addresses to the bookcase and to nature or Trofimov's about "mankind going forward" and "All Russia is our orchard," are undercut by the contrast between the sentiment and the character: Gayev is callous and shallow, the "eternal student" Trofimov never did a stitch of work. He is properly ridiculed and insulted by Lubov for his scant beard and his silly professions of being "above love." One can sympathize with Chekhov's irritation at the pervading gloom imposed by the Moscow production.

Still, I believe, we cannot, in spite of the author, completely dismiss the genuine pathos of the central situation and of the central figure, Lubov Ranevskaya. Whatever one may say about her recklessness in financial matters and her guilt in relation to her lover in France, we must feel her deep attachment to the house and the orchard, to the past and her lost innocence, clearly and unhumorously expressed in the first act on her arrival, again and again at the impending sale of the estate, and finally at the parting from her house: "Oh, my orchard—my dear, sweet, beautiful orchard! . . . My life, my youth, my happiness—Goodbye!" That Gayev, before the final parting, seems to have overcome the sense of loss and even looks forward to his job in the bank and that Lubov acknowledges that her "nerves are better" and that "she sleeps well" testifies to the indestructible spirit of brother and sister, but cannot minimize the sense of loss, the pathos of parting, the nostalgia for happier times. Nor is the conception of Lopahin simple. Chekhov emphasized, in a letter to Konstantin Stanislavsky who was to play the part, that "Lopahin is a decent person in the full sense of the word, and his bearing must be that of a completely dignified and intelligent man." He is not, he says, a profiteering peasant (*kulachok*, October 30, 1903). He admires Lubov and thinks of her with gratitude. He senses the beauty of the poppies in his fields. Even the scene of the abortive encounter with Varya at the end has its quiet pathos in spite of all its awkwardness and the comic touches such as the reference to the broken thermometer. Firs, the old valet, aged eighty-six, may be grotesque in his deafness and his nostalgia for the good old days of serfdom, but the very last scene when we see him abandoned in the locked-up house surely concludes the play on a note of desolation and even despair.

Chekhov, we must conclude, achieved a highly original and even paradoxical blend of comedy and tragedy or rather of farce and pathos. The play gives a social picture firmly set in a specific historical time: the dissolution of the landed gentry, the rise of the peasant, the encroachment of the city; but it does not propound an obvious social thesis. Chekhov, in his tolerance and tenderness, in his distrust of ideologies and heroics, extends his sympathy to all his characters (with the exception of the crudely ambitious valet Yasha). The glow of his humanity, untrammeled by time and place, keeps *The Cherry Orchard* alive in quite different social and political conditions, as it has the universalizing power of great art.

LIVES, WRITINGS, AND CRITICISM
Biographical and critical works are listed only if they are available in English.

GUSTAVE FLAUBERT

LIFE. Born at Rouen, Normandy, on December 12, 1821, to the chief surgeon of the Hôtel Dieu. Flaubert was extremely precocious: by the age of sixteen he was writing stories in the romantic taste, which were published only after his death. In 1840 he went to Paris to study law (he had received his baccalaureate from the local *lycée*), but he failed in his examinations, and in 1843 suffered a sudden nervous breakdown which kept him at home. In 1846 he moved to Croisset, just outside of Rouen on the Seine, where he made his home for the rest of his life, devoting himself to writing. The same year, in Paris, Flaubert met Louise Colet, a minor poetess and lady about town, who became his mistress. In 1849-1851 he visited the Levant, traveling extensively in Greece, Syria, and Egypt. After his return he settled down to the writing of *Madame Bovary*, which took him five full years. *Madame Bovary* was a great popular success. An attempt was made to suppress it, however, and a lawsuit ensued, charging Flaubert with immorality. In 1857 he was acquitted of this charge. The remainder of his life was uneventful. He made occasional trips to Paris, and one trip, in 1860, to Tunisia to see the ruins of Carthage in preparation for the writing of his novel *Salammbô*. Flaubert died at Croisset on May 8, 1880.

CHIEF WRITINGS. *Madame Bovary* (1856); *Salammbô* (1862); *The Sentimental Education* (*L'Éducation sentimentale*, 1869); *The Temptation of St. Anthony* (*La Tentation de Saint Antoine*, 1874); *Three Tales* (*Trois Contes*, 1877), including "A Simple Heart" ("*Un Coeur simple*"); *Bouvard and Pécuchet* (*Bouvard et Pécuchet*, a posthumous novel, unfinished, 1881).

BIOGRAPHY AND CRITICISM. Erich Auerbach, "In the Hôtel de la Mole," in *Mimesis: The Representation of Reality in Western Literature*, translated by Willard Trask (1953); Benjamin F. Bart, *Flaubert* (1967); *Madame Bovary and the Critics*, edited by Benjamin F. Bart (1966); Victor Brombert, *The Novels of Flaubert* (1966); *Gustave Flaubert: Madame Bovary. Backgrounds and Sources: Essays in Criticism*, edited by Paul de Man (1965); Raymond D. Giraud, *The Unheroic Hero in the Novels of Stendhal, Balzac, and Flaubert* (1957); *Flaubert: A Collection of Critical Essays*, edited by Raymond D. Giraud (1964); Alison Fairlie, *Flaubert: Madam Bovary* (1962); Henry James, "Gustave Flaubert," in *Notes on Novelists* (1914); Harry Levin, "Flaubert," in *The Gates of Horn: A Study of Five French Realists* (1963); Percy Lubbock, chapters 5 and 6 in *The Craft of Fiction* (1921); Maurice Nadau, *The Greatness of Flaubert*, translated by Barbara Bray (1972); Georges Poulet, "Flaubert," in *The Metamorphoses of the Circle*, translated by Carley Dawson and Eliott Coleman (1967); Philip Spencer, *Flaubert: A Biography* (1952); Enid Starkie, *Flaubert: The Making of the Master* (1967); Francis Steegmuller, *Flaubert and Madame Bovary* (1939, new ed. 1950); Margaret G. Tillett, *On Reading Flaubert* (1961); Anthony Thorlby, *Gustave Flaubert and the Art of Realism* (1957); Martin Turnell, "Flaubert," in *The Novel in France* (1951).

FYODOR DOSTOEVSKY

LIFE. Fyodor Mikhailovich Dostoevsky, born in Moscow on October 30, 1821. His father was a staff doctor at the Hospital for the Poor. Later he acquired an estate and serfs. In 1839 he was killed by one of his peasants in a quarrel. Dostoevsky was sent to the Military Engineering Academy in St. Petersburg, from which he graduated in 1843. He became a civil servant, a draftsman in the St. Petersburg Engineering Corps, but resigned soon because he feared that he would be transferred to the provinces when his writing was discovered. His first novel, *Poor People* (1846), proved a great success with the critics; his second, *The Double* (1846), which followed immediately, was a failure.

Subsequently, Dostoevsky became involved in the Petrashevsky circle, a secret society of antigovernment and socialist tendencies. He was arrested on April 23, 1849, and condemned to be shot. On December 22 he was led to public execution, but he was reprieved at the last moment and sent to penal servitude in Siberia (near Omsk), where he worked for four years in a stockade, wearing fetters, completely cut off from communications with Russia. On his release in February, 1854, he was assigned as a common soldier to Semipalatinsk, a small town near the Mongolian frontier. There he received several promotions (eventually becoming an ensign); his rank of nobility, forfeited by his sentence, was restored; and he married the widow of a customs official. In July, 1859, Dostoevsky was permitted to return to Russia, and finally, in December, 1859, to St. Petersburg—after ten years of his life had been spent in Siberia.

In the last year of his exile, Dostoevsky had resumed writing, and in 1861, shortly after his return, he founded a review, *Time (Vremya)*. This was suppressed in 1863, though Dostoevsky had changed his political opinions and was now strongly nationalistic and conservative in outlook. He made his first trip to France and England in 1862, and traveled in Europe again in 1863 and 1865, in order to follow a young woman friend, Apollinaria Suslova, and to indulge in gambling. After his wife's death in 1864, and another unsuccessful journalistic venture, *The Epoch (Epokha)*, 1864-1865, Dostoevsky was for a time almost crushed by gambling debts, emotional entanglements, and frequent epileptic seizures. He barely managed to return from Germany in 1865. In the winter of 1866 he wrote *Crime and Punishment*, and before he had finished it, dictated a shorter novel, *The Gambler*, to meet a deadline. He married his secretary, Anna Grigoryevna Snitkina, early in 1867 and left Russia with her to avoid his creditors. For years they wandered over Germany, Italy, and Switzerland, frequently in abject poverty. Their first child died. In 1871, when the initial chapters of *The Possessed* proved a popular success, Dostoevsky returned to St. Petersburg.

He became the editor of a weekly, *The Citizen (Grazhdanin)*, for a short time and then published a periodical written by himself, *The Diary of a Writer* (1876-1881), which won great acclaim. Honors and some prosperity came to him. At a Pushkin anniversary celebrated in Moscow in 1880 he gave the main speech. But soon after his return to St. Petersburg he died, on January 28, 1881, not yet sixty years old.

CHIEF WRITINGS. *Memoirs from the House of the Dead* (1862); *Notes from Underground* (1864); *Crime and Punishment* (1866); *The Idiot* (1869); *The Possessed* (1871-1872); *The Raw Youth* (1875); *The Brothers Karamazov* (1880).

BIOGRAPHY AND CRITICISM. Monroe C. Beardsley, "Dostoyevsky's Metaphor of the 'Underground,'" *Journal of the History of Ideas*, III (June, 1942), 265-290; Maurice Beebe and Christopher Newton, "Dostoevsky in English: A Checklist of Criticism and Translations" in *Modern Fiction Studies* IV (1958); Nikolay N. Berdayev, *Dostoievsky: An Interpretation* (1934, new ed. 1957); R. P. Blackmur, "Studies in Dostoevsky," in *Eleven Essays in the European Novel* (1964); E. H. Carr, *Dostoevsky, 1821–1881: A New Biography* (1931); Richard Curle, *Characters of Dostoevsky: Studies from Four Novels* (1950); *Fyodor Dostoevsky: Notes from Underground*, edited by Robert G. Durgy, translated by Serge Shishkoff, criticism and analysis (1969); Donald Fanger, *Dostoevsky and Romantic Realism* (1965); Joseph Frank, "Nihilism and *Notes from Underground*," in *Sewanee Review* LXIX (1961); Sigmund Freud, "Dostoievski and Parricide," in *Partisan Review* XIV (1945), 530–44; Vyacheslav Ivanov, *Freedom and the Tragic Life: A Study in Dostoevsky* (1952); Robert L. Jackson, *The Underground Man in Russian Literature* (1958), and *Dostoevsky's Quest for Form* (1966); Janko Lavrin, *Dostoevski: A Study* (1947); David Magarshack, *Dostoevsky* (1962); Konstantin Mochulsky, *Dostoevsky: Life and Work*, translated by Michael Minihan (1967); Middleton Murry, *Fyodor Dostoevsky: A Critical Study* (1916); Richard Peace, *Dostoevsky: An Examination of the Major Novels* (1971); Ernest J. Simmons, *Dostoevski, The Making of a Novelist* (1940); George Steiner, *Tolstoy or Dostoevsky* (1959); Victor Terras, *The Young Dostoevsky, 1846–1849* (1969); Edward Wasiolek, *Dostoevsky: The Major Fiction* (1964); *Dostoevsky: A Collection of Critical Essays*, edited by René Wellek (1962); Avrahm Yarmolinsky, *Dostoevsky: A Study in His Ideology* (1921), and *Dostoevsky: A Life* (1934); L. A. Zander, *Dostoev-*

sky, translated by Natalie Duddington (1948); Stefan Zweig, *Three Masters: Balzac, Dickens, Dostoevsky* (1930).

LEO TOLSTOY

LIFE. Born at Yásnaya Polyána, his mother's estate near Tula (about 130 miles south of Moscow), on August 28, 1828. His father was a retired lieutenant colonel; one of his ancestors, the first count, had served Peter the Great as an ambassador. His mother's father was a Russian general in chief. Tolstoy lost both parents early in his life and was brought up by aunts. He went to the University of Kazan between 1844 and 1847, drifted along aimlessly for a few years more, and in 1851 became a cadet in the Caucasus. As an artillery officer he saw action in the wars with the mountain tribes and again, in 1854-1855, during the Crimean War against the French and English. Tolstoy had written fictional reminiscences of his childhood while he was in the Caucasus, and during the Crimean War he wrote war stories which established his literary reputation. For some years he lived on his estate, where he founded and himself taught an extremely "progressive" school for peasant children. He made two trips to western Europe, in 1857 and in 1860-1861. In 1862 he married the daughter of a physician, Sonya Bers, who bore him thirteen children. In the first years of his married life, between 1863 and 1869, he wrote *War and Peace,* and between 1873 and 1877 composed *Anna Karénina*. After this, a religious crisis came over him, which he described in 1879 in *A Confession*. The next years were devoted to the writing of tracts— attacks on orthodoxy, the government, and the cult of art, and elaborations of his own religious creed. Only slowly did Tolstoy return to the writing of fiction. His longest later book was *The Resurrection*. In 1901 Tolstoy was excommunicated. A disagreement with his wife about the nature of the good life and about financial matters sharpened into a conflict over his last will, which finally led to a complete break: he left home in the company of a doctor friend. He caught cold on the train journey south and died in the house of the stationmaster of Astápovo, on November 20, 1910.

CHIEF WRITINGS. *The Cossacks* (1863); *War and Peace* (1865-1869); *Anna Karénina* (1875-1877); *A Confession* (1879); *The Death of Iván Ilyich* (1886); *The Power of Darkness* (1886); *The Kreutzer Sonata* (1889); *Master and Man* (1895); *What Is Art?* (1897); *The Resurrection* (1899); *Hadji Murad* (1896-1904).

BIOGRAPHY AND CRITICISM. John Bayley, *Tolstoy and the Novel* (1962); Isaiah Berlin, *The Hedgehog and the Fox: An Essay on Tolstoy's View of History* (1953); R. F. Christian, *Tolstoy's "War and Peace": A Study* (1962), and *Tolstoy: A Critical Introduction* (1969); Maxim Gorky, *Reminiscences of Tolstoy* (1921); Janko Lavrin, *Tolstoy* (1946); Derrick Leon, *Tolstoy: His Life and Work* (1944); Georg Lukács, "Tolstoy," in *Studies in European Realism*, translated by E. Bone (1950); Thomas Mann, "Goethe and Tolstoy," in *Essays of Three Decades*, translated by H. T. Lowe-Porter (1947); *Tolstoy: A Collection of Critical Essays*, edited by Ralph E. Matlaw (1967); Aylmer Maude, *The Life of Tolstoy* (2 vols, 1908–1910); D. S. Merezhkovsky, *Tolstoy as Man and Artist* (1902); Renato Poggioli, "A Portrait of Tolstoy as Alceste," in *The Phoenix and the Spider* (1957); Philip Rahv, "The Death of Ivan Ilyich and Joseph K." and "Tolstoy: The Green Twig and the Black Trunk," in *Image and Idea* (1949); Theodore Redpath, *Tolstoy* (1960); Ernest J. Simmons, *Leo Tolstoy* (1946), and *An Introduction to Tolstoy's Writings* (1968); Logan Speirs, *Tolstoy and Chekhov* (1971); George Steiner, *Tolstoy or Dostoevsky* (1959); Stefan Zweig, *Adepts in Self-Portraiture (Casanova, Stendhal, Tolstoy)*, translated by E. and C. Paul (1952).

HENRIK IBSEN

LIFE. Born at Skien, in Norway, on March 20, 1828. His family had sunk into poverty and finally complete bankruptcy. In 1844, at the age of sixteen, Ibsen was sent to Grimstad, another small coastal town, as an apothecary's apprentice. There he lived in almost complete isolation and cut himself off from his family, except for his sister Hedvig. In 1850 he managed to get to Oslo (then Christiana) and to enroll at the university. But he never passed his examinations and in the following year left for Bergen, where he had acquired the position of playwright and assistant stage manager at the newly founded Norwegian Theater. Ibsen supplied the small theater with several historical and romantic plays. In 1857 he was appointed artistic director at the Møllergate Theater in Christiana, and a year later he married Susannah Thoresen. *Love's Comedy* (1862) was his first major success on the stage. Ibsen was then deeply affected by Scandinavianism, the movement for the solidarity of the Northern nations, and when in 1864 Norway refused to do anything to support Denmark in her war with Prussia and Austria over Schleswig-Holstein, he was so disgusted with his country that he left it for what he thought would be permanent exile. After that, Ibsen led a life of wandering. He lived in Rome, in Dresden, in Munich, and in smaller summer resorts, and during this time wrote all his later plays. *The Wild Duck* was written in Gossensass, in the Austrian Alps, in 1884. He paid a visit to Norway in 1885, but returned again to Germany. Only in 1891, when he was sixty-three, did Ibsen return to Christiana for good. He was then famous and widely honored, but lived a very retired life. In 1900 he suffered a stroke which made him a complete invalid for the last years of his life. He died on May 23, 1906, at Christiana.

CHIEF WRITINGS. (All of the works listed are plays.) *A Doll's House* (1879); *Ghosts* (1881); *An Enemy of the People* (1882); *The Wild Duck* (1884); *Rosmersholm* (1886); *The Lady from the Sea* (1888); *Hedda Gabler* (1890); *The Master Builder* (1892).

BIOGRAPHY AND CRITICISM. Eric Bentley, "Wagner and Ibsen: A Contrast," in *The Playwright as Thinker* (1946), and "Ibsen, Pro and Con," in *In Search of Theater* (1959); *Contemporary Approaches to Ibsen*, edited by *Alex* Bolckmans (1966); Muriel C. Bradbrook, *Ibsen: The Norwegian* (1948); Robert Brustein, "Henrik Ibsen," in *The Theater of Revolt* (1964); Brian W. Downs, *Ibsen: The Intellectual Background* (1946), and *A Study of Six Plays by Ibsen* (1950); *Ibsen: A Collection of Critical Essays*, edited by Rolf Fjelde (1965); Hans Heiberg, *Ibsen: A Portrait of the Artist*, translated by Joan Tate (1969); Orley I. Holtan, *Mythic Patterns in Ibsen's Last Plays* (1970); Theodore Jorgensen, *Henrik Ibsen: A Study in Art and Personality* (1945); G. Wilson Knight, *Ibsen* (1962); Halvdan Koht, *Life of Ibsen*, translated by E. Haugen and N. E. Santiello (2 vols., 1971); Janko Lavrin, *Ibsen: An Approach* (1950); F. L. Lucas, *The Drama of Ibsen and Strindberg* (1962); James W. McFarlane, *Ibsen and the Temper of Norwegian Literature* (1960), and *Discussions of Henrik Ibsen* (1962), and *Henrik Ibsen: A Critical Anthology* (1970); Michael Meyer, *Ibsen: A Biography* (1971); Kenneth Muir, *Last Periods of Shakespeare, Racine, Ibsen* (1961); John Northam, *Ibsen's Dramatic Method: A Study of the Prose Dramas* (1953); George Bernard Shaw, *The Quintessence of Ibsenism* (1891, 3rd enl. ed., 1913); Peter F. D. Tennant, *Ibsen's Dramatic Technique* (1948); Maurice J. Valency, *The Flower and the Castle: An Introduction to Modern Drama* (1963); Hermann J. Weigand, *The Modern Ibsen* (1925); Raymond Williams, *Modern Tragedy* (1966); A. E. Zucker, *Henrik Ibsen: The Master Builder* (1927).

ANTON CHEKHOV

LIFE. Anton Pavlovich Chekhov, born on January 17, 1860, at Taganrog, a small town on the Sea of Azov. His father was a grocer and haberdasher;

his grandfather, a serf who had bought his freedom. Chekhov's father went bankrupt in 1876, and the family moved to Moscow, leaving Anton to finish school in his home town. After his graduation in 1879, he followed his family to Moscow, where he studied medicine. In order to earn additional money for his family and himself, he started to write humorous sketches and stories for magazines. In 1884 he became a doctor and published his first collection of stories, *Tales of Melpomene*. In the same year he had his first hemorrhage. All the rest of his life he struggled against tuberculosis. His first play, *Ivanov*, was performed in 1887. Three years later, he undertook an arduous journey through Siberia to the island of Sakhalin (north of Japan) and back by boat through the Suez Canal. He saw there the Russian penal settlements and wrote a moving account of his trip in *Sakhalin Island* (1892). In 1898 his play *The Sea Gull* was a great success at the Moscow Art Theater. The next year he moved to Yalta, in the Crimea, and in 1901 married the actress Olga Knipper. He died on July 2, 1904, at Badenweiler in the Black Forest.

CHIEF WRITINGS. Chekhov's stories, which first appeared in scattered magazines, have been collected in many variously titled volumes. The plays were performed in this order: *Ivanov* (1887); *The Sea Gull* (1896); *Uncle Vanya* (1899); *The Three Sisters* (1901); *The Cherry Orchard* (1904); they have been translated by Constance Garnett, 2 vols., 1924.

BIOGRAPHY AND CRITICISM. W. H. Bruford, *Chekhov and His Russia* (1948) and *Anton Chekhov* (1957); Korney Chukovsky, *Chekhov the Man*, trans. by Pauline Rose (1945); Thomas Adam Eekman, *A. Čechov, 1860-1960. Some Essays* (1960); Oliver Elton, "Chekhov" in *Essays and Addresses* (1939); Francis Fergusson, "*Ghosts* and *The Cherry Orchard*," in *The Idea of a Theater* (1949); Anna Heifetz (Sherman), *Chekhov in English: A List of Works by and about Him*, ed. by A. Yarmolinsky (1949); Ronald Hingley, *Chekhov, A Biographical and Critical Study* (1950); *Chekhov: A Collection of Critical Essays*, edited by Robert L. Jackson (1967); David Magarshack, *Chekhov the Dramatist* (1952), and *Chekhov: A Life* (1952); Leon Shestov, *Chekhov and Other Essays*, edited by Sidney Monas (1966); Ernest J. Simmons, *Chekhov: A Biography* (1962); Logan Speirs, *Tolstoy and Chekhov* (1971); L. J. Styan, *Chekhov in Performance: A Commentary on the Major Plays* (1971); Maurice Valency, *The Breaking Spring: The Plays of Anton Chekhov* (1966).

GUSTAVE FLAUBERT
(1821–1880)
Madame Bovary*

Part One

I

We were in class when the headmaster came in, followed by a new boy, not wearing the school uniform, and a school servant carrying a large desk. Those who had been asleep woke up, and every one rose as if just surprised at his work.

The headmaster made a sign to us to sit down. Then, turning to the teacher, he said to him in a low voice:

"Monsieur Roger, here is a pupil whom I recommend to your care; he'll be in the second. If his work and conduct are satisfactory, he will go into one of the upper classes, as becomes his age."

The new boy, standing in the corner behind the door so that he could hardly be seen, was a country lad of about fifteen, and taller than any of us. His hair was cut square on his forehead like a village choir boy; he looked reliable, but very ill at ease. Although he was not broad-shouldered, his short jacket of green cloth with black buttons must have been tight about the armholes, and showed at the opening of the cuffs red wrists accustomed to being bare. His legs, in blue stockings, looked out from beneath yellowish trousers, drawn tight by suspenders. He wore stout, ill-cleaned, hob-nailed boots.

We began reciting the lesson. He listened with all his ears, as attentive as if at a sermon, not daring even to cross his legs or lean on his elbow; and when at two o'clock the bell rang, the master was obliged to tell him to fall into line with the rest of us.

When we came back to work, we were in the habit of throwing our caps on the ground so as to have our hands more free; we used from the door to toss them under the desk, so that they hit against the wall and made a lot of dust: it was the fad of the moment.

But, whether he had not noticed the trick, or did not dare to attempt it, the new boy was still holding his cap on his knees even after prayers were over. It was one of those head-gears of composite order, in which we can find traces of the bear- and the coonskin, the shako, the bowler, and the cotton nightcap; one of those poor things, in fine, whose dumb ugliness has depths of expression, like an imbecile's face. Ovoid and stiffened with whalebone, it began with three circular strips; then came in succession lozenges of velvet and rabbit fur separated by a red band; after that a sort of bag that ended in a cardboard polygon covered with complicated braiding, from which hung, at the end of a long thin cord, small twisted gold threads in the manner of a tassel. The cap was new; its peak shone.

"Rise," said the master.

He stood up; his cap fell. The whole class began to laugh. He stooped to pick it up. A neighbour knocked it down again with his elbow; he picked it up once more.

"Get rid of your helmet," said the master, who liked to joke.

There was a burst of laughter from the boys, which so thoroughly put the poor lad out of countenance that he did not know whether to keep his cap in his hand, leave it on the ground, or put it on his head. He sat down again and placed it on his knee.

"Rise," repeated the master, "and tell me your name."

The new boy articulated in a stammering voice an unintelligible name.

"Again!"

The same sputtering of syllables was heard, drowned by the tittering of the class.

"Louder!" cried the master; "louder!"

The new boy then took a supreme resolution, opened an inordinately large mouth, and shouted at the top of his voice as if calling some one, the word "Charbovari."

A hubbub broke out, rose in *crescendo* with bursts of shrill voices (they yelled, barked, stamped, repeated "Charbovari! Charbovari!"), then died away into single notes, growing quieter only with great difficulty, and now and again suddenly recommencing along the line of a seat from where rose here and there, like a damp cracker going off, a stifled laugh.

However, amid a rain of penalties, order was gradually re-established in the class; and the master having succeeded in catching the name of "Charles Bovary," having had it dictated to him, spelt out, and re-read, at once ordered the poor devil to go and sit down on the punishment form at the foot of the master's desk. He got up, but before going hesitated.

"What are you looking for?" asked the master.

"My c-c-c-cap," said the new boy shyly, casting troubled looks round him.

"Five hundred verses for all the class!" shouted in a furious voice, stopped, like the *Quos ego*,[1] a fresh outburst. "Silence!" continued the master indignantly, wiping his brow with his handkerchief, which he had just taken from his cap. As to you, Bovary, you will conjugate '*ridiculus sum*' twenty times." Then, in a gentler tone, "Come, you'll find your cap again; it hasn't been stolen."

---

1. Neptune becalming the winds in the *Aeneid* (I.135)

Quiet was restored. Heads bent over desks, and the new boy remained for two hours in an exemplary attitude, although from time to time some paper pellet flipped from the tip of a pen came bang in his face. But he wiped his face with one hand and continued motionless, his eyes lowered.

In the evening, at study hall, he pulled out his sleeveguards from his desk, arranged his small belongings, and carefully ruled his paper. We saw him working conscientiously, looking up every word in the dictionary, and taking the greatest pains. Thanks, no doubt, to the willingness he showed, he had not to go down to the class below. But though he knew his rules passably, he lacked all elegance in composition. It was the curé of his village who had taught him his first Latin; his parents, from motives of economy, having sent him to school as late as possible.

His father, Monsieur Charles Denis Bartolomé Bovary, retired assistant-surgeon-major, compromised about 1812 in certain conscription scandals, and forced at this time to leave the service, had taken advantage of his fine figure to get hold of a dowry of sixty thousand francs in the person of a hosier's daughter who had fallen in love with his good looks. He was a fine man, a great talker, making his spurs ring as he walked, wearing whiskers that ran into his moustache, his fingers always garnished with rings; he dressed in loud colours, had the dash of a military man with the easy go of a commercial traveller. Once married, he lived for three or four years on his wife's fortune, dining well, rising late, smoking long porcelain pipes, not coming in at night till after the theatre, and haunting cafés. The father-in-law died, leaving little; he was indignant at this, tried his hand at the textile business, lost some money in it, then retired to the country, where he thought he would make the land pay off. But, as he knew no more about farming than calico, as he rode his horses instead of sending them to plough, drank his cider in bottle instead of selling it in cask, ate the finest poultry in his farmyard, and greased his hunting-boots with the fat of his pigs, he was not long in finding out that he would do better to give up all speculation.

For two hundred francs[2] a year he managed to rent on the border of the provinces of Caux and Picardy, a kind of place half farm, half private house; and here, soured, eaten up with regrets, cursing his luck, jealous of every one, he shut himself up at the age of forty-five, sick of men, he said, and determined to live in peace.

His wife had adored him once on a time; she had loved him with a thousand servilities that had only estranged him the more. Lively

2. It is very difficult to transpose monetary values from 1840 into present-day figures, since relationships between the actual value of the franc, the cost of living, and the relative cost of specific items (such as rent, real estate, etc.) have undergone fundamental changes. One would not be too far off the mark by reading present-day dollars for Flaubert's francs; that would show Madame Bovary destroyed, at the end of the book, by an 8,000-dollar debt.

once, expansive and affectionate, in growing older she had become (after the fashion of wine that, exposed to air, turns to vinegar) ill-tempered, grumbling, irritable. She had suffered so much without complaint at first, when she had seen him going after all the village harlots, and when a score of bad houses sent him back to her at night, weary, stinking drunk. Then her pride revolted. After that she was silent, burying her anger in a dumb stoicism that she maintained till her death. She was constantly going about looking after business matters. She called on the lawyers, the judges, remembered when notes fell due, got them renewed, and at home ironed, sewed, washed, looked after the workmen, paid the accounts, while he, troubling himself about nothing, eternally besotted in a sleepy sulkiness from which he only roused himself to say nasty things to her, sat smoking by the fire and spitting into the cinders.

When she had a child, it had to be sent out to nurse. When he came home, the lad was spoilt as if he were a prince. His mother stuffed him with jam; his father let him run about barefoot, and, playing the philosopher, even said he might as well go about quite naked like the young of animals. As opposed to the maternal ideas, he had a certain virile idea of childhood on which he sought to mould his son, wishing him to be brought up hardily, like a Spartan, to give him a strong constitution. He sent him to bed without any fire, taught him to drink off large draughts of rum and to jeer at religious processions. But, peaceable by nature, the boy responded poorly to his attempts. His mother always kept him near her; she cut out cardboard pictures for him, told him tales, entertained him with monologues full of melancholy gaiety, chatting and fondling in endless baby-talk. In her life's isolation she transferred on the child's head all her scattered, broken little vanities. She dreamed of high station; she already saw him, tall, handsome, clever, settled as an engineer or in the law. She taught him to read, and even on an old piano she had taught him two or three sentimental ballads. But to all this Monsieur Bovary, caring little for arts and letters, said "It was not worth while. Would they ever have the means to send him to a public school, to buy him a practice, or start him in business? Besides, with brashness a man can always make his way in the world." Madame Bovary bit her lips, and the child knocked about the village.

He followed the farm laborers, drove away with clods of earth the ravens that were flying about. He ate blackberries along the hedges, minded the geese with a long switch, went hay-making during harvest, ran about in the woods, played hopscotch under the church porch on rainy days, and at great fêtes begged the beadle to let him toll the bells, that he might hang all his weight on the long rope and feel himself borne upward by it in its swing.

So he grew like an oak; he was strong of hand, ruddy of complexion.

When he was twelve years old his mother had her own way; he began his lessons. The curé took him in hand; but the lessons were so short and irregular that they could not be of much use. They were given at spare moments in the sacristy, standing up, hurriedly, between a baptism and a burial; or else the curé, if he had not to go out, sent for his pupil after the *Angelus*. They went up to his room and settled down; the flies and moths fluttered round the candle. It was close, the child fell asleep, and the good man, beginning to doze with his hands on his stomach, was soon snoring with his mouth wide open. On other occasions, when Monsieur le Curé, on his way back after administering the holy oil to some sick person in the neighborhood, caught sight of Charles playing about the fields, he called him, lectured him for a quarter of an hour, and took advantage of the occasion to make him conjugate his verb at the foot of a tree. The rain interrupted them or an acquaintance passed. All the same he was always pleased with him, and even said the "young man" had a very good memory.

Charles could not go on like this. Madame Bovary took strong steps. Ashamed, or rather tired out, Monsieur Bovary gave in without a struggle, and they waited one year longer, so that the child could take his first communion.

Six months more passed, and the year after Charles was finally sent to school at Rouen. His father took him there towards the end of October, at the time of the St. Romain fair.

It would now be impossible for any of us to remember any thing about him. He was a youth of even temperament, who played in playtime, worked in school-hours, was attentive in class, slept well in the dormitory, and ate well in the refectory. He had for guardian a hardware merchant in the Rue Ganterie, who took him out once a month on Sundays after his shop was shut, sent him for a walk on the quay to look at the boats, and then brought him back to college at seven o'clock before supper. Every Thursday evening he wrote a long letter to his mother with red ink and three wax seals; then he went over his history note-books, or read an old volume of "Anarchasis"[3] that was lying about the study. When he went for walks he talked to the servant, who, like himself, came from the country.

By dint of hard work he kept always about the middle of the class; once even he got an honor mark in natural history. But at the end of his third year his parents withdrew him from the school to make him study medicine, convinced that he could make it to the bachelor's degree by himself.

His mother chose a room for him on the fourth floor of a dyer's she knew, overlooking the Eau-de-Robec.[4] She made arrangements

3. *Voyage du jeune Anarchasis en Grèce* (1788) was a popular account of ancient Greece, by Jean-Jacques Barthélemy (1716–1795).

4. Small river, now covered up, that flows through the poorest neighborhood of Rouen, used as a sewer by the factories that border it, thus suggesting Flaubert's description as *"une ignoble petite Venise."*

for his board, got him furniture, table and two chairs, sent home for an old cherry-tree bedstead, and bought besides a small cast-iron stove with the supply of wood that was to warm her poor child. Then at the end of a week she departed, after a thousand injunctions to be good now that he was going to be left to himself.

The course list that he read on the notice-board stunned him: lectures on anatomy, lectures on pathology, lectures on physiology, lectures on pharmacy, lectures on botany and clinical medicine, and therapeutics, without counting hygiene and materia medica—all names of whose etymologies he was ignorant, and that were to him as so many doors to sanctuaries filled with magnificent darkness.

He understood nothing of it all; it was all very well to listen—he did not follow. Still he worked; he had bound note-books, he attended all the courses, never missed a single lecture. He did his little daily task like a mill-horse, who goes round and round with his eyes bandaged, not knowing what work it is grinding out.

To spare him expense his mother sent him every week by the carrier a piece of veal baked in the oven, with which he lunched when he came back from the hospital, while he sat kicking his feet against the wall. After this he had to run off to lectures, to the operation-room, to the hospital, and return to his home at the other end of the town. In the evening, after the poor dinner of his landlord, he went back to his room and set to work again in his wet clothes, that smoked as he sat in front of the hot stove.

On the fine summer evenings, at the time when the close streets are empty, when the servants are playing shuttle-cock at the doors, he opened his window and leaned out. The river, that makes of this quarter of Rouen a wretched little Venice, flowed beneath him, between the bridges and the railings, yellow, violet, or blue. Working men, kneeling on the banks, washed their bare arms in the water. On poles projecting from the attics, skeins of cotton were drying in the air. Opposite, beyond the roofs, spread the pure sky with the red sun setting. How pleasant it must be at home! How fresh under the beech-tree! And he expanded his nostrils to breathe in the sweet odours of the country which did not reach him.

He grew thin, his figure became taller, his face took a saddened look that made it almost interesting.

Passively, through indifference, he abandoned all the resolutions he had made. Once he missed a lecture; the next day all the lectures; and, enjoying his idleness, little by little he gave up work altogether.

He got into the habit of going to the cafés, and had a passion for dominoes. To shut himself up every evening in the dirty public room, to push about on marble tables the small sheep-bones with black dots, seemed to him a fine proof of his freedom, which raised him in his own esteem. It was beginning to see life, the sweetness of stolen pleasures; and when he entered, he put his hand on the door-handle with a joy almost sensual. Then many things compressed within him expanded; he learned by heart student songs and sang them at gatherings, became enthusiastic about Béranger,[5] learnt how to make punch, and, finally how to make love.

Thanks to these preparatory labors, he failed completely in his examination for his degree of *officier de santé*.[6] He was expected home the same night to celebrate his success.

He started on foot, stopped at the beginning of the village, sent for his mother, and told her all. She excused him, threw the blame of his failure on the injustice of the examiners, encouraged him a little, and took upon herself to set matters straight. It was only five years later that Monsieur Bovary knew the truth; it was old then, and he accepted it. Moreover, he could not believe that a man born of him could be a fool.

So Charles set to work again and crammed for his examination, ceaselessly learning all the old questions by heart. He passed pretty well. What a happy day for his mother! They gave a grand dinner.

Where should he go to practise? To Tostes, where there was only one old doctor. For a long time Madame Bovary had been on the look-out for his death, and the old fellow had barely been packed off when Charles was installed, opposite his place, as his successor.

But it was not everything to have brought up a son, to have had him taught medicine, and discovered Tostes, where he could practise it; he must have a wife. She found him one—the widow of a bailiff at Dieppe, who was forty-five and had an income of twelve hundred francs.

Though she was ugly, as dry as a bone, her face with as many pimples as the spring has buds, Madame Dubuc had no lack of suitors. To attain her ends Madame Bovary had to oust them all, and she even succeeded in very cleverly baffling the intrigues of a pork-butcher backed up by the priests.

Charles had seen in marriage the advent of an easier life, thinking he would be more free to do as he liked with himself and his money. But his wife was master; he had to say this and not say that in company, to fast every Friday, dress as she liked, harass at her bidding those patients who did not pay. She opened his letters, watched his comings and goings, and listened at the partition-wall when women came to consult him in his surgery.

She had to have her chocolate every morning, attentions without end. She constantly complained of her nerves, her chest, her liver.

---

5. Pierre-Jean de Béranger (1780–1857) was an extremely popular writer of songs often exalting the glories of the empire of Napoleon I.

6. The degree of Officier de Santé, instituted during the Revolution, was a kind of second-class medical degree, well below the doctorate. The student was allowed to attend a medical school without having passed the equivalence of the *baccalauréat*. He could only practice in the department in which the diploma had been conferred (Bovary is thus tied down to the vicinity of Rouen) and was not allowed to perform major operations except in the presence of a full-fledged doctor. The diploma was suppressed in 1892.

The noise of footsteps made her ill; when people went away, solitude became odious to her; if they came back, it was doubtless to see her die. When Charles returned in the evening, she stretched forth two long thin arms from beneath the sheets, put them round his neck, and having made him sit down on the edge of the bed, began to talk to him of her troubles: he was neglecting her, he loved another. She had been warned she would be unhappy; and she ended by asking him for a dose of medicine and a little more love.

II

One night towards eleven o'clock they were awakened by the noise of a horse pulling up outside their door. The maid opened the garret-window and parleyed for some time with a man in the street below. He came for the doctor, had a letter for him. Nastasie came downstairs shivering and undid the locks and bolts one after the other. The man left his horse, and, following the servant, suddenly came in behind her. He pulled out from his wool cap with grey topknots a letter wrapped up in a rag and presented it gingerly to Charles, who rested on his elbow on the pillow to read it. Nastasie, standing near the bed, held the light. Madame in modesty had turned to the wall and showed only her back.

This letter, sealed with a small seal in blue wax, begged Monsieur Bovary to come immediately to the farm of the Bertaux to set a broken leg. Now from Tostes to the Bertaux was a good fifteen miles across country by way of Longueville and Saint-Victor. It was a dark night; Madame Bovary junior was afraid of accidents for her husband. So it was decided the stable-boy should go on first; Charles would start three hours later when the moon rose. A boy was to be sent to meet him, in order to show him the way to the farm and open the gates for him.

Towards four o'clock in the morning, Charles, well wrapped up in his cloak, set out for the Bertaux. Still sleepy from the warmth of his bed, he let himself be lulled by the quiet trot of his horse. When it stopped of its own accord in front of those holes surrounded with thorns that are dug on the margin of furrows, Charles awoke with a start, suddenly remembered the broken leg, and tried to call to mind all the fractures he knew. The rain had stopped, day was breaking, and on the branches of the leafless trees birds roosted motionless, their little feathers bristling in the cold morning wind. The flat country stretched as far as eye could see, and the tufts of trees around the farms seemed, at long intervals, like dark violet stains on the vast grey surface, fading on the horizon into the gloom of the sky. Charles from time to time opened his eyes but his mind grew weary, and sleep coming upon him, he soon fell into a doze wherein his recent sensations blending with memories, he became conscious of a double self, at once student and married man, lying in his bed as but now, and crossing the operation theatre as of old.

The warm smell of poultices mingled in his brain with the fresh odour of dew; he heard the iron rings rattling along the curtain-rods of the bed and saw his wife sleeping . . . As he passed Vassonville he came upon a boy sitting on the grass at the edge of a ditch.

"Are you the doctor?" asked the child.

And on Charles's answer he took his wooden shoes in his hands and ran on in front of him.

The *officier de santé,* riding along, gathered from his guide's talk that Monsieur Rouault must be one of the well-to-do farmers. He had broken his leg the evening before on his way home from a Twelfth-night feast at a neighbor's. His wife had been dead for two years. There was only his daughter, who helped him to keep house, with him.

The ruts were becoming deeper; they were approaching the Bertaux. The little farmboy, slipping through a hole in the hedge, disappeared; then he came back to the end of a courtyard to open the gate. The horse slipped on the wet grass; Charles had to stoop to pass under the branches. The watchdogs in their kennels barked, dragging at their chains. As he entered the Bertaux the horse took fright and stumbled.

It was a substantial-looking farm. In the stables, over the top of the open doors, one could see great cart-horses quietly feeding from new racks. Right along the outbuildings extended a large dunghill, smoking at the top, while amidst fowls and turkeys five or six peacocks, the luxury of Cauchois farmyards, were foraging around. The sheepfold was long, the barn high, with walls smooth as a hand. Under the cart-shed were two large carts and four ploughs, with their whips, shafts and harnesses complete, whose fleeces of blue wool were getting soiled by the fine dust that fell from the graneries. The courtyard sloped upwards, planted with trees set out symmetrically, and the chattering noise of a flock of geese was heard near the pond.

A young woman in a blue merino dress with three flounces came to the threshold of the door to receive Monsieur Bovary; she led him to the kitchen, where a large fire was blazing. The servants' breakfast was boiling beside it in small pots of all sizes. Some damp clothes were drying inside the chimney-corner. The shovel, tongs, and the nozzle of the bellows, all of colossal size, shone like polished steel, while along the walls hung many pots and pans in which the clear flame of the hearth, mingling with the first rays of the sun coming in through the window, was mirrored fitfully.

Charles went up to the first floor to see the patient. He found him in his bed, sweating under his bed-clothes, having thrown his cotton nightcap right away from him. He was a fat little man of fifty, with white skin and blue eyes, the fore part of his head bald, and he wore ear-rings. By his side on a chair stood a large decanter of brandy, from which he poured himself out a little from time to time to keep up his spirits; but as soon as he caught sight of the doctor his elation subsided, and instead of swearing, as he had been doing for the last twelve hours, he began to groan feebly.

The fracture was a simple one, without any kind of complication. Charles could not have hoped for an easier case. Then calling to mind the devices of his masters at the bedside of patients, he comforted the sufferer with all sorts of kindly remarks, those caresses of the surgeon that are like the oil they put on scalpels. In order to make some splints a bundle of laths was brought up from the carthouse. Charles selected one, cut it into two pieces and planed it with a fragment of windowpane, while the servant tore up sheets to make bandages, and Mademoiselle Emma tried to sew some pads. As she was a long time before she found her workcase, her father grew impatient; she did not answer, but as she sewed she pricked her fingers, which she then put to her mouth to suck them.

Charles was surprised at the whiteness of her nails. They were shiny, delicate at the tips, more polished than the ivory of Dieppe, and almond-shaped. Yet her hand was not beautiful, perhaps not white enough, and a little hard at the knuckles; besides, it was too long, with no soft inflections in the outlines. Her real beauty was in her eyes. Although brown, they seemed black because of the lashes, and her look came at you frankly, with a candid boldness.

The bandaging over, the doctor was invited by Monsieur Rouault himself to have a bite before he left.

Charles went down into the room on the ground-floor. Knives and forks and silver goblets were laid for two on a little table at the foot of a huge bed that had a canopy of printed cotton with figures representing Turks. There was an odor of iris-root and damp sheets that escaped from a large oak chest opposite the window. On the floor in corners were sacks of flour stuck upright in rows. These were the overflow from the neighboring granary, to which three stone steps led. By way of decoration for the apartment, hanging to a nail in the middle of the wall, whose green paint scaled off from the effects of the saltpeter, was a crayon head of Minerva in a gold frame, underneath which was written in Gothic letters "To my dear Papa."

First they spoke of the patient, then of the weather, of the great cold, of the wolves that infested the fields at night. Mademoiselle Rouault did not at all like the country, especially now that she had to look after the farm almost alone. As the room was chilly, she shivered as she ate. This showed something of her full lips, that she had a habit of biting when silent.

Her neck stood out from a white turned-down collar. Her hair, whose two black folds seemed each of a single piece, so smooth were they, was parted in the middle by a delicate line that curved slightly with the curve of the head; and, just showing the tip of the ear, it was joined behind in a thick chignon, with a wavy movement at the temples that the country doctor saw now for the first time in his life. The upper part of her cheek was rose-coloured. Like a man, she wore a tortoise-shell eyeglass thrust between two buttons of her blouse.

When Charles, after bidding farewell to old Rouault, returned to the room before leaving, he found her standing, her forehead against the window, looking into the garden, where the beanpoles had been knocked down by the wind. She turned around. "Are you looking for something?" she asked.

"My riding crop, if you please," he answered.

He began rummaging on the bed, behind the doors, under the chairs. It had fallen to the ground, between the sacks and the wall. Mademoiselle Emma saw it, and bent over the flour sacks. Charles out of politeness made a dash also, and as he stretched out his arm, at the same moment felt his breast brush against the back of the young girl bending beneath him. She drew herself up, scarlet, and looked at him over her shoulder as she handed him his riding crop.

Instead of returning to the Bertaux in three days as he had promised, he went back the very next day, then regularly twice a week, without counting the visits he paid now and then as if by accident.

Everything, moreover, went well; the patient progressed favorably; and when, at the end of forty-six days, old Rouault was seen trying to walk alone in his "den," Monsieur Bovary began to be looked upon as a man of great capacity. Old Rouault said that he could not have been cured better by the first doctor of Yvetot, or even of Rouen.

As to Charles, he did not stay to ask himself why it was a pleasure to him to go to the Bertaux. Had he done so, he would, no doubt have attributed his zeal to the importance of the case, or perhaps to the money he hoped to make by it. Was it for this, however, that his visits to the farm formed a delightful exception to the barren occupations of his life? On these days he rose early, set off at a gallop, urging on his horse, then got down to wipe his boots in the grass and put on black gloves before entering. He liked seeing himself enter the courtyard, and noticing the gate turn against his shoulder, the cock crow on the wall, the farmboys run to meet him. He liked the granary and the stables; he liked old Rouault, who pressed his hand and called him his saviour; he liked the small wooden shoes of Mademoiselle Emma on the scoured flags of the kitchen—her high heels made her a little taller; and when she walked in front of him, the wooden soles springing up quickly struck with a sharp sound against the leather of her boots.

She always reconducted him to the first step of the porch. When his horse had not yet been brought round she stayed there. They had said "Good-bye"; there was no more talking. The open air wrapped her round, playing with the soft down on the back of her neck, or blew to and fro on her hips her apron-strings, that fluttered like streamers. Once, during a thaw, the bark of the trees in the yard was oozing, the snow melted on the roofs of the buildings; she stood on the threshold, went to fetch her sunshade and opened it. The parasol, made of an iridescent silk that let the sunlight sift through, colored the white skin of her face with shifting reflections. Beneath it, she smiled at the gentle warmth; drops of water fell one by one on the taut silk.

During the first period of Charles's visits to the Bertaux, the younger Madame Bovary never failed to inquire after the invalid, and she had even chosen in the book that she kept on a system of double entry a clean blank page for Monsieur Rouault. But when she heard he had a daughter, she began to make inquiries, and she learnt that Mademoiselle Rouault, brought up at the Ursuline Convent, had received what is called "a good education"; and so knew dancing, geography, drawing, how to embroider and play the piano. That was the last straw.

"So that's why he looks so beaming when he goes to see her," she thought. "That's why he puts on his new waistcoat regardless of the rain. Ah! that woman! that woman!"

And she detested her instinctively. At first she solaced herself by allusions that Charles did not understand, then by casual observations that he let pass for fear of a storm, finally by open apostrophes to which he knew no reply.—Why did he go back to the Bertaux now that Monsieur Rouault was cured and that the bill was still unpaid? Ah! it was because a certain person was there, some one who knew how to talk, to embroider, to be witty. So that was what he liked; he wanted city girls! And she went on:

"Imagine old Rouault's daughter being taken for a city girl! The grandfather was a shepherd and a cousin of theirs barely escaped being sentenced for nearly killing someone in a brawl. Hardly a reason to put on airs, or showing herself in church dressed in silk, like a countess. If it hadn't been for the colza crop last year, the old fellow would have been hard put paying his arrears."

For very weariness Charles left off going to the Bertaux. Héloïse made him swear, his hand on the prayer-book, that he would go there no more, after much sobbing and many kisses, in a great outburst of love. He obeyed then, but the strength of his desire protested against the servility of his conduct; and he thought, with a kind of naïve hypocrisy, that this interdict to see her gave him a sort of right to love her. And then the widow was thin; she had long teeth; wore in all weathers a little black shawl, the edge of which hung down between her shoulder-blades; her bony figure was sheathed in her clothes as if they were a scabbard; they were too short, and displayed her ankles with the laces of her large boots crossed over grey stockings.

Charles's mother came to see them from time to time, but after a few days the daughter-in-law seemed to put her own edge on her, and then, like two knives, they scarified him with their reflections and observations. It was wrong of him to eat so much. Why did he always offer a free drink to everyone who came along? How stubborn of him not to put on flannel underwear!

In the spring it came about that a notary at Ingouville, who managed the widow Dubuc's property, one fine day vanished, taking with him all the money in his office. Héloïse, it is true, still owned, besides a share in a boat valued at six thousand francs, her house in the Rue St. François; and yet, with all this fortune that had been so trumpeted abroad, nothing, excepting perhaps a little furniture and a few clothes, had appeared in the household. The matter had to be gone into. The house at Dieppe was found to be eaten up with mortgages to its foundations; what she had placed with the notary God only knew, and her share in the boat did not exceed three thousand francs. She had lied, the good lady! In his exasperation, Monsieur Bovary the elder, smashing a chair on the stone floor, accused his wife of having caused the misfortune of their son by harnessing him to such a harridan, whose harness wasn't worth her hide. They came to Tostes. Explanations followed. There were scenes. Héloïse in tears, throwing her arms about her husband, conjured him to defend her from his parents. Charles tried to speak up for her. They grew angry and left the house.

But "the blow had struck home." A week after, as she was hanging up some washing in her yard, she was seized with a spitting of blood, and the next day, while Charles had his back turned and was closing the window curtains, she said, "O God!" gave a sigh and fainted. She was dead! What a surprise!

When all was over at the cemetery Charles went home. He found no one downstairs; he went up to the first floor to their room, saw her dress still hanging at the foot of the alcove; then leaning against the writing-table, he stayed until the evening, buried in a sorrowful reverie. She had loved him after all!

III

One morning old Rouault brought Charles the money for setting his leg—seventy-five francs in forty-sou pieces, and a turkey. He had heard of his loss, and consoled him as well as he could.

"I know what it is," said he, clapping him on the shoulder; "I've been through it. When I lost my poor wife, I went into the field to be alone. I fell at the foot of a tree; I cried; I called on God; I talked nonsense to Him. I wanted to be like the moles that I saw on the branches, their insides swarming with maggots, in short, dead, and an end of it. And when I thought that there were others at that very moment, with their wives in their arms, I struck great blows on the earth with my stick. I almost went out of my mind, to the point of not eating; the very idea of going to a café disgusted me—you wouldn't believe it. Well, very slowly, one day following another, a spring on a winter, and an autumn after a summer, this wore away, piece by piece, crumb by crumb; it passed away, it is gone, I should say it has sunk; for something always remains inside, as we would say—a weight here, at one's heart. But since it is the lot of all of us, one must not give way altogether, and, because others have died, want to die too. You must pull yourself together, Monsieur Bovary. It will pass away. Come and see us; my daughter thinks of you time and again, you know, and she says you are forgetting her. Spring will soon be here. We'll have you shoot a rabbit in the field to help you get over your sorrows."

Charles followed his advice. He went back to the Bertaux. He found all as he had left it, that is to say, as it was five months ago. The pear trees were already in blossom, and Farmer Rouault, on his legs again, came and went, making the farm more lively.

Thinking it his duty to heap the greatest attention upon the doctor because of his sad situation, he begged him not to take his hat off, spoke to him in whispers as if he had been ill, and even pretended to be angry because nothing lighter had been prepared for him than for the others, such as a little custard or stewed pears. He told stories. Charles found himself laughing, but the remembrance of his wife suddenly coming back to him depressed him. Coffee was brought in; he thought no more about her.

He thought less of her as he grew accustomed to living alone. The new delight of independence soon made his loneliness bearable. He could now change his meal-times, go in or out without explanation, and when he was very tired stretch himself at full length on his bed. So he nursed and coddled himself and accepted the consolations that were offered him. On the other hand, the death of his wife had not served him ill in his business, since for a month people had been saying, "The poor young man! what a loss!" His name had been talked about, his practice had increased; and, moreover, he could go to the Bertaux just as he liked. He had an aimless hope, and a vague happiness; he thought himself better looking as he brushed his whiskers before the looking-glass.

One day he got there about three o'clock. Everybody was in the fields. He went into the kitchen, but did not at once catch sight of Emma; the outside shutters were closed. Through the chinks of the wood the sun sent across the flooring long fine rays that were broken at the corners of the furniture and trembled along the ceiling. Some flies on the table were crawling up the glasses that had been used, and buzzing as they drowned themselves in the dregs of the cider. The daylight that came in by the chimney made velvet of the soot at the back of the fireplace, and touched with blue the cold cinders. Between the window and the hearth Emma was sewing; she wore no scarf; he could see small drops of perspiration on her bare shoulders.

After the fashion of country folks she asked him to have something to drink. He said no; she insisted, and at last laughingly offered to have a glass of liqueur with him. So she went to fetch a bottle of curacoa from the cupboard, reached down two small glasses, filled one to the brim, poured scarcely anything into the other, and, after having clinked glasses, carried hers to her mouth. As it was almost empty she bent back to drink, her head thrown back, her lips pouting, her neck straining. She laughed at getting none, while with the tip of her tongue passing between her small teeth she licked drop by drop the bottom of her glass.

She sat down again and took up her work, a white cotton stocking she was darning. She worked with her head bent down; she did not speak, nor did Charles. The air coming in under the door blew a little dust over the stone floor; he watched it drift along, and heard nothing but the throbbing in his head and the faint clucking of a hen that had laid an egg in the yard. Emma from time to time cooled her cheeks with the palms of her hands, and cooled these again on the knobs of the huge fire-dogs.

She complained of suffering since the beginning of the spring from giddiness; she asked if sea-baths would do her any good; she began talking of her convent, Charles of his school; words came to them. They went up into her bed-room. She showed him her old music-books, the little prizes she had won, and the oak-leaf crowns, left at the bottom of a cupboard. She spoke to him, too, of her mother, of the country, and even showed him the bed in the garden where, on the first Friday of every month, she gathered flowers to put on her mother's tomb. But their gardener understood nothing about it; servants were so careless. She would have dearly liked, if only for the winter, to live in town, although the length of the fine days made the country perhaps even more wearisome in the summer. And, according to what she was saying, her voice was clear, sharp, or, suddenly all languor, lingering out in modulations that ended almost in murmurs as she spoke to herself, now joyous, opening big naïve eyes, then with her eyelids half closed, her look full of boredom, her thoughts wandering.

Going home at night, Charles went over her words one by one, trying to recall them, to fill out their sense, that he might piece out the life she had lived before he knew her. But he never saw her in his thoughts other than he had seen her the first time, or as he had just left her. Then he asked himself what would become of her—if she would be married, and to whom? Alas! old Rouault was rich, and she!—so beautiful! But Emma's face always rose before his eyes, and a monotone, like the humming of a top, sounded in his ears, "If you should marry after all! if you should marry!" At night he could not sleep; his throat was parched; he was thirsty. He got up to drink from the water-bottle and opened the window. The night was covered with stars, a warm wind blowing in the distance; the dogs were barking. He turned his head towards the Bertaux.

Thinking that, after all, he had nothing to lose, Charles promised himself to ask her in marriage at the earliest opportunity, but each time the fear of not finding the right words sealed his lips.

Old Rouault would not have been sorry to be rid of his daughter, who was of no use to him in the house. In his heart he excused her, thinking her too clever for farming, a calling under the ban of Heaven, since one never saw a millionaire in it. Far from having made a fortune, the old man was losing every year; for if he was good at bargaining and enjoyed the dodges of the trade, he was the poorest of growers or farm managers. He did not willingly take his hands out of his pockets, and did not spare expense for his own comforts, liking to eat and to sleep well, and never to suffer from the cold. He liked old cider, underdone legs of mutton, brandied coffee well beaten up. He took his meals in the kitchen, alone, opposite the fire on a little table brought to him already laid as on the stage.

When, therefore, he perceived that Charles's cheeks grew flushed if near his daughter, which meant that he would propose one of these days, he mulled over the entire matter beforehand. He certainly thought him somewhat weak, not quite the son-in-law he would have liked, but he was said to be well-behaved, prudent with his money as well as learned, and no doubt would not make too many difficulties about the dowry. Now, as old Rouault would soon be forced to sell twenty-two acres of his land as he owed a good deal to the mason, to the harnessmaker, and as the shaft of the cider-press wanted renewing, "If he asks for her," he said to himself, "I'll give her to him."

In the early fall Charles went to spend three days at the Bertaux. The last had passed like the others in procrastinating from hour to hour. Old Rouault was seeing him off; they were walking along a dirt road full of ruts; they were about to part. This was the time. Charles gave himself as far as to the corner of the hedge, and at last, when past it . . .

"Monsieur Rouault," he murmured, "I should like to say something to you."

They stopped. Charles was silent.

"Well, tell me your story. Don't I know all about it?" said old

Rouault, laughing softly.

"Monsieur Rouault—Monsieur Rouault," stammered Charles.

"I ask nothing better," the farmer went on. "Although, no doubt, the little one agrees with me, still we must ask her opinion. So you get off—I'll go back home. If it is 'yes,' you needn't return because of all the people around, and besides it would upset her too much. But so that you may not be biting your fingernails with impatience, I'll open wide the outer shutter of the window against the wall; you can see it from the back by leaning over the hedge."

And he went off.

Charles fastened his horse to a tree; he ran into the road and waited. Half-an-hour passed, then he counted nineteen minutes by his watch. Suddenly a noise was heard against the wall; the shutter had been thrown back; the hook was still quivering.

The next day by nine o'clock he was at the farm. Emma blushed as he entered, and she gave a little forced laugh to hide her embarrassment. Old Rouault embraced his future son-in-law. The discussion of money matters was put off; moreover, there was plenty of time before them, as the marriage could not decently take place till Charles was out of mourning, that is to say, about the spring of the next year.

The winter passed waiting for this. Mademoiselle Rouault was busy with her trousseau. Part of it was ordered at Rouen, and she made herself slips and nightcaps after fashionplates that she borrowed. When Charles visited the farmer, the preparations for the wedding were talked over; they wondered in what room they should have dinner; they dreamed of the number of dishes that would be wanted, and what should be the entrées.

Emma would, on the contrary, have preferred to have a midnight wedding with torches, but old Rouault could not understand such an idea. So there was a wedding at which forty-three persons were present, at which they remained sixteen hours at table, began again the next day, and even carried a little into the following days.

IV

The guests arrived early in carriages, in one-horse chaises, two-wheeled cars, old open gigs, vans with leather curtains, and the young people from the nearer villages in carts, in which they stood up in rows, holding on to the sides so as not to fall, going at a trot and well shaken up. Some came from a distance of thirty miles, from Goderville, from Normanville, and from Cany. All the relatives of both families had been invited, old quarrels had been patched up and near-forgotten acquaintances written to for the occasion.

From time to time one heard the crack of a whip behind the hedge; then the gates opened, a chaise entered. Galloping up to the foot of the steps, it stopped short and emptied its load. They got down from all sides, rubbing knees and stretching arms. The ladies, wearing bonnets, had on dresses in the town fashion, gold watch chains, pelerines with the ends tucked into belts, or little coloured scarfs fastened down behind with a pin, and that left the back of the neck bare. The boys, dressed like their papas, seemed uncomfortable in their new clothes (many that day were wearing their first pair of boots), and by their sides, speaking never a word, wearing the white dress of their first communion lengthened for the occasion, were some big girls of fourteen or sixteen, cousins or elder sisters no doubt, scarlet, bewildered, their hair greasy with rose-pomade, and very much afraid of dirtying their gloves. As there were not enough stable-boys to unharness all the carriages, the gentlemen turned up their sleeves and set about it themselves. According to their different social positions they wore tail-coats, overcoats, shooting-jackets, cutaway-coats: fine tail-coats, redolent of family respectability, that only came out of the wardrobe on state occasions; overcoats with long tails flapping in the wind and round capes and pockets like sacks; shooting-jackets of coarse cloth, generally worn with a cap with a brass-bound peak; very short cutaway-coats with two small buttons in the back, close together like a pair of eyes, and the tails of which seemed cut out of one piece by a carpenter's hatchet. Some, too (but these, you may be sure, would sit at the bottom of the table), wore their best smocks—that is to say, with collars turned down to the shoulders, the back gathered into small plaits and the waist fastened very low down with a stitched belt.

And the shirts stood out from the chests like armour breastplates! Everyone had just had his hair cut; ears stood out from the heads; they had been close-shaven; a few, even, who had had to get up before daybreak, and not been able to see to shave, had diagonal gashes under their noses or cuts the size of a three-franc piece along the jaws, which the fresh air had enflamed during the trip, so that the great white beaming faces were mottled here and there with red spots.

The mairie was a mile and a half from the farm, and they went there on foot, returning in the same way after the ceremony in the church. The procession, first united like one long coloured scarf that undulated across the fields, along the narrow path winding amid the green wheat, soon lengthened out, and broke up into different groups that loitered to talk. The fiddler walked in front with his violin, gay with ribbons at its pegs. Then came the married pair, the relatives, the friends, all following pell-mell; the children stayed behind amusing themselves plucking the bell-flowers from oat-ears, or playing amongst themselves unseen. Emma's dress, too long, trailed a little on the ground; from time to time she stopped to pull it up, and then delicately, with her gloved hands, she picked off the coarse grass and the thistles, while Charles, empty handed, waited till she had finished. Old Rouault, with a new silk hat and the cuffs of his black coat covering his hands up to the nails, gave his arm to Madame Bovary senior. As to Monsieur Bovary senior, who, heartily despising all these people, had come simply in a frockcoat of military cut with one row of buttons—he was exchanging barroom banter with a blond young farmgirl. She bowed, blushed, and did not know what to say. The other wedding guests talked business or played tricks behind each other's backs, egging each other on in advance for the fun that was to come. Those who listened could always catch the squeaking of the fiddler, who went on playing across the fields. When he saw that the rest were far behind he stopped to take breath, slowly rosined his bow, so that the strings should squeak all the louder, then set off again, by turns lowering and raising the neck of his violin, the better to mark time for himself. The noise of the instrument drove away the little birds from afar.

The table was laid under the cart-shed. On it were four roasts of beef, six chicken fricassées, stewed veal, three legs of mutton, and in the middle a fine roast sucking-pig, flanked by four pork sausages with sorrel. At the corners were decanters of brandy. Sweet bottled-cider frothed round the corks, and all the glasses had been filled to the brim with wine beforehand. Large dishes of yellow cream, that trembled with the least shake of the table, had designed on their smooth surface the initials of the newly wedded pair in nonpareil arabesques. A confectioner of Yvetot had been entrusted with the pies and candies. As he had only just started out in the neighborhood, he had taken a lot of trouble, and at dessert he himself brought in a wedding cake that provoked loud cries of wonderment. At its base there was a square of blue cardboard, representing a temple with porticoes, colonnades, and stucco statuettes all round, and in the niches constellations of gilt paper stars; then on the second level was a dungeon of Savoy cake, surrounded by many fortifications in candied angelica, almonds, raisins, and quarters of oranges; and finally, on the upper platform a green field with rocks set in lakes of jam, nutshell boats, and a small Cupid balancing himself in a chocolate swing whose two uprights ended in real roses for balls at the top.

Until night they ate. When any of them were too tired of sitting, they went out for a stroll in the yard, or for a game of darts in the granary, and then returned to table. Some towards the end went to sleep and snored. But with the coffee every one woke up. Then they began songs, showed off tricks, raised heavy weights, competed to see who could pass his head under his arm while keeping a thumb on the table, tried lifting carts on their shoulders, made bawdy jokes, kissed the women. At night when they left, the horses, stuffed up to the nostrils with oats, could hardly be got into the shafts; they kicked, reared, the harness broke, their masters laughed or swore; and all night in the light of the moon along country roads there were runaway carts at full gallop plunging into the ditches, jumping over yard after yard of stones, clambering up the hills, with women leaning out from the tilt to catch hold of the reins.

Those who stayed at the Bertaux spent the night drinking in the kitchen. The children had fallen asleep under the seats.

The bride had begged her father to be spared the usual marriage pleasantries. However, a fishmonger, one of their cousins (who had brought a pair of soles for his wedding present), began to squirt water from his mouth through the keyhole, when old Rouault came up just in time to stop him, and explain to him that the distinguished position of his son-in-law would not allow of such liberties. The cousin was not easily convinced. In his heart he accused old Rouault of being proud, and he joined four or five other guests in a corner, who, through mere chance, had been served the poorer cuts of meat several times over and also considered themselves ill-treated. They were whispering about their host, hoping with covered hints that he would ruin himself.

Madame Bovary, senior, had not opened her mouth all day. She had been consulted neither as to the dress of her daughter-in-law nor as to the arrangement of the feast; she went to bed early. Her husband, instead of following her, sent to Saint-Victor for some cigars, and smoked till daybreak, drinking kirsch-punch, a mixture unknown to the company that added even more to the consideration in which he was held.

Charles, who was anything but quick-witted, did not shine at the wedding. He answered feebly to the puns, *doubles entendres*, compliments, and the customary pleasantries that were dutifully aimed at him as soon as the soup appeared.

The next day, on the other hand, he seemed another man. It was he who might rather have been taken for the virgin of the evening before, whilst the bride gave no sign that revealed anything. The shrewdest did not know what to make of it, and they looked at her when she passed near them with an unbounded concentration of mind. But Charles concealed nothing. He called her "my wife," addressed her by the familiar "tu," asked for her of everyone, looked for her everywhere, and often he dragged her into the yards, where he could be seen from far between the trees, putting his arm round her waist, and walking half-bending over her, ruffling the collar of her blouse with his head.

Two days after the wedding the married pair left. Charles, on account of his patients, could not be away longer. Old Rouault had them driven back in his cart, and himself accompanied them as far as Vassonville. Here he embraced his daughter for the last time, got down, and went his way. When he had gone about a hundred paces he stopped, and as he saw the cart disappearing, its wheels turning in the dust, he gave a deep sigh. Then he remembered his wedding, the old times, the first pregnancy of his wife; he, too, had been very happy the day when he had taken her from her father to his home, and had carried her off riding pillion, trotting through the snow, for it was near Christmas-time, and the country was all white. She held him by one arm, her basket hanging from the other; the wind blew the long lace of her Cauchois headdress so that it sometimes flapped across his mouth, and when he turned his head he saw near him, on his shoulder, her little rosy face, smiling silently under the gold bands of her cap. To warm her hands she put them from time to time in his breast. How long ago it all was! Their son would have been thirty by now. Then he looked back and saw nothing on the road. He felt dreary as an empty house; and tender memories mingling with sad thoughts in his brain, addled by the fumes of the feast, he felt inclined for a moment to take a turn towards the church. As he was afraid, however, that this sight would make him even sadder, he went right away home.

Monsieur and Madame Charles arrived at Tostes about six o'clock. The neighbors came to the windows to see their doctor's new wife.

The old servant presented herself, curtsied to her, apologised for not having dinner ready, and suggested that madame, in the meantime, should look over her house.

v

The brick front was just in a line with the street, or rather the road. Behind the door hung a cloak with a small collar, a bridle, and a black leather cap, and on the floor, in a corner, were a pair of leggings, still covered with dry mud. On the right was the one room that was both dining and sitting room. A canary-yellow paper, relieved at the top by a garland of pale flowers, was puckered everywhere over the badly-stretched canvas; white calico curtains with a red border hung crossways the length of the window; and on the narrow mantelpiece a clock with a head of Hippocrates shone resplendent between two plate candlesticks under oval shades. On the other side of the passage was Charles's consulting-room, a little room about six paces wide, with a table, three chairs, and an office-chair. Volumes of the "Dictionary of Medical Science," uncut, but the binding rather the worse for the successive sales through which they had gone, occupied almost alone the six shelves of a pinewood bookcase. The smell of sauces penetrated through the walls when he saw patients, just as in the kitchen one could hear the people coughing in the consulting-room and recounting their whole histories. Then, opening on the yard, where the stable was, came a large dilapidated room with a stove, now used as a wood-house, cellar, and pantry, full of old rubbish, of empty casks, discarded garden tools, and a mass of dusty things whose use it was impossible to guess.

The garden, longer than wide, ran between two mud walls covered with espaliered apricot trees, to a thorn hedge that separated it from the field. In the middle was a slate sundial on a brick pedestal; four flower-beds with eglantines surrounded symmetrically the more useful vegetable garden. Right at the bottom, under the spruce bushes, a plaster priest was reading his breviary.

Emma went upstairs. The first room was not furnished, but in the second, the conjugal bedroom, was a mahogany bedstead in an alcove with red drapery. A shell-box adorned the chest of drawers, and on the secretary near the window a bouquet of orange blossoms tied with white satin ribbons stood in a bottle. It was a bride's bouquet: the other one's. She looked at it. Charles noticed; he took the bouquet, carried it to the attic, while Emma seated in an armchair (they were putting her things down around her) thought of her bridal flowers packed up in a bandbox, and wondered, dreaming, what would be done with them if she were to die.

During the first days she kept busy thinking about changes in the house. She took the shades off the candlesticks, had new wall-paper put up, the staircase repainted, and seats made in the garden round the sundial; she even inquired how she could get a basin with a jet fountain and fishes. Finally her husband, knowing that she liked to drive out, picked up a second-hand dogcart, which, with new lamps and a splashboard in striped leather, looked almost like a tilbury.

He was happy then, and without a care in the world. A meal together, a walk in the evening on the highroad, a gesture of her hands over her hair, the sight of her straw hat hanging from the window-fastener, and many other things of which he had never suspected how pleasant they could be, now made up the endless round of his happiness. In bed, in the morning, by her side, on the pillow, he watched the sunlight sinking into the down on her fair cheek, half hidden by the ribbons of her nightcap. Seen thus closely, her eyes looked to him enlarged, especially when, on waking up, she opened and shut her eyelids rapidly many times. Black in the shade, dark blue in broad daylight, they had, as it were, depths of successive colors that, more opaque in the center, grew more transparent towards the surface of the eye. His own eyes lost themselves in these depths and he could see himself mirrored in miniature, down to his shoulders, with his scarf round his head and the top of his shirt open. He rose. She came to the window to see him off, and stayed leaning on the sill between two pots of geranium, clad in her dressing-gown hanging loosely about her. Charles, in the street, buckled his spurs, his foot on the mounting stone, while she talked to him from above, picking with her mouth some scrap of flower or leaf that she blew out at him and which, eddying, floating, described semicircles in the air like a bird, caught before it reached the ground in the ill-groomed mane of the old white mare standing motionless at the door. Charles from horseback threw her a kiss; she answered with a nod; she shut the window, and he set off. And then, along the endless dusty ribbon of the highroad, along the deep lanes that the trees bent over as in arbours, along paths where the wheat reached to the knees, with the sun on his back and the morning air in his nostrils, his heart full of the joys of the past night, his mind at rest, his flesh at ease, he went on, re-chewing his happiness, like those who after dinner taste again the truffles which they are digesting.

Until now what good had he had of his life? His time at school, when he remained shut up within the high walls, alone, in the midst of companions richer than he or cleverer at their work, who laughed at his accent, who jeered at his clothes, and whose mothers came to the school with cakes in their muffs? Later on, when he studied medicine, and never had his purse full enough to take out dancing some little work-girl who would have become his mistress? Afterwards, he had lived fourteen months with the widow, whose feet in bed were cold as icicles. But now he had for life this beautiful woman whom he adored. For him the universe did not extend beyond the silky circumference of her petticoat. He reproached himself for not loving her enough; he wanted to see her again, turned back quickly, ran up the stairs with a beating heart. Emma, in her room, was dressing; he came up on tiptoe, kissed her back; she cried out in surprise.

He could not keep from constantly touching her comb, her rings, her scarf; sometimes he gave her great sounding kisses with all his mouth on her cheeks, or else little kisses in a row all along her bare arm from the tip of her fingers up to her shoulder, and she put him away half-smiling, half-annoyed, as one does with a clinging child.

Before marriage she thought herself in love; but since the happiness that should have followed failed to come, she must, she thought, have been mistaken. And Emma tried to find out what one meant exactly in life by the words *bliss, passion, ecstasy,* that had seemed to her so beautiful in books.

VI

She had read "Paul and Virginia,"[7] and she had dreamed of the little bamboo-house, the negro Domingo, the dog Fidèle, but above all of the sweet friendship of some dear little brother, who seeks red fruit for you on trees taller than steeples, or who runs barefoot over the sand, bringing you a bird's nest.

When she was thirteen, her father himself took her to town to

7. *Paul et Virginie* (1784) is a story of the sentimental and tragic love of two young people on the tropical island of Ile de France (today, Mauritius). It was the most popular work of Bernardin de Saint-Pierre (1737–1814).

place her in the convent. They stopped at an inn in the St. Gervais quarter, where, at their supper, they used painted plates that set forth the story of Mademoiselle de la Vallière.[8] The explanatory legends, chipped here and there by the scratching of knives, all glorified religion, the tendernesses of the heart, and the pomps of court.

Far from being bored at first at the convent, she took pleasure in the society of the good sisters, who, to amuse her, took her to the chapel, which one entered from the refectory by a long corridor. She played very little during recreation hours, knew her catechism well, and it was she who always answered the Vicar's difficult questions. Living thus, without ever leaving the warm atmosphere of the class-rooms, and amid these pale-faced women wearing rosaries with brass crosses, she was softly lulled by the mystic languor exhaled in the perfumes of the altar, the freshness of the holy water, and the lights of the tapers. Instead of following mass, she looked at the pious vignettes with their azure borders in her book, and she loved the sick lamb, the sacred heart pierced with sharp arrows, or the poor Jesus sinking beneath the cross he carried. She tried, by way of mortification, to eat nothing a whole day. She puzzled her head to find some vow to fulfil.

When she went to confession, she invented little sins in order that she might stay there longer, kneeling in the shadow, her hands joined, her face against the grating beneath the whispering of the priest. The comparisons of betrothed, husband, celestial lover, and eternal marriage, that recur in sermons, stirred within her soul depths of unexpected sweetness.

In the evening, before prayers, there was some religious reading in the study. On week-nights it was some abstract of sacred history or the Lectures of the Abbé Frayssinous,[9] and on Sundays passages from the "Génie du Christianisme,"[10] as a recreation. How she listened at first to the sonorous lamentations of romantic melancholy re-echoing through the world and eternity! If her childhood had been spent in the shops of a busy city section, she might perhaps have opened her heart to those lyrical invasions of Nature, which usually come to us only through translation in books. But she knew the country too well; she knew the lowing of cattle, the milking, the ploughs. Accustomed to the quieter aspects of life, she turned instead to its tumultuous parts. She loved the sea only for the sake of its storms, and the green only when it was scattered among ruins. She had to gain some personal profit from things and she rejected as

---

8. One of Louis XIV's mistresses, whose mythologized character is familiar to all readers of Alexandre Dumas's *Le Vicomte de Bragelonne* (a sequel to *The Three Musketeers*).

9. Denis de Frayssinous (1765–1841) was a popular preacher who wrote a *Défense du Christianisme* (1825). Under Louis XVIII he became a bishop and minister of ecclesiastical affairs.

10. *Le Génie du Christianisme* (1802) by François-René de Chateaubriand (1768–1848) was an enormously influential book celebrating the truths and beauties of Roman Catholicism, just before Napoleon's concordat with Rome.

useless whatever did not contribute to the immediate satisfaction of her heart's desires—being of a temperament more sentimental than artistic, looking for emotions, not landscapes.

At the convent there was an old maid who came for a week each month to mend the linen. Patronised by the clergy, because she belonged to an ancient family of noblemen ruined by the Revolution, she dined in the refectory at the table of the good sisters, and after the meal chatted with them for a while before going back to her work. The girls often slipped out from the study to go and see her. She knew by heart the love-songs of the last century, and sang them in a low voice as she stitched away. She told stories, gave them news, ran their errands in the town, and on the sly lent the big girls some of the novels, that she always carried in the pockets of her apron, and of which the lady herself swallowed long chapters in the intervals of her work. They were all about love, lovers, sweethearts, persecuted ladies fainting in lonely pavilions, postilions killed at every relay, horses ridden to death on every page, sombre forests, heart-aches, vows, sobs, tears and kisses, little boatrides by moonlight, nightingales in shady groves, gentlemen brave as lions, gentle as lambs, virtuous as no one ever was, always well dressed, and weeping like fountains. For six months, then, a fifteen year old Emma dirtied her hands with the greasy dust of old lending libraries. With Walter Scott, later on, she fell in love with historical events, dreamed of guardrooms, old oak chests and minstrels. She would have liked to live in some old manor-house, like those longwaisted chatelaines who, in the shade of pointed arches, spent their days leaning on the stone, chin in hand, watching a white-plumed knight galloping on his black horse from the distant fields. At this time she had a cult for Mary Stuart and enthusiastic veneration for illustrious or unhappy women. Joan of Arc, Héloïse,[11] Agnès Sorel,[12] the beautiful Ferronière, and Clémence Isaure stood out to her like comets in the dark immensity of history, where also were seen, lost in shadow, and all unconnected, St. Louis[13] with his oak, the dying Bayard,[14] some cruelties of Louis XI,[15] a little of St. Bartholomew's,[16] the plume of the Béarnais, and always the remembrance of the painted plates glorifying Louis XIV.

11. Héloïse was famous for her love affair with the philosopher Abelard (1101–1164).

12. Agnès Sorel (1422–1450) was a mistress of Charles VII, rumored to have been poisoned by the future Louis XI; *"la belle Ferronière"* (died in 1540) was one of François I's mistresses, wife of the lawyer Le Ferron who is said to have contracted syphilis for the mere satisfaction of passing it on to the king; Clémence Isaure is a half-fictional lady from Toulouse (fourteenth century), popularized in a novel by Florian as an incarnation of the mystical poetry of the troubadours.

13. St. Louis was King of France, Louis IX (1215–1270). He led the seventh and eighth crusades. He was can-onized in 1297. According to tradition he dispensed justice under an oak tree at Vincennes (near Paris).

14. Bayard (Pierre du Terrail, seigneur de, 1473–1524) was one of the most famous French captains, distinguishing himself by feats of bravery during the wars of Francis I. He was killed in 1524. Dying, he chided the connétable de Bourbon for his treason in a famous speech.

15. Louis XI was born in 1421 and was king from 1461 to 1483. He ruthlessly suppressed the rebellious noblemen.

16. St. Bartholomew was the massacre of the Protestants ordered by Catherine de Medici in the night of August 23, 1572.

In the music-class, the ballads she sang were all about little angels with golden wings, madonnas, lagunes, gondoliers; harmless-sounding compositions that, in spite of the inanity of the style and the vagueness of the melody, enabled one to catch a glimpse of the tantalizing phantasmagoria of sentimental realities. Some of her companions brought keepsakes given them as new year's gifts to the convent. These had to be hidden; it was quite an undertaking; they were read in the dormitory. Delicately handling the beautiful satin bindings, Emma looked with dazzled eyes at the names of the unknown authors, who had signed their verses for the most part as counts or viscounts.

She trembled as she blew back the thin transparent paper over the engraving and saw it folded in two and fall gently against the page. Here behind the balustrade of a balcony was a young man in a short cloak, holding in his arms a young girl in a white dress who was wearing an alms-bag at her belt; or there were nameless portraits of English ladies with fair curls, who looked at you from under their round straw hats with their large clear eyes. Some could be seen lounging in their carriages, gliding through parks, a grey-hound bounding along ahead of the equipage, driven at a trot by two small postilions in white breeches. Others, dreaming on sofas with an open letter, gazed at the moon through a slightly open window half draped by a black curtain. The innocent ones, a tear on their cheeks, were kissing doves through the bars of a Gothic cage, or, smiling, their heads on one side, were plucking the leaves of a marguerite with their taper fingers, that curved at the tips like peaked shoes. And you, too, were there, Sultans with long pipes reclining beneath arbours in the arms of Bayadères; Giaours, curved swords, fezzes; and you especially, pale landscapes of dithyrambic lands, that often show us at once palm-trees and firs, tigers on the right, a lion to the left, Tartar minarets on the horizon, Roman ruins in the foreground with some kneeling camels besides; the whole framed by a very neat virgin forest, and with a great perpendicular sunbeam trembling in the water, where, sharply edged on a steel-grey background, white swans are swimming here and there.

And the shade of the oil lamp fastened to the wall above Emma's head lighted up all these pictures of the world, that passed before her one by one in the silence of the dormitory, and to the distant noise of some belated carriage still rolling down the Boulevards.

When her mother died she cried much the first few days. She had a funeral picture made with the hair of the deceased, and, in a letter sent to the Bertaux full of sad reflections on life, she asked to be buried later on in the same grave. The old man thought she must be ill, and came to see her. Emma was secretly pleased that she had reached at a first attempt the rare ideal of delicate lives, never attained by mediocre hearts. She let herself meander along with Lamartine, listened to harps on lakes, to all the songs of dying swans, to the falling of the leaves, the pure virgins ascending to heaven, and the voice of the Eternal discoursing down the valleys. She soon grew tired but wouldn't admit it, continued from habit first, then out of vanity, and at last was surprised to feel herself consoled, and with no more sadness at heart than wrinkles on her brow.

The good nuns, who had been so sure of her vocation, perceived with great astonishment that Mademoiselle Rouault seemed to be slipping from them. They had indeed been so lavish to her of prayers, retreats, novenas, and sermons, they had so often preached the respect due to saints and martyrs, and given so much good advice as to the modesty of the body and the salvation of her soul, that she did as tightly reigned horses: she pulled up short and the bit slipped from her teeth. This nature, positive in the midst of its enthusiasms, that had loved the church for the sake of the flowers, and music for the words of the songs, and literature for the passions it excites, rebelled against the mysteries of faith as it had rebelled against discipline, as something alien to her constitution. When her father took her from school, no one was sorry to see her go. The Lady Superior even thought that she had of late been less than reverent toward the community.

Emma, at home once more, first took pleasure in ruling over servants, then grew disgusted with the country and missed her convent. When Charles came to the Bertaux for the first time, she thought herself quite disillusioned, with nothing more to learn, and nothing more to feel.

But the uneasiness of her new position, or perhaps the disturbance caused by the presence of this man, had sufficed to make her believe that she at last felt that wondrous passion which, till then, like a great bird with rose-coloured wings, hung in the splendor of poetic skies;—and now she could not think that the calm in which she lived was the happiness of her dreams.

VII

She thought, sometimes, that, after all, this was the happiest time of her life: the honeymoon, as people called it. To taste the full sweetness of it, it would no doubt have been necessary to fly to those lands with sonorous names where the days after marriage are full of the most suave laziness! In post-chaises behind blue silken curtains, one rides slowly up steep roads, listening to the song of the postilion re-echoed by the mountains, along with the bells of goats and the muffled sound of a waterfall. At sunset on the shores of gulfs one breathes in the perfume of lemon-trees; then in the evening on the villa-terraces above, one looks hand in hand at the stars, making plans for the future. It seemed to her that certain places on earth must bring happiness, as a plant peculiar to the soil, and that cannot thrive elsewhere. Why could not she lean over balconies in Swiss châlets, or enshrine her melancholy in a Scotch cottage, with a husband dressed in a black velvet coat with long tails, and thin shoes, a pointed hat and frills?

Perhaps she would have liked to confide all these things to some one. But how tell an undefinable uneasiness, changing as the clouds, unstable as the winds? Words failed her and, by the same token, the opportunity, the courage.

If Charles had but wished it, if he had guessed, if his look had but once met her thought, it seemed to her that a sudden bounty would have come from her heart, as the fruit falls from a tree when shaken by a hand. But as the intimacy of their life became deeper, the greater became the gulf that kept them apart.

Charles's conversation was commonplace as a street pavement, and every one's ideas trooped through it in their everyday garb, without exciting emotion, laughter, or thought. He had never had the curiosity, he said, while he lived at Rouen, to go to the theatre to see the actors from Paris. He could neither swim, nor fence, nor shoot, and one day he could not explain some term of horsemanship to her that she had come across in a novel.

A man, on the contrary, should he not know everything, excel in manifold activities, initiate you into the energies of passion, the refinements of life, all mysteries? But this one taught nothing, knew nothing, wished nothing. He thought her happy; and she resented this easy calm, this serene heaviness, the very happiness she gave him.

Sometimes she would draw; and it was great amusement to Charles to stand there bolt upright and watch her bend over her paper, with eyes half-closed the better to see her work, or rolling, between her fingers, little bread-pellets. As to the piano, the more quickly her fingers glided over it the more he wondered. She struck the notes with aplomb, and ran from top to bottom of the key-board without a break. Thus shaken up, the old instrument, whose strings buzzed, could be heard at the other end of the village when the window was open, and often the bailiff's clerk, passing along the highroad bareheaded and in slippers, stopped to listen, his sheet of paper in his hand.

Emma, on the other hand, knew how to look after her house. She sent the patients' accounts in well-phrased letters that had no suggestion of a bill. When they had a neighbor to dinner on Sundays, she managed to have some tasty dish, knew how to pile the plums in pyramids on vine-leaves, how to serve jam turned out on a plate, and even spoke of buying finger bowls for dessert. From all this much consideration was extended to Bovary.

Charles finished by rising in his own esteem for possessing such a wife. He showed with pride in the sitting-room two small pencil sketches by her that he had had framed in very large frames, and hung up against the wall-paper by long green cords. People returning from mass saw him standing on his doorstep, wearing beautiful carpet slippers.

He came home late—at ten o'clock, at midnight sometimes. Then he asked for something to eat, and as the servant had gone to bed, Emma waited on him. He took off his coat to dine more at his ease. He told her, one after the other, the people he had met, the villages where he had been, the prescriptions he had written, and, well pleased with himself, he finished the remainder of the boiled beef, peeled the crust of his cheese, munched an apple, finished the wine, and then went to bed, lay on his back and snored.

As he had been for a long time accustomed to wear nightcaps, his handkerchief would not keep down over his ears, so that his hair in the morning was all dishevelled and whitened with the feathers of the pillow, whose strings came untied during the night. He always wore thick boots that had two long creases over the instep running obliquely towards the ankle, while the upper part continued in a straight line as if stretched on a wooden foot. He said that this was quite good enough for someone who lived in the country.

His mother approved of his thrift, for she came to see him as before, after there had been some violent row at her place; and yet the elder Madame Bovary seemed prejudiced against her daughter-in-law. She thought she was living above her means; the wood, sugar and candles vanished as in a large establishment, and the amount of stovewood used in the kitchen would have been enough for twenty-five courses. She straightened the linen chests, and taught her to keep an eye on the butcher when he brought the meat. Emma had to accept these lessons lavished upon her, and the words "daughter" and "mother" were exchanged all day long, accompanied by little quiverings of the lips, each one uttering sweet words in a voice trembling with anger.

In Madame Dubuc's time the old woman felt that she was still the favourite; but now the love of Charles for Emma seemed to her a desertion from her tenderness, an encroachment upon what was hers, and she watched her son's happiness in sad silence, as a ruined man looks through the windows at people dining in his old house. She recalled to him as remembrances her troubles and her sacrifices, and, comparing these with Emma's casual ways, came to the conclusion that it was not reasonable to adore her so exclusively.

Charles knew not what to answer: he respected his mother, and he loved his wife infinitely; he considered the judgment of the one infallible, and yet he thought the conduct of the other irreproachable. When Madame Bovary had gone, he tried timidly and in the same terms to hazard one or two of the more anodyne observations he had heard from his mamma. Emma proved to him with a word that he was mistaken, and sent him off to his patients.

And yet, in accord with theories she believed right, she wanted to experience love with him. By moonlight in the garden she recited all the passionate rhymes she knew by heart, and, sighing, sang to him many melancholy adagios; but she found herself as calm after this as before, and Charles seemed neither more amorous, nor more moved.

When she had thus for a while struck the flint on her heart without getting a spark, incapable, moreover, of understanding what she did not experience or of believing anything that did not take on a conventional form, she persuaded herself without difficulty that Charles's passion was no longer very ardent. His outbursts became regular; he embraced her at certain fixed times. It was one habit among other habits, like a familiar dessert after the monotony of dinner.

A gamekeeper, whom the doctor had cured of a lung infection, had given madame a little Italian greyhound; she took her out walking, for she went out sometimes in order to be alone for a moment, and not to see before her eyes the eternal garden and the dusty road.

She went as far as the beeches of Banneville, near the deserted pavilion which forms an angle on the field side of the wall. Amidst the grass of the ditches grow long reeds with sharp-edged leaves that cut you.

She began by looking round her to see if nothing had changed since she had last been there. She found again in the same places the foxgloves and wallflowers, the beds of nettles growing round the big stones, and the patches of lichen along the three windows, whose shutters, always closed, were rotting away on their rusty iron bars. Her thoughts, aimless at first, wandered at random, like her greyhound, who ran round and round in the fields, yelping after the yellow butterflies, chasing the field-mice, or nibbling the poppies on the edge of a wheatfield. Then gradually her ideas took definite shape, and, sitting on the grass that she dug up with little pricks of her sunshade, Emma repeated to herself:—Why, for Heaven's sake, did I marry?

She asked herself if by some other chance combination it would not have been possible to meet another man; and she tried to imagine what would have been these unrealised events, this different life, this unknown husband. All, surely, could not be like this one. He might have been handsome, witty, distinguished, attractive, like, no doubt, the men her old companions of the convent had married. What were they doing now? In town, among the crowded streets, the buzzing theatres and the lights of the ball-room, they were living lives where the heart expands and the senses blossom out. As for her, her life was cold as a garret facing north, and ennui, the silent spider, was weaving its web in the darkness, in every corner of her heart. She recalled graduation day, when she mounted the platform to receive her little wreaths. With her hair in long plaits, in her white frock and open prunella shoes she had a pretty way, and when she went back to her seat, the gentlemen bent over to congratulate her; the courtyard was full of carriages; farewells were called to her through their windows; the music-master with his violin-case bowed in passing by. How far off all this! How far away!

She called Djali,[17] took her between her knees, and smoothed the long, delicate head, saying, "Come, kiss your mistress, you who are free of cares."

Then noting the melancholy face of the graceful animal, who yawned slowly, she softened, and comparing her to herself, spoke to her aloud as to somebody in pain whom one is consoling.

Occasionally there came gusts of wind, breezes from the sea rolling in one sweep over the whole plateau of the Caux country, which brought to these fields a salt freshness. The rushes, close to the ground, whistled; the branches of the beech trees trembled in a swift rustling, while their crowns, ceaselessly swaying, kept up a deep murmur. Emma drew her shawl round her shoulders and rose.

In the avenue a green light dimmed by the leaves lit up the short moss that crackled softly beneath her feet. The sun was setting; the sky showed red between the branches, and the trunks of the trees, uniform, and planted in a straight line, seemed a brown colonnade standing out against a background of gold. A fear took hold of her; she called Djali, and hurriedly returned to Tostes by the highroad, threw herself into an armchair, and for the rest of the evening did not speak.

But towards the end of September something extraordinary befell her: she was invited by the Marquis d'Andervilliers to Vaubyessard.

Secretary of State under the Restoration, the Marquis, anxious to re-enter political life, had long since been preparing for his candidature to the Chamber of Deputies. In the winter he distributed a great deal of firewood, and in the Conseil Général always enthusiastically demanded new roads for his arrondissement. During the height of the Summer heat he had suffered from an abcess in the mouth, which Charles had cured as if by miracle by giving a timely

17. Djali is the name of the little she-goat in Hugo's *Notre Dame de Paris.*

little touch with the lancet. The steward sent to Tostes to pay for the operation reported in the evening that he had seen some superb cherries in the doctor's little garden. Now cherry-trees did not thrive at Vaubyessard; the Marquis asked Bovary for some offshoots. He made it his business to thank him personally and, on that occasion, saw Emma. He thought she had a pretty figure, and that she did not greet him like a peasant; so that he did not think he was going beyond the bounds of condescension, nor, on the other hand, making a mistake, in inviting the young couple.

One Wednesday at three o'clock, Monsieur and Madame Bovary, seated in their dog-cart, set out for Vaubyessard, with a great trunk strapped on behind and a hat-box in front on the apron. Besides these Charles held a carton between his knees.

They arrived at nightfall, just as the lamps in the park were being lit to show the way for the carriages.

VIII

The château, a modern building in Italian style, with two projecting wings and three flights of steps, lay at the foot of an immense lawn, on which some cows were grazing among clumps of large trees set out at regular intervals, while large beds of arbutus, rhododendron, syringas and snowballs bulged out their irregular clusters of green along the curve of the gravel path. A river flowed under a bridge; through the mist one could distinguish buildings with thatched roofs scattered over the field bordered by two gently-sloping well-timbered hillocks, and in the background amid the trees rose in two parallel lines the coach-houses and stables, all that was left of the ruined old château.

Charles's dog-cart pulled up before the middle flight of steps; servants appeared; the Marquis came forward, and offering his arm to the doctor's wife, conducted her to the vestibule.

It was paved with marble slabs and seemed very lofty; the sound of footsteps and that of voices re-echoed through it as in a church. Opposite rose a straight staircase, and on the left a gallery overlooking the garden led to the billiard room, from where the click of the ivory balls could be heard immediately upon entering. As she crossed it to go to the drawing-room, Emma saw standing round the table men with grave faces, their chins resting on high cravats. They all wore orders, and smiled silently as they made their strokes. On the dark wainscoting of the walls large gold frames bore at the bottom names written in black letters. She read: "Jean-Antoine d'Andervilliers d'Yverbonville, Count de la Vaubyessard and Baron de la Fresnaye, killed at the battle of Coutras[18] on the 20th of October 1587." And on another: "Jean-Antoine-Henry-Guy d'Andervilliers de la Vaubyessard, Admiral of France and Chevalier of

18. Battle of Coutras (in the Gironde) was won by Henri de Navarre against the   Duke de Joyeuse (1587).

the Order of St. Michael, wounded at the battle of the Hougue-Saint-Vaast on the 29th of May 1692; died at Vaubyessard on the 23rd of January 1693." One could hardly make out the next ones, for the light of the lamps lowered over the green cloth threw a dim shadow round the room. Burnishing the horizontal pictures, it broke up in delicate lines among the cracks in the varnish, and from all these great black squares framed in gold stood out here and there some lighter portion of the painting—a pale brow, two eyes that looked at you, wigs resting on the powdered shoulder of red coats, or the buckle of a garter above a well-rounded calf.

The Marquis opened the drawing-room door; one of the ladies (the Marquise herself) came to meet Emma. She made her sit down by her on an ottoman, and began talking to her as amicably as if she had known her a long time. She was a woman of about forty, with fine shoulders, a hook nose, a drawling voice, and on this evening she wore over her brown hair a simple guipure fichu that fell in a point at the back. A blond young woman sat by her side in a high-backed chair, and gentlemen with flowers in their button-holes were talking to ladies round the fire.

At seven dinner was served. The men, who were in the majority, sat down at the first table in the vestibule; the ladies at the second in the dining-room with the Marquis and Marquise.

Emma, on entering, felt herself wrapped round as by a warm breeze, a blending of the perfume of flowers and of the fine linen, of the fumes of the roasts and the odour of the truffles. The candles in the candelabra threw their lights on the silver dish covers; the cut crystal, covered with a fine mist of steam, reflected pale rays of light; bouquets were placed in a row the whole length of the table; and in the large-bordered plates each napkin, arranged after the fashion of a bishop's mitre, held between its two gaping folds a small oval-shaped roll. The red claws of lobsters hung over the dishes; rich fruit in woven baskets was piled up on moss; the quails were dressed in their own plumage, smoke was rising; and in silk stockings, knee-breeches, white cravat, and frilled shirt, the steward, grave as a judge, passed between the shoulders of the guests, offering ready-carved dishes and, with a flick of the spoon, landed on one's plate the piece one had chosen. On the large porcelain stove inlaid with copper baguettes the statue of a woman, draped to the chin, gazed motionless on the crowded room.

Madame Bovary noticed that many ladies had not put their gloves in their glasses.[19]

At the upper end of the table, alone amongst all these women,

---

19. The ladies in the provinces, unlike their Paris counterparts, did not drink wine at public dinner parties, and signified their intention by putting their gloves in their wine-glasses. The fact that they fail to do so suggests to Emma the high degree of sophistication of the company.

bent over his full plate, and his napkin tied round his neck like a child, an old man sat eating, letting drops of gravy drip from his mouth. His eyes were bloodshot, and he wore his hair in a little queue tied with a black ribbon. He was the Marquis's father-in-law, the old Duke de Laverdière, once on a time favourite of the Count d'Artois, in the days of the Marquis de Conflans' hunting-parties at le Vaudreuil, and had been, it was said, the lover of Queen Marie Antoinette, between Monsieur de Coigny and Monsieur de Lauzun. He had lived a life of loud dissipation, full of duels, bets, elopements; he had squandered his fortune and frightened all his family. A servant behind his chair shouted in his ear, in reply to his mutterings, the names of the dishes that he pointed to, and constantly Emma's eyes turned involuntarily to this old man with hanging lips, as to something extraordinary. He had lived at court and slept in the bed of queens!

Iced champagne was poured out. Emma shivered all over as she felt its cold in her mouth. She had never seen pomegranates nor tasted pineapples. Even the powdered sugar seemed to her whiter and finer than elsewhere.

The ladies afterwards retired to their rooms to prepare for the ball.

Emma made her toilette with the fastidious care of an actress on her début. She did her hair according to the directions of the hairdresser, and put on the barège dress spread out upon the bed. Charles's trousers were tight across the belly.

"My trouser-straps will be rather awkward for dancing," he said.

"Dancing?" repeated Emma.

"Yes!"

"Why, you must be mad! They would make fun of you; stay in your place, as it becomes a doctor."

Charles was silent. He walked up and down waiting for Emma to finish dressing.

He saw her from behind in the mirror between two lights. Her black eyes seemed blacker than ever. Her hair, gently undulating towards the ears, shone with a blue lustre; a rose in her chignon trembled on its mobile stalk, with artificial dewdrops on the tip of the leaves. She wore a gown of pale saffron trimmed with three bouquets of pompon roses mixed with green.

Charles came and kissed her on her shoulder.

"Don't touch me!" she cried; "I'll be all rumpled."

One could hear the flourish of the violin and the notes of a horn. She went downstairs restraining herself from running.

Dancing had begun. Guests were arriving and crowding the room. She sat down on a bench near the door.

The quadrille over, the floor was occupied by groups of talking men and by servants in livery bearing large trays. Along the line of seated women painted fans were fluttering, bouquets half-hid smiling faces, and gold-stoppered scent-bottles were turned in half-clenched hands, with white gloves outlining the nail and tightening on the flesh at the wrists. Lace trimmings, diamond brooches, medallion bracelets trembled on blouses, gleamed on breasts, clinked on bare arms. The hair, well smoothed over the temples and knotted at the nape, bore crowns, or bunches, or sprays of myosotis, jasmine, pomegranate blossoms, wheat-sprays and corn-flowers. Calmly seated in their places, mothers with forbidding countenances were wearing red turbans.

Emma's heart beat rather faster when, her partner holding her by the tips of the fingers, she took her place in a line with the dancers, and waited for the first note to start. But her emotion soon vanished, and, swaying to the rhythm of the orchestra, she glided forward with slight movements of the neck. A smile rose to her lips at certain delicate phrases of the violin, that sometimes played alone while the other instruments were silent; one could hear the clear clink of the louis d'or that were being thrown down upon the card-tables in the next room; then all struck in again, the trumpet uttered its sonorous note, feet marked time, skirts swelled and rustled, hands touched and parted; the same eyes that had been lowered returned to gaze at you again.

A few men (some fifteen or so), of twenty-five to forty, scattered here and there among the dancers or talking at the doorways, distinguished themselves from the crowd by a certain family-air, whatever their differences in age, dress, or countenance.

Their clothes, better made, seemed of finer cloth, and their hair, brought forward in curls towards the temples, glossy with more delicate pomades. They had the complexion of wealth,—that clear complexion that is heightened by the pallor of porcelain, the shimmer of satin, the veneer of old furniture, and that a well-ordered diet of exquisite food maintains at its best. Their necks moved easily in their low cravats, their long whiskers fell over their turned-down collars, they wiped their lips upon handkerchiefs with embroidered initials that gave forth a subtle perfume. Those who were beginning to grow old had an air of youth, while there was something mature in the faces of the young. Their indifferent eyes had the appeased expression of daily-satiated passions, and through all their gentleness of manner pierced that peculiar brutality that stems from a steady command over half-tame things, for the exercise of one's strength and the amusement of one's vanity—the handling of thoroughbred horses and the society of loose women.

A few steps from Emma a gentleman in a blue coat was talking of Italy with a pale young woman wearing a parure of pearls. They were praising the width of the columns of St. Peter's, Tivoli,

Vesuvius, Castellamare,[20] and the Cascine,[21] the roses of Genoa, the Coliseum by moonlight. With her other ear Emma was listening to a conversation full of words she did not understand. A circle gathered round a very young man who the week before had beaten "Miss Arabella," and "Romulus," and won two thousand louis jumping a ditch in England. One complained that his racehorses were growing fat; another of the printers' errors that had disfigured the name of his horse.

The atmosphere of the ball was heavy; the lamps were growing dim. Guests were flocking to the billiard-room. A servant got upon a chair and broke the window-panes. At the crash of the glass Madame Bovary turned her head and saw in the garden the faces of peasants pressed against the window looking in at them. Then the memory of the Bertaux came back to her. She saw the farm again, the muddy pond, her father in his apron under the apple-trees, and she saw herself again as formerly, skimming with her finger the cream off the milk-pans in the dairy. But in the splendor of the present hour her past life, so distinct until then, faded away completely, and she almost doubted having lived it. She was there; beyond the ball was only shadow overspreading all the rest. She was eating a maraschino ice that she held with her left hand in a silver-gilt cup, her eyes half-closed, and the spoon between her teeth.

A lady near her dropped her fan. A gentleman was passing.

"Would you be good enough," said the lady, "to pick up my fan that has fallen behind the sofa?"

The gentleman bowed, and as he moved to stretch out his arm, Emma saw the hand of the young woman throw something white, folded in a triangle, into his hat. The gentleman picking up the fan, respectfully offered it to the lady; she thanked him with a nod and breathed in the smell of her bouquet.

After supper, consisting of plenty of Spanish and Rhine wines, bisque and almond-cream soups, Trafalgar puddings and all sorts of cold meats with jellies that trembled in the dishes, the carriages began to leave one after the other. Raising the corners of the muslin curtain, one could see the light of their lanterns glimmering through the darkness. The seats began to empty, some card-players were still left; the musicians were cooling the tips of their fingers on their tongues. Charles was half asleep, his back propped against a door.

At three o'clock the cotillion began. Emma did not know how to waltz. Every one was waltzing, Mademoiselle d'Andervilliers herself and the Marquis; only the guests staying at the castle were still there, about a dozen persons.

One of the waltzers, however, who was addressed as Viscount, and whose low cut waistcoat seemed moulded to his chest, came a

---

20. Castellamare, a port south of Naples.   21. Cascine, a park near Florence.

second time to ask Madame Bovary to dance, assuring her that he would guide her, and that she would get through it very well.

They began slowly, then increased in speed. They turned; all around them was turning, the lamps, the furniture, the wainscoting, the floor, like a disc on a pivot. On passing near the doors the train of Emma's dress caught against his trousers. Their legs intertwined; he looked down at her; she raised her eyes to his. A torpor seized her and she stopped. They started again, at an even faster pace; the Viscount, sweeping her along, disappeared with her to the end of the gallery, where, panting, she almost fell, and for a moment rested her head upon his breast. And then, still turning, but more slowly, he guided her back to her seat. She leaned back against the wall and covered her eyes with her hands.

When she opened them again, in the middle of the drawing-room three waltzers were kneeling before a lady sitting on a stool. She chose the Viscount, and the violin struck up once more.

Every one looked at them. They kept passing by, she with rigid body, her chin bent down, and he always in the same pose, his figure curved, his elbow rounded, his chin thrown forward. That woman knew how to waltz! They kept it up a long time, and tired out all the others.

Then they talked a few moments longer, and after the good-nights, or rather good-mornings, the guests of the château retired to bed.

Charles dragged himself up by the banister. His knees were giving way under him. For five consecutive hours, he had stood bolt upright at the card-tables, watching them play whist, without understanding anything about it, and it was with a deep sigh of relief that he pulled off his boots.

Emma threw a shawl over her shoulders, opened the window, and leant out.

The night was dark; some drops of rain were falling. She breathed in the damp wind that refreshed her eyelids. The music of the ball was still echoing in her ears, and she tried to keep herself awake in order to prolong the illusion of this luxurious life that she would soon have to give up.

Day began to break. She looked long at the windows of the château, trying to guess which were the rooms of all those she had noticed the evening before. She would have wanted to know their lives, to penetrate into them, to blend with them.

But she was shivering with cold. She undressed, and cowered down between the sheets against Charles, who was asleep.

There were a great many people to luncheon. The meal lasted ten minutes; to the doctor's astonishment, no liqueurs were served. Next, Mademoiselle d'Andervilliers collected some rolls in a small basket to take them to the swans on the ornamental waters, and they went for a walk in the hothouses, where strange plants, bristling with hairs, rose in pyramids under hanging vases from where fell, as from overfilled nests of serpents, long green cords interlacing. The orangery, at the other end, led by a covered way to the tenant houses of the château. The Marquis, to amuse the young woman, took her to see the stables. Above the basket-shaped racks porcelain slabs bore the names of the horses in black letters. Each animal in its stall whisked its tail when any one came near and clicked his tongue. The boards of the harness-room shone like the flooring of a drawing-room. The carriage harness was piled up in the middle against two twisted columns, and the bits, the whips, the spurs, the curbs, were lined up in a row all along the wall.

Charles, meanwhile, went to ask a groom to harness his horse. The dog-cart was brought to the foot of the steps, and all the parcels being crammed in, the Bovarys paid their respects to the Marquis and the Marquise and set out again for Tostes.

Emma watched the turning wheels in silence. Charles, on the extreme edge of the seat, held the reins with his arms spread far apart, and the little horse ambled along in the shafts that were too big for him. The loose reins hanging over his crupper were wet with foam, and the box fastened behind bumped regularly against the cart.

They were on the heights of Thibourville when suddenly some horsemen with cigars between their lips passed, laughing. Emma thought she recognised the Viscount, turned back, and caught on the horizon only the movement of the heads rising or falling with the unequal cadence of the trot or gallop.

A mile farther on they had to stop to mend with some string the traces that had broken.

But Charles, giving a last look to the harness, saw something on the ground between his horse's legs, and he picked up a cigar-case with a green silk border and a crest in the centre like the door of a carriage.

"There are even two cigars in it," said he; "they'll do for this evening after dinner."

"Since when do you smoke?" she asked.

"Sometimes, when I get a chance."

He put his find in his pocket and whipped up the nag.

When they reached home the dinner was not ready. Madame lost her temper. Nastasie answered rudely.

"Leave the room!" said Emma. "You are being insolent. I'll dismiss you."

For dinner there was onion soup and a piece of veal with sorrel. Charles, seated opposite Emma, rubbed his hands gleefully.

"How good it is to be at home again!"

Nastasie could be heard crying. He was rather fond of the poor girl. She had formerly, during the wearisome time of his widowhood, kept him company many an evening. She had been his first patient, his oldest acquaintance in the place.

"Have you dismissed her for good?" he asked at last.

"Yes. Who is to prevent me?" she replied.

Then they warmed themselves in the kitchen while their room was being made ready. Charles began to smoke. He smoked with lips protruded, spitting every moment, drawing back at every puff.

"You'll make yourself ill," she said scornfully.

He put down his cigar and ran to swallow a glass of cold water at the pump. Seizing the cigar case, Emma threw it quickly to the back of the cupboard.

The next day was a long one. She walked about her little garden, up and down the same walks, stopping before the beds, before the fruit tree, before the plaster priest, looking with amazement at all these things of the past that she knew so well. How far off the ball seemed already! What was it that thus set so far asunder the morning of the day before yesterday and the evening of to-day? Her journey to Vaubyessard had made a gap in her life, like the huge crevasses that a thunderstorm will sometimes carve in the mountains, in the course of a single night. Still she was resigned. She devoutly put away in her drawers her beautiful dress, down to the satin shoes whose soles were yellowed with the slippery wax of the dancing floor. Her heart resembled them: in its contact with wealth, something had rubbed off on it that could not be removed.

The memory of this ball, then, became an occupation for Emma. Whenever Wednesday came round she said to herself as she awoke, "Ah! I was there a week—a fortnight—three weeks ago." And little by little the faces grew confused in her remembrance. She forgot the tune of the quadrilles; she no longer saw the liveries and the guest-houses so distinctly; some of the details faded but the wistful feeling remained with her.

IX

Often when Charles was out she took from the cupboard, between the folds of the linen where she had left it, the green silk cigar-case.

She looked at it, opened it, and even smelt the odour of the lining, a mixture of verbena and tobacco. Whose was it? . . . The Viscount's? Perhaps it was a present from his mistress. It had been embroidered on some rosewood frame, a pretty piece of furniture, hidden from all eyes, that had occupied many hours, and over which had fallen the soft curls of the pensive worker. A breath of love had passed over the stitches on the canvas; each prick of the needle had fixed there a hope or a memory, and all those inter-woven threads of silk were but the continued extension of the same silent passion. And then one morning the Viscount had taken it away with him. Of what had they spoken when it lay upon the wide-mantelled chimneys between flower-vases and Pompadour clocks? She was at Tostes; he was at Paris now, far away! What was this Paris like? What a boundless name! She repeated it in a low voice, for the mere pleasure of it; it rang in her ears like a great cathedral bell; it shone before her eyes, even on the labels of her jars of pomade.

At night, when the carts passed under her windows, carrying fish to Paris to the tune of "la Marjolaine," she awoke, and listened to the noise of the iron-bound wheels, which, as they gained the country road, was soon deadened by the earth. "They will be there to-morrow!" she said to herself.

And she followed them in thought up and down the hills, cross-ing villages, gliding along the highroads by the light of the stars. At the end of some indefinite distance there was always a confused spot, into which her dream died.

She bought a plan of Paris, and with the tip of her finger on the map she walked about the capital. She went up the boulevards, stopping at every turn, between the lines of the streets, in front of the white squares that represented the houses. At last she would close the lids of her weary eyes, and see in the darkness the gas jets flaring in the wind and the steps of carriages lowered noisily in front of the theatre-entrances.

She subscribed to "La Corbeille," a ladies' magazine, and the "Sylphe des Salons." She devoured, without skipping a word, all the accounts of first nights, races, and soirées, took an interest in the début of a singer, in the opening of a new shop. She knew the latest fashions, the addresses of the best tailors, the days of the Bois and the Opera. In Eugène Sue[22] she studied descriptions of furni-ture; she read Balzac and George Sand,[23] seeking in them imaginary satisfaction for her own desires. She even brought her book to the table, and turned over the pages while Charles ate and talked to her. The memory of the Viscount always cropped up in everything she read. She made comparisons between him and the fictional characters in her books. But the circle of which he was the centre gradually widened round him, and the aureole that he bore, fading from his form and extending beyond his image, lit up her other dreams.

Paris, more vague than the ocean, glimmered before Emma's eyes with a silvery glow. The many lives that stirred amid this tumult

22. Eugène Sue (1804–1857) a popu-lar novelist, extremely successful at that period, both as a writer and as a fashion-able dandy.

23. George Sand (pseudonym of Aurore Dupín), prolific woman novelist (1803–1876).

were, however, divided into parts, classed as distinct pictures. Emma perceived only two or three that hid from her all the rest, and in themselves represented all humanity. The world of ambassadors moved over polished floors in drawing-rooms lined with mirrors, round oval tables covered with velvet and gold-fringed cloths. There were dresses with trains, deep mysteries, anguish hidden beneath smiles. Then came the society of the duchesses; all were pale; all got up at four o'clock; the women, poor angels, wore English point on their petticoats; and the men, their talents hidden under a frivolous appearance, rode horses to death at pleasure parties, spent the summer season at Baden, and ended up, on reaching their forties, by marrying heiresses. In the private rooms of restaurants, where one dines after midnight by the light of wax candles, the colorful crowd of writers and actresses held sway. They were prodigal as kings, full of ambitious ideals and fantastic frenzies. They lived far above all others, among the storms that rage between heaven and earth, partaking of the sublime. As for the rest of the world, it was lost, with no particular place, and as if non-existent. Anyway, the nearer things were the more her thoughts turned away from them. All her immediate surroundings, the wearisome countryside, the petty-bourgeois stupidity, the mediocrity of existence seemed to her the exception, an exception in which she had been caught by a stroke of fate, while beyond stretched as far as eye could see an immense land of joys and passions. In her wistfulness, she confused the sensuous pleasures of luxury with the delights of the heart, elegance of manners with delicacy of sentiment. Did not love, like Indian plants, need a special soil, a special temperature? Sighs by moonlight, long embraces, tears flowing over yielded hands, all the passions of the flesh and the languors of tenderness seemed to her inseparable from the balconies of great castles where life flows idly by, from boudoirs with silken curtains and thick carpets, well-filled flower-stands, a bed on a raised daïs, and from the flashing of precious stones and the golden braids of liveries.

The boy from the post-office who came to groom the mare every morning passed through the passage with his heavy wooden shoes; there were holes in his apron; his feet were bare in his slippers. And this was the groom in knee-breeches with whom she had to be content! His work done, he did not come back again all day, for Charles on his return put up his horse himself, unsaddled it and put on the halter, while the maid brought a bundle of straw and threw it as best she could into the manger.

To replace Nastasie (who finally left Tostes shedding torrents of tears) Emma hired a young girl of fourteen, an orphan with a sweet face. She forbade her wearing cotton caps, taught her to address her in the third person, to bring a glass of water on a plate, to knock before coming into a room, to iron, starch, and to dress her; she wanted to make a lady's-maid of her. The new servant obeyed without a murmur, so as not to be dismissed; and as madame usually left the key in the sideboard, Félicité every evening took a small supply of sugar that she ate alone in her bed after she had said her prayers.

Sometimes in the afternoon she went across the road to chat with the coachmen. Madame stayed upstairs.

She wore an open dressing-gown, that showed under the shawl shaped collar a pleated blouse with three gold buttons. Her belt was a corded girdle with great tassels, and her small wine-red slippers had a large knot of ribbon that fell over her instep. She had bought herself a blotter, writing-case, pen-holder, and envelopes although she had no one to write to; she dusted her shelf, looked at herself in the mirror, picked up a book, and then, dreaming between the lines, let it drop on her knees. She longed to travel or to go back to her convent. She wanted to die, but she also wanted to live in Paris.

Charles trotted over the country-roads in snow and rain. He ate omelettes on farmhouse tables, poked his arm into damp beds, received the tepid spurt of blood-letting in his face, listened to death-rattles, examined basins, turned over a good deal of dirty linen; but every evening he found a blazing fire, his dinner ready, easy-chairs, and a well-dressed woman, charming and so freshly scented that it was impossible to say where the perfume came from; it might have been her skin that communicated its fragrance to her blouse.

She delighted him by numerous attentions; now it was some new way of arranging paper sconces for the candles, a flounce that she altered on her gown, or an extraordinary name for some very simple dish that the servant had spoilt, but that Charles swallowed with pleasure to the last mouthful. At Rouen she saw some ladies who wore a bundle of charms hanging from their watch-chains; she bought some. She wanted for her mantelpiece two large blue glass vases, and some time after an ivory nécessaire with a silver-gilt thimble. The less Charles understood these refinements the more they seduced him. They added something to the pleasure of the senses and to the comfort of his fireside. It was like a golden dust sanding all along the narrow path of his life.

He was well, looked well; his reputation was firmly established. The country-folk loved him because he was not proud. He petted the children, never went to the public-house, and, moreover, his good behavior inspired confidence. He was specially successful with heavy colds and chest ailments. Being much afraid of killing his patients, Charles, in fact, only prescribed sedatives, from time to time an emetic, a footbath, or leeches. It was not that he was afraid of surgery; he bled people copiously like horses, and for the pulling of teeth the strength of his grasp was second to no one.

Finally, to keep up with the times, he subscribed to "La Ruche Médicale," a new journal whose prospectus had been sent him. He read it a little after dinner, but in about five minutes, the warmth of the room added to the effect of his dinner sent him to sleep; and he sat there, his chin on his two hands and his hair spreading like a mane to the foot of the lamp. Emma looked at him and shrugged her shoulders. Why at least, was not her husband one of those silently determined men who work at their books all night, and at last, when at sixty the age of rhumatism was upon them, wear a string of medals on their ill-fitting black coat? She would have wished this name of Bovary, which was hers, to be illustrious, to see it displayed at the booksellers', repeated in the newspapers, known to all France. But Charles had no ambition. An Yvetot doctor whom he had lately met in consultation had somewhat humiliated him at the very bedside of the patient, before the assembled relatives. When, in the evening, Charles told this incident Emma inveighed loudly against his colleague. Charles was much touched. He kissed her forehead with a tear in his eyes. But she was angered with shame; she felt a wild desire to strike him; she went to open the window in the passage and breathed in the fresh air to calm herself.

"What a man! what a man!" she said in a low voice, biting her lips.

She was becoming more irritated with him. As he grew older his manner grew coarser; at dessert he cut the corks of the empty bottles; after eating he cleaned his teeth with his tongue; in eating his soup he made a gurgling noise with every spoonful; and, as he was getting fatter, the puffed-out cheeks seemed to push the eyes, always small, up to the temples.

Sometimes Emma tucked the red borders of his undervest into his waistcoat, rearranged his cravat, and threw away the faded gloves he was going to put on; and this was not, as he fancied, for his sake; it was for herself, by an expansion of selfishness, of nervous irritation. At other times, she told him what she had been reading, some passage in a novel, a new play, or an anecdote from high society found in a newspaper story; for, after all, Charles was someone to talk to, an ever-open ear, an ever-ready approbation. She even confided many a thing to her greyhound! She would have done so to the logs in the fireplace or to the pendulum of the clock.

All the while, however, she was waiting in her heart for something to happen. Like shipwrecked sailors, she turned despairing eyes upon the solitude of her life, seeking afar some white sail in the mists of the horizon. She did not know what this act of fortune would be, what wind would bring it, towards what shore it would drive her, if it would be a rowboat or an ocean liner with three decks, carrying anguish or laden to the gunwales with bliss. But each morning, as she awoke, she hoped it would come that day; she listened to every sound, sprang up with a start, wondered that it did not come; then at sunset, always more saddened, she longed for the next day.

Spring came round. With the first warm weather, when the pear-trees began to blossom, she had fainting-spells.

From the beginning of July she counted off on her fingers how many weeks there were to October, thinking that perhaps the Marquis d'Andervilliers would give another ball at Vaubyessard. But all September passed without letters or visits.

After the shock of this disappointment her heart once more remained empty, and then the same series of identical days recommenced.

So now they would keep following one another, always the same, immovable, and bringing nothing new. Other lives, however flat, had at least the chance of some event. One adventure sometimes brought with it infinite consequences and the scene changed. But nothing happened to her; God had willed it so! The future was a dark corridor, with its door at the end shut tight.

She gave up music. What was the good of playing? Who would hear her? Since she could never, in a velvet gown with short sleeves, striking with her light fingers the ivory keys of an Erard concert piano, feel the murmur of ecstasy envelop her like a breeze, it was not worth while boring herself with practising. Her drawing cardboard and her embroidery she left in the cupboard. What was the use? What was the use? Sewing irritated her.

"I have read everything," she said to herself.

And she sat there, letting the tongs grow red-hot or looking at the rain falling.

How sad she was on Sundays when vespers sounded! She listened with dull attention to each stroke of the cracked bell. A cat slowly walking over some roof put up his back in the pale rays of the sun. The wind on the highroad blew up clouds of dust. A dog sometimes howled in the distance; and the bell, keeping time, continued at regular intervals its monotonous ringing that died away over the fields.

Then the people came out from church. The women had waxed their wooden shoes, the farmers wore new smocks, and with the little bareheaded children skipping along in front of them, all were going home. And till nightfall, five or six men, always the same, stayed playing at corks in front of the large door of the inn.

The winter was severe. Every morning, the windows were covered with rime, and the light that shone through them, dim as through ground-glass, sometimes did not change the whole day long. At four o'clock the lamp had to be lighted.

On fine days she went down into the garden. The dew had left a silver lace on the cabbages with long transparent threads spreading from one to the other. No birds were to be heard; everything seemed asleep, the fruit tree covered with straw, and the vine, like a great sick serpent under the coping of the wall, along which, on drawing near, one saw the many-footed woodlice crawling. Under the spruce by the hedgerow, the curé in the three-cornered hat reading his breviary had lost his right foot, and the very plaster, scaling off with the frost, had left white scabs on his face.

Then she went up again, shut her door, put on coals, and fainting with the heat of the hearth, felt her boredom weigh more heavily than ever. She would have liked to go down and talk to the maid, but a sense of shame restrained her.

Every day at the same time the schoolmaster in a black skull-cap opened the shutters of his house, and the village policeman, wearing his sword over his blouse, passed by. Night and morning the post-horses, three by three, crossed the street to water at the pond. From time to time the bell of a café would tinkle, and when it was windy one could hear the little brass basins that served as signs for the hairdresser's shop creaking on their two rods. The shop was decorated with an old engraving of a fashion-plate stuck against a window-pane and with the wax bust of a woman with yellow hair. He, too, the hairdresser, lamented his wasted calling, his hopeless future, and dreaming of some shop in a big town—at Rouen, for example, overlooking the harbour, near the theatre—he walked up and down all day from the mairie to the church, sombre and waiting for customers. When Madame Bovary looked up, she always saw him there, like a sentinel on duty, with his skull-cap over his ears and his woolen jacket.

Sometimes in the afternoon outside the window of her room, the head of a man appeared, a swarthy head with black whiskers, smiling slowly, with a broad, gentle smile that showed his white teeth. A waltz began, and on the barrel-organ, in a little drawing-room, dancers the size of a finger, women in pink turbans, Tyrolians in jackets, monkeys in frock-coats, gentlemen in knee breeches, turned and turned between the armchairs, the sofas and the tables, reflected in small pieces of mirror that strips of paper held together at the corners. The man turned the handle, looking to the right, to the left and up at the windows. Now and again, while he shot out a long squirt of brown saliva against the milestone, he lifted his instrument with his knee, to relieve his shoulder from the pressure of the hard straps; and now, doleful and drawling, or merry and hurried, the music issued forth from the box, droning through a curtain of pink taffeta underneath an ornate brass grill. They were airs played in other places at the theatres, sung in drawing-rooms, danced to at night under lighted lustres, echoes of the world that reached even to Emma. Endless sarabands ran through her head, and, like an Oriental dancing-girl on the flowers of a carpet, her thoughts leapt with the notes, swung from dream to dream, from sadness to sadness. When the man had caught some pennies in his cap he drew down an old cover of blue cloth, hitched his organ on to his back, and went off with a heavy tread. She watched him going.

But it was above all the meal-times that were unbearable to her, in this small room on the ground-floor, with its smoking stove, its creaking door, the walls that sweated, the damp pavement; all the bitterness of life seemed served up on her plate, and with the smoke of the boiled beef there rose from her secret soul waves of nauseous disgust. Charles was a slow eater; she played with a few nuts, or, leaning on her elbow, amused herself drawing lines along the oil-cloth table-cover with the point of her knife.

She now let everybody in her household go its own way, and the elder Madame Bovary, when she came to spend part of Lent at Tostes, was much surprised at the change. She who was formerly so careful, so dainty, now spent whole days without dressing, wore grey cotton stockings, and used tallow candles to light the house. She kept saying they must be economical since they were not rich, adding that she was very contented, very happy, that Tostes pleased her very much, and other such statements that left her mother-in-law speechless. Besides, Emma no longer seemed inclined to follow her advice; on one occasion, when Madame Bovary had thought fit to maintain that masters ought to keep an eye on the religion of their servants, she had answered with a look so angry and a smile so cold that the old lady preferred to let the matter drop.

Emma was growing difficult, capricious. She ordered dishes for herself, then she did not touch them; one day drank only pure milk, and the next cups of tea by the dozen. Often she persisted in not going out, then, stifling, threw open the windows and put on light dresses. After she had well scolded her maid she gave her presents or sent her out to see neighbors. She sometimes threw beggars all the silver in her purse, although she was by no means tender-hearted or easily accessible to the feelings of others; like most country-bred people, she always retained in her soul something of the horny hardness of the paternal hands.

Towards the end of February old Rouault, in memory of his cure, personally brought a superb turkey to his son-in-law, and stayed three days at Tostes. Charles being with his patients, Emma kept him company. He smoked in the room, spat on the andirons, talked farming, calves, cows, poultry, and municipal council, so that when he left she closed the door on him with a feeling of satisfaction that surprised even herself. Moreover she no longer concealed her contempt for anything or anybody, and at times expressed singular opinions, finding fault with whatever others approved, and approving things perverse and immoral, all of which left her husband wide-eyed.

Would this misery last for ever? Would she never escape from it? Yet she was the equal of all the women who were living happily. She had seen duchesses at Vaubyessard with clumsier waists and commoner ways, and she hated the divine injustice of God. She leant her head against the walls to weep; she longed for lives of adventure, for masked balls, for shameless pleasures that were bound, she thought, to initiate her to ecstacies she had not yet experienced.

She grew pale and suffered from palpitations of the heart. Charles prescribed valerian drops and camphor baths. Everything that was tried only seemed to irritate her the more.

On certain days she chattered with feverish profusion, and this overexcitement was suddenly followed by a state of torpor, in which she remained without speaking, without moving. What then revived her was to pour a bottle of eau-de-cologne over her arms.

As she was constantly complaining about Tostes, Charles fancied that her illness was no doubt due to some local cause, and, struck by this idea, he began to think seriously of setting up practice elsewhere.

From that moment she drank vinegar to lose weight, contracted a sharp little cough, and lost all appetite.

It cost Charles much to give up Tostes after living there four years, just when he was beginning to get somewhere. Yet if it must be! He took her to Rouen to see his old master. It was a nervous condition; she needed a change of air.

After some looking around, Charles discovered that the doctor of a considerable market-town in the arrondissement of Neufchâtel, a former Polish refugee, had vanished a week earlier. Then he wrote to the local pharmacist to ask the size of the population, the distance from the nearest doctor, how much his predecessor had earned in a year, and so forth; and the answer being satisfactory, he made up his mind to move towards the spring, if Emma's health did not improve.

One day when, in view of her departure, she was tidying a drawer, something pricked her finger. It was a wire of her wedding-bouquet. The orange blossoms were yellow with dust and the silver-bordered satin ribbons frayed at the edges. She threw it into the fire. It flared up more quickly than dry straw. Then it was like a red bush in the cinders, slowly shrinking away. She watched it burn. The little pasteboard berries burst, the wire twisted, the gold lace melted; and the shrivelled paper petals, fluttering like black butterflies at the back of the stove, at last flew up the chimney.

When they left Tostes in the month of March, Madame Bovary was pregnant.

Part Two

I

Yonville-l'Abbaye (named after an old Capuchin abbey of which not even the ruins remain), is a market-town some twenty miles from Rouen, between the Abbeville and Beauvais roads. It lies at the foot of a valley watered by the Rieule, a little river that runs into the Andelle after turning three water-mills near its mouth; it contains a few trout and, on Sundays, the village boys entertain themselves by fishing.

Leaving the main road at la Boissière, one reaches the height of les Leux from where the valley comes into view. The river that runs through it has divided the area into two very distinct regions: on the left are pastures, while the right consists of tilled land. The meadow stretches under a bulge of low hills to join at the back with the pasture land of the Bray country, while on the eastern side, the plain, gently rising, broadens out, showing as far as the eye can reach its blond wheatfields. The water, flowing through the grass, divides with a white line the color of the meadows from that of the ploughed fields, and the country is like a great unfolded mantle with a green velvet cape bordered with a fringe of silver.

On the horizon rise the oaks of the forest of Argueil, with the steeps of the Saint-Jean hills scarred from top to bottom with red irregular lines; they are rain-tracks, and these brick-tones standing out in narrow streaks against the grey colour of the mountain are due to the high iron content of the springs that flow beyond in the neighboring country.

These are the confines of Normandy, Picardy, and the Ile-de-France, a mongrel land whose language, like its landscape, is without accent or character. The worst Neufchâtel cheeses in the arrondissement are made here; and, on the other hand, farming is costly because so much manure is needed to enrich this brittle soil, full of sand and stones.

Up to 1835 no practicable road for getting to Yonville existed, but about this time a cross-road was cut, joining the Abbeville to the Amiens highway; it is occasionally used by the Rouen teamsters on their way to Flanders. Yonville-l'Abbaye has remained stationary in spite of its "new outlet." Instead of improving the soil they persist in keeping up the pasture lands, however depreciated they may be in value, and the lazy village, growing away from the plain, has naturally spread riverwards. It is seen from afar sprawling along the banks like a cowherd taking a nap by the side of the river.

At the foot of the hill beyond the bridge begins a roadway, planted with young aspens that leads in a straight line to the first houses in the place. These, fenced in by hedges, are in the middle of courtyards full of straggling buildings, wine-presses, cart-sheds, and distilleries scattered under thick trees, with ladders, poles, or scythes hooked over the branches. The thatched roofs, like fur caps drawn over eyes, reach down over about a third of the low windows, whose coarse convex glasses have bull's eyes in the middle, like the bottom of a bottle. A meagre pear-tree may be found leaning against some plaster wall crossed by black beams, and one enters the ground-floors through a door with a small swing-gate that keeps out the chicks when they pilfer, on the threshold, crumbs of bread steeped in cider. Gradually the courtyards grow narrower, the houses closer together, and the fences disappear; a bundle of ferns swings under a window from the end of a broomstick; there is a blacksmith's forge and then a wheelwright's, with two or three new carts outside that partly block the way. Then across an open space appears a white house at the end of a round lawn ornamented by a Cupid, his finger on his lips. Two cast-iron jars flank the high porch, copper signs gleam on the door. It is the notary's house, the finest in the place.

The church is on the other side of the street, twenty paces farther down, at the entrance of the square. The little graveyard that surrounds it, closed in by a breast-high wall, is so full of graves that the old stones, level with the ground, form a continuous pavement, on which the grass has, by itself, marked out regular green squares. The church was rebuilt during the last years of the reign of Charles X.[24] The wooden roof is beginning to rot from the top, and here and there black hollows appear in the blue paint. Over the door, where the organ should be, is a gallery for the men, with a spiral staircase that reverberates under the weight of their wooden shoes.

The daylight coming through the plain glass windows falls obliquely upon the pews perpendicular to the walls, here and there adorned with a straw mat inscribed, in large letters, with the name of some parishioner. Further on, where the nave grows narrow, the confessional faces a small Madonna, clothed in satin, wearing a tulle veil sprinkled with silver stars and with cheeks stained red like an idol of the Sandwich Islands;[25] finally, a painted copy entitled "The Holy Family, a gift from the Minister of the Interior," flanked

24. Charles X (1757–1836), son of Louis XV, was the last Bourbon king; he was expelled by the July Revolution (1830).

25. Sandwich Islands is the old name for Hawaii. They were named after John Montagu, fourth Earl of Sandwich (1718–1792) who served as first Lord of Admiralty when the islands were discovered.

by four candlesticks, crowns the main altar and rounds off the view.
The choir stalls, of pine wood, have been left unpainted.

The market, that is to say, a tiled roof supported by some twenty
posts, occupies by itself about half the public square of Yonville.
The town hall, constructed "after the designs of a Paris architect,"
is a sort of Greek temple that forms the corner next to the pharmacy. On the ground-floor are three Ionic columns and on the first
floor a gallery with arched windows, while the crowning frieze is
occupied by a Gallic cock, resting one foot upon the Charter[26] and
holding in the other the scales of Justice.

But what catches the eye most of all is Mr. Homais' pharmacy,
right across from the Lion d'Or. In the evening especially its lamp
is lit up and the red and green jars that embellish his shop-front
cast their colored reflection far across the street; beyond them, as in
a Bengal light, the silhouette of the pharmacist can be seen leaning
over his desk. His house is plastered from top to bottom with
inscriptions written in longhand, in round, in lower case: "Vichy,
Seltzer and Barrège waters, depurative gum drops, Raspail patent
medicine, Arabian racahout, Darcet lozenges, Regnault ointment,
trusses, baths, laxative chocolate, etc." And the signboard, which
stretches all the breadth of the shop, bears in gold letters "Homais,
Pharmacist." Then at the back of the shop, behind the great scales
fixed to the counter, the word "Laboratory" appears on a scroll
above a glass door on which, about half-way up, the word Homais is
once more repeated in gold letters on a black ground.

Beyond this there is nothing to see at Yonville. The street (the
only one) a gunshot long and flanked by a few shops on either side
stops short at the turn of the high road. Turning right and following
the foot of the Saint-Jean hills one soon reaches the graveyard.

At the time of the cholera epidemic, a piece of wall was pulled
down and three acres of land purchased in order to make more
room, but the new area is almost deserted; the tombs, as heretofore,
continue to crowd together towards the gate. The keeper, who is at
once gravedigger and church sexton (thus making a double profit
out of the parish corpses), has taken advantage of the unused plot
of ground to plant potatoes. From year to year, however, his small
field grows smaller, and when there is an epidemic, he does not
know whether to rejoice at the deaths or regret the added graves.

"You feed on the dead, Lestiboudois!" the curé told him one
day.

This grim remark made him reflect; it checked him for some
time; but to this day he carries on the cultivation of his little tubers,
and even maintains stoutly that they grow naturally.

Since the events about to be narrated, nothing in fact has
changed at Yonville. The tin tricolour flag still swings at the top of

26. The *Charte constitutionelle de la*
France, basis of the French constitution after the Revolution, bestowed in
1814 by Louis XVIII and revised in
1830, after the downfall of Charles X.

the church-steeple; the two streamers at the novelty store still flutter in the wind; the spongy white lumps, the pharmacist's foetuses, rot more and more in their cloudy alcohol, and above the big door of the inn the old golden lion, faded by rain, still shows passers-by its poodle mane.

On the evening when the Bovarys were to arrive at Yonville, the widow Lefrançois, the landlady of this inn, was so busy that she sweated great drops as she moved her saucepans around. To-morrow was market-day. The meat had to be cut beforehand, the chickens drawn, the soup and coffee made. Moreover, she had the boarders' meal to see to, and that of the doctor, his wife, and their maid; the billiard-room was echoing with bursts of laughter; three millers in the small parlour were calling for brandy; the wood was blazing, the charcoal crackling, and on the long kitchen-table, amid the quarters of raw mutton, rose piles of plates that rattled with the shaking of the block on which spinach was being chopped. From the poultry-yard was heard the screaming of the chickens whom the servant was chasing in order to wring their necks.

A slightly pockmarked man in green leather slippers, and wearing a velvet cap with a gold tassel, was warming his back at the chimney. His face expressed nothing but self-satisfaction, and he appeared as calmly established in life as the gold-finch suspended over his head in its wicker cage: he was the pharmacist.

"Artémise!" shouted the innkeeper, "chop some wood, fill the water bottles, bring some brandy, hurry up! If only I knew what dessert to offer the guests you are expecting! Good heavens! Those furniture-movers are beginning their racket in the billiard-room again; and their van has been left before the front door! The 'Hirondelle' might crash into it when it draws up. Call Polyte and tell him to put it away . . . Imagine, Monsieur Homais, that since morning they have had about fifteen games, and drunk eight pots of cider! . . . Why they'll tear my billiard-cloth to pieces!" she went on, looking at them from a distance, her strainer in her hand.

"That wouldn't be much of a loss," replied Monsieur Homais. "You would buy another."

"Another billiard-table!" exclaimed the widow.

"Since that one is coming to pieces, Madame Lefrançois. I tell you again you are doing yourself harm, much harm! And besides, players now want narrow pockets and heavy cues. They don't play the way they used to, everything is changed! One must keep pace with the times! Just look at Tellier!"

The hostess grew red with anger. The pharmacist added:

"You may say what you like; his table is better than yours; and if one were to think, for example, of getting up a patriotic tournament for Polish independence or for the victims of the Lyon floods . . ."[27]

"It isn't beggars like him that'll frighten us," interrupted the landlady, shrugging her fat shoulders. "Come, come, Monsieur Homais; as long as the 'Lion d'Or' exists people will come to it. We are no fly-by-nights, we have feathered our nest! While one of these days you'll find the 'Café Français' closed with a fine poster on the shutters. Change my billiard-table!" she went on, speaking to herself, "the table that comes in so handy for folding the washing, and on which, in the hunting season, I have slept six visitors! . . . But what can be keeping the slowpoke of a Hivert?"

"Are you waiting for him to serve your gentlemen's dinner?"

"Wait for him! And what about Monsieur Binet? As the clock strikes six you'll see him come in, for he hasn't his equal under the sun for punctuality. He must always have his seat in the small parlour. He'd rather die than eat anywhere else. And he is finicky! and particular about his cider! Not like monsieur Léon; he sometimes comes at seven, or even half-past, and he doesn't so much as look at what he eats. Such a nice young man! Never speaks a cross word!"

"Well, you see, there's a great difference between an educated man and a former army man who is now a tax-collector."

Six o'clock struck. Binet came in.

He was dressed in a blue frock-coat falling in a straight line round his thin body, and his leather cap, with its lappets knotted over the top of his head with string, showed under the turned-up peak a bald forehead, flattened by the constant wearing of a helmet. He wore a black cloth vest, a hair collar, grey trousers, and, all the year round, well-blacked boots, that had two parallel swellings where the big toes protruded. Not a hair stood out from the regular line of fair whiskers, which, encircling his jaws, framed like a garden border his long, wan face, with smallish eyes and a hooked nose. Clever at all games of cards, a good hunter, and writing a fine hand, he had at home a lathe, and amused himself by turning napkin-rings, with which he crammed his house, jealous as an artist and selfish as a bourgeois.

He went to the small parlour, but the three millers had to be got out first, and during the whole time necessary for resetting the table, Binet remained silent in his place near the stove. Then he shut the door and took off his cap as usual.

"Politeness will not wear out his tongue," said the pharmacist, as soon as he was alone with the hostess.

"He never talks more," she replied. "Last week I had two travel-

---

27. The allusion dates the action of the novel as taking place in 1840; during the winter of 1840, the Rhône overflowed with catastrophic results. At the same time, Louis Philippe was under steady attack for his failure to offer sufficient assistance to the victims of the repression that followed the insurrection of Warsaw (1831).

ling salesmen here selling cloth, really a cheerful pair, who spent the night telling jokes. They made me weep with laughter but he, he stood there mute as a fish, never opened his mouth."

"Yes," said the pharmacist, "no imagination, no wit, nothing that makes a man shine in society."

"Yet they say he is a man of means," objected the landlady.

"Of means?" replied the pharmacist. "He? In his own line, perhaps," he added in a calmer tone. And he went on:

"Now, that a businessman with numerous connections, a lawyer, a doctor, a pharmacist, should be thus absent-minded, that they should become whimsical or even peevish, I can understand; such cases are cited in history. But at least it is because they are thinking of something. How often hasn't it happened to me, for instance, to look on my desk for my pen when I had to write out a label, merely to discover, at last, that I had put it behind my ear?"

Madame Lefrançois just then went to the door to see if the "Hirondelle" was not coming. She started. A man dressed in black suddenly came into the kitchen. By the last gleam of the twilight one could see that he was red-faced and powerfully built.

"What can I do for you, Monsieur le curé?" asked the hostess, as she reached down a copper candlestick from the row of candles. "Will you have something to drink? A thimbleful of *Cassis?* A glass of wine?"

The priest declined very politely. He had come for his umbrella, that he had forgotten the other day at the Ernemont convent, and after asking Madame Lefrançois to have it sent to him at the rectory in the evening, he left for the church; the Angelus was ringing.

When the pharmacist no longer heard the noise of his boots along the square, he confessed that he had found the priest's behaviour just now very unbecoming. This refusal to take any refreshment seemed to him the most odious hypocrisy; all priests tippled on the sly, and were trying to bring back the days of the tithe.

The landlady took up the defence of her curé.

"Besides, he could double up four men like you over his knee. Last year he helped our people to bring in the hay, he carried as many as six bales at once, he is so strong."

"Bravo!" said the pharmacist. "Now just send your daughters to confess to such vigorous fellows! I, if I were the Government, I'd have the priests bled once a month. Yes, Madame Lefrançois, every month—a good phlebotomy, in the interests of the police and morals."

"Be quiet, Monsieur Homais. You are a godless man! You have no religion."

The chemist replied:

"I have a religion, my religion, and I even have more than all these others with their mummeries and their juggling. I adore God, on the contrary. I believe in the Supreme Being, in a Creator, whatever he may be. I care little who has placed us here below to fulfill our duties as citizens and parents; but I don't need to go to church to kiss silver plates, and fatten, out of my pocket, a lot of good-for-nothings who live better than we do. For one can know him as well in a wood, in a field, or even contemplating the ethereal heavens like the ancients. My God is the God of Socrates, of Franklin, of Voltaire, and of Béranger! I support the *Profession de Foi du Vicaire savoyard*[28] and the immortal principles of '89! And I can't admit of an old boy of a God who takes walks in his garden with a cane in his hand, who lodges his friends in the belly of whales, dies uttering a cry, and rises again at the end of three days; things absurd in themselves, and completely opposed, moreover, to all physical laws, which proves to us, by the way, that priests have always wallowed in squalid ignorance, and tried to drag whole nations down after them."

He stopped, looked around as if expecting to find an audience, for in his enthusiasm the pharmacist had for a moment fancied himself in the midst of the town council. But the landlady no longer heard him; she was listening to a distant rolling. One could distinguish the noise of a carriage mingled with the clattering of loose horseshoes that beat against the ground, and at last the "Hirondelle" stopped at the door.

It was a yellow box on two large wheels, that, reaching to the tilt, prevented travellers from seeing the road and dirtied their shoulders. The small panes of narrow windows rattled in their frames when the coach was closed, and retained here and there patches of mud amid the old layers of dust, that not even storms of rain had altogether washed away. It was drawn by three horses, the first a leader, and when it came down-hill its lower side jolted against the ground.

Some of the inhabitants of Yonville came out into the square; they all spoke at once, asking for news, for explanations of the delay, for their orders. Hivert did not know whom to answer first. He ran the errands in town for the entire village. He went to the shops and brought back rolls of leather for the shoemaker, old iron for the farrier, a barrel of herrings for his mistress, hats from the hat-shop and wigs from the hairdresser, and all along the road on his return journey he distributed his parcels, throwing them over fences as he stood upright on his seat and shouted at the top of his voice, while his horses went their own way.

An accident had delayed him. Madame Bovary's greyhound had escaped across the field. They had whistled for him a quarter of an

28. *Profession du Foi du Vicaire savoyard* (1762) is Rousseau's declaration of faith in God, a religion of his heart, coupled with a criticism of revealed religion. It is included in Book IV of his pedagogic treatise *Émile* but was frequently reprinted as an independent pamphlet.

hour; Hivert had even gone back a mile and a half expecting every moment to catch sight of her; but they had been forced to resume the journey. Emma had wept, grown angry; she had accused Charles of this misfortune. Monsieur Lheureux, a draper, who happened to be in the coach with her, had tried to console her by a number of examples of lost dogs recognising their masters at the end of long years. He had been told of one, he said, who had come back to Paris from Constantinople. Another had gone one hundred and fifty miles in a straight line, and swum four rivers; and his own father had owned a poodle, which, after twelve years of absence, had all of a sudden jumped on his back in the street as he was going to dine in town.

II

Emma got out first, then Félicité, Monsieur Lheureux, and a nurse, and they had to wake up Charles in his corner, where he had slept soundly since night set in.

Homais introduced himself; he offered his homages to madame and his respects to monsieur; said he was charmed to have been able to render them some slight service, and added cordially that he had taken the liberty to join them at dinner, his wife being away.

When Madame Bovary entered the kitchen she went up to the fireplace. With two fingertips she caught her dress at the knee, and having thus pulled it up to her ankle, held out her black-booted foot to the fire above the revolving leg of mutton. The flame lit up the whole of her, casting its harsh light over the pattern of her gown, the fine pores of her fair skin, and even her eyelids, when she blinked from time to time. A great red glow passed over her with the wind, blowing through the half-open door.

On the other side of the fireplace, a fair-haired young man watched her in silence.

As he was frequently bored at Yonville, where he was a clerk at Maître Guilleumin, the notary, Monsieur Léon Dupuis (the second of the *Lion d'Or*'s daily customers) often delayed his dinner-hour in the hope that some traveller might come to the inn, with whom he could chat in the evening. On the days when his work was done early, he had, for want of something else to do, to come punctually, and endure from soup to cheese a *tête-à-tête* with Binet. It was therefore with delight that he accepted the hostess's suggestion that he should dine in company with the newcomers, and they passed into the large parlour where Madame Lefrançois, hoping to make an impression, had had the table laid for four.

Homais asked to be allowed to keep on his skull-cap, for fear of catching cold; then, turning to his neighbor:

"Madame is no doubt a little fatigued; one gets so frightfully shaken up in our *Hirondelle*."

"That is true," replied Emma; "but moving about always amuses me. I like a change."

"It is so tedious," sighed the clerk, "to be always riveted to the same places."

"If you were like me," said Charles, "constantly obliged to be in the saddle" . . .

"But," Léon went on, addressing himself to Madame Bovary, "nothing, it seems to me, is more pleasant—when one can," he added.

"Moreover," said the pharmacist, "the practice of medicine is not very hard work in our part of the world, for the state of our roads allows us the use of gigs, and generally, as the farmers are well off, they pay pretty well. We have, medically speaking, besides the ordinary cases of enteritis, bronchitis, bilious affections, &c., now and then a few intermittent fevers at harvest-time; but on the whole, little of a serious nature, nothing special to note, unless it be a great deal of scrofula, due, no doubt, to the deplorable hygienic conditions of our peasant dwellings. Ah! you will find many prejudices to combat, Monsieur Bovary, much obstinacy of routine, with which all the efforts of your science will daily come into collision; for people still have recourse to novenas, to relics, to the priest, rather than come straight to the doctor or the pharmacist. The climate, however, is truly not too bad, and we even have a few nonagenarians in our parish. The thermometer (I have made some observations) falls in winter to 4 degrees, and in the hottest season rises to 25 or 30 degrees Centigrade at the outside, which gives us 24 degrees Réaumur as the maximum, or otherwise stated 54 degrees Fahrenheit (English scale), not more. And, as a matter of fact, we are sheltered from the north winds by the forest of Argueil on the one side, from the west winds by the Saint Jean hills on the other; and this heat, moreover, which, on account of the watery vapours given off by the river and the considerable number of cattle in the fields, which, as you know, exhale much ammonia, that is to say, nitrogen, hydrogen, and oxygen (no, nitrogen and hydrogen alone), and which sucking up the humus from the soil, mixing together all those different emanations, unites them into a single bundle, so to speak, and combining with the electricity diffused through the atmosphere, when there is any, might in the long-run, as in tropical countries, engender poisonous fumes,—this heat, I say, finds itself perfectly tempered on the side from where it comes, or rather from where it ought to come, that is the south side, by the south-eastern winds, which, having cooled themselves in crossing the Seine, reach us sometimes all at once like blasts from Russia!"

"Do you at least have some walks in the neighborhood?" continued Madame Bovary, speaking to the young man.

"Oh, very few," he answered. "There is a place they call La Pâture, on the top of the hill, on the edge of the forest. Sometimes, on Sundays, I go and stay there with a book, watching the sunset."

"I think there is nothing so beautiful as sunsets," she resumed; "but especially by the seashore."

"Oh, I love the sea!" said Monsieur Léon.

"And doesn't it seem to you," continued Madame Bovary, "that the mind travels more freely on this limitless expanse, of which the contemplation elevates the soul, gives ideas of the infinite, the ideal?"

"It is the same with mountainous landscapes," continued Léon. "A cousin of mine who travelled in Switzerland last year told me that one could not picture to oneself the poetry of the lakes, the charm of the waterfalls, the gigantic effect of the glaciers. One sees pines of incredible size across torrents, cottages suspended over precipices, and, a thousand feet below one, whole valleys when the clouds open. Such spectacles must stir to enthusiasm, incline to prayer, to ecstasy; and I no longer wonder why a celebrated musician, in order to stimulate his imagination, was in the habit of playing the piano before some imposing view."

"Do you play?" she asked.

"No, but I am very fond of music," he replied.

"Ah! don't you listen to him, Madame Bovary," interrupted Homais, bending over his plate. "That's sheer modesty. Why, my friend, the other day in your room you were singing 'L'Ange Gardien[29] to perfection. I heard you from the laboratory. You articulated with the skill of an actor."

Léon rented a small room at the pharmacist's, on the second floor overlooking the Square. He blushed at the compliment of his landlord, who had already turned to the doctor, and was enumerating to him, one after the other, all the principal inhabitants of Yonville. He was telling anecdotes, giving information; no one knew just how wealthy the notary was and there were, of course, the Tuvaches who put up a considerable front.

Emma continued, "And what music do you prefer?"

"Oh, German music; that which makes you dream."

"Have you been to the opera?"

"Not yet; but I shall go next year, when I'll be living in Paris to get a law degree."

"As I had the honour of putting it to your husband," said the pharmacist, "with regard to this poor Yanoda who has run away, you will find yourself, thanks to his extravagance, in the possession of one of the most comfortable houses of Yonville. Its greatest convenience for a doctor is a door giving on the Walk, where one

29. A sentimental romance written by Mme. Pauline Duchambre, author of several such songs that appeared in the keepsakes.

can go in and out unseen. Moreover, it contains everything that is useful in a household—a laundry, kitchen with pantry, sitting-room, fruit bins, etc. He was a gay dog, who didn't care what he spent. At the end of the garden, by the side of the water, he had an arbour built just for the purpose of drinking beer in summer; and if madame is fond of gardening she will be able . . . "

"My wife doesn't care to," said Charles; "although she has been advised to take exercise, she prefers always sitting in her room reading."

"Just like me," replied Léon. "And indeed, what is better than to sit by one's fireside in the evening with a book, while the wind beats against the window and the lamp is burning? . . ."

"What, indeed?" she said, fixing her large black eyes wide open upon him.

"One thinks of nothing," he continued; "the hours slip by. Without having to move, we walk through the countries of our imagination, and your thought, blending with the fiction, toys with the details, follows the outline of the adventures. It mingles with the characters, and it seems you are living their lives, that your own heart beats in their breast."

"That is true! that is true!" she said.

"Has it ever happened to you," Léon went on, "to discover some vague idea of one's own in a book, some dim image that comes back to you from afar, and as the fullest expression of your own slightest sentiment?"

"I have experienced it," she replied.

"That is why," he said, "I especially love the poets. I think verse more tender than prose, and that it makes one weep more easily."

"Still in the long-run it is tiring," continued Emma, "and now, on the contrary, I have come to love stories that rush breathlessly along, that frighten one. I detest commonplace heroes and moderate feelings, as one finds them in nature."

"You are right," observed the clerk, "since these works fail to touch the heart, they miss, it seems to me, the true end of art. It is so sweet, amid all the disenchantments of life, to be able to dwell in thought upon noble characters, pure affections, and pictures of happiness. For myself, living here far from the world, this is my one distraction. But there is so little to do in Yonville!"

"Like Tostes, no doubt," replied Emma; "and so I always subscribed to a lending library."

"If madame will do me the honor of making use of it," said the pharmacist, who had just caught the last words, "I have at her disposal a library composed of the best authors, Voltaire, Rousseau, Delille,[30] Walter Scott, the 'Echo des Feuilletons'; and in addition I

---

30. Jacques Delille (1738–1813) wrote idyllic descriptive poems; *Les Jardins* (1782) is best known.

receive various periodicals, among them the 'Fanal de Rouen' daily, being privileged to act as its correspondent for the districts of Buchy, Forges, Neufchâtel, Yonville, and vicinity."

They had been at the table for two hours and a half, for Artémise, the maid, listlessly dragged her slippered feet over the tilefloor, brought in the plates one by one, forgot everything, understood nothing and constantly left the door of the billiard-room half open, so that the handle kept beating against the wall with its hooks.

Unconsciously, Léon, while talking, had placed his foot on one of the bars of the chair on which Madame Bovery was sitting. She wore a small blue silk necktie, which held upright, stiff as a ruff, a pleated batiste collar, and with the movements of her head the lower part of her face gently sunk into the linen or rose from it. Thus side by side, while Charles and the pharmacist chatted, they entered into one of those vague conversations where the hazard of all that is said brings you back to the fixed centre of a common sympathy. The Paris theatres, titles of novels, new quadrilles, and the world they did not know; Tostes, where she had lived, and Yonville, where they were; they examined all, talked of everything till the end of dinner.

When coffee was served Félicité left to prepare the room in the new house, and the guests soon rose from the table. Madame Lefrançois was asleep near the cinders, while the stable-boy, lantern in hand, was waiting to show Monsieur and Madame Bovary the way home. Bits of straw stuck in his red hair, and his left leg had a limp. When he had taken in his other hand the curé's umbrella, they started.

The town was asleep; the pillars of the market threw great shadows; the earth was all grey as on a summer's night.

But as the doctor's house was only some fifty paces from the inn, they had to say good-night almost immediately, and the company dispersed.

As soon as she entered the hallway, Emma felt the cold of the plaster fall about her shoulders like damp linen. The walls were new and the wooden stairs creaked. In their bedroom, on the first floor, a whitish light passed through the curtainless windows. She could catch glimpses of tree-tops, and beyond, the fields, half-drowned in the fog that lay like smoke over the course of the river. In the middle of the room, pell-mell, were scattered drawers, bottles, curtain-rods, gilt poles, with mattresses on the chairs and basins on the floor—the two men who had brought the furniture had left everything about carelessly.

This was the fourth time that she had slept in a strange place. The first was the day she went to the convent; the second, of her arrival at Tostes; the third, at Vaubyessard; and this was the fourth; and it so happened that each one had marked in her life a new beginning. She did not believe that things could remain the same in different places, and since the portion of her life that lay behind her had been bad, no doubt that which remained to be lived would be better.

III

The next day, as she was getting up, she saw the clerk on the Place. She had on a dressing-gown. He looked up and bowed. She nodded quickly and reclosed the window.

Léon waited all day for six o'clock in the evening to come, but on going to the inn, he found only Monsieur Binet already seated at the table.

The dinner of the evening before had been a considerable event for him; he had never till then talked for two hours consecutively to a "lady." How then had he been able to express, and in such language, so many things that he could not have said so well before? He was usually shy, and maintained that reserve which partakes at once of modesty and dissimulation. At Yonville, his manners were generally admired. He listened to the opinions of the older people, and seemed to have moderate political views, a rare thing for a young man. Then he had some accomplishments; he painted in water-colours, could read music, and readily talked literature after dinner when he did not play cards. Monsieur Homais respected him for his education; Madame Homais liked him for his good-nature, for he often took the little Homais into the garden—little brats who were always dirty, very much spoilt, and somewhat slow-moving, like their mother. They were looked after by the maid and by Justin, the pharmacist's apprentice, a second cousin of Monsieur Homais, who had been taken into the house out of charity and was also being put to work as a servant.

The druggist proved the best of neighbors. He advised Madame Bovary as to the tradespeople, sent expressly for his own cider merchant, tasted the wine himself, and saw that the casks were properly placed in the cellar; he explained how to stock up cheaply on butter, and made an arrangement with Lestiboudois, the sacristan, who, besides his ecclesiastical and funereal functions, looked after the main gardens at Yonville by the hour or the year, according to the wishes of the customers.

The need of looking after others was not the only thing that urged the pharmacist to such obsequious cordiality; there was a plan underneath it all.

He had infringed the law of the 19th Ventôse, year xi., article 1,[31] which forbade all persons not having a diploma to practise medicine; so that, after certain anonymous denunciations, Homais had

31. Ventôse ("windy") was the sixth month of the calendar established by the French Republic (from February 19 to March 20). The government of the Republic made the new year begin on September 22, 1792; thus the Year xi is 1801, and the 19th Ventôse March 10.

been summoned to Rouen to see the royal prosecutor in his private office; the magistrate receiving him standing up, ermine on shoulder and cap on head. It was in the morning, before the court opened. In the corridors one heard the heavy boots of the gendarmes walking past, and like a far-off noise great locks that were shut. The druggist's ears tingled as if he were about to have a stroke; he saw the depths of dungeons, his family in tears, his shop sold, all the jars dispersed; and he was obliged to enter a café and take a glass of rum and soda water to recover his spirits.

Little by little the memory of this reprimand grew fainter, and he continued, as heretofore, to give anodyne consultations in his back-parlour. But the mayor resented it, his colleagues were jealous, he had everything and everyone to fear; gaining over Monsieur Bovary by his attentions was to earn his gratitude, and prevent his speaking out later on, should he notice anything. So every morning Homais brought him the paper, and often in the afternoon left his shop for a few moments to have a chat with the Doctor.

Charles was depressed: he had no patients. He remained seated for hours without speaking, went into his consulting-room to sleep, or watched his wife sewing. Then for diversion he tried to work as a handyman around the house; he even tried to decorate the attic with some paint that had been left behind by the painters. But money matters worried him. He had spent so much for repairs at Tostes, for madame's toilette, and for the moving, that the whole dowry, over three thousand écus, had slipped away in two years. Then how many things had been spoilt or lost during their move from Tostes to Yonville, without counting the plaster curé, who, thrown out of the carriage by a particularly severe jolt, had broken in a thousand pieces on the pavement of Quincampoix!

A more positive worry came to distract him, namely, the pregnancy of his wife. As the time of birth approached he cherished her more. It was another bond of the flesh between them, and, as it were, a continued sentiment of a more complex union. When he caught sight of her indolent walk or watched her figure filling out over her uncorseted hips, when he had the opportunity to look at her undisturbed taking tired poses in her armchair, then his happiness knew no bounds; he got up, embraced her, passed his hands over her face, called her little mamma, wanted to make her dance, and, half-laughing, half-crying, uttered all kinds of caressing pleasantries that came into his head. The idea of having begotten a child delighted him. Now he wanted nothing more. He knew all there was to know of human life and sat down to enjoy it serenely, his elbows planted on the table as for a good meal.

Emma at first felt a great astonishment; then was anxious to be delivered that she might know what it felt like to be a mother. But not being able to spend as much as she would have liked on a suspended cradle with rose silk curtains, and embroidered caps, in a fit of bitterness she gave up looking for the layette altogether and had it all made by a village seamstress, without choosing or discussing anything.

Thus she did not amuse herself with those preparations that stimulate the tenderness of mothers, and so her affection was perhaps impaired from the start.

As Charles, however, spoke of the baby at every meal, she soon began to think of him more steadily.

She hoped for a son; he would be strong and dark; she would call him George; and this idea of having a male child was like an expected revenge for all her impotence in the past. A man, at least, is free; he can explore all passions and all countries, overcome obstacles, taste of the most distant pleasures. But a woman is always hampered. Being inert as well as pliable, she has against her the weakness of the flesh and the inequity of the law. Like the veil held to her hat by a ribbon, her will flutters in every breeze; she is always drawn by some desire, restrained by some rule of conduct.

She gave birth on a Sunday at about six o'clock, as the sun was rising.

"It is a girl!" said Charles.

She turned her head away and fainted.

Madame Homais, as well as Madame Lefrançois of the Lion d'Or, almost immediately came running in to embrace her. The pharmacist, as a man of discretion, only offered a few provisional felicitations through the half-opened door. He asked to see the child, and thought it well made.

During her recovery, she spent much time seeking a name for her daughter. First she went over all names that have Italian endings, such as Clara, Louisa, Amanda, Atala; she liked Galsuinde pretty well, and Yseult or Léocadie still better. Charles wanted the child to be called after her mother; Emma opposed this. They ran over the calendar from end to end, and then consulted outsiders.

"Monsieur Léon," said the chemist, "with whom I was talking about it the other day, wonders why you do not choose Madeleine. It is very much in fashion just now."

But Monsieur Bovary's mother protested loudly against this name of a sinner. As to Monsieur Homais, he had a preference for all names that recalled some great man, an illustrious fact, or a generous idea, and it was in accordance with this system that he had baptized his four children. Thus Napoleon represented glory and Franklin liberty; Irma was perhaps a concession to romanticism, but Athalie[32] was a homage to the greatest masterpiece of the French stage. For his philosophical convictions did not interfere with his

32. *Athalie* is a tragedy by Jean Racine (1639–1699) written in 1691 for the pupils of Saint-Cyr. Racine had abandoned the regular stage after a spiritual crisis and wrote two sacred tragedies *Esther* and *Athalie* for the young girls of Saint-Cyr.

artistic tastes; in him the thinker did not stifle the man of sentiment; he could make distinctions, make allowances for imagination
and fanaticism. In this tragedy, for example, he found fault with
the ideas, but admired the style; he detested the conception, but
applauded all the details, and loathed the characters while he grew
enthusiastic over their dialogue. When he read the fine passages he
was transported, but when he thought that the Catholics would use
it to their advantage, he was disconsolate; and in this confusion of
sentiments in which he was involved he would have liked both to
crown Racine with both his hands and take him to task for a good
quarter of an hour.

At last Emma remembered that at the château of Vaubyessard
she had heard the Marquise call a young lady Berthe; from that
moment this name was chosen; and as old Rouault could not come,
Monsieur Homais was requested to be godfather. His gifts were all
products from his establishment, to wit: six boxes of jujubes, a
whole jar of racahout, three cakes of marsh-mallow paste, and six
sticks of sugar-candy that he had come across in a cupboard. On the
evening of the ceremony there was a grand dinner; the curé was
present; there was much excitement. Towards liqueur time, Monsieur
Homais began singing "Le Dieu des bonnes gens."[33] Monsieur Léon
sang a barcarolle, and the elder Madame Bovary, who was godmother, a romance of the time of the Empire; finally, M. Bovary,
senior, insisted on having the child brought down, and began bap-
tizing it with a glass of champagne that he poured over its head.
This mockery of the first of the sacraments aroused the indignation
of the Abbé Bournisien; Father Bovary replied by a quotation from
"La Guerre des Dieux";[34] the curé wanted to leave; the ladies implored, Homais interfered; they succeeded in making the priest sit
down again, and he quietly went on with the half-finished coffee in
his saucer.

Monsieur Bovary père stayed at Yonville a month, dazzling the
natives by a superb soldier's cap with silver tassels that he wore in
the morning when he smoked his pipe in the square. Being also in
the habit of drinking a good deal of brandy, he often sent the
servant to the Lion d'Or to buy him a bottle, which was put down
to his son's account, and to perfume his handkerchiefs he used up
his daughter-in-law's whole supply of eau-de-cologne.

The latter did not at all dislike his company. He had knocked
about the world, he talked about Berlin, Vienna, and Strasbourg, of
his soldier times, of his mistresses, of the brilliant dinner-parties he
had attended; then he was amiable, and sometimes even, either on
the stairs or in the garden, would catch her by the waist, exclaiming:

33. "Le Dieu des Bonnes Gens" is a
deistic song by Béranger (see p. 490, n.5).
34. "La Guerre des Dieux" ("The War
of the Gods") is a satirical poem by
Evarite-Désiré Deforge (later Viscount
de Parny, 1753–1814) published in 1799.
It ridicules the Christian religion.

"Charles, you better watch out!"

Then the elder Madame Bovary became alarmed for her son's happiness, and fearing that her husband might in the long run have an immoral influence upon the ideas of the young woman, she speeded up their departure. Perhaps she had more serious reasons for uneasiness. Monsieur Bovary was the man to stop at nothing.

One day Emma was suddenly seized with the desire to see her little girl, who had been put to nurse with the carpenter's wife, and, without looking at the calendar to see whether the six weeks of the Virgin[35] were yet passed, she set out for the Rollets' house, situated at the extreme end of the village, between the highroad and the fields.

It was mid-day, the shutters of the houses were closed, and the slate roofs that glittered beneath the fierce light of the blue sky seemed to strike sparks from the crest of their gables. A heavy wind was blowing; Emma felt weak as she walked; the stones of the pavement hurt her; she was doubtful whether she would not go home again, or enter somewhere to rest.

At that moment Monsieur Léon came out from a neighboring door with a bundle of papers under his arm. He came to greet her, and stood in the shade in front of Lheureux's shop under the projecting grey awning.

Madame Bovary said she was going to see her baby, but that she was getting tired.

"If . . ." said Léon, not daring to go on.

"Have you any business to attend to?" she asked.

And on the clerk's negative answer, she begged him to accompany her. That same evening this was known in Yonville, and Madame Tuvache, the mayor's wife, declared in the presence of her maid that Madame Bovary was jeopardizing her good name.

To get to the nurse's it was necessary to turn to the left on leaving the street, as if heading for the cemetery, and to follow between little houses and yards a small path bordered with privet hedges. They were in bloom, and so were the speedwells, eglantines, thistles, and the sweetbriar that sprang up from the thickets. Through openings in the hedges one could see into the huts, some pig on a dung-heap, or tethered cows rubbing their horns against the trunk of trees. The two, side by side, walked slowly, she leaning upon him, and he restraining his pace, which he regulated by hers; in front of them flies were buzzing in the warm air.

They recognised the house by an old walnut-tree which shaded it. Low and covered with brown tiles, there hung outside it, beneath the attic-window, a string of onions. Faggots upright against a thorn fence surrounded a bed of lettuces, a few square feet of lavender,

35. Originally the six weeks that separate Christmas from Purification (Feb. 2nd); in those days, the normal period of confinement for a woman after childbirth.

and sweet peas strung on sticks. Dirty water was running here and there on the grass, and all round were several indefinite rags, knitted stockings, a red flannel undershirt, and a large sheet of coarse linen spread over the hedge. At the noise of the gate the wet nurse appeared with a baby she was suckling on one arm. With her other hand she was pulling along a poor puny little boy, his face covered with a scrofulous rash, the son of a Rouen hosier, whom his parents, too taken up with their business, left in the country.

"Go in," she said; "your baby is there asleep."

The room on the ground-floor, the only one in the dwelling, had at its farther end, against the wall, a large bed without curtains, while a kneading-trough took up the side by the window, one pane of which was mended with a piece of blue paper. In the corner behind the door, shining hob-nailed shoes stood in a row under the slab of the washstand, near a bottle of oil with a feather stuck in its mouth; a Mathieu Laensberg[36] lay on the dusty mantelpiece amid gunflints, candle-ends, and bits of tinder. Finally, the last extravagance in the room was a picture representing Fame blowing her trumpets, cut out, no doubt, from some perfumer's prospectus and nailed to the wall with six wooden shoe-pegs.

Emma's child was asleep in a wicker-cradle. She took it up in the wrapping that enveloped it and began singing softly as she rocked it to and fro.

Léon walked up and down the room; it seemed strange to him to see this beautiful woman in her silk dress in the midst of all this poverty. Madame Bovary blushed; he turned away, thinking perhaps there had been an impertinent look in his eyes. Then she put back the little girl, who had just thrown up over her collar. The nurse at once came to dry her, protesting that it wouldn't show.

"You should see some of the other tricks she plays on me," she said. "I always seem to be sponging her off. If you would have the goodness to order Camus, the grocer, to let me have a little soap; it would really be more convenient for you, as I needn't trouble you then."

"All right, all right!" said Emma. "Good-bye, Madame Rollet."

And she went out, wiping her shoes at the door.

The woman accompanied her to the end of the garden, complaining all the time of the trouble she had getting up nights.

"I'm so worn out sometimes that I drop asleep on my chair. You could at least give me a pound of ground coffee; that'd last me a month, and I'd take it in the morning with some milk."

After having submitted to her thanks, Madame Bovary left. She had gone a little way down the path when, at the sound of wooden shoes, she turned round. It was the nurse.

36. A farmer's almanac, begun in 1635   in farms and country houses.
by Mathieu Laensberg, frequently found

"What is it?"

Then the peasant woman, taking her aside behind an elm tree, began talking to her of her husband, who with his trade and six francs a year that the captain . . .

"Hurry up with your story," said Emma.

"Well," the nurse went on, heaving sighs between each word, "I'm afraid he'll be put out seeing me have coffee alone, you know men . . ."

"But I just told you you'll get some," Emma repeated; "I will give you some. Leave me alone!"

"Oh, my dear lady! you see, his wounds give him terrible cramps in the chest. He even says that cider weakens him."

"Do make haste, Mère Rollet!"

"Well," the latter continued, making a curtsey, "if it weren't asking too much," and she curtsied once more, "if you would"— and her eyes begged—"a jar of brandy," she said at last, "and I'd rub your little one's feet with it; they're as tender as your tongue."

Once they were rid of the nurse, Emma again took Monsieur Léon's arm. She walked fast for some time, then more slowly, and looking straight in front of her, her eyes rested on the shoulder of the young man, whose frock-coat had a black-velvet collar. His brown hair fell over it, straight and carefully combed. She noticed his nails, which were longer than one wore them in Yonville. It was one of the clerk's chief concerns to trim them, and for this purpose he kept a special knife in his writing-desk.

They returned to Yonville by the water-side. In the warm season the bank, wider than at other times, showed to their foot the garden walls from where a few steps led to the river. It flowed noiselessly, swift, and cold to the eye; long, thin grasses huddled together in it as the current drove them, and spread themselves upon the limpid water like streaming hair. Sometimes at the top of the reeds or on the leaf of a water-lily an insect with fine legs crawled or rested. The sun pierced with a ray the small blue bubbles of the waves that broke successively on the bank; branchless old willows mirrored their grey barks in the water; beyond, all around, the meadows seemed empty. It was the dinner-hour at the farms, and the young woman and her companion heard nothing as they walked but the fall of their steps on the earth of the path, the words they spoke, and the sound of Emma's dress rustling round her.

The walls of the gardens, crested with pieces of broken bottle, were heated like the glass roof of a hothouse. Wallflowers had sprung up between the bricks, and with the tip of her open parasol Madame Bovary, as she passed, made some of their faded flowers crumble into yellow dust, or else a spray of overhanging honeysuckle and clematis would catch in the fringe of the parasol and scrape for a moment over the silk.

They were talking of a troupe of Spanish dancers who were expected shortly at the Rouen theatre.

"Are you going?" she asked.

"If I can," he answered.

Had they nothing else to say to one another? Yet their eyes were full of more serious speech, and while they forced themselves to find trivial phrases, they felt the same languor stealing over them both; it was like the deep, continuous murmur of the soul dominating that of their voices. Surprised with wonder at this strange sweetness, they did not think of speaking of the sensation or of seeking its cause. Future joys are like tropical shores; like a fragrant breeze, they extend their innate softness to the immense inland world of past experience, and we are lulled by this intoxication into forgetting the unseen horizons beyond.

In one place the ground had been trodden down by the cattle; they had to step on large green stones put here and there in the mud. She often stopped a moment to look where to place her foot, and tottering on the stone that shook, her arms outspread, her form bent forward with a look of indecision, she would laugh, afraid of falling into the puddles of water.

When they arrived in front of her garden, Madame Bovary opened the little gate, ran up the steps and disappeared.

Léon returned to his office. His employer was away; he just glanced at the briefs, then cut himself a pen, and finally took up his hat and went out.

He went to La Pâture at the top of the Argueil hills at the beginning of the forest; he stretched out under the pines and watched the sky through his fingers.

"How bored I am!" he said to himself, "how bored I am!"

He thought he was to be pitied for living in this village, with Homais for a friend and Monsieur Guillaumin for master. The latter, entirely absorbed by his business, wearing gold-rimmed spectacles and red whiskers over a white cravat, understood nothing of mental refinements, although he affected a stiff English manner, which in the beginning had impressed the clerk.

As for Madame Homais, she was the best wife in Normandy, gentle as a sheep, loving her children, her father, her mother, her cousins, weeping for others' woes, letting everything go in her household, and detesting corsets; but so slow of movement, such a bore to listen to, so common in appearance, and of such restricted conversation, that although she was thirty and he only twenty, although they slept in rooms next each other and he spoke to her daily, he never thought that she might be a woman to anyone, or that she possessed anything else of her sex than the gown.

And what else was there? Binet, a few shopkeepers, two or three innkeepers, the curé, and, finally, Monsieur Tuvache, the mayor, with his two sons, rich, haughty, obtuse people, who farmed their own lands and had feasts among themselves, devout Christians at that, but altogether unbearable as companions.

But from the general background of all these human faces the figure of Emma stood out isolated and yet farthest off; for between her and him he seemed to sense a vague abyss.

In the beginning he had called on her several times along with the pharmacist. Charles had not appeared particularly anxious to see him again, and Léon did not know what to do between his fear of being indiscreet and the desire for an intimacy that seemed almost impossible.

IV

When the first cold days set in Emma left her bedroom for the parlour, a long, low-ceilinged room, with on the mantelpiece a large bunch of coral spread out against the looking-glass. Seated in her armchair near the window, she could see the villagers pass along the pavement.

Twice a day Léon went from his office to the Lion d'Or. Emma could watch him coming from afar; she leant forward listening, and the young man glided past the curtain, always dressed in the same way, and without turning his head. But in the twilight, when, her chin resting on her left hand, she let her begun embroidery fall on her knees, she often shuddered at the apparition of this shadow suddenly gliding past. She would get up and order the table to be laid.

Monsieur Homais called at dinner-time. Skull-cap in hand, he came in on tiptoe, in order to disturb no one, always repeating the same phrase, "Good evening, everybody." Then, when he had taken his seat at table between them, he asked the doctor about his patients, and the latter consulted him as to the probability of their payment. Next they talked of "what was in the paper." By this hour of the day, Homais knew it almost by heart, and he repeated from beginning to end, including the comments of the journalist, all the stories of individual catastrophes that had occurred in France or abroad. But the subject becoming exhausted, he was not slow in throwing out some remarks on the dishes before him. Sometimes even, half-rising, he delicately pointed out to madame the tenderest morsel, or turning to the maid, gave her some advice on the manipulation of stews and the hygiene of seasoning. He talked aroma, osmazome, juices, and gelatine in a bewildering manner. Moreover, Homais, with his head fuller of recipes than his shop of jars, excelled in making all kinds of preserves, vinegars, and sweet liqueurs; he knew also all the latest inventions in economic stoves, together with the art of preserving cheeses and of curing sick wines.

At eight o'clock Justin came to fetch him to shut up the shop. Then Monsieur Homais gave him a sly look, especially if Félicité was there, for he had noticed that his apprentice was fond of the doctor's house.

"The young man," he said, "is beginning to have ideas, and the devil take me if I don't believe he's in love with your maid!"

But a more serious fault with which he reproached Justin was his constantly listening to conversation. On Sunday, for example, one could not get him out of the parlor, even when Madame Homais called him to fetch the children, who had fallen asleep in the arm-chairs, dragging down with their backs the overwide slip-covers.

Not many people came to the pharmacist's evening parties, his scandal-mongering and political opinions having successfully alienated various persons. The clerk never failed to be there. As soon as he heard the bell he ran to meet Madame Bovary, took her shawl, and put away under the shop-counter the heavy overshoes she wore when it snowed.

First they played some hands at trente-et-un; next Monsieur Homais played écarté with Emma; Léon standing behind her, gave advice. Standing up with his hands on the back of her chair, he saw the teeth of her comb that bit into her chignon. With every movement that she made to throw her cards the right side of her dress was drawn up. From her turned-up hair a dark colour fell over her back, and growing gradually paler, lost itself little by little in the shade. Her dress dropped on both sides of her chair, blowing out into many folds before it spread on the floor. When Léon occasionally felt the sole of his boot resting on it, he drew back as if he had trodden on something alive.

When the game of cards was over, the pharmacist and the Doctor played dominoes, and Emma, changing her place, leant her elbow on the table, turning over the pages of "L'Illustration." She had brought her ladies' journal with her. Léon sat down near her; they looked at the engravings together, and waited for one another at the bottom of the pages. She often begged him to read her the verses; Léon declaimed them in a languid voice, to which he carefully gave a dying fall in the love passages. But the noise of the dominoes annoyed him. Monsieur Homais was strong at the game; he could beat Charles and give him a double-six. Then the three hundred finished, they both stretched in front of the fire, and were soon asleep. The fire was dying out in the cinders; the teapot was empty, Léon was still reading. Emma listened to him, mechanically turning round the lampshade, its gauze decorated with painted clowns in carriages, and tightrope dancers with balancing-poles.

Léon stopped, pointing with a gesture to his sleeping audience; then they talked in low tones, and their conversation seemed the sweeter to them because it was unheard.

Thus a kind of bond was established between them, a constant exchange of books and of romances. Little inclined to jealousy, Monsieur Bovary thought nothing of it.

On his birthday he received a beautiful phrenological head, all marked with figures to the thorax and painted blue. This was a gift of the clerk's. He showed him many other attentions, to the point of running errands for him at Rouen: and a novel having made the mania for cactuses fashionable, Léon bought some for Madame Bovary, bringing them back on his knees in the "Hirondelle," pricking his fingers on their hard spikes.

She had a railed shelf suspended against her window to hold the pots. The clerk, too, had his small hanging garden; they saw each other tending their flowers at their windows.

One of the village windows was even more often occupied; for on Sundays from morning to night, and every morning when the weather was bright, one could see at an attic-window the profile of Monsieur Binet bending over his lathe; its monotonous humming could be heard at the Lion d'Or.

One evening on coming home Léon found in his room a rug in velvet and wool with leaves on a pale ground. He called Madame Homais, Monsieur Homais, Justin, the children, the cook; he spoke of it to his employer; every one wanted to see this rug. Why did the doctor's wife give the clerk presents? It looked odd; and they decided that he must be her lover.

He gave plenty of reason for this belief, so ceaselessly did he talk of her charms and of her wit; so much so, that Binet once roughly interrupted him:

"What do I care since I'm not one of her friends?"

He tortured himself to find out how he could make his declaration to her, and always halting between the fear of displeasing her and the shame of being such a coward, he wept with discouragement and desire. Then he took energetic resolutions, wrote letters that he tore up, put it off to times that he again deferred. Often he set out with the determination to dare all; but this resolution soon deserted him in Emma's presence; and when Charles, dropping in, invited him to jump into his carriage to go with him to see some patient in the neighborhood, he at once accepted, bowed to madame, and left. Wasn't the husband also a part of her after all?

As for Emma, she did not ask herself whether she loved him. Love, she thought, must come suddenly, with great outbursts and lightnings,—a hurricane of the skies, which sweeps down on life, upsets everything, uproots the will like a leaf and carries away the heart as in an abyss. She did not know that on the terrace of houses the rain makes lakes when the pipes are choked, and she would thus have remained safe in her ignorance when she suddenly discovered a rent in the wall.

V

It was a Sunday in February, an afternoon when the snow was falling.

Monsieur and Madame Bovary, Homais, and Monsieur Léon had all gone to see a yarn-mill that was being built in the valley a mile and a half from Yonville. The druggist had taken Napoleon and Athalie to give them some exercise, and Justin accompanied them, carrying the umbrellas over his shoulder.

Nothing, however, could be less worth seeing than this sight. A great piece of waste ground, on which, amid a mass of sand and stones, were scattered a few rusty cogwheels, surrounded by a long rectangular building pierced with numerous little windows. The building was unfinished; the sky could be seen through the beams of the roofing. Attached to the ridgepole of the gable a bunch of straw mixed with corn-ears fluttered its tricoloured ribbons in the wind.

Homais was talking. He explained to the company the future importance of this establishment, computed the strength of the floorings, the thickness of the walls, and regretted extremely not having a yard-stick such as Monsieur Binet possessed for his own special use.

Emma, who had taken his arm, bent lightly against his shoulder, and she looked at the sun's disc shining afar through the mist with pale splendour. She turned; there was Charles. His cap was drawn down over his eyebrows, and his two thick lips were trembling, which added a look of stupidity to his face; his very back, his calm back, was irritating to behold, and she saw all his platitude spelled out right there, on his very coat.

While she was considering him thus, savoring her irritation with a sort of depraved pleasure, Léon made a step forward. The cold that made him pale seemed to add a more gentle languor to his face; between his cravat and his neck the somewhat loose collar of his shirt showed the skin; some of his ear was showing beneath a lock of hair, and his large blue eyes, raised to the clouds, seemed to Emma more limpid and more beautiful than those mountain-lakes which mirror the heavens.

"Look out there!" suddenly cried the pharmacist.

And he ran to his son, who had just jumped into a pile of lime in order to whiten his boots. Overcome by his father's reproaches, Napoleon began to howl, while Justin dried his shoes with a wisp of straw. But a knife was needed; Charles offered his.

"Ah!" she said to herself, "he carries a knife in his pocket like a peasant."

It was beginning to snow and they turned back to Yonville.

In the evening Madame Bovary did not go to her neighbor's, and when Charles had left and she felt herself alone, the comparison again forced itself upon her, almost with the clarity of direct sensation, and with that lengthening of perspective which memory gives to things. Looking from her bed at the bright fire that was burning, she still saw, as she had down there, Léon standing up with one hand bending his cane, and with the other holding Athalie, who was quietly sucking a piece of ice. She thought him charming; she could not tear herself away from him; she recalled his other attitudes on other days, the words he had spoken, the sound of his voice, his whole person; and she repeated, pouting out her lips as if for a kiss:

"Yes, charming! charming! Is he not in love?" . . . she asked herself; "but with whom? . . . With me!"

All the evidence asserted itself at once; her heart leapt. The flame of the fire threw a joyous light upon the ceiling; she turned on her back, stretched out her arms.

Then began the eternal lamentation: "Oh, if Heaven had but willed it! And why not? What prevented it?"

When Charles came home at midnight, she seemed to have just awakened, and as he made a noise undressing, she complained of a headache, then asked casually what had happened that evening.

"Monsieur Léon," he said, "went to his room early."

She could not help smiling, and she fell asleep, her soul filled with a new delight.

The next day, at dusk, she received a visit from Monsieur Lheureux, the owner of the local general store.

He was a smart man, this shopkeeper.

Born in Gascony but bred a Norman, he grafted upon his southern volubility the cunning of the Cauchois. His fat, flabby, beardless face seemed dyed by a decoction of liquorice, and his white hair made even more vivid the keen brilliance of his small black eyes. No one knew what he had been formerly; some said he was a peddler, others that he was a banker at Routot. One thing was certain: he could make complex figurings in his head that would have frightened Binet himself. Polite to obsequiousness, he always held himself with his back bent in the attitude of one who bows or who invites.

After leaving at the door his black-bordered hat, he put down a green cardboard box on the table, and began by complaining to madame, with many civilities, that he should have remained till that day without the benefit of her confidence. A poor shop like his was not made to attract a lady of fashion; he stressed the words; yet she had only to command, and he would undertake to provide her with anything she might wish, whether it be lingerie or knitwear, hats or dresses, for he went to town regularly four times a month. He was connected with the best houses. His name could be mentioned at the "Trois Frères," at the "Barbe d'Or," or at the "Grand Sauvage"; all these gentlemen knew him inside out. To-day, then, he had come to show madame, in passing, various articles he happened to have by an unusual stroke of luck. And he pulled out half-a-dozen embroidered collars from the box.

Madame Bovary examined them.

"I don't need anything," she said.

Then Monsieur Lheureux delicately exhibited three Algerian scarves, several packages of English needles, a pair of straw slippers, and, finally, four eggcups in cocoa-nut wood, carved in open work by convicts. Then, with both hands on the table, his neck stretched out, leaning forward with open mouth, he watched Emma's gaze wander undecided over the merchandise. From time to time, as if to remove some dust, he flicked his nail against the silk of the scarves spread out at full length, and they rustled with a little noise, making the gold spangles of the material sparkle like stars in the greenish twilight.

"How much are they?"

"A mere trifle," he replied, "a mere trifle. But there's no hurry; whenever it's convenient. We are no Jews."

She reflected for a few moments, and ended by again declining Monsieur Lheureux's offer. Showing no concern, he replied:

"Very well! Better luck next time. I have always got on with ladies . . . even if I didn't with my own!"

Emma smiled.

"I wanted to tell you," he went on good-naturedly, after his joke, "that it isn't the money I should trouble about. Why, I could give you some, if need be."

She made a gesture of surprise.

"Ah!" he said quickly and in a low voice, "I shouldn't have to go far to find you some, rely on that."

And he began asking after Père Tellier, the owner of the "Café Français," who was being treated by Monsieur Bovary at the time.

"What's the matter with Père Tellier? He makes the whole house shake with his coughing, and I'm afraid he'll soon need a pine coat rather than a flannel jacket. He certainly lived it up when he was young! These people, madame, they never know when to stop! He burned himself up with brandy. Still it's sad, all the same, to see an acquaintance go."

And while he fastened up his box he discoursed about the doctor's patients.

"It's the weather, no doubt," he said, looking frowningly at the floor, "that causes these illnesses. I myself don't feel just right. One of these days I shall even have to consult the doctor for a pain I have in my back. Well, good-bye, Madame Bovary. At your service; your very humble servant."

And he gently closed the door behind him.

Emma had her dinner served in her bedroom on a tray by the fireside; she took a long time eating; everything seemed wonderful.

"How good I was!" she said to herself, thinking of the scarves.

She heard steps on the stairs. It was Léon. She got up and took from the chest of drawers the first pile of dusters to be hemmed. When he came in she seemed very busy.

The conversation languished; Madame Bovary let it drop every few minutes, while he himself seemed quite embarrassed. Seated on a low chair near the fire, he kept turning the ivory thimble case with his fingers. She stitched on, or from time to time turned down the hem of the cloth with her nail. She did not speak; he was silent, captivated by her silence, as he would have been by her speech.

"Poor fellow!" she thought.

"How have I displeased her?" he asked himself.

At last, however, Léon said that one of these days, he had to go to Rouen on business.

"Your music subscription has expired; shall I renew it?"

"No," she replied.

"Why?"

"Because . . ."

And pursing her lips she slowly drew a long stitch of grey thread. This work irritated Léon. It seemed to roughen the ends of her fingers. A gallant phrase came into his head, but he did not risk it.

"Then you are giving it up?" he went on.

"What?" she asked hurriedly. "Music? Ah! yes! Have I not my house to look after, my husband to attend to, a thousand things, in fact, many duties that must be considered first?"

She looked at the clock. Charles was late. Then she affected anxiety. Two or three times she even repeated, "He is so good!"

The clerk was fond of Monsieur Bovary. But this tenderness on his behalf came as an unpleasant surprise; still, he sang his praise: everyone did, he said, especially the pharmacist.

"Ah! he is a good man," continued Emma.

"Certainly," replied the clerk.

And he began talking of Madame Homais, whose very untidy appearance generally made them laugh.

"What does it matter?" interrupted Emma. "A good housewife does not trouble about her appearance."

Then she relapsed into silence.

It was the same on the following days; her talks, her manners, everything changed. She took interest in the housework, went to church regularly, and looked after her maid with more severity.

She took Berthe away from the nurse. When visitors called, Félicité brought her in, and Madame Bovary undressed her to show off her limbs. She claimed to love children; they were her consolation, her joy, her passion, and she accompanied her caresses with lyrical outbursts that would have reminded any one but the Yonvillians of Sachette[37] in "Notre Dame de Paris."[38]

When Charles came home he found his slippers put to warm near the fire. His waistcoat now never wanted lining, nor his shirt buttons, and it was quite a pleasure to see in the cupboard the nightcaps arranged in piles of the same height. She no longer grumbled as before when asked to take a walk in the garden; what he proposed was always done, although she never anticipated the wishes to which she submitted without a murmur; and when Léon saw him sit by his fireside after dinner, his two hands on his stomach, his two feet on the fender, his cheeks flushed with wine, his eyes moist with happiness, the child crawling along the carpet, and this woman with the slender waist who came behind his armchair to kiss his forehead:

"What madness!" he said to himself. "How could I ever hope to reach her?"

She seemed so virtuous and inaccessible to him that he lost all hope, even the faintest. But, by thus renouncing her, he made her ascend to extraordinary heights. She transcended, in his eyes, those sensuous attributes which were forever out of his reach; and in his heart she rose forever, soaring away from him like a winged apotheosis. It was one of those pure feelings that do not interfere with life, that are cultivated for their rarity, and whose loss would afflict more than their fulfilment rejoices.

Emma grew thinner, her cheeks paler, her face longer. With her black hair, her large eyes, her straight nose, her birdlike walk, and always silent now, did she not seem to be passing through life scarcely touching it, bearing on her brow the slight mark of a sublime destiny? She was so sad and so calm, at once so gentle and so reserved, that near her one came under the spell of an icy charm, as we shudder in churches at the perfume of the flowers mingling with the cold of the marble. Even others could not fail to be impressed. The pharmacist said:

"She is a real lady! She would not be out of place in a sous-préfecture!"

---

37. Sachette ("sackcloth"); Paguette la Chantefleurie is the mother of Agnes, the girl abducted by gypsies who takes the name Esmeralda. She worshipped a shoe of her stolen child.

38. *Notre Dame de Paris* (1831) is a historical novel by Victor Hugo (1802–1885).

The housewives admired her thrift, the patients her politeness, the poor her charity.

But she was eaten up with desires, with rage, with hate. The rigid folds of her dress covered a tormented heart of which her chaste lips never spoke. She was in love with Léon, and sought solitude that she might more easily delight in his image. His physical presence troubled the voluptuousness of this meditation. Emma thrilled at the sound of his step; then in his presence the emotion subsided, and afterwards there remained in her only an immense astonishment that ended in sorrow.

Léon did not know that when he left her in despair she rose after he had gone to see him in the street. She concerned herself about his comings and goings; she watched his face; she invented quite a story to find an excuse for going to his room. She envied the pharmacist's wife for sleeping under the same roof, and her thoughts constantly centered upon this house, like the Lion d'Or pigeons who alighted there to dip their pink feet and white wings in the rainpipes. But the more Emma grew conscious of her love, the more she repressed it, hoping thus to hide and to stifle her true feeling. She would have liked Léon to know, and she imagined circumstances, catastrophes that would make this possible. What restrained her was, no doubt, idleness and fear, as well as a sense of shame. She thought she had repulsed him too much, that the time was past, that all was lost. Then, pride, the joy of being able to say to herself, "I am virtuous," and to look at herself in the mirror striking resigned poses, consoled her a little for the sacrifice she thought she was making.

Then the desires of the flesh, the longing for money, and the melancholy of passion all blended into one suffering, and instead of putting it out of her mind, she made her thoughts cling to it, urging herself to pain and seeking everywhere the opportunity to revive it. A poorly served dish, a half open door would aggravate her; she bewailed the clothes she did not have, the happiness she had missed, her overexalted dreams, her too cramped home.

What exasperated her was that Charles did not seem to be aware of her torment. His conviction that he was making her happy looked to her a stupid insult, and his self-assurance on this point sheer ingratitude. For whom, then, was she being virtuous? Was it not for him, the obstacle to all happiness, the cause of all misery, and, as it were, the sharp clasp of that complex strap that buckled her in all sides?

Thus he became the butt of all the hatred resulting from her frustrations; but all efforts to conquer them augmented her suffering— for this useless humiliation still added to her despair and widened the gap between them. His very gentleness would drive her at times to rebellion. Domestic mediocrity urged her on to wild extravagance, matrimonial tenderness to adulterous desires. She would have liked

Charles to beat her, that she might have a better right to hate him, to revenge herself upon him. She was surprised sometimes at the shocking thoughts that came into her head, and she had to go on smiling, to hear repeated to her at all hours that she was happy, to pretend to be happy and let it be believed.

Yet, at moments, she loathed this hypocrisy. She was tempted to flee somewhere with Léon and try a new life; but at once a dark, shapeless chasm would open within her soul.

"Besides, he no longer loves me," she thought. "What is to become of me? What help can I hope for, what consolation, what relief?"

Such thoughts would leave her shattered, exhausted, frozen, sobbing silently, with flowing tears.

"Why don't you tell monsieur?" the maid asked her when she came in during these crises.

"It is nerves," said Emma. "Don't mention it to him, he would worry."

"Ah! yes," Félicité went on, "you are just like La Guérine, the daughter of Père Guérin, the fisherman at le Pollet,[39] that I used to know at Dieppe before I came to see you. She was so sad, so sad, that to see her standing on the threshold of her house, she looked like a winding-sheet spread out before the door. Her illness, it appears, was a kind of fog that she had in the head, and the doctors could do nothing about it, neither could the priest. When she had a bad spell, she went off by herself to the sea-shore, so that the customs officer, going his rounds, often found her flat on her face, crying on the pebbles. Then, after her marriage, it stopped, they say."

"But with me," replied Emma, "it was after marriage that it began."

VI

One evening when she was sitting by the open window, watching Lestiboudois, the sexton, trim the boxwood, she suddenly heard the Angelus ringing.

It was the beginning of April, when the primroses are in bloom, and a warm wind blows over the newly-turned flower beds, and the gardens, like women, seem to be getting ready for the summer dances. Through the bars of the arbour and away beyond, the river could be seen in the fields, meandering through the grass in sinuous curves. The evening vapors rose between the leafless poplars, touching their outlines with a violet tint, paler and more transparent than a subtle gauze caught amidst their branches. Cattle moved around in the distance; neither their steps nor their lowing could be heard; and the bell, still ringing through the air, kept up its peaceful lamentation.

39. Suburb of Dieppe, where the fishermen live.

This repeated tinkling stirred in the young woman distant memories of her youth and school-days. She remembered the great candlesticks that rose above the vases full of flowers on the altar, and the tabernacle with its small columns. She would have liked to be once more lost in the long line of white veils, marked off here and there by the stiff black hoods of the good sisters bending over their praying-chairs. At mass on Sundays, when she looked up, she saw the gentle face of the Virgin amid the blue smoke of the rising incense. The image awoke a tender emotion in her; she felt limp and helpless, like the down of a bird whirled by the tempest, and it was unconsciously that she went towards the church, ready for any kind of devotion, provided she could humble her soul and lose all sense of selfhood.

On the Square she met Lestiboudois on his way back, for, in order not to lose out on a full day's wages, he preferred to interrupt his gardening-work and go ring the Angelus when it suited him best. Besides, the earlier ringing warned the boys that catechism time had come.

Already a few who had arrived were playing marbles on the stones of the cemetery. Others, astride the wall, swung their legs, trampling with their wooden shoes the large nettles that grew between the little enclosure and the newest graves. This was the only green spot. All the rest was but stones, always covered with a fine dust, in spite of Lestiboudois' broom.

The children played around in their socks, as if they were on their own ground. The shouts of their voices could be heard through the humming of the bell. The noise subsided with the swinging of the great rope that, hanging from the top of the belfry, dragged its end on the ground. Swallows flitted to and fro uttering little cries, cutting the air with the edge of their wings, and swiftly returned to their yellow nests under the eave-tiles of the coping. At the end of the church a lamp was burning, the wick of a night-light hung up in a glass. Seen from a distance, it looked like a white stain trembling in the oil. A long ray of the sun fell across the nave and seemed to darken the lower sides and the corners.

"Where is the priest?" Madame Bovary asked one of the boys, who was entertaining himself by shaking the turnstile in its too loose socket.

"He is coming," he answered.

Indeed, the door of the rectory creaked and the Abbé Bournisien appeared; the children fled in a heap into the church.

"The little brats!" muttered the priest, "always the same!" Then, picking up a ragged catechism on which he had stepped:

"They have respect for nothing!"

But, as soon as he caught sight of Madame Bovary:

"Excuse me," he said; "I did not recognise you."

He thrust the catechism into his pocket, and stopped, balancing the heavy key of the sacristy between his two fingers.

The full light of the setting sun upon his face made the cloth of his cassock, shiny at the elbows and frayed at the hem, seem paler. Grease and tobacco stains ran along his broad chest, following the line of his buttons, growing sparser in the vicinity of his neckcloth, in which rested the massive folds of his red chin; it was dotted with yellow spots that disappeared beneath the coarse hair of his greyish beard. He had just eaten his dinner, and was breathing noisily.

"And how are you?" he added.

"Not well," replied Emma; "I am suffering."

"So do I," answered the priest. "The first heat of the year is hard to bear, isn't it? But, after all, we are born to suffer, as St. Paul says. But, what does Monsieur Bovary think of it?"

"He!" she said with a gesture of contempt.

"What!" he replied, genuinely surprised, "doesn't he prescribe something for you?"

"Ah!" said Emma, "it is no earthly remedy I need."

But the curé time and again was looking into the church, where the kneeling boys were shouldering one another, and tumbling over like packs of cards.

"I should like to know . . ." she went on.

"You look out, Riboudet," the priest cried angrily, "I'll box your ears, you scoundrel!" Then turning to Emma. "He's Boudet the carpenter's son; his parents are well off, and let him do just as he pleases. Yet he could learn quickly if he would, for he is very sharp. And so sometimes for a joke I call him Riboudet (like the road one takes to go to Maromme), and I even say '*Mon* Riboudet.' Ha! ha! '*Mont* Riboudet.' The other day I repeated this little joke to the bishop, and he laughed. Can you imagine? He deigned to laugh. And how is Monsieur Bovary?"

She seemed not to hear him. And he went on . . .

"Always very busy, no doubt; for he and I are certainly the busiest people in the parish. But he is doctor of the body," he added with a thick laugh, "and I of the soul."

She fixed her pleading eyes upon the priest. "Yes," she said, "you solace all sorrows."

"Ah! don't tell me of it, Madame Bovary. This morning I had to go to Bas-Diauville for a cow was all swollen; they thought it was under a spell. All their cows, I don't know how it is . . . But pardon me! Longuemarre and Boudet! Bless me! Will you stop it?"

And he bounded into the church.

The boys were just then clustering round the large desk, climbing over the cantor's footstool, opening the missal; and others on tiptoe were just about to venture into the confessional. But the priest suddenly distributed a shower of blows among them. Seizing them by the collars of their coats, he lifted them from the ground, and deposited them on their knees on the stones of the choir, firmly, as if he meant to plant them there.

"Yes," said he, when he returned to Emma, unfolding his large cotton handkerchief, one corner of which he put between his teeth, "farmers are much to be pitied."

"Others, too," she replied.

"Certainly. Workingmen in the cities, for instance."

"I wasn't thinking of them . . ."

"Oh, but excuse me! I've known housewives there, virtuous women, I assure you, real saints, who didn't even have bread to eat."

"But those," replied Emma, and the corners of her mouth twitched as she spoke, "those, Monsieur le Curé, who have bread and have no . . ."

"Fire in the winter," said the priest.

"Oh, what does it matter?"

"What! What does it matter? It seems to me that when one has firing and food . . . for, after all . . ."

"My God! my God!" she sighed.

"Do you feel unwell?" he asked, approaching her anxiously. "It is indigestion, no doubt? You must get home, Madame Bovary; drink a little tea, that will strengthen you, or else a glass of fresh water with a little moist sugar."

"Why?"

And she looked like one awaking from a dream.

"Well, you see, you were putting your hand to your forehead. I thought you felt faint."

Then, bethinking himself: "But you were asking me something? What was it? I don't remember."

"I? Oh, nothing . . . nothing," Emma repeated.

And the glance she cast round her slowly fell upon the old man in the cassock. They looked at each other face to face without speaking.

"Well then, Madame Bovary," he said at last, "excuse me, but duty comes first as the saying goes; I must look after my brats. The first communion will soon be upon us, and I fear we shall be behind, as ever. So after Ascension Day I regularly keep them an extra hour every Wednesday. Poor children! One cannot lead them too soon into the path of the Lord . . . he himself advised us to do so, through the mouth of his Divine Son. Good health to you, madame; my respects to your husband."

And he went into the church making a genuflexion as soon as he reached the door.

Emma saw him disappear between the double row of benches, walking with heavy tread, his head a little bent over his shoulder, and with his two half-open hands stretched sidewards.

Then she turned on her heel all of one piece, like a statue on a pivot, and went homewards. But the loud voice of the priest, the clear voices of the boys still reached her ears, and pursued her:

"Are you a Christian?"

"Yes, I am a Christian."

"What is a Christian?"

"He who, being baptized . . . baptized . . . baptized . . ."

She climbed the steps of the staircase holding on to the banisters, and when she was in her room threw herself into an arm-chair.

The whitish light of the window-panes was softly wavering. The pieces of furniture seemed more frozen in their places, about to lose themselves in the shadow as in an ocean of darkness. The fire was out, the clock went on ticking, and Emma vaguely wondered at this calm of all things while within herself there was such tumult. But little Berthe was there, between the window and the work-table, tottering on her knitted shoes, and trying to reach the end of her mother's apron-strings.

"Leave me alone," Emma said, pushing her back with her hand.

The little girl soon came up closer against her knees, and leaning on them with her arms, she looked up with her large blue eyes, while a small thread of clear saliva drooled from her lips on to the silk of her apron.

"Leave me alone," repeated the young woman quite angrily.

Her expression frightened the child, who began to scream.

"Will you leave me alone?" she said, forcing her away with her elbow.

Berthe fell at the foot of the chest of drawers against the brass handle; she cut her cheek, blood appeared. Madame Bovary rushed to lift her up, broke the bell-rope, called for the maid with all her might, and she was just going to curse herself when Charles appeared. It was dinner time; he was coming home.

"Look, dear!" said Emma calmly, "the child fell down while she was playing, and she hurt herself."

Charles reassured her; it was only a slight cut, and he went for some adhesive plaster.

Madame Bovary did not go downstairs to the dining-room; she wished to remain alone to look after the child. Then watching her sleep, the little anxiety she still felt gradually wore off, and she seemed very stupid to herself, and very kind to have been so worried just now at so little. Berthe, in fact, no longer cried. Her breathing now imperceptibly raised the cotton covering. Big tears lay in the corner of the half-closed eyelids, through whose lashes one could see two pale sunken pupils; the adhesive plaster on her cheek pulled the skin aside.

"It is very strange," thought Emma, "how ugly this child is!"

When at eleven o'clock Charles came back from the pharmacist's shop, where he had gone after dinner to return the remainder of the plaster, he found his wife standing by the cradle.

"I assure you it's nothing," he said, kissing her on the forehead. "Don't worry, my poor darling; you will make yourself ill."

He had stayed a long time at the pharmacist's. Although he had not seemed much concerned, Homais, nevertheless, had exerted himself to buoy him up, to "raise his spirits." Then they had talked of the various dangers that threaten childhood, of the carelessness of servants. Madame Homais knew what he meant: she still carried on her chest the scars of a load of charcoal that a cook dropped on her when she was a child. Hence that her kind parents took all sorts of precautions. The knives were not sharpened, nor the floors waxed; there were iron gratings in front of the windows and strong bars across the fireplace. In spite of their spirit, the little Homais could not stir without some one watching them; at the slightest cold their father stuffed them with cough-syrups; and until they turned four they all were mercilessly forced to use padded headwear. This, it is true, was a fancy of Madame Homais'; her husband was secretly afflicted by it. Fearing the possible consequences of such compression to the intellectual organs, he even went so far as to say to her:

"Do you want to make them into Caribs or Botocudos?"

Charles, however, had several times tried to interrupt the conversation.

"I would like a word with you," he whispered, addressing the clerk who preceded him on the stairs.

"Can he suspect anything?" Léon asked himself. His heart beat faster, and all sorts of conjectures occured to him.

At last, Charles, having closed the door behind him, begged him to inquire at Rouen after the price of a fine daguerreotype. It was a sentimental surprise he intended for his wife, a delicate attention: his own portrait in black tail coat. But he wanted first to know how much it would cost. It wouldn't cause Monsieur Léon too much trouble to find out, since he went to town almost every week.

Why? Monsieur Homais suspected some love affair, an intrigue. But he was mistaken. Léon was carrying on no flirtations. He was sadder than ever, as Madame Lefrançois saw from the amount of food he left on his plate. To find out more about it she questioned the tax-collector. Binet answered roughly that he wasn't being paid to spy on him.

All the same, his companion's behavior seemed very strange to him, for Léon often threw himself back in his chair, and stretching out his arms, complained vaguely about life.

"It's because you have no distractions," said the collector.

"What distractions?"

"If I were you I'd have a lathe."

"But I don't know how to turn," answered the clerk.

"Ah! that's true," said the other, rubbing his chin with an air of mingled contempt and satisfaction.

Léon was weary of loving without success; moreover, he was beginning to feel that depression caused by the repetition of the same life, with no interest to inspire and no hope to sustain it. He was so bored with Yonville and the Yonvillers, that the sight of certain persons, of certain houses, irritated him beyond endurance; and the pharmacist, good companion though he was, was becoming absolutely unbearable to him. Yet the prospect of a new condition of life frightened as much as it seduced him.

This apprehension soon changed into impatience, and then Paris beckoned from afar with the music of its masked balls, the laughter of the grisettes. Since he was to go to law-school there anyway, why not set out at once? Who prevented him? And, inwardly, he began making preparations; he arranged his occupations beforehand. In his mind, he decorated an apartment. He would lead an artist's life there! He would take guitar lessons! He would have a dressing-gown, a Basque béret, blue velvet slippers! He already admired two crossed foils over his chimney-piece, with a skull on the guitar above them.

The main difficulty was to obtain his mother's consent, though nothing could seem more reasonable. Even his employer advised him to go to some other law office where he could learn more rapidly. Taking a middle course, then, Léon looked for some position as second clerk in Rouen; found none, and at last wrote his mother a long letter full of details, in which he set forth the reasons for going to live in Paris at once. She consented.

He did not hurry. Every day for a month Hivert carried boxes, valises, parcels for him from Yonville to Rouen and from Rouen to Yonville; and when Léon had rounded out his wardrobe, had his three armchairs restuffed, bought a supply of neckties, in a word, had made more preparations than for a trip round the world, he put it off from week to week, until he received a second letter from his mother urging him to leave, since he wanted to pass his examination before the vacation.

When the moment for the farewells had come, Madame Homais wept, Justin sobbed; Homais, as a strong man, concealed his emotion; he wished to carry his friend's overcoat himself as far as the gate of the notary, who was taking Léon to Rouen in his carriage. The latter had just time to bid farewell to Monsieur Bovary.

When he reached the head of the stairs he stopped, he was so out of breath. When he entered, Madame Bovary rose hurriedly.

"It is I again!" said Léon.

"I was sure of it!"

She bit her lips, and a rush of blood flowing under her skin made her red from the roots of her hair to the top of her collar. She remained standing, leaning with her shoulder against the wainscot.

"The doctor is not here?" he went on.

"He is out."

She repeated:

"He is out."

Then there was silence. They looked one at the other, and their thoughts, united in the same agony, clung together like two hearts in a passionate embrace.

"I would like to kiss little Berthe good-bye," said Léon.

Emma went down a few steps and called Félicité.

He threw one long look around him that took in the walls, the shelves, the fireplace, as if to appropriate everything, to carry it with him.

She returned, and the servant brought Berthe, who was swinging an upside down windmill at the end of a string. Léon kissed her several times on the neck.

"Good-bye poor child! good-bye, dear little one! good-bye!" And he gave her back to her mother.

"Take her away," she said.

They remained alone—Madame Bovary, her back turned, her face pressed against a window-pane; Léon held his cap in his hand, tapping it softly against his thigh.

"It is going to rain," said Emma.

"I have a coat," he answered.

"Ah!"

She turned round, her chin lowered, her forehead bent forward. The light covered it to the curve of the eyebrows, like a single piece of marble, without revealing what Emma was seeing on the horizon or what she was thinking within herself.

"Well, good-bye," he sighed.

She raised her head with a quick movement.

"Yes, good-bye . . . go!"

They faced each other; he held out his hand; she hesitated.

"In the English manner, then," she said, offering him her hand and forcing a laugh.

Léon felt it between his fingers, and the very substance of all his being seemed to pass into that moist palm.

He opened his hand; their eyes met again, and he disappeared. When he reached the market-place, he stopped and hid behind a pillar to look for the last time at this white house with the four green blinds. He thought he saw a shadow behind the window in the room; but the curtain, sliding along the rod as though no one were touching it, slowly opened its long oblique folds, that spread out all at once, and thus hung straight and motionless as a plaster wall. Léon ran away.

From afar he saw his employer's buggy in the road, and by it a man in a coarse apron holding the horse. Homais and Monsieur Guillaumin were talking. They were waiting for him.

"Embrace me," said the pharmacist with tears in his eyes. "Here is your coat, my good friend. Mind the cold; take care of yourself; don't overdo it!"

"Come, Léon, jump in," said the notary.

Homais bent over the splash-board, and in a voice broken by sobs uttered these three sad words:

"A pleasant journey!"

"Good-night," said Monsieur Guillaumin. "Go ahead!"

They departed and Homais went home.

Madame Bovary had opened her window that looked out over the garden and watched the clouds. They were gathering round the sunset in the direction of Rouen, and rolling back swiftly in black swirls, behind which the great rays of the sun looked out like the golden arrows of a suspended trophy, while the rest of the empty heavens was white as porcelain. But a gust of wind bowed the poplars, and suddenly the rain fell; it rattled against the green leaves. Then the sun reappeared, the hens clucked, sparrows shook their wings in the damp thickets, and the pools of water on the gravel as they flowed away carried off the pink flowers of an acacia.

"Ah! how far off he must be already!" she thought.

Monsieur Homais, as usual, came at half-past six during dinner.

"Well," said he, "so we've sent off our young friend!"

"So it seems," replied the doctor. Then, turning on his chair: "Any news at home?"

"Nothing much. Only my wife was a little out of sorts this afternoon. You know women—a nothing upsets them, especially my wife. And we shouldn't object to that, since their nervous system is much more fragile than ours."

"Poor Léon!" said Charles. "How will he live at Paris? Will he get used to it?"

Madame Bovary sighed.

"Of course!" said the pharmacist, smacking his lips. "The late night suppers! the masked balls, the champagne—he won't be losing his time, I assure you."

"I don't think he'll go wrong," objected Bovary.

"Nor do I," said Monsieur Homais quickly; "although he'll have to do like the rest for fear of passing for a Jesuit. And you don't know what a life those jokers lead in the Latin quarter, actresses and the rest! Besides, students are thought a great deal of in Paris. Provided they have a few accomplishments, they are received in the best society; there are even ladies of the Faubourg Saint-Germain[40] who fall in love with them, which later gives them opportunities for making very good matches."

"But," said the doctor, "I fear for him that . . . down there . . ."

"You are right," interrupted the pharmacist, "that is the other side of the coin. And you are constantly obliged to keep your hand in your pocket there. Let us say, for instance, you are in a public garden. A fellow appears, well dressed, even wearing a decoration, and whom one would take for a diplomat. He addresses you, you chat with him; he forces himself upon you; offers you a pinch of snuff, or picks up your hat. Then you become more intimate; he takes you to a café, invites you to his countryhouse, introduces you, between two drinks, to all sorts of people; and three-fourths of the time it's only to get hold of your money or involve you in some shady deal"

"That is true," said Charles; "but I was thinking specially of illnesses—of typhoid fever, for example, that attacks students from the provinces."

Emma shuddered.

"Because of the change of diet," continued the pharmacist, "and of the resulting upset for the whole system. And then the water at Paris, don't you know! The dishes at restaurants, all the spiced food, end by heating the blood, and are not worth, whatever people may say of them, a good hearty stew. As for me, I have always preferred home cooking; it is healthier. So when I was studying pharmacy at Rouen, I boarded in a boarding-house; and dined with the professors."

And thus he went on, expounding his general opinions and his personal preferences, until Justin came to fetch him for a mulled egg for a customer.

"Not a moment's peace!" he cried; "always at it! I can't go out for a minute! Like a plough-horse, I have always to be sweating blood and water! What drudgery!" Then, when he was at the door, "By the way, do you know the news?"

"What news?"

"It is very likely," Homais went on, raising his eyebrows and assuming one of his gravest expressions, "that the agricultural fair

40. Faubourg Saint-Germain is the aristocratic quarter of Paris.

of the Seine-Inférieure will be held this year at Yonville-l'Abbaye."

The rumor, at all events, is going the round. This morning the paper alluded to it. It would be of the utmost importance for our district. But we'll talk it over later. I can see, thank you; Justin has the lantern."

VII

The next day was a dreary one for Emma. Everything seemed shrouded in an atmosphere of bleakness that hung darkly over the outward aspect of things, and sorrow blew into her soul with gentle moans, as the winter wind makes in ruined castles. Her reverie was that of things gone forever, the exhaustion that seizes you after everything is done; the pain, in short, caused by the interruption of a familiar motion, the sudden halting of a long drawn out vibration.

As on the return from Vaubyessard, when the quadrilles were running in her head, she was full of a gloomy melancholy, of a numb despair. Léon reappeared, taller, handsomer, more charming, more vague. Though separated from her, he had not left her; he was there, and the walls of the house seemed to hold his shadow. She could not detach her eyes from the carpet where he had walked, from those empty chairs where he had sat. The river still flowed on and slowly drove its ripples along the slippery banks. They had often walked there listening to the murmur of the waves over the moss-covered pebbles. How bright the sun had been! What happy afternoons they had known, alone, in the shade at the end of the garden! He read aloud, bare-headed, sitting on a footstool of dry sticks; the fresh wind of the meadow set trembling the leaves of the book and the nasturtiums of the arbour. Ah! he was gone, the only charm of her life, the only possible hope of joy. Why had she not seized this happiness when it came to her? Why did she not keep him from leaving, beg him on her knees, when he was about to flee from her? And she cursed herself for not having loved Léon. She thirsted for his lips. She wanted to run after him, to throw herself into his arms and say to him, "It is I; I am yours." But Emma recoiled beforehand at the difficulties of the enterprise, and her desires, increased by regret, became only the more acute.

Henceforth the memory of Léon was the center of her boredom; it burnt there more brightly than the fires left by travellers on the snow of a Russian steppe. She threw herself at his image, pressed herself against it; she stirred carefully the dying embers, sought all around her anything that could make it flare; and the most distant reminiscences, like the most immediate occasions, what she experienced as well as what she imagined, her wasted voluptuous desires that were unsatisfied, her projects of happiness that crackled in the wind like dead boughs, her sterile virtue, her lost hopes, the yoke of domesticity,—she gathered it all up, took everything, and made it all serve as fuel for her melancholy.

The flames, however, subsided, either because the supply had exhausted itself, or because it had been piled up too much. Love, little by little, was quelled by absence; regret stifled beneath habit; and the bright fire that had empurpled her pale sky was overspread and faded by degrees. In her slumbering conscience, she took her disgust for her husband for aspirations towards her lover, the burning of hate for the warmth of tenderness; but as the tempest still raged, and as passion burnt itself down to the very cinders, and no help came, no sun rose, there was night on all sides, and she was lost in the terrible cold that pierced her through.

Then the evil days of Tostes began again. She thought herself now far more unhappy; for she had the experience of grief, with the certainty that it would not end.

A woman who had consented to such sacrifices could well allow herself certain whims. She bought a gothic prie-Dieu, and in a month spent fourteen francs on lemons for polishing her nails; she wrote to Rouen for a blue cashmere gown; she chose one of Lheureux's finest scarves, and wore it knotted round her waist over her dressing-gown; thus dressed, she lay stretched out on the couch with closed blinds.

She often changed her hairdo; she did her hair *à la Chinoise*, in flowing curls, in plaited coils; she parted it on one side and rolled it under, like a man's.

She wanted to learn Italian; she bought dictionaries, a grammar, and a supply of white paper. She tried serious reading, history, and philosophy. Sometimes in the night Charles woke up with a start, thinking he was being called to a patient:

"I'm coming," he stammered.

It was the noise of a match Emma had struck to relight the lamp. But her reading fared like her pieces of embroidery, all of which, only just begun, filled her cupboard; she took it up, left it, passed on to other books.

She had attacks in which she could easily have been driven to commit any folly. She maintained one day, to contradict her husband, that she could drink off a large glass of brandy, and, as Charles was stupid enough to dare her to, she swallowed the brandy to the last drop.

In spite of her vaporish airs (as the housewives of Yonville called them), Emma, all the same, never seemed gay, and usually she had at the corners of her mouth that immobile contraction that puckers the faces of old maids, and those of men whose ambition has failed. She was pale all over, white as a sheet; the skin of her nose was drawn at the nostrils, her eyes had a vague look. After discovering three grey hairs on her temples, she talked much of her old age.

She often had spells. One day she even spat blood, and, as Charles fussed round her showing his anxiety . . .

"Bah!" she answered, "what does it matter?"

Charles fled to his study and wept there, both his elbows on the table, sitting in his office chair under the phrenological head.

Then he wrote to his mother to beg her to come, and they had many long consultations together on the subject of Emma.

What should they decide? What was to be done since she rejected all medical treatment?

"Do you know what your wife wants?" replied Madame Bovary senior. "She wants to be forced to occupy herself with some manual work. If she were obliged, like so many others, to earn her living, she wouldn't have these vapors, that come to her from a lot of ideas she stuffs into her head, and from the idleness in which she lives."

"Yet she is always busy," said Charles.

"Ah! always busy at what? Reading novels, bad books, works against religion, and in which they mock at priests in speeches taken from Voltaire. But all that leads you far astray, my poor child. A person who has no religion is bound to go astray."

So it was decided to keep Emma from reading novels. The enterprise did not seem easy. The old lady took it upon herself: She was, when she passed through Rouen, to go herself to the lending library and represent that Emma had discontinued her subscription. Would they not have a right to call in the police if the bookseller persisted all the same in his poisonous trade?

The farewells of mother and daughter-in-law were cold. During the three weeks that they had been together they had not exchanged half-a-dozen words except for the usual questions and greetings when they met at table and in the evening before going to bed.

Madame Bovary left on a Wednesday, the market-day at Yonville.

Since morning, the Square had been crowded by end on end of carts, which, with their shafts in the air, spread all along the line of houses from the church to the inn. On the other side there were canvas booths for the sale of cotton goods, blankets, and woolen stockings, together with harness for horses, and packages of blue ribbon, whose ends fluttered in the wind. The coarse hardware was spread out on the ground between pyramids of eggs and hampers of cheeses showing pieces of sticky straw. Near the wheat threshers clucking hens passed their necks through the bars of flat cages. The crowds piled up in one place and refused to budge; they threatened at times to smash the window of the pharmacy. On

Wednesdays his shop was never empty, and the people pushed in less to buy drugs than for consultations, so great was Homais' reputation in the neighboring villages. His unshakable assurance deeply impresssed the country people. They considered him a greater doctor than all the doctors.

Emma was standing in the open window (she often did so: in the provinces, the window takes the place of the theatre and the promenade) and she amused herself with watching the rustic crowd, when she saw a gentleman in a green velvet coat. Although he was wearing heavy boots, he had on yellow gloves; he was coming towards the doctor's house, followed by a worried looking peasant with lowered head and quite a thoughtful air.

"Can I see the doctor?" he asked Justin, who was talking on the doorsteps with Félicité.

And, mistaking him for a servant of the house, he added,

"Tell him that M. Rodolphe Boulanger *de la* Huchette is here."

It was not out of affectation that the new arrival added "*de la* Huchette" to his name, but to make himself the better known. La Huchette, in fact, was an estate near Yonville, where he had just bought the château and two farms that he cultivated himself, without, however, taking too many pains. He lived as a bachelor, and was supposed to have an income of "at least fifteen thousand francs a year."

Charles came into the room. Monsieur Boulanger introduced his man, who wanted to be bled because he felt "as if ants were crawling all over him."

"It will clear me out," was his answer to all reasonable objections.

So Bovary brought a bandage and a basin, and asked Justin to hold it. Then addressing the peasant, who was already turning pale:

"Don't be scared, my friend."

"No, no, sir," said the other; "go ahead!"

And with an air of bravado he held out his heavy arm. At the prick of the lancet the blood spurted out, splashing against the looking-glass.

"Hold the basin nearer," exclaimed Charles.

"Look!" said the peasant, "one would swear it was a little fountain flowing. How red my blood is! That's a good sign, isn't it?"

"Sometimes," answered the officier de santé, "one feels nothing at first, and them they start fainting, especially when they're strong like this one."

At these words the peasant dropped the lancet-case he was holding back of his chair. A shudder of his shoulders made the chair-back creak. His hat fell off.

"I thought as much," said Bovary, pressing his finger on the vein.

The basin was beginning to tremble in Justin's hands; his knees shook, he turned pale.

"My wife! get my wife!" called Charles.

With one bound she rushed down the staircase.

"Vinegar," he cried. "Lord, two at a time!"

And he was so upset he could hardly put on the compress.

"It is nothing," said Monsieur Boulanger quietly, taking Justin in his arms. He seated him on the table with his back resting against the wall.

Madame Bovary opened the collar of his shirt. The strings of his shirt had got into a knot, and she was for some minutes moving her light fingers about the young fellow's neck. Then she poured some vinegar on her cambric handkerchief; she moistened his temples with little dabs, and then blew delicately upon them.

The ploughman revived, but Justin remained unconscious. His eyeballs disappeared in their whites like blue flowers in milk.

"We must hide this from him," said Charles.

Madame Bovary took the basin to put it under the table. With the movement she made in bending down, her dress (it was a summer dress with four flounces, yellow, long in the waist and wide in the skirt) spread out around on the tiles; and as Emma, stooping, staggered a little in stretching out her arms, the pull of her dress made it hug more closely the line of her bosom. Then she went to fetch a bottle of water, and she was melting some pieces of sugar when the pharmacist arrived. The maid had gone for him at the height of the confusion; seeing his pupil with his eyes open he gave a sigh of relief; then going round him he looked at him from head to foot.

"You fool!" he said, "you're a real fool! A capital idiot! And all that for a little blood-letting! and coming from a fellow who isn't afraid of anything! a real squirrel, climbing to incredible heights in order to steal nuts! You can be proud of yourself! showing a fine talent for the pharmaceutical profession; for, later on, you may be called before the courts of justice in serious circumstances, to enlighten the consciences of the magistrates, and you would have to keep your head then, to reason, show yourself a man, or else pass for an imbecile."

Justin did not answer. The pharmacist went on:

"Who asked you to come? You are always pestering the doctor and madame. Anyway, on Wednesday, I need you in the shop. There are over 20 people there now waiting to be served. I left them just out of concern for you. Get going! hurry! Wait for me there and keep an eye on the jars."

When Justin, who was rearranging his clothes, had gone, they talked for a little while about fainting-fits. Madame Bovary had never fainted.

"That is most unusual for a lady," said Monsieur Boulanger; "but some people are very susceptible. Thus in a duel, I have seen a witness faint away at the mere sound of the loading of pistols."

"As for me," said the pharmacist, "the sight of other people's blood doesn't affect me in the least, but the mere thought of my own flowing would make me faint if I reflected upon it too much."

Monsieur Boulanger, however, dismissed his servant and told him to be quiet, now that his whim was satisfied.

"It gave me the opportunity of making your acquaintance," he added, and he looked at Emma as he said this.

Then he put three francs on the corner of the table, bowed casually, and went out.

He soon had crossed to the other bank of the river (this was his way back to La Huchette), and Emma saw him in the meadow, walking under the poplars, slackening his pace now and then as one who reflects.

"She is nice, very nice, that doctor's wife," he said to himself. "Fine teeth, black eyes, a dainty foot, a figure like a Parisienne's. Where the devil does she come from? Where did that boor ever pick her up?"

Monsieur Rodolphe Boulanger was thirty-four; he combined brutality of temperament with a shrewd judgment, having had much experience with women and being something of a connoisseur. This one had seemed pretty to him; so he kept dreaming about her and her husband.

"I think he is very stupid. She must be tired of him, no doubt. He has dirty nails, and hasn't shaven for three days. While he is trotting after his patients, she sits there mending socks. How bored she gets! How she'd want to be in the city and go dancing every night! Poor little woman! She is gaping after love like a carp on the kitchen table after water. Three gallant words and she'd adore me, I'm sure of it. She'd be tender, charming. Yes; but how get rid of her afterwards?"

The prospect of love's involvements brought to mind, by contrast, his present mistress. She was an actress in Rouen whom he kept, and when he had pondered over this image, even in memory he found himself satiated.

"Madame Bovary," he thought, "is much prettier, much fresher too. Virginie is decidedly beginning to grow fat. Her enthusiasms bore me to tears. And that habit of hers of eating prawns all the time . . . !"

The fields were empty; around him Rodolphe only heard the

noise of the grass as it rubbed against his boots, and the chirping of
the cricket hidden away among the oats. He again saw Emma in
her room, dressed as he had seen her, and he undressed her.

"Oh, I will have her," he cried, smashing, with a blow of his
cane, a clod of earth before him.

At once, he began to consider the strategy. He wondered:

"Where shall we meet? And how? We shall always be having the
brat on our hands, and the maid, the neighbors, the husband, all
sorts of worries. Bah!" he concluded, "it would be too time-
consuming!"

Then he started again:

"But she really has eyes that bore into your heart. And that pale
complexion! And I, who love pale women!"

When he reached the top of the Argueil hills he had made up his
mind.

"All that remains is to create the proper opportunity. Well, I will
call in now and then, I'll send game and poultry; I'll have myself
bled, if need be. We shall become friends; I'll invite them to my
place. Of course!" he added, "the agricultural fair is coming on;
she'll be there, I'll see her. We'll begin boldly, for that's the surest
way."

VIII

At last it came, the much-awaited agricultural fair. Ever since the
morning of the great day, the villagers, on their doorsteps, were
discussing the preparations. The facade of the townhall had been
hung with garlands of ivy; a tent had been erected in a meadow for
the banquet; and in the middle of the Place, in front of the church,
a kind of a small cannon was to announce the arrival of the prefect
and the names of the fortunate farmers who had won prizes. The
National Guard of Buchy (there was none at Yonville) had come
to join the corps of firemen, of whom Binet was captain. On that
day he wore a collar even higher than usual; and, tightly buttoned
in his tunic, his figure was so stiff and motionless that all life
seemed to be confined to his legs, which moved in time with the
music, with a single motion. As there was some rivalry between the
tax-collector and the colonel, both, to show off their talents, drilled
their men separately. The red epaulettes and the black breastplates
kept parading up and down, one after the other; there was no end
to it, and it constantly began again. Never had there been such a
display of pomp. Several citizens had washed down their houses the
evening before; tricolor flags hung from half-open windows; all the
cafés were full; and in the lovely weather the starched caps, the
golden crosses, and the colored neckerchiefs seemed whiter than
snow, shone in the sun, and relieved with their motley colors the
somber monotony of the frock-coats and blue smocks. The neigh-

boring farmers' wives, when they got off their horses, removed the long pin with which they had gathered their dresses tight around them for fear of getting them spattered; while their husbands protected their hats by covering them with handkerchiefs, of which they held one corner in their teeth.

The crowd came into the main street from both ends of the village. People poured in from the lanes, the alleys, the houses; and from time to time one heard the banging of doors closing behind ladies of the town in cotton gloves, who were going out to see the fête. Most admired of all were two long lamp-stands covered with lanterns, that flanked a platform on which the authorities were to sit. Aside from this, a kind of pole had been placed against the four columns of the townhall, each bearing a small standard of greenish cloth, embellished with inscriptions in gold letters. On one was written, "To Commerce"; on the other, "To Agriculture"; on the third, "To Industry"; and on the fourth, "To the Fine Arts".

But the jubilation that brightened all faces seemed to darken that of Madame Lefrançois, the innkeeper. Standing on her kitchen-steps she muttered to herself:

"How stupid! How stupid they are with their canvas booth! Do they think the prefect will be glad to dine down there under a tent like a gipsy? They call all this fussing for the good of the town! As if it helped the town to send to Neufchâtel for the keeper of a cookshop! And for whom? For cowheads! for tramps!"

The pharmacist passed by. He was wearing a frock-coat, nankeen trousers, beaver shoes, and, to everyone's surprise, a hat—a low crowned hat.

"Your servant," he said. "Excuse me, I am in a hurry."

And as the fat widow asked where he was going . . .

"It seems odd to you, doesn't it, I who am always more cooped up in my laboratory than the man's rat in his cheese."

"What cheese?" asked the landlady.

"Oh, nothing, never mind!" Homais continued. "I merely wished to convey to you, Madame Lefrançois, that I usually live at home like a recluse. To-day, however, considering the circumstances, it is necessary . . ."

"Oh, are you going down there?" she said contemptuously.

"Yes, I am going," replied the pharmacist, astonished. "Am I not a member of the Advisory committee?"

Mère Lefrançois looked at him for a few moments, and ended by saying with a smile:

"That's another matter! But is agriculture any of your business? Do you understand anything about it?"

"Certainly I understand it, since I am a pharmacist,—that is to say, a chemist. And the object of chemistry, Madame Lefrançois, being the knowledge of the reciprocal and molecular action of all natural bodies, it follows that agriculture is comprised within its domain. And, in fact, the composition of the manure, the fermentation of liquids, the analyses of gases, and the effects of miasmas, what, I ask you, is all this, if it isn't chemistry, pure and simple?"

The landlady did not answer. Homais went on:

"Do you think that to be an agriculturist it is necessary to have tilled the earth or fattened fowls oneself? It is much more important to know the composition of the substances in question—the geological strata, the atmospheric actions, the quality of the soil, the minerals, the waters, the density of the different bodies, their capillarity, and what not. And one must be master of all the principles of hygiene in order to direct, criticise the construction of buildings, the feeding of animals, the diet of the servants. And, moreover, Madame Lefrançois, one must know botany, be able to distinguish between plants, you understand, which are the wholesome and those that are deleterious, which are unproductive and which nutritive, if it is well to pull them up here and re-sow them there, to propagate some, destroy others; in brief, one must keep pace with science by reading publications and papers, be always on the alert to detect improvements."

The landlady never took her eyes off the "Café Français" and the pharmacist went on:

"Would to God our agriculturists were chemists, or that at least they would pay more attention to the counsels of science. Thus lately I myself wrote a substantial paper, a memoir of over seventy-two pages, entitled, 'Cider, its Manufacture and its Effects, together with some New Reflections on this Subject,' that I sent to the Agricultural Society in Rouen, and which even procured me the honor of being received among its members—Section, Agriculture; Class, Pomology. Well, if my work had been given to the public . . ."

But the pharmacist stopped, so distracted did Madame Lefrançois seem.

"Just look at them!" she said. "It's past comprehension! Such a hash-house!" And with a shrug of the shoulders that stretched out the stitches of her sweater, she pointed with both hands at the rival establishment, from where singing erupted. "Well, it won't last long," she added, "it'll be over before a week."

Homais drew back in surprise. She came down three steps and whispered in his ear:

"What! you didn't know it? They'll foreclose this week. It's Lheureux who does the selling; he killed them off with his notes."

"What a dreadful catastrophe!" exclaimed the pharmacist, who always found expressions that filled all imaginable circumstances.

Then the landlady began telling him this story, that she had heard from Theodore, Monsieur Guillaumin's servant, and although she detested Tellier, she blamed Lheureux. He was "a wheedler, a fawner."

"There!" she said. "Look at him! There he goes down the square; he is greeting Madame Bovary, who's wearing a green hat. And she is on Monsieur Boulanger's arm."

"Madame Bovary!" exclaimed Homais. "I must go at once and pay her my respects. Perhaps she'll be pleased to have a seat in the enclosure under the peristyle." And, without heeding Madame Lefrançois, who was calling him back for more gossip, the pharmacist walked off rapidly with a smile on his face and his walk jauntier than ever, bowing copiously to right and left, and taking up much room with the large tails of his frock-coat that fluttered behind him in the wind.

Rodolphe having caught sight of him from afar, quickened his pace, but Madame Bovary couldn't keep up; so he walked more slowly, and, smiling at her, said roughly:

"It's only to get away from that fat fellow, you know, the pharmacist."

She nudged him with her elbow.

"How shall I understand that?" he asked himself.

And, walking on, he looked at her out of the corner of his eyes.

Her profile was so calm that it revealed nothing.

It stood out in the light from the oval of her hat that was tied with pale ribbons like waving rushes. Her eyes with their long curved lashes looked straight before her, and though wide open, they seemed slightly slanted at the cheek-bones, because of the blood pulsing gently under the delicate skin. A rosy light shone through the partition between her nostrils. Her head was bent upon her shoulder, and the tips of her teeth shone through her lips like pearls.

"Is she making fun of me?" thought Rodolphe.

Emma's gesture, however, had only been meant for a warning; for Monsieur Lheureux was accompanying them, and spoke now and again as if to enter into the conversation.

"What a beautiful day! Everybody is outside! The wind is from the east!"

Neither Madame Bovary nor Rodolphe answered him, but their slightest movement made him draw near saying, "I beg your pardon!" and raising his hat.

When they reached the blacksmith's house, instead of following the road up to the fence, Rodolphe suddenly turned down a path, drawing Madame Bovary with him. He called out:

"Good evening, Monsieur Lheureux! We'll see you soon!"

"How you got rid of him!" she said, laughing.

"Why," he went on, "allow oneself to be intruded upon by others? And as to-day I have the happiness of being with you . . ."

Emma blushed. He did not finish his sentence. Then he talked of the fine weather and of the pleasure of walking on the grass. A few daisies had sprung up again.

"Here are some pretty Easter daisies," he said, "and enough to provide oracles for all the lovers in the vicinity."

He added,

"Shall I pick some? What do you think?"

"Are you in love?" she asked, coughing a little.

"H'm, h'm! who knows?" answered Rodolphe.

The meadow was beginning to fill up, and the housewives were hustling about with their great umbrellas, their baskets, and their babies. One often had to make way for a long file of country girls, servant-maids with blue stockings, flat shoes and silver rings, who smelt of milk when one passed close to them. They walked along holding one another by the hand, and thus they spread over the whole field from the row of open trees to the banquet tent. But this was the judging time, and the farmers one after the other entered a kind of enclosure formed by ropes supported on sticks.

The beasts were there, their noses turned toward the rope, and making a confused line with their unequal rumps. Drowsy pigs were burrowing in the earth with their snouts, calves were lowing and bleating; the cows, one leg folded under them stretched their bellies on the grass, slowly chewing their cud, and blinking their heavy eyelids at the gnats that buzzed around them. Ploughmen with bare arms were holding by the halter prancing stallions that neighed with dilated nostrils looking in the direction of the mares. These stood quietly, stretching out their heads and flowing manes, while their foals rested in their shadow, or sucked them from time to time. And above the long undulation of these crowded bodies one saw some white mane rising in the wind like a wave, or some sharp horns sticking out, and the heads of men running about. Apart, outside the enclosure, a hundred paces off, was a large black bull, muzzled, with an iron ring in its nostrils, and who moved no more than if he had been in bronze. A child in rags was holding him by a rope.

Between the two lines the committee-men were walking with heavy steps, examining each animal, then consulting one another in a low voice. One who seemed of more importance now and then took notes in a book as he walked along. This was the president of the jury, Monsieur Derozerays de la Panville. As soon as he recognised Rodolphe he came forward quickly, and smiling amiably, said:

"What! Monsieur Boulanger, you are deserting us?"

Rodolphe protested that he would come. But when the president had disappeared:

"To tell the truth," he said, "I shall not go. Your company is better than his."

And while poking fun at the show, Rodolphe, to move about more easily, showed the gendarme his blue card, and even stopped now and then in front of some fine beast, which Madame Bovary did not at all admire. He noticed this, and began jeering at the Yonville ladies and their dresses; then he apologised for his own casual attire. It had the inconsistency of things at once commonplace and refined which enchants or exasperates the ordinary man because he suspects that it reveals an unconventional existence, a dubious morality, the affectations of the artist, and, above all, a certain contempt for established conventions. The wind, blowing up his batiste shirt with pleated cuffs revealed a waistcoat of grey linen, and his broad-striped trousers disclosed at the ankle nankeen boots with patent leather gaiters. These were so polished that they reflected the grass. He trampled on horse's dung, one hand in the pocket of his jacket and his straw hat tilted on one side.

"Anyway," he added, "when one lives in the country. . . . ."

"Nothing is worth while," said Emma.

"That is true," replied Rodolphe. "To think that not one of these people is capable of understanding even the cut of a coat!"

Then they talked about provincial mediocrity, of the lives it stifles, the lost illusions.

"No wonder," said Rodolphe, "that I am more and more sinking in gloom."

"You!" she said in astonishment; "I thought you very lighthearted."

"Oh, yes, it seems that way because I know how to wear a mask of mockery in society, and yet, how many a time at the sight of a cemetery by moonlight have I not asked myself whether it were not better to join those sleeping there!"

"Oh! and your friends?" she said. "How can you forget them."

"My friends! What friends? Have I any? Who cares about me?" And he followed up the last words with a kind of hissing whistle.

They were obliged to separate because of a great pile of chairs that a man was carrying behind them. He was so overladen that one could only see the tips of his wooden shoes and the ends of his two outstretched arms. It was Lestiboudois, the gravedigger, who was carrying the church chairs about amongst the people. Alive to all that concerned his interests, he had hit upon this means of turning the agricultural show to his advantage, and his idea was succeeding, for he no longer knew which way to turn. In fact, the villagers, who were tired and hot, quarrelled for these seats, whose straw smelt of incense, and they leant against the thick backs, stained with the wax of candles, with a certain veneration.

Madame Bovary again took Rodolphe's arm; he went on as if speaking to himself:

"Yes, I have missed so many things. Always alone! Ah! if I had some aim in life, if I had met some love, if I had found some one! Oh, how I would have spent all the energy of which I am capable, surmounted everything, overcome everything!"

"Yet it seems to me," said Emma, "that you are not to be pitied."

"Ah! you think so?" said Rodolphe.

"For, after all," she went on, "you are free . . ."

She hesitated,

"Rich . . ."

"Don't mock me," he replied.

And she protested that she was not mocking him, when the sound of a cannon was heard; immediately all began crowding one another towards the village.

It was a false alarm. The prefect seemed not to be coming, and the members of the jury felt much embarrassed, not knowing if they ought to begin the meeting or wait longer.

At last, at the end of the Place a large hired landau appeared, drawn by two thin horses, generously whipped by a coachman in a white hat. Binet had only just time to shout, "Present arms!" and the colonel to imitate him. There was a rush towards the guns; every one pushed forward. A few even forgot their collars.

But the prefectoral coach seemed to sense the trouble, for the two yoked nags, dawdling in their harness, came at a slow trot in front of the townhall at the very moment when the National Guard and firemen deployed, beating time with their boots.

"Present arms!" shouted Binet.

"Halt!" shouted the colonel. "By the left flank, march!"

And after presenting arms, during which the clang of the band, letting loose, rang out like a brass kettle rolling downstairs, all the guns were lowered.

Then was seen stepping down from the carriage a gentleman in a short coat with silver braiding, with bald brow, and wearing a tuft of hair at the back of his head, of a sallow complexion and the most benign of aspects. His eyes, very large and covered by heavy lids, were half-closed to look at the crowd, while at the same time he raised his sharp nose, and forced a smile upon his sunken mouth. He recognised the mayor by his scarf, and explained to him that the prefect was not able to come. He himself was a councillor at the prefecture; then he added a few apologies. Monsieur Tuvache reciprocated with polite compliments, humbly acknowledged by the other; and they remained thus, face to face, their foreheads almost touching, surrounded by members of the jury, the municipal council, the notable personages, the National Guard and the crowd. The councillor pressing his little cocked hat to his breast repeated his greetings, while Tuvache, bent like a bow, also smiled, stammered, tried to say something, protested his devotion to the monarchy and the honor that was being done to Yonville.

Hippolyte, the groom from the inn, took the head of the horses from the coachman, and, limping along with his clubfoot, led them to the door of the "Lion d'Or" where a number of peasants collected to look at the carriage. The drum beat, the howitzer thundered, and the gentlemen one by one mounted the platform, where they sat down in red utrecht velvet arm-chairs that had been lent by Madame Tuvache.

All these people looked alike. Their fair flabby faces, somewhat tanned by the sun, were the color of sweet cider, and their puffy whiskers emerged from stiff collars, kept up by white cravats with broad bows. All the waistcoats were of velvet, double-breasted; all the watches had, at the end of a long ribbon, an oval seal; all rested their two hands on their thighs, carefully stretching the stride of their trousers, whose unspunged glossy cloth shone more brilliantly than the leather of their heavy boots.

The ladies of the company stood at the back under the porch between the pillars, while the common herd was opposite, standing up or sitting on chairs. Lestiboudois had brought there all the chairs that he had moved from the field, and he even kept running back every minute to fetch others from the church. He caused such confusion with this piece of business that one had great difficulty in getting to the small steps of the platform.

"I think," said Monsieur Lheureux to the pharmacist who was heading for his seat, "that they ought to have put up two Venetian masts with something rather severe and rich for ornaments; it would have been a very pretty sight."

"Certainly," replied Homais; "but what can you expect? The mayor took everything on his own shoulders. He hasn't much taste. Poor Tuvache! he is completely devoid of what is called the genius of art."

Meanwhile, Rodolphe and Madame Bovary had ascended to the first floor of the townhall, to the "council-room," and, as it was empty, he suggested that they could enjoy the sight there more comfortably. He fetched three chairs from the round table under the bust of the monarch, and having carried them to one of the windows, they sat down together.

There was commotion on the platform, long whisperings, much parleying. At last the councillor got up. It was known by now that his name was Lieuvain, and in the crowd the name was now passing from lip to lip. After he had reshuffled a few pages, and bent over them to see better, he began:

"Gentlemen! May I be permitted first of all (before addressing you on the object of our meeting to-day, and this sentiment will, I am sure, be shared by you all), may I be permitted, I say, to pay a tribute to the higher administration, to the government, to the monarch, gentlemen, our sovereign, to that beloved king, to whom no branch of public or private prosperity is a matter of indifference, and who directs with a hand at once so firm and wise the chariot of the state amid the incessant perils of a stormy sea, knowing, moreover, how to make peace respected as well as war, industry, commerce, agriculture, and the fine arts."

"I ought," said Rodolphe, "to get back a little further."

"Why?" said Emma.

But at this moment the voice of the councillor rose to an extraordinary pitch. He declaimed—

"This is no longer the time, gentlemen, when civil discord made blood flow in our market squares, when the landowner, the businessman, the working-man himself, lying down to peaceful sleep, trembled lest he should be awakened suddenly by the noise of alarming tocsins, when the most subversive doctrines audaciously sapped foundations . . ."

"Well, some one down there might see me," Rodolphe resumed, "then I should have to invent excuses for a fortnight; and with my bad reputation . . ."

"Oh, you are slandering yourself," said Emma.

"No! It is dreadful, I assure you."

"But, gentlemen," continued the councillor, "if, banishing from my memory the remembrance of these sad pictures, I carry my eyes back to the present situation of our dear country, what do I see there? Everywhere commerce and the arts are flourishing; everywhere new means of communication, like so many new arteries in the body politic, establish within it new relations. Our great industrial centers have recovered all their activity; religion, more consolidated, smiles in all hearts; our ports are full, confidence is born again, and France breathes once more! . . . ."

"Besides," added Rodolphe, "perhaps from the world's point of view they are right."

"How so?" she asked.

"What!" said he. "Don't you know that there are souls constantly tormented? They need by turns to dream and to act, the purest passions and the most turbulent joys, and thus they fling themselves into all sorts of fantasies, of follies."

Then she looked at him as one looks at a traveler who has voyaged over strange lands, and went on:

"We have not even this distraction, we poor women!"

"A sad distraction, for happiness isn't found in it."

"But is it ever found?" she asked.

"Yes; one day it comes," he answered.

"And this is what you have understood," said the councillor. "You, farmers, agricultural laborers! you pacific pioneers of a work that belongs wholly to civilisation! you, men of progress and morality, you have understood, I say, that political storms are even more redoubtable than atmospheric disturbances!"

"A day comes," repeated Rodolphe, "one is near despair. Then the horizon expands; it is as if a voice cried, 'It is here!' You feel the need of confiding the whole of your life, of giving everything, sacrificing everything to this person. There is no need for explanations; one understands each other, having met before in dreams!" (And he looked at her.) "At last, here it is, this treasure so sought after, here before you. It glitters, it flashes; yet one still doubts, one does not believe it; one remains dazzled, as if one went out from darkness into light."

And as he ended Rodolphe suited the action to the word. He passed his hand over his face, like a man about to faint. Then he let it fall on Emma's. She drew hers back. But the councillor was still reading.

"And who would be surprised at it, gentlemen? He only who was so blind, so imprisoned (I do not fear to say it), so imprisoned by the prejudices of another age as still to misunderstand the spirit of our rural populations. Where, indeed, is more patriotism to be found than in the country, greater devotion to the public welfare, in a word, more intelligence? And, gentlemen, I do not mean that superficial intelligence, vain ornament of idle minds, but rather that profound and balanced intelligence that applies itself above all else to useful objects, thus contributing to the good of all, to the common amelioration and to the support of the state, born of respect for law and the practice of duty . . ."

"Ah! again!" said Rodolphe. "Always 'duty.' I am sick of the word. They are a lot of old jackasses in woolen vests and old bigots with foot-warmers and rosaries who constantly drone into our ears

'Duty, duty!' Ah! by Jove! as if one's real duty were not to feel what is great, cherish the beautiful, and not accept all the conventions of society with the hypocrisy it forces upon us."

"Yet . . . yet . . ." objected Madame Bovary.

"No, no! Why cry out against the passions? Are they not the one beautiful thing on earth, the source of heroism, of enthusiasm, of poetry, music, the arts, in a word, of everything?"

"But one must," said Emma, "to some extent bow to the opinion of the world and accept its morality."

"Ah, but there are two moralities," he replied, "the petty one, the morality of small men that constantly keeps changing, but yells itself hoarse; crude and loud like the crowd of imbeciles that you see down there. But the other, the eternal, that is about us and above, like the landscape that surrounds us, and the blue heavens that give us light."

Monsieur Lieuvain had just wiped his mouth with a pocket-handkerchief. He continued:

"It would be presumptuous of me, gentlemen, to point out to you the uses of agriculture. Who supplies our wants, who provides our means of subsistence, if not the farmer? It is the farmer, gentlemen, who sows with laborious hand the fertile furrows of the country, brings forth the wheat, which, being ground, is made into a powder by means of ingenious machinery, issues from there under the name of flour, and is then transported to our cities, soon delivered to the baker, who makes it into food for poor and rich alike. Again, is it not the farmer who fattens his flocks in the pastures in order to provide us with warm clothing? For how should we clothe or nourish ourselves without his labor? And, gentlemen, is it even necessary to go so far for examples? Who has not frequently reflected on all the momentous things that we get out of that modest animal, the ornament of poultry-yards, that provides us at once with a soft pillow for our bed, with succulent flesh for our tables, and eggs? But I should never end if I were to enumerate one after the other all the different products which the earth, well cultivated, like a generous mother, lavishes upon her children. Here it is the vine; elsewhere apple trees for cider; there colza; further, cheeses; and flax; gentlemen, let us not forget flax, which has made such great strides forward these last years and to which I call your special attention!"

He had no need to call it, for all the mouths of the multitude were wide open, as if to drink in his words. Tuvache by his side listened to him with staring eyes. Monsieur Derozerays from time to time softly closed his eyelids, and farther on the pharmacist, with his son Napoleon between his knees, put his hand behind his ear in order not to lose a syllable. The chins of the other members of the jury nodded slowly up and down in their waistcoats in sign of approval. The firemen at the foot of the platform rested on their bayonets; and Binet, motionless, stood with out-turned elbows, the point of his sabre in the air. Perhaps he could hear, but he certainly couldn't see a thing, for the visor of his helmet fell down on his nose. His lieutenant, the youngest son of Monsieur Tuvache, had an even bigger one; it was so large that he could hardly keep it on, in spite of the cotton scarf that peeped out from underneath. He wore a smile of childlike innocence, and his thin pale face, dripping with sweat, expressed satisfaction, some exhaustion and sleepiness.

The square was crowded up to the houses. People were leaning on their elbows at all the windows, others were standing on their doorsteps, and Justin, in front of the pharmacy, seemed fascinated by the spectacle. In spite of the silence Monsieur Lieuvain's voice was lost in the air. It reached you in fragments of phrases, interrupted here and there by the creaking of chairs in the crowd; then, the long bellowing of an ox would suddenly burst forth from behind, or else the bleating of the lambs, who answered one another from street to street. Even the cowherds and shepherds had driven their beasts this far, and one could hear their lowing from time to time, while with their tongues they tore down some scrap of foliage that hung over their muzzles.

Rodolphe had drawn nearer to Emma, and was whispering hurriedly in her ear:

"Doesn't this conspiracy of society revolt you? Is there a single sentiment it does not condemn? The noblest instincts, the purest feelings are persecuted, slandered; and if at length two poor souls do meet, all is organized in such a way as to keep them from becoming one. Yet they will try, they will call to each other. Not in vain, for sooner or later, be it in six or ten years, they will come together in love; for fate has decreed it, and they are born for each other."

His arms were folded across his knees, and thus lifting his face at her from close by, he looked fixedly at her. She noticed in his eyes small golden lines radiating from the black pupils; she even smelt the perfume of the pomade that made his hair glossy. Then something gave way in her; she recalled the Viscount who had waltzed with her at Vaubyessard, and whose beard exhaled a similar scent of vanilla and lemon, and mechanically she half-closed her eyes the better to breathe it in. But in making this movement, as she leant back in her chair, she saw in the distance, right on the line of the horizon, the old diligence the "Hirondelle," that was slowly descending the hill of Leux, dragging after it a long trail of dust. It was in this yellow carriage that Léon had so often come back to her, and by this route down there that he had gone for ever. She fancied she saw him opposite at his window; then all grew confused; clouds gathered; it seemed to her that she was again turning in the waltz under the light of the lustres on the arm of the Viscount, and that Léon was not far away, that he was coming . . . and yet all the time she was conscious of Rodolphe's head by her side. The sweetness of this sensation revived her past desires, and like grains of sand under a gust of wind, they swirled around in the subtle breath of the perfume that diffused over her soul. She breathed deeply several times to drink in the freshness of the ivy round the columns. She took off her gloves and wiped her hands; then she fanned her face with her handkerchief while she kept hearing, through the throbbing of her temples, the murmur of the crowd and the voice of the councillor intoning his phrases.

He was saying:

"Persevere! listen neither to the suggestions of routine, nor to the over-hasty councils of a rash empiricism. Apply yourselves, above all, to the amelioration of the soil, to good manures, to the development of the breeds, whether equine, bovine, ovine, or porcine. May these shows be to you pacific arenas, where the victor in leaving will hold forth a hand to the vanquished, and will fraternise with him in the hope of even greater success. And you, aged servants! humble helpers, whose hard labor no Government up to this day has taken into consideration, receive the reward of your silent virtues, and be assured that the state henceforward has its eye upon you; that it encourages you, protects you; that it will accede to your just demands, and alleviate as much as possible the heavy burden of your painful sacrifices."

Monsieur Lieuvain sat down; Monsieur Derozerays got up, beginning another speech. His was not perhaps so florid as that of the councillor, but it stood out by a more direct style, that is to say, by more specific knowledge and more elevated considerations. Thus the praise of the Government took up less space; religion and agriculture more. He showed the relation between both, and how they had always contributed to civilisation. Rodolphe was talking dreams, forebodings, magnetism with Madame Bovary. Going back to the cradle of society, the orator painted those fierce times when men lived on acorns in the heart of woods. Then they had left off the skins of beasts, had put on cloth, tilled the soil, planted the vine. Was this a good, or wasn't there more harm than good in this discovery? That was the problem to which Monsieur Derozerays addressed himself. From magnetism little by little Rodolphe had come to affinities, and while the president was citing Cincinnatus[41] and his plough, Diocletian[42] planting his cabbages, and the Emperors

---

41. Cincinnatus was a Roman Consul (460 B.C.), who was supposedly called to his office while found plowing.

42. Diocletian (245–313) was Roman emperor from 284 to 305. He resigned in 305 and retired to Salone, (now Split) in Dalmatia, to cultivate his garden.

of China inaugurating the year by the sowing of seed, the young man was explaining to the young woman that these irresistible attractions find their cause in some previous state of existence.

"Take us, for instance," he said, "how did we happen to meet? What chance willed it? It was because across infinite distances, like two streams uniting, our particular inclinations pushed us toward one another."

And he seized her hand; she did not withdraw it.

"First prize for general farming!" announced the president.

"—Just now, for example, when I went to your home . . ."

"To Mr. Bizat of Quincampoix."

"—Did I know I would accompany you?"

"Seventy francs!"

"—A hundred times I tried to leave; yet I followed you and stayed . . ."

"For manures!"

"—As I would stay to-night, to-morrow, all other days, all my life!"

"To Monsieur Caron of Argueil, a gold medal!"

"—For I have never enjoyed anyone's company so much."

"To Monsieur Bain of Givry-Saint-Martin."

"—And I will never forget you."

"For a merino ram . . ."

"—Whereas you will forget me; I'll pass through your life as a mere shadow . . ."

"To Monsieur Belot of Notre-Dame."

"—But no, tell me there can be a place for me in your thoughts, in your life, can't there?"

"Hog! first prize equally divided between Messrs. Lehérissé and Cullembourg, sixty francs!"

Rodolphe was holding her hand on his; it was warm and quivering like a captive dove that wants to fly away; perhaps she was trying to take it away or perhaps she was answering his pressure, at any rate, she moved her fingers; he exclaimed

"Oh, thank you! You do not repulse me! You are kind! You understand that I am yours! Let me see you, let me look at you!"

A gust of wind that blew in at the window ruffled the cloth on the table, and in the square below all the large bonnets rose up like the fluttering wings of white butterflies.

"Use of oil-cakes!" continued the president.

He was hurrying now: "Flemish manure, flax-growing, drainage, long term leases . . . domestic service."

Rodolphe was no longer speaking. They looked at each other. As their desire increased, their dry lips trembled and languidly, effortlessly, their fingers intertwined.

"Catherine Nicaise Elizabeth Leroux, of Sassetot-la-Guerrière, for fifty-four years of service at the same farm, a silver medal—value, twenty-five francs!"

"Where is Catherine Leroux?" repeated the councillor.

She did not appear, and one could hear whispering voices:

"Go ahead!"

"No."

"To the left!"

"Don't be afraid!"

"Oh, how stupid she is!"

"Well, is she there?" cried Tuvache.

"Yes; here she is."

"Then what's she waiting for?"

There came forward on the platform a frightened-looking little old lady who seemed to shrink within her poor clothes. On her feet she wore heavy wooden shoes, and from her hips hung a large blue apron. Her pale face framed in a borderless cap was more wrinkled than a withered russet apple, and from the sleeves of her red jacket looked out two large hands with gnarled joints. The dust from the barns, washing soda and grease from the wool had so encrusted, roughened, hardened them that they seemed dirty, although they had been rinsed in clear water; and by dint of long service they remained half open, as if to bear humble witness of so much suffering endured. Something of monastic rigidity dignified her. No trace of sadness or tenderness weakened her pale face. Having lived so long among animals, she had taken on their silent and tranquil ways. It was the first time that she found herself in the midst of so large a company; and inwardly scared by the flags, the drums, the gentlemen in frock-coats, and the decorations of the councillor, she stood motionless, not knowing whether she should advance or run away, nor why the crowd was cheering and the jury smiling at her. Thus, a half century of servitude confronted these beaming bourgeois.

"Step forward, venerable Catherine Nicaise Elizabeth Leroux!" said the councillor, who had taken the list of prize-winners from the president; and, looking at the piece of paper and the old woman by turns, he repeated in a fatherly tone:

"Step forward, step forward!"

"Are you deaf?" said Tuvache, who was jumping around in his arm-chair; and he began shouting in her ear, "Fifty-four years of service. A silver medal! Twenty-five francs! For you!"

Then, when she had her medal, she looked at it, and a smile of beatitude spread over her face; and as she walked away they could hear her muttering:

"I'll give it to our curé at home, to say some masses for me!"

"What fanaticism!" exclaimed the pharmacist, leaning across to the notary.

The meeting was over, the crowd dispersed, and now that the speeches had been read, everything fell back into place again, and everything into the old grooves; the masters bullied the servants, the servants beat the animals, indolent victors returning to their stables with a green wreath between their horns.

The National Guards, however, had climbed up to the second floor of the townhall; brioches were stuck on their bayonets, and the drummer of the battalion carried a basket with bottles. Madame Bovary took Rodolphe's arm; he saw her home; they separated at her door; then he walked about alone in the meadow while waiting for the banquet to start.

The feast was long, noisy, ill served; the guests were so crowded that they could hardly move their elbows; and the narrow planks that served as benches almost broke under their weight. They ate huge amounts. Each one stuffed himself with all he could lay hands on. Sweat stood on every brow, and a whitish steam, like the vapour of a stream on an autumn morning, floated above the table between the hanging lamps. Rodolphe, leaning against the canvas of the tent, was thinking so intently of Emma that he heard nothing. Behind him on the grass the servants were piling up the dirty plates, his neighbors were talking; he did not answer them; they filled his glass, and there was silence in his thoughts in spite of the noise around him. He was dreaming of what she had said, of the line of her lips; her face, as in a magic mirror, shone on the plates of the shakos, the folds of her gown fell along the walls, and endless days of love unrolled before him in the future.

He saw her again in the evening during the fireworks, but she was with her husband, Madame Homais, and the pharmacist, who was worrying about the danger of stray rockets. Time and again he left the company to give some advice to Binet.

The fireworks sent to Monsieur Tuvache had, through an excess of caution, been locked in his cellar; so the damp powder would not light, and the main piece, that was to represent a dragon biting his tail, failed completely. From time to time, a meagre Roman-candle went off; then the gaping crowd sent up a roar that mingled with the giggling of the women who were being tickled in the darkness. Emma silently nestled against Charles's shoulder; then, raising her chin, she watched the luminous rays of the rockets against the dark sky. Rodolphe gazed at her in the light of the burning lanterns.

One by one, they went out. Stars appeared. A few drops of rain began to fall. She tied her scarf over her bare head.

At this moment the councillor's carriage came out from the inn. His coachman, who was drunk, suddenly fell asleep, and one could see the mass of his body from afar above the hood, framed by the two lanterns, swaying from right to left with the motion of the springs.

"Truly," said the pharmacist, "severe measures should be taken against drunkenness! I should like to see written up weekly at the door of the townhall on a board *ad hoc* the names of all those who during the week got intoxicated on alcohol. Besides, with regard to statistics, one would thus have, as it were, public records that one could refer to if needed . . . But excuse me!"

And he once more ran off to the captain. The latter was returning to see his lathe.

"You might do well," said Homais to him, "to send one of your men, or to go yourself . . ."

"Oh, leave me alone!" answered the tax-collector. "I'm telling you everything is taken care of."

"There is nothing for you to worry about," said the pharmacist, when he returned to his friends. "Monsieur Binet has assured me that all precautions have been taken. No sparks have fallen; the pumps are full. Let's go to bed."

"I can certainly use some sleep," said Madame Homais with a huge yawn. "But never mind; we've had a beautiful day for our fete."

Rodolphe repeated in a low voice, and with a tender look, "Oh, yes! very beautiful!"

And after a final good night, they parted ways.

Two days later, in the "Fanal de Rouen," there was a long article on the show. Homais had composed it on the spur of the moment, the very morning after the banquet.

"Why these festoons, these flowers, these garlands? Whereto was the crowd hurrying, like the waves of a furious sea under the torrents of a tropical sun pouring its heat upon our meadows?"

Then he spoke of the condition of the peasants. Certainly the Government was doing much, but not enough. "Be bold!" he told them; "a thousand reforms are needed; let us carry them out! Then, reporting on the entry of the councillor, he did not forget "the martial spirit of our militia," nor "our dazzling village maidens," nor the "bald-headed elders like patriarchs, some of whom, left over from our immortal phalanxes, still felt their hearts beat at the manly sound of the drums." He cited himself among the first of the members of the jury, and he even called attention in a note to the fact that Monsieur Homais, pharmacist, had sent a memoir on cider to the agricultural society. When he came to the distribution of the prizes, he painted the joy of the prize-winners in dithyrambic strophes. "The father embraced the son, the brother the brother, the husband his wife. More than one showed his humble medal with pride; and no doubt when he got home to his good housewife, he hung it up weeping on the modest walls of his cottage.

"About six o'clock a banquet prepared in the meadow of Monsieur Leigeard brought together the main participants in the festivities. The utmost merriment reigned throughout. Several toasts were proposed: Monsieur Lieuvain, To the king! Monsieur Tuvache, To the prefect! Monsieur Derozerays, To Agriculture! Monsieur Homais, To the twin sisters, Industry and Fine Arts! Monsieur Leplichey, To Improvements! At night some brilliant fireworks suddenly lit up the sky. It was a real kaleidoscope, an operatic scene; and for a moment our little locality might have thought itself transported into the midst of a dream from the 'Thousand and One Nights.'

"Let us state that no untoward event disturbed this family meeting."

And he added: "Only the absence of the clergy was noted. No doubt the priests do not understand progress in the same way. Just as you please, *messieurs de Loyola!*"[43]

IX

Six weeks passed. Rodolphe did not come again. At last one evening he appeared.

The day after the fair he told himself:

"Let's not go back too soon; that would be a mistake."

And at the end of a week he had gone off hunting. After the hunting he first feared that too much time had passed, and then he reasoned thus:

"If she loved me from the first day, impatience must make her love me even more. Let's persist!"

And he knew that his calculation had been right when, on entering the room, he saw Emma turn pale.

She was alone. Night was falling. The small muslin curtain along the windows deepened the twilight, and the gilding of the barometer, on which the rays of the sun fell, shone in the looking-glass between the meshes of the coral.

Rodolphe remained standing, and Emma hardly answered his first conventional phrases.

"I have been busy," he said, "I have been ill."

"Nothing serious?" she cried.

"Well," said Rodolphe, sitting down at her side on a footstool, "no . . . It was because I did not want to come back."

"Why?"

"Can't you guess?"

He looked at her again, but so hard that she lowered her head, blushing. He pursued:

"Emma . . ."

"Monsieur!" she exclaimed, drawing back a little.

"Ah! you see," he replied in a melancholy voice, "that I was right

---

43. Messieurs de Loyola, or Jesuits. Ignatius Loyola (1491–1556), a Spaniard, founded the Order of the Jesuits in 1534. The Jesuits were expelled from France in 1762.

not to come back; for this name, this name that fills my whole soul, and that escaped me, you forbid me its use! Madame Bovary! . . . why, the whole world calls you thus! Moreover, it is not your name; it is the name of another!"

He repeated,

"Of another!"

And he hid his face in his hands.

"Yes, I think of you constantly! . . . The thought of you drives me to despair. Ah! forgive me! . . . I'll go . . . Adieu . . . I'll go far away, so far that you will never hear of me again; yet . . . today . . . I don't know what force made me come here. For one does not struggle against Heaven; it is impossible to resist the smile of angels; one is carried away by the beautiful, the lovely, the adorable."

It was the first time that Emma had heard such words addressed to her, and her pride unfolded languidly in the warmth of this language, like someone stretching in a hot bath.

"But if I didn't come," he continued, "if I couldn't see you, at least I have gazed long on all that surrounds you. At night, every night, I arose; I came here; I watched your house, the roof glimmering in the moon, the trees in the garden swaying before your window, and the little lamp, a gleam shining through the window-panes in the darkness. Ah! you never knew that there, so near you, so far from you, was a poor wretch . . ."

She turned towards him with a sob.

"Oh, you are kind!" she said.

"No, I love you, that is all! You do not doubt that! Tell me; one word, one single word!"

And Rodolphe imperceptibly glided from the footstool to the ground; but a sound of wooden shoes was heard in the kitchen, and he noticed that the door of the room was not closed.

"You would do an act of charity," he went on, rising, "if you accepted to gratify a whim!" It was to visit her home, he wished to see it, and since Madame Bovary could see no objection to this, they both rose just when Charles came in.

"Good morning, doctor," Rodolphe said to him.

Flattered by this unexpected title, Charles launched into elaborate displays of politeness. Of this the other took advantage to pull himself together.

"Madame was speaking to me," he then said, "about her health."

Charles interrupted; she was indeed giving him thousands of worries; her palpitations were beginning again. Then Rodolphe asked if riding would not be helpful.

"Certainly! excellent, just the thing! What a good idea! You ought to try it."

And as she objected that she had no horse, Monsieur Rodolphe offered one. She refused his offer; he did not insist. Then to explain his visit he said that his ploughman, the man of the blood-letting, still suffered from dizziness.

"I'll drop by," said Bovary.

"No, no! I'll send him to you; we'll come; that will be more convenient for you."

"Ah! very good! I thank you."

And as soon as they were alone, "Why don't you accept Monsieur Boulanger's offer? It was so gracious of him."

She seemed to pout, invented a thousand excuses, and finally declared that perhaps it would look odd.

"That's the least of my worries!" said Charles, turning on his heel. "Health first! You are making a mistake."

"Could I go riding without proper clothes?"

"You must order a riding outfit," he answered.

The riding-habit decided her.

When it was ready, Charles wrote to Monsieur Boulanger that his wife was able to accept his invitation and thanked him in advance for his kindness.

The next day at noon Rodolphe appeared at Charles's door with two saddle-horses. One had pink rosettes at his ears and a deerskin side-saddle.

Rodolphe had put on high soft boots, assuming that she had never seen the likes of them. In fact, Emma was charmed with his appearance as he stood on the landing in his great velvet coat and white corduroy breeches. She was ready; she was waiting for him.

Justin escaped from the store to watch her depart, and the pharmacist himself also came out. He was giving Monsieur Boulanger some good advice.

"An accident happens so easily. Be careful! Your horses may be skittish!"

She heard a noise above her; it was Félicité drumming on the window-panes to amuse little Berthe. The child blew her a kiss; her mother answered with a wave of her whip.

"Have a pleasant ride!" cried Monsieur Homais. "Be careful! above all, be careful!"

And he flourished his newspaper as he saw them disappear.

As soon as he felt the ground, Emma's horse set off at a gallop. Rodolphe galloped by her side. Now and then they exchanged a word. With slightly bent head, her hand well up, and her right arm stretched out, she gave herself up to the cadence of the movement that rocked her in her saddle.

At the bottom of the hill Rodolphe gave his horse its head; they set off together at a bound, then at the top suddenly the horses stopped, and her large blue veil fell about her.

It was early in October. There was fog over the land. Hazy clouds hovered on the horizon between the outlines of the hills; others, rent asunder, floated up and disappeared. Sometimes through a rift in the clouds, beneath a ray of sunshine, gleamed from afar the roofs of Yonville, with the gardens at the water's edge, the yards, the walls and the church steeple. Emma half closed her eyes to pick out her house, and never had this poor village where she lived appeared so small. From the height on which they were the whole valley seemed an immense pale lake sending off its vapour into the air. Clumps of trees here and there stood out like black rocks, and the tall lines of the poplars that rose above the mist were like a beach stirred by the wind.

By the side, on the grass between the pines, a brown light shim-mered in the warm atmosphere. The earth, ruddy like the powder of tobacco, deadened the noise of their steps, and as they walked, the horses kicked up fallen pine cones before them.

Rodolphe and Emma thus skirted the woods. She turned away from time to time to avoid his look, and then she saw only the line of pine trunks, whose monotonous succession made her a little giddy. The horses were panting; the leather of the saddles creaked.

Just as they were entering the forest the sun came out.

"God is with us!" said Rodolphe.

"Do you think so?" she said.

"Forward! forward!" he continued.

He clucked with his tongue. The horses set off at a trot.

Long ferns by the roadside caught in Emma's stirrup. Rodolphe leant forward and removed them as they rode along. At other times, to turn aside the branches, he passed close to her, and Emma felt his knee brushing against her leg. The sky was blue now. The leaves no longer stirred. There were spaces full of heather in flower, and patches of purple alternated with the confused tangle of the trees, grey, fawn, or golden colored, according to the nature of their leaves. Often in the thicket one could hear the fluttering of wings, or else the hoarse, soft cry of the ravens flying off amidst the oaks.

They dismounted. Rodolphe fastened up the horses. She walked on in front on the moss between the paths.

But her long dress got in her way, although she held it up by the skirt; and Rodolphe, walking behind her, saw between the black cloth and the black shoe the delicacy of her white stocking, that seemed to him as if it were a part of her nakedness.

She stopped.

"I am tired," she said.

"Come, try some more," he went on. "Courage!"

Some hundred paces further on she stopped again, and through her veil, that fell sideways from her man's hat over her hips, her face appeared in a bluish transparency as if she were floating under azure waves.

"But where are we going?"

He did not answer. She was breathing irregularly. Rodolphe looked round him biting his moustache.

They came to a larger space which had been cleared of undergrowth. They sat down on the trunk of a fallen tree, and Rodolphe began speaking to her of his love.

He did not frighten her at first with compliments. He was calm, serious, melancholy.

Emma listened to him with bowed head, and stirred the bits of wood on the ground with the tip of her foot.

But at the words, "Are not our destinies now forever united?"

"Oh, no!" she replied. "You know they aren't. It is impossible!"

She rose to go. He seized her by the wrist. She stopped. Then, having gazed at him for a few moments with an amorous and moist look, she said hurriedly:

"Well let's not speak of it again! Where are the horses? Let's go back."

He made a gesture of anger and annoyance. She repeated:

"Where are the horses? Where are the horses?"

Then smiling a strange smile, looking straight at her, his teeth set, he advanced with outstretched arms. She recoiled trembling. She stammered:

"Oh, you frighten me! You hurt me! Take me back!"

"If it must be," he went on, his face changing; and he again became respectful, caressing, timid. She gave him her arm. They went back. He said:

"What was the matter with you? Why? I do not understand. You were mistaken, no doubt. In my soul you are as a Madonna on a pedestal, in a place lofty, secure, immaculate. But I cannot live without you! I need your eyes, your voice, your thought! Be my friend, my sister, my angel!"

And he stretched out his arm and caught her by the waist. Gently she tried to disengage herself. He supported her thus as they walked along.

They heard the two horses browsing on the leaves.

"Not quite yet!" said Rodolphe. "Stay a minute longer! Please stay!"

He drew her farther on to a small pool where duckweeds made a greenness on the water. Faded waterlilies lay motionless between the reeds. At the noise of their steps in the grass, frogs jumped away to hide themselves.

"I shouldn't, I shouldn't!" she said. "I am out of my mind listening to you!"

"Why? . . . Emma! Emma!"

"Oh, Rodolphe! . . ." she said slowly and she pressed against his shoulder.

The cloth of her dress clung to the velvet of his coat. She threw back her white neck which swelled in a sigh, and, faltering, weeping, and hiding her face in her hands, with one long shudder, she abandoned herself to him.

The shades of night were falling; the horizontal sun passing between the branches dazzled the eyes. Here and there around her, in the leaves or on the ground, trembled luminous patches, as if humming-birds flying about had scattered their feathers. Silence was everywhere; something sweet seemed to come forth from the trees. She felt her heartbeat return, and the blood coursing through her flesh like a river of milk. Then far away, beyond the wood, on the other hills, she heard a vague prolonged cry, a voice which lingered, and in silence she heard it mingling like music with the last pulsations of her throbbing nerves. Rodolphe, a cigar between his lips, was mending with his penknife one of the two broken bridles.

They returned to Yonville by the same road. On the mud they saw again the traces of their horses side by side, the same thickets, the same stones in the grass; nothing around them seemed changed; and yet for her something had happened more stupendous than if the mountains had moved in their places. Rodolphe now and again bent forward and took her hand to kiss it.

She was charming on horseback—upright, with her slender waist, her knee bent on the mane of her horse, her face somewhat flushed by the fresh air in the red of the evening.

On entering Yonville she made her horse prance in the road.

People looked at her from the windows.

At dinner her husband thought she looked well, but she pretended not to hear him when he inquired about her ride, and she remained sitting there with her elbow at the side of her plate between the two lighted candles.

"Emma!" he said.

"What?"

"Well, I spent the afternoon at Monsieur Alexandre's. He has an old filly, still very fine, just a little broken in the knees, and that could be bought, I am sure, for a hundred crowns." He added, "And thinking it might please you, I have reserved her . . . I bought her . . . Have I done right? Do tell me!"

She nodded her head in assent; then a quarter of an hour later:

"Are you going out to-night?" she asked.

"Yes. Why?"

"Oh, nothing, nothing, dear!"

And as soon as she had got rid of Charles she went and shut herself up in her room.

At first she felt stunned; she saw the trees, the paths, the ditches, Rodolphe, and she again felt the pressure of his arms, while the leaves rustled and the reeds whistled.

But when she saw herself in the mirror she wondered at her face. Never had her eyes been so large, so black, nor so deep. Something subtle about her being transfigured her.

She repeated: "I have a lover! a lover!" delighting at the idea as if a second puberty had come to her. So at last she was to know those joys of love, that fever of happiness of which she had despaired! She was entering upon a marvelous world where all would be passion, ecstasy, delirium. She felt herself surrounded by an endless rapture. A blue space surrounded her and ordinary existence appeared only intermittently between these heights, dark and far away beneath her.

Then she recalled the heroines of the books that she had read, and the lyric legion of these adulterous women began to sing in her memory with the voice of sisters that charmed her. She became herself, as it were, an actual part of these lyrical imaginings; at long last, as she saw herself among those lovers she had so envied, she fulfilled the love-dream of her youth. Besides, Emma felt a satisfaction of revenge. How she had suffered! But she had won out at last, and the love so long pent up erupted in joyous outbursts. She tasted it without remorse, without anxiety, without concern.

The next day brought a new-discovered sweetness. They exchanged vows. She told him of her sorrows. Rodolphe interrupted her with kisses; and she, looking at him through half-closed eyes, asked him to call her again by her name and to say that he loved her. They were in the forest, as yesterday, this time in the hut of some *sabot* makers. The walls were of straw, and the roof so low they had to stoop. They were seated side by side on a bed of dry leaves.

From that day on they wrote to one another regularly every evening. Emma placed her letter at the end of the garden, by the river, in a crack of the wall. Rodolphe came to fetch it, and put another in its place that she always accused of being too short.

One morning, when Charles had gone out before daybreak, she felt the urge to see Rodolphe at once. She would go quickly to La Huchette, stay there an hour, and be back again at Yonville while every one was still asleep. The idea made her breathless with desire, and she soon found herself in the middle of the field, walking with rapid steps, without looking behind her.

Day was just breaking. Emma recognised her lover's house from a distance. Its two dove-tailed weathercocks stood out black against the pale dawn.

Beyond the farmyard there was a separate building that she assumed must be the château. She entered it as if the doors at her approach had opened wide of their own accord. A large straight staircase led up to the corridor. Emma raised the latch of a door, and suddenly at the end of the room she saw a man sleeping. It was Rodolphe. She uttered a cry.

"You here? You here?" he repeated. "How did you manage to come? Ah! your dress is wet."

"I love you!" she answered, winding her arm around his neck.

This first bold attempt having been successful, now every time Charles went out early Emma dressed quickly and slipped on tiptoe down the steps that led to the waterside.

But when the cow plank was taken up, she had to follow the walls alongside the river; the bank was slippery; to keep from falling, she had to catch hold of the tufts of faded wall-flowers. Then she went across ploughed fields, stumbling, her thin shoes sinking in the heavy mud. Her scarf, knotted round her head, fluttered to the wind in the meadows. She was afraid of the oxen; she began to run; she arrived out of breath, with rosy cheeks, and breathing out from her whole person a fresh perfume of sap, of verdure, of the open air. At this hour Rodolphe was still asleep. It was like a spring morning bursting into his room.

The golden curtains along the windows let a heavy, whitish light filter into the room. Emma would find her way gropingly, with blinking eyes, the drops of dew hanging from her hair, making a topaz halo around her face. Rodolphe, laughing, would draw her to him and press her to his breast.

Then she inspected the room, opened the drawers of the tables, combed her hair with his comb, and looked at herself in his shaving mirror. Often she put between her teeth the big pipe that lay on the bedtable, amongst lemons and pieces of sugar near the water bottle.

It took them a good quarter of an hour to say good-bye. Then Emma cried: she would have wished never to leave Rodolphe. Something stronger than herself drew her to him; until, one day, when she arrived unexpectedly, he frowned as one put out.

"What is wrong?" she said. "Are you ill? tell me!"

He ended up declaring earnestly that her visits were too dangerous and that she was compromising herself.

X

Gradually Rodolphe's fears took possession of her. At first, love had intoxicated her, and she had thought of nothing beyond. But now that he was indispensable to her life, she feared losing the smallest part of his love or upsetting him in the least. When she came back from his house, she looked all about her, anxiously watching every form that passed in the horizon, and every village window from which she could be seen. She listened for steps, cries, the noise of the ploughs, and she stopped short, white, and trembling more than the aspen leaves swaying overhead.

One morning as she was thus returning, she suddenly thought she saw the long barrel of a carbine that seemed to be aimed at her. It stuck out sideways from the end of a small barrel half-buried in the grass on the edge of a ditch. Emma, half-fainting with terror, nevertheless walked on, and a man stepped out of the barrel like a Jack-in-the-box jumping out of his cage. He had gaiters buckled up to the knees, his cap pulled down over his eyes; his lips shivered in the cold and his nose was red. It was Captain Binet lying in ambush for wild ducks.

"You ought to have called out long ago!" he exclaimed. "When one sees a gun, one should always give warning."

The tax-collector was thus trying to hide his own fright, for a prefectorial order prohibited duck-hunting except in boats, Monsieur Binet, despite his respect for the laws, was breaking the law and he expected to see the garde champêtre turn up any moment. But this anxiety whetted his pleasure, and, all alone in his barrel, he congratulated himself on his luck and his cleverness.

The sight of Emma seemed to relieve him of a great weight, and he at once opened the conversation.

"Pretty cold, isn't it; it's nippy!"

Emma didn't answer. He pursued:

"You're certainly off to an early start today."

"Yes," she stammered; "I am just coming from the nurse who is keeping my child."

"Ah, yes indeed, yes indeed. As for myself, I am here, just as you see me, since break of day; but the weather is so muggy, that unless one had the bird at the mouth of the gun . . ."

"Good day, Monsieur Binet," she interrupted, turning her back on him.

"Your servant, madame," he replied drily.

And he went back into his barrel.

Emma regretted having left the tax-collector so abruptly. No doubt he would jump to the worst conclusions. The story about the nurse was the weakest possible excuse, for every one at Yonville knew that the Bovary baby had been at home with her parents for a year. Besides, no one was living in this direction; this path led only to La Huchette. Binet, then, could not fail to guess where she came from, and he would not remain silent; he would talk, that was certain. She remained until evening racking her brain with every lie she could think up, but the image of that idiot with his game bag would not leave her.

Seeing her so gloomy, Charles proposed after dinner to take her to the pharmacist by way of distraction, and the first person she caught sight of in the shop was him again, the tax-collector! He was standing in front of the counter, lit up by the gleams of the red jar, saying:

"Could I have half an ounce of vitriol, please?"

"Justin," cried the pharmacist, "bring us the sulphuric acid."

Then to Emma, who was going up to Madame Homais' room, "Don't go up, it's not worth the trouble, she is just coming down. Why not warm yourself by the fire . . . Excuse me . . . Good-day, doctor" (for the pharmacist much enjoyed pronouncing the word "doctor," as if addressing another by it reflected on himself some of the grandeur of the title). "Justin, take care not to upset the mortars! You'd better fetch some chairs from the little room; you know very well that the arm-chairs are not to be taken out of the drawing-room."

And he was just about to put his arm-chair back in its place when Binet asked him for half an ounce of sugar acid.

"Sugar acid!" said the pharmacist contemptuously, "never heard of it! There is no such thing. Perhaps it is Oxalic acid you want. It is Oxalic, isn't it?"

Binet explained that he wanted a corrosive to make himself some copper-water with which to remove rust from his hunting things. Emma shuddered. The pharmacist was saying:

"Indeed, the dampness we're having is certainly not propitious."

"Nevertheless," replied the tax-collector, with a sly look, "some people seem to like it." She was stifling.

"And give me . . ."

"Will he never go?" she thought.

"Half an ounce of resin and turpentine, four ounces of beeswax, and three half ounces of animal charcoal, if you please, to clean the leather of my togs."

The druggist was beginning to cut the wax when Madame Homais appeared with Irma in her arms, Napoleon by her side, and Athalie following. She sat down on the velvet seat by the window, and the boy squatted down on a footstool, while his eldest sister hovered round the jujube box near her papa. The latter was filling funnels and corking phials, sticking on labels, making up parcels. Around him all were silent; only from time to time could one hear the weights jingling in the scales, and a few words of advice from the pharmacist to his apprentice.

"And how is your little girl?" Madame Homais asked suddenly.

"Silence!" exclaimed her husband, who was writing down some

figures on a scratch pad.

"Why didn't you bring her?" she went on in a low voice.

"Hush! hush!" said Emma, pointing a finger at the pharmacist.

But Binet, quite absorbed in checking over his bill, had probably heard nothing. At last he went out. Then Emma, relieved, uttered a deep sigh.

"How heavily you are breathing!" said Madame Homais.

"It is so hot in here," she replied.

So the next day they agreed to arrange their rendezvous. Emma wanted to bribe her servant with a present, but it would be better to find some safe house at Yonville. Rodolphe promised to look for one.

All through the winter, three or four times a week, in the dead of night he came to the garden. Emma had on purpose taken away the key of the gate, letting Charles think it was lost.

To call her, Rodolphe threw a handful of sand at the shutters. She jumped up with a start; but sometimes he had to wait, for Charles had the habit of talking endlessly by the fireside.

She was wild with impatience; if her eyes could have done it, they would have hurled him out of the window. At last she would begin to undress, then take up a book, and go on reading very quietly as if the book amused her. But Charles, who was in bed, would call her to bed.

"Come, now, Emma," he said, "it is time."

"Yes, I am coming," she answered.

Then, as the candles shone in his eyes, he turned to the wall and fell asleep. She escaped, holding her breath, smiling, half undressed.

Rodolphe had a large cloak; he wrapped it around her, and putting his arm round her waist, he drew her without a word to the end of the garden.

It was in the arbour, on the same bench of half rotten sticks where formerly Léon had stared at her so amorously on the summer evenings. She never thought of him now.

The stars shone through the leafless jasmine branches. Behind them they heard the river flowing, and now and again on the bank the rustling of the dry reeds. Masses of deeper darkness stood out here and there in the night and sometimes, shaken with one single motion, they would rise up and sway like immense black waves pressing forward to engulf them. The cold of the nights made them clasp each other more tightly; the sighs of their lips seemed to them deeper; their eyes, that they could hardly see, larger; and in the midst of the silence words softly spoken would fall on their souls with a crystalline sound, that echoed in endless reverberations.

When the night was rainy, they took refuge in the consulting-

room between the cart-shed and the stable. She would light one of
the kitchen candles that she had hidden behind the books. Rodolphe settled down there as if at home. The sight of the library, of
the desk, of the entire room, in fine, would arouse his mirth; and he
could not refrain from making jokes at Charles' expense despite
Emma's embarrassment. She would have liked to see him more serious, and even on occasions more dramatic; as, for example, when
she thought she heard a noise of approaching steps in the alley.

"Some one is coming!" she said.

He blew out the light.

"Have you your pistols?"

"Why?"

"Why, to defend yourself," replied Emma.

"From your husband? Oh, the poor fellow!" And Rodolphe finished his sentence with a gesture that said, "I could crush him with
a flip of my finger."

She was awed at his bravery, although she felt in it a sort of
indecency and a naïve coarseness that scandalised her.

Rodolphe reflected a good deal on the pistol incident. If she had
spoken in earnest, he thought it most ridiculous, even odious; for he
had no reason whatever to hate the good Charles, not exactly being
devoured by jealousy; and in this same connection, Emma had
made him a solemn promise that he did not think in the best of
taste.

Besides, she was becoming dreadfully sentimental. She had insisted on exchanging miniatures; handfuls of hair had been cut off,
and now she was asking for a ring—a real wedding-ring, in token of
eternal union. She often spoke to him of the evening chimes, of the
"voices of nature." Then she talked to him of their respective
mothers. Rodolphe's had died twenty years ago. Emma none the
less consoled him with conventional phrases, like those one would
use with a bereaved child; sometimes she even said to him, gazing at
the moon:

"I am sure that, from up there, both approve our love."

But she was so pretty! He had possessed so few women of similar
ingenuousness. This love without debauchery was a new experience
for him, and, drawing him out of his lazy habits, caressed at once
his pride and his sensuality. Although his bourgeois common sense
disapproved of it, Emma's exaltations, deep down in his heart,
enchanted him, since they were directed his way. Then, sure of her
love, he no longer made an effort, and insensibly his manner
changed.

No longer, did he, as before, find words so tender that they made
her cry, nor passionate caresses that drove her into ecstasy; their
great love, in which she had lived immersed, seemed to run out

beneath her, like the water of a river absorbed by its own bed; and she could see the bottom. She would not believe it; she redoubled in tenderness, and Rodolphe concealed his indifference less and less.

She did not know if she regretted having yielded to him, or whether she did not wish, on the contrary, to love him even more. The humiliation of having given in turned into resentment, tempered by their voluptuous pleasures. It was not tenderness; it was like a continual seduction. He held her fully in his power; she almost feared him.

On the surface, however, things seemed calm enough, Rodolphe having carried out his adultery just as he had wanted; and at the end of six months, when the spring-time came, they were to one another like a married couple, tranquilly keeping up a domestic flame.

It was the time of year when old Rouault sent his turkey in rememberance of the setting of his leg. The present always arrived with a letter. Emma cut the string that tied it to the basket, and read the following lines:

My Dear Children,—I hope this will find you in good health, and that it will be as good as the others, for it seems to me a little more tender, if I may venture to say so, and heavier. But next time, for a change, I'll give you a turkeycock, unless you would prefer a capon; and send me back the hamper, if you please, with the two old ones. I have had an accident with sheds; the coverings flew off one windy night among the trees. The harvest has not been over-good either. Finally, I don't know when I shall come to see you. It is so difficult now to leave the house since I am alone, my poor Emma.

Here there was a break in the lines as if the old fellow had dropped his pen to dream a little while.

"As for myself, I am very well, except for a cold I caught the other day at Yvetot, where I had gone to hire a shepherd, having got rid of mine because no cooking was good enough for his taste. We are to be pitied with rascals like him! Moreover, he was dishonest.

I heard from a peddler who had a tooth pulled out when he passed through your part of the country this winter, that Bovary was as usual working hard. That doesn't surprise me; and he showed me his tooth; we had some coffee together. I asked him if he had seen you, and he said no, but that he had seen two horses in the stables, from which I conclude that business is looking up. So much the better, my dear children, and may God send you every imaginable happiness!

It grieves me not yet to have seen my dear little grand-daughter, Berthe Bovary. I have planted an Orleans plum-tree for her in the garden under your room, and I won't have it touched until we can make jam from it, that I will keep in the cupboard for her when she comes.

Good-bye, my dear children. I kiss you, my girl, you too, my son-in-law, and the little one on both cheeks. I am, with best compliments, your loving father.

THEODORE ROUAULT

She held the coarse paper in her fingers for some minutes. A continuous stream of spelling mistakes ran through the letter, and Emma followed the kindly thought that cackled right through it like a hen half hidden in a hedge of thorns. The writing had been dried with ashes from the hearth, for a little grey powder slipped from the letter on her dress, and she almost thought she saw her father bending over the hearth to take up the tongs. How long since she had been with him, sitting on the footstool in the chimney-corner, where she used to burn the end of a stick in the crackling flame of the sea-sedges! She remembered the summer evenings all full of sunshine. The colts whinnied when one passed by, and galloped, galloped . . . Under her window there was a beehive and at times, the bees wheeling round in the light, struck against her window like rebounding balls of gold. What happiness she had known at that time, what freedom, what hope! What a wealth of illusions! It was all gone now. She had lost them one by one, at every stage in the growth of her soul, in the succession of her conditions; maidenhood, marriage and love—shedding them along her path like a traveller who leaves something of his wealth at every inn along his road.

But who was it, then, who made her so unhappy? What extraordinary catastrophe had destroyed her life? And she raised her head, as if seeking around her for the cause of all that suffering.

An April sunray was dancing on the china in the shelves; the fire burned; beneath her slippers she felt the softness of the carpet; the day was bright, the air warm, and she heard her child shouting with laughter.

In fact, the little girl was just then rolling on the lawn in the new-mown grass. She was lying flat on her stomach at the top of a rick. The maid was holding her by her skirt. Lestiboudois was raking by her side, and every time he came near she bent forward, beating the air with both her arms.

"Bring her to me," said her mother, rushing over to kiss her. "How I love you, my poor child! How I love you!"

Then noticing that the tips of her ears were rather dirty, she rang at once for warm water, and washed her, changed her underwear, her stockings, her shoes, asked a thousand questions about her health, as if on the return from a long journey, and finally, kissing her again and crying a little, she gave her back to the maid, who was dumbfounded at this sudden outburst.

That evening Rodolphe found her more reserved than usual.

"It will blow over," he thought, "a passing whim . . ."

And he missed three successive rendezvous. When he did appear, her attitude was cold, almost contemptuous.

"Ah! you're wasting time, sweetheart!"

And he pretended not to notice her melancholy sighs, nor the handkerchief she pulled out.

Then Emma knew what it was to repent!

She even wondered why she hated Charles; wouldn't it have been better trying to love him? But he offered little hold for these re-awakened sentiments, so she remained rather embarrassed with her sacrificial intentions until the pharmacist provided her with a timely opportunity.

XI

He had recently read a paper praising a new method for curing club-foot, and since he was a partisan of progress, he conceived the patriotic idea that Yonville should show its pioneering spirit by having some club-foot operations performed there.

"Look here," he told Emma, "what do we risk?" and he ticked off on his fingers the advantages of the attempt, "success practically assured, relief and better appearance for the patient, quick fame for the surgeon. Why, for example, should not your husband relieve poor Hippolyte of the 'Lion d'Or'? He is bound to tell all passing travellers about his cure, and then" (Homais lowered his voice and looked round him) "who is to prevent me from sending a short piece on the subject to the paper? And! My God! an article gets around . . . people talk about it . . . it snowballs! And who knows? who knows?"

After all, Bovary might very well succeed. Emma had no reason to suppose he lacked skill, it would be a satisfaction for her to have urged him to a step by which his reputation and fortune would be increased! She only longed to lean on something more solid than love.

Pressed by her and the pharmacist, Charles allowed himself to be persuaded. He sent to Rouen for Dr. Duval's volume, and every evening, with his head between his hands, he embarked on his reading assignment.

While he struggled with the equinus, varus and valgus—that is to say, *katastrephopody, endostrephopody*, and *exostrephopody,* or in other words, the various deviations of the foot, to the inside, outside, or downwards, as well as with *hypostrephopody* and *anas-trephopody* or torsion below and contraction above,—Monsieur Homais was trying out all possible arguments on the stable boy in order to persuade him to submit to the operation.

"At the very most you'll feel a slight pain, a small prick, like a little blood letting, less than the extraction of certain corns."

Hippolyte thought it over, rolling his stupid eyes.

"Anyway," continued the pharmacist, "it is none of my business. I am telling you this for your own sake! out of pure humanity! I would like to see you freed from that hideous caudication as well as that swaying in your lumbar region which, whatever you say, must considerably interfere with the proper performance of your work."

Then Homais represented to him how much more dashing and nimble he would feel afterwards, and even hinted that he would be more likely to please the women; and the stable boy broke into a stupid grin. Then he attacked him through his vanity:

"Come on, act like a man! Think what would have happened if you had been called into the army, and had to fight under our national banner! . . . Ah! Hippolyte!"

And Homais left him, declaring that he could not understand such blindness, such obstinacy, in refusing the benefits of science.

The poor wretch finally gave in, for it was like a conspiracy. Binet, who never interfered with other people's business, Madame Lefrançois, Artémise, the neighbors, even the mayor, Monsieur Tuvache—every one tried to convince him by lecture and reproof; but what finally won him over was that it would cost him nothing. Bovary even undertook to provide the machine for the operation. This generosity was an idea of Emma's, and Charles consented to it, thinking in his heart of hearts that his wife was an angel.

So with the advice of the pharmacist, and after three fresh starts, he had a kind of box made by the carpenter, with the assistance of the locksmith; it weighed about eight pounds, for iron, wood, sheet-iron, leather, screws, and nuts had not been spared.

Yet, to know which of Hippolyte's tendons had to be cut, it was necessary first of all to find out what kind of club-foot he had.

His foot almost formed a straight line with the leg, which, however, did not prevent it from being turned in, so that it was an equinus combined with something of a varus, or else a slight varus with a strong tendency to equinus. But on the equine foot, wide indeed as a horse's hoof, with its horny skin, and large toes, whose black nails resembled the nails of a horse shoe, the cripple ran about like a deer from morn till night. He was constantly to be seen on the Square, jumping round the carts, thrusting his limping foot forwards. He seemed even stronger on that leg than the other. By dint of hard service it had acquired, as it were, moral qualities of patience and energy; and when he was given some heavy work to do, he would support himself on it in preference to the sound one.

Now, as it was an equinus, it was necessary to cut the Achilles tendon first; if need be, the anterior tibial muscle could be seen to afterwards to take care of the varus. For the doctor did not dare to risk both operations at once; he was already sufficiently worried for fear of injuring some important region that he did not know.

Neither Ambroise Paré, applying a ligature to an artery, for the first time since Celsus did it fifteen centuries before; nor Dupuytren, cutting open abscesses through a thick layer of brain; nor Gensoul on first removing the superior maxilla, had hearts that trembled, hands that shook, minds that strained as Monsieur Bovary's when he approached Hippolyte, his tenotomy knife between his fingers. Just as in a hospital, near by on a table lay a heap of lint, with waxed thread, many bandages—a pyramid of bandages—every bandage to be found at the pharmacy. It was Monsieur Homais who since morning had been organising all these preparations, as much to dazzle the multitude as to keep up his illusions. Charles pierced the skin; a dry crackling was heard. The tendon was cut, the operation over. Hippolyte could not believe his eyes: he bent over Bovary's hands to cover them with kisses.

"Come, be calm," said the pharmacist; "later on you will show your gratitude to your benefactor."

And he went down to report the result to five or six bystanders who were waiting in the yard, and who fancied that Hippolyte would reappear walking straight up. Then Charles, having strapped his patient into the machine, went home, where Emma was anxiously waiting for him on the doorstep. She threw herself on his neck; they sat down at the table; he ate much, and at dessert he even wanted to take a cup of coffee, a luxury he only permitted himself on Sundays when there was company.

The evening was charming, full of shared conversation and common dreams. They talked about their future success, of the improvements to be made in their house; with his rising reputation, he saw his comforts increasing, his wife always loving him; and she was happy to refresh herself with a new sentiment, healthier and purer, and to feel at last some tenderness for this poor man who adored her. The thought of Rodolphe for one moment passed through her mind, but her eyes turned again to Charles; she even noticed with surprise that he had rather handsome teeth.

They were in bed when Monsieur Homais, sidestepping the cook, suddenly entered the room, holding in his hand a newly written sheet of paper. It was the article he intended for the "Fanal de Rouen." He brought it them to read.

"You read it," said Bovary.

He read:

" 'Braving the prejudices that still spread over the face of Europe like a net, the light nevertheless begins to penetrate into our country places. Thus on Tuesday our little town of Yonville found itself the scene of a surgical operation which was at the same time an act of loftiest philanthropy. Monsieur Bovary, one of our most distinguished practitioners . . ."

"Oh, that is too much! too much!" said Charles, choking with emotion.

—"But certainly not! far from it! . . . 'operated on a club-foot.' I have not used the scientific term, because you know in newspapers . . . not everyone would understand . . . the masses, after all, must . . ."

"Certainly," said Bovary; "please go on!"

"I proceed," said the pharmacist. " 'Monsieur Bovary, one of our most distinguished practitioners, performed an operation on a club-footed man, one Hippolyte Tautain, stable-man for the last twenty-five years at the hotel of the "Lion d'Or," kept by Widow Lefrancois, at the Place d'Armes. The novelty of the experiment and the general interest in the patient had attracted such a number of people that a crowd gathered on the threshold of the establishment. The operation, moreover, was performed as if by magic, and barely a few drops of blood appeared on the skin, as though to say that the rebellious tendon had at last given way under the efforts of the medical arts. The patient, strangely enough (we affirm it *de visu*) complained of no pain. His condition up to the present time leaves nothing to be desired. Everything tends to show that his convalescence will be brief; and who knows if, at our next village festivity we shall not see our good Hippolyte appear in the midst of a bacchic dance, surrounded by a group of gay companions, and thus bear witness to all assembled, by his spirit and his capers, of his total recovery? Honor, then, to those generous men of science! Honor to those tireless spirits who consecrate their vigils to the improvement and relief of their kind! Honor to them! Hasn't the time come to cry out that the blind shall see, the deaf hear, the lame walk? What fanaticism formerly promised to a few elect, science now accomplishes for all men. We shall keep our readers informed as to the subsequent progression of this remarkable cure.' "

All this did not prevent Mère Lefrançois from coming five days later, scared out of her wits and shouting:

"Help! he is dying! I am going out of my mind!"

Charles rushed to the "Lion d'Or," and the pharmacist, who caught sight of him passing along the Square without a hat, left his shop. He arrived himself breathless, flushed, anxious, and asked from every one who was going up the stairs:

"What can be the matter with our interesting patient?"

The interesting patient was writhing, in dreadful convulsions, so violent that the contraption in which his foot was locked almost beat down the wall.

With many precautions, in order not to disturb the position of the limb, the box was removed, and an awful spectacle came into view. The outlines of the foot disappeared in such a swelling that the entire skin seemed about to burst; moreover, the leg was covered with bruises caused by the famous machine. Hippolyte had abundantly complained, but nobody had paid any attention to him; now they admitted he might have some grounds for protest and he was freed for a few hours. But hardly had the oedema somewhat gone down, that the two specialists thought fit to put back the limb in the machine, strapping it even tighter to speed up matters. At last, three days after, when Hippolyte could not stand it any longer, they once more removed the machine, and were much surprised at the result they saw. A livid tumescence spread over the entire leg, and a black liquid oozed from several blisters. Things had taken a turn for the worse. Hippolyte was getting bored, and Mère Lefrançois had him installed in the little room near the kitchen, so that he might at least have some distraction.

But the tax-collector, who dined there every day, complained bitterly of such companionship. Then Hippolyte was removed to the billiard-room.

He lay there moaning under his heavy blankets, pale and unshaven, with sunken eyes; from time to time he rubbed his sweating head over the fly-covered pillow. Madame Bovary came to see him. She brought him linen for his poultices; she comforted, and encouraged him. Besides, he did not want for company, especially on market days, when farmers around him were hitting the billiard balls around and fencing with the cues while they drank, sang and brawled.

"How are things?" they would say, clapping him on the shoulder. "Ah! not so well from what we hear. But that's your fault. You should do this! do that!"

And then they told him stories of people who had all been cured by other means. Then by way of consolation they added:

"You pamper yourself too much! You should get up; you coddle yourself like a king. Just the same, old boy, you do smell pretty awful!"

Gangrene was indeed spreading higher and higher. It made Bovary ill to think of it. He came every hour, every moment. Hippolyte looked at him with terrified eyes and sobbed:

"When will I be cured?—Oh, please save me! . . . How unhappy I am! . . . How unhappy I am!"

And the doctor left him, prescribing a strict diet.

"Don't listen to him," said Mère Lefrançois. "Haven't they tortured you enough already? You'll grow still weaker. Here! swallow this."

And she gave him some strong broth, a slice of mutton, a piece of bacon, and sometimes small glasses of brandy, that he had not the strength to put to his lips.

The abbé Bournisien, hearing that he was growing worse, asked to see him. He began by pitying his sufferings, declaring at the same time that he ought to rejoice since it was the will of the Lord, and hasten to reconcile himself with Heaven.

"For," said the ecclesiastic in a paternal tone, "you rather neglected your duties; you were rarely seen at divine worship. How many years is it since you approached the holy table? I understand that your work, that the whirl of the world may have distracted you from your salvation. But now the time has come. Yet don't despair. I have known great sinners, who, about to appear before God (you are not yet at this point I know), had implored His mercy, and who certainly died in a truly repenting frame of mind. Let us hope that, like them, you will set us a good example! Thus, as a precaution, what is to prevent you from saying morning and evening a Hail Mary and an Our Father? Yes, do that, for my sake, to oblige me. That won't cost you anything. Will you promise me?"

The poor devil promised. The curé came back day after day. He chatted with the landlady, and even told anecdotes interspersed with jokes and puns that Hippolyte did not understand. Then, as soon as he could, he would return to religious considerations, putting on an appropriate expression.

His zeal seemed to bring results, for the club-foot soon manifested a desire to go on a pilgrimage to Bon-Secours if he were cured; to which Monsieur Bournisien replied that he saw no objection; two precautions were better than one; moreover, it certainly could do no harm.

The pharmacist was incensed by what he called the priest's machinations; they were prejudicial, he said, to Hippolyte's convalescence, and he kept repeating to Madame Lefrançois, "Leave him alone! leave him alone! You're ruining his morale with your mysticism."

But the good woman would no longer listen to him; she blamed him for being the cause of it all. In sheer rebellion, she hung near the patient's bedside a well-filled basin of holy water and a sprig of boxwood.

Religion, however, seemed no more able than surgery to bring relief and the irresistible putrefaction kept spreading from the foot to the groin. It was all very well to vary the potions and change the poultices; the muscles each day rotted more and more; Charles replied by an affirmative nod of the head when Mére Lefrançois asked him if she could not, as a last resort, send for Monsieur Canivet, a famous surgeon from Neufchâtel.

Charles' fifty-year old colleague, a doctor of medicine with a well established practice and a solid self confidence, did not refrain from laughing disdainfully when he had uncovered the leg, gangrened to the knee. Then having flatly declared that it must be amputated, he went off to the pharmacist's to rail at the asses who could have reduced a poor man to such a state. Shaking Monsieur Homais by his coat-button, he shouted for everyone to hear:

"That is what you get from listening to the fads from Paris! What will they come up with next, these gentlemen from the capital! It is like strabismus, chloroform, lithotrity, monstrosities the Government ought to prohibit. But they want to be clever and cram you full of remedies without troubling about the consequences. We are not so clever out here, not we! We are no specialists, no cure-alls, no fancy talkers! We are practitioners; we cure people, and we wouldn't dream of operating on someone who is in perfect health. Straighten club-feet! As if one could straighten club-feet indeed! It is as if one wished to make a hunchback straight!"

Homais suffered as he listened to this discourse, and he concealed his discomfort beneath a courtier's smile; for he needed to humour Monsieur Canivet, whose prescriptions sometimes came as far as Yonville. So he did not take up the defence of Bovary; he did not even make a single remark, and, renouncing his principles, he sacrificed his dignity to the more serious interests of his business.

This thigh amputation by Doctor Canivet was a great event in the village. On that day all the inhabitants got up earlier, and the Grande Rue, crowded as it was, had something lugubrious about it, as though one were preparing for an execution. At the grocers they discussed Hippolyte's illness; the shops did no business, and Madame Tuvache, the mayor's wife, did not stir from her window, such was her impatience to see the surgeon arrive.

He came in his gig, which he drove himself. The springs of the right side had all given way beneath his corpulence and the carriage tilted a little as it rolled along, revealing on the cushion near him a large case covered in red sheep-leather, whose three brass clasps shone grandly.

Like a whirlwind, the doctor entered the porch of the Lion d'Or and, shouting loudly, he ordered to unharness. Then he went into the stable to see that his horse was eating his oats all right; for on arriving at a patient's he first of all looked after his mare and his gig. The habit made people say, "Ah, that Monsieur Canivet, what a character!" but he was the more esteemed for his composure. The universe as a whole might have been blown apart, and he would not have changed the least of his habits.

Homais introduced himself.

"I count on you," said the doctor. "Are you ready? Come along!"

But the pharmacist blushingly confessed that he was too sensitive to witness such an operation.

"When one is a simple spectator," he said, "the imagination, you know, is easily impressed. And then, my nerves are so . . ."

"Bah!" interrupted Canivet; "on the contrary, you seem like the apoplectic type to me. But I am not surprised, for you gentlemen pharmacists are always poking about your kitchens, which must end by spoiling your constitutions. Now just look at me. I get up every day at four o'clock; I shave with cold water (and am never cold). I don't wear flannel underwear, and I never catch cold; my carcass is good enough! I take things in my stride, philosophically, as they come my way. That is why I am not squeamish like you, and it doesn't matter to me whether I carve up a Christian or the first fowl that comes my way. Habit, you'll say . . . mere habit! . . ."

Then, without any consideration for Hippolyte, who was sweating with agony between his sheets, these gentlemen began a conversation, in which the druggist compared the coolness of a surgeon to that of a general; and this comparison was pleasing to Canivet, who held forth on the demands of his art. He looked upon it as a sacred office, although the ordinary practitioners dishonored it. At last, coming back to the patient, he examined the bandages brought by Homais, the same that had appeared for the club-foot, and asked for some one to hold the limb for him. Lestiboudois was sent for, and Monsieur Canivet having turned up his sleeves, passed into the billiard-room, while the druggist stayed with Artémise and the landlady, both whiter than their aprons, and with ears strained towards the door.

Meanwhile, Bovary didn't dare to stir from his house.

He kept downstairs in the sitting-room by the side of the fireless chimney, his chin on his breast, his hands clasped, his eyes staring. "What a misfortune," he thought, "what a disappointment!" Yet, he had taken all possible precautions. Luck must have been against him. All the same, if Hippolyte died later on, he would be considered the murderer. And how would he defend himself against the questions his patients were bound to ask him during his calls? Maybe, after all, he had made some slip. He thought and thought, but nothing came. The most famous surgeons also made mistakes. But no one would ever believe that; on the contrary, people would laugh, jeer! The news would spread as far as Neufchâtel, as Rouen, everywhere! Who could say if his colleagues would not write against him? Polemics would ensue; he would have to answer in the papers. Hippolyte might even prosecute him. He saw himself dishonored, ruined, lost; and his imagination, assailed by numberless hypotheses, tossed amongst them like an empty cask dragged out to sea and pitched about by the waves.

Emma, opposite, watched him; she did not share his humiliation; she felt another—that of having imagined that such a man could have any worth, as if twenty times already she had not sufficiently perceived his mediocrity.

Charles was pacing the room. His boots creaked on the floor.

"Sit down," she said; "you irritate me!"

He sat down again.

How was it that she—she, who was so intelligent—could have allowed herself to be deceived again? Moreover, what madness had driven her to ruin her life by continual sacrifices? She recalled all her instincts of luxury, all the privations of her soul, the sordidness of marriage, of the household, her dreams sinking into the mire like wounded swallows; all that she had longed for, all that she had denied herself, all that she might have had! And for what? for what?

In the midst of the silence that hung over the village a heart-rending cry pierced the air. Bovary turned white as a sheet. She knit her brows with a nervous gesture, then returned to her thought. And it was for him, for this creature, for this man, who understood nothing, who felt nothing! For he sat there as if nothing had happened, not even suspecting that the ridicule of his name would henceforth sully hers as well as his. She had made efforts to love him, and she had repented with tears for having yielded to another!

"But it was perhaps a valgus after all!" exclaimed Bovary suddenly, interrupting his meditations.

At the unexpected shock of this phrase falling on her thought like a leaden bullet on a silver plate, Emma shuddered and raised her head in an effort to find out what he meant to say; and they gazed at one another in silence, almost amazed to see each other, so far sundered were they by their respective states of consciousness. Charles gazed at her with the dull look of a drunken man, while he listened motionless to the last cries of the sufferer, following each other in long-drawn modulations, broken by sharp spasms like the far-off howling of some beast being slaughtered. Emma bit her wan lips, and rolling between her fingers a piece of wood she had peeled from the coral-tree, fixed on Charles the burning glance of her eyes like two arrows of fire about to dart forth. Everything in him irritated her now; his face, his dress, all the things he did not say, his whole person, in short, his existence. She repented of her past virtue as of a crime, and what still remained of it crumbled away beneath the furious blows of her pride. She revelled in all the evil ironies of triumphant adultery. The memory of her lover came back to her with irresistible, dizzying attractions; she threw her whole soul towards this image, carried by renewed passion; and Charles seemed to her as removed from her life, as eternally absent, as incongruous and annihilated, as if he were dying under her very eyes.

There was a sound of steps on the pavement. Charles looked up, and through the lowered blinds he saw Dr. Canivet standing in broad sunshine at the corner of the market, wiping his brow with his handerchief. Homais, behind him, was carrying a large red bag in his hand, and both were going towards the pharmacy.

Then with a feeling of sudden tenderness and discouragement Charles turned to his wife and said:

"Oh, kiss me, my dear!"

"Don't touch me!" she cried, flushed with anger.

"What is it? what is it?" he repeated, in utter bewilderment. "Don't be upset! calm down! You know that I love you . . . come! . . ."

"Stop it!" she cried with a terrible look.

And rushing from the room, Emma closed the door so violently that the barometer fell from the wall and smashed on the floor.

Charles sank back into his arm-chair thoroughly shaken, wondering what could have come over her, imagining it might be some nervous disease, weeping, and vaguely feeling something fatal and incomprehensible was whirling around him.

When Rodolphe came to the garden that evening, he found his mistress waiting for him at the foot of the steps on the lowest stair. They threw their arms round one another, and all their rancor melted like snow beneath the warmth of that kiss.

XII

Their love resumed its course. Often in the middle of the day, Emma would suddenly write to him, then beckon Justin through the window; he quickly untied his apron and flew to La Huchette. Rodolphe would come; she had to tell him again how bored she was, that her husband was odious, her life dreadful.

"What do you expect me to do about it?" he asked one day impatiently.

"Ah, if only you wanted . . ."

She was sitting on the floor between his knees, her hair loosened, staring in a void.

"Wanted what?" said Rodolphe.

She sighed.

"We would go and live elsewhere . . . anywhere . . ."

"Are you out of your mind!" he said laughing. "How could we?"

She mentioned it again; he pretended not to understand, and changed the subject. What he did not understand was all this worry about so simple an affair as love. But she had a motive, a reason that gave added grounds to her attachment.

Her tenderness, in fact, grew daily as her repulsion toward her husband increased. The more she yielded to the one, the more she loathed the other. Never did Charles seem so unattractive, slow-witted, clumsy and vulgar as when she met him after her rendez-vous with Rodolphe. Then while playing the part of the virtuous wife, she would burn with passion at the thought of his head, the black curl falling over the sun-tanned brow; of his figure, both elegant and strong, of the man so experienced in his thought, so impetuous in his desires! It was for him that she filed her nails with a sculptor's care, that there was never enough cold-cream for her skin, nor patchouli for her handkerchiefs. She loaded herself with bracelets, rings, and necklaces. When she expected him, she filled her two large blue glass vases with roses, and prepared herself and her room like a courtesan receiving a prince. The servant was kept busy steadily laundering her linen, and all day Félicité did not stir from the kitchen, where little Justin, who often kept her company, watched her at work.

With his elbows on the long board on which she was ironing, he greedily watched all these women's garments spread out about him, the dimity petticoats, the fichus, the collars, and the drawers with running strings, wide at the hips and narrowing below.

"What is that for?" asked the young boy, passing his hand over the crinoline or the hooks and eyes.

"Why, haven't you ever seen anything?" Félicité answered laughing. "As if your mistress, Madame Homais, didn't wear the same."

"Oh, well, Madame Homais . . ."

And he added thoughtfully,

"Is she a lady like Madame?"

But Félicité grew impatient of seeing him hanging round her. She was six years older than he, and Theodore, Monsieur Guillau-min's servant, was beginning to pay court to her.

"Leave me alone," she said, moving her pot of starch. "You'd better be off and pound almonds; you are always snooping around women. Before you bother with such things, naughty boy, wait till you've got a beard to your chin."

"Oh, don't be cross! I'll go and clean her boots."

And he hurriedly took down Emma's boots from the shelf all coated with mud—the mud of the rendezvous—that crumbled into powder beneath his fingers, and that he watched as it gently rose in a ray of sunlight.

"How scared you are of spoiling them!" said the maid, who wasn't so particular when she cleaned them herself, because if the boots looked slightly worn Madame would give them to her.

Emma kept a number in her cupboard that she squandered one after the other, without Charles allowing himself the slightest observation.

He also spent three hundred francs for a wooden leg that she thought had to be given to Hippolyte. The top was covered with cork, and it had spring joints, a complicated mechanism, covered over by black trowsers ending in a patent-leather boot. But Hippolyte didn't dare use such a handsome leg every day, and he begged Madame Bovary to get him another more convenient one. The doctor, of course, had to pay for this purchase as well.

So little by little the stable-boy returned to work. One saw him running about the village as before, and when Charles heard from afar the tap of the wooden leg on the pavement, he quickly went in another direction.

It was Monsieur Lheureux, the shopkeeper, who had ordered the wooden leg. This provided him with an excuse for visiting Emma. He chatted with her about the new goods from Paris, about a thousand feminine trifles, made himself very obliging and never asked for his money. Emma yielded to this lazy mode of satisfying all her caprices. When she wanted to give Rodolphe a handsome riding-crop from an umbrella store in Rouen, Monsieur Lheureux placed it on her table the very next week.

But the next day he called on her with a bill for two hundred and seventy francs, not counting the centimes. Emma was much embarrassed; all the drawers of the writing-table were empty; they owed over a fortnight's wages to Lestiboudois, six months to the maid, and there were several other bills. Bovary was impatiently waiting to hear from Monsieur Derozeray who was in the habit of settling every year about Midsummer.

She succeeded at first in putting off Lheureux. At last he lost patience; he was being sued; he was short of capital and unless he could collect on some of his accounts, he would be forced to take back all the goods she had received.

"Oh, very well, take them!" said Emma.

"I was only joking," he replied; "the only thing I regret is the riding crop. Well, I'll have to ask Monsieur to return it to me."

"No, no!" she said.

"Ah! I've got you!" thought Lheureux.

And, certain of his discovery, he went out muttering to himself and with his usual low whistle . . .

"Good! we shall see! we shall see!"

She was wondering how to handle the situation when the maid entered and put on the mantelpiece a small roll of blue paper "with the compliments of Monsieur Derozeray." Emma grasped it, tore it open. It contained fifteen napoleons: the account paid in full. Hearing Charles on the stairs, she threw the money to the back of her drawer, and took out the key.

Three days later, Lheureux returned.

"I have a suggestion to make," he said. "If, instead of the sum, agreed on, you would take. . . ."

"Here it is," she said handing him fourteen napoleons.

The shopkeeper was taken aback. Then, to conceal his disappointment, he was profuse in apologies and offers of service, all of which Emma declined; she remained a few moments fingering in the pocket of her apron the two five-franc pieces of change he had returned to her. She told herself she would economise in order to pay back later . . . "Bah!", she thought, "he'll forget all about it."

Besides the riding-crop with its silver-gilt top, Rodolphe had received a signet with the motto *Amor nel cor,* furthermore, a scarf for a muffler, and, finally, a cigar-case exactly like the Viscount's, that Charles had formerly picked up in the road, and that Emma had kept. These presents, however, humiliated him; he refused several; she insisted, and he ended by obeying, thinking her tyrannical and over-exacting.

Then she had strange ideas.

"When midnight strikes," she said, "you must think of me."

And if he confessed that he had not thought of her, there were floods of reproaches that always ended with the eternal question:

"Do you love me?"

"Why, of course I love you," he answered.

"A great deal?"

"Certainly!"

"You haven't loved any others?"

"Did you think you'd got a virgin?" he exclaimed laughing.

Emma cried, and he tried to console her, adorning his protestations with puns.

"Oh," she went on, "I love you! I love you so that I could not live without you, do you see? There are times when I long to see you again, when I am torn by all the anger of love. I ask myself, where is he? Perhaps he is talking to other women. They smile upon him; he approaches. Oh no; no one else pleases you. There are some more beautiful, but I love you best. I know how to love best. I am your servant, your concubine! You are my king, my idol! You are good, you are beautiful, you are clever, you are strong!"

He had so often heard these things said that they did not strike him as original. Emma was like all his mistresses; and the charm of novelty, gradually falling away like a garment, laid bare the eternal monotony of passion, that has always the same shape and the same language. He was unable to see, this man so full of experience, the variety of feelings hidden within the same expressions. Since libertine or venal lips had murmured similar phrases, he only faintly believed in the candor of Emma's; he thought one should beware of exaggerated declarations which only serve to cloak a tepid love; as though the abundance of one's soul did not sometimes overflow with empty metaphors, since no one ever has been able to give the exact measure of his needs, his concepts, or his sorrows. The human tongue is like a cracked cauldron on which we beat out tunes to set a bear dancing when we would make the stars weep with our melodies.

But with the superiority of critical insight of the person who holds back his emotions in any engagement, Rodolphe perceived that there were other pleasures to be exploited in this love. He discarded all modesty as inconvenient. He treated her without consideration. And he made her into something at once malleable and corrupt. It was an idiotic sort of attachment, full of admiration on his side and voluptuousness on hers, a beatitude which left her numb; and her soul sunk deep into this intoxication and drowned in it, all shrivelled up, like the duke of Clarence[44] in his butt of malmsey.

Solely as a result of her amorous practices, Madame Bovary began to change in appearance. Her glances were bolder, her speech freer; she even went as far as to go out walking with Rodolphe, a cigarette in her mouth, "just to scandalize the town"; finally, those who had doubted doubted no longer when they saw her descend one day from the Hirondelle wearing a tight-fitting waistcoat cut like a man's. And Madame Bovary senior who, after a frightful scene with her husband, had come to seek refuge with her son, was not the least scandalized lady in town. Many other things displeased her too: first of all, Charles had not followed her advice in banning novels from the house; then, the "tone" of the house upset her; she allowed herself to make observations, and there were arguments, especially, on one occasion, concerning Felicité.

The previous evening, while crossing the corridor, Madame Bovary senior had come upon her in the company of a man of about forty wearing a brown collar, who on hearing footsteps, had quickly fled from the kitchen. Emma had burst out laughing; but the good woman was furious, declaring that anyone who took morality seriously ought to keep an eye on their servant's behavior.

"What kind of society do you come from?" asked the daughter-in-law, with so impertinent a look that Madame Bovary asked her if

44. The duke of Clarence was the younger brother of King Edward IV of England and the elder brother of Richard Duke of Gloucester. He was condemned to death for treason and, according to rumor, drowned in a butt of malmsey (a sweet aromatic wine) in February 1478. See Shakespeare, *Richard III*, Act 1, sc. 4, l. 155.

she were not perhaps defending her own case.

"Get out!" said the young woman, rising in fury.

"Emma! . . . Mother! . . ." cried Charles, trying to reconcile them.

But both had fled in their exasperation. Emma was stamping her feet as she repeated:

"Oh! what manners! What a peasant!"

He ran to his mother; she was beside herself. She stammered: "How insolent she is! and how flighty! worse perhaps!"

And she was ready to leave at once if the other did not apologise. So Charles went back again to his wife and implored her to give way; he threw himself at her feet; finally, she said:

"Very well! I'll go to her."

And she actually held out her hand to her mother-in-law with the dignity of a marquise as she said:

"Excuse me, madame."

Then, having returned to her room, she threw herself flat on her bed and cried there like a child, her face buried in the pillow.

She and Rodolphe had agreed that in the event of anything extraordinary occurring, she should fasten a small piece of white paper to the blind, so that if by chance he happened to be in Yonville, he could hurry to the lane behind the house. Emma made the signal; she had been waiting three-quarters of an hour when she suddenly caught sight of Rodolphe at the corner of the square. She felt tempted to open the window and call him, but he had already disappeared. She fell back in despair.

Soon, however, it seemed to her that someone was walking on the pavement. It was he, no doubt. She went downstairs, crossed the yard. He was there outside. She threw herself into his arms.

"Watch out!" he said.

"Ah! if only you knew!" she replied.

And she began telling him everything, hurriedly, disjointedly, exaggerating the facts, inventing many, and with so many digressions that he understood nothing at all.

"Come now, my poor angel, be brave, console yourself, be patient!"

"But I have been patient; I have suffered for four years. A love like ours ought to show itself in the face of heaven. They torture me! I can bear it no longer! Save me!"

She clung to Rodolphe. Her eyes, full of tears, flashed like flames beneath a wave; her panting made her breast rise and fall; never had she seemed more lovely, so much so that he lost his head and said:

"What do you want me to do?"

"Take me away," she cried, "carry me off! . . . I beg you!"

She pressed her lips against his mouth, as if to capture the unhoped for consent the moment it was breathed forth in a kiss.

"But . . ." Rodolphe began.

"What?"

"Your little girl!"

She reflected a few moments, then replied:

"We'll take her with us, there is no other way!"

"What a woman!" he said to himself, watching her as she went. For she had run into the garden. Some one was calling her.

On the following days the elder Madame Bovary was much surprised at the change in her daughter-in-law. Emma, in fact, was showing herself more docile, and even carried her deference to the point of asking for a recipe for pickles.

Was it the better to deceive them both? Or did she wish by a sort of voluptuous stoicism to feel the more profoundly the bitterness of the things she was about to leave? But she paid no heed to them; on the contrary, she lived as lost in the anticipated delight of her coming happiness. It was an eternal subject for conversation with Rodolphe. She leant on his shoulder murmuring:

"Think, we will soon be in the mail-coach! Can you imagine? Is it possible? It seems to me that the moment the carriage will start, it will be as if we were rising in a balloon, as if we were setting out for the clouds. Do you know that I count the hours? . . . Don't you?"

Never had Madame Bovary been so beautiful as at this period; she had that indefinable beauty that results from joy, from enthusiasm, from success, and that expresses the harmony between temperament and circumstances. Her cravings, her sorrows, her sensuous pleasures and her ever-young illusions had slowly brought her to full maturity, and she blossomed forth in the fulness of her being, like a flower feeding on manure, on rain, wind and sunshine. Her half-closed eyelids seemed perfectly shaped for the long languid glances that escaped from them; her breathing dilated the fine nostrils and raised the fleshy corners of her mouth, shaded in the light by a slight black down. Some artist skilled in corruption seemed to have devised the shape of her hair as it fell on her neck, coiled in a heavy mass, casually reassembled after being loosened daily in adultery. Her voice now took more mellow inflections, her figure also; something subtle and penetrating escaped even from the folds of her gown and from the line of her foot. Charles thought her exquisite and altogether irresistible, as when they were first married.

When he came home in the middle of the night, he did not dare to wake her. The porcelain night-light threw a round trembling gleam upon the ceiling, and the drawn curtains of the little cot formed as it were a white hut standing out in the shade by the bedside. Charles looked at them. He seemed to hear the light breathing of his child. She would grow big now; every season would bring rapid progress. He already saw her coming from school as the day drew in, laughing, with ink-stains on her jacket, and carrying her basket on her arm. Then she would have to be sent to a boarding-school; that would cost much; how was it to be done? He kept thinking about it. He thought of renting a small farm in the neighborhood, that he would supervise every morning on his way to his patients. He would not spend what he brought in; he would put it in the savings-bank. Then he would invest in some stocks, he didn't know which; besides, his practice would increase; he counted on it, for he wanted Berthe to be well-educated, to be accomplished, to learn to play the piano. Ah! how pretty she would be later on when she was fifteen, when, resembling her mother, she would, like her, wear large straw hats in the summer-time; from a distance they would be taken for two sisters. He pictured her to himself working in the evening by their side beneath the light of the lamp; she would embroider him slippers; she would look after the house; she would fill all the home with her charm and her gaiety. At last, they would think of her marriage; they would find her some good young fellow with a steady business; he would make her happy; this would last for ever.

Emma was not asleep; she pretended to be; and while he dozed off by her side she awakened to other dreams.

To the gallop of four horses she was carried away for a week towards a new land, from where they would never return. They went on and on, their arms entwined, without speaking a word. Often from the top of a mountain there suddenly appeared some splendid city with domes, and bridges, and ships, forests of lemon trees, and cathedrals of white marble, their pointed steeples crowned with storks' nests. The horses slowed down to a walk because of the wide pavement, and on the ground there were bouquets of flowers, offered by women dressed in red. They heard the chiming of bells, the neighing of mules, together with the murmur of guitars and the noise of fountains, whose rising spray refreshed heaps of fruit arranged like a pyramid at the foot of pale statues that smiled beneath playing waters. And then, one night they came to a fishing village, where brown nets were drying in the wind along the cliffs and in front of the huts. It was there that they would stay; they would live in a low, flat-roofed house, shaded by a palm-tree, in the heart of a gulf, by the sea. They would row in gondolas, swing in hammocks, and their existence would be easy and free as their wide silk gowns, warm and star-spangled as the nights they would contemplate. However, in the immensity of this future that she conjured up, nothing specific stood out; the days, all magnificent, resembled each other like waves; and the vision swayed in the horizon, infinite, harmonised, azure, and bathed in sunshine. But the child began to cough in her cot or Bovary snored more loudly, and Emma did not fall asleep till morning, when the dawn whitened the windows, and when little Justin was already in the square taking down the shutters of the pharmacy.

She had sent for Monsieur Lheureux, and had said to him:

"I want a cloak—a large lined cloak with a deep collar."

"You are going on a journey?" he asked.

"No; but . . . never mind. I count on you to get it in a hurry."

He bowed.

"Besides, I shall want," she went on, "a trunk . . . not too heavy . . . a handy size."

"Yes, yes, I understand. About three feet by a foot and a half, as they are being made just now."

"And a travelling bag."

"No question about it," thought Lheureux, "she is up to something."

"And," said Madame Bovary, taking her watch from her belt, "take this; you can pay yourself out of it."

But the shopkeeper protested that it was not necessary; as if he didn't know and trust her. She was being childish!

She insisted, however, on his taking at least the chain, and Lheureux had already put it in his pocket and was going, when she called him back.

"You will leave everything at your place. As to the cloak"—she seemed to be reflecting—"do not bring it either; you can give me the maker's address, and tell him to have it ready for me."

It was the next month that they were to run away. She was to leave Yonville as if she was going on some business to Rouen. Rodolphe would have booked the seats, obtained the passports, and even have written to Paris in order to have the whole mail-coach reserved for them as far as Marseilles, where they would buy a carriage, and go on from there straight by the Genoa road. She would have sent her luggage to Lheureux, from where it would be taken directly to the "Hirondelle," so that no one would have any suspicion. And in all this there never was any allusion to the child. Rodolphe avoided the subject; it may be that he had forgotten about it.

He wished to have two more weeks before him to arrange some affairs; then at the end of a week he wanted two more; then he said he as ill; next he went on a journey. The month of August passed, and, after all these delays, they decided that it was to be irrevocably fixed for the 4th September—a Monday.

At last the Saturday before arrived.

Rodolphe came in the evening earlier than usual.

"Is everything ready?" she asked him.

"Yes."

Then they walked round a garden-bed, and sat down near the terrace on the kerb-stone of the wall.

"You are sad," said Emma.

"No; why?"

And yet he looked at her strangely, though with tenderness.

"Is it because you are going away?" she went on; "because you are leaving behind what is dear to you, your own life? I can understand that . . . But I have nothing in the world! You are everything I have, and I'll be everything to you. I'll be your family, your country; I'll look after you, I'll love you."

"How sweet you are!" he said, taking her in his arms.

"Am I really?" she said with a voluptuous laugh. "Do you love me? Swear it then!"

"Do I love you? Do I? But I adore you, my love!"

The moon, full and purple-colored, was rising right out of the earth at the end of the meadow. It rose quickly between the branches of the poplar trees, partly hidden as by a tattered black curtain. Then it appeared dazzling white, lighting up the empty sky; slowing down, it let fall upon the river a great stain that broke up into an infinity of stars; and the silver sheen seemed to writhe through the very depths like a headless serpent covered with luminous scales; it also resembled some monster candelabra from which sparkling diamonds fell like molten drops. The soft night was about them; masses of shadow filled the branches. Emma, her eyes half closed, breathed in with deep sighs the fresh wind that was blowing. They did not speak, caught as they were in their dream. The tenderness of the old days came back to their hearts, full and silent as the flowing river, with the soft perfume of the syringas, and threw across their memories shadows more immense and more sombre than those of the still willows that lengthened out over the grass. Often some night-animal, hedgehog or weasel, setting out on the hunt, disturbed the lovers, or sometimes they heard a ripe peach fall by itself from the tree.

"Ah! what a lovely night!" said Rodolphe.

"We shall have others," replied Emma.

Then, as if speaking to herself:

"Yes, it will be good to travel. And yet, why should my heart be so heavy? Is it dread of the unknown? The weight of old habits? . . . Or else? No, it is the excess of happiness. How weak I am! You must forgive me!"

"There is still time!" he cried. "Think! You may regret it later!"

"Never!" she cried impetuously.

And, drawing closer to him:

"What ill could come to me? There is no desert, no precipice, no ocean I would not traverse with you. The longer we live together the more it will be like an embrace, every day closer, more complete. There will be nothing to trouble us, no cares, no obstacle. We shall be alone, all to ourselves forever . . . Say something, answer me!"

At regular intervals he answered, "Yes . . . Yes . . ." She had passed her hands through his hair, and she repeated in a childlike voice through her tears:

"Rodolphe! Rodolphe! . . . Sweet little Rodolphe!"

Midnight struck.

"Midnight!" she said. "Come, it is to-morrow. One more day!"

He rose to go; and as if the movement he made had been the signal for their flight, Emma suddenly seemed gay:

"You have the passports?"

"Yes."

"You are forgetting nothing?"

"No."

"Are you sure?"

"Absolutely."

"You'll be waiting for me at the Hotel de Provence, won't you? . . . at noon?"

He nodded.

"Till to-morrow then!" said Emma in a last caress; and she watched him go.

He did not turn round. She ran after him, and, leaning over the water's edge between the bushes:

"Till to-morrow!" she cried.

He was already on the other side of the river and walking fast across the meadow.

After a few moments Rodolphe stopped; and when he saw her with her white gown gradually fade away in the shade like a ghost, his heart beat so wildly that he had to support himself against a tree.

"What a fool I am!" he said, swearing a dreadful oath. "All the same, she was the prettiest mistress ever."

And immediately Emma's beauty, with all the pleasures of their love, came back to him. For a moment he weakened, but then he rebelled against her.

"For, after all," he exclaimed, gesticulating, "I can't exile myself, and with a child on my hands to boot!"

He was saying these things to strengthen his determination.

"And besides, the worries, the cost! No, no, a thousand times no! It would have been too stupid."

XIII

No sooner was Rodolphe at home than he sat down quickly at his desk under the stag's head that hung as a trophy on the wall. But when he had the pen between his fingers, he could think of nothing, so that, resting on his elbows, he began to reflect. Emma seemed to him to have receded into a far-off past, as if the resolution he had taken had suddenly placed an immeasurable distance between them.

In order to recapture something of her presence, he fetched from the cupboard at the bedside an old Rheims cookie-box, in which he usually kept his love letters. An odour of dry dust and withered roses emanated from it. First he saw a handkerchief stained with pale drops. It was a handkerchief of hers. Once when they were walking her nose had bled; he had forgotten it. Near it, almost too large for the box, was Emma's miniature: her dress seemed pretentious to him, and her languishing look in the worst possible taste. Then, from looking at this image and recalling the memory of the original, Emma's features little by little grew confused in his remembrance, as if the living and the painted face, rubbing one against the other, had erased each other. Finally, he read some of her letters; they were full of explanations relating to their journey, short, technical, and urgent, like business notes. He wanted to see the long ones again, those of old times. In order to find them at the bottom of the box, Rodolphe disturbed all the others, and mechanically began rummaging among this mass of papers and things, finding pell-mell bouquets, garters, a black mask, pins, and hair . . . lots of hair! Some dark, some fair, some, catching in the hinges of the box, even broke when he opened it.

Following his memories, he examined the writing and the style of the letters, as varied as their spelling. They were tender or jovial, facetious, melancholy; there were some that asked for love, others that asked for money. A word recalled faces to him, certain gestures, the sound of a voice; sometimes, however, he remembered nothing at all.

All these women, crowding into his consciousness, rather shrank in size, levelled down by the uniformity of his feeling. Seizing the letters at random, he amused himself for a while by letting them cascade from his right into his left hand. At last, bored and weary, Rodolphe took back the box to the cupboard, saying to himself: "What a lot of nonsense!"

Which summed up his opinion; for pleasures, like schoolboys in a school courtyard, had so trampled upon his heart that no green thing was left; whatever entered there, more heedless than children, did not even, like them, leave a name carved upon the wall.

"Come," he said, "let's go."

He wrote:

> Courage, Emma! you must be brave! I don't want to be the one to ruin your life . . .

"After all, that's true," thought Rodolphe. "I am acting in her interest; I am honest."

> Have you carefully weighed your resolution? Do you know to what an abyss I was dragging you, poor angel? No, you don't, I assure you. You were coming confident and fearless, believing in a future happiness . . . Ah! the wretched creatures we are! We nearly lost our minds!

Rodolphe paused to think of some good excuse.

"If I told her that I lost all my money? No! Besides, that would stop nothing. It would all start again later on. As if one could make women like that listen to reason!"

He thought for a moment, then added:

> I shall not forget you, believe me; and I shall forever have a profound devotion for you; but some day, sooner or later, this ardour (such is the fate of human things) would doubtlessly have diminished. Weariness would have been unavoidable, and who knows if I would not even have had the atrocious pain of witnessing your remorse, of sharing it myself, since I would have been its cause? The mere idea of the grief that would come to you tortures me, Emma. Forget me! Why did I ever know you? Why were you so beautiful? Is it my fault? God, no! only fate is to blame!

"That's a word that always helps," he said to himself.

> Ah, if you had been one of those shallow women of which there are so many, I might, out of selfishness, have tried an experiment, in that case without danger for you. But your exquisite sensitivity, at once your charm and your torment, has prevented you from understanding, adorable woman that you are, the falseness of our future position. I myself had not fully realized this till now; I was living in the bliss of this ideal happiness as under the shade of a poisonous tree, without forseeing the consequences.

"She may suspect that it is out of stinginess that I am giving her up . . . But never mind, let's get this over with!"

> This is a cruel world, Emma. Wherever we might have gone, it would have persecuted us. You would have had to put up with indiscreet questions, calumny, contempt, insult perhaps. Imagine you being insulted! It is unbearable! . . . I who would place you on a throne! I who bear with me your memory as a talisman! For I am going to punish myself by exile for all the ill I have done you. I am going away. I don't know where, I am too close to madness to think. Farewell! Continue to be good! Remember the unfortu-

nate man who caused your undoing. Teach my name to your child; let her repeat it in her prayers.

The wicks of the candles flickered. Rodolphe got up to close the window, and when he sat down again:

"I think that covers it. Ah, let me add this for fear she might pursue me here."

I shall be far away when you read these sad lines, for I have wished to flee as quickly as possible to shun the temptation of seeing you again. No weakness! I shall return, and perhaps later on we shall be able to talk coldly of our past love. Adieu!

And there was a last "adieu" divided into two words: "A Dieu!" which he thought in very excellent taste.

"Now how am I to sign?" he asked himself. " 'Yours devotedly?' No! 'Your friend?' Yes, that's it."

YOUR FRIEND.

He re-read his letter and thought it quite good.

"Poor little woman!" he thought tenderly. "She'll think me harder than a rock. There ought to have been some tears on this; but I can't cry; it isn't my fault." Then, having emptied some water into a glass, Rodolphe dipped his finger into it, and let a big drop fall on the paper, making a pale stain on the ink. Then looking for a seal, he came upon the one "*Amor nel cor.*"

"Hardly the right thing under the circumstances . . . But who cares?"

Whereupon he smoked three pipes and went to bed.

Upon arising the next morning—around two o'clock in the afternoon, for he had slept late—Rodolphe had a basket of apricots picked. He put his letter at the bottom under some vine leaves, and at once ordered Girard, his ploughman, to take it with care to Madame Bovary. They used to correspond this way before and he would send her fruit or game according to season.

"If she asks about me," he said, "tell her that I have gone on a journey. You must give the basket to her herself, into her own hands. Get going now, and be careful!"

Girard put on his new smock, knotted his handkerchief round the apricots, and, walking heavily in his hobnailed boots, quietly made his way to Yonville.

When he got to the house, Madame Bovary was arranging a bundle of linen on the kitchen-table with Félicité.

"Here," said the ploughboy, "is something for you from my master."

She was seized with apprehension, and as she sought in her pocket for some small change, she looked at the peasant with haggard eyes, while he himself stared at her with amazement, not understanding how such a small present could stir up such violent emotions. Finally he left. Félicité stayed. She could bear it no longer; she ran into the sitting room as if to take the apricots there, overturned the basket, tore away the leaves, found the letter, opened it, and, as if pursued by some fearful fire, Emma flew in terror to her room.

Charles was there; she saw him; he spoke to her; she heard nothing, and she ran quickly up the stairs, breathless, distraught, crazed, and ever holding this horrible piece of paper, that crackled between her fingers like a plate of sheet-iron. On the second floor she stopped before the closed attic-door.

Then she tried to calm herself; she recalled the letter; she must finish it but she didn't dare. Where and how was she to read it? She would be seen!

"Here," she thought, "I'll be safe here."

Emma pushed open the door and went in.

The slates projected a heavy heat that gripped her temples, stifled her; she dragged herself to the closed window, drew back the bolt, and the dazzling sunlight burst in.

Opposite, beyond the roofs, the open country stretched as far as the eye could reach. Down below, underneath her, the village square was empty; the stones of the pavement glittered, the weathercocks on the houses stood motionless. At the corner of the street, from a lower story, rose a kind of humming with strident modulations. It was Binet turning.

She leant against the window-frame, and re-read the letter with angry sneers. But the more she concentrated on it, the more confused she grew. She could see him, hear him, feel his embrace; the throbbing of her heart, beating irregularly in her breast like the blows of a battering ram, grew faster and faster. She looked about her wishing that the earth might crumble. Why not end it all? What restrained her? She was free. She advanced, looked at the paving-stones, saying to herself, "Jump! jump!"

The ray of light reflected straight from below drew the weight of her body towards the abyss. The ground of the village square seemed to tilt over and climb up the walls, the floor to pitch forward like in a tossing boat. She was right at the edge, almost hanging, surrounded by vast space. The blue of the sky invaded her, the air was whirling in her hollow head; she had but to yield, to let herself be taken; and the humming of the lathe never ceased, like an angry voice calling her.

"My wife! my wife!" cried Charles.

She stopped.

"Where have you gone? Come here!"

The thought that she had just escaped from death almost made her faint with terror. She closed her eyes; then she started at the touch of a hand on her sleeve; it was Félicité.

"Monsieur is waiting for you, madame; the soup is on the table."

And she had to go down! and sit at the table!

She tried to eat. The food choked her. Then she unfolded her napkin as if to examine the darns, and really tried to concentrate on this work, counting the stitches in the linen. Suddenly she remembered the letter. How had she lost it? Where could it be found? But she felt such weariness of spirit that she could not even invent a pretext for leaving the table. Then she became a coward; she was afraid of Charles; he knew all, that was certain! Just then, he said, in an odd tone:

"We are not likely to see Monsieur Rodolphe soon again, it seems."

"Who told you?" she said, shuddering.

"Who told me!" he replied, rather astonished at her abrupt tone. "Why, Girard, whom I met just now at the door of the Café Français. He has gone on a journey, or is about to go."

She could not suppress a sob.

"What is so surprising about that? He goes away like that from time to time for a change, and I certainly can't blame him. A bachelor, and rich as he is! And from what I hear, he isn't exactly starved for pleasures, our friend! he enjoys life. Monsieur Langlois told me . . ."

He stopped for propriety's sake because the maid had just come in.

She collected the apricots that were strewn over the sideboard and put them back in the basket. Charles, unaware that his wife had turned scarlet, had them brought to him, took one, and bit into it.

"Perfect!" he said; "have a taste!"

And he handed her the basket, which she gently put away from her.

"Smell them! Such perfume!" he insisted, moving it back and forth under her nose.

"I am choking," she exclaimed, leaping up.

By sheer willpower, she succeeded in forcing back the spasm.

"It is nothing," she said, "it is nothing! Just nerves. Sit down and eat."

For she dreaded most of all that he would question her, try to help and not leave her to herself.

Charles, to obey her, sat down again, and he spat the stones of the apricots into his hands, afterwards putting them on his plate.

Suddenly a blue tilbury passed across the square at a rapid trot. Emma uttered a cry and fell back rigid on the floor.

After many hesitations, Rodolphe had finally decided to set out for Rouen. Now, as from La Huchette to Buchy there is no other way than by Yonville, he had to go through the village, and Emma had recognised him by the rays of the lanterns, which like lightning flashed through the twilight.

The general commotion which broke out in the house brought the pharmacist over in a hurry. The table, with all the plates, had been knocked over; sauce, meat, knives, the salt, and cruet-stand were strewn over the room; Charles was calling for help; Berthe, scared, was crying; and Félicité, whose hands trembled, was unlacing her mistress, whose whole body shivered convulsively.

"I'll run to my laboratory for some aromatic vinegar," said the pharmacist.

Then as she opened her eyes on smelling the bottle:

"I thought so," he said, "this thing would resuscitate a corpse!"

"Speak to us," said Charles "try to recover! It is Charles, who loves you . . . Do you know me? Look, here is your little girl; kiss her, darling!"

The child stretched out her arms to cling to her mother's neck. But turning away her head, Emma said in a broken voice:

"No, no . . . I want no one!"

She fainted again. They carried her to her bed.

She lay there stretched at full length, her lips apart, her eyelids closed, her hands open, motionless, and white as a waxen image. Two streams of tears flowed from her eyes and fell slowly upon the pillow.

Charles stood at the back of the alcove, and the pharmacist, near him, maintained the meditative silence that is fitting on the serious occasions of life.

"Don't worry," he said, touching his elbow; "I think the paroxysm is past."

"Yes, she is resting a little now," answered Charles, watching her sleep. "Poor girl! poor girl! She has dropped off now!"

Then Homais asked how the accident had occurred. Charles answered that she had been taken ill suddenly while she was eating some apricots.

"Extraordinary!" continued the pharmacist. "It is quite possible that the apricots caused the syncope. Some natures are so sensitive to certain smells; it would even be a very fine question to study both from a pathological and physiological point of view. The priests know all about it; that's why they use aromatics in all their ceremonies. It is to stupefy the senses and to bring on ecstasies,—a thing, moreover, very easy in persons of the weaker sex, who are

more sensitive than we are. Some are reported fainting at the smell
of burnt horn, or fresh bread . . ."

"Be careful not to wake her!" warned Bovary.

But the pharmacist was not to be stopped. "Not only," he resumed, "are human beings subject to such anomalies, but animals
also. You are of course not ignorant of the singularly aphrodisiac
effect produced by the *Nepeta cataria*, vulgarly called catnip, on the
feline race; and, on the other hand, to quote an example whose
authenticity I can vouch for, Bridaux (one of my old schoolmates,
at present established in the Rue Malpalu) owns a dog that falls
into convulsions as soon as you hold out a snuff-box to him. He
often performs the experiment before his friends at his summerhouse in Bois-Guillaume. Could you believe that a simple sternuta-
tive could cause such damage to a quadrupedal organism? Wouldn't
you agree that it is extremely curious?"

"Yes," said Charles, who was not listening.

"It just goes to show," pursued the pharmacist, smiling with
benign self-satisfaction, "the numberless irregularities of the nervous system. With regard to madame, I must say that she has always
seemed extremely susceptible to me. And so I should by no means
recommend to you, my dear friend, any of those so-called remedies
that, under the pretence of attacking the symptoms, attack the
constitution. No, no gratuitous medications! Diet, that is all; sedatives, emollients, dulcifiers. And then, don't you think we ought to
stimulate the imagination?"

"In what way? How?" said Bovary.

"Ah, that is the problem. 'That is the question' (he said it in
English) as I lately read in a newspaper."

But Emma, awaking, cried out:

"The letter! Where is the letter?"

They thought she was delirious; and she was by midnight. Brain-
fever had set in.

For forty-three days Charles did not leave her. He gave up all his
patients; he no longer went to bed; he was constantly feeling her
pulse, applying mustard plasters and cold-water compresses. He sent
Justin as far as Neufchâtel for ice; the ice melted on the way; he
sent him back again. He called Monsieur Canivet into consultation;
he sent for Dr. Larivière, his old master, from Rouen; he was in
despair. What alarmed him most was Emma's prostration, for she
did not speak, did not listen, did not even seem to suffer—as if both
her body and her soul were resting after all their tribulations.

About the middle of October she could sit up in bed supported
by pillows. Charles wept when he saw her eat her first piece of
bread and jam. Her strength returned; she got up for a few hours of
an afternoon, and one day, when she felt better, he tried to take

her, leaning on his arm, for a walk round the garden. The sand of the paths was disappearing beneath the dead leaves; she walked slowly, dragging her slippers, and leaning against Charles's shoulder. She smiled all the time.

They went thus to the end of the garden near the terrace. She drew herself up slowly, shading her eyes with her hand. She looked far off, as far as she could, but on the horizon were only great bonfires of grass smoking on the hills.

"You will tire yourself, darling!" said Bovary.

And, pushing her gently to make her enter the arbour: "Sit down on this seat; you'll be comfortable."

"Oh! no; not there!" she said in a faltering voice.

She was seized with giddiness, and that evening, she suffered a relapse, less specific in character, it is true, and with more complex symptoms. At times it was her heart that troubled her, then her head or her limbs; she had vomitings, in which Charles thought he detected the first signs of cancer.

And, on top of all this, the poor fellow had money troubles!

XIV

To begin with, he did not know how to reimburse Monsieur Homais for all the drugs he had supplied and although, as a doctor, he could have forgone paying for them, he blushed at the thought of such an obligation. Then the expenses of the household, now that the maid was in charge, became staggering. Bills flooded the house; the tradesmen grumbled; Monsieur Lheureux especially harassed him. At the height of Emma's illness, he had taken advantage of the situation to increase his bill; he hurriedly brought the cloak, the travelling-bag, two trunks instead of one, and a number of other things. Charles protested in vain; the shopkeeper rudely replied that the merchandise had been ordered and that he had no intention of taking it back. Besides, it would interfere with madame's convalescence; the doctor had better think it over; in short, he was resolved to sue him rather than give up his rights and take it off his hands. Charles subsequently ordered them sent back to the shop. Félicité forgot and, having other things on his mind, Charles thought no more about it. Monsieur Lheureux did not desist and, alternating threats with whines, he finally forced Bovary into signing him a six months' promissory note. But hardly had he signed the note than a bold idea occurred to him: he meant to borrow a thousand francs from Lheureux. So, with an embarrassed air, he asked if he could get them, adding that it would be for a year, at any interest. Lheureux ran off to his shop, brought back the money, and dictated another note, by which Bovary undertook to pay to his order on the 1st of September next the sum of one thousand and seventy francs, which, with the hundred and eighty already agreed to, made just twelve hundred and fifty. He was thus lending at six per cent in addition to one-fourth for commission; and since the merchandise brought him a good third profit at least, he stood to make one hundred and thirty francs in twelve months. He hoped that the business would not stop there; that the notes would not be paid on time and would have to be renewed, and that his puny little investment, thriving in the doctor's care like a patient in a rest home, would return to him one day considerably plumper, fat enough to burst the bag.

All of Lheureux's enterprises were thriving. He got the franchise for supplying the Neufchâtel hospital with cider; Monsieur Guillaumin promised him some shares in the turf-bogs of Gaumesnil, and he dreamt of establishing a new coach service between Argueil and Rouen, which no doubt would not be long in putting the ramshackle van of the "Lion d'Or" out of business. Travelling faster, at a cheaper rate, and carrying more luggage, it would concentrate into his hands all of Yonville's business.

Charles often wondered how he would ever be able to pay back so much money next year. He tried to think of solutions, such as applying to his father or selling something. But his father would be deaf, and he—he had nothing to sell. He foresaw such difficulties that he quickly dismissed so disagreeable a subject of meditation from his mind. He reproached himself with forgetting Emma, as if, all his thoughts belonging to this woman, it was robbing her of something not to be constantly thinking of her.

It was a severe winter. Madame Bovary's convalescence was slow. On good days they wheeled her arm-chair to the window that overlooked the square, for she now disliked the garden, and the blinds on that side were always down. She wanted her horse to be sold; what she formerly liked now displeased her. The limit of her concerns seemed to be her own health. She stayed in bed taking light meals, rang for the maid to inquire about her tea or merely to chat. The snow on the market-roof threw a white, still light into the room; then the rain began to fall; and every day Emma would wait with a kind of anxiety for the inevitable return of some trifling event that was of little or no concern to her. The most important was the arrival of the "Hirondelle" in the evening. Then the innkeeper would shout and other voices answered, while Hippolyte's lantern, as he took down the luggage from the roof, was like a star in the darkness. At noontime, Charles came home; then he left again; next she took some broth, and towards five o'clock, as night fell, the children coming back from school, dragging their wooden shoes along the pavement, beat with their rulers against the clapper of the shutters.

Around this time of day, Monsieur Bournisien came to see her. He inquired after her health, gave her news, exhorted her to religion in a playful, gossipy tone that was not without charm. The mere sight of his cassock comforted her.

Once, at the height of her illness, she thought she was about to die and asked for communion; and while they were making the preparations in her room for the sacrament, while they were clearing the night table of its medicine bottles and turning it into an altar, and while Félicité was strewing dahlia flowers on the floor, Emma felt some power passing over her that freed her from her pains, from all perception, from all feeling. Her body, relieved, no longer thought; another life was beginning; it seemed to her that her being, mounting toward God, would be annihilated in that love like a burning incense that melts into vapour. The bed-clothes were sprinkled with holy water, the priest drew the white host from the holy pyx and she fainted with celestial joy as she advanced her lips to accept the body of the Saviour presented to her. The curtains of the alcove floated gently round her like clouds, and the rays of the two tapers burning on the night table seemed to shine like dazzling halos. Then she let her head fall back, fancying she heard in space the music of seraphic harps, and perceived in an azure sky, on a golden throne in the midst of saints holding green palms, God the Father, resplendent with majesty, who ordered to earth angels with wings of fire to carry her away in their arms.

This splendid vision dwelt in her memory as the most beautiful thing that it was possible to dream, so that now she strove to recall her sensation; it was still with her, albeit in a less overpowering manner, but with the same profound sweetness. Her soul, tortured by pride, at length found rest in Christian humility, and, tasting the joy of weakness, she saw within herself the destruction of her will opening wide the gates for heavenly grace to conquer her. She realised the existence of a bliss that could replace happiness, another love beyond all loves, without pause and without end, that would grow forever! Amid the illusions of her hope, she saw a state of purity floating above the earth, mingling with heaven. She wanted to become a saint. She bought rosaries and wore holy medals; she wished to have in her room, by the side of her bed, a reliquary set in emeralds that she might kiss it every evening.

The priest was delighted with her new state of mind, although he couldn't help worrying that Emma's excessive fervor might lead to heresy, to extravagance. But not being much versed in these matters once they went beyond a certain point he wrote to Monsieur Boulard, the bishop's bookseller, to send him "something first rate for a lady with a very distinguished mind." With as much concern as if he were shipping kitchen ware to savages, the bookseller made a random package of whatever happened to be current in the religious booktrade at the time. It contained little question and answer manuals, pamphlets written in the brusque tone of Joseph de Maistre,[45] pseudo-novels in rose-coloured bindings and a sugary style, manufactured by sentimental seminarists or penitent blue-stockings.

45. Joseph de Maistre (1753–1821) was the main theorist of Catholic conservatism. His books, *Du Pape* (1819) and *Soirées de Saint-Petersbourg* (1821), de- fended the power of the pope and the sovereign king and argued that the reign of evil on earth has to be curbed by authority.

There were titles such as "Consider carefully: the Man of the World at the Feet of the Virgin Mary, by Monsieur de * * * , decorated with many Orders"; "The Errors of Voltaire, for the Use of the Young," &c.

Madame Bovary's mind was not yet sufficiently clear to apply herself seriously to anything; moreover, she began this reading in too great a hurry. She grew provoked at the doctrines of religion; the arrogance of the polemic writings displeased her by their ferocious attacks on people she did not know; and the secular stories, sprinkled with religious seasoning, seemed to her written in such ignorance of the world, that they rather led her away from the truths she wanted to see confirmed. Nevertheless, she persevered; and when the volume slipped from her hands, she fancied herself seized with the finest Catholic melancholy ever conceived by an ethereal soul.

As for the memory of Rodolphe, she had locked it away in the deepest recesses of her heart, and it remained there solemn and motionless as a pharaoh's mummy in a catacomb. A fragance escaped from this embalmed love, that, penetrating through everything, perfumed with tenderness the immaculate atmosphere in which she longed to live. When she knelt on her Gothic prie-Dieu, she addressed to the Lord the same suave words that she had murmured formerly to her lover in the outpourings of adultery. She was searching for faith; but no delights descended from the heavens, and she arose with aching limbs and the vague feeling that she was being cheated.

Yet she thought this search all the more admirable, and in the pride of her devoutness Emma compared herself to those grand ladies of long ago whose glory she had dreamed of over a portrait of La Vallière, and who, trailing with so much majesty the lace-trimmed trains of their long gowns, retired into solitude to shed at the feet of Christ the tears of hearts that life had wounded.

Then she indulged in excessive charity. She sewed clothes for the poor, she sent wood to women in childbirth; and on coming home one day, Charles found three tramps eating soup in the kitchen. Her little girl, whom her husband had sent back to the nurse during her illness, returned home. She wanted to teach her to read; even Berthe's crying no longer irritated her. She was resigned, universally tolerant. Her speech was full of elevated expressions. She would say:

"Is your stomach-ache any better, my angel?"

The elder Madame Bovary couldn't find fault with anything except perhaps this mania of knitting jackets for orphans instead of mending her own dishtowels; but, harassed with domestic quarrels, the good woman took pleasure in this quiet house, and she even stayed there till after Easter, to escape the sarcasms of old Bovary, who never failed to order a big pork sausage on Good Friday.

Besides the companionship of her mother-in-law, who strengthened her resolutions somewhat by the rigor of her judgment and her stern appearance, Emma almost every day had other visitors: Madame Langlois, Madame Caron, Madame Dubreuil, Madame Tuvache, and regularly from two to five o'clock the sterling Madame Homais who, for her part, had never believed any of the gossip about her neighbor. The Homais children also came to see her, accompanied by Justin. He went up with them to her bedroom, and remained standing near the door without daring to move or to utter a word. Often enough Madame Bovary, taking no heed of him, would start dressing. She began by taking out her comb and tossing her head, in a brusk gesture, and when for the first time the poor boy saw this mass of hair fall in ringlets to her knees, it was as if he entered suddenly into a new and strange world, whose splendour terrified him.

Emma probably did not notice his silent attentions or his timidity. She had no inkling that love, which presumably had left her life forever, was pulsating right there, under that coarse shirt, in that adolescent heart open to the emanations of her beauty. Besides, she now wrapped all things in the same mood of indifference, she combined gentleness of speech with such haughty looks, affected such contradictory ways, that one could no longer distinguish selfishness from charity, or corruption from virtue. One evening, for example, she first got angry with the maid, who had asked to go out, and stammered as she tried to find some pretext; then suddenly:

"So you love him, don't you?" she said.

And without waiting for an answer from Félicité, who was blushing, she added sadly:

"All right! run along, and have a good time!"

In early spring she had the garden all changed around, over Bovary's objections; yet he was pleased to see her at last express some will of her own. She did so more and more as her strength returned. First, she found occasion to expel Mère Rollet, the nurse, who during her convalescence had taken to visiting the kitchen in the company of her two nurslings and her young boarder, whose appetite surpassed that of a cannibal. She cut down on the visits of the Homais family, gradually freed herself from the other visitors, and even went to church less assiduously, to the great approval of the pharmacist, who remarked to her:

"I suspect you were beginning to fall for the priest's sales talk!"

As before, Monsieur Bournisien would drop in every day after catechism class. He preferred to take the air in the "grove," as he called the arbour. This was the time when Charles came home. They were hot; some sweet cider was brought out, and they drank together to madame's complete recovery.

Binet was often there, that is to say, a little lower down against the terrace wall, fishing for crayfish. Bovary invited him to have a drink, and he proved to be a real expert on the uncorking of the stone bottles.

Looking around with utter self-satisfaction, first at his companions, then at the furthest confines of the landscape, he would say:

"You must first hold the bottle perpendicularly on the table, and after the strings are cut, press the cork upwards inch by inch, gently, very gently—the way they handle soda water in restaurants."

But during his demonstration the cider often spurted right into their faces, and the priest, laughing his thick laugh, would never fail to make his little joke:

"Its excellence certainly strikes the eye!"

He was undoubtedly a kindly fellow and one day he was not even scandalised at the pharmacist, who advised Charles to give madame some distraction by taking her to the theatre at Rouen to hear the illustrious tenor, Lagardy. Homais, surprised at this silence, wanted to know his opinion, and the priest declared that he considered music less dangerous for morals than literature.

But the pharmacist took up the defence of letters. The theatre, he contended, served to decry prejudices and, while pretending to amuse, it taught virtue.

"*Castigat ridendo mores*,[46] Monsieur Bournisien! Look at most of Voltaire's tragedies: they contain a wealth of philosophical considerations that make them into a real school of morals and diplomacy for the people."

"I," said Binet, "once saw a play called the 'Gamin de Paris,'[47] in which there is a really fine part of an old general. He settles the account of a rich young fellow who has seduced a working girl, and at the end . . ."

"Of course," pursued Homais, "there is bad literature as there is bad pharmacy, but to condemn in a lump the most important of the fine arts seems to me a stupidity, a Gothic aberration worthy of the abominable times that imprisoned Galileo."[48]

"I know very well," objected the curé, "that there are good works, good authors. Still, the very fact of crowding people of different sexes into the same room, made to look enticing by displays of worldly pomp, these pagan disguises, the makeup, the lights, the effeminate voices, all this must, in the long-run, engender

46. *Castigat ridendo mores:* "It [comedy] reproves the manners, through laughter"—a slogan for comedy invented by the poet Jean de Santeuil (1630–1697), and given to the harlequin Dominique to put it on the curtain of his theater.

47. *Gamin de Paris* is a comedy by Bayard and Vanderbusch performed in 1836 in Paris.

48. Galileo Galilei (1564–1642), the astronomer, was confined to his house in Arcetri (near Florence) after his book propounding the view that the earth circled around the sun was condemned by the Inquisition (in 1633).

a certain mental libertinage, give rise to immodest thoughts and impure temptations. Such, at any rate, is the opinion of all the church fathers. Moreover," he added, suddenly assuming a mystic tone of voice while he rolled a pinch of snuff between his fingers, "if the Church has condemned the theatre, she must be right; we must bow to her decrees."

"Why," asked the druggist, "should she excommunicate actors when formerly they used to take part openly in religious ceremonies? They would play right in the middle of the choir and perform a kind of farce called "mystery plays" that frequently offended against the laws of decency."

The curé merely groaned and the pharmacist persisted:

"It's like in the Bible; you know . . . there are things in it . . . certain details . . . I'd call them downright daring . . . bordering on obscenity!"

And as Monsieur Bournisien signaled his annoyance:

"Ah! you'll admit that it is not a book to place in the hands of a young girl, and I wouldn't at all like it if Athalie . . . ."

"But it is the Protestants, and not we," protested the other impatiently, "who recommend the Bible."

"All the same," said Homais. "I am surprised that in our days, in this century of enlightenment, any one should still persist in proscribing an intellectual relaxation that is inoffensive, morally uplifting, and sometimes even good for the health—isn't that right, doctor?"

"Quite," the doctor replied in a non-committal tone, either because, sharing the same ideas, he wished to offend no one, or else because he simply had no ideas on the subject.

The conversation seemed at an end when the pharmacist thought fit to try a parting shot.

"I've known priests who put on civilian clothes to go watch burlesque shows."

"Come, come!" said the curé.

"Ah yes, I've known some!"

And, separating the words, he repeated:

"I—have—known—some!"

"Well, they did wrong," said Bournisien, prepared to listen to anything with resignation.

"And they didn't stop at that, either!" persisted the pharmacist.

"That's enough! . . . " exclaimed the priest, looking so fierce that the other thought safe to retreat.

"I only mean to say," he replied in a much less aggressive tone, "that tolerance is the surest way to draw people to religion."

"That is true! that is true!" conceded the priest, sitting down again.

But he stayed only a few minutes. Hardly had he left that Monsieur Homais said to the doctor:

"That's what I call a good fight! See how I found his weak spot? I didn't give him much of a chance . . . Now take my advice. Take madame to the theatre, if only to get for once the better of one of these rooks! If someone could keep the store in my absence, I'd go with you. But hurry! Lagardy is only going to give one performance; he's going to play in England for a tremendous fee. From what I hear, he's quite a character. He's simply loaded with money! He travels with three mistresses and a cook. All these great artists burn the candle at both ends; they need to lead a dissolute life to stir the imagination of the public. But they die at the poorhouse, because they don't have the sense to save their money when it comes in. Well, enjoy your dinner! See you to-morrow."

This theatre idea quickly grew in Bovary's mind; he at once communicated it to his wife, who at first refused, alleging the fatigue, the worry, the expense; but, for once, Charles did not give in, so sure was he that this occasion would do her good. He saw nothing to prevent it: his mother had sent three hundred francs he no longer counted on, the current bills were far from staggering and Lheureux's notes were not due for such a long time that he could dismiss them from his mind. Besides, imagining that she was refusing out of consideration for him, he insisted all the more, until she finally consented. The next day at eight o'clock they set out in the "Hirondelle."

The pharmacist, who had nothing whatever to keep him at Yonville but fancied himself to be indispensable, sighed with envy as he saw them go.

"Well, a pleasant journey!" he said to them; "happy mortals that you are!"

Then addressing himself to Emma, who was wearing a blue silk gown with four flounces:

"You are prettier than ever. You'll make quite an impression in Rouen."

The diligence stopped at the "Croix-Rouge" on the Place Beauvoisine. It was a typical provincial inn, with large stables and small bedrooms and chickens in the courtyard, picking at the oats under the muddy gigs of travelling salesmen;—a fine old place, with worm-eaten balconies that creak in the wind on winter nights, always crowded, noisy and full of food, its black tables stained with coffee and brandy, the thick windows yellowed by flies, the napkins spotted with cheap red wine. Like farmboys dressed in Sunday-clothes, the place still reeks of the country; it has a café on the street and a vegetable-garden on the back. Charles at once set out on his errands. He confused stage-boxes and gallery, orchestra seats and regular boxes, asked for explanations which he did not understand, was sent from the box-office to the manager, came back to the inn, returned to the theatre and ended up by crossing the full length of the town, from theatre to outer boulevard, several times.

Madame bought herself a hat, gloves, and a bouquet. Monsieur worried greatly about missing the beginning, and, without having had time to swallow a plate of soup, they arrived at the gates of the theatre well before opening time.

XV

The crowd was lined up against the wall, evenly distributed on both sides of the entrance rails. At the corner of the neighbouring streets huge bills, printed in Gothic letters, announced "Lucie de Lammermoor-Lagardy-Opera &c."[49] The weather was fine, the people hot; sweat trickled among fancy coiffures and pocket handkerchiefs were mopping red foreheads; now and then a warm wind that blew from the river gently stirred the edges of the canvass awnings hanging from the doors of the cafés. A little lower down, however, one was refreshed by a current of icy air that smelt of tallow, leather, and oil, breathed forth from the Rue des Charrettes with its huge, dark warehouses resounding with the noise of rolling barrels.

For fear of seeming ridiculous, Emma first wanted to take a little stroll in the harbor, and Bovary carefully kept clutching the tickets in his trouser pockets, pressed against his stomach.

Her heart began to beat as soon as she reached the entrance hall. She involuntarily smiled with vanity on seeing the crowd rushing to the right by the other corridor while she went up the staircase to the reserved seats. She was as pleased as a child to push the large tapestried door open with her finger; she breathed deeply the dusty smell of the lobbies, and when she was seated in her box she drew herself up with the self-assurance of a duchess.

The theatre was beginning to fill; opera-glasses were taken from their cases, and the subscribers greeted and bowed as they spotted each other at a distance. They sought relief from the pressures of commerce in the arts, but, unable to take their minds off business matters, they still talked about cotton, spirits of wine, or indigo. The placid and meek heads of the old men, with their pale whitish hair and complexion, resembled silver medals tarnished by lead fumes. The young beaux were strutting about in the orchestra, exhibiting their pink or apple-green cravats under their gaping waistcoats; sitting above them, Madame Bovary admired how they leant the tight-drawn palm of their yellow gloves on the golden knobs of their canes.

---

49. *Lucia di Lammermoor* is an opera by Gaetano Donizetti (1797–1848) first performed in Naples in 1835 (in Paris in 1837). It is based on Walter Scott's novel, *The Bride of Lammermoor* (1819). See Introduction, pp. 462–63.

Now the lights of the orchestra were lit; the chandelier, let down from the ceiling, threw the sudden gaiety of its sparkling crystals over the theatre; then the musicians began to file in; and first there was the protracted hubbub of roaring cellos, squeaking violins, blaring trumpets and piping flutes. But three knocks were heard on the stage, a rolling of drums began, the brass instruments played some chords, and the curtain rose, discovering a country-scene.

It was the cross-roads of a wood, with a fountain on the left, shaded by an oak tree. Peasants and lords with tartans over their shoulders were singing a hunting-song in chorus; a captain suddenly appeared, who evoked the spirit of evil by lifting both his arms to heaven. Another followed; they departed, and the hunters started afresh.

She felt herself carried back to the reading of her youth, into the midst of Walter Scott. She seemed to hear through the mist the sound of the Scotch bagpipes re-echoing over the moors. Her remembrance of the novel helping her to understand the libretto, she followed the story phrase by phrase, while the burst of music dispersed the fleeting thoughts that came back to her. She gave herself up to the flow of the melodies, and felt all her being vibrate as if the violin bows were being drawn over her nerves. Her eyes could hardly take in all the costumes, the scenery, the actors, the painted trees that shook whenever someone walked, and the velvet caps, cloaks, swords—all those imaginary things that vibrated in the music as in the atmosphere of another world. But a young woman stepped forward, throwing a purse to a squire in green. She was left alone on the stage, and the flute was heard like the murmur of a fountain or the warbling of birds. Lucie bravely attacked her cavatina in G major. She begged for love, longed for wings. Emma, too, would have liked to flee away from life, locked in a passionate embrace. Suddenly Edgar Lagardy appeared.

He had that splendid pallor that gives something of the majesty of marble to the ardent races of the South. His vigourous form was tightly clad in a brown-coloured doublet; a small chiselled dagger swung against his left thigh, and he rolled languid eyes while flashing his white teeth. They said that a Polish princess having heard him sing one night on the beach at Biarritz, where he used to be a boatsman, had fallen in love with him. She had lost her entire fortune for his sake. He had deserted her for other women, and this sentimental fame did not fail to enhance his artistic reputation. A skilled ham actor, he never forgot to have a phrase on his seductiveness and his sensitive soul inserted in the accounts about him. He had a fine voice, colossal aplomb, more temperament than intelligence, more pathos than lyric feeling; all this made for an admirable charlatan type, in which there was something of the hairdresser as well as of the bullfighter.

From the first scene he brought down the house. He pressed

Lucie in his arms, he left her, he came back, he seemed desperate; he had outbursts of rage, then elegiac gurglings of infinite sweetness, and tones like sobs and kisses escaped from his bare throat. Emma bent forward to see him, scratching the velvet of the box with her nails. Her heart filled with these melodious lamentations that were accompanied by the lugubrious moanings of the double-basses, like the cries of the drowning in the tumult of a tempest. She recognised all the intoxication and the anguish that had brought her close to death. The voice of the prima donna seemed to echo her own conscience, and the whole fictional story seemed to capture something of her own life. But no one on earth had loved her with such love. He had not wept like Edgar that last moonlit night when they had said "Till tomorrow! Till tomorrow! . . ." The theatre rang with cheers; they repeated the entire stretto; the lovers spoke of the flowers on their tomb, of vows, exile, fate, hopes; and when they uttered the final farewell, Emma gave a sharp cry that mingled with the vibrations of the last chords.

"But why," asked Bovary, "is that lord torturing her like that?"

"No, no!" she answered; "he is her lover!"

"Yet he vows vengeance on her family, while the other one who came on before said, 'I love Lucie and she loves me!' Besides, he went off with her father arm in arm. For he certainly is her father, isn't he—the ugly little man with a cock's feather in his hat?"

Despite Emma's explanations, as soon as the recitative duet began in which Gilbert lays bare his abominable machinations to his master Ashton, Charles, seeing the false engagement ring that is to deceive Lucie, thought it was a love-gift sent by Edgar. He confessed, moreover, that he did not understand the story because of the music, which interfered very much with the words.

"What does it matter?" said Emma. "Do be quiet!"

"Yes, but you know," he went on, leaning against her shoulder, "I like to understand things."

"Be quiet! be quiet!" she cried impatiently.

Lucie came on, half supported by her women, a wreath of orange blossoms in her hair, and paler than the white satin of her gown. Emma dreamed of her marriage day; she saw herself at home again among the fields in the little path as they walked to the church. Why didn't she, like this woman, resist and implore? Instead, she had walked joyously and unwittingly towards the abyss . . . Ah! if in the freshness of her beauty, before the degradation of marriage and the disillusions of adultery, she could have anchored her life upon some great, strong heart! Virtue, affection, sensuous pleasure and duty would have combined to give her eternal bliss. But such happiness, she realized, was a lie, a mockery to taunt desire. She knew now how small the passions were that art magnified. So, striving for detachment, Emma resolved to see in this reproduction of her sorrows a mere formal fiction for the entertainment of the eye, and she smiled inwardly in scornful pity when from behind the velvet curtains at the back of the stage a man appeared in a black cloak.

His large Spanish hat fell at a gesture he made, and immediately the instruments and the singers began the sextet. Edgar, flashing with fury, dominated all the others with his clearer voice; Ashton hurled homicidal provocations at him in deep notes; Lucie uttered her shrill lament; Arthur sang modulated asides in a middle register and the deep basso of the minister pealed forth like an organ, while the female voices re-echoed his words in a delightful chorus. They were lined up in one single gesticulating row, breathing forth anger, vengeance, jealousy, terror, mercy and surprise all at once from their open mouths. The outraged lover brandished his naked sword; his lace ruff rose and fell jerkily with the movements of his chest, and he walked from right to left with long strides, clanking against the boards the silver-gilt spurs of his soft, flaring boots. She thought that he must have inexhaustible supplies of love in him to lavish it upon the crowd with such effusion. All her attempts at critical detachment were swept away by the poetic power of the acting, and, drawn to the man by the illusion of the part, she tried to imagine his life—extraordinary, magnificent, notorious, the life that could have been hers if fate had willed it. If only they had met! He would have loved her, they would have travelled together through all the kingdoms of Europe from capital to capital, sharing in his success and in his hardships, picking up the flowers thrown to him, mending his clothes. Every night, hidden behind the golden lattice of her box, she would have drunk in eagerly the expansions of this soul that would have sung for her alone; from the stage, even as he acted, he would have looked at her. A mad idea took possession of her: he was looking at her right now! She longed to run to his arms, to take refuge in his strength, as in the incarnation of love itself, and to say to him, to cry out, "Take me away! carry me with you! let us leave! All my passion and all my dreams are yours!"

The curtain fell.

The smell of gas mingled with the people's breath and the waving fans made the air even more suffocating. Emma wanted to go out; the crowd filled the corridors, and she fell back in her armchair with palpitations that choked her. Charles, fearing that she would faint, ran to the refreshment-room to get a glass of orgeat.

He had great difficulty in getting back to his seat, for as he was holding the glass in his hands, his elbows bumped into someone at every step; he even spilt three-fourths on the shoulders of a Rouen lady in short sleeves, who feeling the cold liquid running down her

back, started to scream like a peacock, as if she were being murdered. Her mill-owner husband lashed out at his clumsiness, and
while she used her handkerchief to wipe off the stains from her
handsome cherry-coloured taffeta gown, he angrily muttered about
indemnity, costs, reimbursement. Charles was quite out of breath
when he finally reached his wife:

"I thought I'd never make it. What a crowd! . . . What a
crowd!"

And he added:

"Just guess whom I met up there! Monsieur Léon!"

"Léon?"

"Himself! He's coming along to pay his respects."

And as he finished these words the ex-clerk of Yonville entered
the box.

He held out his hand with the casual ease of a gentleman; and
Madame Bovary extended hers, yielding no doubt to the pressure of
a stronger will. She had not felt it since that spring evening when
the rain fell upon the green leaves, and they had said good-bye
while standing near the window. But soon recalling herself to the
necessities of the situation, she managed to shake off the torpor of
her memories, and began stammering a few hurried words.

"Ah! good evening . . . What, you here?"

"Silence!" cried a voice from the orchestra, for the third act was
beginning.

"So you are at Rouen?"

"Yes."

"And since when?"

"Be quiet! Throw them out!"

People were looking at them; they fell silent.

But from that moment she listened no more; and the chorus of
the guests, the scene between Ashton and his servant, the grand
duet in D major, all became more distant, as if the instruments had
grown less sonorous and the characters more remote. She remembered the card games at the pharmacist, the walk to the nurse, the
poetry readings in the arbour, the tête-à-têtes by the fireside—all
the sadness of their love, so calm and so protracted, so discreet, so
tender, and that she had nevertheless forgotten. And why had he
come back? What combination of circumstances had brought him
back into her life? He was standing behind her, leaning with his
shoulder against the wall of the box; now and again she felt herself
shudder as she felt the warmth of his breath on her hair.

"Do you find this amusing?" he said, bending over her so closely
that the end of his moustache brushed her cheek.

She replied flippantly:

"Heavens, no! not particularly."

Then he suggested that they leave the theatre and have an ice
somewhere.

"Oh, not yet; let us stay," said Bovary. "Her hair's undone; this is going to be tragic."

But the madness scene did not interest Emma, and she thought the singer was overacting.

"She screams too loud," she said, turning to Charles who was listening.

"Yes . . . perhaps . . . a little," he replied, torn between his genuine enjoyment and his respect for his wife's opinion.

Then Léon sighed:

"Don't you find it hot . . ."

"Unbearably so! Yes!"

"Don't you feel well?" Bovary inquired.

"Yes, I am stifling; let's go."

Monsieur Léon draped her long lace shawl carefully about her shoulders, and the three of them left and sat down near the harbor, on the terrace of a café. First they spoke of her illness, although Emma interrupted Charles from time to time, for fear, she said, of boring Monsieur Léon; and the latter told them that he had come to spend two years in a big Rouen law firm, in order to gain some experience of how business is conducted in Normandy—so different from Paris. Then he inquired after Berthe, the Homais, Mère Lefrançois, and as they had, in the husband's presence, nothing more to say to one another, the conversation soon came to an end.

People coming out of the theatre walked along the pavement, humming or shouting at the top of their voices, "*O bel ange, ma Lucie!*" Then Léon, playing the dilettante, began to talk music. He had seen Tamburini, Rubini, Persiani, Grisi,[50] and, compared with them, Lagardy, despite his grand outbursts, was nowhere.

"Yet," interrupted Charles, who was slowly sipping his rum-sherbet, "they say that he is quite admirable in the last act. I regret leaving before the end, just when I was beginning to enjoy myself."

"Why," said the clerk, "he will soon give another performance."

But Charles replied that they had to leave the next day. "Unless," he added, turning to his wife, "you'd like to stay by yourself, my darling?"

And changing his tactics at the unexpected opportunity that presented itself to his hopes, the young man sang the praises of Lagardy in the last aria. It was really superb, sublime. Then Charles insisted:

"You'll come back on Sunday. Come, make up your mind. If you feel that this is doing you the least bit of good, you shouldn't

50. Antonio Tamburini (1800–1876), Gian-Battista Rubini (1795–1854), Fanny Facchinardi Persiani (who was the first Lucia), and Ciulia Grisi (1811–1869) were all famous Bel-Canto singers who appeared in Paris in the operas of Rossini and Donizetti.

hesitate to stay."

The adjoining tables, however, were emptying; a waiter came and stood discreetly near them. Charles, who understood, took out his purse; the clerk held back his arm, and made a point of leaving two extra pieces of silver that he made chink on the marble.

"I am really sorry," said Bovary," for all the money you are . . ."

The other silenced him with a gesture of affable disdain and, taking his hat, said:

"So, we are agreed, to-morrow at six o'clock?"

Charles explained once more that he could not absent himself longer, but that nothing prevented Emma . . .

"But," she stammered, with a strange smile, "I don't know if I ought . . ."

"Well, you must think it over. Sleep over it and we'll see in the morning."

Then, to Léon, who was walking along with them:

"Now that you are in our part of the world, I hope you'll come and have dinner with us from time to time."

The clerk declared he would not fail to do so, being obliged, moreover, to go to Yonville on some business for his office. And they parted before the passage Saint-Herbland just as the cathedral struck half-past eleven.

Part Three

I

Monsieur Léon, while studying law, had been a fairly assiduous customer at the Chaumière, a dance-hall where he was particularly successful with the grisettes who thought him distinguished looking. He was the best-mannered of the students; he wore his hair neither too long nor too short, didn't spend all his quarter's money on the first day of the month, and kept on good terms with his professors. As for excesses, he had always abstained from them, as much from cowardice as from refinement.

Often when he stayed in his room to read, or else when sitting in the evening under the linden-trees of the Luxembourg,[51] he let his law-code fall to the ground, and the memory of Emma came back to him. But gradually this feeling grew weaker, and other desires took the upperhand, although the original passion still acted through them. For Léon did not lose all hope; there was for him, as it were, a vague promise floating in the future, like a golden fruit suspended from some fantastic tree.

51. Luxembourg refers to the gardens of the Palace of Luxembourg (built between 1615 and 1620 for Marie de Medici). The gardens are open to the public and much frequented by students, as they are near the Sorbonne.

Then, seeing her again after three years of absence, his passion reawakened. He must, he thought, finally make up his mind to possess her. Moreover, his timidity had worn off in the gay company of his student days, and he returned to the provinces in utter contempt of whoever had not set foot on the asphalt of the boulevards. In the presence of a genuine Parisienne, in the house of some famous physician surrounded by honors and luxury, the poor clerk would no doubt have trembled like a child; but here, on the quais of Rouen, with the wife of a small country-doctor, he felt at his ease, sure to shine. Self-confidence depends on environment: one does not speak in the same tone in the drawing room than in the kitchen; and the wealthy woman seems to have about her, to guard her virtue, all her bank-notes, like an armour, in the lining of her corset.

On leaving the Bovarys the night before, Léon had followed them through the streets at a distance; when he saw them enter the Croix-Rouge, he returned home and spent the night planning his strategy.

So the next afternoon about five o'clock he walked into the kitchen of the inn, pale and apprehensive, driven by a coward's resolution that stops at nothing.

"Monsieur isn't in," a servant told him.

This seemed to him a good omen. He went upstairs.

She didn't seem surprised at his arrival; on the contrary, she apologized for having failed to tell him where they were staying.

"Oh, I guessed it!" said Léon.

He pretended he had found her by chance, guided by instinct. When he saw her smile, he tried to repair his blunder by telling her he had spent the morning looking for her in all the hotels in the town.

"So you have made up your mind to stay?" he added.

"Yes," she said, "and I shouldn't have. One should avoid getting used to inaccessible pleasures when one is burdened by so many responsibilities . . ."

"Oh, I can imagine . . ."

"No, you can't, you are not a woman."

But men too had their trials, and the conversation started off by some philosphical considerations. Emma expatiated on the frailty of earthly affections, and the eternal isolation that stifles the human heart.

To show off, or in a naive imitation of this melancholy which stirred his own, the young man declared that he had been dreadfully despondent. He was bored by the law, attracted by other vocations and his mother had never ceased to harrass him in all her letters. As they talked, they stated the reasons for their respective unhappiness with more precision and they felt a shared exaltation in this growing confidence. But they sometimes stopped short of revealing their thought in full, and then sought to invent a phrase that might nevertheless express it. She did not confess her passion for another; he did not say that he had forgotten her.

Perhaps he no longer remembered the suppers with girls after masked balls; and no doubt she did not recollect the rendezvous of old when she ran across the fields in the morning to her lover's house. The noises of the town hardly reached them, and the room seemed small, as if to bring them even closer together in their solitude. Emma, in a dimity dressing gown, leant her chignon against the back of the old arm-chair; the yellow wall-paper formed, as it were, a golden background behind her, and her bare head was reflected in the mirror with the white parting in the middle, the tip of her ears peeping out from the folds of her hair.

"How bad of me!" she said, "you must forgive me for boring you with my eternal complaints."

"No, never, never!"

"If only you knew," she went on, raising to the ceiling her beautiful eyes, in which a tear was trembling, "if only you knew all I dreamed!"

"So did I! Oh, I too have suffered! Often I went out; I went away. I left, dragging myself along the quays, seeking distraction amid the din of the crowd without being able to banish the heaviness that weighed upon me. In an engraver's shop on the boulevard I found an Italian print of one of the Muses. She is draped in a tunic, and she is looking at the moon, with forget-me-nots in her flowing hair. Something continually drove me there, I would stay for hour after hour."

Then, in a trembling voice:

"She looked a little like you."

Madame Bovary turned away her head that he might not see the irrepressible smile she felt rising to her lips.

"Often," he went on, "I wrote you letters that I tore up."

She did not answer. He continued:

"I sometimes fancied that some chance would bring you. I thought I recognised you at street-corners, and I ran after carriages when I saw a shawl or a veil like yours flutter in the window . . ."

She seemed resolved to let him speak without interruption. With arms crossed and her head lowered, she stared at the rosettes on her slippers, and from time to time moved her toes under the satin.

At last she sighed.

"But what I find worst of all is to drag out, as I do, a useless existence. If our pains could be of use to some one, we should find consolation in the thought of the sacrifice."

He started off in praise of virtue, duty, and silent immolation, having himself an incredible longing for self-sacrifice that he could not satisfy.

"What I would like," she said "is to work in a hospital as a nursing Sister."

"Unfortunately," he replied, "no such holy vocations are open to men, and I can think of no profession . . . except perhaps a doctor's . . ."

With a slight shrug of the shoulders, Emma interrupted him to speak of her illness, which had almost killed her. How she regretted her cure! if she had died, she would not now be suffering. Léon was quick to express his own longing for "the quiet of the tomb"; one night, he had even made his will, asking to be buried in that beautiful coverlet with velvet stripes he had received from her. For this was how they would have wished to be, each setting up an ideal to which they were now trying to adapt their past life. Besides, speech is like a rolling machine that always stretches the sentiment it expresses.

But this made-up story of the coverlet made her ask:

"Why?"

"Why?" He hesitated.

"Because I loved you so!"

And congratulating himself at having surmounted the obstacle, Léon watched her face out of the corner of his eye.

It was like the sky when a gust of wind sweeps the clouds away. The mass of darkening sad thoughts lifted from her blue eyes; her whole face shone.

He waited. At last she replied:

"I always suspected it."

Then they went over all the trifling events of that far-off existence, of which the joys and sorrows had just been conjured up by that one word. He remembered the clematis arbour, the dresses she had worn, the furniture of her room, the entire house.

"And our poor cactuses, where are they?"

"The cold killed them this winter."

"How often did I think of them! I see them again as they looked when on summer mornings the sun shone on your blinds, and I saw your two bare arms among the flowers.

"Poor friend!" she said, holding out her hand.

Léon swiftly pressed his lips to it. Then, when he had taken a deep breath:

"In those days, you were like an incomprehensible power to me which held me captive. Once, for instance, I came to see you, but you probably don't remember."

"I do," she said; "go on."

"You were downstairs in the hall, ready to go out, standing on the last stair; you were wearing a hat with small blue flowers; and without being invited, in spite of myself, I went with you. But I grew more and more conscious of my folly every moment, and I kept walking by your side, not daring to follow you completely but unable to leave. When you went into a shop, I waited in the street, and I watched you through the window taking off your gloves and counting the change on the counter. Then you rang at Madame Tuvache's; you were let in, and I stood like an idiot in front of the great heavy door that had closed after you."

Madame Bovary, as she listened to him, wondered that she was so old. All these things reappearing before her seemed to expand her existence; it was like some sentimental immensity to which she returned; and from time to time she said in a low voice, her eyes half closed:

"Yes, it is true . . . it is true . . ."

They heard eight o'clock strike on the different towers that surround the Place Beauvoisine, a neighborhood of schools, churches, and large empty private dwellings. They no longer spoke, but as they looked upon each other, they felt their heads whirl, as if waves of sound had escaped from their fixed glances. They were hand in hand now, and the past, the future, reminiscences and dreams, all were confounded in the sweetness of this ecstasy. Night was darkening over the walls, leaving visible only, half hidden in the shade, the coarse colours of four bills representing scenes from *La Tour de Nesle*,[52] with Spanish and French captions underneath. Through the sash-window they could see a patch of sky between the pointed roofs.

She rose to light two wax-candles on the chest of drawers, then she sat down again.

"Well . . . ?" said Léon.

"Well . . . ?" she replied.

He was wondering how to resume the interrupted conversation, when she said to him:

"How is it that no one until now has ever expressed such sentiments to me?"

The clerk retorted that idealistic natures rarely found understanding. But he had loved her from the very first moment; the thought of their possible happiness filled him with despair. If only they had met earlier, by some stroke of chance, they would have been forever bound together.

"I have sometimes thought of it," she went on.

"What a dream!" murmured Léon.

And fingering gently the blue border of her long white belt, he

52. A melodrama by Alexandre Dumas the elder (1803–1870) and Gaillardet (1832) in which Marie de Bourgogne, famous for her crimes, is the main heroine.

added,

"Who prevents us from starting all over again?"

"No, my friend," she replied; "I am too old . . . You are too young . . . forget me! Others will love you . . . you will love them."

"Not as I love you!"

"What a child you are! Come, let us be sensible, I want it."

She told him again that their love was impossible, that they must remain, as before, like brother and sister to each other.

Was she speaking seriously? No doubt Emma did not herself know, absorbed as she was by the charm of the seduction and the necessity of defending herself; looking tenderly at the young man, she gently repulsed the timid caresses that his trembling hands attempted.

"Ah! forgive me!" he cried, drawing back.

Emma was seized with a vague fear at this shyness, more dangerous to her than the boldness of Rodolphe when he advanced to her open-armed. No man had ever seemed to her so beautiful. His demeanor suggested an exquisite candor. He lowered his long curling eyelashes. The soft skin of his cheek was flushed, she thought, with desire for her, and Emma felt an invincible longing to press her lips to it. Then, leaning towards the clock as if to see the time:

"How late it is!" she exclaimed. "How we have been chattering!"

He understood the hint and took up his hat.

"You made me forget about the opera! And poor Bovary who left me here especially for that! Monsieur Lormeaux, of the Rue Grand-Pont, was to take me and his wife."

And there would be no other opportunity, as she was to leave the next day.

"Really?" said Léon.

"Yes."

"But I must see you again," he went on. "I had something to tell you . . ."

"What?"

"Something . . . important, serious. I cannot possibly let you go like this. If only you knew . . . Listen to me . . . Haven't you understood? Can't you guess?"

"You made yourself very clear" said Emma.

"Ah! you can jest! But you shouldn't. Have mercy, and allow me to see you again . . . only once . . . one single time."

"Well . . ."

She stopped; then, as if changing her mind:

"But not here!"

"Wherever you say."

"Will you . . ."

She seemed to think; then suddenly:

"To-morrow at eleven o'clock in the cathedral."

"I shall be there," he cried, seizing her hands, which she withdrew.

And as they were both standing up, he behind and Emma with lowered head, he stooped over her and pressed long kisses on her neck.

"You are crazy, you are crazy!" she cried between bursts of laughter, as the kisses multiplied.

Then bending his head over her shoulder, he seemed to beg the consent of her eyes, but when they met his, they seemed icy and distant.

Léon took three paces backwards. He stopped on the threshold; then he whispered in a trembling voice:

"Till to-morrow."

She answered with a nod, and vanished like a bird into the next room.

In the evening Emma wrote the clerk an interminable letter, in which she cancelled the rendezvous; all was over between them; they must not, for the sake of their happiness, meet again. But when the letter was finished, as she did not know Léon's address, she was puzzled.

"I'll give it to him myself," she said; "he'll come."

The next morning, humming a tune while he stood on his balcony by the open window, Léon polished his shoes with special care. He put on white trousers, silken socks, a green coat, emptied all the scent he had into his handkerchief, then having had his hair curled, he uncurled it again, in order to give it a more natural elegance.

"It is still too early," he thought, looking at the barber's cuckoo-clock, that pointed to the hour of nine.

He read an old fashion journal, went out, smoked a cigar, walked up three streets, thought the time had come and walked slowly towards the porch of Notre Dame.

It was a beautiful summer morning. Silver sparkled in the window of the jeweler's store and the light, falling obliquely on the cathedral, threw shimmering reflections on the edges of the grey stones; a flock of birds fluttered in the grey sky round the trefoiled turrets; the square, resounding with cries, was fragrant with the flowers that bordered the pavement, roses, jasmines, carnations, narcissus, and tuberoses, unevenly spaced out between moist grasses, catnip, and chickweed for the birds; the fountains gurgled in the center, and under large umbrellas, amidst heaps of piled up mellons, bare-headed flower vendors wrapped bunches of violets in pieces of paper.

The young man took one. It was the first time that he had

bought flowers for a woman, and his breast, as he smelt them, swelled with pride, as if this homage that he meant for another had been reflected upon himself.

But he was afraid of being seen and resolutely entered the church.

The verger was just then standing on the threshold in the middle of the left doorway, under the figure of Salomé dancing, known in Rouen as the "dancing Marianne". He wore a feather cap, a rapier dangled against his leg and he looked more majestic than a cardinal, as shining as a pyx.

He came towards Léon, and, with the bland benign smile of a priest when questioning a child, asked:

"I gather that Monsieur is a visitor in this town? Would Monsieur care to be shown the church?"

"No!" said Léon.

And he first went round the lower aisles. Then he went out to look at the Place. Emma was not coming yet, so he returned as far as the choir.

The nave was reflected in the full fonts together with the base of the arches and some fragments of the stained glass windows. But the reflections of the painted glass, broken by the marble rim, were continued farther on upon the pavement, like a many-coloured carpet. The broad daylight from outside entered the church in three enormous rays through the three opened portals. From time to time a sacristan crossed the far end of the church, making the sidewise genuflection of a hurried worshipper in the direction of the altar. The crystal lustres hung motionless. In the choir a silver lamp was burning, and from the side chapels and dark places of the church sounds like sighs arose, together with the clang of a closing grating that echoed under the lofty vaults.

Léon walked solemnly alongside the walls. Life had never seemed so good to him. She would soon appear, charming and agitated, looking back to see if anyone was watching her—with her flounced dress, her gold eyeglass, her delicate shoes, with all sorts of elegant trifles that he had never been allowed to taste, and with the ineffable seduction of yielding virtue. The church was set around her like a huge boudoir; the arches bent down to shelter in their darkness the avowal of her love; the windows shone resplendent to light up her face, and the censers would burn that she might appear like an angel amid sweet-smelling clouds.

Meanwhile, she did not come. He sat down on a chair, and his eyes fell upon a blue stained window representing boatmen carrying baskets. He looked at it long, attentively, and he counted the scales of the fishes and the button-holes of the doublets, while his thoughts wandered off in search of Emma.

The verger, left to himself, resented the presence of someone who

dared to admire the cathedral without his assistance. He considered
this a shocking way to behave, robbing him of his due, close to
committing sacrilege.

There was a rustle of silk on the pavement, the edge of a hat, a
hooded cape—it was she! Léon rose and ran to meet her.

Emma was pale. She walked hurriedly.

"Read this!" she said, holding out a piece of paper to him. "Oh,
no!"

And she abruptly withdrew her hand to enter the chapel of the
Virgin, where, kneeling on a chair, she began to pray.

The young man was irritated by this display of piety; then he
nevertheless felt a certain charm in seeing her thus lost in devotions
in the middle of a rendezvous, like an Andalusian marquise; then he
grew bored, for she seemed to go on for ever.

Emma prayed, or rather tried to pray, hoping that some sudden
resolution might descend to her from heaven; and to draw down
divine aid she filled her eyes with the splendors of the tabernacle.
She breathed in the perfumes of the full-blown flowers in the large
vases, and listened to the stillness of the church—a stillness that
only heightened the tumult in her own heart.

She rose, and they were about to leave, when the verger quickly
approached:

"Madame is perhaps a stranger here? Madame would like to visit
the church?"

"Oh, no!" the clerk cried.

"Why not?" she said.

For, with her expiring virtue, she clung to the Virgin, the sculp-
tures, the tombs—to anything.

Then, in order to do things right, the verger took them to the
entrance near the square, where, pointing out with his cane a large
circle of black stones, without inscription or carving:

"This," he said majestically, "is the circumference of the beautiful bell of Ambroise. It weighed forty thousand pounds. There was
not its equal in all Europe. The workman who cast it died of
joy . . ."

"Let's go," said Léon.

The old man started off again; then, having got back to the
chapel of the Virgin, he waved his arm in a theatrical gesture of
demonstration, and, prouder than a country squire showing his
orchard, he announced:

"This simple stone covers Pierre de Brézé, lord of Varenne and
of Brissac, grand marshal of Poitou, and governor of Normandy,
who died at the battle of Montlhéry on the 16th of July, 1465."

Léon was furiously biting his lips of impatience.

"And on the right, this gentleman in full armour, on the prancing horse, is his grandson, Louis de Brézé, lord of Breval and of
Montchauvet, Count de Maulevrier, Baron de Mauny, chamberlain

to the king, Knight of the Order, and also governor of Normandy; he died on the 23rd of July, 1531—a Sunday, as the inscription specifies; and below, this figure, about to descend into the tomb, portrays the same person. How could one conceive of a better way to depict the void of human destiny?"

Madame Bovary lifted her eyeglass. Motionless, Léon watched her without even trying to protest, to make a gesture, so discouraged was he by this double display of idle talk and indifference.

Nothing could stop the guide:

"Near him, this kneeling woman who weeps is his spouse, Diane de Poitiers, comtesse de Brézé, duchesse de Valentinois, born in 1499, died in 1566, and to the left, the one with the child is the Holy Virgin. Now if you turn to this side, you will see the tombs of the Ambroise. They were both cardinals and archbishops of Rouen. That one was minister under Louis XII. He did a great deal for the cathedral. In his will he left thirty thousand gold crowns for the poor."

And without ceasing to talk, he pushed them into a chapel crowded with wooden railings; he pushed some aside and discovered a kind of wooden block that looked vaguely like a poorly carved statue.

"It seems hard to believe," he sighed sadly, "but this used to adorn the tomb of Richard Coeur de Lion,[53] King of England and Duke of Normandy. It was the Calvinists, Monsieur, who reduced it to this condition. They were mean enough to bury it in the earth, under the episcopal throne of Monseigneur the bishop. You can see from here the door by which Monseigneur passes to his house. Let's move on to the gargoyle windows."

But Léon hastily extracted some silver coins from his pocket and seized Emma's arm. The verger stood dumbfounded, not able to understand this untimely munificence when there were still so many things for the stranger to see. He called after him:

"Monsieur! The steeple! the steeple!"[54]

"No, thank you!" said Léon.

"You are missing the best! It is four hundred and forty feet high, nine less than the great pyramid of Egypt. It is all cast iron, it . . ."

Léon was fleeing, for it seemed to him that his love, that for nearly two hours had been frozen in the church like the stones, would now vanish like a vapor through that sort of truncated fun-

---

53. Richard Coeur de Lion, the Lion Hearted (born 1175), was king of England from 1189–1199. He died at the siege of the Castle of Châlus.
54. The Cathedral of Rouen built in the Gothic style in stages from the thir-

teenth century to the early sixteenth, got a high cast iron spire (485 feet), which is generally considered a tasteless disfigurement. Construction was begun in 1824 but not finished until 1876.

nel, rectangular cage or open chimney that rises so grotesquely from the cathedral like the extravagant brainchild of some fantastic roofer.

"But where are we going?" she said.

He pushed on without answering, and Madame Bovary was already dipping her finger in the holy water when behind them they heard a panting breath interrupted by the regular sound of a tapping cane. Léon turned around.

"Monsieur!"

"What is it?"

And he recognised the verger, holding under his arms and bracing against his stomach some twenty large volumes, all of them works on the cathedral.

"Idiot!" muttered Léon, rushing out of the church.

A boy was playing on the sidewalk:

"Go and get me a cab!"

The child bounded off like a ball by the rue des Quatre-Vents; then they were alone a few minutes, face to face, and a little embarrassed.

"Oh Léon! Truly . . . I don't know . . . if I should . . ."

She simpered. Then, in a serious tone:

"It's very improper, you know, it isn't done."

"Everybody does it in Paris!" replied the clerk.

This, like a decisive argument, entirely convinced her. She had made up her mind.

But no cab arrived. Léon shuddered at the thought that she might return into the church. At last the cab appeared.

"At least, you should go out by the northern gate," cried the verger, who was left alone on the threshold, "and look at the Ressurection, the Last Judgment, Paradise, King David, and the damned burning in the flames of Hell!"

"Where to, sir?" asked the coachman.

"Anywhere!" said Léon, pushing Emma into the cab.

And the lumbering machine set out.

It went down the Rue Grand-Pont, crossed the Place des Arts, the Quai Napoleon, the Pont Neuf, and stopped short before the statue of Pierre Corneille.

"Go on," cried a voice that came from within.

The cab went on again, and as soon as it reached the Carrefour Lafayette, set off down-hill, and entered the railroad station at a gallop.

"No, straight on!" cried the same voice.

The cab came out by the gate, and soon having reached the Mall, trotted quietly beneath the elm-trees. The coachman wiped his brow, put his leather hat between his knees, and drove his carriage beyond the side alley by the meadow to the margin of the waters.

It went along by the river, along the towing-path paved with sharp pebbles, and for a long while in the direction of Oyssel, beyond the islands.

But suddenly it turned sideways across Quatremares, Sotteville, La Grande-Chaussée, the Rue d'Elbeuf, and made its third halt in front of the Jardin des Plantes.

"Get on, will you?" cried the voice more furiously.

And at once resuming its course, it passed by Saint Sever, by the Quai des Curandiers, the Quai aux Meules, once more over the bridge, by the Place du Champ de Mars, and behind the hospital gardens, where old men in black coats were walking in the sun along the ivy-covered terraces. It went up the Boulevard Bouvreuil, along the Boulevard Cauchoise, then the whole of Mont-Riboudet to the Deville hills.

It came back; and then, without any fixed plan or direction, wandered about at random. The cab was seen at Saint-Pol, at Lescure, at Mont Gargan, at La Rougue-Marc and Place du Gail-lardbois; in the Rue Maladrerie, Rue Dinanderie, before Saint-Romain, Saint-Vivien, Saint-Maclou, Saint-Nicaise—in front of the Customs, at the Basse-Vieille-Tour, the "Trois Pipes," and the Cimetière monumental. From time to time the coachman on his seat cast despairing glances at the passing cafés. He could not understand what furious locomotive urge prevented these people from ever coming to a stop. Time and again he would try, but exclamations of anger would at once burst forth behind him. Then he would whip his two sweating nags, but he no longer bothered dodging bumps in the road; the cab would hook on to things on all sides but he couldn't have cared less, demoralised as he was, almost weeping with thirst, fatigue and despair.

Near the harbor, among the trucks and the barrels, and along the street corners and the sidewalks, bourgeois stared in wonder at this thing unheard of in the provinces: a cab with all blinds drawn that reappeared incessantly, more tightly sealed than a tomb and tossed around like a ship on the waves.

One time, around noon, in the open country, just as the sun beat most fiercely against the old plated lanterns, a bare hand appeared under the yellow canvass curtain, and threw out some scraps of paper that scattered in the wind, alighting further off like white butterflies on a field of red clover all in bloom.

Then, at about six o'clock the carriage stopped in a back street of the Beauvoisine Quarter, and a woman got out, walking with her veil down and without looking back.

II

On reaching the inn, Madame Bovary was surprised not to see

the stage coach. Hivert had waited for her fifty-three minutes, but finally left without her.

Nothing forced her to go, but she had promised to return that same evening. Moreover, Charles expected her, and in her heart she felt already that cowardly docility that is for some women at once the chastisement and atonement of adultery.

She packed her bag quickly, paid her bill, took a cab in the yard, hurrying on the driver, urging him on, every moment inquiring about time and distance traversed. He succeeded in catching up with the Hirondelle as it neared the first houses of Quincampoix.

Hardly was she seated in her corner that she closed her eyes, and opened them at the foot of the hill, when from afar she recognised Félicité, who was on the look-out in front of the blacksmith's. Hivert pulled up his horses, and the maid, reaching up to the window, said in a tone of mystery:

"Madame, you must go at once to Monsieur Homais. It's for something urgent."

The village was silent as usual. At the corner of the streets little pink mounds lay smoking in the air, for this was the time for jam-making, and every one at Yonville prepared his supply on the same day. But in front of the pharmacist's shop one might admire a far larger heap; it surpassed the others with the superiority that a laboratory must have over domestic ovens, a general need over individual fancy.

She went in. The big arm chair had fallen over and even the "Fanal de Rouen" lay on the ground, outspread between two pestles. She pushed open the door of the hall, and in the middle of the kitchen, amid brown jars full of picked currants, powdered and lump sugar, scales on the table and pans on the fire, she saw assembled all the Homais, big and little, with aprons reaching to their chins, and holding forks in their hands. Justin was standing with bowed head, and the pharmacist was screaming:

"Who told you to go fetch it in the *Capharnaum?*"

"What is it? What is the matter?"

"What is it?" replied the pharmacist. "We are making jelly; it is cooking; but it threatens to boil over because there is too much juice, and I ask for another pan. Then this one here, out of laziness, goes to my laboratory, and dares to take the key to the capharnaum from the nail!"

This name had been given to a small room under the eaves, crammed with the tools and the goods of his trade. He often spent long hours there alone, labelling, decanting, and packaging. He looked upon it not as a simple store-room, but as a veritable sanctuary from where the creations of his own hands were to set forth: pills, lotions and potions that would spread far and wide his rising fame. No one in the world was allowed to set foot there, and he revered it to the point of sweeping it himself. If the pharmacy, open to all comers, was the stage where he displayed his pride, the Capharnaum was the refuge where in selfish concentration, Homais indulged in his most relished pursuits. Therefore, Justin's thoughtlessness seemed to him a monstrous piece of irreverence, and, his face redder than the currants, he continued:

"Yes, the key to the Capharnaum! The key that locks up the acids and caustic alkalis! To go and get a spare pan! a pan with a lid! and that I shall perhaps never use! Everything is of importance in the delicate operations of our art! One must maintain the proper distinctions, and not employ for nearly domestic purposes what is destined for pharmaceutical science! It is as if one were to carve a fowl with a scalpel; as if a magistrate . . ."

"Quiet down," Madame Homais was saying.

And Athalie, pulling at his coat, cried:

"Papa! papa!"

"No, leave me alone!" the pharmacist cried, "leave me alone! I tell you, I might as well be running a grocery store. Just keep at it, don't mind me and break everything to pieces! Smash the testtubes, let the leeches loose, burn the marshmallows, put pickles in the medical jars, tear up the bandages!"

"I thought you wanted to . . ."

"In a moment . . . Do you know what risks you took? Didn't you see something in the corner, on the left, on the third shelf? Speak! Answer me! Say something!"

"I . . . don't . . . know . . ." stammered the boy.

"Ah! you don't know! Well, *I* do! You saw a bottle of blue glass sealed with yellow wax, that contains a white powder carefully marked *Dangerous!* And do you know what is in it? Arsenic! And you go and touch it! You take a pan that stands right next to it!"

"Right next to it!" cried Madame Homais, clasping her hands. "Arsenic! You might have poisoned us all."

And the children began to scream as if they already felt dreadful stomach pains.

"Or poison a patient!" continued the pharmacist. "Do you want to see me dragged into court like a common criminal? or taken to the scaffold? As if you didn't know how careful one has to be in handling chemicals, even I who spent my life doing nothing else. Often I am horrified when I think of my responsibility; the Government persecutes us, and the absurd legislation that rules us is a veritable Damocles' sword suspended over our heads."

Emma gave up trying to find out what they wanted her for, and the pharmacist continued without pausing for breath:

"That is how you thank us for the many kindnesses we have shown you! That is how you reward me for the truly paternal care that I lavish on you! Where would you be if I hadn't taken you in hand? What would you be doing? Who provides you with food, education, clothes, and all the means to rise to a respectable level in society? But if you want to get there, you'll have to learn to pull hard at the oars—get callouses on your hands, as they saying goes. *Fabricando fit faber, age quod agis.*" [55]

He was so exasperated he quoted Latin. He would have used Chinese or Greenlandic had he known them, for he was rocked by one of these crises in which the soul reveals all it contains, just as the storm lays bare the ocean from the seaweed on the shore down to the sand on its deepest bottom.

And he went on:

"I am beginning to regret that I ever took you in charge! I would have done a lot better if I'd let you wallow in poverty and filth, where you were born. The best you can hope for is to be a cowhand. You are not fit to be a scientist! You hardly know how to stick on a label! And there you are, dwelling with me snug as a parson, living in clover, taking your ease!"

Emma turned in despair to Madame Homais:

"I was told to come . . . "

"Heavens!" the lady exclaimed in a mournful tone "How am I to tell you? . . . Such a misfortune!"

She could not finish. The pharmacist was thundering:

"Empty it! Clean it! Take it back! And hurry!"

And seizing Justin by the collar of his apron, he shook him so vigorously that a book fell out of his pocket. The boy stooped, but Homais was the quicker, and, having picked up the volume, he stared at it with bulging eyes and open mouth.

"Conjugal . . . love!" he said, slowly separating the two words. "Ah! very good! very good! very pretty! And with illustrations! . . . Truly, this is too much!"

Madame Homais drew near.

"No, don't touch it!"

The children wanted to look at the pictures.

"Leave the room," he said imperiously.

They went out.

First he walked up and down, with the open book in his hand, rolling his eyes, choking, fuming, apoplectic. Then he came straight to his apprentice, and, planting himself in front of him with folded arms:

"So you are blessed with all the vices under the sun, you little wretch? Watch out! you are following a dangerous path! . . . Did

---

55. *Fabricando fit Faber, age quod agis* ("Do what you do"), the artisan becomes proficient through practice; practice what you are supposed to do.

it never occur to you that this infamous book might fall into the hands of my children, kindle a spark in their minds, tarnish the purity of Athalie, corrupt Napoleon! He is close to being a man. Are you quite sure, at least, that they have not read it? Can you certify to me . . ."

"But, Monsieur," said Emma, "you wished to tell me . . ."

"Oh yes, madame . . . your father-in-law is dead."

Indeed, the elder Bovary had suddenly died from a stroke the evening before, as he got up from the table; overanxious to spare Emma's sensitive nerves, Charles had asked Monsieur Homais to break the horrible news to her as carefully as possible.

Homais had meditated at length over his speech; he had rounded, polished it, given it the proper cadence; it was a masterpiece of prudence and transitions, of subtle turns and delicacy; but anger had got the better of rhetoric.

Emma, abandoning all hope to learn any further details, left the pharmacy; for Monsieur Homais had resumed his vituperations. He was growing calmer, however, and was now grumbling in a paternal tone whilst he fanned himself with his skull-cap.

"It is not that I entirely disapprove of the book. The author was a doctor! It contains scientific information that a man might well want to know; I'd go as far as saying that he ought to know. But later . . . later! You should at least wait till you are yourself full-grown, and your character formed."

When Emma knocked at the door, Charles, who was waiting for her, came forward with open arms and said in a tearful voice:

"Ah! my dear wife. . . ."

And he leant over gently to kiss her. But at the contact of his lips the memory of the other returned; she passed her hand over her face and shuddered.

Yet, she answered:

"Yes, I know . . . I know . . ."

He showed her the letter in which his mother told the event without any sentimental hypocrisy. Her only regret was that her husband had not received the consolation of religion; he had died at Doudeville, in the street, at the door of a café after a patriotic dinner with some ex-officers.

Emma gave him back the letter; then at dinner, for appearance's sake, she affected a lack of appetite. But as he urged her to try, she resolutely began eating, while Charles opposite her sat motionless and dejected.

Now and then he raised his head and gave her a long, distressed look. Once he sighed:

"I'd have liked to see him again!"

She was silent. At last, realizing that she must say something:

"How old was your father?" she asked.

"Fifty-eight."

"Ah!"

And that was all.

A quarter of an hour later, he added: "My poor mother! what will become of her now?"

She made a gesture of ignorance.

Seeing her so taciturn, Charles imagined her much affected, and forced himself to say nothing, not to reawaken this sorrow which moved him. And, shaking off his own:

"Did you enjoy yourself yesterday?" he asked.

"Yes."

When the cloth was removed, Bovary did not rise, nor did Emma; and as she looked at him, the monotony of the spectacle drove little by little all pity from her heart. He seemed to her paltry, weak, a nonentity—a sorry creature in every way. How to get rid of him? What an interminable evening! She felt a stupor invading her, as if from opium fumes.

They heard the sharp noise of a wooden leg on the boards of the entrance hall. It was Hippolyte bringing back Emma's luggage.

To put them down, he had to bring around his wooden stump painfully in a quarter circle.

"He doesn't even seem to remember" she thought, looking at the poor devil, whose coarse red hair was wet with perspiration.

Bovary was searching for a coin at the bottom of his purse; he did not seem to realize how humiliating the man's presence was for him, standing there as the living embodiment of his hopeless ineptitude.

"Oh, you have a pretty bouquet," he said, noticing Léon's violets on the mantlepiece.

"Yes," she replied indifferently; "it's a bouquet I bought just now . . . from a beggar-woman."

Charles picked up the flowers and, bathing his tear-stained eyes in their freshness, he delicately sniffed their perfume. She took them quickly from his hand and put them in a glass of water.

The next day the elder Madame Bovary arrived. She and her son spent much time weeping. Pretending to be busy in the house, Emma managed to stay by herself.

The following day, they had to discuss together the arrangements for the period of mourning. They went and sat down with their workboxes by the waterside under the arbor.

Charles was thinking of his father, and was surprised to feel so much affection for this man, whom up till now he thought he cared little about. The older Madame Bovary was thinking of her husband. The worst days of the past seemed enviable to her. All was forgotten beneath the instinctive regret of such a long habit, and from time to time, while sewing, a big tear rolled down her nose and hung suspened there a moment.

Emma was thinking that it was scarcely forty-eight hours since they had been together, far from the world, lost in ecstasy, and not having eyes enough to gaze upon each other. She tried to recall the slightest details of that past day. But the presence of her husband and mother-in-law bothered her. She would have liked to stop hearing and seeing, in order to keep intact the stillness of her love; but, try as she would, the memory would vanish under the impact of outer sensations.

She was removing the lining of a dress, and the strips were scattered around her. Mother Bovary, without looking up, kept her scissors busy, and Charles, in his felt slippers and his old brown coat that he used as a dressing gown, sat in silence with both hands in his pockets; near them Berthe, in a little white apron, was raking the sandwalks with her spade.

Suddenly they saw Monsieur Lheureux, the storekeeper, come in through the gate.

He came to offer his services "on this sad occasion." Emma replied that none were needed, but the shopkeeper wouldn't take no for an answer.

"I beg your pardon," he said, "but I should like to have a word in private."

Then, in a low voice, he added:

"It is about this little matter . . . you know . . ." Charles turned crimson.

"Oh yes . . . of course."

And, in his confusion, he turned to his wife:

"Darling, could you perhaps . . . ?"

She seemed to understand him, for she rose; and Charles said to his mother:

"Nothing important. Some household trifle, I suppose."

Fearing her reproaches, he didn't want her to know about the note.

As soon as they were alone, Monsieur Lheureux began by congratulating Emma outspokenly on the inheritance, then talked of this and that, the fruit trees, the harvest, his own health which had endless ups and downs. He had to work like a devil and, regardless of what people thought, didn't make enough to buy butter for his bread.

Emma let him talk. She had been so dreadfully bored, these last two days!

"And so you're quite well again?" he went on. "Believe me, your husband was in quite a state. He's a good fellow, though we did have a little misunderstanding."

She asked what the misunderstanding was about, for Charles had told her nothing of the dispute about the goods supplied to her.

"As if you didn't know!" exclaimed Lheureux. "It was about your little caprice . . . the trunks."

He had drawn his hat over his eyes, and, with his hands behind his back, smiling and whistling, he looked straight at her in an unbearable manner. Did he suspect anything? She was lost in all kinds of apprehensions. Finally he said:

"We made it up, and I've come to propose still another arrangement."

He offered to renew the note Bovary had signed. The doctor, of course, would do as he pleased; he was not to trouble himself, especially just now, when he would have a lot to attend to.

"It seems to me he'd do well to turn it all over to some one else, —to you for example. With a power of attorney it could be easily managed, and then the two of us could have our little business transactions together . . ."

She did not understand. He did not insist, and brought the conversation back to his trade; it was impossible that Madame didn't need anything. He would send her a black barège, twelve yards, just enough to make a dress.

"The one you've on is good enough for the house, but you want another for calls. I saw that the very moment that I came in. I've got a quick eye for these things!"

He did not send the material, he brought it. Then he came again to take her measurements; he came again on other pretexts, always trying to make himself agreeable, useful, like a vassal serving his master, as Homais might have put it, and never failing to drop a hint about the power of attorney. He never mentioned the note. She didn't think of it; although Charles doubtlessly had mentioned something at the beginning of her convalescence, so many emotions had passed through her head that she no longer remembered it. Besides, she made it a point never to bring up any money questions. Charles' mother seemed surprised at this, and attributed the change in her ways to the religious sentiments she had contracted during her illness.

But as soon as she left, Emma greatly astounded Bovary by her practical good sense. They would have to make inquiries, look into the mortgages, decide whether it would be more advantageous to sell by auction or by other means.

She quoted legal jargon at random, and grand words such as "order", "the future", "foresight". She constantly exaggerated the difficulties of settling his father's affairs; at last, one day she showed him the rough draft of a power of attorney to manage and administer his business, arrange all notes, sign and endorse all bills, pay all sums, etc. She had profited by Lheureux's lessons.

Charles naively asked her where this paper came from.

"From Master Guillaumin."

And with the utmost coolness she added:

"I don't trust him overmuch. Notaries have such a bad reputation. Perhaps we ought to consult . . . But the only person we know . . . There is no one."

"Unless perhaps Léon . . ." replied Charles, who was thinking.

But it was difficult to explain matters by letter. Then she offered to make the journey. He refused. She insisted. It was quite a contest of mutual consideration. At last she exclaimed, in a childish tone of mock-rebellion:

"No, enough, I will!"

"How good you are!" he said, kissing her on the forehead.

The next morning she set out in the "Hirondelle" for Rouen to consult Monsieur Léon, and she stayed there three days.

III

They were three full, exquisite, magnificent days—a true honeymoon. They stayed at the Hôtel-de-Boulogne, on the harbor; and they lived there behind drawn blinds and closed doors, with flowers on the floor, and iced fruit syrups that were brought them early in the morning.

Towards evening they took a covered boat and went to dine on one of the islands.

At this time of the day, one could hear the caulking irons sound against the hulls in the dockyard. Tar smoke rose up between the trees and large oily patches floated on the water, undulating unevenly in the purple sunlight like surfaces of Florentine bronze.

They drifted down among moored ships whose long slanting cables grazed lightly the top of their boat.

The sounds of the city gradually fainted in the distance, the rattling of carriages, the tumult of voices, the yelping of dogs on the decks of barges. She loosened her hat and they landed on their island.

They sat down in the low-ceilinged room of a tavern with black fishing-nets hanging across the door. They ate fried smelts, cream and cherries. They lay down upon the grass, kissed behind the poplar trees; like two Robinson Crusoes, they would gladly have lived forever in this spot; in their bliss, it seemed to them the most magnificent place on earth. It was not the first time that they had seen trees, a blue sky, meadows; or heard the water flow and the wind blow in the branches. But they had never really felt any of this; it was as if nature had not existed before, or had only begun to be beautiful since the gratification of their desires.

At nightfall they returned. The boat glided along the shores of the islands. They stayed below, hidden in darkness, without saying a word. The square-tipped oars sounded against the iron oar-locks; in the stillness, they seemed to mark time like the beat of a metronome, while the rope that trailed behind never ceased its gentle splash against the water.

One night the moon rose, and they did not fail to make fine phrases about how melancholical and poetic it appeared to them. She even began to sing:

> One night, do you remember,
> We were sailing . . .

Her thin musical voice died away over the water; Léon could hear the wind-borne trills pass by him like a fluttering of wings.

She faced him, leaning against the wall of the cabin while the moon shone through the open blinds. Her black dress, falling around her like a fan, made her seem more slender, taller. Her head was raised, her hands clapsed, her eyes turned towards heaven. At times the shadow of the willows hid her completely; then she reappeared suddenly, like a vision in the moonlight.

Léon, on the floor by her side, found under his hand a ribbon of scarlet silk.

The boatman looked at it, and said at last:

"Perhaps it belongs to the party I took out the other day. They were a jolly bunch of ladies and gentlemen, with cakes, champagne, trumpets—everything in style! There was one especially, a tall handsome man with small moustaches, who was the life of the party. They kept asking him 'Come on, Adolphe—or Dodolphe, or something like that—tell us a story . . .'"

She shuddered.

"Don't you feel well?" Léon inquired, coming closer.

"Oh, it's nothing! Just a chill from the cold night air."

"He's another one who seems to have no trouble finding women," the old sailor added softly, intending to pay Léon a compliment.

Then, spitting on his hands, he took the oars again.

Yet the time to part had come. The farewells were sad. He was to send his letters to Mère Rollet, and she gave him such precise instructions about a double envelope that he was much impressed with her shrewdness in love matters.

"So you can guarantee me that everything is in order?" she said with her last kiss.

"Yes, certainly."

"But why," he thought afterwards as he came back through the streets alone, "is she so very anxious to get this power of attorney?"

IV

Léon soon put on superior airs with his friends, avoided their company, and completely neglected his work.

He waited for her letters, read and re-read them. He wrote to her. He called her to mind with all the strength of his desires and of his memories. Instead of lessening with absence, his longing to see her kept growing to the point where, one Saturday morning he escaped from his office.

When, from the summit of the hill, he saw in the valley below the church-spire with its metal flag swinging in the wind, he felt that delight mingled with triumphant vanity and selfish benevolence that millionaires must experience when they come back to their native village.

He went prowling around round her house. A light was burning in the kitchen. He watched for her shadow behind the curtains, but nothing appeared.

Mère Lefrançois, on seeing him, uttered many exclamations. She thought he had grown taller and thinner, while Artémise, on the contrary, thought him stouter and darker.

He ate in the little dining-room, as in the past, but alone, without the tax collector; for Binet, tired of waiting for the "Hirondelle," had definitely moved his meal an hour earlier. Now he dined punctually at five, which didn't keep him from complaining that the rickety old carriage was late.

Léon finally made up his mind, and knocked at the doctor's door. Madame was in her room, and did not come down for a quarter of an hour. The doctor seemed delighted to see him, but he never left the house that evening, nor the next day.

He saw her alone in the evening, very late, behind the garden in the lane;—in the lane, as with the other one! It was a stormy night, and they talked under an umbrella by lightning flashes.

They couldn't bear the thought of parting.

"I'd rather die!" said Emma.

She seized his arm convulsively, and wept.

"Good bye! When shall I see you again?"

They came back again to embrace once more, and it was then that she promised him to find soon, no matter how, some assured way of meeting in freedom at least once a week. Emma was certain to find a way. She was generally in a hopeful frame of mind: the inheritance money was bound to come in soon.

On the strength of it she bought a pair of yellow curtains with large stripes for her room; Monsieur Lheureux had recommended them as a particularly good buy. She dreamt of getting a carpet, and Lheureux, declaring that it wasn't that much of an investment after all, politely undertook to supply her with one. She could no longer do without his services. Twenty times a day she sent for him, and he at once interrupted whatever he was doing, without a murmur. Neither could people understand why Mére Rollet ate at her house every day, and even paid her private visits.

It was about this time, in the early part of the Winter, that a sudden urge to make music seemed to come over her.

One evening when Charles was listening to her, she began the same piece four times over, each time with much vexation, while he, totally oblivious to her mistakes, exclaimed:

"Bravo! . . . Very good! . . . Don't stop. Keep going!"

"Oh, no. It's awful! My fingers are much too rusty!"

The next day he begged her to play for him again.

"Very well, if you wish."

And Charles had to confess that she had slipped a little. She played wrong notes and blundered; then, stopping short:

"Ah! it's no use. I ought to take some lessons, but . . ."

Biting her lip, she added:

"Twenty francs a lesson, that's too expensive!"

"Maybe it is . . . a little," said Charles with a stupid giggle. "But it seems to me that one might be able to do it for less; for there are artists of little reputation, who are often better than the celebrities."

"Find them!" said Emma.

The next day on coming home, he gave her a sly look, and finally could no longer repress what he had to say:

"How stubborn you can be at times! I went to Barfuchéres to-day. Well, Madame Liégard assured me that her three daughters, who go to school at Miséricorde, take lessons at fifty sous apiece, and that from an excellent teacher!"

She shrugged her shoulders and did not open her piano again.

But whenever she passed in front of it (provided Bovary was present), she sighed:

"Ah! my poor piano!"

And whenever someone came to call, she did not fail to inform them that she had given up music, and could not begin again now for important reasons. People would commiserate. What a pity! She had so much talent! They even spoke to Bovary about it. They put him to shame, especially the pharmacist.

"You are wrong. One should never let any natural faculties lie fallow. Besides, just think, my good friend, that by inducing mad-ame to study, you are economising on the subsequent musical ed-ucation of your child. For my own part, I think that mothers ought themselves to instruct their children. It's an idea of Rousseau's, still rather new perhaps, but bound to win out sooner or later, like vaccination and breast-feeding."

So Charles returned once more to this question of the piano. Emma replied bitterly that it would be better to sell it. Poor piano!

it had given his vanity so many satisfactions that to see it go was for Bovary, in an undefinable manner, like Emma's partial suicide.

"If you really want it . . ." he said, "a lesson from time to time wouldn't ruin us after all."

"But lessons," she replied, "are only of use if one persists."

And this is how she managed to obtain her husband's permission to go to town once a week to see her lover. At the end of a month she was even considered to have made considerable progress.

V

She went on Thursdays. She got up and dressed silently, in order not to awaken Charles, who would have reproached her for getting ready too early. Then she walked up and down, stood at the windows, and looked out over the Square. The early dawn was broadening between the pillars of the market, and the pharmacy, still boarded up, showed in the pale light of the dawn the large letters of the signboard.

When the clock pointed to a quarter past seven, she went to the "Lion d'Or," where a yawning Artémise unlocked the door for her. She would poke the fire in Madame's honor, and Emma remained alone in the kitchen. Now and again she went out. Hivert was leisurely harnessing his horses while listening to the Mère Lefrançois who, sticking her head and night cap through a window, was instructing him on his errands and giving him explanations that would have bewildered any one else. Emma tapped her boots on the cobblestones of the yard.

At last, when he had eaten his soup, put on his cloak, lighted his pipe, and grasped his whip, he calmly took his place on the seat.

The "Hirondelle" started at a slow trot, and for about a mile stopped time and again to pick up waiting passengers along the roadside, before their house-gates. Those who had booked seats the night before kept it waiting; some even were still in bed in their houses. Hivert called, shouted, swore; then he got down from his seat and knocked loudly at the doors. The wind blew through the cracked windows.

Gradually, the four benches filled up. The carriage rolled off; rows of apple-trees followed one upon another, and the road between its two long ditches, full of yellow water, rose, constantly narrowing towards the horizon.

Emma knew every inch of the road: after a certain meadow there was a sign post, then a barn or roadmender's hut. Sometimes, in hope of being surprised, she would close her eyes, but she never lost a clear sense of the distance still to be covered.

At last the brick houses began to follow one another more closely, the earth resounded beneath the wheels, the "Hirondelle" glided between the gardens, revealing through an occasional opening, statues, a summer pavillion, trimmed yew trees, a swing. Then all at once, the city came into sight.

Sloping down like an amphitheatre, and drowned in the fog, it overflowed unevenly beyond its bridges. Then the open country mounted again in a monotonous sweep until it touched in the distance the elusive line of the pale sky. Seen thus from above, the whole landscape seemed frozen, like a picture; the anchored ships were massed in one corner, the river curved round the foot of the green hills, and the oblong islands looked like giant fishes lying motionless on the water. The factory chimneys belched forth immense plumes of brown smoke, their tips carried off in the wind. One heard the rumbling of the foundries, mingled with the clear chimes of the churches, dimly outlined in the fog. The leafless trees on the boulevards seemed violet thickets in the midst of the houses, and the roofs, shining from the rain, threw back unequal reflections, according to the heights of the various districts. From time to time a gust of wind would drive the clouds towards the slopes of Saint Catherine, like aerial waves breaking silently against a cliff.

Something seemed to emanate from this mass of human lives that left her dizzy; her heart swelled as though the hundred and twenty thousand souls palpitating there had all at once wafted to her the passions with which her imagination had endowed them. Her love grew in the presence of this vastness, and filled with the tumult of the vague murmuring which rose from below. She poured it out, onto the squares, the avenues, the streets; and the old Norman city spread out before her like some incredible capital, a Babylon into which she was about to enter. She lifted the window with both hands to lean out, drinking in the breeze; the three horses galloped, the stones grated in the mud, the diligence rocked, and Hivert, from afar, hailed the carts on the road, while the well-to-do residents of Bois Guillaume sedately descended the hill to town in their little family carriages.

The coach made a stop at the city gates; Emma undid her overshoes, put on other gloves, rearranged her shawl, and some twenty paces farther she descended from the "Hirondelle."

The town was beginning to awake. Shop-boys in caps were polishing the front windows of the stores, and women, with baskets balanced on their hips, would stand on the street corners calling out from time to time some sonorous cry. She walked with downcast eyes, close to the walls, and smiling with pleasure beneath her lowered black veil.

For fear of being seen, she did not usually take the most direct road. She would plunge into dark alleys, and emerge, all in a sweat, near the little fountain at the beginning of the Rue Nationale. This was the quarter of the theaters, cabarets, and prostitutes. Often, a cart loaded with shaking scenery passed close by her. Waiters in aprons were sprinkling sand on the flagstones between green shrubs. There was a smell of absinthe, cigars and oysters.

She turned a corner; she recognised him by his curling hair that escaped from beneath his hat.

Léon kept on walking ahead of her along the sidewalk. She followed him into the hotel. He went up, opened the door, entered — What an embrace!

Then, after the kisses, the words rushed forth. They told each other the sorrows of the week, the forebodings, the anxiety for the letters; but now everything was forgotten; they gazed at each other with voluptuous laughs, and tender names.

The bed was a large one, made of mahogany and shaped like a boat. The red silk curtains which hung from the ceiling, were gathered together too low, close to the lyre-shaped headboards;—and nothing in the world was so lovely as her brown hair and white skin set off against that deep crimson color, when with a gesture of modesty, she closed her arms and hid her face in her hands.

The warm room, with its subdued carpet, its frivolous ornaments and its soft light, seemed made for the intimacies of passion. The curtain-rods, ending in arrows, the brass pegs and the great balls of the andirons would suddenly light up if a ray of sunlight entered. On the chimney, between the candelabra there were two of those pink shells in which one hears the murmur of the sea when one holds them against one's ear.

How they loved that room, so full of gaiety, despite its somewhat faded splendour! They always found the furniture arranged the same way, and sometimes hairpins, that she had forgotten the Thursday before, under the pedestal of the clock. They lunched by the fireside on a little round table, inlaid with rosewood. Emma carved, put bits on his plate while playing all sorts of coquettish tricks; she would laugh a ringing libertine laugh when the froth from the champagne overflowed the fragile glass onto the rings of her fingers. They were so completely lost in the possession of each other that they thought themselves in their own house, that they would go on living there until separated by death, like an eternally young married couple. They said "our room," "our carpet," she even said "my slippers," referring to the gift Léon had bought to satisfy a whim of hers. They were rose-colored satin, bordered with swansdown. When she sat on his lap, her leg, which was then too short, hung in the air, and the dainty shoe having no back, was held on only by the toes of her bare foot.

He savoured for the first time the inexpressible delights of feminine refinement. He had never encountered this grace of language, this direction in dress, these poses of a weary dove. He admired the exaltation of her soul and the lace on her petticoat. Besides, was she not a "woman of the world", and a married woman! in short a real mistress!

According to her changing moods, in turn meditative and gay, talkative and silent, passionate and langorous, she awakened in him a thousand desires, called up instincts or memories. She was the mistress of all the novels, the heroine of all the dramas, the vague "she" of all the volumes of verse. On her shoulders, he rediscovered the amber color of the "Odalisque au Bain";[56] her waist was long like the feudal chatelaines; she resembled Musset's "Femme Pâle de Barcelone."[57] Above all, she was his Angel.

It often seemed to him that his soul, fleeing toward her, broke like a wave against the contours of her head, and was drawn irrisistibly down into the whiteness of her breast.

He knelt on the ground before her; and resting his elbows on her lap, he would gaze at her smilingly, his face uplifted.

She bent over him, and murmured, as if choking with intoxication:

"Oh! don't move! don't speak! Look at me! There is something so tender that comes from your eyes. It does me so much good!"

She called him child.

"Do you love me, child?"

And she never heard his reply, his lips always rose so fast to find her mouth.

There was a little bronze cupid on the clock, who simpered as he held up his arms under a golden garland. They had laughed at it many a time, but when they had to part everything seemed serious.

Motionless, they looked at each other and kept repeating:

"Till Thursday! . . . Till Thursday! . . ."

Suddenly she would take his head between her hands and kiss him quickly on the forehead while crying "Adieu" and rush down the stairs.

She went next to a hairdresser in the Rue de la Comédie to have her hair arranged. Night would be falling; they lit the gas in the shop.

She heard the bell in the theatre calling the actors to the performance; and she saw white-faced men and women in faded dresses pass by on the other side of the street and enter in at the stage door.

It was hot in the little low-ceilinged room with its stove humming amidst the wigs and pommades. The smell of the tongs together with the oily hands that were manipulating her hair, would soon stupefy her and she would begin to doze a bit in her dressing gown.

56. Famous painting by Jean Auguste Dominique Ingres.

57. Alfred de Musset frequently in-carnates, for Flaubert, the type of stilted romantic sentimentality he despises.

Often, as he did her hair, the man offered her tickets for a masked ball.

Then she left! She remounted the streets; reached the Croix Rouge, retrieved her overshoes which she had hidden under the bench that morning, and settled into her place among the impatient passengers. The other passengers got out at the foot of the hill in order to spare the horses. She remained alone in the carriage.

At every turn, they could see more and more of the city below, forming a luminous mist above the mass of houses. Emma knelt on the cushions, and let her eyes wander over the dazzling light. She sobbed, called to Léon, sent him tender words and kisses which were lost in the wind.

There was a wretched creature on the hillside, who would wander about with his stick right in the midst of the carriages. A mass of rags covered his shoulders, and an old staved-in beaver hat, shaped like a basin, hid his face; but when he took it off he revealed two gaping bloody orbits in the place of eyelids. The flesh hung in red strips; and from them flowed a liquid which congealed into green scales reaching down to his nose with its black nostrils, which kept sniffing convulsively. To speak to you he threw back his head with an idiotic laugh;—then his blueish eyeballs, rolling round and round, would rub against the open wound near the temples.

He sang a little song as he followed the carriages:

> Often the warmth of a summer day
> Makes a young girl dream her heart away.

And all the rest was about birds and sunshine and green leaves.

Sometimes he would appear behind Emma, his head bare. She would draw back with a cry. Hivert liked to tease him. He would advise him to get a booth at the Saint Romain fair, or else ask him, laughing, how his girl friend was.

Often the coach was already in motion when his hat would be thrust violently in at the window, while he clung with his other arm to the footboard, between the spattering of the wheels. His voice, at first weak and quavering, would grow sharp. It lingered into the night like an inarticulate lament of some vague despair; and, heard through the jingling of the horses' bells, the murmuring of the trees, and the rumble of the empty coach, it had something so distant and sad that it filled Emma with dread. It went to the very depths of her soul, like a whirlwind in an abyss, and carried her away to a boundless realm of melancholy. But Hivert, noticing a weight behind, would lash out savagely at the blind man with his whip. The thong lashed his wounds and he fell back into the mud with a shriek.

The passengers in the Hirondelle would all finally drop off to sleep, some with their mouths open, others their chins pressed against their chests, leaning on their neighbor's shoulder, or with their arm passed through the strap, all the time swaying regularly with the jolting of the carriage; and the sight of the lantern, that was swinging back and forth outside and reflecting on the rumps of the shaft horses, penetrated into the coach through the chocolate-colored curtains, throwing blood-red shadows over all those motionless beings within. Emma, drunk with grief, shivered under her coat and felt her feet grow colder and colder, with death in her soul.

Charles at home would be waiting for her; the "Hirondelle" was always late on Thursdays. Madame arrived at last! She scarcely kissed the child. The dinner was not ready, no matter! She excused the cook. The girl now seemed allowed to do just as she liked.

Often her husband, noting her pallor, asked if she were unwell.

"No," said Emma.

"But," he replied, "you seem so strange this evening."

"Oh, it's nothing! nothing!"

There were even days when she had no sooner come in than she went up to her room; and Justin, who would happen to be there, moved about noiselessly, more adroit at helping her than the best of maids. He put the matches ready, the candlestick, a book, arranged her nightgown, turned back the bedclothes.

"All right," she'd say "that's fine, get going!"

For he stood there, his hands hanging down and his eyes wide open, as if enmeshed in the innumerable threads of a sudden reverie.

The following day was frightful, and those that came after still more unbearable, because of her impatience to once again seize her happiness,—this fierce lust, enflamed by recent memories, which on the seventh day would erupt freely within Léon's embraces. His own passion was manifested by continual expressions of wonder and gratitude. Emma tasted this love discreetly, and with all her being, nourished it by every tender device she knew, and trembled a little that some day it might be lost.

She often said to him, with a sweet melancholy in her voice:

"Ah! you too, you will leave me! You will marry! You will be like all the others."

He asked:

"What others?"

"Why, like all men," she replied.

Then added, repulsing him with a languid movement:

"You are all of you wretches!"

One day, as they were talking philosophically of earthly disillusions she happened to mention (in order to provoke his jealousy, or perhaps through some irrisistible urge to confide in him) that in the past, before she knew him, she had loved someone else. "Not like you," she went on quickly, swearing on the head of her child "that nothing had happened."

The young man believed her, but none the less questioned her to find out what kind of a man *He* was.

"He was a ship's captain, my dear."

Was this not preventing any inquiry, and, at the same time, assuming a higher ground because of the aura of fascination which is supposed to surround a man who must have been of warlike nature and accustomed to receive homage?

The clerk then felt the lowliness of his position; he longed for epaulettes, crosses, titles. These things would please her; he suspected as much from her extravagant habits.

However, Emma never mentioned a number of her most extravagant ideas, such as her desire to have a blue tilbury to drive into Rouen, drawn by an English horse and driven by a groom in turned down boots. It was Justin who had inspired her with this whim, by begging her to take him into service as footman; and if the privation of it did not lessen the pleasure of her arrival at each of their weekly rendez-vous, it certainly augmented the bitterness of the return.

Often, when they were talking together of Paris, she would end by murmuring,

"Ah, how happy we could be living there."

"Are we not happy?" the young man would gently ask, passing his hands over her hair.

"Yes, that is true," she said. "I am mad: kiss me!"

To her husband she was more charming than ever. She made him pistachio-creams and played him waltzes after dinner. He thought himself the most fortunate of men, and Emma was without uneasiness, when, suddenly one evening:

"It is Mademoiselle Lempereur, isn't it, who gives you lessons?"

"Yes."

"Well, I saw her just now," Charles went on, "at Madame Liégard's. I spoke to her about you; and she doesn't know you."

This was like a thunderbolt. However, she replied quite naturally:

"She must have forgotten my name."

"But perhaps," said the doctor, "there are several Demoiselles Lempereur at Rouen who are music teachers."

"Possibly!"

Then she added quickly:

"Nevertheless, I have her receipts, here! Look."

And she went to the writing-table, ransacked all the drawers, mixed up the papers, and at last lost her head so completely that Charles earnestly begged her not to take so much trouble about those wretched receipts.

"Oh! I will find them," she said.

And, in fact, on the following Friday, as Charles was putting on one of his boots in the dark closet where his clothes were kept, he felt a piece of paper between the leather and his sock. He took it out and read:

"Received, for three months' lessons and several pieces of music, the sum of sixty-three francs.—FELICIE LEMPEREUR, professor of music."

"How the devil did it get into my boots?"

"It must," she replied, "have fallen from the old box of bills that is on the edge of the shelf."

From that moment on, her existence was one long tissue of lies, in which she wrapped her love as under a veil in order to hide it. It became a need, an obsession, a delight, to such a point that, if she claimed to have walked on the right side of the street the previous day, one could be sure she had walked on the left.

One morning, when she had gone, as usual, rather lightly clothed, it suddenly began to snow, and as Charles was watching the weather from the window, he caught sight of Monsieur Bournisien in the chaise of Monsieur Tuvache, who was driving him to Rouen. Then he went down to give the priest a thick shawl that he was to hand over to Emma as soon as he reached the Croix-Rouge. When he got to the inn, Monsieur Bournisien asked for the wife of the Yonville doctor. The landlady replied that she very rarely came to her establishment. So that evening, when he recognised Madame Bovary in the "Hirondelle," the curé told her his dilemma, without, however, appearing to attach much importance to it, for he began praising a preacher who was doing wonders at the Cathedral, and whom all the ladies were rushing to hear.

Still, even if he had not asked for any explanations, others, later on, might prove less discreet. So she thought it would be a good idea to get out of the coach at the Croix Rouge each time she came so that the good folk of her village seeing her on the stairs would not become suspicious.

One day, however, Monsieur Lheureux met her coming out of the Hôtel de Boulogne on Léon's arm; and she was frightened, thinking he would gossip. He was not such a fool.

But three days after he came to her room, shut the door, and said:

"I must have some money."

She declared she could not give him any. Lheureux began to moan, reminding her of all the favors he had done her.

In fact, of the two bills signed by Charles, Emma up to the present had paid only one. As to the second, the shopkeeper, at her request, had consented to replace it by another, which again had been renewed for a long date. Then he drew from his pocket a list of goods not paid for; to wit, the curtains, the carpet, the material for the arm-chairs, several dresses, and diverse articles of dress, totalling in all a sum of about two thousand francs.

She hung her head; he continued:

"But if you haven't any ready money, you do have some property."

And he called to her attention a miserable little shack situated at Barneville, near Aumale, that brought in almost nothing. It had formerly been part of a small farm sold by Monsieur Bovary senior; for Lheureux knew everything, even down to the number of acres and the names of the neighbors.

"If I were in your place," he said, "I'd get it off my hands, and have some money left over."

She pointed out the difficulty of finding a buyer; he said he thought he could find one; but she asked him how she should manage to sell it.

"Haven't you your power of attorney?" he replied.

The phrase came to her like a breath of fresh air. "Leave me the bill," said Emma.

"Oh, it isn't worth while," answered Lheureux.

He came back the following week boasting that after having gone to a great deal of trouble, he had finally tracked down a certain man named Langlois, who had had his eye on the property for a long time but had never mentioned a price.

"Never mind the price!" she cried.

On the contrary, he said, they must take their time and sound the fellow out. The affair was certainly worth the trouble of a trip, and, as she could not undertake it, he offered to go to the place and bargain with Langlois. On his return he announced that the purchaser proposed four thousand francs.

Emma's heart rose at this news.

"Frankly," he added, "that's a good price."

She drew half the sum at once, and when she was about to pay her account the shopkeeper said:

"It grieves me, it really does, to see you give up such a considerable sum of money as that all at once." She stared at the bank notes and began to dream of the countless rendez-vous with Léon that those two thousand francs represented.

"What! What do you mean!" she stammered.

"Oh!" he went on, laughing good-naturedly, "one puts anything one likes on receipts. Don't you think I know what household affairs are?"

And he looked at her fixedly, while in his hand he held two long papers which he kept sliding between his nails. At last, opening his billfold, he spread out on the table four bills to order, each for a thousand francs.

"Sign these," he said, "and keep it all!"

She cried out, scandalised.

"But if I give you the balance," replied Monsieur Lheureux impudently, "isn't that doing you a service?"

And taking a pen he wrote at the bottom of the account, "Received from Madame Bovary four thousand francs."

"What is there to worry about, since in six months you'll draw the arrears for your cottage, and I don't make the last bill due till after you've been paid?"

Emma was becoming somewhat confused in her calculations and her ears rang as though gold pieces were bursting out of their bags and tinkling onto the floor all around her. At last Lheureux explained that he had a very good friend named Vinçart, a banker in Rouen, who would discount these four bills. Then he himself would hand over to madame the remainder after the actual debt was paid.

But instead of two thousand francs he brought her only eighteen hundred, for his friend Vinçart (which was "only fair") had deducted two hundred francs for commission and discount.

Then he carelessly asked for a receipt.

"You understand . . . in business . . . sometimes . . . And with the date, please don't forget the date."

A whole horizon of new possibilities now opened up before Emma. She was wise enough to set aside three thousand francs, with which the first three bills were paid when they fell due; but the fourth happened to arrive at the house on a Thursday, and a stunned Charles patiently awaited his wife's return for an explanation.

If she had not told him about this note, it was only to spare him such domestic worries; she sat on his lap, caressed him, cooed at him, gave a long enumeration of all the indispensable things that had been got on credit.

"Really, you must confess, considering the number of things, it isn't too expensive."

Charles, at his wit's end, soon had recourse to the eternal Lheureux, who promised to arrange everything if Charles would sign two more notes, one of which was for seven hundred francs and would be payable in three months. To take care of this he wrote his mother a pathetic letter. Instead of sending a reply she came herself; and when Emma wanted to know whether he had got anything out of her:

"Yes," he replied; "but she wants to see the account."

The next morning at daybreak Emma ran to Lheureux to beg him to make out another account for not more than a thousand francs: for to show the one for four thousand it would be necessary to say that she had paid two-thirds, and confess, consequently, the sale of the property, for the transaction had been well handled by the shopkeeper and only came to light later on.

Despite the low price of each article, Madame Bovary senior of course thought the expenditure extravagant.

"Couldn't you do without a carpet? Why did you re-cover the arm-chairs? In my time there was a single arm-chair in a house, for elderly persons,—at any rate it was so at my mother's, who was a respectable woman, I assure you.—Everybody can't be rich! No fortune can hold out against waste! I should be ashamed to pamper myself as you do! And yet I am old. I need looking after . . . and look at this! Look at this! alterations! frills and finery! What is that! silk for lining at two francs; . . . when you get jaconet for ten sous, or even for eight which does just as well!"

Emma lying on a lounge, replied as calmly as she could "Ah! Madame, enough! enough! . . ."

The other went on lecturing her, predicting they would end in the workhouse. But it was Bovary's fault. Luckily he had promised to destroy that power of attorney.

"What?"

"Ah! he swore he would," went on the good woman.

Emma opened the window, called Charles, and the poor fellow was obliged to confess the promise torn from him by his mother.

Emma disappeared, then came back quickly, and majestically handed her a large sheet of paper.

"Thank you," said the old woman. And she threw the power of attorney into the fire.

Emma began to laugh, a strident, piercing, continuous laugh; she had an attack of hysterics.

"Oh! my God!" cried Charles. "Ah! You are in the wrong too! You come here and make scenes with her! . . ."

His mother, shrugging her shoulders, declared it was "all put on."

But Charles, rebelling for the first time, took his wife's part, so that Madame Bovary senior said she would leave. She went the very next day, and on the threshold, as he was trying to detain her, she replied:

"No, no! You love her better than me, and you are right. It is natural. Take care of yourself! . . . for I'm not likely to be back again soon to 'make scenes' as you say."

Charles nevertheless was very crestfallen before Emma, who did not hide the resentment she still felt at his want of confidence, and it needed many prayers before she would consent to another power of attorney. He even accompanied her to Monsieur Guillaumin to have a second one, just like the other, drawn up.

"I know how it is," said the notary; "a man of science can't be worried with the practical details of life."

And Charles felt relieved by this comfortable reflection, which gave his weakness the flattering appearance of higher preoccupation.

How exalted she was the following Thursday at the hotel in their room with Léon! She laughed, cried, sang, sent for sherbets, wanted to smoke cigarettes, seemed to him wild and extravagant, but adorable, superb.

He did not know what combination of forces within her was driving her to throw herself so recklessly after the pleasures of life. She became irritable, greedy, voluptuous. She walked boldly through the streets with him, her head high, unconcerned, she said, about being compromised. At times, however, Emma shuddered at the sudden thought of meeting Rodolphe, for it seemed to her that, although they were separated forever, she was not completely free from the power he held over her.

One night she did not return to Yonville at all. Charles lost his head with anxiety, and little Berthe refusing to go to bed without her mamma, sobbed as though her heart would break. Justin had gone out searching the road at random. Monsieur Homais even had left his pharmacy.

At last, at eleven o'clock, able to bear it no longer, Charles harnessed his chaise, jumped in, whipped up his horse, and reached the Croix-Rouge about two o'clock in the morning. No one there! He thought that the clerk had perhaps seen her; but where did he live? Happily, Charles remembered his employer's address, and rushed off there.

Day was breaking, and he could make out some letters over the door; he knocked. Some one, without opening the door, shouted out the required information and added a generous number of insults concerning people who disturb others in the middle of the night.

The house inhabited by the clerk had neither bell, knocker, nor porter. Charles beat on the shutters with his fists. A policeman happened to pass by; he felt nervous and left.

"What a fool I am" he said. "M. Lormeaux must have asked her to stay to dinner."

The Lormeaux no longer lived in Rouen.

"She probably stayed to look after Madame Dubreuil. Oh, but Madame Dubreuil has been dead these ten months . . . Then where can she be?"

An idea occurred to him. At a café he asked for a Directory, and hurriedly looked for the name of Mademoiselle Lempereur, who turned out to live at No. 74 Rue de la Renelle-des-Maroquiniers.

As he was turning into the street, Emma herself appeared at the other end of it; he threw himself upon her rather than embraced her, crying:

"What kept you yesterday?"

"I was not well."

"What! . . . Where! . . . How! . . ."

She passed her hand over her forehead and answered,

"At Mme. Lempereur's."

"I was sure of it! I was just on my way there."

"Oh!" said Emma. "It's not worth while now. She just stepped out a minute ago; don't get so excited. I will never feel free, you understand, if the slightest delay is going to make you lose your head like this."

This was a sort of permission that she gave herself, so as to get perfect freedom in her escapades. And she took full and free advantage of it. Whenever she was seized with the desire to see Léon, she would set out upon any pretext whatever, and if he were not expecting her that day, she would go to fetch him at his office.

It was a great delight at first, but soon he no longer concealed the truth, which was, that his master complained very much about these interruptions.

"Oh, who cares!" she said, "come along."

And he slipped out.

She wanted him to dress all in black, and grow a pointed beard, to look like the portraits of Louis XIII.[58] She asked to see his rooms and found them lacking in taste. This embarrassed him but she paid no attention; she then advised him to buy curtains like hers, and when he objected to the expense:

"Ah! ah! you hold onto your pennies!" she said laughing.

Each time Léon had to tell her everything that he had done since their last meeting. She asked him for some verses—some verses "for herself," a "love poem" in honor of her. But he never succeeded in getting a rhyme for the second verse; and at last ended by copying a sonnet from a Keepsake.

He did this less from vanity, than simply out of a desire to please her. He never questioned her ideas; he accepted all her tastes; he was becoming her mistress rather than she his. She had tender words and kisses that thrilled his soul. Where could she have learnt this corruption so deep and well masked as to be almost unseizable?

VI

On his trips to see her, Léon often dined at the pharmacist's, and he felt obliged out of politeness to invite him in turn.

"With pleasure!" Monsieur Homais had replied; "besides, I must

58. Louis XIII (born 1601, king 1610–1643) was the father of Louis XIV.

recharge my mind a bit, for I am getting rusty here. We'll go to the theatre, to the restaurant. We'll do the town."

"Oh, my dear!" tenderly murmured Madame Homais, alarmed at the vague perils he was preparing to brave.

"Well, what? Do you think I'm not sufficiently ruining my health living here amid the continual emanations of the pharmacy? But there! That's just like a woman! They are jealous of science, and then are opposed to our taking the most legitimate distractions. No matter! Count upon me. One of these days I shall turn up at Rouen, and we'll paint the town together."

The pharmacist would formerly have taken good care not to use such an expression, but he was cultivating a flippant Parisian manner which he thought very stylish; and, like his neighbor, Madame Bovary, he questioned the clerk avidly about life in the capital; he even used slang in order to impress . . . the "bourgeois", saying "flip", "cool", "sweet", "neat-o", and "I must break it up", for "I must leave."

So one Thursday Emma was surprised to meet Monsieur Homais in the kitchen of the "Lion d'Or," wearing a traveller's costume, that is to say, wrapped in an old cloak which no one knew he had, while he carried a valise in one hand and the foot-warmer of his establishment in the other. He had confided his intentions to no one, for fear of causing the public anxiety by his absence.

The prospect of seeing again the scenes of his youth no doubt excited him for he never stopped talking during the whole trip; the coach had barely stopped when he leaped out in search of Léon; and in vain the clerk struggled to free himself. M. Homais dragged him off to the flashy Cafe de la Normandie, where he entered majestically, without taking off his hat, for he thought it highly provincial to uncover in any public place.

Emma waited for Léon three quarters of an hour. At last she ran to his office, and, lost in all sorts of conjectures, accusing him of indifference, and reproaching herself for her weakness, she spent the afternoon, her face pressed against the window-panes.

At two o'clock they were still at table opposite each other. The large room was emptying; the stove-pipe, in the shape of a palm-tree, spread its gilt leaves over the white ceiling; and near them, just outside the window, in the full sun, a little fountain gurgled into a white basin, where, among the watercress and asparagus, sluggish lobsters stretched out their claws towards a heap of quail lying on their sides.

Homais relished it all. He was more intoxicated by the luxury than by the fine food and drink, but nevertheless, the Pommard wine began to go to his head, and by the time the "omelette au rhum" appeared, he began expounding scandalous theories on women. What attracted him above all else, was "chic." He adored an elegant outfit and hairdo in a well-furnished apartment, and when it came to their physical proportions, he didn't mind them on the plump side.

Léon watched the clock in despair. The pharmacist went on drinking, eating, and talking.

"You must be completely deprived here in Rouen," he said suddenly. "But then the object of your affections doesn't live far away."

And, when the other blushed:

"Come now, be frank. Can you deny that at Yonville . . ."

The young man began to stammer.

"At Madame Bovary's, can you deny that you were courting . . ."

"Whom do you mean?"

"The maid!"

He was not joking; but vanity getting the better of his judgement, Léon protested indignantly in spite of himself. Besides, he only liked dark women.

"I approve of your taste," said the pharmacist; "they have more temperament."

And whispering into his friend's ear, he pointed out the symptoms by which one could detect temperament in a woman. He even launched into an ethnographic digression: the German was romantic, the French woman licentious, the Italian passionate.

"And negresses?" asked the clerk.

"They are for artistic tastes!" said Homais. "Waiter! Two demitasses!"

"Shall we go?" asked Léon, at last reaching the end of his patience.

"Yes" said Homais in English.

But before leaving he wanted to see the proprietor of the establishment and made him a few compliments. Then the young man, to be alone, alleged he had some business engagement.

"Ah! I will escort you," said Homais.

And all the while he was walking through the streets with him he talked of his wife, his children, of their future, and of his business; told him in what a dilapidated condition he had found it, and to what a state of perfection he had now raised it.

When they arrived in front of the Hôtel de Boulogne, Léon left him abruptly, ran up the stairs, and found his mistress almost hysterical.

On hearing the name of the pharmacist, she flew into a passion. Nevertheless, he kept overwhelming her with good reasons; it wasn't his fault; didn't she know Homais? Could she believe that he would prefer his company? But she turned away; he held her back, and falling on his knees, he encircled her waist with his arm, in a pose at once langorous, passionate, and imploring.

She stood there looking at him, her large flashing eyes were serious, almost terrible. Then her tears clouded them over, her pink eyelids lowered, and she gave him her hands. Léon was just pressing them to his lips when a servant appeared to say that someone wanted to see the gentleman.

"You will come back?" she said.

"Yes."

"But when?"

"Immediately."

"It's a trick," said the pharmacist, when he saw Léon. "I wanted to interrupt this visit, that seemed to me to annoy you. Let's go and have a glass of *garus*[59] at Bridoux'."

Léon swore that he must get back to his office. Then the pharmacist began making jokes about legal papers and procedure.

"Forget about Cujas[60] and Barthole[61] a bit, what the Devil! Who's going to stop you? Be a man! Let's go to Bridoux'. You'll see his dog. It's very interesting."

And as the clerk still insisted:

"I'll go with you. I'll read a paper while I wait for you, or thumb through a code."

Léon, bewildered by Emma's anger, Monsieur Homais' chatter, and perhaps, by the heaviness of the luncheon, was undecided, and, as though he were under the spell of the pharmacist who kept repeating:

"Let's go to Bridoux'. It's just by here, in the Rue Malpalu."

Then, out of cowardice, out of stupidity, out of that undefinable necessity that leads us towards those actions we are most set against, he allowed himself to be led off to Bridoux'; they found him in his small courtyard overseeing three workmen who panted as they turned the huge wheel of a selza water machine. Homais gave them some advice; he embraced Bridoux; they drank some garus. Twenty times Léon tried to escape, but the other seized him by the arm saying:

"Wait a minute! I'm coming! We'll go to the Fanal de Rouen' to see the fellows there. I'll introduce you to Thomassin."

He finally got rid of him, however, and flew to the hotel. Emma was gone.

She had just left in exasperation. She detested him now. His failure to come as he had promised she took as an insult, and she looked for other reasons for separating from him: he was incapable

59. A liqueur named after its inventor, Garus.

60. Jacques Cugar (1522–1590) was a famous jurist who interpreted Roman Law in contemporary terms.

61. Barthole, or Bartole, was an early Italian jurist (1313–1357) in Bologna.

of heroism, weak, banal, more spiritless than a woman, avaricious, and timorous as well.

Later when she was calmer, she realized that she had doubtless been unjust to him. But the picking apart of those we love always alienates us from them. One must not touch one's idols, a little of the gilt always comes off on one's fingers.

They gradually began to talk more frequently of matters outside their love, and in the letters that Emma wrote him she spoke of flowers, poetry, the moon and the stars, naïve resources of a waning passion striving to keep itself alive by all external aids. She was constantly promising herself a profound happiness on her next trip; then she confessed to herself that she had felt nothing extraordinary. This disappointment quickly gave way to a new hope, and Emma returned to him more avid and inflamed than before. She undressed brutally, ripping off the thin laces of her corset so violently that they would whistle round her hips like a gliding snake. She went on tiptoe, barefooted, to see once more that the door was locked, then with one movement, she would let her clothes fall at once to the ground;—then, pale and serious, without a word, she would throw herself against his breast with a long shudder.

Yet there was upon that brow covered with cold drops, on those stammering lips, in those wild eyes, in the grip of those arms, something strange, vague and sinister that seemed to Léon to be subtly gliding between them to force them apart.

He did not dare to question her; but finding how experienced she was, he told himself that she must have passed through all the extremes of both pleasure and pain. What had once charmed now frightened him a little. Furthermore, he revolted against the daily increased absorption of his personality into hers. He resented her, because of this constant victory. He even strove not to love her; then, when he heard the creaking of her boots, he felt his courage desert him, like drunkards at the sight of strong liquor.

It is true, she showered him with every sort of attention, from exotic foods, to little coquettish refinements in her dress and languishing glances. She used to bring roses from Yonville hidden in her bosom which she would toss up into his face; she was worried about his health, advised him how he should behave; and in order to bind him closer to her, hoping perhaps that heaven would take her part, she hung a medal of the Virgin round his neck. She inquired like a virtuous mother about his companions. She said to him:

"Don't see them; don't go out; only think of us; love me!"

She would have liked to be able to watch over his life, and the idea occurred to her of having him followed in the streets. Near the hotel there was always a kind of vagabond who accosted travellers, and who would surely not refuse . . . But her pride revolted at this.

"Ah! So what! What does it matter if he betrays me! What do I care?"

One day, when they had parted early and she was returning alone along the boulevard, she saw the walls of her convent; she sat down on a bench in the shade of the elms. How calm her life had been in those days! How she envied her first undefinable sentiments of love which she had tried to construct from the books she read.

The first months of her marriage, her rides in the forest, the viscount who had waltzed with her, and Lagardy singing, all repassed before her eyes . . . And Léon suddenly appeared to her as far off as the others.

"I do love him!" she said to herself.

No matter! She was not happy, she never had been. Why was her life so unsatisfactory, why did everything she leaned on instantly rot and give way? . . . But suppose there existed somewhere some one strong and beautiful, a man of valor, passionate yet refined, the heart of a poet in the form of an angel, a bronze stringed lyre, playing elegiac epithalamia to the heavens, why might she not someday happen on him? What a vain thought! Besides, nothing was worth the trouble of seeking it; everything was a lie. Every smile concealed a yawn of boredom, every joy a curse, every pleasure its own disgust, and the sweetest kisses left upon your lips only the unattainable desire for a greater delight.

A coarse metallic rattle sounded around her, and the convent bell struck four. And it seemed to her that she had been sitting on that bench since the beginning of time. But an infinity of time can be compressed into a minute like a crowd of people into a small space.

Emma lived all absorbed in her passions and worried no more about money matters than an archduchess.

There came a day, however, when a seedy looking man with a red face and a bald head came to her house, saying he had been sent by Monsieur Vinçart of Rouen. He took out the pins that held together the side-pockets of his long green overcoat, stuck them into his sleeve, and politely handed her a paper.

It was a bill for seven hundred francs, signed by her, and which Lheureux, in spite of all his promises had endorsed to Vinçart.

She sent her servant for him. He could not come.

Then the stranger who had remained standing, casting around him to the right and left curious glances which were hidden behind his blond eyebrows, asked with an innocent air:

"What answer am I to take Vinçart?"

"Well!" said Emma, "tell him . . . that I haven't got it . . . I'll pay him next week . . . He must wait . . . yes, next week."

And the fellow went without another word.

But the next day at twelve o'clock she received a summons, and the sight of the stamped paper, on which appeared several times in large letters, "Maître Hereng, bailiff at Buchy," so frightened her that she rushed in all haste to Lheureux. She found him in his shop, tying up a parcel.

"At your service," he said. "What can I do for you?"

But Lheureux continued what he was doing, aided by a young girl of about thirteen, somewhat hunchbacked, who was both his clerk and his servant.

Then, his sabots clattering on the wooden planks of the shop, he mounted in front of Madame Bovary to the second floor and showed her into a narrow closet, where, in a large pine wood desk, lay some ledgers, protected by an iron bar laid horizontally across them and padlocked down. Against the wall, under some remnants of calico, one caught sight of a safe, but of such dimensions that it must contain something besides promisory notes and cash. Monsieur Lheureux, in fact, went in for pawnbroking, and it was there that he had put Madame Bovary's gold chain, together with the earrings of poor old Tellier, who had been forced, at last, to sell his café, and had bought a small grocery store in Quincampoix, where he was dying of catarrh amongst his candles, that were less yellow than his face.

Lheureux sat down in a large cane arm-chair, saying:

"What's new?"

"Look here!"

"Well, what do you want me to do about it?"

Then she lost her temper, reminding him that he had promised not to endorse her notes away. He admitted it.

"But I was pressed myself; they were holding a knife against my throat too."

"And what will happen now?" she went on.

"Oh, it's very simple; a judgment and then a seizure . . . that's about it!"

Emma kept down a desire to strike him, and asked gently if there was no way of quieting Monsieur Vinçart.

"Oh, sure! appease Vinçart, indeed! You don't know him; he's fiercer than an Arab!"

Nevertheless, Monsieur Lheureux had to help her.

"All right then, listen, it seems to me that I've been pretty good to you so far."

And opening one of his ledgers:

"Look!" he said.

Then moving his finger up the page:

"Let's see . . . let's see . . . ! August 3d, two hundred francs . . . June 17th, a hundred and fifty . . . March 23d, forty-six . . . In April . . ."

He stopped, as if afraid of making some mistake.

"I won't even mention the bills signed by Monsieur Bovary, one for seven hundred francs, and another for three hundred. As to the little payments on your account and the interest, I'd never get to the end of the list, I can't figure that high. I'll have nothing more to do with it."

She wept; she even called him "her good Monsieur Lheureux." But he always fell back upon "that rascal Vinçart." Besides, he hadn't a penny, no one was paying him these days, they were eating his coat off his back, a poor shopkeeper like himself couldn't advance money.

Emma was silent, and Monsieur Lheureux, who was biting the feathers of a quill, no doubt became uneasy at her silence, for he went on:

"Perhaps, if something were paid on this, one of these days . . . I might . . ."

"Well," she said, "as soon as the balance on the Barneville property . . ."

"What? . . ."

And on hearing that Langlois had not yet paid he seemed much surprised. Then in a honied voice:

"Then we'll agree, what do you say to . . . ?"

"Oh! Whatever you say!"

On this he closed his eyes to reflect, wrote down a few figures, and saying that this was really going to hurt him, it was a risky affair, that he was "bleeding" himself for her, he wrote out four bills for two hundred and fifty francs each, to fall due month by month.

"Provided that Vinçart will listen to me! However, it's settled. I don't back down on my word. I'm as square as a brick."

Next he carelessly showed her several new goods; not one of which, however, was in his opinion worthy of madame.

"When I think that there's a dress that costs seven cents a yard and guaranteed color-fast! And they actually swallow it all down! Of course you understand one doesn't tell them what it really is!" He hoped by this confession of chicanery towards others to convince her of his honesty with her.

Then he called her back to show her three yards of guipure that he had lately picked up "at a sale."

"Isn't it lovely?" said Lheureux. "It is very much used now for the backs of arm-chairs. It's quite the rage."

And, quicker than a juggler, he wrapped up the guipure in some blue paper and put it in Emma's hands.

"But at least let me know . . ."

"Yes, some other time," he replied, turning on his heel.

That same evening she urged Bovary to write to his mother, to ask her to send at once the whole of the balance due from the father's estate. The mother-in-law replied that she had nothing more: that the liquidation was complete, and, aside from Barneville, there remained for them an income of six hundred francs, that she would pay them punctually.

Madame Bovary then sent bills to two or three patients, and was soon making great use of this method which turned out to be very successful. She was always careful to add a postscript: "Do not mention this to my husband; you know how proud he is . . . forgive my having to . . . your humble servant. . . ." There were a few complaints; she intercepted them.

To get money she began selling her old gloves, her old hats, all sorts of old odds and ends, and she bargained rapaciously, her peasant blood standing her in good stead. Then on her trips to town she searched the second hand stores for nick-nacks which she was sure, if no one else, Monsieur Lheureux would certainly take off her hands. She bought ostrich feathers, Chinese porcelain, and trunks; she borrowed from Félicité, from Madame Lefrançois, from the landlady at the "Croix Rouge," from everybody, no matter where. With the money she at last received from Barneville she paid two bills; the other fifteen hundred francs fell due. She renewed the notes, and then renewed them again!

Sometimes, it is true, she tried to add up her accounts, but the results were always so staggering, she couldn't believe they were possible. Then she would begin over again, soon get confused, leave everything where it was and forget about it.

The house was a dreary place now! Tradesmen were seen leaving it with angry faces. Handkerchiefs hung drying on the stoves, and little Berthe, to the great scandal of Madame Homais, wore stockings with holes in them. If Charles timidly ventured a remark, she would snap back at him savagely that it certainly wasn't her fault!

What was the meaning of all these fits of temper? He explained everything by her old nervous illness, and reproaching himself with having taken her infirmities for faults, accused himself of egotism, and longed to go and take her in his arms.

"Ah, no!" he said to himself; "I would only annoy her."

And he stayed where he was.

After dinner he would walk about alone in the garden; he took little Berthe on his lap and unfolding his medical journal, tried to teach her to read. But the child, who had never had any schooling at all, would soon open wide her large eyes in bewilderment and begin to cry. Then he would comfort her; he fetched water in her watering can to make rivers on the sand path, or broke off branches from the privet hedges to plant trees in the flower beds. This did not spoil the garden much, which was now overgrown with long weeds. They owed Lestiboudois for so many day's wages. Then the child would grow cold and ask for her mother.

"Go call your nurse," said Charles. "You know, my darling, that mama does not like to be disturbed!"

Autumn was setting in, and the leaves were already falling—as they had two years ago when she was ill!—Where would it all end! . . . And he would continue to pace up and down, his hands behind his back.

Madame was in her room. No one was allowed to enter. There she stayed from morning to night, listless and hardly dressed, from time to time lighting a tablet of Turkish incense she had bought at the shop of an Algerian in Rouen. In order to get rid of this sleeping man stretched out beside her at night, she finally managed by continual badgering to relegate him to a room on the third floor; then she would read until morning, lurid novels where there would be scenes of orgies, violence and bloodshed. Often she would be seized by a sudden terror and cry out. Charles would come running.

"Oh! Leave me alone!" she would say.

Or at other times, when she was burnt more fiercely by that inner flame which her adultery kept feeding, panting and overcome with desire, she would throw open the window breathing in the chill air and letting the wind blow back her hair which hung too heavy on her neck, and, looking up at the stars, she would long for the love of a prince. She thought of him, of Léon. She would then have given anything for a single one of those meetings which would appease her.

These were her gala days. She was determined that they should be magnificent! When he could not pay all the expenses himself, she made up the deficit liberally, which happened pretty well every time. He tried to convince her that they would be just as well off somewhere else, in a more modest hotel, but she always found some objection.

One day she drew six small silver-gilt spoons from her bag (they were old Rouault's wedding present), begging him to pawn them at once for her; Léon obeyed, although the errand annoyed him. He was afraid of compromising himself.

Then, on reflection, he began to think that his mistress was beginning to behave rather strangely, and perhaps they were not wrong in wishing to separate him from her.

In fact, some one had sent his mother a long anonymous letter to warn her that he was "ruining himself with a married woman"; and immediately the good woman had visions of the eternal bug-a-boo of every family, that is to say, that vague and terrible creature, the siren, the fantastic monster which makes its home in the treacherous depths of love. She wrote to Maître Dubocage, his employer, who behaved perfectly in the affair. He kept him for three quarters of an hour trying to open his eyes, to warn him of the abyss into which he was falling. Such an intrigue would damage him later on in his career. He implored him to break with her, and, if he would not make this sacrifice in his own interest, to do it at least for his, Dubocage's sake.

Léon finally swore he would not see Emma again; and he reproached himself with not having kept his word, considering all the trouble and reproaches she was likely to bring down on him, not counting the jokes made by his fellow clerks as they sat around the stove in the morning. Besides, he was soon to be head clerk; it was time to settle down. So he gave up his flute, his exalted sentiments, his poetic imagination; for every bourgeois in the flush of his youth, were it but for a day, a moment, has believed himself capable of immense passions, of lofty enterprises. The most mediocre libertine has dreamed of sultanas; every notary bears within him the débris of a poet.

He was bored now when Emma suddenly began to sob on his breast; and his heart, like the people who can only stand a certain amount of music, became drowsy through indifference to the vibrations of a love whose subtleties he could no longer distinguish.

They knew one another too well to experience any of those sudden surprises which multiply the enjoyment of a possession a hundredfold. She was as sick of him as he was weary of her. Emma found again in adultery all the platitudes of marriage.

But how to get rid of him? Then, though she felt humiliated by the sordidity of such a happiness, she clung to it out of habit, or out of degeneration; she pursued it more desperately than ever, destroying every pleasure by always wishing for it to be too great. She blamed Léon for her disappointed hopes, as if he had betrayed her; and she even longed for some catastrophe that would bring about their separation, since she had not the courage to do it herself.

She none the less went on writing him love letters, in keeping with the notion that a woman must write to her lover.

But while writing to him, it was another man she saw, a phantom fashioned out of her most ardent memories, of her favorite books, her strongest desires, and at last he became so real, so tangible, that her heart beat wildly in awe and admiration, though unable to see him distinctly, for, like a god, he was hidden beneath the abundance of his attributes. He dwelt in that azure land where silken ladders swung from balconies in the moonlight, beneath a flower-scented breeze. She felt him near her; he was coming and would ravish her entire being in a kiss. Then she would fall back to earth again shattered; for these vague ecstasies of imaginary love, would exhaust her more than the wildest orgies.

She now felt a constant pain throughout her body. Often she even received summonses, stamped paper that she barely looked at. She would have liked not to be alive, or to be always asleep.

On the day of Mid-Lent she did not return to Yonville; that evening she went to a masked ball. She wore velvet breeches, red stockings, a peruke, and a three-cornered hat cocked over one ear. She danced all night to the wild sounds of the trombones; people gathered around her, and in the morning she found herself on the steps of the theatre together with five or six other masked dancers, dressed as stevadores or sailors, friends of Léon's who were talking about going out to find some supper.

The neighboring cafés were full. They found a dreadful looking restaurant at the harbor, where the proprietor showed them to a little room on the fifth floor.

The men were whispering in a corner, no doubt consulting about expenses. There were a clerk, two medical students, and a shop assistant: what company for her! As to the women, Emma soon perceived from the tone of their voices that most of them probably came from the lowest class. This frightened her, she drew back her chair and lowered her eyes.

The others began to eat; she ate nothing. Her head was on fire, her eyes smarted, and her skin was ice-cold. In her head she seemed to feel the floor of the ball-room rebounding again beneath the rhythmical pulsation of thousands of dancing feet. The smell of punch and cigar smoke made her dizzy. She fainted; they carried her to the window.

Day was breaking, and a large purple stain was spreading across the pale sky in the direction of the St. Catherine hills. The ashen river was shivering in the wind; there was no one on the bridges; the street lamps were going out.

She came to herself, however, and began to think of Berthe asleep at home in the maid's room. But just then a cart loaded with long strips of iron passed by, and made a deafening metallic vibration against the walls of the house.

She abruptly slipped out of the room; removed her costume; told Léon she had to return; and found herself alone at last in the Hôtel de Boulogne. Everything, herself included, was now unbearable to her. She would have liked to take wing like a bird, and fly off far away to become young again in the realms of immaculate purity.

She left the hotel, crossed the Boulevard, the Place Cauchoise, and the Faubourg, as far as an open street that overlooked the park. She walked rapidly, the fresh air calmed her; and, little by little, the faces of the crowd, the masks, the quadrilles, the lights, the supper, those women, all, disappeared like rising mists. Then, reaching the "Croix-Rouge," she threw herself on the bed in her little room on the second floor, where there were pictures of the "Tour de Nesle." At four o'clock Hivert awoke her.

When she got home, Félicité showed her a grey paper stuck behind the clock. She read:

"In virtue of the seizure in execution of a judgment."

What judgment . . . ? As a matter of fact, the evening before another paper had been brought that she had not yet seen, and she was stunned by these words:

"By power of the king, the law, and the courts, Mme. Bovary is hereby ordered . . ."

Then, skipping several lines, she read:

"Within twenty-four hours, at the latest . . ." But what? "To pay the sum of eight thousand francs." There was even written at the bottom of the page, "She will be constrained thereto by every form of law, and notably by a writ of distraint on her furniture and effects."

What should she do? . . . In twenty-four hours; tomorrow! Lheureux, she thought, probably wanted to frighten her again, for, all at once, she saw through his manoeuvres, the reason for his favors. The only thing that reassured her was the extraordinary amount of the figure.

Nevertheless, as a result of buying and not paying, of borrowing, signing notes, and renewing these notes which grew ever larger each time they fell due, she had ended by preparing a capital for Monsieur Lheureux which he was impatiently waiting to collect to use in his own financial speculations.

She went over to his place, assuming an air of indifference.

"Do you know what has happened to me? It's a joke, I'm sure!"

"No."

"What do you mean?"

He slowly turned around, and, folding his arms, said to her:

"Did you think, my dear lady, that I was going to go on to the end of time providing you with merchandise and cash, just for the love of God? I certainly have to get back what I laid out, let's be fair."

She objected to the amount of the debt.

"Ah! Too bad! The court has recognised it! There's a judgment. You've been notified. Besides, it isn't my fault. It's Vinçart's."

"But couldn't you . . . ?"

"No! Not a single thing!"

"But . . . Still . . . let's talk it over."

And she began beating about the bush; she had known nothing about it . . . it was a surprise . . .

"Whose fault is that?" said Lheureux, bowing ironically. "While I'm slaving like a nigger, you go gallivanting about."

"Ah! Don't preach to me!"

"It never does any harm," he replied.

She turned coward; she implored him; she even pressed her pretty white and slender hand against the shopkeeper's knee.

"There, that'll do! Any one'd think you wanted to seduce me!"

"You are a wretch!" she cried.

"Oh, oh! What a fuss you are making!"

"I will show you up. I'll tell my husband . . ."

"All right! I too, I'll show your husband something!"

And Lheureux drew from his strong box the receipt for eighteen hundred francs that she had given him when Vinçart had discounted the bills.

"Do you think," he added, "that he won't catch on to your little theft, the poor dear man?"

She collapsed, more overcome than if felled by the blow of a club. He was walking up and down from the window to the bureau, repeating all the while:

"I'll show him all right . . . I'll show him all right . . . "

Then he approached her, and said in a soft voice:

"It's no fun, I know; but after all it hasn't killed anyone, and, since that is the only way that is left for you paying back my money . . ."

"But where am I to get any?" said Emma, wringing her hands.

"Bah! when one has friends like you!"

And he looked at her with such a knowing and terrible stare, that she shuddered to the very core of her heart.

"I promise you," she said, "I'll sign . . ."

"I've enough of your signatures!"

"I will sell something else . . ."

"Oh come!" he said, shrugging his shoulders. "You've nothing left to sell."

And he called through the peep-hole that looked down into the shop:

"Annette, don't forget the three coupons of No. 14."

The servant appeared; Emma caught the hint and asked how much money would be needed to put a stop to the proceedings.

"It is too late."

"But if I were to bring you several thousand francs, a quarter of the sum, a third, almost all?"

"No; it's no use!"

And he pushed her gently towards the staircase.

"I implore you, Monsieur Lheureux, just a few days more!"

She was sobbing.

"Ah that's good! let's have some tears!"

"You'll drive me to do something desperate!"

"Don't make me laugh!" said he, shutting the door.

VII

She was stoical the next day when Maître Hareng, the bailiff, with two assistants arrived at her house to draw up inventory for the seizure.

They began with Bovary's consulting-room, and did not write down the phrenological head, which was considered an "instrument of his profession"; but in the kitchen they counted the plates, the saucepans, the chairs, the candlesticks, and in the bedroom all the nick-nacks on the wall-shelf. They examined her dresses, the linen, the dressing-room; and her whole existence, to its most intimate details, was stretched out like a cadavre in an autopsy before the eyes of these three men.

Maître Hareng, buttoned up in his thin black coat, wearing a white choker and very tight foot-straps, repeated from time to time:

"Allow me madame? Allow me?"

Often he uttered exclamations:

"Charming! very pretty."

Then he began writing again, dipping his pen into the horn inkstand he carried in his left hand.

When they had done with the rooms they went up to the attic.

She kept a desk there in which Rodolphe's letters were locked. It had to be opened.

"Ah! a correspondence!" said Maître Hareng, with a discreet smile. "But allow me! for I must make sure the box contains nothing else." And he tipped up the papers lightly, as if to let the napoleons fall out. This made her furious to see this coarse hand, with red moist fingers like slugs, touching these pages against which her heart had beaten.

They went at last! Félicité came back. Emma had sent her out to watch for Bovary in order to keep him away, and they hastily installed the man set to guard the seizure, in the attic, where he swore he would not stir.

During the evening Charles seemed to her careworn. Emma watched him with a look of anguish, fancying she saw an accusation in every line of his face. Then, when her eyes wandered over the chimney-piece ornamented with Chinese screens, over the large curtains, the arm-chairs, all those things that had softened the bitterness of her life, remorse seized her, or rather an immense regret, that, far from destroying her passion, rather irritated it. Charles placidly poked the fire, both his feet on the andirons.

Once the man, no doubt bored in his hiding-place, made a slight noise.

"Is any one walking upstairs?" said Charles.

"No," she replied; "it is a window that has been left open, and is banging in the wind."

The next day which was Sunday, she went to Rouen to call on all the brokers whose names she knew. They were either in the country, or away on a trip. She was not discouraged; and those whom she did manage to see she asked for money, insisting that she absolutely had to have it, that she would pay it back. Some laughed in her face; all refused.

At two o'clock she ran to Léon's apartment, and knocked at the door. No one answered. At length he appeared.

"What brings you here?"

"Am I disturbing you?"

"No . . . but . . ." And he admitted that his landlord didn't like his having "women" there.

"I must speak to you," she went on.

Then he took down the key, but she stopped him.

"No, no! Over there, in our home!"

And they went to their room at the Hôtel de Boulogne.

On arriving she drank off a large glass of water. She was very pale. She said to him:

"Léon, I have a favor to ask you."

And, shaking him by both hands which she held tightly in hers, she added:

"Listen, I must have eight thousand francs."

"But you are mad!"

"Not yet."

And thereupon, telling him the story of the seizure, she explained her distress to him; for Charles knew nothing of it; her mother-in-law detested her; old Rouault could do nothing; but he, Léon, he would set about finding this indispensable sum . . .

"But what do you want me . . . ?"

"What a coward you are!" she cried.

Then he said stupidly, "You're making things out to be worse than they are. Your fellow there could probably be quieted with three thousand francs."

All the more reason to try and do something; it was inconceivable that they couldn't find three thousand francs. Besides, Léon could sign the notes instead of her.

"Go! try! you must! run! . . . Oh! Try! try! I will love you so!"

He went out, and came back at the end of an hour, saying, with a solemn face:

"I have been to three people . . . with no success!"

Then they sat there facing each other on either side of the

fireplace, motionless, without speaking. Emma shrugged her shoulders as she tapped her foot impatiently. He heard her murmur:

"If I were in your place I'd certainly find some!"

"Where?"

"At your office."

And she looked at him.

A diabolical determination showed in her burning eyes which were half closed in a lascivious and encouraging manner;—so that the young man felt himself growing weak beneath the mute will of this woman who was urging him to commit a crime. Then he was afraid, and to avoid any explanation he smote his forehead crying:

"Morel is coming back tonight! He will not refuse me, I hope" (this was one of his friends, the son of a very rich merchant); "and I will bring it you to-morrow," he added.

Emma did not seem to welcome this new hope with all the joy he had expected. Did she suspect the lie? He went on, blushing:

"However, if you don't see me by three o'clock, do not wait for me, my darling. I must leave now, forgive me. Good-bye!"

He pressed her hand, but it felt quite lifeless. Emma had no strength left for any sentiment whatever.

Four o'clock struck; and she rose to return to Yonville, mechanically obeying the force of old habits.

The weather was beautiful; it was one of those March days, clear and sharp, when the sun shines in a perfectly white sky. The people of Rouen, dressed in their Sunday-clothes, seemed happy as they strolled by. She reached the Place du Parvis. People were coming out of the cathedral after vespers; the crowd flowed out through the three portals like a river through the three arches of a bridge, and in the middle, more immobile than a rock, stood the verger.

Then she remembered the day when, eager and full of hope, she had entered beneath this large nave, that had opened out before her, less profound than her love; and she walked on weeping beneath her veil, dazed, staggering, almost fainting.

"Look out!" cried a voice issuing from behind a carriage gate which was swinging open.

She stopped to let pass a black horse, prancing between the shafts of a tilbury, driven by a gentleman dressed in sables. Who was it? She knew him . . . The carriage sprang forward and disappeared.

Why, it was he, the Viscount! She turned away; the street was empty. She was so crushed, so sad, that she had to lean against a wall to keep herself from falling.

Then she thought she had been mistaken.

How could she tell? Everything, within herself and without, was abandoning her. She felt that she was lost, that she was wandering about at random within undefinable abysses, and she was almost happy, on reaching the "Croix Rouge," to see the good Homais, who was watching a large box full of pharmaceutical stores being hoisted on to the "Hirondelle"; holding in his hand a silk handkerchief containing six "cheminots" for his wife.

Madame Homais was very fond of these small, heavy rolls shaped like turbans which are eaten during Lent with salt butter: a last relic of Gothic fare, going back, perhaps, to the Crusades, and with which the hardy Normans would stuff themselves in times gone-by, thinking that they saw, illuminated in the golden light of the torches, between the tankards of Hippocras[62] and the gigantic slabs of meat, the heads of Saracens to be devoured. The druggist's wife crunched them up as they had done, heroically, in spite of her wretched teeth; so whenever Homais made a trip to town, he never failed to bring her home some which he bought at the great baker's in the Rue Massacre.

"Charmed to see you," he said, offering Emma a hand to help her into the "Hirondelle."

Then he tied his "cheminots" to the baggage net and remained with his head bare and his arms folded in an attitude pensive and Napoleonic.

But when the blind man appeared as usual at the foot of the hill he exclaimed indignantly:

"I can't understand why the authorities continue to tolerate such criminal occupations! These unfortunate people should be locked up, forced to do some work. I give you my word, Progress marches at a snail's pace! We are paddling about in a state of total barbarism!"

The blind man held out his hat which flapped about in the window as though it were a pocket in the upholstery which had come loose.

"This," said the pharmacist, "is a scrofulous disease."

And though he knew the poor devil, he pretended to see him for the first time, muttering such words as "cornea," "opaque cornea," "sclerotic," "facies," then asked him in a paternal tone:

"My friend, have you suffered long from this dreadful affliction? Instead of getting drunk in the café you would do better to follow a diet."

He advised him to drink good wine, good beer and to eat good roasts of meat. The blind man went on with his song. He actually seemed almost insane. At last Monsieur Homais opened his purse.

"Now there's a sou; give me back two liards: don't forget what I told you, you'll find it does you good."

Hivert openly cast some doubt on its efficacy. But the druggist said that he would cure the man himself with an antiphlogistic salve of his own composition, and he gave his address: "Monsieur

62. Hippocras (Hippocrates, the Greek physician) was an aromatic, highly spiced wine of medieval Europe.

Homais, near the market, everyone knows me."

"All right!" said Hivert, "in payment, you can 'put on your act' for us."

The blind man squatted down on his haunches with his head thrown back, and rolling his greenish eyes and sticking out his tongue, he rubbed his stomach with both hands while uttering a sort of low howl like a famished dog. Emma, overcome with disgust, threw him a five franc piece over her shoulder. It was all her fortune. It seemed like a grand thing to her to throw it away like this.

The coach had already started again when Monsieur Homais suddenly leaned out of the window and shouted:

"No farinacious foods or dairy products, wear woolen clothing next to the skin, and expose the diseased areas to the smoke of juniper berries."

The sight of the familiar things that passed before her eyes gradually diverted Emma from her present suffering. An intolerable fatigue overwhelmed her, and she reached home stupefied, discouraged, almost asleep.

"Let come what may!" she told herself.

Besides, anything could happen. Couldn't some extraordinary event occur at any moment? Lheureux might even die.

At nine o'clock in the morning she was awakened by the sound of voices in the square. A crowd around the market was reading a large bill fixed to one of the posts, and she saw Justin climb on a milepost and tear down the bill. The local policeman had just seized him by the collar. Monsieur Homais came out of his shop, and Mère Lefrançois, in the midst of the crowd, was talking the loudest of all.

"Madame! madame!" cried Félicité, running in, "it's an outrage!"

And the poor girl, all in tears, handed her a yellow paper that she had just torn off the door. Emma read with a glance that her furniture was for sale.

Then they looked at one another in silence. Servant and master had no secrets from each other. At last Félicité whispered:

"If I were you, madame, I'd go see Monsieur Guillaumin."

"You think so?"

The question meant:

"You who know all about the house from the butler, has the master sometimes spoken of me?"

"Yes, you'd do well to go there."

She dressed, put on her black gown, and her cape with jet beads, and that she might not be seen (there was still a crowd on the Square), she took the path by the river, outside the village.

She was out of breath when she reached the notary's gate. The sky was sombre, and a little snow was falling.

At the sound of the bell, Theodore in a red waistcoat appeared on the steps; he came to open the door with a casual air, as if she were an old acquaintance, and showed her into the dining-room.

A large porcelain stove crackled beneath a cactus that filled up the niche in the wall, and in black wood frames against the oak-stained paper hung Steuben's[63] "Esmeralda" and Schopin's "Put-iphar."[64] The ready-laid table, the two silver chafing-dishes, the crystal door-knobs, the parquet and the furniture, all shone with a scrupulous, English cleanliness; the windows were ornamented at each corner with stained glass.

"Now this," thought Emma, "is the kind of dining-room I ought to have."

The notary came in. With his left hand, he pressed his palm-embroidered dressing gown against his body, while with his other hand he quickly took off and replaced his brown velvet skullcap, which he wore jauntily cocked to the right. After circling around his bald cranium, the end of three strains of blond hair stuck out from underneath the cap.

After he had offered her a seat he sat down to breakfast, apologising profusely for his rudeness.

"I have come," she said, "to beg you, sir . . ."

"What, madame? I am listening."

And she began telling him about her situation.

Monsieur Guillaumin knew all about it. He was working in secret partnership with the shopkeeper, who always provided him with the capital for the mortgage loans he was asked to arrange.

So he knew (and better than she herself) the long story of these notes, small at first, bearing the names of several endorsers, made out for long terms and constantly renewed up to the day when, gathering together all the protested notes, the shopkeeper had asked his friend Vinçart to take in his own name all the necessary legal steps to collect the money, not wishing to appear as a shark in the eyes of his fellow-citizens.

She mingled her story with recriminations against Lheureux, to which the notary from time to time gave meaningless replies. Eating his cutlet and drinking his tea, he buried his chin in his sky-blue cravat, into which were thrust two diamond pins, held together by a small gold chain; and he smiled a singular smile, in a sugary, ambiguous fashion. Noticing that her feet were damp:

"Do get closer to the stove," he said, "put your feet up against the porcelain."

She was afraid of dirtying it but the notary replied gallantly:

63. Karl Steuben (1788–1856) was a German history painter. Esmeralda is the gypsy girl in Hugo's *Notre Dame de Paris* (a picture, "Esmeralda et Quasimodo"—the Dwarf—was exhibited in 1839).
64. Schopin was (with a different spelling) the brother of the composer Chopin. Putiphar is the official of the court of Egypt who was Joseph's master—the wife of Putiphar tried to seduce him. The picture represents the seduction scene.

"Pretty things never spoil anything."

Then she tried to appeal to his better feelings and, growing moved herself, she began telling him about the tightness of her household, her worries, her wants. He could understand that—such an elegant woman!—and, without interrupting his lunch, he turned completely round towards her, so that his knee brushed against her boot; the sole was beginning to curl in the heat of the stove.

But when she asked for three thousand francs, his lips drew tight and he said how sorry he was not to have had the management of her capital before, for there were hundreds of ways very convenient, even for a lady, of turning her money to account. In the turf-pits of Gaumesnil or in Le Havre real estate, they could have ventured, with hardly any risk, on some excellent speculations; and he let her consume herself with rage at the thought of the fabulous sums that she would certainly have made.

"How was it," he went on, "that you didn't come to me?"

"I don't know," she said.

"Why not? Did I frighten you so much? It is I, on the contrary, who ought to complain. We hardly know one another; yet I am very devoted to you. You do not doubt that any longer, I hope?"

He held out his hand, took hers, kissed it greedily, then held it on his knee; and he played delicately with her fingers, while muttering thousands of compliments.

His bland voice rustled like a running brook; a light shone in his eyes through the glimmering of his spectacles, and his hand was advancing up Emma's sleeve to press her arm. She felt against her cheek his panting breath. This man was intolerable.

She sprang to her feet and told him:

"Sir, I am waiting."

"For what?" said the notary, who suddenly became very pale.

"This money."

"But . . ."

Then, yielding to an irresistible wave of desire:

"Well then, . . . yes!"

He dragged himself towards her on his knees, regardless of his dressing gown.

"I beg you, stay! I love you!"

He seized her by the waist. Madame Bovary's face flushed purple. She recoiled with a terrible look, exclaiming:

"You shamelessly take advantage of my distress, sir! I am to be pitied—not to be sold."

And she went out.

The notary remained dumbfounded, his eyes fixed on his fine embroidered slippers. They were a love gift, and their sight finally consoled him. Besides, he reflected that such an adventure might have carried him too far.

"The wretch! the scoundrel! . . . what an infamy!" she said to herself, as she fled with nervous steps under the aspens that lined the road. The disappointment of her failure increased the indignation of her outraged modesty; it seemed to her that Providence pursued her implacably, and, strengthening herself in her pride, she had never felt so much esteem for herself nor so much contempt for others. A spirit of warfare transformed her. She would have liked to strike all men, to spit in their faces, to crush them; she kept walking straight on, as quickly as she could, pale, shaking and furious, searching the empty horizon with tear-dimmed eyes, almost rejoicing in the hatred that was choking her.

When she saw her house a numbness came over her. She could not go on; yet she had to. Besides, what escape was there for her? Félicité was waiting for her at the door.

"Well?"

"No!" said Emma.

And for a quarter of an hour the two of them went over the various persons in Yonville who might perhaps be inclined to help her. But each time that Félicité named some one Emma replied:

"Out of the question! they won't!"

"And the master'll soon be in."

"I know that well enough . . . Now leave me alone."

She had tried everything; there was nothing more to be done now; and when Charles came in she would have to tell him:

"Step aside! This rug on which you are walking is no longer ours. In your own house you don't own a chair, a pin, a straw, and it is I, poor man, who have ruined you."

Then there would be a great sob; next he would weep abundantly, and at last, the surprise past, he would forgive her.

"Yes," she murmured, grinding her teeth, "*he* will forgive me, the man I could never forgive for having known me, even if he had a million to spare! . . . Never! never!"

The thought of Bovary's magnanimity exasperated her. He was bound to find out the catastrophe, whether she confessed or not, now, soon, or to-morrow; so there was no escape from the horrible scene and she would have to bear the weight of his generosity. She wanted to return to Lheureux, but what good would it do? To write to her father—it was too late; and perhaps she began to repent now that she had not yielded to the notary, when she heard the trot of a horse in the alley. It was he; he was opening the gate; he was whiter than the plaster wall. Rushing to the stairs, she fled to the Square; and the wife of the mayor, who was talking to Lestiboudois in front of the church, saw her enter the house of the tax-collector.

She hurried off to tell Madame Caron, and the two ladies went up to the attic; hidden behind a sheet strung up on two poles, they stationed themselves comfortably in full command of Binet's room.

He was alone in his garret, busily copying in wood one of those indescribable bits of ivory, composed of crescents, of spheres hollowed out one within the other, the whole as straight as an obelisk, and of no use whatever; and he was beginning on the last piece—he was nearing his goal! In the twilight of the workshop the white dust was flying from his tools like a shower of sparks under the hoofs of a galloping horse; the two wheels were turning, droning; Binet smiled, his chin lowered, his nostrils distended. He seemed lost in the state of complete bliss that only the most menial tasks can offer: distracting the mind by easily overcome obstacles, they satisfy it completely, leading to a fulfilled achievement that leaves no room for dreams beyond.

"Ah! there she is!" exclaimed Madame Tuvache.

But the noise of the lathe made it impossible to hear what she was saying.

At last the two ladies thought they made out the word "francs," and Madame Tuvache whispered in a low voice:

"She's asking for extra time to pay her taxes."

"Apparently!" replied the other.

They saw her walking up and down, examining the napkin-rings, the candlesticks, the banister rails against the walls, while Binet stroked his beard with satisfaction.

"Do you think she wants to order something from him?" said Madame Tuvache.

"Why, he never sells anything," objected her neighbor.

The tax-collector seemed to be listening with wide-open eyes, as if he did not understand. She went on in a tender, suppliant manner. She came nearer to him, her breast heaving; they no longer spoke.

"Is she making advances to him?" said Madame Tuvache.

Binet was scarlet to his very ears. She took hold of his hands.

"Oh, it's too much!"

And no doubt she was suggesting something abominable to him; for the tax-collector—yet he was brave, had fought at Bautzen[65] and at Lützen,[66] had been through the French campaign,[67] and had even been proposed for the Croix de Guerre—suddenly, as at the sight of a serpent, recoiled as far as he could from her, exclaiming:

"Madame! How dare you? . . ."

"Women like that ought to be whipped," said Madame Tuvache.

"But where did she go?" Madame Caron asked. For while they talked, she had vanished out of sight, till they discovered her running up the Grande Rue and turning right as if making for the graveyard, leaving them lost in wonder.

"Mère Rollet," she cried on reaching the nurse's home, "I am choking; unlace me!" She fell sobbing on the bed. Nurse Rollet

---

65. Bautzen (in Saxony, now in Poland, called Budyszin) was the scene of a battle in 1813 where Napoleon defeated the Prussians and Russians.

66. Lützen, in Saxony, was the scene of another battle of Napoleon.

67. The French campaign refers to the battles in France before the Allies captured Paris and forced the abdication of Napoleon and his banishment to Elba in 1814.

covered her with a petticoat and remained standing by her side. Then, as she did not answer, the woman withdrew, took her wheel and began spinning flax.

"Please, stop that!" she murmured, fancying she heard Binet's lathe.

"What's bothering her?" said the nurse to herself. "Why has she come here?"

She had come, impelled by a kind of horror that drove her from her home.

Lying on her back, motionless, and with staring eyes, she saw things but vaguely, although she tried with idiotic persistence to focus her attention on them. She looked at the scaling walls, two logs smoking end to end in the fireplace, and a long spider crawling over her head in a cracked beam. At last she began to collect her thoughts. She remembered—one day, with Léon . . . Oh! how long ago that was—the sun was shining on the river, and the air full of the scent from the clematis . . . Then, carried by her memories as by a rushing torrent, she soon remembered what had happened the day before.

"What time is it?" she asked.

Mère Rollet went out, raised the fingers of her right hand to that side of the sky that was brightest, and came back slowly, saying: "Nearly three."

"Ah! thank you, thank you!"

For he would come, he was bound to. He would have found the money. But he would, perhaps, go down to her house, not guessing where she was, and she told the nurse to run and fetch him.

"Be quick!"

"I'm going, my dear lady, I'm going!"

She wondered now why she had not thought of him from the first. Yesterday he had given his word; he would not break it. And she already saw herself at Lheureux's spreading out her three bank-notes on his desk. Then she would have to invent some story to explain matters to Bovary. What would she tell him?

The nurse, however, was a long time returning. But, as there was no clock in the cot, Emma feared she was perhaps exaggerating the length of time. She began walking round the garden, step by step; she went into the path by the hedge, and returned quickly, hoping that the woman would have come back by another road. At last, weary of waiting, assailed by fears that she thrust from her, no longer conscious whether she had been here a century or a moment, she sat down in a corner, closed her eyes, and stopped her ears. The gate grated; she sprang up. Before she could speak, Mère Rollet told her:

"There is no one at your house!"

"What?"

"He isn't there. And Monsieur is crying. He is calling for you. Everybody is looking for you."

Emma did not answer. She gasped with wild, rolling eyes, while the peasant woman, frightened at her face drew back instinctively, thinking her mad. Suddenly she struck her brow and uttered a cry; for the thought of Rodolphe, like a flash of lightning in a dark night, had struck into her soul. He was so good, so tender, so generous! And besides, should he hesitate to come to her assistance, she would know well enough how one single glance would reawaken their lost love. So she set out towards La Huchette, unaware that she was hastening to offer what had so angered her a while ago, not in the least conscious of her prostitution.

VIII

She asked herself as she walked along, "What am I going to say? How shall I begin?" And as she went on she recognised the thickets, the trees, the sea-rushes on the hill, the château beyond. All the sensations of her first love came back to her, and her poor oppressed heart expanded in the warmth of this tenderness. A warm wind blew in her face; melting snow fell drop by drop from the leave-buds onto the grass.

She entered, as in the past, through the small park-gate, reached the main courtyard, planted with a double row of lindens, their long whispering branches swaying in the wind. The dogs in their kennels barked, but their resounding voices brought no one out.

She went up the large straight staircase with wooden banisters that led to the hallway paved with dusty flagstones, into which a row of doors opened, as in a monastery or an inn. He was at the top, right at the end, on the left. When she placed her fingers on the lock her strength suddenly deserted her. She was afraid, almost wished he would not be there, though this was her only hope, her last chance of salvation. She collected her thoughts for one moment, and, strengthening herself by the feeling of present necessity, went in.

He was sitting in front of the fire, both his feet propped against the mantelpiece, smoking a pipe.

"Oh, it's you!" he said, getting up hurriedly.

"Yes, it is I . . . I have come, Rodolphe, to ask your advice."

And, despite all her efforts, it was impossible for her to open her lips.

"You have not changed; you're as charming as ever!"

"Oh," she replied bitterly, "they are poor charms since you disdained them."

Then he began a long justification of his conduct, excusing himself in vague terms, since he was unable to invent better.

She yielded to his words, still more to his voice and the sight of him, so that she pretended to believe, or perhaps believed, in the pretext he gave for their break; it was a secret on which depended the honor, the very life of a third person.

"Never mind," she said, looking at him sadly. "I have suffered much."

He replied philosophically:

"Life is that way!"

"Has life," Emma went on, "been kind to you at least since our separation?"

"Oh, neither good . . . nor bad."

"Perhaps it would have been better never to have parted."

"Yes, perhaps."

"You think so?" she said, drawing nearer.

Then, with a sigh:

"Oh, Rodolphe! if only you knew! . . . I loved you so!"

It was then that she took his hand, and they remained some time, their fingers intertwined, like that first day at the Agricultural Fair. With a gesture of pride he struggled against this emotion. But sinking upon his breast she told him:

"How did you think I could live without you? One cannot lose the habit of happiness. I was desperate, I thought I was going to die! I'll tell you about it . . . But you, you fled from me!"

With the natural cowardice that characterizes the stronger sex, he had carefully avoided her for the last three years; now Emma persisted, with coaxing little motions of the head, playful and feline:

"I know you love others, you may as well admit it. Oh! I don't blame them, I understand! You seduced them just as you seduced me. You're a man, a real man! you have all it takes to make yourself loved. But we'll start all over, won't we? We'll love each other as before! Look, I am laughing, I am happy! . . . Say something!"

She was irresistible, with a tear trembling in her eye, like a raindrop in a blue flower-cup, after the storm.

He had drawn her upon his knees, and with the back of his hand was caressing her smooth hair; a last ray of the sun was mirrored there, like a golden arrow. She lowered her head; at last he kissed her on the eyelids quite gently with the tips of his lips.

"Why, you have been crying! Why?"

She burst into tears. Rodolphe thought this was an outburst of her love. As she did not speak, he took this silence to be a last remnant of resistance, so he exclaimed:

"Oh, forgive me! You are the only one who really pleases me. I was a fool, a wicked fool! I love you, I'll always love you! What is the matter? Tell me . . ."

He knelt before her.

"Well, Rodolphe . . . I am ruined! You must lend me three thousand francs."

"But . . ." he said, as he slowly rose to his feet, "but . . ." His face assumed a grave expression.

"You know," she went on quickly, "that my husband had entrusted his money to a notary to invest, and he absconded. So we borrowed; the patients don't pay us. Moreover, the estate isn't settled yet; we shall have the money later on. But to-day, for want of three thousand francs, we are to be sold out, right now, this very minute. Counting on your friendship, I have come to you for help."

"Ah!" thought Rodolphe, turning very pale, "so that's what she came for."

At last he said, very calmly:

"My dear lady, I haven't got them."

He did not lie. If he had had it, he would probably have given the money, although it is generally unpleasant to do such fine things: a demand for money being, of all the winds that blow upon love, the coldest and most destructive.

She stared at him in silence for minutes.

"You haven't got them!"

She repeated several times:

"You haven't got them! . . . I ought to have spared myself this last shame. You never loved me. You are no better than the others."

She was losing her head, giving herself away.

Rodolphe interrupted her, declaring he was himself "hard up."

"Oh! I feel sorry for you!" said Emma, "exceedingly sorry!"

And fixing her eyes upon an embossed rifle that shone against its panoply:

"But when one is so poor one doesn't have silver on the butt of one's gun. One doesn't buy a clock inlaid with tortoiseshell," she went on, pointing to the Boulle clock, "nor silver-gilt whistles for one's whips," and she touched them, "nor charms for one's watch. Oh, he has all he needs! even a liqueur-stand in his bedroom; for you pamper yourself, you live well. You have a château, farms, woods; you go hunting; you travel to Paris. Why, if it were but that," she cried, taking up two cuff-links from the mantlepiece, "even for the least of these trifles, one could get money . . . Oh, I don't want anything from you; you can keep them!"

And she flung the links away with such force that their gold chain broke as it struck against the wall.

"But I! I would have given you everything. I would have sold all, worked for you with my hands, I would have begged on the highroads for a smile, for a look, to hear you say 'Thank you!' And you sit there quietly in your arm-chair, as if you had not made me suffer enough already! But for you, and you know it, I might have lived happily. What made you do it? Was it a bet? Yet you loved me . . . you said so. And but a moment ago . . . Ah! it would have been better to have driven me away. My hands are hot with your kisses, and there is the spot on the carpet where at my knees you swore an eternity of love! You made me believe you; for two years you held me in the most magnificent, the sweetest dream! . . . Our plans for the journey, do you remember? Oh, your letter! your letter! it tore my heart! And then when I come back to him— to him, rich, happy, free—to implore the help the first stranger would give, a suppliant, and bringing back to him all my tenderness, he repulses me because it could cost him three thousand francs!"

"I haven't got them," replied Rodolphe, with that perfect calm with which resigned rage covers itself as with a shield.

She went out. The walls trembled, the ceiling was crushing her, and she passed back through the long alley, stumbling against the heaps of dead leaves scattered by the wind. At last she reached the low hedge in front of the gate; she broke her nails against the lock in her haste to open it. Then a hundred paces beyond, breathless, almost falling, she stopped. And now turning round, she once more saw the impassive château, with the park, the gardens, the three courts, and all the windows of the façade.

She remained lost in stupor, and only conscious of herself through the beating of her arteries, that seemed to burst forth like a deafening music filling all the fields. The earth beneath her feet was more yielding than the sea, and the furrows seemed to her immense brown waves breaking into foam. All the memories and ideas that crowded her head seemed to explode at once like a thousand pieces of fireworks. She saw her father, Lheureux's closet, their room at home, another landscape. Madness was coming upon her; she grew afraid, and managed to recover herself, in a confused way, it is true, for she did not remember the cause of her dreadful confusion, namely the money. She suffered only in her love, and felt her soul escaping from her in this memory, as wounded men, dying, feel their life ebb from their bleeding wounds.

Night was falling, crows were flying about.

Suddenly it seemed to her that fiery spheres were exploding in the air like bullets when they strike, and were whirling, whirling, to melt at last upon the snow between the branches of the trees. In the midst of each of them appeared the face of Rodolphe. They multiplied and drew near, they penetrated her. It all disappeared; she recognised the lights of the houses that shone through the fog.

Now her plight, like an abyss, loomed before her. She was panting as if her heart would burst. Then in an ecstasy of heroism, that
made her almost joyous, she ran down the hill, crossed the cow-
plank, the footpath, the alley, the market, and reached the pharmacy. She was about to enter, but at the sound of the bell some one
might come, and slipping in by the gate, holding her breath, feeling
her way along the walls, she went as far as the door of the kitchen,
where a candle was burning on the stove. Justin in his shirt-sleeves
was carrying out a dish.

"Ah! they're eating; let's wait."

He returned; she tapped at the window. He came out.

"The key! the one for upstairs where he keeps the . . ."

"What?"

And he looked at her, astonished at the pallor of her face, that
stood out white against the black background of the night. She
seemed to him extraordinarily beautiful and majestic as a phantom.
Without understanding what she wanted, he had the presentiment
of something terrible.

But she went on quickly in a low voice that was sweet and
melting:

"I want it; give it to me."

As the partition wall was thin, they could hear the clatter of the
forks on the plates in the dining-room.

She pretended that she wanted to kill the rats that kept her from
sleeping.

"I must go ask Monsieur."

"No, stay!"

Then with a casual air:

"Oh, it's not worth bothering him about, I'll tell him myself
later. Come, hold the light for me."

She entered the corridor into which the laboratory door opened.
Against the wall was a key labelled *Capharnaüm*.

"Justin!" called the pharmacist, growing impatient.

"Let's go up."

And he followed her. The key turned in the lock, and she went
straight to the third shelf, so well did her memory guide her, seized
the blue jar, tore out the cork, plunged in her hand, and withdrawing it full of white powder, she ate it greedily.

"Stop!" he cried, throwing himself upon her.

"Quiet! They might hear us . . ."

He was in despair, ready to call out.

"Say nothing, or all the blame will fall on your master."

Then she went home, suddenly calmed, with something of the
serenity of one that has done his duty.

When Charles, thunderstruck at the news of the execution, rushed home, Emma had just gone out. He cried aloud, wept, fainted, but she did not return. Where could she be? He sent Félicité to Homais, to Monsieur Tuvache, to Lheureux, to the "Lion d'Or," everywhere, and in between the waves of his anxiety he saw his reputation destroyed, their fortune lost, Berthe's future ruined. By what?—Not a word! He waited till six in the evening. At last, unable to bear it any longer, and fancying she had gone to Rouen, he set out along the highroad, walked a mile, met no one, again waited, and returned home.

She had come back.

"What happened? . . . Why did you? . . . Tell me . . ."

She sat down at her writing-table and wrote a letter, which she sealed slowly, adding the date and the hour.

Then she said in a solemn tone:

"You are to read it to-morrow; till then, I beg you, don't ask me a single question. No, not one!"

"But . . ."

"Oh, leave me!"

She lay down full length on her bed.

A bitter taste in her mouth awakened her. She saw Charles, and again closed her eyes.

She was studying herself curiously, to detect the first signs of suffering. But no! nothing as yet. She heard the ticking of the clock, the crackling of the fire, and Charles breathing as he stood upright by her bed.

"Ah! it is but a little thing, death!" she thought. "I shall fall asleep and all will be over."

She drank a mouthful of water and turned her face to the wall. The frightful taste of ink persisted.

"I am thirsty; oh! so thirsty," she sighed.

"What is the matter?" said Charles, who was handing her a glass.

"It's nothing . . . Open the window, I'm choking."

She was seized with a sickness so sudden that she had hardly time to draw out her handkerchief from under the pillow.

"Take it away," she said quickly; "throw it away."

He spoke to her; she did not answer. She lay motionless, afraid that the slightest movement might make her vomit. But she felt an icy cold creeping from her feet to her heart.

"Ah! It's beginning," she murmured.

"What did you say?"

She gently rocked her head to and fro in anguish, opening her jaws as if something very heavy were weighing upon her tongue. At eight o'clock the vomiting began again.

Charles noticed that at the bottom of the basin there was a trace of white sediment sticking to the sides of the porcelain.

"This is extraordinary, very strange!" he repeated.

"No!" she loudly replied, "you are mistaken."

Then gently, almost caressingly, he passed his hand over her stomach. She uttered a sharp cry. He recoiled in terror.

Then she began to moan, faintly at first. Her shoulders were shaken by a strong shudder, and she was growing paler than the sheets in which she buried her clenched fists. Her unequal pulse was now almost imperceptible.

Drops of sweat oozed from her face, that had turned blue and rigid as under the effect of a metallic vapor. Her teeth chattered, her dilated eyes looked vaguely about her, and to all questions she replied only with a shake of the head; she even smiled once or twice. Gradually, her moaning grew louder; she couldn't repress a muffled scream; she pretended she felt better and that she'd soon get up. But she was seized with convulsions and cried out:

"God! It's horrible!"

He threw himself on his knees by her bed.

"Tell me! what have you eaten? Answer, for heaven's sake!"

And he looked at her with a tenderness in his eyes such as she had never seen.

"Well, there . . . there . . ." she said in a faltering voice.

He flew to the writing-table, tore open the seal, and read aloud: "Let no one be blamed . . ." He stopped, passed his hands over his eyes, and read it over again.

"What! . . . Help! Help!"

He could only keep repeating the word: "Poisoned! poisoned!" Félicité ran to Homais, who proclaimed it in the market-place; Madame Lefrançois heard it at the "Lion d'Or;" some got up to go and tell their neighbors, and all night the village was on the alert.

Distracted, stammering, reeling, Charles wandered about the room. He knocked against the furniture, tore his hair, and the pharmacist had never believed that there could be so terrible a sight.

He went home to write to Monsieur Canivet and to Doctor Larivière. His mind kept wandering, he had to start over fifteen times. Hippolyte went to Neufchâtel, and Justin so spurred Bovary's horse that he left it foundered and three parts dead by the hill at Bois-Guillaume.

Charles tried to look up his medical dictionary, but could not read it; the lines were jumping before his eyes.

"Be calm," said the pharmacist; "we must administer a powerful antidote. What is the poison?"

Charles showed him the letter. It was arsenic.

"Very well," said Homais, "we must make an analysis."

For he knew that in cases of poisoning an analysis must be made; and the other, who did not understand, answered:

"Oh, do it! Do anything! Save her . . ."

Then going back to her, he sank upon the carpet, and lay there with his head leaning against the edge of her bed, sobbing.

"Don't cry," she said to him. "Soon I won't trouble you any longer."

"Why did you do it? Who made you?"

She replied:

"There was no other way!"

"Weren't you happy? Is it my fault? But I did the best I could!"

"Yes, that's true . . . you're good, not like the others."

And she slowly passed her hand over his hair. The sweetness of this sensation deepened his sadness; he felt his whole being dissolving in despair at the thought that he must lose her, just when she was confessing more love for him than she ever did. He didn't know what to do, felt paralyzed by fear; the need for an immediate decision took away his last bit of self-control.

Emma thought that, at last, she was through with lying, cheating and with the numberless desires that had tortured her. She hated no one now; a twilight dimness was settling upon her thoughts, and, of all earthly noises, Emma heard none but the intermittent lamentations of this poor heart, sweet and remote like the echo of a symphony dying away.

"Bring me the child," she said, raising herself on her elbow.

"You're not feeling worse, are you?" asked Charles.

"No, no!"

The child, serious, and still half-asleep, was carried in on the maid's arm in her long white nightgown, from which her bare feet peeped out. She looked wonderingly at the disordered room, and half-closed her eyes, dazzled by the burning candles on the table. They reminded her, no doubt, of the morning of New Year's day and Mid-Lent, when thus awakened early by candlelight she came to her mother's bed to fetch her presents.

"But where is it, mamma?" she asked.

And as everybody was silent, "But I can't see my little stocking."

Félicité held her over the bed while she still kept looking towards the mantelpiece.

"Did nurse take it away?" she asked.

At the mention of this name, that carried her back to the memory of her adulteries and her calamities, Madame Bovary turned away her head, as at the loathing of another bitterer poison that rose to her mouth. But Berthe remained perched on the bed.

"Oh, how big your eyes are, mamma! How pale you are! how you sweat!"

Her mother looked at her.

"I'm frightened!" cried the child, recoiling.

Emma took her hand to kiss it; the child struggled.

"Enough! Take her away!" cried Charles, who was sobbing at the foot of the bed.

Then the symptoms ceased for a moment; she seemed less agitated; and at every insignificant word she spoke, every time she drew breath a little easier, his hopes revived. At last, when Canivet came in, he threw himself into his arms.

"Ah; it's you. Thank you! How good of you to come. But she's better. See! look at her."

His colleague was by no means of this opinion, and "never beating about the bush"—as he put it—he prescribed an emetic in order to empty the stomach completely.

She soon began vomiting blood. Her lips became drawn. Her limbs were convulsed, her whole body covered with brown spots, and her pulse slipped beneath the fingers like a stretched thread, like a harp-string about to break.

After this she began to scream horribly. She cursed the poison, railed at it, and implored it to be quick, and thrust away with her stiffened arms everything that Charles, in more agony than herself, tried to make her drink. He stood up, his handkerchief to his lips, moaning, weeping, and choked by sobs that shook his whole body. Félicité was running up and down the room. Homais, motionless, uttered great sighs; and Monsieur Canivet, always retaining his self-command, nevertheless began to feel uneasy.

"The devil! yet she has been purged, and since the cause has been removed . . ."

"The effect must cease," said Homais, "that's obvious."

"Oh, save her!" cried Bovary.

And, without listening to the pharmacist, who was still venturing the hypothesis. "It is perhaps a salutary paroxysm," Canivet was about to administer theriaca, when they heard the cracking of a whip; all the windows rattled, and a postchaise drawn by three horses abreast, up to their ears in mud, drove at a gallop round the corner of market. It was Doctor Larivière.

The apparition of a god would not have caused more commotion. Bovary raised his hands; Canivet stopped short; and Homais pulled off his cap long before the doctor had come in.

He belonged to that great school of surgeons created by Bichat,[68] to that generation, now extinct, of philosophical practitioners, who, cherishing their art with a fanatical love, exercised it with enthusiasm and wisdom. Every one in his hospital trembled when he was angry: and his students so revered him that they tried, as soon

---

68. Marie - Françoise - Xavier Bichat (1771–1802) was the author of an *Anat-*   *omie générale.*

as they were themselves in practice, to imitate him as much as possible. They could be found in all the neighboring towns wearing exactly the same merino overcoat and black frock. The doctor's buttoned cuffs slightly covered his fleshy hands—very beautiful hands, never covered by gloves, as though to be more ready to plunge into suffering. Disdainful of honors, of titles, and of academies, hospitable, generous, fatherly to the poor, and practising virtue without believing in it, he would almost have passed for a saint if the keenness of his intellect had not caused him to be feared as a demon. His glance, more penetrating than his scalpels, looked straight into your soul, and would detect any lie, regardless how well hidden. He went through life with the benign dignity that goes with the assurance of talent and wealth, with forty years of a hard-working, blameless life.

He frowned as soon as he had passed the door when he saw the cadaverous face of Emma stretched out on her back with her mouth open. Then, while apparently listening to Canivet, he rubbed his fingers up and down beneath his nostrils, repeating:

"I see, yes, yes . . ."

But he slowly shrugged his shoulders. Bovary watched him; they looked at one another; and this man, accustomed as he was to the sight of pain, could not keep back a tear that fell on his shirt front.

He tried to take Canivet into the next room. Charles followed him.

"She is sinking, isn't she? If we put on poultices? Anything! Oh, think of something, you who have saved so many!"

Charles put both arms around him, and looked at him in anxious supplication, half-fainting against his breast.

"Come, my poor boy, courage! There is nothing more to be done."

And Doctor Larivière turned away.

"You are leaving?"

"I'll be back."

He went out as if to give an order to the coachman, followed by Canivet, who was equally glad to escape from the spectacle of Emma dying.

The pharmacist caught up with them on the Square. He could not by temperament keep away from celebrities, so he begged Monsieur Larivière to do him the signal honor of staying for lunch.

He sent quickly to the "Lion d'Or" for some pigeons; to the butcher's for all the cutlets that could be found; to Tuvache for cream; and to Lestiboudois for eggs; and Homais himself aided in the preparations, while Madame Homais was saying as she tightened her apron-strings:

"I hope you'll forgive us, sir, for in this village, if one is caught unawares . . ."

"Stemmed glasses!" whispered Homais.

"If only we were in the city, I'd be able to find stuffed pig's feet . . ."

"Be quiet . . . Please doctor, à table!"

He thought fit, after the first few mouthfuls, to supply some details about the catastrophe.

"We first had a feeling of siccity in the pharynx, then intolerable pains at the epigastrium, super-purgation, coma."

"But how did she poison herself?"

"I don't know, doctor, and I don't even know where she can have procured the arsenious acid."

Justin, who was just bringing in a pile of plates, began to tremble.

"What's the matter?" said the pharmacist.

At this question the young man dropped the whole lot on the floor with a dreadful crash.

"Imbecile!" cried Homais, "clumsy lout! blockhead! confounded ass!"

But suddenly controlling himself:

"I wished, doctor, to make an analysis, and *primo* I delicately introduced a tube . . ."

"You would have done better," said the physician, "to introduce your fingers into her throat."

His colleague was silent, having just before privately received a severe lecture about his emetic, so that this good Canivet, so arrogant and so verbose at the time of the club-foot, was to-day very modest. He smiled an incessantly approving smile.

Homais dilated in Amphitryonic pride,[69] and the affecting thought of Bovary vaguely contributed to his pleasure by a kind of selfish comparison with his own lot. Moreover, the presence of the surgeon exalted him. He displayed his erudition, spoke effusively about cantharides, upas, the manchineel, adder bites.

"I have even read that various persons have found themselves under toxicological symptoms, and, as it were, paralyzed by blood sausage that had been too strongly smoked. At least, this was stated in a very fine paper prepared by one of our pharmaceutical authorities, one of our masters, the illustrious Cadet de Gassicourt!"[70]

Madame Homais reappeared, carrying one of those shaky machines that are heated with spirits of wine; for Homais liked to make his coffee at the table, having, moreover, torrefied it, pulverised it, and mixed it himself.

---

69. Amphitryonic pride, a host's pride. *Amphitryon* is a comedy by Molière (1668). The verse:
Le véritable Amphitryon
  Est l'Amphitryon où l'on dîne
has become a proverb. It means a man who brings companions to his table, a rich and powerful man whom we flatter.

70. Cadet de Gassicourt (1769–1821) was the pharmacist of Emperor Napoleon I who had considerable trouble under the Restoration because of his liberal ideas.

"*Saccharum*, doctor?" he said, offering sugar.

Then he had all his children brought down, anxious to have the physician's opinion on their constitutions.

At last Monsieur Larivière was about to leave, when Madame Homais asked for a consultation about her husband. He was making his blood too thick by falling asleep every evening after dinner.

"Oh, it isn't his blood I'd call too thick," said the physician.

And, smiling a little at his unnoticed joke, the doctor opened the door. But the shop was full of people; he had the greatest difficulty in getting rid of Monsieur Tuvache, who feared his wife would get pneumonia because she was in the habit of spitting on the ashes; then of Monseiur Binet, who sometimes experienced sudden attacks of great hunger; and of Madame Caron, who suffered from prickling sensations; of Lheureux, who had dizzy spells; of Lestiboudois, who had rheumatism; and of Madame Lefrançois, who had heartburn. At last the three horses started; and it was the general opinion that he had not shown himself at all obliging.

Public attention was distracted by the appearance of Monsieur Bournisien, who was going across the square carrying the holy oil.

Homais, as was due to his principles, compared priests to ravens attracted by the smell of death. The sight of an ecclesiastic was personally disagreeable to him, for the cassock made him think of the shroud, and his dislike of the one matched his fear of the other.

Nevertheless, not shrinking from what he called his "Mission," he returned to Bovary's house with Canivet, who had been strongly urged by Dr. Larivière to make this call; and he would, but for his wife's objections, have taken his two sons with him, in order to accustom them to great occasions; that this might be a lesson, an example, a solemn picture, that should remain in their heads later on.

The room when they went in was full of mournful solemnity. On the work-table, covered over with a white cloth, there were five or six small balls of cotton in a silver dish, near a large crucifix between two lighted candles.

Emma, her chin sunken upon her breast, had her eyes inordinately wide open, and her poor hands wandered over the sheets with that hideous and gentle movement of the dying, that seems as if they already wanted to cover themselves with the shroud. Pale as a statue and with eyes red as fire, Charles, beyond weeping, stood opposite her at the foot of the bed, while the priest, bending one knee, was muttering in a low voice.

She turned her face slowly, and seemed filled with joy on suddenly seeing the violet stole. She was doubtlessly reminded, in this moment of sudden serenity, of the lost bliss of her first mystical flights, mingling with the visions of eternal beatitude that were beginning.

The priest rose to take the crucifix; then she stretched forward her neck like one suffering from thirst, and glueing her lips to the body of the Man-God, she pressed upon it with all her expiring strength the fullest kiss of love that she had ever given. Then he recited the *Misereatur* and the *Indulgentiam*, dipped his right thumb in the oil, and began to give extreme unction. First, upon the eyes, that had so coveted all wordly goods; then upon the nostrils, that had been so greedy of the warm breeze and the scents of love; then upon the mouth, that had spoken lies, moaned in pride and cried out in lust; then upon the hands that had taken delight in the texture of sensuality; and finally upon the soles of the feet, so swift when she had hastened to satisfy her desires, and that would now walk no more.

The curé wiped his fingers, threw the bit of oil-stained cotton into the fire, and came and sat down by the dying woman, to tell her that she must now blend her sufferings with those of Jesus Christ and abandon herself to the divine mercy.

Finishing his exhortations, he tried to place in her hand a blessed candle, symbol of the celestial glory with which she was soon to be surrounded. Emma, too weak, could not close her fingers, and if it hadn't been for Monsieur Bournisien, the taper would have fallen to the ground.

Yet she was no longer quite so pale, and her face had an expression of serenity as if the sacrament had cured her.

The priest did not fail to point this out; he even explained to Bovary that the Lord sometimes prolonged the life of persons when he thought it useful for their salvation; and Charles remembered the day when, so near death, she had received communion. Perhaps there was no need to despair, he thought.

In fact, she looked around her slowly, as one awakening from a dream; then in a distinct voice she asked for her mirror, and remained bent over it for some time, until big tears fell from her eyes. Then she turned away her head with a sigh and fell back upon the pillows.

Her chest soon began heaving rapidly; the whole of her tongue protruded from her mouth; her eyes, as they rolled, grew paler, like the two globes of a lamp that is going out, so that one might have thought her already dead but for the fearful labouring of her ribs, shaken by violent breathing, as if the soul were struggling to free itself. Félicité knelt down before the crucifix, and the pharmacist himself slightly bent his knees, while Monsieur Canivet looked out vaguely at the Square. Bournisien had resumed his praying, his face bowed against the edge of the bed, his long black cassock trailing behind him in the room. Charles was on the other side, on his knees, his arms outstretched towards Emma. He had taken her hands and pressed them, shuddering at every heartbeat, as at the tremors of a falling ruin. As the death-rattle became stronger the priest prayed faster; his prayers mingled with Bovary's stifled sobs, and sometimes all seemed lost in the muffled murmur of the Latin syllables that sounded like a tolling bell.

Suddenly from the pavement outside came the loud noise of wooden shoes and the clattering of a stick; and a voice rose—a raucous voice—that sang

> Often the heat of a summer's day
> Makes a young girl dream her heart away.

Emma raised herself like a galvanised corpse, her hair streaming, her eyes fixed, staring.

> To gather up all the new-cut stalks
> Of wheat left by the scythe's cold swing,
> Nanette bends over as she walks
> Toward the furrows from where they spring.

"The blind man!" she cried.

And Emma began to laugh, an atrocious, frantic, desperate laugh, thinking she saw the hideous face of the poor wretch loom out of the eternal darkness like a menace.

> The wind blew very hard that day
> It blew her petticoat away.

A final spasm threw her back upon the mattress. They all drew near. She had ceased to exist.

IX

Someone's death always causes a kind of stupefaction; so difficult it is to grasp this advent of nothingness and to resign ourselves to the fact that it has actually taken place. But still, when he saw that she did not move, Charles flung himself upon her, crying:

"Farewell! farewell!"

Homais and Canivet dragged him from the room.

"Control yourself!"

"Yes," he said, struggling, "I'll be quiet. I won't do anything. But let me stay. I want to see her. She is my wife!"

And he wept.

"Cry," said the pharmacist; "let nature take its course; that will relieve you."

Weaker than a child, Charles let himself be led downstairs into the sitting-room, and Monsieur Homais soon went home. On the Square he was accosted by the blind man, who, having dragged himself as far as Yonville in the hope of getting the antiphlogistic salve, was asking every passer-by where the pharmacist lived.

"Good heavens, man, as if I didn't have other fish to fry! I can't help it, but you'll have to come back later."

And he hurried into the shop.

He had to write two letters, to prepare a soothing potion for Bovary, to invent some lie that would conceal the poisoning, and work it up into an article for the "Fanal," without counting the people who were waiting to get the news from him; and when the Yonvillers had all heard his story of the arsenic that she had mistaken for sugar in making a vanilla cream, Homais once more returned to Bovary's.

He found him alone (Monsieur Canivet had left), sitting in an arm-chair near the window, staring with a vacant look at the stone floor.

"Well," Homais said, "you ought yourself to fix the hour for the ceremony."

"Why? What ceremony?"

Then, in a stammering, frightened voice:

"Oh, no! not that. No! I want to keep her here."

Homais, to save face, took up a pitcher from the whatnot to water the geraniums.

"Ah! thank you," said Charles; "how kind of you!"

But he did not finish, choked by the flow of memories that Homais' action had released in him.

Then to distract him, Homais thought fit to talk a little about horticulture: plants wanted moisture. Charles bowed his head in approval.

"Besides, we'll soon be having fine weather again."

"Ah!" said Bovary.

The pharmacist, at his wit's end, gently drew aside the small window-curtain.

"Look! there's Monsieur Tuvache passing by."

Charles repeated mechanically:

"Monsieur Tuvache passing by!"

Homais did not dare to bring up the funeral arrangements again; it was the priest who finally convinced him of the necessity to bury Emma.

He shut himself up in his consulting-room, took a pen, and after sobbing for some time, wrote:

"I wish her to be buried in her wedding dress, with white shoes, and a wreath. Her hair is to be spread out over her shoulders. Three coffins, one oak, one mahogany, one of lead. Let no one try to overrule me; I shall have the strength to resist him. She is to be covered with a large piece of green velvet. This is my wish; see that it is done."

The two men were much taken aback by Bovary's romantic ideas. The pharmacist was first to remonstrate with him:

"This velvet seems excessive to me. Besides, think of the expense . . ."

"What's that to you?" cried Charles. "Leave me alone! You didn't love her. Go away!"

The priest took him by the arm for a walk in the garden. He discoursed on the vanity of earthly things. God was very great, very good: one must submit to his decrees without a murmur, even learn to be grateful for one's suffering.

Charles burst into blasphemy:

"I hate your God!"

"The spirit of rebellion is still upon you," sighed the priest.

Bovary was far away. He was striding along by the wall, near the espalier, and he ground his teeth; he raised to heaven looks of malediction, but not so much as a leaf stirred.

A fine rain was falling: Charles, whose chest was bare, at last began to shiver; he went in and sat down in the kitchen.

At six o'clock a noise like a clatter of old iron was heard on the square; it was the "Hirondelle" coming in, and he remained with his forehead pressed against the window-pane, watching all the passengers get out, one after the other. Félicité put down a mattress for him in the drawing-room. He threw himself upon it and fell asleep.

Although a philosopher, Monsieur Homais respected the dead. So bearing poor Charles no grudge, he returned in the evening to sit up with the body, bringing with him three books and a writing-pad for taking notes.

Monsieur Bournisien was there, and two large candles were burning at the head of the bed, which had been taken out of the alcove.

The pharmacist, unable to keep silent, soon began to express some regrets about this "unfortunate young woman," and the priest replied that there was nothing to do now but pray for her.

"Still," Homais insisted, "it is one of two things; either she died in a state of grace (as the Church calls it), and then she doesn't need our prayers; or else she died unrepentant (that is, I believe, the correct technical term), and then . . ."

Bournisien interrupted him, replying testily that it was none the less necessary to pray.

"But," the pharmacist objected, "since God knows all our needs, what can be the good of prayer?"

"What!" the priest exclaimed, "of prayer? Why, aren't you a Christian?"

"I beg your pardon," said Homais; "I admire Christianity. It freed the slaves, brought morality into the world . . ."

"That isn't the point. Look at the texts . . ."

"Oh! oh! As to texts, look at history; everybody knows that the Jesuits have falsified all the texts!"

Charles came in, and advancing towards the bed, slowly drew the curtains.

Emma's head was turned towards her right shoulder, the corner of her mouth, which was open, seemed like a black hole at the lower part of her face; her two thumbs were bent into the palms of her hands; a kind of white dust besprinkled her lashes, and her eyes were beginning to disappear in a viscous pallor, as if covered by a spiderweb. The sheet sunk in from her breast to her knees, and then rose at the tips of her toes, and it seemed to Charles that infinite masses, an enormous load, were weighing upon her.

The church clock struck two. They could hear the loud murmur of the river flowing in the darkness at the foot of the terrace. Monsieur Bournisien noisily blew his nose from time to time, and Homais' pen was scratching over the paper.

"Come, my good friend," he said, "don't stay here; the sight is too much for you."

When Charles had left, the pharmacist and the priest resumed their argument.

"Read Voltaire," said the one, "read D'Holbach, read the *Encyclopédie!*"[71]

"Read the 'Letters of some Portuguese Jews,' "[72] said the other; "read 'The Meaning of Christianity,'[73] by the former magistrate Nicolas."

They grew warm, they grew red, they both talked at once without listening to each other. Bournisien was scandalised at such audacity; Homais marvelled at such stupidity; and they were about to come to blows when Charles suddenly reappeared. He couldn't resist coming upstairs as though he were spellbound.

He stood at the foot of the bed to see her better, and he lost himself in a contemplation so deep that it was no longer painful.

He recalled stories of catalepsy, the marvels of magnetism, and he said to himself that by willing it with all his force he might perhaps succeed in reviving her. Once he even bent towards her, and cried in a low voice, "Emma! Emma!" His strong breathing made the flames of the candles tremble against the wall.

At daybreak the elder Madame Bovary arrived. As he embraced her, Charles burst into another flood of tears. She tried, as the pharmacist had done, to remonstrate with him on the expenses for the funeral. He became so angry that she was silent, and he even

---

71. Paul-Henri Dietrich, baron d' Holbach (1723–1789), friend and disciple of **Diderot, was one of the most outspoken opponents of religion in the French Enlightenment. The *Encyclopédie*, a dictionary of the sciences, arts and letters, edited by Diderot and d'Alembert** (1751–1772) is the intellectual monument of the French Enlightenment, a fountainhead of later secular and agnostic thought.

72. *Letters of Some Portuguese Jews* (1769) refers to a book by the Abbé Antoine Guéné directed against Voltaire.

73. *The Meaning of Christianity* is one of the many books defending Roman Catholicism by Jean-Jacques-Auguste Nicolas (1807–1888).

commissioned her to go to town at once and buy what was necessary.

Charles remained alone the whole afternoon; they had taken Berthe to Madame Homais'; Félicité was in the room upstairs with Madame Lefrançois.

In the evening he had some visitors. He rose and shook hands with them, unable to speak. Then they sat down together, and formed a large semicircle in front of the fire. With lowered head, they crossed and uncrossed their legs, and uttered from time to time a deep sigh. They were bored to tears, yet none would be the first to go.

Homais, when he returned at nine o'clock (for the last two days Homais seemed to have made the public Square his residence), was laden with a supply of camphor, benzoin and aromatic herbs. He also carried a large jar full of chlorine water, to keep off the miasma. Just then the servant, Madame Lefrançois and the elder Madame Bovary were busy getting Emma dressed, and they were drawing down the long stiff veil that covered her to her satin shoes.

Félicité was sobbing:

"Oh, my poor mistress! my poor mistress!"

"Look at her," said the innkeeper, sighing; "how pretty she still is! Now, couldn't you swear she was going to get up in a minute?"

Then they bent over her to put on her wreath. They had to raise the head a little, and a rush of black liquid poured from her mouth, as if she were vomiting.

"Heavens! Watch out for her dress!" cried Madame Lefrançois. "Now, just come and help us," she said to the pharmacist, "or are you afraid?"

"Afraid?" he replied, "I? As if I hadn't seen a lot worse when I was a student at the Hotel-Dieu. We used to make punch in the dissecting room! Nothingness does not frighten a philosopher; I have often said that I intend to leave my body to the hospitals, to serve the cause of science."

On arriving, the curé inquired after Monsieur Bovary and, at Homais' reply, he said:

"Of course, the blow is still too recent."

Then Homais congratulated him on not being exposed, like other people, to the loss of a beloved companion; this lead to a discussion on the celibacy of priests.

"You must admit," said the pharmacist, "that it is against nature for a man to do without women. There have been crimes . . ."

"For Heaven's sake!" exclaimed the priest, "how do you expect an individual who is married to keep the secrets of the confessional, for example?"

Homais attacked confession. Bournisien defended it; he discoursed on the acts of restitution that it brought about. He cited various anecdotes about thieves who had suddenly become honest. Military men on approaching the tribunal of penitence had finally seen the light. At Fribourg there was a minister . . .

His companion had fallen asleep. Then he felt somewhat stifled by the over-heavy atmosphere of the room; he opened the window; this awoke the pharmacist.

"Come, take a pinch of snuff," he told him. "Take it, it'll do you good."

A continual barking was heard in the distance.

"Do you hear that dog howling?" said the pharmacist.

"They smell the dead," replied the priest. "It's like bees; they leave their hives when there is a death in the neighborhood."

Homais failed to object to these prejudices, for he had again dropped asleep. Monsieur Bournisien, stronger than he, went on moving his lips and muttering for some time, then insensibly his chin sank down, he dropped his big black book, and began to snore.

They sat opposite one another, with bulging stomachs, puffed-up faces, and frowning looks, after so much disagreement uniting at last in the same human weakness, and they moved no more than the corpse by their side, that also seemed to be sleeping.

Charles coming in did not wake them. It was the last time; he came to bid her farewell.

The aromatic herbs were still smoking, and spirals of bluish vapour blended at the window with the entering fog. There were few stars, and the night was warm.

The wax of the candles fell in great drops upon the sheets of the bed. Charles watched them burn, straining his eyes in the glare of their yellow flame.

The watered satin of her gown shimmered white as moonlight. Emma was lost beneath it; and it seemed to him that, spreading beyond her own self, she blended confusedly with everything around her—the silence, the night, the passing wind, the damp odors rising from the ground.

Then suddenly he saw her in the garden at Tostes, on a bench against the thorn hedge, or else at Rouen in the streets, on the threshold of their house, in the yard at Bertaux. He again heard the laughter of the happy boys dancing under the appletrees: the room was filled with the perfume of her hair; and her dress rustled in his arms with a crackling noise. It was the same dress she was wearing now!

For a long while he thus recalled all his lost joys, her attitudes, her movements, the sound of her voice. Wave upon wave of despair came over him, like the tides of an overflowing sea.

He was seized by a terrible curiosity. Slowly, with the tips of his fingers, his heart pounding, he lifted her veil. But he uttered a cry of horror that awoke the other two.

They dragged him down into the sitting-room. Then Félicité came up to say that he wanted some of her hair.

"Cut some off," replied the pharmacist.

And as she did not dare to, he himself stepped forward, scissors in hand. He trembled so that he nicked the skin of the temple in several places. At last, stiffening himself against emotion, Homais gave two or three great cuts at random that left white patches amongst that beautiful black hair.

The pharmacist and the curé resumed their original occupations, not without time and again falling asleep—something of which they accused each other whenever they awoke. Monsieur Bournisien sprinkled the room with holy water and Homais threw a little chlorine on the floor.

Félicité had been so considerate as to put on the chest of drawers, for each of them, a bottle of brandy, some cheese, and a large brioche, and about four o'clock in the morning, unable to restrain himself any longer, the pharmacist sighed:

"I must say that I wouldn't mind taking some sustenance."

The priest did not need any persuading; he left to say mass and, upon his return, they ate and drank, chuckling a little without knowing why, stimulated by that vague gaiety that comes upon us after times of sadness. At the last glass the priest said to the pharmacist, as he clapped him on the shoulder:

"We'll end up good friends, you and I."

In the passage downstairs they met the undertaker's men, who were coming in. Then for two hours Charles had to suffer the torture of hearing the hammer resound against the wood. Next day they lowered her into her oak coffin, that was fitted into the other two; but as the bier was too large, they had to fill up the gaps with the wool of a mattress. At last, when the three lids had been planed down, nailed, soldered, it was placed outside in front of the door; the house was thrown open, and the people of Yonville began to flock round.

Old Rouault arrived, and fainted on the square at the sight of the black cloth.

x

He had only received Homais' letter thirty-six hours after the event; and, to cushion the blow, he had worded it in such a manner that it was impossible to make out just what had happened.

First, the old man had been shaken as if struck by apoplexy. Next, he understood that she was not dead, but she might be . . . At last, he had put on his smock, taken his hat, fastened his spurs to his boots, and set out at full speed; and the whole of the way old Rouault, panting, had been devoured by anxiety. He felt so dizzy that he was forced to dismount. He fancied he heard voices around him and thought he was losing his mind.

Day broke. He saw three black hens asleep in a tree. He shuddered, horrified at this omen. Then he promised the Holy Virgin three chasubles for the church, and vowed that he would go barefooted from the cemetery at Bertaux to the chapel of Vassonville.

He entered Maromme calling out ahead at the people of the inn, burst open the door with a thrust of his shoulder, made for a sack of oats and emptied a bottle of sweet cider into the manger; then he remounted his nag, whose feet struck sparks as it galloped along.

He told himself that they would certainly save her; the doctors were bound to discover a remedy. He remembered all the miraculous cures he had been told about.

Then she appeared to him dead: She was there, before his eyes, lying on her back in the middle of the road. He reined in his horse, and the hallucination disappeared.

At Quincampoix, to give himself heart, he drank three cups of coffee one after the other.

He imagined that they had written the wrong name on the letter. He looked for the letter in his pocket, felt it there, but did not dare to open it.

At last he began to think it was all a bad joke, a spiteful farce, somebody's idea of a fine prank; besides, if she were dead, he would have known. It couldn't be! the countryside looked as usual: the sky was blue, the trees swayed; a flock of sheep passed by. He reached the village; they saw him coming, hunched over his horse, whipping it savagely till its saddle-girths dripped with blood.

When he recovered consciousness, he fell, weeping, into Bovary's arms:

"My daughter! Emma! my child! tell me . . ."

The other replied between sobs:

"I don't know! I don't know! It's a curse!"

The pharmacist pulled them apart.

"Spare him the horrible details. I'll tell monsieur all about it. People are coming, show some dignity, for heaven's sake! Let's behave like philosophers."

Poor Charles tried as hard as he could, and repeated several times:

"Yes, be brave . . ."

"Damn it, I'll be brave," cried the old man, "I'll stay with her till the end!"

The bell was tolling. All was ready; they had to start.

Seated together in a stall of the choir, they saw the three chanting choristers continually pass and repass in front of them. The serpent-player was blowing with all his might. Monsieur Bournisien, in full regalia, was singing in a shrill voice. He bowed before the tabernacle, raising his hands, stretched out his arms. Lestiboudois went about the church with his verger's staff. The bier stood near the lectern, between four rows of candles. Charles felt an urge to get up and put them out.

Yet he tried to stir into himself the proper devotional feelings, to throw himself into the hope of a future life in which he would see her again. He tried to convince himself that she had gone on a long journey, far away, for a long time. But when he thought of her lying there, and that it was all over and that they would put her in the earth, he was seized with a fierce, gloomy, desperate rage. It seemed at times that he felt nothing, and he welcomed this lull in his pain, while blaming himself bitterly for being such a scoundrel.

The sharp noise of an iron-tipped stick was heard on the stones, striking them at irregular intervals. It came from the end of the church, and stopped short at the lower aisles. A man in a coarse brown jacket knelt down painfully. It was Hippolyte, the stable-boy at the "Lion d'Or." He had put on his new leg.

One of the choir boys came round the nave taking collection, and the coppers chinked one after the other on the silver plate.

"Oh hurry up!" cried Bovary, angrily throwing him a five-franc piece. "I can't stand it any longer."

The singer thanked him with a deep bow.

They sang, they knelt, they stood up; it was endless! He remembered how once, in the early days of their marriage, they had been to mass together, and they had sat down on the other side, on the right, by the wall. The bell began again. There was a great shuffling of chairs; the pall bearers slipped their three poles under the coffin, and every one left the church.

Then Justin appeared in the doorway of the pharmacy, but retreated suddenly, pale and staggering.

People stood at the windows to see the procession pass by. Charles walked first, as straight as he could. He tried to look brave and nodded to those who joined the crowd, coming from the side streets or from the open doors. The six men, three on either side, walked slowly, panting a little. The priests, the choristers, and the two choir-boys recited the *De profundis*, and their voices echoed over the fields, rising and falling with the shape of the hills. Sometimes they disappeared in the windings of the path; but the great silver cross always remained visible among the trees.

The women followed, wearing black coats with turned-down hoods; each of them carried a large lighted candle, and Charles felt himself grow faint at this continual repetition of prayers and torch-lights, oppressed by the sweetish smell of wax and of cassocks. A fresh breeze was blowing; the rye and colza were turning green and along the roadside, dewdrops hung from the hawthorn hedges. All sorts of joyous sounds filled the air; the jolting of a cart rolling way off in the ruts, the crowing of a cock, repeated again and again, or the gamboling of a foal under the apple-trees. The pure sky was dappled with rosy clouds; a blueish haze hung over the iris-covered cottages. Charles recognized each courtyard as he passed. He remembered mornings like this, when, after visiting a patient, he left one of those houses to return home, to his wife.

The black cloth decorated with silver tears, flapped from time to time in the wind, baring the coffin underneath. The tired bearers walked more slowly, and the bier advanced jerkily, like a boat that pitches with every wave.

They reached the cemetery.

The men went right down to a place in the grass where a grave had been dug. They grouped themselves all round; and while the priest spoke, the red soil thrown up at the sides kept noiselessly slipping down at the corners.

Then, when the four ropes were laid out, the coffin was pushed onto them. He watched it go down; it seemed to go down forever.

At last a thud was heard; the ropes creaked and were drawn up. Then Bournisien took the spade handed to him by Lestiboudois; while his right hand kept sprinkling holy water, he vigorously threw in a spadeful of earth with the left; and the wood of the coffin, struck by the pebbles, gave forth that dread sound that seems to us the reverberation of eternity.

The priest passed the holy water sprinkler to his neighbor, Monsieur Homais. The pharmacist swung it gravely, then handed it to Charles, who sank to his knees and threw in handfuls of earth, crying, "Adieu!" He sent her kisses; he dragged himself towards the grave, as if to engulf himself with her.

They led him away, and he soon grew calmer, feeling perhaps, like the others, a vague satisfaction that it was all over.

Old Rouault on his way back began quietly smoking a pipe, to Homais' silent disapproval. He also noticed that Monsieur Binet had not come, that Tuvache had disappeared after mass, and that Theodore, the notary's servant, wore a blue coat—"as if he couldn't respect customs, and wear a black coat, for Heaven's sake!" And to share his observations with others he went from group to group. They were deploring Emma's death, especially Lheureux, who had not failed to come to the funeral.

"Poor little lady! What a blow for her husband!"

"Can you imagine," the pharmacist replied, "that he would have done away with himself if I hadn't intervened?"

"Such a fine person! To think that I saw her only last Saturday in my store."

"I haven't had leisure," said Homais, "to prepare a few words that I would cast over her tomb."

On getting home, Charles undressed, and old Rouault put on his blue smock. It was new, and as he had repeatedly wiped his eyes on the sleeves during his journey, the dye had stained his face, and traces of tears lined the layer of dust that covered it.

Mother Bovary joined them. All three were silent. At last the old man sighed:

"Do you remember, my friend, I came to Tostes once when you had just lost your first deceased? I consoled you that time. I could think of something to say then, but now . . ."

Then, with a loud groan that shook his whole chest,

"Ah! this is the end for me! I saw my wife go . . . then my son . . . and now today my daughter!"

He wanted to go back at once to Bertaux, saying that he couldn't sleep in this house. He even refused to see his grand-daughter.

"No, no! It would grieve me too much. You'll kiss her many times for me. Good bye . . . You're a good man! And I'll never forget this," he said, slapping his thigh. "Never fear, you shall always have your turkey."

But when he reached the top of the hill he turned back, as he had turned once before on the road of Saint-Victor when he had parted from her. The windows of the village were all ablaze in the slanting rays of the sun that was setting behind the meadow. He put his hand over his eyes, and saw at the horizon a walled enclosure, with black clusters of trees among the white stones; then he went on his way at a gentle trot, for his nag was limping.

Despite their fatigue, Charles and his mother stayed up talking very long that evening. They spoke of the days of the past and of the future. She would come to live at Yonville; she would keep house for him; they would never part again. She was subtly affectionate, rejoicing in her heart at regaining some of the tenderness that had wandered from her for so many years. Midnight struck. The village was silent as usual, and Charles lay awake, never ceasing to think of her.

Rodolphe, who, to distract himself, had been roaming in the woods all day, was quietly asleep in his château; and Léon, away in the city, also slept.

There was another who at that hour was not asleep.

On the grave between the pine-trees a child was on his knees weeping, and his heart, rent by sobs, was panting in the dark under the weight of an immense sorrow, tender as the moon and unfathomable as the night.

The gate suddenly grated. It was Lestiboudois coming to fetch the spade he had forgotten. He recognised Justin climbing over the wall, and knew at last who had been stealing his potatoes.

XI

The next day Charles had the child brought back. She asked for her mamma. They told her she was away; that she would bring her back some toys. Berthe mentioned her again several times, then finally forgot her. The child's gaiety broke Bovary's heart, and he had to put up besides with the intolerable consolations of the pharmacist.

Before long, money troubles started again. Monsieur Lheureux was putting his friend Vinçart back on the warpath, and before long Charles was signing notes for exorbitant amounts. For he would never consent to let the smallest of the things that had belonged to *her* be sold. His mother was exasperated with him; he grew even more angry than she did. He was a changed man. She left the house.

Then every one began to collect what they could. Mademoiselle Lempereur presented a bill for six months' teaching, although Emma had never taken a lesson (despite the receipted bill she had shown Bovary); it was an arrangement between the two women. The lending library demanded three years' subscriptions; Mère Rollet claimed postage for some twenty letters, and when Charles asked for an explanation, she was tactful enough to reply:

"Oh, I know nothing about it. It was her business."

With every debt he paid Charles thought he had reached the end. But others followed ceaselessly.

He tried to collect accounts due him from patients. He was shown the letters his wife had written. Then he had to apologise.

Félicité now wore Madame Bovary's dresses; not all, for he had kept some, and he locked himself up in Emma's room to look at them. Félicité was about her former mistress's height and often, on seeing her from behind, Charles thought she had come back and cried out:

"Oh, stay, don't go away!"

But at Pentecost she ran away from Yonville, carried off by Theodore, stealing all that was left of the wardrobe.

It was about this time that the widow Dupuis had the honor to inform him of the "marriage of Monsieur Léon Dupuis her son, notary at Yvetot, to Mademoiselle Léocadié Lebœuf Bondeville." Charles, among the other congratulations he sent him, wrote this sentence:

"How happy this would have made my poor wife!"

One day when, wandering aimlessly about the house, he had gone up to the attic, he felt a crumpled piece of paper under his slipper. He opened it and read: "Courage, Emma, courage. I would not bring misery into your life." It was Rodolphe's letter, fallen to the ground between the boxes, where it had remained till now, when the wind from the open dormer had blown it toward the door. And Charles stood, motionless and staring, in the very same place where, long ago, Emma, in despair, and paler even than he had thought of dying. At last he discovered a small R at the bottom of the second page. What did this mean? He remembered Rodolphe's attentions, his sudden disappearance, his embarrassed air on two or three subsequent occasions. But the respectful tone of the letter deceived him.

"Perhaps they loved one another platonically," he told himself.

Besides, Charles was not of those who go to the root of things; he shrank from the proofs, and his vague jealousy was lost in the immensity of his sorrow.

Every one, he thought, must have adored her; all men inevitably must have coveted her. This made her seem even more beautiful, and it awoke in him a fierce and persistent desire, which inflamed his despair and grew boundless, since it could never be assuaged.

To please her, as if she were still living, he adopted her taste, her ideas; he bought patent leather boots and took to wearing white cravats. He waxed his moustache and, just like her, signed promissory notes. She corrupted him from beyond the grave.

He was obliged to sell his silver piece by piece; next he sold the drawing-room furniture. All the rooms were stripped; but the bedroom, her own room, remained as before. After his dinner Charles went up there. He pushed the round table in front of the fire, and drew up *her* arm-chair. He sat down facing it. A candle burnt in one of the gilt candlesticks. Berthe, at his side, colored pictures.

He suffered, poor man, at seeing her so badly dressed, with lace-less boots, and the arm-holes of her pinafore torn down to the hips; for the cleaning woman took no care of her. But she was so sweet, so pretty, and her little head bent forward so gracefully, letting her fair hair fall over her rosy cheeks, that an infinite joy came upon him, a happiness mingled with bitterness, like those ill-made wines that taste of resin. He mended her toys, made her puppets from cardboard, or sewed up half-torn dolls. Then, if his eyes fell upon the sewing kit, a ribbon lying about, or even a pin left in a crack of the table, he began to dream, and looked so sad that she became as sad as he.

No one now came to see them, for Justin had run away to Rouen, where he worked in a grocery, and the pharmacist's children saw less and less of the child. In view of the difference in their social positions, Monsieur Homais had chosen to discontinue the former intimacy.

The blind man, whom his salve had not cured, had gone back to the hill of Bois-Guillaume, where he told the travellers of his failure, to such an extent, that Homais when he went to town hid himself behind the curtains of the "Hirondelle" to avoid meeting him. He detested him, and wishing, in the interests of his own reputation, to get rid of him at all costs, he directed against him a secret campaign, that betrayed the depth of his intellect and the baseness of his vanity. Thus, for six consecutive months, one could read in the "Fanal de Rouen" editorials such as these:

"Anyone who has ever wended his way towards the fertile plains of Picardy has, no doubt, remarked, by the Bois-Guillaume hill, an unfortunate wretch suffering from a horrible facial wound. He bothers the passers by, pursues them and levies a regular tax on all travellers. Are we still living in the monstrous times of the Middle Ages, when vagabonds were permitted to display in our public places leprosy and scrofulas they had brought back from the Crusades?"

Or:

"In spite of the laws against vagrancy, the approaches to our great towns continue to be infected by bands of beggars. Some are seen going about alone, and these are, by no means, the least dangerous. Why don't our City Authorities intervene?"

Then Homais invented incidents:

"Yesterday, by the Bois-Guillaume hill, a skittish horse . . ." And then followed the story of an accident caused by the presence of the blind man.

He managed so well that the fellow was locked up. But he was released. He began again, and so did Homais. It was a struggle. Homais won out, for his foe was condemned to lifelong confinement in an asylum.

This success emboldened him, and henceforth there was no longer a dog run over, a barn burnt down, a woman beaten in the parish, of which he did not immediately inform the public, guided always by the love of progress and the hatred of priests. He instituted comparisons between the public and parochial schools to the detriment of the latter; called to mind the massacre of St. Bartholomew *à propos* of a grant of one hundred francs to the church; denounced abuses and kept people on their toes. That was his phrase. Homais was digging and delving; he was becoming dangerous.

However, he was stifling in the narrow limits of journalism, and soon a book, a major work, became a necessity. Then he composed "General Statistics of the Canton of Yonville, followed by Climatological Remarks." The statistics drove him to philosophy. He busied himself with great questions: the social problem, the moral plight of the poorer classes, pisciculture, rubber, railways, &c. He even began to blush at being a bourgeois. He affected bohemian manners, he smoked. He bought two *chic* Pompadour statuettes to adorn his drawing-room.

He by no means gave up his store. On the contrary, he kept well abreast of new discoveries. He followed the great trend towards chocolates; he was the first to introduce *Cho-ca* and *Revalenta* into the Seine-Inférieure. He was enthusiastic about the hydro-electric Pulvermacher health-belts; he wore one himself, and when at night he took off his flannel undershirt, Madame Homais was dazzled by the golden spiral that almost hid him from view. Her ardor would redouble for that man, swaddled more than a Scythian and as resplendent as one of the Magi.

He had fine ideas about Emma's tomb. First he proposed a broken column surmounted by a drapery, next a pyramid, then a Temple of Vesta, a sort of rotunda . . . or else a large pile of ruins. And in all his plans Homais always stuck to the weeping willow, which he looked upon as the indispensable symbol of sorrow.

Charles and he made a journey to Rouen together to look at some tombs, accompanied by an artist, one Vaufrylard, a friend of Bridoux's, who never ceased to make puns. At last, after having examined some hundred drawings, having ordered an estimate and made another journey to Rouen, Charles decided in favor of a mausoleum, whose two principal sides were to be decorated with "a spirit bearing an extinguished torch."

As to the inscription, Homais could think of nothing finer than *Sta viator*,[74] and he got no further; he racked his brain in vain; all that he could come up with was *Sta viator*. At last he hit upon *Amabilem conjugem calcas*,[75] which was adopted.

A strange thing was happening to Bovary: while continually thinking of Emma, he was nevertheless forgetting her. He grew desperate as he felt this image fading from his memory in spite of all efforts to retain it. Yet every night he dreamt of her; it was always the same dream. He approached her, but when he was about to embrace her she fell into decay in his arms.

For a week he was seen going to church in the evening. Monsieur Bournisien even paid him two or three visits, then gave him up. Moreover, the old man was growing bigoted and fanatic, according to Homais. He thundered against the spirit of the age, and never failed, every other week, in his sermon, to recount the death agony of Voltaire, who died devouring his excrements, as every one knows.

In spite of Bovary's thrifty life, he was far from being able to pay off his old debts. Lheureux refused to renew any more notes. Execution became imminent. Then he appealed to his mother, who consented to let him take a mortgage on her property, but with a great

---

74. *Sta viator*, "Stop, traveler."
75. *Amabilem conjugem calcas*, "you
are treading upon the beloved spouse."

many recriminations against Emma; and in return for her sacrifice she asked for a shawl that had escaped from Félicité's raids. Charles refused to give it to her; they quarrelled.

She made the first peace overtures by offering to let the little girl, who could help her in the house, live with her. Charles consented to this, but when the time for parting came, all his courage failed him. Then there was a final, complete break between them.

As his affections vanished, he clung more closely to the love of his child. She worried him, however, for she coughed sometimes, and had red patches on her cheeks.

Across the square, facing his house, the prospering family of the pharmacist was more flourishing and thriving than ever. Napoleon helped him in the laboratory, Athalie embroidered him a skullcap, Irma cut out rounds of paper to cover the preserves, and Franklin recited the tables of Pythagoras by rote, without the slightest hesitation. He was the happiest of fathers, the most fortunate of men.

Not quite, however! A secret ambition devoured him. Homais hankered after the cross of the Legion of Honour. He had plenty of claims to it.

"First, having at the time of the cholera distinguished myself by a boundless devotion; second, by having published, at my expense, various works of public usefulness, such as" (and he recalled his pamphlet entitled, *On Cider, its Manufacture and Effects*, besides observations on the wooly aphis that he had sent to the Academy; his volume of statistics, and down to his pharmaceutical thesis); "without counting that I am a member of several learned societies" (he was member of a single one).

"And if this won't do," he said, turning on his heels, "there always is the assistance I give at fires!"

Homais' next step was trying to win over the Government to his cause. He secretly did the prefect several favors during the elections. He sold, in a word, prostituted himself. He even addressed a petition to the sovereign in which he implored him to "do him justice;" he called him "our good king," and compared him to Henri IV.

And every morning the pharmacist rushed for the paper to see if his nomination appeared. It was never there. At last, unable to bear it any longer, he had a grass plot in his garden designed to represent the Star of the Cross of Honour, with two little strips of grass running from the top to imitate the ribbon. He walked round it with folded arms, meditating on the folly of the Government and the ingratitude of men.

Out of respect, or because he took an almost sensuous pleasure in dragging out his investigations, Charles had not yet opened the secret drawer of Emma's rosewood desk. One day, however, he sat down before it, turned the key, and pressed the spring. All Léon's letters were there. There could be no doubt this time. He devoured them to the very last, ransacked every corner, all the furniture, all the drawers, behind the walls, sobbing and shouting in mad distress. He discovered a box and kicked it open. Rodolphe's portrait flew out at him, from among the pile of love-letters.

People wondered at his despondency. He never went out, saw no one, refused even to visit his patients. Then they said "he shut himself up to drink."

At times, however, someone would climb on the garden hedge, moved by curiosity. They would stare in amazement at this long-bearded, shabbily clothed, wild figure of a man, who wept aloud as he walked up and down.

On summer evenings, he would take his little girl with him to visit the cemetery. They came back at nightfall, when the only light left in the village was that in Binet's window.

He was unable, however, to savor his grief to the full, for he had no one to share it with. He paid visits to Madame Lefrançois to be able to speak of *her*. But the innkeeper only listened with half an ear, having troubles of her own. For Monsieur Lheureux had finally set up his own business, *les Favorites du Commerce*, and Hivert, every one's favorite messenger, threatened to go to work for the competition unless he received higher wages.

One day when he had gone to the market at Argueil to sell his horse—his last resource—he met Rodolphe.

They both turned pale when they caught sight of one another. Rodolphe, who had only sent his card for the funeral, first stammered some apologies, then grew bolder, and even invited Charles (it was in the month of August and very hot) to share a bottle of beer with him at the terrace of a café.

Leaning his elbows on the table, he chewed his cigar as he talked, and Charles was lost in reverie at the sight of the face she had loved. He seemed to find back something of her there. It was quite a shock to him. He would have liked to have been this man.

The other went on talking of agriculture, cattle and fertilizers, filling with banalities all the gaps where an allusion might slip in. Charles was not listening to him; Rodolphe noticed it, and he could follow the sequence of memories that crossed his face. This face gradually reddened; Charles's nostrils fluttered, his lips quivered. For a moment, Charles stared at him in somber fury and Rodolphe, startled and terrified, stopped talking. But soon the same look of mournful weariness returned to his face.

"I can't blame you for it," he said.

Rodolphe remained silent. And Charles, his head in his hands, went on in a broken voice, with the resigned accent of infinite grief:

"No, I can't blame you any longer."

He even made a phrase, the only one he'd ever made:

"Fate willed it this way."

Rodolphe, who had been the agent of this fate, thought him very meek for a man in his situation, comic even and slightly despicable.

The next day Charles sat down on the garden seat under the arbor. Rays of light were straying through the trellis, the vine leaves threw their shadows on the sand, jasmines perfumed the blue air, Spanish flies buzzed round the lilies in bloom, and Charles was panting like an adolescent under the vague desires of love that filled his aching heart.

At seven o'clock little Berthe who had not seen him all afternoon, came to fetch him for dinner.

His head was leaning against the wall, with closed eyes and open mouth, and in his hand was a long tress of black hair.

"Papa, come!"

And thinking he wanted to play, she gave him a gentle push. He fell to the ground. He was dead.

Thirty-six hours later, at the pharmacist's request, Monsieur Canivet arrived. He performed an autopsy, but found nothing.

When everything had been sold, there remained twelve francs and seventy-five centimes, just enough to send Mademoiselle Bovary off to her grandmother. The woman died the same year; and since Rouault was paralyzed, it was an aunt who took charge of her. She is poor, and sends her to a cotton-mill to earn a living.

Since Bovary's death three doctors have succeeded one another in Yonville without any success, so effectively did Homais hasten to eradicate them. He has more customers than there are sinners in hell; the authorities treat him kindly and he has the public on his side.

He has just been given the cross of the Legion of Honor.

FYODOR DOSTOEVSKY

(1821–1881)

Notes from Underground* [1]

Part I

UNDERGROUND

I

I am a sick man. . . . I am a spiteful man. I am an unattractive man. I believe my liver is diseased. However, I know nothing at all about my disease, and do not know for certain what ails me. I don't consult a doctor for it, and never have, though I have a respect for medicine and doctors. Besides, I am extremely superstitious, sufficiently so to respect medicine, anyway (I am well-educated enough not to be superstitious, but I am superstitious). No, I refuse to consult a doctor from spite. That you probably will not understand. Well, I understand it, though. Of course I can't explain who it is precisely that I am mortifying in this case by my spite: I am perfectly well aware that I cannot "pay out" the doctors by not consulting them; I know better than any one that by all this I am only injuring myself and no one else. But still, if I don't consult a doctor it is from spite. My liver is bad, well—let it get worse!

I have been going on like that for a long time—twenty years. Now I am forty. I used to be in the government service, but am no longer. I was a spiteful official. I was rude and took pleasure in being so. I did not take bribes, you see, so I was bound to find a recompense in that, at least. (A poor jest, but I will not scratch it out. I wrote it thinking it would sound very witty; but now that I have seen myself that I only wanted to show off in a despicable way, I will not scratch it out on purpose!)

When petitioners used to come for information to the table at which I sat, I used to grind my teeth at them, and felt intense enjoyment when I succeeded in making anybody unhappy. I almost always did succeed. For the most part they were all timid people—

---

* 1864. Translated by Constance Garnett. Reprinted in full. The punctuation ". . ." does not indicate omissions from this text.

1. The author of the diary and the diary itself are, of course, imaginary. Nevertheless it is clear that such persons as the writer of these notes not only may, but positively must, exist in our society, when we consider the circumstances in the midst of which our society is formed. I have tried to expose to the view of the public more distinctly than is commonly done, one of the characters of the recent past. He is one of the representatives of a generation still living. In this fragment, entitled "Underground," this person introduces himself and his views, and, as it were, tries to explain the causes owing to which he has made his appearance and was bound to make his appearance in our midst. In the second fragment there are added the actual notes of this person concerning certain events in his life. [Author's note.]

of course, they were petitioners. But of the uppish ones there was one officer in particular I could not endure. He simply would not be humble, and clanked his sword in a disgusting way. I carried on a feud with him for eighteen months over that sword. At last I got the better of him. He left off clanking it. That happened in my youth, though.

But do you know, gentlemen, what was the chief point about my spite? Why, the whole point, the real sting of it lay in the fact that continually, even in the moment of the acutest spleen, I was inwardly conscious with shame that I was not only not a spiteful but not even an embittered man, that I was simply scaring sparrows at random and amusing myself by it. I might foam at the mouth, but bring me a doll to play with, give me a cup of tea with sugar in it, and maybe I should be appeased. I might even be genuinely touched, though probably I should grind my teeth at myself afterwards and lie awake at night with shame for months after. That was my way.

I was lying when I said just now that I was a spiteful official. I was lying from spite. I was simply amusing myself with the petitioners and with the officer, and in reality I never could become spiteful. I was conscious every moment in myself of many, very many elements absolutely opposite to that. I felt them positively swarming in me, these opposite elements. I knew that they had been swarming in me all my life and craving some outlet from me, but I would not let them, would not let them, purposely would not let them come out. They tormented me till I was ashamed: they drove me to convulsions and—sickened me, at last, how they sickened me! Now, are not you fancying, gentlemen, that I am expressing remorse for something now, that I am asking your forgiveness for something? I am sure you are fancying that . . . However, I assure you I do not care if you are. . . .

It was not only that I could not become spiteful, I did not know how to become anything: neither spiteful nor kind, neither a rascal nor an honest man, neither a hero nor an insect. Now, I am living out my life in my corner, taunting myself with the spiteful and useless consolation that an intelligent man cannot become anything seriously, and it is only the fool who becomes anything. Yes, a man in the nineteenth century must and morally ought to be pre-eminently a characterless creature; a man of character, an active man is pre-eminently a limited creature. That is my conviction of forty years. I am forty years old now, and you know forty years is a whole lifetime; you know it is extreme old age. To live longer than forty years is bad manners, is vulgar, immoral. Who lives beyond forty? Answer that, sincerely and honestly. I will tell you who do: fools and worthless fellows. I tell all old men that to their face, all these venerable old men, all these silver-haired and reverend seniors! I tell the whole world that to its face! I have a right to say so, for I shall go on living to sixty myself. To seventy! To eighty! . . . Stay, let me take breath. . . .

You imagine no doubt, gentlemen, that I want to amuse you. You are mistaken in that, too. I am by no means such a mirthful person as you imagine, or as you may imagine; however, irritated by all this babble (and I feel that you are irritated) you think fit to ask me who am I—then my answer is, I am a collegiate assessor. I was in the service that I might have something to eat (and solely for that reason), and when last year a distant relation left me six thousand roubles in his will I immediately retired from the service and settled down in my corner. I used to live in this corner before, but now I have settled down in it. My room is a wretched, horrid one in the outskirts of the town. My servant is an old country-woman, ill-natured from stupidity, and, moreover, there is always a nasty smell about her. I am told that the Petersburg climate is bad for me, and that with my small means it is very expensive to live in Petersburg. I know all that better than all these sage and experienced counsellors and monitors. . . . But I am remaining in Petersburg; . . . I am not going away from Petersburg! I am not going away because . . . ech! Why, it is absolutely no matter whether I am going away or not going away.

But what can a decent man speak of with most pleasure?

Answer: Of himself.

Well, so I will talk about myself.

II

I want now to tell you, gentlemen, whether you care to hear it or not, why I could not even become an insect. I tell you solemnly, that I have many times tried to become an insect. But I was not equal even to that. I swear, gentlemen, that to be too conscious is an illness—a real thoroughgoing illness. For man's everyday needs, it would have been quite enough to have the ordinary human consciousness, that is, half or a quarter of the amount which falls to the lot of a cultivated man of our unhappy nineteenth century, especially one who has the fatal ill-luck to inhabit Petersburg, the most theoretical and intentional town on the whole terrestrial globe. (There are intentional and unintentional towns.) It would have been quite enough, for instance, to have the consciousness by which all so-called direct persons and men of action live. I bet you think I am writing all this from affectation, to be witty at the expense of men of action; and what is more, that from ill-bred affectation, I am clanking a sword like my officer. But, gentlemen, whoever can pride himself on his diseases and even swagger over them?

Though, after all, every one does do that; people do pride themselves on their diseases, and I do, may be, more than any one else. We will not dispute it; my contention was absurd. But yet I am firmly persuaded that a great deal of consciousness, every sort of consciousness, in fact, is a disease. I stick to that. Let us leave that, too, for a minute. Tell me this: why does it happen that at the very, yes, at the very moments when I am most capable of feeling every refinement of all that is "good and beautiful," as they used to say at one time, it would, as though of design, happen to me not only to feel but to do such ugly things, such that . . . Well, in short, actions that all, perhaps, commit; but which, as though purposely, occurred to me at the very time when I was most conscious that they ought not to be committed. The more conscious I was of goodness and of all that was "good and beautiful," the more deeply I sank into my mire and the more ready I was to sink in it altogether. But the chief point was that all this was, as it were, not accidental in me, but as though it were bound to be so. It was as though it were my most normal condition, and not in the least disease or depravity, so that at last all desire in me to struggle against this depravity passed. It ended by my almost believing (perhaps actually believing) that this was perhaps my normal condition. But at first, in the beginning, what agonies I endured in that struggle! I did not believe it was the same with other people, and all my life I hid this fact about myself as a secret. I was ashamed (even now, perhaps, I am ashamed): I got to the point of feeling a sort of secret abnormal, despicable enjoyment in returning home to my corner on some disgusting Petersburg night, acutely conscious that that day I had committed a loathsome action again, that what was done could never be undone, and secretly, inwardly gnawing, gnawing at myself for it, tearing and consuming myself till at last the bitterness turned into a sort of shameful accursed sweetness, and at last—into positive real enjoyment! Yes into enjoyment, into enjoyment! I insist upon that. I have spoken of this because I keep wanting to know for a fact whether other people feel such enjoyment? I will explain; the enjoyment was just from the too intense consciousness of one's own degradation; it was from feeling oneself that one had reached the last barrier, that it was horrible, but that it could not be otherwise; that there was no escape for you; that you never could become a different man; that even if time and faith were still left you to change into something different you would most likely not wish to change; or if you did wish to, even then you would do nothing; because perhaps in reality there was nothing for you to change into.

And the worst of it was, and the root of it all, that it was all in accord with the normal fundamental laws of over-acute consciousness, and with the inertia that was the direct result of those laws, and that consequently one was not only unable to change but could do absolutely nothing. Thus it would follow, as the result of acute consciousness, that one is not to blame in being a scoundrel; as though that were any consolation to the scoundrel once he has come to realize that he actually is a scoundrel. But enough. . . . Ech, I have talked a lot of nonsense, but what have I explained? How is enjoyment in this to be explained? But I will explain it. I will get to the bottom of it! That is why I have taken up my pen. . . .

I, for instance, have a great deal of *amour propre*. I am as suspicious and prone to take offence as a hunchback or a dwarf. But upon my word I sometimes have had moments when if I had happened to be slapped in the face I should, perhaps, have been positively glad of it. I say, in earnest, that I should probably have been able to discover even in that a peculiar sort of enjoyment— the enjoyment, of course, of despair; but in despair there are the most intense enjoyments, especially when one is very acutely conscious of the hopelessness of one's position. And when one is slapped in the face—why then the consciousness of being rubbed into a pulp would positively overwhelm one. The worst of it is, look at it which way one will, it still turns out that I was always the most to blame in everything. And what is most humiliating of all, to blame for no fault of my own but, so to say, through the laws of nature. In the first place, to blame because I am cleverer than any of the people surrounding me. (I have always considered myself cleverer than any of the people surrounding me, and sometimes, would you believe it, have been positively ashamed of it. At any rate, I have all my life, as it were, turned my eyes away and never could look people straight in the face.) To blame, finally, because even if I had had magnanimity, I should only have had more suffering from the sense of its uselessness. I should certainly have never been able to do anything from being magnanimous— neither to forgive, for my assailant would perhaps have slapped me from the laws of nature, and one cannot forgive the laws of nature; nor to forget, for even if it were owing to the laws of nature, it is insulting all the same. Finally, even if I had wanted to be anything but magnanimous, had desired on the contrary to revenge myself on my assailant, I could not have revenged myself on any one for anything because I should certainly never have made up my mind to do anything, even if I had been able to. Why should I not have made up my mind? About that in particular I want to say a few words.

III

With people who know how to revenge themselves and to stand up for themselves in general, how is it done? Why, when they are possessed, let us suppose, by the feeling of revenge, then for the time there is nothing else but that feeling left in their whole being. Such a gentleman simply dashes straight for his object like an infuriated bull with its horns down, and nothing but a wall will stop him. (By the way: facing the wall, such gentlemen—that is, the "direct" persons and men of action—are genuinely nonplussed. For them a wall is not an evasion, as for us people who think and consequently do nothing; it is not an excuse for turning aside, an excuse for which we are always very glad, though we scarcely believe in it ourselves, as a rule. No, they are nonplussed in all sincerity. The wall has for them something tranquillizing, morally soothing, final—maybe even something mysterious . . . but of the wall later.)

Well, such a direct person I regard as the real normal man, as his tender mother nature wished to see him when she graciously brought him into being on the earth. I envy such a man till I am green in the face. He is stupid. I am not disputing that, but perhaps the normal man should be stupid, how do you know? Perhaps it is very beautiful, in fact. And I am the more persuaded of that suspicion, if one can call it so, by the fact that if you take, for instance, the antithesis of the normal man, that is, the man of acute consciousness, who has come, of course, not out of the lap of nature but out of a retort (this is almost mysticism, gentlemen, but I suspect this, too), this retort-made man is sometimes so nonplussed in the presence of his antithesis that with all his exaggerated consciousness he genuinely thinks of himself as a mouse and not a man. It may be an acutely conscious mouse, yet it is a mouse, while the other is a man, and therefore, et cætera, et cætera. And the worst of it is, he himself, his very own self, looks on himself as a mouse; no one asks him to do so; and that is an important point. Now let us look at this mouse in action. Let us suppose, for instance, that it feels insulted, too (and it almost always does feel insulted), and wants to revenge itself, too. There may even be a greater accumulation of spite in it than in *l'homme de la nature et de la vérité*.[2] The base and nasty desire to vent that spite on its assailant rankles perhaps even more nastily in it than in *l'homme de la nature et de la vérité*. For through his innate stupidity the latter looks upon his revenge as justice pure and simple; while in consequence of his acute consciousness the mouse does not be-

2. "the man of nature and truth"; Rousseau's description of himself in the *Confessions* (1781–1788), which created an enormous stir because they professed to tell the whole truth about the author and were sometimes self-accusing.

lieve in the justice of it. To come at last to the deed itself, to the very act of revenge. Apart from the one fundamental nastiness the luckless mouse succeeds in creating around it so many other nastinesses in the form of doubts and questions, adds to the one question so many unsettled questions that there inevitably works up around it a sort of fatal brew, a stinking mess, made up of its doubts, emotions, and of the contempt spat upon it by the direct men of action who stand solemnly about it as judges and arbitrators, laughing at it till their healthy sides ache. Of course the only thing left for it is to dismiss all that with a wave of its paw, and, with a smile of assumed contempt in which it does not even itself believe, creep ignominiously into its mouse-hole. There in its nasty, stinking, underground home our insulted, crushed and ridiculed mouse promptly becomes absorbed in cold, malignant and, above all, everlasting spite. For forty years together it will remember its injury down to the smallest, most ignominious details, and every time will add, of itself, details still more ignominious, spitefully teasing and tormenting itself with its own imagination. It will itself be ashamed of its imaginings, but yet it will recall it all, it will go over and over every detail, it will invent unheard of things against itself, pretending that those things might happen, and will forgive nothing. Maybe it will begin to revenge itself, too, but, as it were, piecemeal, in trivial ways, from behind the stove, incognito, without believing either in its own right to vengeance, or in the success of its revenge knowing that from all its efforts at revenge it will suffer a hundred times more than he on whom it revenges itself, while he, I daresay, will not even scratch himself. On its deathbed it will recall it all over again, with interest accumulated over all the years and. . . .

But it is just in that cold, abominable half despair, half belief, in that conscious burying oneself alive for grief in the underworld for forty years, in that acutely recognized and yet partly doubtful hopelessness of one's position, in that hell of unsatisfied desires turned inward, in that fever of oscillations, or resolutions determined for ever and repented of again a minute later—that the savour of that strange enjoyment of which I have spoken lies. It is so subtle, so difficult of analysis, that persons who are a little limited, or even simply persons of strong nerves, will not understand a single atom of it. "Possibly," you will add on your own account with a grin, "people will not understand it either who have never received a slap in the face," and in that way you will politely hint to me that I, too, perhaps, have had the experience of a slap in the face in my life, and so I speak as one who knows. I bet that you are thinking that. But set your minds at rest, gentlemen, I have not received a slap in the face, though it is absolutely a matter of indifference to me what you may think about it. Possibly, I even regret, myself, that I have given so few slaps in the face during my life. But enough . . . not another word on that subject of such extreme interest to you.

I will continue calmly concerning persons with strong nerves who do not understand a certain refinement of enjoyment. Though in certain circumstances these gentlemen bellow their loudest like bulls, though this, let us suppose, does them the greatest credit, yet, as I have said already, confronted with the impossible they subside at once. The impossible means the stone wall! What stone wall? Why, of course, the laws of nature, the deductions of natural science, mathematics. As soon as they prove to you, for instance, that you are descended from a monkey, then it is no use scowling, accept it for a fact. When they prove to you that in reality one drop of your own fat must be dearer to you than a hundred thousand of your fellow-creatures, and that this conclusion is the final solution of all so-called virtues and duties and all such prejudices and fancies, then you have just to accept it, there is no help for it, for twice two is a law of mathematics. Just try refuting it.

"Upon my word," they will shout at you, "it is no use protesting: it is a case of twice two makes four! Nature does not ask your permission, she has nothing to do with your wishes, and whether you like her laws or dislike them, you are bound to accept her as she is, and consequently all her conclusions. A wall, you see, is a wall . . ." and so on, and so on.

Merciful Heavens! but what do I care for the laws of nature and arithmetic, when, for some reason I dislike those laws and the fact that twice two makes four? Of course I cannot break through the wall by battering my head against it if I really have not the strength to knock it down, but I am not going to be reconciled to it simply because it is a stone wall and I have not the strength.

As though such a stone wall really were a consolation, and really did contain some word of conciliation, simply because it is as true as twice two makes four. Oh, absurdity of absurdities! How much better it is to understand it all, to recognize it all, all the impossibilities and the stone wall; not to be reconciled to one of those impossibilities and stone walls if it disgusts you to be reconciled to it; by the way of the most inevitable, logical combinations to reach the most revolting conclusions on the everlasting theme, that even for the stone wall you are yourself somehow to blame, though again it is as clear as day you are not to blame in the least, and therefore grinding your teeth in silent impotence to sink into luxurious inertia, brooding on the fact that there is no one even for you to feel vindictive against, that you have not, and perhaps never will have, an object for your spite, that it is a sleight of hand, a bit of juggling, a card-sharper's trick, that it is simply a mess, no knowing what and no knowing who, but in spite of all these un-certainties and jugglings, still there is an ache in you, and the more you do not know, the worse the ache.

IV

"Ha, ha, ha! You will be finding enjoyment in toothache next," you cry, with a laugh.

"Well? Even in toothache there is enjoyment," I answer. I had toothache for a whole month and I know there is. In that case, of course, people are not spiteful in silence, but moan; but they are not candid moans, they are malignant moans, and the malig-nancy is the whole point. The enjoyment of the sufferer finds expression in those moans; if he did not feel enjoyment in them he would not moan. It is a good example, gentlemen, and I will develop it. Those moans express in the first place all the aimless-ness of your pain, which is so humiliating to your consciousness; the whole legal system of nature on which you spit disdainfully, of course, but from which you suffer all the same while she does not. They express the consciousness that you have no enemy to punish, but that you have pain; the consciousness that in spite of all possible Wagenheims[3] you are in complete slavery to your teeth; that if some one wishes it, your teeth will leave off aching, and if he does not, they will go on aching another three months; and that finally if you are still contumacious and still protest, all that is left you for your own gratification is to thrash yourself or beat your wall with your fist as hard as you can, and absolutely nothing more. Well, these mortal insults, these jeers on the part of some one unknown, end at last in an enjoyment which sometimes reaches the highest degree of voluptuousness. I ask you, gentlemen, listen sometimes to the moans of an educated man of the nineteenth century suffering from toothache, on the second or third day of the attack, when he is beginning to moan, not as he moaned on the first day, that is, not simply because he has toothache, not just as any coarse peasant, but as a man affected by progress and European civilization, a man who is "divorced from the soil and the national elements," as they express it now-a-days. His moans become nasty, disgustingly malignant, and go on for whole days and nights. And of course he knows himself that he is doing himself no sort of good with his moans; he knows better than any one that he is only lacerating and harassing himself and others for nothing; he knows that even the audience before whom he is making his efforts, and his whole family, listen to him with loathing, do not put the

---

3. Wagenheim was apparently a Ger-man who advertised painless dentistry; he may have used hypnosis or auto suggestion.

least faith in him, and inwardly understand that he might moan differently, more simply, without trills and flourishes, and that he is only amusing himself like that from ill-humour, from malignancy. Well, in all these recognitions and disgraces it is that there lies a voluptuous pleasure. As though he would say: "I am worrying you, I am lacerating your hearts, I am keeping every one in the house awake. Well, stay awake then, you, too, feel every minute that I have toothache. I am not a hero to you now, as I tried to seem before, but simply a nasty person, an impostor. Well, so be it, then! I am very glad that you see through me. It is nasty for you to hear my despicable moans: well, let it be nasty; here I will let you have a nastier flourish in a minute. . . ." You do not understand even now, gentlemen? No, it seems our development and our consciousness must go further to understand all the intricacies of this pleasure. You laugh? Delighted. My jests, gentlemen, are of course in bad taste, jerky, involved, lacking self-confidence. But of course that is because I do not respect myself. Can a man of perception respect himself at all?

v

Come, can a man who attempts to find enjoyment in the very feeling of his own degradation possibly have a spark of respect for himself? I am not saying this now from any mawkish kind of remorse. And, indeed, I could never endure saying, "Forgive me, Papa, I won't do it again," not because I am incapable of saying that—on the contrary, perhaps just because I have been too capable of it, and in what a way, too! As though of design I used to get into trouble in cases when I was not to blame in any way. That was the nastiest part of it. At the same time I was genuinely touched and penitent, I used to shed tears and, of course, deceived myself, though I was not acting in the least and there was a sick feeling in my heart at the time. . . . For that one could not blame even the laws of nature, though the laws of nature have continually all my life offended me more than anything. It is loathsome to remember it all, but it was loathsome even then. Of course, a minute or so later I would realize wrathfully that is was all a lie, a revolting lie, an affected lie, that is, all this penitence, this emotion, these vows of reform. You will ask why did I worry myself with such antics: answer, because it was very dull to sit with one's hands folded, and so one began cutting capers. That is really it. Observe yourselves more carefully, gentlemen, then you will understand that it is so. I invented adventures for myself and made up a life, so as at least to live in some way. How many times it has happened to me—well, for instance, to take offence simply on purpose, for nothing; and one knows oneself, of course, that one is offended at nothing, that one is putting it on, but yet one brings oneself, at last to the point of being really offended. All my life I have had an impulse to play such pranks, so that in the end I could not control it in myself. Another time, twice, in fact, I tried hard to be in love. I suffered, too, gentlemen, I assure you. In the depth of my heart there was no faith in my suffering, only a faint stir of mockery, but yet I did suffer, and in the real, orthodox way; I was jealous, beside myself . . . and it was all from *ennui*, gentlemen, all from *ennui*; inertia overcame me. You know the direct, legitimate fruit of consciousness is inertia, that is, conscious sitting-with-the-hands-folded. I have referred to this already. I repeat, I repeat with emphasis: all "direct" persons and men of action are active just because they are stupid and limited. How explain that? I will tell you: in consequence of their limitation they take immediate and secondary causes for primary ones, and in that way persuade themselves more quickly and easily than other people do that they have found an infallible foundation for their activity, and their minds are at ease and you know that is the chief thing. To begin to act, you know, you must first have your mind completely at ease and no trace of doubt left in it. Why, how am I, for example to set my mind at rest? Where are the primary causes on which I am to build? Where are my foundations? Where am I to get them from? I exercise myself in reflection, and consequently with me every primary cause at once draws after itself another still more primary, and so on to infinity. That is just the essence of every sort of consciousness and reflection. It must be a case of the laws of nature again. What is the result of it in the end? Why, just the same. Remember I spoke just now of vengeance. (I am sure you did not take it in.) I said that a man revenges himself because he sees justice in it. Therefore he has found a primary cause, that is, justice. And so he is at rest on all sides, and consequently he carries out his revenge calmly and successfully, being persuaded that he is doing a just and honest thing. But I see no justice in it, I find no sort of virtue in it either, and consequently if I attempt to revenge myself, it is only out of spite. Spite, of course, might overcome everything, all my doubts, and so might serve quite successfully in place of a primary cause, precisely because it is not a cause. But what is to be done if I have not even spite (I began with that just now, you know). In consequence again of those accursed laws of consciousness, anger in me is subject to chemical disintegration. You look into it, the object flies off into air, your reasons evaporate, the criminal is not to be found, the wrong becomes not a wrong but a phantom, something like the toothache, for which no one is to blame, and consequently there is only the same outlet left again—that is, to beat the wall as hard as you can. So you give it up with a wave of the hand because you have not found a fundamental cause. And try letting yourself be carried away by your feelings, blindly, without reflection, without a primary cause, repelling consciousness at least for a time; hate or love, if only not to sit with your hands folded. The day after to-morrow, at the latest, you will begin despising yourself for having knowingly deceived yourself. Result: a soap-bubble and inertia. Oh, gentlemen, do you know, perhaps I consider myself an intelligent man, only because all my life I have been able neither to begin nor to finish anything. Granted I am a babbler, a harmless vexatious babbler, like all of us. But what is to be done if the direct and sole vocation of every intelligent man is babble, that is, the intentional pouring of water through a sieve?

VI

Oh, if I had done nothing simply from laziness! Heavens, how I should have respected myself, then. I should have respected myself because I should at least have been capable of being lazy; there would at least have been one quality, as it were, positive in me, in which I could have believed myself. Question: What is he? Answer: A sluggard; how very pleasant it would have been to hear that of oneself! It would mean that I was positively defined, it would mean that there was something to say about me. "Sluggard"—why, it is a calling and vocation, it is a career. Do not jest, it is so. I should then be a member of the best club by right, and should find my occupation in continually respecting myself. I knew a gentlemen who prided himself all his life on being a connoisseur of Lafitte. He considered this as his positive virtue, and never doubted himself. He died, not simply with a tranquil, but with a triumphant, conscience, and he was quite right, too. Then I should have chosen a career for myself, I should have been a sluggard and a glutton, not a simple one, but, for instance, one with sympathies for everything good and beautiful. How do you like that? I have long had visions of it. That "good and beautiful" weighs heavily on my mind at forty. But that is at forty; then—oh, then it would have been different! I should have found for myself a form of activity in keeping with it, to be precise, drinking to the health of everything "good and beautiful." I should have snatched at every opportunity to drop a tear into my glass and then to drain it to all that is "good and beautiful." I should then have turned everything into the good and the beautiful; in the nastiest, unquestionable trash, I should have sought out the good and the beautiful. I should have exuded tears like a wet sponge. An artist, for instance, paints a picture worthy of Gay.[4] At once I drink to the health of the artist who painted the picture worthy of Gay,

4. Nikolay Nikolaevich Gay (1831–1894), Russian painter of historical pictures who then had a great reputation. His father was a French emigrant.

because I love all that is "good and beautiful." An author has written *What you will:*[5] at once I drink to the health of "what you will" because I love all that is "good and beautiful."

I should claim respect for doing so. I should persecute any one who would not show me respect. I should live at ease, I should die with dignity, why, it is charming, perfectly charming! And what a good round belly I should have grown, what a triple chin I should have established, what a ruby nose I should have coloured for myself, so that every one would have said, looking at me: "Here is an asset! Here is something real and solid!" And, say what you like, it is very agreeable to hear such remarks about oneself in this negative age.

VII

But these are all golden dreams. Oh, tell me, who was it first announced, who was it first proclaimed, that man only does nasty things because he does not know his own interests; and that if he were enlightened, if his eyes were opened to his real normal interests, man would at once cease to do nasty things, would at once become good and noble because, being enlightened and understanding his real advantage, he would see his own advantage in the good and nothing else. and we all know that not one man can, consciously, act against his own interests, consequently, so to say, through necessity, he would begin doing good? Oh, the babe! Oh, the pure, innocent child! Why, in the first place, when in all these thousands of years has there been a time when man has acted only from his own interest? What is to be done with the millions of facts that bear witness that men, *consciously*, that is fully understanding their real interests, have left them in the background and have rushed headlong on another path, to meet peril and danger, compelled to this course by nobody and by nothing, but, as it were, simply disliking the beaten track, and have obstinately, wilfully, struck out another difficult, absurd way, seeking it almost in the darkness. So, I suppose, this obstinacy and perversity were pleasanter to them than any advantage. . . . Advantage! What is advantage? And will you take it upon yourself to define with perfect accuracy in what the advantage of man consists? And what if it so happens that a man's advantage, *sometimes*, not only may, but even must, consist in his desiring in certain cases what is harmful to himself and not advantageous. And if so, if there can be such a case, the whole principle falls into dust. What do you think—are there such cases? You laugh; laugh away, gentlemen, but only answer me: have man's advantages been reckoned up with perfect certainty? Are there not some which not only have

---

5. subtitle of Shakespeare's comedy *Twelfth Night*, generally used on the Continent instead of the main title, which is difficult to translate.

not been included but cannot possibly be included under any classification? You see, you gentlemen have, to the best of my knowledge, taken your whole register of human advantages from the averages of statistical figures and politico-economical formulas. Your advantages are prosperity, wealth, freedom, peace—and so on, and so on. So that the man who should, for instance, go openly and knowingly in opposition to all that list would, to your thinking, and indeed mine, too, of course, be an obscurantist or an absolute madman: would not he? But, you know, this is what is surprising: why does it so happen that all these statisticians, sages and lovers of humanity, when they reckon up human advantages invariably leave out one? They don't even take it into their reckoning in the form in which it should be taken, and the whole reckoning depends upon that. It would be no great matter, they would simply have to take it, this advantage, and add it to the list. But the trouble is, that this strange advantage does not fall under any classification and is not in place in any list. I have a friend for instance . . . Ech! gentlemen, but of course he is your friend, too; and indeed there is no one, no one, to whom he is not a friend! When he prepares for any undertaking this gentleman immediately explains to you, elegantly and clearly, exactly how he must act in accordance with the laws of reason and truth. What is more, he will talk to you with excitement and passion of the true normal interests of man; with irony he will upbraid the shortsighted fools who do not understand their own interests, nor the true significance of virtue; and, within a quarter of an hour, without any sudden outside provocation, but simply through something inside him which is stronger than all his interests, he will go off on quite a different tack—that is, act in direct opposition to what he has just been saying about himself, in opposition to the laws of reason, in opposition to his own advantage, in fact in opposition to everything . . . I warn you that my friend is a compound personality, and therefore it is difficult to blame him as an individual. The fact is, gentlemen, it seems there must really exist something that is dearer to almost every man than his greatest advantages, or (not to be illogical) there is a most advantageous advantage (the very one omitted of which we spoke just now) which is more important and more advantageous than all other advantages, for the sake of which a man if necessary is ready to act in opposition to all laws; that is, in opposition to reason, honour, peace, prosperity—in fact, in opposition to all those excellent and useful things if only he can attain that fundamental, most advantageous advantage which is dearer to him than all. "Yes, but it's advantage all the same" you will retort. But excuse me, I'll make the point clear, and it is not a case of playing upon words. What matters is, that this advantage is remarkable from the very fact that it breaks down all our classifications, and continually shatters every system constructed by lovers of mankind for the benefit of mankind. In fact, it upsets everything. But before I mention this advantage to you, I want to compromise myself personally, and therefore I boldly declare that all these fine systems, all these theories for explaining to mankind their real normal interests, in order that inevitably striving to pursue these interests they may at once become good and noble —are, in my opinion, so far, mere logical exercises! Yes, logical exercises. Why, to maintain this theory of the regeneration of mankind by means of the pursuit of his own advantage is to my mind almost the same thing as . . . as to affirm, for instance, following Buckle,[6] that through civilization mankind becomes softer, and consequently less bloodthirsty and less fitted for warfare. Logically it does seem to follow from his arguments. But man has such a predilection for systems and abstract deductions that he is ready to distort the truth intentionally, he is ready to deny the evidence of his senses only to justify his logic. I take this example because it is the most glaring instance of it. Only look about you: blood is being spilt in streams, and in the merriest way, as though it were champagne. Take the whole of the nineteenth century in which Buckle lived. Take Napoleon—the Great and also the present one. Take North America—the eternal union. Take the farce of Schleswig-Holstein.[7] . . . And what is it that civilization softens in us? The only gain of civilization for mankind is the greater capacity for variety of sensations—and absolutely nothing more. And through the development of this many-sidedness man may come to finding enjoyment in bloodshed. In fact, this has already happened to him. Have you noticed that it is the most civilized gentlemen who have been the subtlest slaughterers, to whom the Attilas[8] and Stenka Razins[9] could not hold a candle, and if they are not so conspicuous as the Attilas and Stenka Razins it is simply because they are so often met with, are so ordinary and have become so familiar to us. In any case civilization has made mankind if not more bloodthirsty, at least more vilely, more loathsomely bloodthirsty. In old days he saw justice in bloodshed and with his conscience at peace exterminated those he thought proper. Now we do think bloodshed abominable and yet we engage in this

6. Henry Thomas Buckle (1821–1862), the author of the *History of Civilization in England* (two volumes, 1857, 1861), which held that all progress is due to the march of mind. There is no moral progress except indirectly, as a result of intellectual enlightenment.

7. Austria and Prussia invaded Denmark and annexed its southernmost part, Schleswig-Holstein, in 1864.

8. Attila (406?–453 A.D.) was king of the Huns (433?–453). In 451 his armies penetrated as far as Orléans, in what today is France. He was defeated in the battle of Châlons on the Catalaunian plains and retired to Hungary. In 452 he led an expedition against Rome.

9. Stenka Razin was a Don Cossack leader who in 1670 conquered many cities along the Volga. He was finally defeated, captured, and executed in 1671.

abomination, and with more energy than ever. Which is worse? Decide that for yourselves. They say that Cleopatra (excuse an instance from Roman history) was fond of sticking gold pins into her slave-girls' breasts and derived gratification from their screams and writhings. You will say that that was in the comparatively barbarous times; that these are barbarous times too, because also, comparatively speaking, pins are stuck in even now; that though man has now learned to see more clearly than in barbarous ages, he is still far from having learnt to act as reason and science would dictate. But yet you are fully convinced that he will be sure to learn when he gets rid of certain old bad habits, and when common sense and science have completely re-educated human nature and turned it in a normal direction. You are confident that then man will cease from *intentional* error and will, so to say, be compelled not to want to set his will against his normal interests. That is not all; then, you say, science itself will teach man (though to my mind it's a superfluous luxury) that he never has really had any caprice or will of his own, and that he himself is something of the nature of a piano-key or the stop of an organ, and that there are, besides, things called the laws of nature; so that everything he does is not done by his willing it, but is done of itself, by the laws of nature. Consequently we have only to discover these laws of nature, and man will no longer have to answer for his actions and life will become exceedingly easy for him. All human actions will then, of course, be tabulated according to these laws, mathematically, like tables of logarithms up to 108,000, and entered in an index; or, better still, there would be published certain edifying works of the nature of encyclopædic lexicons, in which everything will be so clearly calculated and explained that there will be no more incidents or adventures in the world.

Then—this is all what you say—new economic relations will be established, all ready-made and worked out with mathematical exactitude, so that every possible question will vanish in the twinkling of any eye, simply because every possible answer to it will be provided. Then the "Crystal Palace"[10] will be built. Then . . . . In fact, those will be halcyon days. Of course there is no guaranteeing (this is my comment) that it will not be, for instance, frightfully dull then (for what will one have to do when everything will be calculated and tabulated), but on the other hand everything will be extraordinary rational. Of course boredom may lead you to anything. It is boredom sets one sticking golden pins into people, but all that would not matter. What is bad (this is my

10. Dostoevsky has in mind the London Crystal Palace, a structure of glass and iron built in 1851–1854, and at that time admired as the newest wonder of architecture. The nave was five hundred yards long. The building burned down in 1936.

comment again) is that I dare say people will be thankful for the gold pins then. Man is stupid, you know, phenomenally stupid; or rather he is not at all stupid, but he is so ungrateful that you could not find another like him in all creation. I, for instance, would not be in the least surprised if all of a sudden, *à propos* of nothing, in the midst of general prosperity a gentleman with an ignoble, or rather with a reactionary and ironical, countenance were to arise and, putting his arms akimbo, say to us all: "I say, gentlemen, hadn't we better kick over the whole show and scatter rationalism to the winds, simply to send these logarithms to the devil, and to enable us to live once more at our own sweet foolish will!" That again would not matter, but what is annoying is that he would be sure to find followers—such is the nature of man. And all that for the most foolish reason, which, one would think, was hardly worth mentioning: that is, that man everywhere and at all times, whoever he may be, has preferred to act as he chose and not in the least as his reason and advantage dictated. And one may choose what is contrary to one's own interests, and sometimes one *positively ought* (that is my idea). One's own free unfettered choice, one's own caprice, however wild it may be, one's own fancy worked up at times to frenzy—is that very "most advantageous advantage" which we have overlooked, which comes under no classification and against which all systems and theories are continually being shattered to atoms. And how do these wiseacres know that man wants a normal, a virtuous choice? What has made them conceive that man must want a rationally advantageous choice? What man wants is simply *independent* choice, whatever that independence may cost and wherever it may lead. And choice, of course, the devil only knows what choice.

VIII

"Ha! ha! ha! But you know there is no such thing as choice in reality, say what you like," you will interpose with a chuckle. "Science has succeeded in so far analysing man that we know already that choice and what is called freedom of will is nothing else than——"

Stay, gentlemen, I meant to begin with that myself. I confess, I was rather frightened. I was just going to say that the devil only knows what choice depends on, and that perhaps that was a very good thing, but I remembered the teaching of science . . . and pulled myself up. And here you have begun upon it. Indeed, if there really is some day discovered a formula for all our desires and caprices—that is, an explanation of what they depend upon, by what laws they arise, how they develop, what they are aiming at in one case and in another and so on, that is a real mathematical formula—then, most likely, man will at once cease to feel desire, indeed, he will be certain to. For who would want to choose by rule? Besides, he will at once be transformed from a human being into an organ-stop or something of the sort; for what is a man without desires, without freewill and without choice, if not a stop in an organ? What do you think? Let us reckon the chances—can such a thing happen or not?

"H'm!" you decide. "Our choice is usually mistaken from a false view of our advantage. We sometimes choose absolute nonsense because in our foolishness we see in that nonsense the easiest means for attaining a supposed advantage. But when all that is explained and worked out on paper (which is perfectly possible, for it is contemptible and senseless to suppose that some laws of nature man will never understand), then certainly so-called desires will no longer exist. For if a desire should come into conflict with reason we shall then reason and not desire, because it will be impossible retaining our reason to be *senseless* in our desires, and in that way knowingly act against reason and desire to injure ourselves. And as all choice and reasoning can be really calculated —because there will some day be discovered the laws of our so-called freewill—so, joking apart, there may one day be something like a table constructed of them, so that we really shall choose in accordance with it. If, for instance, some day they calculate and prove to me that I make a long nose at some one because I could not help making a long nose at him and that I had to do it in that particular way, what *freedom* is left me, especially if I am a learned man and have taken my degree somewhere? Then I should be able to calculate my whole life for thirty years beforehand. In short, if this could be arranged there would be nothing left for us to do; anyway, we should have to understand that. And, in fact, we ought unwearyingly to repeat to ourselves that at such and such a time and in such and such circumstances nature does not ask our leave; that we have got to take her as she is and not fashion her to suit our fancy, and if we really aspire to formulas and tables of rules, and well, even . . . to the chemical retort, there's no help for it, we must accept the retort too, or else it will be accepted without our consent. . . ."

Yes, but here I come to a stop! Gentlemen, you must excuse me for being over-philosophical; it's the result of forty years underground! Allow me to indulge my fancy. You see, gentlemen, reason is an excellent thing, there's no disputing that, but reason is nothing but reason and satisfies only the rational side of man's nature, while will is a manifestation of the whole life, that is, of the whole human life including reason and all the impulses. And although our life, in this manifestation of it, is often worthless, yet it is life and not simply extracting square roots. Here I, for instance, quite naturally want to live, in order to satisfy all my capacities for life, and not simply my capacity for reasoning, that is, not simply one twentieth of my capacity for life. What does reason know? Reason only knows what it has succeeded in learning (some things, perhaps, it will never learn; this is a poor comfort, but why not say so frankly?) and human nature acts as a whole, with everything that is in it, consciously or unconsciously, and, even if it goes wrong, it lives. I suspect, gentlemen, that you are looking at me with compassion; you tell me again that an enlightened and developed man, such, in short, as the future man will be, cannot consciously desire anything disadvantageous to himself, that that can be proved mathematically. I thoroughly agree, it can—by mathematics. But I repeat for the hundredth time, there is one case, one only, when man may consciously, purposely, desire what is injurious to himself, what is stupid, very stupid—simply in order to have the right to desire for himself even what is very stupid and not to be bound by an obligation to desire only what is sensible. Of course, this very stupid thing, this caprice of ours, may be in reality, gentlemen, more advantageous for us than anything else on earth, especially in certain cases. And in particular it may be more advantageous than any advantage even when it does us obvious harm, and contradicts the soundest conclusions of our reason concerning our advantage—for in any circumstances it preserves for us what is most precious and most important—that is, our personality, our individuality. Some, you see, maintain that this really is the most precious thing for mankind; choice can, of course, if it chooses, be in agreement with reason; and especially if this be not abused but kept within bounds. It is profitable and sometimes even praiseworthy. But very often, and even most often, choice is utterly and stubbornly opposed to reason . . . and . . . and . . . do you know that that, too, is profitable, sometimes even praiseworthy? Gentlemen, let us suppose that man is not stupid. (Indeed one cannot refuse to suppose that, if only from the one consideration, that, if man is stupid, then who is wise?) But if he is not stupid, he is monstrously ungrateful! Phenomenally ungrateful. In fact, I believe that the best definition of man is the ungrateful biped. But that is not all, that is not his worst defect; his worst defect is his perpetual moral obliquity, perpetual—from the days of the Flood to the Schleswig-Holstein period. Moral obliquity and consequently lack of good sense; for it has long been accepted that lack of good sense is due to no other cause than moral obliquity. Put it to the test and cast your eyes upon the history of mankind. What will you see? Is it a grand spectacle?

Grand, if you like. Take the Colossus of Rhodes,[11] for instance, that's worth something. With good reason Mr. Anaevsky testifies of it that some say that it is the work of man's hands, while others maintain that it has been created by nature herself. Is it many-coloured? May be it is many-coloured, too: if one takes the dress uniforms, military and civilian, of all peoples in all ages—that alone is worth something, and if you take the undress uniforms you will never get to the end of it; no historian would be equal to the job. Is it monotonous? May be it's monotonous too: it's fighting and fighting; they are fighting now, they fought first and they fought last—you will admit, that it is almost too monotonous. In short, one may say anything about the history of the world—anything that might enter the most disordered imagination. The only thing one can't say is that it's rational. The very word sticks in one's throat. And, indeed, this is the odd thing that is continually happening: there are continually turning up in life moral and rational persons, sages and lovers of humanity who make it their object to live all their lives as morally and rationally as possible, to be, so to speak, a light to their neighbours simply in order to show them that it is possible to live morally and rationally in this world. And yet we all know that those very people sooner or later have been false to themselves, playing some queer trick, often a most unseemly one. Now I ask you: what can be expected of man since he is a being endowed with such strange qualities? Shower upon him every earthly blessing, drown him in a sea of happiness, so that nothing but bubbles of bliss can be seen on the surface; give him economic prosperity, such that he should have nothing else to do but sleep, eat cakes and busy himself with the continuation of his species, and even then out of sheer ingratitude, sheer spite, man would play you some nasty trick. He would even risk his cakes and would deliberately desire the most fatal rubbish, the most uneconomical absurdity, simply to introduce into all this positive good sense his fatal fantastic element. It is just his fantastic dreams, his vulgar folly that he will desire to retain, simply in order to prove to himself—as though that were so necessary—that men still are men and not the keys of a piano, which the laws of nature threaten to control so completely that soon one will be able to desire nothing but by the calendar. And that is not all: even if man really were nothing but a piano-key, even if this were proved to him by natural science and mathematics, even then he would not become reasonable, but would purposely do something perverse out of simple ingratitude, simply to gain his point. And if he does not find means he will contrive

11. a statue of Helios (Apollo) at Rhodes (an island in the Aegean Sea), about a hundred feet high, which was considered one of the Seven Wonders of the World. It was erected about 290 B.C.

destruction and chaos, will contrive sufferings of all sorts, only to gain his point! He will launch a curse upon the world, and as only man can curse (it is his privilege, the primary distinction between him and other animals), may be by his curse alone he will attain his object—that is, convince himself that he is a man and not a piano-key! If you say that all this, too, can be calculated and tabulated—chaos and darkness and curses, so that the mere possibility of calculating it all beforehand would stop it all, and reason would reassert itself, then man would purposely go mad in order to be rid of reason and gain his point! I believe in it, I answer for it, for the whole work of man really seems to consist in nothing but proving to himself every minute that he is a man and not a piano-key! It may be at the cost of his skin, it may be by cannibalism! And this being so, can one help being tempted to rejoice that it has not yet come off, and that desire still depends on something we don't know?

You will scream at me (that is, if you condescend to do so) that no one is touching my free will, that all they are concerned with is that my will should of itself, of its own free will, coincide with my own normal interests, with the laws of nature and arithmetic.

Good Heavens, gentlemen, what sort of free will is left when we come to tabulation and arithmetic, when it will all be a case of twice two makes four? Twice two makes four without my will. As if free will meant that!

IX

Gentlemen, I am joking, and I know myself that my jokes are not brilliant, but you know one can't take everything as a joke. I am, perhaps, jesting against the grain. Gentlemen, I am tormented by questions; answer them for me. You, for instance, want to cure men of their old habits and reform their will in accordance with science and good sense. But how do you know, not only that it is possible, but also that it is *desirable*, to reform man in that way? And what leads you to the conclusion that man's inclinations *need* reforming? In short, how do you know that such a reformation will be a benefit to man? And to go to the root of the matter, why are you so positively convinced that not to act against his real normal interests guaranteed by the conclusions of reason and arithmetic is certainly always advantageous for man and must always be a law for mankind? So far, you know, this is only your supposition. It may be the law of logic, but not the law of humanity. You think, gentlemen, perhaps that I am mad? Allow me to defend myself. I agree that man is pre-eminently a creative animal, predestined to strive consciously for an object and to engage in engineering—that is, incessantly and eternally to make new roads, *wherever they may lead*. But the reason why he wants sometimes to go off at a tangent may just be that he is *predestined* to make the road, and perhaps, too, that however stupid the "direct" practical man may be, the thought sometimes will occur to him that the road almost always does lead *somewhere,* and that the destination it leads to is less important than the process of making it, and that the chief thing is to save the well-conducted child from despising engineering, and so giving way to the fatal idleness, which, as we all know, is the mother of all the vices. Man likes to make roads and to create, that is a fact beyond dispute. But why has he such a passionate love for destruction and chaos also? Tell me that! But on that point I want to say a couple of words myself. May it not be that he loves chaos and destruction (there can be no disputing that he does sometimes love it) because he is instinctively afraid of attaining his object and completing the edifice he is constructing? Who knows, perhaps he only loves that edifice from a distance, and is by no means in love with it at close quarters; perhaps he only loves building it and does not want to live in it, but will leave it, when completed, for the use of *les animaux domestiques*—such as the ants, the sheep, and so on. Now the ants have quite a different taste. They have a marvellous edifice of that pattern which endures for ever—the ant-heap.

With the ant-heap the respectable race of ants began and with the ant-heap they will probably end, which does the greatest credit to their perseverance and good sense. But man is a frivolous and incongruous creature, and perhaps, like a chess player, loves the process of the game, not the end of it. And who knows (there is no saying with certainty), perhaps the only goal on earth to which mankind is striving lies in this incessant process of attaining, in other words, in life itself, and not in the thing to be attained, which must always be expressed as a formula, as positive as twice two makes four, and such positiveness is not life, gentlemen, but is the beginning of death. Anyway, man has always been afraid of this mathematical certainty, and I am afraid of it now. Granted that man does nothing but seek that mathematical certainty, he traverses oceans, sacrifices his life in the quest, but to succeed, really to find it, he dreads, I assure you. He feels that when he has found it there will be nothing for him to look for. When workmen have finished their work they do at least receive their pay, they go to the tavern, then they are taken to the police-station—and there is occupation for a week. But where can man go? Anyway, one can observe a certain awkwardness about him when he has attained such objects. He loves the process of attaining, but does not quite like to have attained, and that, of course, is very absurd. In fact, man is a comical creature; there seems to be a kind of jest in it all. But yet mathematical certainty is, after all, something insufferable. Twice two makes four seems to me simply a piece of insolence. Twice two makes four is a pert coxcomb who stands with arms akimbo barring your path and spitting. I admit that twice two makes four is an excellent thing, but if we are to give everything its due, twice two makes five is sometimes a very charming thing too.

And why are you so firmly, so triumphantly, convinced that only the normal and the positive—in other words, only what is conducive to welfare—is for the advantage of man? Is not reason in error as regards advantage? Does not man, perhaps, love something besides well-being? Perhaps he is just as fond of suffering? Perhaps suffering is just as great a benefit to him as well-being? Man is sometimes extraordinarily, passionately, in love with suffering, and that is a fact. There is no need to appeal to universal history to prove that; only ask yourself, if you are a man and have lived at all. As far as my personal opinion is concerned, to care only for well-being seems to me positively ill-bred. Whether it's good or bad, it is sometimes very pleasant, too, to smash things. I hold no brief for suffering nor for well-being either. I am standing for . . . my caprice, and for its being guaranteed to me when necessary. Suffering would be out of place in vaudevilles, for instance; I know that. In the "Crystal Palace" it is unthinkable; suffering means doubt, negation, and what would be the good of a crystal palace if there could be any doubt about it? And yet I think man will never renounce real suffering, that is, destruction and chaos. Why, suffering is the sole origin of consciousness. Though I did lay it down at the beginning that consciousness is the greatest misfortune for man, yet I know man prizes it and would not give it up for any satisfaction. Consciousness, for instance, is infinitely superior to twice two makes four. Once you have mathematical certainty there is nothing left to do or to understand. There will be nothing left but to bottle up your five senses and plunge into contemplation. While if you stick to consciousness, even though the same result is attained, you can at least flog yourself at times, and that will, at any rate, liven you up. Reactionary as it is, corporal punishment is better than nothing.

X[12]

You believe in a crystal palace that can never be destroyed—a palace at which one will not be able to put out one's tongue or make a long nose on the sly. And perhaps that is just why I am afraid of this edifice, that it is of crystal and can never be destroyed and that one cannot put one's tongue out at it even on the sly.

12. Section X was badly mutilated by the censor, as Dostoevsky makes clear in the letter to his brother Mikhail, dated March 26, 1864, which is quoted in our introduction.

You see, if it were not a palace, but a hen-house, I might creep into it to avoid getting wet, and yet I would not call the hen-house a palace out of gratitude to it for keeping me dry. You laugh and say that in such circumstances a hen-house is as good as a mansion. Yes, I answer, if one had to live simply to keep out of the rain.

But what is to be done if I have taken it into my head that that is not the only object in life, and that if one must live one had better live in a mansion. That is my choice, my desire. You will only eradicate it when you have changed my preference. Well, do change it, allure me with something else, give me another ideal. But meanwhile I will not take a hen-house for a mansion. The crystal palace may be an idle dream, it may be that it is inconsistent with the laws of nature and that I have invented it only through my own stupidity, through the old-fashioned irrational habits of my generation. But what does it matter to me that it is inconsistent? That makes no difference since it exists in my desires, or rather exists as long as my desires exist. Perhaps you are laughing again? Laugh away; I will put up with any mockery rather than pretend that I am satisfied when I am hungry. I know, anyway, that I will not be put off with a compromise, with a recurring zero, simply because it is consistent with the laws of nature and actually exists. I will not accept as the crown of my desires a block of slum tenements on a lease of a thousand years, and perhaps with a sign-board of Wagenheim the dentist hanging out. Destroy my desires, eradicate my ideals, show me something better, and I will follow you. You will say, perhaps, that it is not worth your trouble; but in that case I can give you the same answer. We are discussing things seriously; but if you won't deign to give me your attention, I will drop your acquaintance. I can retreat into my underground hole.

But while I am alive and have desires I would rather my hand were withered off than bring one brick to such a building! Don't remind me that I have just rejected the crystal palace for the sole reason that one cannot put out one's tongue at it. I did not say because I am so fond of putting my tongue out. Perhaps the thing I resented was, that of all your edifices there has not been one at which one could not put out one's tongue. On the contrary, I would let my tongue be cut off out of gratitude if things could be so arranged that I should lose all desire to put it out. It is not my fault that things cannot be so arranged, and that one must be satisfied with model flats. Then why am I made with such desires? Can I have been constructed simply in order to come to the conclusion that all my construction is a cheat? Can this be my whole purpose? I do not believe it.

But do you know what: I am convinced that we underground folk ought to be kept on a curb. Though we may sit forty years under-

ground without speaking, when we do come out into the light of
day and break out we talk and talk and talk. . . .

XI

The long and the short of it is, gentlemen, that it is better to do
nothing! Better conscious inertia! And so hurrah for underground!
Though I have said that I envy the normal man to the last drop of
my bile, yet I should not care to be in his place such as he is now
(though I shall not cease envying him). No, no; anyway the underground life is more advantageous. There, at any rate, one can. . . .
Oh, but even now I am lying! I am lying because I know myself
that it is not underground that is better, but something different,
quite different, for which I am thirsting, but which I cannot find!
Damn underground!

I will tell you another thing that would be better, and that is,
if I myself believed in anything of what I have just written. I swear
to you, gentlemen, there is not one thing, not one word of what I
have written that I really believe. That is, I believe it, perhaps, but at
the same time I feel and suspect that I am lying like a cobbler.

"Then why have you written all this?" you will say to me. "I ought
to put you underground for forty years without anything to do and
then come to you in your cellar, to find out what stage you have
reached! How can a man be left with nothing to do for forty years?"

"Isn't that shameful, isn't that humiliating?" you will say, perhaps, wagging your heads contemptuously. "You thirst for life and
try to settle the problems of life by a logical tangle. And how persistent, how insolent are your sallies, and at the same time what a
scare you are in! You talk nonsense and are pleased with it; you say
impudent things and are in continual alarm and apologizing for
them. You declare that you are afraid of nothing and at the same
time try to ingratiate yourself in our good opinion. You declare that
you are gnashing your teeth and at the same time you try to be witty
so as to amuse us. You know that your witticisms are not witty, but
you are evidently well satisfied with their literary value. You may,
perhaps, have really suffered, but you have no respect for your own
suffering. You may have sincerity, but you have no modesty; out of
the pettiest vanity you expose your sincerity to publicity and ig-
nominy. You doubtlessly mean to say something, but hide your last
word through fear, because you have not the resolution to utter it,
and only have a cowardly impudence. You boast of consciousness,
but you are not sure of your ground, for though your mind works,
yet your heart is darkened and corrupt, and you cannot have a full,
genuine consciousness without a pure heart. And how intrusive you
are, how you insist and grimace! Lies, lies, lies!"

Of course I have myself made up all the things you say. That,
too, is from underground. I have been for forty years listening to

you through a crack under the floor. I have invented them myself, there was nothing else I could invent. It is no wonder that I have learned it by heart and it has taken a literary form. . .

But can you really be so credulous as to think that I will print all this and give it to you to read too? And another problem: why do I call you "gentlemen," why do I address you as though you really were my readers? Such confessions as I intend to make are never printed nor given to other people to read. Anyway, I am not strong-minded enough for that, and I don't see why I should be. But you see a fancy has occurred to me and I want to realize it at all costs. Let me explain.

Every man has reminiscences which he would not tell to every one, but only to his friends. He has other matters in his mind which he would not reveal even to his friends, but only to himself, and that in secret. But there are other things which a man is afraid to tell even to himself, and every decent man has a number of such things stored away in his mind. The more decent he is, the greater the number of such things in his mind. Anyway, I have only lately determined to remember some of my early adventures. Till now I have always avoided them, even with a certain uneasiness. Now, when I am not only recalling them, but have actually decided to write an account of them, I want to try the experiment whether one can, even with oneself, be perfectly open and not take fright at the whole truth. I will observe, in parenthesis, that Heine[13] says that a true autobiography is almost an impossibility, and that man is bound to lie about himself. He considers that Rousseau certainly told lies about himself in his *Confessions*, and even intentionally lied, out of vanity. I am convinced that Heine is right; I quite understand how sometimes one may, out of sheer vanity, attribute regular crimes to oneself, and indeed I can very well conceive that kind of vanity. But Heine judged of people who made their confessions to the public. I write only for myself, and I wish to declare once and for all that if I write as though I were addressing readers, that is simply because it is easier for me to write in that form. It is a form, an empty form—I shall never have readers. I have made this plain already. . .

I don't wish to be hampered by any restrictions in the compilation of my notes. I shall not attempt any system or method. I will jot things down as I remember them.

But here, perhaps, some one will catch at the word and ask me: if you really don't reckon on readers, why do you make such compacts with yourself—and on paper too—that is, that you won't at-

13. Dostoevsky alludes to *Confessions* (*Geständnisse*, 1854), fragmentary memoirs written by the German poet Heinrich Heine (1797–1856), in which on the very first page Heine speaks of Rousseau as lying and inventing disgraceful incidents about himself for his *Confessions*. (See footnote 2.)

tempt any system or method, that you jot things down as you remember them, and so on, and so on? Why are you explaining? Why do you apologize?

Well, there it is, I answer.

There is a whole psychology in all this, though. Perhaps it is simply that I am a coward. And perhaps that I purposely imagine an audience before me in order that I may be more dignified while I write. There are perhaps thousands of reasons. Again, what is my object precisely in writing? If it is not for the benefit of the public why should I not simply recall these incidents in my own mind without putting them on paper?

Quite so; but yet it is more imposing on paper. There is something more impressive in it; I shall be better able to criticize myself and improve my style. Besides, I shall perhaps obtain actual relief from writing. To-day, for instance, I am particularly oppressed by one memory of a distant past. It came back vividly to my mind a few days ago, and has remained haunting me like an annoying tune that one cannot get rid of. And yet I must get rid of it somehow. I have hundreds of such reminiscences; but at times some one stands out from the hundred and oppresses me. For some reason I believe that if I write it down I should get rid of it. Why not try?

Besides, I am bored, and I never have anything to do. Writing will be a sort of work. They say work makes man kind-hearted and honest. Well, here is a chance for me, anyway.

Snow is falling to-day, yellow and dingy. It fell yesterday, too, and a few days ago. I fancy it is the wet snow that has reminded me of that incident which I cannot shake off now. And so let it be a story *à propos* of the falling snow.

Part II

À PROPOS OF THE WET SNOW

When from dark error's subjugation
My words of passionate exhortation
  Had wrenched thy fainting spirit free;
And writhing prone in thine affliction
Thou didst recall with malediction
  The vice that had encompassed thee:
And when thy slumbering conscience, fretting
  By recollection's torturing flame,
Thou didst reveal the hideous setting
  Of thy life's current ere I came:
When suddenly I saw thee sicken,
  And weeping, hide thine anguished face,
Revolted, maddened, horror-stricken,
  At memories of foul disgrace, etc., etc., etc. . . .
                    NEKRASOV[14] (*translated by Juliet Soskice*)

14. Nikolay A. Nekrasov (1821–1878) was a famous Russian poet and editor of radical sympathies. The poem quoted dates from 1845, and is without title. The poem ends with the lines, "Into my house come bold and free, Its rightful mistress there to be."

I

At that time I was only twenty-four. My life was even then gloomy, ill-regulated, and as solitary as that of a savage. I made friends with no one and positively avoided talking, and buried myself more and more in my hole. At work in the office I never looked at any one, and I was perfectly well aware that my companions looked upon me, not only as a queer fellow, but even looked upon me—I always fancied this—with a sort of loathing. I sometimes wondered why it was that nobody except me fancied that he was looked upon with aversion? One of the clerks had a most repulsive, pock-marked face, which looked positively villainous. I believe I should not have dared to look at any one with such an unsightly countenance. Another had such a very dirty old uniform that there was an unpleasant odor in his proximity. Yet not one of these gentlemen showed the slightest self-consciousness—either about their clothes or their countenance or their character in any way. Neither of them ever imagined that they were looked at with repulsion; if they had imagined it they would not have minded—so long as their superiors did not look at them in that way. It is clear to me now that, owing to my unbounded vanity and to the high standard I set for myself, I often looked at myself with furious discontent, which verged on loathing, and so I inwardly attributed the same feeling to every one. I hated my face, for instance: I thought it disgusting, and even suspected that there was something base in my expression, and so every day when I turned up at the office I tried to behave as independently as possible, and to assume a lofty expression, so that I might not be suspected of being abject. "My face may be ugly," I thought, "but let it be lofty, expressive, and, above all, *extremely* intelligent." But I was positively and painfully certain that it was impossible for my countenance ever to express those qualities. And what was worst of all, I thought it actually stupid looking, and I would have been quite satisfied if I could have looked intelligent. In fact, I would even have put up with looking base if, at the same time, my face could have been thought strikingly intelligent.

Of course, I hated my fellow clerks one and all, and I despised them all, yet at the same time I was, as it were, afraid of them. In fact, it happened at times that I thought more highly of them than of myself. It somehow happened quite suddenly that I alternated between despising them and thinking them superior to myself. A cultivated and decent man cannot be vain without setting a fearfully high standard for himself, and without despising and almost hating himself at certain moments. But whether I despised them or thought them superior I dropped my eyes almost every time I met any one. I even made experiments whether I could face so and so's looking at me, and I was always the first to drop my eyes. This worried me to distraction. I had a sickly dread, too, of being ridiculous, and so had a slavish passion for the conventional in everything external. I loved to fall into the common rut, and had a whole-hearted terror of any kind of eccentricity in myself. But how could I live up to it? I was morbidly sensitive, as a man of our age should be. They were all stupid, and as like one another as so many sheep. Perhaps I was the only one in the office who fancied that I was a coward and a slave, and I fancied it just because I was more highly developed. But it was not only that I fancied it, it really was so. I was a coward and a slave. I say this without the slightest embarrassment. Every decent man of our age must be a coward and a slave. That is his normal condition. Of that I am firmly persuaded. He is made and constructed to that very end. And not only at the present time owing to some casual circumstances, but always, at all times, a decent man is bound to be a coward and a slave. It is the law of nature for all decent people all over the earth. If any one of them happens to be valiant about something, he need not be comforted nor carried away by that; he would show the white feather just the same before something else. That is how it invariably and inevitably ends. Only donkeys and mules are valiant, and they only till they are pushed up to the wall. It is not worth while to pay attention to them for they really are of no consequence.

Another circumstance, too, worried me in those days: that there was no one like me and I was unlike any one else. "I am unique and they are all alike," I thought—and pondered.

From that it is evident that I was still a youngster.

The very opposite sometimes happened. It was loathsome sometimes to go to the office; things reached such a point that I often came home ill. But all at once, *à propos* of nothing, there would come a phase of scepticism and indifference (everything happened in phases to me), and I would laugh myself at my intolerance and fastidiousness, I would reproach myself with being *romantic*. At one time I was unwilling to speak to any one, while at other times I would not only talk, but go to the length of contemplating making friends with them. All my fastidiousness would suddenly, for no rhyme or reason, vanish. Who knows, perhaps I never had really had it, and it had simply been affected, and got out of books. I have not decided that question even now. Once I quite made friends with them, visited their homes, played preference, drank vodka, talked of promotions. . . . But here let me make a digression.

We Russians, speaking generally, have never had those foolish transcendental "romantics"—German, and still more French—on whom nothing produces any effect; if there were an earthquake, if all France perished at the barricades, they would still be the same, they would not even have the decency to affect a change, but would still go on singing their transcendental songs to the hour of their death, because they are fools. We, in Russia, have no fools; that is well known. That is what distinguishes us from foreign lands. Consequently these transcendental natures are not found amongst us in their pure form. The idea that they are is due to our "realistic" journalists and critics of that day, always on the look out for Kostanzhoglos[15] and Uncle Pyotr Ivanichs[16] and foolishly accepting them as our ideal; they have slandered our romantics, taking them for the same transcendental sort as in Germany or France. On the contrary, the characteristics of our "romantics" are absolutely and directly opposed to the transcendental European type, and no European standard can be applied to them. (Allow me to make use of this word "romantic"—an old-fashioned and much respected word which has done good service and is familiar to all). The characteristics of our romantic are to understand everything, *to see everything and to see it often incomparably more clearly than our most realistic minds see it*; to refuse to accept anyone or anything, but at the same time not to despise anything; to give way, to yield, from policy; never to lose sight of a useful practical object (such as rent-free quarters at the government expense, pensions, decorations), to keep their eye on that object through all the enthusiasms and volumes of lyrical poems, and at the same time to preserve "the good and the beautiful" inviolate within them to the hour of their death, and to preserve themselves also, incidentally, like some precious jewel wrapped in cotton wool if only for the benefit of "the good and the beautiful." Our "romantic" is a man of great breadth and the greatest rogue of all our rogues, I assure you. . . . I can assure you from experience, indeed. Of course, that is, if he is intelligent. But what am I saying! The romantic is always intelligent, and I only meant to observe that although we have had foolish romantics they don't count, and they were only so because in the flower of their youth they degenerated into Germans, and to preserve their precious jewel more comfortably, settled somewhere out there—by preference in Weimar or the Black Forest.

I, for instance, genuinely despised my official work and did not openly abuse it simply because I was in it myself and got a salary for it. Anyway, take note, I did not openly abuse it. Our romantic would rather go out of his mind—a thing, however, which very rarely happens—than take to open abuse, unless he had some other

15. Konstanzhoglo is the ideal efficient landowner in the second part of Gogol's novel *Dead Souls* (published posthumously in 1852).

16. Uncle Pyotr Ivanich, a character in Ivan Goncharov's novel *A Common Story* (1847), is a high bureaucrat, a factory owner who teaches lessons of sobriety and good sense to the romantic hero, Alexander Aduyev.

career in view; and he is never kicked out. At most, they would take him to the lunatic asylum as "the King of Spain"[17] if he should go very mad. But it is only the thin, fair people who go out of their minds in Russia. Innumerable "romantics" attain later in life to considerable rank in the service. Their many-sidedness is remarkable! And what a faculty they have for the most contradictory sensations! I was comforted by this thought even in those days, and I am of the same opinion now. That is why there are so many "broad natures" among us who never lose their ideal even in the depths of degradation; and though they never stir a finger for their ideal, though they are arrant thieves and knaves, yet they tearfully cherish their first ideal and are extraordinarily honest at heart. Yes, it is only among us that the most incorrigible rogue can be absolutely and loftily honest at heart without in the least ceasing to be a rogue. I repeat, our romantics, frequently, become such accomplished rascals (I use the term "rascals" affectionately), suddenly display such a sense of reality and practical knowledge that their bewildered superiors and the public generally can only ejaculate in amazement.

Their many-sidedness is really amazing, and goodness knows what it may develop into later on, and what the future has in store for us. It is not a poor material! I do not say this from any foolish or boastful patriotism. But I feel sure that you are again imagining that I am joking. Or perhaps it's just the contrary and you are convinced that I really think so. Anyway, gentlemen, I shall welcome both views as an honour and a special favour. And do forgive my digression.

I did not, of course, maintain friendly relations with my comrades and soon was at loggerheads with them, and in my youth and inexperience I even gave up bowing to them, as though I had cut off all relations. That, however, only happened to me once. As a rule, I was always alone.

In the first place I spent most of my time at home, reading. I tried to stifle all that was continually seething within me by means of external impressions. And the only external means I had was reading. Reading, of course, was a great help—exciting me, giving me pleasure and pain. But at times it bored me fearfully. One longed for movement in spite of everything, and I plunged all at once into dark, underground, loathsome vice of the pettiest kind. My wretched passions were acute, smarting, from my continual, sickly irritability. I had hysterical impulses, with tears and convulsions. I had no resource except reading, that is, there was nothing in my surroundings which I could respect and which attracted me. I was overwhelmed with depression, too; I had a hysterical craving for incongruity and

17. an allusion to Gogol's story "Memoirs of a Madman" (1835). The narrator imagines himself "the King of Spain" and is finally carried off to a lunatic asylum.

for contrast, and so I took to vice. I have not said all this to justify myself. . . . But, no! I am lying. I did want to justify myself. I make that little observation for my own benefit, gentlemen. I don't want to lie. I vowed to myself I would not.

And so, furtively, timidly, in solitude, at night, I indulged in filthy vice, with a feeling of shame which never deserted me, even at the most loathsome moments, and which at such moments nearly made me curse. Already even then I had my underground world in my soul. I was fearfully afraid of being seen, of being met, of being recognized. I visited various obscure haunts.

One night as I was passing a tavern I saw through a lighted window some gentlemen fighting with billiard cues, and saw one of them thrown out of a window. At other times I should have felt very much disgusted, but I was in such a mood at the time, that I actually envied the gentleman thrown out of a window—and I envied him so much that I even went into the tavern and into the billiard-room. "Perhaps," I thought, "I'll have a fight, too, and they'll throw me out of the window."

I was not drunk—but what is one to do—depression will drive a man to such a pitch of hysteria? But nothing happened. It seemed that I was not even equal to being thrown out of the window and I went away without having my fight.

An officer put me in my place from the first moment.

I was standing by the billiard-table and in my ignorance blocking up the way, and he wanted to pass; he took me by the shoulders and without a word—without a warning or explanation—moved me from where I was standing to another spot and passed by as though he had not noticed me. I could have forgiven blows, but I could not forgive his having moved me without noticing me.

Devil knows what I would have given for a real regular quarrel— a more decent, a more *literary* one, so to speak. I had been treated like a fly. This officer was over six foot, while I was a spindly little fellow. But the quarrel was in my hands. I had only to protest and I certainly would have been thrown out of the window. But I changed my mind and preferred to beat a resentful retreat.

I went out of the tavern straight home, confused and troubled, and the next night I went out again with the same lewd intentions, still more furtively, abjectly and miserably than before, as it were, with tears in my eyes—but still I did go out again. Don't imagine, though, it was cowardice made me slink away from the officer: I never have been a coward at heart, though I have always been a coward in action. Don't be in a hurry to laugh—I assure you I can explain it all.

Oh, if only that officer had been one of the sort who would consent to fight a duel! But no, he was one of those gentlemen (alas, long extinct!) who preferred fighting with cues or, like Gogol's Lieutenant Pirogov,[18] appealing to the police. They did not fight duels and would have thought a duel with a civilian like me an utterly unseemly procedure in any case—and they looked upon the duel altogether as something impossible, something free-thinking and French. But they were quite ready to bully, especially when they were over six foot.

I did not slink away through cowardice, but through an unbounded vanity. I was afraid not of his six foot, not of getting a sound thrashing and being thrown out of the window; I should have had physical courage enough, I assure you; but I had not the moral courage. What I was afraid of was that every one present, from the insolent marker down to the lowest little stinking, pimply clerk in a greasy collar, would jeer at me and fail to understand when I began to protest and to address them in literary language. For of the point of honour—not of honour, but of the point of honour (*point d'honneur*)—one cannot speak among us except in literary language. You can't allude to the "point of honour" in ordinary language. I was fully convinced (the sense of reality, in spite of all my romanticism!) that they would all simply split their sides with laughter, and that the officer would not simply beat me, that is, without insulting me, but would certainly prod me in the back with his knee, kick me round the billiard-table, and only then perhaps have pity and drop me out of the window.

Of course, this trivial incident could not with me end in that. I often met that officer afterwards in the street and noticed him very carefully. I am not quite sure whether he recognized me, I imagine not; I judge from certain signs. But I—I stared at him with spite and hatred and so it went on . . . for several years! My resentment grew even deeper with years. At first I began making stealthy inquiries about this officer. It was difficult for me to do so, for I knew no one. But one day I heard some one shout his surname in the street as I was following him at a distance, as though I were tied to him—and so I learnt his surname. Another time I followed him to his flat, and for ten kopecks learned from the porter where he lived, on which storey, whether he lived alone or with others, and so on— in fact, everything one could learn from a porter. One morning, though I had never tried my hand with the pen, it suddenly occurred to me to write a satire on this officer in the form of a novel which would unmask his villainy. I wrote the novel with relish. I did unmask his villainy, I even exaggerated it; at first I so altered his surname that it could easily be recognized, but on second thoughts

18. a character in Gogol's story "The Nevsky Prospekt" (1835). He pays violent court to the wife of a German tradesman and is thrown out by him and his friends. He does not actually call the police.

I changed it, and sent the story to the *Otechestvenniye Zapiski*.[19] But at that time such attacks were not the fashion and my story was not printed. That was a great vexation to me.

Sometimes I was positively choked with resentment. At last I determined to challenge my enemy to a duel. I composed a splendid, charming letter to him, imploring him to apologize to me, and hinting rather plainly at a duel in case of refusal. The letter was so composed that if the officer had had the least understanding of the good and the beautiful he would certainly have flung himself on my neck and have offered me his friendship. And how fine that would have been! How we should have got on together! "He could have shielded me with his higher rank, while I could have improved his mind with my culture, and, well . . . my ideas, and all sorts of things might have happened." Only fancy, this was two years after his insult to me, and my challenge would have been a ridiculous anachronism, in spite of all the ingenuity of my letter in disguising and explaining away the anachronism. But, thank God (to this day I thank the Almighty with tears in my eyes) I did not send the letter to him. Cold shivers run down my back when I think of what might have happened if I had sent it.

And all at once I revenged myself in the simplest way, by a stroke of genius! A brilliant thought suddenly dawned upon me. Sometimes on holidays I used to stroll along the sunny side of the Nevsky[20] about four o'clock in the afternoon. Though it was hardly a stroll so much as a series of innumerable miseries, humiliations and resentments; but no doubt that was just what I wanted. I used to wriggle along in a most unseemly fashion, like an eel, continually moving aside to make way for generals, for officers of the guards and the hussars, or for ladies. At such minutes there used to be a convulsive twinge at my heart, and I used to feel hot all down my back at the mere thought of the wretchedness of my attire, of the wretchedness and abjectness of my little scurrying figure. This was a regular martyrdom, a continual, intolerable humiliation at the thought, which passed into an incessant and direct sensation, that I was a mere fly in the eyes of all this world, a nasty, disgusting fly—more intelligent, more highly developed, more refined in feeling than any of them, of course—but a fly that was continually making way for every one, insulted and injured by every one. Why I inflicted this torture upon myself, why I went to the Nevsky, I don't know. I felt simply drawn there at every possible opportunity.

Already then I began to experience a rush of the enjoyment of

19. *Notes of the Fatherland*, the most famous radical Russian journal, founded in 1839.

20. Nevsky Prospekt, the most elegant main street in St. Petersburg, about three miles long; now called "Prospekt of the 25th October."

which I spoke in the first chapter. After my affair with the officer I felt even more drawn there than before: it was on the Nevsky that I met him most frequently, there I could admire him. He, too, went there chiefly on holidays. He, too, turned out of his path for generals and persons of high rank, and he, too, wriggled between them like an eel; but people, like me, or even better dressed like me, he simply walked over; he made straight for them as though there was nothing but empty space before him, and never, under any circumstances, turned aside. I gloated over my resentment watching him and . . . always resentfully made way for him. It exasperated me that even in the street I could not be on an even footing with him.

"Why must you invariably be the first to move aside?" I kept asking myself in hysterical rage, waking up sometimes at three o'clock in the morning. "Why is it you and not he? There's no regulation about it; there's no written law. Let the making way be equal as it usually is when refined people meet: he moves half-way and you move half-way; you pass with mutual respect."

But that never happened, and I always moved aside, while he did not even notice my making way for him. And lo and behold a bright idea dawned upon me! "What," I thought, "if I meet him and don't move on one side? What if I don't move aside on purpose, even if I knock up against him? How would that be?" This audacious idea took such a hold on me that it gave me no peace. I was dreaming of it continually, horribly, and I purposely went more frequently to the Nevsky in order to picture more vividly how I should do it when I did do it. I was delighted. This intention seemed to me more and more practical and possible.

"Of course I shall not really push him," I thought, already more good-natured in my joy. "I will simply not turn aside, will run up against him, not very violently, but just shouldering each other—just as much as decency permits. I will push against him just as much as he pushes against me." At last I made up my mind completely. But my preparations took a great deal of time. To begin with, when I carried out my plan I should need to be looking rather more decent, and so I had to think of my get-up. "In case of emergency, if, for instance, there were any sort of public scandal (and the public there is of the most *recherché*: the Countess walks there; Prince D. walks there; all the literary world is there), I must be well dressed; that inspires respect and of itself puts us on an equal footing in the eyes of society."

With this object I asked for some of my salary in advance, and bought at Churkin's a pair of black gloves and a decent hat. Black gloves seemed to me both more dignified and *bon ton* than the lemon-coloured ones which I had contemplated at first. "The colour is too gaudy, it looks as though one were trying to be conspicuous," and I did not take the lemon-coloured ones. I had got ready long beforehand a good shirt, with white bone studs; my overcoat was the only thing that held me back. The coat in itself was a very good one, it kept me warm; but it was wadded and it had a raccoon collar which was the height of vulgarity. I had to change the collar at any sacrifice, and to have a beaver one like an officer's. For this purpose I began visiting the Gostiny Dvor[21] and after several attempts I pitched upon a piece of cheap German beaver. Though these German beavers soon grow shabby and look wretched, yet at first they look exceedingly well, and I only needed it for one occasion. I asked the price; even so, it was too expensive. After thinking it over thoroughly I decided to sell my raccoon collar. The rest of the money—a considerable sum for me, I decided to borrow from Anton Antonich Syetochkin, my immediate superior, an unassuming person, though grave and judicious. He never lent money to any one, but I had, on entering the service, been specially recommended to him by an important personage who had got me my berth. I was horribly worried. To borrow from Anton Antonich seemed to me monstrous and shameful. I did not sleep for two or three nights. Indeed, I did not sleep well at that time, I was in a fever; I had a vague sinking at my heart or else a sudden throbbing, throbbing, throbbing! Anton Antonich was surprised at first, then he frowned, then he reflected, and did after all lend me the money, receiving from me a written authorization to take from my salary a fortnight later the sum that he had lent me.

In this way everything was at last ready. The handsome beaver replaced the mean-looking raccoon, and I began by degrees to get to work. It would never have done to act off-hand, at random; the plan had to be carried out skilfully, by degrees. But I must confess that after many efforts I began to despair: we simply could not run into each other. I made every preparation, I was quite determined—it seemed as though we should run into one another directly—and before I knew what I was doing I had stepped aside for him again and he had passed without noticing me. I even prayed as I approached him that God would grant me determination. One time I had made up my mind thoroughly, but it ended in my stumbling and falling at his feet because at the very last instant when I was six inches from him my courage failed me. He very calmly stepped over me, while I flew on one side like a ball. That night I was ill again, feverish and delirious.

And suddenly it ended most happily. The night before I had made up my mind not to carry out my fatal plan and to abandon it all, and

21. originally a guesthouse for foreign merchants; later used for displaying their wares.

with that object I went to the Nevsky for the last time, just to see
how I would abandon it all. Suddenly, three paces from my enemy,
I unexpectedly made up my mind—I closed my eyes, and we ran
full tilt, shoulder to shoulder, against one another! I did not budge
an inch and passed him on a perfectly equal footing! He did not
even look round and pretended not to notice it; but he was only
pretending, I am convinced of that. I am convinced of that to this
day! Of course, I got the worst of it—he was stronger, but that was
not the point. The point was that I had attained my object, I had
kept up my dignity, I had not yielded a step, and had put myself
publicly on an equal social footing with him. I returned home feeling
that I was fully avenged for everything. I was delighted. I was triumphant and sang Italian arias. Of course, I will not describe to
you what happened to me three days later; if you have read my first
chapter you can guess that for yourself. The officer was afterwards
transferred; I have not seen him now for fourteen years. What is
the dear fellow doing now? Whom is he walking over?

II

But the period of my dissipation would end and I always felt very
sick afterwards. It was followed by remorse—I tried to drive it away:
I felt too sick. By degrees, however, I grew used to that too. I grew
used to everything, or rather I voluntarily resigned myself to enduring it. But I had a means of escape that reconciled everything—
that was to find refuge in "the good and the beautiful," in dreams,
of course. I was a terrible dreamer, I would dream for three months
on end, tucked away in my corner, and you may believe me that at
those moments I had no resemblance to the gentleman who, in the
perturbation of his chicken heart, put a collar of German beaver on
his great coat. I suddenly became a hero. I would not have admitted
my six-foot lieutenant even if he had called on me. I could not even
picture him before me then. What were my dreams and how I could
satisfy myself with them—it is hard to say now, but at the time I was
satisfied with them. Though, indeed, even now, I am to some extent
satisfied with them. Dreams were particularly sweet and vivid after
a spell of dissipation; they came with remorse and with tears, with
curses and transports. There were moments of such positive intoxication, of such happiness, that there was not the faintest trace
of irony within me, on my honour. I had faith, hope, love. I believed blindly at such times that by some miracle, by some external
circumstance, all this would suddenly open out, expand; that suddenly a vista of suitable activity—beneficent, good, and, above all,
ready made (what sort of activity I had no idea, but the great thing
was that it should be all ready for me)—would rise up before me—
and I should come out into the light of day, almost riding a white
horse and crowned with laurel. Anything but the foremost place I

could not conceive for myself, and for that very reason I quite contentedly occupied the lowest in reality. Either to be a hero or to grovel in the mud—there was nothing between. That was my ruin, for when I was in the mud I comforted myself with the thought that at other times I was a hero, and the hero was a cloak for the mud: for an ordinary man it was shameful to defile himself, but a hero was too lofty to be utterly defiled, and so he might defile himself. It is worth noting that these attacks of the "good and the beautiful" visited me even during the period of dissipation and just at the times when I was touching bottom. They came in separate spurts, as though reminding me of themselves, but did not banish the dissipation by their appearance. On the contrary, they seemed to add a zest to it by contrast, and were only sufficiently present to serve as an appetizing sauce. That sauce was made up of contradictions and sufferings, of agonizing inward analysis, and all these pangs and pinpricks gave a certain piquancy, even a significance to my dissipation—in fact, completely answered the purpose of an appetizing sauce. There was a certain depth of meaning in it. And I could hardly have resigned myself to the simple, vulgar, direct debauchery of a clerk and have endured all the filthiness of it. What could have allured me about it then and have drawn me at night into the street? No, I had a lofty way of getting out of it all.

And what loving-kindness, oh Lord, what loving-kindness I felt at times in those dreams of mine! in those "flights into the good and the beautiful;" though it was fantastic love, though it was never applied to anything human in reality, yet there was so much of this love that one did not feel afterwards even the impulse to apply it in reality; that would have been superfluous. Everything, however, passed satisfactorily by a lazy and fascinating transition into the sphere of art, that is, into the beautiful forms of life, lying ready, largely stolen from the poets and novelists and adapted to all sorts of needs and uses. I, for instance, was triumphant over every one; every one, of course, was in dust and ashes, and was forced spontaneously to recognize my superiority, and I forgave them all. I was a poet and a grand gentleman, I fell in love; I came in for countless millions and immediately devoted them to humanity, and at the same time I confessed before all the people my shameful deeds, which, of course, were not merely shameful, but had in them much that was "good and beautiful" something in the Manfred[22] style. Every one would kiss me and weep (what idiots they would be if they did not), while I should go barefoot and hungry preaching new ideas and fighting a victorious Austerlitz[23] against the obscurantists. Then the

22. the hero of Lord Byron's verse drama *Manfred* (1817), who was oppressed by a mysterious guilt.

23. a village near Brno, the capital of Moravia, now in Czechoslovakia, where Napoleon defeated the combined Austrian and Russian armies in 1805.

band would play a march, an amnesty would be declared, the Pope would agree to retire from Rome to Brazil; then there would be a ball for the whole of Italy at the Villa Borghese[24] on the shores of the Lake of Como,[25] the Lake of Como being for that purpose transferred to the neighbourhood of Rome; then would come a scene in the bushes, and so on, and so on—as though you did not know all about it? You will say that it is vulgar and contemptible to drag all this into public after all the tears and transports which I have myself confessed. But why is it contemptible? Can you imagine that I am ashamed of it all, and that it was stupider than anything in your life, gentlemen? And I can assure you that some of these fancies were by no means badly composed. . . . It did not all happen on the shores of Lake Como. And yet you are right—it really is vulgar and contemptible. And most contemptible of all it is that now I am attempting to justify myself to you. And even more contemptible than that is my making this remark now. But that's enough, or there will be no end to it: each step will be more contemptible than the last. . . .

I could never stand more than three months of dreaming at a time without feeling an irresistible desire to plunge into society. To plunge into society meant to visit my superior at the office, Anton Antonich Syetochkin. He was the only permanent acquaintance I have had in my life, and wonder at the fact myself now. But I only went to see him when that phase came over me, and when my dreams had reached such a point of bliss that it became essential at once to embrace my fellows and all mankind; and for that purpose I needed, at least, one human being, actually existing. I had to call on Anton Antonich, however, on Tuesday—his at-home day; so I had always to time my passionate desire to embrace humanity so that it might fall on a Tuesday.

This Anton Antonich lived on the fourth storey in a house in Five Corners, in four low-pitched rooms, one smaller than the other, of a particularly frugal and sallow appearance. He had two daughters and their aunt, who used to pour out the tea. Of the daughters one was thirteen and another fourteen, they both had snub noses, and I was awfully shy of them because they were always whispering and giggling together. The master of the house usually sat in his study on a leather couch in front of the table with some grey-headed gentleman, usually a colleague from our office or some other department. I never saw more than two or three visitors there, always the same. They talked about the excise duty; about business in the Senate,[26] about salaries, about promotions, about His Excellency, and the best means of pleasing him, and so on. I had the patience to sit like a fool beside these people for four hours at a stretch, lis-

24. in Rome.
25. on the border of Italy and Switzerland.

26. The Russian Senate was at that time not a parliamentary body, but a high court.

tening to them without knowing what to say to them or venturing to say a word. I became stupefied, several times I felt myself perspiring, I was overcome by a sort of paralysis; but this was pleasant and good for me. On returning home I deferred for a time my desire to embrace all mankind.

I had however one other acquaintance of a sort, Simonov, who was an old schoolfellow. I had a number of schoolfellows, indeed, in Petersburg, but I did not associate with them and had even given up nodding to them in the street. I believe I had transferred into the department I was in simply to avoid their company and to cut off all connection with my hateful childhood. Curses on that school and all those terrible years of penal servitude! In short, I parted from my schoolfellows as soon as I got out into the world. There were two or three left to whom I nodded in the street. One of them was Simonov, who had been in no way distinguished at school, was of a quiet and equable disposition; but I discovered in him a certain independence of character and even honesty. I don't even suppose that he was particularly stupid. I had at one time spent some rather soulful moments with him, but these had not lasted long and had somehow been suddenly clouded over. He was evidently uncomfortable at these reminiscences, and was, I fancy, always afraid that I might take up the same tone again. I suspected that he had an aversion for me, but still I went on going to see him, not being quite certain of it.

And so on one occasion, unable to endure my solitude and knowing that as it was Thursday Anton Antonich's door would be closed, I thought of Simonov. Climbing up to his fourth storey I was thinking that the man disliked me and that it was a mistake to go and see him. But as it always happened that such reflections impelled me, as though purposely, to put myself into a false position, I went in. It was almost a year since I had last seen Simonov.

III

I found two of my old schoolfellows with him. They seemed to be discussing an important matter. All of them took scarcely any notice of my entrance, which was strange, for I had not met them for years. Evidently they looked upon me as something on the level of a common fly. I had not been treated like that even at school, though they all hated me. I knew, of course, that they must despise me now for my lack of success in the service, and for my having let myself sink so low, going about badly dressed and so on—which seemed to them a sign of my incapacity and insignificance. But I had not expected such contempt. Simonov was positively surprised at my turning up. Even in old days he had always seemed surprised at my coming. All this disconcerted me: I sat down, feeling rather miserable, and began listening to what they were saying.

They were engaged in warm and earnest conversation about a farewell dinner which they wanted to arrange for the next day to a comrade of theirs called Zverkov, an officer in the army, who was going away to a distant province. This Zverkov had been all the time at school with me too. I had begun to hate him particularly in the upper grades. In the lower grades he had simply been a pretty, playful boy whom everybody liked. I had hated him, however, even in the lower grades, just because he was a pretty and playful boy. He was always bad at his lessons and got worse and worse as he went on; however, he left with a good certificate, as he had powerful interest. During his last year at school he came in for an estate of two hundred serfs, and as almost all of us were poor he took up a swaggering tone among us. He was vulgar in the extreme, but at the same time he was a good-natured fellow, even in his swaggering. In spite of superficial, fantastic and sham notions of honour and dignity, all but very few of us positively grovelled before Zverkov, and the more so the more he swaggered. And it was not from any interested motive that they grovelled, but simply because he had been favoured by the gifts of nature. Moreover, it was, as it were, an accepted idea among us that Zverkov was a specialist in regard to tact and the social graces. This last fact particularly infuriated me. I hated the abrupt self-confident tone of his voice, his admiration of his own witticisms, which were often frightfully stupid, though he was bold in his language; I hated his handsome, but stupid face (for which I would, however, have gladly exchanged my intelligent one), and the free-and-easy military manners in fashion in the 'forties. I hated the way in which he used to talk of his future conquests of women (he did not venture to begin his attack upon women until he had the epaulettes of an officer, and was looking forward to them with impatience), and boasted of the duels he would constantly be fighting. I remember how I, invariably so taciturn, suddenly fastened upon Zverkov, when one day talking at a leisure moment with his schoolfellows of his future relations with the fair sex, and growing as sportive as a puppy in the sun, he all at once declared that he would not leave a single village girl on his estate unnoticed, that that was his *droit de seigneur*,[27] and that if the peasants dared to protest he would have them all flogged and double the tax on them, the bearded rascals. Our servile rabble applauded, but I attacked him, not from compassion for the girls and their fathers, but simply because they were applauding such an insect. I got the better of him on that occasion, but though Zverkov was stupid he was lively and impudent, and so laughed it off, and in such a way that my victory was not really complete: the laugh was on his side. He got the better of me on several occasions afterwards, but without malice, jestingly,

27. "the right of the master," i.e., to all the women serfs.

casually. I remained angrily and contemptuously silent and would not answer him. When we left school he made advances to me; I did not rebuff them, for I was flattered, but we soon parted and quite naturally. Afterwards I heard of his barrack-room success as a lieutenant, and of the fast life he was leading. Then there came other rumours—of his successes in the service. By then he had taken to cutting me in the street, and I suspected that he was afraid of compromising himself by greeting a personage as insignificant as me. I saw him once in the theatre, in the third tier of boxes. By then he was wearing shoulder-straps. He was twisting and twirling about, ingratiating himself with the daughters of an ancient General. In three years he had gone off considerably, though he was still rather handsome and adroit. One could see that by the time he was thirty he would be corpulent. So it was to this Zverkov that my schoolfellows were going to give a dinner on his departure. They had kept up with him for those three years, though privately they did not consider themselves on an equal footing with him, I am convinced of that.

Of Simonov's two visitors, one was Ferfichkin, a Russianized German—a little fellow with the face of a monkey, a blockhead who was always deriding every one, a very bitter enemy of mine from our days in the lower grades—a vulgar, impudent, swaggering fellow, who affected a most sensitive feeling of personal honour, though, of course, he was a wretched little coward at heart. He was one of those worshippers of Zverkov who made up to the latter from interested motives, and often borrowed money from him. Simonov's other visitor, Trudolyubov, was a person in no way remarkable—a tall young fellow, in the army, with a cold face, fairly honest, though he worshipped success of every sort, and was only capable of thinking of promotion. He was some sort of distant relation of Zverkov's, and this, foolish as it seems, gave him a certain importance among us. He always thought me of no consequence whatever; his behaviour to me, though not quite courteous, was tolerable.

"Well, with seven roubles each," said Trudolyubov, "twenty-one roubles between the three of us, we ought to be able to get a good dinner. Zverkov, of course, won't pay."

"Of course not, since we are inviting him," Simonov decided.

"Can you imagine," Ferfichkin interrupted hotly and conceitedly, like some insolent flunkey boasting of his master the General's decorations, "can you imagine that Zverkov will let us pay alone? He will accept from delicacy, but he will order half a dozen bottles of champagne."

"Do we want half a dozen for the four of us?" observed Trudolyubov, taking notice only of the half dozen.

"So the three of us, with Zverkov for the fourth, twenty-one roubles, at the Hôtel de Paris at five o'clock to-morrow," Simonov, who had been asked to make the arrangements, concluded finally.

"How twenty-one roubles?" I asked in some agitation, with a show of being offended; "if you count me it will not be twenty-one, but twenty-eight roubles."

It seemed to me that to invite myself so suddenly and unexpectedly would be positively graceful, and that they would all be conquered at once and would look at me with respect.

"Do you want to join, too?" Simonov observed, with no appearance of pleasure, seeming to avoid looking at me. He knew me through and through.

It infuriated me that he knew me so thoroughly.

"Why not? I am an old schoolfellow of his, too, I believe, and I must own I feel hurt that you have left me out," I said, boiling over again.

"And where were we to find you?" Ferfichkin put in roughly.

"You never were on good terms with Zverkov," Trudolyubov added, frowning.

But I had already clutched at the idea and would not give it up.

"It seems to me that no one has a right to form an opinion upon that," I retorted in a shaking voice, as though something tremendous had happened. "Perhaps that is just my reason for wishing it now, that I have not always been on good terms with him."

"Oh, there's no making you out . . . with these refinements," Trudolyubov jeered.

"We'll put your name down," Simonov decided, addressing me. "To-morrow at five o'clock at the Hôtel de Paris."

"What about the money?" Ferfichkin began in an undertone, indicating me to Simonov, but he broke off, for even Simonov was embarrassed.

"That will do," said Trudolyubov, getting up. "If he wants to come so much, let him."

"But it's a private thing, between us friends," Ferfichkin said crossly, as he, too, picked up his hat. "It's not an official gathering."

"We do not want at all, perhaps . . ."

They went away. Ferfichkin did not greet me in any way as he went out, Trudolyubov barely nodded. Simonov, with whom I was left *tête-à-tête*, was in a state of vexation and perplexity, and looked at me queerly. He did not sit down and did not ask me to.

"H'm . . . yes . . . to-morrow, then. Will you pay your subscription now? I just ask so as to know," he muttered in embarrassment.

I flushed crimson, and as I did so I remembered that I had owed Simonov fifteen roubles for ages—which I had, indeed, never forgotten, though I had not paid it.

"You will understand, Simonov, that I could have no idea when I came here. . . . I am very much vexed that I have forgotten. . . ."

"All right, all right, that doesn't matter. You can pay to-morrow after the dinner. I simply wanted to know. . . . Please don't . . ."

He broke off and began pacing the room still more vexed. As he walked he began to stamp with his heels.

"Am I keeping you?" I asked, after two minutes of silence.

"Oh!" he said, starting, "that is—to be truthful—yes. I have to go and see some one . . . not far from here," he added in an apologetic voice, somewhat abashed.

"My goodness, why didn't you say so?" I cried, seizing my cap, with an astonishingly free-and-easy air, which was the last thing I should have expected of myself.

"It's close by . . . not two paces away," Simonov repeated, accompanying me to the front door with a fussy air which did not suit him at all. "So five o'clock, punctually, to-morrow," he called down the stairs after me. He was very glad to get rid of me. I was in a fury.

"What possessed me, what possessed me to force myself upon them?" I wondered, grinding my teeth as I strode along the street, "for a scoundrel, a pig like that Zverkov! Of course, I had better not go; of course, I must just snap my fingers at them. I am not bound in any way. I'll send Simonov a note by to-morrow's post. . . ."

But what made me furious was that I knew for certain that I should go, that I should make a point of going; and the more tactless, the more unseemly my going would be, the more certainly I would go.

And there was a positive obstacle to my going: I had no money. All I had was nine roubles, I had to give seven of that to my servant, Apollon, for his monthly wages. That was all I paid him—he had to keep himself.

Not to pay him was impossible, considering his character. But I will talk about that fellow, about that plague of mine, another time.

However, I knew I should go and should not pay him his wages.

That night I had the most hideous dreams. No wonder; all the evening I had been oppressed by memories of my miserable days at school, and I could not shake them off. I was sent to the school by distant relations, upon whom I was dependent and of whom I have heard nothing since—they sent me there a forlorn, silent boy, already crushed by their reproaches, already troubled by doubt, and looking with savage distrust at every one. My schoolfellows met me with spiteful and merciless jibes because I was not like any of them. But I could not endure their taunts; I could not give in to them with the ignoble readiness with which they gave in to one another. I hated them from the first, and shut myself away from every one in

timid, wounded and disproportionate pride. Their coarseness revolted me. They laughed cynically at my face, at my clumsy figure;
and yet what stupid faces they had themselves. In our school the
boys' faces seemed in a special way to degenerate and grow stupider.
How many fine-looking boys came to us! In a few years they became
repulsive. Even at sixteen I wondered at them morosely; even then
I was struck by the pettiness of their thoughts, the stupidity of their
pursuits, their games, their conversations. They had no understanding of such essential things, they took no interest in such striking,
impressive subjects, that I could not help considering them inferior
to myself. It was not wounded vanity that drove me to it, and for
God's sake do not thrust upon me your hackneyed remarks, repeated
to nausea, that "I was only a dreamer," while they even then had
an understanding of life. They understood nothing, they had no
idea of real life, and I swear that that was what made me most indignant with them. On the contrary, the most obvious, striking
reality they accepted with fantastic stupidity and even at that time
were accustomed to respect success. Everything that was just, but
oppressed and looked down upon, they laughed at heartlessly and
shamefully. They took rank for intelligence; even at sixteen they
were already talking about a snug berth. Of course, a great deal of
it was due to their stupidity, to the bad examples with which they
had always been surrounded in their childhood and boyhood. They
were monstrously depraved. Of course a great deal of that, too, was
superficial and an assumption of cynicism; of course there were
glimpses of youth and freshness even in their depravity; but even
that freshness was not attractive, and showed itself in a certain rak-
ishness. I hated them horribly, though perhaps I was worse than
any of them. They repaid me in the same way, and did not conceal
their aversion for me. But by then I did not desire their affection:
on the contrary I continually longed for their humiliation. To escape
from their derision I purposely began to make all the progress I
could with my studies and forced my way to the very top. This
impressed them. Moreover, they all began by degrees to grasp that
I had already read books none of them could read, and understood
things (not forming part of our school curriculum) of which they
had not even heard. They took a savage and sarcastic view of it, but
were morally impressed, especially as the teachers began to notice
me on those grounds. The mockery ceased, but the hostility remained, and cold and strained relations became permanent between
us. In the end I could not put up with it: with years a craving for
society, for friends, developed in me. I attempted to get on friendly
terms with some of my schoolfellows; but somehow or other my
intimacy with them was always strained and soon ended of itself.
Once, indeed, I did have a friend. But I was already a tyrant at

heart; I wanted to exercise unbounded sway over him; I tried to instil into him a contempt for his surroundings; I required of him a disdainful and complete break with those surroundings. I frightened him with my passionate affection; I reduced him to tears, to hysterics. He was a simple and devoted soul; but when he devoted himself to me entirely I began to hate him immediately and repulsed him—as though all I needed him for was to win a victory over him, to subjugate him and nothing else. But I could not subjugate all of them; my friend was not at all like them either, he was, in fact, a rare exception. The first thing I did on leaving school was to give up the special job for which I had been destined so as to break all ties, to curse my past and shake the dust from off my feet. . . . And goodness knows why, after all that, I should go trudging off to Simonov's!

Early next morning I roused myself and jumped out of bed with excitement, as though it were all about to happen at once. But I believed that some radical change in my life was coming, and would inevitably come that day. Owing to its rarity, perhaps, any external event, however trivial, always made me feel as though some radical change in my life were at hand. I went to the office, however, as usual, but sneaked away home two hours earlier to get ready. The great thing, I thought, is not to be the first to arrive, or they will think I am overjoyed at coming. But there were thousands of such great points to consider, and they all agitated and overwhelmed me. I polished my boots a second time with my own hands; nothing in the world would have induced Apollon to clean them twice a day, as he considered that it was more than his duties required of him. I stole the brushes to clean them from the passage, being careful he should not detect it, for fear of his contempt. Then I minutely examined my clothes and thought that everything looked old, worn and threadbare. I had let myself get too slovenly. My uniform, perhaps, was tidy, but I could not go out to dinner in my uniform. The worst of it was that on the knee of my trousers was a big yellow stain. I had a foreboding that that stain would deprive me of nine-tenths of my personal dignity. I knew, too, that it was very bad to think so. "But this is no time for thinking: now I am in for the real thing," I thought, and my heart sank. I knew, too, perfectly well even then, that I was monstrously exaggerating the facts. But how could I help it? I could not control myself and was already shaking with fever. With despair I pictured to myself how coldly and disdainfully that "scoundrel" Zverkov would meet me; with what dull-witted, invincible contempt the blockhead Trudolyubov would look at me; with what impudent rudeness the insect Ferfichkin would snigger at me in order to curry favour with Zverkov; how completely Simonov would take it all in, and how he would despise me for the abjectness of my vanity and lack of spirit—and, worst of all, how paltry, *unliterary*, commonplace it would all be. Of course, the best thing would be not to go at all. But that was most impossible of all: if I feel impelled to do anything, I seem to be pitchforked into it. I should have jeered at myself ever afterwards: "So you funked it, you funked it, you funked the *real thing!*" On the contrary, I passionately longed to show all that "rabble" that I was by no means such a spiritless creature as I seemed to myself. What is more, even in the acutest paroxysm of this cowardly fever, I dreamed of getting the upper hand, of dominating them, carrying them away, making them like me—if only for my "elevation of thought and unmistakable wit." They would abandon Zverkov, he would sit on one side, silent and ashamed, while I should crush him. Then, perhaps, we would be reconciled and drink to our everlasting friendship; but what was most bitter and most humiliating for me was that I knew even then, knew fully and for certain, that I needed nothing of all this really, that I did not really want to crush, to subdue, to attract them, and that I did not care a straw really for the result, even if I did achieve it. Oh, how I prayed for the day to pass quickly! In unutterable anguish I went to the window, opened the movable pane and looked out into the troubled darkness of the thickly falling wet snow. At last my wretched little clock hissed out five. I seized my hat and trying not to look at Apollon, who had been all day expecting his month's wages, but in his foolishness was unwilling to be the first to speak about it, I slipt between him and the door and jumping into a high-class sledge, on which I spent my last half rouble, I drove up in grand style to the Hôtel de Paris.

IV

I had been certain the day before that I should be the first to arrive. But it was not a question of being the first to arrive. Not only were they not there, but I had difficulty in finding our room. The table was not laid even. What did it mean? After a good many questions I elicited from the waiters that the dinner had been ordered not for five, but for six o'clock. This was confirmed at the buffet too. I felt really ashamed to go on questioning them. It was only twenty-five minutes past five. If they changed the dinner hour they ought at least to have let me know—that is what the post is for, and not to have put me in an absurd position in my own eyes and . . . and even before the waiters. I sat down; the servant began laying the table; I felt even more humiliated when he was present. Towards six o'clock they brought in candles, though there were lamps burning in the room. It had not occurred to the waiter, however, to bring them in at once when I arrived. In the next room two gloomy, angry-looking persons were eating their dinners in silence at two different tables. There was a great deal of noise, even shouting, in a room further away; one could hear the laughter of a crowd of people, and nasty little shrieks in French: there were ladies at the dinner. It was sickening, in fact. I rarely passed more unpleasant moments, so much so that when they did arrive all together punctually at six I was overjoyed to see them, as though they were my deliverers, and even forgot that it was incumbent upon me to show resentment.

Zverkov walked in at the head of them; evidently he was the leading spirit. He and all of them were laughing; but, seeing me, Zverkov drew himself up a little, walked up to me deliberately with a slight, rather jaunty bend from the waist. He shook hands with me in a friendly, but not over-friendly, fashion, with a sort of circumspect courtesy like that of a General, as though in giving me his hand he were warding off something. I had imagined, on the contrary, that on coming in he would at once break into his habitual thin, shrill laugh and fall to making his insipid jokes and witticisms. I had been preparing for them ever since the previous day, but I had not expected such condescension, such high-official courtesy. So, then, he felt himself ineffably superior to me in every respect! If he only meant to insult me by that high-official tone, it would not matter, I thought—I could pay him back for it one way or another. But what if, in reality, without the least desire to be offensive, that sheepshead had a notion in earnest that he was superior to me and could only look at me in a patronizing way? The very supposition made me gasp.

"I was surprised to hear of your desire to join us," he began, lisping and drawling, which was something new. "You and I seem to have seen nothing of one another. You fight shy of us. You shouldn't. We are not such terrible people as you think. Well, anyway, I am glad to renew our acquaintance."

And he turned carelessly to put down his hat on the window.

"Have you been waiting long?" Trudolyubov inquired.

"I arrived at five o'clock as you told me yesterday," I answered aloud, with an irritability that threatened an explosion.

"Didn't you let him know that we had changed the hour?" said Trudolyubov to Simonov.

"No, I didn't. I forgot," the latter replied, with no sign of regret, and without even apologizing to me he went off to order the *hors d'œuvres*.

"So you've been here a whole hour? Oh, poor fellow!" Zverkov cried ironically, for to his notions this was bound to be extremely funny. That rascal Ferfichkin followed with his nasty little snigger like a puppy yapping. My position struck him, too, as exquisitely ludicrous and embarrassing.

"It isn't funny at all!" I cried to Ferfichkin, more and more irritated. "It wasn't my fault, but other people's. They neglected to let me know. It was . . . it was . . . it was simply absurd."

"It's not only absurd, but something else as well," muttered Trudolyubov, naïvely taking my part. "You are not hard enough upon it. It was simply rudeness—unintentional, of course. And how could Simonov . . . h'm!"

"If a trick like that had been played on me," observed Ferfichkin, "I should . . ."

"But you should have ordered something for yourself," Zverkov interrupted, "or simply asked for dinner without waiting for us."

"You will allow that I might have done that without your permission," I rapped out. "If I waited, it was . . ."

"Let us sit down, gentlemen," cried Simonov, coming in. "Everything is ready; I can answer for the champagne; it is capitally frozen. . . . You see, I did not know your address, where was I to look for you?" he suddenly turned to me, but again he seemed to avoid looking at me. Evidently he had something against me. It must have been what happened yesterday.

All sat down; I did the same. It was a round table. Trudolyubov was on my left, Simonov on my right. Zverkov was sitting opposite, Ferfichkin next to him, between him and Trudolyubov.

"Tell me, are you . . . in a government office?" Zverkov went on attending to me. Seeing that I was embarrassed he seriously thought that he ought to be friendly to me, and, so to speak, cheer me up.

"Does he want me to throw a bottle at his head?" I thought, in a fury. In my novel surroundings I was unnaturally ready to be irritated.

"In the N—— office," I answered jerkily, with my eyes on my plate.

"And ha-ave you a go-od berth? I say, what ma-a-de you leave your original job?"

"What ma-a-de me was that I wanted to leave my original job," I drawled more than he, hardly able to control myself. Ferfichkin went off into a guffaw. Simonov looked at me ironically. Trudolyubov left off eating and began looking at me with curiosity.

Zverkov winced, but he tried not to notice it.

"And the remuneration?"

"What remuneration?"

"I mean, your sa-a-lary?"

"Why are you cross-examining me?" However, I told him at once what my salary was. I turned horribly red.

"It is not very handsome," Zverkov observed majestically.

"Yes, you can't afford to dine at cafés on that," Ferfichkin added insolently.

"To my thinking it's very poor," Trudolyubov observed gravely.

"And how thin you have grown! How you have changed!" added Zverkov, with a shade of venom in his voice, scanning me and my attire with a sort of insolent compassion.

"Oh, spare his blushes," cried Ferfichkin, sniggering.

"My dear sir, allow me to tell you I am not blushing," I broke out at last; "do you hear? I am dining here, at this café, at my own expense, not at other people's—note that, Mr. Ferfichkin."

"Wha-at? Isn't every one here dining at his own expense? You would seem to be . . ." Ferfichkin flew out at me, turning as red as a lobster, and looking me in the face with fury.

"Tha-at," I answered, feeling I had gone too far, "and I imagine it would be better to talk of something more intelligent."

"You intend to show off your intelligence, I suppose?"

"Don't disturb yourself, that would be quite out of place here."

"Why are you clacking away like that, my good sir, eh? Have you gone out of your wits in your office?"

"Enough, gentlemen, enough!" Zverkov cried, authoritatively.

"How stupid it is!" muttered Simonov.

"It really is stupid. We have met here, a company of friends, for a farewell dinner to a comrade and you carry on an altercation," said Trudolyubov, rudely addressing himself to me alone. "You invited yourself to join us, so don't disturb the general harmony."

"Enough, enough!" cried Zverkov. "Give over, gentlemen, it's out of place. Better let me tell you how I nearly got married the day before yesterday. . . ."

And then followed a burlesque narrative of how this gentleman had almost been married two days before. There was not a word about the marriage, however, but the story was adorned with generals, colonels and gentlemen-in-waiting, while Zverkov almost took the lead among them. It was greeted with approving laughter; Ferfichkin positively squealed.

No one paid any attention to me, and I sat crushed and humiliated.

"Good Heavens, these are not the people for me!" I thought. "And what a fool I have made of myself before them! I let Ferfichkin go too far, though. The brutes imagine they are doing me an honour in letting me sit down with them. They don't understand that it's an honour to them and not to me! I've grown thinner! My clothes! Oh, damn my trousers! Zverkov noticed the yellow stain on the knee as soon as he came in. . . . But what's the use! I must get up at once, this very minute, take my hat and simply go without a word . . . with contempt! And to-morrow I can send a challenge. The scoundrels! As though I cared about the seven roubles. They may think. . . . Damn it! I don't care about the seven roubles. I'll go this minute!"

Of course I remained. I drank sherry and Lafitte by the glassful in my discomfiture. Being unaccustomed to it, I was quickly affected. My annoyance increased as the wine went to my head. I longed all at once to insult them all in a most flagrant manner and then go away. To seize the moment and show what I could do, so that they would say, "He's clever, though he is absurd," and . . . and . . . in fact, damn them all!

I scanned them all insolently with my drowsy eyes. But they seemed to have forgotten me altogether. They were noisy, vociferous, cheerful. Zverkov was talking all the time. I began listening. Zverkov was talking of some exuberant lady whom he had at last led on to declaring her love (of course, he was lying like a horse), and how he had been helped in this affair by an intimate friend of his, a Prince Kolya, an officer in the hussars, who had three thousand serfs.

"And yet this Kolya, who has three thousand serfs, has not put in an appearance here to-night to see you off," I cut in suddenly.

For a minute every one was silent. "You are drunk already." Trudolyubov deigned to notice me at last, glancing contemptuously in my direction. Zverkov, without a word, examined me as though I were an insect. I dropped my eyes. Simonov made haste to fill up the glasses with champagne.

Trudolyubov raised his glass, as did every one else but me.

"Your health and good luck on the journey!" he cried to Zverkov. "To old times, to our future, hurrah!"

They all tossed off their glasses, and crowded round Zverkov to kiss him. I did not move; my full glass stood untouched before me.

"Why, aren't you going to drink it?" roared Trudolyubov, losing patience and turning menacingly to me.

"I want to make a speech separately, on my own account . . . and then I'll drink it, Mr. Trudolyubov."

"Spiteful brute!" muttered Simonov. I drew myself up in my chair and feverishly seized my glass, prepared for something extraordinary, though I did not know myself precisely what I was going to say.

"*Silence!*" cried Ferfichkin. "Now for a display of wit!"

Zverkov waited very gravely, knowing what was coming.

"Mr. Lieutenant Zverkov," I began, "let me tell you that I hate phrases, phrasemongers and men in corsets . . . that's the first point, and there is a second one to follow it."

There was a general stir.

"The second point is: I hate ribaldry and ribald talkers. Especially ribald talkers! The third point: I love justice, truth and honesty." I went on almost mechanically, for I was beginning to shiver with horror myself and had no idea how I came to be talking like this. "I love thought, Monsieur Zverkov; I love true comradeship, on an equal footing and not . . . H'm . . . I love. . . . But, however, why not? I will drink your health, too, Mr. Zverkov. Seduce the Circassian girls, shoot the enemies of the fatherland and . . . and . . . to your health, Monsieur Zverkov!"

Zverkov got up from his seat, bowed to me and said:

"I am very much obliged to you." He was frightfully offended and turned pale.

"Damn the fellow!" roared Trudolyubov, bringing his fist down on the table.

"Well, he wants a punch in the face for that," squealed Ferfichkin.

"We ought to turn him out," muttered Simonov.

"Not a word, gentlemen, not a movement!" cried Zverkov solemnly, checking the general indignation. "I thank you all, but I can show him for myself how much value I attach to his words."

"Mr. Ferfichkin, you will give me satisfaction to-morrow for your words just now!" I said aloud, turning with dignity to Ferfichkin.

"A duel, you mean? Certainly," he answered. But probably I was so ridiculous as I challenged him and it was so out of keeping with my appearance that everyone, including Ferfichkin, was prostrate with laughter.

"Yes, let him alone, of course! He is quite drunk," Trudolyubov said with disgust.

"I shall never forgive myself for letting him join us," Simonov muttered again.

"Now is the time to throw a bottle at their heads," I thought to myself. I picked up the bottle . . . and filled my glass. . . . "No, I'd better sit on to the end," I went on thinking; "you would be pleased, my friends if I went away. Nothing will induce me to go. I'll go on sitting here and drinking to the end, on purpose, as a sign that I don't think you of the slightest consequence. I will go on sitting and drinking, because this is a public-house and I paid my entrance money. I'll sit here and drink, for I look upon you as so many pawns, as inanimate pawns. I'll sit here and drink . . . and sing if I want to, yes, sing, for I have the right to . . . to sing . . . H'm!"

But I did not sing. I simply tried not to look at any of them. I assumed most unconcerned attitudes and waited with impatience for them to speak *first*. But alas, they did not address me! And oh, how I wished, how I wished at that moment to be reconciled to them! It struck eight, at last nine. They moved from the table to the sofa. Zverkov stretched himself on a lounge and put one foot on a round table. Wine was brought there. He did, as a fact, order three bottles on his own account. I, of course, was not invited to join them. They all sat round him on the sofa. They listened to him, almost with reverence. It was evident that they were fond of him. "What for? What for?" I wondered. From time to time they were moved to drunken enthusiasm and kissed each other. They talked of the Caucasus, of the nature of true passion, of snug berths in the service, of the income of an hussar called Podkharzhevsky, whom none of them knew personally, and rejoiced in the largeness of it, of the extraordinary grace and beauty of a Princess D., whom none of them had ever seen; then it came to Shakespeare's being immortal.

I smiled contemptuously and walked up and down the other side of the room, opposite the sofa, from the table to the stove and back again. I tried my very utmost to show them that I could do without them, and yet I purposely made a noise with my boots, thumping with my heels. But it was all in vain. They paid no attention. I had the patience to walk up and down in front of them from eight o'clock till eleven, in the same place, from the table to the stove and back again. "I walk up and down to please myself and no one can prevent me." The waiter who came into the room stopped, from time to time, to look at me. I was somewhat giddy from turning round so often; at moments it seemed to me that I was in delirium. During those three hours I was three times soaked with sweat and dry again. At times, with an intense, acute pang I was stabbed to the heart by the thought that ten years, twenty years, forty years would pass, and that even in forty years I would remember with loathing and humiliation those filthiest, most ludicrous, and most awful moments of my life. No one could have gone out of his way to degrade himself more shamelessly, and I fully realized it, fully, and yet I went on pacing up and down from the table to the stove. "Oh, if you only knew what thoughts and feelings I am capable of, how cultured I am!" I thought at moments, mentally addressing the sofa on which my enemies were sitting. But my enemies behaved as though I were not in the room. Once —only once—they turned towards me, just when Zverkov was talking about Shakespeare, and I suddenly gave a contemptuous laugh. I laughed in such an affected and disgusting way that they all at once broke off their conversation, and silently and gravely for two minutes watched me walking up and down from the table to the stove, *taking no notice of them*. But nothing came of it: they said nothing, and two minutes later they ceased to notice me again. It struck eleven.

"Friends," cried Zverkov getting up from the sofa, "let us all be off now, *there!*"

"Of course, of course," the others assented. I turned sharply to Zverkov. I was so harassed, so exhausted, that I would have cut my throat to put an end to it. I was in a fever; my hair, soaked with perspiration, stuck to my forehead and temples.

"Zverkov, I beg your pardon," I said abruptly and resolutely. "Ferfichkin, yours too, and every one's, every one's: I have insulted you all!"

"Aha! A duel is not in your line, old man," Ferfichkin hissed venomously.

It sent a sharp pang to my heart.

"No, it's not the duel I am afraid of, Ferfichkin! I am ready to fight you to-morrow, after we are reconciled. I insist upon it, in fact, and you cannot refuse. I want to show you that I am not afraid of a duel. You shall fire first and I shall fire into the air."

"He is comforting himself," said Simonov.

"He's simply raving," said Trudolyubov.

"But let us pass. Why are you barring our way? What do you want?" Zverkov answered disdainfully.

They were all flushed, their eyes were bright: they had been drinking heavily.

"I ask for your friendship, Zverkov; I insulted you, but . . ."

"Insulted? *You* insulted *me?* Understand, sir, that you never, under any circumstances, could possibly insult *me.*"

"And that's enough for you. Out of the way!" concluded Trudolyubov.

"Olympia is mine, friends, that's agreed!" cried Zverkov.

"We won't dispute your right, we won't dispute your right," the others answered, laughing.

I stood as though spat upon. The party went noisily out of the room. Trudolyubov struck up some stupid song. Simonov remained behind for a moment to tip the waiters. I suddenly went up to him.

"Simonov! give me six roubles!" I said, with desperate resolution.

He looked at me in extreme amazement, with vacant eyes. He, too, was drunk.

"You don't mean you are coming with us?"

"Yes."

"I've no money," he snapped out, and with a scornful laugh he went out of the room.

I clutched at his overcoat. It was a nightmare.

"Simonov, I saw you had money. Why do you refuse me? Am I a scoundrel? Beware of refusing me: if you knew, if you knew why I am asking! My whole future, my whole plans depend upon it!"

Simonov pulled out the money and almost flung it at me.

"Take it, if you have no sense of shame!" he pronounced pitilessly, and ran to overtake them.

I was left for a moment alone. Disorder, the remains of dinner, a broken wine-glass on the floor, spilt wine, cigarette ends, fumes of drink and delirium in my brain, an agonizing misery in my heart and finally the waiter, who had seen and heard all and was looking inquisitively into my face.

"I am going there!" I cried. "Either they shall all go down on their knees to beg for my friendship, or I will give Zverkov a slap in the face!"

v

"So this is it, this is it at last—contact with real life," I muttered as I ran headlong downstairs. "This is very different from the Pope's leaving Rome and going to Brazil, very different from the ball on Lake Como!"

"You are a scoundrel," a thought flashed through my mind, "if you laugh at this now."

"No matter!" I cried, answering myself. "Now everything is lost!"

There was no trace to be seen of them, but that made no difference—I knew where they had gone.

At the steps was standing a solitary night sledge-driver in a rough peasant coat, powdered over with the still falling, wet, and as it were warm, snow. It was hot and steamy. The little shaggy piebald horse was also covered with snow and coughing, I remember that very well. I made a rush for the roughly made sledge; but as soon as I raised my foot to get into it, the recollection of how Simonov had just given me six roubles seemed to double me up and I tumbled into the sledge like a sack.

"No, I must do a great deal to make up for all that," I cried. "But I will make up for it or perish on the spot this very night. Start!"

We set off. There was a perfect whirl in my head.

"They won't go down on their knees to beg for my friendship. That is a mirage, cheap mirage, revolting, romantic and fantastical —that's another ball on Lake Como. And so I am bound to slap Zverkov's face! It is my duty to. And so it is settled; I am flying to give him a slap in the face. Hurry up!"

The driver tugged at the reins.

"As soon as I go in I'll give it him. Ought I before giving him the slap to say a few words by way of preface? No. I'll simply go in and give it him. They will all be sitting in the drawing-room, and he with Olympia on the sofa. That damned Olympia! She laughed at my looks on one occasion and refused me. I'll pull Olympia's hair, pull Zverkov's ears! No, better one ear, and pull him by it round the room. Maybe they will all begin beating me and will kick me out. That's most likely, indeed. No matter! Anyway, I shall first slap him; the initiative will be mine; and by the laws of honour that is everything: he will be branded and cannot wipe off the slap by any blows, by nothing but a duel. He will be forced to fight. And let them beat me now. Let them, the ungrateful wretches! Trudolyubov will beat me hardest, he is so strong; Ferfichkin will be sure to catch hold sideways and tug at my hair. But no matter, no matter! That's what I am going for. The blockheads will be forced at last to see the tragedy of it all! When they drag me to the door I shall call out to them that in reality they are not worth my little finger. Get on, driver, get on!" I cried to the driver. He started and flicked his whip, I shouted so savagely.

"We shall fight at daybreak, that's a settled thing. I've done with the office. Ferfichkin made a joke about it just now. But where can I get pistols? Nonsense! I'll get my salary in advance and buy them. And powder, and bullets? That's the second's business. And how can it all be done by daybreak? And where am I to get a second? I have no friends. Nonsense!" I cried, lashing myself up more and more. "It's of no consequence! the first person I meet in the street is bound to be my second, just as he would be bound to pull a drowning man out of water. The most eccentric things may happen. Even if I were to ask the director himself to be my second to-morrow, he would be bound to consent, if only from a feeling of chivalry, and to keep the secret! Anton Antonich. . . ."

The fact is, that at that very minute the disgusting absurdity of my plan and the other side of the question was clearer and more vivid to my imagination than it could be to any one on earth. But. . . .

"Get on, driver, get on, you rascal, get on!"

"Ugh, sir!" said the son of toil.

Cold shivers suddenly ran down me.

Wouldn't it be better . . . to go straight home? My God, my God! Why did I invite myself to this dinner yesterday? But no, it's impossible. And my walking up and down for three hours from the table to the stove? No, they, they and no one else must pay for my walking up and down! They must wipe out this dishonour! Drive on!

And what if they give me into custody? They won't dare! They'll be afraid of the scandal. And what if Zverkov is so contemptuous that he refuses to fight a duel? He is sure to; but in that case I'll show them . . . I will turn up at the posting station when he is setting off to-morrow, I'll catch him by the leg, I'll pull off his coat when he gets into the carriage. I'll get my teeth into his hand, I'll bite him. "See what lengths you can drive a desperate man to!"

He may hit me on the head and they may belabour me from behind. I will shout to the assembled multitude: "Look at this young puppy who is driving off to captivate the Circassian girls after letting me spit in his face!"

Of course, after that everything will be over! The office will have vanished off the face of the earth. I shall be arrested, I shall be tried, I shall be dismissed from the service, thrown in prison, sent to Siberia. Never mind! In fifteen years when they let me out of prison I will trudge off to him, a beggar, in rags. I shall find him in some provincial town. He will be married and happy. He will have a grown-up daughter. . . . I shall say to him: "Look, monster, at my hollow cheeks and my rags! I've lost everything—my career, my happiness, art, science, *the woman I loved*, and all through you. Here are pistols. I have come to discharge my pistol and . . . and I . . . forgive you. Then I shall fire into the air and he will hear nothing more of me. . . ."

I was actually on the point of tears, though I knew perfectly well at that moment that all this was out of Pushkin's *Silvio*[28] and Lermontov's *Masquerade*.[29] And all at once I felt horribly ashamed, so ashamed that I stopped the horse, got out of the sledge, and stood still in the snow in the middle of the street. The driver gazed at me, sighing and astonished.

What was I to do? I could not go on there—it was evidently stupid, and I could not leave things as they were, because that would seem as though . . . Heavens, how could I leave things! And after such insults! "No!" I cried, throwing myself into the sledge again. "It is ordained! It is fate! Drive on, drive on!"

And in my impatience I punched the sledge-driver on the back of the neck.

"What are you up to? What are you hitting me for?" the peasant shouted, but he whipped up his nag so that it began kicking.

The wet snow was falling in big flakes; I unbuttoned myself, regardless of it. I forgot everything else, for I had finally decided on the slap, and felt with horror that it was going to happen *now, at once*, and that *no force could stop it*. The deserted street lamps gleamed sullenly in the snowy darkness like torches at a funeral. The snow drifted under my great-coat, under my coat, under my cravat, and melted there. I did not wrap myself up—all was lost, anyway.

At last we arrived. I jumped out, almost unconscious, ran up the steps and began knocking and kicking at the door. I felt fearfully weak, particularly in my legs and my knees. The door was opened

---

28. actually "The Shot" (1830), by the Russian Poet Alexander Pushkin (1799–1837), a story in which the hero, Silvio, finally gives up the idea of re-venging himself for a slap in the face.
29. a verse play (1835) by the poet Mikhail Y. Lermontov (1814–1841).

quickly as though they knew I was coming. As a fact, Simonov had warned them that perhaps another gentleman would arrive, and this was a place in which one had to give notice and to observe certain precautions. It was one of those "millinery establishments" which were abolished by the police a good time ago. By day it really was a shop; but at night, if one had an introduction, one might visit it for other purposes.

I walked rapidly through the dark shop into the familiar drawing-room, where there was only one candle burning, and stood still in amazement: there was no one there. "Where are they?" I asked somebody. But by now, of course, they had separated. Before me was standing a person with a stupid smile, the "madam" herself, who had seen me before. A minute later a door opened and another person came in.

Taking no notice of anything I strode about the room, and, I believe, I talked to myself. I felt as though I had been saved from death and was conscious of this, joyfully, all over: I should have given that slap, I should certainly, certainly have given it! But now they were not here and . . . everything had vanished and changed! I looked round. I could not realize my condition yet. I looked mechanically at the girl who had come in: and had a glimpse of a fresh, young, rather pale face, with straight, dark eyebrows, and with grave, as it were wondering, eyes that attracted me at once; I should have hated her if she had been smiling. I began looking at her more intently and, as it were, with effort. I had not fully collected my thoughts. There was something simple and good-natured in her face, but something strangely grave. I am sure that this stood in her way here, and no one of those fools had noticed her. She could not, however, have been called a beauty, though she was tall, strong-looking, and well built. She was very simply dressed. Something loathsome stirred within me. I went straight up to her.

I chanced to look into the glass. My harassed face struck me as revolting in the extreme, pale, angry, abject, with dishevelled hair. "No matter, I am glad of it," I thought; "I am glad that I shall seem repulsive to her; I like that."

VI

. . . Somewhere behind a screen a clock began wheezing, as though oppressed by something, as though some one were strangling it. After an unnaturally prolonged wheezing there followed a shrill, nasty, and as it were unexpectedly rapid, chime—as though some one were suddenly jumping forward. It struck two. I woke up, though I had indeed not been asleep but lying half conscious.

It was almost completely dark in the narrow, cramped, low-pitched room, cumbered up with an enormous wardrobe and piles of cardboard boxes and all sorts of frippery and litter. The candle end that had been burning on the table was going out and gave a faint flicker from time to time. In a few minutes there would be complete darkness.

I was not long in coming to myself; everything came back to my mind at once, without an effort, as though it had been in ambush to pounce upon me again. And, indeed, even while I was unconscious a point seemed continually to remain in my memory unforgotten, and round it my dreams moved drearily. But strange to say, everything that had happened to me in that day seemed to me now, on waking, to be in the far, far away past, as though I had long, long ago lived all that down.

My head was full of fumes. Something seemed to be hovering over me, rousing me, exciting me, and making me restless. Misery and spite seemed surging up in me again and seeking an outlet. Suddenly I saw beside me two wide open eyes scrutinizing me curiously and persistently. The look in those eyes was coldly detached, sullen, as it were utterly remote; it weighed upon me.

A grim idea came into my brain and passed all over my body, as a horrible sensation, such as one feels when one goes into a damp and mouldy cellar. There was something unnatural in those two eyes, beginning to look at me only now. I recalled, too, that during those two hours I had not said a single word to this creature, and had, in fact, considered it utterly superfluous; in fact, the silence had for some reason gratified me. Now I suddenly realized vividly the hideous idea—revolting as a spider—of vice, which, without love, grossly and shamelessly begins with that in which true love finds its consummation. For a long time we gazed at each other like that, but she did not drop her eyes before mine and her expression did not change, so that at last I felt uncomfortable.

"What is your name?" I asked abruptly, to put an end to it.

"Liza," she answered almost in a whisper, but somehow far from graciously, and she turned her eyes away.

I was silent.

"What weather! The snow . . . it's disgusting!" I said, almost to myself, putting my arm under my head despondently, and gazing at the ceiling.

She made no answer. This was horrible.

"Have you always lived in Petersburg?" I asked a minute later, almost angrily, turning my head slightly towards her.

"No."

"Where do you come from?"

"From Riga," she answered reluctantly.

"Are you a German?"

"No, Russian."

"Have you been here long?"

"Where?"

"In this house?"

"A fortnight."

She spoke more and more jerkily. The candle went out; I could no longer distinguish her face.

"Have you a father and mother?"

"Yes . . . no . . . I have."

"Where are they?"

"There . . . in Riga."

"What are they?"

"Oh, nothing."

"Nothing? Why, what class are they?"

"Tradespeople."

"Have you always lived with them?"

"Yes."

"How old are you?"

"Twenty."

"Why did you leave them?"

"Oh, for no reason."

That answer meant "Let me alone; I feel sick, sad."

We were silent.

God knows why I did not go away. I felt myself more and more sick and dreary. The images of the previous day began of themselves, apart from my will, flitting through my memory in confusion. I suddenly recalled something I had seen that morning when, full of anxious thoughts, I was hurrying to the office.

"I saw them carrying a coffin out yesterday and they nearly dropped it," I suddenly said aloud, not that I desired to open the conversation, but as it were by accident.

"A coffin?"

"Yes, in the Haymarket; they were bringing it up out of a cellar."

"From a cellar?"

"Not from a cellar, but from a basement. Oh, you know . . . down below . . . from a house of ill-fame. It was filthy all round . . . Egg-shells, litter . . . stench. It was loathsome."

Silence.

"A nasty day to be buried," I began, simply to avoid being silent.

"Nasty, in what way?"

"The snow, the wet." (I yawned.)

"It makes no difference," she said suddenly, after a brief silence.

"No, it's horrid." (I yawned again.) "The gravediggers must have sworn at getting drenched by the snow. And there must have been water in the grave."

"Why water in the grave?" she asked, with a sort of curiosity, but speaking even more harshly and abruptly than before.

I suddenly began to feel provoked.

"Why, there must have been water at the bottom a foot deep. You can't dig a dry grave in Volkovo Cemetery."

"Why?"

"Why? Why, the place is waterlogged. It's a regular marsh. So they bury them in water. I've seen it myself . . . many times."

(I had never seen it once, indeed I had never been in Volkovo, and had only heard stories of it.)

"Do you mean to say, you don't mind how you die?"

"But why should I die?" she answered, as though defending herself.

"Why, some day you will die, and you will die just the same as that dead woman. She was . . . a girl like you. She died of consumption."

"A wench would have died in a hospital . . ." (She knows all about it already: she said "wench," not "girl.")

"She was in debt to her madam," I retorted, more and more provoked by the discussion; "and went on earning money for her up to the end, though she was in consumption. Some sledge-drivers standing by were talking about her to some soldiers and telling them so. No doubt they knew her. They were laughing. They were going to meet in a pot-house to drink to her memory."

A great deal of this was my invention. Silence followed, profound silence. She did not stir.

"And is it better to die in a hospital?"

"Isn't it just the same? Besides, why should I die?" she added irritably.

"If not now, a little later."

"Why a little later?"

"Why, indeed? Now you are young, pretty, fresh, you fetch a high price. But after another year of this life you will be very different—you will go off."

"In a year?"

"Anyway, in a year you will be worth less," I continued malignantly. "You will go from here to something lower, another house; a year later—to a third, lower and lower, and in seven years you will come to a basement in the Haymarket. That will be if you were lucky. But it would be much worse if you got some disease, consumption, say . . . and caught a chill, or something or other. It's not easy to get over an illness in your way of life. If you catch anything you may not get rid of it. And so you would die."

"Oh, well, then I shall die," she answered, quite vindictively, and she made a quick movement.

"But one is sorry."

"Sorry for whom?"

"Sorry for life."

Silence.

"Have you been engaged to be married? Eh?"

"What's that to you?"

"Oh, I am not cross-examining you. It's nothing to me. Why are you so cross? Of course you may have had your own troubles. What is it to me? It's simply that I felt sorry."

"Sorry for whom?"

"Sorry for you."

"No need," she whispered hardly audibly, and again made a faint movement.

That incensed me at once. What! I was so gentle with her, and she. . . .

"Why, do you think that you are on the right path?"

"I don't think anything."

"That's what's wrong, that you don't think. Realize it while there is still time. There still is time. You are still young, good-looking; you might love, be married, be happy. . . ."

"Not all married women are happy," she snapped out in the rude abrupt tone she had used at first.

"Not all, of course, but anyway it is much better than the life here. Infinitely better. Besides, with love one can live even without happiness. Even in sorrow life is sweet; life is sweet, however one lives. But here what is there but . . . filth? Phew!"

I turned away with disgust; I was no longer reasoning coldly. I began to feel myself what I was saying and warmed to the subject. I was already longing to expound the cherished ideas I had brooded over in my corner. Something suddenly flared up in me. An object had appeared before me.

"Never mind my being here, I am not an example for you. I am, perhaps, worse than you are. I was drunk when I came here, though," I hastened, however, to say in self-defence. "Besides, a man is no example for a woman. It's a different thing. I may degrade and defile myself, but I am not any one's slave. I come and go, and that's an end of it. I shake it off, and I am a different man. But you are a slave from the start. Yes, a slave! You give up everything, your whole freedom. If you want to break your chains afterwards, you won't be able to: you will be more and more fast in the snares. It is an accursed bondage. I know it. I won't speak of anything else, maybe you won't understand, but tell me: no doubt you are in debt to your madam? There, you see," I added, though she made no answer, but only listened in silence, entirely absorbed, "that's a bondage for you! You will never buy your freedom. They will see to that. It's like selling your soul to the devil. . . . And besides . . . perhaps I, too, am just as unlucky—how do you know

—and wallow in the mud on purpose, out of misery? You know, men take to drink from grief; well, maybe I am here from grief. Come, tell me, what is there good here? Here you and I . . . came together . . . just now and did not say one word to one another all the time, and it was only afterwards you began staring at me like a wild creature, and I at you. Is that loving? Is that how one human being should meet another? It's hideous, that's what it is!"

"Yes!" she assented sharply and hurriedly.

I was positively astounded by the promptitude of this "Yes." So the same thought may have been straying through her mind when she was staring at me just before. So she, too, was capable of certain thoughts? "Damn it all, this was interesting, this was a point of likeness!" I thought, almost rubbing my hands. And indeed it's easy to turn a young soul like that!

It was the exercise of my power that attracted me most.

She turned her head nearer to me, and it seemed to me in the darkness that she propped herself on her arm. Perhaps she was scrutinizing me. How I regretted that I could not see her eyes. I heard her deep breathing.

"Why have you come here?" I asked her, with a note of authority already in my voice.

"Oh, I don't know."

"But how nice it would be to be living in your father's house! It's warm and free; and you have a home of your own."

"But what if it's worse than this?"

"I must take the right tone," flashed through my mind. "I may not get far with sentimentality." But it was only a momentary thought. I swear she really did interest me. Besides, I was exhausted and moody. And cunning so easily goes hand-in-hand with feeling.

"Who denies it!" I hastened to answer. "Anything may happen. I am convinced that some one has wronged you, and that you are more sinned against than sinning. Of course, I know nothing of your story, but it's not likely a girl like you has come here of her own inclination. . . ."

"A girl like me?" she whispered, hardly audibly; but I heard it.

Damn it all, I was flattering her. That was horrid. But perhaps it was a good thing. . . . She was silent.

"See, Liza, I will tell you about myself. If I had had a home from childhood, I shouldn't be what I am now. I often think that. However bad it may be at home, anyway they are your father and mother, and not enemies, strangers. Once a year at least, they'll show their love of you. Anyway, you know you are at home. I grew up without a home; and perhaps that's why I've turned so . . . unfeeling."

I waited again. "Perhaps she doesn't understand," I thought, "and, indeed, it is absurd—it's moralizing."

"If I were a father and had a daughter, I believe I should love my daughter more than my sons, really," I began indirectly, as though talking of something else, to distract her attention. I must confess I blushed.

"Why so?" she asked.

Ah! so she was listening!

"I don't know, Liza. I knew a father who was a stern, austere man, but used to go down on his knees to his daughter, used to kiss her hands, her feet, he couldn't make enough of her, really. When she danced at parties he used to stand for five hours at a stretch, gazing at her. He was mad over her: I understand that! She would fall asleep tired at night, and he would wake to kiss her in her sleep and make the sign of the cross over her. He would go about in a dirty old coat, he was stingy to every one else, but would spend his last penny for her, giving her expensive presents, and it was his greatest delight when she was pleased with what he gave her. Fathers always love their daughters more than the mothers do. Some girls live happily at home! And I believe I should never let my daughters marry."

"What next?" she said, with a faint smile.

"I should be jealous, I really should. To think that she should kiss any one else! That she should love a stranger more than her father! It's painful to imagine it. Of course, that's all nonsense, of course every father would be reasonable at last. But I believe before I should let her marry, I should worry myself to death; I should find fault with all her suitors. But I should end by letting her marry whom she herself loved. The one whom the daughter loves always seems the worst to the father, you know. That is always so. So many family troubles come from that."

"Some are glad to sell their daughters, rather than marrying them honourably."

Ah, so that was it!

"Such a thing, Liza, happens in those accursed families in which there is neither love nor God," I retorted warmly, "and where there is no love, there is no sense either. There are such families, it's true, but I am not speaking of them. You must have seen wickedness in your own family, if you talk like that. Truly, you must have been unlucky. H'm! . . . that sort of thing mostly comes about through poverty."

"And is it any better with the gentry? Even among the poor, honest people live happily."

"H'm . . . yes. Perhaps. Another thing, Liza, man is fond of reckoning up his troubles, but does not count his joys. If he counted them up as he ought, he would see that every lot has enough happiness provided for it. And what if all goes well with the family, if the blessing of God is upon it, if the husband is a good one, loves you, cherishes you, never leaves you! There is happiness in such a family! Even sometimes there is happiness in the midst of sorrow; and indeed sorrow is everywhere. If you marry *you will find out for yourself*. But think of the first years of married life with one you love: what happiness, what happiness there sometimes is in it! And indeed it's the ordinary thing. In those early days even quarrels with one's husband end happily. Some women get up quarrels with their husbands just because they love them. Indeed, I knew a woman like that: she seemed to say that because she loved him, she would torment him and make him feel it. You know that you may torment a man on purpose through love. Women are particularly given to that, thinking to themselves 'I will love him so, I will make so much of him afterwards, that it's no sin to torment him a little now.' And all in the house rejoice in the sight of you, and you are happy and gay and peaceful and honourable. . . . Then there are some women who are jealous. If he went off anywhere—I knew one such woman, she couldn't restrain herself, but would jump up at night and run off on the sly to find out where he was, whether he was with some other woman. That's a pity. And the woman knows herself it's wrong, and her heart fails her and she suffers, but she loves—it's all through love. And how sweet it is to make it up after quarrels, to own herself in the wrong or to forgive him! And they are both so happy all at once—as though they had met anew, been married over again; as though their love had begun afresh. And no one, no one should know what passes between husband and wife if they love one another. And whatever quarrels there may be between them they ought not to call in their own mother to judge between them and tell tales of one another. They are their own judges. Love is a holy mystery and ought to be hidden from all other eyes, whatever happens. That makes it holier and better. They respect one another more, and much is built on respect. And if once there has been love, if they have been married for love, why should love pass away? Surely one can keep it! It is rare that one cannot keep it. And if the husband is kind and straightforward, why should not love last? The first phase of married love will pass, it is true, but then there will come a love that is better still. Then there will be the union of souls, they will have everything in common, there will be no secrets between them. And once they have children, the most difficult times will seem to them happy, so long as there is love and courage. Even toil will be a joy, you may deny yourself bread for your children and even that will be a joy. They will love you for it afterwards; so you are laying by for your future. As the children grow up you feel that you are an example, a support for them; that even after you die your children will always keep your thoughts and feelings, because they have received them from you, they will take on your semblance and likeness. So you see this is a great duty. How can it fail to draw the father and mother nearer? People say it's a trial to have children. Who says that? It is heavenly happiness! Are you fond of little children, Liza? I am awfully fond of them. You know—a little rosy baby boy at your bosom, and what husband's heart is not touched, seeing his wife nursing his child! A plump little rosy baby, sprawling and snuggling, chubby little hands and feet, clean tiny little nails, so tiny that it makes one laugh to look at them; eyes that look as if they understand everything. And while it sucks it clutches at your bosom with its little hand, plays. When its father comes up, the child tears itself away from the bosom, flings itself back, looks at its father, laughs, as though it were fearfully funny and falls to sucking again. Or it will bite its mother's breast when its little teeth are coming, while it looks sideways at her with its little eyes as though to say, 'Look, I am biting!' Is not all that happiness when they are the three together, husband, wife and child? One can forgive a great deal for the sake of such moments. Yes, Liza, one must first learn to live oneself before one blames others!"

"It's by pictures, pictures like that one must get at you," I thought to myself, though I did speak with real feeling, and all at once I flushed crimson. "What if she were suddenly to burst out laughing, what should I do then?" That idea drove me to fury. Towards the end of my speech I really was excited, and now my vanity was somehow wounded. The silence continued. I almost nudged her.

"Why are you——" she began and stopped. But I understood: there was a quiver of something different in her voice, not abrupt, harsh and unyielding as before, but something soft and shamefaced, so shamefaced that I suddenly felt ashamed and guilty.

"What?" I asked, with tender curiosity.

"Why, you . . ."

"What?"

"Why, you . . . speak somehow like a book," she said, and again there was a note of irony in her voice.

That remark sent a pang to my heart. It was not what I was expecting.

I did not understand that she was hiding her feelings under irony, that this is usually the last refuge of modest and chaste-souled people when the privacy of their soul is coarsely and intrusively invaded, and that their pride makes them refuse to surrender till the last moment and shrink from giving expression to their feelings before you. I ought to have guessed the truth from the timidity with which she had repeatedly approached her sarcasm, only bringing herself to utter it at last with an effort. But I did not guess, and an evil feeling took possession of me.

"Wait a bit!" I thought.

VII

"Oh, hush, Liza! How can you talk about being like a book, when it makes even me, an outsider, feel sick? Though I don't look at it as an outsider, for, indeed, it touches me to the heart. . . . Is it possible, is it possible that you do not feel sick at being here yourself? Evidently habit does wonders! God knows what habit can do with any one. Can you seriously think that you will never grow old, that you will always be good-looking, and that they will keep you here for ever and ever? I say nothing of the loathsomeness of the life here. . . . Though let me tell you this about it—about your present life, I mean; here though you are young now, attractive, nice, with soul and feeling, yet you know as soon as I came to myself just now I felt at once sick at being here with you! One can only come here when one is drunk. But if you were anywhere else, living as good people live, I should perhaps be more than attracted by you, should fall in love with you, should be glad of a look from you, let alone a word; I should hang about your door, should go down on my knees to you, should look upon you as my betrothed and think it an honour to be allowed to. I should not dare to have an impure thought about you. But here, you see, I know that I have only to whistle and you have to come with me whether you like it or not. I don't consult your wishes, but you mine. The lowest labourer hires himself as a workman, but he doesn't make a slave of himself altogether; besides, he knows that he will be free again presently. But when are you free? Only think what you are giving up here? What is it you are making a slave of? It is your soul, together with your body; you are selling your soul which you have no right to dispose of! You give your love to be outraged by every drunkard! Love! But that's everything, you know, it's a priceless diamond, it's a maiden's treasure, love—why, a man would be ready to give his soul, to face death to gain that love. But how much is your love worth now? You are sold, all of you, body and soul, and there is no need to strive for love when you can have everything without love. And you know there is no greater insult to a girl than that, do you understand? To be sure, I have heard that they comfort you, poor fools, they let you have lovers of your own here. But you know that's simply a farce, that's simply a sham, it's just laughing at you, and you are taken in by it! Why, do you suppose he really loves you, that lover of yours? I don't believe it. How can he love you when he knows you may be called away from him any minute?

He would be a low fellow if he did! Will he have a grain of respect
for you? What have you in common with him? He laughs at you
and robs you—that is all his love amounts to! You are lucky if he
does not beat you. Very likely he does beat you, too. Ask him, if
you have got one, whether he will marry you. He will laugh in your
face, if he doesn't spit in it or give you a blow—though maybe he
is not worth a bad halfpenny himself. And for what have you ruined
your life, if you come to think of it? For the coffee they give you to
drink and the plentiful meals? But with what object are they feeding
you up? An honest girl couldn't swallow the food, for she would
know what she was being fed for. You are in debt here, and, of
course, you will always be in debt, and you will go on in debt to the
end, till the visitors here begin to scorn you. And that will soon
happen, don't rely upon your youth—all that flies by express train
here, you know. You will be kicked out. And not simply kicked out;
long before that she'll begin nagging at you, scolding you, abusing
you, as though you had not sacrificed your health for her, had not
thrown away your youth and your soul for her benefit, but as though
you had ruined her, beggared her, robbed her. And don't expect
any one to take your part: the others, your companions, will attack
you, too, to win her favour, for all are in slavery here, and have lost
all conscience and pity here long ago. They have become utterly
vile, and nothing on earth is viler, more loathsome, and more insulting than their abuse. And you are laying down everything here, unconditionally, youth and health and beauty and hope, and at twenty-
two you will look like a woman of five-and-thirty, and you will be
lucky if you are not diseased, pray to God for that! No doubt you
are thinking now that you have a gay time and no work to do! Yet
there is no work harder or more dreadful in the world or ever has
been. One would think that the heart alone would be worn out with
tears. And you won't dare to say a word, not half a word when they
drive you away from here; you will go away as though you were to
blame. You will change to another house, then to a third, then
somewhere else, till you come down at last to the Haymarket. There
you will be beaten at every turn; that is good manners there, the
visitors don't know how to be friendly without beating you. You
don't believe that it is so hateful there? Go and look for yourself
some time, you can see with your own eyes. Once, one New Year's
Day, I saw a woman at a door. They had turned her out as a joke,
to give her a taste of the frost because she had been crying so much,
and they shut the door behind her. At nine o'clock in the morning
she was already quite drunk, dishevelled, half-naked, covered with
bruises, her face was powdered, but she had a black-eye, blood was
trickling from her nose and her teeth; some cabman had just given
her a drubbing. She was sitting on the stone steps, a salt fish of some

sort was in her hand; she was crying, wailing something about her
luck and beating with the fish on the steps, and cabmen and drunken
soldiers were crowding in the doorway taunting her. You don't believe that you will ever be like that? I should be sorry to believe it,
too, but how do you know; maybe ten years, eight years ago that
very woman with the salt fish came here fresh as a cherub, innocent, pure, knowing no evil, blushing at every word. Perhaps she was
like you, proud, ready to take offence, not like the others; perhaps
she looked like a queen, and knew what happiness was in store for
the man who should love her and whom she should love. Do you
see how it ended? And what if at that very minute when she was
beating on the filthy steps with that fish, drunken and dishevelled—
what if at that very minute she recalled the pure early days in her
father's house, when she used to go to school and the neighbour's
son watched for her on the way, declaring that he would love her
as long as he lived, that he would devote his life to her, and when
they vowed to love one another for ever and be married as soon as
they were grown up! No, Liza, it would be happy for you if you
were to die soon of consumption in some corner, in some cellar like
that woman just now. In the hospital, do you say? You will be lucky
if they take you, but what if you are still of use to the madam here?
Consumption is a queer disease, it is not like fever. The patient goes
on hoping till the last minute and says he is all right. He deludes
himself. And that just suits your madam. Don't doubt it, that's how
it is; you have sold your soul, and what is more you owe money, so
you daren't say a word. But when you are dying, all will abandon
you, all will turn away from you, for then there will be nothing to
get from you. What's more, they will reproach you for cumbering
the place, for being so long over dying. However you beg you won't
get a drink of water without abuse: 'Whenever are you going off,
you nasty hussy, you won't let us sleep with your moaning, you make
the gentlemen sick.' That's true, I have heard such things said myself. They will thrust you dying into the filthiest corner in the
cellar—in the damp and darkness; what will your thoughts be, lying
there alone? When you die, strange hands will lay you out, with
grumbling and impatience; no one will bless you, no one will sigh
for you, they only want to get rid of you as soon as may be; they
will buy a coffin, take you to the grave as they did that poor woman
to-day, and celebrate your memory at the tavern. In the gravest
sleet, filth, wet snow—no need to put themselves out for you—'Let
her down, Vanyukha; it's just like her luck—even here, she is head-
foremost, the hussy. Shorten the cord, you rascal.' 'It's all right as it
is.' 'All right, is it? Why, she's on her side! She was a fellow-creature,
after all! But, never mind, throw the earth on her.' And they won't

care to waste much time quarrelling over you. They will scatter the wet blue clay as quick as they can and go off to the tavern . . . and there your memory on earth will end; other women have children to go to their graves, fathers, husbands. While for you neither tear, nor sigh, nor remembrance; no one in the whole world will ever come to you, your name will vanish from the face of the earth —as though you had never existed, never been born at all! Nothing but filth and mud, however you knock at your coffin lid at night, when the dead arise, however you cry: 'Let me out, kind people, to live in the light of day! My life was no life at all; my life has been thrown away like a dish-clout; it was drunk away in the tavern at the Haymarket; let me out, kind people, to live in the world again.' "

And I worked myself up to such a pitch that I began to have a lump in my throat myself, and . . . and all at once I stopped, sat up in dismay, and bending over apprehensively, began to listen with a beating heart. I had reason to be troubled.

I had felt for some time that I was turning her soul upside down and rending her heart, and—and the more I was convinced of it, the more eagerly I desired to gain my object as quickly and as effectually as possible. It was the exercise of my skill that carried me away; yet it was not merely sport. . . .

I knew I was speaking stiffly, artificially, even bookishly, in fact, I could not speak except "like a book." But that did not trouble me: I knew, I felt that I should be understood and that this very bookishness might be an assistance. But now, having attained my effect, I was suddenly panic-stricken. Never before had I witnessed such despair! She was lying on her face, thrusting her face into the pillow and clutching it in both hands. Her heart was being torn. Her youthful body was shuddering all over as though in convulsions. Suppressed sobs rent her bosom and suddenly burst out in weeping and wailing, then she pressed closer into the pillow: she did not want any one here, not a living soul, to know of her anguish and her tears. She bit the pillow, bit her hand till it bled (I saw that afterwards), or, thrusting her fingers into her dishevelled hair seemed rigid with the effort of restraint, holding her breath and clenching her teeth. I began saying something, begging her to calm herself, but felt that I did not dare; and all at once, in a sort of cold shiver, almost in terror, began fumbling in the dark, trying hurriedly to get dressed to go. It was dark: though I tried my best I could not finish dressing quickly. Suddenly I felt a box of matches and a candlestick with a whole candle in it. As soon as the room was lighted up, Liza sprang up, sat up in bed, and with a contorted face, with a half insane smile, looked at me almost senselessly. I sat down beside her

and took her hands; she came to herself, made an impulsive movement towards me, would have caught hold of me, but did not dare,
and slowly bowed her head before me.

"Liza, my dear, I was wrong . . . forgive me, my dear," I began,
but she squeezed my hand in her fingers so tightly that I felt I was
saying the wrong thing and stopped.

"This is my address, Liza, come to me."

"I will come," she answered resolutely, her head still bowed.

"But now I am going, good-bye . . . till we meet again."

I got up; she, too, stood up and suddenly flushed all over, gave a
shudder, snatched up a shawl that was lying on a chair and muffled
herself in it to her chin. As she did this she gave another sickly
smile, blushed and looked at me strangely. I felt wretched; I was in
haste to get away—to disappear.

"Wait a minute," she said suddenly, in the passage just at the
doorway, stopping me with her hand on my overcoat. She put down
the candle in hot haste and ran off; evidently she had thought of
something or wanted to show me something. As she ran away she
flushed, her eyes shone, and there was a smile on her lips—what was
the meaning of it? Against my will I waited: she came back a minute
later with an expression that seemed to ask forgiveness for something. In fact, it was not the same face, not the same look as the
evening before: sullen, mistrustful and obstinate. Her eyes now were
imploring, soft, and at the same time trustful, caressing, timid. The
expression with which children look at people they are very fond of,
of whom they are asking a favour. Her eyes were a light hazel, they
were lovely eyes, full of life, and capable of expressing love as well as
sullen hatred.

Making no explanation, as though I, as a sort of higher being,
must understand everything without explanations, she held out a
piece of paper to me. Her whole face was positively beaming at that
instant with naïve, almost childish, triumph. I unfolded it. It was a
letter to her from a medical student or some one of that sort—a
very high-flown and flowery, but extremely respectful, love-letter.
I don't recall the words now, but I remember well that through the
high-flown phrases there was apparent a genuine feeling, which cannot be feigned. When I had finished reading it I met her glowing,
questioning, and childishly impatient eyes fixed upon me. She fastened her eyes upon my face and waited impatiently for what I
should say. In a few words, hurriedly, but with a sort of joy and
pride, she explained to me that she had been to a dance somewhere
in a private house, a family of "very nice people *who knew nothing*,
absolutely nothing, for she had only come here so lately and it had
all happened . . . and she hadn't made up her mind to stay and
was certainly going away as soon as she had paid her debt . . ."

and at that party there had been the student who had danced with her all the evening. He had talked to her, and it turned out that he had known her in old days at Riga when he was a child, they had played together, but a very long time ago—and he knew her parents, but *about this* he knew nothing, nothing whatever, and had no suspicion! And the day after the dance (three days ago) he had sent her that letter through the friend with whom she had gone to the party . . . and . . . well, that was all."

She dropped her shining eyes with a sort of bashfulness as she finished.

The poor girl was keeping that student's letter as a precious treasure, and had run to fetch it, her only treasure, because she did not want me to go away without knowing that she, too, was honestly and genuinely loved; that she, too, was addressed respectfully. No doubt that letter was destined to lie in her box and lead to nothing. But none the less, I am certain that she would keep it all her life as a precious treasure, as her pride and justification, and now at such a minute she had thought of that letter and brought it with naïve pride to raise herself in my eyes that I might see, that I, too, might think well of her. I said nothing, pressed her hand and went out. I so longed to get away. . . . I walked all the way home, in spite of the fact that the melting snow was still falling in heavy flakes. I was exhausted, shattered, in bewilderment. But behind the bewilderment the truth was already gleaming. The loathsome truth.

VIII

It was some time, however, before I consented to recognize that truth. Waking up in the morning after some hours of heavy, leaden sleep, and immediately realizing all that had happened on the previous day, I was positively amazed at my last night's *sentimentality* with Liza, at all those "outcries of horror and pity." "To think of having such an attack of womanish hysteria, pah!" I concluded. And what did I thrust my address upon her for? What if she comes? Let her come, though; it doesn't matter. . . . But *obviously*, that was not now the chief and the most important matter: I had to make haste and at all costs save my reputation in the eyes of Zverkov and Simonov as quickly as possible; that was the chief business. And I was so taken up that morning that I actually forgot all about Liza.

First of all I had at once to repay what I had borrowed the day before from Simonov. I resolved on a desperate measure: to borrow fifteen roubles straight off from Anton Antonich. As luck would have it he was in the best of humours that morning, and gave it to me at once, on the first asking. I was so delighted at this that, as I signed the I O U with a swaggering air, I told him casually that the night before "I had been keeping it up with some friends at the Hôtel de Paris; we were giving a farewell party to a comrade, in fact,

I might say a friend of my childhood, and you know—a desperate rake, fearfully spoilt—of course, he belongs to a good family, and has considerable means, a brilliant career; he is witty, charming, a regular Lovelace, you understand; we drank an extra 'half-dozen' and . . ."

And it went off all right; all this was uttered very easily, unconstrainedly and complacently.

On reaching home I promptly wrote to Simonov.

To this hour I am lost in admiration when I recall the truly gentlemanly, good-humoured, candid tone of my letter. With tact and good-breeding, and, above all, entirely without superfluous words, I blamed myself for all that had happened. I defended myself, "if I really may be allowed to defend myself," by alleging that being utterly unaccustomed to wine, I had been intoxicated with the first glass, which I said, I had drunk before they arrived, while I was waiting for them at the Hôtel de Paris between five and six o'clock. I begged Simonov's pardon especially; I asked him to convey my explanations to all the others, especially to Zverkov, whom "I seemed to remember as though in a dream" I had insulted. I added that I would have called upon all of them myself, but my head ached, and besides I had not the face to. I was particularly pleased with a certain lightness, almost carelessness (strictly within the bounds of politeness, however), which was apparent in my style, and better than any possible arguments, gave them at once to understand that I took rather an independent view of "all that unpleasantness last night;" that I was by no means so utterly crushed as you, my friends, probably imagine; but on the contrary, looked upon it as a gentleman serenely respecting himself should look upon it. "On a young hero's past no censure is cast!"

"There is actually an aristocratic playfulness about it!" I thought admiringly, as I read over the letter. And it's all because I am an intellectual and cultivated man! Another man in my place would not have known how to extricate himself, but here I have got out of it and am as jolly as ever again, and all because I am "a cultivated and educated man of our day." And, indeed, perhaps, everything was due to the wine yesterday. H'm! . . . no, it was not the wine. I did not drink anything at all between five and six when I was waiting for them. I had lied to Simonov; I had lied shamelessly; and indeed I wasn't ashamed now. . . . Hang it all though, the great thing was that I was rid of it.

I put six roubles in the letter, sealed it up, and asked Apollon to take it to Simonov. When he learned that there was money in the letter, Apollon became more respectful and agreed to take it. Towards evening I went out for a walk. My head was still aching and giddy after yesterday. But as evening came on and the twilight grew denser, my impressions and, following them, my thoughts, grew more and more different and confused. Something was not dead within me, in the depths of my heart and conscience it would not die, and it showed itself in acute depression. For the most part I jostled my way through the most crowded business streets, along Myeshchansky Street, along Sadovy Street and in Yusupov Garden. I always liked particularly sauntering along these streets in the dusk, just when there were crowds of working people of all sorts going home from their daily work, with faces looking cross with anxiety. What I liked was just that cheap bustle, that bare prose. On this occasion the jostling of the streets irritated me more than ever. I could not make out what was wrong with me, I could not find the clue, something seemed rising up continually in my soul, painfully, and refusing to be appeased. I returned home completely upset, it was just as though some crime were lying on my conscience.

The thought that Liza was coming worried me continually. It seemed queer to me that of all my recollections of yesterday this tormented me, as it were, especially, as it were, quite separately. Everything else I had quite succeeded in forgetting by the evening; I dismissed it all and was still perfectly satisfied with my letter to Simonov. But on this point I was not satisfied at all. It was as though I were worried only by Liza. "What if she comes," I thought incessantly, "well, it doesn't matter, let her come! H'm! it's horrid that she should see, for instance, how I live. Yesterday I seemed such a hero to her, while now, h'm! It's horrid, though, that I have let myself go so, the room looks like a beggar's. And I brought my-self to go out to dinner in such a suit! And my American leather sofa with the stuffing sticking out. And my dressing-gown, which will not cover me, such tatters, and she will see all this and she will see Apollon. That beast is certain to insult her. He will fasten upon her in order to be rude to me. And I, of course, shall be panic-stricken as usual, I shall begin bowing and scraping before her and pulling my dressing-gown round me, I shall begin smiling, telling lies. Oh, the beastliness! And it isn't the beastliness of it that matters most! There is something more important, more loath-some, viler! Yes, viler! And to put on that dishonest lying mask again!" . . .

When I reached that thought I fired up all at once.

"Why dishonest? How dishonest? I was speaking sincerely last night. I remember there was real feeling in me, too. What I wanted was to excite an honourable feeling in her. . . . Her crying was a good thing, it will have a good effect."

Yet I could not feel at ease. All that evening, even when I had come back home, even after nine o'clock, when I calculated that Liza could not possibly come, she still haunted me, and what was worse, she came back to my mind always in the same position. One moment out of all that had happened last night stood vividly before my imagination; the moment when I struck a match and saw her pale, distorted face, with its look of torture. And what a pitiful, what an unnatural, what a distorted smile she had at that moment! But I did not know then, that fifteen years later I should still in my imagination see Liza, always with the pitiful, distorted, inappropriate smile which was on her face at that minute.

Next day I was ready again to look upon it all as nonsense, due to over-excited nerves, and, above all, as *exaggerated*. I was always conscious of that weak point of mine, and sometimes very much afraid of it. "I exaggerate everything, that is where I go wrong," I repeated to myself every hour. But, however, "Liza will very likely come all the same," was the refrain with which all my reflections ended. I was so uneasy that I sometimes flew into a fury: "She'll come, she is certain to come!" I cried, running about the room, "if not to-day, she will come to-morrow; she'll find me out! The damnable romanticism of these pure hearts! Oh, the vileness—oh, the silliness—oh, the stupidity of these 'wretched sentimental souls!' Why, how fail to understand? How could one fail to understand? . . ."

But at this point I stopped short, and in great confusion, indeed.

And how few, how few words, I thought, in passing, were needed; how little of the idyllic (and affectedly, bookishly, artificially idyllic too) had sufficed to turn a whole human life at once according to my will. That's virginity, to be sure! Freshness of soil!

At times a thought occurred to me, to go to her, "to tell her all," and beg her not to come to me. But this thought stirred such wrath in me that I believed I should have crushed that "damned" Liza if she had chanced to be near me at the time. I should have insulted her, have spat at her, have turned her out, have struck her!

One day passed, however, another and another; she did not come and I began to grow calmer. I felt particularly bold and cheerful after nine o'clock, I even sometimes began dreaming, and rather sweetly: I, for instance, became the salvation of Liza, simply through her coming to me and my talking to her. . . . I develop her, educate her. Finally, I notice that she loves me, loves me passionately. I pretend not to understand (I don't know, however, why I pretend, just for effect, perhaps). At last all confusion, transfigured, trembling and sobbing, she flings herself at my feet and says that I am her saviour, and that she loves me better than anything in the world. I am amazed, but. . . . "Liza," I say, "can you imagine that I have not noticed your love, I saw it all, I divined it, but I did not dare to approach you first, because I had an influence over you and was afraid that you would force yourself, from gratitude, to respond to my love, would try to rouse in your heart a feeling which was perhaps absent, and I did not wish that . . . because it would be tyranny . . . it would be indelicate (in short, I launch off at that point into European, inexplicably lofty subtleties à la George Sand[30]), but now, now you are mine, you are my creation, you are pure, you are good, you are my noble wife.

> 'Into my house come bold and free,
> Its rightful mistress there to be.' "[31]

Then we begin living together, go abroad and so on, and so on. In fact, in the end it seemed vulgar to me myself, and I began putting out my tongue at myself.

Besides, they won't let her out, "the hussy!" I thought. They don't let them go out very readily, especially in the evening (for some reason I fancied she would come in the evening, and at seven o'clock precisely). Though she did say she was not altogether a slave there yet, and had certain rights; so, h'm! Damn it all, she will come, she is sure to come!

It was a good thing, in fact, that Apollon distracted my attention at that time by his rudeness. He drove me beyond all patience! He was the bane of my life, the curse laid upon me by Providence. We had been squabbling continually for years, and I hated him. My God, how I hated him! I believe I had never hated any one in my life as I hated him, especially at some moments. He was an elderly, dignified man, who worked part of his time as a tailor. But for some unknown reason he despised me beyond all measure, and looked down upon me insufferably. Though, indeed, he looked down upon every one. Simply to glance at that flaxen, smoothly brushed head, at the tuft of hair he combed up on his forehead and oiled with sunflower oil, at that dignified mouth, compressed into the shape of the letter V, made one feel one was confronting a man who never doubted of himself. He was a pedant, to the most extreme point, the greatest pedant I had met on earth, and with that had a vanity only befitting Alexander of Macedon. He was in love with every button on his coat, every nail on his fingers—absolutely in love with them, and he looked it! In his behaviour to me he was a perfect tyrant, he spoke very little to me, and if he chanced to glance at me he gave me a firm, majestically self-confident and invariably ironical look that drove me sometimes to fury. He did his work with the air of doing me the greatest favour. Though he did scarcely anything for me, and did not, indeed, consider himself bound to do anything. There could be no doubt that he looked upon me as the greatest fool on earth, and that "he did not get rid of me" was simply that

---

30. pseudonym of the French woman novelist Mme. Aurore Dudevant (1804–1876), famous also as a promoter of feminism.

31. the last lines of the poem by Nekrasov used as the epigraph of Part II of this story.

he could get wages from me every month. He consented to do nothing for me for seven roubles a month. Many sins should be forgiven me for what I suffered from him. My hatred reached such a point that sometimes his very step almost threw me into convulsions. What I loathed particularly was his lisp. His tongue must have been a little too long or something of that sort, for he continually lisped, and seemed to be very proud of it, imagining that it greatly added to his dignity. He spoke in a slow, measured tone, with his hands behind his back and his eyes fixed on the ground. He maddened me particularly when he read aloud the psalms to himself behind his partition. Many a battle I waged over that reading! But he was awfully fond of reading aloud in the evenings, in a slow, even, sing-song voice, as though over the dead. It is interesting that that is how he has ended: he hires himself out to read the psalms over the dead, and at the same time he kills rats and makes blacking. But at that time I could not get rid of him, it was as though he were chemically combined with my existence. Besides, nothing would have induced him to consent to leave me. I could not live in furnished lodgings: my lodging was my private solitude, my shell, my cave, in which I concealed myself from all mankind, and Apollon seemed to me, for some reason, an integral part of that flat, and for seven years I could not turn him away.

To be two or three days behind with his wages, for instance, was impossible. He would have made such a fuss, I should not have known where to hide my head. But I was so exasperated with every one during those days, that I made up my mind for some reason and with some object to *punish* Apollon and not to pay him for a fortnight the wages that were owing him. I had for a long time— for the last two years—been intending to do this, simply in order to teach him not to give himself airs with me, and to show him that if I liked I could withhold his wages. I purposed to say nothing to him about it, and was purposely silent indeed, in order to score off his pride and force him to be the first to speak of his wages. Then I would take the seven roubles out of a drawer, show him I have the money put aside on purpose, but that I won't, I won't, I simply won't pay him his wages, I won't just because that is "what I wish," because "I am master, and it is for me to decide," because he has been disrespectful, because he has been rude; but if he were to ask respectfully I might be softened and give it to him, otherwise he might wait another fortnight, another three weeks, a whole month. . . .

But angry as I was, yet he got the better of me. I could not hold out for four days. He began as he always did begin in such cases, for there had been such cases already, there had been attempts (and it may be observed I knew all this beforehand, I knew his nasty tactics by heart). He would begin by fixing upon me an exceedingly severe stare, keeping it up for several minutes at a time, particularly on meeting me or seeing me out of the house. If I held out and pretended not to notice these stares, he would, still in silence, proceed to further tortures. All at once, *à propos* of nothing, he would walk softly and smoothly into my room, when I was pacing up and down or reading, stand at the door, one hand behind his back and one foot behind the other, and fix upon me a stare more than severe, utterly contemptuous. If I suddenly asked him what he wanted, he would make me no answer, but continue staring at me persistently for some seconds, then, with a peculiar compression of his lips and a most significant air, deliberately turn round and deliberately go back to his room. Two hours later he would come out again and again present himself before me in the same way. It had happened that in my fury I did not even ask him what he wanted, but simply raised my head sharply and imperiously and began staring back at him. So we stared at one another for two minutes; at last he turned with deliberation and dignity and went back again for two hours.

If I were still not brought to reason by all this, but persisted in my revolt, he would suddenly begin sighing while he looked at me, long, deep sighs as though measuring by them the depths of my moral degradation, and, of course, it ended at last by his triumphing completely: I raged and shouted, but still was forced to do what he wanted.

This time the usual staring manœuvres had scarcely begun when I lost my temper and flew at him in a fury. I was irritated beyond endurance apart from him.

"Stay," I cried, in a frenzy, as he was slowly and silently turning, with one hand behind his back, to go to his room, "stay! Come back, come back, I tell you!" and I must have bawled so unnaturally, that he turned round and even looked at me with some wonder. However, he persisted in saying nothing, and that infuriated me.

"How dare you come and look at me like that without being sent for? Answer!"

After looking at me calmly for half a minute, he began turning round again.

"Stay!" I roared, running up to him, "don't stir! There. Answer, now: what did you come in to look at?"

"If you have any order to give me it's my duty to carry it out," he answered, after another silent pause, with a slow, measured lisp, raising his eyebrows and calmly twisting his head from one side to another, all this with exasperating composure.

"That's not what I am asking you about, you torturer!" I shouted, turning crimson with anger. "I'll tell you why you came here myself: you see, I don't give you your wages, you are so proud you don't want to bow down and ask for it, and so you come to punish me with your stupid stares, to worry me and you have no sus . . . pic . . . ion how stupid it is—stupid, stupid, stupid, stupid!" . . .

He would have turned round again without a word, but I seized him.

"Listen," I shouted to him. "Here's the money, do you see, here it is" (I took it out of the table drawer); "here's the seven roubles complete, but you are not going to have it, you . . . are . . . not . . . going . . . to . . . have it until you come respectfully with bowed head to beg my pardon. Do you hear?"

"That cannot be," he answered, with the most unnatural self-confidence.

"It shall be so," I said, "I give you my word of honour, it shall be!"

"And there's nothing for me to beg your pardon for," he went on, as though he had not noticed my exclamations at all. "Why, besides, you called me a 'torturer,' for which I can summon you at the police-station at any time for insulting behaviour."

"Go, summon me," I roared, "go at once, this very minute, this very second! You are a torturer all the same! a torturer!"

But he merely looked at me, then turned, and regardless of my loud calls to him, he walked to his room with an even step and without looking round.

"If it had not been for Liza nothing of this would have happened," I decided inwardly. Then, after waiting a minute, I went myself behind his screen with a dignified and solemn air, though my heart was beating slowly and violently.

"Apollon," I said quietly and emphatically, though I was breathless, "go at once without a minute's delay and fetch the police-officer."

He had meanwhile settled himself at his table, put on his spectacles and taken up some sewing. But, hearing my order, he burst into a guffaw.

"At once, go this minute! Go on, or else you can't imagine what will happen."

"You are certainly out of your mind," he observed, without even raising his head, lisping as deliberately as ever and threading his needle. "Whoever heard of a man sending for the police against himself? And as for being frightened—you are upsetting yourself about nothing, for nothing will come of it."

"Go!" I shrieked, clutching him by the shoulder. I felt I should strike him in a minute.

But I did not notice the door from the passage softly and slowly open at that instant and a figure come in, stop short, and begin staring at us in perplexity. I glanced, nearly swooned with shame, and rushed back to my room. There, clutching at my hair with both hands, I leaned my head against the wall and stood motionless in that position.

Two minutes later I heard Apollon's deliberate footsteps. "There is some woman asking for you," he said, looking at me with peculiar severity. Then he stood aside and let in Liza. He would not go away, but stared at us sarcastically.

"Go away, go away," I commanded in desperation. At that moment my clock began whirring and wheezing and struck seven.

IX

"Into my house come bold and free,
Its rightful mistress there to be."
(From the same poem)

I stood before her crushed, crestfallen, revoltingly confused, and I believe I smiled as I did my utmost to wrap myself in the skirts of my ragged wadded dressing-gown—exactly as I had imagined the scene not long before in a fit of depression. After standing over us for a couple of minutes Apollon went away, but that did not make me more at ease. What made it worse was that she, too, was overwhelmed with confusion, more so, in fact, than I should have expected. At the sight of me, of course.

"Sit down," I said mechanically, moving a chair up to the table, and I sat down on the sofa. She obediently sat down at once and gazed at me open-eyed, evidently expecting something from me at once. This naïveté of expectation drove me to fury, but I restrained myself.

She ought to have tried not to notice, as though everything had been as usual, while instead of that, she . . . and I dimly felt that I should make her pay dearly for *all this*.

"You have found me in a strange position, Liza," I began, stammering and knowing that this was the wrong way to begin. "No, no, don't imagine anything," I cried, seeing that she had suddenly flushed. "I am not ashamed of my poverty. . . . On the contrary I look with pride on my poverty. I am poor but honourable. . . . One can be poor and honourable," I muttered. "However . . . would you like tea?". . .

"No," she was beginning.

"Wait a minute."

I leapt up and ran to Apollon. I had to get out of the room somehow.

"Apollon," I whispered in feverish haste, flinging down before him the seven roubles which had remained all the time in my clenched fist, "here are your wages, you see I give them to you; but for that you must come to my rescue: bring me tea and a dozen rusks from the restaurant. If you won't go, you'll make me a miser-

able man! You don't know what this woman is. . . . This is—
everything! You may be imagining something. . . . But you don't
know what that woman is!" . . .

Apollon, who had already sat down to his work and put on his
spectacles again, at first glanced askance at the money without
speaking or putting down his needle; then, without paying the
slightest attention to me or making any answer he went on busying
himself with his needle, which he had not yet threaded. I waited
before him for three minutes with my arms crossed *à la Napoléon*.
My temples were moist with sweat. I was pale, I felt it. But, thank
God, he must have been moved to pity, looking at me. Having
threaded his needle he deliberately got up from his seat, deliberately
moved back his chair, deliberately took off his spectacles, deliberately counted the money, and finally asking me over his shoulder:
"Shall I get a whole portion?" deliberately walked out of the room.
As I was going back to Liza, the thought occurred to me on the
way: shouldn't I run away just as I was in my dressing-gown, no
matter where, and then let happen what would.

I sat down again. She looked at me uneasily. For some minutes
we were silent.

"I will kill him," I shouted suddenly, striking the table with my
fist so that the ink spurted out of the inkstand.

"What are you saying!" she cried, starting.

"I will kill him! kill him!" I shrieked, suddenly striking the table
in absolute frenzy, and at the same time fully understanding how
stupid it was to be in such a frenzy. "You don't know, Liza, what
that torturer is to me. He is my torturer. . . . He has gone now
to fetch some rusks; he . . ."

And suddenly I burst into tears. It was an hysterical attack. How
ashamed I felt in the midst of my sobs; but still I could not restrain
them.

She was frightened.

"What is the matter? What is wrong?" she cried, fussing about
me.

"Water, give me water, over there!" I muttered in a faint voice,
though I was inwardly conscious that I could have got on very well
without water and without muttering in a faint voice. But I was,
what is called, *putting it on*, to save appearances, though the attack
was a genuine one.

She gave me water, looking at me in bewilderment. At that moment Apollon brought in the tea. It suddenly seemed to me that
this commonplace, prosaic tea was horribly undignified and paltry
after all that had happened, and I blushed crimson. Liza looked at
Apollon with positive alarm. He went out without a glance at
either of us.

"Liza, do you despise me?" I asked, looking at her fixedly, trembling with impatience to know what she was thinking.

She was confused, and did not know what to answer.

"Drink your tea," I said to her angrily. I was angry with myself, but, of course, it was she who would have to pay for it. A horrible spite against her suddenly surged up in my heart; I believe I could have killed her. To revenge myself on her I swore inwardly not to say a word to her all the time. "She is the cause of it all," I thought.

Our silence lasted for five minutes. The tea stood on the table; we did not touch it. I had got to the point of purposely refraining from beginning in order to embarrass her further; it was awkward for her to begin alone. Several times she glanced at me with mournful perplexity. I was obstinately silent. I was, of course, myself the chief sufferer, because I was fully conscious of the disgusting meanness of my spiteful stupidity, and yet at the same time I could not restrain myself.

"I want to . . . get away . . . from there altogether," she began, to break the silence in some way, but, poor girl, that was just what she ought not to have spoken about at such a stupid moment to a man so stupid as I was. My heart positively ached with pity for her tactless and unnecessary straightforwardness. But something hideous at once stifled all compassion in me; it even provoked me to greater venom. I did not care what happened. Another five minutes passed.

"Perhaps I am in your way," she began timidly, hardly audibly, and was getting up.

But as soon as I saw this first impulse of wounded dignity I positively trembled with spite, and at once burst out.

"Why have you come to me, tell me that, please?" I began, gasping for breath and regardless of logical connection in my words. I longed to have it all out at once, at one burst; I did not even trouble how to begin. "Why have you come? Answer, answer," I cried, hardly knowing what I was doing. "I'll tell you, my good girl, why you have come. You've come because I talked sentimental stuff to you then. So now you are soft as butter and longing for fine sentiments again. So you may as well know that I was laughing at you then. And I am laughing at you now. Why are you shuddering? Yes, I was laughing at you! I had been insulted just before, at dinner, by the fellows who came that evening before me. I came to you, meaning to thrash one of them, an officer; but I didn't succeed, I didn't find him; I had to avenge the insult on some one to get back my own again; you turned up, I vented my spleen on you and laughed at you. I had been humiliated, so I wanted to humiliate; I had been treated like a rag, so I wanted to show my power. . . . That's what it was, and you imagined I had come there on purpose to save you. Yes? You imagined that? You imagined that?"

I knew that she would perhaps be muddled and not take it all in exactly, but I knew, too, that she would grasp the gist of it, very well indeed. And so, indeed, she did. She turned white as a handkerchief, tried to say something, and her lips worked painfully; but she sank on a chair as though she had been felled by an axe. And all the time afterwards she listened to me with her lips parted and her eyes wide open, shuddering with awful terror. The cynicism, the cynicism of my words overwhelmed her. . . .

"Save you!" I went on, jumping up from my chair and running up and down the room before her. "Save you from what? But perhaps I am worse than you myself. Why didn't you throw it in my teeth when I was giving you that sermon: 'But what did you come here yourself for? was it to read us a sermon?' Power, power was what I wanted then, sport was what I wanted, I wanted to ring out your tears, your humiliation, your hysteria—that was what I wanted then! Of course, I couldn't keep it up then, because I am a wretched creature, I was frightened, and, the devil knows why, gave you my address in my folly. Afterwards, before I got home, I was cursing and swearing at you because of that address, I hated you already because of the lies I had told you. Because I only like playing with words, only dreaming, but, do you know, what I really want is that you should all go to hell. That is what I want. I want peace; yes, I'd sell the whole world for a farthing, straight off, so long as I was left in peace. Is the world to go to pot, or am I to go without my tea? I say that the world may go to pot for me so long as I always get my tea. Did you know that, or not? Well, anyway, I know that I am a blackguard, a scoundrel, an egoist, a sluggard. Here I have been shuddering for the last three days at the thought of your coming. And do you know what has worried me particularly for these three days? That I posed as such a hero to you, and now you would see me in a wretched torn dressing-gown, beggarly, loathsome. I told you just now that I was not ashamed of my poverty; so you may as well know that I am ashamed of it; I am more ashamed of it than of anything, more afraid of it than of being found out if I were a thief, because I am as vain as though I had been skinned and the very air blowing on me hurts. Surely by now you must realize that I shall never forgive you for having found me in this wretched dressing-gown, just as I was flying at Apollon like a spiteful cur. The saviour, the former hero, was flying like a mangy, unkempt sheep-dog at his lackey, and the lackey was jeering at him! And I shall never forgive you for the tears I could not help shedding before you just now, like some silly woman put to shame! And for what I am confessing to you now, I shall never forgive *you* either! Yes— you must answer for it all because you turned up like this, because

I am a blackguard, because I am the nastiest, stupidest, absurdest and most envious of all the worms on earth, who are not a bit better than I am, but, the devil knows why, are never put to confusion; while I shall always be insulted by every louse, that is my doom! And what is it to me that you don't understand a word of this! And what do I care, what do I care about you, and whether you go to ruin there or not? Do you understand? How I shall hate you now after saying this, for having been here and listening. Why, it's not once in a lifetime a man speaks out like this, and then it is in hysterics! . . . What more do you want? Why do you still stand confronting me, after all this? Why are you worrying me? Why don't you go?"

But at this point a strange thing happened. I was so accustomed to think and imagine everything from books, and to picture everything in the world to myself just as I had made it up in my dreams beforehand, that I could not all at once take in this strange circumstance. What happened was this: Liza, insulted and crushed by me, understood a great deal more than I imagined. She understood from all this what a woman understands first of all, if she feels genuine love, that is, that I was myself unhappy.

The frightened and wounded expression on her face was followed first by a look of sorrowful perplexity. When I began calling myself a scoundrel and a blackguard and my tears flowed (the tirade was accompanied throughout by tears) her whole face worked convulsively. She was on the point of getting up and stopping me; when I finished she took no notice of my shouting: "Why are you here, why don't you go away?" but realized only that it must have been very bitter to me to say all this. Besides, she was so crushed, poor girl; she considered herself infinitely beneath me; how could she feel anger or resentment? She suddenly leapt up from her chair with an irresistible impulse and held out her hands, yearning towards me, though still timid and not daring to stir. . . . At this point there was a revulsion in my heart, too. Then she suddenly rushed to me, threw her arms round me and burst into tears. I, too, could not restrain myself, and sobbed as I never had before.

"They won't let me . . . I can't be good!" I managed to articulate; then I went to the sofa, fell on it face downwards, and sobbed on it for a quarter of an hour in genuine hysterics. She came close to me, put her arms round me and stayed motionless in that position. But the trouble was that the hysterics could not go on for ever, and (I am writing the loathsome truth) lying face downwards on the sofa with my face thrust into my nasty leather pillow, I began by degrees to be aware of a far-away, involuntary but irresistible feeling that it would be awkward now for me to raise my head and look Liza straight in the face. Why was I ashamed? I don't know, but I was ashamed. The thought, too, came into my overwrought brain that our parts now were completely changed, that she was now the heroine, while I was just such a crushed and humiliated creature as she had been before me that night—four days before. . . . And all this came into my mind during the minutes I was lying on my face on the sofa.

My God! surely I was not envious of her then.

I don't know, to this day I cannot decide, and at the time, of course, I was still less able to understand what I was feeling than now. I cannot get on without domineering and tyrannizing over some one, but . . . there is no explaining anything by reasoning and so it is useless to reason.

I conquered myself, however, and raised my head; I had to do so sooner or later . . . and I am convinced to this day that it was just because I was ashamed to look at her that another feeling was suddenly kindled and flamed up in my heart . . . a feeling of mastery and possession. My eyes gleamed with passion, and I gripped her hands tightly. How I hated her and how I was drawn to her at that minute! The one feeling intensified the other. It was almost like an act of vengeance. At first there was a look of amazement, even of terror on her face, but only for one instant. She warmly and rapturously embraced me.

x

A quarter of an hour later I was rushing up and down the room in frenzied impatience, from minute to minute I went up to the screen and peeped through the crack at Liza. She was sitting on the ground with her head leaning against the bed, and must have been crying. But she did not go away, and that irritated me. This time she understood it all. I had insulted her finally, but . . . there's no need to describe it. She realized that my outburst of passion had been simply revenge, a fresh humiliation, and that to my earlier, almost causeless hatred was added a *personal hatred*, born of envy. . . . Though I do not maintain positively that she understood all this distinctly; but she certainly did fully understand that I was a despicable man, and what was worse, incapable of loving her.

I know I shall be told that this is incredible—but it is incredible to be as spiteful and stupid as I was; it may be added that it was strange I should not love her, or at any rate, appreciate her love. Why is it strange? In the first place, by then I was incapable of love, for I repeat, with me loving meant tyrannizing and showing my moral superiority. I have never in my life been able to imagine any other sort of love, and have nowadays come to the point of sometimes thinking that love really consists in the right—freely given by the beloved object—to tyrannize over her.

Even in my underground dreams I did not imagine love except as a struggle. I began it always with hatred and ended it with moral subjugation, and afterwards I never knew what to do with the subjugated object. And what is there to wonder at in that, since I had succeeded in so corrupting myself, since I was so out of touch with "real life," as to have actually thought of reproaching her, and putting her to shame for having come to me to hear "fine sentiments"; and did not even guess that she had come not to hear fine sentiments, but to love me, because to a woman all reformation, all salvation from any sort of ruin, and all moral renewal is included in love and can only show itself in that form.

I did not hate her so much, however, when I was running about the room and peeping through the crack in the screen. I was only insufferably oppressed by her being here. I wanted her to disappear. I wanted "peace," to be left alone in my underground world. Real life oppressed me with its novelty so much that I could hardly breathe.

But several minutes passed and she still remained, without stirring, as though she were unconscious. I had the shamelessness to tap softly at the screen as though to remind her. . . . She started, sprang up, and flew to seek her kerchief, her hat, her coat, as though making her escape from me. . . . Two minutes later she came from behind the screen and looked with heavy eyes at me. I gave a spiteful grin, which was forced, however, to *keep up appearances*, and I turned away from her eyes.

"Good-bye," she said, going towards the door.

I ran up to her, seized her hand, opened it, thrust something in it and closed it again. Then I turned at once and dashed away in haste to the other corner of the room to avoid seeing her, anyway. . . .

I did not mean a moment since to tell a lie—to write that I did this accidentally, not knowing what I was doing through foolishness, through losing my head. But I don't want to lie, and so I will say straight out that I opened her hand and put the money in it . . . from spite. It came into my head to do this while I was running up and down the room and she was sitting behind the screen. But this I can say for certain: though I did that cruel thing purposely, it was not an impulse from the heart, but came from my evil brain. This cruelty was so affected, so purposely made up, so completely a product of the brain, of books, that I could not even keep it up a minute—first I dashed away to avoid seeing her, and then in shame and despair rushed after Liza. I opened the door in the passage and began listening.

"Liza! Liza!" I cried on the stairs, but in a low voice, not boldly.

There was no answer, but I fancied I heard her footsteps, lower down on the stairs.

"Liza!" I cried, more loudly.

No answer. But at that minute I heard the stiff outer glass door open heavily with a creak and slam violently, the sound echoed up the stairs.

She had gone. I went back to my room in hesitation. I felt horribly oppressed.

I stood still at the table, beside the chair on which she had sat and looked aimlessly before me. A minute passed, suddenly I started; straight before me on the table I saw. . . . In short, I saw a crumpled blue five-rouble note, the one I had thrust into her hand a minute before. It was the same note; it could be no other, there was no other in the flat. So she had managed to fling it from her hand on the table at the moment when I had dashed into the further corner.

Well! I might have expected that she would do that. Might I have expected it? No, I was such an egoist, I was so lacking in respect for my fellow-creatures that I could not even imagine she would do so. I could not endure it. A minute later I flew like a madman to dress, flinging on what I could at random and ran headlong after her. She could not have got two hundred paces away when I ran out into the street.

It was a still night and the snow was coming down in masses and falling almost perpendicularly, covering the pavement and the empty street as though with a pillow. There was no one in the street, no sound was to be heard. The street lamps gave a disconsolate and useless glimmer. I ran two hundred paces to the cross-roads and stopped short.

Where had she gone? And why was I running after her?

Why? To fall down before her, to sob with remorse, to kiss her feet, to entreat her forgiveness! I longed for that, my whole breast was being rent to pieces, and never, never shall I recall that minute with indifference. But—what for? I thought. Should I not begin to hate her, perhaps, even to-morrow, just because I had kissed her feet to-day? Should I give her happiness? Had I not recognized that day, for the hundredth time, what I was worth? Should I not torture her?

I stood in the snow, gazing into the troubled darkness and pondered this.

"And will it not be better?" I mused fantastically, afterwards at home, stifling the living pang of my heart with fantastic dreams. "Will it not be better that she should keep the resentment of the insult for ever? Resentment—why, it is purification; it is a most stinging and painful consciousness! To-morrow I should have defiled her soul and have exhausted her heart, while now the feeling of insult will never die in her heart, and however loathsome the filth awaiting her—the feeling of insult will elevate and purify her . . .

by hatred . . . h'm! . . . perhaps, too, by forgiveness. . . . Will all that make things easier for her though? . . ."

And, indeed, I will ask on my own account here, an idle question: which is better—cheap happiness or exalted sufferings? Well, which is better?

So I dreamed as I sat at home that evening, almost dead with the pain in my soul. Never had I endured such suffering and remorse, yet could there have been the faintest doubt when I ran out from my lodging that I should turn back half-way? I never met Liza again and I have heard nothing of her. I will add, too, that I remained for a long time afterwards pleased with the phrase about the benefit from resentment and hatred in spite of the fact that I almost fell ill from misery.

Even now, so many years later, all this is somehow a very evil memory. I have many evil memories now, but . . . hadn't I better end my "Notes" here? I believe I made a mistake in beginning to write them, anyway I have felt ashamed all the time I've been writing this story; so it's hardly literature so much as a corrective punishment. Why, to tell long stories, showing how I have spoiled my life through morally rotting in my corner, through lack of fitting environment, through divorce from real life, and rankling spite in my underground world, would certainly not be interesting; a novel needs a hero, and all the traits for an anti-hero are *expressly* gathered together here, and what matters most, it all produces an unpleasant impression, for we are all divorced from life, we are all cripples, every one of us, more or less. We are so divorced from it that we feel at once a sort of loathing for real life, and so cannot bear to be reminded of it. Why, we have come almost to looking upon real life as an effort, almost as hard labour, and we are all privately agreed that it is better in books. And why do we fuss and fume sometimes? Why are we perverse and ask for something else? We don't know what ourselves. It would be the worse for us if our petulant prayers were answered. Come, try, give any one of us, for instance, a little more independence, untie our hands, widen the spheres of our activity, relax the control and we . . . yes, I assure you . . . we should be begging to be under control again at once. I know that you will very likely be angry with me for that, and will begin shouting and stamping. Speak for yourself, you will say, and for your miseries in your underground holes, and don't dare to say "all of us"—excuse me, gentlemen, I am not justifying myself with that "all of us." As for what concerns me in particular I have only in my life carried to an extreme what you have not dared to carry half-way, and what's more, you have taken your cowardice for good sense, and have found comfort in deceiving yourselves. So that perhaps, after all, there is more life in me than in you. Look into it more carefully! Why, we don't even know what living means now, what it is, and what it is called? Leave us alone without books and we shall be lost and in confusion at once. We shall not know what to join on to, what to cling to, what to love and what to hate, what to respect and what to despise. We are oppressed at being men— men with a real individual flesh and blood, we are ashamed of it, we think it a disgrace and try to contrive to be some sort of impossible generalized man. We are stillborn, and for generations past have been begotten, not by living fathers, and that suits us better and better. We are developing a taste for it. Soon we shall contrive to be born somehow from an idea. But enough; I don't want to write more from "Underground."

(*The notes of this paradoxalist do not end here, however. He could not refrain from going on with them, but it seems to us that we may stop here.*)

LEO TOLSTOY
(1828–1910)
The Death of Iván Ilyich*

I

During an interval in the Melvínski trial in the large building of the Law Courts the members and public prosecutor met in Iván Egórovich Shébek's private room, where the conversation turned on the celebrated Krasóvski case. Fëdor Vasílievich warmly maintained that it was not subject to their jurisdiction, Iván Egórovich maintained the contrary, while Peter Ivánovich, not having entered into the discussion at the start, took no part in it but looked through the *Gazette* which had just been handed in.

"Gentlemen," he said, "Iván Ilyich has died!"

"You don't say!"

"Here, read it yourself," replied Peter Ivánovich, handing Fëdor Vasílievich the paper still damp from the press. Surrounded by a black border were the words: "Praskóvya Fëdorovna Goloviná, with profound sorrow, informs relatives and friends of the demise of her beloved husband Iván Ilyich Golovín, Member of the Court of Justice, which occurred on February the 4th of this year 1882. The funeral will take place on Friday at one o'clock in the afternoon."

* 1886. Translated by Louise and Aylmer Maude. From *The Works of Tolstoy*, Vol. XV, London, Oxford University Press, 1934. Reprinted by permission of the publisher.

Iván Ilyich had been a colleague of the gentlemen present and was liked by them all. He had been ill for some weeks with an illness said to be incurable. His post had been kept open for him, but there had been conjectures that in case of his death Alexéev might receive his appointment, and that either Vínnikov or Shtábel would succeed Alexéev. So on receiving the news of Iván Ilyich's death the first thought of each of the gentlemen in that private room was of the changes and promotions it might occasion among themselves or their acquaintances.

"I shall be sure to get Shtábel's place or Vínnikov's," thought Fëdor Vasílievich. "I was promised that long ago, and the promotion means an extra eight hundred rubles a year for me besides the allowance."

"Now I must apply for my brother-in-law's transfer from Kalúga," thought Peter Ivánovich. "My wife will be very glad, and then she won't be able to say that I never do anything for her relations."

"I thought he would never leave his bed again," said Peter Ivánovich aloud. "It's very sad."

"But what really was the matter with him?"

"The doctors couldn't say—at least they could, but each of them said something different. When last I saw him I thought he was getting better."

"And I haven't been to see him since the holidays. I always meant to go."

"Had he any property?"

"I think his wife had a little—but something quite trifling."

"We shall have to go to see her, but they live so terribly far away."

"Far away from you, you mean. Everything's far away from your place."

"You see, he never can forgive my living on the other side of the river," said Peter Ivánovich, smiling at Shébek. Then, still talking of the distances between different parts of the city, they returned to the Court.

Besides considerations as to the possible transfers and promotions likely to result from Iván Ilyich's death, the mere fact of the death of a near acquaintance aroused, as usual, in all who heard of it the complacent feeling that, "it is he who is dead and not I."

Each one thought or felt, "Well, he's dead but I'm alive!" But the more intimate of Iván Ilyich's acquaintances, his so-called friends, could not help thinking also that they would now have to fulfil the very tiresome demands of propriety by attending the funeral service and paying a visit of condolence to the widow.

Fëdor Vasílievich and Peter Ivánovich had been his nearest acquaintances. Peter Ivánovich had studied law with Iván Ilyich and had considered himself to be under obligations to him.

Having told his wife at dinner-time of Iván Ilyich's death, and of his conjecture that it might be possible to get her brother transferred to their circuit, Peter Ivánovich sacrificed his usual nap, put on his evening clothes, and drove to Iván Ilyich's house.

At the entrance stood a carriage and two cabs. Leaning against the wall in the hall downstairs near the cloak-stand was a coffin-lid covered with cloth of gold, ornamented with gold cord and tassels, that had been polished up with metal powder. Two ladies in black were taking off their fur cloaks. Peter Ivánovich recognized one of them as Iván Ilyich's sister, but the other was a stranger to him. His colleague Schwartz was just coming downstairs, but on seeing Peter Ivánovich enter he stopped and winked at him, as if to say: "Iván Ilyich has made a mess of things—not like you and me."

Schwartz's face with his Piccadilly whiskers, and his slim figure in evening dress, had as usual an air of elegant solemnity which contrasted with the playfulness of his character and had a special piquancy here, or so it seemed to Peter Ivánovich.

Peter Ivánovich allowed the ladies to precede him and slowly followed them upstairs. Schwartz did not come down but remained where he was, and Peter Ivánovich understood that he wanted to arrange where they should play bridge that evening. The ladies went upstairs to the widow's room, and Schwartz with seriously compressed lips but a playful look in his eyes, indicated by a twist of his eyebrows the room to the right where the body lay.

Peter Ivánovich, like everyone else on such occasions, entered feeling uncertain what he would have to do. All he knew was that at such times it is always safe to cross oneself. But he was not quite sure whether one should make obeisances while doing so. He therefore adopted a middle course. On entering the room he began crossing himself and made a slight movement resembling a bow. At the same time, as far as the motion of his head and arm allowed, he surveyed the room. Two young men—apparently nephews, one of whom was a high-school pupil—were leaving the room, crossing themselves as they did so. An old woman was standing motionless, and a lady with strangely arched eyebrows was saying something to her in a whisper. A vigorous, resolute Church Reader, in a frock-coat, was reading something in a loud voice with an expression that precluded any contradiction. The butler's assistant, Gerásim, stepping lightly in front of Peter Ivánovich, was strewing something on the floor. Noticing this, Peter Ivánovich was immediately aware of a faint odour of a decomposing body.

The last time he had called on Iván Ilyich, Peter Ivánovich had seen Gerásim in the study. Iván Ilyich had been particularly fond of him and he was performing the duty of a sick nurse.

Peter Ivánovich continued to make the sign of the cross slightly inclining his head in an intermediate direction between the coffin, the Reader, and the icons on the table in a corner of the room. Afterwards, when it seemed to him that this movement of his arm in crossing himself had gone on too long, he stopped and began to look at the corpse.

The dead man lay, as dead men always lie, in a specially heavy way, his rigid limbs sunk in the soft cushions of the coffin, with the head forever bowed on the pillow. His yellow waxen brow with bald patches over his sunken temples was thrust up in the way peculiar to the dead, the protruding nose seeming to press on the upper lip. He was much changed and had grown even thinner since Peter Ivánovich had last seen him, but, as is always the case with the dead, his face was handsomer and above all more dignified than when he was alive. The expression on the face said that what was necessary had been accomplished, and accomplished rightly. Besides this there was in that expression a reproach and a warning to the living. This warning seemed to Peter Ivánovich out of place, or at least not applicable to him. He felt a certain discomfort and so he hurriedly crossed himself once more and turned and went out of the door—too hurriedly and too regardless of propriety, as he himself was aware.

Schwartz was waiting for him in the adjoining room with legs spread wide apart and both hands toying with his top-hat behind his back. The mere sight of that playful, well-groomed, and elegant figure refreshed Peter Ivánovich. He felt that Schwartz was above all these happenings and would not surrender to any depressing influences. His very look said that this incident of a church service for Iván Ilyich could not be a sufficient reason for infringing the order of the session—in other words, that it would certainly not prevent his unwrapping a new pack of cards and shuffling them that evening while a footman placed four fresh candles on the table: in fact, that there was no reason for supposing that this incident would hinder their spending the evening agreeably. Indeed he said this in a whisper as Peter Ivánovich passed him, proposing that they should meet for a game at Fëdor Vasílievich's. But apparently Peter Ivánovich was not destined to play bridge that evening. Praskóvya Fëdorovna (a short, fat woman who despite all efforts to the contrary had continued to broaden steadily from her shoulders downwards and who had the same extraordinary arched eyebrows as the lady who had been standing by the coffin), dressed all in black, her head covered with lace, came out of her own room with some other ladies, conducted them to the room where the dead body lay, and said: "The service will begin immediately. Please go in."

Schwartz, making an indefinite bow, stood still, evidently neither accepting nor declining this invitation. Praskóvya Fëdorovna recognizing Peter Ivánovich, sighed, went close up to him, took his hand, and said: "I know you were a true friend to Iván Ilyich . . ." and looked at him awaiting some suitable response. And Peter Ivánovich knew that, just as it had been the right thing to cross himself in that room, so what he had to do here was to press her hand, sigh, and say, "Believe me . . ." So he did all this and as he did it felt that the desired result had been achieved: that both he and she were touched.

"Come with me. I want to speak to you before it begins," said the widow. "Give me your arm."

Peter Ivánovich gave her his arm and they went to the inner rooms, passing Schwartz who winked at Peter Ivánovich compassionately.

"That does for our bridge! Don't object if we find another player. Perhaps you can cut in when you do escape," said his playful look.

Peter Ivánovich sighed still more deeply and despondently, and Praskóvya Fëdorovna pressed his arm gratefully. When they reached the drawing-room, upholstered in pink cretonne and lighted by a dim lamp, they sat down at the table—she on a sofa and Peter Ivánovich on a low hassock, the springs of which yielded spasmodically under his weight. Praskóvya Fëdorovna had been on the point of warning him to take another seat, but felt that such a warning was out of keeping with her present condition and so changed her mind. As he sat down on the hassock Peter Ivánovich recalled how Iván Ilyich had arranged this room and had consulted him regarding this pink cretonne with green leaves. The whole room was full of furniture and knick-knacks, and on her way to the sofa the lace of the widow's black shawl caught on the carved edge of the table. Peter Ivánovich rose to detach it, and the springs of the hassock, relieved of his weight, rose also and gave him a push. The widow began detaching her shawl herself, and Peter Ivánovich again sat down, suppressing the rebellious springs of the hassock under him. But the widow had not quite freed herself and Peter Ivánovich got up again, and again the hassock rebelled and even creaked. When this was all over she took out a clean cambric handkerchief and began to weep. The episode with the shawl and the struggle with the hassock had cooled Peter Ivánovich's emotions and he sat there with a sullen look on his face. This awkward situation was interrupted by Sokolóv, Iván Ilyich's butler, who came to report that the plot in the cemetery that Praskóvya Fëdorovna had chosen would cost two hundred rubles. She stopped weeping and, looking at Peter Ivánovich with the air of a victim, remarked in French that it was very hard for her. Peter Ivánovich made a silent gesture signifying his full conviction that it must indeed be so.

"Please smoke," she said in a magnanimous yet crushed voice, and turned to discuss with Sokolóv the price of the plot for the grave.

Peter Ivánovich while lighting his cigarette heard her inquiring very circumstantially into the prices of different plots in the cemetery and finally decide which she would take. When that was done she gave instructions about engaging the choir. Sokolóv then left the room.

"I look after everything myself," she told Peter Ivánovich, shifting the albums that lay on the table; and noticing that the table was endangered by his cigarette-ash, she immediately passed him an ash-tray, saying as she did so: "I consider it an affectation to say that my grief prevents my attending to practical affairs. On the contrary, if anything can—I won't say console me, but—distract me, it is seeing to everything concerning him." She again took out her handkerchief as if preparing to cry, but suddenly, as if mastering her feeling, she shook herself and began to speak calmly. "But there is something I want to talk to you about."

Peter Ivánovich bowed, keeping control of the springs of the hassock, which immediately began quivering under him.

"He suffered terribly the last few days."

"Did he?" said Peter Ivánovich.

"Oh, terribly! He screamed unceasingly, not for minutes but for hours. For the last three days he screamed incessantly. It was unendurable. I cannot understand how I bore it; you could hear him three rooms off. Oh, what I have suffered!"

"Is it possible that he was conscious all that time?" asked Peter Ivánovich.

"Yes," she whispered. "To the last moment. He took leave of us a quarter of an hour before he died, and asked us to take Volódya away."

The thought of the sufferings of this man he had known so intimately, first as a merry little boy, then as a school-mate, and later as a grown-up colleague, suddenly struck Peter Ivánovich with horror, despite an unpleasant consciousness of his own and this woman's dissimulation. He again saw that brow, and that nose pressing down on the lip, and felt afraid for himself.

"Three days of frightful suffering and then death! Why, that might suddenly, at any time, happen to me," he thought, and for a moment felt terrified. But—he did not himself know how—the customary reflection at once occurred to him that this had happened to Iván Ilyich and not to him, and that it should not and could not happen to him, and that to think that it could would be yielding to depression which he ought not to do, as Schwartz's expression plainly showed. After which reflection Peter Ivánovich felt reassured, and began to ask with interest about the details of Iván Ilyich's death, as though death was an accident natural to Iván Ilyich but certainly not to himself.

After many details of the really dreadful physical sufferings Iván Ilyich had endured (which details he learnt only from the effect those sufferings had produced on Praskóvya Fëdorovna's nerves) the widow apparently found it necessary to get to business.

"Oh, Peter Ivánovich, how hard it is! How terribly, terribly hard!" and she again began to weep.

Peter Ivánovich sighed and waited for her to finish blowing her nose. When she had done so he said, "Believe me . . ." and she again began talking and brought out what was evidently her chief concern with him—namely, to question him as to how she could obtain a grant of money from the government on the occasion of her husband's death. She made it appear that she was asking Peter Ivánovich's advice about her pension, but he soon saw that she already knew about that to the minutest detail, more even than he did himself. She knew how much could be got out of the government in consequence of her husband's death, but wanted to find out whether she could not possibly extract something more. Peter Ivánovich tried to think of some means of doing so, but after reflecting for a while and, out of propriety, condemning the government for its niggardliness, he said he thought that nothing more could be got. Then she sighed and evidently began to devise means of getting rid of her visitor. Noticing this, he put out his cigarette, rose, pressed her hand, and went out into the anteroom.

In the dining-room where the clock stood that Iván Ilyich had liked so much and had bought at an antique shop, Peter Ivánovich met a priest and a few acquaintances who had come to attend the service, and he recognized Iván Ilyich's daughter, a handsome young woman. She was in black and her slim figure appeared slimmer than ever. She had a gloomy, determined, almost angry expression, and bowed to Peter Ivánovich as though he were in some way to blame. Behind her, with the same offended look, stood a wealthy young man, an examining magistrate, whom Peter Ivánovich also knew and who was her fiancé, as he had heard. He bowed mournfully to them and was about to pass into the death-chamber, when from under the stairs appeared the figure of Iván Ilyich's schoolboy son, who was extremely like his father. He seemed a little Iván Ilyich, such as Peter Ivánovich remembered when they studied law together. His tear-stained eyes had in them the look that is seen in the eyes of boys of thirteen or fourteen who are not pure-minded.

When he saw Peter Ivánovich he scowled morosely and shamefacedly. Peter Ivánovich nodded to him and entered the death-
chamber. The service began: candles, groans, incense, tears, and
sobs. Peter Ivánovich stood looking gloomily down at his feet. He
did not look once at the dead man, did not yield to any depressing
influence, and was one of the first to leave the room. There was no
one in the anteroom, but Gerásim darted out of the dead man's
room, rummaged with his strong hands among the fur coats to find
Peter Ivánovich's and helped him on with it.

"Well, friend Gerásim," said Peter Ivánovich, so as to say something. "It's a sad affair, isn't it?"

"It's God's will. We shall all come to it some day," said Gerásim,
displaying his teeth—the even, white teeth of a healthy peasant—
and, like a man in the thick of urgent work, he briskly opened the
front door, called the coachman, helped Peter Ivánovich into the
sledge, and sprang back to the porch as if in readiness for what he
had to do next.

Peter Ivánovich found the fresh air particularly pleasant after
the smell of incense, the dead body, and carbolic acid.

"Where to, sir?" asked the coachman.

"It's not too late even now. . . . I'll call round on Fëdor Vasílievich."

He accordingly drove there and found them just finishing the
first rubber, so that it was quite convenient for him to cut in.

II

Iván Ilyich's life had been most simple and most ordinary and
therefore most terrible.

He had been a member of the Court of Justice, and died at the
age of forty-five. His father had been an official who after serving
in various ministries and departments in Petersburg had made the
sort of career which brings men to positions from which by reason
of their long service they cannot be dismissed, though they are
obviously unfit to hold any responsible position, and for whom
therefore posts are specially created, which though fictitious, carry
salaries of from six to ten thousand rubles that are not fictitious,
and in receipt of which they live on to a great age.

Such was the Privy Councillor and superfluous member of various
superfluous institutions, Ilya Epímovich Golovín.

He had three sons, of whom Iván Ilyich was the second. The
eldest son was following in his father's footsteps only in another
department, and was already approaching that stage in the service
at which a similar sinecure would be reached. The third son was a
failure. He had ruined his prospects in a number of positions and
was now serving in the railway department. His father and brothers,
and still more their wives, not merely disliked meeting him, but

avoided remembering his existence unless compelled to do so. His sister had married Baron Greff, a Petersburg official of her father's type. Iván Ilyich was *le phénix de la famille*[1] as people said. He was neither as cold and formal as his elder brother nor as wild as the younger, but was a happy mean between them—an intelligent, polished, lively and agreeable man. He had studied with his younger brother at the School of Law, but the latter had failed to complete the course and was expelled when he was in the fifth class. Iván Ilyich finished the course well. Even when he was at the School of Law he was just what he remained for the rest of his life: a capable, cheerful, good-natured, and sociable man, though strict in the fulfilment of what he considered to be his duty: and he considered his duty to be what was so considered by those in authority. Neither as a boy nor as a man was he a toady, but from early youth was by nature attracted to people of high station as a fly is drawn to the light, assimilating their ways and views of life and establishing friendly relations with them. All the enthusiasms of childhood and youth passed without leaving much trace on him; he succumbed to sensuality, to vanity, and latterly among the highest classes to liberalism, but always within limits which his instinct unfailingly indicated to him as correct.

At school he had done things which had formerly seemed to him very horrid and made him feel disgusted with himself when he did them; but when later on he saw that such actions were done by people of good position and that they did not regard them as wrong, he was able not exactly to regard them as right, but to forget about them entirely or not be at all troubled at remembering them.

Having graduated from the School of Law and qualified for the tenth rank of the civil service, and having received money from his father for his equipment, Iván Ilyich ordered himself clothes at Scharmer's, the fashionable tailor, hung a medallion inscribed *respice finem*[2] on his watch-chain, took leave of his professor and the prince who was patron of the school, had a farewell dinner with his comrades at Donon's first-class restaurant, and with his new and fashionable portmanteau, linen, clothes, shaving and other toilet appliances, and a travelling rug, all purchased at the best shops, he set off for one of the provinces where, through his father's influence, he had been attached to the governor as an official for special service.

In the province Iván Ilyich soon arranged as easy and agreeable a position for himself as he had had at the School of Law. He performed his official tasks, made his career, and at the same time amused himself pleasantly and decorously. Occasionally he paid

1. "the phoenix of the family." The word "phoenix" is used here to mean "rare bird," "prodigy."

2. "Regard the end" (a Latin motto).

official visits to country districts, where he behaved with dignity both to his superiors and inferiors, and performed the duties entrusted to him, which related chiefly to the sectarians,[3] with an exactness and incorruptible honesty of which he could not but feel proud.

In official matters, despite his youth and taste for frivolous gaiety, he was exceedingly reserved, punctilious, and even severe; but in society he was often amusing and witty, and always good-natured, correct in his manner, and *bon enfant*, as the governor and his wife —with whom he was like one of the family—used to say of him.

In the province he had an affair with a lady who made advances to the elegant young lawyer, and there was also a milliner; and there were carousals with aides-de-camp who visited the district, and after-supper visits to a certain outlying street of doubtful reputation; and there was too some obsequiousness to his chief and even to his chief's wife, but all this was done with such a tone of good breeding that no hard names could be applied to it. It all came under the heading of the French saying: "*Il faut que jeunesse se passe.*"[4] It was all done with clean hands, in clean linen, with French phrases, and above all among people of the best society and consequently with the approval of people of rank.

So Iván Ilyich served for five years and then came a change in his official life. The new and reformed judicial institutions were introduced, and new men were needed. Iván Ilyich became such a new man. He was offered the post of Examining Magistrate, and he accepted it though the post was in another province and obliged him to give up the connexions he had formed and to make new ones. His friends met to give him a send-off; they had a group-photograph taken and presented him with a silver cigarette-case, and he set off to his new post.

As examining magistrate Iván Ilyich was just as *comme il faut* and decorous a man, inspiring general respect and capable of separating his official duties from his private life, as he had been when acting as an official on special service. His duties now as examining magistrate were far more interesting and attractive than before. In his former position it had been pleasant to wear an undress uniform made by Scharmer, and to pass through the crowd of petitioners and officials who were timorously awaiting an audience with the governor, and who envied him as with free and easy gait he went straight into his chief's private room to have a cup of tea and a cigarette with him. But not many people had then been directly dependent on him—only police officials and the sectarians

3. the Old Believers, a large group of Russians (about twenty-five million in 1900), members of a sect which originated in a break with the Orthodox Church in the seventeenth century; they were subject to many legal restrictions.
4. Youth must have its fling. [Translator's note.]

when he went on special missions—and he liked to treat them politely, almost as comrades, as if he were letting them feel that he who had the power to crush them was treating them in this simple, friendly way. There were then but few such people. But now, as an examining magistrate, Iván Ilyich felt that everyone without exception, even the most important and self-satisfied, was in his power, and that he need only write a few words on a sheet of paper with a certain heading, and this or that important, self-satisfied person would be brought before him in the role of an accused person or a witness, and if he did not choose to allow him to sit down, would have to stand before him and answer his questions. Iván Ilyich never abused his power; he tried on the contrary to soften its expression, but the consciousness of it and of the possibility of softening its effect, supplied the chief interest and attraction of his office. In his work itself, especially in his examinations, he very soon acquired a method of eliminating all considerations irrelevant to the legal aspect of the case, and reducing even the most complicated case to a form in which it would be presented on paper only in its externals, completely excluding his personal opinion of the matter, while above all observing every prescribed formality. The work was new and Iván Ilyich was one of the first men to apply the new Code of 1864.[5]

On taking up the post of examining magistrate in a new town, he made new acquaintances and connexions, placed himself on a new footing, and assumed a somewhat different tone. He took up an attitude of rather dignified aloofness towards the provincial authorities, but picked out the best circle of legal gentlemen and wealthy gentry living in the town and assumed a tone of slight dissatisfaction with the government, of moderate liberalism, and of enlightened citizenship. At the same time, without at all altering the elegance of his toilet, he ceased shaving his chin and allowed his beard to grow as it pleased.

Iván Ilyich settled down very pleasantly in this new town. The society there, which inclined towards opposition to the governor, was friendly, his salary was larger, and he began to play *vint* [a form of bridge], which he found added not a little to the pleasure of life, for he had a capacity for cards, played good-humouredly, and calculated rapidly and astutely, so that he usually won.

After living there for two years he met his future wife, Praskóvya Fëdorovna Míkhel, who was the most attractive, clever, and brilliant girl of the set in which he moved, and among other amusements and relaxations from his labours as examining magistrate, Iván Ilyich established light and playful relations with her.

While he had been an official on special service he had been ac-

5. The emancipation of the serfs in 1861 was followed by a thorough all-round reform of judicial proceedings. [Translator's note.]

customed to dance, but now as an examining magistrate it was exceptional for him to do so. If he danced now, he did it as if to show that though he served under the reformed order of things, and had reached the fifth official rank, yet when it came to dancing he could do it better than most people. So at the end of an evening he sometimes danced with Praskóvya Fëdorovna, and it was chiefly during these dances that he captivated her. She fell in love with him. Iván Ilyich had at first no definite intention of marrying, but when the girl fell in love with him he said to himself: "Really, why shouldn't I marry?"

Praskóvya Fëdorovna came of a good family, was not bad looking, and had some little property. Iván Ilyich might have aspired to a more brilliant match, but even this was good. He had his salary, and she, he hoped, would have an equal income. She was well connected, and was a sweet, pretty, and thoroughly correct young woman. To say that Iván Ilyich married because he fell in love with Praskóvya Fëdorovna and found that she sympathized with his views of life would be as incorrect as to say that he married because his social circle approved of the match. He was swayed by both these considerations: the marriage gave him personal satisfaction, and at the same time it was considered the right thing by the most highly placed of his associates.

So Iván Ilyich got married.

The preparations for marriage and the beginning of married life, with its conjugal caresses, the new furniture, new crockery, and new linen, were very pleasant until his wife became pregnant—so that Iván Ilyich had begun to think that marriage would not impair the easy, agreeable, gay, and always decorous character of his life, approved of by society and regarded by himself as natural, but would even improve it. But from the first months of his wife's pregnancy, something new, unpleasant, depressing, and unseemly, and from which there was no way of escape, unexpectedly showed itself.

His wife, without any reason—*de gaieté de coeur* as Iván Ilyich expressed it to himself—began to disturb the pleasure and propriety of their life. She began to be jealous without any cause, expected him to devote his whole attention to her, found fault with everything, and made coarse and ill-mannered scenes.

At first Iván Ilyich hoped to escape from the unpleasantness of this state of affairs by the same easy and decorous relation to life that had served him heretofore: he tried to ignore his wife's disagreeable moods, continued to live in his usual easy and pleasant way, invited friends to his house for a game of cards, and also tried going out to his club or spending his evenings with friends. But one day his wife began upbraiding him so vigorously, using such coarse words, and continued to abuse him every time he did not fulfil her demands, so resolutely and with such evident determination not to give way till he submitted—that is, till he stayed at home and was bored just as she was—that he became alarmed. He now realized that matrimony—at any rate with Praskóvya Fëdorovna—was not always conducive to the pleasures and amenities of life, but on the contrary often infringed both comfort and propriety, and that he must therefore entrench himself against such infringement. And Iván Ilyich began to seek for means of doing so. His official duties were the one thing that imposed upon Praskóvya Fëdorovna, and by means of his official work and the duties attached to it he began struggling with his wife to secure his own independence.

With the birth of their child, the attempts to feed it and the various failures in doing so, and with the real and imaginary illnesses of mother and child, in which Iván Ilyich's sympathy was demanded but about which he understood nothing, the need of securing for himself an existence outside his family life became still more imperative.

As his wife grew more irritable and exacting and Iván Ilyich transferred the centre of gravity of his life more and more to his official work, so did he grow to like his work better and became more ambitious than before.

Very soon, within a year of his wedding, Iván Ilyich had realized that marriage, though it may add some comforts to life, is in fact a very intricate and difficult affair towards which in order to perform one's duty, that is, to lead a decorous life approved of by society, one must adopt a definite attitude just as towards one's official duties.

And Iván Ilyich evolved such an attitude towards married life. He only required of it those conveniences—dinner at home, housewife, and bed—which it could give him, and above all that propriety of external forms required by public opinion. For the rest he looked for light-hearted pleasure and propriety, and was very thankful when he found them, but if he met with antagonism and querulousness he at once retired into his separate fenced-off world of official duties, where he found satisfaction.

Iván Ilyich was esteemed a good official, and after three years was made Assistant Public Prosecutor. His new duties, their importance, the possibility of indicting and imprisoning anyone he chose, the publicity his speeches received, and the success he had in all these things, made his work still more attractive.

More children came. His wife became more and more querulous and ill-tempered, but the attitude Iván Ilyich had adopted towards his home life rendered him almost impervious to her grumbling.

After seven years' service in that town he was transferred to another province as Public Prosecutor. They moved, but were short of money and his wife did not like the place they moved to. Though the salary was higher the cost of living was greater, besides which two of their children died and family life became still more unpleasant for him.

Praskóvya Fëdorovna blamed her husband for every inconvenience they encountered in their new home. Most of the conversations between husband and wife, especially as to the children's education, led to topics which recalled former disputes, and those disputes were apt to flare up again at any moment. There remained only those rare periods of amorousness which still came to them at times but did not last long. These were islets at which they anchored for a while and then again set out upon that ocean of veiled hostility which showed itself in their aloofness from one another. This aloofness might have grieved Iván Ilyich had he considered that it ought not to exist, but he now regarded the position as normal, and even made it the goal at which he aimed in family life. His aim was to free himself more and more from those unpleasantnesses and to give them a semblance of harmlessness and propriety. He attained this by spending less and less time with his family, and when obliged to be at home he tried to safeguard his position by the presence of outsiders. The chief thing however was that he had his official duties. The whole interest of his life now centered in the official world and that interest absorbed him. The consciousness of his power, being able to ruin anybody he wished to ruin, the importance, even the external dignity of his entry into court, or meetings with his subordinates, his success with superiors and inferiors, and above all his masterly handling of cases, of which he was conscious—all this gave him pleasure and filled his life, together with chats with his colleagues, dinners, and bridge. So that on the whole Iván Ilyich's life continued to flow as he considered it should do—pleasantly and properly.

So things continued for another seven years. His eldest daughter was already sixteen, another child had died, and only one son was left, a schoolboy and a subject of dissensions. Iván Ilyich wanted to put him in the School of Law, but to spite him Praskóvya Fëdorovna entered him at the High School. The daughter had been educated at home and had turned out well: the boy did not learn badly either.

III

So Iván Ilyich lived for seventeen years after his marriage. He was already a Public Prosecutor of long standing, and had declined several proposed transfers while awaiting a more desirable post, when an unanticipated and unpleasant occurrence quite upset the peaceful course of his life. He was expecting to be offered the post of presiding judge in a University town, but Hoppe somehow came to the front and obtained the appointment instead. Iván Ilyich became irritable, reproached Hoppe, and quarrelled both with him and with his immediate superiors—who became colder to him and again passed him over when other appointments were made.

This was in 1880, the hardest year of Iván Ilyich's life. It was then that it became evident on the one hand that his salary was insufficient for them to live on, and on the other that he had been forgotten, and not only this, but that what was for him the greatest and most cruel injustice appeared to others a quite ordinary occurrence. Even his father did not consider it his duty to help him. Iván Ilyich felt himself abandoned by everyone, and that they regarded his position with a salary of 3,500 rubles as quite normal and even fortunate. He alone knew that with the consciousness of the injustices done him, with his wife's incessant nagging, and with the debts he had contracted by living beyond his means, his position was far from normal.

In order to save money that summer he obtained leave of absence and went with his wife to live in the country at her brother's place.

In the country, without his work, he experienced *ennui* for the first time in his life, and not only *ennui* but intolerable depression, and he decided that it was impossible to go on living like that, and that it was necessary to take energetic measures.

Having passed a sleepless night pacing up and down the veranda, he decided to go to Petersburg and bestir himself, in order to punish those who had failed to appreciate him and to get transferred to another ministry.

Next day, despite many protests from his wife and her brother, he started for Petersburg with the sole object of obtaining a post with a salary of five thousand rubles a year. He was no longer bent on any particular department, or tendency, or kind of activity. All he now wanted was an appointment to another post with a salary of five thousand rubles, either in the administration, in the banks, with the railways, in one of the Empress Márya's Institutions,[6] or even in the customs—but it had to carry with it a salary of five thousand rubles and be in a ministry other than that in which they had failed to appreciate him.

And this quest of Iván Ilyich's was crowned with remarkable and unexpected success. At Kursk an acquaintance of his, F. I. Ilyín, got into the first-class carriage, sat down beside Iván Ilyich, and told him of a telegram just received by the governor of Kursk announcing that a change was about to take place in the ministry: Peter Ivánovich was to be superseded by Iván Semënovich.

The proposed change, apart from its significance for Russia, had

6. reference to the charitable organization founded by the Empress Márya, wife of Paul I, late in the eighteenth century.

a special significance for Iván Ilyich, because by bringing forward a new man, Peter Petróvich, and consequently his friend Zachár Ivánovich, it was highly favourable for Iván Ilyich, since Zachár Ivánovich was a friend and colleague of his.

In Moscow this news was confirmed, and on reaching Petersburg Iván Ilyich found Zachár Ivánovich and received a definite promise of an appointment in his former department of Justice.

A week later he telegraphed to his wife: "Zachár in Miller's place. I shall receive appointment on presentation of report."

Thanks to this change of personnel, Iván Ilyich had unexpectedly obtained an appointment in his former ministry which placed him two stages above his former colleagues besides giving him five thousand rubles salary and three thousand five hundred rubles for expenses connected with his removal. All his ill humour towards his former enemies and the whole department vanished, and Iván Ilyich was completely happy.

He returned to the country more cheerful and contented than he had been for a long time. Praskóvya Fëdorovna also cheered up and a truce was arranged between them. Iván Ilyich told of how he had been fêted by everybody in Petersburg, how all those who had been his enemies were put to shame and now fawned on him, how envious they were of his appointment, and how much everybody in Petersburg had liked him.

Praskóvya Fëdorovna listened to all this and appeared to believe it. She did not contradict anything, but only made plans for their life in the town to which they were going. Iván Ilyich saw with delight that these plans were his plans, that he and his wife agreed, and that, after a stumble, his life was regaining its due and natural character of pleasant lightheartedness and decorum.

Iván Ilyich had come back for a short time only, for he had to take up his new duties on the 10th of September. Moreover, he needed time to settle into the new place, to move all his belongings from the province, and to buy and order many additional things: in a word, to make such arrangements as he had resolved on, which were almost exactly what Praskóvya Fëdorovna too had decided on.

Now that everything had happened so fortunately, and that he and his wife were at one in their aims and moreover saw so little of one another they got on together better than they had done since the first years of marriage. Iván Ilyich had thought of taking his family away with him at once, but the insistence of his wife's brother and her sister-in-law, who had suddenly become particularly amiable and friendly to him and his family, induced him to depart alone.

So he departed, and the cheerful state of mind induced by his success and by the harmony between his wife and himself, the one intensifying the other, did not leave him. He found a delightful house, just the thing both he and his wife had dreamt of. Spacious, lofty reception rooms in the old style, a convenient and dignified study, rooms for his wife and daughter, a study for his son—it might have been specially built for them. Iván Ilyich himself superintended the arrangements, chose the wallpapers, supplemented the furniture (preferably with antiques which he considered particularly *comme il faut*), and supervised the upholstering. Everything progressed and progressed and approached the ideal he had set himself: even when things were only half completed they exceeded his expectations. He saw what a refined and elegant character, free from vulgarity, it would all have when it was ready. On falling asleep he pictured to himself how the reception-room would look. Looking at the yet unfinished drawing-room he could see the fireplace, the screen, the what-not, the little chairs dotted here and there, the dishes and plates on the walls, and the bronzes, as they would be when everything was in place. He was pleased by the thought of how his wife and daughter, who shared his taste in this matter, would be impressed by it. They were certainly not expecting as much. He had been particularly successful in finding, and buying cheaply, antiques which gave a particularly aristocratic character to the whole place. But in his letters he intentionally understated everything in order to be able to surprise them. All this so absorbed him that his new duties—though he liked his official work—interested him less than he had expected. Sometimes he even had moments of absent-mindedness during the Court Sessions, and would consider whether he should have straight or curved cornices for his curtains. He was so interested in it all that he often did things himself, rearranging the furniture, or rehanging the curtains. Once when mounting a step-ladder to show the upholsterer, who did not understand, how he wanted the hangings draped, he made a false step and slipped, but being a strong and agile man he clung on and only knocked his side against the knob of the window frame. The bruised place was painful but the pain soon passed, and he felt particularly bright and well just then. He wrote: "I feel fifteen years younger." He thought he would have everything ready by September, but it dragged on till mid-October. But the result was charming not only in his eyes but to everyone who saw it.

In reality it was just what is usually seen in the houses of people of moderate means who want to appear rich, and therefore succeed only in resembling others like themselves: there were damasks, dark wood, plants, rugs, and dull and polished bronzes—all the things people of a certain class have in order to resemble other people of that class. His house was so like the others that it would never have been noticed, but to him it all seemed to be quite exceptional. He was very happy when he met his family at the station and brought them to the newly furnished house all lit up, where a footman in a white tie opened the door into the hall decorated with plants, and when they went on into the drawing-room and the study uttering exclamations of delight. He conducted them everywhere, drank in their praises eagerly, and beamed with pleasure. At tea that evening, when Praskóvya Fëdorovna among other things asked him about his fall, he laughed, and showed them how he had gone flying and had frightened the upholsterer.

"It's a good thing I'm a bit of an athlete. Another man might have been killed, but I merely knocked myself, just here; it hurts when it's touched, but it's passing off already—it's only a bruise."

So they began living in their new home—in which, as always happens, when they got thoroughly settled in they found they were just one room short—and with the increased income, which as always was just a little (some. five hundred rubles) too little, but it was all very nice.

Things went particularly well at first, before everything was finally arranged and while something had still to be done: this thing bought, that thing ordered, another thing moved, and something else adjusted. Though there were some disputes between husband and wife, they were both so well satisfied and had so much to do that it all passed off without any serious quarrels. When nothing was left to arrange it became rather dull and something seemed to be lacking, but they were then making acquaintances, forming habits, and life was growing fuller.

Iván Ilyich spent his mornings at the law court and came home to dinner, and at first he was generally in a good humour, though he occasionally became irritable just on account of his house. (Every spot on the tablecloth or the upholstery, and every broken window-blind string, irritated him. He had devoted so much trouble to arranging it all that every disturbance of it distressed him.) But on the whole his life ran its course as he believed life should do: easily, pleasantly, and decorously.

He got up at nine, drank his coffee, read the paper, and then put on his undress uniform and went to the law courts. There the harness in which he worked had already been stretched to fit him and he donned it without a hitch: petitioners, inquiries at the chancery, the chancery itself, and the sittings public and administrative. In all this the thing was to exclude everything fresh and vital, which always disturbs the regular course of official business, and to admit only official relations with people, and then only on official grounds. A man would come, for instance, wanting some information. Iván Ilyich, as one in whose sphere the matter did not lie, would have nothing to do with him: but if the man had some business with him in his official capacity, something that could be expressed on officially stamped paper, he would do everything, positively everything he could within the limits of such relations, and in doing so would maintain the semblance of friendly human relations, that is, would observe the courtesies of life. As soon as the official relations ended, so did everything else. Iván Ilyich possessed this capacity to separate his real life from the official side of affairs and not mix the two, in the highest degree, and by long practice and natural aptitude had brought it to such a pitch that sometimes, in the manner of a virtuoso, he would even allow himself to let the human and official relations mingle. He let himself do this just because he felt that he could at any time he chose resume the strictly official attitude again and drop the human relation. And he did it all easily, pleasantly, correctly, and even artistically. In the intervals between the sessions he smoked, drank tea, chatted a little about politics, a little about general topics, a little about cards, but most of all about official appointments. Tired, but with the feelings of a virtuoso—one of the first violins who has played his part in an orchestra with precision—he would return home to find that his wife and daughter had been out paying calls, or had a visitor, and that his son had been to school, had done his homework with his tutor, and was duly learning what is taught at High Schools. Everything was as it should be. After dinner, if they had no visitors, Iván Ilyich sometimes read a book that was being much discussed at the time, and in the evening settled down to work, that is, read official papers, compared the depositions of witnesses, and noted paragraphs of the Code applying to them. This was neither dull nor amusing. It was dull when he might have been playing bridge, but if no bridge was available it was at any rate better than doing nothing or sitting with his wife. Iván Ilyich's chief pleasure was giving little dinners to which he invited men and women of good social position, and just as his drawing-room resembled all other drawing-rooms so did his enjoyable little parties resemble all other such parties.

Once they even gave a dance. Iván Ilyich enjoyed it and everything went off well, except that it led to a violent quarrel with his wife about the cakes and sweets. Praskóvya Fëdorovna had made her own plans, but Iván Ilyich insisted on getting everything from an expensive confectioner and ordered too many cakes, and the quarrel occurred because some of those cakes were left over and the confectioner's bill came to forty-five rubles. It was a great and disagreeable quarrel. Praskóvya Fëdorovna called him "a fool and an imbecile," and he clutched at his head and made angry allusions to divorce.

But the dance itself had been enjoyable. The best people were there, and Iván Ilyich had danced with Princess Trúfonova, a sister of the distinguished founder of the Society "Bear my Burden."

The pleasures connected with his work were pleasures of ambition; his social pleasures were those of vanity; but Iván Ilyich's greatest pleasure was playing bridge. He acknowledged that whatever disagreeable incident happened in his life, the pleasure that beamed like a ray of light above everything else was to sit down to bridge with good players, not noisy partners, and of course to four-handed bridge (with five players it was annoying to have to stand out, though one pretended not to mind), to play a clever and serious game (when the cards allowed it) and then to have supper and drink a glass of wine. After a game of bridge, especially if he had won a little (to win a large sum was unpleasant), Iván Ilyich went to bed in specially good humour.

So they lived. They formed a circle of acquaintances among the best people and were visited by people of importance and by young folk. In their views as to their acquaintances, husband, wife, and daughter were entirely agreed, and tacitly and unanimously kept at arm's length and shook off the various shabby friends and relations who, with much show of affection, gushed into the drawing-room with its Japanese plates on the walls. Soon these shabby friends ceased to obtrude themselves and only the best people remained in the Golovíns' set.

Young men made up to Lisa, and Petríshchev, an examining magistrate and Dmítri Ivánovich Petríshchev's son and sole heir, began to be so attentive to her that Iván Ilyich had already spoken to Praskóvya Fëdorovna about it, and considered whether they should not arrange a party for them, or get up some private theatricals.

So they lived, and all went well, without change, and life flowed pleasantly.

IV

They were all in good health. It could not be called ill health if Iván Ilyich sometimes said that he had a queer taste in his mouth and felt some discomfort in his left side.

But this discomfort increased and, though not exactly painful, grew into a sense of pressure in his side accompanied by ill humour. And his irritability became worse and worse and began to mar the agreeable, easy, and correct life that had established itself in the Golovín family. Quarrels between husband and wife became more and more frequent, and soon the ease and amenity disappeared and even the decorum was barely maintained. Scenes again became frequent, and very few of those islets remained on which husband and wife could meet without an explosion. Praskóvya Fëdorovna now had good reason to say that her husband's temper was trying. With characteristic exaggeration she said he had always had a dreadful temper, and that it had needed all her good nature to put up with it for twenty years. It was true that now the quarrels were started by him. His bursts of temper always came just before dinner, often just as he began to eat his soup. Sometimes he noticed that a plate or dish was chipped, or the food was not right, or his son put his elbow on the table, or his daughter's hair was not done as he liked it, and for all this he blamed Praskóvya Fëdorovna. At first she retorted and said disagreeable things to him, but once or twice he fell into such a rage at the beginning of dinner that she realized it was due to some physical derangement brought on by taking food, and so she restrained herself and did not answer, but only hurried to get the dinner over. She regarded this self-restraint as highly praiseworthy. Having come to the conclusion that her husband had a dreadful temper and made her life miserable, she began to feel sorry for herself, and the more she pitied herself the more she hated her husband. She began to wish he would die; yet she did not want him to die because then his salary would cease. And this irritated her against him still more. She considered herself dreadfully unhappy just because not even his death could save her, and though she concealed her exasperation, that hidden exasperation of hers increased his irritation also.

After one scene in which Iván Ilyich had been particularly unfair and after which he had said in explanation that he certainly was irritable but that it was due to his not being well, she said that if he was ill it should be attended to, and insisted on his going to see a celebrated doctor.

He went. Everything took place as he had expected and as it always does. There was the usual waiting and the important air assumed by the doctor, with which he was so familiar (resembling that which he himself assumed in court), and the sounding and listening, and the questions which called for answers that were foregone conclusions and were evidently unnecessary, and the look of importance which implied that "if only you put yourself in our hands we will arrange everything—we know indubitably how it has to be done, always in the same way for everybody alike." It was all just as it was in the law courts. The doctor put on just the same air towards him as he himself put on towards an accused person.

The doctor said that so-and-so indicated that there was so-and-so inside the patient, but if the investigation of so-and-so did not confirm this, then he must assume that and that. If he assumed that and that, then . . . and so on. To Iván Ilyich only one question was important: was his case serious or not? But the doctor ignored that inappropriate question. From his point of view it was not the one under consideration, the real question was to decide between a floating kidney, chronic catarrh, or appendicitis. It was not a question of Iván Ilyich's life or death, but one between a floating kidney and appendicitis. And that question the doctor solved brilliantly, as it seemed to Iván Ilyich, in favour of the appendix, with the reservation that should an examination of the urine give fresh indications the matter would be reconsidered. All this was just what Iván Ilyich had himself brilliantly accomplished a thousand times in dealing with men on trial. The doctor summed up just as brilliantly, looking over his spectacles triumphantly and even gaily at the accused. From the doctor's summing up Iván Ilyich concluded that things were bad, but that for the doctor, and perhaps for everybody else, it was a matter of indifference, though for him it was bad. And this conclusion struck him painfully, arousing in him a great feeling of pity for himself and of bitterness towards the doctor's indifference to a matter of such importance.

He said nothing of this, but rose, placed the doctor's fee on the table, and remarked with a sigh: "We sick people probably often put inappropriate questions. But tell me, in general, is this complaint dangerous, or not? . . ."

The doctor looked at him sternly over his spectacles with one eye, as if to say: "Prisoner, if you will not keep to the questions put to you, I shall be obliged to have you removed from the court."

"I have already told you what I consider necessary and proper. The analysis may show something more." And the doctor bowed.

Iván Ilyich went out slowly, seated himself disconsolately in his sledge, and drove home. All the way home he was going over what the doctor had said, trying to translate those complicated, obscure, scientific phrases into plain language and find in them an answer to the question: "Is my condition bad? Is it very bad? Or is there as yet nothing much wrong?" And it seemed to him that the meaning of what the doctor had said was that it was very bad. Everything in the streets seemed depressing. The cabmen, the houses, the passers-by, and the shops, were dismal. His ache, this dull gnawing ache that never ceased for a moment, seemed to have acquired a new and more serious significance from the doctor's dubious remarks. Iván Ilyich now watched it with a new and oppressive feeling.

He reached home and began to tell his wife about it. She listened, but in the middle of his account his daughter came in with her hat on, ready to go out with her mother. She sat down reluctantly to listen to this tedious story, but could not stand it long, and her mother too did not hear him to the end.

"Well, I am very glad," she said. "Mind now to take your medicine regularly. Give me the prescription and I'll send Gerásim to the chemist's." And she went to get ready to go out.

While she was in the room Iván Ilyich had hardly taken time to breathe, but he sighed deeply when she left it.

"Well," he thought, "perhaps it isn't so bad after all."

He began taking his medicine and following the doctor's directions, which had been altered after the examination of the urine. But then it happened that there was a contradiction between the indications drawn from the examination of the urine and the symptoms that showed themselves. It turned out that what was happening differed from what the doctor had told him, and that he had either forgotten, or blundered, or hidden something from him. He could not, however, be blamed for that, and Iván Ilyich still obeyed his orders implicitly and at first derived some comfort from doing so.

From the time of his visit to the doctor, Iván Ilyich's chief occupation was the exact fulfilment of the doctor's instructions regarding hygiene and the taking of medicine, and the observation of his pain and his excretions. His chief interests came to be people's ailments and people's health. When sickness, deaths, or recoveries were mentioned in his presence, especially when the illness resembled his own, he listened with agitation which he tried to hide, asked questions, and applied what he heard to his own case.

The pain did not grow less, but Iván Ilyich made efforts to force himself to think that he was better. And he could do this so long as nothing agitated him. But as soon as he had any unpleasantness with his wife, any lack of success in his official work, or held bad cards at bridge, he was at once acutely sensible of his disease. He had formerly borne such mischances, hoping soon to adjust what was wrong, to master it and attain success, or make a grand slam. But now every mischance upset him and plunged him into despair. He would say to himself. "There now, just as I was beginning to get better and the medicine had begun to take effect, comes this accursed misfortune, or unpleasantness . . ." And he was furious with the mishap, or with the people who were causing the unpleasantness and killing him, for he felt that this fury was killing him but could not restrain it. One would have thought that it should have been clear to him that this exasperation with circumstances and people aggravated his illness, and that he ought therefore to ignore unpleasant occurrences. But he drew the very opposite conclusion: he said that he needed peace, and he watched for everything that might disturb it and became irritable at the slightest infringement of it. His condition was rendered worse by the fact that he read medical books and consulted doctors. The progress of his disease was so gradual that he could deceive himself when comparing one day with another—the difference was so slight. But when he consulted the doctors it seemed to him that he was getting worse, and even very rapidly. Yet despite this he was continually consulting them.

That month he went to see another celebrity, who told him almost the same as the first had done but put his questions rather differently, and the interview with this celebrity only increased Iván Ilyich's doubts and fears. A friend of a friend of his, a very good doctor, diagnosed his illness again quite differently from the others, and though he predicted recovery, his questions and suppositions bewildered Iván Ilyich still more and increased his doubts. A homeopathist diagnosed the disease in yet another way, and prescribed medicine which Iván Ilyich took secretly for a week. But after a week, not feeling any improvement and having lost confidence both in the former doctor's treatment and in this one's, he became still more despondent. One day a lady acquaintance mentioned a cure effected by a wonder-working icon. Iván Ilyich caught himself listening attentively and beginning to believe that it had occurred. This incident alarmed him. "Has my mind really weakened to such an extent?" he asked himself. "Nonsense! It's all rubbish. I mustn't give way to nervous fears but having chosen a doctor must keep strictly to his treatment. That is what I will do. Now it's all settled. I won't think about it, but will follow the treatment seriously till summer, and then we shall see. From now there must be no more of this wavering!" This was easy to say but impossible to carry out. The pain in his side oppressed him and seemed to grow worse and more incessant, while the taste in his mouth grew stranger and stranger. It seemed to him that his breath had a disgusting smell, and he was conscious of a loss of appetite and strength. There was no deceiving himself: something terrible, new, and more important than anything before in his life, was taking place within him of which he alone was aware. Those about him did not understand or would not understand it, but thought everything in the world was going on as usual. That tormented Iván Ilyich more than anything. He saw that his household, especially his wife and daughter who were in a perfect whirl of visiting, did not understand anything of it and were annoyed that he was so depressed and so exacting, as if he were to blame for it. Though they tried to disguise it he saw that he was an obstacle in their path, and that his wife had adopted a definite line in regard to his illness and kept to it regardless of anything he said or did. Her attitude was this: "You know," she would say to her friends, "Iván Ilyich can't do as other people do, and keep to the treatment prescribed for him. One day he'll take his drops and keep strictly to his diet and go to bed in good time, but the next day unless I watch him he'll suddenly forget his medicine, eat sturgeon—which is forbidden—and sit up playing cards till one o'clock in the morning."

"Oh, come, when was that?" Iván Ilyich would ask in vexation. "Only once at Peter Ivánovich's."

"And yesterday with Shébek."

"Well, even if I hadn't stayed up, this pain would have kept me awake."

"Be that as it may you'll never get well like that, but will always make us wretched."

Praskóvya Fëdorovna's attitude to Iván Ilyich's illness, as she expressed it both to others and to him, was that it was his own fault and was another of the annoyances he caused her. Iván Ilyich felt that this opinion escaped her involuntarily—but that did not make it easier for him.

At the law courts too, Iván Ilyich noticed, or thought he noticed, a strange attitude towards himself. It sometimes seemed to him that people were watching him inquisitively as a man whose place might soon be vacant. Then again, his friends would suddenly begin to chaff him in a friendly way about his low spirits, as if the awful, horrible, and unheard-of thing that was going on within him, incessantly gnawing at him and irresistibly drawing him away, was a very agreeable subject for jests. Schwartz in particular irritated him by his jocularity, vivacity, and *savoir-faire*, which reminded him of what he himself had been ten years ago.

Friends came to make up a set and they sat down to cards. They dealt, bending the new cards to soften them, and he sorted the diamonds in his hand and found he had seven. His partner said "No trumps" and supported him with two diamonds. What more could be wished for? It ought to be jolly and lively. They would make a grand slam. But suddenly Iván Ilyich was conscious of that gnawing pain, that taste in his mouth, and it seemed ridiculous that in such circumstances he should be pleased to make a grand slam.

He looked at his partner Mikháil Mikháylovich, who rapped the table with his strong hand and instead of snatching up the tricks pushed the cards courteously and indulgently towards Iván Ilyich that he might have the pleasure of gathering them up without the trouble of stretching out his hand for them. "Does he think I am too weak to stretch out my arm?" thought Iván Ilyich, and forgetting what he was doing he over-trumped his partner, missing the grand slam by three tricks. And what was most awful of all was that he saw how upset Mikháil Mikháylovich was about it but did not himself care. And it was dreadful to realize why he did not care.

They all saw that he was suffering, and said: "We can stop if you are tired. Take a rest." Lie down? No, he was not at all tired, and he finished the rubber. All were gloomy and silent. Iván Ilyich felt that he had diffused this gloom over them and could not dispel it. They had supper and went away, and Iván Ilyich was left alone with the consciousness that his life was poisoned and was poisoning the lives of others, and that this poison did not weaken but penetrated more and more deeply into his whole being.

With this consciousness, and with physical pain besides the terror, he must go to bed, often to lie awake the greater part of the night. Next morning he had to get up again, dress, go to the law courts, speak, and write; or if he did not go out, spend at home those twenty-four hours a day each of which was a torture. And he had to live thus all alone on the brink of an abyss, with no one who understood or pitied him.

v

So one month passed and then another. Just before the New Year his brother-in-law came to town and stayed at their house. Iván Ilyich was at the law courts and Praskóvya Fëdorovna had gone shopping. When Iván Ilyich came home and entered his study he found his brother-in-law there—a healthy, florid man—unpacking his portmanteau himself. He raised his head on hearing Iván Ilyich's footsteps and looked up at him for a moment without a word. That stare told Iván everything. His brother-in-law opened his mouth to utter an exclamation of surprise but checked himself, and that action confirmed it all.

"I have changed, eh?"

"Yes, there is a change."

And after that, try as he would to get his brother-in-law to return to the subject of his looks, the latter would say nothing about it. Praskóvya Fëdorovna came home and her brother went out to her. Iván Ilyich locked the door and began to examine himself in the glass, first full face, then in profile. He took up a portrait of himself taken with his wife, and compared it with what he saw in the glass. The change in him was immense. Then he bared his arms to the elbow, looked at them, drew the sleeves down again, sat down on an ottoman, and grew blacker than night.

"No, no, this won't do!" he said to himself, and jumped up, went to the table, took up some law papers and began to read them, but could not continue. He unlocked the door and went into the reception-room. The door leading to the drawing-room was shut. He approached it on tiptoe and listened.

"No, you are exaggerating!" Praskóvya Fëdorovna was saying.

"Exaggerating! Don't you see it? Why, he's a dead man! Look at his eyes—there's no light in them. But what is it that is wrong with him?"

"No one knows. Nikoláevich [that was another doctor] said something, but I don't know what. And Leshchetítsky [this was the celebrated specialist] said quite the contrary . . ."

Iván Ilyich walked away, went to his own room, lay down and began musing: "The kidney, a floating kidney." He recalled all the doctors had told him of how it detached itself and swayed about. And by an effort of imagination he tried to catch that kidney and arrest it and support it. So little was needed for this, it seemed to him. "No, I'll go to see Peter Ivánovich again." [That was the friend whose friend was a doctor.] He rang, ordered the carriage, and got ready to go.

"Where are you going, *Jean?*" asked his wife, with a specially sad and exceptionally kind look.

This exceptionally kind look irritated him. He looked morosely at her.

"I must go to see Peter Ivánovich."

He went to see Peter Ivánovich, and together they went to see his friend, the doctor. He was in, and Iván Ilyich had a long talk with him.

Reviewing the anatomical and physiological details of what in the doctor's opinion was going on inside him, he understood it all.

There was something, a small thing, in the vermiform appendix. It might all come right. Only stimulate the energy of one organ and check the activity of another, then absorption would take place and everything would come right. He got home rather late for dinner, ate his dinner, and conversed cheerfully, but could not for a long time bring himself to go back to work in his room. At last, however, he went to his study and did what was necessary, but the consciousness that he had put something aside—an important, intimate matter which he would revert to when his work was done— never left him. When he had finished his work he remembered that this intimate matter was the thought of his vermiform appendix. But he did not give himself up to it, and went to the drawing-room for tea. There were callers there, including the examining magistrate who was a desirable match for his daughter, and they were conversing, playing the piano, and singing. Iván Ilyich, as Praskóvya Fëdorovna remarked, spent that evening more cheerfully than usual, but he never for a moment forgot that he had postponed the important matter of the appendix. At eleven o'clock he said goodnight and went to his bedroom. Since his illness he had slept alone in a small room next to his study. He undressed and took up a novel by Zola,[7] but instead of reading it he fell into thought, and in his imagination that desired improvement in the vermiform appendix occurred. There was the absorption and evacuation and the re-

7. Émile Zola (1840–1902), French novelist, author of the *Rougon-Macquart* novels (*Nana, Germinal,* and so on). Tolstoy condemned Zola for his naturalistic theories and considered his novels crude and gross.

establishment of normal activity. "Yes, that's it!" he said to himself. "One need only assist nature, that's all." He remembered his medicine, rose, took it, and lay down on his back watching for the beneficent action of the medicine and for it to lessen the pain. "I need only take it regularly and avoid all injurious influences. I am already feeling better, much better." He began touching his side: it was not painful to the touch. "There, I really don't feel it. It's much better already." He put out the light and turned on his side . . . "The appendix is getting better, absorption is occurring." Suddenly he felt the old, familiar, dull, gnawing pain, stubborn and serious. There was the same familiar loathsome taste in his mouth. His heart sank and he felt dazed. "My God! My God!" he muttered. "Again, again! And it will never cease." And suddenly the matter presented itself in a quite different aspect. "Vermiform appendix! Kidney!" he said to himself. "It's not a question of appendix or kidney, but of life and . . . death. Yes, life was there and now it is going, going and I cannot stop it. Yes. Why deceive myself? Isn't it obvious to everyone but me that I'm dying, and that it's only a question of weeks, days . . . it may happen this moment. There was light and now there is darkness. I was here and now I'm going there! Where?" A chill came over him, his breathing ceased, and he felt only the throbbing of his heart.

"When I am not, what will there be? There will be nothing. Then where shall I be when I am no more? Can this be dying? No, I don't want to!" He jumped up and tried to light the candle, felt for it with trembling hands, dropped candle and candlestick on the floor, and fell back on his pillow.

"What's the use? It makes no difference," he said to himself, staring with wide-open eyes into the darkness. "Death. Yes, death. And none of them know or wish to know it, and they have no pity for me. Now they are playing." (He heard through the door the distant sound of a song and its accompaniment.) "It's all the same to them, but they will die too! Fools! I first, and they later, but it will be the same for them. And now they are merry . . . the beasts!"

Anger choked him and he was agonizingly, unbearably miserable. "It is impossible that all men have been doomed to suffer this awful horror!" He raised himself.

"Something must be wrong. I must calm myself—must think it all over from the beginning." And he again began thinking. "Yes, the beginning of my illness: I knocked my side, but I was still quite well that day and the next. It hurt a little, then rather more. I saw the doctors, then followed despondency and anguish, more doctors, and I drew nearer to the abyss. My strength grew less and I kept coming nearer and nearer, and now I have wasted away and there

is no light in my eyes. I think of the appendix—but this is death!
I think of mending the appendix, and all the while here is death!
Can it really be death?" Again terror seized him and he gasped for
breath. He leant down and began feeling for the matches, pressing
with his elbow on the stand beside the bed. It was in his way and
hurt him, he grew furious with it, pressed on it still harder, and
upset it. Breathless and in despair he fell on his back, expecting
death to come immediately.

Meanwhile the visitors were leaving. Praskóvya Fëdorovna was
seeing them off. She heard something fall and came in.

"What has happened?"

"Nothing. I knocked it over accidentally."

She went out and returned with a candle. He lay there panting
heavily, like a man who has run a thousand yards, and stared upwards at her with a fixed look.

"What is it, *Jean?*"

"No . . . o . . . thing. I upset it." ("Why speak of it? She
won't understand," he thought.)

And in truth she did not understand. She picked up the stand,
lit his candle, and hurried away to see another visitor off. When she
came back he still lay on his back, looking upwards.

"What is it? Do you feel worse?"

"Yes."

She shook her head and sat down.

"Do you know, *Jean,* I think we must ask Leshchetísky to come
and see you here."

This meant calling in the famous specialist, regardless of expense.
He smiled malignantly and said "No." She remained a little longer
and then went up to him and kissed his forehead.

While she was kissing him he hated her from the bottom of his
soul and with difficulty refrained from pushing her away.

"Good-night. Please God you'll sleep."

"Yes."

VI

Iván Ilyich saw that he was dying, and he was in continual
despair.

In the depth of his heart he knew he was dying, but not only was
he not accustomed to the thought, he simply did not and could not
grasp it.

The syllogism he had learned from Kiesewetter's *Logic:*[8] "Caius
is a man, men are mortal, therefore Caius is mortal," had always
seemed to him correct as applied to Caius, but certainly not as

8. Karl Kiesewetter (1766–1819)
was a German popularizer of Kant's
philosophy. His *Outline of Logic Ac-*
cording to Kantian Principles (1796)
was widely used in Russian adaptations
as a schoolbook.

applied to himself. That Caius—man in the abstract—was mortal, was perfectly correct, but he was not Caius, not an abstract man, but a creature quite, quite separate from all others. He had been little Ványa, with a mamma and a papa, with Mítya and Volódya, with the toys, a coachman and a nurse, afterwards with Kátenka and with all the joys, griefs, and delights of childhood, boyhood, and youth. What did Caius know of the smell of that striped leather ball Ványa had been so fond of? Had Caius kissed his mother's hand like that, and did the silk of her dress rustle so for Caius? Had he rioted like that at school when the pastry was bad? Had Caius been in love like that? Could Caius preside at a session as he did? Caius really was mortal, and it was right for him to die; but for me, little Ványa, Iván Ilyich, with all my thoughts and emotions, it's altogether a different matter. It cannot be that I ought to die. That would be too terrible."

Such was his feeling.

"If I had to die like Caius I should have known it was so. An inner voice would have told me so, but there was nothing of the sort in me and I and all my friends felt that our case was quite different from that of Caius. And now here it is!" he said to himself. "It can't be. It's impossible! But here it is. How is this? How is one to understand it?"

He could not understand it, and tried to drive this false, incorrect, morbid thought away and to replace it by other proper and healthy thoughts. But that thought, and not the thought only but the reality itself, seemed to come and confront him.

And to replace that thought he called up a succession of others, hoping to find in them some support. He tried to get back into the former current of thoughts that had once screened the thought of death from him. But strange to say, all that had formerly shut off, hidden, and destroyed, his consciousness of death, no longer had that effect. Iván Ilyich now spent most of his time in attempting to re-establish that old current. He would say to himself: "I will take up my duties again—after all I used to live by them." And banishing all doubts he would go to the law courts, enter into conversation with his colleagues, and sit carelessly as was his wont, scanning the crowd with a thoughtful look and leaning both his emaciated arms on the arms of his oak chair; bending over as usual to a colleague and drawing his papers nearer he would interchange whispers with him, and then suddenly raising his eyes and sitting erect would pronounce certain words and open the proceedings. But suddenly in the midst of those proceedings the pain in his side, regardless of the stage the proceedings had reached, would begin its own gnawing work. Iván Ilyich would turn his attention to it and try to drive the thought of it away, but without success. *It* would come and stand before him and look at him, and he would be petrified and the light would die out of his eyes, and he would again begin asking himself whether *It* alone was true. And his colleagues and subordinates would see with surprise and distress that he, the brilliant and subtle judge, was becoming confused and making mistakes. He would shake himself, try to pull himself together, manage somehow to bring the sitting to a close, and return home with the sorrowful consciousness that his judicial labours could not as formerly hide from him what he wanted them to hide, and could not deliver him from *It*. And what was worst of all was that *It* drew his attention to itself not in order to make him take some action but only that he should look at *It*, look it straight in the face: look at it without doing anything, suffer inexpressibly.

And to save himself from this condition Iván Ilyich looked for consolations—new screens—and new screens were found and for a while seemed to save him, but then they immediately fell to pieces or rather became transparent, as if *It* penetrated them and nothing could veil *It*.

In these latter days he would go into the drawing-room he had arranged—that drawing-room where he had fallen and for the sake of which (how bitterly ridiculous it seemed) he had sacrificed his life—for he knew that his illness originated with that knock. He would enter and see that something had scratched the polished table. He would look for the cause of this and find that it was the bronze ornamentation of an album, that had got bent. He would take up the expensive album which he had lovingly arranged, and feel vexed with his daughter and her friends for their untidiness—for the album was torn here and there and some of the photographs turned upside down. He would put it carefully in order and bend the ornamentation back into position. Then it would occur to him to place all those things in another corner of the room, near the plants. He would call the footman, but his daughter or wife would come to help him. They would not agree, and his wife would contradict him, and he would dispute and grow angry. But that was all right, for then he did not think about *It*. *It* was invisible.

But then, when he was moving something himself, his wife would say: "Let the servants do it. You will hurt yourself again." And suddenly *It* would flash through the screen and he would see it. It was just a flash, and he hoped it would disappear, but he would involuntarily pay attention to his side. "It sits there as before, gnawing just the same!" And he could no longer forget *It*, but could distinctly see it looking at him from behind the flowers. "What is it all for?"

"It really is so! I lost my life over that curtain as I might have done when storming a fort. Is that possible? How terrible and how stupid. It can't be true! It can't, but it is."

He would go to his study, lie down, and again be alone with It: face to face with It. And nothing could be done with It except to look at it and shudder.

VII

How it happened it is impossible to say because it came about step by step, unnoticed, but in the third month of Iván Ilyich's illness, his wife, his daughter, his son, his acquaintances, the doctors, the servants, and above all he himself, were aware that the whole interest he had for other people was whether he would soon vacate his place, and at last release the living from the discomfort caused by his presence and be himself released from his sufferings.

He slept less and less. He was given opium and hypodermic injections of morphine, but this did not relieve him. The dull depression he experienced in a somnolent condition at first gave him a little relief, but only as something new, afterwards it became as distressing as the pain itself or even more so.

Special foods were prepared for him by the doctors' orders, but all those foods became increasingly distasteful and disgusting to him.

For his excretions also special arrangements had to be made, and this was a torment to him every time—a torment from the uncleanliness, the unseemliness, and the smell, and from knowing that another person had to take part in it.

But just through this most unpleasant matter, Iván Ilyich obtained comfort. Gerásim, the butler's young assistant, always came in to carry the things out. Gerásim was a clean, fresh peasant lad, grown stout on town food and always cheerful and bright. At first the sight of him, in his clean Russian peasant costume, engaged on that disgusting task embarrassed Iván Ilyich.

Once when he got up from the commode too weak to draw up his trousers, he dropped into a soft armchair and looked with horror at his bare, enfeebled thighs with the muscles so sharply marked on them.

Gerásim with a firm light tread, his heavy boots emitting a pleasant smell of tar and fresh winter air, came in wearing a clean Hessian apron, the sleeves of his print shirt tucked up over his strong bare young arms; and refraining from looking at his sick master out of consideration for his feelings, and restraining the joy of life that beamed from his face, he went up to the commode.

"Gerásim!" said Iván Ilyich in a weak voice.

Gerásim started, evidently afraid he might have committed some blunder, and with a rapid movement turned his fresh, kind, simple young face which just showed the first downy signs of a beard.

"Yes, sir?"

"That must be very unpleasant for you. You must forgive me. I am helpless."

"Oh, why, sir," and Gerásim's eyes beamed and he showed his glistening white teeth, "what's a little trouble? It's a case of illness with you, sir."

And his deft strong hands did their accustomed task, and he went out of the room stepping lightly. Five minutes later he as lightly returned.

Iván Ilyich was still sitting in the same position in the armchair.

"Gerásim," he said when the latter had replaced the freshly-washed utensil. "Please come here and help me." Gerásim went up to him. "Lift me up. It is hard for me to get up, and I have sent Dmítri away."

Gerásim went up to him, grasped his master with his strong arms deftly but gently, in the same way that he stepped—lifted him, supported him with one hand, and with the other drew up his trousers and would have set him down again, but Iván Ilyich asked to be led to the sofa. Gerásim, without an effort and without apparent pressure, led him, almost lifting him, to the sofa and placed him on it.

"Thank you. How easily and well you do it all!"

Gerásim smiled again and turned to leave the room. But Iván Ilyich felt his presence such a comfort that he did not want to let him go.

"One thing more, please move up that chair. No, the other one—under my feet. It is easier for me when my feet are raised."

Gerásim brought the chair, set it down gently in place, and raised Iván Ilyich's legs on to it. It seemed to Iván Ilyich that he felt better while Gerásim was holding up his legs.

"It's better when my legs are higher," he said. "Place that cushion under them."

Gerásim did so. He again lifted the legs and placed them, and again Iván Ilyich felt better while Gerásim held his legs. When he set them down Iván Ilyich fancied he felt worse.

"Gerásim," he said. "Are you busy now?"

"Not at all, sir," said Gerásim, who had learnt from the townsfolk how to speak to gentlefolk.

"What have you still to do?"

"What have I to do? I've done everything except chopping the logs for to-morrow."

"Then hold my legs up a bit higher, can you?"

"Of course I can. Why not?" And Gerásim raised his master's legs higher and Iván Ilyich thought that in that position he did not feel any pain at all.

"And how about the logs?"

"Don't trouble about that, sir. There's plenty of time."

Iván Ilyich told Gerásim to sit down and hold his legs, and began to talk to him. And strange to say it seemed to him that he felt better while Gerásim held his legs up.

After that Iván Ilyich would sometimes call Gerásim and get him to hold his legs on his shoulders, and he liked talking to him. Gerásim did it all easily, willingly, simply, and with a good nature that touched Iván Ilyich. Health, strength, and vitality in other people were offensive to him, but Gerásim's strength and vitality did not mortify but soothed him.

What tormented Iván Ilyich most was the deception, the lie, which for some reason they all accepted, that he was not dying but was simply ill, and that he only need keep quiet and undergo a treatment and then something very good would result. He however knew that do what they would nothing would come of it, only still more agonizing suffering and death. This deception tortured him—their not wishing to admit what they all knew and what he knew, but wanting to lie to him concerning his terrible condition, and wishing and forcing him to participate in that lie. Those lies —lies enacted over him on the eve of his death and destined to degrade this awful, solemn act to the level of their visitings, their curtains, their sturgeon for dinner—were a terrible agony for Iván Ilyich. And strangely enough, many times when they were going through their antics over him he had been within a hairbreadth of calling out to them: "Stop lying! You know and I know that I am dying. Then at least stop lying about it!" But he had never had the spirit to do it. The awful, terrible act of his dying was, he could see, reduced by those about him to the level of a casual, unpleasant, and almost indecorous incident (as if someone entered a drawing-room diffusing an unpleasant odour) and this was done by that very decorum which he had served all his life long. He saw that no one felt for him, because no one even wished to grasp his position. Only Gerásim recognized and pitied him. And so Iván Ilyich felt at ease only with him. He felt comforted when Gerásim supported his legs (sometimes all night long) and refused to go to bed, saying: "Don't you worry, Iván Ilyich. I'll get sleep enough later on," or when he suddenly became familiar and exclaimed: "If you weren't sick it would be another matter, but as it is, why should I grudge a little trouble?" Gerásim alone did not lie; everything showed that he alone understood the facts of the case and did not consider it necessary to disguise them, but simply felt sorry for his emaciated and enfeebled master. Once when Iván Ilyich was sending him away he even said straight out: "We shall all of us die, so why should I grudge a little trouble?"—expressing the fact that he did not think his work burdensome, because he was doing it for a dying man and hoped someone would do the same for him when his time came.

Apart from this lying, or because of it, what most tormented Iván Ilyich was that no one pitied him as he wished to be pitied. At certain moments after prolonged suffering he wished most of all (though he would have been ashamed to confess it) for someone to pity him as a sick child is pitied. He longed to be petted and comforted. He knew he was an important functionary, that he had a beard turning grey, and that therefore what he longed for was impossible, but still he longed for it. And in Gerásim's attitude towards him there was something akin to what he wished for, and so that attitude comforted him. Iván Ilyich wanted to weep, wanted to be petted and cried over, and then his colleague Shébek would come, and instead of weeping and being petted, Iván Ilyich would assume a serious, severe, and profound air, and by force of habit would express his opinion on a decision of the Court of Appeal and would stubbornly insist on that view. This falsity around him and within him did more than anything else to poison his last days.

VIII

It was morning. He knew it was morning because Gerásim had gone, and Peter the footman had come and put out the candles, drawn back one of the curtains, and begun quietly to tidy up. Whether it was morning or evening, Friday or Sunday, made no difference, it was all just the same: the gnawing, unmitigated, agonizing pain, never ceasing for an instant, the consciousness of life inexorably waning but not yet extinguished, the approach of that ever dreaded and hateful Death which was the only reality, and always the same falsity. What were days, weeks, hours, in such a case?

"Will you have some tea, sir?"

"He wants things to be regular, and wishes the gentlefolk to drink tea in the morning," thought Iván Ilyich, and only said "No."

"Wouldn't you like to move onto the sofa, sir?"

"He wants to tidy up the room, and I'm in the way. I am un-cleanliness and disorder," he thought, and said only:

"No, leave me alone."

The man went on bustling about. Iván Ilyich stretched out his hand. Peter came up, ready to help.

"What is it, sir?"

"My watch."

Peter took the watch which was close at hand and gave it to his master.

"Half-past eight. Are they up?"

"No sir, except Vladímir Ivánich" (the son) "who has gone to school. Praskóvya Fëdorovna ordered me to wake her if you asked for her. Shall I do so?"

"No, there's no need to." "Perhaps I'd better have some tea," he thought, and added aloud: "Yes, bring me some tea."

Peter went to the door, but Iván Ilyich dreaded being left alone. "How can I keep him here? Oh yes, my medicine." "Peter, give me my medicine." "Why not? Perhaps it may still do me some good." He took a spoonful and swallowed it. "No, it won't help. It's all tomfoolery, all deception," he decided as soon as he became aware of the familiar, sickly, hopeless taste. "No, I can't believe in it any longer. But the pain, why this pain? If it would only cease just for a moment!" And he moaned. Peter turned towards him. "It's all right. Go and fetch me some tea."

Peter went out. Left alone Iván Ilyich groaned not so much with pain, terrible though that was, as from mental anguish. Always and forever the same, always these endless days and nights. If only it would come quicker! If only *what* would come quicker? Death, darkness? . . . No, no! Anything rather than death!

When Peter returned with the tea on a tray, Iván Ilyich stared at him for a time in perplexity, not realizing who and what he was. Peter was disconcerted by that look and his embarrassment brought Iván Ilyich to himself.

"Oh, tea! All right, put it down. Only help me to wash and put on a clean shirt."

And Iván Ilyich began to wash. With pauses for rest, he washed his hands and then his face, cleaned his teeth, brushed his hair, and looked in the glass. He was terrified by what he saw, especially by the limp way in which his hair clung to his pallid forehead.

While his shirt was being changed he knew that he would be still more frightened at the sight of his body, so he avoided looking at it. Finally he was ready. He drew on a dressing-gown, wrapped himself in a plaid, and sat down in the armchair to take his tea. For a moment he felt refreshed, but as soon as he began to drink the tea he was again aware of the same taste, and the pain also returned. He finished it with an effort, and then lay down stretching out his legs, and dismissed Peter.

Always the same. Now a spark of hope flashes up, then a sea of despair rages, and always pain; always pain, always despair, and always the same. When alone he had a dreadful and distressing desire to call someone, but he knew beforehand that with others present it would be still worse. "Another dose of morphine—to lose consciousness. I will tell him, the doctor, that he must think of something else. It's impossible, impossible, to go on like this."

An hour and another pass like that. But now there is a ring at the door bell. Perhaps it's the doctor? It is. He comes in fresh, hearty, plump, and cheerful, with that look on his face that seems to say: "There now, you're in a panic about something, but we'll arrange it all for you directly!" The doctor knows this expression is out of place here, but he has put it on once for all and can't take it off—like a man who has put on a frock-coat in the morning to pay a round of calls.

The doctor rubs his hands vigorously and reassuringly.

"Brr! How cold it is! There's such a sharp frost; just let me warm myself!" he says, as if it were only a matter of waiting till he was warm, and then he would put everything right.

"Well now, how are you?"

Iván Ilyich feels that the doctor would like to say: "Well, how are our affairs?" but that even he feels that this would not do, and says instead: "What sort of a night have you had?"

Iván Ilyich looks at him as much as to say: "Are you really never ashamed of lying?" But the doctor does not wish to understand this question, and Iván Ilyich says: "Just as terrible as ever. The pain never leaves me and never subsides. If only something . . ."

"Yes, you sick people are always like that. . . . There, now I think I'm warm enough. Even Praskóvya Fëdorovna, who is so particular, could find no fault with my temperature. Well, now I can say good-morning," and the doctor presses his patient's hand.

Then, dropping his former playfulness, he begins with a most serious face to examine the patient, feeling his pulse and taking his temperature, and then begins the sounding and auscultation.

Iván Ilyich knows quite well and definitely that all this is nonsense and pure deception, but when the doctor, getting down on his knee, leans over him, putting his ear first higher then lower, and performs various gymnastic movements over him with a significant expression on his face, Iván Ilyich submits to it all as he used to submit to the speeches of the lawyers, though he knew very well that they were all lying and why they were lying.

The doctor, kneeling on the sofa, is still sounding him when Praskóvya Fëdorovna's silk dress rustles at the door and she is heard scolding Peter for not having let her know of the doctor's arrival.

She comes in, kisses her husband, and at once proceeds to prove that she has been up a long time already, and only owing to a misunderstanding failed to be there when the doctor arrived.

Iván Ilyich looks at her, scans her all over, sets against her the whiteness and plumpness and cleanness of her hands and neck, the gloss of her hair, and the sparkle of her vivacious eyes. He hates her with his whole soul. And the thrill of hatred he feels for her makes him suffer from her touch.

Her attitude towards him and his disease is still the same. Just as the doctor had adopted a certain relation to his patient which he could not abandon, so had she formed one towards him—that he was not doing something he ought to do and was himself to blame, and that she reproached him lovingly for this—and she could not now change that attitude.

"You see he doesn't listen to me and doesn't take his medicine at the proper time. And above all he lies in a position that is no doubt bad for him—with his legs up."

She described how he made Gerásim hold his legs up.

The doctor smiled with a contemptuous affability that said: "What's to be done? These sick people do have foolish fancies of that kind, but we must forgive them."

When the examination was over the doctor looked at his watch, and then Praskóvya Fëdorovna announced to Iván Ilyich that it was of course as he pleased, but she had sent to-day for a celebrated specialist who would examine him and have a consultation with Michael Danílovich (their regular doctor).

"Please don't raise any objections. I am doing this for my own sake," she said ironically, letting it be felt that she was doing it all for his sake and only said this to leave him no right to refuse. He remained silent, knitting his brows. He felt that he was so surrounded and involved in a mesh of falsity that it was hard to unravel anything.

Everything she did for him was entirely for her own sake, and she told him she was doing for herself what she actually was doing for herself, as if that was so incredible that he must understand the opposite.

At half-past eleven the celebrated specialist arrived. Again the sounding began and the significant conversations in his presence and in another room, about the kidneys and the appendix, and the questions and answers, with such an air of importance that again, instead of the real question of life and death which now alone confronted him, the question arose of the kidney and the appendix which were not behaving as they ought to and would now be attacked by Michael Danílovich and the specialist and forced to amend their ways.

The celebrated specialist took leave of him with a serious though not hopeless look, and in reply to the timid question Iván Ilyich, with eyes glistening with fear and hope, put to him as to whether there was a chance of recovery, said that he could not vouch for it but there was a possibility. The look of hope with which Iván Ilyich watched the doctor out was so pathetic that Praskóvya Fëdorovna, seeing it, even wept as she left the room to hand the doctor his fee.

The gleam of hope kindled by the doctor's encouragement did not last long. The same room, the same pictures, curtains, wallpaper, medicine bottles, were all there, and the same aching suffering body, and Iván Ilyich began to moan. They gave him a subcutaneous injection and he sank into oblivion.

It was twilight when he came to. They brought him his dinner and he swallowed some beef tea with difficulty, and then everything was the same again and night was coming on.

After dinner, at seven o'clock, Praskóvya Fëdorovna came into the room in evening dress, her full bosom pushed up by her corset, and with traces of powder on her face. She had reminded him in the morning that they were going to the theatre. Sarah Bernhardt was visiting the town and they had a box, which he had insisted on their taking. Now he had forgotten about it and her toilet offended him, but he concealed his vexation when he remembered that he had himself insisted on their securing a box and going because it would be an instructive and aesthetic pleasure for the children.

Praskóvya Fëdorovna came in, self-satisfied but yet with a rather guilty air. She sat down and asked how he was, but, as he saw, only for the sake of asking and not in order to learn about it, knowing that there was nothing to learn—and then went on to what she really wanted to say: that she would not on any account have gone but that the box had been taken and Helen and their daughter were going, as well as Petríshchev (the examining magistrate, their daughter's fiancé) and that it was out of the question to let them go alone; but that she would have much preferred to sit with him for a while; and he must be sure to follow the doctor's orders while she was away.

"Oh, and Fëdor Petróvich" (the fiancé) "would like to come in. May he? And Lisa?"

"All right."

Their daughter came in in full evening dress, her fresh young flesh exposed (making a show of that very flesh which in his own case caused so much suffering), strong, healthy, evidently in love, and impatient with illness, suffering, and death, because they interfered with her happiness.

Fëdor Petróvich came in too, in evening dress, his hair curled à la Capoul, a tight stiff collar round his long sinewy neck, an enormous white shirt-front and narrow black trousers tightly stretched over his strong thighs. He had one white glove tightly drawn on, and was holding his opera hat in his hand.

Following him the schoolboy crept in unnoticed, in a new uniform, poor little fellow, and wearing gloves. Terribly dark shadows showed under his eyes, the meaning of which Iván Ilyich knew well.

His son had always seemed pathetic to him, and now it was dreadful to see the boy's frightened look of pity. It seemed to Iván Ilyich that Vásya was the only one besides Gerásim who understood and pitied him.

They all sat down and again asked how he was. A silence followed

Lisa asked her mother about the opera-glasses, and there was an altercation between mother and daughter as to who had taken them and where they had been put. This occasioned some unpleasantness.

Fëdor Petróvich inquired of Iván Ilyich whether he had ever seen Sarah Bernhardt. Iván Ilyich did not at first catch the question, but then replied: "No, have you seen her before?"

"Yes, in *Adrienne Lecouvreur*."[9]

Praskóvya Fëdorovna mentioned some rôles in which Sarah Bernhardt was particularly good. Her daughter disagreed. Conversation sprang up as to the elegance and realism of her acting—the sort of conversation that is always repeated and is always the same.

In the midst of the conversation Fëdor Petróvich glanced at Iván Ilyich and became silent. The others also looked at him and grew silent. Iván Ilyich was staring with glittering eyes straight before him, evidently indignant with them. This had to be rectified, but it was impossible to do so. The silence had to be broken, but for a time no one dared to break it and they all became afraid that the conventional deception would suddenly become obvious and the truth become plain to all. Lisa was the first to pluck up courage and break that silence, but by trying to hide what everybody was feeling, she betrayed it.

"Well, if we are going it's time to start," she said, looking at her watch, a present from her father, and with a faint and significant smile at Fëdor Petróvich relating to something known only to them. She got up with a rustle of her dress.

They all rose, said good-night, and went away.

When they had gone it seemed to Iván Ilyich that he felt better; the falsity had gone with them. But the pain remained—that same pain and that same fear that made everything monotonously alike, nothing harder and nothing easier. Everything was worse.

Again minute followed minute and hour followed hour. Everything remained the same and there was no cessation. And the inevitable end of it all became more and more terrible.

"Yes, send Gerásim here," he replied to a question Peter asked.

IX

His wife returned late at night. She came in on tiptoe, but he heard her, opened his eyes, and made haste to close them again. She wished to send Gerásim away and to sit with him herself, but he opened his eyes and said: "No, go away."

"Are you in great pain?"

"Always the same."

"Take some opium."

9. a play (1849) by the French dramatist Eugène Scribe (1791–1861), in which the heroine was a famous actress of the eighteenth century. Tolstoy considered Scribe, who wrote over four hundred plays, a shoddy, commercial playwright.

He agreed and took some. She went away.

Till about three in the morning he was in a state of stupefied misery. It seemed to him that he and his pain were being thrust into a narrow, deep black sack, but though they were pushed further and further in they could not be pushed to the bottom. And this, terrible enough in itself, was accompanied by suffering. He was frightened yet wanted to fall through the sack, he struggled but yet co-operated. And suddenly he broke through, fell, and regained consciousness. Gerásim was sitting at the foot of the bed dozing quietly and patiently, while he himself lay with his emaciated stockinged legs resting on Gerásim's shoulders; the same shaded candle was there and the same unceasing pain.

"Go away, Gerásim," he whispered.

"It's all right, sir. I'll stay a while."

"No. Go away."

He removed his legs from Gerásim's shoulders, turned sideways onto his arm, and felt sorry for himself. He only waited till Gerásim had gone into the next room and then restrained himself no longer but wept like a child. He wept on account of his helplessness, his terrible loneliness, the cruelty of man, the cruelty of God, and the absence of God.

"Why hast Thou done all this? Why hast Thou brought me here? Why, dost Thou torment me so terribly?"

He did not expect an answer and yet wept because there was no answer and could be none. The pain again grew more acute, but he did not stir and did not call. He said to himself: "Go on! Strike me! But what is it for? What have I done to Thee? What is it for?"

Then he grew quiet and not only ceased weeping but even held his breath and became all attention. It was as though he were listening not to an audible voice but to a voice of his soul, to the current of thoughts arising within him.

"What is it you want?" was the first clear conception capable of expression in words, that he heard.

"What do you want? What do you want?" he repeated to himself.

"What do I want? To live and not to suffer," he answered.

And again he listened with such concentrated attention that even his pain did not distract him.

"To live? How?" asked his inner voice.

"Why, to live as I used to—well and pleasantly."

"As you lived before, well and pleasantly?" the voice repeated.

And in imagination he began to recall the best moments of his pleasant life. But strange to say none of those best moments of his pleasant life now seemed at all what they had then seemed—none of them except the first recollections of childhood. There, in childhood, there had been something really pleasant with which it would be possible to live if it could return. But the child who had experienced that happiness existed no longer, it was like a reminiscence of somebody else.

As soon as the period began which had produced the present Iván Ilyich, all that had then seemed joys now melted before his sight and turned into something trivial and often nasty.

And the further he departed from childhood and the nearer he came to the present the more worthless and doubtful were the joys. This began with the School of Law. A little that was really good was still found there—there was light-heartedness, friendship, and hope. But in the upper classes there had already been fewer of such good moments. Then during the first years of his official career, when he was in the service of the Governor, some pleasant moments again occurred: they were the memories of love for a woman. Then all became confused and there was still less of what was good; later on again there was still less that was good, and the further he went the less there was. His marriage, a mere accident, then the disenchantment that followed it, his wife's bad breath and the sensuality and hypocrisy: then that deadly official life and those preoccupations about money, a year of it, and two, and ten, and twenty, and always the same thing. And the longer it lasted the more deadly it became. "It is as if I had been going downhill while I imagined I was going up. And that is really what it was. I was going up in public opinion, but to the same extent life was ebbing away from me. And now it is all done and there is only death."

"Then what does it mean? Why? It can't be that life is so senseless and horrible. But if it really has been so horrible and senseless, why must I die and die in agony? There is something wrong!"

"Maybe I did not live as I ought to have done," it suddenly occurred to him. "But how could that be, when I did everything properly?" he replied, and immediately dismissed from his mind this, the sole solution of all the riddles of life and death, as something quite impossible.

"Then what do you want now? To live? Live how? Live as you lived in the law courts when the usher proclaimed 'The judge is coming!' The judge is coming, the judge!" he repeated to himself. "Here he is, the judge. But I am not guilty!" he exclaimed angrily. "What is it for?" And he ceased crying, but turning his face to the wall continued to ponder on the same question: Why, and for what purpose, is there all this horror? But however much he pondered he found no answer. And whenever the thought occurred to him, as it often did, that it all resulted from his not having lived as he ought to have done, he at once recalled the correctness of his whole life, and dismissed so strange an idea.

x

Another fortnight passed. Iván Ilyich now no longer left his sofa. He would not lie in bed but lay on the sofa, facing the wall nearly all the time. He suffered ever the same unceasing agonies and in his loneliness pondered always on the same insoluble question: "What is this? Can it be that it is Death?" And the inner voice answered: "Yes, it is Death."

"Why these sufferings?" And the voice answered, "For no reason —they just are so." Beyond and besides this there was nothing.

From the very beginning of his illness, ever since he had first been to see the doctor, Iván Ilyich's life had been divided between two contrary and alternating moods: now it was despair and the expectation of this uncomprehended and terrible death, and now hope and an intently interested observation of the functioning of his organs. Now before his eyes there was only a kidney or an intestine that temporarily evaded its duty, and now only that incomprehensible and dreadful death from which it was impossible to escape.

These two states of mind had alternated from the very beginning of his illness, but the further it progressed the more doubtful and fantastic became the conception of the kidney, and the more real the sense of impending death.

He had but to call to mind what he had been three months before and what he was now, to call to mind with what regularity he had been going downhill, for every possibility of hope to be shattered.

Latterly during that loneliness in which he found himself as he lay facing the back of the sofa, a loneliness in the midst of a populous town and surrounded by numerous acquaintances and relations but that yet could not have been more complete anywhere—either at the bottom of the sea or under the earth—during that terrible loneliness Iván Ilyich had lived only in memories of the past. Pictures of his past rose before him one after another. They always began with what was nearest in time and then went back to what was most remote—to his childhood—and rested there. If he thought of the stewed prunes that had been offered him that day, his mind went back to the raw shrivelled French plums of his childhood, their peculiar flavour and the flow of saliva when he sucked their stones, and along with the memory of that taste came a whole series of memories of those days: his nurse, his brother, and their toys. "No, I mustn't think of that. . . . It is too painful," Iván Ilyich said to himself, and brought himself back to the present—to the button on the back of the sofa and the creases in its morocco. "Morocco is expensive, but it does not wear well: there had been a quarrel about it. It was a different kind of quarrel and a different kind of morocco that time when we tore father's portfolio and were punished, and mamma brought us some tarts. . . ." And again his thoughts dwelt on his childhood, and again it was painful and he tried to banish them and fix his mind on something else.

Then again together with that chain of memories another series passed through his mind—of how his illness had progressed and grown worse. There also the further back he looked the more life there had been. There had been more of what was good in life and more of life itself. The two merged together. "Just as the pain went on getting worse and worse, so my life grew worse and worse," he thought. "There is one bright spot there at the back, at the beginning of life, and afterwards all becomes blacker and blacker and proceeds more and more rapidly—in inverse ratio to the square of the distance from death," thought Iván Ilyich. And the example of a stone falling downwards with increasing velocity entered his mind. Life, a series of increasing sufferings, flies further and further towards its end—the most terrible suffering. "I am flying. . . ." He shuddered, shifted himself, and tried to resist, but was already aware that resistance was impossible, and again with eyes weary of gazing but unable to cease seeing what was before them, he stared at the back of the sofa and waited—awaiting that dreadful fall and shock and destruction.

"Resistance is impossible!" he said to himself. "If I could only understand what it is all for! But that too is impossible. An explanation would be possible if it could be said that I have not lived as I ought to. But it is impossible to say that," and he remembered all the legality, correctitude, and propriety of his life. "That at any rate can certainly not be admitted," he thought, and his lips smiled ironically as if someone could see that smile and be taken in by it. "There is no explanation! Agony, death. . . . What for?"

XI

Another two weeks went by in this way and during that fortnight an event occurred that Iván Ilyich and his wife had desired. Petríshchev formally proposed. It happened in the evening. The next day Praskóvya Fëdorovna came into her husband's room considering how best to inform him of it, but that very night there had been a fresh change for the worse in his condition. She found him still lying on the sofa but in a different position. He lay on his back, groaning and staring fixedly straight in front of him.

She began to remind him of his medicines, but he turned his eyes towards her with such a look that she did not finish what she was saying; so great an animosity, to her in particular, did that look express.

"For Christ's sake let me die in peace!" he said.

She would have gone away, but just then their daughter came in and went up to say good morning. He looked at her as he had done at his wife, and in reply to her inquiry about his health said dryly that he would soon free them all of himself. They were both silent and after sitting with him for a while went away.

"Is it our fault?" Lisa said to her mother. "It's as if we were to blame! I am sorry for papa, but why should we be tortured?"

The doctor came at his usual time. Iván Ilyich answered "Yes" and "No," never taking his angry eyes from him, and at last said: "You know you can do nothing for me, so leave me alone."

"We can ease your sufferings."

"You can't even do that. Let me be."

The doctor went into the drawing-room and told Praskóvya Fëdorovna that the case was very serious and that the only resource left was opium to allay her husband's sufferings, which must be terrible.

It was true, as the doctor said, that Iván Ilyich's physical sufferings were terrible, but worse than the physical sufferings were his mental sufferings which were his chief torture.

His mental sufferings were due to the fact that that night, as he looked at Gerásim's sleepy, good-natured face with its prominent cheek-bones, the question suddenly occurred to him: "What if my whole life has really been wrong?"

It occurred to him that what had appeared perfectly impossible before, namely that he had not spent his life as he should have done, might after all be true. It occurred to him that his scarcely perceptible attempts to struggle against what was considered good by the most highly placed people, those scarcely noticeable impulses which he had immediately suppressed, might have been the real thing, and all the rest false. And his professional duties and the whole arrangement of his life and of his family, and all his social and official interests, might all have been false. He tried to defend all those things to himself and suddenly felt the weakness of what he was defending. There was nothing to defend.

"But if that is so," he said to himself, "and I am leaving this life with the consciousness that I have lost all that was given me and it is impossible to rectify it—what then?"

He lay on his back and began to pass his life in review in quite a new way. In the morning when he saw first his footman, then his wife, then his daughter, and then the doctor, their every word and movement confirmed to him the awful truth that had been revealed to him during the night. In them he saw himself—all that for which he had lived—and saw clearly that it was not real at all, but a terrible and huge deception which had hidden both life and death. This consciousness intensified his physical suffering tenfold. He groaned and tossed about, and pulled at his clothing which choked and stifled him. And he hated them on that account.

He was given a large dose of opium and became unconscious, but at noon his sufferings began again. He drove everybody away and tossed from side to side.

His wife came to him and said:

"*Jean*, my dear, do this for me. It can't do any harm and often helps. Healthy people often do it."

He opened his eyes wide.

"What? Take communion? Why? It's unnecessary! However . . ."

She began to cry.

"Yes, do, my dear. I'll send for our priest. He is such a nice man."

"All right. Very well," he muttered.

When the priest came and heard his confession, Iván Ilyich was softened and seemed to feel a relief from his doubts and consequently from his sufferings, and for a moment there came a ray of hope. He again began to think of the vermiform appendix and the possibility of correcting it. He received the sacrament with tears in his eyes.

When they laid him down again afterwards he felt a moment's ease, and the hope that he might live awoke in him again. He began to think of the operation that had been suggested to him. "To live! I want to live!" he said to himself.

His wife came in to congratulate him after his communion, and when uttering the usual conventional words she added:

"You feel better, don't you?"

Without looking at her he said "Yes."

Her dress, her figure, the expression of her face, the tone of her voice, all revealed the same thing. "This is wrong, it is not as it should be. All you have lived for and still live for is falsehood and deception, hiding life and death from you." And as soon as he admitted that thought, his hatred and his agonizing physical suffering again sprang up, and with that suffering a consciousness of the unavoidable, approaching end. And to this was added a new sensation of grinding shooting pain and a feeling of suffocation.

The expression of his face when he uttered that "yes" was dreadful. Having uttered it, he looked her straight in the eyes, turned on his face with a rapidity extraordinary in his weak state and shouted:

"Go away! Go away and leave me alone!"

XII

From that moment the screaming began that continued for three days, and was so terrible that one could not hear it through two closed doors without horror. At the moment he answered his wife he realized that he was lost, that there was no return, that the end had come, the very end, and his doubts were still unsolved and remained doubts.

"Oh! Oh! Oh!" he cried in various intonations. He had begun by screaming "I won't!" and continued screaming on the letter "o."

For three whole days, during which time did not exist for him, he struggled in that black sack into which he was being thrust by an invisible, resistless force. He struggled as a man condemned to death struggles in the hands of the executioner, knowing that he cannot save himself. And every moment he felt that despite all his efforts he was drawing nearer and nearer to what terrified him. He felt that his agony was due to his being thrust into that black hole and still more to his not being able to get right into it. He was hindered from getting into it by his conviction that his life had been a good one. That very justification of his life held him fast and prevented his moving forward, and it caused him most torment of all.

Suddenly some force struck him in the chest and side, making it still harder to breathe, and he fell through the hole and there at the bottom was a light. What had happened to him was like the sensation one sometimes experiences in a railway carriage when one thinks one is going backwards while one is really going forwards and suddenly becomes aware of the real direction.

"Yes, it was all not the right thing," he said to himself, "but that's no matter. It can be done. But what *is* the right thing?" he asked himself, and suddenly grew quiet.

This occurred at the end of the third day, two hours before his death. Just then his schoolboy son had crept softly in and gone up to the bedside. The dying man was still screaming desperately and waving his arms. His hand fell on the boy's head, and the boy caught it, pressed it to his lips, and began to cry.

At that very moment Iván Ilyich fell through and caught sight of the light, and it was revealed to him that though his life had not been what it should have been, this could still be rectified. He asked himself, "What *is* the right thing?" and grew still, listening. Then he felt that someone was kissing his hand. He opened his eyes, looked at his son, and felt sorry for him. His wife came up to him and he glanced at her. She was gazing at him open-mouthed, with undried tears on her nose and cheek and a despairing look on her face. He felt sorry for her too.

"Yes, I am making them wretched," he thought. "They are sorry, but it will be better for them when I die." He wished to say this but had not the strength to utter it. "Besides, why speak? I must act," he thought. With a look at his wife he indicated his son and said: "Take him away . . . sorry for him . . . sorry for you too. . . ." He tried to add, "forgive me," but said "forego" and waved his hand, knowing that He whose understanding mattered would understand.

And suddenly it grew clear to him that what had been oppressing him and would not leave him was all dropping away at once from two sides, from ten sides, and from all sides. He was sorry for them, he must act so as not to hurt them: release them and free himself from these sufferings. "How good and how simple!" he thought. "And the pain?" he asked himself. "What has become of it? Where are you, pain?"

He turned his attention to it.

"Yes, here it is. Well, what of it? Let the pain be."

"And death . . . where is it?"

He sought his former accustomed fear of death and did not find it. "Where is it? What death?" There was no fear because there was no death.

In place of death there was light.

"So that's what it is!" he suddenly exclaimed aloud. "What joy!"

To him all this happened in a single instant, and the meaning of that instant did not change. For those present his agony continued for another two hours. Something rattled in his throat, his emaciated body twitched, then the gasping and rattle became less and less frequent.

"It is finished!" said someone near him.

He heard these words and repeated them in his soul.

"Death is finished," he said to himself. "It is no more!"

He drew in a breath, stopped in the midst of a sigh, stretched out, and died.

HENRIK IBSEN
(1828–1906)
The Wild Duck*

Characters

WERLE, *a merchant, manufacturer, etc.*

GREGERS WERLE, *his son*

OLD EKDAL

HIALMAR EKDAL, *his son, a photographer*

GINA EKDAL, *Hialmar's wife*

HEDVIG, *their daughter, a girl of fourteen*

MRS. SÖRBY, *Werle's housekeeper*

RELLING, *a doctor*

MOLVIK, *student of theology*

GRÅBERG, *Werle's bookkeeper*

PETTERSEN, *Werle's servant*

JENSEN, *a hired waiter*

FLABBY GENTLEMAN

THIN-HAIRED GENTLEMAN

SHORT-SIGHTED GENTLEMAN

SIX OTHER GENTLEMEN, *guests at Werle's dinner-party*

SEVERAL HIRED WAITERS

The first act passes in WERLE'S *house, the remaining acts at* HIALMAR EKDAL'S.

* 1884. Translated by Frances Elizabeth Archer.

Act I

SCENE.—At WERLE'S *house. A richly and comfortably furnished study; bookcases and upholstered furniture; a writing-table, with papers and documents, in the centre of the room; lighted lamps with green shades, giving a subdued light. At the back, open folding-doors with curtains drawn back. Within is seen a large and hand-some room, brilliantly lighted with lamps and branching candle-sticks. In front, on the right (in the study), a small baize door leads into* WERLE'S *office. On the left, in front, a fireplace with a glowing coal fire, and farther back a double door leading into the dining-room.*

WERLE'S *servant,* PETTERSEN, *in livery, and* JENSEN, *the hired waiter, in black, are putting the study in order. In the large room, two or three other hired waiters are moving about, arranging things and lighting more candles. From the dining-room, the hum of conversation and laughter of many voices are heard; a glass is tapped with a knife; silence follows, and a toast is proposed; shouts of* "Bravo!" *and then again a buzz of conversation.*

PETTERSEN. [*Lights a lamp on the chimney-place and places a shade over it*] Listen to them, Jensen! Now the old man's on his legs holding a long palaver about Mrs. Sörby.

JENSEN. [*Pushing forward an armchair*] Is it true, what folks say, that they're—very good friends, eh?

PETTERSEN. Lord knows.

JENSEN. I've heard tell as he's been a lively customer in his day.

PETTERSEN. May be.

JENSEN. And he's giving this spread in honor of his son, they say.

PETTERSEN. Yes. His son came home yesterday.

JENSEN. This is the first time I ever heard as Mr. Werle had a son.

PETTERSEN. Oh, yes, he has a son, right enough. But he's a fixture, as you might say, up at the Höidal works. He's never once come to town all the years I've been in service here.

A WAITER. [*In the doorway of the other room*] Pettersen, here's an old fellow wanting——

PETTERSEN. [*Mutters*] The devil—who's this now?

[OLD EKDAL *appears from the right, in the inner room. He is dressed in a threadbare overcoat with a high collar; he wears woollen mittens and carries in his hand a stick and a fur cap. Under his arm, a brown paper parcel. Dirty red-brown wig and small grey moustache.*]

PETTERSEN. [*Goes towards him*] Good Lord—what do you want here?

EKDAL. [*In the doorway*] Must get into the office, Pettersen.

PETTERSEN. The office was closed an hour ago, and——

EKDAL. So they told me at the front door. But Graberg's in there still. Let me slip in this way, Pettersen; there's a good fellow.

[*Points towards the baize door*] It's not the first time I've come this way.

PETTERSEN. Well, you may pass. [*Opens the door*] But mind you go out again the proper way, for we've got company.

EKDAL. I know, I know—h'm! Thanks, Pettersen, good old friend! Thanks! [*Mutters softly*] Ass!

[*He goes into the office;* PETTERSEN *shuts the door after him.*]

JENSEN. Is he one of the office people?

PETTERSEN. No he's only an outside hand that does odd jobs of copying. But he's been a tip-topper in his day, has old Ekdal.

JENSEN. You can see he's been through a lot.

PETTERSEN. Yes; he was an army officer, you know.

JENSEN. You don't say so?

PETTERSEN. No mistake about it. But then he went into the timber trade or something of the sort. They say he once played Mr. Werle a very nasty trick. They were partners in the Höidal works at the time. Oh, I know old Ekdal well, I do. Many a nip of bitters and bottle of ale we two have drunk at Madame Eriksen's.

JENSEN. He don't look as if he'd much to stand treat with.

PETTERSEN. Why, bless you, Jensen, it's me that stands treat. I always think there's no harm in being a bit civil to folks that have seen better days.

JENSEN. Did he go bankrupt, then?

PETTERSEN. Worse than that. He went to prison.

JENSEN. To prison!

PETTERSEN. Or perhaps it was the Penitentiary. [*Listens*] Sh! They're leaving the table.

[*The dining-room door is thrown open from within by a couple of waiters.* MRS. SÖRBY *comes out conversing with two* GENTLEMEN. *Gradually the whole company follows, amongst them* WERLE. *Last come* HIALMAR EKDAL *and* GREGERS WERLE.]

MRS. SÖRBY. [*In passing, to the servant*] Tell them to serve the coffee in the music-room, Pettersen.

PETTERSEN. Very well, Madam.

[*She goes with the two* GENTLEMEN *into the inner room and thence out to the right.* PETTERSEN *and* JENSEN *go out the same way.*]

FLABBY GENTLEMAN. [*To* THIN-HAIRED GENTLEMAN] Whew! What a dinner!—It was no joke to do it justice!

THIN-HAIRED GENTLEMAN. Oh, with a little good-will one can get through a lot in three hours.

FLABBY GENTLEMAN. Yes, but afterwards, afterwards, my dear Chamberlain![1]

THIRD GENTLEMAN. I hear the coffee and maraschino are to be served in the music-room.

---

1. "Chamberlain" was the non-hereditary honorary title conferred by the King upon men of wealth and position. [Translator's note.]

FLABBY GENTLEMAN. Bravo! Then perhaps Mrs. Sörby will play us something.

THIN-HAIRED GENTLEMAN. [*In a low voice*] I hope Mrs. Sörby mayn't play us a tune we don't like, one of these days!

FLABBY GENTLEMAN. Oh, no, not she! Bertha will never turn against her old friends.

[*They laugh and pass into the inner room.*]

WERLE. [*In a low voice, dejectedly*] I don't think anybody noticed it, Gregers.

GREGERS. [*Looks at him*] Noticed what?

WERLE. Did you not notice it either?

GREGERS. What do you mean?

WERLE. We were thirteen at table.

GREGERS. Indeed? Were there thirteen of us?

WERLE. [*Glances towards* HIALMAR EKDAL] Our usual party is twelve. [*To the others*] This way, gentlemen!

[WERLE *and the others, all except* HIALMAR *and* GREGERS, *go out by the back, to the right.*]

HIALMAR. [*Who has overheard the conversation*] You ought not to have invited me, Gregers.

GREGERS. What! Not ask my best and only friend to a party supposed to be in my honor——?

HIALMAR. But I don't think your father likes it. You see I am quite outside his circle.

GREGERS. So I hear. But I wanted to see you and have a talk with you, and I certainly shan't be staying long.—Ah, we two old schoolfellows have drifted far apart from each other. It must be sixteen or seventeen years since we met.

HIALMAR. Is it so long?

GREGERS. It is indeed. Well, how goes it with you? You look well. You have put on flesh and grown almost stout.

HIALMAR. Well, "stout" is scarcely the word; but I daresay I look a little more of a man than I used to.

GREGERS. Yes, you do; your outer man is in first-rate condition.

HIALMAR. [*In a tone of gloom*] Ah, but the inner man! That is a very different matter, I can tell you! Of course you know of the terrible catastrophe that has befallen me and mine since last we met.

GREGERS. [*More softly*] How are things going with your father now?

HIALMAR. Don't let us talk of it, old fellow. Of course my poor unhappy father lives with me. He hasn't another soul in the world to care for him. But you can understand that this is a miserable subject for me.—Tell me, rather, how you have been getting on up at the works.

GREGERS. I have had a delightfully lonely time of it—plenty of leisure to think and think about things. Come over here; we may as well make ourselves comfortable.

[*He seats himself in an armchair by the fire and draws* HIALMAR *down into another alongside of it.*]

HIALMAR. [*Sentimentally*] After all, Gregers, I thank you for invit-ing me to your father's table, for I take it as a sign that you have got over your feeling against me.

GREGERS. [*Surprised*] How could you imagine I had any feeling against you?

HIALMAR. You had at first, you know.

GREGERS. How at first?

HIALMAR. After the great misfortune. It was natural enough that you should. Your father was within an ace of being drawn into that—well, that terrible business.

GREGERS. Why should that give me any feeling against you? Who can have put that into your head?

HIALMAR. I know it did, Gregers; your father told me so himself.

GREGERS. [*Starts*] My father! Oh, indeed. H'm.—Was that why you never let me hear from you?—not a single word.

HIALMAR. Yes.

GREGERS. Not even when you made up your mind to become a photographer?

HIALMAR. Your father said I had better not write to you at all, about anything.

GREGERS. [*Looking straight before him*] Well, well, perhaps he was right.—But tell me now, Hialmar: are you pretty well satisfied with your present position?

HIALMAR. [*With a little sigh*] Oh, yes, I am; I have really no cause to complain. At first, as you may guess, I felt it a little strange. It was such a totally new state of things for me. But of course my whole circumstances were totally changed. Father's utter, irre-trievable ruin,—the shame and disgrace of it, Gregers——

GREGERS. [*Affected*] Yes, yes; I understand.

HIALMAR. I couldn't think of remaining at college; there wasn't a shilling to spare; on the contrary, there were debts—mainly to your father, I believe——

GREGERS. H'm——

HIALMAR. In short, I thought it best to break, once for all, with my old surroundings and associations. It was your father that spe-cially urged me to it; and since he interested himself so much in me——

GREGERS. My father did?

HIALMAR. Yes, you surely knew that, didn't you? Where do you suppose I found the money to learn photography, and to furnish a studio and make a start? All that cost a pretty penny, I can tell you.

GREGERS. And my father provided the money?

HIALMAR. Yes, my dear fellow, didn't you know? I understood him to say he had written to you about it.

GREGERS. Not a word about his part in the business. He must have forgotten it. Our correspondence has always been purely a business one. So it was my father that——!

HIALMAR. Yes, certainly. He didn't wish it to be generally known; but he it was. And of course it was he, too, that put me in a position to marry. Don't you—don't you know about that either?

GREGERS. No, I haven't heard a word of it. [*Shakes him by the arm*] But, my dear Hialmar, I can't tell you what pleasure all this gives me—pleasure, and self-reproach. I have perhaps done my father injustice after all—in some things. This proves that he has a heart. It shows a sort of compunction——

HIALMAR. Compunction——?

GREGERS. Yes, yes—whatever you like to call it. Oh, I can't tell you how glad I am to hear this of father.—So you are a married man, Hialmar! That is further than I shall ever get. Well, I hope you are happy in your married life?

HIALMAR. Yes, thoroughly happy. She is as good and capable a wife as any man could wish for. And she is by no means without culture.

GREGERS. [*Rather surprised*] No, of course not.

HIALMAR. You see, life is itself an education. Her daily intercourse with me—— And then we know one or two rather remarkable men, who come a good deal about us. I assure you, you would hardly know Gina again.

GREGERS. Gina?

HIALMAR. Yes; had you forgotten that her name was Gina?

GREGERS. Whose name? I haven't the slightest idea——

HIALMAR. Don't you remember that she used to be in service here?

GREGERS. [*Looks at him*] Is it Gina Hansen——?

HIALMAR. Yes, of course it is Gina Hansen.

GREGERS. ——who kept house for us during the last year of my mother's illness?

HIALMAR. Yes, exactly. But, my dear friend, I'm quite sure your father told you that I was married.

GREGERS. [*Who has risen*] Oh, yes, he mentioned it; but not that—— [*Walking about the room*] Stay—perhaps he did— now that I think of it. My father always writes such short letters. [*Half seats himself on the arm of the chair*] Now tell me, Hialmar —this is interesting—how did you come to know Gina—your wife?

HIALMAR. The simplest thing in the world. You know Gina did not stay here long; everything was so much upset at that time, owing to your mother's illness and so forth, that Gina was not equal to it all; so she gave notice and left. That was the year before your mother died—or it may have been the same year.

GREGERS. It was the same year. I was up at the works then. But afterwards——?

HIALMAR. Well, Gina lived at home with her mother, Madame Hansen, an excellent hard-working woman, who kept a little eating-house. She had a room to let, too, a very nice comfortable room.

GREGERS. And I suppose you were lucky enough to secure it?

HIALMAR. Yes; in fact, it was your father that recommended it to me. So it was there, you see, that I really came to know Gina.

GREGERS. And then you got engaged?

HIALMAR Yes. It doesn't take young people long to fall in love——; h'm——

GREGERS. [*Rises and moves about a little*] Tell me: was it after your engagement—was it then that my father—I mean was it then that you began to take up photography?

HIALMAR. Yes, precisely. I wanted to make a start and to set up house as soon as possible; and your father and I agreed that this photography business was the readiest way. Gina thought so, too. Oh, and there was another thing in its favor, by-the-bye: it happened, luckily, that Gina had learnt to retouch.

GREGERS. That chimed in marvellously.

HIALMAR. [*Pleased, rises*] Yes, didn't it? Don't you think it was a marvellous piece of luck?

GREGERS. Oh, unquestionably. My father seems to have been almost a kind of providence for you.

HIALMAR. [*With emotion*] He did not forsake his old friend's son in the hour of his need. For he has a heart, you see.

MRS. SÖRBY [*Enters, arm-in-arm with* WERLE] Nonsense, my dear Mr. Werle; you mustn't stop there any longer staring at all the lights. It's very bad for you.

WERLE. [*Lets go her arm and passes his hand over his eyes*] I daresay you are right.

[PETTERSEN *and* JENSEN *carry round refreshment trays.*]

MRS. SÖRBY. [*To the guests in the other room*] This way, if you please, gentlemen. Whoever wants a glass of punch must be so good as to come in here.

FLABBY GENTLEMAN. [*Comes up to* MRS. SÖRBY] Surely, it isn't possible that you have suspended our cherished right to smoke?

MRS. SÖRBY. Yes. No smoking here, in Mr. Werle's sanctum, Chamberlain.

THIN-HAIRED GENTLEMAN. When did you enact these stringent amendments to the cigar law, Mrs. Sörby?

MRS. SÖRBY. After the last dinner, Chamberlain, when certain persons permitted themselves to overstep the mark.

THIN-HAIRED GENTLEMAN. And may one never overstep the mark a little bit, Madame Bertha? Not the least little bit?

MRS. SÖRBY. Not in any respect whatsoever, Mr. Balle.

[*Most of the guests have assembled in the study; servants hand round glasses of punch.*]

WERLE. [*To* HIALMAR, *who is standing beside a table*] What are you studying so intently, Ekdal?

HIALMAR. Only an album, Mr. Werle.

THIN-HAIRED GENTLEMAN. [*Who is wandering about*] Ah, photographs! They are quite in your line, of course.

FLABBY GENTLEMAN. [*In an armchair*] Haven't you brought any of your own with you?

HIALMAR. No, I haven't.

FLABBY GENTLEMAN. You ought to have; it's very good for the digestion to sit and look at pictures.

THIN-HAIRED GENTLEMAN. And it contributes to the entertainment, you know.

SHORT-SIGHTED GENTLEMAN. And all contributions are thankfully received.

MRS. SÖRBY. The Chamberlains think that when one is invited out to dinner, one ought to exert oneself a little in return, Mr. Ekdal.

FLABBY GENTLEMAN. Where one dines so well, that duty becomes a pleasure.

THIN-HAIRED GENTLEMAN. And when it's a case of the struggle for existence, you know——

MRS. SÖRBY. I quite agree with you!

[*They continue the conversation, with laughter and joking.*]

GREGERS. [*Softly*] You must join in, Hialmar.

HIALMAR. [*Writhing*] What am I to talk about?

FLABBY GENTLEMAN. Don't you think, Mr. Werle, that Tokay may be considered one of the more wholesome sorts of wine?

WERLE. [*By the fire*] I can answer for the Tokay you had today, at any rate; it's one of the very finest seasons. Of course you would notice that.

FLABBY GENTLEMAN. Yes, it had a remarkably delicate flavor.

HIALMAR. [*Shyly*] Is there any difference between the seasons?

FLABBY GENTLEMAN. [*Laughs*] Come! That's good!

WERLE. [*Smiles*] It really doesn't pay to set fine wine before you.

THIN-HAIRED GENTLEMAN. Tokay is like photographs, Mr. Ekdal: they both need sunshine. Am I not right?

HIALMAR. Yes, light is important, no doubt.

MRS. SÖRBY. And it's exactly the same with Chamberlains—they, too, depend very much on sunshine,[2] as the saying is.

2. The "sunshine" of court favor. [Translator's note.]

THIN-HAIRED GENTLEMAN. Oh, fie! That's a very threadbare sarcasm!

SHORT-SIGHTED GENTLEMAN. Mrs. Sörby is coming out——

FLABBY GENTLEMAN. ——and at our expense, too. [*Holds up his finger reprovingly*] Oh, Madame Bertha, Madame Bertha!

MRS. SÖRBY. Yes, and there's not the least doubt that the seasons differ greatly. The old vintages are the finest.

SHORT-SIGHTED GENTLEMAN. Do you reckon me among the old vintages?

MRS. SÖRBY. Oh, far from it.

THIN-HAIRED GENTLEMAN. There now! But me, dear Mrs. Sörby——?

FLABBY GENTLEMAN. Yes, and me? What vintage should you say that we belong to?

MRS. SÖRBY. Why, to the sweet vintages, gentlemen.

[*She sips a glass of punch. The* GENTLEMEN *laugh and flirt with her.*]

WERLE. Mrs. Sörby can always find a loop-hole—when she wants to. Fill your glasses, gentlemen! Pettersen, will you see to it—! Gregers, suppose we have a glass together. [GREGERS *does not move*] Won't you join us, Ekdal? I found no opportunity of drinking with you at table.

[GRÅBERG, *the bookkeeper, looks in at the baize door.*]

GRÅBERG. Excuse me, sir, but I can't get out.

WERLE. Have you been locked in again?

GRÅBERG. Yes, and Flakstad has carried off the keys.

WERLE. Well, you can pass out this way.

GRÅBERG. But there's some one else——

WERLE. All right; come through, both of you. Don't be afraid.

[GRÅBERG *and* OLD EKDAL *come out of the office.*]

WERLE. [*Involuntarily*] Ugh!

[*The laughter and talk among the guests cease.* HIALMAR *starts at the sight of his father, puts down his glass and turns towards the fireplace.*]

EKDAL. [*Does not look up, but makes little bows to both sides as he passes, murmuring*] Beg pardon, come the wrong way. Door locked—door locked. Beg pardon.

[*He and* GRÅBERG *go out by the back, to the right.*]

WERLE. [*Between his teeth*] That idiot Gråberg.

GREGERS. [*Opened-mouthed and staring, to* HIALMAR] Why surely that wasn't——!

FLABBY GENTLEMAN. What's the matter? Who was it?

GREGERS. Oh, nobody; only the bookkeeper and some one with him.

SHORT-SIGHTED GENTLEMAN. [*To* HIALMAR] Did you know that man?

HIALMAR. I don't know—I didn't notice——

FLABBY GENTLEMAN. What the deuce has come over every one? [*He joins another group who are talking softly.*]

MRS. SÖRBY. [*Whispers to the servant*] Give him something to take with him;—something good, mind.

PETTERSEN. [*Nods*] I'll see to it. [*Goes out.*]

GREGERS. [*Softly and with emotion, to* HIALMAR] So that was really he!

HIALMAR. Yes.

GREGERS. And you could stand there and deny that you knew him!

HIALMAR. [*Whispers vehemently*] But how could I——!

GREGERS. ——acknowledge your own father?

HIALMAR. [*With pain*] Oh, if you were in my place—— [*The conversation amongst the guests, which has been carried on in a low tone, now swells into constrained joviality.*]

THIN-HAIRED GENTLEMAN. [*Approaching* HIALMAR *and* GREGERS *in a friendly manner*] Aha! Reviving old college memories, eh? Don't you smoke, Mr. Ekdal? May I give you a light? Oh, by-the-bye, we mustn't——

HIALMAR. No, thank you, I won't——

FLABBY GENTLEMAN. Haven't you a nice little poem you could recite to us, Mr. Ekdal? You used to recite so charmingly.

HIALMAR. I am sorry I can't remember anything.

FLABBY GENTLEMAN. Oh, that's a pity. Well, what shall we do, Balle? [*Both* GENTLEMEN *move away and pass into the other room.*]

HIALMAR. [*Gloomily*] Gregers—I am going! When a man has felt the crushing hand of Fate, you see—— Say good-bye to your father for me.

GREGERS. Yes, yes. Are you going straight home?

HIALMAR. Yes. Why?

GREGERS. Oh, because I may perhaps look in on you later.

HIALMAR. No, you mustn't do that. You must not come to my home. Mine is a melancholy abode, Gregers, especially after a splendid banquet like this. We can always arrange to meet somewhere in the town.

MRS. SÖRBY. [*Who has quietly approached*] Are you going, Ekdal?

HIALMAR. Yes.

MRS. SÖRBY. Remember me to Gina.

HIALMAR. Thanks.

MRS. SÖRBY. And say I am coming up to see her one of these days.

HIALMAR. Yes, thank you. [*To* GREGERS] Stay here; I will slip out unobserved. [*He saunters away, then into the other room, and so out to the right.*]

MRS. SÖRBY. [*Softly to the servant, who has come back*] Well, did you give the old man something?

PETTERSEN. Yes; I sent him off with a bottle of cognac.

MRS. SÖRBY. Oh, you might have thought of something better than that.

PETTERSEN. Oh, no, Mrs. Sörby; cognac is what he likes best in the world.

FLABBY GENTLEMAN. [*In the doorway with a sheet of music in his hand*] Shall we play a duet, Mrs. Sörby?

MRS. SÖRBY. Yes, suppose we do.

THE GUESTS. Bravo, bravo!

[*She goes with all the guests through the back room, out to the right.* GREGERS *remains standing by the fire.* WERLE *is looking for something on the writing-table and appears to wish that* GREGERS *would go; as* GREGERS *does not move,* WERLE *goes towards the door.*]

GREGERS. Father, won't you stay a moment?

WERLE. [*Stops*] What is it?

GREGERS. I must have a word with you.

WERLE. Can it not wait till we are alone?

GREGERS. No, it cannot; for perhaps we shall never be alone together.

WERLE. [*Drawing nearer*] What do you mean by that?

[*During what follows, the pianoforte is faintly heard from the distant music-room.*]

GREGERS. How has that family been allowed to go so miserably to the wall?

WERLE. You mean the Ekdals, I suppose.

GREGERS. Yes, I mean the Ekdals. Lieutenant Ekdal was once so closely associated with you.

WERLE. Much too closely; I have felt that to my cost for many a year. It is thanks to him that I—yes I—have had a kind of slur cast upon my reputation.

GREGERS. [*Softly*] Are you sure that he alone was to blame?

WERLE. Who else do you suppose——?

GREGERS. You and he acted together in that affair of the forests——

WERLE. But was it not Ekdal that drew the map of the tracts we had bought—that fraudulent map! It was he who felled all that timber illegally on Government ground. In fact, the whole management was in his hands. I was quite in the dark as to what Lieutenant Ekdal was doing.

GREGERS. Lieutenant Ekdal himself seems to have been very much in the dark as to what he was doing.

WERLE. That may be. But the fact remains that he was found guilty and I acquitted.

GREGERS. Yes, I know that nothing was proved against you.

WERLE. Acquittal is acquittal. Why do you rake up these old miseries that turned my hair grey before its time? Is that the sort of thing you have been brooding over up there, all these years? I can assure you, Gregers, here in the town the whole story has been forgotten long ago—so far as *I* am concerned.

GREGERS. But that unhappy Ekdal family——

WERLE. What would you have had me do for the people? When Ekdal came out of prison he was a broken-down being, past all help. There are people in the world who dive to the bottom the moment they get a couple of slugs in their body and never come to the surface again. You may take my word for it, Gregers, I have done all I could without positively laying myself open to all sorts of suspicion and gossip——

GREGERS. Suspicion——? Oh, I see.

WERLE. I have given Ekdal copying to do for the office, and I pay him far, far more for it than his work is worth——

GREGERS. [*Without looking at him*] H'm; that I don't doubt.

WERLE. You laugh? Do you think I am not telling you the truth? Well, I certainly can't refer you to my books, for I never enter payments of that sort.

GREGERS. [*Smiles coldly*] No, there are certain payments it is best to keep no account of.

WERLE. [*Taken aback*] What do you mean by that?

GREGERS. [*Mustering up courage*] Have you entered what it cost you to have Hialmar Ekdal taught photography?

WERLE. I? How "entered" it?

GREGERS. I have learnt that it was you who paid for his training. And I have learnt, too, that it was you who enabled him to set up house so comfortably.

WERLE. Well, and yet you talk as though I had done nothing for the Ekdals! I can assure you these people have cost me enough in all conscience.

GREGERS. Have you entered any of these expenses in your books?

WERLE. Why do you ask?

GREGERS. Oh, I have my reasons. Now tell me: when you interested yourself so warmly in your old friend's son—it was just before his marriage, was it not?

WERLE. Why, deuce take it—after all these years, how can I——?

GREGERS. You wrote me a letter about that time—a business letter, of course; and in a postscript you mentioned—quite briefly— that Hialmar Ekdal had married a Miss Hansen.

WERLE. Yes, that was quite right. That was her name.

GREGERS. But you did not mention that this Miss Hansen was Gina Hansen—our former housekeeper.

WERLE. [*With a forced laugh of derision*] No; to tell the truth, it didn't occur to me that you were so particularly interested in our former housekeeper.

GREGERS. No more I was. But [*Lowers his voice*] there were others in this house who were particularly interested in her.

WERLE. What do you mean by that? [*Flaring up*] You are not alluding to me, I hope?

GREGERS. [*Softly but firmly*] Yes, I am alluding to you.

WERLE. And you dare——! You presume to——! How can that ungrateful hound—that photographer fellow—how dare he go making such insinuations!

GREGERS. Hialmar has never breathed a word about this. I don't believe he has the faintest suspicion of such a thing.

WERLE. Then where have you got it from? Who can have put such notions in your head?

GREGERS. My poor unhappy mother told me; and that the very last time I saw her.

WERLE. Your mother! I might have known as much! You and she—you always held together. It was she who turned you against me, from the first.

GREGERS. No, it was all that she had to suffer and submit to, until she broke down and came to such a pitiful end.

WERLE. Oh, she had nothing to suffer or submit to; not more than most people, at all events. But there's no getting on with morbid, overstrained creatures—that I have learnt to my cost.—And you could go on nursing such a suspicion—burrowing into all sorts of old rumors and slanders against your own father! I must say, Gregers, I really think that at your age you might find something more useful to do.

GREGERS. Yes, it is high time.

WERLE. Then perhaps your mind would be easier than it seems to be now. What can be your object in remaining up at the works, year out and year in, drudging away like a common clerk, and not drawing a farthing more than the ordinary monthly wage? It is downright folly.

GREGERS. Ah, if I were only sure of that.

WERLE. I understand you well enough. You want to be independent; you won't be beholden to me for anything. Well, now there happens to be an opportunity for you to become independent, your own master in everything.

GREGERS. Indeed? In what way——?

WERLE. When I wrote you insisting on your coming to town at once—h'm——

GREGERS. Yes, what is it you really want of me? I have been waiting all day to know.

WERLE. I want to propose that you should enter the firm, as partner.

GREGERS. I! Join your firm? As partner?

WERLE. Yes. It would not involve our being constantly together. You could take over the business here in town, and I should move up to the works.

GREGERS. You would?

WERLE. The fact is, I am not so fit for work as I once was. I am obliged to spare my eyes, Gregers; they have begun to trouble me.

GREGERS. They have always been weak.

WERLE. Not as they are now. And, besides, circumstances might possibly make it desirable for me to live up there—for a time, at any rate.

GREGERS. That is certainly quite a new idea to me.

WERLE. Listen, Gregers: there are many things that stand between us; but we are father and son after all. We ought surely to be able to come to some sort of understanding with each other.

GREGERS. Outwardly, you mean, of course?

WERLE. Well, even that would be something. Think it over, Gregers. Don't you think it ought to be possible? Eh?

GREGERS. [*Looking at him coldly*] There is something behind all this.

WERLE. How so?

GREGERS. You want to make use of me in some way.

WERLE. In such a close relationship as ours, the one can always be useful to the other.

GREGERS. Yes, so people say.

WERLE. I want very much to have you at home with me for a time. I am a lonely man, Gregers; I have always felt lonely, all my life through; but most of all now that I am getting up in years. I feel the need of some one about me——

GREGERS. You have Mrs. Sörby.

WERLE. Yes, I have her; and she has become, I may say, almost indispensable to me. She is lively and even-tempered; she brightens up the house; and that is a very great thing for me.

GREGERS. Well, then, you have everything just as you wish it.

WERLE. Yes, but I am afraid it can't last. A woman so situated may easily find herself in a false position, in the eyes of the world. For that matter it does a man no good, either.

GREGERS. Oh, when a man gives such dinners as you give, he can risk a great deal.

WERLE. Yes, but how about the woman, Gregers? I fear she won't accept the situation much longer; and even if she did—even if, out of attachment to me, she were to take her chance of gossip and scandal and all that——? Do you think, Gregers—you with your strong sense of justice——

GREGERS. [*Interrupts him*] Tell me in one word: are you thinking of marrying her?

WERLE. Suppose I were thinking of it? What then?

GREGERS. That's what I say: what then?

WERLE. Should you be inflexibly opposed to it!

GREGERS. Not at all. Not by any means.

WERLE. I was not sure whether your devotion to your mother's memory——

GREGERS. I am not overstrained.

WERLE. Well, whatever you may or may not be, at all events you have lifted a great weight from my mind. I am extremely pleased that I can reckon on your concurrence in this matter.

GREGERS. [*Looking intently at him*] Now I see the use you want to put me to.

WERLE. Use to put you to? What an expression!

GREGERS. Oh, don't let us be nice in our choice of words—not when we are alone together, at any rate. [*With a short laugh*] Well, well. So this is what made it absolutely essential that I should come to town in person. For the sake of Mrs. Sörby, we are to get up a pretence at family life in the house—a tableau of filial affection! That will be something new indeed.

WERLE. How dare you speak in that tone!

GREGERS. Was there ever any family life here? Never since I can remember. But now, forsooth, your plans demand something of the sort. No doubt it will have an excellent effect when it is reported that the son has hastened home, on the wings of filial piety, to the grey-haired father's wedding-feast. What will then remain of all the rumors as to the wrongs the poor dead mother had to submit to? Not a vestige. Her son annihilates them at one stroke.

WERLE. Gregers—I believe there is no one in the world you detest as you do me.

GREGERS. [*Softly*] I have seen you at too close quarters.

WERLE. You have seen me with your mother's eyes. [*Lowers his voice a little*] But you should remember that her eyes were—clouded now and then.

GREGERS [*Quivering*] I see what you are hinting at. But who was to blame for mother's unfortunate weakness? Why, you, and all those——! The last of them was this woman that you palmed off upon Hialmar Ekdal, when you were—— Ugh!

WERLE. [*Shrugs his shoulders*] Word for word as if it were your mother speaking!

GREGERS. [*Without heeding*] And there he is now, with his great, confiding, childlike mind, compassed about with all this treachery —living under the same roof with such a creature and never dreaming that what he calls his home is built upon a lie! [*Comes a step nearer*] When I look back upon your past, I seem to see a battle-field with shattered lives on every hand.

WERLE. I begin to think the chasm that divides us is too wide.

GREGERS. [*Bowing, with self-command*] So I have observed; and therefore I take my hat and go.

WERLE. You are going! Out of the house?

GREGERS. Yes. For at last I see my mission in life.

WERLE. What mission?

GREGERS. You would only laugh if I told you.

WERLE. A lonely man doesn't laugh so easily, Gregers.

GREGERS. [*Pointing towards the background*] Look, father,—the Chamberlains are playing blind-man's-buff with Mrs. Sörby.— Good-night and good-bye.

> [*He goes out by the back to the right. Sounds of laughter and merriment from the company, who are now visible in the outer room.*]

WERLE. [*Muttering contemptuously after* GREGERS] Ha——! Poor wretch—and he says he is not overstrained!

Act II

SCENE—HIALMAR EKDAL'S *studio, a good-sized room, evidently in the top story of the building. On the right, a sloping roof of large panes of glass, half-covered by a blue curtain. In the right-hand corner, at the back, the entrance door; farther forward, on the same side, a door leading to the sitting-room. Two doors on the opposite side, and between them an iron stove. At back, a wide double sliding-door. The studio is plainly but comfortably fitted up and furnished. Between the doors on the right, standing out a little from the wall, a sofa with a table and some chairs; on the table a lighted lamp with a shade; beside the stove an old arm-chair. Photographic instruments and apparatus of different kinds lying about the room. Against the back wall, to the left of the double door, stands a book-case containing a few books, boxes, and bottles of chemicals, instruments, tools, and other objects. Photographs and small articles, such as camel's-hair pencils, paper, and so forth, lie on the table.*

GINA EKDAL *sits on a chair by the table, sewing.* HEDVIG *is sitting on the sofa, with her hands shading her eyes and her thumbs in her ears, reading a book.*

GINA. [*Glances once or twice at* HEDVIG, *as if with secret anxiety; then says*] Hedvig!

> [HEDVIG *does not hear.*]

GINA. [*Repeats more loudly*] Hedvig!

HEDVIG. [*Takes away her hands and looks up*] Yes, mother?

GINA. Hedvig dear, you mustn't sit reading any longer now.

HEDVIG. Oh, mother, mayn't I read a little more? Just a little bit?

GINA. No, no, you must put away your book now. Father doesn't like it; he never reads hisself in the evening.

HEDVIG. [*Shuts the book*] No, father doesn't care much about reading.

GINA. [*Puts aside her sewing and takes up a lead pencil and a little account-book from the table*] Can you remember how much we paid for the butter today?

HEDVIG. It was one crown sixty-five.

GINA. That's right. [*Puts it down*] It's terrible what a lot of butter we get through in this house. Then there was the smoked sausage, and the cheese—let me see—[*Writes*]—and the ham—[*Adds up*] Yes, that makes just——

HEDVIG. And then the beer.

GINA. Yes, to be sure. [*Writes*] How it do mount up! But we can't manage with no less.

HEDVIG. And then you and I didn't need anything hot for dinner, as father was out.

GINA. No; that was so much to the good. And then I took eight crowns fifty for the photographs.

HEDVIG. Really! So much as that?

GINA. Exactly eight crowns fifty.

[*Silence.* GINA *takes up her sewing again;* HEDVIG *takes paper and pencil and begins to draw, shading her eyes with her left hand.*]

HEDVIG. Isn't it jolly to think that father is at Mr. Werle's big dinner-party?

GINA. You know he's not really Mr. Werle's guest. It was the son invited him. [*After a pause*] We have nothing to do with that Mr. Werle.

HEDVIG. I'm longing for father to come home. He promised to ask Mrs. Sörby for something nice for me.

GINA. Yes, there's plenty of good things in that house, I can tell you.

HEDVIG. [*Goes on drawing*] And I believe I'm a little hungry, too.

[OLD EKDAL, *with the paper parcel under his arm and another parcel in his coat pocket, comes in by the entrance door.*]

GINA. How late you are today, grandfather!

EKDAL. They had locked the office door. Had to wait in Gråberg's room. And then they let me through—h'm.

HEDVIG. Did you get some more copying to do, grandfather?

EKDAL. This whole packet. Just look.

GINA. That's capital.

HEDVIG. And you have another parcel in your pocket.

EKDAL. Eh? Oh, never mind, that's nothing. [*Puts his stick away in a corner*] This work will keep me going a long time, Gina. [*Opens one of the sliding-doors in the back wall a little*] Hush! [*Peeps into the room for a moment, then pushes the door carefully to again*] Hee-hee! They're fast asleep, all the lot of them. And she's gone into the basket herself. Hee-hee!

HEDVIG. Are you sure she isn't cold in that basket, grandfather?

EKDAL. Not a bit of it! Cold? With all that straw? [*Goes towards the farther door on the left*] There are matches in here, I suppose.

GINA. The matches is on the drawers.

[EKDAL *goes into his room.*]

HEDVIG. It's nice that grandfather has got all that copying.

GINA. Yes, poor old father; it means a bit of pocket-money for him.

HEDVIG. And he won't be able to sit the whole forenoon down at that horrid Madame Eriksen's.

GINA. No more he won't.   [*Short silence*]

HEDVIG. Do you suppose they are still at the dinner-table?

GINA. Goodness knows; as like as not.

HEDVIG. Think of all the delicious things father is having to eat! I'm certain he'll be in splendid spirits when he comes. Don't you think so, mother?

GINA. Yes; and if only we could tell him that we'd got the room let——

HEDVIG. But we don't need that this evening.

GINA. Oh, we'd be none the worst of it, I can tell you. It's no use to us as it is.

HEDVIG. I mean we don't need it this evening, for father will be in a good humor at any rate. It is best to keep the letting of the room for another time.

GINA. [*Looks across at her*] You like having some good news to tell father when he comes home in the evening?

HEDVIG. Yes; for then things are pleasanter somehow.

GINA. [*Thinking to herself*] Yes, yes, there's something in that.

[OLD EKDAL *comes in again and is going out by the foremost door to the left.*]

GINA. [*Half turning in her chair*] Do you want something out of the kitchen, grandfather?

EKDAL. Yes, yes, I do. Don't you trouble.   [*Goes out*]

GINA. He's not poking away at the fire, is he? [*Waits a moment*] Hedvig, go and see what he's about.

[EKDAL *comes in again with a small jug of steaming hot water.*]

HEDVIG. Have you been getting some hot water, grandfather?

EKDAL. Yes, hot water. Want it for something. Want to write, and the ink has got as thick as porridge—h'm.

GINA. But you'd best have your supper first, grandfather. It's laid in there.

EKDAL. Can't be bothered with supper, Gina. Very busy, I tell you. No one's to come to my room. No one—h'm.

[*He goes into his room;* GINA *and* HEDVIG *look at each other.*]

GINA. [*Softly*] Can you imagine where he's got money from?

HEDVIG. From Gråberg, perhaps.

GINA. Not a bit of it. Gråberg always sends the money to me.

HEDVIG. Then he must have got a bottle on credit somewhere.

GINA. Poor grandfather, who'd give him credit?

HIALMAR EKDAL, *in an overcoat and grey felt hat, comes in from the right.*]

GINA. [*Throws down her sewing and rises*] Why, Ekdal, is that you already?

HEDVIG. [*At the same time, jumping up*] Fancy your coming so soon, father!

HIALMAR. [*Taking off his hat*] Yes, most of the people were coming away.

HEDVIG. So early?

HIALMAR. Yes, it was a dinner-party, you know.

[*Taking off his overcoat*]

GINA. Let me help you.

HEDVIG. Me, too.

[*They draw off his coat;* GINA *hangs it up on the back wall.*]

HEDVIG. Were there many people there, father?

HIALMAR. Oh, no, not many. We were about twelve or fourteen at table.

GINA. And you had some talk with them all?

HIALMAR. Oh, yes, a little; but Gregers took up most of my time.

GINA. Is Gregers as ugly as ever?

HIALMAR. Well, he's not very much to look at. Hasn't the old man come home?

HEDVIG. Yes, grandfather is in his room, writing.

HIALMAR. Did he say anything?

GINA. No, what should he say?

HIALMAR. Didn't he say anything about——? I heard something about his having been with Gråberg. I'll go in and see him for a moment.

GINA. No, no, better not.

HIALMAR. Why not? Did he say he didn't want me to go in?

GINA. I don't think he wants to see nobody this evening——

HEDVIG. [*Making signs*] H'm—h'm!

GINA. [*Not noticing*]——he has been in to fetch hot water——

HIALMAR. Aha! Then he's——

GINA. Yes, I suppose so.

HIALMAR. Oh, God! my poor old white-haired father!—— Well, well; there let him sit and get all the enjoyment he can.

[OLD EKDAL, *in an indoor coat and with a lighted pipe, comes from his room.*]

EKDAL. Got home? Thought it was you I heard talking.

HIALMAR. Yes, I have just come.

EKDAL. You didn't see me, did you?

HIALMAR. No, but they told me you had passed through—so I thought I would follow you.

EKDAL. H'm, good of you, Hialmar.—Who were they, all those fellows?

HIALMAR.—Oh, all sorts of people. There was Chamberlain Flor, and Chamberlain Balle, and Chamberlain Kaspersen and Chamberlain—this, that, and the other—I don't know who all——

EKDAL. [*Nodding*] Hear that, Gina! Chamberlains every one of them!

GINA. Yes, I hear as they're terrible genteel in that house nowadays.

HEDVIG. Did the Chamberlains sing, father? Or did they read aloud?

HIALMAR. No, they only talked nonsense. They wanted me to recite something for them; but I knew better than that.

EKDAL. You weren't to be persuaded, eh?

GINA. Oh, you might have done it.

HIALMAR. No; one mustn't be at everybody's beck and call. [*Walks about the room*] That's not my way, at any rate.

EKDAL. No, no; Hialmar's not to be had for the asking, he isn't.

HIALMAR. I don't see why I should bother myself to entertain people on the rare occasions when I go into society. Let the others exert themselves. These fellows go from one great dinner-table to the next and gorge and guzzle day out and day in. It's for them to bestir themselves and do something in return for all the good feeding they get.

GINA. But you didn't say that?

HIALMAR. [*Humming*] Ho-ho-ho——; faith, I gave them a bit of my mind.

EKDAL. Not the Chamberlains?

HIALMAR. Oh, why not? [*Lightly*] After that, we had a little discussion about Tokay.

EKDAL. Tokay! There's a fine wine for you!

HIALMAR. [*Comes to a standstill*] It may be a fine wine. But of course you know the vintages differ; it all depends on how much sunshine the grapes have had.

GINA. Why, you know everything, Ekdal.

EKDAL. And did they dispute that?

HIALMAR. They tried to; but they were requested to observe that it was just the same with Chamberlains—that with them, too, different batches were of different qualities.

GINA. What things you do think of!

EKDAL. Hee-hee! So they got that in their pipes, too?

HIALMAR. Right in their teeth.

EKDAL. Do you hear that, Gina? He said it right in the very teeth of all the Chamberlains.

GINA. Fancy——! Right in their teeth!

HIALMAR. Yes, but I don't want it talked about. One doesn't speak of such things. The whole affair passed off quite amicably of course. They were nice, genial fellows; I didn't want to wound them—not I!

EKDAL. Right in their teeth, though——!

HEDVIG. [*Caressingly*] How nice it is to see you in a dress-coat! It suits you so well, father.

HIALMAR. Yes, don't you think so? And this one really sits to perfection. It fits almost as if it had been made for me;—a little tight in the arm-holes perhaps;—help me, Hedvig. [*Takes off the coat*] I think I'll put on my jacket. Where is my jacket, Gina?

GINA. Here it is.   [*Brings the jacket and helps him.*]

HIALMAR. That's it! Don't forget to send the coat back to Molvik first thing tomorrow morning.

GINA. [*Laying it away*] I'll be sure and see to it.

HIALMAR. [*Stretching himself*] After all, there's a more homely feeling about this. A free-and-easy indoor costume suits my whole personality better. Don't you think so, Hedvig?

HEDVIG. Yes, father.

HIALMAR. When I loosen my necktie into a pair of flowing ends— like this—eh?

HEDVIG. Yes, that goes so well with your moustache and the sweep of your curls.

HIALMAR. I should not call them curls exactly; I should rather say locks.

HEDVIG. Yes, there are too big for curls.

HIALMAR. Locks describes them better.

HEDVIG. [*After a pause, twitching his jacket*] Father!

HIALMAR. Well, what is it?

HEDVIG. Oh, you know very well.

HIALMAR. No, really I don't——

HEDVIG. [*Half laughing, half whispering*] Oh, yes, father; now don't tease me any longer!

HIALMAR. Why, what do you mean?

HEDVIG. [*Shaking him*] Oh, what nonsense; come, where are they, father? All the good things you promised me, you know?

HIALMAR. Oh—if I haven't forgotten all about them!

HEDVIG. Now you're only teasing me, father! Oh, it's too bad of you! Where have you put them?

HIALMAR. No, I positively forgot to get anything. But wait a little! I have something else for you, Hedvig.

[*Goes and searches in the pockets of the coat.*]

HEDVIG. [*Skipping and clapping her hands*] Oh, mother, mother!

GINA. There, you see; if you only give him time——

HIALMAR. [*With a paper*] Look, here it is.

HEDVIG. That? Why, that's only a paper.

HIALMAR. That is the bill of fare, my dear; the whole bill of fare. Here you see: "Menu"—that means bill of fare.

HEDVIG. Haven't you anything else?

HIALMAR. I forgot the other things, I tell you. But you may take my word for it, these dainties are very unsatisfying. Sit down at the table and read the bill of fare, and then I'll describe to you how the dishes taste. Here you are, Hedvig.

HEDVIG. [*Gulping down her tears*] Thank you. [*She seats herself, but does not read;* GINA *makes signs to her;* HIALMAR *notices it.*]

HIALMAR. [*Pacing up and down the room*] It's monstrous what absurd things the father of a family is expected to think of; and if he forgets the smallest trifle, he is treated to sour faces at once. Well, well, one gets used to that, too. [*Stops near the stove, by the old man's chair*] Have you peeped in there this evening, father?

EKDAL. Yes, to be sure I have. She's gone into the basket.

HIALMAR. Ah, she has gone into the basket. Then she's beginning to get used to it.

EKDAL. Yes; just as I prophesied. But you know there are still a few little things——

HIALMAR. A few improvements, yes.

EKDAL. They've got to be made, you know.

HIALMAR. Yes, let us have a talk about the improvements, father. Come, let us sit on the sofa.

EKDAL. All right. H'm—think I'll just fill my pipe first. Must clean it out, too. H'm.

[*He goes into his room.*]

GINA. [*Smiling to* HIALMAR] His pipe!

HIALMAR. Oh, yes, yes, Gina; let him alone—the poor shipwrecked old man.—Yes, these improvements—we had better get them out of hand tomorrow.

GINA. You'll hardly have time tomorrow, Ekdal.

HEDVIG. [*Interposing*] Oh, yes he will, mother!

GINA. ——for remember them prints that has to be retouched, they've sent for them time after time.

HIALMAR. There now! those prints again! I shall get them finished all right! Have any new orders come in?

GINA. No, worse luck; tomorrow I have nothing but those two sittings, you know.

HIALMAR. Nothing else? Oh, no, if people won't set about things with a will——

GINA. But what more can I do? Don't I advertise in the papers as much as we can afford?

HIALMAR. Yes, the papers, the papers; you see how much good they do. And I suppose no one has been to look at the room either?

GINA. No, not yet.

HIALMAR. That was only to be expected. If people won't keep their eyes open——. Nothing can be done without a real effort, Gina!

HEDVIG. [*Going towards him*] Shall I fetch you the flute, father?

HIALMAR. No; no flute for me; I want no pleasures in this world. [*Pacing about*] Yes, indeed I will work tomorrow; you shall see if I don't. You may be sure I shall work as long as my strength holds out.

GINA. But my dear, good Ekdal, I didn't mean it in that way.

HEDVIG. Father, mayn't I bring in a bottle of beer?

HIALMAR. No, certainly not. I require nothing, nothing——[*Comes to a standstill*] Beer? Was it beer you were talking about?

HEDVIG. [*Cheerfully*] Yes, father; beautiful, fresh beer.

HIALMAR. Well—since you insist upon it, you may bring in a bottle.

GINA. Yes, do; and we'll be nice and cosy.

[HEDVIG *runs towards the kitchen door.*]

HIALMAR. [*By the stove, stops her, looks at her, puts his arm round her neck and presses her to him*] Hedvig, Hedvig!

HEDVIG. [*With tears of joy*] My dear, kind father!

HIALMAR. No, don't call me that. Here have I been feasting at the rich man's table,—battening at the groaning board——! And I couldn't even——!

GINA. [*Sitting at the table*] Oh, nonsense, nonsense, Ekdal.

HIALMAR. It's not nonsense! And yet you mustn't be too hard upon me. You know that I love you for all that.

HEDVIG. [*Throwing her arms round him*] And we love you, oh, so dearly, father!

HIALMAR. And if I am unreasonable once in a while,—why then—you must remember that I am a man beset by a host of cares. There, there! [*Dries his eyes*] No beer at such a moment as this. Give me the flute.

[HEDVIG *runs to the bookcase and fetches it.*]

HIALMAR. Thanks! That's right. With my flute in my hand and you two at my side——ah——!

[HEDVIG *seats herself at the table near* GINA; HIALMAR *paces backwards and forwards, pipes up vigorously and plays a Bohemian peasant dance, but in a slow plaintive tempo, and with sentimental expression.*]

HIALMAR. [*Breaking off the melody, holds out his left hand to* GINA *and says with emotion*] Our roof may be poor and humble, Gina, but it is home. And with all my heart I say: here dwells my happiness.

[*He begins to play again; almost immediately after, a knocking is heard at the entrance door.*]

GINA. [*Rising*] Hush, Ekdal,—I think there's some one at the door.

HIALMAR. [*Laying the flute on the bookcase*] There! Again!

[GINA *goes and opens the door.*]

GREGERS WERLE. [*In the passage*] Excuse me——

GINA. [*Starting back slightly*] Oh!

GREGERS. ——does not Mr. Ekdal, the photographer, live here?

GINA. Yes, he does.

HIALMAR. [*Going towards the door*] Gregers! You here after all? Well, come in then.

GREGERS. [*Coming in*] I told you I would come and look you up.

HIALMAR. But this evening——? Have you left the party?

GREGERS. I have left both the party and my father's house.—Good evening, Mrs. Ekdal. I don't know whether you recognize me?

GINA. Oh, yes; it's not difficult to know young Mr. Werle again.

GREGERS. No, I am like my mother; and no doubt you remember her.

HIALMAR. Left your father's house, did you say?

GREGERS. Yes, I have gone to a hotel.

HIALMAR. Indeed. Well, since you're here, take off your coat and sit down.

GREGERS. Thanks.

[*He takes off his overcoat. He is now dressed in a plain grey suit of a countrified cut.*]

HIALMAR. Here, on the sofa. Make yourself comfortable.

[GREGERS *seats himself on the sofa;* HIALMAR *takes a chair at the table.*]

GREGERS. [*Looking around him*] So these are your quarters, Hialmar —this is your home.

HIALMAR. This is the studio, as you see——

GINA. But it's the largest of our rooms, so we generally sit here.

HIALMAR. We used to live in a better place; but this flat has one great advantage; there are such capital outer rooms——

GINA. And we have a room on the other side of the passage that we can let.

GREGERS. [*To* HIALMAR] Ah—so you have lodgers, too?

HIALMAR. No, not yet. They're not so easy to find, you see; you have to keep your eyes open. [*To* HEDVIG] What about the beer, eh?

[HEDVIG *nods and goes out into the kitchen.*]

GREGERS. So that is your daughter?

HIALMAR. Yes, that is Hedvig.

GREGERS. And she is your only child?

HIALMAR. Yes, the only one. She is the joy of our lives, and—[*lowering his voice*]—at the same time our deepest sorrow, Gregers.

GREGERS. What do you mean?

HIALMAR. She is in serious danger of losing her eyesight.

GREGERS. Becoming blind?

HIALMAR. Yes. Only the first symptoms have appeared as yet, and she may not feel it much for some time. But the doctor has warned us. It is coming, inexorably.

GREGERS. What a terrible misfortune! How do you account for it?

HIALMAR. [*Sighs*] Hereditary, no doubt.

GREGERS. [*Starting*] Hereditary?

GINA. Ekdal's mother had weak eyes.

HIALMAR. Yes, so my father says; I can't remember her.

GREGERS. Poor child! And how does she take it?

HIALMAR. Oh, you can imagine we haven't the heart to tell her of it. She dreams of no danger. Gay and careless and chirping like a little bird, she flutters onward into a life of endless night. [*Overcome*] Oh, it is cruelly hard on me, Gregers.

[HEDVIG *brings a tray with beer and glasses, which she sets upon the table.*]

HIALMAR. [*Stroking her hair*] Thanks, thanks, Hedvig.

[HEDVIG *puts her arm around his neck and whispers in his ear.*]

HIALMAR. No, no bread and butter just now. [*Looks up*] But perhaps you would like some, Gregers.

GREGERS. [*With a gesture of refusal*] No, no, thank you.

HIALMAR. [*Still melancholy*] Well, you can bring in a little all the same. If you have a crust, that is all I want. And plenty of butter on it, mind.

[HEDVIG *nods gaily and goes out into the kitchen again.*]

GREGERS. [*Who has been following her with his eyes*] She seems quite strong and healthy otherwise.

GINA. Yes. In other ways there's nothing amiss with her, thank goodness.

GREGERS. She promises to be very like you, Mrs. Ekdal. How old is she now?

GINA. Hedvig is close on fourteen; her birthday is the day after tomorrow.

GREGERS. She is pretty tall for her age, then.

GINA. Yes, she's shot up wonderful this last year.

GREGERS. It makes one realize one's own age to see these young people growing up.—How long is it now since you were married?

GINA. We've been married—let me see—just on fifteen years.

GREGERS. Is it so long as that?

GINA. [*Becomes attentive; looks at him*] Yes, it is indeed.

HIALMAR. Yes, so it is. Fifteen years all but a few months. [*Changing his tone*] They must have been long years for you, up at the works, Gregers.

GREGERS. They seemed long while I was living them; now they are over, I hardly know how the time has gone.

[OLD EKDAL *comes from his room without his pipe, but with his old-fashioned uniform cap on his head; his gait is somewhat unsteady.*]

EKDAL. Come now, Hialmar, let's sit down and have a good talk about this—h'm—what was it again?

HIALMAR. [*Going towards him*] Father, we have a visitor here— Gregers Werle.—I don't know if you remember him.

EKDAL. [*Looking at* GREGERS, *who has risen*] Werle? Is that the son? What does he want with me?

HIALMAR. Nothing; it's me he has come to see.

EKDAL. Oh! Then there's nothing wrong?

HIALMAR. No, no, of course not.

EKDAL. [*With a large gesture*] Not that I'm afraid, you know; but——

GREGERS. [*Goes over to him*] I bring you a greeting from your old hunting-grounds, Lieutenant Ekdal.

EKDAL. Hunting-grounds?

GREGERS. Yes, up in Höidal, about the works, you know.

EKDAL. Oh, up there. Yes, I knew all those places well in the old days.

GREGERS. You were a great sportsman then.

EKDAL. So I was, I don't deny it. You're looking at my uniform cap. I don't ask anybody's leave to wear it in the house. So long as I don't go out in the streets with it——

[HEDVIG *brings a plate of bread and butter, which she puts upon the table.*]

HIALMAR. Sit down, father, and have a glass of beer. Help yourself, Gregers.

[EKDAL *mutters and stumbles over to the sofa.* GREGERS *seats himself on the chair nearest to him,* HIALMAR *on the other side of* GREGERS. GINA *sits a little way from the table, sewing;* HEDVIG *stands beside her father.*]

GREGERS. Can you remember, Lieutenant Ekdal, how Hialmar and I used to come up and visit you in the summer and at Christmas?

EKDAL. Did you? No, no, no; I don't remember it. But sure enough

I've been a tidy bit of a sportsman in my day. I've shots bears,
too. I've shot nine of 'em, no less.

GREGERS. [*Looking sympathetically at him*] And now you never get
any shooting?

EKDAL. Can't just say that, sir. Get a shot now and then perhaps.
Of course not in the old way. For the woods, you see—the woods,
the woods——! [*Drinks*] Are the woods fine up there now?

GREGERS. Not so fine as in your time. They have been thinned a
good deal.

EKDAL. Thinned? [*More softly, and as if afraid*] It's dangerous work
that. Bad things come of it. The woods revenge themselves.

HIALMAR. [*Filling up his glass*] Come—a little more, father.

GREGERS. How can a man like you—such a man for the open air
—live in the midst of a stuffy town, boxed within four walls?

EKDAL. [*Laughs quietly and glances at* HIALMAR] Oh, it's not so
bad here. Not at all so bad.

GREGERS. But don't you miss all the things that used to be a part
of your very being—the cool sweeping breezes, the free life in
the woods and on the uplands, among beasts and birds——?

EKDAL. [*Smiling*] Hialmar, shall we let him see it?

HIALMAR. [*Hastily and a little embarrassed*] Oh, no, no, father; not
this evening.

GREGERS. What does he want to show me?

HIALMAR. Oh, it's only something—you can see it another time.

GREGERS. [*Continues, to the old man*] You see I have been thinking,
Lieutenant Ekdal, that you should come up with me to the works;
I am sure to be going back soon. No doubt you could get some
copying there, too. And here, you have nothing on earth to
interest you—nothing to liven you up.

EKDAL. [*Stares in astonishment at him*] Have I nothing on earth
to——!

GREGERS. Of course you have Hialmar; but then he has his own
family. And a man like you, who has always had such a passion
for what is free and wild——

EKDAL. [*Thumps the table*] Hialmar, he shall see it!

HIALMAR. Oh, do you think it's worth while, father? It's all dark.

EKDAL. Nonsense; it's moonlight. [*Rises*] He shall see it, I tell you.
Let me pass! Come and help me, Hialmar.

HEDVIG. Oh, yes, do, father!

HIALMAR. [*Rising*] Very well then.

GREGERS. [*To* GINA] What is it?

GINA. Oh, nothing so very wonderful, after all.

[EKDAL *and* HIALMAR *have gone to the back wall and are
each pushing back a side of the sliding door;* HEDVIG *helps
the old man;* GREGERS *remains standing by the sofa;* GINA

*sits still and sews. Through the open doorway a large, deep
irregular garret is seen with odd nooks and corners; a couple
of stove-pipes running through it, from rooms below. There
are skylights through which clear moonbeams shine in on
some parts of the great room; others lie in deep shadow.*]

EKDAL. [*To* GREGERS] You may come close up if you like.

GREGERS. [*Going over to them*] Why, what is it?

EKDAL. Look for yourself. H'm.

HIALMAR. [*Somewhat embarrassed*] This belongs to father, you
understand.

GREGERS. [*At the door, looks into the garret*] Why, you keep poultry,
Lieutenant Ekdal.

EKDAL. Should think we did keep poultry. They've gone to roost
now. But you should just see our fowls by daylight, sir!

HEDVIG. And there's a——

EKDAL. Sh—sh! don't say anything about it yet.

GREGERS. And you have pigeons, too, I see.

EKDAL. Oh, yes, haven't we just got pigeons! They have their nest-
boxes up there under the roof-tree; for pigeons like to roost high,
you see.

HIALMAR. They aren't all common pigeons.

EKDAL. Common! Should think not indeed! We have tumblers and
a pair of pouters, too. But come here! Can you see that hutch
down there by the wall?

GREGERS. Yes; what do you use it for?

EKDAL. That's where the rabbits sleep, sir.

GREGERS. Dear me; so you have rabbits, too?

EKDAL. Yes, you may take my word for it, we have rabbits! He wants
to know if we have rabbits, Hialmar! H'm! But now comes the
thing, let me tell you! Here we have it! Move away, Hedvig.
Stand here; that's right,—and now look down there.—Don't you
see a basket with straw in it?

GREGERS. Yes. And I can see a fowl lying in the basket.

EKDAL. H'm—"a fowl"——

GREGERS. Isn't it a duck?

EKDAL. [*Hurt*] Why, of course it's a duck.

HIALMAR. But what kind of duck, do you think?

HEDVIG. It's not just a common duck——

EKDAL. Sh!

GREGERS. And it's not a Muscovy duck either.

EKDAL. No, Mr.—Werle; it's not a Muscovy duck; for it's a wild
duck!

GREGERS. Is it really? A wild duck?

EKDAL. Yes, that's what it is. That "fowl" as you call it—is the wild
duck. It's our wild duck, sir.

HEDVIG. My wild duck. It belongs to me.

GREGERS. And can it live up here in the garret? Does it thrive?

EKDAL. Of course it has a trough of water to splash about in, you know.

HIALMAR. Fresh water every other day.

GINA. [*Turning towards* HIALMAR] But my dear Ekdal, it's getting icy cold here.

EKDAL. H'm, we had better shut up then. It's as well not to disturb their night's rest, too. Close up, Hedvig.

[HIALMAR *and* HEDVIG *push the garret doors together.*]

EKDAL. Another time you shall see her properly. [*Seats himself in the armchair by the stove*] Oh, they're curious things, these wild ducks, I can tell you.

GREGERS. How did you manage to catch it, Lieutenant Ekdal?

EKDAL. *I* didn't catch it. There's a certain man in this town whom we have to thank for it.

GREGERS. [*Starts slightly*] That man was not my father, was he?

EKDAL. You've hit it. Your father and no one else. H'm.

HIALMAR. Strange that you should guess that, Gregers.

GREGERS. You were telling me that you owed so many things to my father; and so I thought perhaps——

GINA. But we didn't get the duck from Mr. Werle himself——

EKDAL. It's Håkon Werle we have to thank for her, all the same, Gina. [*To* GREGERS] He was shooting from a boat, you see, and he brought her down. But your father's sight is not very good now. H'm; she was only wounded.

GREGERS. Ah! She got a couple of slugs in her body, I suppose.

HIALMAR. Yes, two or three.

HEDVIG. She was hit under the wing, so that she couldn't fly.

GREGERS. And I suppose she dived to the bottom, eh?

EKDAL. [*Sleepily, in a thick voice*] Of course. Always do that, wild ducks do. They shoot to the bottom as deep as they can get, sir —and bite themselves fast in the tangle and seaweed—and all the devil's own mess that grows down there. And they never come up again.

GREGERS. But your wild duck came up again, Lieutenant Ekdal.

EKDAL. He had such an amazingly clever dog, your father had. And that dog—he dived in after the duck and fetched her up again.

GREGERS. [*Who has turned to* HIALMAR] And then she was sent to you here?

HIALMAR. Not at once; at first your father took her home. But she wouldn't thrive there; so Pettersen was told to put an end to her——

EKDAL. [*Half asleep*] H'm—yes—Pettersen—that ass——

HIALMAR. [*Speaking more softly*] That was how we got her, you see;

for father knows Pettersen a little; and when he heard about the wild duck he got him to hand her over to us.

GREGERS. And now she thrives as well as possible in the garret there?

HIALMAR. Yes, wonderfully well. She has got fat. You see, she has lived in there so long now that she has forgotten her natural wild life; and it all depends on that.

GREGERS. You are right there, Hialmar. Be sure you never let her get a glimpse of the sky and the sea——. But I mustn't stay any longer; I think your father is asleep.

HIALMAR. Oh, as for that——

GREGERS. But, by-the-bye——you said you had a room to let—a spare room?

HIALMAR. Yes; what then? Do you know of anybody——?

GREGERS. Can I have that room?

HIALMAR. You?

GINA. Oh, no, Mr. Werle, you——

GREGERS. May I have the room? If so, I'll take possession first thing tomorrow morning.

HIALMAR. Yes, with the greatest pleasure——

GINA. But, Mr. Werle, I'm sure it's not at all the sort of room for you.

HIALMAR. Why, Gina! how can you say that?

GINA. Why, because the room's neither large enough nor light enough, and——

GREGERS. That really doesn't matter, Mrs. Ekdal.

HIALMAR. I call it quite a nice room, and not at all badly furnished either.

GINA. But remember the pair of them underneath.

GREGERS. What pair?

GINA. Well, there's one as has been a tutor——

HIALMAR. That's Molvik—Mr. Molvik, B.A.

GINA. And then there's a doctor, by the name of Relling.

GREGERS. Relling? I know him a little; he practised for a time up in Höidal.

GINA. They're a regular rackety pair, they are. As often as not, they're out on the loose in the evenings; and then they come home at all hours, and they're not always just——

GREGERS. One soon gets used to that sort of thing. I daresay I shall be like the wild duck——

GINA. H'm; I think you ought to sleep upon it first, anyway.

GREGERS. You seem very unwilling to have me in the house, Mrs. Ekdal.

GINA. Oh, no! What makes you think that?

HIALMAR. Well, you really behave strangely about it, Gina. [*To* GREGERS] Then I suppose you intend to remain in the town for the present?

GREGERS. [*Putting on his overcoat*] Yes, now I intend to remain here.

HIALMAR. And yet not at your father's? What do you propose to do, then?

GREGERS. Ah, if I only knew that, Hialmar, I shouldn't be so badly off! But when one has the misfortune to be called Gregers—! "Gregers"—and then "Werle" after it; did you ever hear anything so hideous?

HIALMAR. Oh, I don't think so at all.

GREGERS. Ugh! Bah! I feel I should like to spit upon the fellow that answers to such a name. But when a man is once for all doomed to be Gregers—Werle in this world, as I am——

HIALMAR. [*Laughs*] Ha, ha! If you weren't Gregers Werle, what would you like to be?

GREGERS. If I should choose, I should like best to be a clever dog.

GINA. A dog!

HEDVIG. [*Involuntarily*] Oh, no!

GREGERS. Yes, an amazingly clever dog; one that goes to the bottom after wild ducks when they dive and bite themselves fast in tangle and seaweed, down among the ooze.

HIALMAR. Upon my word now, Gregers—I don't in the least know what you're driving at.

GREGERS. Oh, well, you might not be much the wiser if you did. It's understood, then, that I move in early tomorrow morning. [*To* GINA] I won't give you any trouble; I do everything for myself. [*To* HIALMAR] We can talk about the rest tomorrow.—Goodnight, Mrs. Ekdal. [*Nods to* HEDVIG] Goodnight.

GINA. Goodnight, Mr. Werle.

HEDVIG. Goodnight.

HIALMAR. [*Who has lighted a candle*] Wait a moment; I must show you a light; the stairs are sure to be dark.

[GREGERS *and* HIALMAR *go out by the passage door.*]

GINA. [*Looking straight before her, with her sewing in her lap*] Wasn't that queer-like talk about wanting to be a dog?

HEDVIG. Do you know, mother—I believe he meant something quite different by that.

GINA. Why, what should he mean?

HEDVIG. Oh, I don't know; but it seemed to me he meant something different from what he said—all the time.

GINA. Do you think so? Yes, it was sort of queer.

HIALMAR. [*Comes back*] The lamp was still burning. [*Puts out the candle and sets it down*] Ah, now one can get a mouthful of food at last. [*Begins to eat the bread and butter*] Well, you see, Gina —if only you keep your eyes open——

GINA. How, keep your eyes open——?

HIALMAR. Why, haven't we at last had the luck to get the room let? And just think—to a person like Gregers—a good old friend.

GINA. Well, I don't know what to say about it.

HEDVIG. Oh, mother, you'll see; it'll be such fun!

HIALMAR. You're very strange. You were so bent upon getting the room let before; and now you don't like it.

GINA. Yes, I do, Ekdal; if it had only been to some one else——— But what do you suppose Mr. Werle will say?

HIALMAR. Old Werle? It doesn't concern him.

GINA. But surely you can see that there's something amiss between them again, or the young man wouldn't be leaving home. You know very well those two can't get on with each other.

HIALMAR. Very likely not, but———

GINA. And now Mr. Werle may fancy it's you that has egged him on———

HIALMAR. Let him fancy so, then! Mr. Werle has done a great deal for me; far be it from me to deny it. But that doesn't make me everlastingly dependent upon him.

GINA. But, my dear Ekdal, maybe grandfather'll suffer for it. He may lose the little bit of work he gets from Gråberg.

HIALMAR. I could almost say: so much the better! Is it not humiliating for a man like me to see his grey-haired father treated as a pariah? But now I believe the fulness of time is at hand. [*Takes a fresh piece of bread and butter*] As sure as I have a mission in life, I mean to fulfil it now!

HEDVIG. Oh, yes, father, do!

GINA. Hush! Don't wake him!

HIALMAR. [*More softly*] I will fulfil it, I say. The day shall come when——— And that is why I say it's a good thing we have let the room; for that makes me more independent. The man who has a mission in life must be independent. [*By the armchair, with emotion*] Poor old white-haired father! Rely on your Hialmar. He has broad shoulders—strong shoulders, at any rate. You shall yet wake up some fine day and——— [*To* GINA] Do you not believe it?

GINA. [*Rising*] Yes, of course I do; but in the meantime suppose we see about getting him to bed.

HIALMAR. Yes, come.

[*They take hold of the old man carefully.*]

Act III

SCENE—HIALMAR EKDAL'S *studio. It is morning: the daylight shines through the large window in the slanting roof; the curtain is drawn back.*

HIALMAR *is sitting at the table, busy retouching a photograph;*

several others lie before him. Presently GINA, *wearing her hat and cloak, enters by the passage door; she has a covered basket on her arm.*

HIALMAR. Back already, Gina?

GINA. Oh, yes, one can't let the grass grow under one's feet.
[*Sets her basket on a chair and takes off her things.*]

HIALMAR. Did you look in at Gregers' room?

GINA. Yes, that I did. It's a rare sight, I can tell you; he's made a pretty mess to start off with.

HIALMAR. How so?

GINA. He was determined to do everything for himself, he said; so he sets to work to light the stove, and what must he do but screw down the damper till the whole room is full of smoke. Ugh! There was a smell fit to——

HIALMAR. Well, really!

GINA. But that's not the worst of it; for then he thinks he'll put out the fire, and goes and empties his water-jug into the stove and so makes the whole floor one filthy puddle.

HIALMAR. How annoying!

GINA. I've got the porter's wife to clear up after him, pig that he is! But the room won't be fit to live in till the afternoon.

HIALMAR. What's he doing with himself in the meantime?

GINA. He said he was going out for a little while.

HIALMAR. I looked in upon him, too, for a moment—after you had gone.

GINA. So I heard. You've asked him to lunch.

HIALMAR. Just to a little bit of early lunch, you know. It's his first day—we can hardly do less. You've got something in the house, I suppose?

GINA. I shall have to find something or other.

HIALMAR. And don't cut it too fine, for I fancy Relling and Molvik are coming up, too. I just happened to meet Relling on the stairs, you see; so I had to——

GINA. Oh, are we to have those two as well?

HIALMAR. Good Lord—couple more or less can't make any difference.

OLD EKDAL. [*Opens his door and looks in*] I say, Hialmar—— [*Sees* GINA] Oh!

GINA. Do you want anything, grandfather?

EKDAL. Oh, no, it doesn't matter. H'm! [*Retires again.*]

GINA. [*Takes up the basket*] Be sure you see that he doesn't go out.

HIALMAR. All right, all right. And, Gina, a little herring-salad wouldn't be a bad idea; Relling and Molvik were out on the loose again last night.

GINA. If only they don't come before I'm ready for them——

HIALMAR. No, of course they won't; take your own time.

GINA. Very well; and meanwhile you can be working a bit.

HIALMAR. Well, I am working! I am working as hard as I can!

GINA. Then you'll have that job off your hands, you see.

[*She goes out to the kitchen with her basket.* HIALMAR *sits for a time penciling away at the photograph in an indolent and listless manner.*]

EKDAL. [*Peeps in, looks round the studio and says softly*] Are you busy?

HIALMAR. Yes, I'm toiling at these wretched pictures——

EKDAL. Well, well, never mind,—since you're so busy—h'm!

[*He goes out again; the door stands open.*]

HIALMAR. [*Continues for some time in silence; then he lays down his brush and goes over to the door*] Are you busy, father?

EKDAL. [*In a grumbling tone, within*] If you're busy, I'm busy, too. H'm!

HIALMAR. Oh, very well, then.   [*Goes to his work again.*]

EKDAL. [*Presently, coming to the door again*] H'm; I say, Hialmar, I'm not so very busy, you know.

HIALMAR. I thought you were writing.

EKDAL. Oh, the devil take it! can't Gråberg wait a day or two? After all, it's not a matter of life and death.

HIALMAR. No; and you're not his slave either.

EKDAL. And about that other business in there——

HIALMAR. Just what I was thinking of. Do you want to go in? Shall I open the door for you?

EKDAL. Well, it wouldn't be a bad notion.

HIALMAR. [*Rises*] Then we'd have that off our hands.

EKDAL. Yes, exactly. It's got to be ready first thing tomorrow. It is tomorrow, isn't it? H'm?

HIALMAR. Yes, of course it's tomorrow.

[HIALMAR *and* EKDAL *push aside each his half of the sliding door. The morning sun is shining in through the skylights; some doves are flying about; others sit cooing, upon the perches; the hens are heard clucking now and then, further back in the garret.*]

HIALMAR. There; now you can get to work, father.

EKDAL. [*Goes in*] Aren't you coming, too?

HIALMAR. Well, really, do you know——; I almost think—— [*Sees* GINA *at the kitchen door*] I? No; I haven't time; I must work.— But now for our new contrivance——

[*He pulls a cord, a curtain slips down inside, the lower part consisting of a piece of old sailcloth, the upper part of a stretched fishing net. The floor of the garret is thus no longer visible.*]

HIALMAR. [*Goes to the table*] So! Now, perhaps I can sit in peace for a little while.

GINA. Is he rampaging in there again?

HIALMAR. Would you rather have had him slip down to Madame Eriksen's? [*Seats himself*] Do you want anything? You know you said——

GINA. I only wanted to ask if you think we can lay the table for lunch here?

HIALMAR. Yes; we have no early appointment, I suppose?

GINA. No, I expect no one today except those two sweethearts that are to be taken together.

HIALMAR. Why the deuce couldn't they be taken together another day?

GINA. Don't you know I told them to come in the afternoon, when you are having your nap?

HIALMAR. Oh, that's capital. Very well, let us have lunch here then.

GINA. All right; but there's no hurry about laying the cloth; you can have the table for a good while yet.

HIALMAR. Do you think I am not sticking at my work? I'm at it as hard as I can!

GINA. Then you'll be free later on, you know.

[*Goes out into the kitchen again. Short pause.*]

EKDAL. [*In the garret doorway, behind the net*] Hialmar!

HIALMAR. Well?

EKDAL. Afraid we shall have to move the water-trough, after all.

HIALMAR. What else have I been saying all along?

EKDAL. H'm—h'm—h'm.

[*Goes away from the door again.* HIALMAR *goes on working a little; glances towards the garret and half rises.* HEDVIG *comes in from the kitchen.*]

HIALMAR. [*Sits down again hurriedly*] What do you want?

HEDVIG. I only wanted to come in beside you, father.

HIALMAR. [*After a pause*] What makes you go prying around like that? Perhaps you are told off to watch me?

HEDVIG. No, no.

HIALMAR. What is your mother doing out there?

HEDVIG. Oh, mother's in the middle of making the herring-salad. [*Goes to the table*] Isn't there any little thing I could help you with, father?

HIALMAR. Oh, no. It is right that I should bear the whole burden—— so long as my strength holds out. Set your mind at rest, Hedvig; if only your father keeps his health——

HEDVIG. Oh, no, father! You mustn't talk in that horrid way.
[*She wanders about a little, stops by the doorway and looks into the garret.*]

HIALMAR. Tell me, what is he doing?

HEDVIG. I think he's making a new path to the water-trough.

HIALMAR. He can never manage that by himself! And here am I doomed to sit——!

HEDVIG. [*Goes to him*] Let me take the brush, father; I can do it, quite well.

HIALMAR. Oh, nonsense; you will only hurt your eyes.

HEDVIG. Not a bit. Give me the brush.

HIALMAR. [*Rising*] Well, it won't take more than a minute or two.

HEDVIG. Pooh, what harm can it do then? [*Takes the brush*] There!
[*Seats herself*] I can begin upon this one.

HIALMAR. But mind you don't hurt your eyes! Do you hear? *I* won't be answerable; you do it on your own responsibility—understand that.

HEDVIG. [*Retouching*] Yes, yes, I understand.

HIALMAR. You are quite clever at it, Hedvig. Only a minute or two, you know.
[*He slips through by the edge of the curtain into the garret.* HEDVIG *sits at her work.* HIALMAR *and* EKDAL *are heard disputing inside.*]

HIALMAR. [*Appears behind the net*] I say, Hedvig—give me those pincers that are lying on the shelf. And the chisel. [*Turns away inside*] Now you shall see, father. Just let me show you first what I mean!
[HEDVIG *has fetched the required tools from the shelf and hands them to him through the net.*]

HIALMAR. Ah, thanks. I didn't come a moment too soon.
[*Goes back from the curtain again; they are heard carpentering and talking inside.* HEDVIG *stands looking in at them. A moment later there is a knock at the passage door; she does not notice it.*]

GREGERS WERLE. [*Bareheaded, in indoor dress, enters and stops near the door*] H'm——!

HEDVIG. [*Turns and goes towards him*] Good morning. Please come in.

GREGERS. Thank you. [*Looking towards the garret*] You seem to have workpeople in the house.

HEDVIG. No, it is only father and grandfather. I'll tell them you are here.

GREGERS. No, no, don't do that; I would rather wait a little.
[*Seats himself on the sofa.*]

HEDVIG. It looks so untidy here——

[*Begins to clear away the photographs.*]

GREGERS. Oh, don't take them away. Are those prints that have to be finished off?

HEDVIG. Yes, they are a few I was helping father with.

GREGERS. Please don't let me disturb you.

HEDVIG. Oh, no.

[*She gathers the things to her and sits down to work;* GREGERS *looks at her, meanwhile, in silence.*]

GREGERS. Did the wild duck sleep well last night?

HEDVIG. Yes, I think so, thanks.

GREGERS. [*Turning towards the garret*] It looks quite different by day from what it did last night in the moonlight.

HEDVIG. Yes, it changes ever so much. It looks different in the morning and in the afternoon; and it's different on rainy days from what it is in fine weather. ·

GREGERS. Have you noticed that?

HEDVIG. Yes, how could I help it?

GREGERS. Are you, too, fond of being in there with the wild duck?

HEDVIG. Yes, when I can manage it——

GREGERS. But I suppose you haven't much spare time; you go to school, no doubt.

HEDVIG. No, not now; father is afraid of my hurting my eyes.

GREGERS. Oh; then he reads with you himself?

HEDVIG. Father has promised to read with me; but he has never had time yet.

GREGERS. Then is there nobody else to give you a little help?

HEDVIG. Yes, there is Mr. Molvik; but he is not always exactly— quite——

GREGERS. Sober?

HEDVIG. Yes, I suppose that's it!

GREGERS. Why, then you must have any amount of time on your hands. And in there I suppose it is a sort of world by itself?

HEDVIG. Oh, yes, quite. And there are such lots of wonderful things.

GREGERS. Indeed?

HEDVIG. Yes, there are big cupboards full of books; and a great many of the books have pictures in them.

GREGERS. Aha!

HEDVIG. And there's an old bureau with drawers and flaps, and a big clock with figures that go out and in. But the clock isn't going now.

GREGERS. So time has come to a standstill in there—in the wild duck's domain.

HEDVIG. Yes. And then there's an old paint-box and things of that sort, and all the books.

GREGERS. And you read the books, I suppose?

HEDVIG. Oh, yes, when I get the chance. Most of them are English though, and I don't understand English. But then I look at the pictures.—There is one great big book called "Harrison's History of London."[3] It must be a hundred years old; and there are such heaps of pictures in it. At the beginning there is Death with an hour-glass and a woman. I think that is horrid. But then there are all the other pictures of churches, and castles, and streets, and great ships sailing on the sea.

GREGERS. But tell me, where did all those wonderful things come from?

HEDVIG. Oh, an old sea captain once lived here, and he brought them home with him. They used to call him "The Flying Dutchman." That was curious, because he wasn't a Dutchman at all.

GREGERS. Was he not?

HEDVIG. No. But at last he was drowned at sea, and so he left all those things behind him.

GREGERS. Tell me now—when you are sitting in there looking at the pictures, don't you wish you could travel and see the real world for yourself?

HEDVIG. Oh, no! I mean always to stay at home and help father and mother.

GREGERS. To retouch photographs?

HEDVIG. No, not only that. I should love above everything to learn to engrave pictures like those in the English books.

GREGERS. H'm. What does your father say to that?

HEDVIG. I don't think father likes it; father is strange about such things. Only think, he talks of my learning basket-making and straw-plaiting! But I don't think that would be much good.

GREGERS. Oh, no, I don't think so either.

HEDVIG. But father was right in saying that if I had learnt basket-making I could have made the new basket for the wild duck.

GREGERS. So you could; and it was you that ought to have done it, wasn't it?

HEDVIG. Yes, for it's my wild duck.

GREGERS. Of course it is.

HEDVIG. Yes, it belongs to me. But I lend it to father and grandfather as often as they please.

GREGERS. Indeed? What do they do with it?

HEDVIG. Oh, they look after it, and build places for it, and so on.

GREGERS. I see; for no doubt the wild duck is by far the most distinguished inhabitant of the garret?

HEDVIG. Yes, indeed she is; for she is a real wild fowl, you know.

---

3. *A New and Universal History of the Cities of London and Westminster,* by Walter Harrison, London, 1775, folio. [Translator's note.]

And then she is so much to be pitied; she has no one to care for,
poor thing.

GREGERS. She has no family, as the rabbits have——

HEDVIG. No. The hens, too, many of them, were chickens together;
but she has been taken right away from all her friends. And then
there is so much that is strange about the wild duck. Nobody
knows her, and nobody knows where she came from either.

GREGERS. And she has been down in the depths of the sea.

HEDVIG. [*With a quick glance at him, represses a smile and asks*]
Why do you say "depths of the sea"?

GREGERS. What else should I say?

HEDVIG. You could say "the bottom of the sea."[4]

GREGERS. Oh, mayn't I just as well say the depths of the sea?

HEDVIG. Yes; but it sounds so strange to me when other people
speak of the depths of the sea.

GREGERS. Why so? Tell me why?

HEDVIG. No, I won't; it's so stupid.

GREGERS. Oh, no, I am sure it's not. Do tell me why you smiled.

HEDVIG. Well, this is the reason: whenever I come to realize suddenly—in a flash—what is in there, it always seems to me that
the whole room and everything in it should be called "the depths
of the sea."—But that is so stupid.

GREGERS. You mustn't say that.

HEDVIG. Oh, yes, for you know it is only a garret.

GREGERS. [*Looks fixedly at her*] Are you so sure of that?

HEDVIG. [*Astonished*] That it's a garret?

GREGERS. Are you quite certain of it?

> [HEDVIG *is silent, and looks at him open-mouthed.* GINA
> *comes in from the kitchen with the table things.*]

GREGERS. [*Rising*] I have come in upon you too early.

GINA. Oh, you must be somewhere; and we're nearly ready now, anyway. Clear the table, Hedvig.

> [HEDVIG *clears away her things; she and* GINA *lay the cloth
> during what follows.* GREGERS *seats himself in the armchair
> and turns over an album.*]

GREGERS. I hear you can retouch, Mrs. Ekdal.

GINA. [*With a side glance*] Yes, I can.

GREGERS. That was exceedingly lucky.

GINA. How—lucky?

GREGERS. Since Ekdal took to photography, I mean.

HEDVIG. Mother can take photographs, too.

GINA. Oh, yes; I was bound to learn that.

---

4. Gregers here uses the old-fashioned
expression "havsens bund," while Hedvig would have him use the more commonplace "havets bund" or "havbun-
den." [Translator's note.]

GREGERS. So it is really you that carry on the business, I suppose?

GINA. Yes, when Ekdal hasn't time himself——

GREGERS. He is a great deal taken up with his old father, I daresay.

GINA. Yes; and then you can't expect a man like Ekdal to do nothing but take pictures of Dick, Tom, and Harry.

GREGERS. I quite agree with you; but having once gone in for the thing——

GINA. You can surely understand, Mr. Werle, that Ekdal's not like one of your common photographers.

GREGERS. Of course not; but still——

[A shot is fired within the garret.]

GREGERS [Starting up] What's that?

GINA. Ugh! now they're firing again!

GREGERS. Have they firearms in there?

HEDVIG. They are out shooting.

GREGERS. What! [At the door of the garret] Are you shooting, Hialmar?

HIALMAR. [Inside the net] Are you there? I didn't know; I was so taken up—— [To HEDVIG] Why did you not let us know? [Comes into the studio.]

GREGERS. Do you go shooting in the garret?

HIALMAR. [Showing a double-barrelled pistol] Oh, only with this thing.

GINA. Yes, you and grandfather will do yourselves a mischief some day with that there pigstol.

HIALMAR. [With irritation] I believe I have told you that this kind of firearm is called a pistol.

GINA. Oh, that doesn't make it much better, that I can see.

GREGERS. So you have become a sportsman, too, Hialmar?

HIALMAR. Only a little rabbit-shooting now and then. Mostly to please father, you understand.

GINA. Men are strange beings; they must always have something to pervert theirselves with.

HIALMAR. [Snappishly] Just so; we must always have something to divert ourselves with.

GINA. Yes, that's just what I say.

HIALMAR. H'm. [To GREGERS] You see the garret is fortunately so situated that no one can hear us shooting. [Lays the pistol on the top shelf of the bookcase] Don't touch the pistol, Hedvig! One of the barrels is loaded; remember that.

GREGERS. [Looking through the net] You have a fowling-piece, too, I see.

HIALMAR. That is father's old gun. It's no use now; something has gone wrong with the lock. But it's fun to have it all the same; for we can take it to pieces now and then, and clean and grease it.

and screw it together again.—Of course, it's mostly father that fiddle-faddles with all that sort of thing.

HEDVIG. [*Beside* GREGERS] Now you can see the wild duck properly.

GREGERS. I was just looking at her. One of her wings seems to me to droop a bit.

HEDVIG. Well, no wonder; her wing was broken, you know.

GREGERS. And she trails one foot a little. Isn't that so?

HIALMAR. Perhaps a very little bit.

HEDVIG. Yes, it was by that foot the dog took hold of her.

HIALMAR. But otherwise she hasn't the least thing the matter with her; and that is simply marvellous for a creature that has a charge of shot in her body and has been between a dog's teeth——

GREGERS. [*With a glance at* HEDVIG] ——and that has lain in the depths of the sea—so long.

HEDVIG. [*Smiling*] Yes.

GINA. [*Laying the table*] That blessed wild duck! What a lot of fuss you do make over her.

HIALMAR. H'm;—will lunch soon be ready?

GINA. Yes, directly. Hedvig, you must come and help me now.

[GINA *and* HEDVIG *go out into the kitchen.*]

HIALMAR. [*In a low voice*] I think you had better not stand there looking in at father; he doesn't like it. [GREGERS *moves away from the garret door.*] Besides, I may as well shut up before the others come. [*Claps his hands to drive the fowls back*] Shh—shh, in with you! [*Draws up the curtain and pulls the doors together*] All the contrivances are my own invention. It's really quite amusing to have things of this sort to potter with and to put to rights when they get out of order. And it's absolutely necessary, too; for Gina objects to having rabbits and fowls in the studio.

GREGERS. To be sure; and I suppose the studio is your wife's special department?

HIALMAR. As a rule, I leave the everyday details of business to her; for then I can take refuge in the parlor and give my mind to more important things.

GREGERS. What things may they be, Hialmar?

HIALMAR. I wonder you have not asked that question sooner. But perhaps you haven't heard of the invention?

GREGERS. The invention? No.

HIALMAR. Really? Have you not? Oh, no, out there in the wilds——

GREGERS. So you have invented something, have you?

HIALMAR. It is not quite completed yet; but I am working at it. You can easily imagine that when I resolved to devote myself to photography, it wasn't simply with the idea of taking likenesses of all sorts of commonplace people.

GREGERS. No; your wife was saying the same thing just now.

HIALMAR. I swore that if I consecrated my powers to this handicraft, I would so exalt it that it should become both an art and a science. And to that end I determined to make this great invention.

GREGERS. And what is the nature of the invention? What purpose does it serve?

HIALMAR. Oh, my dear fellow, you mustn't ask for details yet. It takes time, you see. And you must not think that my motive is vanity. It is not for my own sake that I am working. Oh, no; it is my life's mission that stands before me night and day.

GREGERS. What is your life's mission?

HIALMAR. Do you forget the old man with the silver hair?

GREGERS. Your poor father? Well, but what can you do for him?

HIALMAR. I can raise up his self-respect from the dead, by restoring the name of Ekdal to honor and dignity.

GREGERS. Then that is your life's mission?

HIALMAR. Yes. I will rescue the shipwrecked man. For shipwrecked he was, by the very first blast of the storm. Even while those terrible investigations were going on, he was no longer himself. That pistol there—the one we use to shoot rabbits with—has played its part in the tragedy of the house of Ekdal.

GREGERS. The pistol? Indeed?

HIALMAR. When the sentence of imprisonment was passed—he had the pistol in his hand——

GREGERS. Had he——?

HIALMAR. Yes; but he dared not use it. His courage failed him. So broken, so demoralized was he even then! Oh, can you understand it? He, a soldier; he, who had shot nine bears, and who was descended from two lieutenant-colonels—one after the other, of course. Can you understand it, Gregers?

GREGERS. Yes, I understand it well enough.

HIALMAR. I cannot. And once more the pistol played a part in the history of our house. When he had put on the grey clothes and was under lock and key—oh, that was a terrible time for me, I can tell you. I kept the blinds drawn down over both my windows. When I peeped out, I saw the sun shining as if nothing had happened. I could not understand it. I saw people going along the street, laughing and talking about indifferent things. I could not understand it. It seemed to me that the whole of existence must be at a standstill—as if under an eclipse.

GREGERS. I felt that, too, when my mother died.

HIALMAR. It was in such an hour that Hialmar Ekdal pointed the pistol at his own breast.

GREGERS. You, too, thought of——!

HIALMAR. Yes.

GREGERS. But you did not fire?

HIALMAR. No. At the decisive moment I won the victory over myself. I remained in life. But I can assure you it takes some courage
to choose life under circumstances like those.

GREGERS. Well, that depends on how you look at it.

HIALMAR. Yes, indeed, it takes courage. But I am glad I was firm:
for now I shall soon perfect my invention; and Dr. Relling
thinks, as I do myself, that father may be allowed to wear his uniform again. I will demand that as my sole reward.

GREGERS. So that is what he meant about his uniform——?

HIALMAR. Yes, that is what he most yearns for. You can't think
how my heart bleeds for him. Every time we celebrate any little
family festival—Gina's and my wedding-day, or whatever it may
be—in comes the old man in the lieutenant's uniform of happier
days. But if he only hears a knock at the door—for he daren't
show himself to strangers, you know—he hurries back to his room
again as fast as his old legs can carry him. Oh, it's heart-rending
for a son to see such things!

GREGERS. How long do you think it will take you to finish your invention?

HIALMAR. Come now, you mustn't expect me to enter into particulars like that. An invention is not a thing completely under
one's own control. It depends largely on inspiration—on intuition
—and it is almost impossible to predict when the inspiration may
come.

GREGERS. But it's advancing?

HIALMAR. Yes, certainly, it is advancing. I turn it over in my mind
every day; I am full of it. Every afternoon, when I have had my
dinner, I shut myself up in the parlor, where I can ponder undisturbed. But I can't be goaded to it; it's not a bit of good;
Relling says so, too.

GREGERS. And you don't think that all that business in the garret
draws you off and distracts you too much?

HIALMAR. No, no, no; quite the contrary. You mustn't say that. I
cannot be everlastingly absorbed in the same laborious train of
thought. I must have something alongside of it to fill up the time
of waiting. The inspiration, the intuition, you see—when it
comes, it comes, and there's an end of it.

GREGERS. My dear Hialmar, I almost think you have something of
the wild duck in you.

HIALMAR. Something of the wild duck? How do you mean?

GREGERS. You have dived down and bitten yourself fast in the
undergrowth.

HIALMAR. Are you alluding to the well-nigh fatal shot that has
broken my father's wing—and mine, too?

GREGERS. Not exactly to that. I don't say that your wing has been broken; but you have strayed into a poisonous marsh, Hialmar; an insidious disease has taken hold of you, and you have sunk down to die in the dark.

HIALMAR. I? To die in the dark? Look here, Gregers, you must really leave off talking such nonsense.

GREGERS. Don't be afraid; I shall find a way to help you up again. I, too, have a mission in life now; I found it yesterday.

HIALMAR. That's all very well; but you will please leave me out of it. I can assure you that—apart from my very natural melancholy, of course—I am as contented as any one can wish to be.

GREGERS. Your contentment is an effect of the marsh poison.

HIALMAR. Now, my dear Gregers, pray do not go on about disease and poison; I am not used to that sort of talk. In my house nobody ever speaks to me about unpleasant things.

GREGERS. Ah, that I can easily believe.

HIALMAR. It's not good for me, you see. And there are no marsh poisons here, as you express it. The poor photographer's roof is lowly, I know—and my circumstances are narrow. But I am an inventor, and I am the breadwinner of a family. That exalts me above my mean surroundings.—Ah, here comes lunch!

[GINA *and* HEDVIG *bring bottles of ale, a decanter of brandy, glasses, etc. At the same time,* RELLING *and* MOLVIK *enter from the passage; they are both without hat or overcoat.* MOLVIK *is dressed in black.*]

GINA. [*Placing the things upon the table*] Ah, you two have come in the nick of time.

RELLING. Molvik got it into his head that he could smell herring-salad, and then there was no holding him.—Good morning again, Ekdal.

HIALMAR. Gregers, let me introduce you to Mr. Molvik. Doctor—— Oh, you know Relling, don't you?

GREGERS. Yes, slightly.

RELLING. Oh, Mr. Werle, junior! Yes, we two have had one or two little skirmishes up at the Höidal works. You've just moved in?

GREGERS. I moved in this morning.

RELLING. Molvik and I live right under you, so you haven't far to go for the doctor and the clergyman, if you should need anything in that line.

GREGERS. Thanks, it's not quite unlikely, for yesterday we were thirteen at table.

HIALMAR. Oh, come now, don't let us get upon unpleasant subjects again!

RELLING. You may make your mind easy, Ekdal; I'll be hanged if the finger of fate points to you.

HIALMAR. I should hope not, for the sake of my family. But let us sit down now, and eat and drink and be merry.

GREGERS. Shall we not wait for your father?

HIALMAR. No, his lunch will be taken in to him later. Come along! [*The men seat themselves at table, and eat and drink.* GINA *and* HEDVIG *go in and out and wait upon them.*]

RELLING. Molvik was frightfully stewed yesterday, Mrs. Ekdal.

GINA. Really? Yesterday again?

RELLING. Didn't you hear him when I brought him home last night?

GINA. No, I can't say I did.

RELLING. That was a good thing, for Molvik was disgusting last night.

GINA. Is that true, Molvik?

MOLVIK. Let us draw a veil over last night's proceedings. That sort of thing is totally foreign to my better self.

RELLING. [*To* GREGERS] It comes over him like a sort of possession, and then I have to go out on the loose with him. Mr. Molvik is dæmonic, you see.

GREGERS. Dæmonic?

RELLING. Molvik is dæmonic, yes.

GREGERS. H'm.

RELLING. And dæmonic natures are not made to walk straight through the world; they must meander a little now and then.— Well, so you still stick up there at those horrible grimy works?

GREGERS. I have stuck there until now.

RELLING. And did you ever manage to collect that claim you went about presenting?

GREGERS. Claim? [*Understands him*] Ah. I see.

HIALMAR. Have you been presenting claims, Gregers?

GREGERS. Oh, nonsense.

RELLING. Faith, but he has, though! He went around to all the cottars' cabins presenting something he called "the claim of the ideal."

GREGERS. I was young then.

RELLING. You're right; you were very young. And as for the claim of the ideal—you never got it honored while *I* was up there.

GREGERS. Nor since either.

RELLING. Ah, then you've learnt to knock a little discount off, I expect.

GREGERS. Never, when I have a true man to deal with.

HIALMAR. No, I should think not, indeed. A little butter, Gina.

RELLING. And a slice of bacon for Molvik.

MOLVIK. Ugh; not bacon! [*A knock at the garret door.*]

HIALMAR. Open the door, Hedvig; father wants to come out.

[HEDVIG *goes over and opens the door a little way;* EKDAL *en-*

ters with a fresh rabbit-skin; she closes the door after him.]

EKDAL. Good morning, gentlemen! Good sport today. Shot a big one.

HIALMAR. And you've gone and skinned it without waiting for me——!

EKDAL. Salted it, too. It's good tender meat, is rabbit; it's sweet; it tastes like sugar. Good appetite to you, gentlemen!

[*Goes into his room.*]

MOLVIK. [*Rising*] Excuse me——; I can't——; I must get downstairs immediately——

RELLING. Drink some soda water, man!

MOLVIK. [*Hurrying away*] Ugh—ugh!

[*Goes out by the passage door.*]

RELLING. [*To* HIALMAR] Let us drain a glass to the old hunter.

HIALMAR. [*Clinks glasses with him*] To the undaunted sportsman who has looked death in the face!

RELLING. To the grey-haired—— [*Drinks*] By-the-bye, is his hair grey or white?

HIALMAR. Something between the two, I fancy; for that matter, he has very few hairs left of any color.

RELLING. Well, well, one can get through the world with a wig. After all, you are a happy man, Ekdal; you have your noble mission to labor for———

HIALMAR. And I do labor, I can tell you.

RELLING. And then you have your excellent wife, shuffling quietly in and out in her felt slippers, and that seesaw walk of hers, and making everything cosy and comfortable about you.

HIALMAR. Yes, Gina—[*Nods to her*]—you were a good helpmate on the path of life.

GINA. Oh, don't sit there cricketizing me.

RELLING. And your Hedvig, too, Ekdal!

HIALMAR. [*Affected*] The child, yes! The child before everything! Hedvig, come here to me. [*Strokes her hair*] What day is it tomorrow, eh?

HEDVIG. [*Shaking him*] Oh, no, you're not to say anything, father.

HIALMAR. It cuts me to the heart when I think what a poor affair it will be; only a little festivity in the garret——

HEDVIG. Oh, but that's just what I like!

RELLING. Just you wait till the wonderful invention sees the light, Hedvig!

HIALMAR. Yes, indeed—then you shall see——! Hedvig, I have resolved to make your future secure. You shall live in comfort all your days. I will demand—something or other—on your behalf. That shall be the poor inventor's sole reward.

HEDVIG. [*Whispering, with her arms round his neck*] Oh, you dear, kind father!

RELLING. [*To* GREGERS] Come now, don't you find it pleasant, for once in a way, to sit at a well-spread table in a happy family circle?

HIALMAR. Ah, yes, I really prize these social hours.

GREGERS. For my part, I don't thrive in marsh vapors.

RELLING. Marsh vapors?

HIALMAR. Oh, don't begin with that stuff again!

GINA. Goodness knows there's no vapors in this house, Mr. Werle; I give the place a good airing every blessed day.

GREGERS. [*Leaves the table*] No airing you can give will drive out the taint I mean.

HIALMAR. Taint!

GINA. Yes, what do you say to that, Ekdal?

RELLING. Excuse me—may it not be you yourself that have brought the taint from those mines up there?

GREGERS. It is like you to call what I bring into this house a taint.

RELLING. [*Goes up to him*] Look here, Mr. Werle, junior: I have a strong suspicion that you are still carrying about that "claim of the ideal," large as life, in your coat-tail pocket.

GREGERS. I carry it in my breast.

RELLING. Well, wherever you carry it, I advise you not to come dunning us with it here, so long as *I* am on the premises.

GREGERS. And if I do so nonetheless?

RELLING. Then you'll go head-foremost down the stairs; now I've warned you.

HIALMAR [*Rising*] Oh, but Relling——!

GREGERS. Yes, you may turn me out——

GINA. [*Interposing between them*] We can't have that, Relling. But I must say, Mr. Werle, it ill becomes you to talk about vapors and taints, after all the mess you made with your stove.

[*A knock at the passage door.*]

HEDVIG. Mother, there's somebody knocking.

HIALMAR. There now, we're going to have a whole lot of people!

GINA. I'll go—— [*Goes over and opens the door, starts, and draws back*] Oh—oh, dear!

[WERLE, *in a fur coat, advances one step into the room.*]

WERLE. Excuse me, but I think my son is staying here.

GINA. [*With a gulp*] Yes.

HIALMAR. [*Approaching him*] Won't you do us the honor to——?

WERLE. Thank you, I merely wish to speak to my son.

GREGERS. What is it? Here I am.

WERLE. I want a few words with you, in your room.

GREGERS. In my room? Very well—— [*About to go.*]

GINA. No, no, your room's not in a fit state——

WERLE. Well then, out in the passage here; I want to have a few words with you alone.

HIALMAR. You can have them here, sir. Come into the parlor, Relling.

[HIALMAR *and* RELLING *go off to the right.* GINA *takes* HEDVIG *with her into the kitchen.*]

GREGERS. [*After a short pause*] Well, now we are alone.

WERLE. From something you let fall last evening, and from your coming to lodge with the Ekdals, I can't help inferring that you intend to make yourself unpleasant to me in one way or another.

GREGERS. I intend to open Hialmar Ekdal's eyes. He shall see his position as it really is—that is all.

WERLE. Is that the mission in life you spoke of yesterday?

GREGERS. Yes. You have left me no other.

WERLE. Is it I, then, that have crippled your mind, Gregers?

GREGERS. You have crippled my whole life. I am not thinking of all that about mother—— But it's thanks to you that I am continually haunted and harassed by a guilty conscience.

WERLE. Indeed! It is your conscience that troubles you, is it?

GREGERS. I ought to have taken a stand against you when the trap was set for Lieutenant Ekdal. I ought to have cautioned him, for I had a misgiving as to what was in the wind.

WERLE. Yes, that was the time to have spoken.

GREGERS. I did not dare to, I was so cowed and spiritless. I was mortally afraid of you—not only then, but long afterwards.

WERLE. You have got over that fear now, it appears.

GREGERS. Yes, fortunately. The wrong done to old Ekdal, both by me and by—others, can never be undone; but Hialmar I can rescue from all the falsehood and deception that are bringing him to ruin.

WERLE. Do you think that will be doing him a kindness?

GREGERS. I have not the least doubt of it.

WERLE. You think our worthy photographer is the sort of man to appreciate such friendly offices?

GREGERS. Yes, I do.

WERLE. H'm—we shall see.

GREGERS. Besides, if I am to go on living, I must try to find some cure for my sick conscience.

WERLE. It will never be sound. Your conscience has been sickly from childhood. That is a legacy from your mother, Gregers—the only one she left you.

GREGERS. [*With a scornful half-smile*] Have you not yet forgiven her for the mistake you made in supposing she would bring you a fortune?

WERLE. Don't let us wander from the point.—Then you hold to your purpose of setting young Ekdal upon what you imagine to be the right scent?

GREGERS. Yes, that is my fixed resolve.

WERLE. Well, in that case I might have spared myself this visit; for, of course, it is useless to ask whether you will return home with me?

GREGERS. Quite useless.

WERLE. And I suppose you won't enter the firm either?

GREGERS. No.

WERLE. Very good. But as I am thinking of marrying again, your share in the property will fall to you at once.[5]

GREGERS. [*Quickly*] No, I do not want that.

WERLE. You don't want it?

GREGERS. No, I dare not take it, for conscience' sake.

WERLE. [*After a pause*] Are you going up to the works again?

GREGERS. No; I consider myself released from your service.

WERLE. But what are you going to do?

GREGERS. Only to fulfil my mission; nothing more.

WERLE. Well, but afterwards? What are you going to live upon?

GREGERS. I have laid by a little out of my salary.

WERLE. How long will that last?

GREGERS. I think it will last my time.

WERLE. What do you mean?

GREGERS. I shall answer no more questions.

WERLE. Good-bye then, Gregers.

GREGERS. Good-bye.   [WERLE *goes.*]

HIALMAR. [*Peeping in*] He's gone, isn't he?

GREGERS. Yes.

    [HIALMAR *and* RELLING *enter; also* GINA *and* HEDVIG *from the kitchen.*]

RELLING. That luncheon-party was a failure.

GREGERS. Put on your coat, Hialmar; I want you to come for a long walk with me.

HIALMAR. With pleasure. What was it your father wanted? Had it anything to do with me?

GREGERS. Come along. We must have a talk. I'll go and put on my overcoat.

    [*Goes out by the passage door.*]

GINA. You shouldn't go out with him, Ekdal.

5. By Norwegian law, before a widower can marry again, a certain proportion of his property must be settled on his children by his former marriage. [Translator's note.]

RELLING. No, don't you do it. Stay where you are.

HIALMAR. [Gets his hat and overcoat] Oh, nonsense! When a friend of my youth feels impelled to open his mind to me in private——

RELLING. But devil take it——don't you see that the fellow's mad, cracked, demented?

GINA. There, what did I tell you? His mother before him had crazy fits like that sometimes.

HIALMAR. The more need for a friend's watchful eye. [To GINA] Be sure you have dinner ready in good time. Good-bye for the present.

[Goes out by the passage door.]

RELLING. It's a thousand pities the fellow didn't go to hell through one of the Höidal mines.

GINA. Good Lord! what makes you say that?

RELLING. [Muttering] Oh, I have my own reasons.

GINA. Do you think young Werle is really mad?

RELLING. No, worse luck; he's no madder than most other people. But one disease he has certainly got in his system.

GINA. What's the matter with him?

RELLING. Well, I'll tell you, Mrs. Ekdal. He is suffering from an acute attack of integrity.

GINA. Integrity?

HEDVIG. Is that a kind of disease?

RELLING. Yes, it's a national disease; but it only appears sporadically. [Nods to GINA] Thanks for your hospitality.

[He goes out by the passage door.]

GINA. [Moving restlessly to and fro] Ugh, that Gregers Werle—he was always a wretched creature.

HEDVIG. [Standing by the table and looking searchingly at her] I think all this is very strange.

Act IV

SCENE—HIALMAR EKDAL'S studio. A photograph has just been taken; a camera with the cloth over it, a pedestal, two chairs, a folding table, etc., are standing out in the room. Afternoon light; the sun is going down; a little later it begins to grow dusk.

GINA stands in the passage doorway, with a little box and a wet glass plate in her hand, and is speaking to somebody outside.

GINA. Yes, certainly. When I make a promise I keep it. The first dozen shall be ready on Monday. Good afternoon.

[Someone is heard going downstairs. GINA shuts the door, slips the plate into the box and puts it into the covered camera.]

HEDVIG. [*Comes in from the kitchen*] Are they gone?

GINA. [*Tidying up*] Yes, thank goodness, I've got rid of them at last.

HEDVIG. But can you imagine why father hasn't come home yet?

GINA. Are you sure he's not down in Relling's room?

HEDVIG. No, he's not; I ran down the kitchen stair just now and asked.

GINA. And his dinner standing and getting cold, too.

HEDVIG. Yes, I can't understand it. Father's always so careful to be home to dinner!

GINA. Oh, he'll be here directly, you'll see.

HEDVIG. I wish he would come; everything seems so queer today.

GINA. [*Calls out*] There he is!

[HIALMAR EKDAL *comes in at the passage door.*]

HEDVIG. [*Going to him*] Father! Oh, what a time we've been waiting for you!

GINA. [*Glancing sidelong at him*] You've been out a long time, Ekdal.

HIALMAR. [*Without looking at her*] Rather long, yes.

[*He takes off his overcoat;* GINA *and* HEDVIG *go to help him; he motions them away.*]

GINA. Perhaps you've had dinner with Werle?

HIALMAR. [*Hanging up his coat*] No.

GINA. [*Going towards the kitchen door*] Then I'll bring some in for you.

HIALMAR. No; let the dinner alone. I want nothing to eat.

HEDVIG. [*Going nearer to him*] Are you not well, father?

HIALMAR. Well? Oh, yes, well enough. We have had a tiring walk, Gregers and I.

GINA. You didn't ought to have gone so far, Ekdal; you're not used to it.

HIALMAR. H'm; there's many a thing a man must get used to in this world. [*Wanders about the room*] Has any one been here whilst I was out?

GINA. Nobody but the two sweethearts.

HIALMAR. No new orders?

GINA. No, not today.

HEDVIG. There will be some tomorrow, father; you'll see.

HIALMAR. I hope there will, for tomorrow I am going to set to work in real earnest.

HEDVIG. Tomorrow! Don't you remember what day it is tomorrow?

HIALMAR. Oh, yes, by-the-bye———. Well, the day after, then. Henceforth I mean to do everything myself; I shall take all the work into my own hands.

GINA. Why, what can be the good of that, Ekdal? It'll only make your life a burden to you. I can manage the photography all right, and you can go on working at your invention.

HEDVIG. And think of the wild duck, father,—and all the hens and rabbits and——!

HIALMAR. Don't talk to me of all that trash! From tomorrow I will never set foot in the garret again.

HEDVIG. Oh, but father, you promised that we should have a little party——

HIALMAR. H'm, true. Well, then, from the day after tomorrow. I should almost like to wring that cursed wild duck's neck!

HEDVIG. [Shrieks] The wild duck!

GINA. Well, I never!

HEDVIG. [Shaking him] Oh, no, father; you know it's my wild duck!

HIALMAR. That is why I don't do it. I haven't the heart to—for your sake, Hedvig. But in my inmost soul I feel that I ought to do it. I ought not to tolerate under my roof a creature that has been through those hands.

GINA. Why, good gracious, even if grandfather did get it from that poor creature, Pettersen——

HIALMAR. [Wandering about] There are certain claims—what shall I call them?—let me say claims of the ideal—certain obligations, which a man cannot disregard without injury to his soul.

HEDVIG. [Going after him] But think of the wild duck,—the poor wild duck!

HIALMAR. [Stops] I tell you I will spare it—for your sake. Not a hair of its head shall be—I mean, it shall be spared. There are greater problems than that to be dealt with. But you should go out a little now, Hedvig, as usual; it is getting dusk enough for you now.

HEDVIG. No, I don't care about going out now.

HIALMAR. Yes, do; it seems to me your eyes are blinking a great deal; all these vapors in here are bad for you. The air is heavy under this roof.

HEDVIG. Very well, then, I'll run down the kitchen stair and go for a little walk. My cloak and hat?—oh, they're in my own room. Father—be sure you don't do the wild duck any harm while I'm out.

HIALMAR. Not a feather of its head shall be touched. [Draws her to him] You and I, Hedvig—we two——! Well, go along.

[HEDVIG nods to her parents and goes out through the kitchen.]

HIALMAR. [Walks about without looking up] Gina.

GINA. Yes?

HIALMAR. From tomorrow—or, say, from the day after tomorrow—I should like to keep the household account-book myself.

GINA. Do you want to keep the accounts, too, now?

HIALMAR. Yes; or to check the receipts at any rate.

GINA. Lord help us! that's soon done.

HIALMAR. One would hardly think so; at any rate, you seem to make the money go a very long way. [*Stops and looks at her*] How do you manage it?

GINA. It's because me and Hedvig, we need so little.

HIALMAR. Is it the case that father is very liberally paid for the copying he does for Mr. Werle?

GINA. I don't know as he gets anything out of the way. I don't know the rates for that sort of work.

HIALMAR. Well, what does he get, about? Let me hear!

GINA. Oh, it varies; I daresay it'll come to about as much as he costs us, with a little pocket-money over.

HIALMAR. As much as he costs us! And you have never told me this before!

GINA. No, how could I tell you? It pleased you so much to think he got everything from you.

HIALMAR. And he gets it from Mr. Werle.

GINA. Oh, well, he has plenty and to spare, he has.

HIALMAR. Light the lamp for me, please!

GINA. [*Lighting the lamp*] And, of course, we don't know as it's Mr. Werle himself; it may be Gråberg——

HIALMAR. Why attempt such an evasion?

GINA. I don't know; I only thought——

HIALMAR. H'm.

GINA. It wasn't me that got grandfather that copying. It was Bertha, when she used to come about us.

HIALMAR. It seems to me your voice is trembling.

GINA. [*Putting the lamp-shade on*] Is it?

HIALMAR. And your hands are shaking, are they not?

GINA. [*Firmly*] Come right out with it, Ekdal. What has he been saying about me?

HIALMAR. Is it true—can it be true that—that there was an—an understanding between you and Mr. Werle, while you were in service there?

GINA. That's not true. Not at that time. Mr. Werle did come after me, that's a fact. And his wife thought there was something in it, and then she made such a hocus-pocus and hurly-burly, and she hustled me and bustled me about so that I left her service.

HIALMAR. But afterwards, then?

GINA. Well, then I went home. And mother—well, she wasn't the woman you took her for, Ekdal; she kept on worrying and worry ing at me about one thing and another—for Mr. Werle was a widower by that time.

HIALMAR. Well, and then?

GINA. I suppose you've got to know it. He gave me no peace until he'd had his way.

HIALMAR. [*Striking his hands together*] And this is the mother of my child! How could you hide this from me?

GINA. Yes, it was wrong of me; I ought certainly to have told you long ago.

HIALMAR. You should have told me at the very first;—then I should have known the sort of woman you were.

GINA. But would you have married me all the same?

HIALMAR. How can you dream that I would?

GINA. That's just why I didn't dare tell you anything, then. For I'd come to care for you so much, you see; and I couldn't go and make myself utterly miserable——

HIALMAR. [*Walks about*] And this is my Hedvig's mother. And to know that all I see before me—[*Kicks a chair*]—all that I call my home—I owe to a favored predecessor! Oh, that scoundrel Werle!

GINA. Do you repent of the fourteen—the fifteen years we've lived together?

HIALMAR. [*Placing himself in front of her*] Have you not every day, every hour, repented of the spider's-web of deceit you have spun around me? Answer me that! How could you help writhing with penitence and remorse?

GINA. Oh, my dear Ekdal, I've had all I could do to look after the house and get through the day's work——

HIALMAR. Then you never think of reviewing your past?

GINA. No; Heaven knows I'd almost forgotten those old stories.

HIALMAR. Oh, this dull, callous contentment! To me there is something revolting about it. Think of it—never so much as a twinge of remorse!

GINA. But tell me, Ekdal—what would have become of you if you hadn't had a wife like me?

HIALMAR. Like you——!

GINA. Yes; for you know I've always been a bit more practical and wide-awake than you. Of course I'm a year or two older.

HIALMAR. What would have become of me!

GINA. You'd got into all sorts of bad ways when first you met me; that you can't deny.

HIALMAR. "Bad ways" do you call them? Little do you know what a man goes through when he is in grief and despair—especially a man of my fiery temperament.

GINA. Well, well, that may be so. And I've no reason to crow over you, neither; for you turned a moral of a husband, that you did, as soon as ever you had a house and home of your own.—And now we've got everything so nice and cosy about us; and me and Hedvig was just thinking we'd soon be able to let ourselves go a bit, in the way of both food and clothes.

HIALMAR. In the swamp of deceit, yes.

GINA. I wish to goodness that detestable thing had never set his foot inside our doors!

HIALMAR. And I, too, thought my home such a pleasant one. That was a delusion. Where shall I now find the elasticity of spirit to bring my invention into the world of reality? Perhaps it will die with me; and then it will be your past, Gina, that will have killed it.

GINA. [*Nearly crying*] You mustn't say such things, Ekdal. Me, that has only wanted to do the best I could for you, all my days!

HIALMAR. I ask you, what becomes of the breadwinner's dream? When I used to lie in there on the sofa and brood over my invention, I had a clear enough presentiment that it would sap my vitality to the last drop. I felt even then that the day when I held the patent in my hand—that day—would bring my—release. And then it was my dream that you should live on after me, the dead inventor's well-to-do widow.

GINA. [*Drying her tears*] No, you mustn't talk like that, Ekdal. May the Lord never let me see the day I am left a widow!

HIALMAR. Oh, the whole dream has vanished. It is all over now. All over!

[GREGERS WERLE *opens the passage door cautiously and looks in.*]

GREGERS. May I come in?

HIALMAR. Yes, come in.

GREGERS. [*Comes forward, his face beaming with satisfaction, and holds out both his hands to them*] Well, dear friends——! [*Looks from one to the other and whispers to* HIALMAR] Have you not done it yet?

HIALMAR. [*Aloud*] It is done.

GREGERS. It is?

HIALMAR. I have passed through the bitterest moments of my life.

GREGERS. But also, I trust, the most ennobling.

HIALMAR. Well, at any rate, we have got through it for the present.

GINA. God forgive you, Mr. Werle.

GREGERS. [*In great surprise*] But I don't understand this.

HIALMAR. What don't you understand?

GREGERS. After so great a crisis—a crisis that is to be the starting-point of an entirely new life—of a communion founded on truth, and free from all taint of deception——

HIALMAR. Yes, yes, I know; I know that quite well.

GREGERS. I confidently expected, when I entered the room, to find the light of transfiguration shining upon me from both husband and wife. And now I see nothing but dulness, oppression, gloom——

GINA. Oh, is that it? [*Takes off the lamp-shade.*]

GREGERS. You will not understand me, Mrs. Ekdal. Ah, well, you, I suppose, need time to——. But you, Hialmar? Surely you feel a new consecration after the great crisis.

HIALMAR. Yes, of course I do. That is—in a sort of way.

GREGERS. For surely nothing in the world can compare with the joy of forgiving one who has erred and raising her up to oneself in love.

HIALMAR. Do you think a man can so easily throw off the bitter cup I have drained?

GREGERS. No, not a common man, perhaps. But a man like you——!

HIALMAR. Good God! I know that well enough. But you must keep me up to it, Gregers. It takes time, you know.

GREGERS. You have much of the wild duck in you, Hialmar.

[RELLING *has come in at the passage door.*]

RELLING. Oho! is the wild duck to the fore again?

HIALMAR. Yes; Mr. Werle's wing-broken victim.

RELLING. Mr. Werle's——? So it's him you are talking about?

HIALMAR. Him and—ourselves.

RELLING. [*In an undertone to* GREGERS] May the devil fly away with you!

HIALMAR. What is that you are saying?

RELLING. Only uttering a heartfelt wish that this quack-salver would take himself off. If he stays here, he is quite equal to making an utter mess of life, for both of you.

GREGERS. These two will not make a mess of life, Mr. Relling. Of course I won't speak of Hialmar—him we know. But she, too, in her innermost heart, has certainly something loyal and sincere——

GINA. [*Almost crying*] You might have let me alone for what I was, then.

RELLING. [*To* GREGERS] Is it rude to ask what you really want in this house?

GREGERS. To lay the foundations of a true marriage.

RELLING. So you don't think Ekdal's marriage is good enough as it is?

GREGERS. No doubt it is as good a marriage as most others, worse luck. But a true marriage it has yet to become.

HIALMAR. You have never had eyes for the claims of the ideal, Relling.

RELLING. Rubbish, my boy!—but excuse me, Mr. Werle: how many

—in round numbers—how many true marriages have you seen in the course of your life?

GREGERS. Scarcely a single one.

RELLING. Nor I either.

GREGERS. But I have seen innumerable marriages of the opposite kind. And it has been my fate to see at close quarters what ruin such a marriage can work in two human souls.

HIALMAR. A man's whole moral basis may give away beneath his feet; that is the terrible part of it.

RELLING. Well, I can't say I've ever been exactly married, so I don't pretend to speak with authority. But this I know, that the child enters into the marriage problem. And you must leave the child in peace.

HIALMAR. Oh—Hedvig! my poor Hedvig!

RELLING. Yes, you must be good enough to keep Hedvig outside of all this. You two are grown-up people; you are free, in God's name, to make what mess and muddle you please of your life. But you must deal cautiously with Hedvig, I tell you; else you may do her a great injury.

HIALMAR. An injury!

RELLING. Yes, or she may do herself an injury—and perhaps others, too.

GINA. How can you know that, Relling?

HIALMAR. Her sight is in no immediate danger, is it?

RELLING. I am not talking about her sight. Hedvig is at a critical age. She may be getting all sorts of mischief into her head.

GINA. That's true—I've noticed it already! She's taken to carrying on with the fire, out in the kitchen. She calls it playing at house-on-fire. I'm often scared for fear she really sets fire to the house.

RELLING. You see; I thought as much.

GREGERS. [*To* RELLING] But how do you account for that?

RELLING. [*Sullenly*] Her constitution's changing, sir.

HIALMAR. So long as the child has me——! So long as *I* am above ground——!

[*A knock at the door.*]

GINA. Hush, Ekdal; there's some one in the passage. [*Calls out*] Come in!

[MRS. SÖRBY, *in walking dress, comes in.*]

MRS. SÖRBY. Good evening.

GINA. [*Going towards her*] Is it really you, Bertha?

MRS. SÖRBY. Yes, of course it is. But I'm disturbing you, I'm afraid?

HIALMAR. No, not at all; an emissary from that house——

MRS. SÖRBY. [*To* GINA] To tell the truth, I hoped your men-folk would be out at this time. I just ran up to have a little chat with you, and to say good-bye.

GINA. Good-bye? Are you going away, then?

MRS. SÖRBY. Yes, tomorrow morning,—up to Höidal. Mr. Werle started this afternoon. [*Lightly to* GREGERS] He asked me to say good-bye for him.

GINA. Only fancy——!

HIALMAR. So Mr. Werle has gone? And now you are going after him?

MRS. SÖRBY. Yes, what do you say to that, Ekdal?

HIALMAR. I say: beware!

GREGERS. I must explain the situation. My father and Mrs. Sörby are going to be married.

HIALMAR. Going to be married!

GINA. Oh, Bertha! So it's come to that at last!

RELLING. [*His voice quivering a little*] This is surely not true?

MRS. SÖRBY. Yes, my dear Relling, it's true enough.

RELLING. You are going to marry again?

MRS. SÖRBY. Yes, it looks like it. Werle has got a special licence, and we are going to be married quite quietly, up at the works.

GREGERS. Then I must wish you all happiness, like a dutiful stepson.

MRS. SÖRBY. Thank you very much—if you mean what you say. I certainly hope it will lead to happiness, both for Werle and for me.

RELLING. You have every reason to hope that. Mr. Werle never gets drunk—so far as I know; and I don't suppose he's in the habit of thrashing his wives, like the late lamented horse-doctor.

MRS. SÖRBY. Come now, let Sörby rest in peace. He had his good points, too.

RELLING. Mr. Werle has better ones, I have no doubt.

MRS. SÖRBY. He hasn't frittered away all that was good in him, at any rate. The man who does that must take the consequences.

RELLING. I shall go out with Molvik this evening.

MRS. SÖRBY. You mustn't do that, Relling. Don't do it—for my sake.

RELLING. There's nothing else for it. [*To* HIALMAR] If you're going with us, come along.

GINA. No, thank you. Ekdal doesn't go in for that sort of dissertation.

HIALMAR. [*Half aloud, in vexation*] Oh, do hold your tongue!

RELLING. Good-bye, Mrs.—Werle.

[*Goes out through the passage door.*]

GREGERS. [*To* MRS. SÖRBY] You seem to know Dr. Relling pretty intimately.

MRS. SÖRBY. Yes, we have known each other for many years. At one time it seemed as if things might have gone further between us.

GREGERS. It was surely lucky for you that they did not.

MRS. SÖRBY. You may well say that. But I have always been wary of acting on impulse. A woman can't afford absolutely to throw herself away.

GREGERS. Are you not in the least afraid that I may let my father know about this old friendship?

MRS. SÖRBY. Why, of course, I have told him all about it myself.

GREGERS. Indeed?

MRS. SÖRBY. Your father knows every single thing that can, with any truth, be said about me. I have told him all; it was the first thing I did when I saw what was in his mind.

GREGERS. Then you have been franker than most people, I think.

MRS. SÖRBY. I have always been frank. We women find that the best policy.

HIALMAR. What do you say to that, Gina?

GINA. Oh, we're not all alike, us women aren't. Some are made one way, some another.

MRS. SÖRBY. Well, for my part, Gina, I believe it's wisest to do as I've done. And Werle has no secrets either, on his side. That's really the great bond between us, you see. Now he can talk to me as openly as a child. He has never had the chance to do that before. Fancy a man like him, full of health and vigor, passing his whole youth and the best years of his life in listening to nothing but penitential sermons! And very often the sermons had for their text the most imaginary offences—at least so I understand.

GINA. That's true enough.

GREGERS. If you ladies are going to follow up this topic, I had better withdraw.

MRS. SÖRBY. You can stay as far as that's concerned. I shan't say a word more. But I wanted you to know that I had done nothing secretly or in an underhand way. I may seem to have come in for a great piece of luck; and so I have, in a sense. But after all, I don't think I am getting any more than I am giving. I shall stand by him always, and I can tend and care for him as no one else can, now that he is getting helpless.

HIALMAR. Getting helpless?

GREGERS. [To MRS. SÖRBY] Hush, don't speak of that here.

MRS. SÖRBY. There is no disguising it any longer, however much he would like to. He is going blind.

HIALMAR. [Starts] Going blind? That's strange. He, too, going blind!

GINA. Lots of people do.

MRS. SÖRBY. And you can imagine what that means to a business man. Well, I shall try as well as I can to make my eyes take the place of his. But I mustn't stay any longer; I have heaps of things to do.—Oh, by-the-bye, Ekdal, I was to tell you that if there is anything Werle can do for you, you must just apply to Gråberg.

GREGERS. That offer I am sure Hialmar Ekdal will decline with thanks.

MRS. SÖRBY. Indeed? I don't think he used to be so——

GINA. No, Bertha, Ekdal doesn't need anything from Mr. Werle now.

HIALMAR. [*Slowly, and with emphasis*] Will you present my compliments to your future husband and say that I intend very shortly to call upon Mr. Gråberg——

GREGERS. What! You don't really mean that?

HIALMAR. To call upon Mr. Gråberg, I say, and obtain an account of the sum I owe his principal. I will pay that debt of honor—ha ha ha! a debt of honor, let us call it! In any case, I will pay the whole with five per cent interest.

GINA. But, my dear Ekdal, God knows we haven't got the money to do it.

HIALMAR. Be good enough to tell your future husband that I am working assiduously at my invention. Please tell him that what sustains me in this laborious task is the wish to free myself from a torturing burden of debt. That is my reason for proceeding with the invention. The entire profits shall be devoted to releasing me from my pecuniary obligations to your future husband.

MRS. SÖRBY. Something has happened here.

HIALMAR. Yes, you are right.

MRS. SÖRBY. Well, good-bye. I had something else to speak to you about, Gina; but it must keep till another time. Good-bye.

[HIALMAR *and* GREGERS *bow silently.* GINA *follows* MRS. SÖRBY *to the door.*]

HIALMAR. Not beyond the threshold, Gina!

[MRS. SÖRBY *goes;* GINA *shuts the door after her.*]

HIALMAR. There now, Gregers; I have got that burden of debt off my mind.

GREGERS. You soon will, at all events.

HIALMAR. I think my attitude may be called correct.

GREGERS. You are the man I have always taken you for.

HIALMAR. In certain cases, it is impossible to disregard the claim of the ideal. Yet, as the breadwinner of a family, I cannot but writhe and groan under it. I can tell you it is no joke for a man without capital to attempt the repayment of a long-standing obligation, over which, so to speak, the dust of oblivion had gathered. But it cannot be helped: the Man in me demands his rights.

GREGERS. [*Laying his hand on* HIALMAR's *shoulder*] My dear Hialmar—was it not a good thing I came?

HIALMAR. Yes.

GREGERS. Are you not glad to have had your true position made clear to you?

HIALMAR. [*Somewhat impatiently*] Yes, of course I am. But there is one thing that is revolting to my sense of justice.

GREGERS. And what is that?

HIALMAR. It is that—but I don't know whether I ought to express myself so unreservedly about your father.

GREGERS. Say what you please, so far as I am concerned.

HIALMAR. Well, then, is it not exasperating to think that it is not I, but he, who will realize the true marriage?

GREGERS. How can you say such a thing?

HIALMAR. Because it is clearly the case. Isn't the marriage between your father and Mrs. Sörby founded upon complete confidence, upon entire and unreserved candor on both sides? They hide nothing from each other; they keep no secrets in the background; their relation is based, if I may put it so, on mutual confession and absolution.

GREGERS. Well, what then?

HIALMAR. Well, is not that the whole thing? Did you not yourself say this was precisely the difficulty that had to be overcome in order to found a true marriage?

GREGERS. But this is a totally different matter, Hialmar. You surely don't compare either yourself or your wife with those two——? Oh, you understand me well enough.

HIALMAR. Say what you like, there is something in all this that hurts and offends my sense of justice. It really looks as if there were no just providence to rule the world.

GINA. Oh, no, Ekdal; for God's sake don't say such things.

GREGERS. H'm; don't let us get upon those questions.

HIALMAR. And yet, after all, I cannot but recognize the guiding finger of fate. He is going blind.

GINA. Oh, you can't be sure of that.

HIALMAR. There is no doubt about it. At all events there ought not to be; for in that very fact lies the righteous retribution. He has hoodwinked a confiding fellow-creature in days gone by——

GREGERS. I fear he has hoodwinked many.

HIALMAR. And now comes inexorable, mysterious Fate and demands Werle's own eyes.

GINA. Oh, how dare you say such dreadful things! You make me quite scared.

HIALMAR. It is profitable, now and then, to plunge deep into the night side of existence.

[HEDVIG, *in her hat and cloak, comes in by the passage door. She is pleasurably excited and out of breath.*]

GINA. Are you back already?

HEDVIG. Yes, I didn't care to go any farther. It was a good thing, too; for I've just met some one at the door.

HIALMAR. It must have been that Mrs. Sörby.

HEDVIG. Yes.

HIALMAR. [*Walks up and down*] I hope you have seen her for the last time.

[*Silence.* HEDVIG, *discouraged, looks first at one and then at the other, trying to divine their frame of mind.*]

HEDVIG. [*Approaching, coaxingly*] Father.

HIALMAR. Well—what is it, Hedvig?

HEDVIG. Mrs. Sörby had something with her for me.

HIALMAR. [*Stops*] For you?

HEDVIG. Yes. Something for tomorrow.

GINA. Bertha has always given you some little thing on your birthday.

HIALMAR. What is it?

HEDVIG. Oh, you mustn't see it now. Mother is to give it to me tomorrow morning before I'm up.

HIALMAR. What is all this hocus-pocus that I am to be in the dark about?

HEDVIG. [*Quickly*] Oh, no, you may see it if you like. It's a big letter.

[*Takes the letter out of her cloak pocket.*]

HIALMAR. A letter, too?

HEDVIG. Yes, it is only a letter. The rest will come afterwards, I suppose. But fancy—a letter! I've never had a letter before. And there's "Miss" written upon it. [*Reads*] "Miss Hedvig Ekdal." Only fancy—that's me!

HIALMAR. Let me see that letter.

HEDVIG. [*Hands it to him*] There it is.

HIALMAR. That is Mr. Werle's hand.

GINA. Are you sure of that, Ekdal?

HIALMAR. Look for yourself.

GINA. Oh, what do I know about such-like things?

HIALMAR. Hedvig, may I open the letter—and read it?

HEDVIG. Yes, of course you may, if you want to.

GINA. No, not tonight, Ekdal; it's to be kept till tomorrow.

HEDVIG. [*Softly*] Oh, can't you let him read it? It's sure to be something good; and then father will be glad, and everything will be nice again.

HIALMAR. I may open it, then?

HEDVIG. Yes, do, father. I'm so anxious to know what it is.

HIALMAR. Well and good. [*Opens the letter, takes out a paper, reads it through and appears bewildered*] What is this——?

GINA. What does it say?

HEDVIG. Oh, yes, father—tell us!

HIALMAR. Be quiet. [*Reads it through again; he has turned pale, but says with self-control*] It is a deed of gift, Hedvig.

HEDVIG. Is it? What sort of gift am I to have?

HIALMAR. Read for yourself.

[HEDVIG *goes over and reads for a time by the lamp.*]

HIALMAR. [*Half-aloud, clenching his hands*] The eyes! The eyes— and then that letter!

HEDVIG. [*Leaves off reading*] Yes, but it seems to me that it's grand-father that's to have it.

HIALMAR. [*Takes letter from her*] Gina—can you understand this?

GINA. I know nothing whatever about it; tell me what's the matter.

HIALMAR. Mr. Werle writes to Hedvig that her old grandfather need not trouble himself any longer with the copying, but that he can henceforth draw on the office for a hundred crowns a month——

GREGERS. Aha!

HEDVIG. A hundred crowns, mother! I read that.

GINA. What a good thing for grandfather!

HIALMAR. ——a hundred crowns a month so long as he needs it— that means, of course, so long as he lives.

GINA. Well, so he's provided for, poor dear.

HIALMAR. But there is more to come. You didn't read that, Hedvig. Afterwards this gift is to pass on to you.

HEDVIG. To me! The whole of it?

HIALMAR. He says that the same amount is assured to you for the whole of your life. Do you hear that, Gina?

GINA. Yes, I hear.

HEDVIG. Fancy—all that money for me! [*Shakes him*] Father, father, aren't you glad——?

HIALMAR. [*Eluding her*] Glad! [*Walks about*] Oh, what vistas— what perspectives open up before me! It is Hedvig, Hedvig that he showers these benefactions upon!

GINA. Yes, because it's Hedvig's birthday——

HEDVIG. And you'll get it all the same, father! You know quite well I shall give all the money to you and mother.

HIALMAR. To mother, yes! There we have it.

GREGERS. Hialmar, this is a trap he is setting for you.

HIALMAR. Do you think it's another trap?

GREGERS. When he was here this morning he said: Hialmar Ekdal is not the man you imagine him to be.

HIALMAR. Not the man——!

GREGERS. That you shall see, he said.

HIALMAR. He meant you should see that I would let myself be bought off——!

HEDVIG. Oh, mother, what does all this mean?

GINA. Go and take off your things.

[HEDVIG *goes out by the kitchen door, half-crying.*]

GREGERS. Yes, Hialmar—now is the time to show who was right, he or I.

HIALMAR. [*Slowly tears the paper across, lays both pieces on the table and says*] Here is my answer.

GREGERS. Just what I expected.

HIALMAR. [*Goes over to* GINA, *who stands by the stove, and says in a low voice*] Now please make a clean breast of it. If the connection between you and him was quite over when you—came to care for me, as you call it—why did he place us in a position to marry?

GINA. I suppose he thought as he could come and go in our house.

HIALMAR. Only that? Was not he afraid of a possible contingency?

GINA. I don't know what you mean.

HIALMAR. I want to know whether—your child has the right to live under my roof.

GINA. [*Draws herself up; her eyes flash*] You ask that?

HIALMAR. You shall answer me this one question: Does Hedvig belong to me—or——? Well?

GINA. [*Looking at him with cold defiance*] I don't know.

HIALMAR. [*Quivering a little*] You don't know!

GINA. How should *I* know? A creature like me——

HIALMAR. [*Quietly turning away from her*] Then I have nothing more to do in this house.

GREGERS. Take care, Hialmar! Think what you are doing!

HIALMAR. [*Puts on his overcoat*] In this case, there is nothing for a man like me to think twice about.

GREGERS. Yes, indeed, there are endless things to be considered. You three must be together if you are to attain the true frame of mind for self-sacrifice and forgiveness.

HIALMAR. I don't want to attain it. Never, never! My hat! [*Takes his hat*] My home has fallen in ruins about me. [*Bursts into tears*] Gregers, I have no child!

HEDVIG. [*Who has opened the kitchen door*] What is that you're saying? [*Coming to him*] Father, father!

GINA. There, you see!

HIALMAR. Don't come near me, Hedvig! Keep far away. I cannot bear to see you! Oh! those eyes——! Good-bye.

[*Makes for the door.*]

HEDVIG. [*Clinging close to him and screaming loudly*] No! no! Don't leave me!

GINA [*Cries out*] Look at the child, Ekdal! Look at the child!

HIALMAR. I will! I cannot! I must get out—away from all this!
[*He tears himself away from* HEDVIG *and goes out by the
passage door.*]

HEDVIG. [*With despairing eyes*] He is going away from us, mother!
He is going away from us! He will never come back again!

GINA. Don't cry, Hedvig. Father's sure to come back again.

HEDVIG. [*Throws herself sobbing on the sofa*] No, no, he'll never
come home to us any more.

GREGERS. Do you believe I meant all for the best, Mrs. Ekdal?

GINA. Yes, I daresay you did; but God forgive you, all the same.

HEDVIG. [*Lying on the sofa*] Oh, this will kill me! What have I done
to him? Mother, you must fetch him home again!

GINA. Yes, yes, yes; only be quiet, and I'll go out and look for him.
[*Puts on her outdoor things*] Perhaps he's gone in to Relling's.
But you mustn't lie there and cry. Promise me!

HEDVIG. [*Weeping convulsively*] Yes, I'll stop, I'll stop; if only
father comes back!

GREGERS. [*To* GINA, *who is going*] After all, had you not better leave
him to fight out his bitter fight to the end?

GINA. Oh, he can do that afterwards. First of all, we must get the
child quieted.
[*Goes out by the passage door.*]

HEDVIG. [*Sits up and dries her tears*] Now you must tell me what
all this means? Why doesn't father want me any more?

GREGERS. You mustn't ask that till you are a big girl—quite
grown-up.

HEDVIG. [*Sobs*] But I can't go on being as miserable as this till I'm
grown-up.—I think I know what it is.—Perhaps I'm not really
father's child.

GREGERS. [*Uneasily*] How could that be?

HEDVIG. Mother might have found me. And perhaps father has just
got to know it; I've read of such things.

GREGERS. Well, but if it were so——

HEDVIG. I think he might be just as fond of me for all that. Yes,
fonder almost. We got the wild duck in a present, you know,
and I love it so dearly all the same.

GREGERS. [*Turning the conversation*] Ah, the wild duck, by-the-bye!
Let us talk about the wild duck a little, Hedvig.

HEDVIG. The poor wild duck! He doesn't want to see it any more
either. Only think, he wanted to wring its neck!

GREGERS. Oh, he won't do that.

HEDVIG. No; but he said he would like to. And I think it was horrid
of father to say it, for I pray for the wild duck every night and
ask that it may be preserved from death and all that is evil.

GREGERS. [*Looking at her*] Do you say your prayers every night?

HEDVIG. Yes.

GREGERS. Who taught you to do that?

HEDVIG. I myself, one time when father was very ill, and had leeches on his neck and said that death was staring him in the face.

GREGERS. Well?

HEDVIG. Then I prayed for him as I lay in bed, and since then I have always kept it up.

GREGERS. And now you pray for the wild duck, too?

HEDVIG. I thought it was best to bring in the wild duck, for she was so weakly at first.

GREGERS. Do you pray in the morning, too?

HEDVIG. No, of course not.

GREGERS. Why not in the morning as well?

HEDVIG. In the morning it's light, you know, and there's nothing in particular to be afraid of.

GREGERS. And your father was going to wring the neck of the wild duck that you love so dearly?

HEDVIG. No; he said he ought to wring its neck, but he would spare it for my sake; and that was kind of father.

GREGERS. [*Coming a little nearer*] But suppose you were to sacrifice the wild duck of your own free will for his sake.

HEDVIG. [*Rising*] The wild duck!

GREGERS. Suppose you were to make a free-will offering, for his sake, of the dearest treasure you have in the world!

HEDVIG. Do you think that would do any good?

GREGERS. Try it, Hedvig.

HEDVIG. [*Softly, with flashing eyes*] Yes, I will try it.

GREGERS. Have you really the courage for it, do you think?

HEDVIG. I'll ask grandfather to shoot the wild duck for me.

GREGERS. Yes, do. But not a word to your mother about it.

HEDVIG. Why not?

GREGERS. She doesn't understand us.

HEDVIG. The wild duck! I'll try it tomorrow morning.

[GINA *comes in by the passage door.*]

HEDVIG. [*Going towards her*] Did you find him, mother?

GINA. No, but I heard as he had called and taken Relling with him.

GREGERS. Are you sure of that?

GINA. Yes, the porter's wife said so. Molvik went with them, too, she said.

GREGERS. This evening, when his mind so sorely needs to wrestle in solitude——!

GINA. [*Takes off her things*] Yes, men are strange creatures, so they are. The Lord only knows where Relling has dragged him to! I ran over to Madame Eriksen's, but they weren't there.

HEDVIG. [*Struggling to keep back her tears*] Oh, if he should never come home any more!

GREGERS. He will come home again. I shall have news to give him tomorrow; and then you shall see how he comes home. You may rely upon that, Hedvig, and sleep in peace. Good-night.

[*He goes out by the passage door.*]

HEDVIG. [*Throws herself sobbing on* GINA'S *neck*] Mother, mother!

GINA. [*Pats her shoulder and sighs*] Ah, yes; Relling was right, he was. That's what comes of it when crazy creatures go about presenting the claims of the—what-you-may-call-it.

Act V

SCENE—HIALMAR EKDAL'S *studio. Cold, grey morning light. Wet snow lies upon the large panes of the sloping roof-window.*

GINA *comes from the kitchen with an apron and bib on, and carrying a dusting-brush and a duster; she goes towards the sitting-room door. At the same moment* HEDVIG *comes hurriedly in from the passage.*

GINA. [*Stops*] Well?

HEDVIG. Oh, mother, I almost think he's down at Relling's——

GINA. There, you see!

HEDVIG. ——because the porter's wife says she could hear that Relling had two people with him when he came home last night.

GINA. That's just what I thought.

HEDVIG. But it's no use his being there, if he won't come up to us.

GINA. I'll go down and speak to him at all events.

[OLD EKDAL, *in dressing-gown and slippers, and with a lighted pipe, appears at the door of his room.*]

EKDAL. Hialmar—— Isn't Hialmar at home?

GINA. No, he's gone out.

EKDAL. So early? And in such a tearing snowstorm? Well, well; just as he pleases; I can take my morning walk alone.

[*He slides the garret door aside;* HEDVIG *helps him; he goes in; she closes it after him.*]

HEDVIG. [*In an undertone*] Only think, mother, when poor grandfather hears that father is going to leave us.

GINA. Oh, nonsense; grandfather mustn't hear anything about it. It was a heaven's mercy he wasn't at home yesterday in all that hurly-burly.

HEDVIG. Yes, but——

[GREGERS *comes in by the passage door.*]

GREGERS. Well, have you any news of him?

GINA. They say he's down at Relling's.

GREGERS. At Relling's! Has he really been out with those creatures?

GINA. Yes, like enough.

GREGERS. When he ought to have been yearning for solitude, to collect and clear his thoughts——

GINA. Yes, you may well say so.

[RELLING *enters from the passage.*]

HEDVIG. [*Going to him*] Is father in your room?

GINA. [*At the same time*] Is he there?

RELLING. Yes, to be sure he is.

HEDVIG. And you never let us know!

RELLING. Yes, I'm a brute. But in the first place I had to look after the other brute; I mean our dæmonic friend, of course; and then I fell so dead asleep that——

GINA. What does Ekdal say today?

RELLING. He says nothing whatever.

HEDVIG. Doesn't he speak?

RELLING. Not a blessed word.

GREGERS. No, no; I can understand that very well.

GINA. But what's he doing then?

RELLING. He's lying on the sofa, snoring.

GINA. Oh, is he? Yes, Ekdal's a rare one to snore.

HEDVIG. Asleep? Can he sleep?

RELLING. Well, it certainly looks like it.

GREGERS. No wonder, after the spiritual conflict that has rent him——

GINA. And then he's never been used to gadding about out of doors at night.

HEDVIG. Perhaps it's a good thing that he's getting sleep, mother.

GINA. Of course it is; and we must take care we don't wake him up too early. Thank you, Relling. I must get the house cleaned up a bit now, and then—— Come and help me, Hedvig.

[GINA *and* HEDVIG *go into the sitting-room.*]

GREGERS. [*Turning to* RELLING] What is your explanation of the spiritual tumult that is now going on in Hialmar Ekdal?

RELLING. Devil a bit of a spiritual tumult have *I* noticed in him.

GREGERS. What! Not at such a crisis, when his whole life has been placed on a new foundation——? How can you think that such an individuality as Hialmar's——?

RELLING. Oh, individuality—he! If he ever had any tendency to the abnormal development you call individuality, I can assure you it was rooted out of him while he was still in his teens.

GREGERS. That would be strange indeed,—considering the loving care with which he was brought up.

RELLING. By those two high-flown, hysterical maiden aunts, you mean?

GREGERS. Let me tell you that they were women who never forgot the claim of the ideal—but of course you will only jeer at me again.

RELLING. No, I'm in no humor for that. I know all about those ladies; for he has ladled out no end of rhetoric on the subject of his "two soul-mothers." But I don't think he has much to thank them for. Ekdal's misfortune is that in his own circle he has always been looked upon as a shining light——

GREGERS. Not without reason, surely. Look at the depth of his mind!

RELLING. *I* have never discovered it. That his father believed in it I don't so much wonder; the old lieutenant has been an ass all his days.

GREGERS. He has had a child-like mind all his days; that is what you cannot understand.

RELLING. Well, so be it. But then, when our dear, sweet Hialmar went to college, he at once passed for the great light of the future amongst his comrades, too! He was handsome, the rascal—red and white—a shop-girl's dream of manly beauty; and with his superficially emotional temperament, and his sympathetic voice and his talent for declaiming other people's verses and other people's thoughts——

GREGERS. [*Indignantly*] Is it Hialmar Ekdal you are talking about in this strain?

RELLING. Yes, with your permission; I am simply giving you an inside view of the idol you are grovelling before.

GREGERS. I should hardly have thought I was quite stone blind.

RELLING. Yes, you are—or not far from it. You are a sick man, too, you see.

GREGERS. You are right there.

RELLING. Yes. Yours is a complicated case. First of all there is that plaguy integrity-fever; and then—what's worse—you are always in a delirium of hero-worship; you must always have something to adore, outside yourself.

GREGERS. Yes, I must certainly seek it outside myself.

RELLING. But you make such shocking mistakes about every new phœnix you think you have discovered. Here again you have come to a cottar's cabin with your claim of the ideal; and the people of the house are insolvent.

GREGERS. If you don't think better than that of Hialmar Ekdal, what pleasure can you find in being everlastingly with him?

RELLING. Well, you see, I'm supposed to be a sort of doctor—save the mark! I can't but give a hand to the poor sick folk who live under the same roof with me.

GREGERS. Oh, indeed! Hialmar Ekdal is sick, too, is he?

RELLING. Most people are, worse luck.

GREGERS And what remedy are you applying in Hialmar's case?

RELLING. My usual one. I am cultivating the life-illusion[6] in him.

GREGERS. Life-illusion? I didn't catch what you said.

RELLING. Yes, I said illusion. For illusion, you know, is the stimulating principle.

GREGERS. May I ask with what illusion Hialmar is inoculated?

RELLING. No, thank you; I don't betray professional secrets to quacksalvers. You would probably go and muddle his case still more than you have already. But my method is infallible. I have applied it to Molvik as well. I have made him "dæmonic." That's the blister I have to put on his neck.

GREGERS. Is he not really dæmonic, then?

RELLING. What the devil do you mean by dæmonic? It's only a piece of gibberish I've invented to keep up a spark of life in him. But for that, the poor harmless creature would have succumbed to self-contempt and despair many a long year ago. And then the old lieutenant! But he has hit upon his own cure, you see.

GREGERS. Lieutenant Ekdal? What of him?

RELLING. Just think of the old bear-hunter shutting himself up in that dark garret to shoot rabbits! I tell you there is not a happier sportsman in the world than that old man pottering about in there among all that rubbish. The four or five withered Christmas trees he has saved up are the same to him as the whole great fresh Höidal forest; the cock and the hens are big game-birds in the fir-tops; and the rabbits that flop about the garret floor are the bears he has to battle with—the mighty hunter of the mountains!

GREGERS. Poor unfortunate old man! Yes; he has indeed had to narrow the ideals of his youth.

RELLING. While I think of it, Mr. Werle, junior—don't use that foreign word: ideals. We have the excellent native word: lies.

GREGERS. Do you think the two things are related?

RELLING. Yes, just about as closely as typhus and putrid fever.

GREGERS. Dr. Relling, I shall not give up the struggle until I have rescued Hialmar from your clutches!

RELLING. So much the worse for him. Rob the average man of his life-illusion, and you rob him of his happiness at the same stroke. [*To* HEDVIG, *who comes in from the sitting-room*] Well, little wild-duck-mother, I'm just going down to see whether papa is still lying meditating upon that wonderful invention of his.

[*Goes out by passage door.*]

GREGERS. [*Approaches* HEDVIG] I can see by your face that you have not yet done it.

HEDVIG. What? Oh, that about the wild duck! No.

6. "Livslögnen," literally "the life-lie." [Translator's note.]

GREGERS. I suppose your courage failed when the time came.

HEDVIG. No, that wasn't it. But when I awoke this morning and remembered what we had been talking about, it seemed so strange.

GREGERS. Strange?

HEDVIG. Yes, I don't know—— Yesterday evening, at the moment, I thought there was something so delightful about it; but since I have slept and thought of it again, it somehow doesn't seem worth while.

GREGERS. Ah, I thought you could not have grown up quite unharmed in this house.

HEDVIG. I don't care about that, if only father would come up——

GREGERS. Oh, if only your eyes had been opened to that which gives life its value—if you possessed the true, joyous, fearless spirit of sacrifice, you would soon see how he would come up to you.—But I believe in you still, Hedvig.

[*He goes out by the passage door.* HEDVIG *wanders about the room for a time; she is on the point of going into the kitchen when a knock is heard at the garret door.* HEDVIG *goes over and opens it a little;* OLD EKDAL *comes out; she pushes the door to again.*]

EKDAL. H'm, it's not much fun to take one's morning walk alone.

HEDVIG. Wouldn't you like to go shooting, grandfather?

EKDAL. It's not the weather for it today. It's so dark there, you can scarcely see where you're going.

HEDVIG. Do you never want to shoot anything besides the rabbits?

EKDAL. Do you think the rabbits aren't good enough?

HEDVIG. Yes, but what about the wild duck?

EKDAL. Ho-ho! are you afraid I shall shoot your wild duck? Never in the world. Never.

HEDVIG. No, I suppose you couldn't; they say it's very difficult to shoot wild ducks.

EKDAL. Couldn't! Should rather think I could.

HEDVIG. How would you set about it, grandfather?—I don't mean with my wild duck, but with others?

EKDAL. I should take care to shoot them in the breast, you know; that's the surest place. And then you must shoot against the feathers, you see—not the way of the feathers.

HEDVIG. Do they die then, grandfather?

EKDAL. Yes, they die right enough—when you shoot properly. Well, I must go and brush up a bit. H'm—understand—h'm. [*Goes into his room*]

[HEDVIG *waits a little, glances towards the sitting-room door, goes over to the book-case, stands on tip-toe, takes the*

double-barrelled pistol down from the shelf and looks at it.
GINA, with brush and duster, comes from the sitting-room.
HEDVIG hastily lays down the pistol, unobserved.]

GINA. Don't stand raking amongst father's things, Hedvig.

HEDVIG. [*Goes away from the bookcase*] I was only going to tidy up
a little.

GINA. You'd better go into the kitchen and see if the coffee's keeping hot; I'll take his breakfast on a tray, when I go down to him.
[HEDVIG *goes out.* GINA *begins to sweep and clean up the
studio. Presently the passage door is opened with hesitation,
and* HIALMAR EKDAL *looks in. He has on his overcoat, but
not his hat; he is unwashed, and his hair is dishevelled and
unkempt. His eyes are dull and heavy.*]

GINA. [*Standing with the brush in her hand and looking at him*]
Oh, there now, Ekdal—so you've come after all!

HIALMAR. [*Comes in and answers in a toneless voice*] I come—only
to depart again immediately.

GINA. Yes, yes, I suppose so. But, Lord help us! what a sight you
are!

HIALMAR. A sight?

GINA. And your nice winter coat, too! Well, that's done for.

HEDVIG. [*At the kitchen door*] Mother, hadn't I better——? [*Sees*
HIALMAR, *gives a loud scream of joy and runs to him*] Oh, father,
father!

HIALMAR. [*Turns away and makes a gesture of repulsion*] Away,
away, away! [*To* GINA] Keep her away from me, I say!

GINA. [*In a low tone*] Go into the sitting-room, Hedvig.
[HEDVIG *does so without a word.*]

HIALMAR. [*Fussily pulls out the table-drawer*] I must have my books
with me. Where are my books?

GINA. Which books?

HIALMAR. My scientific books, of course; the technical magazines I
require for my invention.

GINA. [*Searches in the bookcase*] Is it these here paper-covered ones?

HIALMAR. Yes, of course.

GINA. [*Lays a heap of magazines on the table*] Shan't I get Hedvig
to cut them for you?

HIALMAR. I don't require to have them cut for me.
[*Short silence.*]

GINA. Then you're still set on leaving us, Ekdal?

HIALMAR. [*Rummaging amongst the books*] Yes, that is a matter of
course, I should think.

GINA. Well, well.

HIALMAR. [*Vehemently*] How can I live here, to be stabbed to the
heart every hour of the day?

GINA. God forgive you for thinking such vile things of me.

HIALMAR. Prove——!

GINA. I think it's you as has got to prove.

HIALMAR. After a past like yours? There are certain claims—I may almost call them claims of the ideal——

GINA. But what about grandfather? What's to become of him, poor dear?

HIALMAR. I know my duty; my helpless father will come with me. I am going out into the town to make arrangements—— H'm— [*Hesitatingly*]—has any one found my hat on the stairs?

GINA. No. Have you lost your hat?

HIALMAR. Of course I had it on when I came in last night; there's no doubt about that; but I couldn't find it this morning.

GINA. Lord help us! where have you been to with those two ne'er-do-wells?

HIALMAR. Oh, don't bother me about trifles. Do you suppose I am in the mood to remember details?

GINA. If only you haven't caught cold, Ekdal——
    [*Goes out into the kitchen.*]

HIALMAR. [*Talks to himself in a low tone of irritation, while he empties the table-drawer*] You're a scoundrel, Relling!—You're a low fellow!—Ah, you shameless tempter!—I wish I could get some one to stick a knife into you!
    [*He lays some old letters on one side, finds the torn document of yesterday, takes it up and looks at the pieces; puts it down hurriedly as* GINA *enters.*]

GINA. [*Sets a tray with coffee, etc., on the table*] Here's a drop of something hot, if you'd fancy it. And there's some bread and butter and a snack of salt meat.

HIALMAR. [*Glancing at the tray*] Salt meat? Never under this roof! It's true I have not had a mouthful of solid food for nearly twenty-four hours; but no matter.—My memoranda! The commencement of my autobiography! What has become of my diary, and all my important papers? [*Opens the sitting-room door but draws back*] She is there, too!

GINA. Good Lord! the child must be somewhere!

HIALMAR. Come out.
    [*He makes room;* HEDVIG *comes, scared, into the studio.*]

HIALMAR. [*With his hand upon the door-handle, says to* GINA] In these, the last moments I spend in my former home, I wish to be spared from interlopers——
    [*Goes into the room.*]

HEDVIG. [*With a bound towards her mother, asks softly, trembling*] Does that mean me?

GINA. Stay out in the kitchen, Hedvig; or, no—you'd best go into your own room. [*Speaks to* HIALMAR *as she goes into him*] Wait a bit, Ekdal; don't rummage so in the drawers; I know where everything is.

HEDVIG. [*Stands a moment immovable, in terror and perplexity, biting her lips to keep back the tears; then she clenches her hands convulsively and says softly*] The wild duck.

[*She steals over and takes the pistol from the shelf, opens the garret door a little way, creeps in and draws the door to after her.* HIALMAR *and* GINA *can be heard disputing in the sitting-room.*]

HIALMAR. [*Comes in with some manuscript books and old loose papers, which he lays upon the table*] That portmanteau is of no use! There are a thousand and one things I must drag with me.

GINA. [*Following with the portmanteau*] Why not leave all the rest for the present and only take a shirt and a pair of woollen drawers with you?

HIALMAR. Whew!—all these exhausting preparations——!
[*Pulls off his overcoat and throws it upon the sofa.*]

GINA. And there's the coffee getting cold.

HIALMAR. H'm.
[*Drinks a mouthful without thinking of it and then another.*]

GINA. [*Dusting the backs of the chairs*] A nice job you'll have to find such another big garret for the rabbits.

HIALMAR. What! Am I to drag all those rabbits with me, too?

GINA. You don't suppose grandfather can get on without his rabbits.

HIALMAR. He must just get used to doing without them. Have not I to sacrifice very much greater things than rabbits?

GINA. [*Dusting the bookcase*] Shall I put the flute in the portmanteau for you?

HIALMAR. No. No flute for me. But give me the pistol!

GINA. Do you want to take the pistol with you?

HIALMAR. Yes. My loaded pistol.

GINA. [*Searching for it*] It's gone. He must have taken it in with him.

HIALMAR. Is he in the garret?

GINA. Yes, of course he's in the garret.

HIALMAR. H'm—poor lonely old man.
[*He takes a piece of bread and butter, eats it, and finishes his cup of coffee.*]

GINA. If we hadn't have let that room, you could have moved in there.

HIALMAR. And continued to live under the same roof with——! Never,—never!

GINA. But couldn't you put up with the sitting-room for a day or two? You could have it all to yourself.

HIALMAR. Never within these walls!

GINA. Well, then, down with Relling and Molvik.

HIALMAR. Don't mention those wretches' names to me! The very thought of them almost takes away my appetite.—Oh, no, I must go out into the storm and the snow-drift,—go from house to house and seek shelter for my father and myself.

GINA. But you've got no hat, Ekdal! You've been and lost your hat, you know.

HIALMAR. Oh, those two brutes, those slaves of all the vices! A hat must be procured. [*Takes another piece of bread and butter*] Some arrangements must be made. For I have no mind to throw away my life, either.

[*Looks for something on the tray.*]

GINA. What are you looking for?

HIALMAR. Butter.

GINA. I'll get some at once. [*Goes out into the kitchen.*]

HIALMAR. [*Calls after her*] Oh, it doesn't matter; dry bread is good enough for me.

GINA. [*Brings a dish of butter*] Look here; this is fresh churned.

[*She pours out another cup of coffee for him; he seats himself on the sofa, spreads more butter on the already buttered bread and eats and drinks awhile in silence.*]

HIALMAR. Could I, without being subject to intrusion—intrusion of any sort—could I live in the sitting-room there for a day or two?

GINA. Yes, to be sure you could, if you only would.

HIALMAR. For I see no possibility of getting all father's things out in such a hurry.

GINA. And, besides, you've surely got to tell him first as you don't mean to live with us others no more.

HIALMAR. [*Pushes away his coffee cup*] Yes, there is that, too; I shall have to lay bare the whole tangled story to him—— I must turn matters over; I must have breathing-time; I cannot take all these burdens on my shoulders in a single day.

GINA. No, especially in such horrible weather as it is outside.

HIALMAR. [*Touching* WERLE's *letter*] I see that paper is still lying about here.

GINA. Yes, I haven't touched it.

HIALMAR. So far as I am concerned it is mere waste paper——

GINA. Well, I have certainly no notion of making any use of it.

HIALMAR. ——but we had better not let it get lost all the same;—in all the upset when I move, it might easily——

GINA. I'll take good care of it, Ekdal.

HIALMAR. The donation is in the first instance made to father, and it rests with him to accept or decline it.

GINA. [*Sighs*] Yes, poor old father——

HIALMAR. To make quite safe—— Where shall I find some gum?

GINA. [*Goes to the bookcase*] Here's the gum-pot.

HIALMAR. And a brush?

GINA. The brush is here, too.   [*Brings him the things.*]

HIALMAR. [*Takes a pair of scissors*] Just a strip of paper at the back ——[*Clips and gums*] Far be it from me to lay hands upon what is not my own—and least of all upon what belongs to a destitute old man—and to—the other as well.—There now. Let it lie there for a time; and when it is dry, take it away. I wish never to see that document again. Never!

[GREGERS WERLE *enters from the passage.*]

GREGERS. [*Somewhat surprised*] What,—are you sitting here, Hialmar?

HIALMAR. [*Rises hurriedly*] I had sunk down from fatigue.

GREGERS. You have been having breakfast, I see.

HIALMAR. The body sometimes makes its claims felt, too.

GREGERS. What have you decided to do?

HIALMAR. For a man like me, there is only one course possible. I am just putting my most important things together. But it takes time, you know.

GINA. [*With a touch of impatience*] Am I to get the room ready for you, or am I to pack your portmanteau?

HIALMAR. [*After a glance of annoyance at* GREGERS] Pack—and get the room ready!

GINA. [*Takes the portmanteau*] Very well; then I'll put in the shirt and the other things.

[*Goes into the sitting-room and draws the door to after her.*]

GREGERS. [*After a short silence*] I never dreamed that this would be the end of it. Do you really feel it a necessity to leave house and home?

HIALMAR. [*Wanders about restlessly*] What would you have me do? —I am not fitted to bear unhappiness, Gregers. I must feel secure and at peace in my surroundings.

GREGERS. But can you not feel that here? Just try it. I should have thought you had firm ground to build upon now—if only you start afresh. And, remember, you have your invention to live for.

HIALMAR. Oh, don't talk about my invention. It's perhaps still in the dim distance.

GREGERS. Indeed!

HIALMAR. Why, great heavens, what would you have me invent? Other people have invented almost everything already. It becomes more and more difficult every day——

GREGERS. And you have devoted so much labor to it.

HIALMAR. It was that blackguard Relling that urged me to it.

GREGERS. Relling?

HIALMAR. Yes, it was he that first made me realize my aptitude for making some notable discovery in photography.

GREGERS. Aha—it was Relling!

HIALMAR. Oh, I have been so truly happy over it! Not so much for the sake of the invention itself, as because Hedvig believed in it —believed in it with a child's whole eagerness of faith.—At least, I have been fool enough to go and imagine that she believed in it.

GREGERS. Can you really think Hedvig has been false towards you?

HIALMAR. I can think anything now. It is Hedvig that stands in my way. She will blot out the sunlight from my whole life.

GREGERS. Hedvig! Is it Hedvig you are talking of? How should she blot out your sunlight?

HIALMAR. [Without answering] How unutterably I have loved that child! How unutterably happy I have felt every time I came home to my humble room, and she flew to meet me, with her sweet little blinking eyes. Oh, confiding fool that I have been! I loved her unutterably;—and I yielded myself up to the dream, the delusion, that she loved me unutterably in return.

GREGERS. Do you call that a delusion?

HIALMAR. How should I know? I can get nothing out of Gina; and besides, she is totally blind to the ideal side of these complications. But to you I feel impelled to open my mind, Gregers. I cannot shake off this frightful doubt—perhaps Hedvig has never really and honestly loved me.

GREGERS. What would you say if she were to give you a proof of her love? [Listens] What's that? I thought I heard the wild duck——?

HIALMAR. It's the wild duck quacking. Father's in the garret.

GREGERS. Is he? [His face lights up with joy] I say, you may yet have proof that your poor misunderstood Hedvig loves you!

HIALMAR. Oh, what proof can she give me? I dare not believe in any assurance from that quarter.

GREGERS. Hedvig does not know what deceit means.

HIALMAR. Oh, Gregers, that is just what I cannot be sure of. Who knows what Gina and that Mrs. Sörby may many a time have sat here whispering and tattling about? And Hedvig usually has her ears open, I can tell you. Perhaps the deed of gift was not such a surprise to her, after all. In fact, I'm not sure but that I noticed something of the sort.

GREGERS. What spirit is this that has taken possession of you?

HIALMAR. I have had my eyes opened. Just you notice;—you'll see, the deed of gift is only a beginning. Mrs. Sörby has always been a good deal taken up with Hedvig, and now she has the power to do whatever she likes for the child. They can take her from me whenever they please.

GREGERS. Hedvig will never, never leave you.

HIALMAR. Don't be so sure of that. If only they beckon to her and throw out a golden bait——! And, oh! I have loved her so unspeakably! I would have counted it my highest happiness to take her tenderly by the hand and lead her, as one leads a timid child through a great dark empty room!—I am cruelly certain now that the poor photographer in his humble attic has never really and truly been anything to her. She has only cunningly contrived to keep on a good footing with him until the time came.

GREGERS. You don't believe that yourself, Hialmar.

HIALMAR. That is just the terrible part of it—I don't know what to believe,—I never can know it. But can you really doubt that it must be as I say? Ho-ho, you have far too much faith in the claim of the ideal, my good Gregers! If those others came, with the glamour of wealth about them, and called to the child:—"Leave him: come to us: here life awaits you——!"

GREGERS. [*Quickly*] Well, what then?

HIALMAR. If I then asked her: Hedvig, are you willing to renounce that life for me? [*Laughs scornfully*] No thank you! You would soon hear what answer I should get.

[*A pistol shot is heard from within the garret.*]

GREGERS. [*Loudly and joyfully*] Hialmar!

HIALMAR. There now; he must needs go shooting, too.

GINA. [*Comes in*] Oh, Ekdal, I can hear grandfather blazing away in the garret by hisself.

HIALMAR. I'll look in——

GREGERS. [*Eagerly, with emotion*] Wait a moment! Do you know what that was?

HIALMAR. Yes, of course I know.

GREGERS. No, you don't know. But *I* do. That was the proof!

HIALMAR. What proof?

GREGERS. It was a child's free-will offering. She has got your father to shoot the wild duck.

HIALMAR. To shoot the wild duck!

GINA. Oh, think of that——!

HIALMAR. What was that for?

GREGERS. She wanted to sacrifice to you her most cherished possession; for then she thought you would surely come to love her again.

HIALMAR. [*Tenderly, with emotion*] Oh, poor child!

GINA. What things she does think of!

GREGERS. She only wanted your love again, Hialmar. She could not live without it.

GINA. [*Struggling with her tears*] There, you can see for yourself, Ekdal.

HIALMAR. Gina, where is she?

GINA. [*Sniffs*] Poor dear, she's sitting out in the kitchen, I dare say.

HIALMAR. [*Goes over, tears open the kitchen door and says*] Hedvig, come, come in to me! [*Looks around*] No, she's not here.

GINA. Then she must be in her own little room.

HIALMAR. [*Without*] No, she's not here either. [*Comes in*] She must have gone out.

GINA. Yes, you wouldn't have her anywheres in the house.

HIALMAR. Oh, if she would only come home quickly, so that I can tell her—— Everything will come right now, Gregers; now I believe we can begin life afresh.

GREGERS. [*Quietly*] I knew it; I knew the child would make amends.

[OLD EKDAL *appears at the door of his room; he is in full uniform and is busy buckling on his sword.*]

HIALMAR. [*Astonished*] Father! Are you there?

GINA. Have you been firing in your room?

EKDAL. [*Resentfully, approaching*] So you go shooting alone, do you, Hialmar?

HIALMAR. [*Excited and confused*] Then it wasn't you that fired that shot in the garret?

EKDAL. Me that fired? H'm.

GREGERS. [*Calls out to* HIALMAR] She has shot the wild duck herself!

HIALMAR. What can it mean? [*Hastens to the garret door, tears it aside, looks in and calls loudly*] Hedvig!

GINA. [*Runs to the door*] Good God, what's that?

HIALMAR. [*Goes in*] She's lying on the floor!

GREGERS. Hedvig! lying on the floor?

[*Goes in to* HIALMAR.]

GINA. [*At the same time*] Hedvig! [*Inside the garret*] No, no, no!

EKDAL. Ho-ho! does she go shooting, too, now?

[HIALMAR, GINA, *and* GREGERS carry HEDVIG *into the studio; in her dangling right hand she holds the pistol fast clasped in her fingers.*]

HIALMAR. [*Distracted*] The pistol has gone off. She has wounded herself. Call for help! Help!

GINA. [*Runs into the passage and calls down*] Relling! Relling! Doctor Relling; come up as quick as you can!

[HIALMAR *and* GREGERS *lay* HEDVIG *down on the sofa.*]

EKDAL. [*Quietly*] The woods avenge themselves.

HIALMAR. [*On his knees beside* HEDVIG] She'll soon come to now. She's coming to——; yes, yes, yes.

GINA. [*Who has come in again*] Where has she hurt herself? I can't see anything——

[RELLING *comes hurriedly, and immediately after him* MOL-VIK; *the latter without his waistcoat and necktie, and with his coat open.*]

RELLING. What's the matter here?

GINA. They say Hedvig has shot herself.

HIALMAR. Come and help us!

RELLING. Shot herself!

[*He pushes the table aside and begins to examine her.*]

HIALMAR. [*Kneeling and looking anxiously up at him*] It can't be dangerous? Speak, Relling! She is scarcely bleeding at all. It can't be dangerous?

RELLING. How did it happen?

HIALMAR. Oh, we don't know——

GINA. She wanted to shoot the wild duck.

RELLING. The wild duck?

HIALMAR. The pistol must have gone off.

RELLING. H'm. Indeed.

EKDAL. The woods avenge themselves. But I'm not afraid, all the same.

[*Goes into the garret and closes the door after him.*]

HIALMAR. Well, Relling,—why don't you say something?

RELLING. The ball has entered the breast.

HIALMAR. Yes, but she's coming to!

RELLING. Surely you can see that Hedvig is dead.

GINA. [*Bursts into tears*] Oh, my child, my child——

GREGERS. [*Huskily*] In the depths of the sea——

HIALMAR. [*Jumps up*] No, no, she must live! Oh, for God's sake, Relling—only a moment—only just till I can tell her how unspeakably I loved her all the time!

RELLING. The bullet has gone through her heart. Internal hemorrhage. Death must have been instantaneous.

HIALMAR. And I! I hunted her from me like an animal! And she crept terrified into the garret and died for love of me! [*Sobbing*] I can never atone to her! I can never tell her——! [*Clenches his hands and cries, upwards*] O thou above——! If thou be indeed! Why hast thou done this thing to me?

GINA. Hush, hush, you mustn't go on that awful way. We had no right to keep her, I suppose.

MOLVIK. The child is not dead, but sleepeth.

RELLING. Bosh.

HIALMAR. [*Becomes calm, goes over to the sofa, folds his arms and looks at* HEDVIG] There she lies so stiff and still.

RELLING. [*Tries to loosen the pistol*] She's holding it so tight, so tight.

GINA. No, no, Relling, don't break her fingers; let the pistol be.

HIALMAR. She shall take it with her.

GINA. Yes, let her. But the child mustn't lie here for a show. She shall go to her own room, so she shall. Help me, Ekdal.

[HIALMAR *and* GINA *take* HEDVIG *between them.*]

HIALMAR. [*As they are carrying her*] Oh, Gina, Gina, can you survive this?

GINA. We must help each other to bear it. For now at least she belongs to both of us.

MOLVIK. [*Stretches out his arms and mumbles*] Blessed be the Lord; to earth thou shalt return; to earth thou shalt return——

RELLING. [*Whispers*] Hold your tongue, you fool; you're drunk.

[HIALMAR *and* GINA *carry the body out through the kitchen door.* RELLING *shuts it after them.* MOLVIK *slinks out into the passage.*]

RELLING. [*Goes over to* GREGERS *and says*] No one shall ever convince me that the pistol went off by accident.

GREGERS. [*Who has stood terrified, with convulsive twitchings*] Who can say how the dreadful thing happened?

RELLING. The powder has burnt the body of her dress. She must have pressed the pistol right against her breast and fired.

GREGERS. Hedvig has not died in vain. Did you not see how sorrow set free what is noble in him?

RELLING. Most people are ennobled by the actual presence of death. But how long do you suppose this nobility will last in him?

GREGERS. Why should it not endure and increase throughout his life?

RELLING. Before a year is over, little Hedvig will be nothing to him but a pretty theme for declamation.

GREGERS. How dare you say that of Hialmar Ekdal?

RELLING. We will talk of this again, when the grass has first withered on her grave. Then you'll hear him spouting about "the child too early torn from her father's heart;" then you'll see him steep himself in a syrup of sentiment and self-admiration and self-pity. Just you wait!

GREGERS. If you are right and I am wrong, then life is not worth living.

RELLING. Oh, life would be quite tolerable, after all, if only we could be rid of the confounded duns that keep on pestering us,

in our poverty, with the claim of the ideal.
GREGERS. [*Looking straight before him*] In that case, I am glad that my destiny is what it is.
RELLING. May I inquire,—what is your destiny?
GREGERS. [*Going*] To be the thirteenth at table.
RELLING. The devil it is.

ANTON CHEKHOV
(1860–1904)
The Cherry Orchard*

Characters

LUBOV ANDREYEVNA RANEVSKAYA, *a landowner*
ANYA, *her seventeen-year-old daughter*
VARYA, *her adopted daughter, twenty-two years old*
LEONID ANDREYEVICH GAYEV, *Mme. Ranevskaya's brother*
YERMOLAY ALEXEYEVICH LOPAHIN, *a merchant*
PYOTR SERGEYEVICH TROFIMOV, *a student*
SIMEONOV-PISHCHIK, *a landowner*
CHARLOTTA IVANOVNA, *a governess*
SEMYON YEPIHODOV, *a clerk*
DUNYASHA, *a maid*
FIRS (pronounced *fierce*), *a manservant, aged eighty-seven*
YASHA, *a young valet*
A TRAMP
STATIONMASTER
POST OFFICE CLERK
GUESTS
SERVANTS

The action takes place on Mme. Ranevskaya's estate.

Act I

A room that is still called the nursery. One of the doors leads into ANYA's room. Dawn, the sun will soon rise. It is May, the cherry trees are in blossom, but it is cold in the orchard; there is a morning frost. The windows are shut. Enter DUNYASHA with a candle, and LOPAHIN with a book in his hand.

LOPAHIN: The train is in, thank God. What time is it?
DUNYASHA: Nearly two. [*Puts out the candle.*] It's light already.

* "The Cherry Orchard," from *The Portable Chekhov*, translated by Avraham Yarmolinsky. Copyright 1947 by The Viking Press, Inc. Reprinted by permission of the publisher.

LOPAHIN: How late is the train, anyway? Two hours at least. [*Yawns and stretches.*] I'm a fine one! What a fool I've made of myself! I came here on purpose to meet them at the station, and then I went and overslept. I fell asleep in my chair. How annoying! You might have waked me ...

DUNYASHA: I thought you'd left. [*Listens.*] I think they're coming!

LOPAHIN: [*Listens.*] No, they've got to get the luggage, and one thing and another ... [*Pause.*] Lubov Andreyevna spent five years abroad, I don't know what she's like now. . . . She's a fine person—lighthearted, simple. I remember when I was a boy of fifteen, my poor father—he had a shop here in the village then—punched me in the face with his fist and made my nose bleed. We'd come into the yard, I don't know what for, and he'd had a drop too much. Lubov Andreyevna, I remember her as if it were yesterday—she was still young and so slim—led me to the wash-basin, in this very room ... in the nursery. "Don't cry, little peasant," she said, "it'll heal in time for your wedding . . ." [*Pause.*] Little peasant ... my father was a peasant, it's true, and here I am in a white waistcoat and yellow shoes. A pig in a pastry shop, you might say. It's true I'm rich. I've got a lot of money. . . . But when you look at it closely, I'm a peasant through and through. [*Pages the book.*] Here I've been reading this book and I didn't understand a word of it. . . . I was reading it and fell asleep ... [*Pause.*]

DUNYASHA: And the dogs were awake all night, they feel that their masters are coming.

LOPAHIN: Dunyasha, why are you so—

DUNYASHA: My hands are trembling. I'm going to faint.

LOPAHIN: You're too soft, Dunyasha. You dress like a lady, and look at the way you do your hair. That's not right. One should remember one's place.

[*Enter* YEPIHODOV *with a bouquet; he wears a jacket and highly polished boots that squeak badly. He drops the bouquet as he comes in.*]

YEPIHODOV: [*Picking up the bouquet.*] Here, the gardener sent these, said you're to put them in the dining room. [*Hands the bouquet to* DUNYASHA.]

LOPAHIN: And bring me some kvass.

DUNYASHA: Yes, sir. [*Exits.*]

YEPIHODOV: There's a frost this morning—three degrees below—and yet the cherries are all in blossom. I cannot approve of our climate. [*Sighs.*] I cannot. Our climate does not activate properly. And, Yermolay Alexeyevich, allow me to make a further remark. The other day I bought myself a pair of boots, and I make bold to assure you, they squeak so that it is really intolerable. What should I grease them with?

LOPAHIN: Oh, get out! I'm fed up with you.

YEPIHODOV: Every day I meet with misfortune. And I don't complain, I've got used to it, I even smile.

[DUNYASHA *enters, hands* LOPAHIN *the kvass.*]

YEPIHODOV: I am leaving [*Stumbles against a chair, which falls over.*] There! [*Triumphantly, as it were.*] There again, you see what sort of circumstance, pardon the expression. . . . It is absolutely phenomenal! [*Exits.*]

DUNYASHA: You know, Yermolay Alexeyevich, I must tell you, Yepihodov has proposed to me.

LOPAHIN: Ah!

DUNYASHA: I simply don't know . . . he's a quiet man, but sometimes when he starts talking, you can't make out what he means. He speaks nicely—and it's touching—but you can't understand it. I sort of like him though, and he is crazy about me. He's an unlucky man . . . every day something happens to him. They tease him about it here . . . they call him, Two-and-Twenty Troubles.

LOPAHIN: [*Listening.*] There! I think they're coming.

DUNYASHA: They *are* coming! What's the matter with me? I feel cold all over.

LOPAHIN: They really are coming. Let's go and meet them. Will she recognize me? We haven't seen each other for five years.

DUNYASHA: [*In a flutter.*] I'm going to faint this minute. . . . Oh, I'm going to faint!

[*Two carriages are heard driving up to the house.* LOPAHIN *and* DUNYASHA *go out quickly. The stage is left empty. There is a noise in the adjoining rooms.* FIRS, *who had driven to the station to meet* LUBOV ANDREYEVNA RANEVSKAYA, *crosses the stage hurriedly, leaning on a stick. He is wearing an old-fashioned livery and a tall hat. He mutters to himself indistinctly. The hubbub offstage increases. A* VOICE: "Come, let's go this way." *Enter* LUBOV ANDREYEVNA, ANYA, *and* CHARLOTTA IVANOVNA *with a pet dog on a leash, all in traveling dresses;* VARYA, *wearing a coat and kerchief;* GAYEV, SIMEONOV-PISHCHIK, LOPAHIN, DUNYASHA *with a bag and an umbrella, servants with luggage. All walk across the room.*]

ANYA: Let's go this way. Do you remember what room this is, Mamma?

MME. RANEVSKAYA: [*Joyfully, through her tears.*] The nursery!

VARYA: How cold it is! My hands are numb. [*To* MME. RANEVSKAYA.] Your rooms are just the same as they were, Mamma, the white one and the violet.

MME. RANEVSKAYA: The nursery! My darling, lovely room! I slept here when I was a child . . . [*Cries.*] And here I am, like a child again! [*Kisses her brother and* VARYA, *and then her brother again.*] Varya's just the same as ever, like a nun. And I recognized Dunyasha. [*Kisses* DUNYASHA.]

GAYEV: The train was two hours late. What do you think of that? What a way to manage things!

CHARLOTTA: [*To* PISHCHIK.] My dog eats nuts, too.

PISHCHIK: [*In amazement.*] You don't say!

[*All go out, except* ANYA *and* DUNYASHA.]

DUNYASHA: We've been waiting for you for hours. [*Takes* ANYA's *hat and coat.*]

ANYA: I didn't sleep on the train for four nights and now I'm frozen . . .

DUNYASHA: It was Lent when you left; there was snow and frost, and now . . . My darling! [*Laughs and kisses her.*] I have been waiting for you, my sweet, my darling! But I must tell you something . . . I can't put it off another minute . . .

ANYA: [*Listlessly.*] What now?

DUNYASHA: The clerk, Yepihodov, proposed to me, just after Easter.

ANYA: There you are, at it again . . . [*Straightening her hair.*] I've lost all my hairpins . . . [*She is staggering with exhaustion.*]

DUNYASHA: Really, I don't know what to think. He loves me—he loves me so!

ANYA: [*Looking toward the door of her room, tenderly.*] My own room, my windows, just as though I'd never been away. I'm home! Tomorrow morning I'll get up and run into the orchard. Oh, if I could only get some sleep. I didn't close my eyes during the whole journey—I was so anxious.

DUNYASHA: Pyotr Sergeyevich came the day before yesterday.

ANYA: [*Joyfully.*] Petya!

DUNYASHA: He's asleep in the bathhouse. He has settled there. He said he was afraid of being in the way. [*Looks at her watch.*] I should wake him, but Miss Varya told me not to. "Don't you wake him," she said.

[*Enter* VARYA *with a bunch of keys at her belt.*]

VARYA: Dunyasha, coffee, and be quick. . . . Mamma's asking for coffee.

DUNYASHA: In a minute. [*Exits.*]

VARYA: Well, thank God, you've come. You're home again. [*Fondling* ANYA.] My darling is here again. My pretty one is back.

ANYA: Oh, what I've been through!

VARYA: I can imagine.

ANYA: When we left, it was Holy Week, it was cold then, and all the way Charlotta chattered and did her tricks. Why did you have to saddle me with Charlotta?

VARYA: You couldn't have traveled all alone, darling—at seventeen!

ANYA: We got to Paris, it was cold there, snowing. My French is dreadful. Mamma lived on the fifth floor; I went up there, and found all kinds of Frenchmen, ladies, an old priest with a book. The place was full of tobacco smoke, and so bleak. Suddenly I felt sorry for Mamma, so sorry, I took her head in my arms and hugged her and couldn't let go of her. Afterward Mamma kept fondling me and crying . . .

VARYA: [*Through tears.*] Don't speak of it . . . don't.

ANYA: She had already sold her villa at Mentone, she had nothing left, nothing. I hadn't a kopeck left either, we had only just enough to get home. And Mamma wouldn't understand! When we had dinner at the stations, she always ordered the most expensive dishes, and tipped the waiters a whole ruble. Charlotta, too. And Yasha kept ordering, too—it was simply awful. You know Yasha's Mamma's footman now, we brought him here with us.

VARYA: Yes, I've seen the blackguard.

ANYA: Well, tell me—have you paid the interest?

VARYA: How could we?

ANYA: Good heavens, good heavens!

VARYA: In August the estate will be put up for sale.

ANYA: My God!

LOPAHIN: [Peeps in at the door and bleats]. Meh-h-h. [Disappears.]

VARYA: [Through tears.] What I couldn't do to him! [Shakes her fist threateningly.]

ANYA: [Embracing VARYA, gently.] Varya, has he proposed to you? [VARYA shakes her head.] But he loves you. Why don't you come to an understanding? What are you waiting for?

VARYA: Oh, I don't think anything will ever come of it. He's too busy, he has no time for me . . . pays no attention to me. I've washed my hands of him—I can't bear the sight of him. They all talk about our getting married, they all congratulate me—and all the time there's really nothing to it—it's all like a dream. [In another tone.] You have a new brooch—like a bee.

ANYA: [Sadly.] Mamma bought it. [She goes into her own room and speaks gaily like a child.] And you know, in Paris I went up in a balloon.

VARYA: My darling's home, my pretty one is back! [DUNYASHA returns with the coffeepot and prepares coffee. VARYA stands at the door of ANYA's room.] All day long, darling, as I go about the house, I keep dreaming. If only we could marry you off to a rich man, I should feel at ease. Then I would go into a convent, and afterward to Kiev, to Moscow . . . I would spend my life going from one holy place to another . . . I'd go on and on. . . . What a blessing that would be!

ANYA: The birds are singing in the orchard. What time is it?

VARYA: It must be after two. Time you were asleep, darling. [Goes into ANYA's room.] What a blessing that would be! [YASHA enters with a plaid and a traveling bag, crosses the stage.]

YASHA: [Finically.] May I pass this way, please?

DUNYASHA: A person could hardly recognize you, Yasha. Your stay aboard has certainly done wonders for you.

YASHA: Hm-m . . . and who are you?

DUNYASHA: When you went away I was that high—[Indicating with her hand.] I'm Dunyasha—Fyodor Kozoyedev's daughter. Don't you remember?

YASHA: Hm! What a peach! [He looks round and embraces her. She cries out and drops a saucer. YASHA leaves quickly.]

VARYA: [In the doorway, in a tone of annoyance.] What's going on here?

DUNYASHA: [Through tears.] I've broken a saucer.

VARYA: Well, that's good luck.

ANYA: [Coming out of her room.] We ought to warn Mamma that Petya's here.

VARYA: I left orders not to wake him.

ANYA: [Musingly.] Six years ago father died. A month later brother

Grisha was drowned in the river. . . . Such a pretty little boy he was—only seven. It was more than Mamma could bear, so she went away, went away without looking back . . . [*Shudders.*] How well I understand her, if she only knew! [*Pauses.*] And Petya Trofimov was Grisha's tutor, he may remind her of it all . . .

[*Enter* FIRS, *wearing a jacket and a white waistcoat. He goes up to the coffeepot.*]

FIRS: [*Anxiously.*] The mistress will have her coffee here. [*Puts on white gloves.*] Is the coffee ready? [*Sternly, to* DUNYASHA.] Here, you! And where's the cream?

DUNYASHA: Oh, my God! [*Exits quickly.*]

FIRS: [*Fussing over the coffeepot.*] Hah! the addlehead! [*Mutters to himself.*] Home from Paris. And the old master used to go to Paris too . . . by carriage. [*Laughs.*]

VARYA: What is it, Firs?

FIRS: What is your pleasure, Miss? [*Joyfully.*] My mistress has come home, and I've seen her at last! Now I can die. [*Weeps with joy.*]

[*Enter* MME. RANEVSKAYA, GAYEV, *and* SIMEONOV-PISHCHIK. *The latter is wearing a tight-waisted, pleated coat of fine cloth, and full trousers.* GAYEV, *as he comes in, goes through the motions of a billiard player with his arms and body.*]

MME. RANEVSKAYA: Let's see, how does it go? Yellow ball in the corner! Bank shot in the side pocket!

GAYEV: I'll tip it in the corner! There was a time, Sister, when you and I used to sleep in this very room and now I'm fifty-one, strange as it may seem.

LOPAHIN: Yes, time flies.

GAYEV: Who?

LOPAHIN: I say, time flies.

GAYEV: It smells of patchouli here.

ANYA: I'm going to bed. Good night, Mamma. [*Kisses her mother.*]

MME. RANEVSKAYA: My darling child! [*Kisses her hands.*] Are you happy to be home? I can't come to my senses.

ANYA: Good night, Uncle.

GAYEV: [*Kissing her face and hands.*] God bless you, how like your mother you are! [*To his sister.*] At her age, Luba, you were just like her.

[ANYA *shakes hands with* LOPAHIN *and* PISHCHIK, *then goes out, shutting the door behind her.*]

MME. RANEVSKAYA: She's very tired.

PISHCHIK: Well, it was a long journey.

VARYA: [*To* LOPAHIN *and* PISHCHIK.] How about it, gentlemen? It's past two o'clock—isn't it time for you to go?

MME. RANEVSKAYA: [*Laughs.*] You're just the same as ever, Varya. [*Draws her close and kisses her.*] I'll have my coffee and then we'll all go. [FIRS *puts a small cushion under her feet.*] Thank you, my dear. I've got used to coffee. I drink it day and night. Thanks, my dear old man. [*Kisses him.*]

VARYA: I'd better see if all the luggage has been brought in. [*Exits.*]

MME. RANEVSKAYA: Can it really be I sitting here? [*Laughs.*] I feel like dancing, waving my arms about. [*Covers her face with her hands.*] But maybe I am dreaming! God knows I love my country, I love it tenderly; I couldn't look out of the window in the train, I kept crying so. [*Through tears.*] But I must have my coffee. Thank you, Firs, thank you, dear old man. I'm so happy that you're still alive.

FIRS: Day before yesterday.

GAYEV: He's hard of hearing.

LOPAHIN: I must go soon, I'm leaving for Kharkov about five o'clock. How annoying! I'd like to have a good look at you, talk to you. . . . You're just as splendid as ever.

PISHCHIK: [*Breathing heavily.*] She's even better-looking. . . . Dressed in the latest Paris fashion. . . . Perish my carriage and all its four wheels. . . .

LOPAHIN: Your brother, Leonid Andreyevich, says I'm a vulgarian and an exploiter. But it's all the same to me—let him talk. I only want you to trust me as you used to. I want you to look at me with your touching, wonderful eyes, as you used to. Dear God! My father was a serf of your father's and grandfather's, but you, you yourself, did so much for me once . . . so much . . . that I've forgotten all about that; I love you as though you were my sister —even more.

MME. RANEVSKAYA: I can't sit still, I simply can't. [*Jumps up and walks about in violent agitation.*] This joy is too much for me. . . . Laugh at me, I'm silly! My own darling bookcase! My darling table! [*Kisses it.*]

GAYEV: While you were away, nurse died.

MME. RANEVSKAYA: [*Sits down and takes her coffee.*] Yes, God rest her soul; they wrote me about it.

GAYEV: And Anastasy is dead. Petrushka Kossoy has left me and has gone into town to work for the police inspector. [*Takes a box of sweets out of his pocket and begins to suck one.*]

PISHCHIK: My daughter Dashenka sends her regards.

LOPAHIN: I'd like to tell you something very pleasant—cheering. [*Glancing at his watch.*] I am leaving directly. There isn't much time to talk. But I will put it in a few words. As you know, your cherry orchard is to be sold to pay your debts. The sale is to be on the twenty-second of August; but don't you worry, my dear, you may sleep in peace; there is a way out. Here is my plan. Give me your attention! Your estate is only fifteen miles from the town; the railway runs close by it; and if the cherry orchard and the land along the riverbank were cut up into lots and these leased for summer cottages, you would have an income of at least 25,000 rubles a year out of it.

GAYEV: Excuse me. . . . What nonsense.

MME. RANEVSKAYA: I don't quite understand you, Yermolay Alexeyevich.

LOPAHIN: You will get an annual rent of at least ten rubles per acre, and if you advertise at once, I'll give you any guarantee you like that you won't have a square foot of ground left by autumn, all the lots will be snapped up. In short, congratulations, you're saved. The location is splendid—by that deep river. . . . Only, of course, the ground must be cleared . . . all the old buildings, for instance, must be torn down, and this house, too, which is useless, and, of course, the old cherry orchard must be cut down.

MME. RANEVSKAYA: Cut down? My dear, forgive me, but you don't know what you're talking about. If there's one thing that's interesting—indeed, remarkable—in the whole province, it's precisely our cherry orchard.

LOPAHIN: The only remarkable thing about this orchard is that it's a very large one. There's a crop of cherries every other year, and you can't do anything with them; no one buys them.

GAYEV: This orchard is even mentioned in the encyclopedia.

LOPAHIN: [*Glancing at his watch.*] If we can't think of a way out, if we don't come to a decision, on the twenty-second of August the cherry orchard and the whole estate will be sold at auction. Make up your minds! There's no other way out—I swear. None, none.

FIRS: In the old days, forty or fifty years ago, the cherries were dried, soaked, pickled, and made into jam, and we used to—

GAYEV: Keep still, Firs.

FIRS: And the dried cherries would be shipped by the cartload. It meant a lot of money! And in those days the dried cherries were soft and juicy, sweet, fragrant. . . . They knew the way to do it, then.

MME. RANEVSKAYA: And why don't they do it that way now?

FIRS: They've forgotten. Nobody remembers it.

PISHCHIK: [*To* MME. RANEVSKAYA.] What's doing in Paris? Eh? Did you eat frogs there?

MME. RANEVSKAYA: I ate crocodiles.

PISHCHIK: Just imagine!

LOPAHIN: There used to be only landowners and peasants in the country, but now these summer people have appeared on the scene. . . . All the towns, even the small ones, are surrounded by these summer cottages; and in another twenty years, no doubt, the summer population will have grown enormously. Now the summer resident only drinks tea on his porch, but maybe he'll take to working his acre, too, and then your cherry orchard will be a rich, happy, luxuriant place.

GAYEV: [*Indignantly.*] Poppycock!

[*Enter* VARYA *and* YASHA.]

VARYA: There are two telegrams for you, Mamma dear. [*Picks a key from the bunch at her belt and noisily opens an old-fashioned bookcase.*] Here they are.

MME. RANEVSKAYA: They're from Paris. [*Tears them up without reading them.*] I'm through with Paris.

GAYEV: Do you know, Luba, how old this bookcase is? Last week I pulled out the bottom drawer and there I found the date burnt in it. It was made exactly a hundred years ago. Think of that! We could celebrate its centenary. True, it's an inanimate object, but nevertheless, a bookcase . . .

PISHCHIK: [*Amazed.*] A hundred years! Just imagine!

GAYEV: Yes. [*Tapping it.*] That's something. . . . Dear, honored bookcase, hail to you who for more than a century have served the glorious ideals of goodness and justice! Your silent summons to fruitful toil has never weakened in all those hundred years [*through tears*], sustaining, through successive generations of our family, courage and faith in a better future, and fostering in us ideals of goodness and social consciousness. . . . [*Pauses.*]

LOPAHIN: Yes . . .

MME. RANEVSKAYA: You haven't changed a bit, Leonid.

GAYEV: [*Somewhat embarrassed.*] I'll play it off the red in the corner! Tip it in the side pocket!

LOPAHIN: [*Looking at his watch.*] Well, it's time for me to go . . .

YASHA: [*Handing a pillbox to* MME. RANEVSKAYA.] Perhaps you'll take your pills now.

PISHCHIK: One shouldn't take medicines, dearest lady, they do neither harm nor good. . . . Give them here, my valued friend. [*Takes the pillbox, pours the pills into his palm, blows on them, puts them in his mouth, and washes them down with some kvass.*] There!

MME. RANEVSKAYA: [*Frightened.*] You must be mad!

PISHCHIK: I've taken all the pills.

LOPAHIN: What a glutton!
[*All laugh.*]

FIRS: The gentleman visited us in Easter week, ate half a bucket of pickles, he did . . . [*Mumbles.*]

MME. RANEVSKAYA: What's he saying?

VARYA: He's been mumbling like that for the last three years—we're used to it.

YASHA: His declining years!
[CHARLOTTA IVANOVNA, *very thin, tightly laced, dressed in white, a lorgnette at her waist, crosses the stage.*]

LOPAHIN: Forgive me, Charlotta Ivanovna, I've not had time to greet you. [*Tries to kiss her hand.*]

CHARLOTTA: [*Pulling away her hand.*] If I let you kiss my hand, you'll be wanting to kiss my elbow next, and then my shoulder.

LOPAHIN: I've no luck today. [*All laugh.*] Charlotta Ivanovna, show us a trick.

MME. RANEVSKAYA: Yes, Charlotta, do a trick for us.

CHARLOTTA: I don't see the need. I want to sleep. [*Exits.*]

LOPAHIN: In three weeks we'll meet again. [*Kisses* MME. RANEVSKAYA's *hand.*] Good-bye till then. Time's up. [*To* GAYEV.] Bye-bye. [*Kisses* PISHCHIK.] Bye-bye. [*Shakes hands with* VARYA, *then with* FIRS *and* YASHA.] I hate to leave. [*To* MME. RANEVSKAYA.] If you make up your mind about the cottages, let me know; I'll get you a loan of 50,000 rubles. Think it over seriously.

VARYA: [*Crossly.*] Will you never go!

LOPAHIN: I'm going, I'm going. [*Exits.*]

GAYEV: The vulgarian. But, excuse me . . . Varya's going to marry him, he's Varya's fiancé.

VARYA: You talk too much, Uncle.

MME. RANEVSKAYA: Well, Varya, it would make me happy. He's a good man.

PISHCHIK: Yes, one must admit, he's a most estimable man. And my Dashenka . . . she too says that . . . she says . . . lots of things. [*Snores; but wakes up at once.*] All the same, my valued friend, could you oblige me . . . with a loan of 240 rubles? I must pay the interest on the mortgage tomorrow.

VARYA: [*Alarmed.*] We can't, we can't!

MME. RANEVSKAYA: I really haven't any money.

PISHCHIK: It'll turn up. [*Laughs.*] I never lose hope, I thought everything was lost, that I was done for, when lo and behold, the railway ran through my land . . . and I was paid for it. . . . And something else will turn up again, if not today, then tomorrow . . . Dashenka will win two hundred thousand . . . she's got a lottery ticket.

MME. RANEVSKAYA: I've had my coffee, now let's go to bed.

FIRS: [*Brushes off* GAYEV; *admonishingly.*] You've got the wrong trousers on again. What am I to do with you?

VARYA: [*Softly.*] Anya's asleep. [*Gently opens the window.*] The sun's up now, it's not a bit cold. Look, Mamma dear, what wonderful trees. And heavens, what air! The starlings are singing!

GAYEV: [*Opens the other window.*] The orchard is all white. You've not forgotten it? Luba? That's the long alley that runs straight, straight as an arrow; how it shines on moonlight nights, do you remember? You've not forgotten?

MME. RANEVSKAYA: [*Looking out of the window into the orchard.*] Oh, my childhood, my innocent childhood. I used to sleep in this nursery—I used to look out into the orchard, happiness waked with me every morning, the orchard was just the same then . . . nothing has changed. [*Laughs with joy.*] All, all white! Oh, my orchard! After the dark, rainy autumn and the cold winter, you are young again, and full of happiness, the heavenly angels have not left you. . . . If I could free my chest and my shoulders from this rock that weighs on me, if I could only forget the past!

GAYEV: Yes, and the orchard will be sold to pay our debts, strange as it may seem.

MME. RANEVSKAYA: Look! There is our poor mother walking in the orchard . . . all in white . . . [*Laughs with joy.*] It is she!

GAYEV: Where?

VARYA: What are you saying, Mamma dear!

MME. RANEVSKAYA: There's no one there, I just imagined it. To the right, where the path turns toward the arbor, there's a little white tree, leaning over, that looks like a woman . . .

[TROFIMOV *enters, wearing a shabby student's uniform and spectacles.*]

MME. RANEVSKAYA: What an amazing orchard! White masses of blossom, the blue sky . . .

TROFIMOV: Lubov Andreyevna! [*She looks round at him.*] I just want to pay my respects to you, then I'll leave at once. [*Kisses her hand ardently.*] I was told to wait until morning, but I hadn't the patience . . . [MME. RANEVSKAYA *looks at him, perplexed.*]

VARYA: [*Through tears.*] This is Petya Trofimov.

TROFIMOV: Petya Trofimov, formerly your Grisha's tutor. . . . Can I have changed so much? [MME. RANEVSKAYA *embraces him and weeps quietly.*]

GAYEV: [*Embarrassed.*] Don't, don't, Luba.

VARYA: [*Crying.*] I told you, Petya, to wait until tomorrow.

MME. RANEVSKAYA: My Grisha . . . my little boy . . . Grisha . . . my son.

VARYA: What can one do, Mamma dear, it's God's will.

TROFIMOV: [*Softly, through tears.*] There . . . there.

MME. RANEVSKAYA: [*Weeping quietly.*] My little boy was lost . . . drowned. Why? Why, my friend? [*More quietly.*] Anya's asleep in there, and here I am talking so loudly . . . making all this noise. . . . But tell me, Petya, why do you look so badly? Why have you aged so?

TROFIMOV: A mangy master, a peasant woman in the train called me.

MME. RANEVSKAYA: You were just a boy then, a dear little student, and now your hair's thin—and you're wearing glasses! Is it possible you're still a student? [*Goes toward the door.*]

TROFIMOV: I suppose I'm a perpetual student.

MME. RANEVSKAYA: [*Kisses her brother, then* VARYA.] Now, go to bed. . . . You have aged, too, Leonid.

PISHCHIK: [*Follows her.*] So now we turn in. Oh, my gout! I'm staying the night here . . . Lubov Andreyevna, my angel, tomorrow morning . . . I do need 240 rubles.

GAYEV: He keeps at it.

PISHCHIK: I'll pay it back, dear . . . it's a trifling sum.

MME. RANEVSKAYA: All right, Leonid will give it to you. Give it to him, Leonid.

GAYEV: Me give it to him! That's a good one!

MME. RANEVSKAYA: It can't be helped. Give it to him! He needs it. He'll pay it back.

[MME. RANEVSKAYA, TROFIMOV, PISHCHIK, *and* FIRS *go out;* GAYEV, VARYA, *and* YASHA *remain.*]

GAYEV: Sister hasn't got out of the habit of throwing money around. [*To* YASHA.] Go away, my good fellow, you smell of the barnyard.

YASHA: [*With a grin.*] And you, Leonid Andreyevich, are just the same as ever.

GAYEV: Who? [*To* VARYA.] What did he say?

VARYA: [*To* YASHA.] Your mother's come from the village; she's been sitting in the servants' room since yesterday, waiting to see you.

YASHA: Botheration!

VARYA: You should be ashamed of yourself!

YASHA: She's all I needed! She could have come tomorrow. [*Exits.*]

VARYA: Mamma is just the same as ever; she hasn't changed a bit. If she had her own way, she'd keep nothing for herself.

GAYEV: Yes . . . [*Pauses.*] If a great many remedies are offered for some disease, it means it is incurable; I keep thinking and racking my brains; I have many remedies, ever so many, and that really means none. It would be fine if we came in for a legacy; it would be fine if we married off our Anya to a very rich man; or we might go to Yaroslavl and try our luck with our aunt, the Countess. She's very rich, you know . . .

VARYA: [*Weeping.*] If only God would help us!

GAYEV: Stop bawling. Aunt's very rich, but she doesn't like us. In the first place, Sister married a lawyer who was no nobleman . . . [ANYA *appears in the doorway.*] She married beneath her, and it can't be said that her behavior has been very exemplary. She's good, kind, sweet, and I love her, but no matter what extenuating circumstances you may adduce, there's no denying that she has no morals. You sense it in her least gesture.

VARYA: [*In a whisper.*] Anya's in the doorway.

GAYEV: Who? [*Pauses.*] It's queer, something got into my right eye—my eyes are going back on me. . . . And on Thursday, when I was in the circuit court—

[*Enter* ANYA.]

VARYA: Why aren't you asleep, Anya?

ANYA: I can't get to sleep, I just can't.

GAYEV: My little pet! [*Kisses* ANYA's *face and hands.*] My child! [*Weeps.*] You are not my niece, you're my angel! You're everything to me. Believe me, believe—

ANYA: I believe you, Uncle. Everyone loves you and respects you . . . but, Uncle dear, you must keep still. . . . You must. What were you saying just now about my mother? Your own sister? What made you say that?

GAYEV: Yes, yes . . . [*Covers his face with her hand.*] Really, that was awful! Good God! Heaven help me! Just now I made a speech to the bookcase . . . so stupid! And only after I was through, I saw how stupid it was.

VARYA: It's true, Uncle dear, you ought to keep still. Just don't talk, that's all.

ANYA: If you could only keep still, it would make things easier for you, too.

GAYEV: I'll keep still. [*Kisses* ANYA's *and* VARYA's *hands.*] I will. But now about business. On Thursday I was in court; well, there were a number of us there, and we began talking of one thing and another, and this and that, and do you know, I believe it will be possible to raise a loan on a promissory note to pay the interest at the bank.

VARYA: If only God would help us!

GAYEV: On Tuesday I'll go and see about it again. [*To* VARYA.] Stop bawling. [*To* ANYA.] Your mamma will talk to Lopahin, and he, of course, will not refuse her . . . and as soon as you're rested, you'll go to Yaroslavl to the Countess, your great-aunt. So we'll be working in three directions at once, and the thing is in the bag. We'll pay the interest—I'm sure of it. [*Puts a candy in his mouth.*] I swear on my honor, I swear by anything you like, the estate shan't be sold. [*Excitedly.*] I swear by my own happiness! Here's my hand on it, you can call me a swindler and a scoundrel if I let it come to an auction! I swear by my whole being.

ANYA: [*Relieved and quite happy again.*] How good you are,

Uncle, and how clever! [*Embraces him.*] Now I'm at peace, quite at peace, I'm happy.

[*Enter* FIRS.]

FIRS: [*Reproachfully.*] Leonid Andreyevich, have you no fear of God? When are you going to bed?

GAYEV: Directly, directly. Go away, Firs, I'll ... yes, I will undress myself. Now, children, 'nightie-'nightie. We'll consider details tomorrow, but now go to sleep. [*Kisses* ANYA *and* VARYA.] I am a man of the eighties; they have nothing good to say of that period nowadays. Nevertheless, in the course of my life, I have suffered not a little for my convictions. It's not for nothing that the peasant loves me; one should know the peasant; one should know from which—

ANYA: There you go again, Uncle.

VARYA: Uncle dear, be quiet.

FIRS: [*Angrily.*] Leonid Andreyevich!

GAYEV: I'm coming, I'm coming! Go to bed! Double bank shot in the side pocket! Here goes a clean shot ...

[*Exits,* FIRS *hobbling after him.*]

ANYA: I am at peace now. I don't want to go to Yaroslavl—I don't like my great-aunt, but still, I am at peace, thanks to Uncle. [*Sits down.*]

VARYA: We must get some sleep. I'm going now. While you were away, something unpleasant happened. In the old servants' quarters, there are only the old people as you know; Yefim, Polya, Yevstigney, and Karp, too. They began letting all sorts of rascals in to spend the night. ... I didn't say anything. Then I heard they'd been spreading a report that I gave them nothing but dried peas to eat—out of stinginess, you know ... and it was all Yevstigney's doing. ... All right, I thought, if that's how it is, I thought, just wait. I sent for Yevstigney ... [*Yawns.*] He comes. ... "How's this, Yevstigney?" I say, "You fool ..." [*Looking at* ANYA.] Anichka! [*Pauses.*] She's asleep. [*Puts her arm around* ANYA.] Come to your little bed. ... Come ... [*Leads her.*] My darling has fallen asleep. ... Come.

[*They go out. Far away beyond the orchard, a shepherd is piping.* TROFIMOV *crosses the stage and, seeing* VARYA *and* ANYA, *stands still.*]

VARYA: Sh! She's asleep ... asleep. ... Come, darling.

ANYA: [*Softly, half-asleep.*] I'm so tired. Those bells ... Uncle ... dear. ... Mamma and Uncle ...

VARYA: Come, my precious, come along. [*They go into* ANYA'S *room.*]

TROFIMOV: [*With emotion.*] My sunshine, my spring!

Act II

A meadow. An old, long-abandoned, lopsided little chapel; near it a well, large slabs, which had apparently once served as tombstones, and an old bench. In the background the road to the Gayev estate. To one side poplars loom darkly, where the cherry orchard begins. In the distance a row of telegraph poles, and far off, on the hori-

zon, the faint outline of a large city which is seen only in fine, clear weather. The sun will soon be setting. CHARLOTTA, YASHA, and DUNYASHA are seated on the bench. YEPIHODOV stands near and plays a guitar. All are pensive. CHARLOTTA wears an old peaked cap. She has taken a gun from her shoulder and is straightening the buckle on the strap.

CHARLOTTA: [*Musingly.*] I haven't a real passport, I don't know how old I am, and I always feel that I am very young. When I was a little girl, my father and mother used to go from fair to fair and give performances, very good ones. And I used to do the *salto mortale*, and all sorts of other tricks. And when papa and mamma died, a German lady adopted me and began to educate me. Very good. I grew up and became a governess. But where I come from and who am I, I don't know. . . . Who were my parents? Perhaps they weren't even married. . . . I don't know . . . [*Takes a cucumber out of her pocket and eats it.*] I don't know a thing. [*Pause.*] One wants so much to talk, and there isn't anyone to talk to. . . . I haven't anybody.

YEPIHODOV: [*Plays the guitar and sings.*] "What care I for the jarring world? What's friend or foe to me? . . ." How agreeable it is to play the mandolin.

DUNYASHA: That's a guitar, not a mandolin. [*Looks in a hand mirror and powders her face.*]

YEPIHODOV: To a madman in love it's a mandolin. [*Sings.*] "Would that the heart were warmed by the fire of mutual love!" [YASHA *joins in.*]

CHARLOTTA: How abominably these people sing. Pfui! Like jackals!

DUNYASHA: [*To* YASHA.] How wonderful it must be though to have stayed abroad!

YASHA: Ah, yes, of course, I cannot but agree with you there. [*Yawns and lights a cigar.*]

YEPIHODOV: Naturally. Abroad, everything has long since achieved full perplexion.

YASHA: That goes without saying.

YEPIHODOV: I'm a cultivated man, I read all kinds of remarkable books. And yet I can never make out what direction I should take, what is it that I want, properly speaking. Should I live, or should I shoot myself, properly speaking? Nevertheless, I always carry a revolver about me. . . . Here it is . . . [*Shows revolver.*]

CHARLOTTA: I've finished. I'm going. [*Puts the gun over her shoulder.*] You are a very clever man, Yepihodov, and a very terrible one; women must be crazy about you. Br-r-r! [*Starts to go.*] These clever men are all so stupid; there's no one for me to talk to . . . always alone, alone, I haven't a soul . . . and who I am, and why I am, nobody knows. [*Exits unhurriedly.*]

YEPIHODOV: Properly speaking and letting other subjects alone, I must say regarding myself, among other things, that fate treats me mercilessly, like a storm treats a small boat. If I am mistaken, let us say, why then do I wake up this morning, and there on my chest is a spider of enormous dimensions . . . like this . . . [*Indicates with both hands.*] Again, I take up a pitcher of kvass to have a drink, and in it there is something unseemly to the highest degree, something like a cockroach. [*Pause.*] Have you read Buckle?[1] [*Pause.*] I wish to have a word with you, Avdotya Fyodorovna, if I may trouble you.

DUNYASHA: Well, go ahead.

YEPIHODOV: I wish to speak with you alone. [*Sighs.*]

DUNYASHA: [*Embarrassed.*] Very well. Only first bring me my little cape. You'll find it near the wardrobe. It's rather damp here.

YEPIHODOV: Certainly, ma'am; I will fetch it, ma'am. Now I know what to do with my revolver. [*Takes the guitar and goes off playing it.*]

YASHA: Two-and-Twenty Troubles! An awful fool, between you and me. [*Yawns.*]

DUNYASHA: I hope to God he doesn't shoot himself! [*Pause.*] I've become so nervous, I'm always fretting. I was still a little girl when I was taken into the big house, I am quite unused to the simple life now, and my hands are white, as white as a lady's. I've become so soft, so delicate, so refined, I'm afraid of everything. It's so terrifying; and if you deceive me, Yasha, I don't know what will happen to my nerves. [YASHA *kisses her.*]

YASHA: You're a peach! Of course, a girl should never forget herself; and what I dislike more than anything is when a girl don't behave properly.

DUNYASHA: I've fallen passionately in love with you; you're educated—you have something to say about everything. [*Pause.*]

YASHA: [*Yawns.*] Yes, ma'am. Now the way I look at it, if a girl loves someone, it means she is immoral. [*Pause.*] It's agreeable smoking a cigar in the fresh air. [*Listens.*] Someone's coming this way. . . . It's our madam and the others. [DUNYASHA *embraces him impulsively.*] You go home, as though you'd been to the river to bathe; go by the little path, or else they'll run into you and suspect me of having arranged to meet you here. I can't stand that sort of thing.

DUNYASHA: [*Coughing softly.*] Your cigar's made my head ache. [*Exits.* YASHA *remains standing near the chapel. Enter* MME. RANEVSKAYA, GAYEV, *and* LOPAHIN.]

LOPAHIN: You must make up your mind once and for all—there's no time to lose. It's quite a simple question, you know. Do you agree to lease your land for summer cottages or not? Answer in one word, yes or no; only one word!

MME. RANEVSKAYA: Who's been smoking such abominable cigars here? [*Sits down.*]

GAYEV: Now that the railway line is so near, it's made things very convenient. [*Sits down.*] Here we've been able to have lunch in town. Yellow ball in the side pocket! I feel like going into the house and playing just one game.

MME. RANEVSKAYA: You can do that later.

LOPAHIN: Only one word! [*Imploringly.*] Do give me an answer!

GAYEV: [*Yawning.*] Who?

MME. RANEVSKAYA: [*Looks into her purse.*] Yesterday I had a lot

---

1. Henry Thomas Buckle (1821–1862) wrote a *History of Civilization in England* (1857–1861) which was considered daringly materialistic and free thinking.

of money and now my purse is almost empty. My poor Varya tries to economize by feeding us just milk soup; in the kitchen the old people get nothing but dried peas to eat, while I squander money thoughtlessly. [*Drops the purse, scattering gold pieces.*] You see, there they go . . . [*Shows vexation.*]

YASHA: Allow me—I'll pick them up. [*Picks up the money.*]

MME. RANEVSKAYA: Be so kind. Yasha. And why did I go to lunch in town? That nasty restaurant, with its music and the tablecloth smelling of soap. . . . Why drink so much, Leonid? Why eat so much? Why talk so much? Today again you talked a lot, and all so inappropriately about the seventies, about the decadents.[2] And to whom? Talking to waiters about decadents!

LOPAHIN: Yes.

GAYEV: [*Waving his hand.*] I'm incorrigible; that's obvious. [*Irritably, to* YASHA.] Why do you keep dancing about in front of me?

YASHA: [*Laughs.*] I can't hear your voice without laughing—

GAYEV: Either he or I—

MME. RANEVSKAYA: Go away, Yasha; run along.

YASHA: [*Handing* MME. RANEVSKAYA *her purse.*] I'm going at once. [*Hardly able to suppress his laughter.*] This minute. [*Exits.*]

LOPAHIN: That rich man, Deriganov, wants to buy your estate. They say he's coming to the auction himself.

MME. RANEVSKAYA: Where did you hear that?

LOPAHIN: That's what they are saying in town.

GAYEV: Our aunt in Yaroslavl has promised to help; but when she will send the money, and how much, no one knows.

LOPAHIN: How much will she send? A hundred thousand? Two hundred?

MME. RANEVSKAYA: Oh, well, ten or fifteen thousand; and we'll have to be grateful for that.

LOPAHIN: Forgive me, but such frivolous people as you are, so queer and unbusinesslike—I never met in my life. One tells you in plain language that your estate is up for sale, and you don't seem to take it in.

MME. RANEVSKAYA: What are we to do? Tell us what to do.

LOPAHIN: I do tell you, every day; every day I say the same thing! You must lease the cherry orchard and the land for summer cottages, you must do it and as soon as possible—right away. The auction is close at hand. Please understand! Once you've decided to have the cottages, you can raise as much money as you like, and you're saved.

MME. RANEVSKAYA: Cottages—summer people—forgive me, but it's all so vulgar.

GAYEV: I agree with you absolutely.

LOPAHIN: I shall either burst into tears or scream or faint! I can't stand it! You've worn me out! [*To* GAYEV.] You're an old woman!

GAYEV: Who?

LOPAHIN: An old woman! [*Gets up to go.*]

---

2. A group of French poets (Mallarmé is today the most famous) of the 1880's were labeled "decadents" by their ene- mies and sometimes adopted the name themselves, proud of their refinement and sensitivity.

MME. RANEVSKAYA: [*Alarmed.*] No, don't go! Please stay, I beg you, my dear. Perhaps we shall think of something.

LOPAHIN: What is there to think of?

MME. RANEVSKAYA: Don't go, I beg you. With you here it's more cheerful anyway. [*Pause.*] I keep expecting something to happen, it's as though the house were going to crash about our ears.

GAYEV: [*In deep thought.*] Bank shot in the corner.... Three cushions in the side pocket....

MME. RANEVSKAYA: We have been great sinners ...

LOPAHIN: What sins could you have committed?

GAYEV: [*Putting a candy in his mouth.*] They say I've eaten up my fortune in candy! [*Laughs.*]

MME. RANEVSKAYA: Oh, my sins! I've squandered money away recklessly, like a lunatic, and I married a man who made nothing but debts. My husband drank himself to death on champagne, he was a terrific drinker. And then, to my sorrow, I fell in love with another man, and I lived with him. And just then—that was my first punishment—a blow on the head: my little boy was drowned here in the river. And I went abroad, went away forever ... never to come back, never to see this river again ... I closed my eyes and ran, out of my mind.... But he followed me, piti-less, brutal. I bought a villa near Mentone, because he fell ill there; and for three years, day and night, I knew no peace, no rest. The sick man wore me out, he sucked my soul dry. Then last year, when the villa was sold to pay my debts, I went to Paris, and there he robbed me, abandoned me, took up with another woman, I tried to poison myself—it was stupid, so shameful—and then suddenly I felt drawn back to Russia, back to my own country, to my little girl. [*Wipes her tears away.*] Lord, Lord! Be merciful, forgive me my sins—don't punish me anymore! [*Takes a telegram out of her pocket.*] This came today from Paris—he begs me to forgive him, implores me to go back ... [*Tears up the telegram.*] Do I hear music? [*Listens.*]

GAYEV: That's our famous Jewish band, you remember? Four vio-lins, a flute, and a double bass.

MME. RANEVSKAYA: Does it still exist? We ought to send for them some evening and have a party.

LOPAHIN: [*Listens.*] I don't hear anything. [*Hums softly.*] "The Germans for a fee will Frenchify a Russian." [*Laughs.*] I saw a play at the theater yesterday—awfully funny.

MME. RANEVSKAYA: There was probably nothing funny about it. You shouldn't go to see plays, you should look at yourselves more often. How drab your lives are—how full of unnecessary talk.

LOPAHIN: That's true; come to think of it, we do live like fools. [*Pause.*] My pop was a peasant, an idiot; he understood nothing, never taught me anything, all he did was beat me when he was drunk, and always with a stick. Fundamentally, I'm just the same kind of blockhead and idiot. I was never taught anything—I have a terrible handwriting. I write so that I feel ashamed before people, like a pig.

MME. RANEVSKAYA: You should get married, my friend.

LOPAHIN: Yes . . . that's true.

MME. RANEVSKAYA: To our Varya, she's a good girl.

LOPAHIN: Yes.

MME. RANEVSKAYA: She's a girl who comes of simple people, she works all day long; and above all, she loves you. Besides, you've liked her for a long time now.

LOPAHIN: Well, I've nothing against it. She's a good girl. [*Pause.*]

GAYEV: I've been offered a place in the bank—6,000 a year. Have you heard?

MME. RANEVSKAYA: You're not up to it. Stay where you are.

   [FIRS *enters, carrying an overcoat.*]

FIRS: [*To* GAYEV.] Please put this on, sir, it's damp.

GAYEV: [*Putting it on.*] I'm fed up with you, brother.

FIRS: Never mind. This morning you drove off without saying a word. [*Looks him over.*]

MME. RANEVSKAYA: How you've aged, Firs.

FIRS: I beg your pardon?

LOPAHIN: The lady says you've aged.

FIRS: I've lived a long time; they were arranging my wedding and your papa wasn't born yet. [*Laughs.*] When freedom came I was already head footman. I wouldn't consent to be set free then; I stayed on with the master . . . [*Pause.*] I remember they were all very happy, but why they were happy, they didn't know themselves.

LOPAHIN: It was fine in the old days! At least there was flogging!

FIRS: [*Not hearing.*] Of course. The peasants kept to the masters, the masters kept to the peasants; but now they've all gone their own ways, and there's no making out anything.

GAYEV: Be quiet, Firs. I must go to town tomorrow. They've promised to introduce me to a general who might let us have a loan.

LOPAHIN: Nothing will come of that. You won't even be able to pay the interest, you can be certain of that.

MME. RANEVSKAYA: He's raving, there isn't any general. [*Enter* TROFIMOV, ANYA, *and* VARYA.]

GAYEV: Here come our young people.

ANYA: There's Mamma, on the bench.

MME. RANEVSKAYA: [*Tenderly.*] Come here, come along, my darlings. [*Embraces* ANYA *and* VARYA.] If you only knew how I love you both! Sit beside me—there, like that. [*All sit down.*]

LOPAHIN: Our perpetual student is always with the young ladies.

TROFIMOV: That's not any of your business.

LOPAHIN: He'll soon be fifty, and he's still a student!

TROFIMOV: Stop your silly jokes.

LOPAHIN: What are you so cross about, you queer bird?

TROFIMOV: Oh, leave me alone.

LOPAHIN: [*Laughs.*] Allow me to ask you, what do you think of me?

TROFIMOV: What I think of you, Yermolay Alexeyevich, is this: you are a rich man who will soon be a millionaire. Well, just as a beast of prey, which devours everything that comes in its way, is necessary for the process of metabolism to go on, so you, too, are necessary. [*All laugh.*]

VARYA: Better tell us something about the planets, Petya.

MME. RANEVSKAYA: No, let's go on with yesterday's conversation.

TROFIMOV: What was it about?

GAYEV: About man's pride.

TROFIMOV: Yesterday we talked a long time, but we came to no conclusion. There is something mystical about man's pride in your sense of the word. Perhaps you're right, from your own point of view. But if you reason simply, without going into subtleties, then what call is there for pride? Is there any sense in it, if man is so poor a thing physiologically, and if, in the great majority of cases, he is coarse, stupid, profoundly unhappy? We should stop admiring ourselves. We should work, and that's all.

GAYEV: You die, anyway.

TROFIMOV: Who knows? And what does it mean—to die? Perhaps man has a hundred senses, and at his death only the five we know perish, while the other ninety-five remain alive.

MME. RANEVSKAYA: How clever you are, Petya!

LOPAHIN: [*Ironically.*] Awfully clever!

TROFIMOV: Mankind goes forward, developing its powers. Everything that is now unattainable for it will one day come within man's reach and be clear to him; only we must work, helping with all our might those who seek the truth. Here among us in Russia only the very few work as yet. The great majority of the intelligentsia, as far as I can see, seek nothing, do nothing, are totally unfit for work of any kind. They call themselves the intelligentsia, yet they are uncivil to their servants, treat the peasants like animals, are poor students, never read anything serious, do absolutely nothing at all, only talk about science, and have little appreciation of the arts. They are all solemn, have grim faces, they all philosophize and talk of weighty matters. And meanwhile the vast majority of us, ninety-nine out of a hundred, live like savages. At the least provocation—a punch in the jaw, and curses. They eat disgustingly, sleep in filth and stuffiness, bedbugs everywhere, stench and damp and moral slovenliness. And obviously, the only purpose of all our fine talk is to hoodwink ourselves and others. Show me where the public nurseries are that we've heard so much about, and the libraries. We read about them in novels, but in reality they don't exist, there is nothing but dirt, vulgarity, and Asiatic backwardness. I don't like very solemn faces, I'm afraid of them, I'm afraid of serious conversations. We'd do better to keep quiet for a while.

LOPAHIN: Do you know, I get up at five o'clock in the morning, and I work from morning till night; and I'm always handling money, my own and other people's, and I see what people around me are really like. You've only to start doing anything to see how few honest, decent people there are. Sometimes when I lie awake at night, I think: "Oh, Lord, thou hast given us immense forests, boundless fields, the widest horizons, and living in their midst, we ourselves ought really to be giants."

MME. RANEVSKAYA: Now you want giants! They're only good in fairy tales; otherwise they're frightening.

[YEPIHODOV *crosses the stage at the rear, playing the guitar.*]

MME. RANEVSKAYA: [*Pensively.*] There goes Yepihodov.

GAYEV: Ladies and gentlemen, the sun has set.

TROFIMOV: Yes.

GAYEV: [*In a low voice, declaiming as it were.*] Oh, Nature, wondrous Nature, you shine with eternal radiance, beautiful and indifferent! You, whom we call our mother, unite within yourself life and death! You animate and destroy!

VARYA: [*Pleadingly.*] Uncle dear!

ANYA: Uncle, again!

TROFIMOV: You'd better bank the yellow ball in the side pocket.

GAYEV: I'm silent, I'm silent . . .

[*All sit plunged in thought. Stillness reigns. Only* FIRS'S *muttering is audible. Suddenly a distant sound is heard, coming from the sky as it were, the sound of a snapping string, mournfully dying away.*]

MME. RANEVSKAYA: What was that?

LOPAHIN: I don't know. Somewhere far away, in the pits, a bucket's broken loose; but somewhere very far away.

GAYEV: Or it might be some sort of bird, perhaps a heron.

TROFIMOV: Or an owl . . .

MME. RANEVSKAYA: [*Shudders.*] It's weird, somehow. [*Pause.*]

FIRS: Before the calamity the same thing happened—the owl screeched, and the samovar hummed all the time.

GAYEV: Before what calamity?

FIRS: Before the Freedom.³ [*Pause.*]

MME. RANEVSKAYA: Come, my friends, let's be going. It's getting dark. [*To* ANYA.] You have tears in your eyes. What is it, my little one? [*Embraces her.*]

ANYA: I don't know, Mamma; it's nothing.

TROFIMOV: Somebody's coming.

[*A* TRAMP *appears, wearing a shabby white cap and an overcoat. He is slightly drunk.*]

TRAMP: Allow me to inquire, will this short cut take me to the station?

GAYEV: It will. Just follow that road.

TRAMP: My heartfelt thanks. [*Coughing.*] The weather is glorious. [*Recites.*] "My brother, my suffering brother.⁴ . . . Go down to the Volga!⁵ Whose groans . . .?' [*To* VARYA.] Mademoiselle, won't you spare 30 kopecks for a hungry Russian?

VARYA: [*Frightened, cries out.*]

LOPAHIN: [*Angrily.*] Even panhandling has its proprieties.

MME. RANEVSKAYA: [*Scared.*] Here, take this. [*Fumbles in her purse.*] I haven't any silver . . . never mind, here's a gold piece.

TRAMP: My heartfelt thanks. [*Exits. Laughter.*]

VARYA: [*Frightened.*] I'm leaving. I'm leaving. . . . Oh, Mamma dear, at home the servants have nothing to eat, and you gave him a gold piece!

---

3. refers to the emancipation of the serfs in 1861.

4. from a poem by Syomon Nadson (1862–1887).

5. comes from a poem by Nikolay Nekrasov (1821–1878).

MME. RANEVSKAYA: What are you going to do with me? I'm such a fool. When we get home, I'll give you everything I have. Yermolay Alexeyevich, you'll lend me some more . . .

LOPAHIN: Yes, ma'am.

MME. RANEVSKAYA: Come, ladies and gentlemen, it's time to be going. Oh! Varya, we've settled all about your marriage. Congratulations!

VARYA: [Through tears.] Really, Mamma, that's not a joking matter.

LOPAHIN: "Aurelia, get thee to a nunnery, go . . ."[6]

GAYEV: And do you know, my hands are trembling: I haven't played billiards in a long time.

LOPAHIN: "Aurelia, nymph, in your orisons, remember me!"[6]

MME. RANEVSKAYA: Let's go, it's almost suppertime.

VARYA: He frightened me! My heart's pounding.

LOPAHIN: Let me remind you, ladies and gentlemen, on the twenty-second of August the cherry orchard will be up for sale. Think about that! Think!

[All except TROFIMOV and ANYA go out.]

ANYA: [Laughs.] I'm grateful to that tramp, he frightened Varya and so we're alone.

TROFIMOV: Varya's afraid we'll fall in love with each other all of a sudden. She hasn't left us alone for days. Her narrow mind can't grasp that we're above love. To avoid the petty and illusory, everything that prevents us from being free and happy—that is the goal and meaning of our life. Forward! Do not fall behind, friends!

ANYA: [Strikes her hands together.] How well you speak! [Pause.] It's wonderful here today.

TROFIMOV: Yes, the weather's glorious.

ANYA: What have you done to me, Petya? Why don't I love the cherry orchard as I used to? I loved it so tenderly. It seemed to me there was no spot on earth lovelier than our orchard.

TROFIMOV: All Russia is our orchard. Our land is vast and beautiful, there are many wonderful places in it. [Pause.] Think of it, Anya, your grandfather, your great-grandfather and all your ancestors were serf owners, owners of living souls, and aren't human beings looking at you from every tree in the orchard, from every leaf, from every trunk? Don't you hear voices? Oh, it's terrifying! Your orchard is a fearful place, and when you pass through it in the evening or at night, the old bark on the trees gleams faintly, and the cherry trees seem to be dreaming of things that happened a hundred, two hundred years ago and to be tormented by painful visions. What is there to say? We're at least two hundred years behind, we've really achieved nothing yet, we have no definite attitude to the past, we only philosophize, complain of the blues, or drink vodka. It's all so clear: in order to live in the present, we should first redeem our past,

6. Lopahin makes comic use of Hamlet's meeting with Ophelia (in the Russian distorted to "Okhmelia"). Hamlet, seeing her approaching, says: "Nymph, in thy orisons / Be all my sins remembered." (Act III, sc. 1, ll. 89–90), and later, suspecting her of spying for her father, sends her off with "Get thee to a nunnery" (l. 121).

finish with it, and we can expiate it only by suffering, only by extraordinary, unceasing labor. Realize that, Anya.

ANYA: The house in which we live has long ceased to be our own, and I will leave it, I give you my word.

TROFIMOV: If you have the keys, fling them into the well and go away. Be free as the wind.

ANYA: [*In ecstasy.*] How well you put that!

TROFIMOV: Believe me, Anya, believe me! I'm not yet thirty, I'm young, I'm still a student—but I've already suffered so much. In winter I'm hungry, sick, harassed, poor as a beggar, and where hasn't Fate driven me? Where haven't I been? And yet always, every moment of the day and night, my soul is filled with inexplicable premonitions. . . . I have a premonition of happiness, Anya. . . . I see it already!

ANYA: [*Pensively.*] The moon is rising.

[YEPIHODOV *is heard playing the same mournful tune on the guitar. The moon rises. Somewhere near the poplars* VARYA *is looking for* ANYA *and calling,* "Anya, where are you?"]

TROFIMOV: Yes, the moon is rising. [*Pause.*] There it is, happiness, it's approaching, it's coming nearer and nearer, I can already hear its footsteps. And if we don't see it, if we don't know it, what does it matter? Others will!

VARYA'S VOICE: Anya! Where are you?

TROFIMOV: That Varya again! [*Angrily.*] It's revolting!

ANYA: Never mind, let's go down to the river. It's lovely there.

TROFIMOV: Come on. [*They go.*]

VARYA'S VOICE: Anya! Anya!

Act III

A drawing room separated by an arch from a ballroom. Evening. Chandelier burning. The Jewish band is heard playing in the anteroom. In the ballroom they are dancing the Grand Rond. PISHCHIK *is heard calling,* "Promenade à une paire." PISHCHIK *and* CHARLOTTA, TROFIMOV *and* MME. RANEVSKAYA, ANYA *and the* POST OFFICE CLERK, VARYA *and the* STATIONMASTER, *and others enter the drawing room in couples.* DUNYASHA *is in the last couple.* VARYA *weeps quietly, wiping her tears as she dances. All parade through drawing room.* PISHCHIK *calling,* "Grand rond, balancez!" *and* "Les cavaliers à genoux et remerciez vos dames!" FIRS, *wearing a dress coat, brings in soda water on a tray.* PISHCHIK *and* TROFIMOV *enter the drawing room.*

PISHCHIK: I have high blood pressure; I've already had two strokes. Dancing's hard work for me; but as they say, "If you run with the pack, you can bark or not, but at least wag your tail." Still, I'm as strong as a horse. My late lamented father, who would have his joke, God rest his soul, used to say, talking about our origin, that the ancient line of the Simeonov-Pishchiks was descended from the very horse that Caligula had made a senator. [*Sits down.*] But the trouble is, I have no money. A hungry dog believes in nothing but meat. [*Snores, and wakes up at once.*] It's the same with me—I can think of nothing but money.

TROFIMOV: You know, there *is* something equine about your figure.

PISHCHIK: Well, a horse is a fine animal—one can sell a horse.

[*Sound of billiards being played in an ·adjoining room.* VARYA *appears in the archway.*]

TROFIMOV: [*Teasing her.*] Madam Lopahina! Madam Lopahina!

VARYA: [*Angrily.*] Mangy master!

TROFIMOV: Yes, I am a mangy master and I'm proud of it.

VARYA: [*Reflecting bitterly.*] Here we've hired musicians, and what shall we pay them with? [*Exits.*]

TROFIMOV: [*To* PISHCHIK.] If the energy you have spent during your lifetime looking for money to pay interest had gone into something else, in the end you could have turned the world upside down.

PISHCHIK: Nietzsche, the philosopher, the greatest, most famous of men, that colossal intellect, says in his works that it is permissible to forge banknotes.

TROFIMOV: Have you read Nietzsche?

PISHCHIK: Well . . . Dashenka told me. . . . And now I've got to the point where forging banknotes is the only way out for me. . . . The day after tomorrow I have to pay 310 rubles—I already have 130 . . . [*Feels in his pockets. In alarm.*] The money's gone! I've lost my money! [*Through tears.*] Where's my money? [*Joyfully.*] Here it is! Inside the lining . . . I'm all in a sweat . . .

[*Enter* MME. RANEVSKAYA *and* CHARLOTTA.]

MME. RANEVSKAYA: [*Hums the "Lezginka."*] Why isn't Leonid back yet? What is he doing in town? [*To* DUNYASHA.] Dunyasha, offer the musicians tea.

TROFIMOV: The auction hasn't taken place, most likely.

MME. RANEVSKAYA: It's the wrong time to have the band, and the wrong time to give a dance. Well, never mind. [*Sits down and hums softly.*]

CHARLOTTA: [*Hands* PISHCHIK *a pack of cards.*] Here is a pack of cards. Think of any card you like.

PISHCHIK: I've thought of one.

CHARLOTTA: Shuffle the pack now. That's right. Give it here, my dear Mr. Pishchik. *Eins, zwei, drei!*[7] Now look for it—it's in your side pocket.

PISHCHIK: [*Taking the card out of his pocket.*] The eight of spades! Perfectly right! Just imagine!

CHARLOTTA: [*holding the pack of cards in her hands. To* TROFIMOV.] Quickly, name the top card.

TROFIMOV: Well, let's see—the queen of spades.

CHARLOTTA: Right! [*To* PISHCHIK.] Now name the top card.

PISHCHIK: The ace of hearts.

CHARLOTTA: Right! [*Claps her hands and the pack of cards disappears.*] Ah, what lovely weather it is today! [*A mysterious feminine voice, which seems to come from under the floor, answers her:* "Oh, yes, it's magnificent weather, madam."] You are my best ideal. [*Voice:* "And I find you pleasing too, madam."]

7. German for "one, two, three."

STATIONMASTER: [*Applauding.*] The lady ventriloquist, bravo!

PISHCHIK: [*Amazed.*] Just imagine! Enchanting Charlotta Ivanovna, I'm simply in love with you.

CHARLOTTA: In love? [*Shrugs her shoulders.*] Are you capable of love? *Guter Mensch, aber schlechter Musikant!*[8]

TROFIMOV: [*Claps* PISHCHIK *on the shoulder.*] You old horse, you!

CHARLOTTA: Attention please! One more trick! [*Takes a plaid from a chair.*] Here is a very good plaid; I want to sell it. [*Shaking it out.*] Does anyone want to buy it?

PISHCHIK: [*In amazement.*] Just imagine!

CHARLOTTA: *Eins, zwei, drei!* [*Raises the plaid quickly, behind it stands* ANYA. *She curtsies, runs to her mother, embraces her, and runs back into the ballroom, amid general enthusiasm.*]

MME. RANEVSKAYA: [*Applauds.*] Bravo! Bravo!

CHARLOTTA: Now again! *Eins, zwei, drei!* [*Lifts the plaid; behind it stands* VARYA, *bowing.*]

PISHCHIK: [*In amazement.*] Just imagine!

CHARLOTTA: The end! [*Throws the plaid at* PISHCHIK, *curtsies, and runs into the ballroom.*]

PISHCHIK: [*Running after her.*] The rascal! What a woman, what a woman! [*Exits.*]

MME. RANEVSKAYA: And Leonid still isn't here. What is he doing in town so long? I don't understand. It must be all over by now. Either the estate has been sold, or the auction hasn't taken place. Why keep us in suspense so long?

VARYA: [*Trying to console her.*] Uncle's bought it, I feel sure of that.

TROFIMOV: [*Mockingly.*] Oh, yes!

VARYA: Great-aunt sent him an authorization to buy it in her name, and to transfer the debt. She's doing it for Anya's sake. And I'm sure that God will help us, and Uncle will buy it.

MME. RANEVSKAYA: Great-aunt sent fifteen thousand to buy the estate in her name, she doesn't trust us, but that's not even enough to pay the interest. [*Covers her face with her hands.*] Today my fate will be decided, my fate—

TROFIMOV: [*Teasing* VARYA.] Madam Lopahina!

VARYA: [*Angrily.*] Perpetual student! Twice already you've been expelled from the university.

MME. RANEVSKAYA: Why are you so cross, Varya? He's teasing you about Lopahin. Well, what of it? If you want to marry Lopahin, go ahead. He's a good man, and interesting; if you don't want to, don't. Nobody's compelling you, my pet!

VARYA: Frankly, Mamma dear, I take this thing seriously; he's a good man and I like him.

MME. RANEVSKAYA: All right then, marry him. I don't know what you're waiting for.

VARYA: But, Mamma, I can't propose to him myself. For the last two years, everyone's been talking to me about him—talking. But he either keeps silent, or else cracks jokes. I understand; he's

8. ("A good man, but a bad musician") usually quoted in the plural: *"Gute Leute, schlechte Musikanten."* It comes from *Das Buch le Grand* (1826) of German poet Heinrich Heine (1799–1856). Here it suggests that Pishchik may be a good man but a bad lover.

growing rich, he's absorbed in business—he has no time for me. If I had money, even a little, say, 100 rubles, I'd throw everything up and go far away—I'd go into a nunnery.

TROFIMOV: What a blessing . . .

VARYA: A student ought to be intelligent. [*Softly, with tears in her voice.*] How homely you've grown, Petya! How old you look! [*To* MME. RANEVSKAYA, *with dry eyes.*] But I can't live without work, Mamma dear; I must keep busy every minute.

[*Enter* YASHA.]

YASHA: [*Hardly restraining his laughter.*] Yepihodov has broken a billiard cue! [*Exits.*]

VARYA: Why is Yepihodov here? Who allowed him to play billiards? I don't understand these people! [*Exits.*]

MME. RANEVSKAYA: Don't tease her, Petya. She's unhappy enough without that.

TROFIMOV: She bustles so—and meddles in other people's business. All summer long she's given Anya and me no peace. She's afraid of a love affair between us. What business is it of hers? Besides, I've given no grounds for it, and I'm far from such vulgarity. We are above love.

MME. RANEVSKAYA: And I suppose I'm beneath love? [*Anxiously.*] What can be keeping Leonid? If I only knew whether the estate has been sold or not. Such a calamity seems so incredible to me that I don't know what to think—I feel lost. . . . I could scream. . . . I could do something stupid. . . . Save me, Petya, tell me something, talk to me!

TROFIMOV: Whether the estate is sold today or not, isn't it all one? That's all done with long ago—there's no turning back, the path is overgrown. Calm yourself, my dear. You mustn't deceive yourself. For once in your life you must face the truth.

MME. RANEVSKAYA: What truth? You can see the truth, you can tell it from falsehood, but I seem to have lost my eyesight, I see nothing. You settle every great problem so boldly, but tell me, my dear boy, isn't it because you're young, because you don't yet know what one of your problems means in terms of suffering? You look ahead fearlessly, but isn't it because you don't see and don't expect anything dreadful, because life is still hidden from your young eyes? You're bolder, more honest, more profound than we are, but think hard, show just a bit of magnanimity, spare me. After all, I was born here, my father and mother lived here, and my grandfather; I love this house. Without the cherry orchard, my life has no meaning for me, and if it really must be sold, then sell me with the orchard. [*Embraces* TROFIMOV, *kisses him on the forehead.*] My son was drowned here. [*Weeps.*] Pity me, you good, kind fellow!

TROFIMOV: You know, I feel for you with all my heart.

MME. RANEVSKAYA: But that should have been said differently, so differently! [*Takes out her handkerchief—a telegram falls on the floor.*] My heart is so heavy today—you can't imagine! The noise here upsets me—my inmost being trembles at every sound—I'm shaking all over. But I can't go into my own room; I'm afraid to be alone. Don't condemn me, Petya. . . . I love you as though you were one of us, I would gladly let you marry Anya—I swear I would—only, my dear boy, you must study—you must take your degree—you do nothing, you let yourself be tossed by Fate from place to place—it's so strange. It's true, isn't it? And you should do something about your beard, to make it grow somehow! [*Laughs.*] You're so funny!

TROFIMOV: [*Picks up the telegram.*] I've no wish to be a dandy.

MME. RANEVSKAYA: That's a telegram from Paris. I get one every day. One yesterday and one today. That savage is ill again—he's in trouble again. He begs forgiveness, implores me to go to him, and really I ought to go to Paris to be near him. Your face is stern, Petya; but what is there to do, my dear boy? What am I to do? He's ill, he's alone and unhappy, and who is to look after him, who is to keep him from doing the wrong thing, who is to give him his medicine on time? And why hide it or keep still about it—I love him! That's clear. I love him, love him! He's a millstone round my neck, he'll drag me to the bottom, but I love that stone, I can't live without it. [*Presses* TROFIMOV's *hand.*] Don't think badly of me. Petya, and don't say anything, don't say . . .

TROFIMOV: [*Through tears.*] Forgive me my frankness in heaven's name; but, you know, he robbed you!

MME. RANEVSKAYA: No, no, no, you mustn't say such things! [*Covers her ears.*]

TROFIMOV: But he's a scoundrel! You're the only one who doesn't know it. He's a petty scoundrel—a nonentity!

MME. RANEVSKAYA: [*Controlling her anger.*] You are twenty-six or twenty-seven years old, but you're still a schoolboy.

TROFIMOV: That may be.

MME. RANEVSKAYA: You should be a man at your age. You should understand people who love—and ought to be in love yourself. You ought to fall in love! [*Angrily.*] Yes, yes! And it's not purity in you, it's prudishness, you're simple a queer fish, a comical freak!

TROFIMOV: [*Horrified.*] What is she saying?

MME. RANEVSKAYA: "I am above love!" You're not above love, but simply, as our Firs says, you're an addlehead. At your age not to have a mistress!

TROFIMOV: [*Horrified.*] This is frightful! What is she saying! [*Goes rapidly into the ballroom, clutching his head.*] It's frightful—I can't stand it, I won't stay! [*Exits, but returns at once.*] All is over between us! [*Exits into anteroom.*]

MME. RANEVSKAYA: [*Shouts after him.*] Petya! Wait! You absurd fellow, I was joking. Petya!

[*Sound of somebody running quickly downstairs and suddenly falling down with a crash.* ANYA *and* VARYA *scream. Sound of laughter a moment later.*]

MME. RANEVSKAYA: What's happened?

[ANYA *runs in.*]

ANYA: [*Laughing.*] Petya's fallen downstairs! [*Runs out.*]

MME. RANEVSKAYA: What a queer bird that Petya is!

[STATIONMASTER, *standing in the middle of the ballroom,*

recites Alexey Tolstoy's "Magdalene,"[9] *to which all listen, but after a few lines, the sound of a waltz is heard from the anteroom and the reading breaks off. All dance.* TROFIMOV, ANYA, VARYA, *and* MME. RANEVSKAYA *enter from the anteroom.*]

MME. RANEVSKAYA: Petya, you pure soul, please forgive me. . . . Let's dance.

[*Dances with* PETYA. ANYA *and* VARYA *dance.* FIRS *enters, puts his stick down by the side door.* YASHA *enters from the drawing room and watches the dancers.*]

YASHA: Well, Grandfather?

FIRS: I'm not feeling well. In the old days it was generals, barons, and admirals that were dancing at our balls, and now we have to send for the Post Office Clerk and the Stationmaster, and even they aren't too glad to come. I feel kind of shaky. The old master that's gone, their grandfather, dosed everyone with sealing wax, whatever ailed 'em. I've been taking sealing wax every day for twenty years or more. Perhaps that's what's kept me alive.

YASHA: I'm fed up with you, Grandpop. [*Yawns.*] It's time you croaked.

FIRS: Oh, you addlehead! [*Mumbles.*]

[TROFIMOV *and* MME. RANEVSKAYA *dance from the ballroom into the drawing room.*]

MME. RANEVSKAYA: *Merci.* I'll sit down a while. [*Sits down.*] I'm tired.

[*Enter* ANYA.]

ANYA: [*Excitedly.*] There was a man in the kitchen just now who said the cherry orchard was sold today.

MME. RANEVSKAYA: Sold to whom?

ANYA: He didn't say. He's gone. [*Dances off with* TROFIMOV.]

YASHA: It was some old man gabbing, a stranger.

FIRS: And Leonid Andreyevich isn't back yet, he hasn't come. And he's wearing his lightweight between-season overcoat; like enough, he'll catch cold. Ah, when they're young they're green.

MME. RANEVSKAYA: This is killing me. Go, Yasha, find out to whom it has been sold.

YASHA: But the old man left long ago. [*Laughs.*]

MME. RANEVSKAYA: What are you laughing at? What are you pleased about?

YASHA: That Yepihodov is such a funny one. A funny fellow, Two-and-Twenty Troubles!

MME. RANEVSKAYA: Firs, if the estate is sold, where will you go?

FIRS: I'll go where you tell me.

MME. RANEVSKAYA: Why do you look like that? Are you ill? You ought to go to bed.

FIRS: Yes! [*With a snigger.*] Me go to bed, and who's to hand

---

9. called "The Sinning Woman" in Russian, begins thus:
A bustling crowd with happy laughter, with twangling lutes and clashing cymbals
with flowers and foliage all around the colonnaded portico.
Alexey Tolstoy (1817–1875) was a distant relative of Leo Tolstoy, popular in his time as a dramatist and poet.

things round? Who's to see to things? I'm the only one in the whole house.

YASHA: [*To* MME. RANEVSKAYA.] Lubov Andreyevna, allow me to ask a favor of you, be so kind! If you go back to Paris, take me with you, I beg you. It's positively impossible for me to stay here. [*Looking around; sotto voce.*] What's the use of talking? You see for yourself, it's an uncivilized country, the people have no morals, and then the boredom! The food in the kitchen's revolting, and besides there's this Firs wanders about mumbling all sorts of inappropriate words. Take me with you, be so kind!

[*Enter* PISHCHIK.]

PISHCHIK: May I have the pleasure of a waltz with you, charming lady? [MME. RANEVSKAYA *accepts.*] All the same, enchanting lady, you must let me have 180 rubles. . . . You must let me have [*dancing*] just one hundred and eighty rubles. [*They pass into the ballroom.*]

YASHA: [*Hums softly.*] "Oh, wilt thou understand the tumult in my soul?"

[*In the ballroom a figure in a gray top hat and checked trousers is jumping about and waving its arms; shouts: "Bravo, Charlotta Ivanovna!"*]

DUNYASHA: [*Stopping to powder her face; to* FIRS.] The young miss has ordered me to dance. There are so many gentlemen and not enough ladies. But dancing makes me dizzy, my heart begins to beat fast, Firs Nikolayevich. The Post Office Clerk said something to me just now that quite took my breath away. [*Music stops.*]

FIRS: What did he say?

DUNYASHA: "You're like a flower," he said.

YASHA: [*Yawns.*] What ignorance. [*Exits.*]

DUNYASHA: "Like a flower!" I'm such a delicate girl. I simply adore pretty speeches.

FIRS: You'll come to a bad end.

[*Enter* YEPIHODOV.]

YEPIHODOV: [*To* DUNYASHA.] You have no wish to see me, Avdotya Fyodorovna . . . as though I was some sort of insect. [*Sighs.*] Ah, life!

DUNYASHA: What is it you want?

YEPIHODOV: Indubitably you may be right. [*Sighs.*] But of course, if one looks at it from the point of view, if I may be allowed to say so, and apologizing for my frankness, you have completely reduced me to a state of mind. I know my fate. Every day some calamity befalls me, and I grew used to it long ago, so that I look upon my fate with a smile. You gave me your word, and though I—

DUNYASHA: Let's talk about it later, please. But just now leave me alone, I am daydreaming. [*Plays with a fan.*]

YEPIHODOV: A misfortune befalls me every day; and if I may be allowed to say so, I merely smile, I even laugh.

[*Enter* VARYA.]

VARYA: [*To* YEPIHODOV.] Are you still here? What an impertinent fellow you are really! Run along, Dunyasha. [*To* YEPIHODOV.]

Either you're playing billiards and breaking a cue, or you're wandering about the drawing room as though you were a guest.

YEPIHODOV: You cannot, permit me to remark, penalize me.

VARYA: I'm not penalizing you; I'm just telling you. You merely wander from place to place, and don't do your work. We keep you as a clerk, but heaven knows what for.

YEPIHODOV: [*Offended.*] Whether I work or whether I walk, whether I eat or whether I play billiards, is a matter to be discussed only by persons of understanding and of mature years.

VARYA: [*Enraged.*] You dare say that to me—you dare? You mean to say I've no understanding? Get out of here at once! This minute!

YEPIHODOV: [*Scared.*] I beg you to express yourself delicately.

VARYA: [*Beside herself.*] Clear out this minute! Out with you!

[YEPIHODOV *goes toward the door,* VARYA *following.*]

VARYA: Two-and-Twenty Troubles! Get out—don't let me set eyes on you again!

[*Exit* YEPIHODOV. *His voice is heard behind the door:* "I shall lodge a complaint against you!"]

VARYA: Oh, you're coming back? [*She seizes the stick left near door by* FIRS.] Well, come then . . . come . . . I'll show you. . . . Ah, you're coming? You're coming? . . . Come . . . [*Swings the stick just as* LOPAHIN *enters.*]

LOPAHIN: Thank you kindly.

VARYA: [*Angrily and mockingly.*] I'm sorry.

LOPAHIN: It's nothing. Thank you kindly for your charming reception.

VARYA: Don't mention it. [*Walks away, looks back and asks softly.*] I didn't hurt you, did I?

LOPAHIN: Oh, no, not at all. I shall have a large bump, though.

[*Voices from the ballroom:* "Lopahin is here! Lopahin!"]

[*Enter* PISHCHIK.]

PISHCHIK: My eyes do see, my ears do hear! [*Kisses* LOPAHIN.]

LOPAHIN: You smell of cognac, my dear friends. And we've been celebrating here, too.

[*Enter* MME. RANEVSKAYA.]

MME. RANEVSKAYA: Is that you, Yermolay Alexeyevich? What kept you so long? Where's Leonid?

LOPAHIN: Leonid Andreyevich arrived with me. He's coming.

MME. RANEVSKAYA: Well, what happened? Did the sale take place? Speak!

LOPAHIN: [*Embarrassed, fearful of revealing his joy.*] The sale was over at four o'clock. We missed the train—had to wait till half-past nine. [*Sighing heavily.*] Ugh. I'm a little dizzy.

[*Enter* GAYEV. *In his right hand he holds parcels, with his left he is wiping away his tears.*]

MME. RANEVSKAYA: Well, Leonid? What news? [*Impatiently, through tears.*] Be quick, for God's sake!

GAYEV: [*Not answering, simply waves his hand. Weeping, to* FIRS.] Here, take these; anchovies, Kerch herrings . . . I haven't eaten all day. What I've been through! [*The click of billiard balls comes through the open door of the billiard room and*

YASHA's *voice is heard:* "Seven and eighteen!" GAYEV's *expression changes, he no longer weeps.*] I'm terribly tired. Firs, help me change. [*Exits, followed by* FIRS.]

PISHCHIK: How about the sale? Tell us what happened.

MME. RANEVSKAYA: Is the cherry orchard sold?

LOPAHIN: Sold.

MME. RANEVSKAYA: Who bought it?

LOPAHIN: I bought it.

> [*Pause.* MME. RANEVSKAYA *is overcome. She would fall to the floor, were it not for the chair and table near which she stands.* VARYA *takes the keys from her belt, flings them on the floor in the middle of the drawing room and goes out.*]

LOPAHIN: I bought it. Wait a bit, ladies and gentlemen, please, my head is swimming, I can't talk. [*Laughs.*] We got to the auction and Deriganov was there already. Leonid Andreyevich had only 15,000 and straight off Deriganov bid 30,000 over and above the mortgage. I saw how the land lay, got into the fight, bid 40,000. He bid 45,000. I bid fifty-five. He kept adding five thousands, I ten. Well . . . it came to an end. I bid ninety above the mortgage and the estate was knocked down to me. Now the cherry orchard's mine! Mine! [*Laughs uproariously.*] Lord! God in Heaven! The cherry orchard's mine! Tell me that I'm drunk—out of my mind—that it's all a dream. [*Stamps his feet.*] Don't laugh at me! If my father and my grandfather could rise from their graves and see all that has happened—how their Yermolay, who used to be flogged, their half-literate Yermolay, who used to run about barefoot in winter, how that very Yermolay has bought the most magnificent estate in the world. I bought the estate where my father and grandfather were slaves, where they weren't even allowed to enter the kitchen. I'm asleep—it's only a dream—I only imagine it. . . . It's the fruit of your imagination, wrapped in the darkness of the unknown! [*Picks up the keys, smiling genially.*] She threw down the keys, wants to show she's no longer mistress here. [*Jingles keys.*] Well, no matter. [*The band is warming up.*] Hey, musicians! Strike up! I want to hear you! Come, everybody, and see how Yermolay Lopahin will lay the ax to the cherry orchard and how the trees will fall to the ground. We will build summer cottages there, and our grandsons and great-grandsons will see a new life here. Music! Strike up!

> [*The band starts to play.* MME RANEVSKAYA *has sunk into a chair and is weeping bitterly.*]

LOPAHIN: [*Reproachfully.*] Why, why didn't you listen to me? My dear friend, my poor friend, you can't bring it back now. [*Tearfully.*] Oh, if only this were over quickly! Oh, if only our wretched, disordered life were changed!

PISHCHIK: [*Takes him by the arm; sotto voce.*] She's crying. Let's go into the ballroom. Let her be alone. Come. [*Takes his arm and leads him into the ballroom.*]

LOPAHIN: What's the matter? Musicians, play so I can hear you! Let me have things the way I want them. [*Ironically.*] Here comes the new master, the owner of the cherry orchard.

[*Accidentally he trips over a little table, almost upsetting the candelabra.*] I can pay for everything. *Exits with* PISHCHIK.]

[MME. RANEVSKAYA, *alone, sits huddled up, weeping bitterly. Music plays softly. Enter* ANYA *and* TROFIMOV *quickly.* ANYA *goes to her mother and falls on her knees before her.* TROFIMOV *stands in the doorway.*]

ANYA: Mamma, Mamma, you're crying! Dear, kind, good Mamma, my precious, I love you, I bless you! The cherry orchard is sold, it's gone, that's true, quite true. But don't cry, Mamma, life is still before you, you still have your kind, pure heart. Let us go, let us go away from here, darling. We will plant a new orchard, even more luxuriant than this one. You will see it, you will understand, and like the sun at evening, joy—deep, tranquil joy—will sink into your soul, and you will smile, Mamma. Come, darling, let us go.

Act IV

Scene as in Act I. No window curtains or pictures, only a little furniture, piled up in a corner, as if for sale. A sense of emptiness. Near the outer door and at the back, suitcases, bundles, etc., are piled up. A door open on the left and the voices of VARYA *and* ANYA *are heard.* LOPAHIN *stands waiting.* YASHA *holds a tray with glasses full of champagne.* YEPIHODOV *in the anteroom is tying up a box. Behind the scene a hum of voices: peasants have come to say good-bye. Voice of* GAYEV: "Thanks, brothers, thank you."

YASHA: The country folk have come to say good-bye. In my opinion, Yermolay Alexeyevich, they are kindly souls, but there's nothing in their heads.

[*The hum dies away. Enter* MME. RANEVSKAYA *and* GAYEV. *She is not crying, but is pale, her face twitches and she cannot speak.*]

GAYEV: You gave them your purse, Luba. That won't do! That won't do!

MME. RANEVSKAYA: I couldn't help it! I couldn't! [*They go out.*]

LOPAHIN: [*Calls after them.*] Please, I beg you, have a glass at parting. I didn't think of bringing any champagne from town and at the station I could find only one bottle. Please, won't you? [*Pause.*] What's the matter, ladies and gentlemen, don't you want any? [*Moves away from the door.*] If I'd known, I wouldn't have bought it. Well, then I won't drink any, either. [YASHA *carefully sets the tray down on a chair*.] At least you have a glass, Yasha.

YASHA: Here's to the travelers! And good luck to those that stay! [*Drinks.*] This champagne isn't the real stuff, I can assure you.

LOPAHIN: Eight rubles a bottle. [*Pause.*] It's devilishly cold here.

YASHA: They didn't light the stoves today—it wasn't worth it, since we're leaving. [*Laughs.*]

LOPAHIN: Why are you laughing?

YASHA: It's just that I'm pleased.

LOPAHIN: It's October, yet it's as still and sunny as though it were summer. Good weather for building. [*Looks at his watch, and speaks off.*] Bear in mind, ladies and gentlemen, the train goes in forty-seven minutes, so you ought to start for the station in twenty minutes. Better hurry up!

[*Enter* TROFIMOV, *wearing an overcoat.*]

TROFIMOV: I think it's time to start. The carriages are at the door. The devil only knows what's become of my rubbers; they've disappeared. [*Calling off.*] Anya! My rubbers are gone. I can't find them.

LOPAHIN: I've got to go to Kharkov. I'll take the same train you do. I'll spend the winter in Kharkov. I've been hanging round here with you, till I'm worn out with loafing. I can't live without work—I don't know what to do with my hands, they dangle as if they didn't belong to me.

TROFIMOV: Well, we'll soon be gone, then you can go on with your useful labors again.

LOPAHIN: Have a glass.

TROFIMOV: No, I won't.

LOPAHIN: So you're going to Moscow now?

TROFIMOV: Yes, I'll see them into town, and tomorrow I'll go on to Moscow.

LOPAHIN: Well, I'll wager the professors aren't giving any lectures, they're waiting for you to come.

TROFIMOV: That's none of your business.

LOPAHIN: Just how many years have you been at the university?

TROFIMOV: Can't you think of something new? Your joke's stale and flat. [*Looking for his rubbers.*] We'll probably never see each other again, so allow me to give you a piece of advice at parting: don't wave your hands about! Get out of the habit. And another thing: building bungalows, figuring that summer residents will eventually become small farmers, figuring like that is just another form of waving your hands about. . . . Never mind, I love you anyway; you have fine, delicate fingers, like an artist; you have a fine, delicate soul.

LOPAHIN: [*Embracing him.*] Good-bye, my dear fellow. Thank you for everything. Let me give you some money for the journey, if you need it.

TROFIMOV: What for? I don't need it.

LOPAHIN: But you haven't any.

TROFIMOV: Yes, I have, thank you. I got some money for a translation—here it is in my pocket. [*Anxiously.*] But where are my rubbers?

VARYA: [*From the next room.*] Here! Take the nasty things. [*Flings a pair of rubbers onto the stage.*]

TROFIMOV: What are you so cross about, Varya? Hm . . . and these are not my rubbers.

LOPAHIN: I sowed three thousand acres of poppies in the spring, and now I've made 40,000 on them, clear profit; and when my poppies were in bloom, what a picture it was! So, as I say, I made 40,000; and I am offering you a loan because I can afford it. Why turn up your nose at it? I'm a peasant—I speak bluntly.

TROFIMOV: Your father was a peasant, mine was a druggist—that proves absolutely nothing whatever [LOPAHIN *takes out his wallet.*] Don't, put that away! If you were to offer me two hundred thousand, I wouldn't take it. I'm a free man. And everything that all of you, rich and poor alike, value so highly and hold so dear hasn't the slightest power over me. It's like so much fluff floating in the air. I can get on without you, I can pass you by, I'm strong and proud. Mankind is moving toward the highest truth, toward the highest happiness possible on earth, and I am in the front ranks.

LOPAHIN: Will you get there?

TROFIMOV: I will. [*Pause.*] I will get there, or I will show others the way to get there.

[*The sound of axes chopping down trees is heard in the distance.*]

LOPAHIN: Well, good-bye, my dear fellow. It's time to leave. We turn up our noses at one another, but life goes on just the same. When I'm working hard, without resting, my mind is easier, and it seems to me that I, too, know why I exist. But how many people are there in Russia, brother, who exist nobody knows why? Well, it doesn't matter. That's not what makes the wheels go round. They say Leonid Andreyevich has taken a position in the bank, 6,000 rubles a year. Only, of course, he won't stick to it, he's too lazy. . . .

ANYA: [*In the doorway.*] Mamma begs you not to start cutting down the cherry trees until she's gone.

TROFIMOV: Really, you should have more tact! [*Exits.*]

LOPAHIN: Right away—right away! Those men . . . [*Exits.*]

ANYA: Has Firs been taken to the hospital?

YASHA: I told them this morning. They must have taken him.

ANYA: [*To* YEPIHODOV, *who crosses the room.*] Yepihodov, please find out if Firs has been taken to the hospital.

YASHA: [*Offended.*] I told Yegor this morning. Why ask a dozen times?

YEPIHODOV: The aged Firs, in my definitive opinion, is beyond mending. It's time he was gathered to his fathers. And I can only envy him. [*Puts a suitcase down on a hat box and crushes it.*] There now, of course. I knew it! [*Exits.*]

YASHA: [*Mockingly.*] Two-and-Twenty Troubles!

VARYA: [*Through the door.*] Has Firs been taken to the hospital?

ANYA: Yes.

VARYA: Then why wasn't the note for the doctor taken too?

ANYA: Oh! Then someone must take it to him. [*Exits.*]

VARYA: [*From adjoining room.*] Where's Yasha? Tell him his mother's come and wants to say good-bye.

YASHA: [*Waves his hand.*] She tries my patience.

[DUNYASHA *has been occupied with the luggage. Seeing* YASHA *alone, she goes up to him.*]

DUNYASHA: You might just give me one little look, Yasha. You're going away. . . . You're leaving me . . . [*Weeps and throws herself on his neck.*]

YASHA: What's there to cry about? [*Drinks champagne.*] In six days I shall be in Paris again. Tomorrow we get into an express train and off we go, that's the last you'll see of us. . . . I can scarcely believe it. *Vive la France!* It don't suit me here, I just can't live here. That's all there is to it. I'm fed up with the ignorance here, I've had enough of it. [*Drinks champagne.*] What's there to cry about? Behave yourself properly, and you'll have no cause to cry.

DUNYASHA: [*Powders her face, looking in pocket mirror.*] Do send me a letter from Paris. You know I loved you, Yasha, how I loved you! I'm a delicate creature, Yasha.

YASHA: Somebody's coming! [*Busies himself with the luggage; hums softly.*]

[*Enter* MME. RANEVSKAYA, GAYEV, ANYA, *and* CHARLOTTA.]

GAYEV: We ought to be leaving. We haven't much time. [*Looks at* YASHA.] Who smells of herring?

MME. RANEVSKAYA: In about ten minutes we should be getting into the carriages. [*Looks around the room.*] Good-bye, dear old home, good-bye, grandfather. Winter will pass, spring will come, you will no longer be here, they will have torn you down. How much these walls have seen! [*Kisses* ANYA *warmly.*] My treasure, how radiant you look! Your eyes are sparkling like diamonds. Are you glad? Very?

ANYA: [*Gaily.*] Very glad. A new life is beginning, Mamma.

GAYEV: Well, really, everything is all right now. Before the cherry orchard was sold, we all fretted and suffered; but afterward, when the question was settled finally and irrevocably, we all calmed down, and even felt quite cheerful. I'm a bank employee now, a financier. The yellow ball in the side pocket! And anyhow, you are looking better, Luba, there's no doubt of that.

MME. RANEVSKAYA: Yes, my nerves are better, that's true. [*She is handed her hat and coat.*] I sleep well. Carry out my things, Yasha. It's time. [*To* ANYA.] We shall soon see each other again, my little girl. I'm going to Paris, I'll live there on the money your great-aunt sent us to buy the estate with—long live Auntie! But that money won't last long.

ANYA: You'll come back soon, soon, Mamma, won't you? Meanwhile I'll study. I'll pass my high school examination, and then I'll go to work and help you. We'll read all kinds of books together, Mamma, won't we? [*Kisses her mother's hands.*] We'll read in the autumn evenings, we'll read lots of books, and a new wonderful world will open up before us. [*Falls into a revery.*] Mamma, do come back.

MME. RANEVSKAYA: I will come back, my precious. [*Embraces her daughter. Enter* LOPAHIN *and* CHARLOTTA *who is humming softly.*]

GAYEV: Charlotta's happy: she's singing.

CHARLOTTA: [*Picks up a bundle and holds it like a baby in swaddling clothes.*] Bye, baby, bye. [*A baby is heard crying:* "Wah! Wah!"] Hush, hush, my pet, my little one. ["Wah! Wah!"] I'm so sorry for you! [*Throws the bundle down.*] You will find me a position, won't you? I can't go on like this.

LOPAHIN: We'll find one for you, Charlotta Ivanovna, don't worry.

GAYEV: Everyone's leaving us. Varya's going away. We've suddenly become of no use.

CHARLOTTA: There's no place for me to live in town, I must go away. [*Hums.*]

    [*Enter* PISHCHIK.]

LOPAHIN: There's nature's masterpiece!

PISHCHIK: [*Gasping.*] Oh . . . let me get my breath . . . I'm in agony. . . . Esteemed friends . . . Give me a drink of water. . . .

GAYEV: Wants some money, I suppose. No, thank you . . . I'll keep out of harm's way. [*Exits.*]

PISHCHIK: It's a long while since I've been to see you, most charming lady. [*To* LOPAHIN.] So you are here . . . glad to see you, you intellectual giant . . . There . . . [*Gives* LOPAHIN *money.*] Here's 400 rubles, and I still owe you 840.

LOPAHIN: [*Shrugging his shoulders in bewilderment.*] I must be dreaming. . . . Where did you get it?

PISHCHIK: Wait a minute . . . it's hot. . . . A most extraordinary event! Some Englishmen came to my place and found some sort of white clay on my land . . . [*To* MME. RANEVSKAYA.] And 400 for you . . . most lovely . . . most wonderful . . . [*Hands her the money.*] The rest later. [*Drinks water.*] A young man in the train was telling me just now that a great philosopher recommends jumping off roofs. "Jump!" says he; "that's the long and the short of it!" [*In amazement.*] Just imagine! Some more water!

LOPAHIN: What Englishmen?

PISHCHIK: I leased them the tract with the clay on it for twenty-four years. . . . And now, forgive me, I can't stay. . . . I must be dashing on. . . . I'm going over to Znoikov . . . to Kardamanov . . . I owe them all money . . . [*Drinks water.*] Good-bye, everybody . . . I'll look in on Thursday . . .

MME. RANEVSKAYA: We're just moving into town; and tomorrow I go abroad.

PISHCHIK: [*Upset.*] What? Why into town? That's why the furniture is like that . . . and the suitcases. . . . Well, never mind! [*Through tears.*] Never mind . . . men of colossal intellect, these Englishmen. . . . Never mind . . . Be happy. God will come to your help. . . . Never mind . . . everything in this world comes to an end. [*Kisses* MME. RANEVSKAYA's *hand.*] If the rumor reaches you that it's all up with me, remember this old . . . horse, and say: "Once there lived a certain . . . Simeonov-Pishchik . . . the kingdom of Heaven be his. . . ." Glorious weather! . . . Yes . . . [*Exits, in great confusion, but at once returns and says in the doorway.*] My daughter Dashenka sends her regards. [*Exits.*]

MME. RANEVSKAYA: Now we can go. I leave with two cares weighing on me. The first is poor old Firs. [*Glancing at her watch.*] We still have about five minutes.

ANYA: Mamma, Firs has already been taken to the hospital. Yasha sent him there this morning.

MME. RANEVSKAYA: My other worry is Varya. She's used to getting up early and working; and now, with no work to do, she is like a fish out of water. She has grown thin and pale, and keeps crying, poor soul. [*Pause.*] You know this very well, Yermolay Alexeyevich; I dreamed of seeing her married to you, and it looked as though that's how it would be. [*Whispers to* ANYA, *who nods to* CHARLOTTA *and both go out.*] She loves you. You find her attractive. I don't know, I don't know why it is you seem to avoid each other; I can't understand it.

LOPAHIN: To tell you the truth, I don't understand it myself. It's all a puzzle. If there's still time, I'm ready now, at once. Let's settle it straight off, and have done with it! Without you, I feel I'll never be able to propose.

MME. RANEVSKAYA: That's splendid. After all, it will only take a minute. I'll call her at once. . . .

LOPAHIN: And luckily, here's champagne, too. [*Looks at the glasses.*] Empty! Somebody's drunk it all. [*Yasha coughs.*] That's what you might call guzzling . . .

MME. RANEVSKAYA: [*Animatedly.*] Excellent! We'll go and leave you alone. Yasha, *allez!* I'll call her. [*At the door.*] Varya, leave everything and come here. Come! [*Exits with* YASHA.]

LOPAHIN: [*Looking at his watch.*] Yes . . . [*Pause behind the door, smothered laughter and whispering; at last, enter* VARYA.]

VARYA: [*Looking over the luggage in leisurely fashion.*] Strange, I can't find it . . .

LOPAHIN: What are you looking for?

VARYA: Packed it myself, and I don't remember . . . [*Pause.*]

LOPAHIN: Where are you going now, Varya?

VARYA: I? To the Ragulins'. I've arranged to take charge there—as housekeeper, if you like.

LOPAHIN: At Yashnevo? About fifty miles from here. [*Pause.*] Well, life in this house is ended!

VARYA: [*Examining luggage.*] Where is it? Perhaps I put it in the chest. Yes, life in this house is ended. . . . There will be no more of it.

LOPAHIN: And I'm just off to Kharkov—by this next train. I've a lot to do there. I'm leaving Yepihodov here . . . I've taken him on.

VARYA: Oh!

LOPAHIN: Last year at this time, it was snowing, if you remember, but now it's sunny and there's no wind. It's cold, though. . . . It must be three below.

VARYA: I didn't look. [*Pause.*] And besides, our thermometer's broken. [*Pause. Voice from the yard:* "Yermolay Alexeyevich!"]

LOPAHIN: [*As if he had been waiting for the call.*] This minute! [*Exits quickly.*]

[VARYA *sits on the floor and sobs quietly, her head on a bundle of clothes. Enter* MME. RANEVSKAYA *cautiously.*]

MME. RANEVSKAYA: Well? [*Pause.*] We must be going.

VARYA: [*Wiping her eyes.*] Yes, it's time, Mamma dear. I'll be able to get to the Ragulins' today, if only we don't miss the train.

MME. RANEVSKAYA: [*At the door.*] Anya, put your things on. [*Enter* ANYA, GAYEV, CHARLOTTA. GAYEV *wears a heavy overcoat with a hood. Enter servants and coachmen.* YEPIHODOV *bustles about the luggage.*]

MME. RANEVSKAYA: Now we can start on our journey.

ANYA: [*Joyfully.*] On our journey!

GAYEV: My friends, my dear, cherished friends, leaving this house forever, can I be silent? Can I, at leave-taking, refrain from giving utterance to those emotions that now fill my being?

ANYA: [*Imploringly.*] Uncle!

VARYA: Uncle, Uncle dear, don't.

GAYEV: [*Forlornly.*] I'll bank the yellow in the side pocket . . . I'll be silent . . .

    [*Enter* TROFIMOV, *then* LOPAHIN.]

TROFIMOV: Well, ladies and gentlemen, it's time to leave.

LOPAHIN: Yepihodov, my coat.

MME. RANEVSKAYA: I'll sit down just a minute. It seems as though I'd never before seen what the walls of this house were like, the ceilings, and now I look at them hungrily, with such tender affection.

GAYEV: I remember when I was six years old sitting on that window sill on Whitsunday, watching my father going to church.

MME. RANEVSKAYA: Has everything been taken?

LOPAHIN: I think so. [*Putting on his overcoat.*] Yepihodov, see that everything's in order.

YEPIHODOV: [*In a husky voice.*] You needn't worry, Yermolay Alexeyevich.

LOPAHIN: What's the matter with your voice?

YEPIHODOV: I just had a drink of water. I must have swallowed something.

YASHA: [*Contemptuously.*] What ignorance!

MME. RANEVSKAYA: When we're gone, not a soul will be left here.

LOPAHIN: Until the spring.

    [VARYA *pulls an umbrella out of a bundle, as though about to hit someone with it.* LOPAHIN *pretends to be frightened.*]

VARYA: Come, come, I had no such idea!

TROFIMOV: Ladies and gentlemen, let's get into the carriages—it's time. The train will be in directly.

VARYA: Petya, there they are, your rubbers, by that trunk. [*Tearfully.*] And what dirty old things they are!

TROFIMOV: [*Puts on rubbers.*] Let's go, ladies and gentlemen.

GAYEV: [*Greatly upset, afraid of breaking down.*] The train . . . the station. . . . Three cushions in the side pocket, I'll bank this one in the corner . . .

MME. RANEVSKAYA: Let's go.

LOPAHIN: Are we all here? No one in there? [*Locks the side door on the left.*] There are some things stored here, better lock up. Let us go!

ANYA: Good-bye, old house! Good-bye, old life!

TROFIMOV: Hail to you, new life!

    [*Exits with* ANYA. VARYA *looks round the room and goes out slowly.* YASHA *and* CHARLOTTA *with her dog go out.*]

LOPAHIN: And so, until the spring. Go along, friends . . . Bye-bye! [*Exits.*]

[MME. RANEVSKAYA *and* GAYEV *remain alone. As though they had been waiting for this, they throw themselves on each other's necks, and break into subdued, restrained sobs, afraid of being overheard.*]

GAYEV: [*In despair.*] My sister! My sister!

MME. RANEVSKAYA: Oh, my orchard—my dear, sweet, beautiful orchard! My life, my youth, my happiness—good-bye! Good-bye! [*Voice of* ANYA, *gay and summoning:* "Mamma!" *Voice of* TROFIMOV, *gay and excited:* "Halloo!"]

MME. RANEVSKAYA: One last look at the walls, at the windows. . . . Our poor mother loved to walk about this room . . .

GAYEV: My sister, my sister! [*Voice of* ANYA: "Mamma!" *Voice of* TROFIMOV: "Halloo!"]

MME. RANEVSKAYA: We're coming.

[*They go out. The stage is empty. The sound of doors being locked, of carriages driving away. Then silence. In the stillness is heard the muffled sound of the ax striking a tree, a mournful, lonely sound.*

Footsteps are heard. FIRS *appears in the doorway on the right. He is dressed as usual in a jacket and white waistcoat and wears slippers. He is ill.*]

FIRS: [*Goes to the door, tries the handle.*] Locked! They've gone . . . [*Sits down on the sofa.*] They've forgotten me. . . . Never mind . . . I'll sit here a bit . . . I'll wager Leonid Andreyevich hasn't put his fur coat on, he's gone off in his light overcoat . . . [*Sighs anxiously.*] I didn't keep an eye on him. . . . Ah, when they're young, they're green . . . [*Mumbles something indistinguishable.*] Life has gone by as if I had never lived. [*Lies down.*] I'll lie down a while. . . . There's no strength left in you, old fellow; nothing is left, nothing. Ah, you addlehead! [*Lies motionless. A distant sound is heard coming from the sky, as it were, the sound of a snapping string mournfully dying away. All is still again, and nothing is heard but the strokes of the ax against a tree far away in the orchard.*]

Masterpieces of the
Modern World

EDITED BY

KENNETH DOUGLAS
Formerly of Yale University

World literature has it in its power to convey condensed experience from
one land to another.—ALEXANDER SOLZHENITSYN.

The earlier sections of this anthology are made up of literary works that, over the centuries, have held the attention and aroused the enthusiasm of generation after generation of readers. A great piece of writing is consecrated as such, it has been said, by the fact that it remains an all-time best seller: the *Iliad*, *Hamlet* and, less remotely, *Madame Bovary*, the *Cherry Orchard*. For the contemporary and almost contemporary period we do not have this criterion. We must make our bets here and now, when the "verdict of posterity" can be only anticipated. Yet the situation is by no means hopeless: Every writer represented here has at least been widely read and his work submitted to admiring analysis.

Let us begin by attempting to isolate the features most commonly found in twentieth-century writing. This calls for a certain retrospect, particularly in the direction of France during the latter half of the nineteenth century. The outstanding feature of the period was the prestige accorded science, and the attempt, on the part of men engaged in other activities, to share in that prestige. Philosophy, far from challenging the pretensions of the scientists, sought to build on them. Zola raised the claim of scientific validity for the novel; and even poetry, with the Parnassian school, clung to the visible, and recognized that science had dispelled man's dream of his own importance, of a universe where his longings met with a response. Thus the objective presentation of things threatened to discredit the subjective viewpoint and, along with it, the individual—who was, however, constitutionally incapable of forgetting his own petty little worries and becoming the impassive scientific observer.

But that is only half the story, and the other half must be presented here. For this acceptance of scientific dogma aroused resentment and provoked counteraffirmations. In the literary domain, poets were the first to react—doubtless because the poem is less cumbersome and less firmly shackled to externals than the novel, and its publication requires much less capital than the staging of a play. Now poetry, it has been suggested, inevitably tends toward one or another sister art; it aspires if not to the condition of painting then to that of music. Reacting against the dominant visual bias, the new poets declared that it could not be poetry's central task to do what painting could achieve so much more easily: to depict. They sought after subtler relations in poetry than the description of objects and their spatial disposition could provide, relations that would hint at the totality and the meaningfulness of experience—which, unperceived, were slipping past the noses of the scientist and his more lowly ally, the plain, blunt man. The analogy with the suggestive power of music was unavoidable: in music each note, indifferent in itself, acquires its importance from the melodic line, and harmonies and harmonics surround that core of meaning with a fringe of significance that yet remains undefinable. But there is also an alternative way of leaving the everyday world of plain, blunt things behind. One may isolate the object entirely, transforming it as the photograph of an ash tray, when enlarged to fill a whole screen, transforms the ash tray. Loosed from all connection with its functions, imperiously commanding our attention, the object may exert on us an uncanny fascination, like some idol or totem. This focusing on the object is one aspect of Rimbaud's poetry, and it has been exploited most thoroughly by the surrealists of our century.

So, more self-consciously than in previous ages, literature set out to explore itself, to discover its own essence and to widen its boundaries. The naturalistic novelists enlarged them with respect to the social group. The symbolists added, not the already familiar domain of subjective fantasy, but that obscure zone where inner and outer worlds, in some mysterious fashion, at least seem to coincide.

But in art there are no recipes, except for failure. Like all others, this symbolist approach to literature was beset by pitfalls. The spirit sometimes chose to move elsewhere, leaving behind it merely the accessories of symbolism. In that case the symbolist literary work remained plunged in subjectivism (Ernest Renan called the symbolist poets "children sucking their thumbs") and appeared to be the ultimate in artificiality and willful obscurity. Once again the new writers—approximately at the dawning of the twentieth century—would have to find new paths, they would aim at a new simplicity, perhaps a greater humility, and strive vigorously to establish communication with others. Faithfulness to the spirit required unfaithfulness to established forms.

One tendency of the romantic period continued into the latter half of the nineteenth century and, indeed, persists today. That is the feeling, on the part of many writers, despite their own (usually) middle-class origins, that between themselves and the middle classes, or bourgeoisie, or Philistines, a great gulf is fixed. These writers feel that no part is allotted them in society as it is constituted, and that reigning values are fraudulent or trivial, while their own meet with nothing but incomprehension. The writers themselves, in turn, are accused of nihilism, of ingratitude, of loss of nerve, of decadence, and of many other sins. Nihilism, of course, there may be—and the rest. But the question should be raised whether literature and even language itself are not *inevitably* subversive. If something is to remain unchanged, it should not be mentioned—not even praised. For to praise is to focus attention upon it, to drag it into the light of consciousness. Once that has been done, it is fair game for blame as well as praise, for termites and despoiling. On the other hand, to cease to talk, to cease to conjure up imaginary worlds, possible and impossible, would mean, surely, to be no longer human. The only status quo for human beings is, in literature as in life, the questionableness of every status quo. The challenge, to use Arnold Toynbee's term, should be welcomed, for how, otherwise, could there be response?

CHARLES BAUDELAIRE

Baudelaire set out deliberately to startle the bourgeois. His collection of poems bears the gaudy title *Flowers of Evil (Les Fleurs du mal)*, and includes litanies to Satan and several poems which in 1857, the year of the volume's publication, were banned as obscene. Yet Baudelaire's tactics, and his deep-rooted instinct, aimed far beyond mere sensationalism: the reader was to be startled so that he would be forced to realize his *involvement*. If one were to judge exclusively by the accusations of turpitude hurled in the poem-preface against his readers and himself, Baudelaire would appear to reject utterly the notion of a literature for consumers only, for the uncommitted aesthete. His work would seem rather a literature for *sinners* only, for those who, like himself, were seriously involved, and recognized their guilt:

Obtuseness, error, sin, and niggardliness
Possess our minds and drive our bodies hard,
And we nourish our lovely moments of remorse,
As beggars give sustenance to their own vermin.

"Our," "we"—poet and reader are accomplices in vileness. And so it goes unrelentingly on to the famous last line, which T. S. Eliot adopted in *The Waste Land*:

Hypocritical reader,—my fellow, —and my brother!

This, then, is Baudelaire's equivalent to Gulliver in the stables; in this way he repels, yet holds, his reader. In the process, it will be seen, he has enlarged the subject matter of poetry. For one thing, the landscape has changed. The lakes and mountain settings dear to the French romantics, Baudelaire replaces with an urban scene: Paris. He knows the Paris of debauch and crime ("En-chanted evening falls, the crimi-nal's friend"), of the poor ("How often have I followed these little old women"), of the frustrated passing encounter ("Oh, you whom I'd have loved, oh, you who knew!"). His po-etry embraces the "utterly im-possible" topic, notably in "A Carcass," a poem which many have found revolting, though it is only a more circumstantial version of the thoughts that oc-cupy Shakespeare's Hamlet with the skull of Yorick in his hand. It was this poem that encour-aged the painter Cézanne in his long toil; and that Rainer Maria Rilke, struggling to master though not to blunt his hyper-sensitivity, hailed as redemption, through art, of repugnant reality.

A Carcass (Une Charogne) *

Do you remember the thing we saw, dear soul, on that gentle summer morning? At a bend of the path a vile carcass on a peb-bly river bed, its legs in the air like a lustful woman, consumed and exuding poisons, exposed in careless, shameless fashion, its belly filled with effluvia. The sun shone on this corruption, as though to cook it to a turn, and to give back to Nature all she had joined together. And the sky saw how the haughty carcass blossomed out like a flower. The stench was so overpowering, you thought that you would faint on the grass. The flies kept buzzing over the decaying belly from which there emerged black regi-ments of larvae that flowed like a dense liquid along these living rags.

All this sank and rose again

* 1857. The poem is translated in full.

like a wave, or shot upwards, crackling; the body might have been thought to live, swollen with an uncertain breath, and to multiply. And this world emitted a strange music, as of running water and of wind, or the grain that a winnower in a rhythmic motion shakes and turns in his sieve.

The shapes were dissolving and were no more than a dream, an outline that comes slowly on the forgotten canvas, and that the artist finishes only from memory.

Behind the rocks an uneasy bitch looked at us with an angry eye, waiting for the moment to seize once again the portion of the skeleton she had dropped.

And yet you too will come to be like this filth, this ghastly infection, star of my eyes, my nature's sun, you, my angel and my passion! Yes, such you will be, oh, queen of all graces, after the last rites, when you go, beneath grass and luxuriant vegetation, to molder amid the bones.

Then, my beauty! tell the vermin that will eat you with kisses that I have preserved the shape and the divine essence of my decayed loves!

This extension of poetry's domain was not toward the outside only. Baudelaire also probed within his own self, including its least flattering aspects, with a boldness and acumen that anticipated the discoveries of psychoanalysis. The fascination that Baudelaire has exerted of recent years over so many, both French and foreign, is connected with this self-unveiling: his readers are won over not alone by the incantation of his verses but by the fact that they are meeting a man who like themselves has sensed despair, and disgust and infantile urges, and who, also, has made a largely futile attempt to order his existence.

These fresh prospectings into the world outside and the world inside were felt as a unity by Baudelaire, both in actual fact and on the theoretical level. The enunciation of the theory is to be found in the poem "Correspondences"—and it would be difficult to name any other lines that so remarkably map out the aims of literature for a hundred years ahead.

Correspondences (Correspondances)*

Nature is a temple whose living pillars at times give out confused speech; there man traverses forests of symbols which watch him with a look of kinship.

Like long echoes which far off are blended into a deep and shadowy oneness, vast as the night and as light's regions, perfumes, colors and sounds give each other answer.

There are perfumes cool as children's flesh, tender as oboes, green as grasslands,—and others, corrupt, rich and triumphant, with the expansiveness of infinite things, like amber, musk, benjamin and incense, which sing the transports of the spirit and senses.

While the sestet of this sonnet treats of synesthesia (the rendering of an object so as to affect one of the five senses in terms of another), the theme of the first quatrain is of incomparably greater importance. Here Baudelaire asserts the interrelatedness of all things, the presence of universal analogy. Science, in those positivistic mid-century days, was coming to be accepted as a substitute for religion, as a religion in itself. Against this trend, Baudelaire reaffirmed that the individual consciousness is unique and irreplaceable, for the sciences do not and cannot concern themselves with the *total impact* of

* 1857. The poem is translated in full.

experience. And precisely this, Baudelaire insisted, is the artist's task: to evoke and clarify the experiences of the individual consciousness, with its wealth of overtones and gossamer cross-paths and its transcendence of time and space. He was inspired, beyond a doubt, by his readings in the occult, but he profoundly felt the truth that we, and the external world also, are "members one of another."

Thus opposites meet in Baudelaire—cruelty and tenderness, lofty flights and black despair, debauch and spiritual longing; and the note of foreboding is perhaps never entirely absent. But he represents even blasphemies and curses, transfigured in the work of great artists, as an appeal to the Eternal. This was his own endeavor, to ennoble by his art a pitiful existence:

Oh, wastrel monk! When shall
    I learn to make
Of my sad misery's living
    spectacle
The labor of my hands, the
    adoration of my eyes?

Baudelaire's theory of artistic creation called for a cold-blooded mastery and calculation of effects, and at the same time for sensitivity to all those components of personality, demonic or ethereal, which the conventional social self represses or ignores. "Like a perfect chemist and like a hallowed soul" expresses the union of qualities he sought in his creative work; while "Spleen and Ideal" ("Spleen et Idéal"), the title of the opening section of *Flowers of Evil*, names the warring forces that made this union difficult of accomplishment. As he expressed it in prose: "In every man, at every moment, there are two simultaneous urges, one directed to God, the other to Satan."

Such was Baudelaire, predecessor and inspirer of the symbolist poets in France, Russia, Germany, and elsewhere; a blasphemer in whom some Catholics see a profoundly Catholic poet; a dandy who could assert that his poems concerned only the aesthetic sensibilities and yet confess, more privately, that in them he had placed his "entire heart."

ARTHUR RIMBAUD

Rimbaud has perhaps outraged even more sensibilities than Baudelaire. They both offended the backers of the established order in letters and in life, but Rimbaud has been a stumbling block even for the aesthetes of the avant-garde; his example unceasingly calls into question their values also. Those for whom nothing but literature matters must accommodate themselves to a youth of exceptional genius who scornfully tossed aside literature and, along with it, the belief that it could achieve anything worthy of a man's attention. The subsequent silence of Rimbaud is as much a part of the meaning of his career as the explosion of his teens.

Like many adolescent boys, he combined refractoriness and sensitivity, both of which, with him, were pushed to the extreme. In one sense, it is correct to say that his work is extraordinarily mature, but his genius nevertheless bears the stamp of youth. Everything came to him so astonishingly early that, exempt from the usual slow processes of emotional and cultural maturation, it strikes us like some elemental force. Here is the image-making faculty at its rawest and most torrential.

Subjected during his childhood to the rule of a domineering and narrowly pious mother, whose influence he was never completely to shake off, he expresses himself in many of the earlier poems, still written in the usual syllabic meters of French, with an extreme exacerbation. He flouts all the decencies and taboos of respectable middle-class family life and reveals his kinship with wall-scribblers at the same stage of development. Yet even the most trivial infringements of the social code, as he presents them, have a quality of force, urgency—authenticity, it would not be too much to say—that is unique; and sometimes themes as unpromising as the satisfaction of bodily needs or the removal of head-lice yield magnificent poems. Yet not all is rebellion. He could escape, too, from a constricting environment—although to the end of his days he always found the way back to his home and people—and find balm, relatively speaking, in the intensely emotional, sensuous experience of union with nature.

His flight from the conditioning of school and family was but the first step in a voyage of discovery. "Drunken Boat" maps out the course. Its first two stanzas record the poet's liberation from utilitarian, commercial considerations. His journey is an abandonment to the currents of river and sea. The booty

he seeks, like the speaker in Tennyson's "Ulysses," is experience, sensations, reality. Men can only hinder him, but the universe appears disposed to give him aid. As conscious control is progressively lost, with the "rudder and grappling-anchor" of the third paragraph, below, he bathes in "the Poem of the Sea," where genuine love is found. The torrent of hallucinatory images rises to a climax. Yet at last a note of surfeit can be heard, and of longing for Europe's "ancient parapets."

In the original French, this poem makes a startling impact. The images—which are stated, never developed—jostle each other for room and disappear, as though shaken in a kaleidoscope. If we succeed in fixing on one of them for a moment, it may prove to have a lurid, disturbing quality that increases the sense of estrangement. Familiar landmarks are gone, the whole lexicon seethes uncontrollably around us. Yet, on the other hand, the author cannot be accused of mental derangement. Not only is each individual alexandrine of an impeccably classical cut; together they build a severe and simple structure. This lack of control is under control, this dementia is precociously planned, the ocean boils within a mind that has not lost its bearings. Rimbaud, as he himself had announced, *cultivated* insanity. The insane do not need to do so. He ran grave risks, but returned from the voyage—just as, throughout his life, he returned home from every journey.

Drunken Boat (*Le Bateau ivre*) *

As I descended the impassive Streams, I felt myself no longer guided by the haulers: screeching Redskins had taken them for targets, nailing them naked to the colored stakes. I was heedless of all the ships' crews, carriers of Flemish grains or English cottons. When all the uproar around my haulers had ended, the Streams let me descend wherever I would.

In the raging tide-rips of last winter, deafer than the minds of children, I sped on! And the unmoored Peninsulas never withstood more triumphant hullabaloos. The tempest blessed my maritime awakenings. Lighter than a cork I danced on the waters that are called eternal victim-spinners, for ten nights, without regretting the foolish eye of the beacons!

Sweeter than for children the flesh of sour apples, the green water penetrated my hull of pine-wood and stains of blue wines and vomitings washed me, scattering rudder and grappling-anchor. And from that moment, I bathed myself in the Poem of the Sea, infused with stars, and latescent,[1] devouring the green azures where, pale and entranced flotsam, a pensive drowned man, sometimes, descends; where, dyeing all of a sudden the blue-nesses, deliriums and slow rhythms beneath daylight's crimson glows, stronger than liquor, vaster than your lyres, ferment the bitter russet splotches of love!

I know the skies that burst into lightning flashes, and the waterspouts and the surf and the currents; I know the evening, the dawn exalted like a people of doves, and at times I have seen what man believed he saw. I have seen the low sun stained with mystic horrors lighting up with long purple coagulations, similar to actors in age-old dramas, the waters revolving far away their shutter-tremors.[2] I have dreamed the green night with dazzling snows, kisses that rise slowly to the eyes of the seas, the circulation of the unimaginable saps and the yellow and blue awakening of the singing phosphoruses. I have followed for months entire the surge, like hysterical cow-byres, in its assault of the reefs, without reflecting that the luminous feet of the Maries[3] could curb the muzzle of the wheezy Oceans! I have collided, do you know? with unbelievable Floridas mixing, among the flowers, eyes of panthers with the skins of men, rainbows stretched like bridles, beneath the horizon of the seas, on glaucous[4] herds. I have seen marshes ferment, enormous weirs in which a whole Leviathan[5] rots among the reeds, cataracts of water in the midst of calm seas, and the distances

---

* Written in 1871; published in 1883. The poem is translated in full.

1. not in French dictionaries. It may be derived from *latex*, a word denoting the milky juice of plants, or from *latere*, "to lurk"; or it may be intended for "lactescent."

2. caused by the wind blowing over the water.

3. perhaps a reference to Mary Magdalene, Mary of Cleophas, and Mary Salome, who according to Provençal legend landed at the place on the Mediterranean coast of France now called Les Saintes-Maries-de-la-Mer. It is the goal of an annual pilgrimage for European gypsies.

4. sea-green.

5. a monster mentioned in the Book of Job, usually identified as the whale.

plunging into the abysses! Glaciers, silvery suns, pearly waters, skies of embers, hideous strandings at the head of dusky gulfs where giant serpents devoured by bugs fall from tortuous trees with black perfumes!

I would have liked to show the children these dorados of the blue water, these goldfish, these singing fish. Foams of flowers have cradled my driftings, and ineffable winds have lent me wings, at moments. Sometimes, a martyr weary of the poles and zones, the sea, whose sob made my rocking gentle, raised to me its flowers of shade with yellow suckers and I remained like a woman on her knees, a peninsula tossing on my shores the quarrels and the droppings of clamorous birds with light-colored eyes, and I was sailing on when across my frail bonds drowned men descended backwards to sleep . . .[6]

Now I, a boat lost under the hair of the coves, thrown by the hurricane into the birdless ether, I whose carcass, intoxicated with water, the Monitors[7] and the Hanse[8] sailing ships would not have fished out, free, smoking, manned by purple mists, I who pierced the sky glowing red like a wall which bears, an exquisite jam for the good poets, lichens of sun and snots of azure; I who

ran, spotted with electric crescents, a mad plank, escorted by the black sea-horses, when the Julies[9] with bludgeon strokes brought down in collapse the ultramarine skies with their ardent funnels; I who trembled, hearing whimper fifty leagues off the rut of Behemoths[10] and the dense Maelstroms,[11] eternal weaver of blue immobilities, I regret Europe with its ancient parapets! I have seen sidereal[12] archipelagoes! And islands whose delirious skies are open to him who sails: Is it in these bottomless nights that you sleep and are exiled, million birds of gold, oh future Vigor?

But, true, I have wept too much! The Dawns are harrowing. Every moon is atrocious and every sun is bitter: pungent love has swollen me with intoxicating torpors. Oh, may my keel shatter! May I go to the sea!

If I long for a water of Europe, it is the black, cold puddle where towards the balmy twilight a crouching child full of sorrows launches a boat frail as a May butterfly.

I can no longer, bathed in your languors, waves, cross the wake of the carriers of cottons, nor traverse the pride of the flags and pennants, nor swim beneath the horrible eyes of the prison-ships!

Typical again of Rimbaud's attitude are the last three stanzas, expressing first of all a revulsion: "The Dawns are harrowing. . . . every sun is bitter." He voices the ultimate Dionysian urge, he would escape utterly from the limits of

6. Rimbaud's punctuation. Nothing has been omitted at this point.

7. ironclad warships with one or more revolving turrets for large-caliber guns. Named after the first such vessel, which was used against the *Merrimac* in 1862 by the Union forces.

8. the medieval Hanseatic League, a

mercantile federation of North German cities.

9. plural of "July."

10. Mentioned in the Book of Job, the Behemoth is usually identified as the hippopotamus.

11. whirlpools.

12. starry.

self: "Oh, may my keel shatter! May I go to the sea!" Then he turns back once more to Europe, to his own childhood, and in the final stanza admits defeat. Commerce, nationhood, a utilitarian and restrictive society, have triumphed. As has often been pointed out, Rimbaud's own career is here prefigured: the return home, first from European wanderings, and later from the East and Africa, where he faced reality as he had come to see it, abandoning literature, which could not satisfy the demands he had made on it, and making a living through commerce. This was the "gnarled reality" on which he had to fasten his grip.

The literary distinction of Rimbaud lies in the visionary quality of his work. Some would classify him as one of the supreme demiurges, or creators of imaginary universes, in contrast to those poets who celebrate the revealed truth of divine creation or who themselves struggle to perceive the truth. The surrealists, during the twentieth century, have found in him a predecessor who opened the floodgates of the subconscious and far transcended the limitations of the ordinary waking mind. They can find in him, too, an indifference to the reader's comfort and a subordination of the petty question, Is this comprehensible? to the untrammeled rights of free creativity. Rimbaud did not, however, adhere to the surrealist doctrine that writing must be automatic and uncontrolled. In his search for concision and force of expression, he revised with the greatest care.

Rimbaud attempted to use poetry as a way to truth. To the subjective imaginings of the romantic poets, he opposed his own kind of objective poetry—a record made, so-to-speak, impassively, of the extraordinary phantasmagoria invading the consciousness, particularly when the poet has made himself a "seer by a long, immense, and deliberate derangement of all the senses." This was to be hallucination not for its own sake, but as a means to knowledge. And the poet's knowledge was to benefit all men. For the poet is Prometheus; he is "responsible for all humanity, even for the *animals*."

Rimbaud is represented here by selections from his *A Season in Hell*. The text is written in prose (although a number of sections contain poems), in the first person, and is autobiographical. But this is highly idiosyncratic autobiography, which totally bewildered one of its earliest readers, Madame Rimbaud, who had nothing in her background, outlook, or minimal education permitting her to understand so startling a piece of reportage from the borderlands, or depths, of the human psyche.

We must accept with unquestioning faith the response Rimbaud gave to his mother's bafflement: "It means exactly what I've said, literally and completely, in all respects." However, there are at least two things one must recognize before attempting to comprehend Rimbaud's work. The first is that Rimbaud, in his own eyes, was not just another entry in the literary sweepstakes. After personally seeing to the publication of *A Season in Hell,* he did nothing further to make known his other poems. His goal was that of every occultist: to insinuate or batter his way to that one source from which springs the whole diversity of phenomena, and to make this inexhaustible core of strength his own strength. As he asks in his "Drunken Boat," "Is it in these bottomless nights that you sleep and are exiled, million birds of gold, oh future Vigor?" He had spent a season in hell and lived to tell the tale.

A Season in Hell begins with an overview in which Rimbaud acknowledges having resorted to drugs and vice, though foreseeing the cost in suffering. His aim had been to smash through the matchboard façade and poky pretenses of commonplace pseudoreality in order to embrace the truth. The search led him far from the terrestrial paradise of his innocent childhood. What, he wonders, had made that paradise possible? The answer somehow comes to him that it had been inspired by "Charity." But a demon brusquely intrudes upon this insight to tell him that by his lusts, egoism, and indulgence in the capital sins he has damned himself. And the poet informs us that the rest of the book will consist of a "few hideous pages of the journal of my damned soul."

The first selection is called "Alchemy of the Word." The term alchemy describes the endeavor to transmute, at the end of immensely painstaking, hazardous manipulations, lead or some other common substance into gold. The vocabulary of alchemy is also used allegorically, as by the seventeenth-century German cobbler and mystic Jakob Boehme, to describe the freeing of the human soul from dross and corruption and its restoration to pristine purity. It has been maintained that the two processes must advance in lockstep. Thus any person attempting to obtain gold, without at the same time submitting himself to the ascetic discipline of self-purification, would encounter only failure, impoverishment, and final disaster. Rimbaud, unlike the Swedish dramatist Strindberg, never involved himself in alchemy's "practical" side. Nor did he attain to any considerable acquaintance with the extensive literature of alchemy. But works of popularization were readily available in the France of his day, enabling him to acquire the vocabulary of and theoretical familiarity with the stages of alchemical transmutation. The associated moral and spiritual interpretations also lay open before him, and the text of *A Season in Hell* makes it clear they were not overlooked.

In the full text, "Alchemy of the Word" is a second heading surmounted by the main heading "Deliriums II." The preceding piece is "Deliriums I," which has the subordinate heading "The Foolish Virgin—The Infernal Bridegroom." These descriptive labels apply—in that same order, be it noted—to the older poet Paul Verlaine (1844–1896) and to Rimbaud himself. Verlaine, a man of great poetic gifts, a heavy drinker, and unable to withstand the least temptation, had left his young wife to live tempestuously with Rimbaud in Paris, London, and Brussels. The younger but far stronger-willed Rimbaud soon asserted his ascendancy but could not establish any tolerable *modus vivendi* for their joint existence. The end came when Verlaine purchased a revolver and shot Rimbaud in the wrist, a crime for which he served a prison sentence in Belgium. "Deliriums I" is put in the mouth of the "foolish virgin" (Verlaine), who tearfully complains of "her" enslavement to the "infernal bridegroom" (Rimbaud), with his callous, sadistic, and unpredictably arbitrary behavior and desperate search for superhuman powers.

"Deliriums II—Alchemy of the Word" turns from these shared follies to report on Rimbaud's dedication, in total isolation, to his vast artistic and more than artistic ambitions. Rejecting what hitherto had been accepted, accepting whatever had been excluded, or so he imagined, Rimbaud sought to invent a new language that would speak simultaneously to all the senses and so make a reality of the mere pronouncements to be found in Baudelaire's sonnet "Correspondences" (p. 997 above). "Alchemy of the Word" provides samples of such poetic attempts, but their author now admits that his break with the past was less complete than he had hoped. Nevertheless, he at last came to experience his essential self as a particle of light in nature's universal radiance.

This bliss did not endure. His health was threatened, terrors beset him. So he relinquished power and beauty as the objects of his unsparing quest and turned to "Happiness." Visual and audible reminders then came to him from the consoling Christian faith of his childhood. He cites an example of the simple, evocative poetry he now is able to write, and he proclaims his new, true relationship with beauty.

The two remaining selections, "Morning" and "Goodbye," conclude *A Season in Hell.* "Morning" looks back on his sojourn in hell as a thing of the past, and looks forward to a new life of labor and circumspection. The demons that afflict the spirit will be banished, together with every earthly tyrant, and earthly progress will go hand in hand with true religious insight. "Goodbye" evokes the dread metropolis where millions live in the degrading poverty that the poet himself had known. It recalls, too, but in order to dismiss them, the excessive esthetic ambitions and the striving for occult powers that had brought him close to ruin. Now he must discover his duty on earth and opt for a livelihood. "Gnarled reality" must be grasped. Having set aside the old lies and substanceless imaginings, the poet believes that he will be able "to possess the truth in a soul and a body."

Since this prose and these poems are variously peremptory, brusque, and allusive, they present the reader with stumbling blocks—to which the veil of translation unavoidably adds. It has seemed appropriate, consequently, to provide notes that at times can do no more than formulate conjectures. As for a persistent theme that may be detected in these annotations, the reader is reminded of the title of Rimbaud's presumed masterpiece, the strayed and never rediscovered *La Chasse spirituelle*. Whatever its contents may have been, it is avowedly the account of a spiritual quest.

AUGUST STRINDBERG

August Strindberg responded vibrantly to many significant manifestations in the literary and intellectual life of his day and, since that time, has through his writings exerted an influence on every major movement in literature and the drama. Indebted to him are expressionism, the literary exploitation of Freudian theories, surrealism, existentialism, and the theater of the absurd. Both George Bernard Shaw and Eugene O'Neill made known their intense admiration for his achievements. Among the elements by which Strindberg himself was affected were Shakespeare's historical plays and naturalism, with its emulation of the deterministic outlook of science and a concern for social problems. He moved through a Nietzschean individualism to a renewed interest in religion, especially of a nonconfessional kind, embracing Asian doctrines he did not study in depth and putting together a synthesis of his own. He tried to obtain gold by alchemical means and set out to refute the established scientific concept of the elements. After symbolism had been adapted to stage purposes by the Belgian writer Maurice Maeter-linck (1862–1949), Strindberg acknowledged the Belgian's influence and followed his example.

Since Strindberg's dramatic work totals fifty-eight plays, only the most schematic hints as to its nature are possible here. His first great play was *Master Olof*, situated in Sweden at the time of the Reformation. Written in 1872, it was subjected to a process of revision that lasted into 1881. From 1899 on, Strindberg, encouraged by a successful staging of *Master Olof*, wrote a whole series of historical plays which, in the estimation of one critic, are unique in meriting consideration alongside Shakespeare's Tudor dramas.

The years 1886–1889 witnessed the writing of naturalistic plays, including those constantly revived works *The Father* (1887) and *Miss Julie* (1888). From the vantage point of our later day, we can see that these two plays, with the pattern-repetitive psychological determinism of the former and the mounting hysteria of Miss Julie, anticipate altogether remarkably the theories later propounded by Sigmund Freud (1856–1939). The next phase of dramatic activity, though it extended only from 1898 to 1902, resulted in no fewer than eighteen plays. These included, in addition to the historical dramas, plays that may be classified as realistic, expressionistic, and allegorical. And, finally, there are the five "chamber plays"— *The Ghost Sonata* among them —that Strindberg wrote in 1907 and 1909 for his own Intimate Theater in Stockholm.

The fifty-eight plays do not nearly fill the fifty-five volumes of Strindberg's collected works —beside which must be set the volumes of a lavish correspondence. For him, living and writing were not watertight compartments but the two faces of one whole, each mirroring and penetrating the other in an unending reflective and refractive barrage. Even he himself had to confess, at times, his inability to distinguish between the real and the fictitious. Nor does the fact that some works are largely autobiographical (*Inferno*, for instance, which recounts the hallucinatory experiences of the 1890's) permit one to assume that fictional embroiderings have been excluded. The fictions, conversely, lead us back to their author's real existence, and on occasion he depicts the blackness of a situation in such scrupulous detail that we suspect a burlesque intention. In any event, the author never permits us to forget him.

All this proliferation and diversity have indeed their center in the Strindbergian ego, an ego of no mean proportions hidden and yet revealed under the voluminous folds of its magician's cloak. Cruel to the pretensions and self-esteem of others, he himself was abnormally sensitive to slights. Impelled to expose himself to attack, he was cowardly in confronting and anticipating it. For instance, while a respected functionary of the Royal Library, he published a highly satirical novel, *The Red Room* (1879), that created a great stir. During the relatively tranquil earlier years of his first marriage, he brought on himself a charge of blasphemy with the first volume of *Married* (1884), and with the second volume, published the following year, he incurred the reputation, which subsequent publications only strengthened, of being a fanatical antifeminist. He saw himself as pursued by, initially, a cabal of "denatured" Swedish women and, later, by a world-wide conspiracy of such creatures. This, however, was but one aspect of his lifelong tendency to look on himself as a figure of heroic proportions but an outcast, an Ishmael, son of the banished Hagar, handmaiden of the patriarch Abraham. (His own mother had been a servant.) His situation, self-interpreted, may be said to resemble the bastard's lot: tolerated on the fringes of wealth and power but with no heritage of his own except—like Edmund in Shakespeare's *King Lear*—the capacity to dream of or plan a mighty conquest.

The Ghost Sonata, in view of its allusive nature (Strindberg called it "a world of intimations"), has been provided with a more than usually large number of interpretative footnotes. They signal passages that allude to such major themes or motifs as repetition, viewed as undesirable, stagnation, and vampirism, and call attention to other passages that proclaim free will and individual initiative to be mainly or entirely self-deceptions. Here it is important to stress the title of the work. While authors in some instances, and critics more frequently, allege that a piece of writing owes its structure to some musical form, Strindberg quite convincingly, though simply, justifies the *Sonata* of his title. The musical analogy extends beyond the tripartite form, ABA, of the three scenes, it also substitutes for any psychological link between subscene and subscene a first use, the repeated use, and the dropping of a theme. While this repetition underlines a gloomy interpretation of human existence, a conciliatory note is sounded, indeed is actually sung by the Student at the very end. For this, too, there is a musical parallel.

Nevertheless, the characters are not musical phrases but the ghosts or the paradigm of human beings. But, just as music is found to utter things too indefinite or too close to ourselves to permit their expression in words (see Proust's treatment of "the little phrase" in the selection from *Swann's Way* reproduced below, pp. 1174–1203), these personages are able to convey things that rarely survive the clear but withering light of consciousness. These characters, too, like the ghosts in the classical Hades or the damned of Dante's *Inferno*, are hampered neither by the polite conventions of everyday life nor by the Freudian "censor" at the service of the superego. The musical analogy still functions, however, as support for the assertion that the level of the individual subconscious or unconscious does not dominate the play. There is the common thread pulling all together, as the Old Man declares, and this has the consequence of placing the accent on a linked destiny in which all share, whether within the con-

fines of this particular work or made universally applicable to human life. So—we may set aside the details of the elaborate cosmic scheme that Strindberg expounded elsewhere—the author has labored successfully to exemplify the "We are members one of another" of Saint Paul and the notion of one-in-all and all-in-one affirmed by so many Asian scriptures.

LUIGI PIRANDELLO

Pirandello at no time shared the extravagant hopes voiced by the youthful Rimbaud. He saw all things as garish, kaleidoscopic, hallucinatory, inextricably entangled, and irremediably ambiguous. An unbeliever, he gives the lie to the notion, dear to the believer, that a basic despair unfits a man for goal-oriented activity. Not only was he a prolific writer, but in his plays specifically he created his own genre, his own theater, and a public, beyond Italian shores as well as at home, that was able to appreciate his work.

His success is bound up with a courageous refusal to accept the standard routines of middle-class theater and with the adoption of startling, even bewildering innovations which, to a considerable extent, were also the revival of age-old theatrical devices and situations. Plausibility flies out of the window, and there is no attempt to render the implausible more palatable by a shrewd measuring of the dosage. With the rapid, firecracker-like eruptions of unforeseeable occurrences, of reversals of fortune or behavior, that mark his plays, Pirandello calls into existence something akin to the Italian Renaissance's improvisatory

Commedia dell'Arte (he calls one play *Tonight We Improvise*) and to the Roman comedies of Plautus, most familiar to today's audiences in the form of the musical *A Funny Thing Happened on the Way to the Forum*.

Yet this sophisticated, highly educated man did not simply purvey popular theatrical concoctions. He had his own attitude to life. Disabused without being cynical, he saw men as fraudulent not alone in their surface pretensions. What lay behind the surface was no less shoddy, uncertain, and vacillating. One mask, one facet of the personality, was replaced by another. There was no center that could impose a genuine order. Many of his personages are bitterly aware of their own incoherence, and their self-examination is both persistent and fruitless. Or it may occur that one especially lucid character acts as spokesman for the author. Even then, the feverish ratiocination and the eruptions of a multicolored unreality that thrill and amaze the theater public do not hide his sadness.

Pirandello's career proceeded from poetry through novels (seven of them) and short stories (they fill fifteen volumes) to plays. In every genre he began with his native Sicilian settings, and he translated several of his works into Sicilian dialect. But his most distinctive gifts required the greater complexity of thought and feeling associated with personages of less restricted horizons, and to such personages he turned, particularly in the three plays most frequently performed today: *Right You Are* (*If You Think So*), *Henry IV*, and *Six Characters in Search of an Author*. The first of these exemplifies his skepticism concerning "truth." A family newly arrived in town shocks the natives and arouses their impertinent curiosity by its unorthodox living arrangements. It is discovered, through much prying, that the family's members cannot even agree on what their relationship to one another is though they are content to live with this ambiguity, or would be, were it not for their neighbors' shamelessness. Properly directed and performed, with brio, with rapierlike thrusts and a compelling drive, this play can transport audiences into a frenzy of intellectual excitement.

The "Six Characters" are, as the play's title declares, looking for an author. Restless, unhappy embryos of an act of literary conception that has never reached fulfillment in a completed work, they invade a stage where a play by Pirandello is being rehearsed and demand to be incarnated by the actors. The actors make the attempt, but their dissatisfaction with the unusually raw material that is offered them, and the characters' own disapproval of the actors' substitution of standardized banalities for the uniqueness of the events that make up the whole of the characters' shadow existence, constitute—in the form of a fiasco—a Pirandellian tour de force. He imprisons his audience in an avowed unreality that nevertheless seems to cast an intense (if fitful) light on the audience's own emotional and ideological world.

Henry IV may be regarded as

the most massively successful embodiment of Pirandello's concern with the unanswerable question: What is Truth? Unlike Pilate, he could never wash his hands of it. The hero in this play has fallen from a horse and struck his head while participating in a pageant in the role of the medieval German emperor Henry IV. He emerges from unconsciousness but not from the role, and since he is wealthy he is able, with the connivance of friends and hirelings, to maintain it. This is the basic datum—but, since Pirandello is the author, the play bursts from these bonds. The ultimate sequence of reversals might be summarized as: role seen as role, role become reality, role again seen as role but not abandoned, role abandoned, role seen as role yet—for at this juncture something irremediable occurs—unwillingly reassumed. The hero remains locked forever, and consciously so, within a senseless farce. A similar forced wearing of a mask is performed by the French mime, Marcel Marceau: What had been tried on in jest becomes an inescapable destiny.

Pirandello did not comment on politics or social movements, but his writings make it plain that he looked on society as a burden inflicted upon the individual, with which he has to come to terms. He himself had been the obedient son of a father who derived his income from sulphur mines in Sicily. Never was he more disastrously obedient than in 1894, when he accepted as his wife a young woman he had not previously known, the daughter of his father's business partner. After

some years of marriage, and with the collapse of the sulphur mining venture, Signora Pirandello's mind became affected. She raged against her husband with an insane jealousy nothing could assuage—though he handed over to her all his earnings, keeping only enough for streetcar fare. Even when her hostility turned also against their daughter, he decided not to have his wife institutionalized. The situation was terminated only with her death in 1918.

The close relationship between this tortured domesticity and Pirandello's fascination by the polar opposites appearance and reality can hardly be denied. In view of accusations that he took a perverse delight in holding up to mockery the normal and respectable, it is important to point out that he was in fact an ethical and deeply responsible person who metamorphosed his own pain into an impressive body of work that has led to a renewed understanding of theater as theater.

THOMAS MANN

The painter Cézanne put such passion and tenacity into his lifelong struggle with the problems of painting technique that even the layman, as he moves through an exhibition of Cézanne's work, may be gripped by a modified access to this passion. A similar intensity characterizes Thomas Mann, but in his case the impelling force is the desire to comprehend. Though all writers surely possess it to some extent, there are few outside the ranks of the philosophers in whom it so triumphantly overrides other considerations. One may perfectly well grant a restricted validity to the view that Mann's writings are "boring," another way of saying that in his eagerness to get to the root of a matter, even if doing so means exploring every possible facet under every possible illumination, he often shows little regard for a frivolous and short-winded reader's expectation of entertainment. But this "boringness" largely loses its unfavorable aspects when made to take its place in the totality of Mann's aims and achievements.

Mann exhibits qualities which are not a necessary part of the imaginative writer's equipment. As the fine flower of the tradition of the German burgher, with its respect for learning and the things of the spirit, he made his own an awe-inspiring erudition, and at the same time became, in a nontrivial sense, a genuine sophisticate. Without relinquishing the German burgher's virtues, Mann grew to be a citizen of the world. Rooted in his milieu and origins, he is yet, somewhat like Joyce, outside them. The literatures of Germany and the rest of Europe, philosophy, history, music, psychology, all contributed to make of Mann a mirror of his age.

"Much study is a weariness of the flesh," and sophistication, a late stage in any culture, threatens to collapse in a loss of the vital urge. Mann was acutely conscious of this danger, partly because of his absorption in the pessimistic philosophy of Schopenhauer, in Nietzsche's analysis of the nineteenth century's "nihilism," and in the music of Wagner, which Nietzsche denounced as an enervating poison. But this cultural experience bore fruit on the soil of lived experience—it can flourish nowhere else—which for Mann included family tragedy.

At about the age of twenty-three, he started to write *Buddenbrooks* (1900), a two-volume novel that certainly stands on its own merits. The original bears the subtitle *Decay of a Family (Verfall einer Familie)*, and the novel inextricably incorporates elements of the history of his own family, which was established in business at the old Hanse town of Lübeck, close to the Baltic. The magnificent instinctive self-assurance and the mental health that had been the Voltairian grandfather's have yielded, in the grandson Thomas Buddenbrooks, to doubts and sickly hesitations. Schopenhauer's *The World as Will and Idea* has for him a morbid fascination. His brother Christian grows up to be a harmless but unemployable eccentric. Hanno, the son of Thomas Buddenbrooks and last of the whole line, has an aversion from life and longing for death that exceeds his father's. To this longing he abandons himself, improvising on the piano melodies that end in a repeated, structureless series of sounds, and dies before his school days are over.

This novel embodies the central problem of the earlier Thomas Mann, a problem which continued to put forth offshoots in later years. On the one side he sees bourgeois obtuseness, health, and adaptation to the coarse demands of everyday reality, on the other the sensitivity and insight of the artist, a precious gift indeed, but sickly, a menace to itself and the body public. Mann did not contemplate this unfortunate dichotomy from the outside; it was his intimate conflict, for he knew himself to be a burgher and an artist also. The short story "Tonio Kröger" (1903) gives perhaps the most direct expression to this dilemma, while "Death in Venice" ("Der Tod in Venedig," 1913) associates love of beauty and a genuine artistic accomplishment with morbidity, perversion, and death.

The great panoramic novel *The Magic Mountain (Der Zauberberg*, 1924) is a detailed account of the preoccupations and conversations of wealthy tubercular patients in a Swiss sanitarium. More essentially, it is a survey and critique of occidental civilization prior to the catastrophe of World War I, a regretful but definitive "goodbye to all that."

Mann, quite admirably and without repudiating his past and his roots, continued to grow throughout his career, and his sympathies embraced a great deal more than the sad lot of the artist in a Philistine society. After reviewing what had been his own world, in *The Magic Mountain*, he tried in the four novels taking the biblical Joseph for their hero to plunge into the mythical past, to conjure up and grasp a prerational world view. Politically, too, Mann grew with the years, neither clinging obstinately to a dead past nor riding, like an aging adolescent, some hollow "wave of the future."

Here, to represent his work, we have chosen "Felix Krull,"

written at a moment when the pressures on the dedicated, industrious author had somewhat abated. For once he was happily able to throw to the winds the vast moral burden of being human in an inhuman world. The artist as swindler, the swindler as artist—Mann's wholehearted "ja" in this story to this equation conveys itself to us in a great burst of buoyant irreverence, with an effect akin, possibly, to that of the satyr play with which the Greek dramatists rounded off each cycle of three tragedies.

Mann, however, wrote this tale in mid-career. He continued to regard it as an unfinished fragment, to be taken up again. This he did, much later, expanding it to a two-volume novel of the same name that remained, however, even then unfinished. There are some hilarious scenes, and the "Lust am Fabulieren" (delight in tale spinning) which had never deserted Mann supports him here also. Nevertheless, erudition runs away with him, and the delight that he perhaps took in it himself is less likely to be shared. The challenge of the early fragment, with its bounce and brilliance, remains.

RAINER MARIA RILKE

Rilke's life was an immense *task*. Endowed with a morbid sensitivity and a dubious gift of facility that might have led to disaster in life or in art, he conquered both dangers. He lived, someone has said, the aesthetic life to the full. And so he did, but only in the sense that he submitted himself to a rigorous discipline, aiming at no ivory-tower or coterie art, but at the elucidation of man's role in the world.

This "aesthete," then, this wanderer, this lifelong accepter of hospitality from the titled and wealthy, this husband too respectful of his wife's individuality to share a hearth with her—how far too easy it is to mock at Rilke!—had the good fortune or the skill to insure himself the proper material conditions for the fulfillment of his task, in spite of his apparent drifting and his slight financial resources. Residing at different periods in Germany, France, and Switzerland, with visits to Scandinavia, Italy, Spain, Russia, and his native Austria-Hungary, he made himself a truly European poet. The first World War, shattering European unity, shattered his peace of mind also, and not until several years after the war's close did he succeed in finding once again release of his poetic powers, which then flooded out to complete the *Duino Elegies* (*Duineser Elegien*, 1923), fragmentarily given him ten years before, and to call into being their pendant, the *Sonnets to Orpheus* (*Die Sonnette an Orpheus*, 1923).

The *Duino Elegies*, as befits the name, form a lament, but of a very special kind. Their slow modulations conjure up a picture of man ill at ease in the universe. "The sick animal," Nietzsche had called man, and the second elegy finds similarly that "Everything is agreed to remain silent concerning us, in part / as shameful perhaps and in part as an unutterable hope." It is in order to throw some light on the latter possibility that the elegiac form has been adopted, for, says one of the Orpheus sonnets, "Rejoicing *knows*, and longing tells its story,— / only lament learns still . . ."

The ninth of the ten elegies represents the climax of Rilke's long search for the meaning of human life; now he is able to glimpse the goal. This *once* that we live on earth will never *not* have been—but we can neither retain it nor bequeath it to another. Yet, possessing language, we are the only beings who can transmute the material thing and the transitory event into an enduring immateriality. Man can fulfill the hope of the earth by allowing the earth to arise once more, "invisible." In his *Elegies* and *Sonnets to Orpheus*, Rilke joins those who voice the poet's confidence in the supreme importance of his strivings. Almost to the word, he concurs with the French symbolist poet Stéphane Mallarmé, for whom literature was "the Orphic explanation of the earth," and who maintained, both humorously and more than humorously, "with an ineradicable, doubtless, writer's prejudice," that all things were destined to lead to a book.

MARCEL PROUST

Apart from one or two early works and a handful of essays, Marcel Proust put all he had to say into one novel of immense length, whose final volumes did not appear until after his death. Naturally enough, the subject matter treated, rather than the fundamental aim, drew the attention of the first readers of Proust, and since the complete work was not available (nor indeed written), they can readily be forgiven their oversights. The basic theme and its subsidiaries are actually indicated in the opening pages of *Remembrance of Things Past (À la Recherche du temps perdu,* 1913-1927), as the whole is called, but only by a miracle of divination could anyone else have developed them.

Remembrance of Things Past is a chronicle of society; that is to say, of the fashionable world, with its rulers and climbers, and also the valets, coachmen, maid-servants, and panders who enable it to revolve. For quite a while it was a favored sport, among fashionable people, to guess at the real salon hostess or elderly reprobate hidden behind the fictitious name—and Proust did of course make use of the many exotic personalities he had encountered during his extensive social peregrinations.

Yet as volume succeeded volume, it became apparent that Proust was evolving something very different from an entertaining exposure of high life. The dimensions of his undertaking made it, first of all, a valuable portrait of a whole segment of society, in the wider sense. And as his characters pirouetted and struck their poses, rose or declined in the social scale, it became clear, too, that here was no static tableau, but the history, over perhaps forty years, of the individuals making up a so-called elite and of the sub-groups which battled for prestige—the history of their rise, triumphs, and decay. Here is the justification for the quite exceptional length of Proust's novel: being a work of art, it must not

simply affirm that time is slipping by, and with it all things; the conviction of this evanescence must seize hold of us.

This sense of transitoriness extends also to Proust's characters; psychologically, they have no solid, integrating core of personality. Their desires crystallize for a while around some beloved person, but the crystals dissolve. However, in the game of love which has so great a role in these idle lives, one principle, "the intermissions of the heart," provides for an oscillating consistency that may extend over many years. "He" loves "her," but she is cold to his advances. One day she receives him more kindly. At once she is devalued in his eyes, having lost the unattainableness, the promise of an unrealizable bliss, which has perhaps constituted for him her only charm. So now it is his turn to become indifferent, while she as a consequence loves and suffers.

"Vanity of vanities; all is vanity." Proust echoes and expands this cry of the Preacher in Ecclesiastes. Or, to borrow the terminology of existentialist philosophy, he spreads before our eyes a dreadful panorama of "inauthentic existence," and those who search for traditional consolations will be tempted to denounce his pessimism. Any interpretation of the book, however, must take into account Marcel, the central character and the narrator of the whole. His presence and his quest give a unity to what otherwise, indeed, might appear as an unrelieved chronicle of dissolution.

Two strands woven together will eventually, we may assume,

enable Marcel to bridge the gulf that separates him from salvation. One strand is his longing to become a writer, an ambition which for long years, because of lethargy and the failure to find his own road, he never seriously attempts to realize; the other is his longing to escape from the bondage of time (one might say "fear of death" instead, but Marcel never puts it that way), and his discovery of a key that opens the door to eternity. For him, that is. There is no record of anyone else even having bothered to try the key in whose efficacy Marcel has such unquestioning faith.

How does one escape from time? The answer involves an understanding of the two types of memory distinguished by Proust—voluntary and involuntary. Voluntary memory is the everyday kind. I can recall, for example, that at the age of twelve I spent the summer at the seaside. Far more intimately bound up with the root of things is involuntary memory, which may be aroused for example by our smelling some scent which many years before was associated with some happening. These gusts of memory, thus unpredictably aroused, fill Marcel with a pure joy, such as he has never felt when living in the present. But they are only the first glimpse of light peeping through from behind the door to salvation, and hard work and mental discipline are needed if ever the door is to be forced open. Marcel often shrinks from the effort required to penetrate, by way of this first summons from the past, into the sunken, paradisiacal world of his own dead years. When success is attained, the result is like the Japanese paper flower, a tiny pellet which when placed in water unfolds until it covers the whole surface. The image, which is Proust's own, might well serve to characterize his sentences also, those gently unfolding, interminable sentences which so amazingly combine the relaxed, dreamy quality of reminiscence and the acute vision of a man intellectually disciplined and in deadly earnest.

Proust does not entirely abandon the present in favor of the past, for the only access to this past is through the present. The immateriality of the joy accompanying involuntary memory rests on the fact that it is experience of a relation whose two terms are the past and the present. There is a kind of metaphor, in which the past finds expression in the forms of the present. The same penchant for telescoping various periods in time explains why Proust devotes page after page to the etymology of place names, why he sees the villagers as living incarnations of the statues in the village's Romanesque church. Odette, similarly, has stepped out of a Botticelli painting, and a footman at Mme. de Saint-Euverte's "is" a Mantegna. The present is linked to and justified by the past, for in this way the fatuous or boorish, contingent and nonessential living person is taken up into a hierarchy of archetypes which are outside time, immune from change. In the same way the snobbery of Proust and of Marcel can be explained. The Duchesse de Guermantes is the living distillation of centuries of French history. How could Marcel fail to adore her!

The arts too are an attempt to escape from the accidental and to unveil essence, and Proust therefore has a great deal to say about literature, music, and painting. In the passage we print here, taken from the first volume of the work, *Swann's Way (Du Côté de chez Swann,* 1913), an initial attempt is made to record the effect produced by, or rather the truth of things as they stand revealed in, a little musical phrase. For Swann, this phrase embodies his love for Odette, but in itself it is not indifferent or fortuitous; he had been attracted to it for its own sake and had on numerous occasions persuaded Odette to play it for him. However, Swann, the central character of this first part of the novel, is only a man of the world, an aesthete and dilettante, and proves incapable of the persistent mental and moral effort which alone could enable him to approximate in words the message made known through the phrase of music. Swann must yield his place to Marcel, a man who has not sold his soul for "the pomps and vanities of this wicked world," before the ultimate in elucidation can be achieved. And behind Marcel is Proust himself, who accomplished the destiny that Marcel, at the novel's end, has only begun really to make his own.

ANDRÉ GIDE

The serpent was the most subtle of the beasts of the field, we read in Genesis, and that is the guise under which André Gide has appeared to some. *An Evildoer* is the title of a book written by a father who accused Gide of having led to his son's ruin. There are obviously other things to be said about him, or he would scarcely have been awarded a Nobel prize in his old age. But even those favorably disposed to Gide will be ready to admit that the quality of deviousness distinguishes his character.

Gide was a distinguished, and much more than a distinguished, man of letters, and his writings and personal example have had an incalculable influence over many young men for more than half a century. In France his reputation is now somewhat overshadowed, but this is the unavoidable consequence of his having for so long played a prominent part in French intellectual life. Yet he may still hold a message for a youthful elite in one of the advanced or advancing countries, encouraging them to resist pressures to conform and urging them to develop an individual life style.

Gide was far from being a simple hedonist or aesthete. The son of a Protestant father and a Catholic mother, he thought that this mixed origin explained the warring impulses he felt within him. Accompanying a strong, and deviant, sexual urge, which first found release with Arab boys in France's North African possessions, was a sense of devotion to the woman he married, a first cousin. It was a strange relationship—and not only because the marriage, without the topic even once being discussed by man and wife, remained unconsummated. In rather parallel fashion his celebration of pagan freedoms, and freedom from guilt feelings, was counterbalanced by an emotional reverence for the Christ of the New Testament.

The sophisticated literary circles of late nineteenth-century France looked on Christianity (which for most Frenchmen meant Catholicism and nothing else) as an anachronism doomed in fairly short order to disappear. It was this assumption that disappeared, and from the late eighties on there were many "conversions," as they were called, though usually it was a baptized but nonpracticing Catholic who came to see his nominal faith as a truly revealed religion. Among those returning to the fold were a number of prominent literary men. So it was not surprising that Gide should be viewed as a desirable convert, and that from time to time a discreet allusion should be dropped, in his presence, to the haven that awaited him.

Whether or not Gide ever seriously entertained the idea of yielding to these blandishments, he did not respond to them rudely or with a categorical rejection. But when he learned that rumors of his impending conversion were being circulated, he decided that something needed to be done. What he did was to retell the parable of the prodigal son. Situating the story within a "frame," he imagines himself represented as kneeling, like the medieval donor of a religious painting, in a corner of the canvas, his eyes filled with tears. In reality, however, he has reserved for himself "le beau rôle," the title part. This returned prodigal is not so much repentant as discouraged and depressed. When his mother suggests that he marry, he answers almost as though for him life was effectively over. Any bride his mother fancies will do.

Gide radically alters the New Testament parable by introducing a third, younger brother. To this brother, who idolizes him, the prodigal confesses that only a failure of nerve had induced him to return home. The hunger, the defeats, and the humiliations have been too much for him. Yet, in a sense, all is not lost. Confident that he is of tougher fiber, the younger brother accepts the older brother's blessing and vanishes into the darkness to make his way alone.

To understand the "lesson" that this parable offered the men of Gide's own generation, the conversation with the older brother is particularly important. Gide erects a basic ideological barrier between the two brothers, going far beyond the fraternal rivalry and ill-feeling that the Bible story hints at. The prodigal had felt, and still believes, that only the man with the daring to shake off his inherited burden of advantages and responsibilities, and to plunge into the unknown, can win true riches. The elder brother, on the other hand, proudly accepts his place in the established order with its conventional wisdom—which, in his eyes, is unchallengeable truth.

By portraying an establishment figure in this unsympathetic light, Gide informs the would-be soul-savers, and the public at large, that his considered answer to the proselytizers is an icy "no." He does not accept as the legitimate administrator of the interests on earth of the loving heavenly Father a harsh authoritarian and disciplinarian who sees men as fundamentally evil, to be kept within bounds only by means of menaces and punishment.

The belief in the total depravity of man is not, properly speaking, orthodox Christian doctrine. But in France a highly authoritarian trend, at bottom political rather than religious, was making itself heard, and its leaders would gladly have enlisted the Church in the service of their political goals. Their hatred of all undisciplined religiosity, of a "sentimental" personal attachment to Christ, for instance, knew no bounds. The perpetual threat of chaos required a ruthless repression of unchanneled impulse. Gide, on his side, was not a whit less certain that all regimentation is the death of the spirit.

Many of Gide's works, like this variation on a Bible story, are short but distinctive. Bulkiest is his *Journal*, which he maintained over a long period of time. Elements of his life omitted from it are discussed in the autobiographical *Si le grain ne meurt* (*Unless It Die*) and in shorter autobiographical essays. His fiction includes *L'Immoraliste* (*The Immoralist*) and *La Porte étroite* (*Strait Is the Gate*), both written in the 1900's and with marked autobiographical overtones. *Les Caves du Vatican* (*Lafcadio's Adventures*) is a highly accomplished piece of satirical pyrotechnics, and *Les Faux-Monnayeurs* (*The Counterfeiters*) is constructed of mirrors that reflect mirrors. That is to say, many characters write of intimate matters on pages that fall into the hands of other characters. Gide raised these glints and gleanings to an even higher dimension of complexity by publishing the diary he had kept while working on the book. His writings are filled with fascinating problems for literary commentators and literary psychologists, and his scrupulous handling of the French language delights the connoisseur.

FRANZ KAFKA

It is not unusual to introduce Kafka in such a fashion that all but the boldest are frightened away from his writings. For tactical reasons, therefore, but also because it is true, let us begin by saying that Kafka's works are meticulously detailed accounts of happenings within the three dimensions and the time element of everyday reality. To see in the mind's eye what is represented as occurring presents no problem at all.

The dialogue, also, follows strictly all the normal rules of syntax; the sentences do not even approach those of Thomas Mann in complexity, the vocabulary is much more restricted than his. A great deal of this discourse, however, is of the "he said and she said" variety; that is, it records statements previously made by characters not present, perhaps reporting actions of yet other characters, or of personages who do not appear at all, or even passing on rumors and conflicting rumors. And nothing, and no one, is ever pinned down, a circumstance which is bound to give rise to bafflement and frustration.

The narrative sections, too, quite frequently expend their lucidity on the reporting of highly improbable or extremely curious incidents. Couples sink to the floor in loving embraces whose embarrassing interruption the circumstances make almost inevitable; mysterious agencies, inconclusively discussed by one or more characters, impinge on the hero decisively, yet in a way which leaves the purport of their intervention far from clear.

The result is that the reader tends to oscillate between the bafflement already alluded to and the search for, even the discovery of, a solution. But the very proponent of this solution may come to see that he has been unjustifiably dogmatic, while those who deny that any solution can be found slip all too easily, a little later, into some one-sided dogmatism of their own.

Most trenchantly characterizing this uneasy pendulum movement to which Kafka drives us is a phrase of Sartre's: "Kafka, or the impossibility of transcendence." For Kafka, unlike the positivists and the horizonless men of every age, saw this world of ours as a system incomplete in itself, traversed by fissures through which we glimpse something that for a moment seems to hold out the promise of a transcendent justification of all things and of ourselves. But then the vision disappears, and we fall back on the patchwork of immanence, of mundane reality. According to the religious interpretation of his work made by his biographer and friend Max Brod, Kafka depicts the world as it is—disconcerting, harsh, incurably ambiguous, the site of our logically undemonstrable conviction that God is good, but not of direct acquaintanceship with God—and does not share the view that a spiritual explanation of reality should try to win recruits by depicting the world as it is not. Yet according to another interpreter, Kafka mocks at the claims of the mystics and of religion in general.

Kafka's career as a whole was powerfully affected by the fact that he was a Jew. To be a Jew is to experience the impact of society in a way concerning which too few non-Jews trouble to inform themselves. Sooner or later the Jewish child is impressed, possibly as the result of some jeering remark or abusive epithet, with the sense of his *difference* from others, a difference about which nothing can be done. It does not stop there. The child learns that in the eyes of others the Jews are to blame, for anything or everything, and that he himself is guilty with the rest. But when such accusations from outside are repeated often enough, they arouse a sense of guilt within, also. Thus are born the conflicting impulses to admit guilt, yet to rebel against the unspecified and unproven accusation, proudly to refuse the assimilation which is denied and yet to long for it and strive toward it.

It should be mentioned, too, that Kafka's sense of guilt derived not only from these social pressures but also from his emotional involvement with his father, of whom he stood in awe and whose magnificent competence (so Franz Kafka saw it) contrasted with his own unreadiness to shoulder the burdens of marriage and a career. His first short story, "The Judgment" ("Das Urteil," 1913) most directly reveals the ambivalence of his attitude toward his father. Rebellion and repentance are intermingled. The story was written without a moment's hesitation in the course of one night, and the writing of the last sentence, very significantly, as Kafka told Brod, was accompanied by a sense of powerful sexual release.

Kafka's work is a great deal more, however, than an ingenious veiled portrayal of what it means to be a Jew in Western society. It does not affect us solely as the reflection of the situation of a minority to which we may not ourselves belong. For the suggestion may be advanced that the Jew, or the Wandering Jew, has come to be the archetype of Western man. The Jewish diaspora, the scattering of a people over the face of the earth, can be taken as the symbol of two things: of the increased uprootedness of individuals and populations all over the world, and of the state of consciousness induced by this separation from old values, old places, and old beloved objects.

"The Metamorphosis" ("Die Verwandlung," 1912) is the masterful and haunting expansion of a term of abuse. A human being is contemptuously called a louse, an insect. And usually that's all there is to it. Except that something remains—the wound, the sense of having been depreciated or degraded. Perhaps even an element of fear lurks in some crevice of the psyche, especially when the psyche is that of a child. Who knows, at what tender age, what dread transformations may sometimes occur!

Transformation is a common literary motif. Sometimes the fanciful and poetic predominated; sometimes the horrible. Here the horrible has the upper hand. It pounds at us all the more relentlessly because of the matter-of-fact tone used and the precise and circumstantial detailing of the embarrassments and physical difficulties that beset the transformed Gregor Samsa. Nor does he enjoy the privilege of suffering in isolation. The family is at once drawn in, and so is Gregor's employer, to whom the family is indebted. Gregor's uncomplaining readiness to support the entire family and the quiet sacrifice of his personal desires—all this goes unrecognized. The faults he attributes to himself and the sense of guilt they have instilled, built up to intolerable proportions by the massive disapproval of society and family —of his father, to be precise— set a gulf between him and human kind. Step by step, whatever is human recedes from him.

The peak of tension in this quietly told drama is reached when the father begins to pelt Gregor with apples. To this painful dilemma there can be only one solution. It happens, and at once. The family—sister, mother, and father—is bathed in light and joy; they experience a genuine renewal, for the monster is dead.

Few readers will fail to sense the persistent echo that this tale arouses in them. We were all once ten-year-olds; we still are a little. We do not have Kafka's gift for dredging up, in mythical form, the fears that afflicted us then, but we can recognize them when Kafka brings them to the light of day.

ISAAC BASHEVIS SINGER

The Yiddish language, in which I. B. Singer writes his books, is approximately one thousand years old. Basically German (though not standard modern German) in grammatical structure and vocabulary, but containing many Hebrew words and adding, subsequently, others from Russian, Polish and, most recently, English, this language mirrors the circumstances under which Jews lived during that long period.

Originating in the Rhineland and along the Danube, the language traveled eastward as its speakers fled the pogroms that had begun as an accompaniment to the First Crusade (1096). Thus the Jews of Eastern Europe, the Ashkenazi, spoke Yiddish, that is, Jewish German. (The Sephardic Jews, similarly, who were expelled from Spain in the late fifteenth century, have maintained until today, in their "exile" in the eastern Mediterranean, a form of medieval Spanish as their language.)

In English translation, the best-known Yiddish writer is undoubtedly Shalom Aleichem, who died in Brooklyn in 1916— the earlier migrations to the East were matched, in the late nineteenth and twentieth centuries, by migrations to the west. Renewed fame has come to him, throughout the United States and the world, because of the successful musical *Fiddler on the Roof*, which is based on his stories of Tevyeh the dairyman.

Isaac Bashevis Singer, born in 1904, had a briefer experience in the now vanished world of Eastern Jewry. But he nevertheless was deeply immersed in it. His father was a rabbi in a small town near Warsaw and was extremely poor, since he begrudged the time it would have taken him to learn Russian and thus qualify for recognition by the Russian authorities. He preferred to devote his time, when no other demands were made on it, to the study of the Torah (the Pentateuch, the first five books of the Bible). The elder Singer subsequently moved to a poor district in Warsaw. But Isaac spent the later war years with his mother's family in Bilgoray, near Lublin, where the food supplies were better. The boy's grandfather had been a highly esteemed rabbi, whose religious learning was matched by a commanding presence and practical competence. And he often heard tales of the glorious past that had revolved around his grandfather.

I. B. Singer, separated while still quite a young man from the narrow, but also intense and remarkably variegated life of Polish Jewry, still lives intensely in this world in his imagination, and this attitude is the driving force behind his creativity. In his short stories he ranges over every aspect of Jewish life. That the supernatural has a special allure for him is of little wonder, since the boy heard constant talk about "spirits of the dead that possess the bodies of the living, souls reincarnated as animals, houses inhabited by hobgoblins, cellars haunted by demons." Though he will not be pinned down concerning precise details, even today I. B. Singer avows his belief in spiritual entities of which the scientific rationalist knows nothing. His tales, including those he has written for children, make use of the elements of folklore and superstition for which he himself had been so avid. He has also written a number of novels, one of them situated in the seventeenth century, whose aim it is to paint a broad panorama of Jewish life. More recently he has placed some of his fiction in the United States, but he limits himself to dealing with Jewish immigrants, the people he knows best.

For a direct, nonfictional account of his boyhood years, one may read *A Day of Pleasure* (1969) or the partially overlapping *In My Father's Court* (1966). This does not refer, of course, to a royal or ducal court, or even the busy, populous "court" of a Hasidic rabbi, adulated by his followers and attracting countless hangers-on. It was simply his father the rabbi in his function as judge or conciliator in disputes that arose between members of his congregation, or others, who then came to him and undertook to abide by his decision. The book introduces the reader to well-established patterns of thinking and behavior that are nevertheless quite astounding, on occasion, and which in the main are, no doubt, strategies that tended to preserve individual and group existence during the centuries of compressed and ever-threatened

existence in the ghettos. For a more disabused, less fond reflection of the life of this same family, with its ineffectual male head and his more energetic, more skeptical spouse, one can turn to *Of a World That Is No More* (1970), by I. J. Singer, the older-by-eleven-years brother of I. B. Singer. This brother detested his sixty-hour school week, was an unenthusiastic student of the Torah, and loved the open fields, horses, and handicrafts, all inappropriate interests for the son of a Rabbi.

The story reprinted here, "The Gentleman from Cracow," testifies to the Evil One's maleficent powers—which extend far beyond the individual and can wreak havoc on a whole town. The story unfolds in its own picturesque, gripping way; as a piece of fiction it requires no commentary here. It is more important to point out that whole communities of Jews in Eastern Europe sometimes *were* eliminated. The refusal of any individual to conform to the accepted laws and mores was potentially too dangerous to be tolerated, and was looked on as apostasy and treason. Gradually, as the danger lessened, some sought to adapt to the non-Jewish world and hankered after a secular education. What had been the bliss of the Sabbath and the inexhaustible riches of the Torah became an intolerably irksome network of prohibitions and ritual requirements. The worm, if not the serpent Satan, had entered the fruit, and one fateful step led to another: Gentile dress and ways were adopted and, as in this story, cards were played and men and women actually danced together. Disaster on earth, the traditionalists believed, would be the direct expression of the Divine anger. Singer is also sensitive, however, to the psychological problems confronting the innovators, to their irrational fears and guilt feelings at having broken with tradition. He himself had listened to the skeptical remarks of his older brother and had been swayed by them. Consequently, though situated in a shadowy past, this legend reveals something of Singer's own doubts and ambivalences. He is a figure bridging two generations, two continents, and two irreconcilable outlooks on life.

BERTOLT BRECHT

Brecht must be considered one of the most imaginative and powerful playwrights of our time. "Song of a Scribbler of Plays" ("Lied des Stückeschreibers") tells us something of how he conceived his task. "I am a scribbler of plays," he declares. "I present what I have seen"—how human beings are sold and bartered; how men stand idly in the street and wait, sometimes hopeful, sometimes dejected; how people set traps for one another; what they say to each other, mother to son, wife to husband, undertaker to dying man—"I report it all."

In calling himself a scribbler rather than a playwright, Brecht assumes an anti-intellectual, unsophisticated attitude that is somewhat deceptive. For in the same "Song" he admits that he adapted the plays of other countries and other times, testing their techniques and absorbing whatever he felt he could utilize.

It is one of the many paradoxes in Brecht's life that his very originality grew out of his ability to take not only life itself but also literature as a source of inspiration—adapting, adopting, parodying, or satirizing what he found. Villon's ballads, the chronicles of the Thirty Years' War, religious hymns, the German classical authors, Goethe and Schiller, Japanese Nō plays, the Bible, all served him and contributed to his work. But this "scribbler" made them his own, thanks to the admirable adroitness with which he handled the German language. With the might of his poetry—which fluctuated between moving lyricism and crude comedy, biting criticism and sheer delight in existence—he transcended his conscious didactic intentions to achieve, to the accompaniment of stirring biblical echoes, a forthright excoriation of the rich and exaltation of the poor.

Brecht's life and work are both filled with seemingly irreconcilable features. Perhaps they account for the intensity and ever-surprising liveliness of his writing. There is naïveté and sophistication; a glorification of individuality and the subordination of the individual to a common cause; skepticism and a deep trust in simple folk; acceptance of myth and an insistence on rationality, science, and progress; a world of light fantasy and another of crass realism. Though painfully concerned with the economic problems of the day, the playwright is equally aware of the insignificance of the moment, in a world where men are transients who leave few traces. "We know that we are provisional. And after us will come: nothing worth mentioning." In spite of his desire to be engagé, a socially and politically committed ("engaged") writer, at a time when that word was still unknown, and to be a good Communist militant, neither the poet nor his work ever proved entirely acceptable to the Communists. But it was, nevertheless, the Communist sector of postwar divided Germany that at last offered him a stage suited to his plays, such as he had never known during the years of his American exile from the Nazis. Here it was—with the Berliner Ensemble that his wife Helene Weigel founded in 1949—that he laid the foundations for a fame that the western world had previously denied him.

As a dramatic author, Brecht ranged from experimental expressionism to serious musicals, whose high-spirited rhythms were so deceptive and so alluring that even audiences antagonistic to their "messages" eagerly applauded them; from didactic plays repeating the "Party line" to serious drama. At first he composed his own tunes for the ballads with which his plays are interspersed, but soon he sought the help of Kurt Weill, Paul Hindemith, and Hanns Eissler. Receptive to all that was new, he took his place in the vanguard time and again. The "epic" style of theater that was developed in Germany after World War I, with its insertion of narrative and film into dramatic dialogue and its defiance of the Aristotelian unities of time and action, so captivated him that he became its outstanding representative. Yet other plays fore-shadow the recent "theatre of the Absurd."

The playwright's profound interest in technique led him not only to study the drama of other ages and countries but also to write theoretical essays that prescribed a non-Aristotelian theater and rejected such supposedly essential elements as empathy, catharsis, unity of action, and psychological motivation of character. But he was too skilled a playwright and too experienced a man of the theater to be guided exclusively by any theory. His book *Staging in Progress*, as we might call his *Theaterarbeit*, written in collaboration with the staff of the Berliner Ensemble, demonstrates how he submitted his theories to an unceasing revision. In practical terms, his main aim as a dramatist and director was to establish an aesthetic distance between the audience and what was happening on the stage. This distancing sought to bar any emotional involvement on the part of the spectator and to provoke instead his intellectual awareness and comprehension. The style of acting called for is in direct opposition to the "method acting" prevalent in the United States, and this may explain why Brecht's plays have been less successful in the States than in European countries.

While Brecht's openly didactic period is not without interest, on the whole we must judge it arid. The years of the playwright's maturity, which coincided with his exile (1933-1948), brought forth his greatest theatrical masterpieces, though the earlier *Threepenny Opera*, thanks in 1923 part to the beguiling music of

Kurt Weill, had brought him international fame and recognition. *Galileo*, written in 1938 and 1939, *Mother Courage and Her Children* (1939), *The Good Woman of Setzuan* (1938-1940), *Herr Puntila and His Man Matti* (1940-1941), and *The Caucasian Chalk Circle* (1943-1945) assure him a place among the great playwrights.

In these plays of his maturity, Brecht abandoned both the rigid didacticism and the anarchical romantic characters of his youth in favor of universal man presented in his pathetic struggle against all the forces that crush him and deprive him of a fully human existence. These enemies include war and poverty, political irresponsibility and arbitrary decisions. Rousseau's theme of the basic goodness of man and his corruption by society seems to pervade all of Brecht's work. As he presents him, man wants to be good. Man finds it difficult to be bad but, confronting corruption and greed, deprivation and suffering, he uses in sheer self-defense the weapons of his oppressors and sometimes stifles his natural feeling of pity. Thus Mother Courage, underneath her crust of greed and shrewd opportunism, remains the unselfish, afflicted mother. Shen-Te, the good woman of Setzuan, is ruthless against her exploiters in order to secure her child's future.

Brecht's distaste for "psychological" drama and his belief in man's innate goodness, covered over though it be by the corruption of society, often led him to depict his characters as split personalities, veering between extreme kindness and extreme meanness, or even between two seemingly contradictory masks. In the early *Man Is Man*, the protagonist is tricked into assuming another's name. His entire personality is changed; trusting simplicity yields to domineering cruelty. Herr Puntila has antithetical attitudes, character, and beliefs, depending upon whether he is drunk or sober. The good woman of Setzuan repeatedly dons the mask of a "visiting cousin" who, in contrast to her own unselfish nature, is shrewd and calculating. With Galileo and Mother Courage one might be justified in speaking of schizoid personalities, were it not that Brecht's plays reflect rather the cleavage between the spirit —which desires the good—and the flesh—whose selfish desires conjure up the bad. This emerges most clearly, perhaps, in *Saint Joan of the Stockyards*. The King of the stockyards, parodying Goethe's Faust, refers to the two souls that rend his breast.

Only in *The Caucasian Chalk Circle* does the playwright separate these two warring souls and embody them in two women, the vain and totally selfish Governor's wife and Grusha the maid, unselfish, infinitely faithful and kind. The stage is set for one of the most enchanting fairy tales. The bad woman, fleeing the beleaguered city, spends her time choosing clothes and abandons her child. The good woman finds that "the seductive power of goodness" is "terrible." Yet she shuns no danger or hardship to protect the other woman's child, and is even ready to abandon her hope of reunion with the man she loves. After peace has been restored, the Governor's wife again seeks her child, but for purely selfish reasons.

In Brecht's world, the law usually favors the rich. One might expect that the Governor's wife, rich and corrupt and, also, the child's actual mother, would win her case. But in this fairy tale, with its wholly bad and wholly good characters, a good fairy in the person of Azdak appears to ensure that rightness and goodness shall triumph. Grusha the maid keeps the child and departs with the man she loves. Obviously, they will live happily ever after. In its moving simplicity the love of Grusha and her soldier stands out even more strongly against the background of war and political intrigue.

Viewed technically, this play is epic theater at its best, with the narrator seated at one side of the stage, with its songs and significant dialogues. The Prologue reveals that the original play was Chinese. The story is enacted to entertain the State Reconstruction Commission that has come to consider the rebuilding of a shattered Caucasian village community. The play must reflect the problems to be solved, and that is why the old legend is transformed. The narrator voices the hope that, in the shadow of the Soviet tractors, the old poet will hold his own. He is convinced that the old and the new wisdom will mix admirably. And this is Brecht's own view. His greatness lies in the fact that he has been able to embody both the soul of reality and the soul of poetry.

JEAN-PAUL SARTRE

Sartre is one of those rare authors who have been outstandingly successful in a great variety of genres. His publications embrace short stories, novels, plays, essays, psychology, philosophy, and public affairs. It would be misleading, however, not to indicate that, despite his prodigious literary activities and, probably, the many thousands of pages he has written but not published, he has not been equally active in every type of writing all the time. His five short stories all appeared in the 1930's. There was one prewar novel, *Nausea,* and in the 1950's he abandoned a novel, *Roads to Liberty,* after publishing the first three volumes. He has totally repudiated the 728 pages of *Being and Nothingness,* the philosophical work that aroused an extraordinary furor immediately after World War II and which, with the backing of several consistently successful plays, brought him world fame. The one thing that has remained constant, in this flood of words so diversely used, is the flood itself. It is in this sense that Sartre ironically gave the title *The Words* to a sketch of his early years.

No adequate account of this immense production can be given here. It is important to realize, however, that the reader whose interests are purely literary can gain only a fragmentary view of Sartre as writer, publicist, and ideologue. To complete the picture, he would have to plow through many pages that use several technical vocabularies and strange terms coined by Sartre himself. *Existentialism* was not his invention, actually, and it has also been applied, with excessive liberality, to the thinking of the German philosopher Martin Heidegger and of many others whose theories cannot possibly all be reconciled. Sartre's outlook, unlike Heidegger's, was rigidly dualistic. He maintained, in *Being and Nothingness*, that man had been regarded by philosophers and psychologists from the outside as though he were an object, and that previous attempts to deal with man's inwardness had actually smuggled the object inside him, in a disguised form. But the object is simply what it is, knowing no past and hoping for and fearing no future. Man, on the contrary, is divided against himself, looking backward and forward, and imagining how the present could be changed into what it is not (*néantiser*, "to nihilize," is Sartre's word for this procedure). Each man's project, no matter how varied the methods and envisaged goal may be, is fundamentally the endeavor to realize himself fully, like a solid object, but at the same time to realize, or be conscious, that he has become an unconscious object. He would thus have welded into unity the essence of the object and the existence of the subject. But this aim is self-contradictory, hence impossible, and man—to quote the last phrase of *Being and Nothingness*—"is a useless passion."

There are, on the path to this conclusion, many fascinating psychological analyses of great originality and depth. Some commentators have declared a number of the book's individual parts to be more impressive than the whole, and they find Sartre more successful as a psychologist than on the metaphysical level.

For Sartre today, existentialism is but a trend, petit bourgeois in origin (since Sartre, its originator, is a petit bourgeois), within the one great ideology of the last hundred years and more: Marxism. Today, even when the psychology of one individual is at the center of his attention, he no longer finds it valid to consider this individual apart from the immediate social group and the wider society in which he has grown up and still lives.

One immense change that has taken place in Sartre's outlook can be simply stated. He had declared, in *Being and Nothingness*, that man was totally free— even though, as he paradoxically put it, man was "condemned to be free" and "free to commit himself." Now Sartre holds that man's freedom is but a nuance within societal patterns, whether these be firmly established, undergoing significant modification, or on the way out. However, freedom is no less precious and essential, because of that.

Yet Sartre's philosophical acumen is matched by the ability to create men and women within the matrix of a fictional work. In the story, "The Room," included here, the first character to appear is Mme. Darbédat. In order to escape her husband's noisy rampagings, she has taken refuge in a mysterious illness. Nevertheless, she does her best to make a pattern out of her memories, moods, and emotions, so that she may incarnate that fine flower of bourgeois culture, the lady.

Sartre has always found it easier to treat the bourgeoise with some measure of indulgence, since she too, like her servants, like workers, convicts, and conscripts, can be regarded as a victim of the bourgeois system. But he has no mercy on the male, the bourgeois, in whom he sees the exploiter.

M. Darbédat, her husband, leads an inauthentic existence, lying to himself as well as to other people. His insane son-in-law, he maintains, must be put away. But this is for Pierre's own good, not because it would eliminate from M. Darbédat's own life an embarrassment and a scandal. As for Eve, his daughter and Pierre's wife, she is committing the unpardonable sin of "being different," by refusing to adopt her father's solution of the problem. No one, in his view, has the right not to be normal, not to share the joys of normal folk.

Eve is desperately trying to live inside her husband's world. The attempt is futile, for he inhabits not a world, but a jumble of incoherent fancies. She cannot go insane along with him, for insanity is not togetherness. Thus, gesture by gesture, thought after thought, this latter part of the story moves inexorably toward frustration.

Yet more is to be required of Eve's love for her husband. She knows that he is doomed to sink into a vegetablelike immobility. Contemplating the sleeping Pierre, she says, "I'll kill you before that."

Many years ago, Sartre announced that he would undertake an "existential psychoanalysis" of Gustave Flaubert, while revealing on a number of occasions that he did not esteem the man behind the novels. In *L'Idiot de la famille* he has re-

cently begun to carry out this promise. Two volumes, two thousand pages, perhaps one million words, lead us to the time when Flaubert published *Madame Bovary*, his first novel. In this connection, too, there has been a radical change in Sartre's outlook. First of all, the book could be written as currently conceived only because there is a huge amount of material available on Flaubert's childhood and the circumstances surrounding it. Reversing the old-fashioned deterministic practice of using an author's works simply as documents that throw light on the man, Sartre maintains that a man's life may enable us to understand better his writings, which realize in fantasy possibilities that the real world denies. But Sartre is not content merely to stand the old practice on its head. Utilizing the abundant materials and allowing himself, too, interpretative leaps that a cautious academic scholar would not even dream of, he works out and concretely exemplifies a method that flows in both directions: from milieu to individual, from individual to milieu. In this way, Sartre believes, it is possible to converge upon the complex truth of a man (a child, first of all) as society molds him, and also to illuminate more powerfully just what the individual has done with the measure of freedom that is his lot.

A study of these crushing dimensions is not going to be thoroughly read by very many people. It is conceivable, however, that the model Sartre has provided will significantly influence writers in the fields of literary history, social and political history, and sociology. In this way it may come to influence, at a considerable number of removes, and perhaps affecting public affairs as well as scholarly fields, the lives of people to whom the very name of Sartre is unknown. At all events, the serious investigator owes it to himself to examine whether he has anything to learn from this extraordinary work.

ALBERT CAMUS

Though Camus was a mature, established writer and recipient of the Nobel Prize for Literature at the time of his death in an automobile crash, it is nevertheless hard to shake off the feeling that his life's work had not been fully rounded out. Perhaps this is due to the shocking suddenness of his death, which was felt as a personal loss by many who had never known him. Perhaps he had arrived at a hiatus in his career, and stood on the verge of deciding, or discovering, in what direction he would next proceed. Or it may be that his writings themselves reveal him as a man dumbfounded, on the one hand, by the beauty of the world: a North African landscape shimmering in the heat, the swimmer's plunge and resurfacing in the sunlight, the unproblematical sensualities of growing up in the popular quarters of a French North African city. But the hideous, too, was a shock whose tremors refused to subside: shock at the callousness of men and at the yet grimmer reality of death and disease, to which even innocent children fall victim. Camus, though a professed unbeliever, neverthe-less voiced his sense of outrage in terms that recall the questioning of Job and *The Brothers Karamazov* of Dostoevsky, along with countless others throughout history: How can unmerited suffering be reconciled with the existence of a God who is both all-powerful and good?

This questioning, or accusation, emerges most clearly at one stage of what is, in terms of length, Camus' most ambitious work, when a priest gives the orthodox Christian answer to this difficulty but fails to convince his hearer. The Plague—which, Camus insists, is a chronicle and not a novel—is related in the first person by a doctor who witnesses the outbreak and ravages of pestilence in a town which, because of this, is segregated from the rest of the country. The onset, worsening, and slow ebb of the malady form the setting against which men play their varied parts, which range from selfless dedication to a devil-may-care attitude that might have brought about the deaths of all. Some critics regard the work as that rare literary phenomenon in modern times, a piece of allegorical writing. The plague-bringing rats would then be the Nazis, and the isolated town would represent France or Nazi-occupied Europe. However, it is impossible to demonstrate that Camus' fiction and historical reality coincide in every essential feature. No one in the town, not even the most frivolous individual, was actually on the side of the rats. The situation in France under Nazi domination was distressingly different.

Dostoevskian questions had

already been posed by Camus in his first novel, *The Stranger*, published in 1942. As in *The Brothers Karamazov*, a man is shot and an innocent man is absurdly convicted of the deed. Though innocent of his father's murder, Dimitrof was condemned because of a series of events that seemed to point to him as the culprit. Meursault, hero of *The Stranger*, did actually commit murder, but one might say that the deed was done "in all innocence." It was a reflex movement that, in the glaring heat of noon, made him reach for the revolver in his pocket when the Arab's knife flashed menacingly.

On legal grounds Meursault should have been acquitted, since he had acted in self-defense. But what rendered him suspect and intolerable was his general behavior, which threatened to expose the duplicity of accepted mores. The first slip had been his failure to weep during his mother's funeral. Society, acting as judge, could not understand this individual who did not pay homage to the forces of the universal cliché. Condemned to death for his strangeness, the stranger is turned in on himself and forced to reflect as he has never reflected before. He emerges from his anguished pondering still in rebellion against his fate but able to rejoice in the "tender indifference" of the natural world, with its stars, night odors, salty air.

The hero's previous attitude (nothing "made sense," it "didn't matter") is an essential component, and does much to explain the success of the book. The failure of this strang-

er to understand, to respect, to abide by the conventional petty hypocrisies that keep society moving smoothly in the old grooves, make of him an exemplar of "alienated" or "turned off" youth, just as, within the limits of possibility of time and place, he had become a dropout. The number of Meursaults in circulation was to multiply mightily, after the end of World War II.

The Myth of Sisyphus, also published in 1942, restates in a more theoretical way what *The Stranger* had expressed in novelistic terms. Sisyphus, condemned by the gods to a labor of utter futility, was for Camus the archetype of the "absurd hero." But his Sisyphus, in a sense, escapes his punishment. Knowing that his work is in vain, that the boulder, once he has pushed it to the mountain top, will inevitably roll to the bottom, Sisyphus joyously carries out his repetitive task. "One ought to be Sisyphus, and happy," that is the lesson to be drawn. Camus finds happiness in activity and in a full and sensuous union with the world. Yet one question continues to obtrude itself. In this godless universe, where "everything is permitted," that is, where man is not held back by fear of divine retribution, is everything, indeed, permitted? This Dostoevskian question pursues Camus through novels, essays, and plays until he reaches the conclusion that man, in relation to his fellow man, can sin.

The Fall (1957), which once more takes up this problem of man's guilt and the extent of his freedom, again reminds us of *The Brothers Karamazov*, especially of the chapter on the Grand Inquisitor. The narrator and protagonist identifies himself as a "judge-penitent" and confesses to a life filled with self-love and vanity: "I, I, I is the refrain of my whole life." Vanity has led to duplicity, for the self-created image of self established a role that must be maintained and that must be acknowledged by others. The more virtuous this image, in terms of what society expects, the greater the applause that will be won. Yet the individual, basking in the warmth of this applause, may be situated at a far remove from any reality corresponding to the image. But he continues to live his lie, to play the role assigned to him partly by himself and partly by others, until something occurs that shatters his complacency.

The "I" of this novel is not unique; it is really "we." And this is generally true of Camus' highly stylized characters. They remain lifelike, nevertheless; though we do not expect to meet any individual so generically simplified, like a clown or a personage from the commedia dell' arte, these characters nonetheless possess stark reality.

"The Renegade" is also a narrative in the first person. This is the most savage and the most impressive of the stories that make up *Exile and the Kingdom* (published in 1958). In it Camus has created a masklike living thing that is horrifyingly real. A slave speaks, and the story centers around the problem of man's freedom. In this "renegade," slavery seems to be innate. His changes of allegiance leave him ever both slave and prisoner. It

matters little that one of his masters is the god of love and the other a god of hatred. His dedication to the god of love has led him to flee the confines of the seminary and to set himself up as a missionary among the most cruel savages. Eager to accept suffering and torture in the service of his lord, he believes that the faith radiating from him will conquer his oppressors. The actuality is very different.

In their harsh city of salt, these silent savages, dressed in black, are his undoubted masters. So he abandons the god of love (in actual fact, nothing of the sort but only the means by which he sought to establish his own domination) and pays homage to the Fetish, the god of hatred. Here, he believes, is "the principle of the world." Once more he is disappointed. The god of malice and hatred also turns out to be vulnerable. Soldiers arrive; they punish the worshippers of the Fetish. The missionary-turned-slave can achieve no second apostasy that would place him on the side of the big batallions. His tongueless mouth is stuffed with salt, and he dies a slave. Free men cannot be renegades because they have no masters. He who wanted to enslave others with the power of his word remains tongueless and can express his pain only in animal-like grunts and cries.

The technique used by Camus in telling this story is rather extraordinary. It is an interior monologue. There is not even the nameless interlocutor of *The Fall*. Part of the story is a flashback. As he lies in wait for the new missionary, whom he has decided to kill, the renegade recapitulates his life. But though the flashback ends when, seemingly, he shoots the new missionary, the story goes on, Ramblingly, and between grunts of pain, the renegade finally acknowledges that the power of the sorcerer has been vanquished by the power of the soldiers, who are in the service of the god of love. Power replaces power, and the renegade's feeble gesture of aid has changed nothing. He dies, his mouth filled with salt. It is a bleak and despairing tale that Camus relates. We might do well to look back to his Sisyphus, happy in the recognition of the futility of his labor, in no man's service and rewarded by none.

ALEXANDER SOLZHENITSYN

More than great talent is required to produce a great writer in Russia. It also takes great courage. Under both czar and commissar, the Russian authorities have always seen writers as a threat—who, as Nikita Khrushchev put it, would form "a second government," if means were not found to control them. The greater the writer, of course, the more considerable the threat. Pushkin, Dostoevsky, Tolstoy under the old regime, Gorky, Pasternak, Solzhenitsyn under the new—these are but six of the writers whose peace of mind and freedom to write, or freedom of movement, or physical freedom, were in greater or lesser degree denied. If a writer did not possess quite extraordinary toughness of mind and character, he was (and is) likely to yield, and find his lot eased by

the status symbols and tangible rewards that the state can bestow. Others, with greater dignity, have preferred to write for themselves alone, making no attempt to publish. Some writers emigrated. And there have been suicides. Of those who have waged a constant struggle, in spite of rebuffs, pillorying, and defamation, to obtain publication in their own land, Solzhenitsyn is an outstanding example.

While still a child, he had a strong literary urge. For financial and practical reasons, however, he majored at the university in physics and mathematics, and during the war years—he was twenty-one years old when World War II broke out— served with great distinction in the artillery. His downfall was brought about by imprudent criticism, expressed in his private correspondence, of "the mustachioed one," whom the authorities readily identified as Stalin. His eight-year sentence began with sojourns in various camps, but he was transferred to a special institute for scientifically trained prisoners. This provided him with the background for his novel *The First Circle*. Transferred to a camp for political prisoners in Kazakhstan, he worked with his hands, and acquired the background for *One Day in the Life of Ivan Denisovich*. Upon completion of his prison sentence he was exiled for life to an area in southern Kazakhstan, where he taught physics and mathematics to primary school pupils. Some time after Stalin's death in 1953 he was moved to a cancer clinic where, despite his apparently terminal condition, he was cured. This experience enabled him to write *The Cancer Ward*. In 1957 he was declared innocent of the charges that had led to his imprisonment.

During his years in camp he had composed poetry in his head, and after his release he wrote prose to satisfy his inner urge with no thought that he could ever hope for publication. This absence of an outlet became terribly burdensome to him. By 1961, relying on the general signs of a thaw in internal conditions and on a bold speech by Alexander Tvardovsky, the poet who edited the periodical *Novy Mir*, he took the grave risk of sending off the manuscript of *One Day*. Tvardovsky, surmounting all the hurdles placed in his way, succeeded one year later in publishing the "first work" of this forty-four-year-old author. The novel at once became a sensation all over Russia, with people queueing up at the public libraries to enter their names on the waiting list for it. In 1963, Solzhenitsyn was still allowed to publish "Matryona's House" and one other story. But the climate was already changing. To this day, no other piece of writing by Solzhenitsyn has been published in Russia. His personal archives were seized, and he was expelled from the Writers' Union. When he was awarded the Nobel Prize for Literature in 1970, the campaign of defamation against him intensified.

Samizdat, which literally means "self-publication," has attained considerable dimensions in Russia. It means the under-cover circulation of manuscripts, usually in typewritten form, to trustworthy individuals. In this way thousands of Russians have been able to read the text of Solzhenitsyn's two novels, *The First Circle* and *The Cancer Ward*. Manuscripts were also smuggled abroad, where the two works were published in Russian and in numerous translations. The smuggling was done without Solzhenitsyn's knowledge and against his wishes. *One Day in the Life of Ivan Denisovich* recounts the devices used by an illiterate prisoner (his "crime" had been to have fallen into German hands during the war—all repatriated prisoners of war were ipso facto suspect) to survive and, when possible, to do a little better than survive, in bleak, subzero prison camp conditions. There are some things he will not do, and thus he is able to maintain the difficult balance that insures both survival and continued self-respect. This is a victory of the human spirit over tyranny, meanness, and planned debasement. The writing is entirely realistic, there are no rhetorical or sentimental flights, no moral is specifically drawn. For Solzhenitsyn, too, this is a victory: of sobriety, firmness, control, and of a steady vision that neither overlooks pettiness nor fails to see grandeur beneath prison rags.

Dante placed the souls of distinguished pagans in the first, relatively pleasant, circle of his hell. Similarly, the skilled inhabitants of the special research institute, that other *First Circle*, are spared the worst features of the prison camps. They are carrying out work of the highest importance, in which Stalin takes a personal interest. Believing that the human voice is no less unique than the thumb print, they succeed in breaking down recordings of telephone conversations so as to identify the speaker with reasonable certainty—or, at all events, with all the certainty Stalin required. The imprisoned scientists and linguists are of all types. Some remain dedicated Communists, although in disgrace; with impassioned arguments they justify the "reason of State" that brushes aside ethical qualms. Others are implacably hostile, and would suffer any fate rather than further the plans of a despot. Yet all, willy-nilly, are dragged in to serve his designs.

Everything is subservient to the dictator, Stalin, with his tigerish yellow eyes. The novel contains a portrait of the sick, aged monster, alone at the center of his own web. It is a remarkable tribute to Solzhenitsyn's power to rise above hatred and notions of revenge that even in this instance we are made aware of the humanity allied to the inhumanity. The book, while dramatic in its unfolding, and exciting in terms of personal clashes and conflicts, also possesses a striking spatial quality. We have the sense that the whole panorama or, better, the whole geometrically organized, dynamic mandala of Stalinist Russia is displayed before us.

There is a greater adversary in *The Cancer Ward*: death. In writing this work Solzhenitsyn, who himself had lingered at death's threshold, not only challenged comparison with Tolstoy's *Death of Iván Ilyich*, he had a more ambitious aim, since all the patients of a cancer ward, with their differing backgrounds and temperaments and levels of education, face the same ultimate antagonist. There is the Stalinist bureaucrat, both officially and personally committed to "looking on the bright side of things," and thus lost in lies and self-deceit. There is the central character who, like Solzhenitsyn himself, wins the battle against death.

The secretary of the Nobel Prize Committee has said that Mother Russia is central in Solzhenitsyn's work, and he names Matryona as one embodiment of that figure. "Matryona's House" excellently exemplifies the qualities of Solzhenitsyn's writing. He is not interested in new novelistic techniques, in any fanciful departures from the solid traditions of the Russian novel. (From his own very different conception of literature Vladimir Nabokov, the émigré author of *Lolita*, judges him to be "a mediocre writer.") He approaches the writer's task with the thoroughness in preparation, as in execution, of a scientist engaged on a major research project or of an artillery officer aware of the disaster that might result from the least oversight. Short story though it is, "Matryona's House" has the unhurrying pace, the scrupulousness in choice of detail, the eventual partial crises before the final crisis, and the time for reflection that follows, that suggest the breadth and weightiness of a novel. In musical terms, Solzhenitsyn favors *adagio* and *andante* over *prestissimo* and *allegro molto vivace*.

The citation that accompanied the award of the Nobel Prize was fortunately phrased: "For the ethical force with which he has pursued the indispensable traditions of Russian literature." In surveying the twists and turns that have marked the course of literature over the most recent decades, one might hazard the guess that an ethical standpoint may be more and more unashamedly adopted in the years ahead. In that or in any event, Solzhenitsyn's Matryona will be borne in mind, she of whom he declares in conclusion that

> She was that righteous one without whom, according to the proverb, no village can stand.
> Nor any city.
> Nor our whole land.

August 1914, the first volume of the projected multivolume novel recreating the Russia of World War I and the early revolutionary years, was published in Russian—but outside Russia —in 1971. (Solzhenitsyn no longer insists that publication abroad occurs without any collaboration from him.) "The general concept of the novel," he has written, "came to my mind in 1936, when I was just leaving secondary school. Since then I have never departed from it, regarding it as the chief artistic design of my life." He envisages it as requiring twenty years, but "probably I will not live to finish it." As for his earlier books, they are secondary, "a result of the oddities of my life story."

The massive work inaugurated by *August 1914* raises the curtain on an immense panorama of Russia, both social and ideological. The style ranges from the poetic and evocative to the precisely naturalistic and technical. While employing many old-fashioned procedures, it also utilizes such modernistic devices as excerpts from the press and brief film scenarios (John Dos Passos's trilogy *U.S.A.* was influential here.) Historical events are merged with Solzhenitsyn's own inventions, and actual historical personages interact with fictional characters.

The work inevitably faces comparison with Tolstoy's *War and Peace*. But that is not all. Solzhenitsyn, it is clear, challenges his readers to measure him against the greatest, and does so from the novel's first page: "In the early sunlight the whole of the Caucasus range . . . could be seen." This is the setting, too, of Aeschylus's *Prometheus Bound*. There, at "the world's limit," Might and Violence, the servitors of the new tyrant Zeus, supervise the nailing of Prometheus to a crag. Prometheus, himself a god, has stolen the fire of the gods for the benefit of mankind. •

As day progresses, and as Solzhenitsyn's travelers advance, the rising vapors that announce a blazing summer day obscure the base of the mountain chain. Then the upper reaches become indistinguishable from clouds until, finally, the heat haze obliterates them altogether. The travelers move on as though "hemmed in by rounded foothills: the Camel, the Bull, the bare-topped Snake, and the thickly wooded Iron Hill."

The "selva obscura," the dark wood of Dante, and the leopard, lion, and she-wolf that bar his way in the first canto of the *Inferno*, have surely been evoked.

"Our revels now are ended," wrote Shakespeare, in the fourth act of his late play, *The Tempest*, and the following lines predict that "like the baseless fabric of this vision" not only the "cloud-capped towers" and "gorgeous palaces" but "the great globe itself . . . shall dissolve." In audacious antithesis, it is at the very outset of his toweringly ambitious work that Solzhenitsyn conjures up a like evanescence. At this stage its exact symbolic significance cannot be divined. Perhaps the Renaissance world of Shakespeare and—quite assuredly!—the technological modern age will be transcended by a newer and also older vision, a more nearly total concatenation, of individual, society, history, nature, and cosmos.

LIVES, WRITINGS, AND CRITICISM
Biographical and critical works are listed only if they are available in English.

CHARLES BAUDELAIRE
LIFE. Born in Paris on April 9, 1821. In 1828 his widowed mother married Jacques Aupick, later to become a general and an ambassador. Throughout his life Baudelaire remained greatly attached to his mother and detested his stepfather. His independent behavior having caused alarm, in 1841 he was dispatched on a voyage to the tropics. The following year saw the beginning of his lifelong liaison with Jeanne Duval, a mulatto woman, and of his frequent changes of residence in Paris. Disturbed by his extravagance, the family in 1844 placed him under a financial tutelage which was never to be lifted. The revolutionary disturbances of 1848 awakened his enthusiasm, though later he expressed reactionary political views. The same year he published the first of his many translations from Edgar Allan Poe. His long-heralded collection of poems *Flowers of Evil* (*Les Fleurs du mal*), which at last appeared in 1857, was judged to contain matter offensive to morals: author and publisher were fined, and obliged to omit six poems. Baudelaire, who had probably acquired a venereal infection many years before, noted in 1862 that he had felt on his forehead "the breeze from imbecility's wing." Two years later he left Paris, and his creditors, for Brussels. There, in 1866, he was stricken with aphasia and hemiplegia, and he was brought back to Paris. After prolonged suffering he died in his mother's arms, on August 31, 1867. He was interred beside the body of General Aupick.

CHIEF WRITINGS. *Flowers of Evil* (*Les Fleurs du mal*, 1857), translated by Lewis Piaget Shanks (1931), George Dillon and Edna St. Vincent Millay (1936), C. F. McIntyre (1947), Geoffrey Wagner (1949), Roy Campbell (1952), William Aggeler (1954), Francis Duke (1961), and selected and edited by Martiel and Jackson Mathews (rev. ed. 1963); *Artificial Paradises* (*Les Paradis artificiels*, 1860); *Aesthetic Curiosities* (*Curiosités esthétiques*, 1868); *Little Poems in Prose* (*Petits Poèmes en prose*, 1869), translated by A. Crowley (1928) and James Huneker (1929); *Romantic Art* (*L'Art romantique*, 1869); *Posthumous Works and Unedited Correspondence* (*Œuvres posthumes et correspondances inédites*, 1887), including material translated by Christopher Isherwood as *Intimate Journals* (1930); *Baudelaire as a Literary Critic* (1964), translated and edited by Lois B. and Francis E. Hyslop, Jr.; *Painter of Modern Life and Other Writings on Art* (1964), edited by Jonathan Mayne.

BIOGRAPHY AND CRITICISM. François Porché, *Charles Baudelaire* (1928); Peter Quennell, *Baudelaire and the Symbolists* (1929); S. A. Rhodes, *The Cult of Beauty in Charles Baudelaire* (1929); Enid Starkie, *Baudelaire* (1933); Margaret Gilman, *Baudelaire the Critic* (1943); Joseph D. Bennett, *Baudelaire, a Criticism* (1944); Marcel Raymond, *From Baudelaire to Surrealism* (1949); Jean-Paul Sartre, *Baudelaire* (1950); P. M. Jones, *Baudelaire* (1952); Martin Turnell, *Baudelaire* (1954); D. J. Mossop, *Baudelaire's Tragic Hero* (1961); Henri Peyre (ed.), *Baudelaire* (1962); and Pierre

Emmanuel, *Baudelaire: The Paradox of Redemptive Satanism* (1970).

ARTHUR RIMBAUD

LIFE. Jean Nicholas Arthur Rimbaud was born on October 20, 1854, in Charleville, a town of northeastern France. He proved to be an unusually gifted student, and was encouraged in his literary tastes and endeavors, and also in his revolutionary ardor, by Georges Izambard, his teacher. In 1870 he made the first of his flights from home, and spent ten days in jail as a vagrant. The following year, the poet Paul Verlaine invited Rimbaud to Paris. It was the beginning of a stormy relationship. Together they visited London and Brussels, where, in 1873, Verlaine shot Rimbaud through the wrist and was sentenced to two years' imprisonment. In the same year, at the age of nineteen, Rimbaud gave up the writing of poetry. He found his way to many parts of Europe, to Cyprus, to Java, and to Aden, where he worked for an exporting firm, later moving to Harar, in Abyssinia. As an independent trader he went on expeditions in Abyssinia, and engaged in gunrunning, but it cannot be definitely established that he trafficked in slaves. Falling ill in 1891, he returned to France, and his leg, which was in horrible condition, was amputated at Marseilles. He died on November 10, 1891.

CHIEF WRITINGS. *A Season in Hell* (*Une Saison en enfer*, 1873), translated by Delmore Schwartz (2nd ed. 1940), Norman Cameron (1950); *Illuminations* (*Les Illuminations*, 1887), partially translated by Louise Varèse in *Prose Poems from The Illuminations* (1946); *Complete Poems* (*Poésies complètes*, 1895); *Complete Works* (*OEuvres complètes*, 1946); *Works* (*OEuvres*, 1950). Other translations are to be found in Lionel Abel, *Some Poems of Rimbaud* (1939); Norman Cameron, *Selected Verse Poems* (1942); *Complete Works with Selected Letters*, translated by Wallace Fowlie (1966).

BIOGRAPHY AND CRITICISM. Peter Quennell, *Baudelaire and the Symbolists* (1929); Konrad Bercovici, *Savage Prodigal* (1948); Marcel Raymond, *From Baudelaire to Surrealism* (1949); W. M. Frohock, *Rimbaud's Poetic Practice* (1963); Gwendolyn Bays, *The Orphic Vision* (1964); Wallace Fowlie, *Rimbaud* (1966); and Enid Starkie, *Arthur Rimbaud* (revised edition, 1968).

AUGUST STRINDBERG

LIFE. Strindberg was born in Stockholm in 1849 to a father of upper-class origins who was then living in financially distressed circumstances with a former domestic servant. He had married her only a short while before the birth of this child, the fourth of eleven children. Though the boy was highly intelligent and did well at school, he dropped out of the university, repelled by the milieu and embarrassed by his poverty. He began to write for the theater, and at the age of twenty-one was awarded a prize by the Swedish Academy. For eight years (1874–1882) a post in the Royal Library gave him social status and a livelihood. However, an underlying compulsion to brand himself an outsider was revealed in his bitingly sarcastic novel *The Red Room* (1879).

In the 1880's he proclaimed his left-wing sympathies, his atheism, and his adherence to naturalistic doctrines in literature. Toward the end of that decade, having become acquainted with the works of Friedrich Nietzsche (1844–1901), he moved toward a heroic individualism. During the 1890's, while living in Paris, he spent a great deal of time endeavoring to transmute "baser" substances into gold and in trying to prove that the so-called elements were actually compounds. He was hospitalized with severe injuries to his hands. During this period he was beset by frightening hallucinations. A record of this phase of his life is found in his *Inferno* (1898).

Although Strindberg moved in the direction of religious belief, he stopped short of adherence to Catholicism, or to any other creed. But it was a natural extension of his occult concerns that he should incorporate the Eastern doctrine of reincarnation into his view of things.

The last years of his life were spent in Sweden, and were marked by a renewal of the sensitivity to social ills that he had expressed in the 1880s. He died in 1912 of cancer of the stomach.

A significant source of turmoil in Strindberg's chaotic yet astonishingly productive existence was his difficulty in living either with or without a wife. Each of his three marriages ended in divorce—predictably, one might say, since he insisted that all three, ambitious and career-minded women, should content themselves with the roles of wife and mother. He gave vent to a fascination with and dread of women in much of his writing; e.g., in the plays *The Father* (1887) and *Dance of Death* (1901). In the 1890's he even came to believe that an international cabal of women was conspiring against him.

CHIEF WRITINGS. Plays: *Six Plays* (1955); *Selected History Plays*, 5 vols. (1955–59); *Three Plays* (1958); *Miss Julie and Other Plays* (1960); *Five Plays* (1960); *The Road to Damascus: A Trilogy* (1960); *Seven Plays* (1960); *The Chamber Plays* (1962); *The Plays of Strindberg*, vol. I (1964); *Selected Plays* (1964); *World Historical Plays* (1970). Other Works:

Legends: Autobiographical Sketches (1912); *The People of Hemsö* (1959), also translated as *The Natives of Hemsö* (1965); *Letters of Strindberg to Harriet Bosse* (1959); *A Madman's Defense* (1967), also translated as *A Madman's Manifesto* (1971); *Inferno* (1962), also translated in *Inferno, Alone, and Other Writings* (1968); *From an Occult Diary, Marriage with Harriet* (1965); *The Son of a Servant* (1966); *The Red Room* (1967); *The Scapegoat* (1967); *The Strindberg Reader* (1968).

BIOGRAPHY AND CRITICISM. Joan Bulman, *Strindberg and Shakespeare* (1933); G. A. Campbell, *Strindberg* (1933); Frida Strindberg (Frieda Uhl), *Marriage with Genius* (2d ed., 1940); Eric Bentley, *The Playwright as Thinker* (1946, 1955); Brita M. E. Mortensen and B. W. Downs, *Strindberg: An Introduction to His Life and Work* (1949); Elizabeth Sprigge, *The Strange Life of August Strindberg* (1949); Martin Lamm, *Modern Drama* (1952); Otto Heller, *Prophets of Dissent* (1960); Harry Levin, *The Power of Darkness* (1960); Alrik Gustafson, *A History of Swedish Literature* (1961); John Stewart Collis, *Marriage and Genius* (1963); Maurice Valency, *The Flower and the Castle* (1963); C. E. Dahlström, *Strindberg's Dramatic Expressionism* (2d ed., 1965); Robert Brustein, *The Theatre of Revolt* (1966); Carl Reinhold Smedmark (ed.) *Essays on Strindberg* (1966); Eric O. Johannesson, *The Novels of August Strindberg* (1968); Martin Lamm, *August Strindberg* (1971).

LUIGI PIRANDELLO

LIFE. Pirandello was born in Girgenti, Sicily, in 1867. Having convinced his father that he had no head for business, he went off to study at the University of Rome, later transferring to the University of Bonn, in Germany. He wrote his Ph.D. dissertation on the dialect of his native town. He married in 1894 and settled in Rome. For ten years he was able to write without having to earn a livelihood, since his father gave him a generous allowance. The failure of the family business put an end to that, and for many years Pirandello taught in Rome at the equivalent of a normal school for women. His home life was made burdensome by his wife's increasingly serious mental derangement. She died in 1918. Pirandello achieved fame as a playwright about 1920, and thereupon gave up his teaching position. He traveled in Italy and elsewhere in Europe, and in America, with a theatrical troupe that performed his own plays. In 1934 he was awarded the Nobel Prize for Literature. He died in 1936.

CHIEF WRITINGS. *Naked Masks: Five Plays* (1922, 1952); *Each in His Own Way, and Two Other Plays* (1923); *The One-Act Plays* (1928); *The Old and the Young,* 2 volumes (1928); *As You Desire Me* (1931); *Horse in the Moon, Twelve Short Stories* (1932); *Tonight We Improvise* (1932); *One, None and a Hundred Thousand: A Novel* (1933); *The Naked Truth, and Eleven Other Stories* (1934); *Better Think Twice About It and Twelve Other Stories* (1935); *Six Characters in Search of an Author* (1935); *The Outcast: A Novel* (1935); *The Medals and Other Stories* (1939); *Right You Are* (1954); *When Someone Is Somebody* (1956); *The Mountain Giants* (1958); *Short Stories* (1959); *To Clothe the Naked, and Two Other Plays* (1962); *Pirandello's One-Act Plays* (1964); *The Late Mattia Pascal* (1923, 1964); *Short Stories* (1965).

BIOGRAPHY AND CRITICISM. John Palmer, *Studies in the Contemporary Theater* (1927); Stark Young, *Immortal Shadows* (1948); Francis Fergusson, *The Idea of a Theater* (1949); Lander MacClintock, *The Age of Pirandello* (1951); Thomas Bishop, *Pirandello and the French Theater* (1960); Walter Starkie, *Luigi Pirandello, 1867–1936,* third revised edition (1965); Oscar Büdel, *Pirandello* (1966); Glauco Cambon (ed.), *Pirandello: A Collection of Essays* (1967); and Domenico Vittorini, *The Drama of Luigi Pirandello* (1957, 1969).

THOMAS MANN

LIFE. Born on June 6, 1875, in the old Hanse town of Lubeck, where his father was a grain merchant. His mother was of German-Brazilian extraction. Upon the death of the father, the family moved to Munich. Here Mann worked for an insurance company, and for the satirical and literary weekly *Simplicissimus,* and attended the university without taking a degree. The writing of *Buddenbrooks* was begun during a stay in Rome. He continued to live in Munich until 1933, but after the Nazis came into power he settled in Switzerland, where he edited the periodical *Mass und Wert.* He moved to the United States in 1938, and became a citizen. At the time of his death, in 1955, he was living in Switzerland. He was awarded the Nobel prize in 1929.

CHIEF WRITINGS. *Buddenbrooks* (1900); "Tonio Kröger" (1903); *Royal Highness (Königliche Hoheit,* 1909); *Death in Venice (Der Tod in Venedig,* 1913); *The Reflections of a Non-Political Man (Betrachtungen eines Unpolitischen,* 1918); *Of the German Republic (Von deutscher Republik,* 1923); *The Magic Mountain (Der Zauberberg,* 1924); *Mario and the Magician (Mario und der Zauberer,* 1929); *Joseph and His Brethren (Jo-*

seph und seine Brüder, 4 vols., 1933–1944); *Lotte in Weimar* (1939), translated as *The Beloved Returns* (1940); *Doctor Faustus* (*Doktor Faustus*, 1947); *The Holy Sinner* (*Der Erwählte*, 1951); *Confessions of Felix Krull, Confidence Man* (*Bekenntnisse des Hochstaplers Felix Krull*, 1954). Other volumes of translations are *Stories of Three Decades* (1936); *Selected Essays* (1941); *Order of the Day* (1942); *Essays of Three Decades* (1946); *The Thomas Mann Reader*, edited by J. W. Angell (1950); and *Letters of Thomas Mann*, edited by Richard and Clara Winston (1970).

BIOGRAPHY AND CRITICISM. James Cleugh, *Thomas Mann: A Study* (1933); H. J. Weigand, *Thomas Mann's Novel Der Zauberberg* (1933); J. G. Brennan, *Thomas Mann's World* (1942); Charles Neider (ed.), *The Stature of Thomas Mann* (1947); Henry Hatfield, *Thomas Mann* (1951); John Maurice Lindsay, *Thomas Mann* (1954); Klaus W. Jonas, *Fifty Years of Thomas Mann Studies, A Bibliography of Criticism* (1955); R. H. Thomas, *Thomas Mann: The Mediation of Art* (1956); F. Kaufmann, *Thomas Mann: The World as Will and Representation* (1957); Thomas Mann, *A Sketch of My Life*, rev. ed. (1960); Erich Heller, *Thomas Mann, Ironic German* (1961); Henry C. Hatfield (ed.), *Thomas Mann* (1961), and *Thomas Mann: A Collection of Critical Essays* (1964); Hans Burgin and Hans-Otto Mayer, *Thomas Mann: A Chronicle of His Life* (1969); Erich Kahler, *The Orbit of Thomas Mann* (1969); André Von Gronicka, *Thomas Mann: Profile and Perspectives* (1970); and Arnold Bauer, *Thomas Mann* (1971).

RAINER MARIA RILKE

LIFE. Born in Prague, Austria-Hungary, on December 4, 1875, of Bohemian and Alsatian stock. The family had strong military traditions, and between 1886 and 1891 the sensitive boy spent utterly wretched years in the military academies of Sankt Pölten and Weisskirchen. Abandoning the prospect of a military career, he attended the commercial school at Linz for a year, and then was allowed to study the humanities at the universities of Prague and Munich. From 1899 on, he traveled extensively. He made two trips to Russia, in 1899 and 1900, meeting Tolstoy and acquiring a lively interest in Russian language and literature. He next spent two years in an artists' colony at Worpswede, near Bremen, Germany, and there met Clara Westhoff, a sculptress, whom he married in 1901. A daughter was born in 1902, but henceforth Rilke and his wife never again lived for any long period together. Rilke was frequently a guest at the houses of titled and wealthy people, and for a while, in

1905–1906, he acted as secretary to the sculptor Rodin, whom he revered. In 1912, at the castle of Duino, which is situated overlooking the Adriatic not far from Trieste (then Austrian territory), Rilke first conceived his *Duino Elegies* (*Duineser Elegien*). But inspiration deserted him, the war of 1914–1918 numbed his spirit, and not until 1922, at Muzot, his residence in French Switzerland, did the *Elegies* "write themselves" in the space of eight days, preceded and followed by the totally unexpected gift of the *Sonnets to Orpheus* (*Die Sonnette an Orpheus*), first and second parts. On December 29, 1926, the poet died, after considerable suffering, of myeloid leukemia. Its first symptom was the improper healing of the scratch of a rose thorn. He had been plucking roses to give to a young girl whose visit he expected.

CHIEF WRITINGS. *Stories of God* (*Geschichten vom lieben Gott*, 1900), translated by M. D. Herter Norton and Nora Purtscher-Wydenbruck (1932); *The Book of Pictures* (*Das Buch der Bilder*, 1902, and enlarged edition, 1906); *Auguste Rodin* (1903); *The Book of Hours* (*Das Stundenbuch*, 1905), translated in part by Babette Deutsch in *Poems from the Book of Hours* (1941); *The Tale of the Love and Death of Cornet Christopher Rilke* (*Die Weise von Liebe und Tod des Cornets Christoph Rilke*, 1906), translated by M. D. Herter Norton (1932); *New Poems* (*Neue Gedichte*), 2 vols., 1907–1908; *The Notebooks of Malte Laurids Brigge* (*Die Aufzeichnungen des Malte Laurids Brigge*, 1910), translated by M. D. Herter Norton (1949); *Duino Elegies* (*Duineser Elegien*, 1923), translated by J. B. Leishman and Stephen Spender (1939); *Sonnets to Orpheus* (*Die Sonnette an Orpheus*, 1923), translated by M. D. Herter Norton (1942). See also *Sonnets to Orpheus* [and] *Duino Elegies*, translated by Jessie Lemont (1945). For other translations see Richard von Mises, *Rilke in English: A Tentative Bibliography* (1947).

BIOGRAPHY AND CRITICISM. F. Olivero, *Rainer Maria Rilke* (1931); E. C. Mason, *Rilke's Apotheosis* (1938); W. Rose and C. G. Houston (eds.), *Rainer Maria Rilke: Aspects of His Mind and Poetry* (1938); E. M. Butler, *Rainer Maria Rilke* (1941); C. M. Bowra, *The Heritage of Symbolism* (1943); Nora Purtscher, *Rilke, Man and Poet* (1949); F. W. van Heerikhuizen, *Rainer Maria Rilke* (1952); H. E. Holthusen, *Rainer Maria Rilke* (1952); H. W. Belmore, *Rilke's Craftsmanship* (1954); Geoffrey H. Hartman, *The Unmediated Vision* (1954); H. W. Belmore, *Rilke's Craftsmanship* (1955); W. L. Graff, *Rainer Maria Rilke* (1956); H. Frederic Peters, *Rainer Maria Rilke* (1960); Romano Guardini, *Rilke's Duino Elegies* (1961); Eudo C.

Mason, *Rilke, Europe and the English-speaking World* (1961); J. R. von Salis, *Rainer Maria Rilke: The Years in Switzerland* (1964); and Priscilla Shaw, *Rilke, Valéry and Yeats* (1964).

MARCEL PROUST

LIFE. Born on July 10, 1871, to a successful Parisian doctor and a Jewish mother. When Proust was nine years old, it became evident that he was asthmatic. Very much attached to his mother, he was thoroughly spoiled by both parents, since his doctor-father decided that this was the wisest course. He studied erratically and moved in the best of society, frequenting among other salons that of Mme. de Caillavet, where he met Anatole France and later found support for his zeal in the Dreyfus cause. He made many friends, with whom he later corresponded extensively. Summers were spent not far from Chartres at Illiers, the Combray of the novel, or at Cabourg, which he renamed Balbec, on the Normandy coast. In 1900 he paid a visit to Venice, and acquired a liking for Ruskin. The death of his father in 1904 and his mother in 1905, and the increasing severity of his asthma, led him to withdraw from society. Henceforth he lived in a cork-lined room, the windows tight shut to keep out the pollen of plants, and he wrote generally at night. Often he wrote in bed, lying flat on his back and holding the paper in the air. The first volume of his long novel was originally printed at his own expense, and initially attracted little attention. Before his death, which occurred on November 18, 1922, he was able to complete his immense project, though not to revise the final part.

CHIEF WRITINGS. *Pleasures and Regrets* (*Les Plaisirs et les jours*, 1896); *Remembrance of Things Past* (*À la Recherche du temps perdu*, 1913–1927); *Sketches and Miscellanies* (*Pastiches et mélanges*, 1919); *Chronicles* (*Chroniques*, 1927); *Letters* (*Correspondance*, 6 vols., 1930–1936); *Jean Santeuil* (1952); *Contre Sainte-Beuve* (1954). Another volume of translations is *Marcel Proust: A Selection from His Miscellaneous Writings*, edited by Gerard Hopkins (1948); and *Letters*, translated by Mina Curtis (1966).

BIOGRAPHY AND CRITICISM. Léon Pierre-Quint, *Marcel Proust, His Life and Work* (1927); J. W. Krutch, *Five Masters* (1930); G. E. Lemaître, *Four French Novelists* (1938); Derrick Leon, *Introduction to Proust* (1940); Harold March, *The Two Worlds of Marcel Proust* (1948); F. C. Green, *The Mind of Proust* (1949); André Maurois, *Proust, Portrait of a Genius* (1950); Charlotte Haldane, *Proust* (1951); P. A. Spalding, *A Reader's Handbook to Proust* (1951); Walter A. Strauss, *Proust and Literature* (1957); Richard H. Barker, *Marcel Proust: A Biography* (1958); George D. Painter, *Proust, The Early Years* (1959); René Girard (ed.), George D. Painter, *Proust, The Early Years* (1959); René Girard (ed.), *Proust: A Collection of Critical Essays* (1962); Milton Hindus, *Reader's Guide to Marcel Proust* (1962); Margaret Mein, *Proust's Challenge to Time* (1962); Howard Moss, *The Magic Lantern of Marcel Proust* (1962); William S. Bell, *Proust's Nocturnal Muse* (1963); Roger Shattuck, *Proust's Binoculars* (1963); Leo Bersani, *Marcel Proust* (1965); George D. Painter, *Proust: The Later Years* (1965); Germaine Brée, *Marcel Proust and Deliverance from Time* (revised edition, 1969); and Peter Quennel (ed.), *Marcel Proust 1871–1922* (1970).

ANDRÉ GIDE

LIFE. Born on November 22, 1869, in Paris, to Protestant parents (his mother's family had recently been converted from Catholicism). His father died in 1880. He received an irregular education, attending the École Alsacienne for some time but also studying with private tutors. During the 1890's he frequented the gathering places of the symbolists, among them the salon of Stéphane Mallarmé, but felt ill at ease, owing to his piety, his awkwardness, and his slowness of speech. A trip to North Africa in the autumn of 1893 revolutionized his existence. He became seriously ill at Biskra, and during his convalescence fell in love with earthly delights—see his *Fruits of the Earth* (*Les Nourritures terrestres*), *The Immoralist* (*L'Immoraliste*), and the autobiographical *If It Die* (*Si le Grain ne meurt*). At this time he broke with symbolist literary ideals. On returning to Paris in 1895 he married his cousin Emmanuèle. Thereafter he divided his life between his two estates (in Normandy and in Paris) and extensive travels in Europe and North Africa. During World War I he spent some time working with Belgian refugees. A journey to the Congo led him to expose the abuses that occurred there, and in the early 1930's he announced his adherence to communism. But this new faith did not survive the test of a journey to Russia. A highly controversial career was crowned by the award of the Nobel prize in 1947. With his wide and penetrating reading, his sympathy for the young, his readiness to encourage budding talents, and his preaching of self-realization, Gide exercised a great influence in France and other European countries. Recently there has been increased interest in his writings in the United States. He died on February 19, 1951.

CHIEF WRITINGS. *Marshlands* (*Paludes*, 1895), translated by G. D. Painter in *Marshlands and Prometheus Misbound* (1953); *Fruits of the Earth* (*Les Nourritures terrestres*, 1897),

translated by Dorothy Bussy (1949);
Prometheus Misbound (Le Prométhée mal enchaîné, 1899), translated by
G. D. Painter in *Marshlands and Prometheus Misbound* (1953); *The Immoralist (L'Immoraliste*, 1902), translated by Dorothy Bussy (1930); *Saül* (1903), translated by Dorothy Bussy in *Return of the Prodigal . . . Saul* (1953); *Return of the Prodigal (Le Retour de l'enfant prodigue*, 1907), translated by Dorothy Bussy in *Return of the Prodigal . . . Saul* (1953); *Strait Is the Gate (La Porte étroite*, 1909), translated by Dorothy Bussy (1924); *Isabelle* (1911), translated by Dorothy Bussy in *Two Symphonies* (1931); *Corydon* (1911), translated by Hugh Gibb (1950); *The Vatican Swindle (Les Caves du Vatican*, 1914), translated by Dorothy Bussy as *Lafcadio's Adventures* (1927); *The Pastoral Symphony (La Symphonie pastorale*, 1919), translated by Dorothy Bussy in *Two Symphonies* (1931); *The Counterfeiters (Les Faux-monnayeurs*, 1925), translated by Dorothy Bussy (1928), and in 1951 published in one volume with *Journal of the Counterfeiters (Journal des faux-monnayeurs*, 1926), translated by Justin O'Brien; *If It Die (Si le Grain ne meurt*, 1926), translated by Dorothy Bussy (1935); *The Journals, 1889–1949* (1939–1950), translated by Justin O'Brien, 4 vols. (1947–1951); *Theseus (Thésée*, 1946), translated by John Russell in *Two Legends: Œdipus and Theseus* (1950); *Et nunc manet in te* (1947), translated by Justin O'Brien as *Madeleine* (1952); André Gide and Paul Valéry, *Self-Portraits: The Gide-Valéry Letters*, translated by June Guicharnaud (1966).

BIOGRAPHY AND CRITICISM. Montgomery Belgion, *Our Present Philosophy of Life* (1929); Léon Pierre-Quint, *André Gide: His Life and His Work* (1934); G. E. Lemaître, *Four French Novelists* (1938); Klaus Mann, *André Gide and the Crisis of Modern Thought* (1943); Van Meter Ames, *André Gide* (1947); Harold March, *André Gide and the Hound of Heaven* (1951); G. D. Painter, *André Gide* (1952); L. Thomas, *André Gide* (1952); Justin O'Brien, *Portrait of André Gide* (1953); J. C. McLaren, *The Theatre of André Gide* (1953); R. Martin du Gard, *Recollections of André Gide* (1953); Germaine Brée, *André Gide* (1962); Jean Delay, *The Youth of André Gide* (1963); Ralph Freedman, *The Lyrical Novel* (1963); J. G. Brennan, *Three Philosophical Novelists* (1964); Wallace Fowlie, *André Gide: His Life and Art* (1965); George D. Painter, *André Gide: A Critical Biography* (1968); Albert J. Guerard, *André Gide* (revised edition, 1969); G. W. Ireland, *André Gide: A Study of His Creative Writings* (1970); David Littlejohn (ed.), *Gide: A Collection of Critical Essays* (1970).

FRANZ KAFKA

LIFE. Born on July 3, 1883, in Prague, then an important town of the Austro-Hungarian Empire. The son of a well-to-do middle-class Jewish merchant, he studied at the German University in Prague, obtaining his law degree in 1906. He then worked for many years in the workmen's insurance division of an insurance company that had official state backing. He was much impressed by his father and his father's satisfactory adjustment to life in the role of breadwinner and head of a family, and was troubled by a sense of his own contrasting inadequacy. For several years he entertained the idea of marriage; and he became engaged, but the projected marriage did not take place. In 1923 he met Dora Dymant, descendant of a prominent Eastern Jewish family, an excellent Hebrew scholar and a gifted actress. At the end of July he left Prague and established himself with her in Berlin. "I found an idyll," writes Max Brod of his visits to him there. "At last I saw my friend in a happy frame of mind; his physical condition however had grown worse." He had had several attacks of tuberculosis, and died, after considerable suffering, on June 3, 1924.

CHIEF WRITINGS. "The Judgment" ("Das Urteil," 1913), and "In the Penal Colony" ("In der Strafkolonie," 1919), translated in *The Penal Colony* (1948); *The Trial (Der Prozess,* 1925); *The Castle (Das Schloss,* 1926); *America (Amerika,* 1927); *Collected Works (Gesammelte Schriften,* 1935–1937); *The Diaries (Tagebücher,* 1951), translated (from the unpublished manuscript) by Joseph Kresh, 2 vols. (1948–1949); *Letters to Milena (Briefe an Milena,* 1952). Other translations are available in *Parables in German and English* (1947); *Selected Short Stories,* translated by Willa and Edwin Muir (1952); *Wedding Preparations in the Country, and Other Posthumous Writings,* translated by Ernest Kaiser and Eithne Wilkins (1954).

BIOGRAPHY AND CRITICISM. For biography see Max Brod, *Franz Kafka* (1947); G. Janouch, *Conversations with Kafka* (1953, 1971). For criticism see Paul Goodman, *Kafka's Prayer* (1947); Charles Neider, *Kafka: His Mind and Art* (1949); Antel Flores and Homer Swanda (eds.), *Franz Kafka Today* (1958); Ronald D. Gray (ed.), *Kafka* (1963); Mark Spilka, *Dickens and Kafka* (1963); Angel Flores (ed.), *The Kafka Problem* (1946, 1963); Margarete Buber-Neumann, *Mistress to Kafka: The Life and Death of Milena* (1966); Heinz Politzer, *Franz Kafka: Parable and Paradox* (1962, revised and enlarged edition, 1967); Martin Greenberg, *The Terror of Art: Kafka and Modern Literature* (1968); and Herbert Tauber, *Franz Kafka: An Interpretation of His Works* (1968).

ISAAC BASHEVIS SINGER

LIFE. Singer was born in Russian Poland in 1904, the son of a poor rabbi. The family moved to Warsaw while he was still a very small boy. In 1917 his mother took him and her other young children to live with relatives in the small town of Bilgoray, returning with them to Warsaw when the war ended. The older brother, I. J. Singer, left the strict confines of orthodox Judaism to establish himself as a writer, and in the early twenties Isaac Bashevis Singer followed him. At first he wrote in Hebrew, but soon changed to Yiddish. In 1935 he emigrated to the United States, separating from his first wife—who, with their son, found her way to Russia and later to Israel. Singer was married again in 1940, to a former resident of Munich. While he continues to write in Yiddish, he pays very close attention to the translation of his works into English.

CHIEF WRITINGS. *The Family Moskat* (1950); *Gimpel the Fool and Other Stories* (1957); *The Magician of Lublin* (1960); *The Spinoza of Market Street* (1961); *The Slave* (1962); *Short Friday and Other Stories* (1964); *In My Father's Court* (1966); *The Manor* (1967); *The Estate* (1969); *A Day of Pleasure: Stories of a Boy Growing Up in Warsaw* (1969); *Enemies: A Love Story* (1972).

BIOGRAPHY AND CRITICISM. Marcia Allentuck (ed.), *The Achievement of Isaac Bashevis Singer* (1969); Irving Malin, *Isaac Bashevis Singer* (1972); Irving Malin (ed.), *Critical Views of Isaac Bashevis Singer* (1972).

BERTOLT BRECHT

LIFE. Brecht was born in Augsburg, Germany, on February 10, 1898. His first literary efforts were published when he was sixteen. During World War I, his study of medicine in Munich was interrupted by service in a military hospital. With the return of peace he set out to make his way as a free-lance writer. An early play was performed in 1922, and was awarded a prize. Two years later he moved to Berlin, and at once plunged into the theatrical life of the capital. He wrote many plays and worked actively at embodying them on the stage. The Nazi accession to power meant exile for him, for his left-wing views were no secret and as a Jew his life was in danger. After eight years spent in various European countries he found his way to the United States in 1941. Few of his works were performed, and the name of Brecht remained generally unknown. He returned to Europe in 1947, adopted Austrian citizenship but settled in the German People's Republic (East Germany). He died in East Berlin on August 14, 1958.

CHIEF WRITINGS. *Selected Poems* (1959); *Poems on the Theatre* (1961); *Seven Plays* (1961); *Tales from the Calendar* (1961); *Mother Courage and Her Children* (1963); *Baal, A Man's a Man, The Elephant Calf* (1964); *Brecht on Theatre* (1964); *The Threepenny Opera* (1964); *The Jewish Wife and Other Short Plays* (1965); *The Jungle of the Cities and Other Plays* (1965), *The Messinghauf Dialogues* (1965); *The Mother* (1965); *The Caucasian Chalk Circle* (1966); *Edward II: A Chronicle Play* (1966); *Galileo* (1966); *The Good Woman of Setzuan* (1966); *Manual of Piety* (1966).

BIOGRAPHY AND CRITICISM. John Willett, *The Theatre of Bertolt Brecht* (1959); Martin Esslin, *Brecht, The Man and His Work* (1960); R. Gray, *Bertolt Brecht* (1961); Peter Demetz (ed.), *Brecht: A Collection of Critical Essays* (1962); David I. Grossvogel, *Four Playwrights and a Postscript* (1962); Walter Weideli, *The Art of Bertolt Brecht* (1963); Frederick Ewen, *Bertolt Brecht: His Life, His Art, and His Times* (1967); Charles R. Lyons, *Bertolt Brecht: The Despair and the Polemic* (1968).

JEAN-PAUL SARTRE

LIFE. Sartre was born in Paris on June 21, 1905. His father, an officer in the French Navy, died while Sartre was still an infant, and his mother took him to live with her family. Sartre's mother remarried in 1916. After two years in a provincial secondary school, Sartre spent the rest of his schooldays in Paris, going on to study at the University of Paris. He became a secondary-school teacher. He was able to spend one year's leave of absence in Berlin. Made prisoner by the Germans after the French collapse of 1940, Sartre was released fairly soon and returned to teaching. He took part in the Resistance as a writer, though not as an activist, and became famous in 1943 with the performance of *The Flies* (*Les Mouches*) and the extraordinary success of his massive philosophical work *Being and Nothingness* (*L'Être et le Néant*). He gave up teaching the following year, and in 1945 founded the periodical *Les Temps Modernes*. Since then he has continued to write on philosophical, psychological, political, and topical matters, and has written many plays. His one postwar novel, *Roads to Freedom* (*Les Chemins de la Liberté*, 1945 and following years) remains unfinished. In 1962 he published the first volume of his autobiography, *The Words* (*Les Mots*), which deals with his childhood in grandfather Schweitzer's household. In 1964 he was awarded but refused to accept the Nobel Prize.

CHIEF WRITINGS. *Nausea* (*La Nausée*, 1938), translated by Lloyd Alexander (1949); *The Wall* (*Le Mur*, 1939), translated also as *Intimacy and Other Stories* by Lloyd Alexander (1948); *Outline of a Theory of the Emotions* (*Esquisse d'une Théorie des Émotions*,

1940), translated by Bernard Frechtman (1948); *The Flies (Les Mouches,*
1942), translated by Stuart Gilbert
(1947); *Being and Nothingness
(L'Être et le Néant,* 1943), translated
by Hazel E. Barnes (1956); *No Exit
(Huis-Clos,* 1944), translated by Stuart
Gilbert (1947); *The Age of Reason,
The Reprieve,* and *Troubled Sleep
(L'Âge du Raison, Le Sursis,* and *La
Mort dans l'Âme,* constituting three
parts of *Les Chemins de la Liberté,*
1945–1949), translated by Eric Sutton
(1947) and by Gerard Hopkins (1950);
*Existentialism (L'Existentialisme est un
Humanisme,* 1946), translated by Bernard Frechtman (1947); *Baudelaire*
(1947), translated by Martin Turnell
(1950); *Saint Genet, Actor and Martyr*
(1952), translated by Bernard Frechtman (1962); *Literary Essays* (1957);
*The Devil and the Good Lord, and Two
Other Plays* (1960); *The Condemned
of Altona* (1961); *Sartre on Cuba*
(1961); *The Words (Les Mots,* 1962),
translated by Bernard Frechtman
(1964); *The Problem of Method*
(1963); *Saint Genet, Actor and Martyr*
(1968); *Situations* (1965); *Literary
and Philosophical Essays* (1966); *The
Communists and Peace* (1968); *The
Ghost of Stalin* (1968); *On Genocide*
(1968).

BIOGRAPHY AND CRITICISM. Peter J.
Dempsey, *The Psychology of Sartre*
(1950); Hazel Barnes, *The Literature
of Possibility* (1959); Robert Cham-
pigny, *Stages on Sartre's Way, 1938–
1952* (1959); Wilfrid Desan, *The
Tragic Finale: An Essay on the Philosophy of Jean-Paul Sartre* (revised edition, 1960); Norman H. Greene, *Jean-
Paul Sartre: The Existentialist Ethic*
(1960); Iris Murdoch, *Sartre: Ro-
mantic Rationalist* (1960); Philip
Thody, *Jean-Paul Sartre: A Literary
and Political Study* (1960); Fredric
Jameson, *Sartre: The Origin of a Style*
(1961); Edith Kern (ed.), *Sartre: A
Collection of Critical Essays* (1962);
René Marill-Albérès, *Jean-Paul Sartre,
Philosopher without Faith* (1964);
Mary Warnock, *The Philosophy of Sar-
tre* (1965); Eugene H. Falk, *Types of
Thematic Structure* (1967); George H.
Bauer, *Sartre and the Artist* (1969);
Dorothy McCall, *The Theatre of Jean-
Paul Sartre* (1969); James F. Sheri-
dan, *Sartre: The Radical Conversion*
(1969); Edith Kern, *Existential
Thought and Fictional Technique*
(1970); Benjamin Suhl, *Jean-Paul
Sartre: The Philosopher as Literary
Critic* (1970).

ALBERT CAMUS

LIFE. Camus was born in Mondovi,
Algeria, on November 7, 1913, to a
working-class family. The father was
killed early in World War I, and the
mother, who was Spanish, moved to the
city of Algiers. The boy grew up talking
the mixed dialect—French, Spanish,
Arabic—of the streets. A schoolteacher
who took a special interest in Camus
arranged for a scholarship to secondary
school. After several years of university
work, Camus turned to journalism,
joined the Communist Party but stayed
a member less than three years, and became very active in the theater. He
moved to Paris in 1940. He first attracted wide attention as a writer in
1942 for the underground newspaper
Combat, and after the war he continued
to write editorials for it. His total work
brought him the Nobel prize in 1957.
He died on January 4, 1960, in a car
accident.

CHIEF WRITINGS. *The Stranger
(L'Étranger,* 1942); *The Myth of Sis-
yphus (Le mythe de Sisyphe,* 1942);
The Plague (La Peste, 1948); *The
Rebel (L'homme révolté,* 1954); *The
Fall (La chute,* 1957); *Exile and the
Kingdom (L'exil et la royaume,* 1958);
Caligula and Other Plays (1958); *Pos-
sessed* (1960); *Resistance, Rebellion,
and Death* (1960); *Notebook 1935–
1942; Notebook, 1942–1951* (1965);
Lyrical and Critical Essays (1968); *A
Happy Death* (previously unpublished
earlier version of *The Stranger*) (1972).

BIOGRAPHY AND CRITICISM. Albert
Maquet, *Albert Camus: An Invincible
Summer* (1958); John Cruickshank,
*Albert Camus and the Literature of Re-
volt* (1959); Philip Thody, *Albert Camus* (1959); Thomas Hanna, *The
Thought and Art of Albert Camus*
(1959); and *Lyrical Existentialists*
(1962); Germaine Brée, *Albert Camus*
(1961) and *Camus: A Collection of
Critical Essays* (1961); Adele King,
Albert Camus (1964); Phillip H. Rhein,
Albert Camus (1969); Maurice Fried-
man, *The Problematic Rebel* (revised
edition, 1970); Conor C. O'Brien, *Albert Camus: Of Europe and Africa*
(1970); Jean Onimus, *Albert Camus
and Christianity* (1970); and Germaine
Brée, *Camus and Sartre* (1972).

ALEXANDER SOLZHENITSYN

LIFE. Solzhenitsyn was born in Kis-
lovodsk in 1918. His father, who was
an artillery officer on the German
front, had died earlier that year. The
boy grew up in Rostov-on-Don, in poor
circumstances. Though keenly interested
in literature, he studied mathematics and
physics at Rostov University. Upon
graduation in 1941 he was immediately
drafted into the army and, in 1942,
sent to take an intensive course at an
artillery school. He served in the front
lines with an artillery-position-finding
company until his arrest in February
1945. For having referred disrespect-
fully to Stalin, he was sentenced to eight
years' imprisonment.

After spending about one year in
various camps, Solzhenitsyn was transferred to a research institute on the

outskirts of Moscow, where the highly trained prisoners were engaged in advanced research. Then, in 1950, he was sent to a camp for political prisoners in Kazakhstan. After completion of his term of imprisonment he was exiled for life to an area in southern Kazakhstan, where he earned his living by teaching mathematics and physics at the elementary level. By 1953 he was suffering from a severe case of cancer, but this yielded to treatment in a cancer clinic in Tashkent. He was "rehabilitated," declared to have been unjustly condemned, in 1956, and with the lifting of his exile he settled in Ryazan. After considerable negotiations behind the scenes, his novel *One Day in the Life of Ivan Denisovich* was published in the periodical *Novy Mir*. The following year two short stories appeared, but after that official pressures made it impossible to publish anything further by Solzhenitsyn. His personal papers were seized by the authorities, and in 1969 he was expelled from the Union of Soviet Writers. The award of the Nobel Prize for Literature in 1970 was a signal for additional official and officially inspired attacks on Solzhenitsyn. He did not consider traveling to Stockholm to receive the award, for he feared that, if ever he should leave Russia, he would not be allowed to return.

CHIEF WRITINGS. *One Day in the Life of Ivan Denisovich* (1963); *The First Circle* (1968); *The Cancer Ward* (1968, 1969); *The Love Girl and the Innocent* (1970); *For the Good of the Cause* (1970); *We Never Make Mistakes* (1963, 1971); *Stories and Prose Poems* (1971); *August 1914* (1972).

BIOGRAPHY AND CRITICISM. Mikhailo Mikhailov, *Russian Themes* (1968); Leopold Labedz (ed.), *Solzhenitsyn: A Documentary Record* (1970); Michael Scammell, *Solzhenitsyn: A Biography* (1971); Helen Muchnic, *Russian Writers* (1972); David Burg and George Feifer, *Solzhenitsyn: A Biography* (1972).

CHARLES BAUDELAIRE
(1821–1867)

Flowers of Evil (Les Fleurs du mal) *

Transcendence

Over the valleys, over the meres
Woods and mountains, clouds and seas,
Beyond the sun, beyond the breeze,
Beyond the bourne of starrèd spheres,

Escape, my spirit, swift and free:
A swimmer revelling in the surge.
From deep immensities emerge
With virile voiceless ecstasy.

From foul miasmas swiftly race,
Breathe deeply of a purer air
And drink, O draught divine and rare,
The limpid light of lucent space!

* From *Flowers of Evil* by Charles Baudelaire, translated by Florence Louie Freedman. Copyright 1966 by Dufour Editions, Inc. Reprinted by permission of the publisher.

12. *lucent space!:* See Baudelaire's similar declaration, in an article discussing Richard Wagner's opera *Tannhäuser:* "I felt myself freed from the bonds of gravity. . . . Then I realized to the full the idea of a soul moving in a luminous environment, of an ecstasy consisting of delight and knowledge." Since he also speaks, in a letter to Wagner, of having experienced "the pride and climactic joy of understanding, of letting myself be penetrated and invaded, in a truly sensual delight resembling that of rising in the air or of revolving in the sea," it is hardly advisable to interpret this poem in purely spiritual or mystical terms.

Behind are misery and spleen,
Those burdens life in darkness bore,
Happy is he whose flights explore   15
Pastures vivid and serene!

He whose thoughts can rise on wings
That soar like larks to dawn-washed skies,
Who understands, as free he flies,
The speech of flowers and voiceless things!   20

20. *voiceless things!*: Compare the sonnet "Correspondences," of which a prose translation is given in the Introduction, p. 997.

The Beacons

Rubens, Lethean garden of indolence,
Pillow of flesh where love lies passively
But life is eager with the turbulence
Of sky-borne airs or sea-streams in the sea;

Da Vinci, mirror sombre and profound,   5
Where gentle angels, smiling and benign,
Are charged with mystery in regions bound
By shadowy gloom of glacier and pine;

Rembrandt, sad hospital with murmurs filled,
Embellished only with a crucifix,   10
Where prayers obscenely sobbed are never stilled,
Whose gloom a fleeting winter sunbeam licks;

Great Michael Angelo, dim that demesne
Of Hercules and Christ, where rigid stand
Powerful phantoms, in the twilight seen   15
Tearing their shrouds with tensely stiffened hand;

A boxer's rage and fawn-like impudence,
The charms of knaves and rascals mustering,
Weak jaundiced man whose hauteur is immense—
Puget, the convict's melancholy king;   20

1. *Rubens: Peter Paul Rubens* (1577–1640), a highly successful Flemish painter who carried out diplomatic missions for the French queen.

5. *Da Vinci:* Leonardo da Vinci (1452–1519), Florentine painter and sculptor, a man of immense scientific knowledge and curiosity.

9. *Rembrandt:* Rembrandt Harmenszoon van Rijn (1606–1669), Dutch painter and etcher.

13. *Michael Angelo:* Michelangelo Buonarroti (1475–1564), Italian sculptor, painter, architect, and poet.

20. *Puget:* Pierre Puget (1620–1694), French sculptor, architect, and painter. The "boxer" of the poem may have been suggested by Puget's statue of Milo of Crotona. As for "convict," as a long-time resident of Toulon, on France's Mediterranean coast, the artist had ample opportunity to study those unfortunates condemned to row in the galleys.

Watteau, a fête for the nobility
Who stray like butterflies in radiance,
Cool airy scene, where lustres vividly
Light Folly's triumph in the whirling dance;

Goya, a world of nightmare, strange and crude,   25
Foetuses cooked on witches' Sabbath fires,
Crones peering into mirrors, children nude,
Adjusting stockings, rousing fiends' desires;

Delacroix, lake of blood, firs evergreen,
Where sinful angels haunt each gloomy glade,   30
Where fanfares strange drift through the cloudy scene
And, like a stifled sigh of Weber, fade:

These curses, blasphemies, plaints that entreat,
These transports, tears, *Te Deums*, this repine,
Echoes a thousand labyrinths repeat,   35
For mortal hearts are opium divine!

A cry voiced by a thousand sentinels,
An order that a thousand throats have passed,
A beacon on a thousand citadels,
A call of hunters lost in forests vast!   40

O Lord, here is our testimony! gauge
By this the measure of our dignity—
This wild lament echoing from age to age,
Stilled at the bourne of your eternity.

21. *Watteau:* Jean Antoine Watteau
(1684–1721), French painter and engraver.
25. *Goya:* Francisco Goya y Lucientes
(1746–1828), Spanish painter and graphic
artist.
29. *Delacroix:* Eugène Delacroix (1799–
1863), French painter, considered to be
the leader of the romantic school of painting. See below the note to line 14 of
"Former Life," and also. below, note on
the title of "Don Juan in Hell."
32. *Weber:* Carl Maria von Weber
(1786–1826), German romantic composer.
33–44. *These curses . . . your eternity:*
The last three stanzas of the poem enun-
ciate the aesthetic and religious message
of romanticism, namely, that poets,
painters, and musicians utter humanity's
longing to attain to the Divine.

Former Life

Long have I dwelt beneath vast porticos
Tinted by ocean suns with flaming dyes,
Where noble columns of majestic size,
Like basalt grottoes in the dusk arose.

The billows, mirrors of resplendent skies,
In solemn mystery at daylight's close,

Mingled their splendid music with the glows
Of sunset fires reflected by my eyes.

There have I lived in tranquil ecstasy,
Amid the radiance, the skies, the waves,   10
While perfume-saturated, naked slaves

With palm-awakened breezes solaced me,
Their only care to probe, the while I languish,
The grievous secret of my haunting anguish.

14. *grievous secret:* such as could be
seen in the eyes of the female figures in
Delacroix's paintings, according to Baudelaire. He expressed this view in an
article dealing with the artist's work.

Don Juan in Hell*

When to the Stygian stream, to pay his fees
Don Juan came, and gave them on that shore
To Charon, proud-eyed as Antisthenes,
A strong-armed, vengeful beggar seized each oar.

With gaping gowns revealing drooping breasts,   5
Women were writhing under sombre skies,
As they, like droves of sacrificial beasts,
Pursued him with their long and anguished cries.

His wages, Sganarelle laughing, sought to claim,
The while Don Luis trembling, showed the dead   10
Roaming those shores, the son who, without shame,
So insolently mocked his agèd head.

Black-robed Elvira, shivering, chaste and thin,
Near him, her lover once, her faithless spouse,
Seemed to implore a farewell smile wherein   15
Would shine the sweetness of his early vows.

In armour, rigid, tall, a man of stone
Cleft, at the helm, the darkly flowing tide;
But leaning on his sword, remote, alone,
The hero calmly watched the waters glide.   20

* A source of Baudelaire's inspiration
may have been two paintings by Delacroix, "The Shipwreck of Don Juan" and
"Dante and Virgil in Hell."
  1. *Stygian stream:* the Styx, river flowing around Hades.
  3. *Charon:* ferrier of souls across the
river Styx. *Antisthenes:* founded (ca. 380
B.C.) the Cynic school of philosophy in
Athens.
  9. *Sganarelle:* Don Juan's servant in
Molière's play *Don Juan* (1665).
  17. *a man of stone:* Don Juan had
killed the Commander, the father of a
woman he loved. The statue of the Commander, mockingly invited to dinner by
Don Juan, accepted the invitation and
arrived to drag Don Juan down to hell.

Beauty

I'm fair, O mortals, fair! a stone-wrought dream!
And this, my breast, where all are bruised in turn,
Is formed that poets may a passion learn,
Silent as matter, deathless and supreme.

Throned, a mysterious sphinx, in azure deep,   5
My heart of snow with swan's pure white combines;
I hate all movement for displacing lines,
And never do I laugh and never weep.

Poets, before my every pose sublime
Bringing to mind the noblest statuary,   10
In earnest study will expend their time;

For I, to charm each docile devotee,
Have mirrors that enhance beauty's delight:
My eyes, my glorious eyes of quenchless light!

The Giantess

When Nature daily with a wild excess
Scattered her monstrous offspring on the scene,
I might, beside a youthful giantess
Have fawned, the pampered kitten of a queen.

I might have loved her body and soul to see,   5
In terrible frolics vastly grow in size;
To wonder if her heart flamed sombrely
Behind the mists that floated in her eyes;

To explore her splendid limbs, relaxed, at ease;
To climb the slopes of her enormous knees;   10
And when, by summer's savage suns oppressed,

She, stretched across the land, lay calm and still,
To sleep uncaring, shadowed by her breast,
Just like a hamlet sheltered by a hill.

Tresses

O tresses curling round your neck so fair!
O locks! O subtle perfumes I inhale!
Rapture! To fill tonight our secret lair
With memories asleep within this hair;
I long, in the air, to shake it like a veil!   5

Languorous Asia, Africa's tropic heat,
A whole world, distant, strange and almost lost,

Lives in these depths, this forest fragrant, sweet;
As others float on music's rhythmic beat,
My soul, Belovèd, is on your perfume tossed.   10

And thus, where trees and men in strength supreme,
Swoon languidly in sultry torrid heat,
Strong tresses, bear me like a surging stream!
You hide, O ebony sea, a dazzling dream
Where sails and oarsmen, masts and pennants meet—   15

An echoing harbour where my soul can hold
Unmeasured draughts of perfume, colour, sound;
Where vessels drift through opalescent gold,
Vast arms outspread, the glory to enfold
Of hot clear skies eternal and profound.   20

My hand shall plunge, while rapture fills my sense,
In these dark waves which those far seas enclose,
This surge shall bear my subtle spirit hence
To you once more, O lavish indolence!
Eternal cradle of embalmed repose!   25

O blue-black hair, cool shadowy tent unfurled,
You yield to me the skies, round, vast and far;
Here, on the down of tresses rich and curled,
I swoon, I drown within a fragrant world
Of aromatic oils and musk and tar.   30

For long! For ever! In your hair shall gleam
The rubies, sapphires, pearls, strewn there by me
To make my love's demands seem less extreme:
For are you not the oasis where I dream,
My gourd brimmed full with wines of memory?   35

Reversibility*

Angel of gladness, do you know despair,
Shame and remorse and weariness and tears,
Those nights of terror filled with tenuous fears,
Those hearts, like crumpled paper, squeezed by care?
Angel of gladness, do you know despair?   5

---

* The theological meaning of the word *reversibility* is the possibility that sinners may benefit from the merits accumulated by the saints and other pious people. Baudelaire sent this poem, unsigned but clearly recognizable as his, to Madame Sabatier, a lady he had already made aware of his tender feelings. Here, while letting her know that he does not seek a physical relationship, he declares that her angelic qualities serve to redeem the hatred, despair, and sickness that had been threatening him.

Angel of goodness, do you know of hate,
Fists clenched in darkness, tears that are as gall,
When vengeance drumming its infernal call
Commands our powers and is obdurate?
Angel of goodness, do you know of hate?   10

Angel of health, know you of Fever's prey
Filling the dreary hospitals, a throng
Like broken exiles faltering along,
With trembling lips, seeking the sun's least ray?
Angel of health, know you of Fever's prey?   15

Angel of beauty, do you know those lines,
Those signs of ageing, and the ghastly pain
Of seeing love by secret horror slain
In eyes where ours had drunk of passion's wines?
Angel of beauty, do you know those lines?   20

Angel of fortune, joy and sanity,
King David might have craved for health afresh
From emanations of your magic flesh;
I, angel, beg but this: Ah! pray for me,
Angel of fortune, joy and sanity!   25

Colloquy

You are an autumn sky, flushed and serene;
Yet sadness in me rises like the sea,
And, ebbing, leaves my lips morose with spleen,
Its acrid ooze, in bitter memory.

Gently your hand explores my ravished breast;   5
You search, belovèd, a desecrated shrine;
Women, with tooth and claw, have doomed your quest,—
You seek a heart! Wild beasts have gorged on mine.

My heart is a mansion wrecked by savage crowds;
They swill there, kill there, tear each other's hair!   10
—Your naked bosom, perfumed air enshrouds!—

O Beauty, scourge of souls, you crave your share!
Then let your eyes, flaming like torch-lit feasts,
Consume these shreds neglected by the beasts.

1. *autumn sky*: The poem is addressed to a young actress, Marie Daubrun. The autumnal mood should be understood as being the poet's own.

12. *Beauty*: The same concept finds expression in the poem "Beauty," printed above. Far from being a healer, Beauty destroys her devotees.

Cats*

Lovers in thrall and scholars stern, controlled,
Both cherish when their years of ripeness come
Strong, docile cats, the darlings of the home,
Who too are sedentary and dread the cold.

Enticed by learning and voluptuousness,   5
Silence and awful darkness serve their needs;
Erebus might have used them as his steeds
If bondage could have quelled ther haughtiness.

Musing, they pose in noble attitudes
Like sphinxes stretched in secret solitudes   10
Who seem to sleep in an eternal dream;

With magic sparks their fertile loins abound,
And flecks of gold like tiny sand-grains gleam
Faintly within their eyes, strange and profound.

* This, one of three cat poems written among artists and literary men.
by Baudelaire, was inspired by a cat 7. *Erebus*: the darkest region of Hades.
named Rosalie, who had many admirers

Music*

So often music bears me like a sea
    Toward my pallid star,
Beneath domed cloud, through air's infinity,
    I voyage afar;

With chest extended, breath each lung swift fills   5
    Like wind-swelled sails,
I scale the backs of breakers, clustered hills
    That darkness veils;

All passions in my soul their conflicts wage,
    A shuddering vessel I!   10
The splendid wind, the mighty tempest's rage,

    Over the whirlpool high
Are rocking me. At times calm seas are there—
    Mirrors of my despair!

* Compare the poem "Transcendence," the vileness and constricting meannesses
printed above. The poems are akin in of everyday life.
invoking the possibility of soaring above

Spleen*

I'm like a king whose realm is wet and cold,
Wealthy yet powerless, young and yet so old,
Who, when his toadies' sycophancy palls,
Turns to his dogs and favourite animals.
Nothing diverts him, hunting, falconry,   5
Nor those who die before his balcony.
However droll the ballads of his clown,
This callous invalid maintains his frown;
His lilied bed might well be in a tomb,
And Prince-enamoured women all assume   10
Vainly their lewdest garments to beguile
This youthful skeleton and win a smile.
The sage who makes him rich fails in the rôle
Of heeler to corruption in his soul;
Even in blood-baths Roman might designed,   15
Which ageing tyrants often call to mind,
He could not warm this corpse, for thick and slow
Within those veins, green Lethean waters flow.

* In the second edition (1861) of *Flowers of Evil*, Baudelaire grouped some eighty-five poems under the sectional title "Spleen and Ideal." Four separate poems are entitled "Spleen." The word, borrowed from the English, served to characterize the morose outlook on life that French people attributed to eccentric English gentlemen or "milords."
3. *sycophancy:* gross flattery, toadying. Derived from two Greek words that mean "sweet speaking."

Spleen

When, like a lid, the lowering heavens weigh
Upon the spirit tortured by its plight,
And when, from the horizon's rim, a day
Emerges darker, sadder than the night;

When earth becomes a humid dungeon where   5
Hope flutters like a bat unceasingly,
Striking the roof and walls and everywhere
Buffeting head and wings despairingly;

When wide-spread showers seem to constitute
A prison where the bars are formed of rain,   10
Where hosts of spiders, infamous and mute,
Are spinning webs deep down within the brain;

12. *within the brain:* These three stanzas have described the mental affliction known as ennui. Its outcome is the "Anguish" whose impingement is related in the two remaining stanzas.

Bells suddenly and furiously toll,
Hurling toward the sky their frightful plaint,
Sounding as though a lost and homeless soul   15
Stubbornly moaned its desolate complaint.

And without sound, no music and no drums,
Long lines of hearses through my spirit drag;
Hope, vanquished, weeps; and tyrant Anguish comes
To hoist upon my skull her night-black flag.   20

Heautontimoroumenos*
(The Self Torturer)

To J. G. F.†

I shall strike you without rage,
A butcher's blow, and feel no shock,
Strike you as Moses struck the rock,
That, from your eyes, I may assuage

My fierce Saharan thirst; your fears   5
Shall mingle with your suffering,
While hope shall buoy my load of longing
On the torrent of your tears

Like a vessel on the sea.
And, in my heart, a precious sound,   10
Your sobs, like music, shall resound—
Drums to the charge, inspiring me!

Am I not a strident note
Within the cosmic symphony,
Thanks to voracious Irony   15
That gnaws and shakes me by the throat?

Her shriek is in my voice itself,
Black poison is my blood through her,
I am the mirror sinister
Wherein the shrew regards herself!   20

---

* This is the title of a comedy by Terence, the Roman writer of comedies. It
was performed in 163 B.C. Baudelaire may
also have encountered the word in the
writings of Thomas de Quincey (1785–
1859), author of *Confessions of an English Opium-Eater*, who describes the
"valetudinarian" as "the most imaginable
heautontimoroumenos, aggravating and
sustaining . . . every symptom that would
else perhaps . . . become evanescent."

† It is not certain what name is referred to by these initials.
13 ff. *Am I not* . . . : The preceding
stanzas look forward to the torture of
another human being. This fourth stanza
is the first to justify the poem's title.
17 ff. *Her shriek* . . . : This stanza was
suggested by an engraving in which Goya
represented a man and woman tied together with cords, and attacked by a
monstrous bird.

I am the wound, and I the knife,
I am the cheek, the vicious smack,
I am the limbs and I the rack,
The life and taker of the life!

A vampire, it's my heart I drain;   25
Forsaken, I eternally
Am doomed to bitter mockery
And never can I smile again!

21. *I am the wound:* In a note written by Baudelaire for his translation of Edgar Allan Poe's *Tales,* he refers to the "primitive force" of "natural Perversity, which unceasingly makes man both murderer and suicide, assassin and executioner."

28. *never can I smile again!:* This may have been suggested by Poe's poem "The Haunted Palace," which contains the lines, "A hideous throng rush out for ever/And laugh, but smile no more."

Women Accursed*

Like cattle ruminating on the sand,
Gazing where in the distance sky meets sea,
Each, as she seeks the other's foot or hand,
Feels faint with joy and bitter ecstasy.

Some, sharing secrets they delight to tell,   5
In woods alive with river melodies,
Recalling timid childhood, fondly spell
Long cherished names upon the bark of trees;

Others, like solemn sisters, pace the verge
Of craggy places filled with apparitions   10
Where once Saint Antony, like lava's surge,
Saw naked, purple breasts of his temptations;

And some, where resinous torches flare, have prayed
In ancient pagan caves, silent and deep,
For cooling of their lusts, seeking your aid,   15
O Bacchus who can lull remorse to sleep!

Others, enthralled by scapulars, append
To flowing robes a hidden whip; in vain
Through lonely nights in sombre woods, they blend
The froth of pleasure with the tears of pain.   20

O virgins, demons, monsters, martyrs—you
Whose yearning spirits scorn reality,

* In general French usage, the title of Baudelaire's poem, "Femmes damnées," has come to mean Lesbians. The poem was one of six declared to be obscene in 1857. The court ordered them suppressed.
11. *Saint Antony:* This hermit (251–356), the founder of monasticism within the Eastern Church, was renowned for the large number of temptations he had succeeded in resisting.
17. *scapulars:* The scapular is a sleeveless monastic garment that hangs loosely from the shoulders.

Sad nymphs devout and dedicated, who
With sobs and cries pursue infinity—

My soul, poor sisters, joins you in your hell!   25
Deep insight pity to my love imparts,
For pangs and lusts nothing can ever quell,
For passion's quenchless flooding of your hearts!

A Voyage to Cythera*

My heart, as though a bird flying elated,
Hovered around the vessel's rigging, free;
Beneath clear skies the ship plunged joyously,
A sea-borne angel sun-intoxicated.

What gloomy isle is this? Cythera's land,   5
In song and fable famed as fair and brave,
Trite Eldorado ageing bachelors crave;
See, after all, how dismal is this strand.

Isle of the heart's sweet secret plenitude!
The ghost of time-famed Venus lingers there,   10
Haunting your seas like perfume everywhere,
Sating the soul with love and lassitude.

Green-myrtled isle where flowers lushly grow,
The quenchless source of all men's veneration,
Where sighs from hearts consumed by adoration   15
Drift, like the scent of roses as they blow

Or cooing of the ring-doves, timelessly!
Barren was Cythera beyond surmise,
A stony desert torn by strident cries;
Yet I, a thing most strange could faintly see!   20

No temple this, shadowed by leafy trees,
To which a flower-loving priestess came,
Her body with her secret zeal aflame,
Her gown the plaything of the passing breeze;

But there, as we so closely drifted by   25
Our great white sails scattered the birds in fear,
We saw a three-branched gallows, stark and clear,
Whose outline like a cypress cleft the sky.

---

* Cythera, an island lying to the north-west of Crete, was dedicated to the goddess Aphrodite. Thus the name came to be used, in poetic language, to designate the haunts of lovers. Watteau (1684–1721) painted two famous canvases, both now in the Louvre, entitled "The Embarcation for Cythera."

Ferocious birds, perching upon their prey,
A man but lately hanged, pecked greedily;
Their hideous beaks, like tools tore viciously
At strips of bleeding flesh foul with decay;   30

The eyes were holes, inward the belly fell,
Heavy intestines flowed about the thighs;
These savage brutes, gorging upon their prize,
Had, with their beaks, castrated it as well.   35

Beneath its feet, wild beasts, eager and grim,
With snouts upraised were prowling restlessly;
The executioner, one appeared to be,
The smaller ones, his aids, surrounding him.   40

Child of this fair-skied Cythera, whose doom
Was to endure in silence all these insults
In expiation of your shameful cults
And sins that have forbidden you the tomb—

Poor gruesome corpse, your pangs are mine! Again   45
I felt—your dangling limbs before my eyes—
As though a vomit on my teeth, arise,
Bitter as gall, familiar floods of pain.

Sad wretch of tender memory! afresh,
Confronting you, I felt the beak, the jaw—   50
The raven and the panther, come to claw
As frenziedly as always at my flesh.

The sky was fair and undisturbed the sea,
But all for me was blood-stained, all was cloud;
Alas! henceforth I felt, as in a shroud,   55
My heart enfolded in this allegory.

Venus! I saw upon your island's dust,
A gallows, symbol of myself, my fate!
O Lord! Give me the strength to contemplate
My body and my soul without disgust!   60

Meditation*

Hush, O my sorrow, be serene and still!
You longed for dusk, it comes, see it is there!

* This is a late poem, not printed until several months after the publication of the second edition of *Flowers of Evil* in 1861. As he had stated in a letter to his mother, the poet was indeed alone at this time, "without friends, without a mistress, without a dog or a cat to whom I might complain."

Darkness enshrouds the town with evening's chill,
Bringing to some relief, to others care.

Now, while the common herd with common will,
Lashed on by pleasure, ruthless overseer,
Would wrench remorse from every tawdry thrill,
My sorrow, take my hand. Ah! stay not here.

Come far from these! See long-lost years on high,
Outmoded, lean from balconies of sky;
Regret, rise smiling from the deep, unspent;

The sun sink low beneath the vaulted height;
And, while a shroud trails from the Orient,
Hear, dearest, hear, the foot-fall of the Night!

ARTHUR RIMBAUD
(1854–1891)

A Season in Hell (Une saison en enfer) *

Deliriums

II

Alchemy of the Word

Back to myself. The story of one of my follies.[1]

For a long time I boasted of possessing all possible landscapes,[2] and found ridiculous the celebrities of modern painting and poetry.

I loved idiotic paintings,[3] frieze panels, stage-sets, jugglers' back-drops, signs, popular colored prints, old-fashioned literature, Church Latin, badly-spelled pornography, the novels of our grandmothers, fairy tales, children's storybooks, old operas, silly refrains, ingenuous rhythms.

I dreamed of crusades, voyages of discovery of which there is no record, republics with no history, long-forgotten religious wars, revo-

---

* Arthur Rimbaud. *A Season in Hell*, translated by Delmore Schwartz. Copyright 1939 by New Directions Publishing Corporation. Reprinted by permission of New Directions Publishing Corporation.

1. On the draft of the poem Rimbaud wrote, "Now I can say that art is just stupidity."

2. Through acquiring the faculties of a seer.

3. This paragraph strongly appealed to the French surrealists of the 1920s, since they shared the tastes listed here and also despised the work of all establishment writers and artists.

lutions in customs, the migration of races and continents: I believed in every magic.[4]

I discovered the color of the vowels![5]—A black, *E* white, *I* red, *O* blue, *U* green.—I regulated the form and movement of each consonant,[6] and, with the rhythms of instinct, I imagined that I had invented a poetic language accessible, sooner or later, to all the senses. I reserved the rights of translation.

This was at first an exercise. I wrote down silences, nights, I put down the inexpressible.[7] I defined frenzies.

* * *

Far from the birds,[8] the herds, the farmer's daughters,
Kneeling upon the heath beside the brook
Ringed by soft hazel trees and a warm green mist
What did I drink? what dream, that afternoon?

What could I drink beside the river Oise
—Elms without voice, turf without flowers, sky overcast!—
Drink from those yellow gourds, far from the hut
Dear to me? Some golden liquor,[9] bringing sweat.

I made a sorry ad for a village saloon.
—A storm thrashed through the clouds. At night
The woodland waters sank in virgin sands,
The wind of God cast icicles on pools;

Weeping, I saw the gold,—and could not drink.[10]

* * *

4. The word must be understood in the most intensely literal fashion—and, as everywhere in these pages, the declaration must be accepted as an exact account of Rimbaud's outlook during the time dealt with.

5. As recorded in his sonnet "Vowels." The colors have been traced back to a children's alphabet book that Rimbaud had had when he was a small boy. It has also been pointed out that the successive stages in the alchemical transformation allegedly have these colors, and in this order.

6. There is no similar poem on the consonants. Rimbaud presumably means that his poetic instinct revealed to him the latent forces waiting, within each consonant, to be released.

7. At the time he was undertaking such "exercises," Rimbaud indeed believed they were successful. But note, also, both the initial reference to his "follies" and the later dismissal of the "old poetic

rubbish" from which he had not fully emancipated himself.

8. This is either a different version, or a recollection both incomplete and divergent, of the poem "Tear," which he had written in 1872. The eleven-syllable line used reveals the influence of Paul Verlaine who, going against the traditional French preference for the more equilibrated line with an even number of syllables, cherished the floating and nebulous effects that, in the absence of a too pronounced regularity, he was able to achieve.

9. This, it has been suggested, is the *aurum potabile* or liquid gold of the alchemists. To drink it ensured one's longevity.

10. This line, far more strongly than do the roughly equivalent lines of the original poem, underscores the bitter contrast between the transcendent goal seemingly within reach and the failure to attain it.

At four in the morning[11] in summer
Love is still fast asleep,
And the groves still exhale the fragrance
  Of the holiday evening.

Down below, in their immense workyard,
In the sun of the Hesperides,[12]
The Carpenters—in shirt-sleeves—
  Already are moving.

In their deserts of moss, quietly,
They prepare the precious ceilings
  On which the city
Will paint a false heaven.

O, for these Workmen, the charming
Subjects of a King of Babylon,
Venus! abandon a moment the Lovers
  Whose hearts are enthroned.

   O Queen of Shepherds,
  Bring the laborers brandy
  That their powers may be steady
While waiting for the noonday swim.

*   *   *

The old poetic rubbish played an important part in my alchemy of words.

I accustomed myself to plain hallucination:[13] I saw quite plainly a mosque where a factory stood, a group of drums played by angels, open carriages on the sky's boulevards, a drawing-room at the bottom of a lake; monsters, mysteries; the title of a vaudeville song raised horrors before me.

Then I would explain my magic sophistries with the hallucination of words!

I ended up by finding sacred the disorder of my spirit. I was indolent, prey to a sluggish fever: I envied the happiness of beasts,—caterpillars, representing the innocence of limbo, moles, the slumber of virginity.

My disposition grew embittered. I said goodbye to the world in what might be called ballads:

---

11. Another poem written in 1872, "A Good Thought in the Morning." The present version has a considerable number of textual variants.

12. Greek name for the Canary Islands.
13. Another paragraph written as though to order for the surrealists of the 1920s.

SONG OF THE HIGHEST TOWER[14]

May they come, may they come,
The days which enchant us.

Patient so long,
I forgot forever.
Fear and suffering
Are lifted away.
And the unwholesome thirst
Darkens my blood.

May they come, may they come,
The days which enchant us.

Like the meadow,
Left untended,
Overgrown, florid
With fragrance and rye,
Amid the harsh hum
Of filthy flies.

May they come, may they come,
The days which enchant us.

I loved the desert, burnt orchards, second-hand shops, tepid drinks. I dragged myself to the sun, the god of fire.[15]

"General, if you still have an old cannon[16] on your ruined ramparts, bombard us with hunks of dry earth. Fire on the show windows of splendid shops! and on the salons! Make the city eat its dust. Oxydize the gargoyles. Fill boudoirs with burning powder of rubies[17] . . ."

Oh! the little gnat drunk at the tavern urinal,[18] in love with the borage, which a ray of light dissolves!

14. The original poem was written in 1872 and contained six six-line stanzas. The present version has variants and, notably, the threefold use of the refrain is an innovation.
15. The translator's eye skipped a line here. The complete sentence might be translated: "I dragged myself through the stinking alleyways and with eyes closed offered myself to the sun, the god of fire." For Rimbaud, the symbolic and emotional significance of the light, of the sun, was very great.
16. Such as the cannon reposing in Rimbaud's native town of Charleville. The poet, who at one period set out to shock the town's respectable citizens with his foul language, unkempt appearance and unorthodox behavior, here provides a sample of his rebellious state of mind.
17. This dream of destruction culminates gloriously in arson, with tongues of fire like red jewels.
18. The poet now condemns his earlier attitude. Such is the power of light that a single ray suffices to annihilate either a gnat or the self-deceiving pretensions of a loutish youth.

HUNGER[19]

If I have any taste, it is hardly
For more than earth and stones,
I always breakfast on air,
On rock, on coal, on iron.

Go, my hungers. Graze, my hungers,
  The field of sounds.
—Suck the vivid venom
  Of sour weeds.

Eat stones that have been cracked,
The old stones from churches;
The shingle of ancient floods,
Bread planted in gray valleys.

       *   *   *

The wolf[20] howled under the leaves,
Spitting out the fine feathers
Of his meal of poultry:
Like him, I consume myself.

The greens and the fruits
Wait only to be taken;
Yet the hedge spider
Only eats violets.

May I sleep! may I boil
At the altars of Solomon.
The broth brims over the rust,
And mingles with Kedron.[21]

    Finally, O happiness, O reason, I stripped the sky of blue, which
is dismal,[22] and I lived as the gold spark of the radiance that is

19. This both echoes and diverges
markedly from the poem "Feasts of
Hunger."
20. This is an accurate copy of the
poem "The Wolf Howled." The first of
these two poems conjures up a purely
mineral realm and diet, while the second
identifies the poet with a predatory beast,
who ultimately is self-consumed, and then
with the predatory spider who, with his
insistence on "planning ahead," neglects
the nourishment lying all around. The
third stanza offers up the poet as sacrifice in the Temple of King Solomon the
all-wise. Finally, the last shred of identity dissolved (compare the "Drunken
Boat" with its "Oh, may my keel shatter! May I go to the sea!"), the poet is
one with the elements.
21. River flowing by Jerusalem and
entering the Dead Sea.
22. The word in the French original is
noir, "black." The azure of the sky may
be the last and most subtle of all opaci-
ties, but it too must be brushed aside so
that essential truth may shine forth and
absorb the individual into its radiance.
The poem that follows celebrates this
transformation.

nature. I derived from joy an expression as comic and wild as possible:[23]

* * *

I have regained[24] it!
What? Eternity.
It is the fusion
    Of sun and ocean.[25]

O immortal soul,
Obey your vow,[26]
Despite the empty dark
And the blazing day.

Thus you work free
Of human supports,
Of vulgar transports!
You soar like the ...

Never hope,
No *orietur*.[27]
Science, patience,
Torture is sure.

No more tomorrow,[28]
Satin-like embers,[29]
    Your ardor
    Is duty.

I have regained it!
—What?—Eternity.
It is the fusion
    Of sun and ocean.

* * *

23. In numerous accounts of escape from the "mind-forged manacles" into spiritual liberation, the outward sign of liberation is recorded as being hearty laughter. This is especially true in Zen Buddhism, of which Rimbaud could not have had any direct knowledge.

24. This differs so considerably from the poem "Eternity" that it must be regarded as a reworking of this original.

25. Eternity is not necessarily something other than time or the products of time. Here it is sensed as embodied, not in the sun and ocean commonsensically perceived as being respectively "up there" and "down below," but in their "fusion"—no less real for being inconceivable.

26. Fusion of the opposites day-night, light-dark, can be experienced only as a consequence of ascetic dedication, such as that referred to in the following stanza.

27. On this level, the practice of petitionary prayer has been left behind.

28. For this would be to experience time as separated from Eternity.

29. Compare the "refining fire" through which Dante describes himself as passing. A related quotation from Dante's *Divine Comedy* is used by T. S. Eliot very near the end of his poem *The Waste Land.* But it is possible that Rimbaud had in mind some technical alchemical term.

I became a fabulous opera: I saw that all beings are fatally attracted to happiness: action is not life,[30] but a way of dissipating one's strength, an enervation. Morality is weakness[31] of the brain.

To every being, several *other* lives seemed to me to be due. This gentleman does not know what he is doing: he is an angel. This family is a litter of dogs. In the cases of several men, I conversed with a moment of their other lives.—Thus, I have been in love with a pig.[32]

None of the sophistries of madness,—the madness which must be locked up,—have been forgotten by me: I could repeat them all, I know the system.

My health was in danger. Terror was approaching. I would fall into a sleep lasting several days, and when up again I went on with the most despondent dreams. I was ripe for death,[33] and by a road full of dangers, my weakness was leading to the ends of the earth, to Kimmeria,[34] fatherland of darkness and whirlwinds.

I had to travel to distract the sorceries collected in my brain. On the sea, which I loved as if it had to cleanse me of defilement, I saw the consoling Cross arise. I had been condemned by the rainbow.[35] Happiness[36] was my doom, my remorse, my worm; my life would always be much too prodigious to be devoted to power and beauty.

Happiness! Its tooth, kind unto death, warned me at cockcrow,[37] —*ad matutinum*,[38] at *Christus venit*,—in the most sombre cities:

* * *

O seasons, O castles![39]
What soul is flawless?

I made the magic study
Of happiness no one escapes.

---

30. All premeditated or willful individual action sets one apart from the universal harmony.

31. The context makes it plain that this is no anticipation of Friedrich Nietzsche's (1844–1901) theories of a morality for slaves and a very different code for the strong. Like calculated action, preformulated rules attempt to interfere with the universal concord. The superior man, as Confucius expressed it, "simply does what seems right to him at the time."

32. It is impossible to avoid identifying this "pig" with Rimbaud's debauched companion, the poet Paul Verlaine.

33. Yet it is a sign of invincible creative vigor that the appalling conditions described in these two paragraphs guide the poet to a phrase of extraordinary beauty: "J'étais mûr pour le trépas, et par une route de dangers ma faiblesse me

menait aux confins du monde et de la Cimmérie, patrie de l'ombre et des tourbillons."

34. The Greeks believed that this was an always misty and cloudy land at the earth's extreme confines.

35. Both are traditional religious symbols.

36. This has replaced, as an ultimate goal, the power and beauty named at the end of the sentence.

37. Probably a reference to Peter's denial of Christ (Luke 22:34, 61).

38. Matins, the morning mass.

39. A variant of the poem "O Seasons, O Castles." The opening evocation of the boundless, never-ending round of the seasons and of all sanctuarylike castle enclosures is, here only, contrasted with the flawed human soul. This does not occur when the first line is later twice repeated as a refrain.

O hail it every time
The Gallic cock[40] sings out.

Ah, I'll want nothing more;
It has taken charge of my life.

This charm[41] has taken soul and flesh
And quieted their conflicts.

O seasons, O castles!

The hour of flight, alas!
Will be the hour of death.[42]

O seasons, O castles!

* * *

That's what happened. Today I know how to greet beauty.

---

40. Condensed within this expression are the freshness of dawning day, so often experienced by the vagrant Rimbaud, the dawning of the world era initiated by Christ's sacrifice, an awareness of the national community (the cock being a traditional symbol for France), and the poet's own role as a singer. All these connotations are carried over into the following couplet.

41. The French *charme*, derived like the English word from the Latin *carmen*, retains more of the Latin meaning: not

only song, but also incantation, magic spell. The poet may be saying that his poetic faculty is no longer harnessed to a laborious individual effort, since now it is or will be linked to flesh, spirit, and the national community.

42. This couplet is a highly significant addition to the original poem. Its imprecision gives to the prediction an even more ominous ring. The most immediate interpretation appears to be that the loss of the "charm," of the poetic gift, will mean the death of the poet himself.

Morning

Had I not *once* a youth pleasant, heroic, fabulous enough to write on leaves of gold: too much luck! Through what crime, what error have I earned my present weakness? You who maintain that some animals sob sorrowfully, that the sick despair, that the dead have bad dreams, try to tell the story of my downfall and my slumber. I myself can no more explain myself than the beggar with his continual *Pater* and *Ave Maria*. *I no longer know how to speak.*

Yet today I think I have finished the story of my hell. It was indeed hell;[1] the ancient one, whose gates were opened by the Son of Man.

From the same desert, during the same night, my tired eyes always awake to the silver star, always, even though the Kings of

---

1. The notion of a descent into hell is common to antiquity (Ulysses, Aeneas) and to Christianity. It has been used to

signify death to the old way of life ("the old Adam") and rebirth into a transformed existence.

Life, the three Magi,[2] heart, soul, and mind are not moved. When will we go, beyond the beaches and the mountains, to greet the birth of the new task,[3] the new wisdom, the flight of tyrants and demons, the end of superstition; to adore—the first ones!—Christmas on Earth?

The song of the skies, the march of peoples![4] Slaves, let us not curse life.

2. These wise men from the East, alerted by the shining of a new star, arrived in Bethlehem to do homage and offer gifts to the infant Christ. Here Rimbaud provides an allegorical interpretation of the three personages: heart, soul, and mind must unite in adoration to make possible what will be the first genuine celebration of Christmas on earth.

3. Only effort and wisdom jointly can

visualize and accomplish what must be done. Similarly, on the side of what must be put to rout, tyrants and demons have long been lending each other indispensable support.

4. Once again Rimbaud asserts the existence of a bond between true religion and earthly progress. The final warning counsels today's "slaves" not to give way to despair.

Goodbye

Autumn already!—But why regret[1] an everlasting sun, if we are engaged in the discovery of the divine light,—far from people who die with the seasons.[2]

Autumn. Our bark, steering toward the motionless fogs, turns toward the port of misery, the enormous city[3] whose sky is mud-stained and fiery. Ah, the stinking rags, the rain-soaked bread, the drunkenness, the thousand loves which crucified me. She will never stop, then, that ghoulish queen[4] of millions of dead souls and bodies, *who will be judged.*[5] I see myself again, my skin eaten by dirt and plague, my hair and arm-pits full of worms, and still larger worms in my heart, stretched out among the unknown who are without age, without feeling ... I could have died there ... Horrible vision! I detest misery.

And I distrust winter because it is the season of comfort![6]— Sometimes in the sky I see endless beaches covered with white and joyous nations. A great golden vessel above me waves its many-colored pennants in the breezes of morning. I have created all festivals, all triumphs, all dramas. I have tried to invent new flowers, new stars, new flesh, new languages. I thought to acquire supernatural powers. Well! I must bury my imagination and my memories! A glorious reputation as an artist and story-teller kicked away![7]

1. In the sense of "to miss, to look back longingly at."

2. The natural course of human life proceeds from birth through maturity to death. But other than and redeeming this, which is the lot of every animal, is the quest for the "divine light."

3. Rimbaud, like George Orwell, had been "down and out in London and Paris" and, at least for short periods, had experienced the sufferings he goes on to

enumerate.

4. Presumably, death.

5. Namely, the souls and bodies.

6. Rimbaud does not regard warm bourgeois domesticity as a satisfying refuge.

7. It is a matter of dispute whether Rimbaud means any literary career whatsoever, or only the sort of literary activity characterized above.

I! I who called myself mage[8] or angel, freed from all morality, I am driven back to the soil, with a duty to seek and rough actuality to grasp! Peasant![9]

Am I mistaken? would charity[10] be the sister of death to me?

In the end, I will ask to be pardoned for having fed myself on lies. And now let us go.

But not a single friendly hand![11] for where would I find help?

* * *

Yes, the new epoch is at best very difficult.

For I can say that I have won out: the grinding of the teeth, the hissing of fire, and the foul breathing have lessened. All miserable memories are fading. My last regrets are packed away,—the jealousy[12] of beggars, of bandits, of the friends of death, the backward of all sorts.—You damned souls, suppose I revenged myself!

One must be absolutely modern.[13]

No more hymns: hold the gains already won. What a hard night! The dried blood smokes on my face, and I have nothing behind me but this horrible bush![14] ... The battle of the spirit is as brutal as the battle of men; but the vision of justice is the pleasure of God alone.

But now it is evening.[15] Let us accept every inflow of vigor and genuine tenderness.[16] And at dawn, armed with an eager patience,[17] we shall enter the splendid cities.

What did I say about a friendly hand! One great advantage is that I can laugh at the old false loves, and put to shame those lying couples,—I saw the hell of woman[18] down there;—and I shall be permitted *to possess the truth in a soul and a body.*

April–August 1873

8. Or magus, plural magi, a miracle worker.

9. The French peasant, as he was represented, for instance, in the stories of Guy de Maupassant (1850–1893), was meanly and graspingly materialistic. Rimbaud had, too, the example of his mother, who clung tenaciously to the family farm.

10. Elsewhere, the poet varies the relationship of these words, speaking of death as a Sister of Charity.

11. Rimbaud's uncompromising and sometimes repellent behavior had alienated many, and discouraged even those who wished him well. It is also highly probable that he could not think of a single person able to aid him in the perilous situation he was traversing.

12. Rimbaud had expressed his envy of criminals and social outcasts of every kind, and also of illiterates.

13. As the following declarations make clear, Rimbaud saw no possibility of a return to a past conceived on conventionally pious lines.

14. This, most probably, is the tree of the knowledge of good and evil that had flourished in the Garden of Eden. To his distress, the poet saw the world split, in the Christian era, between the opposing forces of good and evil. He looked back nostalgically to a more primitive but unified period in human history.

15. In the sense, not of coming repose, but of vigil (French *veille*) and vigilance.

16. Yet once more the poet affirms the concord of forces often regarded as antithetical.

17. A quality signally lacking in Rimbaud himself. This sentence is magnificent: "Et, à l'aurore, armés d'une ardente patience, nous entrerons aux splendides villes."

18. Rimbaud had expressed his awareness of the shackled, frustrated existences forced upon women, and anticipated a day when women would make a splendid and unpredictable contribution to poetry.

AUGUST STRINDBERG

1849–1912

The Ghost Sonata (Spöksonaten) *

Characters

THE OLD MAN, *Hummel, a company director*
THE STUDENT, *Arkenholtz*
THE MILKMAID, *an apparition*
THE CARETAKER'S WIFE
THE CARETAKER
THE LADY IN BLACK, *the daughter of the Caretaker's Wife and the Dead Man. Also referred to as the Dark Lady*
THE COLONEL
THE MUMMY, *the Colonel's wife*
THE GIRL, *the Colonel's daughter, actually the daughter of the Old Man*
THE ARISTOCRAT, *Baron Skanskorg. Engaged to the Lady in Black*
JOHANSSON, *the Old Man's servant*
BENGTSSON, *the Colonel's servant*
THE FIANCÉE, *a white-haired old woman, once betrothed to the Old Man*
THE COOK
A MAIDSERVANT
BEGGARS

Scene I

Outside the house. The corner of the façade of a modern house, showing the ground floor above, and the street in front. The ground floor terminates on the right in the Round Room, above which, on the first floor, is a balcony with a flagstaff. The windows of the Round Room face the street in front of the house, and at the corner look onto the suggestion of a side-street running towards the back. At the beginning of the scene the blinds of the Round Room are down. When, later, they are raised, the white marble statue of a young woman can be seen, surrounded with palms and brightly lighted by rays of sunshine.

To the left of the Round Room is the Hyacinth Room; its

---

* From *Six Plays by Strindberg*, Doubleday Anchor Books, 1955. Translated by Elizabeth Sprigge. Reprinted by permission of Collins-Knowlton-Wing, Inc. Copyright © 1955, 1960, 1962 by Elizabeth Sprigge.

Strindberg first thought of calling the play *Kama-Loka*, a term he had happened upon in some theosophical work. It signifies the realm occupied by spirits who are a prey to their own passions. The actual title reflects the author's conscious choice of a musical structure for his play, whose three scenes represent the sonata structure ABA, followed by a "coda." The underlying piece of music was conceived as being Beethoven's sonata opus 31, no. 2 in D major.

window filled with pots of hyacinths, blue, white and pink. Further left, at the back, is an imposing double front door with laurels in tubs on either side of it. The doors are wide open, showing a staircase of white marble with a banister of mahogany and brass. To the left of the front door is another ground-floor window, with a window-mirror.[1] *On the balcony rail in the corner above the Round Room are a blue silk quilt and two white pillows. The windows to the left of this are hung with white sheets.*[2]

In the foreground, in front of the house, is a green bench; to the right a street drinking-fountain, to the left an advertisement column.

It is a bright Sunday morning, and as the curtain rises the bells of several churches, some near, some far away, are ringing.

On the staircase the LADY IN BLACK *stands motionless.*

The CARETAKER'S WIFE *sweeps the doorstep, then polishes the brass on the door and waters the laurels.*

In a wheel-chair by the advertisement column sits the OLD MAN, *reading a newspaper. His hair and beard are white and he wears spectacles.*

The MILKMAID[3] *comes round the corner on the right, carrying milk bottles in a wire basket. She is wearing a summer dress with brown shoes, black stockings and a white cap. She takes off her cap and hangs it on the fountain, wipes the perspiration from her forehead, washes her hands and arranges her hair, using the water as a mirror.*

A steamship bell is heard, and now and then the silence is broken by the deep notes of an organ in a nearby church.

After a few moments, when all is silent and the MILKMAID *has finished her toilet, the* STUDENT *enters from the left. He has had a sleepless night and is unshaven. He goes straight up to the fountain. There is a pause before he speaks.*

STUDENT. May I have the cup? [*The* MILKMAID *clutches the cup to her.*] Haven't you finished yet? [*The* MILKMAID *looks at him with horror.*]

OLD MAN [*to himself*] Who's he talking to? I don't see anybody. Is he crazy? [*He goes on watching them in great astonishment.*]

STUDENT [*to the* MILKMAID]. What are you staring at? Do I look so terrible? Well, I've had no sleep, and of course you think I've been making a night of it. . . . [*The* MILKMAID *stays just as she is.*] You think I've been drinking, eh? Do I smell of liquor? [*The* MILKMAID *does not change.*] I haven't shaved, I know. Give me a drink of water, girl. I've earned it. [*Pause.*] Oh well, I suppose I'll have to tell you. I spent the whole night dressing wounds and looking after the injured. You see, I was there when that house collapsed[4] last night. Now you know. [*The* MILKMAID *rinses the*

---

1. "Set at an angle inside the window, so as to show what is going on in the street" [translator's note].

2. "Sign of mourning" [translator's note].

3. She is described as an "apparition" in the list of characters.

4. This is the first of many evocations of houses under construction, enduring, decaying, and collapsing or being wrecked—and this first mention refers to a collapse.

cup and gives him a drink.] Thanks. [*The* MILKMAID *stands motionless. Slowly.*] Will you do me a great favor? [*Pause.*] The thing is, my eyes, as you can see, are inflamed, but my hands have been touching wounds and corpses, so it would be dangerous to put them near my eyes. Will you take my handkerchief— it's quite clean—and dip it in the fresh water and bathe my eyes? Will you do this? Will you play the good Samaritan? [*The* MILKMAID *hesitates, but does as he bids.*] Thank you, my dear. [*He takes out his purse. She makes a gesture of refusal.*] Forgive my stupidity, but I'm only half-awake. . . . [*The* MILKMAID *disappears.*]

OLD MAN [*to the* STUDENT]. Excuse me speaking to you, but I heard you say you were at the scene of the accident last night. I was just reading about it in the paper.

STUDENT. Is it in the paper already?

OLD MAN. The whole thing, including your portrait. But they regret that they have been unable to find out the name of the splendid young student. . . .

STUDENT. Really? [*Glances at the paper.*] Yes, that's me. Well I never!

OLD MAN. Who was it you were talking to just now?

STUDENT. Didn't you see? [*Pause.*]

OLD MAN. Would it be impertinent to inquire—what in fact your name is?

STUDENT. What would be the point? I don't care for publicity. If you get any praise, there's always disapproval too. The art of running people down has been developed to such a pitch. . . . Besides, I don't want any reward.

OLD MAN. You're well off, perhaps.

STUDENT. No, indeed. On the contrary, I'm very poor.

OLD MAN. Do you know, it seems to me I've heard your voice before. When I was young I had a friend who pronounced certain words just as you do. I've never met anyone else with quite that pronunciation. Only him—and you. Are you by any chance related to Mr. Arkenholtz,[5] the merchant?

STUDENT. He was my father.

OLD MAN. Strange are the paths of fate. I saw you when you were an infant, under very painful circumstances.

STUDENT. Yes, I understand I came into the world in the middle of a bankruptcy.[6]

OLD MAN. Just that.

STUDENT. Perhaps I might ask your name.

OLD MAN. I am Mr. Hummel.[7]

---

5. Not long before there has been a biblical reference, to the "good Samaritan" of the New Testament parable. The name Arkenholtz may be intended to suggest the Ark in which Noah preserved mankind from destruction, or the Ark of the Covenant constructed by the Israelites at the command of the Almighty and carried by them everywhere in their wan-

derings.

6. Strindberg's own birth occurred at a time of great financial stringency for the family.

7. The German word for bumblebee. Like this insect, Mr. Hummel wandered widely and found sustenance in every flower.

STUDENT. Are you the? . . . I remember that . . .

OLD MAN. Have you often heard my name mentioned in your family?

STUDENT. Yes.

OLD MAN. And mentioned perhaps with a certain aversion? [*The* STUDENT *is silent.*] Yes, I can imagine it. You were told, I suppose, that I was the man who ruined your father? All who ruin themselves through foolish speculations consider they were ruined by those they couldn't fool. [*Pause.*] Now these are the facts. Your father robbed me of seventeen thousand crowns—the whole of my savings at that time.

STUDENT. It's queer that the same story can be told in two such different ways.

OLD MAN. You surely don't believe I'm telling you what isn't true?

STUDENT. What am I to believe? My father didn't lie.

OLD MAN. That is so true. A father never lies.[8] But I too am a father, and so it follows . . .

STUDENT. What are you driving at?

OLD MAN. I saved your father from disaster, and he repaid me with all the frightful hatred that is born of an obligation to be grateful.[9] He taught his family to speak ill of me.

STUDENT. Perhaps you made him ungrateful by poisoning your help with unnecessary humiliation.

OLD MAN. All help is humiliating, sir.

STUDENT. What do you want[10] from me?

OLD MAN. I'm not asking for the money, but if you will render me a few small services, I shall consider myself well paid. You see that I am a cripple. Some say it is my own fault; others lay the blame on my parents. I prefer to blame life itself, with its pitfalls. For if you escape one snare, you fall headlong into another. In any case, I am unable to climb stairs or ring doorbells, and that is why I am asking you to help me.

STUDENT. What can I do?

OLD MAN. To begin with, push my chair so that I can read those playbills. I want to see what is on tonight.

STUDENT [*pushing the chair*]. Haven't you got an attendant?

OLD MAN. Yes, but he has gone on an errand. He'll be back soon. Are you a medical student?

STUDENT. No, I am studying languages, but I don't know at all what I'm going to do.

OLD MAN. Aha! Are you good at mathematics?

STUDENT. Yes, fairly.

OLD MAN. Good. Perhaps you would like a job.

STUDENT. Yes, why not?

8. This sly dig at conventional pieties precedes the unmasking of other shams that constitute the so-called real world.

9. Strindberg himself found this obligation irksome. On one occasion he even complained, in writing, that people from whom he had borrowed money had been sponging on him. And he was humiliated and resentful when friends launched a public appeal for funds for his support.

10. The Student's question shows that he has accepted the truth of the Old Man's story and that he now admits an obligation to him.

OLD MAN. Splendid. [*He studies the playbills.*] They are doing *The Valkyrie* for the matinée. That means the Colonel will be there[11] with his daughter, and as he always sits at the end of the sixth row, I'll put you next to him. Go to that telephone kiosk please and order a ticket for seat eighty-two in the sixth row.

STUDENT. Am I to go to the Opera in the middle of the day?

OLD MAN. Yes. Do as I tell you and things will go well with you. I want to see you happy, rich and honored. Your début last night as the brave rescuer will make you famous by tomorrow and then your name will be worth something.

STUDENT [*going to the telephone kiosk*]. What an odd adventure!

OLD MAN. Are you a gambler?[12]

STUDENT. Yes, unfortunately.

OLD MAN. We'll make it fortunately. Go on now, telephone. [*The* STUDENT *goes. The* OLD MAN *reads his paper. The* LADY IN BLACK *comes out on to the pavement and talks to the* CARETAKER'S WIFE. *The* OLD MAN *listens, but the audience hears nothing. The* STUDENT *returns.*] Did you fix it up?

STUDENT. It's done.

OLD MAN. You see that house?

STUDENT. Yes, I've been looking at it a lot. I passed it yesterday when the sun was shining on the windowpanes, and I imagined all the beauty and elegance there must be inside. I said to my companion: "Think of living up there in the top flat, with a beautiful young wife, two pretty little children and an income of twenty thousand crowns a year."

OLD MAN. So that's what you said. That's what you said. Well, well! I too am very fond of this house.

STUDENT. Do you speculate in houses?

OLD MAN. Mm—yes. But not in the way you mean.

STUDENT. Do you know the people who live here?

OLD MAN. Every one of them. At my age one knows everybody, and their parents and grandparents too, and one's always related[13] to them in some way or other. I am just eighty, but no one knows me—not really. I take an interest in human destiny.[14] [*The blinds of the Round Room are drawn up. The* COLONEL *is seen, wearing mufti. He looks at the thermometer outside one of the windows, then turns back into the room and stands in front of the marble statue.*] Look, that's the Colonel, whom you will sit next to this afternoon.

STUDENT. Is he—the Colonel? I don't understand any of this, but it's like a fairy story.

11. The first direct revelation of the Old Man's apparent omniscience and of his power drive.

12. Strindberg, though he did not gamble, was greatly addicted to the search for "hidden meanings" in any casual occurrence.

13. This enunciates another important factor in the play. There are multiple blood ties, some not generally known, that link the characters, and some of these ties were created by secret liaisons. Later there is a reference to a homosexual attraction, and there are also bonds of one sort or another arising from criminal activities.

14. Another hint that the Old Man is far more than the decrepit figure he appears to be.

OLD MAN. My whole life's like a book of fairy stories,[15] sir. And although the stories are different, they are held together by one thread, and the main theme constantly recurs.

STUDENT. Who is that marble statue of?

OLD MAN. That, naturally, is his wife.

STUDENT. Was she such a wonderful person?

OLD MAN. Er . . . yes.

STUDENT. Tell me.

OLD MAN. We can't judge people, young man. If I were to tell you that she left him, that he beat her, that she returned to him and married him a second time,[16] and that now she is sitting inside there like a mummy, worshipping her own statue—then you would think me crazy.

STUDENT. I don't understand.

OLD MAN. I didn't think you would. Well, then we have the window with the hyacinths.[17] His daughter lives there. She has gone out for a ride, but she will be home soon.

STUDENT. And who is the dark lady talking to the caretaker?

OLD MAN. Well, that's a bit complicated, but it is connected with the dead man,[18] up there where you see the white sheets.

STUDENT. Why, who was he?

OLD MAN. A human being like you or me, but the most conspicuous thing about him was his vanity. If you were a Sunday child,[19] you would see him presently come out of that door to look at the Consulate flag flying at half-mast. He was, you understand, a Consul, and he reveled in coronets and lions and plumed hats and colored ribbons.

STUDENT. Sunday child, you say? I'm told I was born on a Sunday.

OLD MAN. No, were you really? I might have known it. I saw it from the color of your eyes. Then you can see what others can't. Have you noticed that?

STUDENT. I don't know what others do see, but at times. . . . Oh, but one doesn't talk of such things!

OLD MAN. I was almost sure of it. But you can talk to me, because I understand such things.

STUDENT. Yesterday, for instance . . . I was drawn to that obscure little street where later on the house collapsed. I went there and stopped in front of that building which I had never seen before. Then I noticed a crack in the wall. . . . I heard the floor boards snapping. . . . I dashed over and picked up a child that was passing under the wall. . . . The next moment the house collapsed. I was saved, but in my arms, which I thought held the child, was nothing at all.

OLD MAN. Yes, yes, just as I thought. Tell me something. Why

15. The Old Man voices Strindberg's own conviction that life has the qualities of fiction, and that seemingly unrelated matters are actually closely connected.

16. Recurrence, or repetition, is a theme built into the structure of the play. Another theme touched on here is that of stagnation.

17. The symbolism of these flowers is explained in Scene 3.

18. Though not listed in the cast of characters, he appears later in this scene.

19. Children born on Sunday were credited with possessing the gift of second sight, the ability to see apparitions.

were you gesticulating that way just now by the fountain? And why were you talking to yourself?

STUDENT. Didn't you see the milkmaid I was talking to?

OLD MAN [*in horror*]. Milkmaid?

STUDENT. Surely. The girl who handed me the cup.

OLD MAN. Really? So that's what was going on. Ah well, I haven't second sight, but there are things I can do. [THE FIANCÉE *is now seen to sit down by the window which has the window-mirror.*] Look at that old woman in the window. Do you see her? Well, she was my fiancée once, sixty years ago. I was twenty. Don't be alarmed. She doesn't recognize me. We see one another every day, and it makes no impression on me, although once we vowed to love one another eternally. Eternally!

STUDENT. How foolish you were in those days! We never talk to our girls like that.

OLD MAN. Forgive us, young man. We didn't know any better. But can you see that that old woman was once young and beautiful?

STUDENT. It doesn't show. And yet there's some charm in her looks. I can't see her eyes.

[*The* CARETAKER'S WIFE *comes out with a basket of chopped fir branches.*[20]]

OLD MAN. Ah, the caretaker's wife! That dark lady is her daughter by the dead man. That's why her husband was given the job of caretaker. But the dark lady has a suitor, who is an aristocrat with great expectations. He is in the process of getting a divorce— from his present wife, you understand. She's presenting him with a stone mansion in order to be rid of him. This aristocratic suitor is the son-in-law of the dead man, and you can see his bedclothes being aired on the balcony upstairs. It is complicated, I must say.

STUDENT. It's fearfully complicated.

OLD MAN. Yes, that it is, internally and externally, although it looks quite simple.

STUDENT. But then who was the dead man?

OLD MAN. You asked me that just now, and I answered. If you were to look round the corner, where the tradesmen's entrance is, you would see a lot of poor people whom he used to help—when it suited him.

STUDENT. He was a kind man then.

OLD MAN. Yes—sometimes.

STUDENT. Not always?

OLD MAN. No-o. That's the way of people. Now, sir, will you push my chair a little, so that it gets into the sun. I'm horribly cold. When you're never able to move about, the blood congeals. I'm going to die soon, I know that, but I have a few things to do first. Take my hand and feel how cold I am.

STUDENT [*taking it*]. Yes, inconceivably. [*He shrinks back, trying in vain to free his hand.*]

20. "It was customary in Sweden to strew the ground with these for a funeral"   [translator's note].

OLD MAN. Don't leave me. I am tired now and lonely, but I haven't always been like this, you know. I have an enormously long life behind me, enormously long. I have made people unhappy and people have made me unhappy—the one cancels out the other—but before I die I want to see you happy. Our fates are entwined through your father—and other things.

STUDENT. Let go of my hand. You are taking all my strength. You are freezing me. What do you want with me?

OLD MAN. [*letting go*]. Be patient and you shall see and understand. Here comes the young lady. [*They watch the* GIRL *approaching, though the audience cannot yet see her.*]

STUDENT. The Colonel's daughter?

OLD MAN. His daughter—yes. Look at her. Have you ever seen such a masterpiece?

STUDENT. She is like the marble statue in there.

OLD MAN. That's her mother, you know.

STUDENT. You are right. Never have I seen such a woman of woman born. Happy the man who may lead her to the altar and his home.

OLD MAN. You can see it. Not everyone recognizes her beauty. So, then, it is written.[21]

[*The* GIRL *enters, wearing an English riding habit. Without noticing anyone she walks slowly to the door, where she stops to say a few words to the* CARETAKER'S WIFE. *Then she goes into the house. The* STUDENT *covers his eyes with his hand.*]

OLD MAN. Are you weeping?

STUDENT. In the face of what's hopeless there can be nothing but despair.

OLD MAN. I can open doors and hearts, if only I find an arm to do my will. Serve me and you shall have power.

STUDENT. Is it a bargain? Am I to sell my soul?

OLD MAN. Sell nothing. Listen. All my life I have *taken.* Now I have a craving to give—give. But no one will accept. I am rich, very rich, but I have no heirs, except for a good-for-nothing who torments the life out of me. Become my son. Inherit me while I am still alive. Enjoy life so that I can watch, at least from a distance.

STUDENT. What am I to do?

OLD MAN. First go to *The Valkyrie.*

STUDENT. That's settled. What else?

OLD MAN. This evening you must be in there—in the Round Room.

STUDENT. How am I to get there?

OLD MAN. By way of *The Valkyrie.*

STUDENT. Why have you chosen me as your medium? Did you know me before?

OLD MAN. Yes, of course. I have had my eye on you for a long time.

21. It is foreordained. The following interchange underlines this sense of being a pawn in a far-ranging plan conceived by some invisible, irresistible power.

But now look up there at the balcony. The maid is hoisting the flag to half-mast for the Consul. And now she is turning the bed-clothes. Do you see that blue quilt? It was made for two to sleep under, but now it covers only one. [*The* GIRL, *having changed her dress, appears in the window and waters the hyacinths.*] There is my little girl. Look at her, look! She is talking to the flowers. Is she not like that blue hyacinth herself? She gives them drink—nothing but pure water, and they transform the water into color and fragrance. Now here comes the Colonel with the newspaper. He is showing her the bit about the house that collapsed. Now he's pointing to your portrait. She's not indifferent. She's reading of your brave deed. . . .

I believe it's clouding over. If it turns to rain I shall be in a pretty fix, unless Johansson comes back soon. [*It grows cloudy and dark. The* FIANCÉE *at the window-mirror closes her window.*] Now my fiancée is closing the window. Seventy-nine years old. The window-mirror is the only mirror she uses, because in it she sees not herself, but the world outside—in two directions. But the world can see her; she hasn't thought of that. Anyhow she's a handsome old woman.

[*Now the* DEAD MAN, *wrapped in a winding sheet, comes out of the door.*]

STUDENT. Good God, what do I see?

OLD MAN. What do you see?

STUDENT. Don't *you* see? There, in the doorway, the dead man?

OLD MAN. I see nothing, but I expected this. Tell me.

STUDENT. He is coming out into the street. [*Pause.*] Now he is turning his head and looking up at the flag.

OLD MAN. What did I tell you? You may be sure he'll count the wreaths and read the visiting cards. Woe to him who's missing.

STUDENT. Now he's turning the corner.

OLD MAN. He's gone to count the poor at the back door. The poor are in the nature of a decoration, you see. "Followed by the blessings of many." Well, he's not going to have my blessing. Between ourselves he was a great scoundrel.

STUDENT. But charitable.

OLD MAN. A charitable scoundrel, always thinking of his grand funeral. When he knew his end was near, he cheated the State out of fifty thousand crowns. Now his daughter has relations with another woman's husband and is wondering about the Will. Yes, the scoundrel can hear every word we're saying, and he's welcome to it. Ah, here comes Johansson! [JOHANSSON *enters.*] Report! [JOHANSSON *speaks, but the audience does not hear.*] Not at home, eh? You are an ass. And the telegram? Nothing? Go on. . . . At six this evening? That's good. Special edition, you say? With his name in full. Arkenholtz, a student, born . . . parents . . . That's splendid. . . . I think it's beginning to rain. . . . What did he say about it? So—so. He wouldn't? Well, he must. Here comes the aristocrat. Push me round the corner, Johansson, so I can hear what the poor are saying. And, Arkenholtz, you wait for me here. Understand? [*To* JOHANSSON.] Hurry up now, hurry up.

[JOHANSSON *wheels the chair round the corner. The* STUDENT *remains watching the* GIRL, *who is now loosening the earth round the hyacinths. The* ARISTOCRAT, *wearing mourning, comes in and speaks to the* DARK LADY, *who has been walking to and fro on the pavement.*]

ARISTOCRAT. But what can we do about it? We shall have to wait.

LADY. I can't wait.

ARISTOCRAT. You can't? Well then, go into the country.[22]

LADY. I don't want to do that.

ARISTOCRAT. Come over here or they will hear what we are saying. [*They move towards the advertisement column and continue their conversation inaudibly.* JOHANSSON *returns.*]

JOHANSSON [*to the* STUDENT.] My master asks you not to forget that other thing, sir.

STUDENT [*hesitating.*] Look here . . . first of all tell me . . . who is your master?

JOHANSSON. Well, he's so many things, and he has been everything.

STUDENT. Is he a wise man?

JOHANSSON. Depends what that is. He says all his life he's been looking for a Sunday child, but that may not be true.

STUDENT. What does he want? He's grasping, isn't he?

JOHANSSON. It's power he wants. The whole day long he rides round in his chariot like the god Thor[23] himself. He looks at houses, pulls them down, opens up new streets, builds squares . . . But he breaks into houses too, sneaks through windows, plays havoc with human destinies, kills his enemies—and never forgives. Can you imagine it, sir? This miserable cripple was once a Don Juan—although he always lost his women.

STUDENT. How do you account for that?

JOHANSSON. You see he's so cunning he makes the women leave him when he's tired of them. But what he's most like now is a horse-thief in the human market. He steals human beings in all sorts of different ways. He literally stole me out of the hands of the law. Well, as a matter of fact I'd made a slip—hm, yes—and only he knew about it. Instead of getting me put in gaol, he turned me into a slave. I slave—for my food alone, and that's none of the best.

STUDENT. Then what is it he means to do in this house?

JOHANSSON. I'm not going to talk about that. It's too complicated.

STUDENT. I think I'd better get away[24] from it all.

[*The* GIRL *drops a bracelet out the window.*]

JOHANSSON. Look! The young lady has dropped her bracelet out of the window. [*The* STUDENT *goes slowly over, picks up the bracelet and returns it to the* GIRL, *who thanks him stiffly. The* STUDENT *goes back to* JOHANSSON.] So you mean to get away.

---

22. This suggests that the Lady is pregnant.

23. The Scandinavian god of thunder, who carried a hammer.

24. The Student dismisses this prudent notion because of what he takes to be a sign of encouragement from the girl.

That's not so easy as you think, once he's got you in his net. And he's afraid of nothing between heaven and earth—yes, of one thing he is—of one person rather. . . .

STUDENT. Don't tell me. I think perhaps I know.

JOHANSSON. How can you know?

STUDENT. I'm guessing. Is it a little milkmaid he's afraid of?

JOHANSSON. He turns his head the other way whenever he meets a milk cart. Besides, he talks in his sleep. It seems he was once in Hamburg. . . .

STUDENT. Can one trust this man?

JOHANSSON. You can trust him—to do anything.

STUDENT. What's he doing now round the corner?

JOHANSSON. Listening to the poor. Sowing a little word, loosening one stone at a time, till the house falls down——[25]metaphorically speaking. You see I'm an educated man. I was once a book-seller. . . . Do you still mean to go away?

STUDENT. I don't like to be ungrateful. He saved my father once, and now he only asks a small service in return.

JOHANSSON. What is that?

STUDENT. I am to go to *The Valkyrie.*

JOHANSSON. That's beyond me. But he's always up to new tricks. Look at him now, talking to that policeman. He is always thick with the police. He uses them, gets them involved in his interests, holds them with false promises and expectations, while all the time he's pumping them. You'll see that before the day is over he'll be received in the Round Room.

STUDENT. What does he want there? What connection has he[26] with the Colonel?

JOHANSSON. I think I can guess, but I'm not sure. You'll see for yourself once you're in there.

STUDENT. I shall never be in there.

JOHANSSON. That depends on yourself. Go to *The Valkyrie.*

STUDENT. Is that the way?

JOHANSSON. Yes, if he said so. Look. Look at him in his war chariot, drawn in triumph by the beggars, who get nothing for their pains but the hint of a treat at his funeral.

[*The* OLD MAN *appears standing up in his wheel-chair, drawn by one of the beggars and followed by the rest.*]

OLD MAN. Hail the noble youth who, at the risk of his own life, saved so many others in yesterday's accident. Three cheers for Arkenholtz! [*The* BEGGARS *bare their heads but do not cheer. The* GIRL *at the window waves her handkerchief. The* COLONEL *gazes from the window of the Round Room. The* OLD WOMAN *rises at her window. The* MAID *on the balcony hoists the flag to the top.*] Clap your hands, citizens. True, it is Sunday, but the

25. Destruction, together with Creation and Preservation, form a divine trinity in Hindu thought.

26. Notice the number of connections mentioned but left unexplained or only partly explained. As in a detective novel, tension is built up by arousing our curiosity but deferring its satisfaction. Again, as in a detective novel, this is a sealed-off house, or world. Nothing exists outside it or unconnected with it.

ass in the pit[27] and the ear in the corn field[28] will absolve us. And although I am not a Sunday child, I have the gift of prophecy and also that of healing. Once I brought a drowned person back to life. That was in Hamburg on a Sunday morning just like this. . . .

[*The* MILKMAID *enters, seen only by the* STUDENT *and the* OLD MAN. *She raises her arms like one who is drowning and gazes fixedly at the* OLD MAN. *He sits down, then crumples up, stricken with horror.*]

Johansson! Take me away! Quick! . . . Arkenholtz, don't forget *The Valkyrie.*

STUDENT. What is all this?

JOHANSSON. We shall see. We shall see.

Scene II

Inside the Round Room. At the back is a white porcelain stove. On either side of it are a mirror, a pendulum clock and candelabra. On the right of the stove is the entrance to the hall beyond which is a glimpse of a room furnished in green and mahogany. On the left of the stove is the door to a cupboard, papered like the wall. The statue, shaded by palms, has a curtain which can be drawn to conceal it.

A door on the left leads into the Hyacinth Room, where the GIRL *sits reading.*

The back of the COLONEL *can be seen, as he sits in the Green Room, writing.*

BENGTSSON, *the Colonel's servant, comes in from the hall. He is wearing livery, and is followed by* JOHANSSON, *dressed as a waiter.*

BENGTSSON. Now you'll have to serve the tea, Johansson, while I take the coats. Have you ever done it before?

JOHANSSON. It's true I push a war chariot in the daytime, as you know, but in the evenings I go as a waiter to receptions and so forth. It's always been my dream to get into this house. They're queer people here, aren't they?

BENGTSSON. Ye-es. A bit out of the ordinary anyhow.

JOHANSSON. Is it to be a musical party or what?

BENGTSSON. The usual ghost supper, as we call it. They drink tea and don't say a word—or else the Colonel does all the talking. And they crunch their biscuits, all at the same time. It sounds like rats in an attic.

JOHANSSON. Why do you call it the ghost supper?

BENGTSSON. They look like ghosts. And they've kept this up for twenty years, always the same people saying the same things or saying nothing at all for fear of being found out.

JOHANSSON. Isn't there a mistress of the house?

27. Jesus defended his disciples' right to pick ears of corn on the sabbath by saying that even a sheep (not an ass) may be rescued from a pit on the Sabbath (Matthew 12:11).

28. See Mark 2:25–28; Matthew 12:1–8; Luke 6:1–5.

BENGTSSON. Oh yes, but she's crazy. She sits in a cupboard because her eyes can't bear the light. [*He points to the papered door.*] She sits in there.

JOHANSSON. In there?

BENGTSSON. Well, I told you they were a bit out of the ordinary.

JOHANSSON. But then—what does she look like?

BENGTSSON. Like a mummy. Do you want to have a look at her? [*He opens the door.*] There she is.

The figure of the COLONEL'S WIFE *is seen, white and shrivelled into a* MUMMY.]

JOHANSSON. Oh my God!

MUMMY. [*babbling*]. Why do you open the door? Haven't I told you to keep it closed?

BENGTSSON [*in a wheedling tone.*] Ta, ta, ta, ta. Be a good girl now, then you'll get something nice. Pretty Polly.²⁹

MUMMY [*parrot-like.*] Pretty Polly. Are you there, Jacob? Currrrr!

BENGTSSON. She thinks she's a parrot, and maybe she's right. [*To the* MUMMY.] Whistle for us, Polly. [*The* MUMMY *whistles.*]

JOHANSSON. Well, I've seen a few things in my day, but this beats everything.

BENGTSSON. You see, when a house gets old, it grows moldy, and when people stay a long time together and torment each other they go mad. The mistress of the house—shut up, Polly!—that mummy there, has been living here for forty years—same husband, same furniture, same relatives, same friends. [*He closes the papered door.*] And the goings-on in this house—well, they're beyond me. Look at that statue—that's her when she was young.

JOHANSSON. Good Lord! Is that the mummy?

BENGTSSON. Yes. It's enough to make you weep. And somehow, carried away by her own imagination or something, she's got to be a bit like a parrot—the way she talks and the way she can't stand cripples or sick people. She can't stand the sight of her own daughter, because she's sick.

JOHANSSON. Is the young lady sick?

BENGTSSON. Didn't you know that?

JOHANSSON. No. And the Colonel, who is he?

BENGTSSON. You'll see.

JOHANSSON [*looking at the statue.*] It's horrible to think that . . . How old is she now?

BENGTSSON. Nobody knows. But it's said that when she was thirty-five she looked nineteen, and that's what she made the Colonel believe³⁰ she was—here in this very house. Do you know what that black Japanese screen by the couch is for? They call it the death-screen, and when someone's going to die, they put it round —same as in a hospital.

JOHANSSON. What a horrible house! And the student was longing to get in, as if it were paradise.

---

29. She identifies herself with a parrot, that is, is reduced to repeating lifelessly what has already been said.

30. This element of deception is at the very origin of the situation.

BENGTSSON. What student? Oh, I know. The one who's coming here this evening. The Colonel and the young lady happened to meet him at the Opera, and both of them took a fancy to him. Hm. Now it's my turn to ask questions. Who is your master—the man in the wheelchair?

JOHANSSON. Well, he er . . . Is he coming here too?

BENGTSSON. He hasn't been invited.

JOHANSSON. He'll come uninvited—if need be.

[*The* OLD MAN *appears in the hall on crutches, wearing a frock-coat and top-hat. He steals forward and listens.*]

BENGTSSON. He's a regular old devil, isn't he?

JOHANSSON. Up to the ears.

BENGTSSON. He looks like old Nick himself.

JOHANSSON. And he must be a wizard too, for he goes through locked doors.[31]

[*The* OLD MAN *comes forward and takes hold of* JOHANSSON *by the ear.*]

OLD MAN. Rascal—take care! [*To* BENGTSSON.] Tell the Colonel I am here.

BENGTSSON. But we are expecting guests.

OLD MAN. I know. But my visit is as good as expected, if not exactly looked forward to.

BENGTSSON. I see. What name shall I say? Mr. Hummel?

OLD MAN. Exactly. Yes. [BENGTSSON *crosses the hall to the Green Room, the door of which he closes behind him. To* JOHANSSON.] Get out! [JOHANSSON *hesitates.*] Get out! [JOHANSSON *disappears into the hall. The* OLD MAN *inspects the room and stops in front of the statue in much astonishment.*] Amelia! It is she—she!

MUMMY. [*from the cupboard*]. Prrr-etty Polly. [*The* OLD MAN *starts.*]

OLD MAN. What was that? Is there a parrot in the room? I don't see it.

MUMMY Are you there, Jacob?

OLD MAN. The house is haunted.

MUMMY. Jacob!

OLD MAN. I'm scared. So these are the kind of secrets they guard in this house. [*With his back turned to the cupboard he stands looking at a portrait.*] There he is—he!

[*The* MUMMY *comes out behind the* OLD MAN *and gives a pull at his wig.*]

MUMMY. Currrrr! Is it . . . ? Currrrr!

OLD MAN [*jumping out of his skin.*] God in heaven! Who is it?

MUMMY [*in a natural voice.*] Is it Jacob?

OLD MAN. Yes, my name is Jacob.

MUMMY [*with emotion.*] And my name is Amelia.

OLD MAN. No, no, no . . . Oh my God!

MUMMY. That's how I look. Yes. [*Pointing to the statue.*] And that's how I *did* look. Life opens one's eyes, does it not? I live

---

31. Another hint that the Old Man has supernatural powers.

mostly in the cupboard to avoid seeing and being seen. . . . But, Jacob, what do you want here?

OLD MAN. My child. Our child.

MUMMY There she is.

OLD MAN. Where?

MUMMY. There—in the Hyacinth Room.

OLD MAN [*looking at the* GIRL]. Yes, that is she. [*Pause.*] And what about her father—the Colonel, I mean—your husband?

MUMMY. Once, when I was angry with him, I told him everything.

OLD MAN. Well . . .?

MUMMY. He didn't believe me. He just said: "That's what all wives say when they want to murder their husbands."[32] It was a terrible crime none the less. It has falsified his whole life—his family tree too. Sometimes I take a look in the Peerage, and then I say to myself: Here she is, going about with a false birth certificate like some servant girl, and for such things people are sent to the reformatory.

OLD MAN. Many do it. I seem to remember your own date of birth was given incorrectly.

MUMMY. My mother made me do that. I was not to blame. And in our crime, *you* played the biggest part.

OLD MAN. No. Your husband caused that crime, when he took my fiancée from me. I was born one who cannot forgive until he has punished. That was to me an imperative duty—and is so still.

MUMMY. What are you expecting to find in this house? What do you want? How did you get in? Is it to do with my daughter? If you touch her, you shall die.

OLD MAN. I mean well by her.

MUMMY. Then you must spare her father.

OLD MAN. No.

MUMMY. Then you shall die. In this room, behind that screen.

OLD MAN. That may be. But I can't let go once I've got my teeth into a thing.

MUMMY. You want to marry her to that student. Why? He is nothing and has nothing.

OLD MAN. He will be rich, through me.

MUMMY Have you been invited here tonight?

OLD MAN. No, but I propose to get myself an invitation to this ghost supper.

MUMMY. Do you know who is coming?

OLD MAN. Not exactly.

MUMMY. The Baron. The man who lives up above—whose father-in-law was buried this afternoon.

OLD MAN. The man who is getting a divorce in order to marry the daughter of the Caretaker's Wife . . . The man who used to be —your lover.

MUMMY. Another guest will be your former fiancée, who was seduced by my husband.

---

32. This device was used by the wife in Strindberg's play *The Father* to drive her husband insane. Strindberg had tor- tured himself by surmising that his children by his first wife might be the offspring of another man.

OLD MAN. A select gathering.

MUMMY. Oh God, if only we might die, might die!

OLD MAN. Then why have you stayed together?

MUMMY. Crime and secrets and guilt bind us together. We have broken our bonds and gone our own ways, times without number, but we are always drawn together again.

OLD MAN. I think the Colonel is coming.

MUMMY. Then I will go in to Adèle. [*Pause.*] Jacob, mind what you do. Spare him. [*Pause. She goes into the Hyacinth Room and disappears.*]

[*The* COLONEL *enters, cold and reserved, with a letter in his hand.*]

COLONEL. Be seated, please. [*Slowly the* OLD MAN *sits down. Pause. The* COLONEL *stares at him.*] You wrote this letter, sir?

OLD MAN. I did.

COLONEL. Your name is Hummel?

OLD MAN. It is. [*Pause.*]

COLONEL. As I understand, you have bought in all my unpaid promissory notes. I can only conclude that I am in your hands. What do you want?

OLD MAN. I want payment, in one way or another.

COLONEL. In what way?

OLD MAN. A very simple one. Let us not mention the money. Just bear with me in your house as a guest.

COLONEL. If so little will satisfy you . . .

OLD MAN. Thank you.

COLONEL. What else?

OLD MAN. Dismiss Bengtsson.

COLONEL. Why should I do that? My devoted servant, who has been with me a lifetime, who has the national medal for long and faithful service—why should I do that?

OLD MAN. That's how you see him—full of excellent qualities. He is not the man he appears to be.

COLONEL. Who is?

OLD MAN. [*taken aback.*] True. But Bengtsson must go.

COLONEL. Are you going to run my house?

OLD MAN. Yes. Since everything here belongs to me—furniture, curtains, dinner service, linen . . . and more too.

COLONEL. How do you mean—more?

OLD MAN. Everything. I own everything here. It is mine.

COLONEL. Very well, it is yours. But my family escutcheon[33] and my good name remain my own.

OLD MAN. No, not even those. [*Pause.*] You are not a nobleman.

COLONEL. How dare you!

OLD MAN. [*producing a document.*] If you read this extract from *The Armorial Gazette,* you will see that the family whose name you are using has been extinct for a hundred years.

COLONEL. I have heard rumors to this effect, but I inherited the

33. Shield on which armorial bearings are depicted. Here the term is used fig- uratively for the noble family itself.

name from my father. [*Reads.*] It is true. You are right. I am not a nobleman. Then I must take off my signet ring. It is true, it belongs to you. [*Gives it to him.*] There you are.

OLD MAN. [*pocketing the ring.*] Now we will continue. You are not a Colonel either.

COLONEL. I am not . . .?

OLD MAN. No. You once held the temporary rank of Colonel in the American Volunteer Force, but after the war in Cuba and the reorganization of the Army, all such titles were abolished.

COLONEL. Is this true?

OLD MAN [*indicating his pocket.*] Do you want to read it?

COLONEL. No, that's not necessary. Who are you, and what right have you to sit there stripping me in this fashion?

OLD MAN. You will see. But as far as stripping you goes . . . do you know who you are?

COLONEL. How dare you?

OLD MAN. Take off that wig and have a look at yourself in the mirror. But take your teeth out at the same time and shave off your moustache. Let Bengtsson unlace your metal stays and perhaps a certain X.Y.Z. a lackey, will recognize himself. The fellow who was a cupboard lover in a certain kitchen . . . [*The* COLONEL *reaches for the bell on the table, but* HUMMEL *checks him.*] Don't touch that bell, and don't call Bengtsson. If you do, I'll have him arrested. [*Pause.*] And now the guests are beginning to arrive. Keep your composure and we will continue to play our old parts for a while.

COLONEL. Who are you? I recognize your voice and eyes.

OLD MAN. Don't try to find out. Keep silent and obey.

[*The* STUDENT *enters and bows to the* COLONEL.]

STUDENT. How do you do, sir.

COLONEL. Welcome to my house, young man. Your splendid behavior at that great disaster has brought your name to everybody's lips, and I count it an honor to receive you in my home.

STUDENT. My humble descent, sir . . . your illustrious name and noble birth. . . .

COLONEL. May I introduce Mr. Arkenholtz—Mr. Hummel. If you will join the ladies in here, Mr. Arkenholtz—I must conclude my conversation with Mr. Hummel. [*He shows the* STUDENT *into the Hyacinth Room, where he remains visible, talking shyly to the* GIRL.] A splendid young man, musical, sings, writes poetry. If he only had blue blood in him, if he were of the same station, I don't think I should object . . .

OLD MAN. To what?

COLONEL. To my daughter . . .

OLD MAN. Your daughter! But apropos of that, why does she spend all her time in there?

COLONEL. She insists on being in the Hyacinth Room except when she is out-of-doors. It's a peculiarity of hers. Ah, here comes Miss Beatrice von Holsteinkrona—a charming woman, a pillar of the Church, with just enough money of her own to suit her birth and position.

OLD MAN [*to himself.*] My fiancée.

[*The* FIANCÉE *enters, looking a little crazy.*]

COLONEL. Miss Holsteinkrona—Mr. Hummel. [*The* FIANCÉE *curtseys and takes a seat. The* ARISTOCRAT *enters and seats himself. He wears mourning and looks mysterious.*] Baron Skanskorg . . .

OLD MAN [*aside, without rising.*] That's the jewel-thief, I think. [*To the* COLONEL.] If you bring in the Mummy, the party will be complete.

COLONEL [*at the door of the Hyacinth Room.*] Polly!

MUMMY [*entering*] Currrrr . . . !

COLONEL. Are the young people to come in too?

OLD MAN. No, not the young people. They shall be spared. [*They all sit silent in a circle.*]

COLONEL. Shall we have the tea brought in?

OLD MAN. What's the use? No one wants tea. Why should we pretend about it?

COLONEL. Then shall we talk?

OLD MAN. Talk of the weather, which we know? Inquire about each other's health, which we know just as well. I prefer silence—then one can hear thoughts and see the past. Silence cannot hide anything—but words can. I read the other day that differences of language originated among savages for the purpose of keeping one tribe's secrets hidden from another. Every language therefore is a code, and he who finds the key can understand every language in the world. But this does not prevent secrets from being exposed without a key, specially when there is a question of paternity to be proved. Proof in a Court of Law is another matter. Two false witnesses suffice to prove anything about which they are agreed, but one does not take witnesses along on the kind of explorations I have in mind. Nature herself has instilled in human beings a sense of modesty which tries to hide what should be hidden, but we slip into situations unintentionally, and by chance sometimes the deepest secret is divulged—the mask torn from the impostor, the villain exposed. . . . [*Pause. All look at each other in silence.*] What a silence there is now! [*Long silence.*] Here, for instance, in this honorable house, in this elegant home, where beauty, wealth and culture are united. . . . [*Long silence.*] All of us now sitting here know who we are—do we not? There's no need for me to tell you. And you know me, although you pretend ignorance. [*He indicates the Hyacinth Room.*] In there is my daughter. *Mine*—you know that too. She had lost the desire to live, without knowing why. The fact is she was withering away in this air charged with crime and deceit and falseness of every kind. That is why I looked for a friend for her in whose company she might enjoy the light and warmth of noble deeds. [*Long silence.*] That was my mission in this house: to pull up the weeds, to expose the crimes, to settle all accounts so that those young people might start afresh in this home, which is my gift to them. [*Long silence.*] Now I am going to grant safe-conduct, to each of you in his and her proper time and turn. Whoever stays I shall have arrested. [*Long silence.*] Do you hear

the clock ticking like a death-watch beetle in the wall? Do you
hear what it says? "It's time, it's time, it's time." When it
strikes, in a few moments, your time will be up. Then you can
go, but not before. It's raising its arm against you before it
strikes. Listen! It is warning you. "The clock can strike." And I
can strike too. [*He strikes the table with one of his crutches.*]
Do you hear? [*Silence. The* MUMMY *goes up to the clock and
stops it, then speaks in a normal and serious voice.*]

MUMMY. But I can stop time in its course. I can wipe out the past
and undo what is done. But not with bribes, not with threats—
only through suffering and repentance. [*She goes up to the* OLD
MAN.] We are miserable human beings, that we know. We have
erred and we have sinned, we like all the rest. We are not what
we seem, because at bottom we are better than ourselves, since
we detest our sins. But when you, Jacob Hummel, with your false
name, choose to sit in judgment over us, you prove yourself worse
than us miserable sinners. For you are not the one you appear to
be. You are a thief of human souls. You stole me once with false
promises. You murdered the Consul who was buried today; you
strangled him with debts. You have stolen the student, binding
him by the pretence of a claim on his father, who never owed
you a farthing. [*Having tried to rise and speak, the* OLD MAN
*sinks back in his chair and crumples up more and more as she
goes on.*] But there is one dark spot in your life which I am not
quite sure about, although I have my suspicions. I think Bengtsson knows. [*She rings the bell on the table.*]

OLD MAN. No, not Bengtsson, not him.

MUMMY. So he does know. [*She rings again. The* MILKMAID
appears in the hallway door, unseen by all but the OLD MAN, *who
shrinks back in horror. The* MILKMAID *vanishes as* BENGTSSON
enters.] Do you know this man, Bengtsson?

BENGTSSON. Yes, I know him and he knows me. Life, as you are
aware, has its ups and downs. I have been in his service; another
time he was in mine. For two whole years he was a sponger in my
kitchen. As he had to be away by three, the dinner was got ready
at two, and the family had to eat the warmed-up leavings of that
brute. He drank the soup stock, which the cook then filled up
with water. He sat out there like a vampire,[34] sucking the
marrow out of the house, so that we became like skeletons. And
he nearly got us put in prison when we called the cook a thief.
Later I met the man in Hamburg under another name. He was a
usurer then, a blood-sucker. But while he was there he was
charged with having lured a young girl out on to the ice so as to
drown her, because she had seen him commit a crime he was
afraid would be discovered. . . . [*The* MUMMY *passes her hand
over the* OLD MAN's *face.*]

MUMMY. *This* is you. Now give up the notes and the Will.
[JOHANSSON *appears in the hallway door and watches the scene

34. This replaces the less offensive   Hummel.
bumblebee image suggested by the name

with great interest, knowing he is now to be freed from slavery. The OLD MAN *produces a bundle of papers and throws it on the table. The* MUMMY *goes over and strokes his back.*] Parrot. Are you there, Jacob?

OLD MAN [*like a parrot.*] Jacob is here. Pretty Polly.[35] Currrrr!

MUMMY. May the clock strike?

OLD MAN [*with a clucking sound.*] The clock may strike. [*Imitating a cuckoo clock.*] Cuckoo, cuckoo, cuckoo. . . . [*The* MUMMY *opens the cupboard door.*]

MUMMY. Now the clock has struck. Rise, and enter the cupboard where I have spent twenty years repenting our crime. A rope is hanging there, which you can take as the one with which you strangled the Consul, and with which you meant to strangle your benefactor. . . . Go! [*The* OLD MAN *goes in to the cupboard. The* MUMMY *closes the door.*] Bengtsson! Put up the screen—the death-screen. [BENGTSSON *places the screen in front of the door.*] It is finished. God have mercy on his soul.

ALL. Amen. [*Long silence.*]

[*The* GIRL *and the* STUDENT *appear in the Hyacinth Room. She has a harp, on which he plays a prelude, and then accompanies the* STUDENT'S *recitation.*]

STUDENT. I saw the sun. To me it seemed
that I beheld the Hidden.
Men must reap what they have sown;
blest is he whose deeds are good.
Deeds which you have wrought in fury,
cannot in evil find redress.
Comfort him you have distressed
with loving-kindness—this will heal.
No fear has he who does no ill.
Sweet is innocence.

Scene III

Inside the Hyacinth Room. *The general effect of the room is exotic and oriental. There are hyacinths everywhere, of every color, some in pots, some with the bulbs in glass vases and the roots going down into the water.*

On top of the tiled stove is a large seated Buddha, in whose lap rests a bulb from which rises the stem of a shallot (Allium ascalonicum), bearing its globular cluster of white, starlike flowers.

On the right is an open door, leading into the Round Room, where the COLONEL *and the* MUMMY *are seated, inactive and silent. A part of the death-screen is also visible.*

On the left is a door to the pantry and kitchen.

The STUDENT *and the* GIRL *(Adèle) are beside the table; he standing, she seated with her harp.*

35. The Old Man, on the point of attaining final victory, is now defeated and entangled in his own past. Therefore he takes over the repetitive role of the Mummy, who has escaped by seeing the possibility of salvation "through suffering and repentance."

GIRL. Now sing to my flowers.

STUDENT. Is this the flower of your soul?

GIRL. The one and only. Do you too love the hyacinth?

STUDENT. I love it above all other flowers—its virginal shape rising straight and slender out of the bulb, resting on the water and sending its pure white roots down into the colorless fluid. I love its colors; the snow-white, pure as innocence, the yellow honey-sweet, the youthful pink, the ripe red, but best of all the blue—the dewy blue, deep-eyed and full of faith. I love them all, more than gold or pearls. I have loved them ever since I was a child, have worshipped them because they have all the fine qualities I lack. . . . And yet . . .

GIRL. Go on.

STUDENT. My love is not returned, for these beautiful blossoms hate me.

GIRL. How do you mean?

STUDENT. Their fragrance, strong and pure as the early winds of spring which have passed over melting snows, confuses my senses, deafens me, blinds me, thrusts me out of the room, bombards me with poisoned arrows that wound my heart and set my head on fire. Do you know the legend of that flower?

GIRL. Tell it to me.

STUDENT. First its meaning. The bulb is the earth, resting on the water or buried in the soil. Then the stalk rises, straight as the axis of the world, and at the top are the six-pointed star-flowers.

GIRL. Above the earth—the stars. Oh, that is wonderful! Where did you learn this? How did you find it out?

STUDENT. Let me think. . . . In your eyes. And so, you see, it is an image of the Cosmos. This is why Buddha[36] sits holding the earth-bulb, his eyes brooding as he watches it grow, outward and upward, transforming itself into a heaven. This poor earth will become a heaven. It is for this that Buddha waits.

GIRL. I see it now. Is not the snowflake six-pointed too like the hyacinth flower?

STUDENT. You are right. The snowflakes must be falling stars.

GIRL. And the snowdrop is a snow-star, grown out of snow.

STUDENT. But the largest and most beautiful of all the stars in the firmament, the golden-red Sirius, is the narcissus with its gold and red chalice and its six white rays.

GIRL. Have you seen the shallot in bloom?

STUDENT. Indeed I have. It bears its blossoms within a ball, a globe like the celestial one, strewn with white stars.

GIRL. Oh how glorious! Whose thought was that?

STUDENT. Yours.

GIRL. Yours.

STUDENT. Ours. We have given birth to it together. We are wedded.

GIRL. Not yet.

STUDENT. What's still to do?

36. The flower traditionally associated with Buddha is the lotus, which also grows on the surface of the water.

GIRL. Waiting, ordeals, patience.

STUDENT. Very well. Put me to the test. [*Pause.*] Tell me. Why do your parents sit in there so silently, not saying a single word?

GIRL. Because they have nothing to say to each other, and because neither believes what the other says. This is how my father puts it: What's the point of talking, when neither of us can fool the other?[37]

STUDENT. What a horrible thing to hear!

GIRL. Here comes the Cook. Look at her, how big and fat she is. [*They watch the* COOK, *although the audience cannot yet see her.*]

STUDENT. What does she want?

GIRL. To ask me about the dinner. I have to do the housekeeping as my mother's ill.

STUDENT. What have we to do with the kitchen?

GIRL. We must eat. Look at the Cook. I can't bear the sight of her.

STUDENT. Who is that ogress?

GIRL. She belongs to the Hummel family of vampires. She is eating us.

STUDENT. Why don't you dismiss her?

GIRL. She won't go. We have no control over her. We've got her for our sins. Can't you see that we are pining and wasting away?[38]

STUDENT. Don't you get enough to eat?

GIRL. Yes, we get many dishes, but all the strength has gone. She boils the nourishment out of the meat and gives us the fibre and water, while she drinks the stock herself. And when there's a roast, she first boils out the marrow, eats the gravy and drinks the juices herself. Everything she touches loses its savor. It's as if she sucked with her eyes. We get the grounds when she has drunk the coffee. She drinks the wine and fills the bottles up with water.

STUDENT. Send her packing.

GIRL. We can't.

STUDENT. Why not?

GIRL. We don't know. She won't go. No one has any control over her. She has taken all our strength from us.

STUDENT. May I get rid of her?

GIRL. No. It must be as it is. Here she is. She will ask me what is to be for dinner. I shall tell her. She will make objections and get her own way.

STUDENT. Let her do the ordering herself then.

GIRL. She won't do that.

STUDENT. What an extraordinary house! It is bewitched.

GIRL. Yes. But now she is turning back, because she has seen you.

---

37. Reciprocal deceit and pretense are presented as the base that makes conversation possible.

38. Strindberg sometimes complained that the food set before him did not nourish him properly. The Cook is, among other things, his highly personal version of the class struggle—with victory, it would seem, lying inevitably within the grasp of the "underclass," as he called it.

THE COOK [*in the doorway.*] No, that wasn't the reason. [*She grins, showing all her teeth.*]

STUDENT. Get out!

COOK. When it suits me. [*Pause.*] It does suit me now. [*She disappears.*]

GIRL. Don't lose your temper. Practise patience. She is one of the ordeals we have to go through in this house. You see, we have a housemaid too, whom we have to clean up after.

STUDENT. I am done for. *Cor in æthere.*[39] Music!

GIRL. Wait.

STUDENT. Music!

GIRL. Patience. This room is called the room of ordeals. It looks beautiful, but it is full of defects.

STUDENT. Really? Well, such things must be seen to. It is very beautiful, but a little cold. Why don't you have a fire?

GIRL. Because it smokes.

STUDENT. Can't you have the chimney swept?

GIRL. It doesn't help. You see that writing-desk there?

STUDENT. An unusually fine piece.

GIRL. But it wobbles.[40] Every day I put a piece of cork under that leg and every day the housemaid takes it away when she sweeps and I have to cut a new piece. The penholder is covered with ink every morning and so is the inkstand. I have to clean them up every morning after that woman, as sure as the sun rises. [*Pause.*] What's the worst job you can think of?

STUDENT. To count the washing. Ugh!

GIRL. That I have to do. Ugh!

STUDENT. What else?

GIRL. To be waked in the middle of the night and have to get up and see to the window, which the housemaid has left banging.

STUDENT. What else?

GIRL. To get up on a ladder and tie the cord on the damper[41] which the housemaid has torn off.

STUDENT. What else?

GIRL. To sweep after her, to dust after her, to light the fire in the stove when all she's done is throw in some wood. To see to the damper, to wipe the glasses, to lay the table over again, to open the bottles, to see that the rooms are aired, to remake my bed, to rinse the water-bottle when it's green with sediment, to buy matches and soap which are always lacking, to wipe the chimneys and trim the wicks to keep the lamps from smoking—and so that they don't go out when we have company, I have to fill them myself. . . .

STUDENT. Music!

39. Latin for "A horn is heard in the air."

40. Strindberg was abnormally sensitive to the least flaw in everyday domestic arrangements.

41. "Damper to the big stove" [translator's note].

GIRL. Wait. The labor comes first. The labor of keeping the dirt of life at a distance.

STUDENT. But you are wealthy and have two servants.

GIRL. It doesn't help. Even if we had three. Living is hard work, and sometimes I grow tired. [*Pause.*] Think then if there were a nursery as well.

STUDENT. The greatest of joys.

GIRL. And the costliest. Is life worth so much hardship?

STUDENT. That must depend on the reward you expect for your labors. I would not shrink from anything to win your hand.

GIRL. Don't say that. You can never have me.

STUDENT. Why not?

GIRL. You mustn't ask. [*Pause.*]

STUDENT. You dropped your bracelet out of the window. . . .

GIRL. Because my hand has grown so thin. [*Pause. The* COOK *appears with a Japanese bottle in her hand.*] There she is—the one who devours me and all of us.

STUDENT. What has she in her hand?

GIRL. It is the bottle of coloring matter that has letters like scorpions on it. It is the soy which turns water into soup and takes the place of gravy. She makes cabbage soup with it—and mock-turtle soup too.

STUDENT [*to* COOK.] Get out!

COOK. You drain us of sap, and we drain you. We take the blood and leave you the water, but colored . . . colored. I am going now, but all the same I shall stay, as long as I please. [*She goes out.*]

STUDENT. Why did Bengtsson get a medal?

GIRL. For his great merits.

STUDENT. Has he no defects?

GIRL. Yes, great ones. But you don't get a medal for them. [*They smile.*]

STUDENT. You have many secrets in this house.

GIRL. As in all others. Permit us to keep ours.

STUDENT. Don't you approve of candor?

GIRL. Yes—within reason.

STUDENT. Sometimes I'm seized with a raging desire to say all I think. But I know the world would go to pieces if one were completely candid. [*Pause.*] I went to a funeral the other day . . . in church. It was very solemn and beautiful.

GIRL. Was it Mr. Hummel's?

STUDENT. My false benefactor's—yes. At the head of the coffin stood an old friend of the deceased. He carried the mace. I was deeply impressed by the dignified manner and moving words of the clergyman. I cried. We all cried. Afterwards we went to a tavern, and there I learned that the man with the mace had been in love with the dead man's son. . . . [*The* GIRL *stares at him,*

42. What the Student had taken as a sign of encouragement was a trivial mis- hap—and a hook baited by Destiny.

trying to understand.] And that the dead man had borrowed money from his son's admirer. [*Pause.*] Next day the clergyman was arrested for embezzling the church funds. A pretty story.

GIRL. Oh . . . ! [*Pause.*]

STUDENT. Do you know how I am thinking about you now?

GIRL. Don't tell me, or I shall die.

STUDENT. I must, or I shall die.

GIRL. It is in asylums that people say everything they think.

STUDENT. Exactly. My father finished up in an asylum.

GIRL. Was he ill?

STUDENT. No, he was well, but he was mad. You see, he broke out once—in these circumstances. Like all of us, he was surrounded with a circle of acquaintances; he called them friends for short. They were a lot of rotters, of course, as most people are, but he had to have some society—he couldn't get on all alone. Well, as you know, in everyday life no one tells people what he thinks of them, and he didn't either. He knew perfectly well what frauds they were—he'd sounded the depths of their deceit—but as he was a wise and well-bred man, he was always courteous to them. Then one day he gave a big party. It was in the evening and he was tired by the day's work and by the strain of holding his tongue and at the same time talking rubbish with his guests. . . . [*The* GIRL *is frightened.*] Well, at the dinner table he rapped for silence, raised his glass, and began to speak. Then something loosed the trigger. He made an enormous speech in which he stripped the whole company naked, one after the other, and told them of all their treachery. Then, tired out, he sat down on the table and told them all to go to hell.

GIRL. Oh!

STUDENT. I was there, and I shall never forget what happened then. Father and Mother came to blows, the guests rushed for the door . . . and my father was taken to a madhouse, where he died. [*Pause.*] Water that is still too long stagnates, and so it is in this house too. There is something stagnating here. And yet I thought it was paradise itself that first time I saw you coming in here. There I stood that Sunday morning, gazing in. I saw a Colonel who was no Colonel. I had a benefactor who was a thief and had to hang himself. I saw a mummy who was not a mummy and an old maid—what of the maidenhood, by the way? Where is beauty to be found? In nature, and in my own mind, when it is in its Sunday clothes. Where are honor and faith? In fairy-tales and children's fancies. Where is anything that fulfills its promise? In my imagination. Now your flowers have poisoned me and I have given the poison back to you. I asked you to become my wife in a home full of poetry and song and music. Then the Cook came. . . . *Sursum Corda!*[43] Try once more to strike fire

---

43. Latin for "Lift up your hearts" or "Be of good cheer." They are the first words in the Preface of the Mass.

and glory out of the golden harp. Try, I beg you, I implore you on my knees. [*Pause.*] Then I will do it myself. [*He picks up the harp, but the strings give no sound.*] It is dumb and deaf. To think that the most beautiful flowers are so poisonous, are the most poisonous. The curse lies over the whole of creation, over life itself. Why will you not be my bride? Because the very life-spring within you is sick . . . now I can feel that vampire in the kitchen beginning to suck me. I believe she is a Lamia,[44] one of those that suck the blood of children. It is always in the kitchen quarters that the seed-leaves of the children are nipped, if it has not already happened in the bedroom. There are poisons that destroy the sight and poisons that open the eyes. I seem to have been born with the latter kind, for I cannot see what is ugly as beautiful, nor call evil good. I cannot. Jesus Christ descended into hell. That was His pilgrimage on earth[45]—to this mad-house, this prison, this charnel-house, this earth. And the madmen killed Him when He wanted to set them free; but the robber they let go. The robber[46] always gets the sympathy. Woe! Woe to us all. Saviour of the world, save us! We perish. [*And now the* GIRL *has drooped, and it is seen that she is dying. She rings.* BENGTSSON *enters.*]

GIRL. Bring the screen. Quick, I am dying. [BENGTSSON *comes back with the screen, opens it and arranges it in front of the* GIRL.]

STUDENT. The Liberator is coming. Welcome, pale and gentle one. Sleep, you lovely, innocent, doomed creature, suffering for no fault of your own. Sleep without dreaming, and when you wake again . . . may you be greeted by a sun that does not burn, in a home without dust, by friends without stain, by a love without flaw. You wise and gentle Buddha, sitting there waiting for a Heaven to sprout from the earth, grant us patience in our ordeal and purity of will, so that this hope may not be confounded. [*The strings of the harp hum softly and a white light fills the room.*]

I saw the sun. To me it seemed
that I beheld the Hidden.
Men must reap what they have sown,
blest is he whose deeds are good.
Deeds which you have wrought in fury,
cannot in evil find redress.
Comfort him you have distressed
with loving-kindness—this will heal.
No fear has he who does no ill.
Sweet is innocence.

[*A faint moaning is heard behind the screen.*] You poor little child, child of this world of illusion, guilt, suffering and death,

---

44. A vampirelike creature of classical antiquity, having the head and breast of a woman and the body of a serpent.

45. Elsewhere Strindberg has presented earth as purgatory, here he sees it as hell.

46. Barabbas, released by Pilate, whereas Jesus was scourged and taken away to be crucified (Mark 15:7–15).

this world of endless change, disappointment, and pain. May the Lord of Heaven be merciful to you upon your journey.

[*The room disappears. Böcklin's picture* The Island of the Dead[47] *is seen in the distance, and from the island comes music, soft, sweet, and melancholy.*]

47. The Swiss-German painter Arnold Böcklin (1827–1901) is remembered today above all for this picture, which represents, in somber tones, the vessel conveying the dead on its passage to the island. Copies of this picture and of its companion piece, *The Island of the Living*, flanked the proscenium arch of Strindberg's Intimate Theater.

LUIGI PIRANDELLO

(1867–1936)

Henry IV*

A Tragedy in Three Acts

Characters

HENRY IV[1]
THE MARCHIONESS MATILDA SPINA
FRIDA, *her daughter*
CHARLES DI NOLLI, *the young Marquis*
BARON TITO BELCREDI
DOCTOR DIONYSIUS GENONI

HAROLD (FRANK)
LANDOLPH (LOLO)
ORDULPH (MOMO)
BERTHOLD (FINO)

} *The four private counsellors (The names in brackets are nicknames)*

JOHN, *the old waiter*
THE TWO VALETS IN COSTUME

A Solitary Villa in Italy in Our Own Time

* From *Naked Masks: Five Plays* by Luigi Pirandello. Translated by Edward Storer. Edited by Eric Bentley. Copyright 1922, 1952, by E. P. Dutton & Co., Inc. Renewal, 1950, by Stefano, Fausto, and Lietta Pirandello. Dutton Paperback Edition. Reprinted by permission of E. P. Dutton & Co., Inc.

1. German emperor, 1065–1106. During a reign filled with conflict, his greatest antagonist was Gregory VII, pope from 1073 to 1085. Twice excommunicated, Henry had on one occasion, at Canossa, to wait three days in the snow before Gregory received and pardoned him.

Act I

Salon in the villa, furnished and decorated so as to look exactly like the throne room of Henry IV in the royal residence at Goslar.[2] *Among the antique decorations there are two modern life-size portraits in oil painting. They are placed against the back wall, and mounted in a wooden stand that runs the whole length of the wall. (It is wide and protrudes, so that it is like a large bench.) One of the paintings is on the right; the other on the left of the throne, which is in the middle of the wall and divides the stand.*[3]

The Imperial chair and Baldachin.[3]

The two portraits represent a lady and a gentleman, both young, dressed up in carnival costumes: one as "Henry IV," the other as the "Marchioness Matilda of Tuscany."[4] *Exits to right and left.*

When the curtain goes up, the two valets jump down, as if surprised, from the stand on which they have been lying, and go and take their positions, as rigid as statues, on either side below the throne with their halberds in their hands. Soon after, from the second exit, right, enter HAROLD, LANDOLPH, ORDULPH *and* BERTHOLD, *young men employed by the* MARQUIS CHARLES DI NOLLI *to play the part of "Secret Counsellors" at the court of "Henry IV." They are, therefore, dressed like German knights of the XIth century.* BERTHOLD, *nicknamed Fino, is just entering on his duties for the first time. His companions are telling him what he has to do and amusing themselves at his expense. The scene is to be played rapidly and vivaciously.*

LANDOLPH [*to* BERTHOLD *as if explaining*]. And this is the throne room.

HAROLD. At Goslar.

ORDULPH. Or at the castle in the Hartz, if you prefer.

HAROLD. Or at Wurms.

LANDOLPH. According as to what's doing, it jumps about with us, now here, now there.

ORDULPH. In Saxony.

HAROLD. In Lombardy.

LANDOLPH. On the Rhine.

ONE OF THE VALETS [*without moving, just opening his lips*]. I say . . .

HAROLD [*turning round*]. What is it?

FIRST VALET [*like a statue*]. Is he coming in or not? [*He alludes to* HENRY IV.]

ORDULPH. No, no, he's asleep. You needn't worry.

SECOND VALET [*releasing his pose, taking a long breath and going to lie down again on the stand*]. You might have told us at once.

FIRST VALET [*going over to* HAROLD]. Have you got a match, please?

---

2. The permanent capital of Henry IV.
3. A fixed canopy.

4. Henry's lifelong enemy, she owned the castle at Canossa.

LANDOLPH. What? You can't smoke a pipe here, you know.

FIRST VALET [*while* HAROLD *offers him a light*]. No; a cigarette. [*Lights his cigarette and lies down again on the stand.*]

BERTHOLD [*who has been looking on in amazement, walking round the room, regarding the costumes of the others*]. I say . . . this room . . . these costumes . . . Which Henry IV is it? I don't quite get it. Is he Henry IV of France or not? [*At this* LANDOLPH, HAROLD, *and* ORDULPH, *burst out laughing.*]

LANDOLPH [*still laughing; and pointing to* BERTHOLD *as if inviting the others to make fun of him*]. Henry of France he says: ha! ha!

ORDULPH. He thought it was the king of France!

HAROLD. Henry IV of Germany, my boy: the Salian dynasty![5]

ORDULPH. The great and tragic Emperor!

LANDOLPH. He of Canossa. Every day we carry on here the terrible war between Church and State, by Jove.

ORDULPH. The Empire against the Papacy!

HAROLD. Anti-popes against the Pope!

LANDOLPH. Kings against anti-kings!

ORDULPH. War on the Saxons!

HAROLD. And all the rebel Princes!

LANDOLPH. Against the Emperor's own sons!

BERTHOLD [*covering his head with his hands to protect himself against this avalanche of information*]. I understand! I understand! Naturally, I didn't get the idea at first. I'm right then: these aren't costumes of the XVIth century?

HAROLD. XVIth century be hanged!

ORDULPH. We're somewhere between a thousand and eleven hundred.

LANDOLPH. Work it out for yourself: if we are before Canossa on the 25th of January, 1071 . . .[6]

BERTHOLD [*more confused than ever*]. Oh my God! What a mess I've made of it!

ORDULPH. Well, just slightly, if you supposed you were at the French court.

BERTHOLD. All that historical stuff I've swatted up!

LANDOLPH. My dear boy, it's four hundred years earlier.

BERTHOLD [*getting angry*]. Good Heavens! You ought to have told me it was Germany and not France. I can't tell you how many books I've read in the last fifteen days.

HAROLD. But I say, surely you knew that poor Tito was Adalbert of Bremen,[7] here?

BERTHOLD. Not a damned bit!

LANDOLPH. Well, don't you see how it is? When Tito died, the Marquis Di Nolli . . .

BERTHOLD. Oh, it was he, was it? He might have told me.

HAROLD. Perhaps he thought you knew.

LANDOLPH. He didn't want to engage anyone else in substitution.

---

5. Line of German emperors, in power from 1024 to 1125.

6. 1077 is the correct date.

7. Archbishop, appointed by Henry III, and regent until Henry IV came of age in 1066.

He thought the remaining three of us would do. But *he* began to cry out: "With Adalbert driven away . . .":[8] because, you see, he didn't imagine poor Tito was dead; but that, as Bishop Adalbert, the rival bishops of Cologne and Mayence had driven him off . . .

BERTHOLD [*taking his head in his hand*]. But I don't know a word of what you're talking about.

ORDULPH. So much the worse for you, my boy!

HAROLD. But the trouble is that not even we know who you are.

BERTHOLD. What? Not even you? You don't know who I'm supposed to be?

ORDULPH. Hum! "Berthold."

BERTHOLD. But which Berthold? And why Berthold?

LANDOLPH [*solemnly imitating* HENRY IV]. "They've driven Adalbert away from me. Well then, I want Berthold! I want Berthold!" That's what he said.

HAROLD. We three looked one another in the eyes: who's got to be Berthold?

ORDULPH. And so here you are, "Berthold," my dear fellow!

LANDOLPH. I'm afraid you will make a bit of a mess of it.

BERTHOLD [*indignant, getting ready to go*]. Ah, no! Thanks very much, but I'm off! I'm out of this!

HAROLD [*restraining him with the other two, amid laughter*]. Steady now! Don't get excited!

LANDOLPH. Cheer up, my dear fellow! We don't any of us know who we are really. He's Harold; he's Ordulph! I'm Landolph! That's the way he calls us. We've got used to it. But who are we? Names of the period! Yours, too, is a name of the period: Berthold! Only one of us, poor Tito, had got a really decent part, as you can read in history: that of the Bishop of Bremen. He was just like a real bishop. Tito did it awfully well, poor chap!

HAROLD. Look at the study he put into it!

LANDOLPH. Why, he even ordered his Majesty about, opposed his views, guided and counselled him. We're "secret counsellors"—in a manner of speaking only; because it is written in history that Henry IV was hated by the upper aristocracy for surrounding himself at court with young men of the bourgeoisie.

ORDULPH. Us, that is.

LANDOLPH. Yes, small devoted vassals, a bit dissolute and very gay . . .

BERTHOLD. So I've got to be gay as well?

HAROLD. I should say so! Same as we are!

ORDULPH. And it isn't too easy, you know.

LANDOLPH. It's a pity; because the way we're got up, we could do a fine historical reconstruction. There's any amount of material in the story of Henry IV. But, as a matter of fact, we do nothing. We have the form without the content. We're worse than the real secret counsellors of Henry IV; because certainly no one had given them a part to play—at any rate, they didn't feel they had a part to play. It was their life. They looked after their own interests at

---

8. On acceding to the throne in 1066, Henry had been obliged to dismiss him.

the expense of others, sold investitures and—what not! We stop here in this magnificent court—for what?—Just doing nothing. We're like so many puppets hung on the wall, waiting for someone to come and move us or make us talk.

HAROLD. Ah, no, old sport, not quite that! We've got to give the proper answer, you know. There's trouble if he asks you something and you don't chip in with the cue.

LANDOLPH. Yes, that's true.

BERTHOLD. Don't rub it in too hard! How the devil am I to give him the proper answer, if I've swatted up Henry IV of France, and now he turns out to be Henry IV of Germany? [*The other three laugh.*]

HAROLD. You'd better start and prepare yourself at once.

ORDULPH. We'll help you out.

HAROLD. We've got any amount of books on the subject. A brief run through the main points will do to begin with.

ORDULPH. At any rate, you must have got some sort of general idea.

HAROLD. Look here! [*Turns him around and shows him the portrait of the Marchioness Matilda on the wall.*] Who's that?

BERTHOLD [*looking at it*]. That? Well, the thing seems to me somewhat out of place, anyway: two modern paintings in the midst of all this respectable antiquity!

HAROLD. You're right! They weren't there in the beginning. There are two niches there behind the pictures. They were going to put up two statues in the style of the period. Then the places were covered with those canvases there.

LANDOLPH [*interrupting and continuing*]. They would certainly be out of place if they really were paintings!

BERTHOLD. What are they, if they aren't paintings?

LANDOLPH. Go and touch them! Pictures all right . . . but for him! [*Makes a mysterious gesture to the right, alluding to* HENRY IV.] . . . who never touches them! . . .

BERTHOLD. No? What are they for him?

LANDOLPH. Well, I'm only supposing, you know; but I imagine I'm about right. They're images such as . . . well—such as a mirror might throw back. Do you understand? That one there represents himself, as he is in this throne room, which is all in the style of the period. What's there to marvel at? If we put you before a mirror, won't you see yourself, alive, but dressed up in ancient costume? Well, it's as if there were two mirrors there, which cast back living images in the midst of a world which, as you well see, when you have lived with us, comes to life too.

BERTHOLD. I say, look here . . . I've no particular desire to go mad here.

HAROLD. Go mad, be hanged! You'll have a fine time!

BERTHOLD. Tell me this: how have you all managed to become so learned?

LANDOLPH. My dear fellow, you can't go back over 800 years of history without picking up a bit of experience.

HAROLD. Come on! Come on! You'll see how quickly you get into it!

ORDULPH. You'll learn wisdom, too, at this school.

BERTHOLD. Well, for Heaven's sake, help me a bit! Give me the main lines, anyway.

HAROLD. Leave it to us. We'll do it all between us.

LANDOLPH. We'll put your wires on you and fix you up like a first-class marionette. Come along! [THEY *take him by the arm to lead him away.*]

BERTHOLD [*stopping and looking at the portrait on the wall*]. Wait a minute! You haven't told me who that is. The Emperor's wife?

HAROLD. No! The Emperor's wife is Bertha of Susa, the sister of Amadeus II of Savoy.

ORDULPH. And the Emperor, who wants to be young with us, can't stand her, and wants to put her away.

LANDOLPH. That is his most ferocious enemy: Matilda, Marchioness of Tuscany.

BERTHOLD. Ah, I've got it: the one who gave hospitality to the Pope!

LANDOLPH. Exactly: at Canossa!

ORDULPH. Pope Gregory VII!

HAROLD. Our *bête noir!* Come on! come on! [*All four move toward the right to go out, when, from the left, the old servant* JOHN *enters in evening dress.*]

JOHN [*quickly, anxiously*]. Hss! Hss! Frank! Lolo!

HAROLD [*turning round*]. What is it?

BERTHOLD [*marvelling at seeing a man in modern clothes enter the throne room*]. Oh! I say, this is a bit too much, this chap here!

LANDOLPH. A man of the XXth century, here! Oh, go away! [THEY *run over to him, pretending to menace him and throw him out.*]

ORDULPH [*heroically*]. Messenger of Gregory VII, away!

HAROLD. Away! Away!

JOHN [*annoyed, defending himself*]. Oh, stop it! Stop it, I tell you!

ORDULPH. No, you can't set foot here!

HAROLD. Out with him!

LANDOLPH [*to* BERTHOLD]. Magic, you know! He's a demon conjured up by the Wizard of Rome! Out with your swords! [*Makes as if to draw a sword.*]

JOHN [*shouting*]. Stop it, will you? Don't play the fool with me! The Marquis has arrived with some friends . . .

LANDOLPH. Good! Good! Are there ladies too?

ORDULPH. Old or young?

JOHN. There are two gentlemen.

HAROLD. But the ladies, the ladies, who are they?

JOHN. The Marchioness and her daughter.

LANDOLPH [*surprised*]. What do you say?

ORDULPH. The Marchioness?

JOHN. The Marchioness! The Marchioness!

HAROLD. Who are the gentlemen?

JOHN. I don't know.

HAROLD [*to* BERTHOLD]. They're coming to bring us a message from the Pope, do you see?

ORDULPH. All messengers of Gregory VII! What fun!

JOHN. Will you let me speak, or not?

ORDULPH. Come on then!

JOHN. One of the two gentlemen is a doctor, I fancy.

LANDOLPH. Oh, I see, one of the usual doctors.

HAROLD. Bravo Berthold, you'll bring us luck!

LANDOLPH. You wait and see how we'll manage this doctor!

BERTHOLD. It looks as if I were going to get into a nice mess right away.

JOHN. If the gentlemen would allow me to speak . . . they want to come here into the throne room.

LANDOLPH [*surprised*]. What? She? The Marchioness here?

HAROLD. Then this is something quite different! No play-acting this time!

LANDOLPH. We'll have a real tragedy: that's what!

BERTHOLD [*curious*]. Why? Why?

ORDULPH [*pointing to the portrait*]. She is that person there, don't you understand?

LANDOLPH. The daughter is the fiancée of the Marquis. But what have they come for, I should like to know?

ORDULPH. If he sees her, there'll be trouble.

LANDOLPH. Perhaps he won't recognize her any more.

JOHN. You must keep him there, if he should wake up . . .

ORDULPH. Easier said than done, by Jove!

HAROLD. You know what he's like!

JOHN. —even by force, if necessary! Those are my orders. Go on! Go on!

HAROLD. Yes, because who knows if he hasn't already wakened up?

ORDULPH. Come on then!

LANDOLPH [*going towards* JOHN *with the others*]. You'll tell us later what it all means.

JOHN [*shouting after them*]. Close the door there, and hide the key! That other door too. [*Pointing to the other door on right.*]

JOHN [*to the* TWO VALETS]. Be off, you two! There! [*Pointing to exit right.*] Close the door after you, and hide the key!

[*The* TWO VALETS *go out by the first door on right.* JOHN *moves over to the left to show in:* DONNA MATILDA SPINA, *the young* MARCHIONESS FRIDA, DR. DIONYSIUS GENONI, *the* BARON TITO BELCREDI *and the young* MARQUIS CHARLES DI NOLLI, *who, as master of the house, enters last.*

DONNA MATILDA SPINA is about 45, still handsome, although there are too patent signs of her attempts to remedy the ravages of time with make-up. Her head is thus rather like a Walkyrie.[9] *This facial make-up contrasts with her beautiful sad mouth. A widow for many years, she now has as her friend the* BARON TITO BELCREDI, *whom neither she nor anyone else takes seriously—at least so it would appear.*

What TITO BELCREDI *really is for her at bottom, he alone knows; and he is, therefore, entitled to laugh, if his friend feels the need of pretending not to know. He can always laugh at the jests which the beautiful Marchioness makes with the others at his expense. He is slim, prematurely gray, and young-*

---

9. In Germanic mythology, female creature who rode over battlefields and gath- ered up spirits of dead warriors.

er than she is. *His head is bird-like in shape. He would be a very vivacious person, if his ductile agility (which among other things makes him a redoubtable swordsman) were not enclosed in a sheath of Arab-like laziness, which is revealed in his strange, nasal drawn-out voice.*

FRIDA, *the daughter of the Marchioness is* 19. *She is sad; because her imperious and too beautiful mother puts her in the shade, and provokes facile gossip against her daughter as well as against herself. Fortunately for her, she is engaged to the* MARQUIS CHARLES DI NOLLI.

CHARLES DI NOLLI *is a stiff young man, very indulgent towards others, but sure of himself for what he amounts to in the world. He is worried about all the responsibilities which he believes weigh on him. He is dressed in deep mourning for the recent death of his mother.*

DR. DIONYSIUS GENONI *has a bold rubicund Satyr-like face, prominent eyes, a pointed beard (which is silvery and shiny) and elegant manners. He is nearly bald. All enter in a state of perturbation, almost as if afraid, and all (except* DI NOLLI) *looking curiously about the room. At first, they speak sotto voce.*]

DI NOLLI [*to* JOHN]. Have you given the orders properly?

JOHN. Yes, my Lord; don't be anxious about that.

BELCREDI. Ah, magnificent! magnificent!

DOCTOR. How extremely interesting! Even in the surroundings his raving madness—is perfectly taken into account!

DONNA MATILDA [*glancing round for her portrait, discovers it, and goes up close to it*]. Ah! Here it is! [*Going back to admire it, while mixed emotions stir within her.*] Yes ... yes ... [*Calls her daughter* FRIDA.]

FRIDA. Ah, your portrait!

DONNA MATILDA. No, no ... look again; it's you, not I, there!

DI NOLLI. Yes, it's quite true. I told you so. I ...

DONNA MATILDA. But I would never have believed it! [*Shaking as if with a chill.*] What a strange feeling it gives one! [*Then looking at her daughter.*] Frida, what's the matter? [*She pulls her to her side, and slips an arm round her waist.*] Come: don't you see yourself in me there?

FRIDA. Well, I really ...

DONNA MATILDA. Don't you think so? Don't you, really? [*Turning to* BELCREDI.] Look at it, Tito! Speak up, man!

BELCREDI [*without looking*]. Ah, no! I shan't look at it. For me, *a priori*, certainly not!

DONNA MATILDA. Stupid! You think you are paying me a compliment! [*Turning to* DOCTOR GENONI.] What do you say, Doctor? Do say something, please!

DOCTOR [*makes a movement to go near to the picture*].

BELCREDI [*with his back turned, pretending to attract his attention secretly*].—Hss! No, Doctor! For the love of Heaven, have nothing to do with it!

DOCTOR [*getting bewildered and smiling*]. And why shouldn't I?

DONNA MATILDA. Don't listen to him! Come here! He's insufferable!

FRIDA. He acts the fool by profession, didn't you know that?

BELCREDI [*to the* DOCTOR, *seeing him go over*]. Look at your feet, Doctor! Mind where you're going!

DOCTOR. Why?

BELCREDI. Be careful you don't put your foot in it!

DOCTOR [*laughing feebly*]. No, no. After all, it seems to me there's no reason to be astonished at the fact that a daughter should resemble her mother!

BELCREDI. Hullo! Hullo! He's done it now; he's said it.

DONNA MATILDA [*with exaggerated anger, advancing towards* BELCREDI]. What's the matter? What he said? What has he done?

DOCTOR [*candidly*]. Well, isn't it so?

BELCREDI [*answering the* MARCHIONESS]. I said there was nothing to be astounded at—and you are astounded! And why so, then, if the thing is so simple and natural for you now?

DONNA MATILDA [*still more angry*]. Fool! fool! It's just because it is so natural! Just because it isn't my daughter who is there. [*Pointing to the canvas.*] That is my portrait; and to find my daughter there instead of me fills me with astonishment, an astonishment which, I beg you to believe, is sincere. I forbid you to cast doubts on it.

FRIDA [*slowly and wearily*]. My God! It's always like this . . . rows over nothing . . .

BELCREDI [*also slowly, looking dejected, in accents of apology*]. I cast no doubt on anything! I noticed from the beginning that you haven't shared your mother's astonishment; or, if something did astonish you, it was because the likeness between you and the portrait seemed so strong.

DONNA MATILDA. Naturally! She cannot recognize herself in me as I was at her age; while I, there, can very well recognize myself in her as she is now!

DOCTOR. Quite right! Because a portrait is always there fixed in the twinkling of an eye: for the young lady something far away and without memories, while, for the Marchioness, it can bring back everything: movements, gestures, looks, smiles, a whole heap of things . . .

DONNA MATILDA. Exactly!

DOCTOR [*continuing, turning towards her*]. Naturally enough, you can live all these old sensations again in your daughter.

DONNA MATILDA. He always spoils every innocent pleasure for me, every touch I have of spontaneous sentiment! He does it merely to annoy me.

DOCTOR [*frightened at the disturbance he has caused, adopts a professorial tone*]. Likeness, dear Baron, is often the result of imponderable things. So one explains that . . .

BELCREDI [*interrupting the discourse*]. Somebody will soon be finding a likeness between you and me, my dear Professor!

DI NOLLI. Oh! let's finish with this, please! [*Points to the two doors on the right, as a warning that there is someone there who may be listening.*] We've wasted too much time as it is!

FRIDA. As one might expect when *he's* present. [*Alludes to* BELCREDI.]

DI NOLLI. Enough! The Doctor is here; and we have come for a very serious purpose which you all know is important for me.

DOCTOR. Yes, that is so! But now, first of all, let's try to get some points down exactly. Excuse me, Marchioness, will you tell me why your portrait is here? Did you present it to him then?

DONNA MATILDA. No, not at all. How could I have given it to him? I was just like Frida then—and not even engaged. I gave it to him three or four years after the accident. I gave it to him because his mother wished it so much . . . [*Points to* DI NOLLI.]

DOCTOR. She was his sister? [*Alludes to* HENRY IV.]

DI NOLLI. Yes, Doctor; and our coming here is a debt we pay to my mother who has been dead for more than a month. Instead of being here, she and I [*Indicating Frida.*] ought to be traveling together . . .

DOCTOR. . . . taking a cure of quite a different kind!

DI NOLLI. —Hum! Mother died in the firm conviction that her adored brother was just about to be cured.

DOCTOR. And can't you tell me, if you please, how she inferred this?

DI NOLLI. The conviction would appear to have derived from certain strange remarks which he made, a little before mother died.

DOCTOR. Oh, remarks! . . . Ah! . . . It would be extremely useful for me to have those remarks, word for word, if possible.

DI NOLLI. I can't remember them. I know that mother returned awfully upset from her last visit with him. On her death-bed, she made me promise that I would never neglect him, that I would have doctors see him, and examine him.

DOCTOR. Um! Um! Let me see! let me see! Sometimes very small reasons determine . . . and this portrait here then? . . .

DONNA MATILDA. For Heaven's sake, Doctor, don't attach excessive importance to this. It made an impression on me because I had not seen it for so many years!

DOCTOR. If you please, quietly, quietly . . .

DI NOLLI. —Well, yes, it must be about fifteen years ago.

DONNA MATILDA. More, more: eighteen!

DOCTOR. Forgive me, but you don't quite know what I'm trying to get at. I attach a very great importance to these two portraits . . . They were painted, naturally, prior to the famous—and most regrettable pageant, weren't they?

DONNA MATILDA. Of course!

DOCTOR. That is . . . when he was quite in his right mind—that's what I've been trying to say. Was it his suggestion that they should be painted?

DONNA MATILDA. Lots of the people who took part in the pageant had theirs done as a souvenir . . .

BELCREDI. I had mine done—as "Charles of Anjou!"[10]

10. (1246–85). Founder of the line of Anjou.

DONNA MATILDA. . . . as soon as the costumes were ready.

BELCREDI. As a matter of fact, it was proposed that the whole lot of us should be hung together in a gallery of the villa where the pageant took place. But in the end, everybody wanted to keep his own portrait.

DONNA MATILDA. And I gave him this portrait of me without very much regret . . . since his mother . . . [*Indicates* DI NOLLI.]

DOCTOR. You don't remember if it was he who asked for it?

DONNA MATILDA. Ah, that I don't remember . . . Maybe it was his sister, wanting to help out . . .

DOCTOR. One other thing: was it his idea, this pageant?

BELCREDI [*at once*]. No, no, it was mine!

DOCTOR. If you please . . .

DONNA MATILDA. Don't listen to him! It was poor Belassi's idea.

BELCREDI. Belassi! What had he got to do with it?

DONNA MATILDA. Count Belassi, who died, poor fellow, two or three months after . . .

BELCREDI. But if Belasi wasn't there when . . .

DI NOLLI. Excuse me, Doctor; but is it really necessary to establish whose the original idea was?

DOCTOR. It would help me, certainly!

BELCREDI. I tell you the idea was mine? There's nothing to be proud of in it, seeing what the result's been. Look here, Doctor, it was like this. One evening, in the first days of November, I was looking at an illustrated German review in the club. I was merely glancing at the pictures, because I can't read German. There was a picture of the Kaiser, at some University town where he had been a student . . . I don't remember which.

DOCTOR. Bonn, Bonn!

BELCREDI. —You are right: Bonn! He was on horseback, dressed up in one of those ancient German student guild-costumes, followed by a procession of noble students, also in costume. The picture gave me the idea. Already someone at the club had spoken of a pageant for the forthcoming carnival. So I had the notion that each of us should choose for this Tower of Babel pageant to represent some character: a king, an emperor, a prince, with his queen, empress, or lady, alongside of him—and all on horseback. The suggestion was at once accepted.

DONNA MATILDA. I had my invitation from Belassi.

BELCREDI. Well, he wasn't speaking the truth! That's all I can say, if he told you the idea was his. He wasn't even at the club the evening I made the suggestion, just as he [*Meaning* HENRY IV.] wasn't there either.

DOCTOR. So he chose the character of Henry IV?

DONNA MATILDA. Because I . . . thinking of my name, and not giving the choice any importance, said I would be the Marchioness Matilda of Tuscany.

DOCTOR. I . . . don't understand the relation between the two.

DONNA MATILDA. —Neither did I, to begin with, when he said that in that case he would be at my feet like Henry IV at Canossa. I had heard of Canossa of course; but to tell the truth, I'd forgotten most of the story; and I remember I received a curious impression when I had to get up my part, and found that I was the faithful and zealous friend of Pope Gregory VII in deadly enmity with the Emperor of Germany. Then I understood why, since I had chosen to represent his implacable enemy, he wanted to be near me in the pageant as Henry IV.

DOCTOR. Ah, perhaps because . . .

BELCREDI. —Good Heavens, Doctor, because he was then paying furious court to her! [*Indicates the* MARCHIONESS.] And she, naturally . . .

DONNA MATILDA. Naturally? Not naturally at all . . .

BELCREDI [*pointing to her*]. She shouldn't stand him . . .

DONNA MATILDA. —No, that isn't true! I didn't dislike him. Not at all! But for me, when a man begins to want to be taken seriously, well . . .

BELCREDI [*continuing for her*]. He gives you the clearest proof of his stupidity.

DONNA MATILDA. No, dear; not in this case; because he was never a fool like you.

BELCREDI. Anyway, I've never asked you to take me seriously.

DONNA MATILDA. Yes, I know. But with him one couldn't joke. [*Changing her tone and speaking to the* DOCTOR.] One of the many misfortunes which happen to us women, Doctor, is to see before us every now and again a pair of eyes glaring at us with a contained intense promise of eternal devotion. [*Bursts out laughing.*] There is nothing quite so funny. If men could only see themselves with that eternal look of fidelity in their faces! I've always thought it comic; then more even than now. But I want to make a confession—I can do so after twenty years or more. When I laughed at him then, it was partly out of fear. One might have almost believed a promise from those eyes of his. But it would have been very dangerous.

DOCTOR [*with lively interest*]. Ah! ah! This is most interesting! Very dangerous, you say?

DONNA MATILDA. Yes, because he was very different from the others. And then, I am . . . well . . . what shall I say? . . . a little impatient of all that is pondered, or tedious. But I was too young then, and a woman. I had the bit between my teeth. It would have required more courage than I felt I possessed. So I laughed at him too—with remorse, to spite myself, indeed; since I saw that my own laugh mingled with those of all the others—the other fools—who made fun of him.

BELCREDI. My own case, more or less!

DONNA MATILDA. You make people laugh at you, my dear, with your trick of always humiliating yourself. It was quite a different affair with him. There's a vast difference. And you—you know—people laugh in your face!

BELCREDI. Well, that's better than behind one's back!

DOCTOR. Let's get to the facts. He was then already somewhat exalted, if I understand rightly.

BELCREDI. Yes, but in a curious fashion, Doctor.

DOCTOR. How?

BELCREDI. Well, cold-bloodedly so to speak.

DONNA MATILDA. Not at all! It was like this, Doctor! He was a bit strange, certainly; but only because he was fond of life: eccentric, there!

BELCREDI. I don't say he simulated exaltation. On the contrary, he was often genuinely exalted. But I could swear, Doctor, that he saw himself at once in his own exaltation. Moreover, I'm certain it made him suffer. Sometimes he had the most comical fits of rage against himself.

DOCTOR. Yes?

DONNA MATILDA. That is true.

BELCREDI [*to* DONNA MATILDA]. And why? [*To the* DOCTOR.] Evidently, because that immediate lucidity that comes from acting, assuming a part, at once put him out of key with his own feelings, which seemed to him not exactly false, but like something he was obliged to give the value there and then of—what shall I say—of an act of intelligence, to make up for that sincere cordial warmth he felt lacking. So he improvised, exaggerated, let himself go, so as to distract and forget himself. He appeared inconstant, fatuous, and —yes—even ridiculous, sometimes.

DOCTOR. And may we say unsociable?

BELCREDI. No, not at all. He was famous for getting up things: *tableaux vivants*,[11] dances, theatrical performances for charity: all for the fun of the thing, of course. He was a jolly good actor, you know!

DI NOLLI. Madness has made a superb actor of him.

BELCREDI. —Why, so he was even in the old days. When the accident happened, after the horse fell . . .

DOCTOR. Hit the back of his head, didn't he?

DONNA MATILDA. Oh, it was horrible! He was beside me! I saw him between the horse's hoofs! It was rearing!

BELCREDI. None of us thought it was anything serious at first. There was a stop in the pageant, a bit of disorder. People wanted to know what had happened. But they'd already taken him off to the villa.

DONNA MATILDA. There wasn't the least sign of a wound, not a drop of blood.

BELCREDI. We thought he had merely fainted.

DONNA MATILDA. But two hours afterwards . . .

BELCREDI. He reappeared in the drawing-room of the villa . . . that is what I wanted to say . . .

DONNA MATILDA. My God! What a face he had. I saw the whole thing at once!

11. People in costume, grouped to resemble a famous painting.

BELCREDI. No, no! that isn't true. Nobody saw it, Doctor, believe me!

DONNA MATILDA. Doubtless, because you were all like mad folk.

BELCREDI. Everybody was pretending to act his part for a joke. It was a regular Babel.

DONNA MATILDA. And you can imagine, Doctor, what terror struck into us when we understood that he, on the contrary, was playing his part in deadly earnest . . .

DOCTOR. Oh, he was there too, was he?

BELCREDI. Of course! He came straight into the midst of us. We thought he'd quite recovered, and was pretending, fooling, like all the rest of us . . . only doing it rather better; because, as I say, he knew how to act.

DONNA MATILDA. Some of them began to hit him with their whips and fans and sticks.

BELCREDI. And then—as a king, he was armed, of course—he drew out his sword and menaced two or three of us . . . It was a terrible moment, I can assure you!

DONNA MATILDA. I shall never forget that scene—all our masked faces hideous and terrified gazing at him, at that terrible mask of his face, which was no longer a mask, but madness, madness personified.

BELCREDI. He was Henry IV, Henry IV in person, in a moment of fury.

DONNA MATILDA. He'd got into it all the detail and minute preparation of a month's careful study. And it all burned and blazed there in the terrible obsession which lit his face.

DOCTOR. Yes, that is quite natural, of course. The momentary obsession of a dilettante became fixed, owing to the fall and the damage to the brain.

BELCREDI [*to* FRIDA *and* DI NOLLI]. You see the kind of jokes life can play on us. [*To* DI NOLLI.] You were four or five years old. [*To* FRIDA.] Your mother imagines you've taken her place there in that portrait; when, at the time, she had not the remotest idea that she would bring you into the world. My hair is already grey; and he—look at him—[*Points to portrait*]—ha! A smack on the head, and he never moves again: Henry IV for ever!

DOCTOR [*seeking to draw the attention of the others, looking learned and imposing*]. —Well, well, then it comes, we may say, to this . . . [*Suddenly the first exit to right, the one nearest footlights, opens, and* BERTHOLD *enters all excited.*]

BERTHOLD [*rushing in*]. I say! I say! [*Stops for a moment, arrested by the astonishment which his appearance has caused in the others.*]

FRIDA [*running away terrified*]. Oh dear! oh dear! it's he, it's . . .

DONNA MATILDA [*covering her face with her hands so as not to see*]. Is it, is it he?

DI NOLLI. No, no, what are you talking about? Be calm!

DOCTOR. Who is it then?

BELCREDI. One of our masqueraders.

DI NOLLI. He is one of the four youths we keep here to help him out in his madness . . .

BERTHOLD. I beg your pardon, Marquis . . .

DI NOLLI. Pardon be damned! I gave orders that the doors were to be closed, and that nobody should be allowed to enter.

BERTHOLD. Yes, sir, but I can't stand it any longer, and I ask you to let me go away this very minute.

DI NOLLI. Oh, you're the new valet, are you? You were supposed to begin this morning, weren't you?

BERTHOLD. Yes, sir, and I can't stand it, I can't bear it.

DONNA MATILDA [*to* DI NOLLI *excitedly*]. What? Then he's not so calm as you said?

BERTHOLD [*quickly*]. —No, no, my lady, it isn't he; it's my companions. You say "help him out with his madness," Marquis; but they don't do anything of the kind. They're the real madmen. I come here for the first time, and instead of helping me . . .

[LANDOLPH *and* HAROLD *come in from the same door, but hesitate on the threshold.*]

LANDOLPH. Excuse me?

HAROLD. May I come in, my Lord?

DI NOLLI. Come in! What's the matter? What are you all doing?

FRIDA. Oh God! I'm frightened! I'm going to run away. [*Makes towards exit at left.*]

DI NOLLI [*restraining her at once*]. No, no, Frida!

LANDOLPH. My Lord, this fool here . . . [*Indicates* BERTHOLD.]

BERTHOLD [*protesting*]. Ah, no thanks, my friends, no thanks! I'm not stopping here! I'm off!

LANDOLPH. What do you mean—you're not stopping here?

HAROLD. He's ruined everything, my Lord, running away in here!

LANDOLPH. He's made him quite mad. We can't keep him in there any longer. He's given orders that he's to be arrested; and he wants to "judge" him at once from the throne: What is to be done?

DI NOLLI. Shut the door, man! Shut the door! Go and close that door! [LANDOLPH *goes over to close it.*]

HAROLD. Ordulph, alone, won't be able to keep him there.

LANDOLPH. —My Lord, perhaps if we could announce the visitors at once, it would turn his thoughts. Have the gentlemen thought under what pretext they will present themselves to him?

DI NOLLI. —It's all been arranged! [*To the* DOCTOR.] If you, Doctor, think it well to see him at once. . . .

FRIDA. I'm not coming! I'm not coming! I'll keep out of this. You too, mother, for Heaven's sake, come away with me!

DOCTOR. —I say . . . I suppose he's not armed, is he?

DI NOLLI. —Nonsense! Of course not. [*To* FRIDA.] Frida, you know this is childish of you. You wanted to come!

FRIDA. I didn't at all. It was mother's idea.

DONNA MATILDA. And I'm quite ready to see him. What are we going to do?

BELCREDI. Must we absolutely dress up in some fashion or other?

LANDOLPH. —Absolutely essential, indispensable, sir. Alas! as you see . . . [*Shows his costume*], there'd be awful trouble if he saw you gentlemen in modern dress.

HAROLD. He would think it was some diabolical masquerade.

DI NOLLI. As these men seem to be in costume to you, so we appear to be in costume to him, in these modern clothes of ours.

LANDOLPH. It wouldn't matter so much if he wouldn't suppose it to be the work of his mortal enemy.

BELCREDI. Pope Gregory VII?

LANDOLPH. Precisely. He calls him "a pagan."

BELCREDI. The Pope a pagan? Not bad that!

LANDOLPH. —Yes, sir,—and a man who calls up the dead! He accuses him of all the diabolical arts. He's terribly afraid of him.

DOCTOR. Persecution mania!

HAROLD. He'd be simply furious.

DI NOLLI [*to* BELCREDI]. But there's no need for you to be there, you know. It's sufficient for the Doctor to see him.

DOCTOR. —What do you mean? . . . I? Alone?

DI NOLLI. —But they are there. [*Indicates the three young men.*]

DOCTOR. I don't mean that . . . I mean if the Marchioness . . .

DONNA MATILDA. Of course. I mean to see him too, naturally. I want to see him again.

FRIDA. Oh, why, mother, why? Do come away with me, I implore you!

DONNA MATILDA [*imperiously*]. Let me do as I wish! I came here for this purpose! [*To* LANDOLPH.] I shall be "Adelaide," the mother.

LANDOLPH. Excellent! The mother of the Empress Bertha. Good! It will be enough if her Ladyship wears the ducal crown and puts on a mantel that will hide her other clothes entirely. [*To* HAROLD.] Off you go, Harold!

HAROLD. Wait a moment! And this gentleman here? . . . [*Alludes to the* DOCTOR.]

DOCTOR. —Ah yes . . . we decided I was to be . . . the Bishop of Cluny, Hugh of Cluny!

HAROLD. The gentleman means the Abbot. Very good! Hugh of Cluny.[12]

LANDOLPH. —He's often been here before!

DOCTOR [*amazed*]. —What? Been here before?

LANDOLPH. —Don't be alarmed! I mean that it's an easily prepared disguise . . .

HAROLD. We've made use of it on other occasions, you see!

DOCTOR. But . . .

LANDOLPH. Oh, no there's no risk of his remembering. He pays more attention to the dress than to the person.

DONNA MATILDA. That's fortunate for me too then.

DI NOLLI. Frida, you and I'll get along. Come on, Tito!

BELCREDI. Ah no. If she [*Indicates the* MARCHIONESS.] stops here, so do I!

DONNA MATILDA. But I don't need you at all.

12. Godfather of Henry IV.

BELCREDI. You may not need me, but I should like to see him again myself. Mayn't I?

LANDOLPH. Well, perhaps it would be better if there were three.

HAROLD. How is the gentleman to be dressed then?

BELCREDI. Oh, try and find some easy costume for me.

LANDOLPH [*to* HAROLD]. Hum! Yes . . . he'd better be from Cluny too.

BELCREDI. What do you mean—from Cluny?

LANDOLPH. A Benedictine's habit of the Abbey of Cluny. He can be in attendance on Monsignor. [*To* HAROLD.] Off you go! [*To* BERTHOLD.] And you too get away and keep out of sight all today. No, wait a bit! [*To* BERTHOLD.] You bring here the costumes he will give you. [*To* HAROLD.] You go at once and announce the visit of the "Duchess Adelaide" and "Monsignor Hugh of Cluny." Do you understand? [HAROLD *and* BERTHOLD *go off by the first door on the right.*]

DI NOLLI. We'll retire now. [*Goes off with* FRIDA, *left.*]

DOCTOR. Shall I be a *persona grata*[13] to him, as Hugh of Cluny?

LANDOLPH. Oh, rather! Don't worry about that! Monsignor has always been received here with great respect. You too, my Lady, he will be glad to see. He never forgets that it was owing to the intercession of you two that he was admitted to the Castle of Canossa and the presence of Gregory VII, who didn't want to receive him.

BELCREDI. And what do I do?

LANDOLPH. You stand a little apart, respectfully: that's all.

DONNA MATILDA [*irritated, nervous*]. You would do well to go away, you know.

BELCREDI [*slowly, spitefully*]. How upset you seem! . . .

DONNA MATILDA [*proudly*]. I am as I am. Leave me alone!

[BERTHOLD *comes in with the costumes.*]

LANDOLPH [*seeing him enter*]. Ah, the costumes: here they are. This mantle is for the Marchioness . . .

DONNA MATILDA. Wait a minute! I'll take off my hat. [*Does so and gives it to* BERTHOLD.]

LANDOLPH. Put it down there! [*Then to the* MARCHIONESS, *while he offers to put the ducal crown on her head.*] Allow me!

DONNA MATILDA. Dear, dear! Isn't there a mirror here?

LANDOLPH. Yes, there's one there [*Points to the door on the left.*] If the Marchioness would rather put it on herself . . .

DONNA MATILDA. Yes, yes, that will be better. Give it to me! [*Takes up her hat and goes off with* BERTHOLD, *who carries the cloak and the crown.*]

BELCREDI. Well, I must say, I never thought I should be a Benedictine monk! By the way, this business must cost an awful lot of money.

THE DOCTOR. Like any other fantasy, naturally!

BELCREDI. Well, there's a fortune to go upon.

LANDOLPH. We have got there a whole wardrobe of costumes of the

13. Person declared to be officially acceptable.

period, copied to perfection from old models. This is my special job. I get them from the best theatrical costumers. They cost lots of money. [DONNA MATILDA *re-enters, wearing mantle and crown.*]

BELCREDI [*at once, in admiration*]. Oh magnificent! Oh, truly regal!

DONNA MATILDA [*looking at* BELCREDI *and bursting out into laughter*]. Oh no, no! Take it off! You're impossible. You look like an ostrich dressed up as a monk.

BELCREDI. Well, how about the Doctor?

THE DOCTOR. I don't think I looked so bad, do I?

DONNA MATILDA. No; the Doctor's all right . . . but you are too funny for words.

THE DOCTOR. Do you have many receptions here then?

LANDOLPH. It depends. He often gives orders that such and such a person appear before him. Then we have to find someone who will take the part. Women too . . .

DONNA MATILDA [*hurt, but trying to hide the fact*]. Ah, women too?

LANDOLPH. Oh, yes; many at first.

BELCREDI [*laughing*]. Oh, that's great! In costume, like the Marchioness?

LANDOLPH. Oh well, you know, women of the kind that lend themselves to . . .

BELCREDI. Ah, I see! [*Perfidiously to the* MARCHIONESS.] Look out, you know he's becoming dangerous for you.

[*The second door on the right opens, and* HAROLD *appears making first of all a discreet sign that all conversation should cease.*]

HAROLD. His Majesty, the Emperor!

[*The* TWO VALETS *enter first, and go and stand on either side of the throne. Then* HENRY IV *comes in between* ORDULPH *and* HAROLD, *who keep a little in the rear respectfully.*

HENRY IV *is about 50 and very pale. The hair on the back of his head is already grey; over the temples and forehead it appears blond, owing to its having been tinted in an evident and puerile fashion. On his cheek bones he has two small, doll-like dabs of color, that stand out prominently against the rest of his tragic pallor. He is wearing a penitent's sack over his regal habit, as at Canossa. His eyes have a fixed look which is dreadful to see, and this expression is in strained contrast with the sackcloth.* ORDULPH *carries the Imperial crown;* HAROLD, *the sceptre with eagle, and the globe with the cross.*]

HENRY IV [*bowing first to* DONNA MATILDA *and afterwards to the* DOCTOR]. My lady . . . Monsignor . . . [*Then he looks at* BELCREDI *and seems about to greet him too; when, suddenly, he turns to* LANDOLPH, *who has approached him, and asks him sotto voce and with diffidence.*] Is that Peter Damiani?[14]

LANDOLPH. No, Sire. He is a monk from Cluny who is accompanying the Abbot.

---

14. Cardinal-bishop of Ostia. He had tried to compel Henry IV to take back his first wife.

HENRY IV [*looks again at* BELCREDI *with increasing mistrust, and then noticing that he appears embarrassed and keeps glancing at* DONNA MATILDA *and the* DOCTOR, *stands upright and cries out*]. No, it's Peter Damiani! It's no use, father, your looking at the Duchess. [*Then turning quickly to* DONNA MATILDA *and the* DOCTOR *as though to ward off a danger*.] I swear it! I swear that my heart is changed towards your daughter. I confess that if he [*Indicates* BELCREDI.] hadn't come to forbid it in the name of Pope Alexander, I'd have repudiated her. Yes, yes, there were people ready to favour the repudiation: the Bishop of Mayence would have done it for a matter of one hundred and twenty farms. [*Looks at* LANDOLPH *a little perplexed and adds*.] But I mustn't speak ill of the bishops at this moment! [*More humbly to* BELCREDI.] I am grateful to you, believe me, I am grateful to you for the hindrance you put in my way!—God knows, my life's been all made of humiliations: my mother,[15] Adalbert, Tribur,[16] Goslar! And now this sackcloth you see me wearing! [*Changes tone suddenly and speaks like one who goes over his part in a parenthesis of astuteness*.] It doesn't matter: clarity of ideas, perspicacity, firmness and patience under adversity that's the thing. [*Then turning to all and speaking solemnly*.] I know how to make amends for the mistakes I have made; and I can humiliate myself even before you, Peter Damiani. [*Bows profoundly to him and remains curved. Then a suspicion is born in him which he is obliged to utter in menacing tones, almost against his will*.] Was it not perhaps you who started that obscene rumor that my holy mother had illicit relations with the Bishop of Augusta?

BELCREDI [*since* HENRY IV *has his finger pointed at him*]. No, no, it wasn't I . . .

HENRY IV [*straightening up*]. Not true, not true? Infamy! [*Looks at him and then adds*.] I didn't think you capable of it! [*Goes to the* DOCTOR *and plucks his sleeve, while winking at him knowingly*.] Always the same, Monsignor, those bishops, always the same!

HAROLD [*softly, whispering as if to help out the doctor*]. Yes, yes, the rapacious bishops!

THE DOCTOR [*to* HAROLD, *trying to keep it up*]. Ah, yes, those fellows . . . ah yes . . .

HENRY IV. Nothing satisfies them! I was a little boy, Monsignor . . . One passes the time, playing even, when, without knowing it, one is a king.—I was six years old; and they tore me away from my mother, and made use of me against her without my knowing anything about it . . . always profaning, always stealing, stealing! . . . One greedier than the other . . . Hanno[17] worse than Stephen![18] Stephen worse than Hanno!

LANDOLPH [*sotto voce, persuasively, to call his attention*]. Majesty!

15. She had served as his first regent.
16. There Henry had been forced by the nobles and clergy of Saxony to seek Pope Gregory's pardon.

17. Archbishop of Cologne, Henry's second regent.
18. Probably Pope Stephen IX.

HENRY IV [*turning round quickly*]. Ah yes . . . this isn't the moment to speak ill of the bishops. But this infamy against my mother, Monsignor, is too much. [*Looks at the* MARCHIONESS *and grows tender.*] And I can't even weep for her, Lady . . . I appeal to you who have a mother's heart! She came here to see me from her convent a month ago . . . They had told me she was dead! [*Sustained pause full of feeling. Then smiling sadly.*] I can't weep for her; because if you are here now, and I am like this [*Shows the sackcloth he is wearing.*] it means I am twenty-six years old!

HAROLD. And that she is therefore alive, Majesty! . . .

ORDULPH. Still in her convent!

HENRY IV [*looking at them*]. Ah yes! And I can postpone my grief to another time. [*Shows the* MARCHIONESS *almost with coquetry the tint he has given to his hair.*] Look! I am still fair . . . [*Then slowly as if in confidence.*] For you . . . there's no need! But little exterior details do help! A matter of time, Monsignor, do you understand me? [*Turns to the* MARCHIONESS *and notices her hair.*] Ah, but I see that you too, Duchess . . . Italian, eh? [*As much as to say "false"; but without any indignation, indeed rather with malicious admiration.*] Heaven forbid that I should show disgust or surprise! Nobody cares to recognize that obscure and fatal power which sets limits to our will. But I say, if one is born and one dies . . . Did you want to be born, Monsignor? I didn't! And in both cases, independently of our wills, so many things happen we would wish didn't happen, and to which we resign ourselves as best we can! . . .

DOCTOR [*merely to make a remark, while studying* HENRY IV *carefully*]. Alas! Yes, alas!

HENRY IV. It's like this: When we are not resigned, out come our desires. A woman wants to be a man . . . an old man would be young again. Desires, ridiculous fixed ideas of course—But reflect! Monsignor, those other desires are not less ridiculous: I mean, those desires where the will is kept within the limits of the possible. Not one of us can lie or pretend. We're all fixed in good faith in a certain concept of ourselves. However, Monsignor, while you keep yourself in order, holding on with both your hands to your holy habit, there slips down from your sleeves, there peels off from you like . . . like a serpent . . . something you don't notice: life, Monsignor! [*Turns to the* MARCHIONESS.] Has it never happened to you, my Lady, to find a different self in yourself? Have you always been the same? My God! One day . . . how was it, how was it you were able to commit this or that action? [*Fixes her so intently in the eyes as almost to make her blanch.*] Yes, that particular action, that very one: we understand each other! But don't be afraid: I shall reveal it to none. And you, Peter Damiani, how could you be a friend of that man? . . .

LANDOLPH. Majesty!

HENRY IV [*at once*]. No, I won't name him! [*Turning to* BELCREDI.] What did you think of him? But we all of us cling tight to our conceptions of ourselves, just as he who is growing old dyes his hair. What does it matter that this dyed hair of mine isn't a reality for you, if it *is*, to some extent, for me?—you, you, my Lady, certainly don't dye your hair to deceive the others, nor even yourself; but only to cheat your own image a little before the looking-glass. I do it for a joke! You do it seriously! But I assure you that you too, Madam, are in masquerade, though it be in all seriousness; and I am not speaking of the venerable crown on your brows or the ducal mantle. I am speaking only of the memory you wish to fix in yourself of your fair complexion one day when it pleased you—or of your dark complexion, if you were dark: the fading image of your youth! For you, Peter Damiani, on the contrary, the memory of what you have been, of what you have done, seems to you a recognition of past realities that remain within you like a dream. I'm in the same case too: with so many inexplicable memories—like dreams! Ah! . . . There's nothing to marvel at in it, Peter Damiani! Tomorrow it will be the same thing with our life of today! [*Suddenly getting excited and taking hold of his sackcloth.*] This sackcloth here . . . [*Beginning to take it off with a gesture of almost ferocious joy while the* THREE VALETS *run over to him, frightened, as if to prevent his doing so.*] Ah, my God! [*Draws back and throws off sackcloth.*] Tomorrow, at Bressanone, twenty-seven German and Lombard bishops will sign with me the act of deposition of Gregory VII! No Pope at all! Just a false monk!

ORDULPH [*with the other three*]. Majesty! Majesty! In God's name! . . .

HAROLD [*inviting him to put on the sackcloth again*]. Listen to what he says, Majesty!

LANDOLPH. Monsignor is here with the Duchess to intercede in your favor. [*Makes secret signs to the* DOCTOR *to say something at once.*]

DOCTOR [*foolishly*]. Ah yes . . . yes . . . we are here to intercede . . .

HENRY IV [*repenting at once, almost terrified, allowing the three to put on the sackcloth again, and pulling it down over him with his own hands*]. Pardon . . . yes . . . yes . . . pardon, Monsignor: forgive me, my Lady . . . I swear to you I feel the whole weight of the anathema. [*Bends himself, takes his face between his hands, as though waiting for something to crush him. Then changing tone, but without moving, says softly to* LANDOLPH, HAROLD *and* ORDULPH.] But I don't know why I cannot be humble before that man there! [*Indicates* BELCREDI.]

LANDOLPH [*sotto voce*]. But why, Majesty, do you insist on believing he is Peter Damiani, when he isn't, at all?

HENRY IV [*looking at him timorously*]. He isn't Peter Damiani?

HAROLD. No, no, he is a poor monk, Majesty.

HENRY IV [*sadly with a touch of exasperation*]. Ah! None of us can estimate what we do when we do it from instinct . . . You perhaps, Madam, can understand me better than the others, since you are a woman and a Duchess. This is a solemn and decisive moment. I could, you know, accept the assistance of the Lombard bishops, arrest the Pope, lock him up here in the castle, run to Rome and

elect an anti-Pope; offer alliance to Robert Guiscard[19]—and Gregory VII would be lost! I resist the temptation; and, believe me, I
am wise in doing so. I feel the atmosphere of our times and the
majesty of one who knows how to be what he ought to be! a
Pope! Do you feel inclined to laugh at me, seeing me like this?
You would be foolish to do so; for you don't understand the political wisdom which makes this penitent's sack advisable. The parts
may be changed tomorrow. What would you do then? Would
you laugh to see the Pope a prisoner? No! It would come to the
same thing: I dressed as a penitent, today; he, as prisoner tomorrow! But woe to him who doesn't know how to wear his mask, be he
king or Pope!—Perhaps he is a bit too cruel! No! Yes, yes, maybe!—
You remember, my Lady, how your daughter Bertha, for whom,
I repeat, my feelings have changed [*Turns to* BELCREDI *and shouts
to his face as if he were being contradicted by him.*]—Yes, changed
on account of the affection and devotion she showed me in that
terrible moment . . . [*Then once again to the* MARCHIONESS.] . . .
you remember how she came with me, my Lady, followed me like
a beggar and passed two nights out in the open, in the snow?[20]
You are her mother! Doesn't this touch your mother's heart?
Doesn't this urge you to pity, so that you will beg His Holiness for
pardon, beg him to receive us?

DONNA MATILDA [*trembling, with feeble voice*]. Yes, yes, at once . . .

DOCTOR. It shall be done!

HENRY IV. And one thing more! [*Draws them in to listen to him.*]
It isn't enough that he should receive me! You know he can do
everything—everything. I tell you! He can even call up the dead.
[*Touches his chest.*] Behold me! Do you see me? There is no magic
art unknown to him. Well, Monsignor, my Lady, my torment is
really this: that whether here or there [*Pointing to his portrait almost in fear.*] I can't free myself from this magic. I am a penitent
now, you see, and I swear to you I shall remain so until he receives me. But you two, when the excommunication is taken off,
must ask the Pope to do this thing he can so easily do: to take me
away from that; [*Indicating the portrait again.*] and let me live
wholly and freely my miserable life. A man can't always be twenty-
six, my Lady. I ask this of you for your daughter's sake too; that
I may love her as she deserves to be loved, well disposed as I am
now, all tender towards her for her pity. There: it's all there! I
am in your hands! [*Bows.*] My Lady! Monsignor!

[*He goes off, bowing grandly, through the door by which he
entered, leaving everyone stupefied, and the* MARCHIONESS *so
profoundly touched, that no sooner has he gone than she
breaks out into sobs and sits down almost fainting.*]

CURTAIN

19. A Norman prince, allied with Gregory VII.

20. Outside the castle of Canossa, in
1077.

Act II

Another room of the villa, adjoining the throne room. Its furniture is antique and severe. Principal exit at rear in the background. To the left, two windows looking on the garden. To the right, a door opening into the throne room.

Late afternoon of the same day.

DONNA MATILDA, *the* DOCTOR *and* BELCREDI *are on the stage engaged in conversation; but* DONNA MATILDA *stands to one side, evidently annoyed at what the other two are saying; although she cannot help listening, because, in her agitated state, everything interests her in spite of herself. The talk of the other two attracts her attention, because she instinctively feels the need for calm at the moment.*

BELCREDI. It may be as you say, Doctor, but that was my impression.

DOCTOR. I won't contradict you; but, believe me, it is only . . . an impression.

BELCREDI. Pardon me, but he even said so, and quite clearly [*Turning to the* MARCHIONESS.] Didn't he, Marchioness?

DONNA MATILDA [*turning round*]. What did he say? . . . [*Then not agreeing.*] Oh yes . . . but not for the reason you think!

DOCTOR. He was alluding to the costumes we had slipped on . . . Your cloak [*Indicating the* MARCHIONESS.] our Benedictine habits . . . But all this is childish!

DONNA MATILDA [*turning quickly, indignant*]. Childish? What do you mean, Doctor?

DOCTOR. From one point of view, it is—I beg you to let me say so, Marchioness! Yet, on the other hand, it is much more complicated than you can imagine.

DONNA MATILDA. To me, on the contrary, it is perfectly clear!

DOCTOR [*with a smile of pity of the competent person towards those who do not understand*]. We must take into account the peculiar psychology of madmen; which, you must know, enables us to be certain that they observe things and can, for instance, easily detect people who are disguised; can in fact recognize the disguise and yet believe in it; just as children do, for whom disguise is both play and reality. That is why I used the word childish. But the thing is extremely complicated, inasmuch as he must be perfectly aware of being an image to himself and for himself—that image there, in fact! [*Alluding to the portrait in the throne room, and pointing to the left.*]

BELCREDI. That's what he said!

DOCTOR. Very well then— An image before which other images, ours, have appeared: understand? Now he, in his acute and perfectly lucid delirium, was able to detect at once a difference between his image and ours: that is, he saw that ours were make-believes. So he suspected us; because all madmen are armed with a special diffidence. But that's all there is to it! Our make-believe, built up all round his, did not seem pitiful to him. While his seemed all the more tragic to us, in that he, as if in defiance—understand?—and induced by his suspicion, wanted to show us up merely as a joke. That was also partly the case with him, in coming before us with painted cheeks and hair, and saying he had done it on purpose for a jest.

DONNA MATILDA [*impatiently*]. No, it's not that, Doctor. It's not like that! It's not like that!

DOCTOR. Why isn't it, may I ask?

DONNA MATILDA [*with decision but trembling*]. I am perfectly certain he recognized me!

DOCTOR. It's not possible . . . it's not possible!

BELCREDI [*at the same time*]. Of course not!

DONNA MATILDA [*more than ever determined, almost convulsively*]. I tell you, he recognized me! When he came close up to speak to me—looking in my eyes, right into my eyes—he recognized me!

BELCREDI. But he was talking of your daughter!

DONNA MATILDA. That's not true! He was talking of me! Of me!

BELCREDI. Yes, perhaps, when he said . . .

DONNA MATILDA [*letting herself go*]. About my dyed hair! But didn't you notice that he added at once: "or the memory of your dark hair, if you were dark"? He remembered perfectly well that I was dark—then!

BELCREDI. Nonsense! nonsense!

DONNA MATILDA [*not listening to him, turning to the* DOCTOR]. My hair, Doctor, is really dark—like my daughter's! That's why he spoke of her.

BELCREDI. But he doesn't even know your daughter! He's never seen her!

DONNA MATILDA. Exactly! Oh, you never understand anything! By my daughter, stupid, he meant me—as I was then!

BELCREDI. Oh, this is catching! This is catching, this madness!

DONNA MATILDA [*softly, with contempt*]. Fool!

BELCREDI. Excuse me, were you ever his wife? Your daughter is his wife—in his delirium: Bertha of Susa.

DONNA MATILDA. Exactly! Because I, no longer dark—as he remembered me—but *fair*, introduced myself as "Adelaide," the mother. My daughter doesn't exist for him: he's never seen her—you said so yourself! So how can he know whether she's fair or dark?

BELCREDI. But he said dark, speaking generally, just as anyone who wants to recall, whether fair or dark, a memory of youth in the color of the hair! And you, as usual, begin to imagine things! Doctor, you said I ought not to have come! It's she who ought not to have come!

DONNA MATILDA [*upset for a moment by* BELCREDI's *remark, recovers herself. Then with a touch of anger, because doubtful*]. No, no . . . he spoke of me . . . He spoke all the time to me, with me, of me . . .

BELCREDI. That's not bad! He didn't leave me a moment's breathing space and you say he was talking all the time to you? Unless you think he was alluding to you too, when he was talking to Peter Damiani!

DONNA MATILDA [*defiantly, almost exceeding the limits of courteous discussion*]. Who knows? Can you tell me why, from the outset, he showed a strong dislike for you, for you alone? [*From the tone of the question, the expected answer must almost explicitly be: "because he understands you are my lover."* BELCREDI *feels this so well that he remains silent and can say nothing.*]

DOCTOR. The reason may also be found in the fact that only the visit of the Duchess Adelaide and the Abbot of Cluny was announced to him. Finding a third person present, who had not been announced, at once his suspicions . . .

BELCREDI. Yes, exactly! His suspicion made him see an enemy in me: Peter Damiani! But she's got it into her head, that he recognized her . . .

DONNA MATILDA. There's no doubt about it! I could see it from his eyes, doctor. You know, there's a way of looking that leaves no doubt whatever . . . Perhaps it was only for an instant, but I am sure!

DOCTOR. It is not impossible: a lucid moment . . .

DONNA MATILDA. Yes, perhaps . . . And then his speech seemed to me full of regret for his and my youth—for the horrible thing that happened to him, that has held him in that disguise from which he has never been able to free himself, and from which he longs to be free—he said so himself!

BELCREDI. Yes, so as to be able to make love to your daughter, or you, as you believe—having been touched by your pity.

DONNA MATILDA. Which is very great, I would ask you to believe.

BELCREDI. As one can see, Marchioness; so much so that a miracle-worker might expect a miracle from it!

DOCTOR. Will you let me speak? I don't work miracles, because I am a doctor and not a miracle-worker. I listened very intently to all he said; and I repeat that that certain analogical elasticity, common to all systematized delirium, is evidently with him much . . . what shall I say?—much relaxed! The elements, that is, of his delirium no longer hold together. It seems to me he has lost the equilibrium of his second personality and sudden recollections drag him—and this is very comforting—not from a state of incipient apathy, but rather from a morbid inclination to reflective melancholy, which shows a . . . a very considerable cerebral activity. Very comforting, I repeat! Now if, by this violent trick we've planned . . .

DONNA MATILDA [*turning to the window, in the tone of a sick person complaining*]. But how is it that the motor has not returned? It's three hours and a half since . . .

DOCTOR. What do you say?

DONNA MATILDA. The motor, Doctor! It's more than three hours and a half . . .

DOCTOR [*taking out his watch and looking at it*]. Yes, more than four hours, by this!

DONNA MATILDA. It could have reached here an hour ago at least! But, as usual . . .

BELCREDI. Perhaps they can't find the dress . . .

DONNA MATILDA. But I explained exactly where it was! [*Impatiently.*] And Frida . . . where is Frida?

BELCREDI [*looking out of the window*]. Perhaps she is in the garden with Charles . . .

DOCTOR. He'll talk her out of her fright.

BELCREDI. She's not afraid, Doctor; don't you believe it: the thing bores her rather . . .

DONNA MATILDA. Just don't ask anything of her! I know what she's like.

DOCTOR. Let's wait patiently. Anyhow, it will soon be over, and it has to be in the evening . . . It will only be the matter of a moment! If we can succeed in rousing him, as I was saying, and in breaking at one go the threads—already slack—which still bind him to this fiction of his, giving him back what he himself asks for—you remember, he said: "one cannot always be twenty-six years old, madam!" if we can give him freedom from this torment, which even *he* feels is a torment, then if he is able to recover at one bound the sensation of the distance of time . . .

BELCREDI [*quickly*]. He'll be cured! [*Then emphatically with irony.*] We'll pull him out of it all!

DOCTOR. Yes, we may hope to set him going again, like a watch which has stopped at a certain hour . . . just as if we had our watches in our hands and were waiting for that other watch to go again.—A shake—so—and let's hope it'll tell the time again after its long stop. [*At this point the* MARQUIS CHARLES DI NOLLI *enters from the principal entrance.*]

DONNA MATILDA. Oh, Charles! . . . And Frida? Where is she?

DI NOLLI. She'll be here in a moment.

DOCTOR. Has the motor arrived?

DI NOLLI. Yes.

DONNA MATILDA. Yes? Has the dress come?

DI NOLLI. It's been here some time.

DOCTOR. Good! Good!

DONNA MATILDA [*trembling*]. Where is she? Where's Frida?

DI NOLLI [*shrugging his shoulders and smiling sadly, like one lending himself unwillingly to an untimely joke*]. You'll see, you'll see! . . . [*Pointing towards the hall.*] Here she is! . . . [BERTHOLD *appears at the threshold of the hall, and announces with solemnity.*]

BERTHOLD. Her Highness the Countess Matilda of Canossa! [FRIDA *enters, magnificent and beautiful, arrayed in the robes of her mother as "Countess Matilda of Tuscany," so that she is a living copy of the portrait in the throne room.*]

FRIDA [*passing* BERTHOLD, *who is bowing, says to him with disdain*]. Of Tuscany, of Tuscany! Canossa is just one of my castles!

BELCREDI [*in admiration*]. Look! Look! She seems another person . . .

DONNA MATILDA. One would say it were I! Look!—Why, Frida, look! She's exactly my portrait, alive!

DOCTOR. Yes, yes . . . Perfect! Perfect! The portrait, to the life.

BELCREDI. Yes, there's no question about it. She *is* the portrait! Magnificent!

FRIDA. Don't make me laugh, or I shall burst! I say, mother, what a tiny waist you had? I had to squeeze so to get into this!

DONNA MATILDA [*arranging her dress a little*]. Wait! . . . Keep still! . . . These pleats . . . is it really so tight?

FRIDA. I'm suffocating! I implore you, to be quick! . . .

DOCTOR. But we must wait till it's evening!

FRIDA. No, no, I can't hold out till evening!

DONNA MATILDA. Why did you put it on so soon?

FRIDA. The moment I saw it, the temptation was irresistible . . .

DONNA MATILDA. At least you could have called me, or have had someone help you! It's still all crumpled.

FRIDA. So I saw, mother; but they are old creases; they won't come out.

DOCTOR. It doesn't matter, Marchioness! The illusion is perfect. [*Then coming nearer and asking her to come in front of her daughter, without hiding her.*] If you please, stay there, there . . . at a certain distance . . . now a little more forward . . .

BELCREDI. For the feeling of the distance of time . . .

DONNA MATILDA [*slightly turning to him*]. Twenty years after! A disaster! A tragedy!

BELCREDI. Now don't let's exaggerate!

DOCTOR [*embarrassed, trying to save the situation*]. No, no! I meant the dress . . . so as to see . . . You know . . .

BELCREDI [*laughing*]. Oh, as for the dress, Doctor, it isn't a matter of twenty years! It's eight hundred! An abyss! Do you really want to shove him across it [*Pointing first to* FRIDA *and then to* MARCHIONESS.] from there to here? But you'll have to pick him up in pieces with a basket! Just think now: for us it is a matter of twenty years, a couple of dresses, and a masquerade. But, if, as you say, Doctor, time has stopped for and around him: if he lives there [*Pointing to* FRIDA.] with her, eight hundred years ago . . . I repeat: the giddiness of the jump will be such, that finding himself suddenly among us . . . [*The* DOCTOR *shakes his head in dissent.*] You don't think so?

DOCTOR. No, because life, my dear baron, can take up its rhythms. This—our life—will at once become real also to him; and will pull him up directly, wresting from him suddenly the illusion, and showing him that the eight hundred years, as you say, are only twenty! It will be like one of those tricks, such as the leap into space, for instance, of the Masonic rite, which appears to be heaven knows how far, and is only a step down the stairs.

BELCREDI. Ah! An idea! Yes! Look at Frida and the Marchioness, doctor! Which is more advanced in time? We old people, Doctor! The young ones think they are more ahead; but it isn't true: we are more ahead, because time belongs to us more than to them.

DOCTOR. If the past didn't alienate us . . .

BELCREDI. It doesn't matter at all! How does it alienate us? They [*Pointing to* FRIDA *and* DI NOLLI.] have still to do what we have accomplished, Doctor: to grow old, doing the same foolish things, more or less, as we did . . . This is the illusion: that one comes forward through a door to life. It isn't so! As soon as one is born, one starts dying; therefore, he who started first is the most advanced of all. The youngest of us is father Adam! Look there: [*Pointing to* FRIDA.] eight hundred years younger than all of us—the Countess Matilda of Tuscany. [*He makes her a deep bow.*]

DI NOLLI. I say, Tito, don't start joking.

BELCREDI. Oh, you think I am joking? . . .

DI NOLLI. Of course, of course . . . all the time.

BELCREDI. Impossible! I've even dressed up as a Benedictine . . .

DI NOLLI. Yes, but for a serious purpose.

BELCREDI. Well, exactly. If it has been serious for the others . . . for Frida, now, for instance. [*Then turning to the* DOCTOR.] I swear, Doctor, I don't yet understand what you want to do.

DOCTOR [*annoyed*]. You'll see! Let me do as I wish . . . At present you see the Marchioness still dressed as . . .

BELCREDI. Oh, she also . . . has to masquerade?

DOCTOR. Of course! of course! In another dress that's in there ready to be used when it comes into his head he sees the Countess Matilda of Canossa before him.

FRIDA [*while talking quietly to* DI NOLLI *notices the doctor's mistake*]. Of Tuscany, of Tuscany!

DOCTOR. It's all the same!

BELCREDI. Oh, I see! He'll be faced by two of them . . .

DOCTOR. Two, precisely! And then . . .

FRIDA [*calling him aside*]. Come here, doctor! Listen!

DOCTOR. Here I am! [*Goes near the two young people and pretends to give some explanations to them.*]

BELCREDI [*softly to* DONNA MATILDA]. I say, this is getting rather strong, you know!

DONNA MATILDA [*looking him firmly in the face*]. What?

BELCREDI. Does it really interest you as much as all that—to make you willing to take part in . . . ? For a woman this is simply enormous! . . .

DONNA MATILDA. Yes, for an ordinary woman.

BELCREDI. Oh, no, my dear, for all women,—in a question like this! It's an abnegation.

DONNA MATILDA. I owe it to him.

BELCREDI. Don't lie! You know well enough it's not hurting you!

DONNA MATILDA. Well, then, where does the abnegation come in?

BELCREDI. Just enough to prevent you losing caste in other people's eyes—and just enough to offend me! . . .

DONNA MATILDA. But who is worrying about you now?

DI NOLLI [*coming forward*]. It's all right. It's all right. That's what we'll do! [*Turning toward* BERTHOLD.] Here you, go and call one of those fellows!

BERTHOLD. At once! [*Exit.*]

DONNA MATILDA. But first of all we've got to pretend that we are going away.

DI NOLLI. Exactly! I'll see to that . . . [*To* BELCREDI.] you don't mind staying here?

BELCREDI [*ironically*]. Oh, no, I don't mind, I don't mind! . . .

DI NOLLI. We must look out not to make him suspicious again, you know.

BELCREDI. Oh, Lord! *He* doesn't amount to anything!

DOCTOR. He must believe absolutely that we've gone away. [LANDOLPH *followed by* BERTHOLD *enters from the right.*]

LANDOLPH. May I come in?

DI NOLLI. Come in! Come in! I say—your name's Lolo, isn't it?

LANDOLPH. Lolo, or Landolph, just as you like!

DI NOLLI. Well, look here: the Doctor and the Marchioness are leaving, at once.

LANDOLPH. Very well. All we've got to say is that they have been able to obtain the permission for the reception from His Holiness. He's in there in his own apartments repenting of all he said—and in an awful state to have the pardon! Would you mind coming a minute? . . . If you would, just for a minute . . . put on the dress again . . .

DOCTOR. Why, of course, with pleasure . . .

LANDOLPH. Might I be allowed to make a suggestion? Why not add that the Marchioness of Tuscany has interceded with the Pope that he should be received?

DONNA MATILDA. You see, he has recognized me!

LANDOLPH. Forgive me . . . I don't know my history very well. I am sure you gentlemen know it much better! But I thought it was believed that Henry IV had a secret passion for the Marchioness of Tuscany.

DONNA MATILDA [*at once*]. Nothing of the kind! Nothing of the kind!

LANDOLPH. That's what I thought! But he says he's loved her . . . he's always saying it . . . And now he fears that her indignation for this secret love of his will work him harm with the Pope.

BELCREDI. We must let him understand that this aversion no longer exists.

LANDOLPH. Exactly! Of course!

DONNA MATILDA [*to* BELCREDI]. History says—I don't know whether you know it or not—that the Pope gave way to the supplications of the Marchioness Matilda and the Abbot of Cluny. And I may say, my dear Belcredi, that I intended to take advantage of this fact—at the time of the pageant—to show him my feelings were not so hostile to him as he supposed.

BELCREDI. You are most faithful to history, Marchioness . . .

LANDOLPH. Well then, the Marchioness could spare herself a double disguise and present herself with Monsignor [*Indicating the* DOCTOR.] as the Marchioness of Tuscany.

DOCTOR [*quickly, energetically*]. No, no! That won't do at all. It would ruin everything. The impression from the conformation must be a sudden one, give a shock! No, no, Marchioness, you will appear again as the Duchess Adelaide, the mother of the Empress. And then we'll go away. This is most necessary: that he should know we've gone away. Come on! Don't let's waste any more time! There's a lot to prepare.

[*Exeunt the* DOCTOR, DONNA MATILDA, *and* LANDOLPH, *right.*]

FRIDA. I am beginning to feel afraid again.

DI NOLLI. Again, Frida?

FRIDA. It would have been better if I had seen him before.

DI NOLLI. There's nothing to be frightened of, really.

FRIDA. He isn't furious, is he?

DI NOLLI. Of course not! he's quite calm.

BELCREDI [*with ironic sentimental affectation*]. Melancholy! Didn't you hear that he loves you?

FRIDA. Thanks! That's just why I am afraid.

BELCREDI. He won't do you any harm.

DI NOLLI. It'll only last a minute . . .

FRIDA. Yes, but there in the dark with him . . .

DI NOLLI. Only for a moment; and I will be near you, and all the others behind the door ready to run in. As soon as you see your mother, your part will be finished . . .

BELCREDI. I'm afraid of a different thing: that we're wasting our time . . .

DI NOLLI. Don't begin again! The remedy seems a sound one to me.

FRIDA. I think so too! I feel it! I'm all trembling!

BELCREDI. But, mad people, my dear friends—though they don't know it, alas—have this felicity which we don't take into account . . .

DI NOLLI [*interrupting, annoyed*]. What felicity? Nonsense!

BELCREDI [*forcefully*]. They don't reason!

DI NOLLI. What's reasoning got to do with it, anyway?

BELCREDI. Don't you call it reasoning that he will have to do—according to us—when he sees her [*Indicates* FRIDA.] and her mother? We've reasoned it all out, surely!

DI NOLLI. Nothing of the kind: no reasoning at all! We put before him a double image of his own fantasy, or fiction, as the doctor says.

BELCREDI [*suddenly*]. I say, I've never understood why they take degrees in medicine.

DI NOLLI [*amazed*]. Who?

BELCREDI. The alienists!

DI NOLLI. What ought they to take degrees in, then?

FRIDA. If they are alienists, in what else should they take degrees?

BELCREDI. In law, of course! All a matter of talk! The more they talk, the more highly they are considered. "Analogous elasticity," "the sensation of distance in time!" And the first thing they tell you is that they don't work miracles—when a miracle's just what is wanted! But they know that the more they say they are not miracle-workers, the more folk believe in their seriousness!

BERTHOLD [*who has been looking through the keyhole of the door on right*]. There they are! There they are! They're coming in here.

DI NOLLI. Are they?

BERTHOLD. He wants to come with them . . . Yes! . . . He's coming too!

DI NOLLI. Let's get away, then! Let's get away, at once! [*To* BERTHOLD.] You stop here!

BERTHOLD. Must I?

[*Without answering him,* DI NOLLI, FRIDA, *and* BELCREDI *go out by the main exit, leaving* BERTHOLD *surprised. The door on the right opens, and* LANDOLPH *enters first, bowing. Then* DONNA MATILDA *comes in, with mantle and ducal crown as in the first act; also the* DOCTOR *as the* ABBOT OF CLUNY. HENRY IV *is among them in royal dress.* ORDULPH *and* HAROLD *enter last of all.*]

HENRY IV [*following up what he has been saying in the other room*]. And now I will ask you a question: how can I be astute, if you think me obstinate?

DOCTOR. No, no, not obstinate!

HENRY IV [*smiling, pleased*]. Then you think me really astute?

DOCTOR. No, no, neither obstinate, nor astute.

HENRY IV [*with benevolent irony*]. Monsignor, if obstinacy is not a vice which can go with astuteness, I hoped that in denying me the former, you would at least allow me a little of the latter. I can assure you I have great need of it. But if you want to keep it all for yourself . . .

DOCTOR. I? I? Do I seem astute to you?

HENRY IV. No. Monsignor! What do you say? Not in the least! Perhaps in this case, I may seem a little obstinate to you [*Cutting short to speak to* DONNA MATILDA.] With your permission: a word in confidence to the Duchess. [*Leads her aside and asks her very earnestly.*] Is your daughter really dear to you?

DONNA MATILDA [*dismayed*]. Why, yes, certainly . . .

HENRY IV. Do you wish me to compensate her with all my love, with all my devotion, for the grave wrongs I have done her—though you must not believe all the stories my enemies tell about my dissoluteness!

DONNA MATILDA. No, no, I don't believe them. I never have believed such stories.

HENRY IV. Well, then are you willing?

DONNA MATILDA [*confused*]. What?

HENRY IV. That I return to love your daughter again? [*Looks at her and adds, in a mysterious tone of warning.*] You mustn't be a friend of the Marchioness of Tuscany!

DONNA MATILDA. I tell you again that she has begged and tried not less than ourselves to obtain your pardon . . .

HENRY IV [*softly, but excitedly*]. Don't tell me that! Don't say that to me! Don't you see the effect it has on me, my Lady?

DONNA MATILDA [*looks a him; then very softly as if in confidence*]. You love her still?

HENRY IV [*puzzled*]. Still? Still, you say? You know, then? But nobody knows! Nobody must know!

DONNA MATILDA. But perhaps she knows, if she has begged so hard for you!

HENRY IV [*looks at her and says*]. And you love your daughter? [*Brief pause. He turns to the* DOCTOR *with laughing accents.*] Ah, Monsignor, it's strange how little I think of my wife! It may be a sin, but I swear to you that I hardly feel her at all in my heart. What is stranger is that her own mother scarcely feels her in her heart. Confess, my Lady, that she amounts to very little for you. [*Turning to* DOCTOR.] She talks to me of that other woman, insistently, insistently, I don't know why! . . .

LANDOLPH [*humbly*]. Maybe, Majesty, it is to disabuse you of some ideas you have had about the Marchioness of Tuscany. [*Then, dismayed at having allowed himself this observation, adds.*] I mean just now, of course . . .

HENRY IV. You too maintain that she has been friendly to me?

LANDOLPH. Yes, at the moment, Majesty.

DONNA MATILDA. Exactly! Exactly! . . .

HENRY IV. I understand. That is to say, you don't believe I love her. I see! I see! Nobody's ever believed it, nobody's ever thought it. Better so, then! But enough, enough! [*Turns to the* DOCTOR *with changed expression.*] Monsignor, you see? The reasons the Pope has had for revoking the excommunication have got nothing at all to do with the reasons for which he excommunicated me originally. Tell Pope Gregory we shall meet again at Brixen. And you, Madame, should you chance to meet your daughter in the courtyard of the castle of your friend the Marchioness, ask her to visit me. We shall see if I succeed in keeping her close beside me as wife and Empress. Many women have presented themselves here already assuring me that they were she. And I thought to have her—yes, I tried sometimes—there's no shame in it, with one's wife!—But when they said they were Bertha, and they were from Susa, all of them—I can't think why—started laughing! [*Confidentially.*] Understand?—in bed—I undressed—so did she—yes, by God, undressed—a man and a woman—it's natural after all! Like that, we don't bother much about who we are. And one's dress is like a phantom that hovers always near one. Oh, Monsignor, phantoms in general are nothing more than trifling disorders of the spirit: images we cannot contain within the bounds of sleep. They reveal themselves even when we are awake, and they frighten us. I . . . ah . . . I am always afraid when, at night time, I see disordered images before me. Sometimes I am even afraid of my own blood pulsing loudly in my arteries in the silence of night, like the sound of a distant step in a lonely corridor! . . . But, forgive me! I have kept you standing too long already. I thank you, my Lady, I thank you, Monsignor. [DONNA MATILDA *and the* DOCTOR *go off bowing. As soon as they have gone,* HENRY IV *suddenly changes his tone.*] Buffoons, buffoons! One can play any tune on them! And that other fellow . . . Pietro Damiani! . . . Caught him out perfectly! He's afraid to appear before me again. [*Moves up and down excitedly while saying this; then sees* BER-

THOLD, *and points him out to the other three valets.*] Oh, look at
this imbecile watching me with his mouth wide open! [*Shakes
him.*] Don't you understand? Don't you see, idiot, how I treat
them, how I play the fool with them, make them appear before me
just as I wish? Miserable, frightened clowns that they are! And you
[*Addressing the* VALETS.] are amazed that I tear off their ridiculous
masks now, just as if it wasn't I who had made them mask themselves to satisfy this taste of mine for playing the madman!

LANDOLPH — HAROLD — ORDULPH [*bewildered, looking at one
another*]. What? What does he say? What?

HENRY IV [*answers them imperiously*]. Enough! enough! Let's stop
it. I'm tired of it. [*Then as if the thought left him no peace.*] By
God! The impudence! To come here along with her lover! . . .
And pretending to do it out of pity? So as not to infuriate a poor
devil already out of the world, out of time, out of life! If it hadn't
been supposed to be done out of pity, one can well imagine that
fellow wouldn't have allowed it. Those people expect others to
behave as they wish all the time. And, of course, there's nothing
arrogant in that! Oh, no! Oh, no! It's merely their way of thinking, of feeling, of seeing. Everybody has his own way of thinking;
you fellows, too. Yours is that of a flock of sheep—miserable,
feeble, uncertain . . . But those others take advantage of this and
make you accept their way of thinking; or, at least, they suppose
they do; because, after all, what do they succeed in imposing on
you? Words, words which anyone can interpret in his own manner! That's the way public opinion is formed! And it's a bad look
out for a man who finds himself labelled one day with one of these
words which everyone repeats; for example "madman," or "imbecile." Don't you think it is rather hard for a man to keep quiet,
when he knows that there is a fellow going about trying to persuade everybody that he is as he sees him, trying to fix him in
other people's opinion as a "madman"—according to him? Now
I am talking seriously! Before I hurt my head, falling from my
horse . . . [*Stops suddenly, noticing the dismay of the four young
men.*] What's the matter with you? [*Imitates their amazed looks.*]
What? Am I, or am I not, mad? Oh, yes! I'm mad all right! [*He
becomes terrible.*] Well, then, by God, down on your knees, down
on your knees! [*Makes them go down on their knees one by one.*]
I order you to go down on your knees before me! And touch the
ground three times with your foreheads! Down, down! That's the
way you've got to be before madmen! [*Then annoyed with their
facile humiliation.*] Get up, sheep! You obeyed me, didn't you?
You might have put the strait jacket on me! . . . Crush a man with
the weight of a word—it's nothing—a fly! all our life is crushed
by the weight of words: the weight of the dead. Look at me here:
can you really suppose that Henry IV is still alive? All the same,
I speak, and order you live men about! Do you think it's a joke that
the dead continue to live?—Yes, *here* it's a joke! But get out into
the live world!—Ah, you say: what a beautiful sunrise—for us! All
time is before us!—Dawn! We will do what we like with this day—.

Ah, yes! To Hell with tradition, the old conventions! Well, go on! You will do nothing but repeat the old, old words, while you imagine you are living! [*Goes up to* BERTHOLD *who has now become quite stupid*] You don't understand a word of this do you? What's your name?

BERTHOLD. I? . . . What? . . . Berthold . . .

HENRY IV. Poor Berthold! What's your name here?

BERTHOLD. I . . . I . . . my name is Fino.

HENRY IV [*feeling the warning and critical glances of the others, turns to them to reduce them to silence*]. Fino?

BERTHOLD. Fino Pagliuca, sire.

HENRY IV [*turning to* LANDOLPH]. I've heard you call each other by your nick-names often enough! Your name is Lolo isn't it?

LANDOLPH. Yes, sire . . . [*Then with a sense of immense joy.*] Oh Lord! Oh Lord! Then he is not mad . . .

HENRY IV [*brusquely*]. What?

LANDOLPH [*hesitating*]. No . . . I said . . .

HENRY IV. Not mad, any more. No. Don't you see? We're having a joke on those that think I am mad! [*To* HAROLD.] I say, boy, your name's Franco . . . [*To* ORDULPH] And yours . . .

ORDULPH. Momo.

HENRY IV. Momo, Momo . . . A nice name that!

LANDOLPH. So he isn't . . .

HENRY IV. What are you talking about? Of course not! Let's have a jolly, good laugh! . . . [*Laughs.*] Ah! . . . Ah! . . . Ah! . . .

LANDOLPH — HAROLD — ORDULPH [*looking at each other half happy and half dismayed*]. Then he's cured! . . . he's all right! . . .

HENRY IV. Silence! Silence! . . . [*To* BERTHOLD.] Why don't you laugh? Are you offended? I didn't mean it especially for you. It's convenient for everybody to insist that certain people are mad, so they can be shut up. Do you know why? Because it's impossible to hear them speak! What shall I say of these people who've just gone away? That one is a whore, another a libertine, another a swindler . . . don't you think so? You can't believe a word he says . . . don't you think so?—By the way, they all listen to me terrified. And why are they terrified, if what I say isn't true? Of course, you can't believe what madmen say—yet, at the same time, they stand there with their eyes wide open with terror!—Why? Tell me, tell me, why?—You see I'm quite calm now!

BERTHOLD. But perhaps, they think that . . .

HENRY IV. No, no, my dear fellow! Look me well in the eyes! . . . I don't say that it's true—nothing is true, Berthold! But . . . look me in the eyes!

BERTHOLD. Well . . .

HENRY IV. You see? You see? . . . You have terror in your own eyes now because I seem mad to you! There's the proof of it! [*Laughs.*]

LANDOLPH [*coming forward in the name of the others, exasperated*]. What proof?

HENRY IV. Your being so dismayed because now I seem again mad to you. You have thought me mad up to now, haven't you? You feel that this dismay of yours can become terror too—something to dash away the ground from under your feet and deprive you of the air you breathe! Do you know what it means to find yourselves face to face with a madman—with one who shakes the foundations of all you have built up in yourselves, your logic, the logic of all your constructions? Madmen, lucky folk! construct without logic, or rather with a logic that flies like a feather. Voluble! Voluble! Today like this and tomorrow—who knows? You say: "This cannot be"; but for them everything can be. You say: "This isn't true!" And why? Because it doesn't seem true to you, or you, or you . . . [*Indicates the three of them in succession.*] . . . and to a hundred thousand others! One must see what seems true to these hundred thousand others who are not supposed to be mad! What a magnificent spectacle they afford, when they reason! What flowers of logic they scatter! I know that when I was a child, I thought the moon in the pond was real. How many things I thought real! I believed everything I was told—and I was happy! Because it's a terrible thing if you don't hold on to that which seems true to you today—to that which will seem true to you tomorrow, even if it is the opposite of that which seemed true to you yesterday. I would never wish you to think, as I have done, on this horrible thing which really drives one mad: that if you were beside another and looking into his eyes—as I one day looked into somebody's eyes—you might as well be a beggar before a door never to be opened to you; for he who does enter there will never be you, but someone unknown to you with his own different and impenetrable world . . . [*Long pause. Darkness gathers in the room, increasing the sense of strangeness and consternation in which the four young men are involved.* HENRY IV *remains aloof, pondering on the misery which is not only his, but everybody's. Then he pulls himself up, and says in an ordinary tone.*] It's getting dark here . . .

ORDULPH. Shall I go for a lamp?

HENRY IV [*ironically*]. The lamp, yes the lamp! . . . Do you suppose I don't know that as soon as I turn my back with my oil lamp to go to bed, you turn on the electric light for yourselves, here, and even there, in the throne room? I pretend not to see it!

ORDULPH. Well, then, shall I turn it on now?

HENRY IV. No, it would blind me! I want my lamp!

ORDULPH. It's ready here behind the door. [*Goes to the main exit, opens the door, goes out for a moment, and returns with an ancient lamp which is held by a ring at the top.*]

HENRY IV. Ah, a little light! Sit there around the table, no, not like that; in an elegant, easy, manner! . . . [*To* HAROLD.] Yes, you, like that! [*Poses him.*] [*Then to* BERTHOLD.] You, so! . . . and I, here! [*Sits opposite them.*] We could do with a little decorative moonlight. It's very useful for us, the moonlight. I feel a real necessity for it, and pass a lot of time looking up at the moon from my window. Who would think, to look at her that she knows that eight hundred years have passed, and that I, seated at the window, cannot really be Henry IV gazing at the moon like any poor devil? But, look, look! See what a magnificent night scene we have here: the emperor surrounded by his faithful counsellors! . . . How do you like it?

LANDOLPH [*softly to* HAROLD, *so as not to break the enchantment*]. And to think it wasn't true!

HENRY IV. True? What wasn't true?

LANDOLPH [*timidly as if to excuse himself*]. No . . . I mean . . . I was saying this morning to him [*Indicates* BERTHOLD.]—he has just entered on service here—I was saying: what a pity that dressed like this and with so many beautiful costumes in the wardrobe . . . and with a room like that . . . [*Indicates the throne room.*]

HENRY IV. Well? what's the pity?

LANDOLPH. Well . . . that we didn't know . . .

HENRY IV. That it was all done in jest, this comedy?

LANDOLPH. Because we thought that . . .

HAROLD [*coming to his assistance*]. Yes . . . that it was done seriously!

HENRY IV. What do you say? Doesn't it seem serious to you?

LANDOLPH. But if you say that . . .

HENRY IV. I say that—you are fools! You ought to have known how to create a fantasy for yourselves, not to act it for me, or anyone coming to see me; but naturally, simply, day by day, before nobody, feeling yourselves alive in the history of the eleventh century, here at the court of your emperor, Henry IV! You, Ordulph [*Taking him by the arm.*], alive in the castle of Goslar, waking up in the morning, getting out of bed, and entering straightway into the dream, clothing yourself in the dream that would be no more a dream, because you would have lived it, felt it all alive in you. You would have drunk it in with the air you breathed; yet knowing all the time that it was a dream, so you could better enjoy the privilege afforded you of having to do nothing else but live this dream, this far off and yet actual dream! And to think that at a distance of eight centuries from this remote age of ours, so colored and so sepulchral, the men of the twentieth century are torturing themselves in ceaseless anxiety to know how their fates and fortunes will work out! Whereas you are already in history with me . . .

LANDOLPH. Yes, yes, very good!

HENRY IV. . . . Everything determined, everything settled!

ORDULPH. Yes, yes!

HENRY IV. And sad as is my lot, hideous as some of the events are, bitter the struggles and troublous the time—still all history! All history that cannot change, understand? All fixed for ever! And you could have admired at your ease how every effect followed obediently its cause with perfect logic, how every event took place precisely and coherently in each minute particular! The pleasure, the pleasure of history, in fact, which is so great, was yours.

LANDOLPH. Beautiful, beautiful!

HENRY IV. Beautiful, but it's finished! Now that you know, I could not do it any more! [*Takes his lamp to go to bed.*] Neither could you, if up to now you haven't understood the reason of it! I am sick of it now. [*Almost to himself with violent contained rage.*] By God, I'll make her sorry she came here! Dressed herself up as a mother-in-law for me . . . ! And he as an abbot . . . ! And they bring a doctor with them to study me . . . ! Who knows if they don't hope to cure me? . . . Clowns . . . ! I'd like to smack one of them at least in the face: yes, that one—a famous swordsman, they say! . . . He'll kill me . . . Well, we'll see, we'll see! . . . [*A knock at the door.*] Who is it?

THE VOICE OF JOHN. Deo Gratias!

HAROLD [*very pleased at the chance for another joke*]. Oh, it's John, it's old John, who comes every night to play the monk.

ORDULPH [*rubbing his hands*]. Yes, yes! Let's make him do it!

HENRY IV [*at once, severely*]. Fool, why? Just to play a joke on a poor old man who does it for love of me?

LANDOLPH [*to* ORDULPH]. It has to be as if it were true.

HENRY IV. Exactly, as if true! Because, only so, truth is not a jest [*Opens the door and admits* JOHN *dressed as a humble friar with a roll of parchment under his arm.*] Come in, come in, father! [*Then assuming a tone of tragic gravity and deep resentment.*] All the documents of my life and reign favorable to me were destroyed deliberately by my enemies. One only has escaped destruction, this, my life, written by a humble monk who is devoted to me. And you would laugh at him! [*Turns affectionately to* JOHN, *and invites him to sit down at the table.*] Sit down, father, sit down! Have the lamp near you! [*Puts the lamp near him.*] Write! Write!

JOHN [*opens the parchment and prepares to write from dictation*]. I am ready, your Majesty!

HENRY IV [*dictating*]. "The decree of peace proclaimed at Mayence helped the poor and the good, while it damaged the powerful and the bad. [*Curtain begins to fall.*] It brought wealth to the former, hunger and misery to the latter . . ."

CURTAIN

Act III

The throne room so dark that the wall at the bottom is hardly seen. The canvases of the two portraits have been taken away; and, within their frames, FRIDA, *dressed as the "Marchioness of Tuscany," and* CHARLES DI NOLLI, *as "Henry IV," have taken the exact positions of the portraits.*

For a moment, after the raising of curtain, the stage is empty. Then the door on the left opens; and HENRY IV, *holding the lamp by the ring on top of it, enters. He looks back to speak to the four young men, who, with* JOHN, *are presumedly in the adjoining hall, as at the end of the second act.*

HENRY IV. No, stay where you are, stay where you are. I shall manage all right by myself. Good night! [*Closes the door and walks,* very sad and tired, across the hall towards the second door on the right, which leads into his apartments.]

FRIDA [*as soon as she sees that he has just passed the throne, whispers from the niche like one who is on the point of fainting away with fright*]. Henry . . .

HENRY IV [*stopping at the voice, as if someone had stabbed him traitorously in the back, turns a terror-stricken face towards the wall at the bottom of the room; raising an arm instinctively, as if to defend himself and ward off a blow*]. Who is calling me? [*It is not a question, but an exclamation vibrating with terror, which does not expect a reply from the darkness and the terrible silence of the hall, which suddenly fills him with the suspicion that he is really mad.*]

FRIDA [*at his shudder of terror, is herself not less frightened at the part she is playing, and repeats a little more loudly*]. Henry! . . . [*But, although she wishes to act the part as they have given it to her, she stretches her head a little out of frame towards the other frame.*]

HENRY IV [*gives a dreadful cry; lets the lamp fall from his hands to cover his head with his arms, and makes a movement as if to run away*].

FRIDA [*jumping from the frame on to the stand and shouting like a mad woman*]. Henry! . . . Henry! . . . I'm afraid! . . . I'm terrified! . . .

[*And while* DI NOLLI *jumps in turn on to the stand and thence to the floor and runs to* FRIDA *who, on the verge of fainting, continues to cry out, the* DOCTOR, DONNA MATILDA, *also dressed as "Matilda of Tuscany,"* TITO BELCREDI. LANDOLPH, BERTHOLD *and* JOHN *enter the hall from the doors on the right and on the left. One of them turns on the light: a strange light coming from lamps hidden in the ceiling so that only the upper part of the stage is well lighted. The others without taking notice of* HENRY IV, *who looks on astonished by the unexpected inrush, after the moment of terror which still causes him to tremble, run anxiously to support and comfort the still shaking* FRIDA, *who is moaning in the arms of her fiancé. All are speaking at the same time.*]

DI NOLLI. No, no, Frida . . . Here I am . . . I am beside you!

DOCTOR [*coming with the others*]. Enough! Enough! There's nothing more to be done! . . .

DONNA MATILDA. He is cured, Frida. Look! He is cured! Don't you see?

DI NOLLI [*astonished*]. Cured?

BELCREDI. It was only for fun! Be calm!

FRIDA. No! I am afraid! I am afraid!

DONNA MATILDA. Afraid of what? Look at him! He was never mad at all! . . .

DI NOLLI. That isn't true! What are you saying? Cured?

DOCTOR. It appears so. I should say so . . .

BELCREDI. Yes, yes! They have told us so. [*Pointing to the four young men.*]

DONNA MATILDA. Yes, for a long time! He has confided in them, told them the truth!

DI NOLLI [*now more indignant than astonished*]. But what does it mean? If, up to a short time ago . . . ?

BELCREDI. Hum! He was acting, to take you in and also us, who in good faith . . .

DI NOLLI. Is it possible? To deceive his sister, also, right up to the time of her death?

HENRY IV [*remains apart, peering at one and now at the other under the accusation and the mockery of what all believe to be a cruel joke of his, which is now revealed. He has shown by the flashing of his eyes that he is meditating a revenge, which his violent contempt prevents him from defining clearly, as yet. Stung to the quick and with a clear idea of accepting the fiction they have insidiously worked up as true, he bursts forth at this point*]. Go on, I say! Go on!

DI NOLLI [*astonished at the cry*]. Go on! What do you mean?

HENRY IV. It isn't *your* sister only that is dead!

DI NOLLI. My sister? Yours, I say, whom you compelled up to the last moment, to present herself here as your mother Agnes!

HENRY IV. And was she not *your* mother?

DI NOLLI. My mother? Certainly my mother!

HENRY IV. But your mother is dead for me, *old and far away!* You have just got down now from there. [*Pointing to the frame from which he jumped down.*] And how do you know whether I have not wept her long in secret, dressed even as I am?

DONNA MATILDA [*dismayed, looking at the others*]. What does he say? [*Much impressed, observing him.*] Quietly! quietly, for Heaven's sake!

HENRY IV. What do I say? I ask all of you if Agnes was not the mother of Henry IV? [*Turns to* FRIDA *as if she were really the "Marchioness of Tuscany."*] You, Marchioness, it seems to me, ought to know.

FRIDA [*still frightened, draws closer to* DI NOLLI]. No, no, I don't know. Not I!

DOCTOR. It's the madness returning. . . . Quiet now, everybody!

BELCREDI [*indignant*]. Madness indeed, Doctor! He's acting again! . . .

HENRY IV [*suddenly*]. I? You have emptied those two frames over there, and he stands before my eyes as Henry IV . . .

BELCREDI. We've had enough of this joke now.

HENRY IV. Who said joke?

DOCTOR [*loudly to* BELCREDI]. Don't excite him, for the love of God!

BELCREDI [*without lending an ear to him, but speaking louder*]. But they have said so [*Pointing again to the four young men.*], they, they!

HENRY IV [*turning around and looking at them*]. You? Did you say it was all a joke?

LANDOLPH [*timid and embarrassed*]. No . . . really we said that you were cured.

BELCREDI. Look here! Enough of this! [*To* DONNA MATILDA.] Doesn't it seem to you that the sight of him, [*Pointing to* DI NOLLI.] Marchioness, and that of your daughter dressed so, is becoming an intolerable puerility?

DONNA MATILDA. Oh, be quiet! What does the dress matter, if he is cured?

HENRY IV. Cured, yes! I am cured! [*To* BELCREDI.] ah, but not to let it end this way all at once, as you suppose! [*Attacks him.*] Do you know that for twenty years nobody has ever dared to appear before me here like you and that gentleman? [*Pointing to the* DOCTOR.]

BELCREDI. Of course I know it. As a matter of fact, I too appeared before you this morning dressed . . .

HENRY IV. As a monk, yes!

BELCREDI. And you took me for Peter Damiani! And I didn't even laugh, believing, in fact, that . . .

HENRY IV. That I was mad! Does it make you laugh seeing her like that, now that I am cured? And yet you might have remembered that in my eyes her appearance now . . . [*Interrupts himself with a gesture of contempt.*] Ah! [*Suddenly turns to the* DOCTOR.] You are a doctor, aren't you?

DOCTOR. Yes.

HENRY IV. And you also took part in dressing her up as the Marchioness of Tuscany? To prepare a counterjoke for me here, eh?

DONNA MATILDA [*impetuously*]. No, no! What do you say? It was done for you! I did it for your sake.

DOCTOR [*quickly*]. To attempt, to try, not knowing . . .

HENRY IV [*cutting him short.* I understand. I say counter-joke, in his case [*Indicates* BELCREDI.] because he believes that I have been carrying on a jest . . .

BELCREDI. But excuse me, what do you mean? You say yourself you are cured.

HENRY IV. Let me speak! [*To the* DOCTOR.] Do you know, Doctor, that for a moment you ran the risk of making me mad again? By God, to make the portraits speak; to make them jump alive out of their frames . . .

DOCTOR. But you saw that all of us ran in at once, as soon as they told us . . .

HENRY IV. Certainly! [*Contemplates* FRIDA *and* DI NOLLI, *and then looks at the* MARCHIONESS, *and finally at his own costume.*] The combination is very beautiful . . . Two couples . . . Very good, very good, Doctor! For a madman, not bad! . . . [*With a slight wave of his hand to* BELCREDI.] It seems to him now to be a carnival out of season, eh? [*Turns to look at him.*] We'll get rid now of this masquerade costume of mine, so that I may come away with you. What do you say?

BELCREDI. With me? With us?

HENRY IV. Where shall we go? To the Club? In dress coats and with white ties? Or shall both of us go to the Marchioness' house?

BELCREDI. Wherever you like! Do you want to remain here still, to continue—alone—what was nothing but the unfortunate joke of a day of carnival? It is really incredible, incredible how you have been able to do all this, freed from the disaster that befell you!

HENRY IV. Yes, you see how it was! The fact is that falling from my horse and striking my head as I did, I was really mad for I know not how long . . .

DOCTOR. Ah! Did it last long?

HENRY IV [*very quickly to the* DOCTOR]. Yes, Doctor, a long time! I think it must have been about twelve years. [*Then suddenly turning to speak to* BELCREDI.] Thus I saw nothing, my dear fellow, of all that, after that day of carnival, happened for you but not for me: how things changed, how my friends deceived me, how my place was taken by another, and all the rest of it! And suppose my place had been taken in the heart of the woman I loved? . . . And how should I know who was dead or who had disappeared? . . . All this, you know, wasn't exactly a jest for me, as it seems to you . . .

BELCREDI. No, no! I don't mean that if you please. I mean after . . .

HENRY IV. Ah, yes? After? One day [*Stops and addresses the* DOCTOR.]—A most interesting case, Doctor! Study me well! Study me carefully! [*Trembles while speaking.*] All by itself, who knows how, one day the trouble here [*Touches his forehead.*] mended. Little by little, I open my eyes, and at first I don't know whether I am asleep or awake. Then I know I am awake. I touch this thing and that; I see clearly again . . . Ah!—then, as *he* says [*Alludes to* BELCREDI.] away, away with this masquerade, this incubus! Let's open the windows, breathe life once again! Away! Away! Let's run out! [*Suddenly pulling himself up.*] But where? And to do what? To show myself to all, secretly, as Henry IV, not like this, but arm in arm with you, among my dear friends?

BELCREDI. What are you saying?

DONNA MATILDA. Who could think it? It's not to be imagined. It was an accident.

HENRY IV. They all said I was mad before. [*To* BELCREDI.] And you know it! You were more ferocious than any one against those who tried to defend me.

BELCREDI. Oh, that was only a joke!

HENRY IV. Look at my hair! [*Shows him the hair on the nape of his neck.*]

BELCREDI. But mine is grey too!

HENRY IV. Yes, with this difference: that mine went grey here, as Henry IV, do you understand? And I never knew it! I perceived it all of a sudden, one day, when I opened my eyes; and I was terrified because I understood at once that not only had my hair gone grey, but that I was all grey, inside; that everything had fallen to pieces, that everything was finished; and I was going to arrive hungry as a wolf, at a banquet which had already been cleared away . . .

BELCREDI. Yes, but, what about the others? . . .

HENRY IV [*quickly*]. Ah, yes, I know! They couldn't wait until I was cured, not even those, who, behind my back, pricked my saddled horse till it bled. . . .

DI NOLLI [*agitated*]. What, what?

HENRY IV. Yes, treacherously, to make it rear and cause me to fall.

DONNA MATILDA [*quickly, in horror*]. This is the first time I knew that.

HENRY IV. That was also a joke, probably!

DONNA MATILDA. But who did it? Who was behind us, then?

HENRY IV. It doesn't matter who it was. All those that went on feasting and were ready to leave me their scrapings, Marchioness, of miserable pity, or some dirty remnant of remorse in the filthy plate! Thanks! [*Turning quickly to the* DOCTOR.] Now, Doctor, the case must be absolutely new in the history of madness; I preferred to remain mad—since I found everything ready and at my disposal for this new exquisite fantasy. I would live it—this madness of mine—with the most lucid consciousness; and thus revenge myself on the brutality of a stone which had dented my head. The solitude—this solitude—squalid and empty as it appeared to me when I opened my eyes again— I determined to deck it out with all the colors and splendors of that far off day of carnival, when you [*Looks at* DONNA MATILDA *and points* FRIDA *out to her.*]—when you, Marchioness, triumphed. So I would oblige all those who were around me to follow, by God, at my orders that famous pageant which had been—for you and not for me—the jest of a day. I would make it become—for ever—no more a joke but a reality, the reality of a real madness: here, all in masquerade, with throne room, and these my four secret counsellors: secret and, of course, traitors. [*He turns quickly towards them.*] I should like to know what you have gained by revealing the fact that I was cured! If I am cured, there's no longer any need of you, and you will be discharged! To give anyone one's confidence . . . that is really the act of a madman. But now I accuse you in my turn. [*Turning to othe others.*] Do you know? They thought [*Alludes to the* VALETS.] they could make fun of me too with you. [*Bursts out laughing. The others laugh, but shamefacedly, except* DONNA MATILDA.]

BELCREDI [*to* DI NOLLI]. Well, imagine that . . . That's not bad . . .

DI NOLLI [*to the* FOUR YOUNG MEN]. You?

HENRY IV. We must pardon them. This dress [*Plucking his dress*]. which is for me the evident, involuntary caricature of that other continuous, everlasting masquerade, of which we are the involuntary puppets [*Indicates* BELCREDI.], when, without knowing it, we mask ourselves with that which we appear to be . . . ah, that dress of theirs, this masquerade of theirs, of course, we must forgive it them, since they do not yet see it is identical with themselves . . . [*Turning again to* BELCREDI.] You know, it is quite easy to get accustomed to it. One walks about as a tragic character, just as if it were nothing . . . [*Imitates the tragic manner.*] in a room like this . . . Look here, doctor! I remember a priest, certainly Irish, a nice-looking priest, who was sleeping in the sun one November day, with his arm on the corner of the bench of a public garden.

He was lost in the golden delight of the mild sunny air which must have seemed for him almost summery. One may be sure that in that moment he did not know any more that he was a priest, or even where he was. He was dreaming . . . A little boy passed with a flower in his hand. He touched the priest with it here on the neck. I saw him open his laughing eyes, while all his mouth smiled with the beauty of his dream. He was forgetful of everything . . . But all at once, he pulled himself together, and stretched out his priest's cassock; and there came back to his eyes the same seriousness which you have seen in mine; because the Irish priests defend the seriousness of their Catholic faith with the same zeal with which I defend the sacred rights of hereditary monarchy! I am cured, gentlemen: because I can act the madman to perfection, here; and I do it very quietly, I'm only sorry for you that have to live your madness so agitatedly, without knowing it or seeing it.

BELCREDI. It comes to this, then, that it is we who are mad. That's what it is!

HENRY IV [*containing his irritation*]. But if you weren't mad, both you and she [*Indicating the* MARCHIONESS.] would you have come here to see me?

BELCREDI. To tell the truth, I came here believing that you were the madman.

HENRY IV [*suddenly indicating the* MARCHIONESS]. And she?

BELCREDI. Ah, as for her . . . I can't say. I see she is all fascinated by your words, by this *conscious* madness of yours. [*Turns to her.*] Dressed as you are [*Speaking to her.*], you could even remain here to live it out, Marchioness.

DONNA MATILDA. You are insolent!

HENRY IV [*conciliatingly*]. No, Marchioness, what he means to say is that the miracle would be complete, according to him, with you here, who—as the Marchioness of Tuscany, you well know,—could not be my friend, save, as at Canossa, to give me a little pity . . .

BELCREDI. Or even more than a little! She said so herself!

HENRY IV [*to the* MARCHIONESS, *continuing*]. And even, shall we say, a little remorse! . . .

BELCREDI. Yes, that too she has admitted.

DONNA MATILDA [*angry*]. Now look here . . .

HENRY IV [*quickly, to placate her*]. Don't bother about him! Don't mind him! Let him go on infuriating me—though the Doctor's told him not to. [*Turns to* BELCREDI.] But do you suppose I am going to trouble myself any more about what happened between us—the share you had in my misfortune with her [*Indicates the* MARCHIONESS *to him and pointing* BELCREDI *out to her.*] the part he has now in your life? This is my life! Quite a different thing from your life! Your life, the life in which you have grown old—I have not lived that life. [*To* DONNA MATILDA.] Was this what you wanted to show me with this sacrifice of yours, dressing yourself up like this, according to the Doctor's idea? Excellently done, Doctor! Oh, an excellent idea:—"As we were then, eh? and as we are now?" But I am not a madman according to your way of think-ing, Doctor. I know very well that that man there [*Indicates* DI NOLLI.] cannot be me; because I am Henry IV, and have been, these twenty years, cast in this eternal masquerade. She has lived these years! [*Indicates the* MARCHIONESS.] She has enjoyed them and has become—look at her!—a woman I can no longer recog-nize. It is so that I knew her! [*Points to* FRIDA *and draws near her.*] This is the Marchioness I know, always this one! . . . You seem a lot of children to be so easily frightened by me . . . [*To* FRIDA.] And you're frightened too, little girl, aren't you, by the jest that they made you take part in—though they didn't under-stand it wouldn't be the jest they meant it to be, for me? Oh miracle of miracles! Prodigy of prodigies! The dream alive in you! More than alive in you! It was an image that wavered there and they've made you come to life! Oh, mine! You're mine, mine, mine, in my own right! [HE *holds her in his arms, laughing like a madman, while all stand still terrified. Then as they advance to tear* FRIDA *from his arms, he becomes furious, terrible and cries im-periously to his* VALETS.] Hold them! Hold them! I order you to hold them!

> [*The* FOUR YOUNG MEN *amazed, yet fascinated, move to ex-ecute his orders, automatically, and seize* DI NOLLI, *the* DOC-TOR, *and* BELCREDI.]

BELCREDI [*freeing himself*]. Leave her alone! Leave her alone! You're no madman!

HENRY IV [*in a flash draws the sword from the side of* LANDOLPH, *who is close to him*]. I'm not mad, eh! Take that, you! . . . [*Drives sword into him. A cry of horror goes up. All rush over to assist* BELCREDI, *crying out together.*]

DI NOLLI. Has he wounded you?

BERTHOLD. Yes, yes, seriously!

DOCTOR. I told you so!

FRIDA. Oh God, oh God!

DI NOLLI. Frida, come here!

DONNA MATILDA. He's mad, mad!

DI NOLLI. Hold him!

BELCREDI [*while* THEY *take him away by the left exit,* HE *protests as he is borne out*]. No, no, you're not mad! You're not mad. He's not mad!

> [THEY *go out by the left amid cries and excitement. After a moment, one hears a still sharper, more piercing cry from* DONNA MATILDA, *and then, silence.*]

HENRY IV [*who has remained on the stage between* LANDOLPH, HAROLD *and* ORDULPH, *with his eyes almost starting out of his head, terri-fied by the life of his own masquerade which has driven him to crime.*] Now, yes . . . we'll have to [*Calls his* VALETS *around him as if to protect him.*] here we are . . . together . . . for ever!

CURTAIN

THOMAS MANN
(1875–1955)
Felix Krull*

As I take my pen in hand, in ample leisure and complete retirement —in sound health too, though tired, so very tired that I shall hardly be able to proceed save in small stages and with frequent pauses for rest—as I take up my pen, then, to commit my confessions to the long-suffering paper, in the neat and pleasing calligraphy of which I a master, I own to a fleeting misgiving on the score of my own fitness for the task in hand. Am I, I ask myself, equipped by previous training for this intellectual enterprise? However, since every word that I have to say concerns solely my own personal and peculiar experiences, errors, and passions and hence should be entirely within my compass; so the only doubt which can arise is whether I command the necessary tact and gifts of expression, and in my view these are less the fruit of a regular course of study than of natural parts and a favourable atmosphere in youth. For the latter I have not lacked; I come of an upper-class if somewhat loose-living home, and my sister Olympia and I had the benefit for some months of the ministrations of a Fräulein from Vevey[1]—though it is true that she had to leave, in consequence of a rivalry between her and my mother, of which my father was the object. My godfather Maggotson, with whom I was in daily and intimate contact, was an artist of considerable merit; everybody in the little town called him professor, though that enviable title was his more by courtesy than by right. My father, his size and obesity notwithstanding, had great personal charm, and he always laid stress upon lucid and well-chosen language. There was French blood in the family from the grandmother's side and he himself had spent some of his young years in France—he used to say that he knew Paris like his waistcoat pocket. His French pronunciation was excellent and he was fond of introducing into his conversation little expressions like "*C'est ça*," "*épatant*," "*parfaitement*," "*à mon goût*,"[2] and so on. Up till the end of his life he was a great favourite with the female sex. I have said all this of course by way of preface and somewhat out of the due order of my tale. As for myself I have a natural

---

* Reprinted from *Stories of Three Decades* by Thomas Mann and translated by H. T. Lowe-Porter. Copyright 1936 and renewed 1964 by Alfred A. Knopf, Inc. Reprinted by permission of the publisher.

1. nursemaid from a small town on Lake Geneva.
2. "That's right, splendid, precisely, to my liking."

instinct for good form, upon which throughout my career of fraud I have always been able to rely, as my story will only too abundantly show. I think therefore that I may commit it to writing without further misgivings on this score. I am resolved to practise the utmost candour, regardless whether I incur the reproach of vanity or shamelessness—for what moral value or significance can confessions like mine possess if they have not the value of perfect sincerity?

The Rhine valley brought me forth—that region favoured of heaven, mild and without ruggedness either in its climate or in the nature of its soil, abounding in cities and villages peopled by a blithe and laughter-loving folk—truly of all the regions of the earth it must be one of the sweetest. Here on these slopes exposed to the southern sun and sheltered from rude winds by the hills of the Rhine valley lie those flourishing resorts the very sound of whose names makes the heart of the toper to laugh: Rüdesheim,[3] Johannisberg, Rauenthal—and here too that most estimable little town where forty years ago I saw the light. It lies slightly westward of the bend made by the river at Mainz. Containing some four thousand souls, it is famous for its wine-cellars and is one of the chief landing-places for the steamers which ply up and down the Rhine. Thus the gay city of Mainz was very near, the Taunus baths patronized by high society, Homburg, Langenschwalbach, and Schlangenbad. This last we could reach by a half-hour's journey on a narrow-gauge road; and how often in the pleasant time of year did we make excursions thither, my parents, my sister Olympia, and I, by train, by carriage, or by boat! Many other excursions we made too, in all directions, for everywhere nature smiled and the hand of man and his fertile brain had spread out pleasures for our delectation. I can still see my father, clad in his comfortable summer suit with a pattern of small checks, as he used to sit with us in the arbour of some inn garden, rather far off the table, for his paunch prevented him from drawing up close, wrapt in enjoyment of a dish of prawns washed down with golden wine. Often my godfather Maggotson was with us, looking at the scene through his big round glasses and absorbing great and small into his artist soul.

My poor father was the proprietor of the firm of Engelbert Krull, makers of the now extinct brand of sparkling wine called Lorley Extra Cuvée. The cellars of the firm lay on the Rhine not far from the landing-stage, and often as a lad I used to play in the cool vaults or follow the stone-paved lanes that led in all directions among the high-tiered shelves, meditating upon the army of bottles that lay in slanting rows upon their sides. "There you lie," I would apostrophize them—though of course at that time I had no power to put my thoughts into apposite words—"there you lie in this sub-

3. All these places produce well-known Rhine wines.

terranean twilight and within you there is clearing and mellowing
that bubbling golden sap which shall make so many pairs of eyes to
sparkle and so many hearts to throb with heightened zest. You are
not much to look at now; but one day you will mount up to the
light and be arrayed in festal splendour and there will be parties
and weddings and little celebrations in private rooms and your corks
will pop up to the ceiling and kindle mirth and levity and desire in
the hearts of men."—Some such ideas as these the boy strove to
express; and so much at least was true, that the firm of Engelbert
Krull laid great stress upon the exterior of their wares, those last
touches which in the trade are known as the coiffure. The compressed corks were fastened with silver wire and gold cords sealed
with purple wax, yes, actually a stately round seal such as one sees
on documents. The necks were wrapped in a fullness of silver foil
and on the swelling body was a flaring label with gilt flourishes
round the edge. This label had been concocted by my godfather
Maggotson. It bore several coats of arms and stars, my father's monogram, and the name of the brand: Lorley Extra Cuvée, all in gilt
letters, and a female figure arrayed in a few spangles and a necklace,
sitting on the top of a rock with her legs crossed, combing her
flowing hair. But unfortunately it appears that the quality of the
wine did not correspond to the splendour of its setting-out. "Krull,"
I have heard my godfather say, "I have the greatest respect for you
personally; but really the police ought to condemn your wine. A
week ago I was foolish enough to drink half a bottle and my constitution has not yet recovered from the shock. What sort of stuff do
you dose it with—petroleum, fusel oil? Anyhow, it's poison. You
ought to be afraid to sell it." My poor father's was a soft nature, he
could not bear hard words and was always thrown into a distress.
"It's all right for you to joke, Maggotson," he would answer, gently
caressing his belly with his finger-tips, as was his habit, "but there is
such a prejudice against the domestic product, I have to keep down
the price and make the public believe it is getting something for its
money. Anyhow, the competition is so fierce that I shall not be able
to go on for long." Thus my poor father.

Our villa was a charming little property seated on a slope commanding a view of the Rhine. The front garden ran downhill and
rejoiced in many crockeryware adornments: dwarfs, toadstools, and
animals in lifelike poses; there was a looking-glass ball on a stand,
which grotesquely distorted the faces of the passers-by; an æolian
harp,[4] several grottoes, and a fountain whose spray made an ingenious design in the air while silver-fish swam in the basin. As for
our domestic interior, it was after my father's heart, who above all
things liked comfort and good cheer. Cosy nooks invited one to sit
down; there was a real spinning-wheel in one corner, and endless trifles and knick-knacks. Mussel-shells, glass boxes, bottles of smelling-

---

4. Box with strings that are set vibrating by the wind.

salts stood about on étagères[5] and velvet-topped tables. A multiplicity of down cushions in silk-embroidered covers were distributed on sofas and day-beds, for my father loved to lie soft. The curtain-rods were halberds,[6] and the portières[7] very jolly, made of coloured beads and rushes, which look quite like a solid door, but you can pass through without lifting your hand, when they fall behind you with a whispering sound. Above the wind-screen was an ingenious device which played the first bar of "Wine, Women, and Song" in a pleasing little tinkle whenever the door opened or shut.

Such was the home upon which, on a mild rainy Sunday in May, I first opened my eyes. From now on I mean to follow the order of events and not run ahead of my story. If report tells true, the birth was slow and difficult and did not come to pass without help from the family doctor, whose name was Mecum. It appears that I—if I may use the first person to refer to that far-away and foreign little being—was extremely inactive and made no attempt to second my mother's efforts, showing no zeal to enter a world which I was yet to love with such an ardent love. However, I was a healthy and well-formed infant and throve at the breast of my excellent wet-nurse in a way to encourage the liveliest hopes for my future. Yet the most mature reflection inclines me to associate this reluctance to exchange the darkness of the womb for the light of day with the extraordinary gift and passion for sleep which has been mine all my life. They tell me that I was a quiet child, that I did not cry and break the peace, but was given to sleep and napping, to a degree most comfortable to my nurses. And however great my subsequent love of the world, which caused me to mingle in it in all sorts of guises and to attach it to myself by all possible means, yet I feel that in night and slumber always my true home was to be found. Even without physical fatigue I have always fallen asleep with the greatest ease and enjoyment, lost myself in far and dreamless forgetfulness, and waked after ten or twelve or even fourteen hours' oblivion more refreshed and gratified than even by all the satisfactions and successes of my waking hours. Is there a contradiction here between this love of sleep and my great urge towards life and love of which it will be in place to speak hereafter? I have said that I have concentrated much thought upon this matter and several times I have had the clearest perception that there is no contradiction but rather a hidden connection and correspondence. And it is the fact that now, when I have aged and grown weary so that I feel none of my old irresistible compulsion towards the society of men, but live in complete retirement, only now is my power of sleep impaired, so that I am in a sense a stranger to it, my slumbers being short and light and fleeting; whereas even in the prison—where there was much opportunity—I slept better than in the soft beds of the most

5. open shelves for bric-a-brac.
6. weapons consisting of an elaborate

7. hangings that cover a doorway.
axlike blade mounted on a shaft.

luxurious hotels. But I am fallen into my old error of getting ahead of my story.

Often enough I heard from my parents' lips that I was a Sunday child; and though I was brought up to despise all forms of superstition I have always thought there was some significance in the fact, taken in connection with my Christian name of Felix (for so I was christened, after my godfather Maggotson) and my physical fineness and sense of well-being. Yes, I have always believed that I was *felix*, a favoured child of the gods; and I may say that, on the whole, events do not show me to have been mistaken in this lively conviction. Indeed, it is peculiarly characteristic of my career that whatever misfortune and suffering it may have held always seemed like a divergence from the natural order, a cloud, as it were, through which my native sunniness continued to shine.—After which digression into the abstract I will once more return to depict in its broad outlines the scene of my early youth.

A child full of fantasy, I afforded the family much amusement by my imaginative flights. I have often been told, and seem still to remember, how when I was still in dresses it pleased me to pretend that I was the Kaiser. In this game I would persist for hours at a time. Sitting in my little go-cart, which my nurse would push about the garden or the lower floors of the house, I would draw down my mouth as far as I could, so that my upper lip was lengthened out of all proportion, and blink my eyes slowly until what with the strain and the strength of my feelings they would presently grow red and fill with tears. Quite overcome with the burden of my age and dignity I would sit silent in my go-cart, my nurse having been instructed to tell all the passers-by how things stood, for I should have taken it hard had they failed to fall in with my whim. "This is the Kaiser I am pushing about here," she would say, carrying her hand to her temple in an awkward salute; and everybody would pay me homage. My godfather Maggotson, who loved his joke, would play up to me in every way. "Look, there he goes, the hoary old hero!" he would say, with an exaggeratedly deep obeisance. Then he would pretend to be the populace and stand beside my path tossing his hat in the air, his stick, even his glasses, shouting: "Hurrah, hurrah!" and laughing fit to kill himself when out of the excess of my emotions the tears would roll down my long-drawn face.

I used to play the same sort of game when I was much older and could no longer expect my elders to fall in with them. I did not miss their co-operation, glorying as I did in my free and incommunicable flights of imagination. I awoke one morning, for instance, filled with the idea that I was a prince, a prince eighteen years old, named Karl; and prince I remained all day long, for the inestimable advantage of this kind of game was that it never needed to be interrupted, not even during the almost insupportable hours which I spent at school. I moved about clothed in a sort of amiable aloofness, holding lively imaginary converse with my governor or adjutant; and the secret of my own superiority which I hugged to my breast filled me with a perfectly indescribable pride and joy. What a glorious gift is the fancy, what subtle satisfactions it affords! The boys I knew, being ignorant of this priceless advantage which I possessed, seemed to me dull and limited louts indeed, unable to enter the kingdom where I was at home at no cost to myself and simply by an act of the will. They were all very simple fellows, with coarse hair and red hands. They would have had a hard time indeed convincing themselves that they were princes—and very foolish they would have looked. Whereas my hair was as silken-soft as one seldom sees it in boys, and light in colour; together with my blue-grey eyes it formed a fascinating contrast to the golden brownness of my skin, so that I hovered on the border-line between blond and brunet and might have been considered either. I had good hands and early began to care for them: well-shaped without being too narrow, never clammy, but dry and just warm enough to be pleasant. The finger-nails too were the kind that it is a pleasure to look at. And my voice, even before it changed, had an ingratiating note and could fall so flatteringly upon the ear that I liked above all things to listen to it myself when I was alone and could blissfully engage in long, plausible, but quite meaningless colloquies[8] with my aide-de-camp, accompanying them with extravagant gestures and attitudes. Such, then, were the physical advantages which I possessed; but these things are mostly very intangible, well-nigh impossible to put into words even for one equipped with a high degree of literary skill, and only recognizable in their effects. However that may be, I could not for long have disguised from myself that I was made of finer stuff than my schoolmates, and take no shame to myself for frankly admitting that such was the case. It is nothing to me to be accused of conceit; I should need to be either a fool or a hypocrite to write myself down an average person when I am but honouring the truth in repeating that I am made of finer stuff.

I grew up very much by myself, for my sister Olympia was several years older than I; and indulged as pastime in various mental quiddities,[9] of which I will cite one or two. I had taken it into my head to study that mysterious force the human will and to practise in myself how far it was capable of extension into regions considered beyond human powers. It is a well-known fact that the muscles controlling the pupils of our eyes react involuntarily in accordance with the strength of the light upon them. I decided to test whether this reaction could be brought under control of the will. I would stand before my mirror and concentrate all my powers upon the effort to expand or contract my pupils. And I protest that these obstinate efforts were actually crowned with success. At first, while I stood bathed in perspiration, my colour coming and going, there would be

8. conversations, conferences.   9. subtle distinctions, oddities.

an irregular flicker and fluctuation. But by practice I actually succeeded in narrowing the pupils to the merest points and then expanding them to great round pools of blackness. The fearful joy I felt at this result was actually accompanied by a physical shuddering before the mysteries of our human nature.

It was at this time, too, I often amused myself by a sort of introspection which even today has not lost all charm for me. I would inquire of myself: which is better, to see the world small or to see it large? The significance of the question was this: great men, I thought, field-marshals, statesmen, conquerors, and leading spirits generally that rise above the mass of mankind must be so constituted as to see the world small, like a chess-board, else they would never command the necessary ruthlessness to regulate the common weal and woe according to their own will. Yet it was quite possible, on the other hand, that such a diminishing point of view, as it were, might lead to one doing nothing at all. For if you saw the world and human beings in it as small and insignificant and were early persuaded that nothing was worth while, you could easily sink into indifference and indolence and contemptuously prefer your own peace of mind to any influence you might exert upon the spirits of men. And added to that your own supine detachment from mankind would certainly give offence and cut you off still further from any success you might have had in despite of yourself. Then is it better, I would next inquire, to think of the world and human nature as great, glorious, and important, worthy the expenditure of every effort to the end of achieving some meed of esteem and good report? Yet again, how easily can such a point of view lead to self-detraction and loss of confidence, so that the fickle world passes you by with a smile as a simpleton, in favour of more self-confident lovers! Though on the other hand such genuine credulity and artlessness has its good side too, since men cannot but be flattered by the way you look up to them; and if you devote yourself to making this impression, it will give weight and seriousness to your life, lend it meaning in your own eyes, and lead to your advancement. In this wise would I speculate and weigh the pros and cons; but always it has lain in my nature to take up the second position, seeing the world and mankind as great and glorious phenomena, capable of affording such priceless satisfactions that no effort on my part could seem disproportionate to the rewards I might reap.

Ideas of this kind were certainly calculated to isolate me from my schoolmates and companions, who of course spent their time in more commonplace and traditional occupations. But it is also a fact that these boys, most of whose fathers were either civil servants or the owners of vineyards, were instructed to avoid my society. I early discovered this, for on inviting one of them to our home he made no bones of telling me that he had been forbidden to associate with me because my family were not respectable. The experience not only wounded my pride but made me covet an intercourse which otherwise I could not have craved. But there is no doubt that the current opinion about our household and the goings-on there was in large measure justified.

I have referred above to the disturbance in our family circle due to the presence of our Fräulein from Vevey. My poor father was infatuated with this girl and ran after her until he succeeded in gaining his ends, or so it seemed, for dissensions arose between him and my mother and he departed for Mainz, where he remained for several weeks restoring his equilibrium with the joys of a bachelor life. My mother took entirely the wrong course, I am convinced, in treating my poor father with such a lack of consideration. She was a woman of insignificant mental parts; but what was more to the point, her human weaknesses were no less apparent than his own. My sister Olympia, a fat and fleshly-minded creature who later went on the stage and had some small success there, took after her in this respect—the difference between them and my poor father being that theirs was a heavy and sensual greed of pleasure, whereas his follies were never without a certain ease and grace. Mother and daughter lived in unusual intimacy—I recall once seeing my mother measure Olympia's thigh with a tape-measure, which gave me to think for several hours. Another time, when I was old enough to have some intuitive understanding of such matters though no words to express them in, I watched unseen and saw my mother and sister flirting with a young painter who was doing some work about the house. He was a dark-eyed lad in a white smock and they painted upon him a green moustache with his own paint. In the end they roused him to such a pitch that they fled giggling up the attic stair and he pursued them thither. My parents bored each other to tears and got relief by filling the house with guests from Mainz and Wiesbaden so that our house was the scene of a continual round of gaieties. It was a promiscuous crew who frequented these gatherings: actors and actresses, young business men, the sickly young infantry lieutenant who later proposed to my sister; a Jewish banker with a wife whose charms gushed appallingly out of her jet-spangled frock; a journalist in a velvet waistcoat with a lock of hair falling over his brow, who every time brought along a new wife. They would arrive for seven o'clock dinner, and the feasting, the dancing and piano-playing, the skylarking and shrieks of laughter would go on all night. Particularly at carnival-time and the vintage season the waves of pleasure rose very high. My father, who was very clever in such things, would set off the most splendid fireworks in the garden; all the company would be masked and unearthly light would play upon the crockery dwarfs. All restraint was abandoned. At that time it was my sorry lot to attend the high school of our little town; and often I would go down to the dining-room at seven o'clock or half past with face new-washed, to eat my breakfast and find the guests still at their after-dinner coffee, rumpled, sallow, and hollow-eyed, blinking at the daylight; they would receive me into their midst with shoutings.

When still quite young I was allowed with my sister Olympia to take part in the festivities. Even when alone we always set a good table, and my father drank champagne mixed with soda-water. But at these parties there were endless courses prepared by a chef from Wiesbaden with the assistance of our own cook: the most tempting succession of sweets, savouries, and ices. Lorley Extra Cuvée flowed in streams, but many good wines were served as well. I was particularly fond of the bouquet of Berncasteler Doctor. Later in life I made acquaintance with many of the noblest wines and could order Grand Vin Château Margaux or Grand Cru Mouton-Rothschild, two very fine wines, as to the manner born.

I love to call up the picture of my father as he presided at the head of the table, with his white imperial, and his belly confined in a white silk waistcoat. His voice was weak and sometimes he would be seized by self-consciousness and look down at his plate. Yet his enjoyment was to be read in his eyes and in his shining red face. "*C'est épatant*," he would say. "*Parfaitement*"—and with his fingers, which curved backwards at the tips, he would give delicate touches to the table-service. My mother and sister meanwhile were abandoned to a gross and soulless gluttony, between courses flirting with their table-mates behind their fans.

After dinner, when the gas-chandeliers began to be wreathed in smoke, came dancing and forfeit-playing. When the evening was advanced I used to be sent to bed; but as sleep, in that din, was out of the question, I would wrap myself in my red woollen coverlet and in this becoming disguise return to the feast, where I was received with cries of joy from all the females. Refreshments such as wine jellies, lemonade, punch, herring salad, were served in relays until the morning coffee. The dance was free and untrammelled, the games of forfeits were pretext for much kissing and caressing; the ladies bent over the backs of their chairs to give the gentlemen stimulating glimpses into the bosoms of their frocks; and the climax of the evening arrived when some humorist turned out the gas and there was a general scramble in the dark.

These parties were undoubtedly the cause of the unfavourable criticism which spread about the town; but according to the reports which came to my ears it was their economic aspect that was the target for gossip. For it was only too well known that my father's business was at a desperate pass and that the dining and wining and fireworks must give it the *coup de grâce*.[10] I was sensitive enough to feel the hostile atmosphere when I was still very young; it united, as I have said, with certain peculiarities of my own character to give me on the whole a great deal of pain. The more cordially, then, did

10. death blow.

I appreciate an incident which took place at about this time; I set it down here with peculiar pleasure.

I was eight years old when my family and I spent some weeks one summer at the famous and neighboring resort of Langenschwalbach. My father took mud baths for his gout, and my mother and sister made themselves talked about for the size and shape of their hats. Of the society we frequented there is little good to be said. The residential class, as usual, avoided us. The better-class guests kept themselves to themselves as they usually do; and such society as we could get had not much to recommend it. Yet I liked Langenschwalbach and later on often made such resorts the scene of my operations. The tranquil, well-regulated existence and the sight of aristocratic and well-groomed people in the gardens and on the tennis courts satisfied an inward craving of my soul. But the strongest attraction of all was the daily concert given by a well-trained orchestra to the guests of the cure. Though I never attained to skill in any branch of the art I was a fanatical lover of music; even as a child I could not tear myself away from the pretty little pavilion where a becomingly uniformed band played selections and potpourris under the direction of their gypsy leader. Hours on end I would crouch on the steps of that little temple of art, enchanted to my very marrow by the ordered succession of sweet sounds and watching with rapture every motion of the musicians as they attacked their instruments. In particular I was thrilled by the gestures of the violinists and when I went home I delighted my parents with an imitation performed on two sticks, one long and one short. The swinging movement of the left arm in producing a soulful tone, the soft gliding motion from one position to the next, the dexterity of the fingering in virtuoso passages and cadenzas, the fine and supple bowing of the right wrist, the cheek cuddled in such utter abandonment to the violin—all this I succeeded in reproducing so faithfully that the family, especially my father, burst into enthusiastic applause. And being in good spirits due to the beneficial effect of the baths, he conceived the following little joke, with the connivance of the long-haired and almost speechless little bandmaster. They bought a small cheap violin and plentifully smeared the bow with vaseline. As a rule not much attention was paid to my appearance; but now I was arrayed in a pretty sailor suit with gilt buttons and lanyard all complete, also silk stockings and shiny patent-leather shoes. And one Sunday I took my place at the side of the little conductor during the afternoon promenade concert and assisted in the performance of a Hungarian dance, doing with my violin and my vaselined bow what I had done with my two sticks. My success was tremendous. The public, gentle and simple, streamed up from all sides and assembled before the pavilion to look at the infant prodigy. My pale face, my utter absorption in my task, the lock of hair falling over my brow, my childish hands and wrists in the full, tapering sleeves of the pretty blue sailor suit—in short, my whole touching and astonishing little figure captured all hearts. When I finished with a full sweep of the bow across all the fiddle-strings, the garden resounded with applause and delighted cries from male and female throats. The bandmaster stowed my bow and fiddle safely away and I was set down on the ground, where I was overwhelmed with praises and caresses. The most aristocratic ladies and gentlemen stroked my hair, patted my cheeks and hands, called me an angel child and an amazing little devil. An old Russian princess in violet silk and white side-curls took my head between her beringed hands and kissed my brow, all beaded as it was with perspiration. Then in a pitch of enthusiasm she snatched a lyre-shaped diamond brooch from her throat and with a perfect torrent of ecstatic French pinned it on the front of my blouse. My family approached and my father made excuses for the defects of my playing on the score of my tender years. I was escorted to the confectioner's, where at three different tables I was regaled with chocolate and cream cakes. The scions of the noble family of Siebenklingen, whom I had admired from afar while they regarded me with cold disdain, came up and asked me to play croquet, and while our parents drank coffee together I went off with the children in the seventh heaven of delight, my diamond brooch upon my blouse. That was one of the happiest days of my life, perhaps quite the happiest. The cry was set up that I should play again; actually the management of the Casino approached my father and asked for an encore; but he refused, saying that he had only permitted me to play by way of exception and that repeated public appearances were not consistent with my social position. And besides our stay in Bad Langenschwalbach was drawing to a close.

I wish now to speak of my godfather Maggotson, by no means an ordinary man. He was short and thickset in build, with thin and prematurely grey hair, which he wore parted over one ear and brushed across his crown. He was clean-shaven, with a hooked nose and thin, compressed lips, and wore large round glasses with celluloid rims. His face was further remarkable for the fact that it was bald above the eyes, having no brows to speak of; also for the somewhat acidulous disposition it betrayed—to which, indeed, he was wont to give expression in words, as for instance in his cynical explanation of the name he bore. "Nature," he would say, "is full of corruption and blow-flies, and I am her offspring. Therefore am I called Maggotson. But as for why I am called Felix, that God alone knows." He came from Cologne, where he had once moved in the best social circles and often acted as carnival steward. But for reasons which remained obscure he had been obliged to leave Cologne; he had gone into retirement in our little town, where he very soon —a considerable time before my birth—became an intimate of our household. At all our evening companies he was a regular and indispensable guest and in high favour with young and old. He would purse his lips and fix the ladies through his round glasses, with appraising eyes, until they would screech for mercy, putting their hands before their faces and begging him to turn away his gaze. Apparently they feared the penetrating artist eye; but he, it would seem, did not share in their awe of his calling, and not infrequently made ironic allusions to the nature of artists. "Phidias,"[11] he would say, "also called Pheidias, was a man of more than average gifts—as might perhaps be gathered from the fact that he was convicted for theft and put in jail at Athens for having appropriated to his own use the gold and ivory entrusted to him for his statue of Athena. But Pericles,[12] who had discovered him, had him set free, thereby proving himself to be a connoisseur not only of art but of artists as well; and Phidias—or Pheidias—went to Olympia, where he was commissioned to make the great chryselephantine[13] statue of the Olympian Zeus. But what did he do? He stole the gold and ivory again—and there in the prison at Olympia he died. An extraordinary combination, my friends. But that is the way people are. They want people to be talented—which is already something out of the ordinary. But when it comes to the other qualities which go with the talents—and perhaps are essential to them—oh, no, they don't care for these at all, they refuse to have any understanding of them." Thus my godfather. I have set down his remarks verbatim because he repeated them so often that I know them by heart.

I have said that we lived on terms of mutual regard; yes, I believe that I enjoyed his especial favour, and often as I grew older it was my especial delight to serve as his model, dressing up in all sorts of costumes, of which he possessed a large and varied collection. His studio was a sort of lumber-room with a large window under the roof of a little house standing by itself down on the Rhine. He rented this house and lived in it with an old serving-woman, and there I would pose for him hours at a time, perched on a rude model-throne while he brushed and scraped and painted away. Several times I sat for him in the nude for a large picture with a Greek mythological subject, destined to adorn the dining-room of a wine-dealer in Mainz. When I did this my godfather was not chary of his praise; and indeed I was a little like a young god, slender, graceful, yet powerful in build, with a golden skin and proportions that lacked little of perfection. If there was a fault it lay in that my legs were a little too short; but my godfather consoled me for this defect by saying that Goethe,[14] that prince of the intellect, had been short-legged too and certainly had never been hampered thereby.

11. fifth-century Greek sculptor.
12. Athenian statesman of the fifth century.
13. overlaid with gold and ivory.

14. Johann Wolfgang von Goethe (1749–1832), German poet, novelist, and dramatist.

The hours devoted to these sittings form an especial chapter in my memory. Yet I enjoyed even more, I think, the "dressing up" itself; and that took place not only in the studio but at our house as well. Often when my godfather was to sup with us he would send up a large bundle of costumes, wigs, and accessories and try them all on me after the meal, sketching any particularly good effect on the lid of a pasteboard box. "He has a head for costumes," he would say, meaning that everything became me, and that in each disguise which I assumed I looked better and more natural than in the last. I might appear as a Roman flute-player in a short smock, a wreath of roses twined in my black locks; as an English page in snug-fitting satin with lace collar and plumed hat; as a Spanish bullfighter in spangled jacket and large round sombrero; as a youthful abbé of the Watteau[15] period, with cap and bands, mantle and buckled shoes; as an Austrian officer in white military tunic with sash and dagger; or as a German mountaineer in leather shorts and hobnailed boots, with the bock's-beard stuck in his green felt hat—whatever the costume, the mirror assured me that I was born to wear it, and my audience declared that I looked to the life exactly the person whom I aimed to represent. My godfather even asserted that with the aid of costume and wig I seemed able to put on not only whatever social rank or national characteristics I chose, but that I could actually adapt myself to any given period or century. For each age, my godfather would say, imparts to its children its own physiognomical stamp; whereas I, in the costume of a Florentine dandy of the end of the Middle Ages, could look as though I had stepped from a contemporary portrait, and yet be no less convincing in the full-bottomed wig which was the fashionable ideal of a later century.—Ah, those were glorious hours! But when they were over and I resumed my dull and ordinary dress, how stale, flat, and unprofitable seemed all the world by contrast, in what deep dejection did I spend the rest of the evening!

Of my godfather I shall say no more in this place. Later on, at the end of my strenuous career, this extraordinary man intervened decisively in my destiny and saved me from despair.

I search my mind for further impressions of my youth, and am reminded at once of the day when I first attended the theatre, at Wiesbaden, with my parents. I should interpolate here that in what I have so far set down I have not too anxiously adhered to the chronological order but have treated my younger days as a whole and moved freely within them from episode to episode. When I posed to my godfather as a Greek god I was sixteen or seventeen years old and thus no longer a child, though very backwards at school. But my first visit to the theatre fell in my fourteenth year—though even so my physical and mental maturity, as will presently be seen, was well advanced and my sensitiveness to certain classes of

15. French painter (1684–1721).

impressions much keener than is ordinarily the case. What I saw that evening made the strongest impression on me and gave me food for perennial reflection.

We had first visited a Viennese café, where I drank sweet punch and my father imbibed absinthe through a straw—and this already was calculated to stir me to my depths. But how put into words the fever which possessed me when we drove in a droshky[16] to the theatre and entered the lighted auditorium with its tiers of boxes? The women fanning their bosoms in the balcony, the men leaning over their chairs to chat; the hum and buzz of conversation in the stalls where we presently took our seats; the odours which streamed from hair and clothing to mingle with that of the illuminating gas; the confusion of sounds as the orchestra tuned up; the voluptuous frescoes displaying whole cascades of rosy foreshortenings—certainly all this could not but spur my youthful senses and prepare my mind for all the extraordinary scenes to follow. I had never before save in church seen so many people gathered together; and this playhouse, with its impressively complex seating-arrangements and its elevated stage where the elect, in brilliant costumes and to musical accompaniment, performed their dialogues and dances and developed the activities required by the plot—certainly all that was in my eyes a church where pleasure was the god; where men in need of edification gathered in the darkness to gaze upwards openmouthed at a sphere of bright perfection where each saw embodied the desire of his heart.

The piece was an unpretentious offering to the comic muse—I have even forgotten its name. Its scene was laid in Paris, which delighted my poor father's heart, and it centred round the figure of an idle young attaché, the traditional fascinator and lady-killer, played by the highly popular leading man, whose name was Müller-Rosé. I heard his real name from my father, who rejoiced in his personal acquaintance, and the picture of this man will remain forever in my memory. He is probably old and worn-out by now, like me, but at that time his power to dazzle all the world, myself included, made upon me so strong an impression that it belongs to the decisive experiences of my life. I say to dazzle, and it will be seen hereafter how much meaning I would convey by that word. But first I will essay to set down from my still very lively recollections the impression which Müller-Rosé made upon me. On his first entrance he was dressed all in black—yet he radiated brilliance. He was supposed to come from some resort of the gay world and to be slightly intoxicated—a state which he knew how to counterfeit to perfection, yet without any suggestion of grossness. He wore a black cloak with a satin lining, patent-leather shoes, evening dress, white kid gloves, and a top hat which sat far back on his glistening locks, arranged in the then fashionable military parting, which ran all the

16. four-wheeled open vehicle, used in Russia.

way to the back of the neck. And every article of all this was so irreproachable, so well-pressed, and sat with a flawless perfection such as in real life could not endure above a quarter of an hour and made him seem like a being from another world. In particular the top hat, light-heartedly askew on his head, was the very pattern and mirror of what a top hat should be, without one grain of dust and with the most beautiful reflections, exactly as though they had been painted on. And this superb figure had a face to match, of a rosy fineness like wax, with almond-shaped, black-rimmed eyes, a small, short, straight nose and an extremely clear-cut, coral-red mouth and a little black moustache, even as though it were drawn with a paint-brush, following the outline of his arched upper lip. Reeling with a supple poise such as drunken men in everyday life do not possess, he gave his hat and stick to an attendant, slipped out of his cloak, and stood there in full evening fig,[17] with diamond studs in his pleated shirt-front. As he drew off his gloves, laughing and rattling on in a silvery voice, you could see that his hands were white as milk outside and adorned with diamond rings, but inside pink like his face. He stood before the footlights at one side of the stage and trilled the first verse of a song all about what a wonderful life it was to be an attaché and a favourite with the ladies. Then he spread out his arms and snapped his fingers and waltzed apparently delirious with bliss over to the other side of the stage, where he sang the second verse and made his exit. Being recalled by loud applause, he sang the third and last verse in front of the prompter's box. And then with easy grace he began unfolding his rôle as called for by the plot. He was supposed to be very rich, which in itself lent his figure an almost magical charm. He appeared in a succession of "changes": immaculate white sports clothes with a red belt; a full-dress, slightly outré[18] uniform—yes, in one delicate and hair-raising situation, pale-blue silk underdrawers. The complications of the plot were audacious, adventurous, and risqué by turns. One saw him at the feet of a countess, at a champagne supper with two predatory[19] daughters of joy, and standing with raised pistol confronting his fatuous rival in a duel. And not one of these elegant but strenuous occupations had power to derange one fold of his shirt-front, extinguish any of the brilliance of his top hat, or deepen the delicate tint of his complexion. He moved so easily within the frame of the musical and dramatic conventions that they seemed, so far from restricting him, to release him from the limitations of everyday life. He seemed pervaded to the finger-tips by a magic which we know how to express only by the vague and inadequate word "talent"—the exercise of which obviously gave him as much pleasure as it did us. He would fit his fingers round the silver crook of his cane, would let his hands glide into his trouser pockets, and

17. In "soup and fish," evening dress.
18. exaggerated, excessive, in dubious

taste.
19. rapacious, grasping.

these actions, even his getting out of a chair, his very exits and entrances, had a quality of conscious gratification which filled the heart of the beholder with joy. Yes, that was it: Müller-Rosé heightened our joy of life—if the phrase is adequate to express that feeling, mingled of pain and pleasure, envy, yearning, hope, and irresistible love which the sight of the consummately charming can kindle in the human soul.

The public in the stalls was composed of middle-class citizens and their wives, clerks, one-year service men, and little girls in blouses; and despite the rapture of my own sensations I was able and eager to look about me and interpret the feelings of the audience. On all these faces sat a look of almost silly bliss. They were rapt in self-forgetful absorption, a smile played about their lips, sweeter and more lively in the little shop-girls, more brooding and dreamy in the grown-up women, while on the faces of the men it expressed the benevolent admiration which simple fathers feel in the presence of sons who have passed beyond their own sphere and realized the dreams of their youth. As for the clerks and the young soldiers, everything stood wide open in their upturned faces—eyes, mouths, nostrils, everything. And their smiles seemed to be saying: "Suppose it was us, standing up there in our underdrawers—how should we be making out? And look how he knows how to behave with those shameless hussies, just as though he were no better than they!"—When Müller-Rosé left the stage a power seemed to have gone out of the audience, all their shoulders sagged. When he stormed triumphantly from the back-stage to the footlights, holding a note with arms outspread, every bosom seemed to heave in his direction and the ladies' satin bodices creaked at the seams. Yes, as we sat there in the darkness we were like a swarm of night-flying insects rushing blind, dumb, and drunken into the flame.

My father was royally entertained. He had followed the French custom and carried hat and stick into the theatre with him. When the curtain fell he put on the one and with the other banged on the floor loud and long. "*C'est épatant*," said he several times, quite weak with enthusiasm. At last it was all over and we were outside in the lobby, among a crowd of clerks who were quite uplifted and trying to walk, talk, and hold their canes like the hero of the evening. My father said to me: "Come along, let's go and shake hands with him. Good Lord, weren't we on pretty good terms once, Müller and I? He will be delighted to see me again." So we instructed our ladies to wait for us in the vestibule and went off to pay our respects. We passed through the director's box, next the stage and already dark, then through a little door and behind the scenes. Stage-hands were clearing away in the eerie darkness. A little creature in red livery, who had been a lift-boy in the play, stood leaning against the wall sunk in reverie. My poor father pinched her playfully where her figure was amplest and asked her the way to the

dressing-rooms, which she pointed out with rather an ill grace. We
went through a whitewashed corridor, where uncovered gas-jets
flared in the confined air. From behind several doors issued loud
laughter or angry voices, and my father gestured with his thumb to
call my attention to them as we went on. At the end of the narrow
passage he knocked on the last door, laying his ear to his knuckle.
From within came a gruff shout: "Who's there?" or "What the
devil do you want?" or words to that effect. "May I come in?"
asked my father in reply, whereupon the voice instructed him to do
something else with which I would not sully the pages of my narrative. My father smiled his deprecating little smile and called
through the door: "Müller, it's Krull, Engelbert Krull. I suppose I
may shake you by the hand, after all these years?" There was a
laugh from inside and the voice said: "Oh, so it's you, old horse!
Always on the hunt for some sport, eh?" And as we opened the
door it went on: "I suppose you won't take any harm from my
nakedness!" We went in. I shall never forget the disgusting sight
that offered itself to my boyish eyes.

Müller-Rosé was seated at a grubby dressing-table in front of a
dusty and speckled mirror with side wings. He had nothing on but a
pair of grey tricot drawers, and a man in shirt-sleeves was massaging
his back, the sweat running down his own face. The actor's visage
glistened with salve and he was busy wiping it off with a towel
already stiff with rouge and grease paint. Half of his countenance
still had the rosy coating which had made him radiant on the stage
but now looked merely pink and silly beside the cheesy pallor of the
man's natural complexion. He had taken off the chestnut-brown wig
and I saw that he was red-haired. One of his eyes still had deep
black shadows beneath it and metallic dust clung to the lashes; the
other was inflamed and watery and leered up at us with an inde-
scribably *gamin*[20] expression. All this I might have borne. But not
the pimples with which Müller-Rosé's back, chest, shoulders, and
upper arms were thickly strewn. They were horrible pimples, red-
rimmed, suppurating, some of them even bleeding; even today I
cannot repress a shudder at the thought of them. I find that our
capacity for disgust is in direct proportion to our capacity for enjoyment, to our eagerness for the pleasures which this world can give.
A cool and indifferent nature could never be so shaken by disgust as
I was at that moment. Worst of all was the air of the room, compounded of sweat and exhalations from the pots and jars and sticks
of grease paint which strewed the table. At first I thought I could
not stand it above a minute without being sick.

However, I stood and looked—but I can add nothing to this
description of Müller-Rosé's dressing-room. Perhaps I should
reproach myself for having so little that is objective to report of my

20. ragamuffin, street Arab.

first visit to a theatre—if I were not writing primarily for my own amusement and only secondarily for any public I may have. I am not bent on sustaining any dramatic suspense, leaving such effects to the writers of imaginative tales, who must contrive to give their inventions the beautiful and symmetrical proportions of a work of art—whereas my material is derived from my own experiences alone and I feel I may dispose it as seems to me good. Thus I shall linger upon such events as were of especial value or significance to me, neglecting no necessary detail to bring them out; passing over more lightly those of less personal moment. I have well-nigh forgotten what passed between my father and Müller-Rosé on that occasion —probably because other matters took my attention. For it is undoubtedly true that we receive stronger impressions through the senses than through the mind. I recall that the singer—though surely the applause which had greeted him that evening must have left him in no great doubt as to his triumph—kept asking my father whether it had "gone over" or how well it had "gone over." I perfectly understood how he felt. I have even a vague memory of some rather ordinary turns of phrase which he wove into the conversation, as for instance, in reply to some insinuation of my father's: "Shut your jaw—" then adding in the same breath: "over a quid of tobacco, there's some on the stand." But, as I said, I lent but half an ear to this or other specimens of his mental quality, being altogether taken up by my own sense impressions.

"So this, then"—ran my thoughts—"this pimpled and smeary individual is the charmer at whom the indistinguished masses were just now gazing up blissful-eyed! This repulsive worm is the reality of the glorious butterfly in whom all those deluded onlookers thought to see realized all their own secret dreams of beauty, grace, and perfection! He is just like one of those disgusting little creatures which have the power of being phosphorescent in the evening." But the grown-up people in the audience, who on the whole must know about life and who yet were so frightfully eager to be deceived, must they not have been aware of the deception? Or did they just privately not consider it one? And that is quite possible. For when you come to think about it, which is the "real" shape of the glowworm: the insignificant little creature crawling about on the flat of your hand, or the poetic spark that swims through the summer night? Who would presume to say? Rather call up the picture you saw before: the swarm of moths and gnats, rushing blindly and irresistibly into the flame. With what unanimity in the work of self-delusion! What can it be, then, but that such an instinctive need as this is implanted by God Himself in the heart of man, to satisfy which the Müller-Rosés are created? Here beyond a doubt is operative in life a wise and indispensable economy, in the service of which such men are kept and rewarded. How much admiration is his due for the success which he achieved tonight and achieves every night! Let us then smother what disgust we feel, in the realization that he knows all about his frightful pimples and yet—with the help of grease paint, lighting, music, and distance—can move before his audience with such complete assurance as to make them see in him their heart's ideal and thereby endlessly to enliven and edify them. And more: let us ask ourselves what it was that urged this miserable mountebank to learn the art of transfiguring himself nightly. What are the secret sources of the charm which possessed him and radiated from his finger-tips? The question needs but to be asked to be answered: who does not know the magic, the ineffable sweetness—for which any words we have are all too pale—of the power which teaches the glow-worm to light the night? This man could not hear too often nor too emphatically that his performance gave pleasure, pleasure beyond the ordinary. It was the yearning of all his being towards the host of yearning souls, it was that inspired and winged his art. He gave us joy of life, we in our turn sated his craving for applause; and was this not a mutual satisfaction, a true marriage of desires?

The above lines indicate the main current of the thoughts which surged through my eager and overheated brain as I sat there in Müller-Rosé's dressing-room, yes, and for days and weeks afterwards possessed my musings and my dreams. And always they were accompanied by emotions so profound and shattering, such a drunkenness of yearning, hope, and joy, that even today, despite my great fatigue, the memory of them makes my heart beat faster. In those days my feelings were of such violence that they threatened to burst my frame; often they made me somewhat ailing and thus served me as a pretext for stopping away from school.

It would be superfluous to dwell upon the reasons for my growing aversion to this odious institution. I am only able to live when my mind and my fancy are completely free; and thus it is that the memory of my years in prison is actually less hateful to me than those of the ostensibly more honourable bond of slavery and fear which chafed my sensitive boyish soul when I was forced to attend at the ugly little white box of a school-building down in the town. Add to these feelings the isolation from which I suffered, the grounds of which I have set forth above, and it will surprise nobody that I early had the idea of taking more holidays than the law allowed.

And in carrying out my idea another game I had long practised was of signal service to me: that of imitating my father's handwriting. A father is the natural and nearest model for the growing boy striving to adapt himself to the adult world. Physical structure as well as the more mysterious bond between them incline the boy to admire all that in the parent of which he is still incapable himself and to strive to imitate it—or rather it is perhaps his very admiration which unconsciously leads him to develop along the lines which the laws of inheritance have laid down. At the time when I was still digging great pothooks in my slate I already dreamed of guiding a steel pen with my father's swiftness and skill; and how many scraps of paper I covered later on with efforts to copy his hand from memory, my fingers arranged round the pen in the same delicate fashion as his. His writing was not in fact very hard to imitate, for my poor father wrote a childish hand, like a copybook, quite undeveloped, its only peculiarity being that the letters were very tiny and prolonged immoderately by hairlines in a way I have never seen anywhere else. This mannerism I soon mastered to the life. In contrast to the angular Gothic character of the script the signature, *E. Krull*, had a Latin *ductus*.[21] It was surrounded by a perfect cloud of flourishes, which at first sight looked difficult to copy, but were in reality so simple in conception that I succeeded almost better with the signature than with anything else. The lower half of the *E* made a bold curve to the right, in whose open lap, as it were, the remaining syllable was neatly nestled. A second flourish rose from the *u*, embracing everything before it, cutting the curve of the *E* in two places and ending in an *s*-shaped down-stroke flanked like the curve of the *E* with rows of dots. The whole signature was higher than it was long, it was both naïve and bizarre; thus it lent itself so well to my purpose that in the end the inventor of it could not himself have distinguished between my products and his own.

Of course I very soon made practical use of a gift which had been acquired solely for my amusement. I employed it to gain my mental freedom—as follows: "My son Felix," I wrote, "had severe cramps on the 7th of this month and had to stop away from school. Regretfully yours, E. Krull." Or: "An infected sore on the gum as well as a sprained right arm obliged my son Felix to keep his bed from the 10th to the 14th. Regret his not having been able to attend school. Faithfully yours, E. Krull." My efforts being crowned with success, nothing hindered me from spending the school hours of one day or even of several roaming about outside the town, lying stretched in the leafy, whispering shade of some green pasture, dreaming the dreams peculiar to my youth and state. Sometimes I hid in the ruins of the old episcopal seat on the Rhine; sometimes, even, in winter and rough weather in the hospitable studio of my godfather, who indeed chid me for my conduct, but in tones which showed that he had a certain sympathy with the motives which led to it.

But now and again it came about that I lay in bed at home—and

21. flowing quality.

not always, as I have explained above, without any justification. It is a favourite theory of mine that every deception which has not a higher truth at its root but is simply a barefaced lie is by the very fact so gross and palpable that nobody can fail to see through it. Only one kind of lie has a chance of being effective: that which is quite undeserving of the name of deceit, being but the product of a lively imagination which has not yet entered wholly into the realm of the actual and acquired those tangible signs by which alone it can be estimated at its proper worth. True, I was a sturdy boy, who never aside from the usual childish ails had anything the matter with him. Yet when one morning I decided to avoid trouble and suffering by stopping in bed I was by no means practising a gross perversion of the actual situation. For why should I have gone to meet trouble, when I possessed the means of rendering powerless at will the army of my oppressors? The higher truth actually was that the tension and depression due to my imaginative flights was not seldom so overpowering that they became actual suffering; together with my fear of what the day might bring forth they were enough to produce a basis of solid fact for my pretences to rest upon. I needed to put no strain upon myself to command the sympathy and concern of my people and the family doctor.

On a certain day, when the need for freedom and the possession of my own soul had become overpowering, I began with producing my symptoms with myself as sole audience. The extreme limit of the hour for rising was overpassed in dreams; breakfast had been brought in and was cooling on the table downstairs; all the stupid louts in town were on their dull schoolward way; daily life had begun, and I was irretrievably committed to a course of rebellion against my taskmasters. The audacity of my conduct was enough to make my heart flutter and my cheek turn pale. I noted that my finger-nails had taken on a bluish tint. The morning was cold and I needed to throw off the covers for only a few moments and to lie relaxed—when I had brought on a most convincing attack of shivers and teeth-chattering. All that I am saying is of course highly indicative of my character and temperament. I have always been very sensitive, susceptible, and in need of cherishing; and everything I have accomplished in life has been the result of self-conquest—yes, to be regarded as a moral achievement of a high order. If it were otherwise I should never, either then or later, have succeeded by mere voluntary relaxation of mind and body in producing the appearance of physical suffering and thus in inclining those about me to tenderness and concern. To counterfeit illness effectively could never be within the powers of the coarse-grained man. But anybody who is made of finer stuff—if I may be pardoned for repeating the phrase—is always, though he may never be ill in the rude sense of the word, on familiar terms with suffering and can control its symptoms by intuition.

I closed my eyes and then opened them to their widest extent, making them look appealing and plaintive. I knew without the aid of a glass that my hair was rumpled from sleep and fell in damp strands on my brow. My face being already pale, I made it look sunken by a device of my own, drawing in the cheeks and holding them imperceptibly with the teeth from inside. This made my chin look longer too and gave me the appearance of having got thin over-night. A dilating of the nostrils and an almost painful twitching of the muscles at the corners of the eyes contributed to the effect. I put my basin on a chair by my bed, folded my blue-nailed fingers across my breast, chattered my teeth from time to time, and thus awaited the moment when somebody should come to look me up.

That would not be too early; my parents loved to lie abed and it might be two or three school hours had passed before it became known that I was still in the house. Then my mother came upstairs and into the room and asked if I were ill. I looked at her large-eyed, as though in my dazed condition it was hard for me to tell who she was. Then I said yes, I thought I must be ill. What was the matter? Oh, my head, and the ache in my bones—"and why am I so cold?" I went on, in a monotonous voice, articulating with difficulty and tossing myself from side to side of the bed. My mother looked sym-pathetic. I do not believe that she took my sufferings very seriously, but as her sensibilities were very much in excess of her reason she could not bring herself to spoil the game but instead joined in and began to support me in my performance. "Poor child," she said, laying her forefinger on my cheek and shaking her head in pity, "don't you want something to eat?" I declined with a shudder, pressing my chin on my chest. The iron consistency of my perform-ance sobered her somewhat; she was startled out of her enjoyment of the game, for that anybody should on such grounds refrain from food and drink was quite beyond her. She looked at me with a growing sense of reality. When she had got so far I assisted her to a decision by a display of art as arduous as it was effective. Starting up in bed with fitful and shuddering motions I drew my basin towards me and bent over it with frightful twitchings and contor-tions of my whole body, such as could not be witnessed without sympathetic convulsions by anyone not possessed of a heart of stone. "Nothing in me," I gasped between my writhings, lifting my wry and wasted face from the basin. "Gave it all up in the night"; and then I nerved myself to a protracted climax of such gaspings and chokings that it seemed I should never again get my breath. My mother held my head and repeatedly called me by my name in anxious and urgent tones, to bring me to myself. When my limbs began at length to relax, "I will send for Dusing!" she cried, and ran out of the room. Exhausted but with an indescribable and joyful sense of satisfaction, I fell back upon my pillows.

How often had I imagined to myself such a scene, how often passed through all its stages in my mind before I ventured to put it into operation! I hope that I may be understood when I say that I felt as though I were in a joyful dream when for the first time I put it into practice and achieved a complete success. It is not everybody can do such a thing. One may dream of it—but one does not do it. Suppose, a man thinks, that something awful were to happen to me: if I were to fall in a faint or blood were to burst out of my nose, or if I were to have some kind of seizure—then how suddenly the world's harsh unconcern would turn into attention, sympathy, and tardy remorse! But the flesh is obtusely strong and enduring, it holds out long after the mind has felt the need of sympathy and care; it will not manifest the alarming tangible symptoms which would make everybody imagine himself in a like state of suffering and speak with admonishing voice to the conscience of the world. But I—I had produced these symptoms, as effectively as though I had had nothing to do with their appearance. I had improved upon nature, realized a dream; and he alone who has tried to create a compelling and effective reality out of nothing, out of sheer inward knowledge and contemplation—in short, out of a combination of nothing but fantasy and his own personality—he alone can understand the strange and dreamlike satisfaction with which I rested from my creative task.

An hour later came Medical Inspector Dusing. He had been our family physician ever since the death of old Dr. Mecum, the practitioner who had ushered me into the world. Dr. Dusing was tall and stooped, with an awkward carriage and bristling mouse-coloured hair. He was constantly either caressing his long nose with thumb and forefinger or else rubbing his large bony hands. This man might have been dangerous to my enterprise. Not, I think, through his professional ability, which I believe to have been meagre—though indeed a genuine scholar serving science with single mind and heart for its own sake would have been easiest of all to deceive. No, but Dr. Dusing might have seen through me by virtue of a certain crude knowledge of human frailty which he possessed and which is often the whole stock-in-trade of inferior natures. This unworthy follower of Esculapius[22] was both stupid and striving and had been appointed to office through personal influence, adroit exploitation of wine-house acquaintances, and the receipt of patronage; he was always driving to Wiesbaden to further his interests in the exercise of his office. It was very telling that he did not keep to the rule of

---

22. (or Aesculapius) Roman god of medicine and healing.

first come, first served in his waiting-room, but took the more influential patients first, leaving the simpler ones to sit. His manner
towards the former class was obsequious, towards the latter harsh
and cynical, often betraying that he did not believe in their complaints. I am convinced that he would not have stopped at any lie,
corruption, or bribery which would ingratiate him with his superiors
or recommend him as a zealous party man with the ruling powers;
such behaviour was consistent with the shrewd practical sense which
in default of higher qualifications he relied upon to see him to his
goal. My poor father's position was already very dubious; yet as a
taxpayer and a business man he belonged to the influential classes
of the town, and Dr. Dusing naturally wished to stand well with
such a client. It is even possible that the wretched man enjoyed corruption for corruption's sake and found that a sufficient reason for
conniving at my fraud. In any case, he would come in and sit down
at my bedside with the usual phrases, saying: "Well, well, what's all
this?" or "What have we here?" and the moment would come
when a wink, a smile, or a significant little pause would indicate to
me that we were partners in deception at the little game of sham-
ming sick—"school-sick," as he was pleased to call it. Never did I
make the smallest return to his advances. Not out of caution, for he
would probably not have betrayed me, but out of pride and the genuine contempt I felt for him. I only looked more dismal and helpless, my cheeks grew hollower, my breathing shorter and more
difficult, my mouth more lax, at each attempt he made to seduce
me. I was quite prepared to go through another attack of vomiting
if needs must; and so persistently did I fail to understand his
worldly wisdom that in the end he had to abandon that line of
attack in favour of a more strictly professional one.

That presented some difficulty. First because he was actually
stupid; and second because the clinical picture I presented was very
general and indefinite in its character. He thumped my chest and
listened to me all over, peered into my throat by means of the
handle of a tablespoon, gave me great discomfort by taking my temperature, and finally for better or worse was driven to pass judgment. "Just the megrims,"[23] said he. "Nothing to worry about.
The usual attack. And our young friend's tummy always acts in
sympathy. He must be quiet, see no visitors, he must not talk,
better lie in a darkened room. I'll write a prescription—a little caf-
feine and citric acid will do no harm, it's always the best thing." If
there were any cases of flu in the town, he would say: "Flu, my
dear lady, with a gastric complication. That is what our young
friend has caught. Not much inflammation of the passages as yet;
still there is some. Do you notice any, my child? Do you feel like

23. morbid low spirits.

coughing? There is a little fever too; it will probably increase in the course of the day. The pulse is rapid and irregular." And he could think of nothing more, save to prescribe a certain bitter-sweet tonic wine from the chemist's. I was nothing loth; I found it most soothing and comforting, now that the battle had been won.

Indeed, the doctor's calling is not different from any other: its practitioners are for the most part ordinary empty-headed folk, ready to see what is not there and to deny the obvious. Any untrained person, if he loves and has knowledge of the flesh, is their superior and in the mysteries of the art can lead them by the nose. The inflammation of the air passages was something I had not thought of, so I had not included it in my performance. But once I had forced the doctor to drop the theory of "school-sickness," he had to fall back on flu, and to that end had to assume that my throat was irritated and my tonsils swollen, which was just as little the case as the other. He was quite right about the fever—though the fact entirely disproved his first diagnosis by presenting a genuine clinical phenomenon. Medical science teaches that fever can only be caused by the infection of the blood through some agency or other and that fever on other than physical grounds does not exist. That is absurd. My readers will be as convinced as I am myself that I was not ill in the ordinary sense when Inspector Dusing examined me. But I was highly excited; I had concentrated my whole being upon an act of the will; I was drunk with the intensity of my own performance in the rôle of parodying nature—a performance which had to be masterly lest it become ridiculous; I was delirious with the alternate tension and relaxation necessary to give actuality in my own eyes and others' to a condition which did not exist; and all this so heightened and enhanced my organic processes that the doctor could actually read the result off the thermometer. The same explanation applies to the pulse. When the Inspector's head lay on my chest and I inhaled the animal odour of his dry grey hair, I had it in my power to feel a violent reaction that made my heart beat fast and unevenly. And as for my stomach, Dr. Dusing always said that it was affected, whatever other diagnosis he produced; and it was true enough that the organ was uncommonly sensitive, pulsing and contracting with every stir of feeling, so that where others under stress of circumstances speak of a throbbing heart, I might always speak of a throbbing stomach. Of this phenomenon the doctor was aware and he was not a little impressed by it.

So he prescribed his acid drops or his tonic wine and stopped awhile gossiping with my mother; I lay meantime breathing short-windedly through my flaccid[24] lips and looking vacantly at the ceiling. My father would probably come in, too, and look at me with

24. limp, flabby.

an embarrassed self-conscious air, avoiding my eye. He would take occasion to consult the doctor about his gout. Then I was left alone, to spend the day—perhaps two or three days—on short commons (which I did not mind, because they made the food taste better) and in peace and freedom, given over to dreams of the brilliant future. When my youthful appetite rebelled at the diet of rusks[25] and gruel, I would slip out of my bed, open my writing-desk, and resort to the store of chocolate which nearly always lay there.

Where did I get my chocolate? It came into my possession in a strange, almost a fantastic way. On a corner of the busiest street in our little city there was an excellent delicatessen shop, a branch, if I mistake not, of a Wiesbaden firm. It supplied the wants of the best society and was most attractive. My way to school led me past this shop and many times I had entered it with a small coin in my hand to buy cheap sweets, such as fruit drops or barley sugar. But one day on going in I found it empty, not only of purchasers but also of attendants. There was a little bell on a spring over the door, and this had rung as I entered; but either the inner room was empty or the occupants did not hear the bell—I was and remained alone. And at first the emptiness surprised and startled me, it even gave me an uncanny feeling; but presently I began to look about me, for never before had I been able to contemplate undisturbed the delights of such a spot. It was a narrow room, with a rather high ceiling, and crammed from top to bottom with goodies. There were rows and rows of hams, sausages of all shapes and colours—white, yellow, red, and black; fat and lean and round and long—lines of tins and conserves, cocoas and teas, bright translucent glasses of honey, marmalade, and jam; bottles plump and bottles slender, filled with liqueurs and punch—all these things crowded the shelves from floor to ceiling. Then there were glass show-cases where smoked mackerel, lampreys, flounders, and eels were displayed on platters to tempt the appetite. There were dishes of Italian salad, lobsters spreading their claws on blocks of ice, sprats pressed flat and gleaming goldenly from opened boxes; choice fruits—garden strawberries and grapes beautiful as though they came from the Promised Land; tiers of sardine tins and those fascinating little white earthenware jars of caviar and *foie gras*. Plump chickens dangled their necks from the top shelf, and there were trays of cooked meats, ham, tongue, beef, and veal, smoked salmon and breast of goose, with the slender slicing-knife lying ready to hand. There were all sorts of cheeses under glass bells, brick-red, milk-white, and marbled, also the creamy ones that ooze in a golden wave out of their silver foil. Artichokes, bundles of asparagus, truffles, little liver sau-

25. zwieback.

sages in silver paper—all these things lay heaped in rich abundance; while on other tables stood open tin boxes full of fine biscuits, spice cakes piled in criss-cross layers, and glass urns full of dessert bon-bons and crystallized fruits.

I stood transfixed. Holding my breath and cocking my ears I drank in the enchanting atmosphere of the place and the medley of odours from chocolate and smoked fish and earthy truffles. My fancy ran riot with memories of fairy-stories of the paradise of chil-dren, of underground treasure-chambers where children born on Sunday might enter and fill their pockets with precious stones. It seemed like a dream; everyday laws and dull regulations were all sus-pended, one might give free rein to one's desires and let fancy rove in blissful unrestraint. I was seized with such a fever of desire on beholding this paradise of plenty entirely given over to my single person that I felt my very limbs to twitch. It took great self-control not to burst out in a pæan of jubilation at so much richness and so much freedom. I spoke into the silence, saying: "Good day" in quite a loud voice; I can still remember how the strained tones of my voice died away into the stillness. No one answered. And the water ran into my mouth in streams at that very moment. One quick and noiseless step and I stood beside one of the laden tables. I made one rapturous grab into the nearest glass urn, slipped my fistful of pralines into my coat pocket, gained the door, and by another second was round the corner of the street.

No doubt I shall be accused of common theft. I will not deny the accusation, I will simply retreat and not confront anyone who chooses to take the paltry word into his mouth. But the word—the poor, cheap, worn-out word, which does violence to all the finer meanings of life—is one thing, and quite another the living, prime-val, and absolute deed, forever shining with newness and originality. It is only out of habit and sheer mental indolence that we come to regard them as the same thing. And the truth is that the word, as used to describe or characterize a deed, is no better than one of these wire fly-killers that always miss the fly. Moreover, whenever it is a question of an act, it is not the what nor the why that matters (although the second is the more important), but simply and solely the who. Whatever I have done and committed, it has always been first of all *my* deed, not Tom's, Dick's, or Harry's: and though I have had to swallow, especially at the hands of the law, having the same name applied to me as to ten thousand others, I have always rebelled against such an unnatural comparison, in the unshakable conviction that I am a favourite of the powers that be and actually compact of different flesh and blood. The reader will forgive me this excursion into the abstract, and it may be that it ill becomes me, for I have no training or warrant for that kind of metaphysical thought. But I consider it my duty either to reconcile him so far as possible with the idiosyncrasies of my existence or else to prevent him from reading further.

When I got home I went up to my room, still in my overcoat, spread my treasure-trove out on my table, and examined it. I almost disbelieved that it was still there—for how often do not priceless things come to us in our dreams, yet when we wake our hands are empty. Imagine my lively joy—like that of a man waking from such a dream to find his treasure materialized on his bed-quilt—in examining my bonbons! They were of the best quality, wrapped in silver paper, filled with sweet liqueur and flavoured creams; but it was not alone their quality that enraptured me; even more it was the winning over of my dream treasure into my waking hand that made up the sum of my delight—a delight too great for me not to think of repeating it as occasion offered. Whatever the explanation—I did not cudgel my brains to find one—the shop proved to be often open and unwatched at the noon hour, as I could tell by strolling slowly past the door with my school-satchel on my back. I would return and go in, having learned to open the door so softly that the little bell did not jingle. By way of precaution I would say: "Good day"—and then take what was nearest, never too much, always with wise moderation, a handful of bonbons, a tablet of chocolate, a slice of cake—very probably nothing was ever missed. But these dream-like occasions on which I clutched with open hand the sweets of life were accompanied by such an expansion of my whole personality that they gave me anew the sensations with which certain trains of thought and introspection had already made me familiar.

At this point—though not without having laid aside the flowing pen to pause and collect my thoughts—I wish to enter at more length with my unknown reader upon a theme already glanced at earlier in these confessions. Let me say at once that such a reader will be disappointed if he expects from me any lightness of tone or lewdness of expression. No, for the dictates of morality and good form demand that discretion and sobriety be united with the candour which I promised at the outset of my enterprise. Pleasure in the salacious for its own sake, though an almost universal fault, has always been incomprehensible to me, and verbal excesses of this kind I have always found the most repulsive of all, since they are the cheapest and have not the excuse of passion. People laugh and joke about these matters precisely as though they were dealing with the simplest and most amusing subject in the world, whereas the exact opposite is the truth; and to talk of them in that loose and airy way is to surrender to the whinnyings of the mob the most important and mysterious concern of nature and of life. But to my confession.

First of all I must make it clear that the above-mentioned concern began very early to play a rôle with me, to occupy my thoughts, shape my fancies, and form the content of my childish enterprises—long, that is, before I had any words for it or could possibly form any general ideas of its nature or bearing. For a considerable time, that is, I regarded my tendency to such thoughts and the lively pleasure I had in them to be private and personal to myself. Nobody else, I thought, would understand them, and it was in fact advisable not to talk of them at all. Lacking any other means of description, I grouped all my emotions and fancies together under the heading of "the great joy" or "the best of all" and guarded them as a priceless secret. And thanks to this jealous reserve, thanks also to my isolation, and to a third cause to which I shall presently come, I long remained in this state of intellectual ignorance which so little corresponded to the liveliness of my senses. For as far back as I can remember, this "great joy" took up a commanding position in my inner life—indeed it probably began to do so farther back than my conscious memory extends. For small children are to that extent "innocent" in that they are unconscious; but that they are so in the sense of angelic purity is without doubt a sentimental superstition which would not stand the test of an objective examination. For myself, at least, I have it from an unexceptionable source, that even at my nurse's breast I displayed the clearest evidence of certain feelings—and this tradition has always seemed highly credible to me, as indicative of the eagerness of my nature.

In fact my penchant for the pleasures of love bordered on the extraordinary; even today it is my conviction that it far exceeded the usual measure. That this was so I had early grounds for suspecting; but my suspicions were converted to certainty on the evidence of that person who told me of my susceptible behaviour while still at the breast. With this person I sustained for several years a secret relationship. I refer to our housemaid Genoveva, who had been with us from a child and was in the beginning of her thirties when I reached sixteen. She was the daughter of a sergeant-major and had for a long time been engaged to the station-master at a little station between Frankfurt and Nieder-Lahnstein. She had a good deal of feeling for the refinements of life, and although she performed all the hard work of the house her position was as much housekeeper as servant. The marriage was—for lack of money—only a distant prospect; and the long waiting must have been a genuine hardship to the poor girl. In person she was a well-developed blonde with a lively green eye and mincing ways. But despite the prospect of spending her best years in renunciation she never listened to proposals from a lower sphere of society—advances from soldiers, working-men, or such people—for she did not reckon herself with common folk, feeling disgust for their speech and the way they smelt. The case was different with the son of the house, who aroused her approbation as he developed, and might give her the feeling that in satisfying him she both as it were performed a domestic duty and also improved her own station in society. Thus it happened that my desires did not encounter any serious resistance. I need not go into great detail—the episode had the usual features, too well known to be of interest to a cultured audience.

One evening my godfather Maggotson had supped with us, and we had spent the evening trying on costumes. When I went up to bed it happened—very likely so contrived by her—that I met Genoveva at the door of my attic room. We stopped to talk, by degrees moved over into the room itself, and ended by occupying it together for the night. I well remember my mood: it was one of gloom, disillusion, and boredom such as often seized upon me at the end of an evening devoted to the exercise of my "head for costumes"—only this time even more severe than usual. I had resumed my ordinary garb with loathing, I had the impulse to tear it off—but not the desire to forget my misery in slumber. For it seemed to me that the only possible consolation was to be found in Genoveva's arms—yes, to tell the whole truth, I felt that in complete intimacy with her I should find the continuation and consummation of my brilliant evening and the proper goal of my ramblings through my godfather's wardrobe of costumes. However that may be, at least the soul-satisfying, unimaginable delight I discovered on Genoveva's white, well-nourished breast defies all description. I cried out for very bliss, I felt myself mounting heavenwards. And it was not of a selfish nature, my desire: for so I was constructed that it was kindled only by the mutual joy of Genoveva.

Of course every possibility of comparison is out of the question; I can neither demonstrate nor disprove, but I was then and am now convinced that with me the satisfaction of love is twice as sweet and twice as poignant as with the average man. But it would be doing me an injustice to conclude that on the score of my unusual endowment I became a libertine and lady-killer. My difficult and dangerous life made great demands on my powers of concentration—I had to take care not to exhaust myself. I have observed that with some the act of love is a trifle which they perfunctorily discharge and go their way as though nothing had happened. As for me, the tribute which I paid was so great as to leave me for the time quite vacant and empty of the power to act. True, I have often exceeded, for the flesh is weak and I found my amorous requirements only too easily met. But in the end and on the whole I was of a temper too manly and too serious not to be called back from sensual relaxation to a necessary and healthful austerity. Moreover, the purely physical satisfaction is surely the grosser part of that which I had as a child instinctively called "the great joy." It enervates by satisfying us all too completely; it makes us bad lovers of the world, because on the one hand it robs life of its bloom and enchantment and on the other it impoverishes our own power to charm, since only he who desires is amiable, not he who is sated. For my part, I know many kinds of satisfaction finer and more subtle than the crude act which after all is but a limited and illusory satisfaction of appetite; and I am convinced that he has but a crude notion of enjoyment whose activities are directed only and immediately to the definite goal. My desires were always upon a broader, larger, and more general scale; they found the sweetest feeding where others might not seek; they were never precisely defined or specialized—and for this reason among others it was that despite my special aptitude I remained so long innocent and unconscious, yes, actually my whole life long a child and dreamer.

And herewith I leave a subject in dealing with which I believe I have not for a moment transgressed the canons of propriety and good taste, and hasten forwards to the tragic moment which terminated my sojourn under my parents' roof, and formed the turning-point of my career. I begin by mentioning the betrothal of my sister Olympia to Second Lieutenant Deibel of the second Nassau regiment No. 88, stationed in Mainz. The betrothal was attended by celebrations on a grand scale but led up to no other consequences. For the stress of circumstances proved too much for it; it was broken off and my sister—after the collapse of our family life—went on the stage. Deibel was a sickly young man, very ignorant of life. He was a constant guest at our parties, where, heated by dancing, forfeit-playing, and Berncasteler Doctor and fired by the judicious glimpses of their charms vouchsafed by the ladies of our household, he fell wildly in love with Olympia. With the concupiscence of weak-chested persons the world over, and probably overestimating our position and consequence, he actually one evening went on his knees and, almost shedding tears in his ardour, implored her to be his. To this day I do not understand how Olympia had the face to accept him, for certainly she did not respond to the feelings he professed and was doubtless informed by my mother of the true state of our affairs. But she probably thought it was high time to be sure of some refuge, no matter how frail, from the oncoming storm; she may even have thought that her engagement to an officer in the army, however poor his prospects, might delay the catastrophe. My poor father was appealed to for his consent and gave it with an embarrassed air and not much to say; whereupon the family event was communicated to the assembled guests, who received the news with loud acclaim and baptized it, so to say, with streams of Lorley

Extra Cuvée. After that, Lieutenant Deibel came almost daily to our house from Mainz, and did no little damage to his health by constant attendance upon the object of his sickly desire. I once entered the room where the betrothed pair had been for some little time alone and found him looking so distracted and moribund that I am convinced the turn which affairs presently took was for him a piece of unmixed good fortune.

As for me, my mind was occupied in these weeks almost wholly with the fascinating subject of the change of name which my sister's marriage would entail upon her. I remember that I envied her almost to bitterness. She who for so long had been called Olympia Krull would sign herself in future Olympia Deibel—and that fact alone possessed all the charm of novelty. How tiresome it is to sign all one's life long the same name to letters and papers! The hand grows paralysed with irritation and disgust—what a pleasurable refreshment and stimulation then of the whole being comes of being able to give oneself a new name and to hear oneself addressed by it! It seemed to me a positive advantage which the female sex has over the male that at least once in life the opportunity is afforded of this tonic and restorative—whereas to the male any change is as good as forbidden by law. I, personally, not having been born to lead the flabby and protected existence of the great bourgeois class, have often overstepped a prohibition which ran counter both to my safety and my dislike of the humdrum and everyday. I displayed in the process, if I may say so, a very pretty gift of invention; and there was a peculiar easy grace in the act whereby I, for the first time in my life, laid aside like a soiled and worn-out garment the name to which I was born, to assume another which for elegance and euphony far surpassed that of Lieutenant Deibel.

But in the midst of the betrothal episode events had taken their course, and ruin—to express myself poetically—knocked with harsh knuckles upon the door of our home. Those malicious rumours about my poor father's business, the studied avoidance we suffered from all and sundry, the gossip about our domestic affairs—all these were most cruelly confirmed by the event, to the unlovely satisfaction of the croakers. The consuming public had more and more refrained from buying our brand of wine. Lowering the price of course did not improve the product, nor did the alluring design produced against his better judgment by my good-natured godfather have any effect in staying the disaster. Ruin fell upon my poor father in the spring of my eighteenth year.

I was of course at that time entirely lacking in business sense— nor am I now any better off in that respect, since my own career, based on imagination and self-discipline, gave me no commercial training. Accordingly I refrain from trying my pen on a subject of which I have no knowledge and from burdening the reader with an account of the misfortunes of the Lorley wine company. But I feel impelled to give expression to the great sympathy which in these last months I felt for my father. He sank more and more into a speechless melancholy and would sit somewhere about the house with his head bent and the fingers of his right hand gently stroking his rounded belly, ceaselessly and rapidly blinking his eyes. He made frequent pathetic trips to Mainz, probably to try to get hold of some money; he would return from these excursions greatly dejected, wiping his face and eyes with a little batiste handkerchief. It was only at the evening parties, which we still held in our villa, when he sat at table with his napkin tied round his neck, his guests about him, and his glass in his hand, presiding over the feast, that anything like comfort revisited him. Yet in the course of one such evening there occurred a most unpleasant quarrel between my poor father and the Jewish banker, husband of the jet-laden female. He, as I then learned, was one of the most hardened cut-throats who ever lured harried and unwary business folk into their nets. Very soon thereafter came that serious and ominous day—yet for me refreshing in its novel excitement—when the factory and business premises of my father did not open and a group of cold-eyed, tight-lipped gentlemen appeared at our villa to attach our possessions. My poor father, in the choicest of phrases, had declared his bankruptcy before the courts and appended to his declaration that naïve and flourishing signature of his which I so well knew how to imitate; and with due solemnity proceedings in bankruptcy were instituted.

On that day our disgrace gave me occasion to stop away from school—and I may say here that it was never granted me to finish my course. This was firstly due to my never having troubled to conceal my aversion to the despotism and dullness which characterized that institution, and secondly because our domestic circumstances and ultimate disruption filled the masters with venom and contempt. At the Easter holidays after my poor father's failure they refused to give me my leaving-certificate, thus offering me the alternative of putting up with an inferior position unsuited to my age or of leaving the school and losing the advantages of a certificate. In the joyful consciousness that my native parts were adequate to make up for the loss of such extremely limited advantages, I chose the latter course.

Our financial collapse was complete; it became clear that my poor father had put if off so long and involved himself so deeply in the toils of the usurers only because he was aware that when the crash came it would reduce him to beggary. Everything came under the hammer: the warehouses (but who wanted to buy so notoriously bad a product as my father's wine?), the real estate—that is, the cellars and our villa, laden as those were with mortgages to two-thirds of their value, the interest on which had not been paid for years; the dwarfs, the toadstools and crockery animals in the gardens —yes, the glass ball and the æolian harp went the same sad way. The inside of the house was stripped of every charm: the spinning-wheel, the down cushions, the glass boxes and smelling-bottles all went at public auction, not even the halberds over the windows and the glass bead curtains were spared, and if the little device over the ventilator that played "Wine, Women, and Song" when the door was opened, still jingled unmindful of the desolation, it was only because it had not been noticed by its legal owners.

One could scarcely say at first that my father looked like a broken man. His face even expressed a certain satisfaction that his affairs, having passed beyond his own competence, now found themselves in such good hands; and since the bank which had purchased our property let us for very pity remain for the present within its bare walls, we still had a roof over our heads. Temperamentally easy-going and good-natured, he could not credit his fellow human beings with being so puritanically cruel as to reject him utterly; he was simple enough to try to form a local company with himself as director. His proposals were brusquely repulsed, as also other efforts he made to re-establish himself in life—though if he had been successful he would doubtless have proceeded upon his old courses of feastings and fireworks. But when everything failed he at last recognized the fact; and probably considering that he was in the way of us others, who might make better headway without him, he resolved to make an end of himself.

Five months had passed since the beginning of the bankruptcy proceedings; it was early autumn. Since Easter I had not gone back to school and was enjoying my temporary freedom and lack of prospects. We had gathered in our bare dining-room, my mother, my sister Olympia, and I, to eat our meagre meal, and were waiting for the head of the family. But when we had finished our soup and he did not appear, we sent Olympia, who had always been his favourite, to summon him. She had been gone scarcely three minutes when we heard her give a prolonged scream and then run still screaming upstairs and down and then distractedly up again. Frightened to my very marrow and ready for the worst, I went to my father's room. There he lay, upon the floor, with his clothing opened; his hand was resting upon the roundness of his belly, and beside him lay the fatal shining thing with which he had shot himself in his gentle heart. Our maid Genoveva and I lifted him to the sofa, and while she ran for the doctor, my sister Olympia still rushed screaming through the house, and my mother out of very fear would not venture out of the dining-room, I stood beside the earthly husk of my progenitor, now growing cold, with my hand over my eyes, and paid him the abundant tribute of my tears.

RAINER MARIA RILKE
(1875–1926)
Duino Elegies (Duineser Elegien)*

Third Elegy

To sing the Belovèd is one thing. Another, alas! is
to celebrate that hidden, guilty river-god of the blood.
He, whom she knows from afar, her young lover, what does he know
of that Lord of Pleasure, who, before his love had stilled him,
often from loneliness, often as if she did not exist,   5
would uplift his god-head, O, from what unknown depths, dripping,
rousing the night with his interminable uproar.
O the Neptune within our blood, O his terrible trident!
O the dark blast of his breast from his curved conch-shell!
Listen, how the night grows fluted and hollow. You stars,   10
is it not from you that the lover's delight in the loved one's
face arises? Does not his innermost insight
in her pure face come from the purest star?

It was not you, alas, nor was it his mother
who bent his brows into an arch so expectant.   15
Not for you, maiden who loves him, not for you did
his lips begin to curve in that more fruitful contour.
Do you really believe your gentle approach could have so
convulsed him, you, who wander like the dawn-wind?
It was you who shook his heart; but more ancient terrors   20
rushed into him in that shattering contact.
Call him . . . You cannot wholly call him from those dark
    companions.
He *will* free himself, he escapes them; lightly he dwells in
the home of your heart and accepts it and begins again there.
But did he begin himself, ever?   25

* 1923. From *Sonnets to Orpheus* [and] *Duino Elegies*, translated by Jessie Lemont, New York, The Fine Editions Press, copyright 1945 by Jessie Lemont. The third and ninth elegies are reprinted in their entirety. The punctuation ". . ." does not indicate omissions from the text.

Mother, to you who began his life, he was the little one;
To you he was new, you arched over those young eyes
the friendly world and averted the strange one.
Where, O where are the years when you, simply
with your slender figure, concealed the surging chaos?   30
You hid so much from him; the nightly-distrusted chamber
you made harmless, and in your heart's great refuge
there was more human space than the night-space around him.
Not in the darkness, no, in your nearer presence
you placed the night-light and it shone as though out of friend-
    ship.   35
Nowhere was there a creak you could not explain with a smile, as
though you had long known *when* the floor would behave thus . . .
And he listened to you and was quieted. So much it availed,
gently, your coming; his tall cloaked Fate stepped
behind the wardrobe and his restless future vanished   40
into the lightly shifting folds of the curtain.

And he himself was comforted, as he lay there
under drowsy eye-lids, your light figure,
sweetly releasing the feeling of coming sleep,
appeared to be guarding . . . But *within*, who could resist,   45
prevent, within him, the flood of origins?
Alas, there *was* no caution in that sleeper; sleeping,
but dreaming, and feverish: what he embarked on!
He, so young, so timid, how he was entangled
in the ever on-creeping tendrils of inner event,   50
already twisted into patterns, to throttle growths, to preying
forms of animals? How he gave himself up to it— Loved.

Loved his inner universe, his interior wilderness,
this jungle within him, among whose silent ruins
green-lit, his heart stood. Loved, left it, went into his   55
own roots, and out into violent beginning
where his tiny birth was already outlived. Descended
lovingly into the older blood, the crevasses
where Frightfulness lay, still gorged with his fathers.
And each terror knew him, winked, as if with understanding.   60
Yes, Horror smiled at him . . . Seldom did you,
Mother, smile so tenderly. How could he
not love that which smiled at him? He loved it
before you, for, even while you bore him, it was
dissolved in the water that makes the seed lighter.   65

See, we do not love like the flowers, for a single
season only: when we love, immemorial
sap mounts in our arms. O maiden, it is

this: that we have loved *within* us, not one, of the
future, but all the innumerable brewing;   70
not only the one child, but even the fathers, who like
mountain-ruins rest in our depths; even the dry
river-bed of former mothers—; even the whole
soundless landscape under its clouded
or cloudless destiny—: *this*, maiden, was before your existence.   75

And you yourself, what do you know,—you have conjured
long past times in your lover. What feelings
welled up from those bygone beings. What women
hated you there. What sinister men you
roused in his youthful veins? Dead children were   80
trying to reach you . . . O gently, gently,
show him daily a loving, dependable task done,—
guide him close to the garden, give him
transcendent nights . . .
            Hold him   85

Ninth Elegy

Why when this span of life might drift away,
as laurel, a little darker than all
the surrounding green, with tiny waves on the edges
of every leaf (like the wind's smile)—: why then
must we be human, and shunning Fate,   5
long for Fate? . . . O, not because happiness *is*
the precipitate benefit of a near loss.
Not out of curiosity, not for the sake of the heart,
that also could be in the laurel . . .
But because to be here is so much, and because   10
all the world around us, so fleeting, seems to need us,
to strangely concern us. Us, the most fleeting.
Once everything, only once. Once and no more. And we also
once. Never again. But this
having been once, though once only,   15
to have been once on Earth,—can it ever be blotted out?

And so we press on, striving toward attainment,
striving to hold it within our mere hands,
in the overfilled sight, and in the speechless heart.
Striving to become it— To whom to give it? We would love   20
to hold it all forever . . . Alas, in the other event,
O, what can be taken Beyond? Not the perception
learned here so slowly, and nothing that occurs here: Nothing.

But the sorrow— But all the hardness of life,
the long experience of love,—also the more   25
inexpressible things. But later
under the stars, what then? *They* are *indeed* inexpressible.
For the wanderer does not bring from the mountain-slope
a handful of earth to the valley, inexpressible earth, but only
a word he has gathered—pure, the gold and blue   30
gentian. Are we, perhaps, *here*, only to say: House.
Bridge. Fountain. Gate. Jug. Fruit-tree. Window.—
at most: Pillar. Tower . . . But to *say*,—you understand,
O to *say*, with an intensity the things themselves never
hoped to achieve. Is it not the secret guile   35
of this silent earth, which urges lovers
in their passion to be enchanted by each other?
Threshold: how much it means
for two lovers, that they should be wearing their own
worn threshold a little, they too, after the many before,   40
and before the many to come . . . lightly.

Here is the time for the *Legend. Here* is its home.
Speak and understand. More than ever
the things that we live with are falling away,
are dispossessed and replaced by an act without plan.   45
A concealed act, that is readily disrupted as soon as
the inner energy awakes and takes a new form.
Between the beats our heart
lives on, as between the teeth,
the tongue nevertheless   50
still continues to praise.

Praise the world to the Angel, not the inexpressible: you
cannot impress him with the splendour you have felt in all the
    world,
where he profoundly feels, you are only a novice. Show him
some simple thing, remoulded by age after age   55
till it lives, in our hands and our eyes, as a part of ourselves.
Tell him these things. He would be more astounded than you were
by the rope-maker in Rome or by the potter on the Nile.
Show him how joyous a thing can be, how innocent, and ours;
how the wailing lament clearly unfolds into form,   60

52. *the Angel:* The angel of Rilke,
in the *Elegies*, has little to do with
the Christian conception, but is a
being of immense power who moves
freely between the visible and invisible
worlds. Men could not support his immediate presence.

serves as a thing, or dies in a thing,—and fades in the beyond
like the melody of a violin. And these living things
that are departing, understand when you praise them; fleeting,
they believe they will be saved by us, the most fleeting of all.
They wish us to wholly change them within our invisible hearts   65
into—O endlessly—into ourselves! Whosoever we are.

Earth, is not this what you wish: an *invisible*
rebirth in us? Is it not your dream
to be once invisible?—Earth! invisible!
What is your urgent command, if not transformation?   70
Earth, you belovèd. O, believe me, you need
your Springtime no longer to win me: one
O, one only, even one is too much for my blood.
I have been unutterably yours from time immemorial.
Ever, you were in the right, and your holiest inspiration   75
is friendly Death.
See, I live. Wherefore? Neither childhood nor future
are growing less . . . Overflowing existence
leaps within my heart.

MARCEL PROUST
(1871–1922)
Remembrance of Things Past
(À la Recherche du temps perdu)*

It was at the Marquise de Saint-Euverte's, on the last, for that
season, of the evenings on which she invited people to listen to the
musicians who would serve, later on, for her charity concerts. Swann,
who had intended to go to each of the previous evenings in turn,
but had never been able to make up his mind, received, while he
was dressing for this party, a visit from the Baron de Charlus, who
came with an offer to go with him to the Marquise's, if his company
could be of any use in helping Swann not to feel quite so bored
when he got there, to be a little less unhappy. But Swann had thanked
him with:

"You can't conceive how glad I should be of your company. But
the greatest pleasure that you can give me will be if you will go

---

instead to see Odette.[1] You know what a splendid influence you have over her. I don't suppose she'll be going anywhere this evening, unless she goes to see her old dressmaker, and I'm sure she would be delighted if you went with her there. In any case, you'll find her at home before then. Try to keep her amused, and also to give her a little sound advice. If you could arrange something for tomorrow which would please her, something that we could all three do together. Try to put out a feeler, too, for the summer; see if there's anything she wants to do, a cruise that we might all three take; anything you can think of. I don't count upon seeing her tonight, myself; still if she would like me to come, or if you find a loophole, you've only to send me a line at Mme. de Saint-Euverte's up till midnight; after that I shall be here. Ever so many thanks for all you are doing for me—you know what I feel about you!"

His friend promised to go and do as Swann wished as soon as he had deposited him at the door of the Saint-Euverte house, where he arrived soothed by the thought that M. de Charlus would be spending the evening in the Rue La Pérouse,[2] but in a state of melancholy indifference to everything that did not involve Odette, and in particular to the details of fashionable life, a state which invested them with the charm that is to be found in anything which, being no longer an object of our desire, appears to us in its own guise. On alighting from his carriage, in the foreground of that fictitious summary of their domestic existence which hostesses are pleased to offer to their guests on ceremonial occasions, and in which they shew a great regard for accuracy of costume and setting, Swann was amused to discover the heirs and successors of Balzac's[3] 'tigers'[4] —now 'grooms'—who normally followed their mistress when she walked abroad, but now, hatted and booted, were posted out of doors, in front of the house on the gravelled drive, or outside the stables, as gardeners might be drawn up for inspection at the ends of their several flower-beds. The peculiar tendency which he had always had to look for analogies between living people and the portraits in galleries reasserted itself here, but in a more positive and more general form; it was society as a whole, now that he was detached from it, which presented itself to him in a series of pictures. In the cloak-room, into which, in the old days, when he was still a man of fashion, he would have gone in his overcoat, to emerge from it in evening dress, but without any impression of what had occurred there, his mind having been, during the minute or two that

---

1. Charles Swann had paid court to Odette de Crécy, a woman of rather doubtful antecedents, and she had become his mistress. Not, however, until she showed indifference and avoided him did Swann, who hitherto had imagined his emotions to be in perfect control, fall hopelessly in love with her.

2. Odette lived on this street.

3. Honoré de Balzac (1799–1850), French novelist, whose novels are known collectively as the *Human Comedy*.

4. grooms, footmen.

he had spent in it, either still at the party which he had just left, or already at the party into which he was just about to be ushered, he now noticed, for the first time, roused by the unexpected arrival of so belated a guest, the scattered pack of splendid effortless animals, the enormous footmen who were drowsing here and there upon benches and chests, until, pointing their noble greyhound profiles, they towered upon their feet and gathered in a circle round about him.

One of them, of a particularly ferocious aspect, and not unlike the headsman in certain Renaissance pictures which represent executions, tortures, and the like, advanced upon him with an implacable air to take his 'things.' But the harshness of his steely glare was compensated by the softness of his cotton gloves, so effectively that, as he approached Swann, he seemed to be exhibiting at once an utter contempt for his person and the most tender regard for his hat. He took it with a care to which the precision of his movements imparted something that was almost overfastidious, and with a delicacy that was rendered almost touching by the evidence of his splendid strength. Then he passed it to one of his satellites, a novice and timid, who was expressing the panic that overpowered him by casting furious glances in every direction, and displayed all the dumb agitation of a wild animal in the first hours of its captivity.

A few feet away, a strapping great lad in livery stood musing, motionless, statuesque, useless, like that purely decorative warrior whom one sees in the most tumultuous of Mantegna's[5] paintings, lost in dreams, leaning upon his shield, while all around him are fighting and bloodshed and death; detached from the group of his companions who were thronging about Swann, he seemed as determined to remain unconcerned in the scene, which he followed vaguely with his cruel, greenish eyes, as if it had been the Massacre of the Innocents or the Martyrdom of Saint James. He seemed precisely to have sprung from that vanished race—if, indeed, it ever existed, save in the reredos of San Zeno[6] and the frescoes of the Eremitani,[7] where Swann had come in contact with it, and where it still dreams—fruit of the impregnation of a classical statue by some one of the Master's[8] Paduan models, or of Albert Dürer's[9] Saxons. And the locks of his reddish hair, crinkled by nature, but glued to his head by brilliantine, were treated broadly as they are in that Greek sculpture which the Mantuan painter never ceased to study, and which, if in its creator's purpose it represents but man, manages at least to extract from man's simple outlines such a variety of richness, borrowed, as it were, from the whole of animated nature, that a head of hair, by the glossy

---

5. Andrea Mantegna (1431–1506), Italian painter, died at Mantua. Such figures can be seen in the paintings named at the end of this sentence, which are among the frescoes the artist painted in the two churches mentioned in the following sentence.
6. a church in Verona.
7. the church of San Agestino degli Eremitani in Padua.
8. Mantegna's.
9. German painter (1471–1528).

undulation and beak-like points of its curls, or in the overlaying of the florid triple diadem of its brushed tresses, can suggest at once a bunch of seaweed, a brood of fledgling doves, a bed of hyacinths and a serpent's writhing back. Others again, no less colossal, were disposed upon the steps of a monumental staircase which, by their decorative presence and marmorean immobility, was made worthy to be named, like that god-crowned ascent in the Palace of the Doges,[10] the 'Staircase of the Giants,' and on which Swann now set foot, saddened by the thought that Odette had never climbed it. Ah, with what joy would he, on the other hand, have raced up the dark, evil-smelling, breakneck flights to the little dressmaker's, in whose attic he would so gladly have paid the price of a weekly stage-box at the Opera for the right to spend the evening there when Odette came, and other days too, for the privilege of talking about her, of living among people whom she was in the habit of seeing when he was not there, and who, on that account, seemed to keep secret among themselves some part of the life of his mistress more real, more inaccessible and more mysterious than anything that he knew. Whereas upon that pestilential, enviable staircase to the old dressmaker's, since there was no other, no service stair in the building, one saw in the evening outside every door an empty, unwashed milk-can set out, in readiness for the morning round, upon the doormat; on the despicable, enormous staircase which Swann was at that moment climbing, on either side of him, at different levels, before each anfractuosity[11] made in its walls by the window of the porter's lodge or the entrance to a set of rooms, representing the departments of indoor service which they controlled, and doing homage for them to the guests, a gate-keeper, a major-domo, a steward (worthy men who spent the rest of the week in semi-independence in their own domains, dined there by themselves like small shop-keepers, and might tomorrow lapse to the plebeian service of some successful doctor or industrial magnate), scrupulous in carrying out to the letter all the instructions that had been heaped upon them before they were allowed to don the brilliant livery which they wore only at long intervals, and in which they did not feel altogether at their ease, stood each in the arcade of his doorway, their splendid pomp tempered by a democratic good-fellowship, like saints in their niches, and a gigantic usher, dressed Swiss Guard fashion, like the beadle in a church, struck the pavement with his staff as each fresh arrival passed him. Coming to the top of the staircase, up which he had been followed by a servant with a pallid countenance and a small pigtail clubbed at the back of his head, like one of Goya's[12] sacristans or a tabellion[13] in an old play, Swann passed by an office in which the lackeys, seated like notaries before their massive registers,

---

10. The Doge was the elected ruler of Venice (697–1797).
11. channel, crevice, or passage full of windings and turnings.

12. Francisco Goya (1746–1828), Spanish painter.
13. notary or scrivener.

rose solemnly to their feet and inscribed his name. He next crossed a little hall which—just as certain rooms are arranged by their owners to serve as the setting for a single work of art (from which they take their name), and, in their studied bareness, contain nothing else besides—displayed to him as he entered it, like some priceless effigy by Benvenuto Cellini[14] of an armed watchman, a young footman, his body slightly bent forward, rearing above his crimson gorget[15] an even more crimson face, from which seemed to burst forth torrents of fire, timidity and zeal, who, as he pierced the Aubusson tapestries[16] that screened the door of the room in which the music was being given with his impetuous, vigilant, desperate gaze, appeared, with a soldierly impassibility or a supernatural faith —an allegory of alarums, incarnation of alertness, commemoration of a riot—to be looking out, angel or sentinel, from the tower of dungeon or cathedral, for the approach of the enemy or for the hour of Judgment. Swann had now only to enter the concert-room, the doors of which were thrown open to him by an usher loaded with chains, who bowed low before him as though tendering to him the keys of a conquered city. But he thought of the house in which at that very moment he might have been, if Odette had but permitted, and the remembered glimpse of an empty milk-can upon a door-mat wrung his heart.

He speedily recovered his sense of the general ugliness of the human male when, on the other side of the tapestry curtain, the spectacle of the servants gave place to that of the guests. But even this ugliness of faces, which of course were mostly familiar to him, seemed something new and uncanny, now that their features,—instead of being to him symbols of practical utility in the identification of this or that man, who until then had represented merely so many pleasures to be sought-after, boredoms to be avoided, or courtesies to be acknowledged—were at rest, measurable by aesthetic co-ordinates alone, in the autonomy of their curves and angles. And in these men, in the thick of whom Swann now found himself packed, there was nothing (even to the monocle which many of them wore, and which, previously, would, at the most, have enabled Swann to say that so-and-so wore a monocle) which, no longer restricted to the general connotation of a habit, the same in all of them, did not now strike him with a sense of individuality in each. Perhaps because he did not regard General de Froberville and the Marquis de Bréauté, who were talking together just inside the door, as anything more than two figures in a picture, whereas they were the old and useful friends who had put him up for the Jockey Club[17] and had supported him in duels, the General's monocle, stuck like a shell-splinter in his

14. Florentine engraver, sculptor and goldsmith (1500–1571). See the section on the Renaissance.

15. a piece of armor for the throat.

16. woven at Aubusson, in the *département* of Creuse, France.

17. a highly exclusive club which organizes race meetings.

common, scarred, victorious, overbearing face, in the middle of a forehead which it left half-blinded, like the single-eyed flashing front of the Cyclops,[18] appeared to Swann as a monstrous wound which it might have been glorious to receive but which it was certainly not decent to expose, while that which M. de Bréauté wore, as a festive badge, with his pearl-grey gloves, his crush hat and white tie, substituting it for the familiar pair of glasses (as Swann himself did) when he went out to places, bore, glued to its other side, like a specimen prepared on a slide for the microscope, an infinitesimal gaze that swarmed with friendly feeling and never ceased to twinkle at the loftiness of ceilings, the delightfulness of parties, the interestingness of programmes and the excellence of refreshments.

"Hallo! you here! why, it's ages since I've seen you," the General greeted Swann and, noticing the look of strain on his face and concluding that it was perhaps a serious illness that had kept him away, went on, "You're looking well, old man!" while M. de Bréauté turned with, "My dear fellow, what on earth are you doing here?" to a 'society novelist' who had just fitted into the angle of eyebrow and cheek his own monocle, the sole instrument that he used in his psychological investigations and remorseless analyses of character, and who now replied, with an air of mystery and importance, rolling the 'r';—"I am observing!"

The Marquis de Forestelle's monocle was minute and rimless, and, by enforcing an incessant and painful contraction of the eye over which it was incrusted like a superfluous cartilage, the presence of which there was inexplicable and its substance unimaginable, it gave to his face a melancholy refinement, and led women to suppose him capable of suffering terribly when in love. But that of M. de Saint-Candé, girdled, like Saturn, with an enormous ring, was the centre of gravity of a face which composed itself afresh every moment in relation to the glass, while his thrusting red nose and swollen sarcastic lips endeavoured by their grimaces to rise to the level of the steady flame of wit that sparkled in the polished disk, and saw itself preferred to the most ravishing eyes in the world by the smart, depraved young women whom it set dreaming of artificial charms and a refinement of sensual bliss; and then, behind him, M. de Palancy, who with his huge carp's head and goggling eyes moved slowly up and down the stream of festive gatherings, unlocking his great mandibles[19] at every moment as though in search of his orientation, had the air of carrying about upon his person only an accidental and perhaps purely symbolical fragment of the glass wall of his aquarium, a part intended to suggest the whole which recalled to Swann, a fervent admirer of Giotto's[20] Vices and Virtues at Padua, that In-

---

18. in Homer's *Odyssey*, a giant with but one eye in the middle of his forehead.

19. here, the upper and lower jaws.
20. Giotto di Bondone (1266?–1336?), Florentine painter.

justice by whose side a leafy bough evokes the idea of the forests that enshroud his secret lair.

Swann had gone forward into the room, under pressure from Mme. de Saint-Euverte and in order to listen to an aria from *Orfeo*[21] which was being rendered on the flute, and had taken up a position in a corner from which, unfortunately, his horizon was bounded by two ladies of 'uncertain' age, seated side by side, the Marquise de Cambremer and the Vicomtesse de Franquetot, who, because they were cousins, used to spend their time at parties in wandering through the rooms, each clutching her bag and followed by her daughter, hunting for one another like people at a railway station, and could never be at rest until they had reserved, by marking them with their fans or handkerchiefs, two adjacent chairs; Mme. de Cambremer, since she knew scarcely anyone, being all the more glad of a companion, while Mme. de Franquetot, who, on the contrary, was extremely popular, thought it effective and original to shew all her fine friends that she preferred to their company that of an obscure country cousin with whom she had childish memories in common. Filled with ironical melancholy, Swann watched them as they listened to the pianoforte intermezzo (Liszt's[22] 'Saint Francis preaching to the birds') which came after the flute, and followed the virtuoso in his dizzy flight; Mme. de Franquetot anxiously, her eyes starting from her head, as though the keys over which his fingers skipped with such agility were a series of trapezes, from any one of which he might come crashing, a hundred feet, to the ground, stealing now and then a glance of astonishment and unbelief at her companion, as who should say: "It isn't possible, I would never have believed that a human being could do all that!"; Mme. de Cambremer, as a woman who had received a sound musical education, beating time with her head—transformed for the nonce into the pendulum of a metronome, the sweep and rapidity of whose movements from one shoulder to the other (performed with that look of wild abandonment in her eye which a sufferer shews who is no longer able to analyse his pain, nor anxious to master it, and says merely "I can't help it") so increased that at every moment her diamond earrings caught in the trimming of her bodice, and she was obliged to put straight the bunch of black grapes which she had in her hair, though without any interruption of her constantly accelerated motion. On the other side (and a little way in front) of Mme. de Franquetot was the Marquise de Gallardon, absorbed in her favourite meditation, namely, upon her own kinship with the Guermantes family,[23] from which she derived both publicly and in private a good deal of glory not unmingled with shame, the

21. an opera (1762) with music by Christoph Willibald Gluck (1714–1787).

22. Franz Liszt (1811–1886), Hungarian composer.

23. in Proust's novel, an aristocratic family of the greatest eminence.

most brilliant ornaments of that house remaining somewhat aloof from her, perhaps because she was just a tiresome old woman, or because she was a scandalous old woman, or because she came of an inferior branch of the family, or very possibly for no reason at all. When she found herself seated next to some one whom she did not know, as she was at this moment next to Mme. de Franquetot, she suffered acutely from the feeling that her own consciousness of her Guermantes connection could not be made externally manifest in visible characters, like those which, in the mosaics in Byzantine churches, placed one beneath another, inscribe in a vertical column by the side of some Sacred Personage the words which he is supposed to be uttering. At this moment she was pondering the fact that she had never received an invitation, or even a call, from her young cousin the Princesse des Laumes,[24] during the six years that had already elapsed since the latter's marriage. The thought filled her with anger—and with pride; for, by virtue of having told everyone who expressed surprise at never seeing her at Mme. des Laumes's, that it was because of the risk of meeting the Princesse Mathilde[25] there—a degradation which her own family, the truest and bluest of Legitimists,[26] would never have forgiven her, she had come gradually to believe that this actually was the reason for her not visiting her young cousin. She remembered, it is true, that she had several times inquired of Mme. des Laumes how they might contrive to meet, but she remembered it only in a confused way, and besides did more than neutralise this slightly humiliating reminiscence by murmuring, "After all, it isn't for me to take the first step; I am at least twenty years older than she is." And fortified by these unspoken words she flung her shoulders proudly back until they seemed to part company with her bust, while her head, which lay almost horizontally upon them, made one think of the 'stuck-on' head of a pheasant which is brought to the table regally adorned with its feathers. Not that she in the least degree resembled a pheasant, having been endowed by nature with a short and squat and masculine figure; but successive mortifications had given her a backward tilt, such as one may observe in trees which have taken root on the very edge of a precipice and are forced to grow backwards to preserve their balance. Since she was obliged, in order to console herself for not being quite on a level with the rest of the Guermantes, to repeat to herself incessantly that it was owing to the uncompromising rigidity of her principles and pride that she saw so little of them, the constant iteration had gradually remoulded her body, and had given her a sort of 'bearing' which was accepted by the plebeian as a sign of breeding,

---

24. later, on the death of her father-in-law, to be known as the Duchesse de Guermantes.

25. a Bonaparte princess. This real-life personage appears as a character in Proust's novel.

26. royalists.

and even kindled, at times, a momentary spark in the jaded eyes of old gentlemen in clubs. Had anyone subjected Mme. de Gallardon's conversation to that form of analysis which by noting the relative frequency of its several terms would furnish him with the key to a ciphered message, he would at once have remarked that no expression, not even the commonest forms of speech, occurred in it nearly so often as "at my cousins the Guermantes'," "at my aunt Guermantes's," "Elzéar de Guermantes's health," "my cousin Guermantes's box." If anyone spoke to her of a distinguished personage, she would reply that, although she was not personally acquainted with him, she had seen him hundreds of times at her aunt Guermantes's, but she would utter this reply in so icy a tone, with such a hollow sound, that it was at once quite clear that if she did not know the celebrity personally that was because of all the obstinate, ineradicable principles against which her arching shoulders were stretched back to rest, as on one of those ladders on which gymnastic instructors make us 'extend' so as to develop the expansion of our chests.

At this moment the Princesse des Laumes, who had not been expected to appear at Mme. de Saint-Euverte's that evening, did in fact arrive. To shew that she did not wish any special attention, in a house to which she had come by an act of condescension, to be paid to her superior rank, she had entered the room with her arms pressed close to her sides, even when there was no crowd to be squeezed through, no one attempting to get past her; staying purposely at the back, with the air of being in her proper place, like a king who stands in the waiting procession at the doors of a theatre where the management have not been warned of his coming; and strictly limiting her field of vision—so as not to seem to be advertising her presence and claiming the consideration that was her due—to the study of a pattern in the carpet or of her own skirt, she stood there on the spot which had struck her as the most modest (and from which, as she very well knew, a cry of rapture from Mme. de Saint-Euverte would extricate her as soon as her presence there was noticed), next to Mme. de Cambremer, whom, however, she did not know. She observed the dumb-show by which her neighbour was expressing her passion for music, but she refrained from copying it. This was not to say that, for once that she had consented to spend a few minutes in Mme. de Saint-Euverte's house, the Princesse des Laumes would not have wished (so that the act of politeness to her hostess which she had performed by coming might, so to speak, 'count double') to shew herself as friendly and obliging as possible. But she had a natural horror of what she called 'exaggerating,' and always made a point of letting people see that she 'simply must not' indulge in any display of emotion that was not in keeping with the tone of the circle in which she moved, although such displays never failed to make an impression upon her, by virtue of that spirit of imitation, akin to timidity, which is developed in the most self-confident persons, by contact with an unfamiliar environment, even though it be inferior to their own. She began to ask herself whether these gesticulations might not, perhaps, be a necessary concomitant of the piece of music that was being played, a piece which, it might be, was in a different category from all the music that she had ever heard before; and whether to abstain from them was not a sign of her own inability to understand the music, and of discourtesy towards the lady of the house; with the result that, in order to express by a compromise both of her contradictory inclinations in turn, at one moment she would merely straighten her shoulder-straps or feel in her golden hair for the little balls of coral or of pink enamel, frosted with tiny diamonds, which formed its simple but effective ornament, studying, with a cold interest, her impassioned neighbour, while at another she would beat time for a few bars with her fan, but, so as not to forfeit her independence, she would beat a different time from the pianist's. When he had finished the Liszt Intermezzo and had begun a Prelude by Chopin,[27] Mme. de Cambremer turned to Mme. de Franquetot with a tender smile, full of intimate reminiscence, as well as of satisfaction (that of a competent judge) with the performance. She had been taught in her girlhood to fondle and cherish those long-necked, sinuous creatures, the phrases of Chopin, so free, so flexible, so tactile, which begin by seeking their ultimate resting-place somewhere beyond and far wide of the direction in which they started, the point which one might have expected them to reach, phrases which divert themselves in those fantastic bypaths only to return more deliberately—with a more premeditated reaction, with more precision, as on a crystal bowl which, if you strike it, will ring and throb until you cry aloud in anguish—to clutch at one's heart.

Brought up in a provincial household with few friends or visitors, hardly ever invited to a ball, she had fuddled her mind, in the solitude of her old manor-house, over setting the pace, now crawling-slow, now passionate, whirling, breathless, for all those imaginary waltzing couples, gathering them like flowers, leaving the ball-room for a moment to listen, where the wind sighed among the pine-trees, on the shore of the lake, and seeing him of a sudden advancing towards her, more different from anything one had ever dreamed of than earthly lovers are, a slender young man, whose voice was resonant and strange and false, in white gloves. But nowadays the old-fashioned beauty of this music seemed to have become a trifle stale. Having forfeited, some years back, the esteem of 'really musical' people, it had lost its distinction and its charm, and even those whose

27. Frédéric Chopin (1810–1849), Polish composer.

taste was frankly bad had ceased to find in it more than a moderate pleasure to which they hardly liked to confess. Mme. de Cambremer cast a furtive glance behind her. She knew that her young daughter-in-law (full of respect for her new and noble family, except in such matters as related to the intellect, upon which, having 'got as far' as Harmony and the Greek alphabet, she was specially enlightened) despised Chopin, and fell quite ill when she heard him played. But finding herself free from the scrutiny of this Wagnerian, who was sitting, at some distance, in a group of her own contemporaries, Mme. de Cambremer let herself drift upon a stream of exquisite memories and sensations. The Princesse des Laumes was touched also. Though without any natural gift for music, she had received, some fifteen years earlier, the instruction which a music-mistress of the Faubourg Saint-Germain,[28] a woman of genius who had been, towards the end of her life, reduced to penury, had started, at seventy, to give to the daughters and granddaughters of her old pupils. This lady was now dead. But her method, an echo of her charming touch, came to life now and then in the fingers of her pupils, even of those who had been in other respects quite mediocre, had given up music, and hardly ever opened a piano. And so Mme. des Laumes could let her head sway to and fro, fully aware of the cause, with a perfect appreciation of the manner in which the pianist was rendering this Prelude, since she knew it by heart. The closing notes of the phrase that he had begun sounded already on her lips. And she murmured "How charming it is!" with a stress on the opening consonants of the adjective, a token of her refinement by which she felt her lips so romantically compressed, like the petals of a beautiful, budding flower, that she instinctively brought her eyes into harmony, illuminating them for a moment with a vague and sentimental gaze. Meanwhile Mme. de Gallardon had arrived at the point of saying to herself how annoying it was that she had so few opportunities of meeting the Princesse des Laumes, for she meant to teach her a lesson by not acknowledging her bow. She did not know that her cousin was in the room. A movement of Mme. de Franquetot's head disclosed the Princess. At once Mme. de Gallardon dashed towards her, upsetting all her neighbours; although determined to preserve a distant and glacial manner which should remind everyone present that she had no desire to remain on friendly terms with a person in whose house one might find oneself, any day, cheek by jowl with the Princesse Mathilde, and to whom it was not her duty to make advances since she was not 'of her generation,' she felt bound to modify this air of dignity and reserve by some non-committal remark which would justify her overture and would force the Princess to engage in conversation; and so, when she reached her cousin, Mme.

28. the aristocratic district of Paris.

de Gallardon, with a stern countenance and one hand thrust out as though she were trying to 'force' a card, began with "How is your husband?" in the same anxious tone that she would have used if the Prince had been seriously ill. The Princess, breaking into a laugh which was one of her characteristics, and was intended at once to shew the rest of an assembly that she was making fun of some one and also to enhance her own beauty by concentrating her features around her animated lips and sparkling eyes, answered: "Why, he's never been better in his life!" And she went on laughing.

Mme. de Gallardon then drew herself up and, chilling her expression still further, perhaps because she was still uneasy about the Prince's health, said to her cousin:

"Oriane" (at once Mme. des Laumes looked with amused astonishment towards an invisible third, whom she seemed to call to witness that she had never authorised Mme. de Gallardon to use her Christian name), "I should be so pleased if you would look in, just for a minute, tomorrow evening, to hear a quintet, with the clarinet, by Mozart. I should like to have your opinion of it."

She seemed not so much to be issuing an invitation as to be asking a favour, and to want the Princess's opinion of the Mozart quintet just as though it had been a dish invented by a new cook, whose talent it was most important that an epicure should come to judge.

"But I know that quintet quite well. I can tell you now—that I adore it."

"You know, my husband isn't at all well; it's his liver. He would like so much to see you," Mme. de Gallardon resumed, making it now a corporal work of charity for the Princess to appear at her party.

The Princess never liked to tell people that she would not go to their houses. Every day she would write to express her regret at having been kept away—by the sudden arrival of her husband's mother, by an invitation from his brother, by the Opera, by some excursion to the country—from some party to which she had never for a moment dreamed of going. In this way she gave many people the satisfaction of feeling that she was on intimate terms with them, that she would gladly have come to their houses, and that she had been prevented from doing so only by some princely occurrence which they were flattered to find competing with their own humble entertainment. And then, as she belonged to that witty 'Guermantes set' —in which there survived something of the alert mentality, stripped of all commonplace phrases and conventional sentiments, which dated from Mérimée,[29] and found its final expression in the plays of Meilhac and Halévy[30]—she adapted its formula so as to suit even

---

29. Prosper Mérimée (1803–1870), French writer and intimate of the Empress Eugénie.

30. Henry Meilhac (1831–1897) and Ludovic Halévy (1834–1884) collaborated in the writing of many comedies and operettas.

her social engagements, transposed it into the courtesy which was always struggling to be positive and precise, to approximate itself to the plain truth. She would never develop at any length to a hostess the expression of her anxiety to be present at her party; she found it more pleasant to disclose to her all the various little incidents on which it would depend whether it was or was not possible for her to come.

"Listen, and I'll explain," she began to Mme. de Gallardon. "Tomorrow evening I must go to a friend of mine, who has been pestering me to fix a day for ages. If she takes us to the theatre afterwards, then I can't possibly come to you, much as I should love to; but if we just stay in the house, I know there won't be anyone else there, so I can slip away."

"Tell me, have you seen your friend M. Swann?"

"No! my precious Charles! I never knew he was here. Where is he? I must catch his eye."

"It's a funny thing that he should come to old Saint-Euverte's," Mme. de Gallardon went on. "Oh, I know he's very clever," meaning by that 'very cunning,' "but that makes no difference; fancy a Jew here, and she the sister and sister-in-law of two Archbishops."

"I am ashamed to confess that I am not in the least shocked," said the Princesse des Laumes.

"I know he's a converted Jew, and all that, and his parents and grandparents before him. But they do say that the converted ones are worse about their religion than the practising ones, that it's all just a pretence; is that true, d'you think?"

"I can throw no light at all on the matter."

The pianist, who was 'down' to play two pieces by Chopin, after finishing the Prelude had at once attacked a Polonaise. But once Mme. de Gallardon had informed her cousin that Swann was in the room, Chopin himself might have risen from the grave and played all his works in turn without Mme. des Laumes's paying him the slightest attention. She belonged to that one of the two divisions of the human race in which the untiring curiosity which the other half feels about the people whom it does not know is replaced by an unfailing interest in the people whom it does. As with many women of the Faubourg Saint-Germain, the presence, in any room in which she might find herself, of another member of her set, even although she had nothing in particular to say to him, would occupy her mind to the exclusion of every other consideration. From that moment, in the hope that Swann would catch sight of her, the Princess could do nothing but (like a tame white mouse when a lump of sugar is put down before its nose and then taken away) turn her face, in which were crowded a thousand signs of intimate connivance, none of them with the least relevance to the sentiment underlying Chopin's music, in the direction where Swann was, and, if he moved, divert accordingly the course of her magnetic smile.

"Oriane, don't be angry with me," resumed Mme. de Gallardon, who could never restrain herself from sacrificing her highest social ambitions, and the hope that she might one day emerge into a light that would dazzle the world, to the immediate and secret satisfaction of saying something disagreeable, "people do say about your M. Swann that he's the sort of man one can't have in the house; is that true?"

"Why, you, of all people, ought to know that it's true," replied the Princesse des Laumes, "for you must have asked him a hundred times, and he's never been to your house once."

And leaving her cousin mortified afresh, she broke out again into a laugh which scandalised everyone who was trying to listen to the music, but attracted the attention of Mme. de Saint-Euverte, who had stayed, out of politeness, near the piano, and caught sight of the Princess now for the first time. Mme. de Saint-Euverte was all the more delighted to see Mme. des Laumes, as she imagined her to be still at Guermantes,[31] looking after her father-in-law, who was ill.

"My dear Princess, you here?"

"Yes, I tucked myself away in a corner, and I've been hearing such lovely things."

"What, you've been in the room quite a time?"

"Oh, yes, quite a long time, which seemed very short; it was only long because I couldn't see you."

Mme. de Saint-Euverte offered her own chair to the Princess, who declined it with:

"Oh, please, no! Why should you? It doesn't matter in the least where I sit." And deliberately picking out, so as the better to display the simplicity of a really great lady, a low seat without a back: "There now, that hassock, that's all I want. It will make me keep my back straight. Oh! Good heavens, I'm making a noise again; they'll be telling you to have me 'chucked out'."

Meanwhile, the pianist having doubled his speed, the emotion of the music-lovers was reaching its climax, a servant was handing refreshments about on a salver, and was making the spoons rattle, and, as on every other 'party-night,' Mme. de Saint-Euverte was making signs to him, which he never saw, to leave the room. A recent bride, who had been told that a young woman ought never to appear bored, was smiling vigorously, trying to catch her hostess's eye so as to flash a token of her gratitude for the other's having 'thought of her' in connection with so delightful an entertainment. And yet, although she remained more calm than Mme. de Franquetot,

31. country seat of the Guermantes family.

it was not without some uneasiness that she followed the flying fingers; what alarmed her being not the pianist's fate but the piano's, on which a lighted candle, jumping at each *fortissimo*, threatened, if not to set its shade on fire, at least to spill wax upon the ebony. At last she could contain herself no longer, and, running up the two steps of the platform on which the piano stood, flung herself on the candle to adjust its sconce. But scarcely had her hand come within reach of it when, on a final chord, the piece finished, and the pianist rose to his feet. Nevertheless the bold initiative shewn by this young woman and the moment of blushing confusion between her and the pianist which resulted from it, produced an impression that was favourable on the whole.

"Did you see what that girl did just now, Princess?" asked General de Froberville, who had come up to Mme. des Laumes as her hostess left her for a moment. "Odd, wasn't it? Is she one of the performers?"

"No, she's a little Mme. de Cambremer," replied the Princess carelessly, and then, with more animation: "I am only repeating what I heard just now, myself; I haven't the faintest notion who said it, it was some one behind me who said that they were neighbours of Mme. de Saint-Euverte in the country, but I don't believe anyone knows them, really. They must be 'country cousins'! By the way, I don't know whether you're particularly 'well-up' in the brilliant society which we see before us, because I've no idea who all these astonishing people can be. What do you suppose they do with themselves when they're not at Mme. de Saint-Euverte's parties? She must have ordered them in with the musicians and the chairs and the food. 'Universal providers,' you know. You must admit, they're rather splendid, General. But can she really have the courage to hire the same 'supers' every week? It isn't possible!"

"Oh, but Cambremer is quite a good name; old, too," protested the General.

"I see no objection to its being old," the Princess answered dryly, "but whatever else it is it's not euphonious," she went on, isolating the word euphonious as though between inverted commas, a little affectation to which the Guermantes set were addicted.

"You think not, eh! She's a regular little peach, though," said the General, whose eyes never strayed from Mme. de Cambremer. "Don't you agree with me, Princess?"

"She thrusts herself forward too much; I think, in so young a woman, that's not very nice—for I don't suppose she's my generation," replied Mme. des Laumes (the last word being common, it appeared, to Gallardon and Guermantes). And then, seeing that M. de Froberville was still gazing at Mme. de Cambremer, she added, half out of malice towards the lady, half wishing to oblige the

General. "Not very nice . . . for her husband! I am sorry that I do not know her, since she seems to attract you so much; I might have introduced you to her," said the Princess, who, if she had known the young woman, would most probably have done nothing of the sort. "And now I must say good night, because one of my friends is having a birthday party, and I must go and wish her many happy returns," she explained, modestly and with truth, reducing the fashionable gathering to which she was going to the simple proportions of a ceremony which would be boring in the extreme, but at which she was obliged to be present, and there would be something touching about her appearance. "Besides, I must pick up Basin.[32] While I've been here, he's gone to see those friends of his —you know them too, I'm sure—who are called after a bridge—oh, yes, the Iénas."[33]

"It was a battle before it was a bridge, Princess; it was a victory!" said the General. "I mean to say, to an old soldier like me," he went on, wiping his monocle and replacing it, as though he were laying a fresh dressing on the raw wound underneath, while the Princess instinctively looked away, "that Empire nobility, well, of course, it's not the same thing, but, after all, taking it as it is, it's very fine of its kind; they were people who really did fight like heroes."

"But I have the deepest respect for heroes," the Princess assented, though with a faint trace of irony. "If I don't go with Basin to see this Princesse d'Iéna, it isn't for that, at all; it's simply because I don't know them. Basin knows them; he worships them. Oh, no, it's not what you think; he's not in love with her. I've nothing to set my face against! Besides, what good has it ever done when I have set my face against them?" she queried sadly, for the whole world knew that, ever since the day upon which the Prince des Laumes had married his fascinating cousin, he had been consistently unfaithful to her. "Anyhow, it isn't that at all. They're people he has known for ever so long, they do him very well, and that suits me down to the ground. But I must tell you what he's told me about their house; it's quite enough. Can you imagine it, all their furniture is 'Empire'!"

"But, my dear Princess, that's only natural; it belonged to their grandparents."

"I don't quite say it didn't, but that doesn't make it any less ugly. I quite understand that people can't always have nice things, but at least they needn't have things that are merely grotesque. What do you say? I can think of nothing more devastating, more utterly smug than that hideous style—cabinets covered all over with swans' heads, like bath-taps!"

---

32. baptismal name of her husband, the Prince des Laumes, later Duc de Guermantes.

33. Titles dating from the Napoleonic epoch were scorned by the old aristocracy.

"But I believe, all the same, that they've got some lovely things; why, they must have that famous mosaic table on which the Treaty of . . ."

"Oh, I don't deny, they may have things that are interesting enough from the historic point of view. But things like that can't, ever, be beautiful . . . because they're simply horrible! I've got things like that myself, that came to Basin from the Montesquious.[34] Only, they're up in the attics at Guermantes, where nobody ever sees them. But, after all, that's not the point, I would fly to see them, with Basin; I would even go to see them among all their sphinxes and brasses, if I knew them, but—I don't know them! D'you know, I was always taught, when I was a little girl, that it was not polite to call on people one didn't know." She assumed a tone of childish gravity. "And so I am just doing what I was taught to do. Can't you see those good people, with a totally strange woman bursting into their house? Why, I might get a most hostile reception."

And she coquettishly enhanced the charm of the smile which the idea had brought to her lips, by giving to her blue eyes, which were fixed on the General, a gentle, dreamy expression.

"My dear Princess, you know that they'ld be simply wild with joy."

"No, why?" she inquired, with the utmost vivacity, either so as to seem unaware that it would be because she was one of the first ladies in France, or so as to have the pleasure of hearing the General tell her so. "Why? How can you tell? Perhaps they would think it the most unpleasant thing that could possibly happen. I know nothing about them, but if they're anything like me, I find it quite boring enough to see the people I do know; I'm sure if I had to see people I didn't know as well, even if they had 'fought like heroes,' I should go stark mad. Besides, except when it's an old friend like you, whom one knows quite apart from that, I'm not sure that 'heroism' takes one very far in society. It's often quite boring enough to have to give a dinner-party, but if one had to offer one's arm to Spartacus,[35] to let him take one down . . . ! Really, no; it would never be Vercingetorix[36] I should send for, to make a fourteenth. I feel sure, I should keep him for really big 'crushes.' And as I never give any . . ."

"Ah! Princess, it's easy to see you're not a Guermantes for nothing. You have your share of it, all right, the 'wit of the Guermantes'!"

"But people always talk about the wit of *the* Guermantes; I never could make out why. Do you really know any *others* who have it?" she rallied him, with a rippling flow of laughter, her features concentrated, yoked to the service of her animation, her eyes sparkling,

34. The noble family of Montesquiou actually exists.
35. killed in 71 B.C. after heading a revolt of slaves against the Roman authority.
36. executed 46 B.C. He led a confederation of Gallic tribes in resistance to Julius Caesar.

blazing with a radiant sunshine of gaiety which could be kindled only by such speeches—even if the Princess had to make them herself— as were in praise of her wit or of her beauty. "Look, there's Swann talking to your Cambremer woman; over there, beside old Saint-Euverte, don't you see him? Ask him to introduce you. But hurry up, he seems to be just going!"

"Did you notice how dreadfully ill he's looking?" asked the General.

"My precious Charles? Ah, he's coming at last; I was beginning to think he didn't want to see me!"

Swann was extremely fond of the Princesse des Laumes, and the sight of her recalled to him Guermantes, a property close to Combray,[37] and all that country which he so dearly loved and had ceased to visit, so as not to be separated from Odette. Slipping into the manner, half-artistic, half-amorous—with which he could always manage to amuse the Princess—a manner which came to him quite naturally whenever he dipped for a moment into the old social atmosphere, and wishing also to express in words, for his own satisfaction, the longing that he felt for the country:

"Ah!" he exclaimed, or rather intoned, in such a way as to be audible at once to Mme. de Saint-Euverte, to whom he spoke, and to Mme. des Laumes, for whom he was speaking, "Behold our charming Princess! See, she has came up on purpose from Guermantes to hear Saint Francis[38] preach to the birds, and has only just had time, like a dear little titmouse, to go and pick a few little hips and haws and put them in her hair; there are even some drops of dew upon them still, a little of the hoar-frost which must be making the Duchess, down there, shiver. It is very pretty indeed, my dear Princess."

"What! The Princess came up on purpose from Guermantes? But that's too wonderful! I never knew; I'm quite bewildered," Mme. de Saint-Euverte protested with quaint simplicity, being but little accustomed to Swann's way of speaking. And then, examining the Princess's headdress, "Why, you're quite right; it is copied from . . . what shall I say, not chestnuts, no—oh, it's a delightful idea, but how can the Princess have known what was going to be on my programme? The musicians didn't tell me, even."

Swann, who was accustomed, when he was with a woman whom he had kept up the habit of addressing in terms of gallantry, to pay her delicate compliments which most other people would not and need not understand, did not condescend to explain to Mme. de Saint-Euverte that he had been speaking metaphorically. As for the Princess, she was in fits of laughter, both because Swann's wit was highly

37. Swann's country estate was situated near this (fictitious) village.

38. St. Francis of Assisi (1182–1226). founder of the Franciscan order of monks.

appreciated by her set, and because she could never hear a compliment addressed to herself without finding it exquisitely subtle and irresistibly amusing.

"Indeed! I'm delighted, Charles, if my little hips and haws meet with your approval. But tell me, why did you bow to that Cambremer person, are you also her neighbour in the country?"

Mme. de Saint-Euverte, seeing that the Princess seemed quite happy talking to Swann, had drifted away.

"But you are, yourself, Princess!"

"I! Why, they must have 'countries' everywhere, those creatures! Don't I wish I had!"

"No, not the Cambremers; her own people. She was a Legrandin, and used to come to Combray. I don't know whether you are aware that you are Comtesse de Combray, and that the Chapter[39] owes you a due."

"I don't know what the Chapter owes me, but I do know that I'm 'touched' for a hundred francs every year, by the Curé,[40] which is a due that I could very well do without. But surely these Cambremers have rather a startling name. It ends just in time, but it ends badly!"[41] she said with a laugh.

"It begins no better."[42] Swann took the point.

"Yes; that double abbreviation!"

"Some one very angry and very proper who didn't dare to finish the first word."

"But since he couldn't stop himself beginning the second, he'd have done better to finish the first and be done with it. We are indulging in the most refined form of humour, my dear Charles, in the very best of taste—but how tiresome it is that I never see you now," she went on in a coaxing tone, "I do so love talking to you. Just imagine, I could not make that idiot Froberville see that there was anything funny about the name Cambremer. Do agree that life is a dreadful business. It's only when I see you that I stop feeling bored."

Which was probably not true. But Swann and the Princess had the same way of looking at the little things of life—the effect, if not the cause of which was a close analogy between their modes of expression and even of pronunciation. This similarity was not striking because no two things could have been more unlike than their voices. But if one took the trouble to imagine Swann's utterances divested of the sonority that enwrapped them, of the moustache from under which they emerged, one found that they were the same phrases,

---

39. of the church at Combray.
40. the parish priest.
41. The last syllable of the name is the beginning of the vulgar French word *merde*.

42. General Cambronne (1770–1842) uttered the same word (*merde*) when he refused to surrender to the English at Waterloo, so it is called "Cambronne's word."

the same inflexions, that they had the 'tone' of the Guermantes set. On important matters, Swann and the Princess had not an idea in common. But since Swann had become so melancholy, and was always in that trembling condition which precedes a flood of tears, he had the same need to speak about his grief that a murderer has to tell some one about his crime. And when he heard the Princess say that life was a dreadful business, he felt as much comforted as if she had spoken to him of Odette.

"Yes, life is a dreadful business! We must meet more often, my dear friend. What is so nice about you is that you are not cheerful. We could spend a most pleasant evening together."

"I'm sure we could; why not come down to Guermantes? My mother-in-law would be wild with joy. It's supposed to be very ugly down there, but I must say, I find the neighbourhood not at all unattractive; I have a horror of 'picturesque spots'."

"I know it well, it's delightful!" replied Swann. "It's almost too beautiful, too much alive for me just at present; it's a country to be happy in. It's perhaps because I have lived there, but things there speak to me so. As soon as a breath of wind gets up, and the cornfields begin to stir, I feel that some one is going to appear suddenly, that I am going to hear some news; and those little houses by the water's edge . . . I should be quite wretched!"

"Oh! my dearest Charles, do take care; there's that appalling Rampillon woman; she's seen me; hide me somewhere, do tell me again, quickly, what it was that happened to her: I get so mixed up; she's just married off her daughter, or her lover (I never can remember)—perhaps both—to each other! Oh, no, I remember now, she's been dropped by her Prince . . . Pretend to be talking, so that the poor old Berenice[43] sha'n't come and invite me to dinner. Anyhow, I'm going. Listen, my dearest Charles, now that I have seen you, once in a blue moon, won't you let me carry you off and take you to the Princesse de Parme's, who would be so pleased to see you (you know), and Basin too, for that matter, he's meeting me there. If one didn't get news of you, sometimes, from Mémé[44] . . . Remember, I never see you at all now!"

Swann declined. Having told M. de Charlus that, on leaving Mme. de Saint-Euverte's, he would go straight home, he did not care to run the risk, by going on now to the Princesse de Parme's, of missing a message which he had, all the time, been hoping to see brought in to him by one of the footmen, during the party, and which he was perhaps going to find left with his own porter, at home.

"Poor Swann," said Mme. des Laumes that night to her husband; "he is always charming, but he does look so dreadfully unhappy.

43. In Racine's play of that name (1670), Queen Berenice is rejected by the Emperor Titus.
44. nickname of M. de Charlus.

You will see for yourself, for he has promised to dine with us one of these days. I do feel that it's really absurd that a man of his intelligence should let himself be made to suffer by a creature of that kind, who isn't even interesting, for they tell me she's an absolute idiot!" she concluded with the wisdom invariably shewn by people who, not being in love themselves, feel that a clever man ought to be unhappy only about such persons as are worth his while; which is rather like being astonished that anyone should condescend to die of cholera at the bidding of so insignificant a creature as the common bacillus.

Swann now wished to go home, but, just as he was making his escape, General de Froberville caught him and asked for an introduction to Mme. de Cambremer, and he was obliged to go back into the room to look for her.

"I say, Swann, I'ld rather be married to that little woman than killed by savages, what do you say?"

The words 'killed by savages' pierced Swann's aching heart; and at once he felt the need of continuing the conversation. "Ah!" he began, "some fine lives have been lost in that way . . . There was, you remember, that explorer whose remains Dumont d'Urville[45] brought back, La Pérouse . . ." (and he was at once happy again, as though he had named Odette). "He was a fine character, and interests me very much, does La Pérouse," he ended sadly.

"Oh, yes, of course, La Pérouse," said the General. "It's quite a well known name. There's a street called that."

"Do you know anyone in the Rue La Pérouse?" asked Swann excitedly.

"Only Mme. de Chanlivault, the sister of that good fellow Chaussepierre. She gave a most amusing theatre-party the other evening. That's a house that will be really smart some day, you'll see!"

"Oh, so she lives in the Rue La Pérouse. It's attractive; I like that street; it's so sombre."

"Indeed it isn't. You can't have been in it for a long time; it's not at all sombre now; they're beginning to build all round there."

When Swann did finally introduce M. de Froberville to the young Mme. de Cambremer, since it was the first time that she had heard the General's name, she hastily outlined upon her lips the smile of joy and surprise with which she would have greeted him if she had never, in the whole of her life, heard anything else; for, as she did not yet know all the friends of her new family, whenever anyone was presented to her, she assumed that he must be one of them, and thinking that she would shew her tact by appearing to have heard 'such a lot about him' since her marriage, she would hold out

45. French navigator (1780–1842) who discovered the remains of Jean-François de La Pérouse (1741–1788), massacred by the natives of Vanikoro, in Polynesia.

her hand with an air of hesitation which was meant as a proof at once of the inculcated reserve which she had to overcome and of the spontaneous friendliness which successfully overcame it. And so her parents-in-law, whom she still regarded as the most eminent pair in France, declared that she was an angel; all the more that they preferred to appear, in marrying her to their son, to have yielded to the attraction rather of her natural charm than of her considerable fortune.

"It's easy to see that you're a musician heart and soul, Madame," said the General, alluding to the incident of the candle.

Meanwhile the concert had begun again, and Swann saw that he could not now go before the end of the new number. He suffered greatly from being shut up among all these people whose stupidity and absurdities wounded him all the more cruelly since, being ignorant of his love, incapable, had they known of it, of taking any interest, or of doing more than smile at it as at some childish joke, or deplore it as an act of insanity, they made it appear to him in the aspect of a subjective state which existed for himself alone, whose reality there was nothing external to confirm; he suffered overwhelmingly, to the point at which even the sound of the instruments made him want to cry, from having to prolong his exile in this place to which Odette would never come, in which no one, nothing, was aware of her existence, from which she was entirely absent.

But suddenly it was as though she had entered, and this apparition tore him with such anguish that his hand rose impulsively to his heart. What had happened was that the violin had risen to a series of high notes, on which it rested as though expecting something, an expectancy which it prolonged without ceasing to hold on to the notes, in the exaltation with which it already saw the expected object approaching, and with a desperate effort to continue until its arrival, to welcome it before itself expired, to keep the way open for a moment longer, with all its remaining strength, that the stranger might enter in, as one holds a door open that would otherwise automatically close. And before Swann had had time to understand what was happening, to think: "It is the little phrase from Vinteuil's sonata.[46] I mustn't listen!", all his memories of the days when Odette had been in love with him, which he had succeeded, up till that evening, in keeping invisible in the depths of his being, deceived by this sudden reflection of a season of love, whose sun, they supposed, had dawned again, had awakened from their slumber, had taken wing and risen to sing maddeningly in his ears, without pity for his present desolation, the forgotten strains of happiness.

In place of the abstract expressions "the time when I was happy,"

---

46. Swann had "fallen in love" with a phrase from this sonata (fictitious, Vinteuil is a character of the novel) and had come to make of it the leitmotif of his relationship with Odette.

"the time when I was loved," which he had often used until then, and without much suffering, for his intelligence had not embodied in them anything of the past save fictitious extracts which preserved none of the reality, he now recovered everything that had fixed unalterably the peculiar, volatile essence of that lost happiness; he could see it all; the snowy, curled petals of the chrysanthemum which she had tossed after him into his carriage, which he had kept pressed to his lips—the address 'Maison Dorée,' embossed on the note-paper on which he had read "My hand trembles so as I write to you," the frowning contraction of her eyebrows when she said pleadingly: "You won't let it be very long before you send for me?"; he could smell the heated iron of the barber whom he used to have in to singe his hair while Loredan[47] went to fetch the little working girl;[48] could feel the torrents of rain which fell so often that spring, the ice-cold homeward drive in his victoria, by moonlight; all the network of mental habits, of seasonable impressions, of sensory reactions, which had extended over a series of weeks its uniform meshes, by which his body now found itself inextricably held. At that time he had been satisfying a sensual curiosity to know what were the pleasures of those people who lived for love alone. He had supposed that he could stop there, that he would not be obliged to learn their sorrows also; how small a thing the actual charm of Odette was now in comparison with that formidable terror which extended it like a cloudy halo all around her, that enormous anguish of not knowing at every hour of the day and night what she had been doing, of not possessing her wholly, at all times and in all places! Alas, he recalled the accents in which she had exclaimed: "But I can see you at any time; I am always free!"—she, who was never free now; the interest, the curiosity that she had shewn in his life, her passionate desire that he should do her the favour—of which it was he who, then, had felt suspicious, as of a possibly tedious waste of his time and disturbance of his arrangements—of granting her access to his study; how she had been obliged to beg that he would let her take him to the Verdurins'; and, when he did allow her to come to him once a month, how she had first, before he would let himself be swayed, had to repeat what a joy it would be to her, that custom of their seeing each other daily, for which she had longed at a time when to him it had seemed only a tiresome distraction, for which, since that time, she had conceived a distaste and had definitely broken herself of it, while it had become for him so insatiable, so dolorous a need. Little had he suspected how truly he spoke when, on their third meeting, as she repeated: "But why don't you let me come to you oftener?" he had

47. Swann's coachman.
48. It had been Swann's practice to dally with her in the earlier part of the evening, before going on to see

Odette at the Verdurins', a wealthy and socially ambitious couple, in whose house Odette spent almost every evening.

told her, laughing, and in a vein of gallantry, that it was for fear of forming a hopeless passion. Now, alas, it still happened at times that she wrote to him from a restaurant or hotel, on paper which bore a printed address, but printed in letters of fire that seared his heart. "Written from the Hôtel Vouillemont. What on earth can she have gone there for? With whom? What happened there?" He remembered the gas-jets that were being extinguished along the Boulevard des Italiens when he had met her, when all hope was gone,[49] among the errant shades upon that night which had seemed to him almost supernatural and which now (that night of a period when he had not even to ask himself whether he would be annoying her by looking for her and by finding her, so certain was he that she knew no greater happiness than to see him and to let him take her home) belonged indeed to a mysterious world to which one never may return again once its doors are closed. And Swann could distinguish, standing, motionless, before that scene of happiness in which it lived again, a wretched figure which filled him with such pity, because he did not at first recognise who it was, that he must lower his head, lest anyone should observe that his eyes were filled with tears. It was himself.

When he had realised this, his pity ceased; he was jealous, now, of that other self whom she had loved, he was jealous of those men of whom he had so often said, without much suffering: "Perhaps she's in love with them," now that he had exchanged the vague idea of loving, in which there is no love, for the petals of the chrysanthemum and the 'letter-heading' of the Maison d'Or; for they were full of love. And then, his anguish becoming too keen, he passed his hand over his forehead, let the monocle drop from his eye, and wiped its glass. And doubtless, if he had caught sight of himself at that moment, he would have added to the collection of the monocles which he had already identified, this one which he removed, like an importunate, worrying thought, from his head, while from its misty surface, with his handkerchief, he sought to obliterate his cares.

There are in the music of the violin—if one does not see the instrument itself, and so cannot relate what one hears to its form, which modifies the fullness of the sound—accents which are so closely akin to those of certain contralto voices, that one has the illusion that a singer has taken her place amid the orchestra. One raises one's eyes; one sees only the wooden case, magical as a Chinese box; but, at moments, one is still tricked by the deceiving appeal of the Siren; at times, too, one believes that one is listening to a captive spirit, struggling in the darkness of its masterful box, a box quivering with enchantment, like a devil immersed in a stoup of holy water; some-

---

49. Swann, having arrived too late to find Odette at the Verdurins', had sought her long and fruitlessly in cafés and restaurants.

times, again, it is in the air, at large, like a pure and supernatural creature that reveals to the ear, as it passes, its invisible message.

As though the musicians were not nearly so much playing the little phrase as performing the rites on which it insisted before it would consent to appear, as proceeding to utter the incantations necessary to procure, and to prolong for a few moments, the miracle of its apparition, Swann, who was no more able now to see it than if it had belonged to a world of ultra-violet light, who experienced something like the refreshing sense of a metamorphosis in the momentary blindness with which he had been struck as he approached it, Swann felt that it was present, like a protective goddess, a confidant of his love, who, so as to be able to come to him through the crowd, and to draw him aside to speak to him, had disguised herself in this sweeping cloak of sound. And as she passed him, light, soothing, as softly murmured as the perfume of a flower, telling him what she had to say, every word of which he closely scanned, sorry to see them fly away so fast, he made involuntarily with his lips the motion of kissing, as it went by him, the harmonious, fleeting form.

He felt that he was no longer in exile and alone since she, who addressed herself to him, spoke to him in a whisper of Odette. For he had no longer, as of old, the impression that Odette and he were not known to the little phrase. Had it not often been the witness of their joys? True that, as often, it had warned him of their frailty. And indeed, whereas, in that distant time, he had divined an element of suffering in its smile, in its limpid and disillusioned intonation, tonight he found there rather the charm of a resignation that was almost gay. Of those sorrows, of which the little phrase had spoken to him then, which he had seen it—without his being touched by them himself—carry past him, smiling, on its sinuous and rapid course, of those sorrows which were now become his own, without his having any hope of being, ever, delivered from them, it seemed to say to him, as once it had said of his happiness: "What does all that matter; it is all nothing." And Swann's thoughts were borne for the first time on a wave of pity and tenderness towards that Vinteuil, towards that unknown, exalted brother who also must have suffered so greatly; what could his life have been? From the depths of what well of sorrow could he have drawn that god-like strength, that unlimited power of creation?

When it was the little phrase that spoke to him of the vanity of his sufferings, Swann found a sweetness in that very wisdom which, but a little while back, had seemed to him intolerable when he thought that he could read it on the faces of indifferent strangers, who would regard his love as a digression that was without importance. 'Twas because the little phrase, unlike them, whatever opinion it might hold on the short duration of these states of the soul, saw in them something not, as everyone else saw, less serious than the events of everyday life, but, on the contrary, so far superior to everyday life as to be alone worthy of the trouble of expressing it. Those graces of an intimate sorrow, 'twas them that the phrase endeavoured to imitate, to create anew; and even their essence, for all that it consists in being incommunicable and in appearing trivial to everyone save him who has experience of them, the little phrase had captured, had rendered visible. So much so that it made their value be confessed, their divine sweetness be tasted by all those same onlookers—provided only that they were in any sense musical—who, the next moment, would ignore, would disown them in real life, in every individual love that came into being beneath their eyes. Doubtless the form in which it had codified those graces could not be analysed into any logical elements. But ever since, more than a year before, discovering to him many of the riches of his own soul, the love of music had been born, and for a time at least had dwelt in him, Swann had regarded musical *motifs* as actual ideas, of another world, of another order, ideas veiled in shadows, unknown, impenetrable by the human mind, which none the less were perfectly distinct one from another, unequal among themselves in value and in significance. When, after that first evening at the Verdurins', he had had the little phrase played over to him again, and had sought to disentangle from his confused impressions how it was that, like a perfume or a caress, it swept over and enveloped him, he had observed that it was to the closeness of the intervals between the five notes which composed it and to the constant repetition of two of them that was due that impression of a frigid, a contracted sweetness; but in reality he knew that he was basing this conclusion not upon the phrase itself, but merely upon certain equivalents, substituted (for his mind's convenience) for the mysterious entity of which he had become aware, before ever he knew the Verdurins, at the earlier party, when for the first time he had heard the sonata played. He knew that his memory of the piano falsified still further the perspective in which he saw the music, that the field open to the musician is not a miserable stave of seven notes, but an immeasurable keyboard (still, almost all of it, unknown), on which, here and there only, separated by the gross darkness of its unexplored tracts, some few among the millions of keys, keys of tenderness, of passion, of courage, of serenity, which compose it, each one differing from all the rest as one universe differs from another, have been discovered by certain great artists who do us the service, when they awaken in us the emotion corresponding to the theme which they have found, of shewing us what richness, what variety lies hidden, unknown to us, in that great black impenetrable night, discouraging exploration, of our soul, which we have been content to regard as valueless and waste and void. Vinteuil had been one of those musicians. In his little phrase, albeit it presented to the mind's eye a clouded surface, there was contained, one felt, a matter so consistent, so explicit, to which the phrase gave so new, so original a force, that those who had once heard it preserved the memory of it in the treasure-chamber of their minds. Swann would repair to it as to a conception of love and happiness, of which at once he knew as well in what respects it was peculiar as he would know of the *Princesse de Clèves*,[50] or of *René*,[51] should either of those titles occur to him. Even when he was not thinking of the little phrase, it existed, latent, in his mind, in the same way as certain other conceptions without material equivalent, such as our notions of light, of sound, of perspective, of bodily desire, the rich possessions wherewith our inner temple is diversified and adorned. Perhaps we shall lose them, perhaps they will be obliterated, if we return to nothing in the dust. But so long as we are alive, we can no more bring ourselves to a state in which we shall not have known them than we can with regard to any material object, than we can, for example, doubt the luminosity of a lamp that has just been lighted, in view of the changed aspect of everything in the room, from which has vanished even the memory of the darkness. In that way Vinteuil's phrase, like some theme, say, in *Tristan*,[52] which represents to us also a certain acquisition of sentiment, has espoused our mortal state, had endued a vesture of humanity that was affecting enough. Its destiny was linked, for the future, with that of the human soul, of which it was one of the special, the most distinctive ornaments. Perhaps it is not-being that is the true state, and all our dream of life is without existence; but, if so, we feel that it must be that these phrases of music, these conceptions which exist in relation to our dream, are nothing either. We shall perish, but we have for our hostages these divine captives who shall follow and share our fate. And death in their company is something less bitter, less inglorious, perhaps even less certain.

So Swann was not mistaken in believing that the phrase of the sonata did, really, exist. Human as it was from this point of view, it belonged, none the less, to an order of supernatural creatures whom we have never seen, but whom, in spite of that, we recognise and acclaim with rapture when some explorer of the unseen contrives to coax one forth, to bring it down from that divine world to which he has access to shine for a brief moment in the firmament of ours. This was what Vinteuil had done for the little phrase. Swann felt that the composer had been content (with the musical instruments at his disposal) to draw aside its veil, to make it visible, following

50. novel by Mme. de La Fayette (1634–1692).

51. short novel by François-René de Chateaubriand (1768–1848). See pp.

379ff. in this volume.

52. *Tristan and Isolde* (1865) by Richard Wagner (1813–1883).

and respecting its outlines with a hand so loving, so prudent, so delicate and so sure, that the sound altered at every moment, blunting itself to indicate a shadow, springing back into life when it must follow the curve of some more bold projection. And one proof that Swann was not mistaken when he believed in the real existence of this phrase, was that anyone with an ear at all delicate for music would at once have detected the imposture had Vinteuil, endowed with less power to see and to render its forms, sought to dissemble (by adding a line, here and there, of his own invention) the dimness of his vision or the feebleness of his hand.

The phrase had disappeared. Swann knew that it would come again at the end of the last movement, after a long passage which Mme. Verdurin's pianist always 'skipped.' There were in this passage some admirable ideas which Swann had not distinguished on first hearing the sonata, and which he now perceived, as if they had, in the cloakroom of his memory, divested themselves of their uniform disguise of novelty. Swann listened to all the scattered themes which entered into the composition of the phrase, as its premises enter into the inevitable conclusion of a syllogism;[53] he was assisting at the mystery of its birth. "Audacity," he exclaimed to himself, "as inspired, perhaps, as a Lavoisier's[54] or an Ampère's,[55] the audacity of a Vinteuil making experiment, discovering the secret laws that govern an unknown force, driving across a region unexplored towards the one possible goal the invisible team in which he has placed his trust and which he never may discern!" How charming the dialogue which Swann now heard between piano and violin, at the beginning of the last passage. The suppression of human speech, so far from letting fancy reign there uncontrolled (as one might have thought), had eliminated it altogether. Never was spoken language of such inflexible necessity, never had it known questions so pertinent, such obvious replies. At first the piano complained alone, like a bird deserted by its mate; the violin heard and answered it, as from a neighbouring tree. It was as at the first beginning of the world, as if there were not yet but these twain upon the earth, or rather in this world closed against all the rest, so fashioned by the logic of its creator that in it there should never be any but themselves; the world of this sonata. Was it a bird, was it the soul, not yet made perfect, of the little phrase, was it a fairy, invisibly somewhere lamenting, whose plaint the piano heard and tenderly repeated? Its cries were so sudden that the violinist must snatch up his bow and race to catch them as they came. Marvellous bird! The violinist seemed to wish to charm,

53. in logic, a type of formal argument consisting of three propositions.
54. Antoine Lavoisier (1743–1794), French chemist who established the law of the conservation of matter.

55. André Marie Ampère (1775–1836), French mathematician and physicist who discovered the fundamental law of electrodynamics.

to tame, to woo, to win it. Already it had passed into his soul, already the little phrase which it evoked shook like a medium's the body of the violinist, 'possessed' indeed. Swann knew that the phrase was going to speak to him once again. And his personality was now so divided that the strain of waiting for the imminent moment when he would find himself face to face, once more with the phrase, convulsed him in one of those sobs which a fine line of poetry or a piece of alarming news will wring from us, not when we are alone, but when we repeat one or the other to a friend, in whom we see ourselves reflected, like a third person, whose probable emotion softens him. It reappeared, but this time to remain poised in the air, and to sport there for a moment only, as though immobile, and shortly to expire. And so Swann lost nothing of the precious time for which it lingered. It was still there, like an iridescent bubble that floats for a while unbroken. As a rainbow, when its brightness fades, seems to subside, then soars again and, before it is extinguished, is glorified with greater splendour than it has ever shewn; so to the two colours which the phrase had hitherto allowed to appear it added others now, chords shot with every hue in the prism, and made them sing. Swann dared not move, and would have liked to compel all the other people in the room to remain still also, as if the slightest movement might embarrass the magic presence, supernatural, delicious, frail, that would so easily vanish. But no one, as it happened, dreamed of speaking. The ineffable utterance of one solitary man, absent, perhaps dead (Swann did not know whether Vinteuil were still alive), breathed out above the rites of those two hierophants, sufficed to arrest the attention of three hundred minds, and made of that stage on which a soul was thus called into being one of the noblest altars on which a supernatural ceremony could be performed. It followed that, when the phrase at last was finished, and only its fragmentary echoes floated among the subsequent themes which had already taken its place, if Swann at first was annoyed to see the Comtesse de Monteriender, famed for her imbecilities, lean over towards him to confide in him her impressions, before even the sonata had come to an end; he could not refrain from smiling, and perhaps also found an underlying sense, which she was incapable of perceiving, in the words that she used. Dazzled by the virtuosity of the performers, the Comtesse exclaimed to Swann: "It's astonishing! I have never seen anything to beat it . . ." But a scrupulous regard for accuracy making her correct her first assertion, she added the reservation: "anything to beat it . . . since the table-turning!"

From that evening, Swann understood that the feeling which Odette had once had for him would never revive, that his hopes of happiness would not be realised now. And the days on which, by a lucky chance, she had once more shewn herself kind and loving to him, or if she had paid him any attention, he recorded those apparent and misleading signs of a slight movement on her part towards him with the same tender and sceptical solicitude, the desperate joy that people reveal who, when they are nursing a friend in the last days of an incurable malady, relate, as significant facts of infinite value: "Yesterday he went through his accounts himself, and actually corrected a mistake that we had made in adding them up; he ate an egg today and seemed quite to enjoy it, if he digests it properly we shall try him with a cutlet tomorrow"—although they themselves know that these things are meaningless on the eve of an inevitable death. No doubt Swann was assured that if he had now been living at a distance from Odette he would gradually have lost all interest in her, so that he would have been glad to learn that she was leaving Paris for ever; he would have had the courage to remain there; but he had not the courage to go.

ANDRÉ GIDE

(1869–1951)

The Return of the Prodigal Son (Retour de l'enfant prodigue) *

As was done in old triptychs,[1] I have painted here, for my secret pleasure, the parable[2] told to us by Our Lord Jesus Christ. Leaving

* Reprinted from *French Stories*, edited and translated by Wallace Fowlie. Copyright © 1960 by Bantam Books, Inc. All rights reserved. Original story copyright © 1949 by Editions Gallimard. Reprinted with permission of the publishers.

1. sets of three painted or sculptured panels, often placed behind the altar.

2. A certain man had two sons: And the younger of them said to his father, Father, give me the portion of goods that falleth to me. And he divided unto them his living.

And not many days after the younger son gathered all together, and took his journey into a far country, and there wasted his substance with riotous living. And when he had spent all, there arose a mighty famine in that land; and he began to be in want. And he went and joined himself to a citizen of that country; and he sent him into the fields to feed swine. And he would fain have filled his belly with the husks that the swine did eat: and no man gave unto him.

And when he came to himself, he said, How many hired servants of my father's have bread enough and to spare, and I perish with hunger! I will arise and go to my father, and will say unto him, Father, I have sinned against heaven, and before thee, and am no more worthy to be called thy son: make me as one of thy hired servants.

And he arose, and came to his father. But when he was yet a great way off, his father saw him, and had compassion, and ran, and fell on his neck, and kissed him. And the son said unto him, Father, I have sinned against heaven, and in thy sight, and am no more worthy to be called thy son.

But the father said to his servants, Bring forth the best robe, and put it on him; and put a ring on his hand, and shoes on his feet: and bring hither the fatted calf, and kill it; and let us eat, and be merry: For this my son was dead, and is alive again; he was lost, and is found. And they began to be merry.

Now his elder son was in the field: and as he came and drew nigh to the scattered and indistinct the double inspiration which moves me, I have not tried to prove the victory of any god over me—or my victory. And yet, if the reader demands of me some expression of piety, he will not perhaps look for it in vain in my painting, where, like a donor in the corner of the picture, I am kneeling, a pendant to the prodigal son, smiling like him and also like him, my face soaked with tears.

The Prodigal Son

When, after a long absence, tired of his fancies and as if fallen out of love with himself, the prodigal son, from the depths of that destitution he sought, thinks of his father's face; of that not too small room where his mother used to bend over his bed; of that garden, watered with a running stream, but enclosed and from which he had always wanted to escape; of his thrifty older brother whom he never loved, but who still holds, in the expectation of his return, that part of his fortune which, as a prodigal, he was not able to squander—the boy confesses to himself that he did not find happiness, nor even succeed in prolonging very much that disorderly excitement which he sought in place of happiness. "Ah!" he thinks, "if my father, after first being angry with me, believed me dead, perhaps, in spite of my sins, he would rejoice at seeing me again. Ah, if I go back to him very humbly, my head bowed and covered with ashes, and if, bending down before him and saying to him: 'Father, I have sinned against heaven, and before you,' what shall I do if, raising me with his hand, he says, 'Come into the house, my son'?" And already the boy is piously on his way.

When from the top of the hill he sees at last the smoking roofs of the house, it is evening. But he waits for the shadows of night in order to veil somewhat his poverty. In the distance he hears his father's voice. His knees give way. He falls and covers his face with his hands because he is ashamed of his shame, and yet he knows that he is the lawful son. He is hungry. In a fold of his tattered cloak he has only one handful of those sweet acorns which were his food, as they were the food of the swine he herded. He sees the preparations for supper. He makes out his mother coming on to the

house, he heard musick and dancing. And he called one of the servants, and asked what these things meant. And he said unto him, Thy brother is come; and thy father hath killed the fatted calf, because he hath received him safe and sound. And he was angry, and would not go in: therefore came his father out, and intreated him.

And he answering said to his father, Lo, these many years do I serve thee, neither transgressed I at any time thy commandment; and yet thou never gavest me a kid, that I might make merry with my friends: but as soon as this thy son was come, which hath devoured thy living with harlots, thou hast killed for him the fatted calf.

And he said unto him, Son, thou art ever with me, and all that I have is thine. It was meet that we should make merry, and be glad: for this thy brother was dead, and is alive again; and was lost, and is found (Luke 15:11–22).

doorstep. . . . He can hold back no longer. He runs down the hill and comes into the courtyard where his dog, failing to recognize him, barks. He tries to speak to the servants. But they are suspicious and move away in order to warn the master. Here he is!

Doubtless he was expecting his prodigal son, because he recognizes him immediately. He opens his arms. The boy then kneels before him, and hiding his forehead with one arm, he raises his right hand for pardon:

"Father! Father! I have gravely sinned against heaven and against you. I am not worthy to be called your son. But at least, like one of your servants, the humblest, let me live in a corner of our house."

The father raises him and embraces him.

"My son, blessed is this day when you come back to me!" And his joy weeps as it overflows his heart. He raises his head from his son's brow which he was kissing, and turns toward his servants:

"Bring forth the best robe. Put shoes on his feet, and a precious ring on his finger. Look in our stables for the fattest calf and kill it. Prepare a joyful feast, for my son whom I thought dead is alive."

And as the news spreads rapidly, he hastens. He does not want another to say:

"Mother, the son we wept for has returned to us."

Everyone's joy mounting up like a hymn troubles the older son. He sits down at the common table because his father invites him and urges him forcibly. Alone, among all the guests, for even the humblest servant is invited, he shows an angry expression. To the repentant sinner why is there more honor than to himself, who has never sinned? He esteems order more than love. If he consents to appear at the feast, it is because by giving credit to his brother, he can lend him joy for one evening. It is also because his father and mother have promised him to rebuke the prodigal tomorrow, and because he himself is preparing to admonish him seriously.

The torches send up their smoke toward heaven. The meal is over. The servants have cleared the tables. Now, in the night, when not a breath is stirring, soul after soul, in the weary house, goes to sleep. And yet, in the room next to the prodigal's, I know a boy, his younger brother, who throughout the night until dawn will try in vain to sleep.

The Father's Reprimand

Lord, like a child I kneel before You today, my face soaked with tears. If I remember and transcribe here your compelling parable, it is because I know who your prodigal child was. I see myself in him. At times I hear in myself and repeat in secret those words which, from the depth of his great distress, You have him cry:

"How many hirelings of my father have bread enough and to spare, and I perish with hunger!"

I imagine the father's embrace, and in the warmth of such love my heart melts. I imagine an earlier distress, and even—ah! I imagine all kinds of things. This I believe: I am the very one whose heart beats when, from the top of the hill, he sees again the blue roofs of the house he left. What keeps me then from running toward my home and going in?—I am expected. I can see the fatted calf they are preparing. . . . Stop! Do not set up the feast too quickly!—Prodigal son, I am thinking of you. Tell me first what your Father said to you the next day, after the feast of welcome. Ah! even if the elder son prompts you, Father, let me hear your voice sometimes through his words!

"My son, why did you leave me?"

"Did I really leave you? Father, are you not everywhere? Never did I cease loving you."

"Let us not split hairs. I had a house which kept you in. It was built for you. Generations worked so that in it your soul could find shelter, luxury worthy of it, comfort and occupation. Why did you, the heir, the son, escape from the House?"

"Because the House shut me in. The House is not You, Father."

"It is I who built it, and for you."

"Ah! you did not say that, my brother did. You built the whole world, the House and what is not the House. The House was built by others. In your name, I know, but by others."

"Man needs a roof under which he can lay his head. Proud boy! Do you think you can sleep in the open?"

"Do you need pride to do that? Some poorer than I have done so."

"They are the poor. You are not poor. No one can give up his wealth. I had made you rich above all men."

"Father, you know that when I left, I took with me all the riches I could. What do I care about goods that cannot be carried away?"

"All that fortune you took away, you have spent recklessly."

"I changed your gold into pleasures, your precepts into fantasy, my chastity into poetry, and my austerity into desires."

"Was it for that your thrifty parents strove to instill into you so much virtue?"

"So that I should burn with a brighter flame perhaps, being kindled by a new fervor."

"Think of that pure flame Moses saw on the sacred bush. It shone, but without consuming."

"I have known love which consumes."

"The love which I want to teach you, refreshes. After a short time, what did you have left, prodigal son?"

"The memory of those pleasures."

"And the destitution which comes after them."

"In that destitution, I felt close to you, Father."

"Was poverty needed to drive you back to me?"

"I do not know. I do not know. It was in the dryness of the desert that I loved my thirst more."

"Your poverty made you feel more deeply the value of riches."

"No, not that! Can't you understand me, Father? My heart, emptied of everything, became filled with love. At the cost of all my goods, I bought fervor."

"Were you happy, then, far from me?"

"I did not feel far from you."

"Then, what made you come back? Tell me."

"I don't know. Laziness perhaps."

"Laziness, my son? What! Wasn't it love?"

"Father, I have told you. I never loved you better than in the desert. But each morning I was tired of looking for my subsistence. In the House, at least there is food to eat."

"Yes, servants look after that. So, what brought you back was hunger."

"Cowardice also perhaps, and sickness. . . . In the end, that food I was never sure of finding weakened me. Because I fed on wild fruit and locusts and honey. I grew less and less able to stand the discomfort which at first quickened my fervor. At night, when I was cold, I thought of my tucked-in bed in my father's house. When I fasted, I thought of my father's home where the abundance of food served always exceeded my hunger. I weakened; I didn't feel enough courage, enough strength to struggle much longer and yet . . ."

"So yesterday's fatted calf seemed good to you?"

The prodigal son throws himself down sobbing, with his face against the ground.

"Father! Father! The wild taste of sweet acorns is still in my mouth, in spite of everything. Nothing could blot out their savor."

"Poor child!" says the father as he raises him up. "I spoke to you perhaps too harshly. Your brother wanted me to. Here it is he who makes the law. It is he who charged me to say to you: 'Outside of the House, there is no salvation for you.' But listen. It was I who made you. I know what is in you. I know what sent you out on your wanderings. I was waiting for you at the end of the road. If you had called me . . . I was there."

"Father! might I then have found you without coming back?"

"If you felt weak, you did well to come back. Go now. Go back to the room I had prepared for you. Enough for today. Rest. Tomorrow you will speak with your brother."

The Elder Brother's Reprimand

The prodigal son first tries to bluster.

"Big brother," he begins, "we aren't very much alike. Brother, we aren't alike at all."

The elder brother says:

"It's your fault."

"Why mine?"

"Because I live by order. Whatever differs from it is the fruit or the seed of pride."

"Am I different only in my faults?"

"Only call quality what brings you back to order, and curtail all the rest."

"It is that mutilation I fear. What you plan to suppress comes also from the Father."

"Not suppress—curtail, I said."

"I understand. All the same, that is how I curtailed my virtues."

"And that is also why now I still see them in you. You must exaggerate them. Understand me. It is not a diminution of yourself, but an exaltation I propose, in which the most diverse, the most unruly elements of your flesh and your spirit must join together harmoniously, in which the worst in you must nourish the best, in which the best must submit to . . ."

"It was exaltation which I also sought and found in the desert— and perhaps not very different from the one you propose to me."

"To tell the truth, I wanted to impose it on you."

"Our Father did not speak so harshly."

"I know what the Father said to you. It was vague. He no longer expresses himself very clearly, so that he can be made to say what one wants. But I understand his thought very well. With the servants, I am the one interpreter, and who wants to understand the Father must listen to me."

"I understand him quite easily without you."

"You thought you did. But you understood incorrectly. There are not several ways of understanding the Father. There are not several ways of listening to him. There are not several ways of loving him, so that we may be united in his love."

"In his House."

"This love brings one back here. You see this, for you have come back. Tell me now, what impelled you to leave?"

"I felt too clearly that the House is not the entire universe. I myself am not completely in the boy you wanted me to be. I could not help imagining other cultures, other lands, and roads by which to reach them, roads not yet traced. I imagined in myself the new being which I felt rushing down those roads. I ran away."

"Think what could have happened if, like you, I had deserted our

Father's House. Servants and thieves would have pillaged all our goods."

"That would not have mattered to me, since I was catching sight of other goods . . ."

"Which your pride exaggerated. My brother, indiscipline is over. You will learn, if you don't yet know it, out of what chaos man has emerged. He has just barely emerged. With all of his artless weight, he falls back into it as soon as the Spirit no longer supports him above it. Do not learn this at your own expense. The well-ordered elements which make up your being wait only for an acquiescence, a weakening on your part in order to return to anarchy . . . But what you will never know is the length of time that was needed for man to elaborate man. Now that we have the model, let us keep it. 'Hold that fast which thou hast,' says the Spirit to the Angel of the Church, and He adds, 'that no man taketh thy crown.'[3] The *which thou hast* is your crown, that royalty over others and over yourself. The usurper lies in wait for your crown. He is everywhere. He prowls around you and in you. *Hold fast*, my brother! Hold fast."

"Too long ago I let go my hold. And now I cannot close my hand over my own wealth."

"Yes, you can. I will help you. I have watched over your wealth during your absence."

"And moreover, I know those words of the Spirit. You did not quote them all."

"You are right. It goes on: 'Him that overcometh will I make a pillar in the temple of my God, and he shall go no more out.' "[4]

" 'And he shall go no more out.' That is precisely what terrifies me."

"If it is for his happiness."

"Oh! I understand. But I had been in that temple . . ."

"You found you were wrong to have left, since you wanted to return."

"I know, I know. I am back now. I agree."

"What good can you look for elsewhere, which here you do not find in abundance? Or better—here alone your wealth is to be found."

"I know that you kept my riches for me."

"The part of your fortune which you did not squander, namely that part which is common to all of us: the property."

"Then do I personally own nothing else?"

"Yes. That special allotment of gifts which perhaps our Father will still consent to grant you."

"That is all I want. I agree to own only that."

"How proud you are! You will not be consulted. Between you and me, that portion is risky. I would advise your giving it up. It

<hr>

3. Revelation 3:11. 4. Revelation 3:12.

was that allotment of personal gifts which already brought on your downfall. That was the wealth you squandered immediately."

"The other kind I couldn't take with me."

"Therefore you will find it intact. Enough for today. Find rest now in the House."

"That suits me well, for I am tired."

"Then blessed be your fatigue! Now go and sleep. Tomorrow your mother will speak to you."

The Mother

Prodigal son, whose mind still rebels against the words of your brother, let your heart now speak. How sweet it is, as you lie at the feet of your mother, with your head hidden on her lap, to feel her caressing hand bow your stubborn neck!

"Why did you leave me for so long a time?"

And since you answer only with tears:

"Why weep now, my son? You have been given back to me. In waiting for you, I have shed all my tears."

"Were you still waiting for me?"

"Never did I give up hoping for you. Before going to sleep, every evening I would think: if he returns tonight, will he be able to open the door? And it took me a long time to fall asleep. Every morning, before I was totally awake, I would think: isn't it today he will come back? Then I prayed. I prayed so hard that it was not possible for you not to come back."

"Your prayers forced me to come back."

"Don't smile because of me, my child."

"Oh mother, I have come back to you very humble. See how I place my forehead lower than your heart! There is not one of my thoughts of yesterday which does not become empty today. When close to you, I can hardly understand why I left the house."

"You will not leave it again?"

"I cannot leave it again."

"What then attracted you outside?"

"I don't want to think of it any more. Nothing . . . Myself . . ."

"Did you think then that you would be happy away from us?"

"I was not looking for happiness."

"What were you looking for?"

"I was looking for . . . who I was."

"Oh! son of your parents, and brother among your brothers."

"I was not like my brothers. Let's not talk any more about it. I have come back now."

"Yes, let's talk of it further. Do not believe that your brothers are so unlike you."

"Henceforth my one care is to be like all of you."

"You say that as if with resignation."

"Nothing is more fatiguing than to realize one's difference. Finally my wandering tired me out."

"You have aged, that is true."

"I have suffered."

"My poor child! Doubtless your bed was not made every evening, nor the table set for all your meals?"

"I ate what I found and often it was green or spoiled fruit which my hunger made into food."

"At least did you suffer only from hunger?"

"The sun at mid-day, the cold wind in the heart of the night, the shifting sand of the desert, the thorns which made my feet bloody, nothing of all that stopped me, but—I didn't tell this to my brother —I had to serve . . ."

"Why did you conceal it?"

"Bad masters who harmed me bodily, exasperated my pride, and gave me barely enough to eat. That is when I thought: 'Serving for the sake of serving! . . .' In dreams I saw my house, and I came home."

The prodigal son again lowers his head and his mother caresses it tenderly.

"What are you going to do now?"

"I have told you. Try to become like my big brother, look after our property, like him choose a wife . . ."

"You have doubtless someone in mind, as you say that."

"Oh, anyone at all will be my first preference, as soon as you have chosen her. Do as you did for my brother."

"I should have preferred someone you love."

"What does it matter? My heart had made a choice. I renounce the pride which took me far away from you. Help me in my choice. I submit, I tell you. And I will have my children submit also. In that way, my adventure will not seem pointless to me."

"Listen to me. There is at this moment a child you could take on already as a charge."

"What do you mean and of whom are you speaking?"

"Of your younger brother who was not ten when you left, whom you hardly recognized, but who . . ."

"Go on, mother! What are you worried about now?"

"In whom you might well have recognized yourself because he is like what you were when you left."

"Like me?"

"Like what you were, I said, not yet, alas, what you have become."

"What he will become."

"What you must make him become immediately. Speak to him. He will listen to you, doubtless, you the prodigal. Tell him what disappointment you met on your way. Spare him . . ."

"But what causes you such alarm about my brother? Perhaps simply a resemblance of features . . ."

"No, no! the resemblance between you two is deeper. I worry now for him about what first did not worry me enough for you. He reads too much, and doesn't always prefer good books."

"Is that all it is?"

"He is often perched on the highest part of the garden, from where, as you know, you can see the countryside over the walls."

"I remember. Is that all?"

"He spends less time with us than in the farm."

"Ah! what does he do there?"

"Nothing wrong. But it is not the farmers he stays with, it is the farm hands who are as different from us as possible and those who are not from this country. There is one in particular, who comes from some distance, and who tells him stories.

"Ah! the swineherd."

"Yes. Did you know him? . . . Your brother each evening in order to listen to him, follows him into the pigsties. He comes back only for dinner, but with no appetite, and his clothes reeking. Remonstrances have no effect. He stiffens under constraint. On certain mornings, at dawn, before any of us are up, he runs off to accompany that swineherd to the gate when he is leading off his herd to graze."

"He knows he must not leave."

"You knew also! One day he will escape from me, I am sure. One day he will leave . . ."

"No, I will speak to him, mother. Don't be alarmed."

"I know he will listen to a great deal from you. Did you see how he watched you that first evening, with what prestige your rags were covered, and the purple robe your father put on you! I was afraid that in his mind he will confuse one with the other, and that he is attracted first by the rags. But now this idea seems ridiculous to me. For if you, my child, had been able to foresee such unhappiness, you would not have left us, would you?"

"I don't know now how I was able to leave you, you who are my mother."

"Well, tell him all that."

"I will tell him that tomorrow evening. Now kiss me on my forehead as you used to when I was small and you watched me fall asleep. I am sleepy."

"Go to bed. I am going to pray for all of you."

Dialogue with the Younger Brother

Beside the prodigal's, there is a room not too small, with bare walls. The prodigal, a lamp in his hand, comes close to the bed were his younger brother is lying, his face toward the wall. He begins in a low voice, so as not to disturb him if the boy is sleeping.

"I would like to talk to you, brother."

"What is stopping you?"

"I thought you were sleeping."

"I don't have to sleep in order to dream."

"You were dreaming? Of what?"

"What do you care? If I can't understand my dreams, I don't think you will be able to explain them to me."

"Are they that subtle, then? If you told them to me, I would try."

"Do you choose your dreams? Mine are what they want to be, and are freer than I . . . What have you come here for? Why are you disturbing me in my sleep?"

"You aren't sleeping, and I'm here to speak gently to you."

"What have you to say to me?"

"Nothing, if that is the tone you take."

"Then goodbye."

The prodigal goes toward the door, but puts the lamp on the floor so that the room is barely lighted. Then, coming back, he sits on the edge of the bed and in the dark strokes for a long time the boy's forehead which is kept turned away.

"You answer me more gruffly than I ever did your brother. Yet I too rebelled against him."

The stubborn boy suddenly sat up.

"Tell me, is it my brother that sent you?"

"No, not he, but our mother."

"So, you wouldn't have come of your own accord."

"But I came as a friend."

Half sitting up on his bed, the boy looks straight at the prodigal.

"How could one of my family be my friend?"

"You are mistaken about our brother . . ."

"Don't speak to me about him! I hate him. My whole heart cries out against him. He's the reason for my answering you gruffly."

"Explain why."

"You wouldn't understand."

"Tell me just the same."

The prodigal rocks his brother in his arms and already the boy begins to yield.

"The evening you returned, I couldn't sleep. All night I kept thinking: I had another brother, and I didn't know it. . . . That is why my heart beat so hard when, in the courtyard of our house, I saw you come covered with glory."

"Alas, I was covered then with rags."

"Yes, I saw you. You were already glorious. And I saw what our father did. He put a ring on your finger, a ring the like of which our brother does not have. I did not want to question anyone about you. All that I knew was that you had come from very far away, and that your eyes, at table . . ."

"Were you at the feast?"

"Oh! I know you did not see me. During the whole meal you looked far off without seeing anything. And it was all right when on the second evening you spoke with our father, but on the third . . ."

"Go on."

"Ah! you could have said to me at least one word of love!"

"You were expecting me then?"

"Impatiently! Do you think I would hate our brother so much if you had not gone to talk with him that evening and for so long? What did you find to say to each other? You certainly know, if you are like me, that you can have nothing in common with him."

"I had behaved very wrongly toward him."

"Is that possible?"

"At any rate toward our father and mother. You know that I ran away from home."

"Yes, I know. A long time ago, wasn't it?"

"When I was about your age."

"Ah! And that's what you call behaving wrong?"

"Yes, it was wrong, it was my sin."

"When you left, did you feel you were doing wrong?"

"No, I felt duty-bound to leave."

"What has happened since then to change your first truth into an error?"

"I suffered."

"And is that what makes you say: I did wrong?"

"No, not exactly. That is what made me reflect."

"Then, before, you didn't reflect?"

"Yes, but my weak reason let itself be conquered by my desires."

"As later by your suffering. So that today you have come back . . . conquered."

"No, not exactly—resigned."

"At any rate, you have given up being what you wanted to be."

"What my pride persuaded me to be."

The boy remains silent a moment, then suddenly cries with a sob:

"Brother! I am the boy you were when you left. Tell me. Did you find nothing but disappointments on your wanderings? Is all that I imagine outside and different from here, only an illusion? All the newness I feel in me, is that madness? Tell me, what did you meet on your way that seemed so tragic? Oh! what made you come back?"

"The freedom I was looking for, I lost. When captive, I had to serve."

"I am captive here."

"Yes, but I mean serving bad masters. Here you are serving your parents."

"Ah! serving for the sake of serving! At least don't we have the freedom of choosing our bondage?"

"I had hoped for that. As far as my feet carried me, I walked, like Saul in search of his she-asses, in search of my desire. But there where a kingdom was waiting for him, I found wretchedness. And yet . . ."

"Didn't you mistake the road?"

"I walked straight ahead."

"Are you sure? And yet there are still other kingdoms, and lands without kings, to discover."

"Who told you?"

"I know it, I feel it. I have already the impression of being the lord over them."

"Proud boy!"

"Ah! ah! that's something our brother said to you. Why do you repeat it to me now? Why didn't you keep that pride? You would not have come back."

"Then I would never have known you."

"Yes, yes, out there where I would have joined you, you would have recognized me as your brother. It seems to me even that I am leaving in order to find you."

"That you are leaving?"

"Haven't you understood? Aren't you yourself encouraging me to leave?"

"I wanted to spare your returning, but by sparing your departure."

"No, no, don't tell me that. No, you don't mean that. You yourself left like a conqueror, didn't you?"

"And that is what made my bondage seem harder to me."

"Then, why did you give in to it? Were you already so tired?"

"No, not then. But I had doubts."

"What do you mean?"

"Doubts about everything, about myself. I wanted to stop and settle down somewhere. The comfort which this master promised me was a temptation . . . Yes, I feel it clearly now. I failed."

The prodigal bows his head and hides his face in his hands.

"But at first?"

"I had walked for a long time through large tracts of wild country."

"The desert?"

"It wasn't always the desert."

"What were you looking for there?"

"I myself do not understand now."

"Get up from my bed. Look, on the table beside it, there, near that torn book."

"I see a pomegranate split open."

"The swineherd brought it to me the other evening, after he had not been back for three days."

"Yes, it is a wild pomegranate."

"I know. It is almost unbearably bitter. And yet I feel, if I were sufficiently thirsty, I would bite into it."

"Ah! now I can tell you. That is the thirst I was looking for in the desert."

"A thirst which that sour fruit alone can quench . . ."

"No, but it makes you love that thirst."

"Do you know where it can be picked?"

"In a small deserted orchard you reach before evening. No longer does any wall separate it from the desert. A stream flowed through it. Some half-ripe fruit hung from the branches."

"What fruit?"

"The same which grows in our garden, but wild. It had been very hot all day."

"Listen. Do you know why I was expecting you this evening? I am leaving before the end of the night. Tonight, this night, as soon as it grows pale . . . I have girded my loins. Tonight I have kept on my sandals."

"So, what I was not able to do, you will do?"

"You opened the way for me, and it will help me to think of you."

"It is for me to admire you, and for you to forget me, on the contrary. What are you taking with you?"

"You know that as the youngest, I have no share in the inheritance. I am taking nothing."

"That is better."

"What are you looking at through the window?"

"The garden where our dead forefathers are sleeping."

"Brother . . ." (and the boy, who has gotten out of bed, puts, around the prodigal's neck, his arm which has become as tender as his voice)—"Come with me."

"Leave me! leave me! I am staying to console our mother. Without me you will be braver. It is time now. The sky turns pale. Go without making any noise. Come! kiss me, my young brother, you are taking with you all my hopes. Be strong. Forget us. Forget me. May you never come back . . . Go down quietly, I am holding the lamp . . ."

"Ah! give me your hand as far as the door."

"Be careful of the steps as you go down."

FRANZ KAFKA
(1883–1924)
The Metamorphosis (Die Verwandlung) *

As Gregor Samsa awoke one morning from uneasy dreams he found himself transformed in his bed into a gigantic insect. He was lying on his hard, as it were armor-plated, back and when he lifted his head a little he could see his dome-like brown belly divided into stiff arched segments on top of which the bed quilt could hardly keep in position and was about to slide off completely. His numerous legs, which were pitifully thin compared to the rest of his bulk, waved helplessly before his eyes.

What has happened to me? he thought. It was no dream. His room, a regular human bedroom, only rather too small, lay quiet between the four familiar walls. Above the table on which a collection of cloth samples was unpacked and spread out—Samsa was a commercial traveler—hung the picture which he had recently cut out of an illustrated magazine and put into a pretty gilt frame. It showed a lady, with a fur cap on and a fur stole, sitting upright and holding out to the spectator a huge fur muff into which the whole of her forearm had vanished!

Gregor's eyes turned next to the window, and the overcast sky—one could hear rain drops beating on the window gutter—made him quite melancholy. What about sleeping a little longer and forgetting all this nonsense, he thought, but it could not be done, for he was accustomed to sleep on his right side and in his present condition he could not turn himself over. However violently he forced himself towards his right side he always rolled on to his back again. He tried it at least a hundred times, shutting his eyes to keep from seeing his struggling legs, and only desisted when he began to feel in his side a faint dull ache he had never experienced before.

Oh God, he thought, what an exhausting job I've picked on! Traveling about day in, day out. It's much more irritating work than doing the actual business in the office, and on top of that there's the trouble of constant traveling, of worrying about train connections, the bed and irregular meals, casual acquaintances that are always new and never become intimate friends. The devil take it all! He felt a slight itching up on his belly; slowly pushed himself on his back nearer to the top of the bed so that he could lift his head more easily; identified the itching place which was surrounded by many small white spots the nature of which he could not understand and made to touch it with a leg, but drew the leg back immediately, for the contact made a cold shiver run through him.

He slid down again into his former position. This getting up

* 1916. Reprinted by permission of Schocken Books Inc. from *The Penal Colony* by Franz Kafka. Copyright © 1948 by Schocken Books Inc., New York. Translated by Willa and Edwin Muir.

early, he thought, makes one quite stupid. A man needs his sleep. Other commercials live like harem women. For instance, when I come back to the hotel of a morning to write up the orders I've got, these others are only sitting down to breakfast. Let me just try that with my chief; I'd be sacked on the spot. Anyhow, that might be quite a good thing for me, who can tell? If I didn't have to hold my hand because of my parents I'd have given notice long ago, I'd have gone to the chief and told him exactly what I think of him. That would knock him endways from his desk! It's a queer way of doing, too, this sitting on high at a desk and talking down to employees, especially when they have to come quite near because the chief is hard of hearing. Well, there's still hope; once I've saved enough money to pay back my parents' debts to him—that should take another five or six years—I'll do it without fail. I'll cut myself completely loose then. For the moment, though, I'd better get up, since my train goes at five.

He looked at the alarm clock ticking on the chest. Heavenly Father! he thought. It was half-past six o'clock and the hands were quietly moving on, it was even past the half-hour, it was getting on toward a quarter to seven. Had the alarm clock not gone off? From the bed one could see that it had been properly set for four o'clock; of course it must have gone off. Yes, but was it possible to sleep quietly through that ear-splitting noise? Well, he had not slept quietly, yet apparently all the more soundly for that. But what was he to do now? The next train went at seven o'clock; to catch that he would need to hurry like mad and his samples weren't even packed up, and he himself wasn't feeling particularly fresh and active. And even if he did catch the train he wouldn't avoid a row with the chief, since the firm's porter would have been waiting for the five o'clock train and would have long since reported his failure to turn up. The porter was a creature of the chief's, spineless and stupid. Well, supposing he were to say he was sick? But that would be most unpleasant and would look suspicious, since during his five years' employment he had not been ill once. The chief himself would be sure to come with the sick-insurance doctor, would reproach his parents with their son's laziness and would cut all excuses short by referring to the insurance doctor, who of course regarded all mankind as perfectly healthy malingerers. And would he be so far wrong on this occasion? Gregor really felt quite well, apart from a drowsiness that was utterly superfluous after such a long sleep, and he was even unusually hungry.

As all this was running through his mind at top speed without his being able to decide to leave his bed—the alarm clock had just struck a quarter to seven—there came a cautious tap at the door behind the head of his bed. "Gregor," said a voice—it was his mother's—"it's a quarter to seven. Hadn't you a train to catch?" That gentle voice! Gregor had a shock as he heard his own voice answering hers, unmistakably his own voice, it was true, but with a persistent horrible twittering squeak behind it like an undertone, that left the words in their clear shape only for the first moment and then rose up reverberating round them to destroy their sense, so that one could not be sure one had heard them rightly. Gregor wanted to answer at length and explain everything, but in the circumstances he confined himself to saying: "Yes, yes, thank you, Mother, I'm getting up now." The wooden door between them must have kept the change in his voice from being noticeable outside, for his mother contented herself with this statement and shuffled away. Yet this brief exchange of words had made the other members of the family aware that Gregor was still in the house, as they had not expected, and at one of the side doors his father was already knocking, gently, yet with his fist. "Gregor, Gregor," he called, "what's the matter with you?" And after a little while he called again in a deeper voice: "Gregor! Gregor!" At the other side door his sister was saying in a low, plaintive tone: "Gregor? Aren't you well? Are you needing anything?" He answered them both at once: "I'm just ready," and did his best to make his voice sound as normal as possible by enunciating the words very clearly and leaving long pauses between them. So his father went back to his breakfast, but his sister whispered: "Gregor, open the door, do." However, he was not thinking of opening the door, and felt thankful for the prudent habit he had acquired in traveling of locking all doors during the night, even at home.

His immediate intention was to get up quietly without being disturbed, to put on his clothes and above all eat his breakfast, and only then to consider what else was to be done, since in bed, he was well aware, his meditations would come to no sensible conclusion. He remembered that often enough in bed he had felt small aches and pains, probably caused by awkward postures, which had proved purely imaginary once he got up, and he looked forward eagerly to seeing this morning's delusions gradually fall away. That the change in his voice was nothing but the precursor of a severe chill, a standing ailment of commercial travelers, he had not the least possible doubt.

To get rid of the quilt was quite easy; he had only to inflate himself a little and it fell off by itself. But the next move was difficult, especially because he was so uncommonly broad. He would have needed arms and hands to hoist himself up; instead he had only the numerous little legs which never stopped waving in all directions and which he could not control in the least. When he tried to bend one of them it was the first to stretch itself straight; and did he succeed at last in making it do what he wanted, all the other legs meanwhile waved the more wildly in a high degree of unpleasant agitation. "But what's the use of lying idle in bed," said Gregor to himself.

He thought that he might get out of bed with the lower part of his body first, but this lower part, which he had not yet seen and of which he could form no clear conception, proved too difficult to move: it shifted so slowly; and when finally, almost wild with annoyance, he gathered his forces together and thrust out recklessly, he had miscalculated the direction and bumped heavily against the lower end of the bed, and the stinging pain he felt informed him that precisely this lower part of his body was at the moment probably the most sensitive.

So he tried to get the top part of himself out first, and cautiously moved his head towards the edge of the bed. That proved easy enough, and despite its breadth and mass the bulk of his body at last slowly followed the movement of his head. Still, when he finally got his head free over the edge of the bed he felt too scared to go on advancing, for after all if he let himself fall in this way it would take a miracle to keep his head from being injured. And at all costs he must not lose consciousness now, precisely now; he would rather stay in bed.

But when after a repetition of the same efforts he lay in his former position again, sighing, and watched his little legs struggling against each other more wildly than ever, if that were possible, and saw no way of bringing any order into this arbitrary confusion, he told himself again that it was impossible to stay in bed and that the most sensible course was to risk everything for the smallest hope of getting away from it. At the same time he did not forget meanwhile to remind himself that cool reflection, the coolest possible, was much better than desperate resolves. In such moments he focused his eyes as sharply as possible on the window, but, unfortunately, the prospect of the morning fog, which muffled even the other side of the narrow street, brought him little encouragement and comfort. "Seven o'clock already," he said to himself when the alarm clock chimed again, "seven o'clock already and still such a thick fog." And for a little while he lay quiet, breathing lightly, as if perhaps expecting such complete repose to restore all things to their real and normal condition.

But then he said to himself: "Before it strikes a quarter past seven I must be quite out of this bed, without fail. Anyhow, by that time someone will have come from the office to ask for me, since it opens before seven." And he set himself to rocking his whole body at once in a regular rhythm, with the idea of swinging it out of the bed. If he tipped himself out in that way he could keep his head from injury by lifting it at an acute angle when he fell. His back seemed to be hard and was not likely to suffer from a fall on the carpet. His biggest worry was the loud crash he would not be able to help making, which would probably cause anxiety, if not terror, behind all the doors. Still, he must take the risk.

When he was already half out of the bed—the new method was more a game than an effort, for he needed only to hitch himself across by rocking to and fro—it struck him how simple it would be if he could get help. Two strong people—he thought of his father and the servant girl—would be amply sufficient; they would only have to thrust their arms under his convex back, lever him out of the bed, bend down with their burden and then be patient enough to let him turn himself right over on the the floor, where it was to be hoped his legs would then find their proper function. Well, ignoring the fact that the doors were all locked, ought he really to call for help? In spite of his misery he could not suppress a smile at the very idea of it.

He had got so far that he could barely keep his equilibrium when he rocked himself strongly, and he would have to nerve himself very soon for the final decision since in five minutes' time it would be a quarter past seven—when the front door bell rang. "That's someone from the office," he said to himself, and grew almost rigid, while his little legs only jigged about all the faster. For a moment everything stayed quiet. "They're not going to open the door," said Gregor to himself, catching at some kind of irrational hope. But then of course the servant girl went as usual to the door with her heavy tread and opened it. Gregor needed only to hear the first good morning of the visitor to know immediately who it was—the chief clerk himself. What a fate, to be condemned to work for a firm where the smallest omission at once gave rise to the gravest suspicion! Were all employees in a body nothing but scoundrels, was there not among them one single loyal devoted man who, had he wasted only an hour or so of the firm's time in a morning, was so tormented by conscience as to be driven out of his mind and actually incapable of leaving his bed? Wouldn't it really have been sufficient to send an apprentice to inquire—if any inquiry were necessary at all—did the chief clerk himself have to come and thus indicate to the entire family, an innocent family, that this suspicious circumstance could be investigated by no one less versed in affairs than himself? And more through the agitation caused by these reflections than through any act of will Gregor swung himself out of bed with all his strength. There was a loud thump, but it was not really a crash. His fall was broken to some extent by the carpet, his back, too, was less stiff than he thought, and so there was merely a dull thud, not so very startling. Only he had not lifted his head carefully enough and had hit it; he turned it and rubbed it on the carpet in pain and irritation.

"That was something falling down in there," said the chief clerk in the next room to the left. Gregor tried to suppose to himself that something like what had happened to him today might some day happen to the chief clerk; one really could not deny that it was possible. But as if in brusque reply to this supposition the chief clerk took a couple of firm steps in the next-door room and his patent leather boots creaked. From the right-hand room his sister was whispering to inform him of the situation: "Gregor, the chief clerk's here." "I know," muttered Gregor to himself; but he didn't dare to make his voice loud enough for his sister to hear it.

"Gregor," said his father now from the left-hand room, "the chief clerk has come and wants to know why you didn't catch the early train. We don't know what to say to him. Besides, he wants to talk to you in person. So open the door, please. He will be good enough to excuse the untidiness of your room." "Good morning, Mr. Samsa," the chief clerk was calling amiably meanwhile. "He's not well," said his mother to the visitor, while his father was still speaking through the door, "he's not well, sir, believe me. What else would make him miss a train! The boy thinks about nothing but his work. It makes me almost cross the way he never goes out in the evenings; he's been here the last eight days and has stayed at home every single evening. He just sits there quietly at the table reading a newspaper or looking through railway timetables. The only amusement he gets is doing fretwork. For instance, he spent two or three evenings cutting out a little picture frame; you would be surprised to see how pretty it is; it's hanging in his room; you'll see it in a minute when Gregor opens the door. I must say I'm glad you've come, sir; we should never have got him to unlock the door by ourselves; he's so obstinate; and I'm sure he's unwell, though he wouldn't have it to be so this morning." "I'm just coming," said Gregor slowly and carefully, not moving an inch for fear of losing one word of the conversation. "I can't think of any other explanation, madam," said the chief clerk, "I hope it's nothing serious. Although on the other hand I must say that we men of business— fortunately or unfortunately—very often simply have to ignore any slight indisposition, since business must be attended to." "Well, can the chief clerk come in now?" asked Gregor's father impatiently, again knocking on the door. "No," said Gregor. In the left-hand room a painful silence followed this refusal, in the right-hand room his sister began to sob.

Why didn't his sister join the others? She was probably newly out of bed and hadn't even begun to put on her clothes yet. Well, why was she crying? Because he wouldn't get up and let the chief clerk in, because he was in danger of losing his job, and because the chief would begin dunning his parents again for the old debts? Surely these were things one didn't need to worry about for the present. Gregor was still at home and not in the least thinking of deserting the family. At the moment, true, he was lying on the carpet and no one who knew the condition he was in could seriously expect him to admit the chief clerk. But for such a small discourtesy, which could plausibly be explained away somehow later on, Gregor could hardly be dismissed on the spot. And it seemed to Gregor that it would be much more sensible to leave him in

peace for the present than to trouble him with tears and entreaties. Still, of course, their uncertainty bewildered them all and
excused their behavior.

"Mr. Samsa," the chief clerk called now in a louder voice, "what's
the matter with you? Here you are, barricading yourself in your
room, giving only 'yes' and 'no' for answers, causing your parents a
lot of unnecessary trouble and neglecting—I mention this only in
passing—neglecting your business duties in an incredible fashion. I
am speaking here in the name of your parents and of your chief,
and I beg you quite seriously to give me an immediate and precise
explanation. You amaze me, you amaze me. I thought you were a
quiet, dependable person, and now all at once you seem bent on
making a disgraceful exhibition of yourself. The chief did hint to
me early this morning a possible explanation for your disappearance
—with reference to the cash payments that were entrusted to you
recently—but I almost pledged my solemn word of honor that this
could not be so. But now that I see how incredibly obstinate you
are, I no longer have the slightest desire to take your part at all. And
your position in the firm is not so unassailable. I came with the
intention of telling you all this in private, but since you are wasting
my time so needlessly I don't see why your parents shouldn't hear
it too. For some time past your work has been most unsatisfactory;
this is not the season of the year for a business boom, of course,
we admit that, but a season of the year for doing no business at
all, that does not exist, Mr. Samsa, must not exist."

"But, sir," cried Gregor, beside himself and in his agitation forgetting everything else, "I'm just going to open the door this very
minute. A slight illness, an attack of giddiness, has kept me from
getting up. I'm still lying in bed. But I feel all right again. I'm
getting out of bed now. Just give me a moment or two longer!
I'm not quite so well as I thought. But I'm all right, really. How a
thing like that can suddenly strike one down! Only last night I was
quite well, my parents can tell you, or rather I did have a slight presentiment. I must have showed some sign of it. Why didn't I report
it at the office! But one always thinks that an indisposition can be
got over without staying in the house. Oh sir, do spare my parents!
All that you're reproaching me with now has no foundation; no one
has ever said a word to me about it. Perhaps you haven't looked at the
last orders I sent in. Anyhow, I can still catch the eight o'clock train,
I'm much the better for my few hours' rest. Don't let me detain you
here, sir; I'll be attending to business very soon, and do be good
enough to tell the chief so and to make my excuses to him!"

And while all this was tumbling out pell-mell and Gregor hardly
knew what he was saying, he had reached the chest quite easily,
perhaps because of the practice he had had in bed, and was now

trying to lever himself upright by means of it. He meant actually to open the door, actually to show himself and speak to the chief clerk; he was eager to find out what the others, after all their insistence, would say at the sight of him. If they were horrified then the responsibility was no longer his and he could stay quiet. But if they took it calmly, then he had no reason either to be upset, and could really get to the station for the eight o'clock train if he hurried. At first he slipped down a few times from the polished surface of the chest, but at length with a last heave he stood upright; he paid no more attention to the pains in the lower part of his body, however they smarted. Then he let himself fall against the back of a near-by chair, and clung with his little legs to the edges of it. That brought him into control of himself again and he stopped speaking, for now he could listen to what the chief clerk was saying.

"Did you understand a word of it?" the chief clerk was asking; "surely he can't be trying to make fools of us?" "Oh dear," cried his mother, in tears, "perhaps he's terribly ill and we're tormenting him. Grete! Grete!" she called out then. "Yes Mother?" called his sister from the other side. They were calling to each other across Gregor's room. "You must go this minute for the doctor. Gregor is ill. Go for the doctor, quick. Did you hear how he was speaking?" "That was no human voice," said the chief clerk in a voice noticeably low beside the shrillness of the mother's. "Anna! Anna!" his father was calling through the hall to the kitchen, clapping his hands, "get a locksmith at once!" And the two girls were already running through the hall with a swish of skirts—how could his sister have got dressed so quickly?—and were tearing the front door open. There was no sound of its closing again; they had evidently left it open, as one does in houses where some great misfortune has happened.

But Gregor was now much calmer. The words he uttered were no longer understandable, apparently, although they seemed clear enough to him, even clearer than before, perhaps because his ear had grown accustomed to the sound of them. Yet at any rate people now believed that something was wrong with him, and were ready to help him. The positive certainty with which these first measures had been taken comforted him. He felt himself drawn once more into the human circle and hoped for great and remarkable results from both the doctor and the locksmith, without really distinguishing precisely between them. To make his voice as clear as possible for the decisive conversation that was now imminent he coughed a little, as quietly as he could, of course, since this noise too might not sound like a human cough for all he was able to judge. In the next room meanwhile there was complete silence. Perhaps his parents were sitting at the table with the chief clerk, whispering, perhaps they were all leaning against the door and listening.

Slowly Gregor pushed the chair towards the door, then let go of it, caught hold of the door for support—the soles at the end of his little legs were somewhat sticky—and rested against it for a moment after his efforts. Then he set himself to turning the key in the lock with his mouth. It seemed, unhappily, that he hadn't really any teeth—what could he grip the key with?—but on the other hand his jaws were certainly very strong; with their help he did manage to set the key in motion, heedless of the fact that he was undoubtedly damaging them somewhere, since a brown fluid issued from his mouth, flowed over the key and dripped on the floor. "Just listen to that," said the chief clerk next door; "he's turning the key." That was a great encouragement to Gregor; but they should all have shouted encouragement to him, his father and mother too: "Go on, Gregor," they should have called out, "keep going, hold on to that key!" And in the belief that they were all following his efforts intently, he clenched his jaws recklessly on the key with all the force at his command. As the turning of the key progressed he circled round the lock, holding on now only with his mouth, pushing on the key, as required, or pulling it down again with all the weight of his body. The louder click of the finally yielding lock literally quickened Gregor. With a deep breath of relief he said to himself: "So I didn't need the locksmith," and laid his head on the handle to open the door wide.

Since he had to pull the door towards him, he was still invisible when it was really wide open. He had to edge himself slowly round the near half of the double door, and to do it very carefully if he was not to fall plump upon his back just on the threshold. He was still carrying out this difficult manoeuvre, with no time to observe anything else, when he heard the chief clerk utter a loud "Oh!"— it sounded like a gust of wind—and now he could see the man, standing as he was nearest to the door, clapping one hand before his open mouth and slowly backing away as if driven by some invisible steady pressure. His mother—in spite of the chief clerk's being there her hair was still undone and sticking up in all directions— first clasped her hands and looked at his father, then took two steps towards Gregor and fell on the floor among her outspread skirts, her face quite hidden on her breast. His father knotted his fist with a fierce expression on his face as if he meant to knock Gregor back into his room, then looked uncertainly round the living room, covered his eyes with his hands and wept till his great chest heaved.

Gregor did not go now into the living room, but leaned against the inside of the firmly shut wing of the door, so that only half his body was visible and his head above it bending sideways to look at the others. The light had meanwhile strengthened; on the other side of the street one could see clearly a section of the endlessly long, dark gray building opposite—it was a hospital—abruptly punctuated by its row of regular windows; the rain was still falling, but only in large singly discernible and literally singly splashing drops. The breakfast dishes were set out on the table lavishly, for breakfast was the most important meal of the day to Gregor's father, who lingered it out for hours over various newspapers. Right opposite Gregor on the wall hung a photograph of himself on military service, as a lieutenant, hand on sword, a carefree smile on his face, inviting one to respect his uniform and military bearing. The door leading to the hall was open, and one could see that the front door stood open too, showing the landing beyond and the beginning of the stairs going down.

"Well," said Gregor, knowing perfectly that he was the only one who had retained any composure, "I'll put my clothes on at once, pack up my samples and start off. Will you only let me go? You see, sir, I'm not obstinate, and I'm willing to work; traveling is a hard life, but I couldn't live without it. Where are you going, sir? To the office? Yes? Will you give a true account of all this? One can be temporarily incapacitated, but that's just the moment for remembering former services and bearing in mind that later on, when the incapacity has been got over, one will certainly work with all the more industry and concentration. I'm loyally bound to serve the chief, you know that very well. Besides, I have to provide for my parents and my sister. I'm in great difficulties, but I'll get out of them again. Don't make things any worse for me than they are. Stand up for me in the firm. Travelers are not popular there, I know. People think they earn sacks of money and just have a good time. A prejudice there's no particular reason for revising. But you, sir, have a more comprehensive view of affairs than the rest of the staff, yes, let me tell you in confidence, a more comprehensive view than the chief himself, who, being the owner, lets his judgment easily be swayed against one of his employees. And you know very well that the traveler, who is never seen in the office almost the whole year round, can so easily fall a victim to gossip and ill luck and unfounded complaints, which he mostly knows nothing about, except when he comes back exhausted from his rounds, and only then suffers in person from their evil consequences, which he can no longer trace back to the original causes. Sir, sir, don't go away without a word to me to show that you think me in the right at least to some extent!"

But at Gregor's very first words the chief clerk had already backed away and only stared at him with parted lips over one twitching shoulder. And while Gregor was speaking he did not stand still one moment but stole away towards the door, without taking his eyes off Gregor, yet only an inch at a time, as if obeying some secret injunction to leave the room. He was already at the hall, and the suddenness with which he took his last step out of the living room would have made one believe he had burned the sole of his foot. Once in the hall he stretched his right arm before him towards the staircase, as if some supernatural power were waiting there to deliver him.

Gregor perceived that the chief clerk must on no account be allowed to go away in this frame of mind if his position in the firm were not to be endangered to the utmost. His parents did not understand this so well; they had convinced themselves in the course of years that Gregor was settled for life in this firm, and besides they were so preoccupied with their immediate troubles that all foresight had forsaken them. Yet Gregor had this foresight. The chief clerk must be detained, soothed, persuaded and finally won over; the whole future of Gregor and his family depended on it! If only his sister had been there! She was intelligent; she had begun to cry while Gregor was still lying quietly on his back. And no doubt the chief clerk, so partial to ladies, would have been guided by her; she would have shut the door of the flat and in the hall talked him out of his horror. But she was not there, and Gregor would have to handle the situation himself. And without remembering that he was still unaware what powers of movement he possessed, without even remembering that his words in all possibility, indeed in all likelihood, would again be unintelligible, he let go the wing of the door, pushed himself through the opening, started to walk towards the chief clerk, who was already ridiculously clinging with both hands to the railing on the landing; but immediately, as he was feeling for a support, he fell down with a little cry upon all his numerous legs. Hardly was he down when he experienced for the first time this morning a sense of physical comfort; his legs had firm ground under them; they were completely obedient, as he noted with joy; they even strove to carry him forward in whatever direction he chose; and he was inclined to believe that a final relief from all his sufferings was at hand. But in the same moment as he found himself on the floor, rocking with suppressed eagerness to move, not far from his mother, indeed just in front of her, she, who had seemed so completely crushed, sprang all at once to her feet, her arms and fingers outspread, cried: "Help, for God's sake, help!" bent her head down as if to see Gregor better, yet on the contrary kept backing senselessly away; had quite forgotten that the laden table stood behind her; sat upon it hastily, as if in absence of mind, when she bumped into it; and seemed altogether unaware that the big coffee pot beside her was upset and pouring coffee in a flood over the carpet.

"Mother, Mother," said Gregor in a low voice, and looked up at her. The chief clerk, for the moment, had quite slipped from his mind; instead, he could not resist snapping his jaws together at the sight of the streaming coffee. That made his mother scream again, she fled from the table and fell into the arms of his father, who hastened to catch her. But Gregor had now no time to spare for his parents; the chief clerk was already on the stairs; with his chin on the banisters he was taking one last backward look. Gregor made a spring, to be as sure as possible of overtaking him; the chief clerk must have divined his intention, for he leaped down several steps and vanished; he was still yelling "Ugh!" and it echoed through the whole staircase.

Unfortunately, the flight of the chief clerk seemed completely to upset Gregor's father, who had remained relatively calm until now, for instead of running after the man himself, or at least not hindering Gregor in his pursuit, he seized in his right hand the walking stick which the chief clerk had left behind on a chair, together with a hat and greatcoat, snatched in his left hand a large newspaper from the table and began stamping his feet and flourishing the stick and the newspaper to drive Gregor back into his room. No entreaty of Gregor's availed, indeed no entreaty was even understood, however humbly he bent his head his father only stamped on the floor the more loudly. Behind his father his mother had torn open a window, despite the cold weather, and was leaning far out of it with her face in her hands. A strong draught set in from the street to the staircase, the window curtains blew in, the newspapers on the table fluttered, stray pages whisked over the floor. Pitilessly Gregor's father drove him back, hissing and crying "Shoo!" like a savage. But Gregor was quite unpracticed in walking backwards, it really was a slow business. If he only had a chance to turn round he could get back to his room at once, but he was afraid of exasperating his father by the slowness of such a rotation and at any moment the stick in his father's hand might hit him a fatal blow on the back or on the head. In the end, however, nothing else was left for him to do since to his horror he observed that in moving backwards he could not even control the direction he took; and so, keeping an anxious eye on his father all the time over his shoulder, he began to turn round as quickly as he could, which was in reality very slowly. Perhaps his father noted his good intentions, for he did not interfere except every now and then to help him in the manoeuvre from a distance with the point of the stick. If only he would have stopped making that unbearable hissing noise! It made Gregor quite lose his head. He had turned almost completely round when the hissing noise so distracted him that he even turned a little the wrong way again. But when at last his head was fortunately right in front of the doorway, it appeared that his body was too broad simply to get through the opening. His father, of course, in his present mood was far from thinking of such a thing as opening the other half of the door, to let Gregor have enough space. He had merely the fixed idea of driving Gregor back into his room as quickly as possible. He would never have suffered Gregor to make the circumstantial preparations for standing up on end and perhaps slipping his way through the door. Maybe he was now making more noise than ever to urge Gregor forward, as if no obstacle impeded him; to Gregor, anyhow, the noise in his rear sounded no longer like the voice of one single father; this was really no joke, and Gregor thrust himself —come what might—into the doorway. One side of his body rose up, he was tilted at an angle in the doorway, his flank was quite bruised, horrid blotches stained the white door, soon he was stuck fast and, left to himself, could not have moved at all, his legs on one side fluttered trembling in the air, those on the other were crushed painfully to the floor—when from behind his father gave him a strong push which was literally a deliverance and he flew far into the room, bleeding freely. The door was slammed behind him with the stick, and then at last there was silence.

II

Not until it was twilight did Gregor awake out of a deep sleep, more like a swoon than a sleep. He would certainly have waked up of his own accord not much later, for he felt himself sufficiently rested and well-slept, but it seemed to him as if a fleeting step and a cautious shutting of the door leading into the hall had aroused him. The electric lights in the street cast a pale sheen here and there on the ceiling and the upper surfaces of the furniture, but down below, where he lay, it was dark. Slowly, awkwardly trying out his feelers, which he now first learned to appreciate, he pushed his way to the door to see what had been happening there. His left side felt like one single long, unpleasantly tense scar, and he had actually to limp on his two rows of legs. One little leg, moreover, had been severely damaged in the course of that morning's events— it was almost a miracle that only one had been damaged—and trailed uselessly behind him.

He had reached the door before he discovered what had really drawn him to it: the smell of food. For there stood a basin filled with fresh milk in which floated little sops of white bread. He could almost have laughed with joy, since he was now still hungrier than in the morning, and he dipped his head almost over the eyes straight into the milk. But soon in disappointment he withdrew it again; not only did he find it difficult to feed because of his tender left side—and he could only feed with the palpitating collaboration of his whole body—he did not like the milk either, although milk had been his favorite drink and that was certainly why his sister had set it there for him, indeed it was almost with repulsion that he turned away from the basin and crawled back to the middle of the room.

He could see through the crack of the door that the gas was turned on in the living room, but while usually at this time his father made a habit of reading the afternoon newspaper in a loud voice to his mother and occasionally to his sister as well, not a sound was now to be heard. Well, perhaps his father had recently given up this habit of reading aloud, which his sister had mentioned so often in conversation and in her letters. But there was the same silence all around, although the flat was certainly not empty of occupants. "What a quiet life our family has been leading," said Gregor to himself, and as he sat there motionless staring into the darkness he felt great pride in the fact that he had been able to provide such a life for his parents and sister in such a fine flat. But what if all the quiet, the comfort, the contentment were now to end in horror? To keep himself from being lost in such thoughts Gregor took refuge in movement and crawled up and down the room.

Once during the long evening one of the side doors was opened a little and quickly shut again, later the other side door too; someone had apparently wanted to come in and then thought better of it. Gregor now stationed himself immediately before the living room door, determined to persuade any hesitating visitor to come in or at least to discover who it might be; but the door was not opened again and he waited in vain. In the early morning, when the doors were locked, they had all wanted to come in, now that he had opened one door and the other had apparently been opened during the day, no one came in and even the keys were on the other side of the doors.

It was late at night before the gas went out in the living room, and Gregor could easily tell that his parents and his sister had all stayed awake until then, for he could clearly hear the three of them stealing away on tiptoe. No one was likely to visit him, not until the morning, that was certain; so he had plenty of time to meditate at his leisure on how he was to arrange his life afresh. But the lofty, empty room in which he had to lie flat on the floor filled him with an apprehension he could not account for, since it had been his very own room for the past five years—and with a half-unconscious action, not without a slight feeling of shame, he scuttled under the sofa, where he felt comfortable at once, although his back was a little cramped and he could not lift his head up, and his only regret was that his body was too broad to get the whole of it under the sofa.

He stayed there all night, spending the time partly in a light slumber, from which his hunger kept waking him up with a start, and partly in worrying and sketching vague hopes, which all led to the same conclusion, that he must lie low for the present and, by exercising patience and the utmost consideration, help the family to bear the inconvenience he was bound to cause them in his present condition.

Very early in the morning, it was still almost night, Gregor had the chance to test the strength of his new resolutions, for his sister, nearly fully dressed, opened the door from the hall and peered in. She did not see him at once, yet when she caught sight of him under the sofa—well, he had to be somewhere, he couldn't have flown away, could he?—she was so startled that without being able to help it she slammed the door shut again. But as if regretting her behavior she opened the door again immediately and came in on tiptoe, as if she were visiting an invalid or even a stranger. Gregor had pushed his head forward to the very edge of the sofa and watched her. Would she notice that he had left the milk standing, and not for lack of hunger, and would she bring in some other kind of food more to his taste? If she did not do it of her own accord, he would rather starve than draw her attention to the fact, although he felt a wild impulse to dart out from under the sofa, throw himself at her feet and beg her for something to eat. But his sister at once noticed, with surprise, that the basin was still full, except for a little milk that had been spilt all around it, she lifted it immediately, not with her bare hands, true, but with a cloth and carried it away. Gregor was wildly curious to know what she would bring instead, and made various speculations about it. Yet what she actually did next, in the goodness of her heart, he could never have guessed at. To find out what he liked she brought him a whole selection of food, all set out on an old newspaper. There were old, half-decayed vegetables, bones from last night's supper covered with a white sauce that had thickened; some raisins and almonds; a piece of cheese that Gregor would have called uneatable two days ago; a dry roll of bread, a buttered roll, and a roll both buttered and salted. Besides all that, she set down again the same basin, into which she had poured some water, and which was apparently to be reserved for his exclusive use. And with fine tact, knowing that Gregor would not eat in her presence, she withdrew quickly and even turned the key, to let him understand that he could take his ease as much as he liked. Gregor's legs all whizzed towards the food. His wounds must have healed completely, moreover, for he felt no disability, which amazed him and made him reflect how more than a month ago he had cut one finger a little with a knife and had still suffered pain from the wound only the day before yesterday. Am I less sensitive now? he thought, and sucked greedily at the cheese, which above all the other edibles attracted him at once and strongly. One after another and with tears of satisfaction in his eyes he quickly devoured the cheese, the vegetables and the sauce; the fresh food, on the other hand, had no charms for him, he could not even stand the smell of it and actually dragged away to some little distance the things he could eat. He had long finished his meal and was only lying lazily on the same spot when his sister turned the key slowly as a sign for him to retreat. That roused him at once, although he was nearly asleep, and he hurried under the sofa again. But it took considerable self-control for him to stay under the sofa, even for the short time his sister was in the room, since the large meal had swollen his body somewhat and he was so cramped he could hardly breathe. Slight attacks of breathlessness afflicted him and his eyes were starting a little out of his head as he watched his unsuspecting sister sweeping together with a broom not only the remains of what he had eaten but even the things he had not touched, as if these were now of no use to anyone, and hastily shoveling it all into a bucket, which she covered with a wooden lid and carried away. Hardly had she turned her back when Gregor came from under the sofa and stretched and puffed himself out.

In this manner Gregor was fed, once in the early morning while his parents and the servant girl were still asleep, and a second time after they had all had their midday dinner, for then his parents took a short nap and the servant girl could be sent out on some errand or other by his sister. Not that they would have wanted him to starve, of course, but perhaps they could not have borne to know more about his feeding than from hearsay, perhaps too his sister wanted to spare them such little anxieties wherever possible, since they had quite enough to bear as it was.

Under what pretext the doctor and the locksmith had been got rid of on that first morning Gregor could not discover, for since what he said was not understood by the others it never struck any of them, not even his sister, that he could understand what they said, and so whenever his sister came into his room he had to content himself with hearing her utter only a sigh now and then and an occasional appeal to the saints. Later on, when she had got a little used to the situation—of course she could never get completely used to it—she sometimes threw out a remark which was kindly meant or could be so interpreted. "Well, he liked his dinner today," she would say when Gregor had made a good clearance of his food; and when he had not eaten, which gradually happened more and more often, she would say almost sadly: "Everything's been left standing again."

But although Gregor could get no news directly, he overheard a lot from the neighboring rooms, and as soon as voices were audible, he would run to the door of the room concerned and press his whole body against it. In the first few days especially there was no conversation that did not refer to him somehow, even if only indirectly. For two whole days there were family consultations at every mealtime about what should be done; but also between meals the same subject was discussed, for there were always at least two members of the family at home, since no one wanted to be alone in the flat and to leave it quite empty was unthinkable. And on the very first of these days the household cook—it was not quite clear what and how much she knew of the situation—went down on her knees to his mother and begged leave to go, and when she departed, a quarter of an hour later, gave thanks for her dismissal with tears in her eyes as if for the greatest benefit that could have been conferred on her, and without any prompting swore a solemn oath that she would never say a single word to anyone about what had happened.

Now Gregor's sister had to cook too, helping her mother; true, the cooking did not amount to much, for they ate scarcely anything. Gregor was always hearing one of the family vainly urging another to eat and getting no answer but: "Thanks, I've had all I want," or something similar. Perhaps they drank nothing either. Time and again his sister kept asking his father if he wouldn't like some beer and offered kindly to go and fetch it herself, and when he made no answer suggested that she could ask the concierge to fetch it, so that he need feel no sense of obligation, but then a round "No" came from his father and no more was said about it.

In the course of that very first day Gregor's father explained the family's financial position and prospects to both his mother and his sister. Now and then he rose from the table to get some voucher or memorandum out of the small safe he had rescued from the collapse of his business five years earlier. One could hear him opening the complicated lock and rustling papers out and shutting it again. This statement made by his father was the first cheerful information Gregor had heard since his imprisonment. He had been of the opinion that nothing at all was left over from his father's business, at least his father had never said anything to the contrary, and of course he had not asked him directly. At that time Gregor's sole desire was to do his utmost to help the family to forget as soon as possible the catastrophe which had overwhelmed the business and thrown them all into a state of complete despair. And so he had set to work with unusual ardor and almost overnight had become a commercial traveler instead of a little clerk, with of course much greater chances of earning money, and his success was immediately translated into good round coin which he could lay on the table for his amazed and happy family. These had been fine times, and they had never recurred, at least not with the same sense of glory, although later on Gregor had earned so much money that he was able to meet the expenses of the whole household and did so. They had simply got used to it, both the family and Gregor; the money was gratefully accepted and gladly given, but there was no special uprush of warm feeling. With his sister alone had he remained intimate, and it was a secret plan of his that she, who loved music, unlike himself, and could play movingly on the violin, should be sent next year to study at the Conservatorium, despite the great expense that would entail, which must be made up in some other way. During his brief visits home the Conservatorium was often mentioned in the talks he had with his sister, but always merely as a beautiful dream which could never come true, and his parents discouraged even these innocent references to it; yet Gregor had made up his mind firmly about it and meant to announce the fact with due solemnity on Christmas Day.

Such were the thoughts, completely futile in his present condition, that went through his head as he stood clinging upright to the door and listening. Sometimes out of sheer weariness he had to give up listening and let his head fall negligently against the door, but he always had to pull himself together again at once, for even the slight sound his head made was audible next door and brought all conversation to a stop. "What can he be doing now?" his father would say after a while, obviously turning towards the door, and only then would the interrupted conversation gradually be set going again.

Gregor was now informed as amply as he could wish—for his father tended to repeat himself in his explanations, partly because it was a long time since he had handled such matters and partly because his mother could not always grasp things at once—that a certain amount of investments, a very small amount it was true, had survived the wreck of their fortunes and had even increased a little because the dividends had not been touched meanwhile. And besides that, the money Gregor brought home every month—he had kept only a few dollars for himself—had never been quite used up and now amounted to a small capital sum. Behind the door Gregor nodded his head eagerly, rejoiced at this evidence of unexpected thrift and foresight. True, he could really have paid off some more of his father's debts to the chief with this extra money, and so brought much nearer the day on which he could quit his job, but doubtless it was better the way his father had arranged it.

Yet this capital was by no means sufficient to let the family live on the interest of it; for one year, perhaps, or at the most two, they could live on the principal, that was all. It was simply a sum that ought not to be touched and should be kept for a rainy day; money for living expenses would have to be earned. Now his father was still hale enough but an old man, and he had done no work for the past five years and could not be expected to do much; during these five years, the first years of leisure in his laborious though unsuccessful life, he had grown rather fat and become sluggish. And Gregor's old mother, how was she to earn a living with her asthma, which troubled her even when she walked through the flat and kept her lying on a sofa every other day panting for breath beside an open window? And was his sister to earn her bread, she who was still a child of seventeen and whose life hitherto had been so pleasant, consisting as it did in dressing herself nicely, sleeping long, helping in the housekeeping, going out to a few modest entertainments and above all playing the violin? At first whenever the need for earning money was mentioned Gregor let go his hold on the door and threw himself down on the cool leather sofa beside it, he felt so hot with shame and grief.

Often he just lay there the long nights through without sleeping at all, scrabbling for hours on the leather. Or he nerved himself to the great effort of pushing an armchair to the window, then crawled up over the window sill and, braced against the chair, leaned against the window panes, obviously in some recollection of the sense of freedom that looking out of a window always used to give him. For in reality day by day things that were even a little way off were growing dimmer to his sight; the hospital across the street, which he used to execrate for being all too often before his eyes, was now quite beyond his range of vision, and if he had not known that he lived in Charlotte Street, a quiet street but still a city street, he might have believed that his window gave on a desert waste where gray sky and gray land blended indistinguishably into each other. His quick-witted sister only needed to observe twice that the armchair stood by the window; after that whenever she had tidied the room she always pushed the chair back to the same place at the window and even left the inner casements open.

If he could have spoken to her and thanked her for all she had to do for him, he could have borne her ministrations better; as it was, they oppressed him. She certainly tried to make as light as possible of whatever was disagreeable in her task, and as time went on she succeeded, of course, more and more, but time brought more enlightenment to Gregor too. The very way she came in distressed him. Hardly was she in the room when she rushed to the window, without even taking time to shut the door, careful as she was usually to shield the sight of Gregor's room from the others, and as if she were almost suffocating tore the casements open with hasty fingers, standing then in the open draught for a while even in the bitterest cold and drawing deep breaths. This noisy scurry of hers upset Gregor twice a day; he would crouch trembling under the sofa all the time, knowing quite well that she would certainly have spared him such a disturbance had she found it at all possible to stay in his presence without opening the window.

On one occasion, about a month after Gregor's metamorphosis, when there was surely no reason for her to be still startled at his appearance, she came a little earlier than usual and found him gazing out of the window, quite motionless, and thus well placed to look like a bogey. Gregor would not have been surprised had she not come in at all, for she could not immediately open the window while he was there, but not only did she retreat, she jumped back as if in alarm and banged the door shut; a stranger might well have thought that he had been lying in wait for her there meaning to bite her. Of course he hid himself under the sofa at once, but he had to wait until midday before she came again, and she seemed more ill at ease than usual. This made him realize how repulsive the sight of him still was to her, and that it was bound to go on being repulsive, and what an effort it must cost her not to run away even from the sight of the small portion of his body that stuck out from under the sofa. In order to spare her that, therefore, one day he carried a sheet on his back to the sofa—it cost him four hours' labor—and arranged it there in such a way as to hide him completely, so that even if she were to bend down she could not see him. Had she considered the sheet unnecessary, she would certainly have stripped it off the sofa again, for it was clear enough that this curtaining and confining of himself was not likely to conduce to Gregor's comfort, but she left it where it was, and Gregor even fancied that he caught a thankful glance from her eye when he lifted the sheet carefully a very little with his head to see how she was taking the new arrangement.

For the first fortnight his parents could not bring themselves to the point of entering his room, and he often heard them expressing their appreciation of his sister's activities, whereas formerly they had frequently scolded her for being as they thought a somewhat useless daughter. But now, both of them often waited outside the door, his father and his mother, while his sister tidied his room, and as soon as she came out she had to tell them exactly how things were in the room, what Gregor had eaten, how he had conducted himself this time and whether there was not perhaps some slight improvement in his condition. His mother, moreover, began relatively soon to want to visit him, but his father and sister dissuaded her at first with arguments which Gregor listened to very attentively and altogether approved. Later, however, she had to be held back by main force, and when she cried out: "Do let me in to Gregor, he is my unfortunate son! Can't you understand that I must go to him?" Gregor thought that it might be well to have her come in, not every day, of course, but perhaps once a week; she understood things, after all, much better than his sister, who was only a child despite the efforts she was making and had perhaps taken on so difficult a task merely out of childish thoughtlessness.

Gregor's desire to see his mother was soon fulfilled. During the daytime he did not want to show himself at the window, out of consideration for his parents, but he could not crawl very far around the few square yards of floor space he had, nor could be bear lying quietly at rest all during the night, while he was fast losing any interest he had ever taken in food, so that for mere recreation he had formed the habit of crawling crisscross over the walls and ceiling. He especially enjoyed hanging suspended from the ceiling; it was much better than lying on the floor; one could breathe more freely; one's body swung and rocked lightly; and in the almost blissful absorption induced by this suspension it could happen to his own surprise that he let go and fell plump on the floor. Yet he now had his body much better under control than formerly, and even such a big fall did him no harm. His sister at once remarked the new distraction Gregor had found for himself—he left traces behind him of the sticky stuff on his soles wherever he crawled—and she got the idea in her head of giving him as wide a field as possible to crawl in and of removing the pieces of furniture that hindered him, above all the chest of drawers and the writing desk. But that was more than she could manage all by herself; she did not dare ask her father to help her; and as for the servant girl, a young creature of sixteen who had had the courage to stay on after the cook's departure, she could not be asked to help, for she had begged as an especial favor that she might keep the kitchen door locked and open it only on a definite summons; so there was nothing left but to apply to her mother at an hour when her father was out. And the old lady did come, with exclamations of joyful eagerness, which, however, died away at the door of Gregor's room. Gregor's sister, of course, went in first, to see that everything was in order before letting his mother enter. In great haste Gregor pulled the sheet lower and rucked it more in folds so that it really looked as if it had been thrown accidentally over the sofa. And this time he did not peer out from under it; he renounced the pleasure of seeing his mother on this occasion and was only glad that she had come at all. "Come in, he's out of sight," said his sister, obviously leading her mother in by the hand. Gregor could now hear the two women struggling to shift the heavy old chest from its place, and his sister claiming the greater part of the labor for herself, without listening to the admonitions of her mother who feared she might overstrain herself. It took a long time. After at least a quarter of an hour's tugging his mother objected that the chest had better be left where it was, for in the first place it was too heavy and could never be got out before his father came home, and standing in the middle of the room like that it would only hamper Gregor's movements, while in the second place it was not at all certain that removing the furniture would be doing a service to Gregor. She was inclined to think to the contrary; the sight of the naked walls made her own heart heavy, and why shouldn't Gregor have the same feeling, considering that he had been used to his furniture for so long and might feel forlorn without it. "And doesn't it look," she concluded in a low voice—in fact she had been almost whispering all the time as if to avoid letting Gregor, whose exact whereabouts she did not know, hear even the tones of her voice, for she was convinced that he could not understand her words—"doesn't it look as if we were showing him, by taking away his furniture, that we have given up hope of his ever getting better and are just leaving him coldly to himself? I think it would be best to keep his room exactly as it has always been, so that when he comes back to us he will find everything unchanged and be able all the more easily to forget what has happened in between."

On hearing these words from his mother Gregor realized that the lack of all direct human speech for the past two months together with the monotony of family life must have confused his mind, otherwise he could not account for the fact that he had quite earnestly looked forward to having his room emptied of furnishing. Did he really want his warm room, so comfortably fitted with old family furniture, to be turned into a naked den in which he would certainly be able to crawl unhampered in all directions but at the price of shedding simultaneously all recollection of his human background? He had indeed been so near the brink of forgetfulness that only the voice of his mother, which he had not heard for so long, had drawn him back from it. Nothing should be taken out of his room; everything must stay as it was; he could not dispense with the good influence of the furniture on his state of mind; and even if the furniture did hamper him in his senseless crawling round and round, that was no drawback but a great advantage.

Unfortunately his sister was of the contrary opinion; she had grown accustomed, and not without reason, to consider herself an expert in Gregor's affairs as against her parents, and so her mother's advice was now enough to make her determined on the removal not only of the chest and the writing desk, which had been her first intention, but of all the furniture except the indispensable sofa. This determination was not, of course, merely the outcome of childish recalcitrance and of the self-confidence she had recently developed so unexpectedly and at such cost; she had in fact perceived that Gregor needed a lot of space to crawl about in, while on the other hand he never used the furniture at all, so far as could be seen. Another factor might have been also the enthusiastic temperament of an adolescent girl, which seeks to indulge itself on every opportunity

and which now tempted Grete to exaggerate the horror of her brother's circumstances in order that she might do all the more for him.
In a room where Gregor lorded it all alone over empty walls no one
save herself was likely ever to set foot.

And so she was not to be moved from her resolve by her mother,
who seemed moreover to be ill at ease in Gregor's room and therefore unsure of herself, was soon reduced to silence and helped her
daughter as best she could to push the chest outside. Now, Gregor
could do without the chest, if need be, but the writing desk he must
retain. As soon as the two women had got the chest out of his room,
groaning as they pushed it, Gregor stuck his head out from under
the sofa to see how he might intervene as kindly and cautiously as
possible. But as bad luck would have it, his mother was the first to
return, leaving Grete clasping the chest in the room next door where
she was trying to shift it all by herself, without of course moving it
from the spot. His mother however was not accustomed to the sight
of him, it might sicken her and so in alarm Gregor backed quickly
to the other end of the sofa, yet could not prevent the sheet from
swaying a little in front. That was enough to put her on the alert.
She paused, stood still for a moment and then went back to Grete.

Although Gregor kept reassuring himself that nothing out of the
way was happening, but only a few bits of furniture were being
changed round, he soon had to admit that all this trotting to and
fro of the two women, their little ejaculations and the scraping of
furniture along the floor affected him like a vast disturbance coming
from all sides at once, and however much he tucked in his head and
legs and cowered to the very floor he was bound to confess that
he would not be able to stand it for long. They were clearing his
room out; taking away everything he loved; the chest in which he
kept his fret saw and other tools was already dragged off; they were
now loosening the writing desk which had almost sunk into the floor,
the desk at which he had done all his homework when he was at
the commercial academy, at the grammar school before that, and,
yes, even at the primary school—he had no more time to waste in
weighing the good intentions of the two women, whose existence he
had by now almost forgotten, for they were so exhausted that they
were laboring in silence and nothing could be heard but the heavy
scuffling of their feet.

And so he rushed out—the women were just leaning against the
writing desk in the next room to give themselves a breather—and
four times changed his direction, since he really did not know what
to rescue first, then on the wall opposite, which was already otherwise
cleared, he was struck by the picture of the lady muffled in so much
fur and quickly crawled up to it and pressed himself to the glass,
which was a good surface to hold on to and comforted his hot belly

This picture at least, which was entirely hidden beneath him, was going to be removed by nobody. He turned his head towards the door of the living room so as to observe the women when they came back.

They had not allowed themselves much of a rest and were already coming; Grete had twined her arm round her mother and was almost supporting her. "Well, what shall we take now?" said Grete, looking round. Her eyes met Gregor's from the wall. She kept her composure, presumably because of her mother, bent her head down to her mother, to keep her from looking up, and said, although in a fluttering, unpremeditated voice: "Come, hadn't we better go back to the living room for a moment?" Her intentions were clear enough to Gregor, she wanted to bestow her mother in safety and then chase him down from the wall. Well, just let her try it! He clung to his picture and would not give it up. He would rather fly in Grete's face.

But Grete's words had succeeded in disquieting her mother, who took a step to one side, caught sight of the huge brown mass on the flowered wallpaper, and before she was really conscious that what she saw was Gregor screamed in a loud, hoarse voice: "Oh God, oh God!" fell with outspread arms over the sofa as if giving up and did not move. "Gregor!" cried his sister, shaking her fist and glaring at him. This was the first time she had directly addressed him since his metamorphosis. She ran into the next room for some aromatic essence with which to rouse her mother from her fainting fit. Gregor wanted to help too—there was still time to rescue the picture—but he was stuck fast to the glass and had to tear himself loose; he then ran after his sister into the next room as if he could advise her, as he used to do; but then had to stand helplessly behind her; she meanwhile searched among various small bottles and when she turned round started in alarm at the sight of him; one bottle fell on the floor and broke; a splinter of glass cut Gregor's face and some kind of corrosive medicine splashed him; without pausing a moment longer Grete gathered up all the bottles she could carry and ran to her mother with them; she banged the door shut with her foot. Gregor was now cut off from his mother, who was perhaps nearly dying because of him; he dared not open the door for fear of frightening away his sister, who had to stay with her mother; there was nothing he could do but wait; and harassed by self-reproach and worry he began now to crawl to and fro, over everything, walls, furniture and ceiling, and finally in his despair, when the whole room seemed to be reeling round him, fell down on to the middle of the big table.

A little while elapsed, Gregor was still lying there feebly and all around was quiet, perhaps that was a good omen. Then the doorbell rang. The servant girl was of course locked in her kitchen, and Grete would have to open the door. It was his father. "What's been happening?" were his first words; Grete's face must have told him everything. Grete answered in a muffled voice, apparently hiding her head on his breast: "Mother has been fainting, but she's better now. Gregor's broken loose." "Just what I expected," said his father, "just what I've been telling you, but you women would never listen." It was clear to Gregor that his father had taken the worst interpretation of Grete's all too brief statement and was assuming that Gregor had been guilty of some violent act. Therefore Gregor must now try to propitiate his father, since he had neither time nor means for an explanation. And so he fled to the door of his own room and crouched against it, to let his father see as soon as he came in from the hall that his son had the good intention of getting back into his room immediately and that it was not necessary to drive him there, but that if only the door were opened he would disappear at once.

Yet his father was not in the mood to perceive such fine distinctions. "Ah!" he cried as soon as he appeared, in a tone which sounded at once angry and exultant. Gregor drew his head back from the door and lifted it to look at his father. Truly, this was not the father he had imagined to himself; admittedly he had been too absorbed of late in his new recreation of crawling over the ceiling to take the same interest as before in what was happening elsewhere in the flat, and he ought really to be prepared for some changes. And yet, and yet, could that be his father? The man who used to lie wearily sunk in bed whenever Gregor set out on a business journey; who welcomed him back of an evening lying in a long chair in a dressing gown; who could not really rise to his feet but only lifted his arms in greeting, and on the rare occasions when he did go out with his family, on one or two Sundays a year and on high holidays, walked between Gregor and his mother, who were slow walkers anyhow, even more slowly than they did, muffled in his old greatcoat, shuffling laboriously forward with the help of his crook-handled stick which he set down most cautiously at every step and, whenever he wanted to say anything, nearly always came to a full stop and gathered his escort around him? Now he was standing there in fine shape; dressed in a smart blue uniform with gold buttons, such as bank messengers wear; his strong double chin bulged over the stiff high collar of his jacket; from under his bushy eyebrows his black eyes darted fresh and penetrating glances; his onetime tangled white hair had been combed flat on either side of a shining and carefully exact parting. He pitched his cap, which bore a gold monogram, probably the badge of some bank, in a wide sweep across the whole room on to a sofa and with the tail-ends of his jacket thrown back, his hands in his trouser pockets, advanced with a grim visage towards Gregor. Likely enough he did not himself know what he meant to do, at any rate he lifted his feet uncommonly high, and Gregor was dumbfounded at the enormous size of his shoe soles. But Gregor could not risk standing up to him, aware as he had been from the very first day of his new life that his father believed only the severest measures suitable for dealing with him. And so he ran before his father, stopping when he stopped and scuttling forward again when his father made any kind of move. In this way they circled the room several times without anything decisive happening, indeed the whole operation did not even look like a pursuit because it was carried out so slowly. And so Gregor did not leave the floor, for he feared that his father might take as a piece of peculiar wickedness any excursion of his over the walls or the ceiling. All the same, he could not stay this course much longer, for while his father took one step he had to carry out a whole series of movements. He was already beginning to feel breathless, just as in his former life his lungs had not been very dependable. As he was staggering along, trying to concentrate his energy on running, hardly keeping his eyes open; in his dazed state never even thinking of any other escape than simply going forward; and having almost forgotten that the walls were free to him, which in this room were well provided with finely carved pieces of furniture full of knobs and crevices—suddenly something lightly flung landed close behind him and rolled before him. It was an apple; a second apple followed immediately; Gregor came to a stop in alarm; there was no point in running on, for his father was determined to bombard him. He had filled his pockets with fruit from the dish on the sideboard and was now shying apple after apple, without taking particularly good aim for the moment. The small red apples rolled about the floor as if magnetized and cannoned into each other. An apple thrown without much force grazed Gregor's back and glanced off harmlessly. But another following immediately landed right on his back and sank in; Gregor wanted to drag himself forward, as if this startling, incredible pain could be left behind him; but he felt as if nailed to the spot and flattened himself out in a complete derangement of all his senses. With his last conscious look he saw the door of his room being torn open and his mother rushing out ahead of his screaming sister, in her underbodice, for her daughter had loosened her clothing to let her breathe more freely and recover from her swoon, he saw his mother rushing towards his father, leaving one after another behind her on the floor her loosened petticoats, stumbling over her petticoats straight to his father and embracing him, in complete union with him—but here Gregor's sight began to fail—with her hands clasped round his father's neck as she begged for her son's life.

III

The serious injury done to Gregor, which disabled him for more than a month—the apple went on sticking in his body as a visible reminder, since no one ventured to remove it—seemed to have made even his father recollect that Gregor was a member of the family, despite his present unfortunate and repulsive shape, and ought not to be treated as an enemy, that, on the contrary, family duty required the suppression of disgust and the exercise of patience, nothing but patience.

And although his injury had impaired, probably for ever, his powers of movement, and for the time being it took him long, long minutes to creep across his room like an old invalid—there was no question now of crawling up the wall—yet in his own opinion he was sufficiently compensated for this worsening of his condition by the fact that towards evening the living-room door, which he used to watch intently for an hour or two beforehand, was always thrown open, so that lying in the darkness of his room, invisible to the family, he could see them all at the lamp-lit table and listen to their talk, by general consent as it were, very different from his earlier eavesdropping.

True, their intercourse lacked the lively character of former times, which he had always called to mind with a certain wistfulness in the small hotel bedrooms where he had been wont to throw himself down, tired out, on damp bedding. They were now mostly very silent. Soon after supper his father would fall asleep in his armchair; his mother and sister would admonish each other to be silent; his mother, bending low over the lamp, stitched at fine sewing for an underwear firm; his sister, who had taken a job as a salesgirl, was learning shorthand and French in the evenings on the chance of bettering herself. Sometimes his father woke up, and as if quite unaware that he had been sleeping said to his mother: "What a lot of sewing you're doing today!" and at once fell asleep again, while the two women exchanged a tired smile.

With a kind of mulishness his father persisted in keeping his uniform on even in the house; his dressing gown hung uselessly on its peg and he slept fully dressed where he sat, as if he were ready for service at any moment and even here only at the beck and call of his superior. As a result, his uniform, which was not brand-new to start with, began to look dirty, despite all the loving care of the mother and sister to keep it clean, and Gregor often spent whole evenings gazing at the many greasy spots on the garment, gleaming with gold buttons always in a high state of polish, in which the old man sat sleeping in extreme discomfort and yet quite peacefully.

As soon as the clock struck ten his mother tried to rouse his father with gentle words and to persuade him after that to get into bed, for sitting there he could not have a proper sleep and that was what he needed most, since he had to go on duty at six. But with the mulishness that had obsessed him since he became a bank messenger he always insisted on staying longer at the table, although he regularly fell asleep again and in the end only with the greatest trouble could be got out of his armchair and into his bed. However insistently Gregor's mother and sister kept urging him with gentle reminders, he would go on slowly shaking his head for a quarter of an hour, keeping his eyes shut, and refuse to get to his feet. The mother plucked at his sleeve, whispering endearments in his ear, the sister left her lessons to come to her mother's help, but Gregor's father was not to be caught. He would only sink down deeper in his chair. Not until the two women hoisted him up by the armpits did he open his eyes and look at them both, one after the other, usually with the remark: "This is a life. This is the peace and quiet of my old age." And leaning on the two of them he would heave himself up, with difficulty, as if he were a great burden to himself, suffer them to lead him as far as the door and then wave them off and go on alone, while the mother abandoned her needlework and the sister her pen in order to run after him and help him farther.

Who could find time, in this overworked and tired-out family, to bother about Gregor more than was absolutely needful? The household was reduced more and more; the servant girl was turned off; a gigantic bony charwoman with white hair flying round her head came in morning and evening to do the rough work; everything else was done by Gregor's mother, as well as great piles of sewing. Even various family ornaments, which his mother and sister used to wear with pride at parties and celebrations, had to be sold, as Gregor discovered of an evening from hearing them all discuss the prices obtained. But what they lamented most was the fact that they could not leave the flat which was much too big for their present circumstances, because they could not think of any way to shift Gregor. Yet Gregor saw well enough that consideration for him was not the main difficulty preventing the removal, for they could have easily shifted him in some suitable box with a few air holes in it; what really kept them from moving into another flat was rather their own complete hopelessness and the belief that they had been singled out for a misfortune such as had never happened to any of their relations or acquaintances. They fulfilled to the uttermost all that the world demands of poor people, the father fetched breakfast for the small clerks in the bank, the mother devoted her energy to making underwear for strangers, the sister trotted to and fro behind the counter at the behest of customers, but more than this they had not the strength to do. And the wound in Gregor's back began to nag at him afresh when his mother and sister, after getting his father into bed, came back again, left their work lying, drew close to each other and sat cheek to cheek; when his mother, pointing towards his room, said: "Shut that door now, Grete," and he was left again in darkness, while next door the women mingled their tears or perhaps sat dry-eyed staring at the table.

Gregor hardly slept at all by night or by day. He was often haunted by the idea that next time the door opened he would take the family's affairs in hand again just as he used to do; once more, after this long interval, there appeared in his thoughts the figures of the chief and the chief clerk, the commercial travelers and the apprentices, the porter who was so dull-witted, two or three friends in other firms, a chambermaid in one of the rural hotels, a sweet and fleeting memory, a cashier in a milliner's shop, whom he had wooed earnestly but too slowly—they all appeared, together with strangers or people he had quite forgotten, but instead of helping him and his family they were one and all unapproachable and he was glad when they vanished. At other times he would not be in the mood to bother about his family, he was only filled with rage at the way they were neglecting him, and although he had no clear idea of what he might care to eat he would make plans for getting into the larder to take the food that was after all his due, even if he were not hungry. His sister no longer took thought to bring him what might especially please him, but in the morning and at noon before she went to business hurriedly pushed into his room with her foot any food that was available, and in the evening cleared it out again with one sweep of the broom, heedless of whether it had been merely tasted, or—as most frequently happened—left untouched. The cleaning of his room, which she now did always in the evenings, could not have been more hastily done. Streaks of dirt stretched along the walls, here and there lay balls of dust and filth. At first Gregor used to station himself in some particularly filthy corner when his sister arrived, in order to reproach her with it, so to speak. But he could have sat there for weeks without getting her to make any improvement; she could see the dirt as well as he did, but she had simply made up her mind to leave it alone. And yet, with a touchiness that was new to her, which seemed anyhow to have infected the whole family, she jealously guarded her claim to be the sole caretaker of Gregor's room. His mother once subjected his room to a thorough cleaning, which was achieved only by means of several buckets of water—all this dampness of course upset Gregor too and he lay widespread, sulky and motionless on the sofa—but she was well punished for it. Hardly had his sister noticed the changed aspect of his room that evening than she rushed in high dudgeon into the living room and, despite the imploringly raised hands of her mother, burst into a storm of weeping, while her parents—her father had of course been startled out of his chair—looked on at first in helpless amazement; then they too began to go into action; the father reproached the mother on his right for not having left the cleaning of Gregor's room to his sister; shrieked at the sister on his left that never again was she to be allowed to clean Gregor's room; while the mother tried to pull the father into his bedroom, since he was beyond himself with agitation; the sister, shaken with sobs, then beat upon the table with her small fists; and Gregor hissed loudly with rage because not one of them thought of shutting the door to spare him such a spectacle and so much noise.

Still, even if the sister, exhausted by her daily work, had grown tired of looking after Gregor as she did formerly, there was no need for his mother's intervention or for Gregor's being neglected at all. The charwoman was there. This old widow, whose strong bony frame had enabled her to survive the worst a long life could offer, by no means recoiled from Gregor. Without being in the least curious she had once by chance opened the door of his room and at the sight of Gregor, who, taken by surprise, began to rush to and fro although no one was chasing him, merely stood there with her arms folded. From that time she never failed to open his door a little for a moment, morning and evening, to have a look at him. At first she even used to call him to her, with words which apparently she took to be friendly, such as: "Come along, then, you old dung beetle!" or "Look at the old dung beetle, then!" To such allocutions Gregor made no answer, but stayed motionless where he was, as if the door had never been opened. Instead of being allowed to disturb him so senselessly whenever the whim took her, she should rather have been ordered to clean out his room daily, that charwoman! Once, early in the morning—heavy rain was lashing on the windowpanes, perhaps a sign that spring was on the way—Gregor was so exasperated when she began addressing him again that he ran at her, as if to attack her, although slowly and feebly enough. But the charwoman instead of showing fright merely lifted high a chair that happened to be beside the door, and as she stood there with her mouth wide open it was clear that she meant to shut it only when she brought the chair down on Gregor's back. "So you're not coming any nearer?" she asked, as Gregor turned away again, and quietly put the chair back into the corner.

Gregor was now eating hardly anything. Only when he happened to pass the food laid out for him did he take a bit of something in his mouth as a pastime, kept it there for an hour at a time and usually spat it out again. At first he thought it was chagrin over the state of his room that prevented him from eating, yet he soon got used to the various changes in his room. It had become a habit in the family to push into his room things there was no room for elsewhere, and there were plenty of these now, since one of the rooms had been let to three lodgers. These serious gentlemen—all three of them with full beards, as Gregor once observed through a crack in the door—had a passion for order, not only in their own room but,

since they were now members of the household, in all its arrangements, especially in the kitchen. Superfluous, not to say dirty, objects they could not bear. Besides, they had brought with them most
of the furnishings they needed. For this reason many things could
be dispensed with that it was no use trying to sell but that should
not be thrown away either. All of them found their way into Gregor's
room. The ash can likewise and the kitchen garbage can. Anything
that was not needed for the moment was simply flung into Gregor's
room by the charwoman, who did everything in a hurry; fortunately
Gregor usually saw only the object, whatever it was, and the hand
that held it. Perhaps she intended to take the things away again
as time and opportunity offered, or to collect them until she could
throw them all out in a heap, but in fact they just lay wherever
she happened to throw them, except when Gregor pushed his way
through the junk heap and shifted it somewhat, at first out of necessity, because he had not room enough to crawl, but later with increasing enjoyment, although after such excursions, being sad and
weary to death, he would lie motionless for hours. And since the
lodgers often ate their supper at home in the common living room,
the living-room door stayed shut many an evening, yet Gregor reconciled himself quite easily to the shutting of the door, for often
enough on evenings when it was opened he had disregarded it entirely and lain in the darkest corner of his room, quite unnoticed by
the family. But on one occasion the charwoman left the door open
a little and it stayed ajar even when the lodgers came in for supper
and the lamp was lit. They set themselves at the top end of the
table where formerly Gregor and his father and mother had eaten
their meals, unfolded their napkins and took knife and fork in hand.
At once his mother appeared in the other doorway with a dish of
meat and close behind her his sister with a dish of potatoes piled high.
The food steamed with a thick vapor. The lodgers bent over the food
set before them as if to scrutinize it before eating, in fact the man in
the middle, who seemed to pass for an authority with the other two,
cut a piece of meat as it lay on the dish, obviously to discover if it were
tender or should be sent back to the kitchen. He showed satisfaction,
and Gregor's mother and sister, who had been watching anxiously,
breathed freely and began to smile.

The family itself took its meals in the kitchen. None the less,
Gregor's father came into the living room before going into the kitch-
en and with one prolonged bow, cap in hand, made a round of the
table. The lodgers all stood up and murmured something in their
beards. When they were alone again they ate their food in almost
complete silence. It seemed remarkable to Gregor that among the
various noises coming from the table he could always distinguish the
sound of their masticating teeth, as if this were a sign to Gregor

that one needed teeth in order to eat, and that with toothless jaws even of the finest make one could do nothing. "I'm hungry enough," said Gregor sadly to himself, "but not for that kind of food. How these lodgers are stuffing themselves, and here am I dying of starvation!"

On that very evening—during the whole of his time there Gregor could not remember ever having heard the violin—the sound of violin-playing came from the kitchen. The lodgers had already finished their supper, the one in the middle had brought out a newspaper and given the other two a page apiece, and now they were leaning back at ease reading and smoking. When the violin began to play they pricked up their ears, got to their feet, and went on tiptoe to the hall door where they stood huddled together. Their movements must have been heard in the kitchen, for Gregor's father called out: "Is the violin-playing disturbing you, gentlemen? It can be stopped at once." "On the contrary," said the middle lodger, "could not Fräulein Samsa come and play in this room, beside us, where it is much more convenient and comfortable?" "Oh certainly," cried Gregor's father, as if he were the violin-player. The lodgers came back into the living room and waited. Presently Gregor's father arrived with the music stand, his mother carrying the music and his sister with the violin. His sister quietly made everything ready to start playing; his parents, who had never let rooms before and so had an exaggerated idea of the courtesy due to lodgers, did not venture to sit down on their own chairs; his father leaned against the door, the right hand thrust between two buttons of his livery coat, which was formally buttoned up; but his mother was offered a chair by one of the lodgers and, since she left the chair just where he had happened to put it, sat down in a corner to one side.

Gregor's sister began to play; the father and mother, from either side, intently watched the movements of her hands. Gregor, attracted by the playing, ventured to move forward a little until his head was actually inside the living room. He felt hardly any surprise at his growing lack of consideration for the others; there had been a time when he prided himself on being considerate. And yet just on this occasion he had more reason than ever to hide himself, since owing to the amount of dust which lay thick in his room and rose into the air at the slightest movement, he too was covered with dust; fluff and hair and remnants of food trailed with him, caught on his back and along his sides; his indifference to everything was much too great for him to turn on his back and scrape himself clean on the carpet, as once he had done several times a day. And in spite of his condition, no shame deterred him from advancing a little over the spotless floor of the living room.

To be sure, no one was aware of him. The family was entirely absorbed in the violin-playing; the lodgers, however, who first of all had stationed themselves, hands in pockets, much too close behind the music stand so that they could all have read the music, which must have bothered his sister, had soon retreated to the window, half-whispering with downbent heads, and stayed there while his father turned an anxious eye on them. Indeed, they were making it more than obvious that they had been disappointed in their expectation of hearing good or enjoyable violin-playing, that they had had more than enough of the performance and only out of courtesy suffered a continued disturbance of their peace. From the way they all kept blowing the smoke of their cigars high in the air through nose and mouth one could divine their irritation. And yet Gregor's sister was playing so beautifully. Her face leaned sideways, intently and sadly her eyes followed the notes of music. Gregor crawled a little farther forward and lowered his head to the ground so that it might be possible for his eyes to meet hers. Was he an animal, that music had such an effect upon him? He felt as if the way were opening before him to the unknown nourishment he craved. He was determined to push forward till he reached his sister, to pull at her skirt and so let her know that she was to come into his room with her violin, for no one here appreciated her playing as he would appreciate it. He would never let her out of his room, at least, not so long as he lived; his frightful appearance would become, for the first time, useful to him; he would watch all the doors of his room at once and spit at intruders; but his sister should need no constraint, she should stay with him of her own free will; she should sit beside him on the sofa, bend down her ear to him and hear him confide that he had had the firm intention of sending her to the Conservatorium, and that, but for his mishap, last Christmas—surely Christmas was long past?—he would have announced it to everybody without allowing a single objection. After this confession his sister would be so touched that she would burst into tears, and Gregor would then raise himself to her shoulder and kiss her on the neck, which, now that she went to business, she kept free of any ribbon or collar.

"Mr. Samsa!" cried the middle lodger, to Gregor's father, and pointed, without wasting any more words, at Gregor, now working himself slowly forwards. The violin fell silent, the middle lodger first smiled to his friends with a shake of the head and then looked at Gregor again. Instead of driving Gregor out, his father seemed to think it more needful to begin by soothing down the lodgers, although they were not at all agitated and apparently found Gregor more entertaining than the violin-playing. He hurried towards them and spreading out his arms, tried to urge them back into their own room and at the same time to block their view of Gregor. They now began to be really a little angry, one could not tell whether because of the old man's behavior or because it had just dawned on them that all unwittingly they had such a neighbor as Gregor next door. They demanded explanations of his father, they waved their arms like him, tugged uneasily at their beards, and only with reluctance backed towards their room. Meanwhile Gregor's sister, who stood there as if lost when her playing was so abruptly broken off, came to life again, pulled herself together all at once after standing for a while holding violin and bow in nervelessly hanging hands and staring at her music, pushed her violin into the lap of her mother, who was still sitting in her chair fighting asthmatically for breath, and ran into the lodgers' room to which they were now being shepherded by her father rather more quickly than before. One could see the pillows and blankets on the beds flying under her accustomed fingers and being laid in order. Before the lodgers had actually reached their room she had finished making the beds and slipped out.

The old man seemed once more to be so possessed by his mulish self-assertiveness that he was forgetting all the respect he should show to his lodgers. He kept driving them on and driving them on until in the very door of the bedroom the middle lodger stamped his foot loudly on the floor and so brought him to a halt. "I beg to announce," said the lodger, lifting one hand and looking also at Gregor's mother and sister, "that because of the disgusting conditions prevailing in this household and family"—here he spat on the floor with emphatic brevity—"I give you notice on the spot. Naturally I won't pay you a penny for the days I have lived here, on the contrary I shall consider bringing an action for damages against you, based on claims—believe me—that will be easily susceptible of proof." He ceased and stared straight in front of him, as if he expected something. In fact his two friends at once rushed into the breach with these words: "And we too give notice on the spot." On that he seized the door-handle and shut the door with a slam.

Gregor's father, groping with his hands, staggered forward and fell into his chair; it looked as if he were stretching himself there for his ordinary evening nap, but the marked jerkings of his head, which was as if uncontrollable, showed that he was far from asleep. Gregor had simply stayed quietly all the time on the spot where the lodgers had espied him. Disappointment at the failure of his plan, perhaps also the weakness arising from extreme hunger, made it impossible for him to move. He feared, with a fair degree of certainty, that at any moment the general tension would discharge itself in a combined attack upon him, and he lay waiting. He did not react even to the noise made by the violin as it fell off his mother's lap from under her trembling fingers and gave out a resonant note.

"My dear parents," said his sister, slapping her hand on the table by way of introduction, "things can't go on like this. Perhaps you don't realize that, but I do. I won't utter my brother's name in the presence of this creature, and so all I say is: we must try to get rid of it. We've tried to look after it and to put up with it as far as is humanly possible, and I don't think anyone could reproach us in the slightest."

"She is more than right," said Gregor's father to himself. His mother, who was still choking for lack of breath, began to cough hollowly into her hand with a wild look in her eyes.

His sister rushed over to her and held her forehead. His father's thoughts seemed to have lost their vagueness at Grete's words, he sat more upright, fingering his service cap that lay among the plates still lying on the table from the lodgers' supper, and from time to time looked at the still form of Gregor.

"We must try to get rid of it," his sister now said explicitly to her father, since her mother was coughing too much to hear a word, "it will be the death of both of you, I can see that coming. When one has to work as hard as we do, all of us, one can't stand this continual torment at home on top of it. At least I can't stand it any longer." And she burst into such a passion of sobbing that her tears dropped on her mother's face, where she wiped them off mechanically.

"My dear," said the old man sympathetically, and with evident understanding, "but what can we do?"

Gregor's sister merely shrugged her shoulders to indicate the feeling of helplessness that had now overmastered her during her weeping fit, in contrast to her former confidence.

"If he could understand us," said her father, half questioningly; Grete, still sobbing, vehemently waved a hand to show how unthinkable that was.

"If he could understand us," repeated the old man, shutting his eyes to consider his daughter's conviction that understanding was impossible, "then perhaps we might come to some agreement with him. But as it is—"

"He must go," cried Gregor's sister, "that's the only solution, Father. You must just try to get rid of the idea that this is Gregor. The fact that we've believed it for so long is the root of all our trouble. But how can it be Gregor? If this were Gregor, he would have realized long ago that human beings can't live with such a creature, and he'd have gone away on his own accord. Then we wouldn't have any brother, but we'd be able to go on living and keep his memory in honor. As it is, this creature persecutes us, drives away our lodgers, obviously wants the whole apartment to himself and would have us all sleep in the gutter. Just look, Father," she shrieked all at once, "he's at it again!" And in an access of panic that was quite incomprehensible to Gregor she even quitted her mother, literally thrusting the chair from her as if she would rather sacrifice her mother than stay so near to Gregor, and rushed behind her father, who also rose up, being simply upset by her agitation, and half-spread his arms out as if to protect her.

Yet Gregor had not the slightest intention of frightening anyone, far less his sister. He had only begun to turn round in order to crawl back to his room, but it was certainly a startling operation to watch, since because of his disabled condition he could not execute the difficult turning movements except by lifting his head and then bracing it against the floor over and over again. He paused and looked round. His good intentions seemed to have been recognized; the alarm had only been momentary. Now they were all watching him in melancholy silence. His mother lay in her chair, her legs stiffly outstretched and pressed together, her eyes almost closing for sheer weariness; his father and his sister were sitting beside each other, his sister's arm around the old man's neck.

Perhaps I can go on turning round now, thought Gregor, and began his labors again. He could not stop himself from panting with the effort, and had to pause now and then to take breath. Nor did anyone harass him, he was left entirely to himself. When he had completed the turn-round he began at once to crawl straight back. He was amazed at the distance separating him from his room and could not understand how in his weak state he had managed to accomplish the same journey so recently, almost without remarking it. Intent on crawling as fast as possible, he barely noticed that not a single word, not an ejaculation from his family, interfered with his progress. Only when he was already in the doorway did he turn his head round, not completely, for his neck muscles were getting stiff, but enough to see that nothing had changed behind him except that his sister had risen to her feet. His last glance fell on his mother, who was not quite overcome by sleep.

Hardly was he well inside his room when the door was hastily pushed shut, bolted and locked. The sudden noise in his rear startled him so much that his little legs gave beneath him. It was his sister who had shown such haste. She had been standing ready waiting and had made a light spring forward, Gregor had not even heard her coming, and she cried "At last!" to her parents as she turned the key in the lock.

"And what now?" said Gregor to himself, looking round in the darkness. Soon he made the discovery that he was now unable to stir a limb. This did not surprise him, rather it seemed unnatural that he should ever actually have been able to move on these feeble little legs. Otherwise he felt relatively comfortable. True, his whole body was aching, but it seemed that the pain was gradually growing less and would finally pass away. The rotting apple in his back and the inflamed area around it, all covered with soft dust, already hardly troubled him. He thought of his family with tenderness and love. The decision that he must disappear was one that he held to even more strongly than his sister, if that were possible. In this state of vacant and peaceful meditation he remained until the tower clock struck three in the morning. The first broadening of light in the world outside the window entered his consciousness once more. Then his head sank to the floor of its own accord and from his nostrils came the last faint flicker of his breath.

When the charwoman arrived early in the morning—what between her strength and her impatience she slammed all the doors so loudly, never mind how often she had been begged not to do so, that no one in the whole apartment could enjoy any quiet sleep after her arrival—she noticed nothing unusual as she took her customary peep into Gregor's room. She thought he was lying motionless on purpose, pretending to be in the sulks; she credited him with every kind of intelligence. Since she happened to have the long-handled broom in her hand she tried to tickle him up with it from the doorway. When that too produced no reaction she felt provoked and poked at him a little harder, and only when she had pushed him along the floor without meeting any resistance was her attention aroused. It did not take her long to establish the truth of the matter, and her eyes widened, she let out a whistle, yet did not waste much time over it but tore open the door of the Samsas' bedroom and yelled into the darkness at the top of her voice: "Just look at this, it's dead; it's lying here dead and done for!"

Mr. and Mrs. Samsa started up in their double bed and before they realized the nature of the charwoman's announcement had some difficulty in overcoming the shock of it. But then they got out of bed quickly, one on either side, Mr. Samsa throwing a blanket over his shoulders, Mrs. Samsa in nothing but her nightgown; in this array they entered Gregor's room. Meanwhile the door of the living room opened, too, where Grete had been sleeping since the advent of the lodgers; she was completely dressed as if she had not been to bed, which seemed to be confirmed also by the paleness of her face. "Dead?" said Mrs. Samsa, looking questioningly at the charwoman, although she could have investigated for herself, and the fact was obvious enough without investigation. "I should say so," said the charwoman, proving her words by pushing Gregor's corpse a long way to one side with her broomstick. Mrs. Samsa made a movement as if to stop her, but checked it. "Well," said Mr. Samsa, "now thanks be to God." He crossed himself, and the three women followed his example. Grete, whose eyes never left the corpse, said: "Just see how thin he was. It's such a long time since he's eaten anything. The food came out again just as it went in." Indeed,

Gregor's body was completely flat and dry, as could only now be seen when it was no longer supported by the legs and nothing prevented one from looking closely at it.

"Come in beside us, Grete, for a little while," said Mrs. Samsa with a tremulous smile, and Grete, not without looking back at the corpse, followed her parents into their bedroom. The charwoman shut the door and opened the window wide. Although it was so early in the morning a certain softness was perceptible in the fresh air. After all, it was already the end of March.

The three lodgers emerged from their room and were surprised to see no breakfast; they had been forgotten. "Where's our breakfast?" said the middle lodger peevishly to the charwoman. But she put her finger to her lips and hastily, without a word, indicated by gestures that they should go into Gregor's room. They did so and stood, their hands in the pockets of their somewhat shabby coats, around Gregor's corpse in the room where it was now fully light.

At that the door of the Samsas' bedroom opened and Mr. Samsa appeared in his uniform, his wife on one arm, his daughter on the other. They all looked a little as if they had been crying; from time to time Grete hid her face on her father's arm.

"Leave my house at once!" said Mr. Samsa, and pointed to the door without disengaging himself from the women. "What do you mean by that?" said the middle lodger, taken somewhat aback, with a feeble smile. The two others put their hands behind them and kept rubbing them together, as if in gleeful expectation of a fine set-to in which they were bound to come off the winners. "I mean just what I say," answered Mr. Samsa, and advanced in a straight line with his two companions towards the lodger. He stood his ground at first quietly, looking at the floor as if his thoughts were taking a new pattern in his head. "Then let us go, by all means," he said, and looked up at Mr. Samsa as if in a sudden access of humility he were expecting some renewed sanction for this decision. Mr. Samsa merely nodded briefly once or twice with meaning eyes. Upon that the lodger really did go with long strides into the hall, his two friends had been listening and had quite stopped rubbing their hands for some moments and now went scuttling after him as if afraid that Mr. Samsa might get into the hall before them and cut them off from their leader. In the hall they all three took their hats from the rack, their sticks from the umbrella stand, bowed in silence and quitted the apartment. With a suspiciousness which proved quite unfounded Mr. Samsa and the two women followed them out to the landing; leaning over the banister they watched the three figures slowly but surely going down the long stairs, vanishing from sight at a certain turn of the staircase on every floor and coming into view again after a moment or so; the more they dwindled, the more the Samsa family's interest in them dwindled, and when a butcher's boy met them and passed them on the stairs coming up proudly with a tray on his head, Mr. Samsa and the two women soon left the landing and as if a burden had been lifted from them went back into their apartment.

They decided to spend this day in resting and going for a stroll; they had not only deserved such a respite from work, but absolutely needed it. And so they sat down at the table and wrote three notes of excuse, Mr. Samsa to his board of management, Mrs. Samsa to her employer and Grete to the head of her firm. While they were writing, the charwoman came in to say that she was going now, since her morning's work was finished. At first they only nodded without looking up, but as she kept hovering there they eyed her irritably. "Well?" said Mr. Samsa. The charwoman stood grinning in the doorway as if she had good news to impart to the family but meant not to say a word unless properly questioned. The small ostrich feather standing upright on her hat, which had annoyed Mr. Samsa ever since she was engaged, was waving gaily in all directions. "Well, what is it then?" asked Mrs. Samsa, who obtained more respect from the charwoman than the others. "Oh," said the charwoman, giggling so amiably that she could not at once continue, "just this, you don't need to bother about how to get rid of the thing next door. It's been seen to already." Mrs. Samsa and Grete bent over their letters again, as if preoccupied; Mr. Samsa, who perceived that she was eager to begin describing it all in detail, stopped her with a decisive hand. But since she was not allowed to tell her story, she remembered the great hurry she was in, being obviously deeply huffed: "Bye, everybody," she said, whirling off violently, and departed with a frightful slamming of doors.

"She'll be given notice tonight," said Mr. Samsa, but neither from his wife nor his daughter did he get any answer, for the charwoman seemed to have shattered again the composure they had barely achieved. They rose, went to the window and stayed there, clasping each other tight. Mr. Samsa turned in his chair to look at them and quietly observed them for a little. Then he called out: "Come along, now, do. Let bygones by bygones. And you might have some consideration for me." The two of them complied at once, hastened to him, caressed him and quickly finished their letters.

Then they all three left the apartment together, which was more than they had done for months, and went by tram into the open country outside the town. The tram, in which they were the only passengers, was filled with warm sunshine. Leaning comfortably back in their seats they canvassed their prospects for the future, and it appeared on closer inspection that these were not at all bad, for the jobs they had got, which so far they had never really discussed with each other, were all three admirable and likely to lead to better things later on. The greatest immediate improvement in their condition would of course arise from moving to another house; they wanted to take a smaller and cheaper but also better situated and more easily run apartment than the one they had, which Gregor had selected. While they were thus conversing, it struck both Mr. and Mrs. Samsa, almost at the same moment, as they became aware of their daughter's increasing vivacity, that in spite of all the sorrow of recent times, which had made her cheeks pale, she had bloomed into a pretty girl with a good figure. They grew quieter and half unconsciously exchanged glances of complete agreement, having come to the conclusion that it would soon be time to find a good husband for her. And it was like a confirmation of their new dreams and excellent intentions that at the end of their journey their daughter sprang to her feet first and stretched her young body.

ISAAC BASHEVIS SINGER
(1904–)

The Gentleman from Cracow*

I

Amid thick forests and deep swamps, on the slope of a hill, level at the summit, lay the village of Frampol. Nobody knew who had founded it, or why just there. Goats grazed among the tombstones which were already sunk in the ground of the cemetery. In the community house there was a parchment with a chronicle on it, but the first page was missing and the writing had faded. Legends were current among the people, tales of wicked intrigue concerning a mad nobleman, a lascivious lady, a Jewish scholar, and a wild dog. But their true origin was lost in the past.

Peasants who tilled the surrounding countryside were poor; the land was stubborn. In the village, the Jews were impoverished; their roofs were straw, their floors dirt. In summer many of them wore no shoes, and in cold weather they wrapped their feet in rags or wore sandals made of straw.

Rabbi Ozer, although renowned for his erudition, received a salary of only eighteen groszy a week. The assistant rabbi, besides

* From *Gimpel the Fool*, translated by Martha Glicklich and Elaine Gottlieb. Copyright © 1957 by Isaac Bashevis Singer. Reprinted with the permission of Farrar, Straus and Giroux.

being ritual slaughterer, was teacher, matchmaker, bath attendant, and poorhouse nurse as well. Even those villagers who were considered wealthy knew little of luxury. They wore cotton gabardines, tied about their waists with string, and tasted meat only on the Sabbath. Gold coin was rarely seen in Frampol.

But the inhabitants of Frampol had been blessed with fine children. The boys grew tall and strong, the girls handsome. It was a mixed blessing, however, for the young men left to marry girls from other towns, while their sisters, who had no dowries, remained unwed. Yet despite everything, inexplicably, though the food was scarce and the water foul, the children continued to thrive.

Then, one summer, there was a drought. Even the oldest peasants could not recall a calamity such as this one. No rain fell. The corn was parched and stunted. There was scarcely anything worth harvesting. Not until the few sheaves of wheat had been cut and gathered did the rain come, and with it hail which destroyed whatever grain the drought had spared. Locusts huge as birds came in the wake of the storm; human voices were said to issue from their throats. They flew at the eyes of the peasants who tried to drive them away. That year there was no fair, for everything had been lost. Neither the peasants nor the Jews of Frampol had food. Although there was grain in the large towns, no one could buy it.

Just when all hope had been abandoned and the entire town was about to go begging, a miracle occurred. A carriage, drawn by eight spirited horses, came into Frampol. The villagers expected its occupant to be a Christian gentleman, but it was a Jew, a young man between the ages of twenty and thirty, who alighted. Tall and pale, with a round black beard and fiery dark eyes, he wore a sable hat, silver-buckled shoes, and a beaver-trimmed caftan.[1] Around his waist was a green silk sash. Aroused, the entire town rushed to get a glimpse of the stranger. This is the story he told: He was a doctor, a widower from Cracow. His wife, the daughter of a wealthy merchant, had died with their baby in childbirth.

Overwhelmed, the villagers asked why he had come to Frampol. It was on the advice of a Wonder Rabbi, he told them. The melancholy he had known after his wife's death, would, the rabbi assured him, disappear in Frampol. From the poorhouse the beggars came, crowding about him as he distributed alms—three groszy, six grozy, half-gulden pieces. The stranger was clearly a gift from Heaven, and Frampol was not destined to vanish. The beggars hurried to the baker for bread, and the baker sent to Zamosc for a sack of flour.

"One sack?" the young doctor asked. "Why that won't last a single day. I will order a wagonload, and not only flour, but cornmeal also."

1. A long garment with long sleeves and a girdle.

"But we have no money," the village elders explained.

"God willing, you will repay me when times are good," and saying this, the stranger produced a purse crammed with golden ducats. Frampol rejoiced as he counted out the coins.

The next day, wagons filled with flour, buckwheat, barley, millet, and beans, drove into Frampol. News of the village's good fortune reached the ears of the peasants, and they came to the Jews, to buy goods, as the Egyptians had once come to Joseph. Being without money, they paid in kind; as a result, there was meat in town. Now the ovens burned once more; the pots were full. Smoke rose from the chimneys, sending the odors of roast chicken and goose, onion and garlic, fresh bread and pastry, into the evening air. The villagers returned to their occupations; shoemakers mended shoes; tailors picked up their rusted shears and irons.

The evenings were warm and the sky clear, though the Feast of the Tabernacles had already passed. The stars seemed unusually large. Even the birds were awake, and they chirped and warbled as though in mid-summer. The stranger from Cracow had taken the best room at the inn, and his dinner consisted of broiled duck, marchpane,[2] and twisted bread. Apricots and Hungarian wine were his dessert. Six candles adorned the table. One evening after dinner, the doctor from Cracow entered the large public room where some of the more inquisitive townspeople had gathered and asked, "Would anyone care for a game of cards?"

"But it isn't Chanukah[3] yet," they answered in surprise.

"Why wait for Chanukah? I'll put up a gulden for every groszy."

A few of the more frivolous men were willing to try their luck, and it turned out to be good. A groszy meant a gulden, and one gulden became thirty. Anyone played who wished to do so. Everybody won. But the stranger did not seem distressed. Banknotes and coins of silver and gold covered the table. Women and girls crowded into the room, and it seemed as though the gleam of the gold before them was reflected in their eyes. They gasped in wonderment. Never before in Frampol had such things happened. Mothers cautioned their daughters to take pains with their hair, and allowed them to dress in holiday clothes. The girl who found favor in the eyes of the young doctor would be fortunate; he was not one to require a dowry.

II

The next morning, matchmakers called on him, each extolling the virtues of the girl he represented. The doctor invited them to be

2. Marzipan.
3. The Jewish "Feast of Lights," commemorating the rededication of the Temple in Jerusalem by Judas Maccabaeus and his brothers in 165 B.C.

seated, served them honey cake, macaroons, nuts, and mead, and announced, "From each of you I get exactly the same story: Your client is beautiful and clever and possesses every possible distinction. But how can I know which of you is telling the truth? I want the finest of them all as my wife. Here is what I suggest: Let there be a ball to which all the eligible young women are invited. By observing their appearance and behavior, I shall be able to choose among them. Then the marriage contract will be drawn and the wedding arranged."

The matchmakers were astounded. Old Mendel was the first to find words. "A ball? That sort of thing is all right for rich Gentiles, but we Jews have not indulged in such festivities since the destruction of the Temple—except when the Law prescribes it for certain holidays."

"Isn't every Jew obliged to marry off his daughters?" asked the doctor.

"But the girls have no appropriate clothes," another matchmaker protested. "Because of the drought they would have to go in rags."

"I will see that they all have clothes. I'll order enough silk, wool, velvet, and linen from Zamosc to outfit every girl. Let the ball take place. Let it be one that Frampol will never forget."

"But where can we hold it?" another matchmaker interjected. "The hall where we used to hold weddings has burned down, and our cottages are too small."

"There's the market place," the gentleman from Cracow suggested.

"But it is already the month of Heshvan. Any day now, it will turn cold."

"We'll choose a warm night when the moon is out. Don't worry about it."

To all the numerous objections of the matchmakers, the stranger had an answer ready. Finally they agreed to consult the elders. The doctor said he was in no hurry, he would await their decision. During the entire discussion, he had been carrying on a game of chess with one of the town's cleverest young men, while munching raisins.

The elders were incredulous when they heard what had been proposed. But the young girls were excited. The young men approved also. The mothers pretended to hesitate, but finally gave their consent. When a delegation of the older men sought out Rabbi Ozer for his approval, he was outraged.

"What kind of charlatan is this?" he shouted. "Frampol is not Cracow. All we need is a ball! Heaven forbid that we bring down a plague, and innocent infants be made to pay for our frivolity!"

But the more practical of the men reasoned with the rabbi, saying, "Our daughters walk around barefoot and in tatters now. He will provide them with shoes and clothing. If one of them should please him he would marry her and settle here. Certainly that is to our advantage. The synagogue needs a new roof. The windowpanes of the house of study are broken, the bathhouse is badly in need of repairs. In the poorhouse the sick lie on bundles of rotting straw."

"All this is true. But suppose we sin?"

"Everything will be done according to the Law, Rabbi. You can trust us."

Taking down the book of the Law, Rabbi Ozer leafed through it. Occasionally he stopped to study a page, and then, finally, after sighing and hesitating, he consented. Was there any choice? He himself had received no salary for six months.

As soon as the rabbi had given his consent there was a great display of activity. The dry goods merchants traveled immediately to Zamosc and Yanev, returning with cloth and leather paid for by the gentleman from Cracow. The tailors and seamstresses worked day and night; the cobblers left their benches only to pray. The young women, all anticipation, were in a feverish state. Vaguely remembered dance steps were tried out. They baked cakes and other pastries, and used up their stores of jams and preserves which they had been keeping in readiness for illness. The Frampol musicians were equally active. Cymbals, fiddles, and bagpipes, long forgotten and neglected, had to be dusted off and tuned. Gaiety infected even the very old, for it was rumored that the elegant doctor planned a banquet for the poor where alms would be distributed.

The eligible girls were wholly concerned wth self-improvement. They scrubbed their skin and arranged their hair, a few even visited the ritual bath to bathe among the married women. In the evenings, faces flushed, eyes sparkling, they met at each other's houses, to tell stories and ask riddles. It was difficult for them, and for their mothers as well, to sleep at night. Fathers sighed as they slept. And suddenly the young girls of Frampol seemed so attractive that the young men who had contemplated marrying outside of town fell in love with them. Although the young men still sat in the study-house poring over the Talmud,[4] its wisdom no longer penetrated to them. It was the ball alone that they spoke of now, only the ball that occupied their thoughts.

The doctor from Cracow also enjoyed himself. He changed his clothes several times daily. First it was a silk coat worn with pompommed slippers, then a woolen caftan with high boots. At one meal he wore a pelerine[5] trimmed with beaver tails, and at the next a cape embroidered with flowers and leaves. He breakfasted on roast pigeon which he washed down with dry wine. For lunch he ordered

---

4. The collection of commentaries on oral laws dating from postbiblical times.   5. Cloak.

egg noodles and blintzes, and he was audacious enough to eat Sabbath pudding on weekdays. He never attended prayer, but instead played all sorts of games: cards, goats and wolves, coin-pitching. Having finished lunch, he would drive through the neighborhood with his coachman. The peasants would lift their hats as he passed, and bow almost to the ground. One day he strolled through Frampol with a gold-headed cane. Women crowded to the windows to observe him, and boys, following after him, picked up the rock candy he tossed them. In the evenings he and his companions, gay young men, drank wine until all hours. Rabbi Ozer constantly warned his flock that they walked a downhill path led by the Evil One, but they paid no attention to him. Their minds and hearts were completely possessed by the ball, which would be held at the market place in the middle of that month, at the time of the full moon.

III

At the edge of town, in a small valley close to a swamp, stood a hut no larger than a chicken coop. Its floor was dirt, its window was boarded; and the roof, because it was covered with green and yellow moss, made one think of a bird's nest that had been forsaken. Heaps of garbage were strewn before the hut, and lime ditches furrowed the soggy earth. Amidst the refuse there was an occasional chair without a seat, a jug missing an ear, a table without legs. Every type of broom, bone, and rag seemed to be rotting there. This was where Lipa the Ragpicker lived iwth his daughter, Hodle. While his first wife was alive, Lipa had been a respected merchant in Frampol where he occupied a pew at the east wall of the synagogue. But after his wife had drowned herself in the river, his condition declined rapidly. He took to drink, associated with the town's worst element, and soon ended up bankrupt.

His second wife, a beggar woman from Yanev, bore him a daughter whom she left behind when she deserted him for non-support. Unconcerned about his wife's departure, Lipa allowed the child to shift for herself. Each week he spent a few days collecting rags from the garbage. The rest of the time he was in the tavern. Although the innkeeper's wife scolded him, she received only abusive answers in reply. Lipa had his success among the men as a tale-spinner. He attracted business to the place with his fantastic yarns about witches and windmills and devils and goblins. He could also recite Polish and Ukrainian rhymes and had a knack for telling jokes. The innkeeper allowed him to occupy a place near the stove, and from time to time he was given a bowl of soup and a piece of bread. Old friends, remembering Lipa's former affluence, occasionally presented him with a pair of pants, a threadbare coat, or a shirt. He accepted everything ungraciously. He even stuck out his tongue at his benefactors as they turned away from him.

As in the saying, "Like father, like son," Hodle inherited the vices of both parents—her drunken father, her begging mother. By the time she was six, she had won a reputation as a glutton and thief. Barefoot and half-naked, she roamed the town, entering houses and raiding the larders of those who were not home. She preyed on chickens and ducks, cut their throats with glass, and ate them. Although the inhabitants of Frampol had often warned her father that he was rearing a wanton, the information did not seem to bother him. He seldom spoke to her and she did not even call him father. When she was twelve, her lasciviousness became a matter of discussion among the women. Gypsies visited her shack, and it was rumored that she devoured the meat of cats and dogs, in fact, every kind of carcass. Tall and lean, with red hair and green eyes, she went barefoot summer and winter, and her skirts were made of colored scraps discarded by the seamstresses. She was feared by mothers who said she wove spells that blighted the young. The village elders who admonished her received brazen answers. She had the shrewdness of a bastard, the quick tongue of an adder, and when attacked by street urchins, did not hesitate to strike back. Particularly skilled in swearing, she had an unlimited repertoire. It was like her to call out, "Pox on your tongue and gangrene in your eyes," or, possibly, "May you rot till the skunks run from your smell."

Occasionally her curses were effective, and the town grew wary of incurring her anger. But as she matured she tended to avoid the town proper, and the time came when she was almost forgotten. But on the day that the Frampol merchants, in preparation for the ball, distributed cloth and leather among the town's young women, Hodle reappeared. She was now about seventeen, fully grown, though still in short skirts; her face was freckled, and her hair disheveled. Beads, such as those worn by gypsies, encircled her throat, and on her wrists were bracelets made from wolves' teeth. Pushing her way through the crowd, she demanded her share. There was nothing left but a few odds and ends, which were given to her. Furious with her allotment, she hastened home with it. Those who had seen what had happened laughed, "Look who's going to the ball! What a pretty picture she'll make!"

At last the shoemakers and tailors were done; every dress fit, every shoe was right. The days were miraculously warm, and the nights as luminous as the evenings of Pentecost. It was the morning star that, on the day of the ball, woke the entire town. Tables and benches lined one side of the market. The cooks had already roasted calves, sheep, goats, geese, ducks, and chicken, and had baked sponge and raisin cakes, braided bread and rolls, onion biscuits, and ginger bread. There were mead and be:r and a barrel of Hungarian wine that had been brought by the wine dealer. When the children arrived they brought the bows and arrows with which they were accustomed to play at the Omer feast, as well as their Purim rattles and Torah flags. Even the doctor's horses were decorated with willow branches and autumn flowers, and the coachmen paraded them through the town. Apprentices left their work, and yeshiva[6] students their volumes of the Talmud. And despite Rabbi Ozer's injunction against the young matrons' attending the ball, they dressed in their wedding gowns and went, arriving with the young girls, who also came in white, each bearing a candle in her hand as though she were a bridesmaid. The band had already begun to play, and the music was lively. Rabbi Ozer alone was not present, having locked himself in his study. His maidservant had gone to the ball, leaving him to himself. He knew no good could come of such behavior, but there was nothing he could do to prevent it.

By late afternoon all the girls had gathered in the market place, surrounded by the townspeople. Drums were beaten. Jesters performed. The girls danced; first a quadrille, then a scissor dance. Next it was Kozack, and finally the Dance of Anger. Now the moon appeared, although the sun had not yet set. It was time for the gentleman from Cracow. He entered on a white mare, flanked by bodyguards and his best man. He wore a large-plumed hat, and silver buttons flashed on his green coat. A sword hung at his side, and his shiny boots rested in the stirrups. He resembled a gentleman off to war with his entourage. Silently he sat in his saddle, watching the girls as they danced. How graceful they were, how charmingly they moved! But one who did not dance was the daughter of Lipa the Ragpicker. She stood to one side, ignored by them all.

IV

The setting sun, remarkably large, stared down angrily like a heavenly eye upon the Frampol market place. Never before had Frampol seen such a sunset. Like rivers of burning sulphur, fiery clouds streamed across the heavens, assuming the shapes of elephants, lions, snakes, and monsters. They seemed to be waging a battle in the sky, devouring one another, spitting, breathing fire. It almost seemed to be the River of Fire they watched, where demons tortured the evil-doers amidst glowing coals and heaps of ashes. The moon swelled, became vast, blood-red, spotted, scarred, and gave off little light. The evening grew very dark, dissolving even the stars. The young men fetched torches, and a barrel of burning pitch was

6. School for advanced studies.

prepared. Shadows danced back and forth as though attending a ball of their own. Around the market place the houses seemed to vibrate; roofs quivered, chimneys shook. Such gaiety and intoxication had never before been known in Frampol. Everyone, for the first time in months, had eaten and drunk sufficiently. Even the animals participated in the merry-making. Horses neighed, cows mooed, and the few roosters that had survived the slaughter of the fowl crowed. Flocks of crows and strange birds flew in to pick at the leavings. Fireflies illumined the darkness, and lightning flashed on the horizon. But there was no thunder. A weird circular light glowed in the sky for a few moments and then suddenly plummeted toward the horizon, a crimson tail behind it, resembling a burning rod. Then, as everyone stared in wonder at the sky, the gentleman frim Cracow spoke: "Listen to me. I have wonderful things to tell you, but let no one be overcome by joy. Men, take hold of your wives. Young men, look to your girls. You see in me the wealthiest man in the entire world. Money is sand to me, and diamonds are pebbles. I come from the land of Ophir, where King Solomon found the gold for his temple. I dwell in the palace of the Queen of Sheba. My coach is solid gold, its wheels inlaid with sapphires, with axles of ivory, its lamps studded with rubies and emeralds, opals and amethysts. The Ruler of the Ten Lost Tribes of Israel knows of your miseries, and he has sent me to be your benefactor. But there is one condition. Tonight, every virgin must marry. I will provide a dowry of ten thousand ducats for each maiden, as well as a string of pearls that will hang to her knees. But make haste. Every girl must have a husband before the clocks strike twelve."

The crowd was hushed. It was as quiet as New Year's Day before the blowing of the ram's horn. One could hear the buzzing of a fly.

Then one old man called out, "But that's impossible. The girls are not even engaged!"

"Let them become engaged."

"To whom?"

"We can draw lots," the gentleman from Cracow replied. "Whoever is to be married will have his or her name written on a card. Mine also. And then we shall draw to see who is meant for whom."

"But a girl must wait seven days. She must have the prescribed ablutions."

"Let the sin be on me. She needn't wait."

Despite the protestations of the old men and their wives, a sheet of paper was torn into pieces, and on each piece the name of a young man or young woman was written by a scribe. The town's beadle, now in the service of the gentleman from Cracow, drew from one skullcap the names of the young men, and from another those of the young women, chanting their names to the same tune with which he called up members of the congregation for the reading of the Torah.

"Nahum, son of Katriel, betrothed to Yentel, daughter of Nathan. Solomon, son of Cov Baer, betrothed to Tryna, daughter of Jonah Lieb." The assortment was a strange one, but since in the night all sheep are black, the matches seemed reasonable enough. After each drawing, the newly engaged couple, hand in hand, approached the doctor to collect the dowry and wedding gift. As he had promised, the gentleman from Cracow gave each the stipulated sum of ducats, and on the neck of each bride he hung a strand of pearls. Now the mothers, unable to restrain their joy, began to dance and shout. The fathers stood by, bewildered. When the girls lifted their dresses to catch the gold coins given by the doctor, their legs and underclothing were exposed, which sent the men into paroxysms of lust. Fiddles screeched, drums pounded, trumpets blared. The uproar was deafening. Twelve-year-old boys were mated with "spinsters" of nineteen. The sons of substantial citizens took the daughters of paupers as brides; midgets were coupled with giants, beauties with cripples. On the last two slips appeared the names of the gentleman from Cracow and Hodle, the daughter of Lipa the Ragpicker.

The same old man who had called out previously said, "Woe unto us, the girl is a harlot."

"Come to me, Hodle, come to your bridegroom," the doctor bade.

Hodle, her hair in two long braids, dressed in a calico skirt, and with sandals on her feet, did not wait to be asked twice. As soon as she had been called she walked to where the gentleman from Cracow sat on his mare, and fell to her knees. She prostrated herself seven times before him.

"Is it true, what that old fool says?" her prospective husband asked her.

"Yes, my lord, it is so."

"Have you sinned only with Jews or with Gentiles as well?"

"With both."

"Was it for bread?"

"No. For the sheer pleasure."

"How old were you when you started?"

"Not quite ten."

"Are you sorry for what you have done?"

"No."

"Why not?"

"Why should I be?" she answered shamelessly.

"You don't fear the tortures of hell?"

"I fear nothing—not even God. There is no God."

Once more the old man began to scream, "Woe to us, woe to us, Jews! A fire is upon us, burning, Jews, Satan's fire. Save your souls. Jews. Flee, before it is too late!"

"Gag him," the gentleman from Cracow commanded.

The guards seized the old man and gagged him. The doctor leading Hodle by the hand, began to dance. Now, as though the powers of darkness had been summoned, the rain and hail began to fall; flashes of lightning were accompanied by mighty thunderclaps. But, heedless of the storm, pious men and women embraced without shame, dancing and shouting as though possessed. Even the old were affected. In the furor, dresses were ripped, shoes shaken off, hats, wigs and skullcaps trampled in the mud. Sashes, slipping to the ground, twisted there like snakes. Suddenly there was a terrific crash. A huge bolt of lightning had simultaneously struck the synagogue, the study house, and the ritual bath. The whole town was on fire.

Now at last the deluded people realized that there was no natural origin to these occurrences. Although the rain continued to fall and even increased in intensity, the fire was not extinguished. An eerie light glowed in the market place. Those few prudent individuals who tried to disengage themselves from the demented crowd were crushed to earth and trampled.

And then the gentleman from Cracow revealed his true identity. He was no longer the young man the villagers had welcomed, but a creature covered with scales, with an eye in his chest, and on his forehead a horn that rotated at great speed. His arms were covered with hair, thorns, and elflocks, and his tail was a mass of live serpents, for he was none other than Ketev Mriri, Chief of the Devils.

Witches, werewolves, imps, demons, and hobgoblins plummeted from the sky, some on brooms, others on hoops, still others on spiders. Osnath, the daughter of Machlath, her fiery hair loosened in the wind, her breasts bare and thighs exposed, leaped from chimney to chimney, and skated along the eaves. Namah, Hurmizah the daughter of Aff, and many other she-devils did all sorts of somersaults. Satan himself gave away the bridegroom, while four evil spirits held the poles of the canopy, which had turned into writhing pythons. Four dogs escorted the groom. Hodle's dress fell from her and she stood naked. Her breasts hung down to her navel and her feet were webbed. Her hair was a wilderness of worms and caterpillars. The groom held out a triangular ring and, instead of saying, "With this ring be thou consecrated to me according to the laws of

Moses and Israel," he said, "With this ring, be thou desecrated to me according to the blasphemy of Korah and Ishmael." And instead of wishing the pair good luck, the evil spirits called out, "Bad luck," and they began to chant:

> *"The curse of Eve, the Mark of Cain,*
> *the cunning of the snake, unite the twain."*

Screaming for the last time, the old man clutched at his head and died. Ketev Mriri began his eulogy:

> *"Devil's dung and Satan's spell*
> *Bring his ghost to roast in hell."*

v

In the middle of the night, old Rabbi Ozer awoke. Since he was a holy man, the fire which was consuming the town had no power over his house. Sitting up in bed he looked about, wondering if dawn were already breaking. But it was neither day nor night without. The sky was a fiery red, and from the distance came a clamor of shouts and songs that resembled the howling of wild beasts. At first, recalling nothing, the old man wondered what was going on. "Has the world come to an end? Or have I failed to hear the ram's horn heralding the Messiah? Has He arrived?" Washing his hands, he put on his slippers and overcoat and went out.

The town was unrecognizable. Where houses had been, only chimneys stood. Mounds of coal smoldered here and there. He called the beadle, but there was no answer. With his cane, the rabbi went searching for his flock.

"Where are you, Jews, where are you?" he called piteously.

The earth scorched his feet, but he did not slacken his pace. Mad dogs and strange beings attacked him, but he wielded his cane against them. His sorrow was so great that he felt no fear. Where the market place used to be, a terrible sight met him. There was nothing but one great swamp, full of mud, slime, and ashes. Floundering in mud up to their waists, a crowd of naked people went through the movements of dance. At first, the rabbi mistook the weirdly moving figures for devils, and was about to recite the chapter, "Let there be contentment," and other passages dealing with exorcism, when he recognized the men of his town. Only then did he remember the doctor from Cracow, and the rabbi cried out bitterly, "Jews, for the sake of God, save your souls! You are in the hands of Satan!"

But the townspeople, too entranced to heed his cries, continued their frenzied movements for a long time, jumping like frogs, shaking as though with fever. With hair uncovered and breasts bare, the women laughed, cried and swayed. Catching a yeshiva boy by the sidelocks, a girl pulled him to her lap. A woman tugged at the beard of a strange man. Old men and women were immersed in slime up to their loins. They scarcely looked alive.

Relentlessly, the rabbi urged the people to resist evil. Reciting the Torah and other holy books, as well as incantations and the several names of God, he succeeded in rousing some of them. Soon others responded. The rabbi had helped the first man from the mire, then that one assisted the next, and so on. Most of them had recovered by the time the morning star appeared. Perhaps the spirits of their forebears had interceded, for although many had sinned, only one man had died this night in the market place square.

Now the men were appalled, realizing that the devil had bewitched them, had dragged them through muck; and they wept.

"Where is our money?" the girls wailed, "And our gold and our jewelry? Where is our clothing? What happened to the wine, the mead, the wedding gifts?"

But everything had turned to mud; the town of Frampol, stripped and ruined, had become a swamp. Its inhabitants were mud-splashed, denuded, monstrous. For a moment, forgetting their grief, they laughed at each other. The hair of the girls had turned into elflocks, and bats were entangled there. The young men had grown gray and wrinkled; the old were yellow as corpses. In their midst lay the old man who had died. Crimson with shame, the sun rose.

"Let us rend our clothes in mourning," one man called, but his words evoked laughter, for all were naked.

"We are doomed, my sisters," lamented a woman.

"Let us drown ourselves in the river," a girl shrieked. "Why go on living?"

One of the yeshiva boys said, "Let us strangle ourselves with our sashes."

"Brothers, we are lost. Let us blaspheme God," said a horse dealer.

"Have you lost your minds, Jews?" cried Rabbi Ozer, "Repent, before it is too late. You have fallen into Satan's snare, but it is my fault, I take the sin upon myself. I am the guilty one. I will be your scapegoat, and you shall remain clean."

"This is madness!" one of the scholars protested, "God forbid that there be so many sins on your holy head!"

"Do not worry abut that. My shoulders are broad. I should have had more foresight. I was blind not to realize that the Cracow doctor was the Evil One. And when the shepherd is blind, the flock goes astray. It is I who deserve the punishment, the curses."

"Rabbi, what shall we do? We have no homes, no bed clothes, nothing. Woe to us, to our bodies and to our souls."

"Our babies!" cried the young matrons. "Let us hurry to them!"

But it was the infants who had been the real victims of the passion for gold that had caused the inhabitants of Frampol to transgress. The infants' cribs were burned, their little bones were charred. The mothers stooped to pick up little hands, feet, skulls. The wailing and crying lasted long, but how long can a whole town weep? The gravedigger gathered the bones and carried them to the cemetery. Half the town began the prescribed seven days of mourning. But all fasted, for there was no food anywhere.

But the compassion of the Jews is well known, and when the neighboring town of Yanev learned what had happened, clothing, bed linen, bread, cheese, and dishes were collected and sent to Frampol. Timber merchants brought logs for building. A rich man offered credit. The next day the reconstruction of the town was begun. Although work is forbidden to those in mourning, Rabbi Ozer issued a verdict that this was an exceptional case: the lives of the people were in danger. Miraculously, the weather remained mild; no snow fell. Never before had there been such diligence in Frampol. The inhabitants built and prayed, mixed lime with sand, and recited psalms. The women worked with the men, while girls, forgetting their fastidiousness, helped also. Scholars and men of high position assisted. Peasants from the surrounding villages, hearing of the catastrophe, took the old and infirm into their homes. They also brought wood, potatoes, cabbages, onions and other food. Priests and bishops from Lublin, hearing of events that suggested witchcraft, came to examine witnesses. As the scribe recorded the names of those living in Frampol, Hodle, the daughter of Lipa the Ragpicker, was suddenly remembered. But when the townspeople went to where her hut had been, they found the hill covered with weeds and bramble, silent save for the cries of crows and cats; there was no indication that human beings had ever dwelt there.

Then it was understood that Hodle was in truth Lilith,[7] and that the host of the netherworld had come to Frampol because of her. After their investigations, the clergymen from Lublin, greatly astonished at what they had seen and heard, returned home. A few days later, the day before the Sabbath, Rabbi Ozer died. The entire

---

7. In Talmudic legend, a female demon, or Adam's first wife who, having refused to recognize his superior position, abandoned him and was transformed into a demon.

town attended his funeral, and the town preacher said a eulogy for him.

In time, a new rabbi came to the community, and a new town arose. The old people died, the mounds in the cemetery sifted down, and the monuments slowly sank. But the story, signed by trustworthy witnesses, can still be read in the parchment chronicle.

And the events in the story brought their epilogue: the lust for gold had been stifled in Frampol; it was never rekindled. From generation to generation the people remained paupers. A gold coin became an abomination in Frampol, and even silver was looked at askance. Whenever a shoemaker or tailor asked too high a price for his work he was told, "Go to the gentleman from Cracow and he will give you buckets of gold."

And on the grave of Rabbi Ozer, in the memorial chapel, there burns an eternal light. A white pigeon is often seen on the roof: the sainted spirit of Rabbi Ozer.

BERTOLT BRECHT
(1898–1956)
The Caucasian Chalk Circle*
English version by Eric Bentley

Characters

OLD MAN, *on the right*	GEORGI ABASHWILL, the Governor
PEASANT WOMAN, *on the right*	NATELLA, *the Governor's wife*
YOUNG PEASANT	MICHAEL, *their son*
A VERY YOUNG WORKER	SHALVA, *an Adjutant*
OLD MAN, *on the left*	ARSEN KAZBEKA, *a fat prince*
PEASANT WOMAN, *on the left*	MESSENGER, *from the Capital*
AGRICULTURIST KATO	NIKO MIKADZE and
GIRL TRACTORIST	MIKA LOLADZE, *Doctors*
WOUNDED SOLDIER	SIMON SHASHAVA, *a soldier*
THE DELEGATE *from the capital*	GRUSHA VASHNADZE,
THE STORY TELLER	*a kitchen maid*
OLD PEASANT, *with the milk*	INVALID

* Written in 1944-1945.

Copyright © 1947, 1948, 1961, 1963 by Eric Bentley, Prologue Copyright © 1959 by Eric Bentley. Reprinted by permission of the University of Minnesota Press.

This adaptation, commissioned and approved by Bertolt Brecht, is based on the German MS of 1946. A German version very close to this MS was published in a supplement to *Sinn und Form*, 1949. My English text has now appeared in three versions. Maja Apelman collaborated on the first one (copyrighted 1947, 1948). The second and third were respectively copyrighted in 1961 and 1963.

—E.B., New York, 1963

CORPORAL *and* PRIVATE

PEASANT *and his wife*

LAVRENTI VASHNADZE,
  Grusha's brother

ANIKO, *his wife*

PEASANT WOMAN, *for a while*
  Grusha's mother-in-law

JUSSUP, *her son*

MONK

AZDAK, *village recorder*

SHAUWA, *a policeman*

GRAND DUKE

DOCTOR

LIMPING MAN

BLACKMAILER

LUDOVICA

INNKEEPER, *her father-in-law*

STABLEBOY

POOR OLD PEASANT WOMAN

IRAKLI, *her brother-in-law,*
  a bandit

THREE WEALTHY FARMERS

ILLO SHUBOLADZE *and*
  SANDRO OBOLADZE, *lawyers*

OLD MARRIED COUPLE

SOLDIERS, SERVANTS, PEASANTS, BEGGARS, MUSICIANS, MERCHANTS,
  NOBLES, ARCHITECTS

Prologue

[*Among the ruins of a war-ravaged Caucasian village the
members of two Kolkhoz¹ villages, mostly women and older
men, are sitting in a circle, smoking and drinking wine. With
them is a* DELEGATE *of the state Reconstruction Commission
from Nuka, the capital.*]

PEASANT WOMAN, *left.* [*Pointing*] In those hills over there we stopped
  three Nazi tanks, but the apple orchard was already destroyed.

OLD MAN, *right.* Our beautiful dairy farm: a ruin.

GIRL TRACTORIST. I laid the fire, Comrade.

  [*Pause*]

DELEGATE. Now listen to the report. Delegates from the goat-breed-
  ing Kolkhoz "Rosa Luxemburg" have been to Nuka. When Hit-
  ler's armies approached, the Kolkhoz had moved its goat-herds
  further east on orders from the authorities. They are now thinking of returning. Their delegates have investigated the village and
  the land and found a lot of it destroyed.

  [DELEGATES *on right nod.*]

  The neighboring fruit-culture Kolkhoz [*To the left*] "Galinsk" is
  proposing to use the former grazing land of Kolkhoz "Rosa Luxemburg," a valley with scanty growth of grass, for orchards and
  vineyards. As a delegate of the Reconstruction Commission, I
  request that the two Kolkhoz villages decide between themselves whether Kolkhoz "Rosa Luxemburg" shall return here or
  not.

OLD MAN, *right.* First of all, I want to protest against the restriction

---

1. *Kolkhoz:* a collective farm in the Soviet Union.

of time for discussion. We of Kolkhoz "Rosa Luxemburg"[2] have spent three days and three nights getting here. And now discussion is limited to half a day.

WOUNDED SOLDIER, *left*. Comrade, we haven't as many villages as we used to have. We haven't as many hands. We haven't as much time.

GIRL TRACTORIST. All pleasures have to be rationed. Tobacco is rationed, and wine. Discussion should be rationed.

OLD MAN, *right*. [*Sighing*] Death to the fascist! But I will come to the point and explain why we want our valley back. There are a great many reasons, but I'll begin with one of the simplest. Makina Abakidze, unpack the goat cheese.

    [A PEASANT WOMAN *from right takes from a basket an enormous cheese wrapped in a cloth. Applause and laughter.*]

Help yourselves, Comrades, start in!

OLD MAN, *left*. [*Suspiciously*] Is this a way of influencing us?

OLD MAN, *right*. [*Amid laughter*] How could it be a way of influencing you, Surab, you valley-thief? Everyone knows you will take the cheese and the valley, too. [*Laughter*] All I expect from you is an honest answer. Do you like the cheese?

OLD MAN, *left*. The answer is: yes.

OLD MAN, *right*. Really. [*Bitterly*] I ought to have known you know nothing about cheese.

OLD MAN, *left*. Why not? When I tell you I like it?

OLD MAN, *right*. Because you can't like it. Because it's not what it was in the old days. And why not? Because our goats don't like the new grass as they did the old. Cheese is not cheese because grass is not grass, that's the thing. Please put that in your report.

OLD MAN, *left*. But your cheese is· excellent.

OLD MAN, *right*. It isn't excellent. It's just passable. The new grazing land is no good, whatever the young people may say. One can't live there. It doesn't even smell of morning in the morning.

    [*Several people laugh.*]

DELEGATE. Don't mind their laughing: they understand you. Comrades, why does one love one's country? Because the bread tastes better there, the air smells better, voices sound stronger, the sky is higher, the ground is easier to walk on. Isn't that so?

OLD MAN, *right*. The valley has belonged to us from all eternity.

SOLDIER, *left*. What does *that* mean—from all eternity? Nothing belongs to anyone from all eternity. When you were young you didn't even belong to yourself. You belonged to the Kazbeki[3] princes.

2. Rosa Luxemburg (1870–1919), member of the German Socialist movement, for whom one of the Kolkhozes is named. She protested against World War I and, with Karl Liebknecht, was responsible for the 1919 revolution in Berlin.

3. *Kazbeki:* Kazbek is a mountain peak in the Central Caucasus.

OLD MAN, *right*. Doesn't it make a difference, though, what kind of trees stand next to the house you are born in? Or what kind of neighbors you have? Doesn't that make a difference? We want to go back just to have you as our neighbors, valley-thieves! Now you can all laugh again.

OLD MAN, *left*. [*Laughing*] Then why don't you listen to what your neighbor, Kato Wachtang, our agriculturist, has to say about the valley?

PEASANT WOMAN, *right*. We've not said all there is to be said about our valley. By no means. Not all the houses are destroyed. As for the dairy farm, at least the foundation wall is still standing.

DELEGATE. You can claim State support—here and there—you know that. I have suggestions here in my pocket.

PEASANT WOMAN, *right*. Comrade Specialist, we haven't come here to bargain. I can't take your cap and hand you another, and say "This one's better." The other one might *be* better; but you *like* yours better.

GIRL TRACTORIST. A piece of land is not a cap—not in our country, Comrade.

DELEGATE. Don't get angry. It's true we have to consider a piece of land as a tool to produce something useful, but it's also true that we must recognize love for a particular piece of land. As far as I'm concerned. I'd like to find out more exactly what you [*to those on the left*] want to do with the valley.

OTHERS. Yes, let Kato speak.

DELEGATE. Comrade Agriculturist!

KATO. [*Rising; she's in military uniform.*] Comrades, last winter, while we were fighting in these hills here as Partisans, we discussed how, after the expulsion of the Germans, we could build up our fruit culture to ten times its original size. I've prepared a plan for an irrigation project. By means of a cofferdam on our mountain lake, 300 hectares[4] of unfertile land can be irrigated. Our Kolkhoz could not only cultivate more fruit, but also have vineyards. The project, however, would pay only if the disputed valley of Kolkhoz "Galinsk" were also included. Here are the calculations. [*She hands the* DELEGATE *a briefcase.*]

OLD MAN, *right*. Write into a report that our Kolkhoz plans to start a new stud farm.

GIRL TRACTORIST. Comrades, the project was conceived during days and nights when we had to take cover in the mountains. We were often without ammunition for our half-dozen rifles. Even getting a pencil was difficult.

[*Applause from both sides*]

OLD MAN, *right*. Our thanks to the Comrades of Kolkhoz "Galinsk" and all who have defended our country!

---

4. A hectare is not quite two and one half acres.

[*They shake hands and embrace.*]

PEASANT WOMAN, *left.* In doing this our thought was that our soldiers—both your men and our men—should return to a still more
productive homeland.

GIRL TRACTORIST. As the poet Mayakovsky said: "The home of the
Soviet people shall also be the home of Reason!"[5]

[*The* DELEGATES *including the* OLD MAN *have got up, and with
the* DELEGATE *specified proceed to study the Agriculturist's
drawings . . . exclamations such as: "Why is the altitude of
all 22 meters?"—"This rock must be blown up"—"Actually,
all they need is cement and dynamite"—"They force the
water to come down here, that's clever!"*]

VERY YOUNG WORKER, *right.* [*To* OLD MAN, *right*] They're going to
irrigate all the fields between the hills, look at that, Aleko!

OLD MAN, *right.* I'm not going to look. I knew the project would be
good. I won't have a revolver aimed at my chest.

DELEGATE. But they only want to aim a pencil at your chest.

[*Laughter*]

OLD MAN, *right.* [*Gets up gloomily, and walks over to look at the
drawings.*] These valley-thieves know only too well that we can't
resist machines and projects in this country

PEASANT WOMAN, *right.* Aleko Bereshwili, you have a weakness for
new projects. That's well known.

DELEGATE. What about my report? May I write that you will all
support the cession of your old valley in the interests of this project
when you get back to your Kolkhoz?

PEASANT WOMAN, *right.* I will. What about you, Aleko?

OLD MAN, *right.* [*Bent over drawings*] I suggest that you give us copies
of the drawings to take along.

PEASANT WOMAN, *right.* Then we can sit down and eat. Once he has
the drawings and he's ready to discuss them, the matter is settled.
I know him. And it will be the same with the rest of us.

[DELEGATES *laughingly embrace again.*]

OLD MAN, *left.* Long live the Kolkhoz "Rosa Luxemburg" and much
luck to your horse-breeding project!

PEASANT WOMAN, *left.* In honor of the visit of the delegates from
Kolkhoz "Rosa Luxemburg" and of the Specialist, the plan is that
we all hear a presentation of the Story Teller Arkadi Tscheidse.

[*Applause.* GIRL TRACTORIST *has gone off to bring the* STORY
TELLER.]

PEASANT WOMAN, *right.* Comrades, your entertainment had better
be good. We're going to pay for it with a valley.

PEASANT WOMAN, *left.* Arkadi Tscheidse knows about our discussion. He's promised to perform something that has a bearing on
the problem.

5. Mayakovsky (1894-1930) was a prominent avant garde, revolutionary writer
who committed suicide.

KATO. We wired to Tiflis three times. The whole thing nearly fell through at the last minute because his driver had a cold.

PEASANT WOMAN, *left.* Arkadi Tscheidse knows 21,000 lines of verse.

OLD MAN, *left.* It's very difficult to get him. You and the Planning Commission should see to it that you get him to come North more often, Comrade.

DELEGATE. We are more interested in economics, I'm afraid.

OLD MAN, *left.* [Smiling] You arrange the redistribution of vines and tractors, why not of songs?

> [*Enter the* STORY TELLER *Arkadi Tscheidse, led by* GIRL TRAC-
> TORIST. *He is a well-built man of simple manners, accompa-
> nied by four* MUSICIANS *with their instruments. The* ARTISTS
> *are greeted with applause.*]

GIRL TRACTORIST. This is the Comrade Specialist, Arkadi.

> [*The* STORY TELLER *greets them all.*]

DELEGATE. I'm honored to make your acquaintance. I heard about your songs when I was a boy at school. Will it be one of the old legends?

THE STORY TELLER. A very old one. It's called The Chalk Circle and comes from the Chinese. But we'll do it, of course, in a changed version. Comrades, it's an honor for me to entertain you after a difficult debate. We hope you will find that the voice of the old poet also sounds well in the shadow of Soviet tractors. It may be a mistake to mix different wines, but old and new wisdom mix admirably. Now I hope we'll get something to eat before the performance begins—it would certainly help.

VOICES. Surely. Everyone into the Club House!

> [*While everyone begins to move, the* DELEGATE *turns to the*
> GIRL TRACTORIST.]

DELEGATE. I hope it won't take long. I've got to get back tonight.

GIRL TRACTORIST. How long will it last, Arkadi? The Comrade Spe-cialist must get back to Tiflis tonight.

THE STORY TELLER. [*Casually*] It's actually two stories. An hour or two.

GIRL TRACTORIST. [*Confidentially*] Couldn't you make it shorter?

THE STORY TELLER. No.

VOICE. Arkadi Tscheidse's performance will take place here in the square after the meal.

> [*And they all go happily to eat.*]

1. The Noble Child

[*As the lights go up, the* STORY TELLER *is seen sitting on the
floor, a black sheepskin cloak round his shoulders, and a litt'e
well-thumbed notebook in his hand. A small group of listeners
—the chorus—sits with him. The manner of his recitation
makes it clear that he has told his story over and over again.
He mechanically fingers the pages, seldom looking at them.*]

> *With appropriate gestures, he gives the signal for each scene to begin.*]

THE STORY TELLER. In olden times, in a bloody time,
There ruled in a Caucasian city—
Men called it City of the Damned—
A governor.
His name was Georgi Abashwili.
He was rich as Croesus[6]
He had a beautiful wife
He had a healthy baby.
No other governor in Grusinia[7]
Had so many horses in his stable
So many beggars in his doorstep
So many soldiers in his service
So many petitioners in his courtyard.
Georgi Abashwili—how shall I describe him to you?
He enjoyed his life.
On the morning of Easter Sunday
The governor and his family went to church.

> [*At the left a large doorway, at the right an even larger gateway.* BEGGARS *and* PETITIONERS *pour from the gateway, holding up thin children, crutches, and petitions. They are followed by* IRONSHIRTS, *and then, expensively dressed, the* GOVERNOR'S FAMILY.]

BEGGARS AND PETITIONERS. Mercy! Mercy, Your Grace! The taxes are too high.
—I lost my leg in the Persian War, where can I get . . .
—My brother is innocent, Your Grace, a misunderstanding . . .
—The child is starving in my arms!
—Our petition is for our son's discharge from the army, our last remaining son!
—Please, Your Grace, the water inspector takes bribes.

> [*One* SERVANT *collects the petitions, another distributes coins from a purse.* SOLDIERS *push the* CROWD *back, lashing at them with thick leather whips.*]

THE SOLDIER. Get back! Clear the church door!

> [*Behind the* GOVERNOR, *his* WIFE, *and the* ADJUTANT, *the* GOVERNOR'S CHILD *is brought through the gateway in an ornate carriage.*]

THE CROWD.
—The baby!
—I can't see it, don't shove so hard!

---

6. Croesus, whose wealth is proverbial, was the last king of Lydia in Asia Minor, in the sixth century B.C.

7. Grusinia is a name used variously for Georgia and for a province in eastern Georgia.

—God bless the child, Your Grace!

THE STORY TELLER. [*While the* CROWD *is driven back with whips*]
For the first time on that Easter Sunday, the people saw the Governor's heir.

Two doctors never moved from the noble child, apple of the Governor's eye.

Even the mighty Prince Kazbeki bows before him at the church door.

[*A* FAT PRINCE *steps forward and greets the family.*]

THE FAT PRINCE. Happy Easter, Natella Abashwili! What a day! When it was raining last night, I thought to myself, gloomy holidays! But this morning the sky was gay. I love a gay sky, a simple heart, Natella Abaswili. And little Michael is a governor from head to foot! Tititi! [*He tickles the child.*]

THE GOVERNOR'S WIFE. What do you think, Arsen, at last Georgi has decided to start building the wing on the east side. All those wretched slums are to be torn down to make room for the garden.

THE FAT PRINCE. Good news after so much bad! What's the latest on the war, Brother Georgi?

[*The* GOVERNOR *indicates a lack of interest.*]

THE FAT PRINCE. Strategical retreat, I hear. Well, minor reverses are to be expected. Sometimes things go well, sometimes not. Such is war. Doesn't mean a thing, does it?

THE GOVERNOR'S WIFE. He's coughing. Georgi, did you hear?

[*She speaks sharply to the* DOCTORS, *two dignified men standing close to the little carriage.*]
He's coughing!

THE FIRST DOCTOR. [*To the* SECOND] May I remind you, Niko Mikadze, that I was against the lukewarm bath? [*To the* GOVERNOR'S WIFE] There's been a little error over warming the bath water, Your Grace.

THE SECOND DOCTOR. [*Equally polite*] Mika Loladze, I'm afraid I can't agree with you. The temperature of the bath water was exactly what our great, beloved Mishiko Oboladze prescribed. More likely a slight draft during the night, Your Grace.

THE GOVERNOR'S WIFE. But do pay more attention to him. He looks feverish, Georgi.

THE FIRST DOCTOR. [*Bending over the child*] No cause for alarm, Your Grace. The bath water will be warmer. It won't occur again.

THE SECOND DOCTOR. [*With a venomous glance at the* FIRST] I won't forget that, my dear Mika Loladze. No cause for concern, Your Grace.

THE FAT PRINCE. Well, well, well! I always say: "A pain in my liver? Then the doctor gets fifty strokes on the soles of his feet." We live in a decadent age. In the old days one said: "Off with his head!"

THE GOVERNOR'S WIFE. Let's go into church. Very likely it's the draft here.

> [*The procession of* FAMILY *and* SERVANTS *turns into the doorway. The* FAT PRINCE *follows, but the* GOVERNOR *is kept back by the* ADJUTANT, *a handsome young man. When the* CROWD *of* PETITIONERS *has been driven off, a young dust-stained* RIDER, *his arm in a sling, remains behind.*]

THE ADJUTANT. [*Pointing at the* RIDER, *who steps forward*] Won't you hear the messenger from the capital, Your Excellency? He arrived this morning. With confidential papers.

THE GOVERNOR. Not before Service, Shalva. But did you hear Brother Kazbeki wish me a happy Easter? Which is all very well, but I don't believe it did rain last night.

THE ADJUTANT. [*Nodding*] We must investigate.

THE GOVERNOR. Yes, at once. Tomorrow.

> [*They pass through the doorway. The* RIDER, *who has waited in vain for an audience, turns sharply round and, muttering a curse, goes off. Only one of the palace guards—*SIMON SHAS-HAVA—*remains at the door.*]

THE STORY TELLER.
The city is still.
Pigeons strut in the church square.
A soldier of the Palace Guard
Is joking with a kitchen maid
As she comes up from the river with a bundle.

> [*With a bundle made of large green leaves under her arm.*]

SIMON. What, the young lady is not in church? Shirking?

GRUSHA. I was dressed to go. But they needed another goose for the banquet. And they asked me to get it. I know about geese.

SIMON. A goose? [*He feigns suspicion.*] I'd like to see that goose. [GRUSHA *does not understand.*] One has to be on one's guard with women. "I only went for a fish," they tell you, but it turns out to be something else.

GRUSHA. [*Walking resolutely toward him and showing him the goose*] There! If it isn't a fifteen-pound goose stuffed full of corn, I'll eat the feathers.

SIMON. A queen of a goose! The Governor himself will eat it. So the young lady has been down to the river again?

GRUSHA. Yes, at the poultry farm.

SIMON. Really? At the poultry farm, down by the river . . . not higher up maybe? Near those willows?

GRUSHA. I only go to the willows to wash the linen.

SIMON. [*Insinuatingly*] Exactly.

GRUSHA. Exactly what?

SIMON. [*Winking*] Exactly that.

GRUSHA. Why shouldn't I wash the linen by the willows?

SIMON. [*With exaggerated laughter*] "Why shouldn't I wash the linen by the willows!" That's good, really good!

GRUSHA. I don't understand the soldier. What's so good about it?

SIMON. [*Slyly*] "If something I know someone learns, she'll grow hot and cold by turns!"

GRUSHA. I don't know what I could learn about those willows.

SIMON. Not even if there was a bush opposite? That one could see everything from? Everything that goes on there when a certain person is—"washing linen"

CRUSHA. What does go on? Won't the soldier say what he means and have done?

SIMON. Something goes on. And something can be seen.

GRUSHA. Could the soldier mean I dip my toes in the water when it is hot? There is nothing else.

SIMON. More. Your toes. And more.

GRUSHA. More what? At most my foot?

SIMON. Your foot. And a little more. [*He laughs heartily.*]

GRUSHA. [*Angrily*] Simon Shashava, you ought to be ashamed of yourself! To sit in a bush on a hot day and wait till someone comes and dips her leg in the river! And I bet you bring a friend along too! [*She runs off.*]

SIMON. [*Shouting after her*] I didn't bring any friend along!

[*As the* STORY TELLER *resumes his tale, the* SOLDIER *steps into the doorway as though to listen to the service.*]

STORY TELLER. The city lies still
But why are there armed men?
The Governor's palace is at peace
But why is it a fortress?
And the Governor returned to his palace
And the fortress was a trap
And the goose was plucked and roasted
But the goose was not eaten this time
And noon was no longer the hour to eat:
Noon was the hour to die.

[*From the doorway at the left the* FAT PRINCE *quickly appears, stands still, looks around. Before the gateway at the right two* IRONSHIRTS *are squatting and playing dice. The* FAT PRINCE *sees them, walks slowly past, making a sign to them. They rise: one goes through the gateway, the other goes off at the right. Muffled voices are heard from various directions in the rear: "To your posts!" The palace is surrounded. The* FAT PRINCE *quickly goes off. Church bells in the distance. Enter, through the doorway, the* GOVERNOR'S FAMILY *and* PROCESSION, *returning from church.*]

THE GOVERNOR'S WIFE. [*Passing the* ADJUTANT] It's impossible to

live in such a slum. But Georgi, of course, will only build for
his little Michael. Never for me! Michael is all! All for Michael!

[*The* PROCESSION *turns into the gateway. Again the* ADJUTANT
lingers behind. He waits. Enter the WOUNDED RIDER *from the
doorway. Two* IRONSHIRTS *of the palace guard have taken up
positions by the gateway.*]

THE ADJUTANT. [*To the* RIDER] The Governor does not wish to receive military reports before dinner—especially if they're depressing, as I assume. In the afternoon His Excellency will confer with
prominent architects. They're coming to dinner too. And here they
are!

[*Enter* THREE GENTLEMEN *through the doorway.*]

Go in the kitchen and get yourself something to eat, my friend.

[*As the* RIDER *goes, the* ADJUTANT *greets the* ARCHITECTS.]

Gentlemen, His Excellency expects you at dinner. He will devote
all his time to you and your great new plans. Come!

ONE OF THE ARCHITECTS. We marvel that His Excellency intends to
build. There are disquieting rumors that the war in Persia has
taken a turn for the worse.

THE ADJUTANT. All the more reason to build! There's nothing to
those rumors anyway. Persia is a long way off, and the garrison
here would let itself be hacked to bits for its Governor.

[*Noise from the palace. The shrill scream of a woman. Someone is shouting orders. Dumbfounded, the* ADJUTANT *moves
toward the gateway. An* IRONSHIRT *steps out, points his lance
at him.*]

What's this? Put down that lance, you dog.

ONE OF THE ARCHITECTS. It's the Princes! Don't you know the
Princes met last night in the capital? And they're against the
Grand Duke and his Governors? Gentlemen, we'd better make
ourselves scarce.

[*They rush off. The* ADJUTANT *remains helplessly behind.*]

THE ADJUTANT. [*Furiously to the* PALACE GUARD] Down with those
lances! Don't you see the Governor's life is threatened?

[*The* IRONSHIRTS *of the Palace Guard refuse to obey. They
stare coldly and indifferently at the* ADJUTANT *and follow the
next events without interest.*]

THE STORY TELLER. O blindness of the great!
They go their way like gods,
Great over bent backs,
Sure of hired fists,
Trusting in the power
Which has lasted so long.
But long is not forever.
O change from age to age!
Thou hope of the people!

[*Enter the* GOVERNOR, *through the gateway, between two* SOL-
DIERS *armed to the teeth. He is in chains. His face is gray.*]

Up, great sir, deign to walk upright!
From your palace, the eyes of many foes follow you!
And now you don't need an architect, a carpenter will do.
You won't be moving into a new palace
But into a little hole in the ground.
Look about you once more, blind man!

[*The arrested man looks round.*]

Does all you had please you?
Between the Easter mass and the Easter meal
You are walking to a place whence no one returns.

[*The* GOVERNOR *is led off. A horn sounds an alarm. Noise
behind the gateway.*]

When the house of a great one collapses
Many little ones are slain.
Those who had no share in the good fortunes of the mighty
Often have a share in their misfortunes.
The plunging wagon
Drags the sweating oxen down with it
Into the abyss.

[*The* SERVANTS *come rushing through the gateway in panic.*]

THE SERVANTS. [*Among themselves*]
—The baskets!
—Take them all into the third courtyard! Food for five days!
—The mistress has fainted! Someone must carry her down.
—She must get away.
—What about us? We'll be slaughtered like chickens, as always.
—Goodness, what'll happen? There's bloodshed already in the
city, they say.
—Nonsense, the Governor has just been asked to appear at a
Princes' meeting. All very correct. Everything'll be ironed out. I
heard this on the best authority. . . .

[*The two* DOCTORS *rush into the courtyard.*]

THE FIRST DOCTOR. [*Trying to restrain the other*] Niko Mikadze, it
is your duty as a doctor to attend Natella Abashwili.

THE SECOND DOCTOR. My duty! It's yours!

THE FIRST DOCTOR. Whose turn is it to look after the child today,
Niko Mikadze, yours or mine?

THE SECOND DOCTOR. Do you really think, Nika Loladze, I'm going
to stay a minute longer in this accursed house on that little brat's
account?

[*They start fighting. All one hears is: "You neglect your duty!"
and "Duty, my foot!" Then the* SECOND DOCTOR *knocks the
FIRST down.*]

Go to hell!   [*Exit.*]

[*Enter the* SOLDIER, SIMON SHASHAVA. *He searches in the crowd for* GRUSHA.]

SIMON. Grusha! There you are at last! What are you going to do?

GRUSHA. Nothing. If worst comes to worst, I've a brother in the mountains. How about you?

SIMON. Forget about me. [*Formally again*] Grusha Vashnadze, your wish to know my plans fills me with satisfaction. I've been ordered to accompany Madam Natella Abashwili as her guard.

GRUSHA. But hasn't the Palace Guard mutinied?

SIMON. [*Seriously*] That's a fact.

GRUSHA. Isn't it dangerous to go with her?

SIMON. In Tiflis, they say: Isn't the stabbing dangerous for the knife?

GRUSHA. You're not a knife, you're a man, Simon Shashava, what has that woman to do with you?

SIMON. That woman has nothing to do with me. I have my orders, and I go.

GRUSHA. The soldier is pigheaded: he is getting himself into danger for nothing—nothing at all. I must get into the third courtyard, I'm in a hurry.

SIMON. Since we're both in a hurry we shouldn't quarrel. You need time for a good quarrel. May I ask if the young lady still has parents?

GRUSHA. No, just a brother.

SIMON. As time is short—my second question is this: Is the young lady as healthy as a fish in water?

GRUSHA. I may have a pain in the right shoulder once in a while. Otherwise I'm strong enough for my job. No one has complained. So far.

SIMON. That's well known. When it's Easter Sunday, and the question arises who'll run for the goose all the same, she'll be the one. My third question is this: Is the young lady impatient? Does she want apples in winter?

GRUSHA. Impatient? No. But if a man goes to war without any reason and then no message comes—that's bad.

SIMON. A message will come. And now my final question . . .

GRUSHA. Simon Shashava, I must get to the third courtyard at once. My answer is yes.

SIMON. [*Very embarrassed*] Haste, they say, is the wind that blows down the scaffolding. But they also say: The rich don't know what haste is. I'm from . . .

GRUSHA. Kutsk . . .

SIMON. So the young lady has been inquiring about me? I'm healthy, I have no dependents. I make ten piasters a month, as paymaster twenty piasters, and I'm asking—very sincerely—for your hand.

GRUSHA. Simon Shashava, it suits me well.

SIMON. [*Taking from his neck a thin chain with a little cross on it*]
My mother gave me this cross, Grusha Vashnadze. The chain is
is silver. Please wear it.

GRUSHA. Many thanks, Simon.

SIMON. [*Hangs it round her neck*] It would be better for the young
lady to go to the third courtyard now. Or there'll be difficulties.
Anyway, I must harness the horses. The young lady will understand?

GRUSHA. Yes, Simon.

[*They stand undecided.*]

SIMON. I'll just take the mistress to the troops that have stayed loyal.
When the war's over, I'll be back. In two weeks. Or three. I hope
my intended won't get tired, awaiting my return.

GRUSHA. Simon Shashava, I shall wait for you.
Go calmly into battle, soldier
The bloody battle, the bitter battle
From which not everyone returns:
When you return I shall be there.
I shall be waiting for you under the green elm
I shall be waiting for you under the bare elm
I shall wait until the last soldier has returned
And longer.
When you come back from the battle
No boots will stand at my door
The pillow beside mine will be empty
And my mouth will be unkissed.
When you return, when you return
You will be able to say: It is just as it was.

SIMON. I thank you, Grusha Vashnadze. And goodbye!
[*He bows low before her. She does the same before him.
Then she runs quickly off without looking round. Enter the*
ADJUTANT *from the gateway.*]

THE ADJUTANT. [*Harshly*] Harness the horses to the carriage! Don't
stand there doing nothing, louse!
[SIMON SHASHAVA *stands to attention and goes off. Two* SERV-
ANTS *crowd from the gateway, bent low under huge trunks.
Behind them, supported by her* WOMEN, *stumbles* NATELLA
ABASHWILI. *She is followed by a* WOMAN *carrying the* CHILD.]

THE GOVERNOR'S WIFE. I hardly know if my head's still on. Where's
Michael? Don't hold him so clumsily. Pile the trunks onto the
carriage. Shalva, is there no news from the city?

THE ADJUTANT. None. All's quiet so far, but there's not a minute
to lose. No room for all these trunks in the carriage. Pick out what
you need. [*Exit quickly.*]

THE GOVERNOR'S WIFE. Only essentials! Quick, open the trunks!
I'll tell you what I need. [*The trunks are lowered and opened.*

She points at some brocade dresses.] The green one! And, of course, the one with the fur trimming. Where are Niko Mikadze and Mika Loladze? I've suddenly got the most terrible migraine again. It always starts in the temples.

[*Enter* GRUSHA.]

Taking your time, eh? Go at once and get the hot water bottles!

[GRUSHA *runs off, returns later with hot water bottles; the* GOVERNOR'S WIFE *orders her about by signs.*]

Don't tear the sleeves.

A YOUNG WOMAN. Pardon, madam, no harm has come to the dress.

THE GOVERNOR'S WIFE. Because I stopped you. I've been watching you for a long time. Nothing in your head but making eyes at Shalva Tzereteli. I'll kill you, you bitch! [*She beats the woman.*]

THE ADJUTANT. [*appearing in the gateway*] Please make haste. Natella Abashwili. Firing has broken out in the city. [*Exit.*]

THE GOVERNOR'S WIFE. [*Letting go of the* YOUNG WOMAN] Oh dear, do you think they'll lay hands on us? Why should they? Why? [*She herself begins to rummage in the trunks.*] How's Michael? Asleep?

THE WOMAN WITH THE CHILD. Yes, madam.

THE GOVERNOR'S WIFE. Then put him down a moment and get my little saffron-colored boots from the bedroom. I need them for the green dress.

[*The* WOMAN *puts down the* CHILD *and goes off.*]

Just look how these things have been packed! No love! No understanding! If you don't give them every order yourself . . . At such moments you realize what kind of servants you have! They gorge themselves at your expense, and never a word of gratitude! I'll remember this.

THE ADJUTANT. [*Entering, very excited*] Natella, you must leave at once!

THE GOVERNOR'S WIFE. Why? I've got to take this silver dress—it cost a thousand piasters. And that one there, and where's the wine-colored one?

THE ADJUTANT. [*Trying to pull her away*] Riots have broken out! We must leave at once. Where's the baby?

THE GOVERNOR'S WIFE. [*Calling to the* YOUNG WOMAN *who was holding the baby*] Maro, get the baby ready! Where on earth are you?

THE ADJUTANT. [*Leaving*] We'll probably have to leave the carriage behind and go ahead on horseback.

[*The* GOVERNOR'S WIFE *rummages again among her dresses, throws some onto the heap of chosen clothes, then takes them off again. Noises, drums are heard. The* YOUNG WOMAN *who was beaten creeps away. The sky begins to grow red.*]

THE GOVERNOR'S WIFE. [*Rummaging desperately*] I simply cannot find the wine-colored dress. Take the whole pile to the carriage.

Where's Asja? And why hasn't Maro come back? Have you all gone crazy?

THE ADJUTANT. [*Returning*] Quick! Quick!

THE GOVERNOR'S WIFE. [*To the* FIRST WOMAN] Run! Just throw them into the carriage!

THE ADJUTANT. We're not taking the carriage. And if you don't come now, I'll ride off on my own.

THE GOVERNOR'S WIFE. [*As the* FIRST WOMAN *can't carry everything*] Where's that bitch Asja? [*The* ADJUTANT *pulls her away.*] Maro, bring the baby! [*To the* FIRST WOMAN] Go and look for Masha. No, first take the dresses to the carriage. Such nonsense! I wouldn't dream of going on horseback!

> [*Turning round, she sees the red sky, and starts back rigid. The fire burns. She is pulled out by the* ADJUTANT. *Shaking, the* FIRST WOMAN *follows with the dresses.*]

MARO. [*From the doorway, with the boots*] Madam! [*She sees the trunks and dresses and runs toward the baby, picks it up, and holds it a moment.*] They left it behind, the beasts. [*She hands it to* GRUSHA.] Hold it a moment. [*She runs off, following the* GOVERNOR'S WIFE.]

> [*Enter* SERVANTS *from the gateway.*]

THE COOK. Well, so they've actually gone. Without the food wagons, and not a minute too early. It's time for us to clear out.

A GROOM. This'll be an unhealthy neighborhood for quite a while. [*To one of the* WOMEN] Suliko, take a few blankets and wait for me in the foal stables.

GRUSHA. What have they done with the governor?

THE GROOM. [*Gesturing throat cutting*] Ffffft.

A FAT WOMAN. [*Seeing the gesture and becoming hysterical*] Oh dear, oh dear, oh dear, oh dear! Our master Georgi Abashwili! A picture of health he was, at the Morning Mass—and now! Oh, take me away, we're all lost, we must die in sin like our master, Georgi Abashwili!

THE OTHER WOMAN. [*Soothing her*] Calm down, Nina! You'll be taken to safety. You've never hurt a fly.

THE FAT WOMAN. [*Being led out*] Oh dear, oh dear, oh dear! Quick! Let's all get out before they come, before they come!

A YOUNG WOMAN. Nina takes it more to heart than the mistress, that's a fact. They even have to have their weeping done for them.

THE COOK. We'd better get out, all of us.

ANOTHER WOMAN. [*Glancing back*] That must be the East Gate burning.

THE YOUNG WOMAN. [*Seeing the* CHILD *in* GRUSHA'S *arms*] The baby! What are you doing with it?

GRUSHA. It got left behind.

THE YOUNG WOMAN. She simply left it there. Michael, who was kept out of all the drafts!

[*The* SERVANTS *gather round the* CHILD.]

GRUSHA. He's waking up.

THE GROOM. Better put him down, I tell you. I'd rather not think what'd happen to anybody who was found with that baby.

THE COOK. That's right. Once they get started, they'll kill each other off, whole families at a time. Let's go.

[*Exeunt all but* GRUSHA, *with the* CHILD *on her arm, and two* WOMEN.]

THE TWO WOMEN. Didn't you hear? Better put him down.

GRUSHA. The nurse asked me to hold him a moment.

THE OLDER WOMAN. She's not coming back, you simpleton.

THE YOUNGER WOMAN. Keep your hands off it.

THE OLDER WOMAN. [*Amiably*] Grusha, you're a good soul, but you're not very bright, and you know it. I tell you, if he had the plague he couldn't be more dangerous.

GRUSHA. [*stubbornly*] He hasn't got the plague. He looks at me! He's human!

THE OLDER WOMAN. Don't look at *him*. You're a fool—the kind that always gets put upon. A person need only say, "Run for the salad, you have the longest legs," and you run. My husband has an ox cart—you can come with us if you hurry! Lord, by now the whole neighborhood must be in flames.

[*Both* WOMEN *leave, sighing. After some hesitation,* GRUSHA *puts the sleeping* CHILD *down, looks at it for a moment, then takes a brocade blanket from the heap of clothes and covers it. Then both* WOMEN *return, dragging bundles.* GRUSHA *starts guiltily away from the* CHILD *and walks a few steps to one side.*]

THE YOUNGER WOMAN. Haven't you packed anything yet? There isn't much time, you know. The Ironshirts will be here from the barracks.

GRUSHA. Coming.

[*She runs through the doorway. Both* WOMEN *go to the gateway and wait. The sound of horses is heard. They flee, screaming. Enter the* FAT PRINCE *with drunken* IRONSHIRTS. *One of them carries the governor's head on a lance.*]

THE FAT PRINCE. Here! In the middle!

[*One* SOLDIER *climbs onto the other's back, takes the head, holds it tentatively over the door.*]

That's not the middle. Farther to the right. That's it. What I do, my friends, I do well.

[*While, with hammer and nail, the* SOLDIER *fastens the head to the wall by its hair.*]

This morning at the church door I said to Georgi Abashwili: "I love a clear sky." Actually, I prefer the lightning that comes out of a clear sky. Yes, indeed. It's a pity they took the brat along, though, I need him, urgently.

[*Exit with* IRONSHIRTS *through the gateway. Trampling of horses again. Enter* GRUSHA *through the doorway looking cautiously about her. Clearly she has waited for the* IRONSHIRTS *to go. Carrying a bundle, she walks toward the gateway. At the last moment, she turns to see if the* CHILD *is still there. Catching sight of the head over the doorway, she screams. Horrified, she picks up her bundle again, and is about to leave when the* STORY TELLER *starts to speak. She stands rooted to the spot.*]

THE STORY TELLER. As she was standing between courtyard and gate,
She heard or she thought she heard a low voice calling.
The child called to her,
Not whining, but calling quite sensibly,
Or so it seemed to her.
"Woman," it said, "help me."
And it went on, not whining, but saying quite sensibly:
"Know, woman, he who hears not a cry for help
But passes by with troubled ears will never hear
The gentle call of a lover nor the blackbird at dawn
Nor the happy sigh of the tired grape-picker as the Angelus rings."

[*She walks a few steps toward the* CHILD *and bends over it.*]
Hearing this she went back for one more look at the child:
Only to sit with him for a moment or two,
Only till someone should come,
His mother, or anyone.

[*Leaning on a trunk, she sits facing the* CHILD.]
Only till she would have to leave, for the danger was too great,
The city was full of flame and crying.

[*The light grows dimmer, as though evening and night were coming on.*]
Fearful is the seductive power of goodness!

[GRUSHA *now settles down to watch over the* CHILD *through the night. Once, she lights a small lamp to look at it. Once, she tucks it in with a coat. From time to time she listens and looks to see whether someone is coming.*]
And she sat with the child a long time,
Till evening came, till night came, till dawn came.
She sat too long, too long she saw
The soft breathing, the small clenched fists,
Till toward morning the seduction was complete
And she rose, and bent down and, sighing, took the child
And carried it away.

[*She does what the* STORY TELLER *says as he describes it.*]
As if it was stolen goods she picked it up.

As if she was a thief she crept away.

2. *The Flight into the Northern Mountains*

THE STORY TELLER. When Grusha Vashnadze left the city
  On the Grusinian highway
  On the way to the Northern Mountains
  She sang a song, she bought some milk.
THE CHORUS. How will this human child escape
  The bloodhounds, the trap-setters?
  Into the deserted mountains she journeyed
  Along the Grusinian highway he journeyed
  She sang a song, she bought some milk.

> [GRUSHA VASHNADZE *walks on. On her back she carries the*
> CHILD *in a sack, in one hand is a large stick, in the other a*
> *bundle. She sings.*]

The Song of the Four Generals

  Four generals
  Set out for Iran.
  With the first one, war did not agree.
  The second never won a victory.
  For the third the weather never was right.
  For the fourth the men would never fight.
  Four generals
  And not a single man!

  Sosso Robakidse
  Went marching to Iran
  With him the war did so agree
  He soon had won a victory.
  For him the weather was always right.
  For him the men would always fight.
  Sosso Robakidse,
  He is our man!

> [*A peasant's cottage appears.*]

GRUSHA. [*To the* CHILD] Noontime is meal time. Now we'll sit hopefully in the grass, while the good Grusha goes and buys a little
  pitcher of milk.

> [*She lays the* CHILD *down and knocks at the cottage door. An*
> OLD MAN *opens it.*]

Grandfather, could I have a little pitcher of milk? And a corn
  cake, maybe?
THE OLD MAN. Milk? We have no milk. The soldiers from the city
  have our goats. Go to the soldiers if you want milk.
GRUSHA. But grandfather, you must have a little pitcher of milk
  for a baby?

THE OLD MAN. And for a God-bless-you, eh?

GRUSHA. Who said anything about a God-bless-you? [*She shows her purse*]. We'll pay like princes. "Head in the clouds, backside in the water."

[*The* PEASANT *goes off, grumbling, for milk.*]

How much for the milk?

THE OLD MAN. Three piasters. Milk has gone up.

GRUSHA. Three piasters for this little drop?

[*Without a word the* OLD MAN *shuts the door in her face.*]

Michael, did you hear that? Three piasters! We can't afford it! [*She goes back, sits down again, and gives the* CHILD *her breast.*] Suck. Think of the three piasters. There's nothing there, but you think you're drinking, and that's something. [*Shaking her head, she sees that the child isn't sucking any more. She gets up, walks back to the door, and knocks again.*]

Open, grandfather, we'll pay. [*Softly*] May lightning strike you!

[*When the* OLD MAN *appears.*]

I thought it would be half a piaster. But the baby must be fed. How about one piaster for that little drop?

THE OLD MAN. Two.

GRUSHA. Don't shut the door again.

[*She fishes a long time in her bag.*]

Here are two piasters. The milk better be good. I still have two days' journey ahead of me. It's a murderous business you have here—and sinful, too!

THE OLD MAN. Kill the soldiers if you want milk.

GRUSHA. [*Giving the* CHILD *some milk*] This is an expensive joke. Take a sip, Michael, it's a week's pay. Around here they think we earned our money just sitting around. Oh, Michael, Michael, you're a nice little load for a girl to take on!

[*Uneasy, she gets up, puts the* CHILD *on her back, and walks on. The* OLD MAN, *grumbling, picks up the pitcher and looks after her unmoved.*]

THE STORY TELLER. As Grusha Vashnadze went northward
The Princes' Ironshirts went after her.

THE CHORUS. How will the barefoot girl escape the Ironshirts,
The bloodhounds, the trap-setters?
They hunt even by night.
Pursuers never tire.
Butchers sleep little.

[*Two* IRONSHIRTS *are trudging along the highway.*]

THE CORPORAL. You'll never amount to anything, blockhead, your heart's not in it. Your senior officer sees this in little things. Yesterday, when I made the fat gal, yes, you grabbed her husband as commanded, and you did kick him in the stomach, at my request, but did you *enjoy* it, like a loyal Private, or were you just doing your duty? I've kept an eye on you, blockhead, you're a hollow reed and a tinkling cymbal, you won't get promoted.

[*They walk a while in silence.*]

Don't think I've forgotten how insubordinate you are, either. Stop limping! I forbid you to limp! You limp because I sold the horses, and I sold the horses because I'd never have got that price again. You limp to show me you don't like marching. I know you. It won't help. You wait. Sing!

THE TWO IRONSHIRTS. [*Singing*] Sadly to war I went my way
Leaving my loved one at her door.
My friends will keep her honor safe
Till from the war I'm back once more.

THE CORPORAL. Louder!

THE TWO IRONSHIRTS. [*Singing*] When 'neath a headstone I shall be
My love a little earth will bring:
"Here rest the feet that oft would run to me
And here the arms that oft to me would cling."

[*They begin to walk again in silence.*]

THE CORPORAL. A good soldier has his heart and soul in it. When he receives an order, he gets a hard on, and when he drives his lance into the enemy's guts, he comes. [*He shouts for joy.*] He lets himself be torn to bits for his superior officer, and as he lies dying he takes note that his corporal is nodding approval, and that is reward enough, it's his dearest wish. You won't get any nod of approval, but you'll croak all right. Christ, how'm I to get my hands on the Governor's bastard with the help of a fool like you!

[*They stay on stage behind.*]

THE STORY TELLER. When Grusha Vashnadze came to the river Sirra
Flight grew too much for her, the helpless child too heavy.
In the cornfields the rosy dawn
Is cold to the sleepless one, only cold.
The gay clatter of the milk cans in the farmyard where the smoke rises
Is only a threat to the fugitive.
She who carries the child feels its weight and little more.

[GRUSHA *stops in front of a farm. A* FAT PEASANT WOMAN *is carrying a milk can through the door.* GRUSHA *waits until she has gone in, then approaches the house cautiously.*]

GRUSHA. [*To the* CHILD] Now you've wet yourself again, and you know I've no linen. Michael, this is where we part company. It's far enough from the city. They wouldn't want you so much that they'd follow you all *this* way, little good-for-nothing. The peasant woman is kind, and can't you just smell the milk? [*She bends down to lay the* CHILD *on the threshold.*] So farewell, Michael, I'll forget how you kicked me in the back all night to make me walk faster. And you can forget the meager fare—it was meant well. I'd like to have kept you—your nose is so tiny—but it can't be. I'd have shown you your first rabbit, I'd have trained you to keep dry, but now I must turn around. My sweetheart the soldier might be back soon, and suppose he didn't find me? You can't ask that, can you?

[*She creeps up to the door and lays the* CHILD *on the threshold. Then, hiding behind a tree, she waits until the* PEASANT WOMAN *opens the door and sees the bundle.*]

THE PEASANT WOMAN. Good heavens, what's this? Husband!

THE PEASANT. What is it? Let me finish my soup.

THE PEASANT WOMAN. [*To the* CHILD] Where's your mother then? Haven't you got one? It's a boy. Fine linen. He's from a good family, you can see that. And they just leave him on our doorstep. Oh, these are times!

THE PEASANT. If they think we're going to feed it, they're wrong. You can take it to the priest in the village. That's the best we can do.

THE PEASANT WOMAN. What'll the priest do with him? He needs a mother. There, he's waking up. Don't you think we could keep him, though?

THE PEASANT. [*Shouting*] No!

THE PEASANT WOMAN. I could lay him in the corner by the armchair. All I need is a crib. I can take him into the fields with me. See him laughing? Husband, we have a roof over our heads. We can do it. Not another word out of you!

[*She carries the* CHILD *into the house. The* PEASANT *follows protesting.* GRUSHA *steps out from behind the tree, laughs, and hurries off in the opposite direction.*]

THE STORY TELLER. Why so cheerful, making for home?

THE CHORUS. Because the child has won new parents with a laugh,
Because I'm rid of the little one, I'm cheerful.

THE STORY TELLER. And why so sad?

THE CHORUS. Because I'm single and free, I'm sad
Like someone who's been robbed
Someone who's newly poor.

[*She walks for a short while, then meets the* TWO IRONSHIRTS, *who point their lances at her.*]

THE CORPORAL. Lady, you are running straight into the arms of the Armed Forces. Where are you coming from? And when? Are you having illicit relations with the enemy? Where is he hiding? What movements is he making in your rear? How about the hills? How about the valleys? How are your stockings secured?

[GRUSHA *stands there frightened.*]

Don't be scared, we always withdraw if necessary . . . what, blockhead? I always withdraw. In that respect at least, I can be relied on. Why are you staring like that at my lance? In the field no soldier drops his lance, that's a rule. Learn it by heart, blockhead. Now, lady, where are you headed?

GRUSHA. To meet my intended, one Simon Shashava, of the Palace Guard in Nuka.

THE CORPORAL. Simon Shashava? Sure, I know him. He gave me the key so I could look you up once in a while. Blockhead, we are getting to be unpopular. We must make her realize we have honorable intentions. Lady, behind apparent frivolity I conceal a serious nature, so let me tell you officially: I want a child from you.

[GRUSHA *utters a little scream.*]

Blockhead, she understood me. Uh-huh, isn't it a sweet shock? "Then first I must take the noodles out of the oven, Officer. Then first I must change my torn shirt, Colonel." But away with jokes, away with my lance! We are looking for a baby. A baby from a good family. Have you heard of such a baby, from the city, dressed in fine linen, and suddenly turning up here?

GRUSHA. No, I haven't heard a thing. [*Suddenly she turns round and runs back, panic-stricken. The* IRONSHIRTS *glance at each other, then follow her, cursing.*]

THE STORY TELLER. Run, kind girl! The killers are coming!
Help the helpless babe, helpless girl!
And so she runs!

THE CHORUS. In the bloodiest times
There are kind people.

[*As* GRUSHA *rushes into the cottage, the* PEASANT WOMAN *is bending over the* CHILD'S *crib.*]

GRUSHA. Hide him. Quick! The Ironshirts are coming! I laid him on your doorstep. But he isn't mine. He's from a good family.

THE PEASANT WOMAN. Who's coming? What Ironshirts?

GRUSHA. Don't ask questions. The Ironshirts that are looking for it.

THE PEASANT WOMAN. They've no business in my house. But I must have a little talk with you, it seems.

GRUSHA. Take off the fine linen. It'll give us away.

THE PEASANT WOMAN. Linen, my foot! In this house I make the decisions! "You can't vomit in *my* room!" Why did you abandon it? It's a sin.

GRUSHA. [*Looking out of the window*] Look, they're coming out from behind those trees! I shouldn't have run away, it made them angry. Oh, what shall I do?

THE PEASANT WOMAN. [*Looking out of the window and suddenly starting with fear*] Gracious! Ironshirts!

GRUSHA. They're after the baby.

THE PEASANT WOMAN. Suppose they come in!

GRUSHA. You mustn't give him to them. Say he's yours.

THE PEASANT WOMAN. Yes.

GRUSHA. They'll run him through if you hand him over.

THE PEASANT WOMAN. But suppose they ask for it? The silver for the harvest is in the house.

GRUSHA. If you let them have him, they'll run him through, right here in this room! You've got to say he's yours!

THE PEASANT WOMAN. Yes. But what if they don't believe me?

GRUSHA. You must be firm.

THE PEASANT WOMAN. They'll burn the roof over our heads.

GRUSHA. That's why you must say he's yours. His name's Michael. But I shouldn't have told you.

[*The* PEASANT WOMAN *nods.*]

Don't nod like that. And don't tremble—they'll notice.

THE PEASANT WOMAN. Yes.

GRUSHA. And stop saying yes, I can't stand it. [*She shakes the* WOMAN.] Don't you have any children?

THE PEASANT WOMAN. [*Muttering*] He's in the war.

GRUSHA. Then maybe *he's* an Ironshirt? Do you want *him* to run children through with a lance? You'd bawl him out. "No fooling with lances in *my* house!" you'd shout, "is that what I've reared you for? Wash your neck before you speak to your mother!"

THE PEASANT WOMAN. That's true, he couldn't get away with anything around here!

GRUSHA. So you'll say he's yours?

THE PEASANT WOMAN. Yes.

GRUSHA. Look! They're coming!

[*There is a knocking at the door. The women don't answer. Enter* IRONSHIRTS. *The* PEASANT WOMAN *bows low.*]

THE CORPORAL. Well, here she is. What did I tell you? What a nose I have! I *smelt* her. Lady, I have a question for you. Why did you run away? What did you think I would do to you? I'll bet it was something dirty. Confess!

GRUSHA. [*While the* PEASANT WOMAN *bows again and again*] I'd left some milk on the stove, and I suddenly remembered it.

THE CORPORAL. Or maybe you imagined I looked at you in a dirty way? Like there could be something between us? A lewd sort of look, know what I mean?

GRUSHA. I didn't see it.

THE CORPORAL. But it's possible, huh? You admit that much. After all, I might be a pig. I'll be frank with you: I could think of all sorts of things if we were alone. [*To the* PEASANT WOMAN] Shouldn't you be busy in the yard? Feeding the hens?

THE PEASANT WOMAN. [*Falling suddenly to her knees*] Soldier, I didn't know a thing about it. Please don't burn the roof over our heads.

THE CORPORAL. What are you talking about?

THE PEASANT WOMAN. I had nothing to do with it. She left it on my doorstep, I swear it!

THE CORPORAL. [*Suddenly seeing the* CHILD *and whistling*] Ah, so
there's a little something in the crib! Blockhead, I smell a thousand
piasters. Take the old girl outside and hold on to her. It looks
like I have a little cross-examining to do.

> [*The* PEASANT WOMAN *lets herself be led out by the* PRIVATE
> *without a word.*]

So, you've got the child I wanted from you! [*He walks toward the
crib.*]

GRUSHA. Officer, he's mine. He's not the one you're after.

THE CORPORAL. I'll just take a look. [*He bends over the crib.* GRUSHA
looks round in despair.]

GRUSHA. He's mine! He's mine!

THE CORPORAL. Fine linen!

> [GRUSHA *dashes at him to pull him away. He throws her off
> and again bends over the crib. Again looking round in despair,
> she sees a log of wood, seizes it, and hits the* CORPORAL *over
> the head from behind. The* CORPORAL *collapses. She quickly
> picks up the* CHILD *and rushes off.*]

THE STORY TELLER. And in her flight from the Ironshirts
After twenty-two days of journeying
At the foot of the Janga-Tu Glacier
Grusha Vashnadze decided to adopt the child.

THE CHORUS. The helpless girl adopted the helpless child.

> [GRUSHA *squats over a half-frozen stream to get the* CHILD
> *water in the hollow of her hand.*]

GRUSHA. Since no one else will take you, son,
I must take you.
Since no one else will take you, son,
You must take me.
O black day in a lean, lean year,
The trip was long, the milk was dear,
My legs are tired, my feet are sore:
But I wouldn't be without you any more.
I'll throw your silken shirt away.
And dress you in rags and tatters.
I'll wash you, son, and christen you in glacier water.
We'll see it through together.

> [*She has taken off the* CHILD's *fine linen and wrapped it in
> a rag.*]

THE STORY TELLER. When Grusha Vashnadze
Pursued by the Ironshirts
Came to the bridge on the glacier
Leading to the villages of the Eastern Slope
She sang the Song of the Rotten Bridge
And risked two lives.

> [*A wind has risen. The bridge on the glacier is visible in the*

dark. *One rope is broken and half the bridge is hanging down the abyss.* MERCHANTS, *two* MEN, *and a* WOMAN, *stand undecided before the bridge as* GRUSHA *and the* CHILD *arrive. One* MAN *is trying to catch the hanging rope with a stick.*]

THE FIRST MAN. Take your time, young woman. You won't get across here anyway.

GRUSHA. But I *have* to get the baby to the east side. To my brother's place.

THE MERCHANT WOMAN. Have to? How d'you mean, "have to"? I have to get there, too—because I have to buy carpets in Atum—carpets a woman had to sell because her husband had to die. But can *I* do what I have to? Can she? Andrei's been fishing for that rope for hours. And I ask you, how are we going to fasten it, even if he gets it up?

THE FIRST MAN. [*Listening*] Hush, I think I hear something.

GRUSHA. The bridge isn't quite rotted through. I think I'll try it.

THE MERCHANT WOMAN. *I* wouldn't—if the devil himself were after me. It's suicide.

THE FIRST MAN. [*Shouting*] Hi!

GRUSHA. Don't shout! [*To the* MERCHANT WOMAN] Tell him not to shout.

THE FIRST MAN. But there's someone down there calling. Maybe they've lost their way.

THE MERCHANT WOMAN. Why shouldn't he shout? Is there something funny about you? Are they after you?

GRUSHA. All right, I'll tell. The Ironshirts are after me. I knocked one down.

THE SECOND MAN. Hide our merchandise!

[*The* WOMAN *hides a sack behind a rock.*]

THE FIRST MAN. Why didn't you say so right away? [*To the others*] If they catch her they'll make mincemeat out of her!

GRUSHA. Get out of my way. I've got to cross that bridge.

THE SECOND MAN. You can't. The precipice is two thousand feet deep.

THE FIRST MAN. Even with the rope it'd be no use. We could hold it up with our hands. But then we'd have to do the same for the Ironshirts.

GRUSHA. Go away.

[*There are calls from the distance: "Hi, up there!"*]

THE MERCHANT WOMAN. They're getting near. But you can't take the child on that bridge. It's sure to break. And look!

[GRUSHA *looks down into the abyss. The* IRONSHIRTS *are heard calling again from below.*]

THE SECOND MAN. Two thousand feet!

GRUSHA. But those men are worse.

THE FIRST MAN. You can't do it. Think of the baby. Risk your life but not a child's.

THE SECOND MAN. With the child she's that much heavier!

THE MERCHANT WOMAN. Maybe she's *really* got to get across. Give *me* the baby. I'll hide it. Cross the bridge alone!

GRUSHA. I won't. We belong together. [*To the* CHILD] "Live together, die together." [*She sings.*]

> The Song of the Rotten Bridge
>
> Deep is the abyss, son,
> I see the weak bridge sway
> But it's not for us, son,
> To choose the way.
>
> The way I know
> Is the one you must tread,
> And all you will eat
> Is my bit of bread.
>
> Of every four pieces
> You shall have three.
> Would that I knew
> How big they will be!

Get out of my way, I'll try it without the rope.

THE MERCHANT WOMAN. You are tempting God!

[*There are shouts from below.*]

GRUSHA. Please, throw that stick away, or they'll get the rope and follow me. [*Pressing the* CHILD *to her, she steps onto the swaying bridge. The* MERCHANT WOMAN *screams when it looks as though the bridge is about to collapse. But* GRUSHA *walks on and reaches the far side.*]

THE FIRST MAN. She made it!

THE MERCHANT WOMAN. [*Who has fallen on her knees and begun to pray, angrily*] I still think it was a sin.

[*The* IRONSHIRTS *appear; the* CORPORAL's *head is bandaged.*]

THE CORPORAL. Seen a woman with a child?

THE FIRST MAN. [*While the* SECOND MAN *throws the stick into the abyss*] Yes, there! But the bridge won't carry you!

THE CORPORAL. You'll pay for this, blockhead!

GRUSHA, *from the far bank laughs and shows the* CHILD *to the* IRONSHIRTS. *She walks on. The wind blows.*]

GRUSHA. [*Turning to the* CHILD] You mustn't be afraid of the wind. He's a poor thing too. He has to push the clouds along and he gets quite cold doing it.

[*Snow starts falling.*]

And the snow isn't so bad, either, Michael. It covers the little fir trees so they won't die in winter. Let me sing you a little song. [*She sings.*]

The Song of the Child

Your father is a bandit
A harlot the mother who bore you.
Yet honorable men
Shall kneel down before you.

Food to the baby horses
The tiger's son will take.
The mothers will get milk
From the son of the snake.

3. In the Northern Mountains

THE STORY TELLER. Seven days the sister, Grusha Vashnadze,
Journeyed across the glacier
And down the slopes she journeyed.
"When I enter my brother's house," she thought
"He will rise and embrace me."
"Is that you, sister?" he will say,
"I have long expected you.
This is my dear wife,
And this is my farm, come to me by marriage,
With eleven horses and thirty-one cows. Sit down.
Sit down with your child at our table and eat."
The brother's house was in a lovely valley.
When the sister came to the brother,
She was ill from walking.
The brother rose from the table.

[A FAT PEASANT COUPLE *rise from the table.* LAVRENTI VASH-NADZE *still has a napkin round his neck, as* GRUSHA, *pale and supported by a* SERVANT, *enters with the* CHILD.]

LAVRENTI. Where've you come from, Grusha?

GRUSHA. [*Feebly*] Across the Janga-Tu Pass, Lavrenti.

THE SERVANT. I found her in front of the hay barn. She has a baby with her.

THE SISTER-IN-LAW. Go and groom the mare.

[*Exit the* SERVANT.]

LAVRENTI. This is my wife Aniko.

THE SISTER-IN-LAW. I thought you were in service in Nuka.

GRUSHA. [*Barely able to stand*] Yes, I was.

THE SISTER-IN-LAW. Wasn't it a good job? We were told it was.

GRUSHA. The Governor got killed.

LAVRENTI. Yes, we heard there were riots. Your aunt told us. Remember, Aniko?

THE SISTER-IN-LAW. Here with us, it's very quiet. City people always want something going on. [*She walks toward the door, calling.*] Sosso, Sosso, don't take the cake out of the oven yet, d'you hear? Where on earth are you? [*Exit, calling.*]

LAVRENTI. [*Quietly, quickly*] Is there a father? [*As she shakes her head*] I thought not. We must think up something. She's religious.

THE SISTER-IN-LAW. [*Returning*] Those servants! [*To* GRUSHA] You have a child.

GRUSHA. It's mine. [*She collapses.* LAVRENTI *rushes to her assistance.*]

THE SISTER-IN-LAW. Heavens, she's ill—what are we going to do?

LAVRENTI. [*Escorting her to a bench near the stove*] Sit down, sit. I think it's just weakness, Aniko.

THE SISTER-IN-LAW. As long as it's not scarlet fever!

LAVRENTI. She'd have spots if it was. It's only weakness. Don't worry, Aniko. [*To* GRUSHA] Better, sitting down?

THE SISTER-IN-LAW. Is the child hers?

GRUSHA. Yes, mine.

LAVRENTI. She's on her way to her husband.

THE SISTER-IN-LAW. I see. Your meat's getting cold.
　　[LAVRENTI *sits down and begins to eat.*]
Cold food's not good for you, the fat mustn't get cold, you know your stomach's your weak spot. [*To* GRUSHA] If your husband's not in the city, where is he?

LIVRENTI. She got married on the other side of the mountain, she says.

THE SISTER-IN-LAW. On the other side of the mountain. I see. [*She also sits down to eat.*]

GRUSHA. I think I should lie down somewhere, Lavrenti.

THE SISTER-IN-LAW. If it's consumption we'll all get it. [*She goes on cross-examining her.*] Has your husband got a farm?

GRUSHA. He's a soldier.

LAVRENTI. But he's coming into a farm—a small one—from his father.

THE SISTER-IN-LAW. Isn't he in the war? Why not?

GRUSHA. [*With effort*] Yes, he's in the war.

THE SISTER-IN-LAW. Then why d'you want to go to the farm?

LAVRENTI. When he comes back from the war, he'll return to his farm.

THE SISTER-IN-LAW. But you're going there now?

LAVRENTI. Yes, to wait for him.

THE SISTER-IN-LAW. [*Calling shrilly*] Sosso, the cake!

GRUSHA. [*Murmuring feverishly*] A farm—a soldier—waiting—sit down, eat.

THE SISTER-IN-LAW. It's scarlet fever.

GRUSHA. [*Starting up*] Yes, he's got a farm!

LAVRENTI. I think it's just weakness, Aniko. Would you look after the cake yourself, dear?

THE SISTER-IN-LAW. But when will he come back if war's broken out again as people say? [*She waddles off, shouting.*] Sosso! Where on earth are you? Sosso!

LAVRENTI. [*Getting up quickly and going to* GRUSHA] You'll get a bed in a minute. She has a good heart. But wait till after supper.

GRUSHA. [*Holding out the* CHILD *to him*] Take him.

LAVRENTI. [*Taking it and looking around*] But you can't stay here long with the child. She's religious, you see.

[GRUSHA *collapses.* LAVRENTI *catches her.*]

THE STORY TELLER. The sister was so ill,

The cowardly brother had to give her shelter.

Summer departed, winter came.

The winter was long, the winter was short

People mustn't know anything,

Rats mustn't bite,

Spring mustn't come.

[GRUSHA *sits over the weaving loom in a workroom. She and the* CHILD, *who is squatting on the floor, are wrapped in blankets. She sings.*]

The Song of the Center

GRUSHA. [*Sings*]

And the lover started to leave

And his betrothed ran pleading after him

Pleading and weeping, weeping and teaching:

"Dearest mine, dearest mine

When you go to war as now you do

When you fight the foe as soon you will

Don't lead with the front line

And don't push with the rear line

At the front is red fire

In the rear is red smoke

Stay in the war's center

Stay near the standard bearer

The first always die

The last are also hit

Those in the center come home."

Michael, we must be clever. If we make ourselves as small as cockroaches, the sister-in-law will forget we're in the house, and then we can stay till the snow melts.

[*Enter* LAVRENTI. *He sits down beside his sister.*]

LAVRENTI. Why are you sitting there muffled up like coachmen, you two? Is it too cold in the room?

GRUSHA. [*Hastily removing one shawl*] It's not too cold, Lavrenti.

LAVRENTI. If it's too cold, you shouldn't be sitting here with the child. Aniko would never forgive herself! [*Pause*] I hope our priest didn't question you about the child?

GRUSHA. He did, but I didn't tell him anything.

LAVRENTI. That's good. I wanted to speak to you about Aniko. She has a good heart but she's very, very sensitive. People need only mention our farm and she's worried. She takes everything hard, you see. One time our milkmaid went to church with a hole in her stocking. Ever since, Aniko has worn two pairs of stockings in church. It's the old family in her. [*He listens.*] Are you sure there are no rats around? If there are rats, you couldn't live here. [*There are sounds as of dripping from the roof.*] What's that dripping?

GRUSHA. It must be a barrel leaking.

LAVRENTI. Yes, it must be a barrel. You've been here six months, haven't you? Was I talking about Aniko? [*They listen again to the snow melting.*] You can't imagine how worried she gets about your soldier-husband. "Suppose he comes back and can't find her!" she says and lies awake. "He can't come before the spring," I tell her. The dear woman! [*The drops begin to fall faster.*] When d'you think he'll come? What do you think? [GRUSHA *is silent.*] Not before the spring, you agree? [GRUSHA *is silent.*] You don't believe he'll come at all? [GRUSHA *is silent.*] But when the spring comes and the snow melts here and on the passes, you can't stay on. They may come and look for you. There's already talk of an illegitimate child. [*The "glockenspiel" of the falling drops has grown faster and steadier.*] Grusha, the snow is melting on the roof. Spring is here.

GRUSHA. Yes.

LAVRENTI. [*Eagerly*] I'll tell you what we'll do. You need a place to go, and, because of the child [*He sighs.*], you have to have a husband, so people won't talk. Now I've made cautious inquiries to see if we can find you a husband. Grusha, I *have* one. I talked to a peasant woman who has a son. Just the other side of the mountain. A small farm. And she's willing.

GRUSHA. But I *can't* marry! I must wait for Simon Shashava.

LAVRENTI. Of course. That's all been taken care of. You don't need a man in bed—you need a man on paper. And I've found you one. The son of this peasant woman is going to die. Isn't that wonderful? He's at his last gasp. And all in line with our story—a husband from the other side of the mountain! And when you met him he was at the last gasp. So you're a widow. What do you say?

GRUSHA. It's true I could use a document with stamps on it for Michael.

LAVRENTI. Stamps make all the difference. Without something in writing the Shah couldn't prove he's a Shah. And you'll have a place to live.

GRUSHA. How much does the peasant woman want?

LAVRENTI. Four hundred piasters.

GRUSHA. Where will you find it?

LAVRENTI. [*Guiltily*] Aniko's milk money.

GRUSHA. No one would know us there. I'll do it.

LAVRENTI. [*Getting up*] I'll let the peasant woman know.
      [*Quick exit.*]

GRUSHA. Michael, you cause a lot of fuss. I came to you as the pear tree comes to the sparrows. And because a Christian bends down and picks up a crust of bread so nothing will go to waste. Michael, it would have been better had I walked quickly away on that Easter Sunday in Nuka in the second courtyard. Now I am a fool.

THE STORY TELLER.
      The bridegroom was lying on his deathbed when the bride arrived.
      The bridegroom's mother was waiting at the door, telling her to hurry.
      The bride brought a child along.
      The witness hid it during the wedding.
      [*On one side the bed. Under the mosquito net lies a very sick* MAN. GRUSHA *is pulled in at a run by her future* MOTHER-IN-LAW. *They are followed by* LAVRENTI *and the* CHILD.]

THE MOTHER-IN-LAW. Quick! Quick! Or he'll die on us before the wedding. [*To* LAVRENTI] I was never told she had a child already.

LAVRENTI. What difference does it make? [*Pointing toward the dying man*] It can't matter to him—in his condition.

THE MOTHER-IN-LAW. To him? But *I'll* never survive the shame! We are honest people. [*She begins to weep.*] My Jussup doesn't have to marry a girl with a child!

LAVRENTI. All right, make it another two hundred piasters. You'll have it in writing that the farm will go to you: but she'll have the right to live here for two years.

THE MOTHER-IN-LAW. [*Drying her tears*] It'll hardly cover the funeral expenses. I hope she'll really lend a hand with the work. And what's happened to the monk? He must have slipped out through the kitchen window. We'll have the whole village round our necks when they hear Jussup's end is come! Oh dear! I'll run and get the monk. But he mustn't see the child!

LAVRENTI. I'll take care he doesn't. But why only a monk? Why not a priest?

THE MOTHER-IN-LAW. Oh, he's just as good. I only made one mistake:

I paid half his fee in advance. Enough to send him to the tavern.
I only hope . . . [*She runs off.*]

LAVRENTI. She saved on the priest, the wretch! Hired a cheap monk.

GRUSHA. You *will* send Simon Shashava over to see me if he turns
up after all?

LAVRENTI. Yes. [*Pointing at the* SICK MAN] Won't you take a look
at him? [GRUSHA, *taking* MICHAEL *to her, shakes her head.*] He's
not moving an eyelid. I hope we aren't too late.

> [*They listen. On the opposite side enter* NEIGHBORS *who look
> around and take up positions against the walls, thus forming
> another wall near the bed, yet leaving an opening so that the
> bed can be seen. They start murmuring prayers. Enter the*
> MOTHER-IN-LAW *with a* MONK. *Showing some annoyance and
> surprise, she bows to the* GUESTS.]

THE MOTHER-IN-LAW. I hope you won't mind waiting a few moments? My son's bride has just arrived from the city. An emergency wedding is about to be celebrated. [*To the* MONK *in the
bedroom.*] I might have known you couldn't keep your trap shut.
[*To* GRUSHA.] The wedding can take place at once. Here's the
license. I myself and the bride's brother,

> [LAVRENTI *tries to hide in the background, after having quietly
> taken* MICHAEL *back from* GRUSHA. *The* MOTHER-IN-LAW
> *waves him away.*]

who will be here in a moment, are the witnesses.

> [GRUSHA *has bowed to the* MONK. *They go to the bed. The*
> MOTHER-IN-LAW *lifts the mosquito net. The* MONK *starts reel-
> ing off the marriage ceremony in Latin. Meanwhile, the*
> MOTHER-IN-LAW *beckons to* LAVRENTI *to get rid of the* CHILD,
> *but fearing that it will cry he draws its attention to the cere-
> mony.* GRUSHA *glances once at the* CHILD, *and* LAVRENTI *waves
> the* CHILD's *hand in a greeting.*]

THE MONK. Are you prepared to be a faithful, obedient, and good
wife to this man, and to cleave to him until death you do part?

GRUSHA. [*Looking at the* CHILD] I am.

THE MONK. [*To the* SICK PEASANT] And are you prepared to be a good
and loving husband to your wife until death you do part? [*As the*
SICK PEASANT *does not answer, the* MONK *looks inquiringly around.*]

THE MOTHER-IN-LAW. Of course he is! Didn't you hear him say yes?

THE MONK. All right. We declare the marriage contracted! How about
extreme unction?

THE MOTHER-IN-LAW. Nothing doing! The wedding cost quite
enough. Now I must take care of the mourners. [*To* LAVRENTI]
Did we say seven hundred?

LAVRENTI. Six hundred. [*He pays.*] Now I don't want to sit with
the guests and get to know people. So farewell, Grusha, and if my
widowed sister comes to visit me, she'll get a welcome from my

wife, or I'll show my teeth. [*Nods, gives the* CHILD *to* GRUSHA, *and leaves. The* MOURNERS *glance after him without interest.*]

THE MONK. May one ask where this child comes from?

THE MOTHER-IN-LAW. Is there a child? I don't see a child. And you don't see a child either—you understand? Or it may turn out I saw all sorts of things in the tavern! Now come on.

[*After* GRUSHA *has put the* CHILD *down and told him to be quiet, they move over left;* GRUSHA *is introduced to the* NEIGHBORS.]

This is my daughter-in-law. She arrived just in time fo find dear Jussup still alive.

ONE WOMAN. He's been ill now a whole year, hasn't he? When our Vassili was drafted he was there to say goodbye.

ANOTHER WOMAN. Such things are terrible for a farm. The corn all ripe and the farmer in bed! It'll really be a blessing if he doesn't suffer too long, I say.

THE FIRST WOMAN. [*Confidentially*] You know why we thought he'd taken to his bed? Because of the draft! And now his end is come!

THE MOTHER-IN-LAW. Sit yourselves down, please! And have some cakes!

[*She beckons to* GRUSHA *and both women go into the bedroom, where they pick up the cake pans off the floor. The* GUESTS, *among them the* MONK, *sit on the floor and begin conversing in subdued voices.*]

ONE PEASANT. [*To whom the* MONK *has handed the bottle which he has taken from his soutane*] There's a child, you say! How can that have happened to Jussup?

A WOMAN. She was certainly lucky to get herself hitched, with him so sick!

THE MOTHER-IN-LAW. They're gossiping already. And gorging themselves on the funeral cakes at the same time! If he doesn't die today, I'll have to bake some more tomorrow!

GRUSHA. I'll bake them for you.

THE MOTHER-IN-LAW. Yesterday some horsemen rode by, and I went out to see who it was. When I came in again he was lying there like a corpse! So I sent for you. It can't take much longer. [*She listens.*]

THE MONK. Dear wedding and funeral guests! Deeply touched, we stand before a bed of death and marriage. The bride gets a veil; the groom, a shroud: how varied, my children, are the fates of men! Alas! One man dies and has a roof over his head, and the other is married and the flesh turns to dust from which it was made. Amen.

THE MOTHER-IN-LAW. He's getting his own back. I shouldn't have hired such a cheap one. It's what you'd expect. A more expensive monk would behave himself. In Sura there's one with a real air of sanctity about him, but of course he charges a fortune. A fifty-piaster monk like that has no dignity, and as for piety, just fifty piasters' worth and no more! When I came to get him in the tavern he'd just made a speech, and he was shouting: "The war is over, beware of the peace!" We must go in.

GRUSHA. [*Giving* MICHAEL *a cake*] Eat this cake, and keep nice and still, Michael.

> [*The two women offer cakes to the* GUESTS. *The* DYING MAN *sits up in bed. He puts his head out from under the mosquito net, stares at the two women, then sinks back again. The* MONK *takes two bottles from his soutane and offers them to the* PEASANT *beside him. Enter three* MUSICIANS *who are greeted with a sly wink by the monk.*]

THE MOTHER-IN-LAW. [*To the* MUSICIANS] What are you doing here? With instruments?

ONE MUSICIAN. Brother Anastasius here [*Pointing at the* MONK] told us there was a wedding on.

THE MOTHER-IN-LAW. What? You brought them? Three more on my neck! Don't you know there's a dying man in the next room?

THE MONK. A very tempting assignment for a musician: something that could be either a subdued Wedding March or a spirited Funeral Dance.

THE MOTHER-IN-LAW. Well, you might as well play. Nobody can stop you eating in any case.

> [*The* MUSICIANS *play a potpourri. The women serve cakes.*]

THE MONK. The trumpet sounds like a whining baby. And you, little drum, what have you got to tell the world?

THE DRUNKEN PEASANT. [*Beside the* MONK, *sings*]
Miss Roundass took the old old man
And said that marriage was the thing
To everyone who met'er.
She later withdrew from the contract because
Candles are better.

> [*The* MOTHER-IN-LAW *throws the* DRUNKEN PEASANT *out. The music stops. The* GUESTS *are embarrassed.*]

THE GUESTS. [*Loudly*]
—Have you heard? The Grand Duke is back! But the Princes are against him.
—They say the Shah of Persia has lent him a great army to restore order in Grusinia.
—But how is that possible? The Shah of Persia is the enemy . . .
—The enemy of Grusinia, you donkey, not the enemy of the Grand Duke!
—In any case, the war's over, so our soldiers are coming back.

> [GRUSHA *drops a cake pan.* GUESTS *help her pick up the cake.*]

AN OLD WOMAN. [*To* GRUSHA] Are you feeling bad? It's just excitement about dear Jussup. Sit down and rest a while, my dear.

[GRUSHA *staggers.*]

THE GUESTS. Now everything'll be the way it was. Only the taxes'll go up because now we'll have to pay for the war.

GRUSHA. [*Weakly*] Did someone say the soldiers are back?

A MAN. I did.

GRUSHA. It can't be true.

THE FIRST MAN. [*To a* WOMAN] Show her the shawl. We bought it from a soldier. It's from Persia.

GRUSHA. [*Looking at the shawl*] They are here. [*She gets up, takes a step, kneels down in prayer, takes the silver cross and chain out of her blouse, and kisses it.*]

THE MOTHER-IN-LAW. [*While the* GUESTS *silently watch* GRUSHA] What's the matter with you? Aren't you going to look after our guests? What's all this city nonsense got to do with us?

THE GUESTS. [*Resuming conversation while* GRUSHA *remains in prayer*]
—You can buy Persian saddles from the soldiers too. Though many want crutches in exchange for them.
—The big shots on one side can win a war, the soldiers on both sides lose it.
—Anyway, the war's over. It's something they can't draft you any more.

[*The* DYING MAN *sits bolt upright in bed. He listens.*]
—What we need is two weeks of good weather.
—Our pear trees are hardly bearing a thing this year.

THE MOTHER-IN-LAW. [*Offering cakes*] Have some more cakes and welcome! There are more!

[*The* MOTHER-IN-LAW *goes to the bedroom with the empty cake pans. Unaware of the* DYING MAN, *she is bending down to pick up another tray when he begins to talk in a hoarse voice.*]

THE PEASANT. How many more cakes are you going to stuff down their throats? Think I'm a goldmine?

[*The* MOTHER-IN-LAW *starts, stares at him aghast, while he climbs out from behind the mosquito net.*]

THE FIRST WOMAN. [*Talking kindly to* GRUSHA *in the next room*] Has the young wife got someone at the front?

A MAN. It's good news that they're on their way home, huh?

THE PEASANT. Don't stare at me like that! Where's this wife you've hung round my neck?

[*Receiving no answer, he climbs out of bed and in his night-shirt staggers into the other room. Trembling, she follows him with the cake pan.*]

THE GUESTS. [*Seeing him and shrieking*] Good God! Jussup!

[*Everyone leaps up in alarm. The women rush to the door.* GRUSHA, *still on her knees, turns round and stares at the* MAN.]

THE PEASANT. A funeral supper! You'd enjoy that, wouldn't you? Get out before I throw you out! [*As the* GUESTS *stampede from the house, gloomily to* GRUSHA] I've upset the apple cart, huh? [*Receiving no answer, he turns round and takes a cake from the pan which his mother is holding.*]

THE STORY TELLER. O confusion! The wife discovers she has a husband. By day there's the child, by night there's the husband. The lover is on his way both day and night. Husband and wife look at each other. The bedroom is small.

> [*Near the bed the* PEASANT *is sitting in a high wooden bathtub, naked; the* MOTHER-IN-LAW *is pouring water from a pitcher. Opposite,* GRUSHA *cowers with* MICHAEL, *who is playing at mending straw mats.*]

THE PEASANT. [*To his mother*] That's her work, not yours. Where's she hiding out now?

THE MOTHER-IN-LAW. [*Calling*] Grusha! The peasant wants you!

GRUSHA. [*To* MICHAEL] There are still two holes to mend.

THE PEASANT. [*When* GRUSHA *approaches*] Scrub my back!

GRUSHA. Can't the peasant do it himself?

THE PEASANT. "Can't the peasant do it himself?" Get the brush! To hell with you! Are you the wife here? Or are you a visitor? [*To the* MOTHER-IN-LAW] It's too cold!

THE MOTHER-IN-LAW. I'll run for hot water.

GRUSHA. Let me go.

THE PEASANT. You stay here.

> [*The* MOTHER-IN-LAW *exits.*]

Rub harder. And no shirking. You've seen a naked fellow before. That child didn't come out of thin air.

GRUSHA. The child was not conceived in joy, if that's what the peasant means.

THE PEASANT. [*Turning and grinning*] You don't look the type.

> [GRUSHA *stops scrubbing him, starts back. Enter the* MOTHER-IN-LAW.]

THE PEASANT. A nice thing you've hung around my neck! A simpleton for a wife!

THE MOTHER-IN-LAW. She just isn't co-operative.

THE PEASANT. Pour—but go easy! Ow! Go easy, I said. [*To* GRUSHA] Maybe you did something wrong in the city . . . I wouldn't be surprised. Why else should you be here? But I won't talk about that. I've not said a word about the illegitimate object you brought into my house either. But my patience has limits! It's against nature. [*To the* MOTHER-IN-LAW] More! [*To* GRUSHA] And even if your soldier does come back, you're married.

GRUSHA. Yes.

THE PEASANT. But your soldier won't come back. Don't you believe it.

GRUSHA. No.

THE PEASANT. You're cheating me. You're my wife and you're not my wife. Where you lie, nothing lies, and yet no other woman can lie there. When I go to work in the morning I'm tired—when I lie down at night I'm awake as the devil. God has given you sex—and what d'you do? I don't have ten piasters to buy myself a woman in the city. Besides, it's a long way. Woman weeds the fields and opens up her legs, that's what our calendar says. D'you hear?

GRUSHA. [*Quietly*] Yes. I didn't mean to cheat you out of it.

THE PEASANT. She didn't mean to cheat me out of it! Pour some more water! [*The* MOTHER-IN-LAW *pours.*] Ow!

THE STORY TELLER. As she sat by the stream to wash the linen
She saw his image in the water
And his face grew dimmer with the passing moons.
As she raised herself to wring the linen
She heard his voice from the murmuring maple
And his voice grew fainter with the passing moons.
Evasions and sighs grew more numerous,
Tears and sweat flowed.
With the passing moons the child grew up.

> [GRUSHA *sits by a stream, dipping linen into the water. In the rear, a few* CHILDREN *are standing.*]

GRUSHA. [*To* MICHAEL] You can play with them, Michael, but don't let them boss you around just because you're the littlest. [MICHAEL *nods and joins the* CHILDREN. *They start playing.*]

THE BIGGEST BOY. Today it's the Heads-Off Game. [*To a* FAT BOY] You're the Prince and you laugh. [*To* MICHAEL] You're the Governor. [*To a* GIRL] You're the Governor's wife and you cry when his head's cut off. And I do the cutting. [*He shows his wooden sword.*] With this. First, they lead the Governor into the yard. The Prince walks in front. The Governor's wife comes last.

> [*They form a procession. The* FAT BOY *is first and laughs. Then comes* MICHAEL, *then the* BIGGEST BOY, *and then the* GIRL, *who weeps.*]

MICHAEL. [*Standing still*] Me cut off head!

THE BIGGEST BOY. That's my job. You're the littlest. The Governor's the easy part. All you do is kneel down and get your head cut off—simple.

MICHAEL. Me want sword!

THE BIGGEST BOY. It's mine! [*He gives him a kick.*]

THE GIRL. [*Shouting to* GRUSHA] He won't play his part!

GRUSHA. [*Laughing*] Even the little duck is a swimmer, they say.

THE BIGGEST BOY. You can be the Prince if you can laugh. [MICHAEL *shakes his head.*]

THE FAT BOY. I laugh best. Let him cut off the head just once. Then you do it, then me.

[*Reluctantly, the* BIGGEST BOY *hands* MICHAEL *the wooden sword and kneels down. The* FAT BOY *sits down, slaps his thigh, and laughs with all his might. The* GIRL *weeps loudly.* MICHAEL *swings the big sword and "cuts off" the head. In doing so, he topples over.*]

THE BIGGEST BOY. Hey! I'll show you how to cut heads off!

[MICHAEL *runs away. The* CHILDREN *run after him.* GRUSHA *laughs, following them with her eyes. On looking back she sees* SIMON SHASHAVA *standing on the opposite bank. He wears a shabby uniform.*]

GRUSHA. Simon!

SIMON. Is that Grusha Vashnadze?

GRUSHA. Simon!

SIMON. [*Formally*] A good morning to the young lady. I hope she is well.

GRUSHA. [*Getting up gaily and bowing low*] A good morning to the soldier. God be thanked he has returned in good health.

SIMON. They found better fish, so they didn't eat me, said the haddock.

GRUSHA. Courage, said the kitchen boy. Good luck, said the hero.

SIMON. How are things here? Was the winter bearable? The neighbor considerate?

GRUSHA. The winter was a trifle rough, the neighbor as usual, Simon.

SIMON. May one ask if a certain person still dips her foot in the water when rinsing the linen?

GRUSHA. The answer is no. Because of the eyes in the bushes.

SIMON. The young lady is speaking of soldiers. Here stands a paymaster.

GRUSHA. A job worth twenty piasters?

SIMON. And lodgings.

GRUSHA. [*With tears in her eyes*] Behind the barracks under the date trees.

SIMON. Yes, there. A certain person has kept her eyes open.

GRUSHA. She has, Simon.

SIMON. And has not forgotten?

[GRUSHA *shakes her head.*]

So the door is still on its hinges as they say?

[GRUSHA *looks at him in silence and shakes her head again.*]

What's this? Is something not as it should be?

GRUSHA. Simon Shashava, I can never return to Nuka. Something has happened.

SIMON. What can have happened?

GRUSHA. For one thing, I knocked an Ironshirt down.

SIMON. Grusha Vashnadze must have had her reasons for that.

GRUSHA. Simon Shashava, I am no longer called what I used to be called.

SIMON. [*After a pause*] I do not understand.

GRUSHA. When do women change their names, Simon? Let me explain. Nothing stands between us. Everything is just as it was. You must believe that.

SIMON. Nothing stands between us and yet there's something?

GRUSHA. How can I explain it so fast and with the stream between us? Couldn't you cross the bridge there?

SIMON. Maybe it's no longer necessary.

GRUSHA. It's very necessary. Come over on this side, Simon. Quick!

SIMON. Does the young lady wish to say someone has come too late?

> [GRUSHA *looks up at him in despair, her face streaming with tears.* SIMON *stares before him. He picks up a piece of wood and starts cutting it.*]

THE STORY TELLER. So many words are said, so many left unsaid.

The soldier has come

Where he comes from, he does not say.

Hear what he thought and did not say:

"The battle began, gray at dawn, grew bloody at noon.

The first man fell in front of me, the second behind me, the third at my side.

I trod on the first, left the second behind, the third was run through by the captain.

One of my brothers died by steel, the other by smoke.

My neck caught fire, my hands froze in my gloves, my toes in my socks.

I fed on aspen buds, I drank maple juice, I slept on stone, in water."

SIMON. I see a cap in the grass. Is there a little one already?

GRUSHA. There is, Simon. How could I conceal the fact? But please don't worry, it is not mine.

SIMON. When the wind once starts to blow, they say, it blows through every cranny. The wife need say no more.

> [GRUSHA *looks into her lap and is silent.*]

THE STORY TELLER. There was yearning but there was no waiting.

The oath is broken. Neither could say why.

Hear what she thought but did not say:

"While you fought in the battle, soldier,

The bloody battle, the bitter battle

I found a helpless infant

I had not the heart to destroy him

I had to care for a creature that was lost

I had to stoop for breadcrumbs on the floor

I had to break myself for that which was not mine

That which was other people's.

Someone must help!

For the little tree needs water

The lamb loses its way when the shepherd is asleep
And its cry is unheard!"

SIMON. Give me back the cross I gave you. Better still, throw it in the
stream. [*He turns to go.*]

GRUSHA. [*Getting up*] Simon Shashava, don't go away! He isn't mine!
He isn't mine! [*She hears the* CHILDREN *calling.*] What's the matter, children?

VOICES. Soldiers! And they're taking Michael away!

> [GRUSHA *stands aghast as two* IRONSHIRTS, *with* MICHAEL *be-
> tween them, come toward her.*]

ONE OF THE IRONSHIRTS. Are you Grusha?

> [*She nods.*]

Is this your child?

GRUSHA. Yes.

> [SIMON *goes.*]

Simon!

THE IRONSHIRT. We have orders, in the name of the law, to take this
child, found in your custody, back to the city. It is suspected that
the child is Michael Abashwili, son and heir of the late Governor
Georgi Abashwili, and his wife, Natella Abashwili. Here is the
document and the seal. [*They lead the* CHILD *away.*]

GRUSHA. [*Running after them, shouting*] Leave him here. Please! He's
mine!

THE STORY TELLER. The ironshirts took the child, the beloved child.
The unhappy girl followed them to the city, the dreaded city.
She who had borne him demanded the child.
She who had raised him faced trial.
Who will decide the case?
To whom will the child be assigned?
Who will the judge be? A good judge? A bad?
The city was in flames.
In the judge's seat sat Azdak.[9]

4. The Story of the Judge

THE STORY TELLER. Hear the story of the judge
How he turned judge, how he passed judgment, what kind of judge
he was.
On that Easter Sunday of the great revolt, when the Grand Duke
was overthrown
And his Governor Abashwili, father of our child, lost his head
The Village Scrivener Azdak found a fugitive in the woods and hid
him in his hut.

> [AZDAK, *in rags and slightly drunk, is helping an* OLD BEGGAR
> *into his cottage.*]

9. The name AZDAK should be accented on the second syllable [Bentley's note].

AZDAK. Stop snorting, you're not a horse. And it won't do you any good with the police, to run like a snotty nose in April. Stand still, I say. [*He catches the* OLD MAN, *who has marched into the cottage as if he'd like to go through the wall.*] Sit down. Feed. Here's a hunk of cheese. [*From under some rags, in a chest, he fishes out some cheese, and the* OLD MAN *greedily begins to eat.*] Haven't eaten in a long time, huh? [*The* OLD MAN *growls.*] Why were you running like that, asshole? The cop wouldn't even have seen you.

THE OLD MAN. Had to! Had to!

AZDAK. Blue Funk? [*The* OLD MAN *stares, uncomprehending.*] Cold feet? Panic? Don't lick your chops like a Grand Duke. Or an old sow. I can't stand it. We have to accept respectable stinkers as God made them, but not you! I once heard of a senior judge who farted at a public dinner to show an independent spirit! Watching you eat like that gives me the most awful ideas. Why don't you say something? [*Sharply*] Show me your hand. Can't you hear? [*The* OLD MAN *slowly puts out his hand.*] White! So you're not a beggar at all! A fraud, a walking swindle! And I'm hiding you from the cops as though you were an honest man! Why were you running like that if you're a landowner? For that's what you are. Don't deny it! I see it in your guilty face! [*He gets up.*] Get out! [*The* OLD MAN *looks at him uncertainly.*] What are you waiting for, peasant-flogger?

THE OLD MAN. Pursued. Need undivided attention. Make proposition . . .

AZDAK. Make what? A proposition? Well, if that isn't the height of insolence. He's making me a proposition! The bitten man scratches his fingers bloody, and the leech that's biting him makes him a proposition! Get out, I tell you!

THE OLD MAN. Understand point of view! Persuasion! Pay hundred thousand piasters one night! Yes?

AZDAK. What, you think you can buy me? For a hundred thousand piasters? Let's say a hundred and fifty thousand. Where are they?

THE OLD MAN. Have not them here. Of course. Will be sent. Hope do not doubt.

AZDAK. Doubt very much. Get out!

[*The* OLD MAN *gets up, waddles to the door. A* VOICE *is heard off stage.*]

A VOICE. Azdak!

[*The* OLD MAN *turns, waddles to the opposite corner, stands still.*]

AZDAK. [*Calling out*] I'm not in! [*He walks to door.*] So you're sniffing around here again, Shauwa?

POLICEMAN SHAUWA. [*Reproachfully*] You've caught another rabbit, Azdak. And you promised me it wouldn't happen again!

AZDAK. [*Severely*] Shauwa, don't talk about things you don't understand. The rabbit is a dangerous and destructive beast. It feeds on plants, especially on the species of plants known as weeds. It must therefore be exterminated.

SHAUWA. Azdak, don't be so hard on me. I'll lose my job if I don't arrest you. I know you have a good heart.

AZDAK. I do not have a good heart! How often must I tell you I'm a man of intellect?

SHAUWA. [*Slyly*] I know, Azdak. You're a superior person. You say so yourself. I'm just a Christian and an ignoramus. So I ask you: When one of the Prince's rabbits is stolen, and I'm a policeman, what should I do with the offending party?

AZDAK. Shauwa, Shauwa, shame on you. You stand and ask me a question, than which nothing could be more seductive. It's like you were a woman—let's say that bad girl Nunowna, and you showed me your thigh—Nunowna's thigh, that would be—and asked me: "What shall I do with my thigh, it itches?" Is she as innocent as she pretends? Of course not. I catch a rabbit, but you catch a man. Man is made in God's image. Not so a rabbit, you know that. I'm a rabbit-eater, but you're a man-eater, Shauwa. And God will pass judgment on you. Shauwa, go home and repent. No, stop, there's something . . . [*He looks at the* OLD MAN *who stands trembling in the corner.*] No, it's nothing. Go home and repent. [*He slams the door behind* SHAUWA.] Now you're surprised, huh? Surprised I didn't hand you over? I couldn't hand over a bedbug to that animal. It goes against the grain. Now don't tremble because of a cop! So old and still so scared? Finish your cheese, but eat it like a poor man, or else they'll still catch you. Must I even explain how a poor man behaves? [*He pushes him down, and then gives him back the cheese.*] That box is the table. Lay your elbows on the table. Now, encircle the cheese on the plate like it might be snatched from you at any moment—what right have you to be safe, huh?—now, hold your knife like an undersized sickle, and give your cheese a troubled look because, like all beautiful things, it's already fading away. [AZDAK *watches him.*] They're after you, which speaks in your favor, but how can we be sure they're not mistaken about you? In Tiflis one time they hanged a landowner, a Turk, who could prove he quartered his peasants instead of merely cutting them in half, as is the custom, and he squeezed twice the usual amount of taxes out of them, his zeal was above suspicion. And yet they hanged him like a common criminal—because he was a Turk—a thing he couldn't do much about. What injustice! He got onto the gallows by a sheer fluke. In short, I don't trust you.

THE STORY TELLER. Thus Azdak gave the old beggar a bed,
And learned that old beggar was the old butcher, the Grand Duke himself,

And was ashamed.

He denounced himself and ordered the policeman to take him to Nuka, to court, to be judged.

[*In the court of justice three* IRONSHIRTS *sit drinking. From a beam hangs a man in judge's robes. Enter* AZDAK, *in chains, dragging* SHAUWA *behind him.*]

AZDAK. [*Shouting*] I've helped the Grand Duke, the Grand Thief, the Grand Butcher, to escape! In the name of justice I ask to be severely judged in public trial!

THE FIRST IRONSHIRT. Who's this queer bird?

SHAUWA. That's our Village Scrivener, Azdak.

AZDAK. I am contemptible! I am a traitor! A branded criminal! Tell them, flat-foot, how I insisted on being chained up and brought to the capital. Because I sheltered the Grand Duke, the Grand Swindler, by mistake. And how I found out afterwards. See the marked man denounce himself! Tell them how I forced you to walk with me half the night to clear the whole thing up.

SHAUWA. And all by threats. That wasn't nice of you, Azdak.

AZDAK. Shut your mouth, Shauwa. You don't understand. A new age is upon us! It'll go thundering over you. You're finished. The police will be wiped out—poof! Everything will be gone into, everything will be brought into the open. The guilty will give themselves up. Why? They couldn't escape the people in any case. [*To* SHAUWA] Tell them how I shouted all along Shoemaker Street: [*With big gestures, looking at the* IRONSHIRTS] "In my ignorance I let the Grand Swindler escape! So tear me to pieces, brothers!" I wanted to get it in first.

THE FIRST IRONSHIRT. And what did your brothers answer?

SHAUWA. They comforted him in Butcher Street, and they laughed themselves sick in Shoemaker Street. That's all.

AZDAK. But with you it's different. I can see you're men of iron. Brothers, where's the judge? I must be tried.

THE FIRST IRONSHIRT. [*Pointing at the hanged man*] There's the judge. And please stop "brothering" us. It's rather a sore spot this evening.

AZDAK. "There's the judge." An answer never heard in Grusinia before. Townsman, where's His Excellency the Governor? [*Pointing to the floor*] There's His Excellency, stranger. Where's the Chief Tax Collector? Where's the official Recruiting officer? The Patriarch? The Chief of Police? There, there, there—all there. Brothers I expected no less of you.

THE SECOND IRONSHIRT. What? *What* was it you expected, funny man?

AZDAK. What happened in Persia, brother, what happened in Persia?

THE SECOND IRONSHIRT. What did happen in Persia?

AZDAK. Everybody was hanged. Viziers, tax collectors. Everybody.

Forty years ago now. My grandfather, a remarkable man by the way,
saw it all. For three whole days. Everywhere.

THE SECOND IRONSHIRT. And who ruled when the Vizier was hanged?

AZDAK. A peasant ruled when the Vizier was hanged.

THE SECOND IRONSHIRT. And who commanded the army?

AZDAK. A soldier, a soldier.

THE SECOND IRONSHIRT. And who paid the wages?

AZDAK. A dyer. A dyer paid the wages.

THE SECOND IRONSHIRT. Wasn't it a weaver, maybe?

THE FIRST IRONSHIRT. And why did all this happen, Persian?

AZDAK. Why did all this happen? Must there be a special reason?
Why do you scratch yourself, brother? War! Too long a war! And
no justice! My grandfather brought back a song that tells how it
was. I will sing it for you. With my friend the policeman. [*To*
SHAUWA] And hold the rope tight. It's very suitable. [*He sings,
with* SHAUWA *holding the rope tight around him.*]

The Song of Injustice in Persia

Why don't our sons bleed any more? Why don't our daughters
weep?
Why do only the slaughter-house cattle have blood in their veins?
Why do only the willows shed tears on Lake Urmi?
The king must have a new province, the peasant must give up his
savings.
That the roof of the world might be conquered, the roof of the cot-
tage is torn down.
Our men are carried to the ends of the earth, so that great ones
can eat at home.
The soldiers kill each other, the marshals salute each other.
They bite the widow's tax money to see if it's good, their swords
break.
The battle was lost, the helmets were paid for.
[*Refrain*] Is it so? Is it so?

SHAUWA. [*Refrain*] Yes, yes, yes, yes, yes it's so.

AZDAK. Do you want to hear the rest of it?

[*The* FIRST IRONSHIRT *nods.*]

THE SECOND IRONSHIRT. [*To* SHAUWA] Did he teach you that song?

SHAUWA. Yes, only my voice isn't very good.

THE SECOND IRONSHIRT. No. [*To* AZDAK] Go on singing.

AZDAK. The second verse is about the peace. [*He sings.*]
The offices are packed, the streets overflow with officials.
The rivers jump their banks and ravage the fields.
Those who cannot let down their own trousers rule countries.
They can't count up to four, but they devour eight courses.
The corn farmers, looking round for buyers, see only the starving.
The weavers go home from their looms in rags.

[*Refrain*] Is it so? Is it so?

SHAUWA. [*Refrain*] Yes, yes, yes, yes, yes it's so.

AZDAK. That's why our sons don't bleed any more, that's why our daughters don't weep.

That's why only the slaughter-house cattle have blood in their veins,

And only the willows shed tears by Lake Urmi toward morning.

THE FIRST IRONSHIRT. Are you going to sing that song here in town?

AZDAK. Sure. What's wrong with it?

THE FIRST IRONSHIRT. Have you noticed that the sky's getting red?

[*Turning round,* AZDAK *sees the sky red with fire.*]

It's the people's quarters. On the outskirts of town. The carpet weavers have caught the "Persian Sickness," too. And they've been asking if Prince Kazbeki isn't eating too many courses. This morning they strung up the city judge. As for us we beat them to pulp. We were paid one hundred piasters per man, you understand?

AZDAK. [*After a pause*] I understand. [*He glances shyly round and, creeping away, sits down in a corner, his head in his hands.*]

THE IRONSHIRTS. [*To each other*]—If there ever was a trouble-maker it's him.

—He must've come to the capital to fish in the troubled waters.

SHAUWA. Oh, I don't think he's a really bad character, gentlemen. Steals a few chickens here and there. And maybe a rabbit.

THE SECOND IRONSHIRT. [*Approaching* AZDAK] Came to fish in the troubled waters, huh?

AZDAK. [*Looking up*] I don't know why I came.

THE SECOND IRONSHIRT. Are you in with the carpet weavers maybe?

[AZDAK *shakes his head.*]

How about that song?

AZDAK. From my grandfather. A silly and ignorant man.

THE SECOND IRONSHIRT. Right. And how about the dyer who paid the wages?

AZDAK. [*Muttering*] That was in Persia.

THE FIRST IRONSHIRT. And this denouncing of yourself? Because you didn't hang the Grand Duke with your own hands?

AZDAK. Didn't I tell you I let him run? [*He creeps farther away and sits on the floor.*]

SHAUWA. I can swear to that: he let him run.

[*The* IRONSHIRTS *burst out laughing and slap* SHAUWA *on the back.* AZDAK *laughs loudest. They slap* AZDAK *too, and unchain him. They all start drinking as the* FAT PRANCE *enters with a* YOUNG MAN.]

THE FIRST IRONSHIRT. [*To* AZDAK, *pointing at the* FAT PRINCE] There's your "new age" for you!

[*More laughter*]

THE FAT PRINCE. Well, my friends, what is there to laugh about?

Permit me a serious word. Yesterday morning the Princes of Grusinia overthrew the war-mongering government of the Grand Duke and did away with his Governors. Unfortunately the Grand Duke himself escaped. In this fateful hour our carpet weavers, those eternal trouble-makers, had the effrontery to stir up a rebellion and hang the universally loved city judge, our dear Illo Orbeliani. Ts—ts—ts. My friends, we need peace, peace, peace in Grusinia! And justice! So I've brought along my dear nephew Bizergan Kazbeki. He'll be the new judge, hm? A very gifted fellow. What do you say? I want your opinion. Let the people decide!

THE SECOND IRONSHIRT. Does this mean *we* elect the judge?

THE FAT PRINCE. Precisely. Let the people propose some very gifted fellow! Confer among yourselves, my friends.

[*The* IRONSHIRTS *confer.*]

Don't worry, my little fox. The job's yours. And when we catch the Grand Duke we won't have to kiss this rabble's ass any longer.

THE IRONSHIRTS. [*Between themselves*]—Very funny: they're wetting their pants because they haven't caught the Grand Duke. —When the outlook isn't so bright, they say: "My friends!" and "Let the people decide!" —Now he even wants justice for Grusinia! But fun is fun as long as it lasts!

[*Pointing at* AZDAK] —He knows all about justice. Hey, rascal, would you like this nephew fellow to be the judge?

AZDAK. Are you asking me? You're not asking *me*?!

THE FIRST IRONSHIRT. Why not? Anything for a laugh!

AZDAK. You'd like to test him to the marrow, correct? Have you a criminal on hand? An experienced one? So the candidate can show what he knows?

THE SECOND IRONSHIRT. Let's see. We do have a couple of doctors downstairs. Let's use them.

AZDAK. Oh, no, that's no good, we can't take real criminals till we're sure the judge will be appointed. He may be dumb, but he must be appointed, or the Law is violated. And the Law is a sensitive organ. I's like the spleen, you mustn't hit it—that would be fatal. Of course you can hang those two without violating the Law, because there was no judge in the vicinity. But Judgment, when pronounced, must be pronounced with absolute gravity—it's all such nonsense. Suppose, for instance, a judge jails a woman—let's say she's stolen a corn cake to feed her child—and this judge isn't wearing his robes—or maybe he's scratching himself while passing sentence and half his body is uncovered—a man's thigh *will* itch once in a while—the sentence this judge passes is a disgrace and the Law is violated. In short it would be easier for a judge's robe and a judge's hat to pass judgment than for a man with no robe and no hat. If you don't treat it with respect, the Law just disappears on you. Now you don't try out a bottle of wine by offering it to a dog; you'd only lose your wine.

THE FIRST IRONSHIRT. Then what do you suggest, hair-splitter?

AZDAK. I'll be the defendant.

THE FIRST IRONSHIRT. You? [*He bursts out laughing.*]

THE FAT PRINCE. What have you decided?

THE FIRST IRONSHIRT. We've decided to stage a rehearsal. Our friend here will be the defendant. Let the candidate be the judge and sit there.

THE FAT PRINCE. It isn't customary, but why not? [*To the* NEPHEW.] A mere formality, my little fox. What have I taught you? Who got there first—the slow runner or the fast?

THE NEPHEW. The silent runner, Uncle Arsen.

[*The* NEPHEW *takes the chair. The* IRONSHIRTS *and the* FAT PRINCE *sit on the steps. Enter* AZDAK, *mimicking the gait of the Grand Duke.*]

AZDAK. [*In the Grand Duke's accent*] Is any here knows me? Am Grand Duke.

THE IRONSHIRTS.
—What is he?
—The Grand Duke. He knows him, too.
—Fine. So get on with the trial.

AZDAK. Listen! Am accused instigating war? Ridiculous! Am saying ridiculous! That enough? If not, have brought lawyers. Believe five hundred. [*He points behind him, pretending to be surrounded by lawyers.*] Requisition all available seats for lawyers! [*The* IRONSHIRTS *laugh; the* FAT PRINCE *joins in.*]

THE NEPHEW. [*To the* IRONSHIRTS] You really wish me to try this case?

I find it rather unusual. From the taste angle, I mean.

THE FIRST IRONSHIRT. Let's go!

THE FAT PRINCE. [*Smiling*] Let him have it, my little fox!

THE NEPHEW. All right. People of Grusinia versus Grand Duke. Defendant, what have you got to say for yourself?

AZDAK. Plenty. Naturally, have read war lost. Only started on the advice of patriots. Like Uncle Arsen Kazbeki. Call Uncle Arsen as witness.

THE FAT PRINCE. [*To the* IRONSHIRTS, *delightedly*] What a screwball!

THE NEPHEW. Motion rejected. One cannot be arraigned for declaring a war, which every ruler has to do once in a while, but only for running a war badly.

AZDAK. Rubbish! Did not run it at all! Had it run! Had it run by Princes! Naturally, they messed it up.

THE NEPHEW. Do you by any chance deny having been commander-in-chief?

AZDAK. Not at all! Always *was* commander-in-chief. At birth shouted at wet nurse. Was trained drop turds in toilet, grew accustomed to command. Always commanded officials rob my cash box. Officers flog soldiers only on command. Landowners sleep with peasants' wives only on strictest command. Uncle Arsen here grew his belly at *my* command!

THE IRONSHIRTS. [*Clapping*] He's good! Long live the Grand Duke!

THE FAT PRINCE. Answer him, my little fox. I'm with you.

THE NEPHEW. I shall answer him according to the dignity of the law. Defendant, preserve the dignity of the law!

AZDAK. Agreed. Command you to proceed with the trial!

THE NEPHEW. It is not your place to command me. You claim that the Princes forced you to declare war. How can you claim, then, that they—er—"messed it up"?

AZDAK. Did not send enough people. Embezzled funds. Sent sick horses. During attack, drinking in whore house. Call Uncle Arsen as witness.

THE NEPHEW. Are you making the outrageous suggestion that the Princes of this country did not fight?

AZDAK. No. Princes fought. Fought for war contracts.

THE FAT PRINCE. [*Jumping up*] That's too much! This man talks like a carpet weaver!

AZDAK. Really? I told nothing but the truth.

THE FAT PRINCE. Hang him! Hang him!

THE FIRST IRONSHIRT. [*Pulling the* PRINCE *down*] Keep quiet! Go on, Excellency!

THE NEPHEW. Quiet! I now render a verdict: You must be hanged! By the neck! Having lost war!

AZDAK. Young man, seriously advise not fall publicly into jerky clipped manner of speech. Cannot be employed as watchdog if howl like wolf. Got it? If people realize Princes speak same language as Grand Duke, may hang Grand Duke *and Princes*, huh? By the way, must overrule verdict. Reason? War lost, but not for Princes. Princes won their war. Got 3,863,000 piasters for horses not delivered, 8,240,000 piasters for food supplies not produced. Are therefore victors. War lost only for Grusinia, which as such is not present in this court.

THE FAT PRINCE. I think that will do, my friends. [*To* AZDAK] You can withdraw, funny man. [*To the* IRONSHIRTS] You may now ratify the new judge's appointment, my friends.

THE FIRST IRONSHIRT. Yes, we can. Take down the judge's gown.

[*One* IRONSHIRT *climbs on the back of the other, pulls the gown off the hanged man.*]

[*To the* NEPHEW] Now you run away so the right ass can get on the right chair. [*To* AZDAK] Step forward! Go to the judge's seat! now sit in it [AZDAK *steps up, bows, and sits down.*] The judge was always a rascal! Now the rascal shall be a judge! [*The judge's gown is placed round his shoulders, the hat on his head.*] And what a judge!

THE STORY TELLER. And there was civil war in the land.

The mighty were not safe.

And Azdak was made a judge by the Ironshirts.

And Azdak remained a judge for two years.

THE STORY TELLER AND CHORUS. When the towns were set afire

And rivers of blood rose higher and higher,

Cockroaches crawled out of every crack.

And the court was full of schemers

And the church of foul blasphemers.

In the judge's cassock sat Azdak.

> [AZDAK *sits in the judge's chair, peeling an apple.* SHAUWA *is sweeping out the hall. On one side an* INVALID *in a wheelchair. Opposite, a* YOUNG MAN *accused of blackmail. An* IRONSHIRT *stands guard, holding the* IRONSHIRT'S *banner.*]

AZDAK. In consideration of the large number of cases, the Court today will hear two cases at a time. Before I open the proceedings, a short announcement—I accept. [*He stretches out his hand. The* BLACKMAILER *is the only one to produce any money. He hands it to* AZDAK.] I reserve the right to punish one of the parties for contempt of court. [*He glances at the* INVALID.] You [*To the* DOCTOR] are a doctor, and you [*To the* INVALID] are bringing a complaint against him. Is the doctor responsible for your condition?

THE INVALID. Yes. I had a stroke on his account.

AZDAK. That would be professional negligence.

THE INVALID. Worse than negligence. I gave this man money for his studies. So far, he hasn't paid me back a cent. It was when I heard he was treating a patient free that I had my stroke.

AZDAK. Rightly. [*To a* LIMPING MAN] And what are you doing here?

THE LIMPING MAN. I'm the patient, your honor.

AZDAK. He treated your leg for nothing?

THE LIMPING MAN. The wrong leg! My rheumatism was in the left leg, and he operated on the right. That's why I limp now.

AZDAK. And you were treated free?

THE INVALID. A five-hundred-piaster operation free! For nothing! For God-bless-you! And I paid for this man's studies! [*To the* DOCTOR] Did they teach you to operate free?

THE DOCTOR. Your Honor, it is actually the custom to demand the fee before the operation, as the patient is more willing to pay before an operation than after. Which is only human. In the case in question I was convinced, when I started the operation, that my servant had already received the fee. In this I was mistaken.

THE INVALID. He was mistaken! A good doctor doesn't make mistakes!

He examines before he operates!

AZDAK. That's right. [*To* SHAUWA] Public Prosecutor, what's the other case about?

SHAUWA. [*Busily sweeping*] Blackmail.

THE BLACKMAILER. High Court of Justice, I'm innocent. I only wanted to find out from the landowner concerned if he really *had* raped his niece. He informed me very politely that this was not the case, and gave me the money only so I could pay for my uncle's studies.

AZDAK. Hm. [*To the* DOCTOR] You, on the other hand, can cite no extenuating circumstances for your offense, huh?

THE DOCTOR. Except that to err is human.

AZDAK. And you are aware that in money matters a good doctor is a highly responsible person? I once heard of a doctor who got a thousand piasters for a sprained finger by remarking that sprains have something to do with blood circulation, which after all a less good doctor might have overlooked, and who, on another occasion made a real gold mine out of a somewhat disordered gall bladder, he treated it with such loving care. You have no excuse, Doctor. The corn merchant, Uxu, had his son study medicine to get some knowledge of trade, our medical schools are so good. [*To the* BLACKMAILER] What's the landowner's name?

SHAUWA. He doesn't want it mentioned.

AZDAK. In that case I will pass judgment. The Court considers the blackmail proved. And you [*To the* INVALID] are sentenced to a fine of one thousand piasters. If you have a second stroke, the doctor will have to treat you free. Even if he has to amputate. [*To the* LIMPING MAN.] As compensation, you will receive a bottle of rubbing alcohol. [*To the* BLACKMAILER] You are sentenced to hand over half the proceeds of your deal to the Public Prosecutor to keep the landowner's name secret. You are advised, moreover, to study medicine—you seem well suited to that calling. [*To the* DOCTOR] You have perpetrated an unpardonable error in the practice of your profession: you are acquitted. Next cases!

THE STORY TELLER AND CHORUS. Men won't do much for a shilling.
For a pound they may be willing.
For 20 pounds the verdict's in the sack.
As for the many, all too many,
Those who've only got a penny—
They've one single, sole recourse: Azdak.

[*Enter* AZDAK *from the caravansary on the highroad, followed by an old bearded* INNKEEPER. *The judge's chair is carried by a* STABLEMAN *and* SHAUWA. *An* IRONSHIRT, *with a banner, takes up his position.*]

AZDAK. Put me down. Then we'll get some air, maybe even a good stiff breeze from the lemon grove there. It does justice good to be done in the open: the wind blows her skirts up and you can see what she's got. Shauwa, we've been eating too much. These official journeys are exhausting. [*To the* INNKEEPER] It's a question of your daughter-in-law?

THE INNKEEPER. Your Worship, it's a question of the family honor. I wish to bring an action on behalf of my son, who's on business on the other side of the mountain. This is the offending stableman, and here's my daughter-in-law.

[*Enter the* DAUGHTER-IN-LAW, *a voluptuous wench. She is veiled.*]

AZDAK. [*Sitting down*] I accept. [*Sighing, the* INNKEEPER *hands him some money.*] Good. Now the formalities are disposed of. This is a case of rape?

THE INNKEEPER. Your Honor, I caught the fellow in the act. Ludovica was in the straw on the stable floor.

AZDAK. Quite right, the stable. Lovely horses! I specially liked the little roan.

THE INNKEEPER. The first thing I did, of course, was to question Ludovica. On my son's behalf.

AZDAK. [*Seriously*] I said I specially liked the little roan.

THE INNKEEPER. [*Coldly*] Really? Ludovica confessed the stableman took her against her will.

AZDAK. Take your veil off, Ludovica.

[*She does so.*]

Ludovica, you please the Court. Tell us how it happened.

LUDOVICA. [*Well-schooled*] When I entered the stable to see the new foal the stableman said to me on his own accord: "It's hot today!" and laid his hand on my left breast. I said to him: "Don't do that!" But he continued to handle me indecently, which provoked my anger. Before I realized his sinful intentions, he got much closer. It was all over when my father-in-law entered and accidentally trod on me.

THE INNKEEPER. [*Explaining*] On my son's behalf.

AZDAK. [*To the* STABLEMAN] You admit you started it?

THE STABLEMAN. Yes.

AZDAK. Ludovica, you like to eat sweet things?

LUDOVICA. Yes, sunflower seeds!

AZDAK. You like to lie a long time in the bathtub?

LUDOVICA. Half an hour or so.

AZDAK. Public Prosecutor, drop your knife—there—on the ground.

[SHAUWA *does so.*]

Ludovica, pick up that knife.

[LUDOVICA, *swaying her hips, does so.*]

See that? [*He points at her.*] The way it moves? The rape is now proven. By eating too much—sweet things, especially—by lying too long in warm water, by laziness and too soft a skin, you have

raped that unfortunate man. Think you can run around with a behind like that and get away with it in court? This is a case of
intentional assault with a dangerous weapon! You are sentenced to
hand over to the Court the little roan which your father liked to
ride "on his son's behalf." And now, come with me to the stables,
so the Court may inspect the scene of the crime, Ludovica.

THE STORY TELLER AND CHORUS. When the sharks the sharks devour
Little fishes have their hour.
For a while the load is off their back.
On Grusinia's highways faring
Fixed-up scales of justice bearing
Strode the poor man's magistrate: Azdak.

And he gave to the forsaken
All that from the rich he'd taken.
And a bodyguard of roughnecks was Azdak's.
And our good and evil man, he
Smiled upon Grusinia's Granny.
His emblem was a tear in sealing wax.

All mankind should love each other
But when visiting your brother
Take an ax along and hold it fast.
Not in theory but in practice
Miracles are wrought with axes
And the age of miracles is not past.

> [AZDAK's *judge's chair is in a tavern. Three* RICH FARMERS
> *stand before* AZDAK. SHAUWA *brings him wine. In a corner
> stands an* OLD PEASANT WOMAN. *In the open doorway, and
> outside, stand* VILLAGERS *looking on. An* IRONSHIRT *stands
> guard with a banner.*]

AZDAK. The Public Prosecutor has the floor.

SHAUWA. It concerns a cow. For five weeks the defendant has had a
cow in her stable, the property of the farmer Suru. She was also
found to be in possession of a stolen ham, and a number of cows
belonging to Shutoff were killed after he asked the defendant to
pay the rent on a piece of land.

THE FARMERS.
—It's a matter of my ham, Your Honor.
—It's a matter of my cow, Your Honor.
—It's a matter of my land, Your Honor.

AZDAK. Well, Granny, what have you got to say to all this?

THE OLD WOMAN. Your Honor, one night toward morning, five weeks
ago, there was a knock at my door, and outside stood a bearded
man with a cow. "My dear woman," he said, "I am the miracle-
working Saint Banditus and because your son has been killed in

the war, I bring you this cow as a souvenir. Take good care of it."

THE FARMERS.

—The robber, Irakli, Your Honor!

—Her brother-in-law, Your Honor!

—The cow-thief!

—The incendiary!

—He must be beheaded!

[*Outside, a* WOMAN *screams. The* CROWD *grows restless, retreats. Enter the* BANDIT IRAKLI *with a huge ax.*]

THE BANDIT. A very good evening, dear friends! A glass of vodka!

THE FARMERS. [*Crossing themselves*] Irakli!

AZDAK. Public Prosecutor, a glass of vodka for our guest. And who are you?

THE BANDIT. I'm a wandering hermit, Your Honor. Thanks for the gracious gift. [*He empties the glass which* SHAUWA *has brought.*] Another!

AZDAK. I am Azdak. [*He gets up and bows. The* BANDIT *also bows.*] The Court welcomes the foreign hermit. Go on with your story, Granny.

THE OLD WOMAN. Your Honor, that first night I didn't yet know Saint Banditus could work miracles, it was only the cow. But one night, a few days later, the farmer's servants came to take the cow away again. Then they turned round in front of my door and went off without the cow. And bumps as big as a fist sprouted on their heads. So I knew that Saint Banditus had changed their hearts and turned them into friendly people.

[*The* BANDIT *roars with laughter.*]

THE FIRST FARMER. I know what changed them.

AZDAK. That's fine. You can tell us later. Continue.

THE OLD WOMAN. Your Honor, the next one to become a good man was the farmer Shutoff—a devil, as everyone knows. But Saint Banditus arranged it so he let me off the rent on the little piece of land.

THE SECOND FARMER. Because my cows were killed in the field.

[*The* BANDIT *laughs.*]

THE OLD WOMAN. [*Answering* AZDAK's *sign to continue*] Then one morning the ham came flying in at my window. It hit me in the small of the back. I'm still lame, Your Honor, look. [*She limps a few steps.*]

[*The* BANDIT *laughs.*]

Your Honor, was there ever a time when a poor old woman could get a ham *without* a miracle?

[*The* BANDIT *starts sobbing.*]

AZDAK. [*Rising from his chair*] Granny, that's a question that strikes straight at the Court's heart. Be so kind as to sit here.

[*The* OLD WOMAN, *hesitating, sits in the judge's chair.*]

AZDAK. [*Sits on the floor, glass in hand, reciting*] Granny
We could almost call you Granny Grusinia
The Woebegone
The Bereaved Mother
Whose sons have gone to war
Receiving the present of a cow
She bursts out crying.
When she is beaten
She remains hopeful.
When she's not beaten
She's surprised.
On us
Who are already damned
May you render a merciful verdict
Granny Grusinia!

[*Bellowing at* THE FARMERS] Admit you don't believe in miracles
you atheists! Each of you is sentenced to pay five hundred piasters
For godlessness! Get out!
    [*The* FARMERS *slink out.*]
And you Granny, and you [*To the* BANDIT] *pious man, empty a*
pitcher of wine with the Public Prosecutor and Azdak
THE STORY TELLER AND CHORUS. And he broke the rules to save them.
Broken law like bread he gave them,
Brought them to shore upon his crooked back.
At long last the poor and lowly
Had someone who was not too holy
To be bribed by empty hands: Azdak.

For two years it was his pleasure
To give the beasts of prey short measure:
He became a wolf to fight the pack.
From All Hallows to All Hallows[10]
On his chair beside the gallows
Dispensing justice in his fashion sat Azdak.
THE STORY TELLER. But the era of disorder came to an end.
The Grand Duke returned.
The Governor's wife returned.
A trial was held.
Many died.
The people's quarters burned anew.
And fear seized Azdak.
    [AZDAK's *judge's chair stands again in the court of justice.*
    AZDAK *sits on the floor, shaving and talking to* SHAUWA. *Noises*
    outside. In the rear the FAT PRINCE's *head is carried by on a*
    lance.]

10. *All Hallows:* All Souls' Day, November 1.

AZDAK. Shauwa, the days of your slavery are numbered, maybe even the minutes. For a long time now I have held you in the iron curb of reason, and it has torn your mouth till it bleeds. I have lashed you with reasonable arguments, I have manhandled you with logic. You are by nature a weak man, and if one slyly throws an argument in your path, you *have* to snap it up, you can't resist. It is your nature to lick the hand of some superior being. But superior beings can be of very different kinds. And now, with your liberation, you will soon be able to follow your natural inclinations, which are low. You will be able to follow your infallible instinct, which teaches you to plant your fat heel on the faces of men. Gone is the era of confusion and disorder, which I find described in the Song of Chaos. Let us now sing that song together in memory of those terrible days. Sit down and don't do violence to the music. Don't be afraid. It sounds all right. And it has a fine refrain. [*He sings.*]

The Song of Chaos

Sister, hide your face! Brother, take your knife!
The times are out of joint!
Big men are full of complaint
And small men full of joy.
The city says:
"Let us drive the strong ones from our midst!"
Offices are raided. Lists of serfs are destroyed.
They have set Master's nose to the grindstone.
They who lived in the dark have seen the light.
The ebony poor box is broken.
Sesnem wood is sawed up for beds.
Who had no bread have barns full.
Who begged for alms of corn now mete it out.
SHAUWA. [*Refrain*] Oh, oh, oh, oh.
AZDAK. [*Refrain*] Where are you, General, where are you?
Please, please, please, restore order!
The nobleman's son can no longer be recognized;
The lady's child becomes the son of her slave.
The councilors meet in a shed.
Once, this man was barely allowed to sleep on the wall;
Now, he stretches his limbs in a bed.
Once, this man rowed a boat; now, he owns ships.
Their owner looks for them, but they're his no longer.
Five men are sent on a journey by their master.
"Go yourself," they say, "we have arrived."
SHAUWA. [*Refrain*] Oh, oh, oh, oh.
AZDAK. [*Refrain*] Where are you, General, where are you?
Please, please, please, restore order!
Yes, so it might have been, had order been neglected much longer.

But now the Grand Duke has returned to the capital, and the Persians have lent him an army to restore order with. The suburbs are already aflame. Go and get me the big book I always sit on.

[SHAUWA *brings the big book from the judge's chair.* AZDAK *opens it.*]

This is the Statute Book and I've always used it, as you can testify. Now I'd better look in this book and see what they can do to me. I've let the down-and-outs get away with murder, and I'll have to pay for it. I helped poverty onto its skinny legs, so they'll hang me for drunkenness. I peeped into the rich man's pocket, which is bad taste. And I can't hide anywhere—everybody knows me because I've helped everybody.

SHAUWA. Someone's coming!

AZDAK. [*In panic, he walks trembling to the chair.*] It's the end. And now they'd enjoy seeing what a Great Man I am. I'll deprive them of that pleasure. I'll beg on my knees for mercy. Spittle will slobber down my chin. The fear of death is in me.

[*Enter* NATELLA ABASHWILI, *the* GOVERNOR'S WIFE, *followed by the* ADJUTANT *and an* IRONSHIRT.]

THE GOVERNOR'S WIFE. What sort of a creature is that, Shalva?

AZDAK. A willing one, Your Highness, a man ready to oblige.

THE ADJUTANT. Natella Abashwili, wife of the late Governor, has just returned. She is looking for her two-year-old son, Michael. She has been informed that the child was carried off to the mountains by a former servant.

AZDAK. The child will be brought back, Your Highness, at your service.

THE ADJUTANT. They say that the person in question is passing it off as her own.

AZDAK. She will be beheaded, Your Highness, at your service.

THE ADJUTANT. That is all.

THE GOVERNOR'S WIFE. [*Leaving*] I don't like that man.

AZDAK. [*Following her to door, bowing*] At your service, Your Highness, it will all be arranged.

5. *The Chalk Circle*

THE STORY TELLER. Hear now the story of the trial
Concerning Governor Abashwili's child
And the establishing of the true mother
By the famous test of the Chalk Circle.

[*The court of justice in Nuka.* IRONSHIRTS *lead* MICHAEL *across stage and out at the back.* IRONSHIRTS *hold* GRUSHA *back with their lances under the gateway until the* CHILD *has been led through. Then she is admitted. She is accompanied by the former governor's* COOK. *Distant noises and a fire-red sky.*]

GRUSHA. [*Trying to hide*] He's brave, he can wash himself now.

THE COOK. You're lucky. It's not a real judge. It's Azdak, a drunk who doesn't know what he's doing. The biggest thieves have got by through him. Because he gets everything mixed up and the rich never offer him big enough bribes, the likes of us sometimes do pretty well.

GRUSHA. I *need* luck right now.

THE COOK. Touch wood. [*She crosses herself.*] I'd better offer up another prayer that the judge may be drunk. [*She prays with motionless lips, while* GRUSHA *looks around, in vain, for the child.*] Why must you hold on to him at any price if he isn't yours? In days like these?

GRUSHA. He's mine. I brought him up.

THE COOK. Have you never thought what'd happen when she came back?

GRUSHA. At first I thought I'd give him to her. Then I thought she wouldn't come back.

THE COOK. And even a borrowed coat keeps a man warm, hm?

[GRUSHA *nods.*]

I'll swear to anything for you. You're a decent girl. [*She sees the soldier* SIMON SHASHAVA *approaching.*] You've done wrong by Simon, though. I've been talking with him. He just can't understand.

GRUSHA. [*Unaware of* SIMON's *presence*] Right now I can't be bothered whether he understands or not!

THE COOK. He knows the child isn't yours, but you married and not free "till death you do part"—he can't understand *that.*

[GRUSHA *sees* SIMON *and greets him.*]

SIMON. [*Gloomily*] I wish the lady to know I will swear I am the father of the child.

GRUSHA. [*Low*] Thank you, Simon.

SIMON. At the same time I wish the lady to know my hands are not tied—nor are hers.

THE COOK. You needn't have said that. You know she's married.

SIMON. And it needs no rubbing in.

[*Enter an* IRONSHIRT.]

THE IRONSHIRT. Where's the judge? Has anyone seen the judge?

ANOTHER IRONSHIRT. [*Stepping forward*] The judge isn't here yet. Nothing but a bed and a pitcher in the whole house!

[*Exeunt* IRONSHIRTS.]

THE COOK. I hope nothing has happened to him. With any other judge you'd have about as much chance as a chicken has teeth.

GRUSHA. [*Who has turned away and covered her face*] Stand in front of me. I shouldn't have come to Nuka. If I run into the Ironshirt, the one I hit over the head . . .

[*She screams. An* IRONSHIRT *had stopped and, turning his back, had been listening to her. He now wheels around. It is the* CORPORAL, *and he has a huge scar across his face.*]

THE IRONSHIRT. [*In the gateway*] What's the matter, Shotta? Do you know her?

THE CORPORAL. [*After staring for some time*] No.

THE IRONSHIRT. She's the one who stole the Abashwili child, or so they say. If you know anything about it you can make some money, Shotta.

[*Exit the* CORPORAL, *cursing.*]

THE COOK. Was it him? [GRUSHA *nods.*] I think he'll keep his mouth shut, or he'd be admitting he was after the child.

GRUSHA. I'd almost forgotten him.

[*Enter the* GOVERNOR'S WIFE, *followed by the* ADJUTANT *and two* LAWYERS.]

THE GOVERNOR'S WIFE. At least there are no common people here, thank God. I can't stand their smell. It always gives me migraine.

THE FIRST LAWYER. Madam, I must ask you to be careful what you say until we have another judge.

THE GOVERNOR'S WIFE. But I didn't say anything, Illo Shuboladze. I love the people with their simple straightforward minds. It's only that their smell brings on my migraine.

THE SECOND LAWYER. There won't be many spectators. The whole population is sitting at home behind locked doors because of the riots on the outskirts of town.

THE GOVERNOR'S WIFE. [*Looking at* GRUSHA] Is that the creature?

THE FIRST LAWYER. Please, most gracious Natella Abashwili, abstain from invective until it is certain the Grand Duke has appointed a new judge and we're rid of the present one, who's about the lowest fellow ever seen in judge's gown. Things are all set to move, you see.

[*Enter* IRONSHIRTS *from the courtyard.*]

THE COOK. Her Grace would pull your hair out on the spot if she didn't know Azdak is for the poor. He goes by the face.

[IRONSHIRTS *begin fastening a rope to a beam.* AZDAK, *in chains, is led in, followed by* SHAUWA, *also in chains. The three* FARMERS *bring up the rear.*]

AN IRONSHIRT. Trying to run away, were you? [*He strikes* AZDAK.]

ONE FARMER. Off with his judge's gown before we string him up!

[IRONSHIRTS *and* FARMERS *tear off* AZDAK's *gown. His torn underwear is visible. Then someone kicks him.*]

AN IRONSHIRT. [*Pushing him into someone else*] If you want a heap of justice, here it is!

[*Accompanied by shouts of "You take it!" and "Let me have him, Brother!" they throw* AZDAK *back and forth until he collapses. Then he is lifted up and dragged under the noose.*]

THE GOVERNOR'S WIFE. [*Who, during this "Ball-game" has clapped her hands hysterically*] I disliked that man from the moment I first saw him.

AZDAK. [*Covered with blood, panting*] I can't see. Give me a rag.

AN IRONSHIRT. What is it you want to see?

AZDAK. You, you dogs! [*He wipes the blood out of his eyes with his shirt.*] Good morning, dogs! How goes it, dogs! How's the dog world? Does it smell good? Got another boot for me to lick? Are you back at each other's throats, dogs?

> [*Accompanied by a* CORPORAL, *a dust-covered* RIDER *enters. He takes some documents from a leather case, looks at them, then interrupts.*]

THE RIDER. Stop! I bring a dispatch from the Grand Duke, containing the latest appointments.

THE CORPORAL. [*Bellowing*] Atten-shun!

THE RIDER. Of the new judge it says: "We appoint a man whom we have to thank for saving a life indispensable to the country's welfare—a certain Azdak of Nuka." Which is he?

SHAUWA. [*Pointing*] That's him, Your Excellency.

THE CORPORAL. [*Bellowing*] What's going on here?

AN IRONSHIRT. I beg to report that His Honor Azdak was already His Honor Azdak, but on these farmer's denunciation was pronounced the Grand Duke's enemy.

THE CORPORAL. [*Pointing at the* FARMERS] March them off! [*They are marched off. They bow all the time.*] See to it that His Honor Azdak is exposed to no more violence.

> [*Exeunt* RIDER *and* CORPORAL.]

THE COOK. [*To* SHAUWA] She clapped her hands! I hope he saw it!

THE FIRST LAWYER. It's a catastrophe.

> [AZDAK *has fainted. Coming to, he is dressed again in judge's robes. He walks, swaying, toward the* IRONSHIRTS.]

AN IRONSHIRT. What does Your Honor desire?

AZDAK. Nothing, fellow dogs, or just an occasional boot to lick. [*To* SHAUWA] I pardon you. [*He is unchained.*] Get me some red wine, the sweet kind. [SHAUWA *stumbles off.*] Get out of here, I've got to judge a case.

> [*Exeunt* IRONSHIRTS. SHAUWA *returns with a pitcher of wine.* AZDAK *gulps it down.*]

Something for my backside. [SHAUWA *brings the Statute Book, puts it on the judge's chair.* AZDAK *sits on it.*] I accept.

> [*The* PROSECUTORS, *among whom a worried council has been held, smile with relief. They whisper.*]

THE COOK. Oh dear!

SIMON. A well can't be filled with dew, they say.

THE LAWYERS. [*Approaching* AZDAK, *who stands up, expectantly*] A quite ridiculous case, Your Honor. The accused has abducted a child and refuses to hand it over.

AZDAK. [*Stretching out his hand, glancing at* GRUSHA] A most attractive person. [*He fingers the money, then sits down, satisfied.*] I declare the proceedings open and demand the whole truth. [*To* GRUSHA] Especially from you.

THE FIRST LAWYER. High Court of Justice! Blood, as the popular saying goes, is thicker than water. This old adage . . .

AZDAK. [*Interrupting*] The Court wants to know the lawyers' fee.

THE FIRST LAWYER. [*Surprised*] I beg your pardon?

[AZDAK, *smiling, rubs his thumb and index finger.*]

Oh, I see. Five hundred piasters, Your Honor, to answer the Court's somewhat unusual question.

AZDAK. Did you hear? The question is unusual. I ask it because I listen in quite a different way when I know you're good.

THE FIRST LAWYER. [*Bowing*] Thank you, Your Honor. High Court of Justice, of all ties the ties of blood are strongest. Mother and child—is there a more intimate relationship? Can one tear a child from its mother? High Court of Justice, she has conceived it in the holy ecstasies of love. She has carried it in her womb. She has fed it with her blood. She has borne it with pain. High Court of Justice, it has been observed that even the wild tigress, robbed of her young, roams restless through the mountains, shrunk to a shadow. Nature herself . . .

AZDAK. [*Interrupting, to* GRUSHA] What's your answer to all this and anything else that lawyer might have to say?

GRUSHA. He's mine.

AZDAK. Is that all? I hope you can prove it. Why should I assign the child to you in any case?

GRUSHA. I brought him up like the priest says "according to my best knowledge and conscience." I always found him something to eat. Most of the time he had a roof over his head. And I went to such trouble for him. I had expenses too. I didn't look out for my own comfort. I brought the child up to be friendly with everyone, and from the beginning taught him to work. As well as he could, that is. He's still very little.

THE FIRST LAWYER. Your Honor, it is significant that the girl herself doesn't claim any tie of blood between her and the child.

AZDAK. The Court takes note of that.

THE FIRST LAWYER. Thank you, Your Honor. And now permit a woman bowed in sorrow—who has already lost her husband and now has also to fear the loss of her child—to address a few words to you. The gracious Natella Abashwili is . . .

THE GOVERNOR'S WIFE. [*Quietly*] A most cruel fate, Sir, forces me to describe to you the tortures of a bereaved mother's soul, the anxiety, the sleepless nights, the . . .

THE SECOND LAWYER. [*Bursting out*] It's outrageous the way this woman is being treated! Her husband's palace is closed to her! The revenue of her estates is blocked, and she is cold-bloodedly told that it's tied to the heir. She can't do a thing without that child. She can't even pay her lawyers! [*To the* FIRST LAWYER, *who, desperate about this outburst, makes frantic gestures to keep him from speaking.*] Dear Illo Shuboladze, surely it can be divulged now that the Abashwili estates are at stake?

THE FIRST LAWYER. Please, Honored Sandro Oboladze! We agreed ... [*To* AZDAK] Of course it is correct that the trial will also decide if our noble client can dispose of the Abashwili estates, which are rather extensive. I say "also" advisedly, for in the foreground stands the human tragedy of a mother, as Natella Abashwili very properly explained in the first words of her moving statement. Even if Michael Abashwili were not heir to the estates, he would still be the dearly beloved child of my client.

AZDAK. Stop! The Court is touched by the mention of estates. It's a proof of human feeling.

THE SECOND LAWYER. Thanks, Your Honor. Dear Illo Shuboladze, we can prove in any case that the woman who took the child is not the child's mother. Permit me to lay before the Court the bare facts. High Court of Justice, by an unfortunate chain of circumstances, Michael Abashwili was left behind on that Easter Sunday while his mother was making her escape. Grusha, a palace kitchen maid, was seen with the baby ...

THE COOK. All her mistress was thinking of was what dresses she'd take along!

THE SECOND LAWYER. [*Unmoved*] Nearly a year later Grusha turned up in a mountain village with a baby and there entered into the state of matrimony with ...

AZDAK. How did you get to that mountain village?

GRUSHA. On foot, Your Honor. And it was mine.

SIMON. I am the father, Your Honor.

THE COOK. I used to look after it for them, Your Honor. For five piasters.

THE SECOND LAWYER. This man is engaged to Grusha, High Court of Justice: his testimony is not trustworthy.

AZDAK. Are you the man she married in the mountain village?

SIMON. No, Your Honor, she married a peasant.

AZDAK. [*To* GRUSHA] Why? [*Pointing at* SIMON] Is he no good in bed? Tell the truth.

GRUSHA. We didn't get that far. I married because of the baby. So it'd have a roof over his head. [*Pointing at* SIMON] He was in the war, Your Honor.

AZDAK. And now he wants you back again, huh?

SIMON. I wish to state in evidence ...

GRUSHA. [*Angrily*] I am no longer free, Your Honor.

AZDAK. And the child, you claim, comes from whoring?

[GRUSHA *doesn't answer.*]

I'm going to ask you a question: What kind of child is it? Is it a ragged little bastard or from a well-to-do family?

GRUSHA. [*Angrily*] He's just an ordinary child.

AZDAK. I mean—did he have refined features from the beginning?

GRUSHA. He had a nose on his face.

AZDAK. A very significant comment! It has been said of me that I went out one time and sniffed at a rosebush before rendering a verdict—tricks like that are needed nowadays. Well, I'll make it short, and not listen to any more lies. [*To* GRUSHA] Especially not yours. [*To all the accused*] I can imagine what you've cooked up to cheat me! I know you people. You're swindlers.

GRUSHA. [*Suddenly*] I can understand your wanting to cut it short, now I've seen what you accepted!

AZDAK. Shut up! Did I accept anything from you?

GRUSHA. [*While the* COOK *tries to restrain her*] I haven't got anything.

AZDAK. True. Quite true. From starvelings I never get a thing. I might just as well starve, myself. You want justice, but do you want to pay for it, hm? When you go to a butcher you know you have to pay, but you people go to a judge as if you were going to a funeral supper.

SIMON. [*Loudly*] When the horse was shod, the horse-fly held out its leg, as the saying is.

AZDAK. [*Eagerly accepting the challenge*] Better a treasure in manure than a stone in a mountain stream.

SIMON. A fine day. Let's go fishing, said the angler to the worm.

AZDAK. I'm my own master, said the servant, and cut off his foot.

SIMON. I love you as a father, said the Czar to the peasants, and had the Czarevitch's head chopped off.

AZDAK. A fool's worst enemy is himself.

SIMON. However, a fart has no nose.

AZDAK. Fined ten piasters for indecent language in court! That'll teach you what justice is.

GRUSHA. [*Furiously*] A fine kind of justice! You play fast and loose with us because we don't talk as refined as that crowd with their lawyers!

AZDAK. That's true. You people are too dumb. It's only right you should get it in the neck.

GRUSHA. You want to hand the child over to her, and she wouldn't even know how to keep it dry, she's so "refined"! You know about as much about justice as I do!

AZDAK. There's something in that. I'm an ignorant man. Haven't even a decent pair of pants on under this gown. Look! With me, everything goes for food and drink—I was educated at a convent. Incidentally, I'll fine you ten piasters for contempt of court. And you're a very silly girl, to turn me against you, instead of making eyes at me and wiggling your backside a little to keep me in a good temper. Twenty piasters!

GRUSHA. Even if it was thirty, I'd tell you what I think of your jus-tice, you drunken onion! [*Incoherently*] How dare you talk to me like the cracked Isaiah on the church window? As if you were some-body? For you weren't born to this. You weren't born to rap your own mother on the knuckles if she swipes a little bowl of salt someplace. Aren't you ashamed of yourself when you see how I tremble before you? You've made yourself their servant so no one will take their houses from them—houses they had stolen! Since when have houses belonged to the bedbugs? But you're on the watch, or they couldn't drag our men into their wars! You bribe-taker!

> [AZDAK *half gets up, starts beaming. With his little hammer he half-heartedly knocks on the table as if to get silence. As* GRUSHA'S *scolding continues, he only beats time with his hammer.*]

I've no respect for you. No more than for a thief or a bandit with a knife! You can do what you want. You can take the child away from me, a hundred against one, but I tell you one thing: only extortioners should be chosen for a profession like yours, and men who rape children! As punishment! Yes, let *them* sit in judgment on their fellow creatures. It is worse than to hang from the gallows.

AZDAK. [*Sitting down*] Now it'll be thirty! And I won't go on squab-bling with you—we're not in a tavern. What'd happen to my dig-nity as a judge? Anyway, I've lost interest in your case. Where's the couple who wanted a divorce? [*To* SHAUWA] Bring 'em in. This case is adjourned for fifteen minutes.

THE FIRST LAWYER. [*To the* GOVERNOR'S WIFE] Even without using the rest of the evidence, Madam, we have the verdict in the bag.

THE COOK. [*To* GRUSHA] You've gone and spoiled your chances with him. You won't get the child now.

THE GOVERNOR'S WIFE. Shalva, my smelling salts!

> [*Enter a* VERY OLD COUPLE.]

AZDAK. I accept.

> [*The* OLD COUPLE *don't understand.*]

I hear you want to be divorced. How long have you been together?

THE OLD WOMAN. Forty years, Your Honor.

AZDAK. And why do you want a divorce?

THE OLD MAN. We don't like each other, Your Honor.

AZDAK. Since when?

THE OLD WOMAN. Oh, from the very beginning, Your Honor.

AZDAK. I'll think about your request and render my verdict when I'm through with the other case.

> [SHAUWA *leads them back.*]

I need the child. [*He beckons* GRUSHA *to and bends not unkindly toward her.*] I've noticed you have a soft spot for justice. I don't believe he's your child, but if he *were* yours, woman, wouldn't you want him to be rich? You'd only have to say he wasn't yours, and he'd have a palace and many horses in his stable and many beggars on his doorstep and many soldiers in his service and many petitioners in his courtyard, wouldn't he? What do you say—don't you want him to be rich?

[GRUSHA *is silent.*]

THE STORY TELLER. Hear now what the angry girl thought but did not say:

Had he golden shoes to wear
He'd be cruel as a bear.
Evil would his life disgrace.
He'd laugh in my face.
Carrying a heart of flint
Is too troublesome a stint.
Being powerful and bad
Is hard on a lad.

Then let hunger be his foe!
Hungry men and women, no
Let him fear the darksome night
But not daylight!

AZDAK. I think I understand you, woman.

GRUSHA. [*Suddenly and loudly*] I won't give him up. I've raised him, and he knows me.

[*Enter* SHAUWA *with the* CHILD.]

THE GOVERNOR'S WIFE. It's in rags!

GRUSHA. That's not true. But I wasn't given time to put his good shirt on.

THE GOVERNOR'S WIFE. It must have been in a pigsty.

GRUSHA. [*Furiously*] I'm not a pig, but there are some who are! Where did you leave your baby?

THE GOVERNOR'S WIFE. I'll show you, you vulgar creature! [*She is about to throw herself on* GRUSHA, *but is restrained by her* LAWYERS.] She's a criminal, she must be whipped. Immediately!

THE SECOND LAWYER. [*Holding his hand over her mouth*] Natella Abashwili, you promised . . . Your Honor, the plaintiff's nerves.

AZDAK. Plaintiff and defendant! The Court has listened to your case, and has come to no decision as to who the real mother is, therefore, I, the judge, am obliged to *choose* a mother for the child. I'll make a test. Shauwa, get a piece of chalk and draw a circle on the floor.

[SHAUWA *does so.*]

Now place the child in the center.

[SHAUWA *puts* MICHAEL, *who smiles at* GRUSHA, *in the center of the circle.*]

Stand near the circle, both of you.

[*The* GOVERNOR'S WIFE *and* GRUSHA *step up to the circle.*
Now each of you take the child by one hand.
[*They do so.*]
The true mother is she who can pull the child out of the circle.

THE SECOND LAWYER. [*Quickly*] High Court of Justice, I object! The fate of the great Abashwili estates, which are tied to the child, as the heir, should not be made dependent on such a doubtful duel. In addition, my client does not command the strength of this person, who is accustomed to physical work.

AZDAK. She looks pretty well fed to me. Pull!

[*The* GOVERNOR'S WIFE *pulls the* CHILD *out of the circle on her side;* GRUSHA *has let go and stands aghast.*]
What's the matter with you? You didn't pull!

GRUSHA. I didn't hold on to him.

THE FIRST LAWYER. [*Congratulating the* GOVERNOR'S WIFE] What did I say! The ties of blood!

GRUSHA. [*Running to* AZDAK] Your Honor, I take back everything I said against you. I ask your forgiveness. But could I keep him till he can speak all the words? He knows a few.

AZDAK. Don't influence the Court. I bet you only know about twenty words yourself. All right, I'll make the test once more, just be to certain.

[*The two women take up their positions again.*]
Pull!

[*Again* GRUSHA *lets go of the* CHILD.]

GRUSHA. [*In despair*] I brought him up! Shall I also tear him to pieces? I can't!

AZDAK. [*Rising*] And in this manner the Court has established the true mother. [*To* GRUSHA] Take your child and be off. I advise you not to stay in the city with him. [*To the* GOVERNOR'S WIFE] And you disappear before I fine you for fraud. Your estates fall to the city. They'll be converted into a playground for the children. They need one, and I've decided it shall be called after me: Azdak's Garden.

[*The* GOVERNOR'S WIFE *has fainted and is carried out by the* LAWYERS *and the* ADJUTANT. GRUSHA *stands motionless.* SHAUWA *leads the* CHILD *toward her.*]
Now I'll take off this judge's gown—it's grown too hot for me. I'm not cut out for a hero. In token of farewell I invite you all to a little dance outside on the meadow. Oh, I'd almost forgotten something in my excitement . . . to sign the divorce decree.

[*Using the judge's chair as a table, he writes something on a piece of paper, and prepares to leave. Dance music has started.*]

SHAUWA. [*Having read what is on the paper*] But that's not right. You've not divorced the old people. You've divorced Grusha!

AZDAK. Have I divorced the wrong couple? What a pity! And I never retract! If I did, how could we keep order in the land? [*To the* OLD COUPLE] I'll invite you to my party instead. You don't mind dancing with each other, do you? [*To* GRUSHA *and* SIMON] I've got forty piasters coming from you.

SIMON. [*Pulling out his purse*] Cheap at the price, Your Honor. And many thanks.

AZDAK. [*Pocketing the cash*] I'll be needing this.

GRUSHA. [*To* MICHAEL] So we'd better leave the city tonight, Michael? [*To* SIMON] You like him?

SIMON. With my respects, I like him.

GRUSHA. Now I can tell you: I took him because on that Easter Sunday I got engaged to you. So he's a child of love. Michael, let's dance.

> [*She dances with* MICHAEL, SIMON *dances with the* COOK, *the* OLD COUPLE *with each other.* AZDAK *stands lost in thought. The dancers soon hide him from view. Occasionally he is seen, but less and less as more couples join the dance.*]

THE STORY TELLER. And after that evening Azdak vanished and was never seen again.

The people of Grusinia did not forget him but long remembered
The period of his judging as a brief golden age,
Almost an age of justice.

> [*All the couples dance off.* AZDAK *has disappeared.*]

But you, you who have listened to the Story of the Chalk Circle,
Take note what men of old concluded:
That what there is shall go to those who are good for it,
Children to the motherly, that they prosper,
Carts to good drivers, that they be driven well,
The valley to the waterers, that it yield fruit.

JEAN-PAUL SARTRE

(1905–)

The Room (La Chambre) *

I

MME. DARBÉDAT held a *rahat-loukoum*[1] between her fingers. She brought it carefully to her lips and held her breath, afraid that the fine dust of sugar that powdered it would blow away. "Just right," she told herself. She bit quickly into its glassy flesh and a scent of

* Jean-Paul Sartre, *The Room*, translated by Lloyd Alexander. Copyright 1948 by New Directions Publishing Corporation. Reprinted by permission of New Directions Publishing Corporation.
1. Also called Turkish delight.

stagnation filled her mouth. "Odd how illness sharpens the sensations." She began to think of mosques, of obsequious Orientals (she had been to Algeria for her honeymoon) and her pale lips started in a smile: the *rahat-loukoum* was obsequious too.

Several times she had to pass the palm of her hand over the pages of her book, for in spite of the precaution she had taken they were covered with a thin coat of white powder. Her hand made the little grains of sugar slide and roll, grating on the smooth paper: "That makes me think of Arcachon, when I used to read on the beach." She had spent the summer of 1907 at the seashore. Then she wore a big straw hat with a green ribbon; she sat close to the jetty, with a novel by Gyp or Colette Yver. The wind made swirls of sand rain down upon her knees, and from time to time she had to shake the book, holding it by the corners. It was the same sensation: only the grains of sand were dry while the small bits of sugar stuck a little to the ends of her fingers. Again she saw a band of pearl grey sky above a black sea. "Eve wasn't born yet." She felt herself all weighted down with memories and precious as a coffer of sandal-wood. The name of the book she used to read suddenly came back to mind: it was called *Petite Madame*, not at all boring. But ever since an unknown illness had confined her to her room she preferred memoirs and historical works.

She hoped that suffering, heavy readings, a vigilant attention to her memories and the most exquisite sensations would ripen her as a lovely hothouse fruit.

She thought, with some annoyance, that her husband would soon be knocking at her door. On other days of the week he came only in the evening, kissed her brow in silence and read *Le Temps*,[2] sitting in the armchair across from her. But Thursday was M. Darbédat's *day*: he spent an hour with his daughter, generally from three to four. Before going he stopped in to see his wife and both discussed their son-in-law with bitterness. These Thursday conversations, predictable to their slightest detail, exhausted Mme. Darbédat. M. Darbédat filled the quiet room with his presence. He never sat, but walked in circles about the room. Each of his outbursts wounded Mme. Darbédat like a glass splintering. This particular Thursday was worse than usual: at the thought that it would soon be necessary to repeat Eve's confessions to her husband, and to see his great terrifying body convulse with fury, Mme. Darbédat broke out in a sweat. She picked up a *loukoum* from the saucer, studied it for a while with hesitation, then sadly set it down: she did not like her husband to see her eating *loukoums*.

She heard a knock and started up. "Come in," she said weakly.

M. Darbédat entered on tiptoe. "I'm going to see Eve," he said,

2. A "semigovernmental" Paris daily paper which was not allowed to con- tinue publication after the liberation of France from Nazi domination.

as he did every Thursday. Mme. Darbédat smiled at him. "Give her a kiss for me."

M. Darbédat did not answer and his forehead wrinkled worriedly: every Thursday at the same time, a muffled irritation mingled with the load of his digestion. "I'll stop in and see Franchot after leaving her, I wish he'd talk to her seriously and try to convince her."

He had made frequent visits to Dr. Franchot. But in vain. Mme. Darbédat raised her eyebrows. Before, when she was well, she shrugged her shoulders. But since sickness had weighted down her body, she replaced the gestures which would have tired her by plays of emotion in the face: she said *yes* with her eyes, *no* with the corners of her mouth: she raised her eyebrows instead of her shoulders.

"There should be some way to take him away from her by force."

"I told you already it was impossible. And besides, the law is very poorly drawn up. Only the other day Franchot was telling me that they have a tremendous amount of trouble with the families: people who can't make up their mind, who want to keep the patient at home; the doctors' hands are tied. They can give their advice, period. That's all. He would," he went on, "have to make a public scandal or else she would have to ask to have him put away herself."

"And that," said Mme. Darbédat, "isn't going to happen tomorrow."

"No." He turned to the mirror and began to comb his fingers through his beard. Mme. Darbédat looked at the powerful red neck of her husband without affection.

"If she keeps on," said M. Darbédat, "she'll be crazier than he is. It's terribly unhealthy. She doesn't leave his side, she only goes out to see you. She has no visitors. The air in their room is simply unbreathable. She never opens the window because Pierre doesn't want it open. As if you should ask a sick man. I believe they burn incense, some rubbish in a little pan, you'd think it was a church. Really, sometimes I wonder . . . she's got a funny look in her eyes, you know."

"I haven't noticed," Mme. Darbédat said. "I find her quite normal. She looks sad, obviously."

"She has a face like an unburied corpse. Does she sleep? Does she eat? But we aren't supposed to ask her about those things. But I should think that with a fellow like Pierre next to her, she wouldn't sleep a wink all night." He shrugged his shoulders. "What I find amazing is that we, her parents, don't have the right to protect her against herself. Understand that Pierre would be much better cared for by Franchot. There's a big park. And besides, I think," he added, smiling a little, "he'd get along much better with people of his own type. People like that are children, you have to leave them alone with each other; they form a sort of freemasonry. That's

where he should have been put the first day and for his own good,
I'd say. Of course it's in his own best interest."

After a moment, he added, "I tell you I don't like to know she's
alone with Pierre, especially at night. Suppose something happened.
Pierre has a very sly way about him."

"I don't know," Mme. Darbédat said, "if there's any reason to
worry. He always looked like that. He always seemed to be making
fun of the world. Poor boy," she sighed, "to have had his pride and
then come to that. He thought he was cleverer than all of us. He
had a way of saying 'You're right' simply to end the argument . . .
It's a blessing for him that he can't see the state he's in."

She recalled with displeasure the long, ironic face, always turned
a little to the side. During the first days of Eve's marriage, Mme.
Darbédat asked nothing more than a little intimacy with her son-
in-law. But he had discouraged her: he almost never spoke, he
always agreed quickly and absentmindedly.

M. Darbédat pursued his idea. "Franchot let me visit his place,"
he said. "It was magnificent. The patients have private rooms with
leather armchairs, if you please, and day-beds. You know, they have
a tennis court and they're going to build a swimming pool."

He was planted before the window, looking out, rocking a little
on his bent legs. Suddenly he turned lithely on his heel, shoulders
lowered, hands in his pockets. Mme. Darbédat felt she was going to
start perspiring: it was the same thing every time: now he was
pacing back and forth like a bear in a cage and his shoes squeaked
at every step.

"Please, please won't you sit down. You're tiring me." Hesitating,
she added, "I have something important to tell you."

M. Darbédat sat in the armchair and put his hands on his knees;
a slight chill ran up Mme. Darbédat's spine: the time had come,
she had to speak.

"You know," she said with an embarrassed cough, "I saw Eve on
Tuesday."

"Yes."

"We talked about a lot of things, she was very nice, she hadn't
been so confiding for a long time. Then I questioned her a little, I
got her to talk about Pierre. Well, I found out," she added, again
embarrassed, "that she is *very* attached to him."

"I know that too damned well," said M. Darbédat.

He irritated Mme. Darbédat a little: she always had to explain
things in such detail. Mme. Darbédat dreamed of living in the company of fine and sensitive people who would understand her slightest word.

"But I mean," she went on, "that she is attached to him *differently* than we imagined."

M. Darbédat rolled furious, anxious eyes, as he always did when he never completely grasped the sense of an allusion or something new.

"What does that all mean?"

"Charles," said Mme. Darbédat, "don't tire me. You should understand a mother has difficulty in telling certain things."

"I don't understand a damned word of anything you say," M. Darbédat said with irritation. "You can't mean . . ."

"Yes," she said.

"They're still. . . now, still . . .?"

"Yes! Yes! Yes!" she said, in three annoyed and dry little jolts.

M. Darbédat spread his arms, lowered his head and was silent.

"Charles," his wife said, worriedly, "I shouldn't have told you. But I couldn't keep it to myself."

"Our child," he said slowly. "With this madman! He doesn't even recognize her any more. He calls her Agatha. She must have lost all sense of her own dignity."

He raised his head and looked at his wife severely. "You're sure you aren't mistaken?"

"No possible doubt. Like you," she added quickly, "I couldn't believe her and I still can't. The mere idea of being touched by that wretch . . . So . . ." she sighed, "I suppose that's how he holds on to her."

"Do you remember what I told you," M. Darbédat said, "when he came to ask for her hand? I told you and I thought he pleased Eve *too much*. You wouldn't believe me." He struck the table suddenly, blushing violently. "It's perversity! He takes her in his arms, kisses her and calls her Agatha, selling her on a lot of nonsense about flying statues and God knows what else! Without a word from her! But what in heaven's name's between those two? Let her be sorry for him, let her put him in a sanatorium and see him every day,—fine. But I never thought . . . I considered her a widow. Listen, Jeannette," he said gravely, "I'm going to speak frankly to you; if she had any sense, I'd rather see her take a lover!"

"Be quiet, Charles!" Mme. Darbédat cried.

M. Darbédat wearily took his hat and the cane he had left on the stool. "After what you've just told me," he concluded, "I don't have much hope left. In any case, I'll have a talk with her because it's my duty."

Mme. Darbédat wished he would go quickly.

"You know," she said to encourage him, "I think Eve is more headstrong than . . . than anything. She knows he's incurable but she's obstinate, she doesn't want to be in the wrong."

M. Darbédat stroked his beard absently.

"Headstrong? Maybe so. If you're right, she'll finally get tired of it. He's not always pleasant and he doesn't have much to say. When I say hello to him he gives me a flabby handshake and doesn't say a word. As soon as they're alone, I think they go back to his obsessions: she tells me sometimes he screams as though his throat were being cut because of his hallucinations. He sees statues. They frighten him because they buzz. He says they fly around and make fishy eyes at him."

He put on his gloves and continued, "She'll get tired of it, I'm not saying she won't. But suppose she goes crazy before that? I wish she'd go out a little, see the world: she'd meet some nice young man—well, someone like Schroeder, an engineer with Simplon, somebody with a future, she could see him a little here and there and she'd get used to the idea of making a new life for herself."

Mme. Darbédat did not answer, afraid of starting the conversation up again. Her husband bent over her.

"So," he said, "I've got to be on my way."

"Goodbye, Papa," Mme. Darbédat said, lifting her forehead up to him. "Kiss her for me and tell her for me she's a poor dear."

Once her husband had gone, Mme. Darbédat let herself drift to the bottom of the armchair and closed her eyes, exhausted. "What vitality," she thought reproachfully. As soon as she got a little strength back, she quietly stretched out her pale hand and took a *loukoum* from the saucer, groping for it without opening her eyes.

Eve lived with her husband on the sixth floor of an old building on the Rue du Bac. M. Darbédat slowly climbed the 112 steps of the stairway. He was not even out of breath when he pushed the bell. He remembered with satisfaction the words of Mlle. Dormoy: "Charles, for your age, you're simply marvelous." Never did he feel himself stronger and healthier than on Thursday, especially after these invigorating climbs.

Eve opened the door: that's right, she doesn't have a maid. No girls *can* stay with her. I can put myself in their place. He kissed her. "Hello, poor darling."

Eve greeted him with a certain coldness.

"You look a little pale," M. Darbédat said, touching her cheek. "You don't get enough exercise."

There was a moment of silence.

"Is Mamma well?" Eve asked.

"Not good, not too bad. You saw her Tuesday? Well, she's just the same. Your Aunt Louise came to see her yesterday, that pleased her. She likes to have visitors, but they can't stay too long. Aunt Louise came to Paris for that mortgage business. I think I told you about it, a very odd sort of affair. She stopped in at the office to ask my advice. I told her there was only one thing to do: sell. She found a taker, by the way: Bretonnel! You remember Bretonnel. He's retired from business now."

He stopped suddenly: Eve was hardly listening. He thought sadly that nothing interested her any more. It's like the books. Before you had to tear them away from her. Now she doesn't even read any more.

"How is Pierre?"

"Well," Eve said. "Do you want to see him?"

"Of course," M. Darbédat said gaily, "I'd like to pay him a little call."

He was full of compassion for this poor young man, but he could not see him without repugnance. *I detest unhealthy people.* Obviously, it was not Pierre's fault: his heredity was terribly loaded down. M. Darbédat sighed: *All the precautions are taken in vain, you find out those things too late.* No, Pierre was not responsible. But still he had always carried that fault in him; it formed the base of his character; it wasn't like cancer or tuberculosis, something you could always put aside when you wanted to judge a man as he is. His nervous grace, the subtlety which pleased Eve so much when he was courting her were the flowers of madness. He was already mad when he married her only you couldn't tell.

It makes you wonder, thought M. Darbédat, *where responsibility begins, or rather, where it ends.* In any case, he was always analysing himself too much, always turned in on himself. But was it the cause or effect of his sickness? He followed his daughter through a long, dim corridor.

"This apartment is too big for you," he said. "You ought to move out."

"You say that every time, Papa," Eve answered, "but I've already told you Pierre doesn't want to leave his room."

Eve was amazing. Enough to make you wonder if she realized her husband's state. He was insane enough to be in a strait-jacket and she respected his decisions and advice as if he still had good sense.

"What I'm saying is for your own good." M. Darbédat went on, somewhat annoyed, "It seems to me that if I were a woman I'd be afraid of these badly lighted old rooms. I'd like to see you in a bright apartment, the kind they're putting up near Auteuil, three airy little rooms. They lowered the rents because they couldn't find any tenants; this would be just the time."

Eve quietly turned the doorknob and they entered the room. M. Darbédat's throat tightened at the heavy odor of incense. The curtains were drawn. In the shadows he made out a thin neck above the back of an armchair: Pierre's back was turned. He was eating.

"Hello, Pierre," M. Darbédat said, raising his voice. "How are we today?" He drew near him: the sick man was seated in front of a small table: he looked sly.

"I see we had soft boiled eggs," M. Darbédat said, raising his voice higher. "That's good!"

"I'm not deaf," Pierre said quietly.

Irritated, M. Darbédat turned his eyes toward Eve as his witness. But Eve gave him a hard glance and was silent. M. Darbédat realized he had hurt her. Too bad for her. It was impossible to find just the right tone for this boy. He had less sense than a child of four and Eve wanted him treated like a man. M. Darbédat could not keep himself from waiting with impatience for the moment when all this ridiculous business would be finished. Sick people annoyed him a little—especially madmen because they were wrong. Poor Pierre, for example, was wrong all along the line, he couldn't speak a reasonable word and yet it would be useless to expect the least humility from him, or even temporary recognition of his errors.

Eve cleared away the eggshells and the cup. She put a knife and fork in front of Pierre.

"What's he going to eat now," M. Darbédat said jovially.

"A steak."

Pierre had taken the fork and held it in the ends of his long, pale fingers. He inspected it minutely and then gave a slight laugh.

"I can't use it this time," he murmured, setting it down, "I was warned."

Eve came in and looked at the fork with passionate interest.

"Agatha," Pierre said, "give me another one."

Eve obeyed and Pierre began to eat. She had taken the suspect fork and held it tightly in her hands, her eyes never leaving it; she seemed to make a violent effort. How suspicious all their gestures and relationships are! thought M. Darbédat.

He was uneasy.

"Be careful, Pierre, take it by the middle because of the prongs."

Eve sighed and laid the fork on the serving table. M. Darbédat felt his gall rising. He did not think it well to give in to all this poor man's whims—even from Pierre's viewpoint it was pernicious. Franchot had said: "One must never enter the delirium of a madman." Instead of giving him another fork, it would have been better to have reasoned quietly and made him understand that the first was like all the others.

He went to the serving table, took the fork ostentatiously and tested the prongs with a light finger. Then he turned to Pierre. But the latter was cutting his meat peacefully: he gave his father-in-law a gentle, inexpressive glance.

"I'd like to have a little talk with you," M. Darbédat said to Eve.

She followed him docilely into the salon. Sitting on the couch, M. Darbédat realized he had kept the fork in his hand. He threw it on the table.

"It's much better here," he said.

"I never come here."

"All right to smoke?"

"Of course, Papa," Eve said hurriedly. "Do you want a cigar?"

M. Darbédat preferred to roll a cigarette. He thought eagerly of the discussion he was about to begin. Speaking to Pierre he felt as embarrassed about his reason as a giant about his strength when playing with a child. All his qualities of clarity, sharpness, precision, turned against him; *I must confess it's somewhat the same with my poor Jeannette.* Certainly Mme. Darbédat was not insane, but this illness had . . . stultified her. Eve, on the other hand, took after her father . . . a straight, logical nature; discussion with her was a pleasure; *that's why I don't want them to ruin her.* M. Darbédat raised his eyes. Once again he wanted to see the fine intelligent features of his daughter. He was disappointed with this face; once so reasonable and transparent, there was now something clouded and opaque in it. Eve had always been beautiful. M. Darbédat noticed she was made up with great care, almost with pomp. She had blued her eyelids and put mascara on her long lashes. This violent and perfect make-up made a painful impression on her father.

"You're green beneath your rouge," he told her. "I'm afraid you're getting sick. And the way you make yourself up now! You used to be so discreet."

Eve did not answer and for an embarrassed moment M. Darbédat considered this brilliant, worn-out face beneath the heavy mass of black hair. He thought she looked like a tragedian. *I even know who she looks like. That woman . . . that Roumanian who played* Phèdre[3] *in French at the Mur d'Orange.* He regretted having made so disagreeable a remark: *It escaped me! Better not worry her with little things.*

"Excuse me," he said smiling. "you know I'm an old purist. I don't like all these creams and paints women stick on their face today. But I'm in the wrong. You must live in your time."

Eve smiled amiably at him. M. Darbédat lit a cigarette and drew several puffs.

"My child," he began, "I wanted to talk with you: the two of us are going to talk the way we used to. Come, sit down and listen to me nicely; you must have confidence in your old Papa."

"I'd rather stand," Eve said. "What did you want to tell me?"

"I am going to ask you a single question," M. Darbédat said a little more dryly. "Where will all this lead you?"

"All this?" Eve asked astonished.

"Yes . . . all this whole life you've made for yourself. Listen," he went on, "don't think I don't understand you (he had a sudden illumination) but what you want to do is beyond human strength. You want to live solely by imagination, isn't that it? You don't want to admit he's sick. You don't want to see the Pierre of today,

---

3. A French classical tragedy, first performed in 1677, by Jean Racine (1639–1699). The performance seen by M. Darbédat took place in the Roman amphitheater in the town of Orange, several miles to the north of Avignon.

do you? You have eyes only for the Pierre of before. My dear, my darling little girl, it's an impossible bet to win," M. Darbédat continued. "Now I'm going to tell you a story which perhaps you don't know. When we were at Sables-d'Olonne—you were three years old —your mother made the acquaintance of a charming young woman with a superb little boy, You played on the beach with this little boy, you were thick as thieves, you were engaged to marry him. A while later, in Paris, your mother wanted to see this young woman again; she was told she had had a terrible accident. That fine little boy's head was cut off by a car. They told your mother, 'Go and see her, but above all don't talk to her about the death of her child, she *will not* believe he is dead.' Your mother went, she found a half-mad creature: she lived as though her boy was still alive; she spoke to him, she set his place at the table. She lived in such a state of nervous tension that after six months they had to take her away by force to a sanatorium where she was obliged to stay three years. No, my child," M. Darbédat said, shaking his head, "these things are impossible. It would have been better if she had recognized the truth courageously. She would have suffered once, then time would have erased with its sponge. There is nothing like looking things in the face, believe me."

"You're wrong," Eve said with effort. "I know very well that Pierre is . . ."

The word did not escape. She held herself very straight and put her hands on the back of the armchair: there was something dry and ugly in the lower part of her face.

"So . . .?" asked M. Darbédat, astonished.

"So . . .?"

"You . . .?"

"I love him as he is," said Eve rapidly and with an irritated look.

"Not true," M. Darbédat said forcefully. "It isn't true: you don't love him, you can't love him. You can only feel that way about a healthy, normal person. You pity Pierre, I don't doubt it, and surely you have the memory of three years of happiness he gave you. But don't tell me you love him. I won't believe you."

Eve remained wordless, staring at the carpet absently.

"You could at least answer me," M. Darbédat said coldly. "Don't think this conversation has been any less painful for me than it has for you."

"More than you think."

"Well then, if you love him," he cried, exasperated, "it is a great misfortune for you, for me and for your poor mother because I'm going to tell you something I would rather have hidden from you: before three years Pierre will be sunk in complete dementia, he'll be like a beast."

He watched his daughter with hard eyes: he was angry at her for having compelled him, by stubbornness, to make this painful revelation.

Eve was motionless; she did not so much as raise her eyes.

"I knew."

"Who told you?" he asked stupified.

"Franchot. I knew six months ago."

"And I told him to be careful with you," said M. Darbédat with bitterness. "Maybe it's better. But under those circumstances you must understand that it would be unpardonable to keep Pierre with you. The struggle you have undertaken is doomed to failure, his illness won't spare him. If there were something to be done, if we could save him by care, I'd say yes. But look: you're pretty, intelligent, gay, you're destroying yourself willingly and without profit. I know you've been admirable, but now it's over . . . done, you've done your duty and more; now it would be immoral to continue. We also have duties to ourselves, child. And then you aren't thinking about us. You must," he repeated, hammering the words, "send Pierre to Franchot's clinic. Leave this apartment where you've had nothing but sorrow and come home to us. If you want to be useful and ease the sufferings of someone else, you have your mother. The poor woman is cared for by nurses, she needs someone closer to her, and *she*," he added, "can appreciate what you do for her and be grateful."

There was a long silence. M. Darbédat heard Pierre singing in the next room. It was hardly a song, rather a sort of sharp, hasty recitative. M. Drabédat raised his eyes to his daughter.

"It's no then?"

"Pierre will stay with me," she said quietly. "I get along well with him."

"By living like an animal all day long?"

Eve smiled and shot a glance at her father, strange, mocking and almost gay. *It's true*. M. Darbédat thought furiously, *that's not all they do; they sleep together.*

"You are completely mad," he said, rising.

Eve smiled sadly and murmured, as if to herself, "Not enough so."

"Not enough? I can only tell you one thing, my child. You frighten me.

He kissed her hastily and left. Going down the stairs he thought: *we should send out two strong-arm men who'd take the poor imbecile away and stick him under a shower without asking his advice on the matter.*

It was a fine autumn day, calm and without mystery; the sunlight gilded the faces of the passers-by. M. Darbédat was struck with the simplicity of the faces; some weather-beaten, others smooth, but they all reflected the happiness and cares with which he was so familiar.

I know exactly what I resent in Eve, he told himself, entering the Boulevard St. Germain. *I resent her living outside the limits of human nature. Pierre is no longer a human being: in all the care and all the love she gives him she deprives human beings of a little. We don't have the right to refuse ourselves to the world; no matter what, we live in society.*

He watched the faces of the passers-by with sympathy; he loved their clear, serious looks. In these sunlit streets, in the midst of mankind, one felt secure, as in the midst of a large family.

A woman stopped in front of an open-air display counter. She was holding a little girl by the hand.

"What's that?" the little girl asked, pointing to a radio set.

"Mustn't touch," her mother said. "It's a radio; it plays music.'

They stood for a moment without speaking, in ecstasy. Touched, M. Darbédat bent down to the little girl and smiled.

II

"HE's gone." The door closed with a dry snap. Eve was alone in the salon. *I wish he'd die.*

She twisted her hands around the back of the armchair: she had just remembered her father's eyes. M. Darbédat had bent over Pierre with a competent air; he had said "That's good!" the way someone says when they speak to invalids. He had looked and Pierre's face had been painted in the depths of his sharp, bulging eyes. *I hate him when he looks at him because I think he sees him.*

Eve's hands slid along the armchair and she turned to the window. She was dazzled. The room was filled with sunlight, it was everywhere, in pale splotches on the rug, in the air like a blinding dust. Eve was not accustomed to this diligent, indiscreet light which darted from everywhere, scouring all the corners, rubbing the furniture like a busy housewife and making it glisten. However, she went to the window and raised the muslin curtain which hung against the pane. Just at that moment M. Darbédat left the building; Eve suddenly caught sight of his broad shoulders. He raised his head and looked at the sky, blinking, then with the stride of a young man he walked away. *He's straining himself*, thought Eve, *soon he'll have a stitch in the side.* She hardly hated him any longer: there was so little in that head; only the tiny worry of appearing young. Yet rage took her again when she saw him turn the corner of the Boulevard St. Germain and disappear. *He's thinking about Pierre.* A little of their life had escaped from the closed room and was being dragged through the streets, in the sun, among the people. *Can they never forget about us?*

The Rue du Bac was almost deserted. An old lady crossed the street with mincing steps; three girls passed, laughing. Then men, strong, serious men carrying briefcases and talking among themselves. *Normal people,* thought Eve, astonished at finding such a powerful hatred in herself. A handsome, fleshy woman ran heavily toward an elegant gentleman. He took her in his arms and kissed her on the mouth. Eve gave a hard laugh and let the curtain fall.

Pierre sang no more but the woman on the fourth floor was playing the piano; she played a Chopin Etude. Eve felt calmer; she took a step toward Pierre's room but stopped almost immediately and leaned against the wall in anguish; each time she left the room, she was panic-stricken at the thought of going back. Yet she knew she could live nowhere else: she loved the room. She looked around it with cold curiosity as if to gain a little time: this shadowless, odorless room where she waited for her courage to return. *You'd think it was a dentist's waiting room.* Armchairs of pink silk, the divan, the tabourets were somber and discreet, a little fatherly; man's best friends. Eve imagined those grave gentlemen dressed in light suits, all like the ones she saw at the window, entering the room, continuing a conversation already begun. They did not even take time to reconnoiter, but advanced with firm step to the middle of the room; one of them, letting his hand drag behind him like a wake in passing knocked over cushions, objects on the table, and was never disturbed by their contact. And when a piece of furniture was in their way, these poised men, far from making a detour to avoid it, quietly changed its place. Finally they sat down, still plunged in their conversation, without even glancing behind them. A *living-room* for *normal people,* thought Eve. She stared at the knob of the closed door and anguish clutched her throat: *I must go back. I never leave him alone so long.* She would have to open the door, then stand for a moment on the threshold, trying to accustom her eyes to the shadow and the room would push her back with all its strength. Eve would have to triumph over this resistance and enter all the way into the heart of the room. Suddenly she wanted violently to see Pierre; she would have liked to make fun of M. Darbédat with him. But Pierre had no need of her; Eve could not foresee the welcome he had in store for her. Suddenly she thought with a sort of pride that she had no place anywhere. *Normal people think I belong with them. But I couldn't stay an hour among them. I need to live out there, on the other side of the wall. But they don't want me out there.*

A profound change was taking place around her. The light had grown old and greying: it was heavy, like the water in a vase of flowers that hasn't been changed since the day before. In this aged light Eve found a melancholy she had long forgotten: the melancholy of an autumn afternoon that was ending. She looked around

her, hesitant, almost timid: all that was so far away: there was neither day nor night nor season nor melancholy in the room. She
vaguely recalled autumns long past, autumns of her childhood, then
suddenly she stiffened: she was afraid of memories.

She heard Pierre's voice. "Agatha! Where are you?"

"Coming!" she cried.

She opened the door and entered the room.

THE heavy odor of incense filled her mouth and nostrils as she
opened her eyes and stretched out her hands—for a long time the
perfume and the gloom had meant nothing more to her than a
single element, acrid and heavy, as simple, as familiar as water, air
or fire—and she prudently advanced toward a pale stain which
seemed to float in the fog. It was Pierre's face: Pierre's clothing (he
dressed in black ever since he had been sick) melted in obscurity.
Pierre had thrown back his head and closed his eyes. He was handsome. Eve looked at his long, curved lashes, then sat close to him on
the low chair. *He seems to be suffering,* she thought. Little by little
her eyes grew used to the darkness. The bureau emerged first, then
the bed, then Pierre's personal things: scissors, the pot of glue,
books, the herbarium which shed its leaves onto the rug near the
armchair.

"Agatha?"

Pierre had opened his eyes. He was watching her, smiling. "You
know, that fork?" he said. "I did it to frighten that fellow. There
was *almost* nothing the matter with it."

Eve's apprehensions faded and she gave a light laugh. "You succeeded," she said, "You drove him completely out of his mind."

Pierre smiled. "Did you see? He played with it a long time, he
held it right in his hands. The trouble is," he said, "they don't
know how to take hold of things; they grab them."

"That's right," Eve said.

Pierre tapped the palm of his left hand lightly with the index of
his right.

"They take with that. They reach out their fingers and when they
catch hold of something they crack down on it to knock it out."

He spoke rapidly and hardly moving his lips; he looked puzzled.

"I wonder what they want," he said at last, "that fellow has
already been here. Why did they send him to me? If they wanted
to know what I'm doing all they have to do is read it on the screen,
they don't even need to leave the house. They make mistakes. They
have the power but they make mistakes. I never make any, that's
my trump card. *Hoffka!*" he said. He shook his long hands before
his forehead. "The bitch Hoffka, Paffka! Suffka! Do you want any
more?"

"Is it the bell?" asked Eve.

"Yes. It's gone." He went on severely. "This fellow, he's just a subordinate. You know him, you went into the living room with him."

Eve did not answer.

"What did he want?" asked Pierre. "He must have told you."

She hesitated an instant, then answered brutally. "He wanted you locked up."

When the truth was told quietly to Pierre he distrusted it. He had to be dealt with violently in order to daze and paralyze his suspicions. Eve preferred to brutalize him rather than lie: when she lied and he acted as if he believed it she could not avoid a very slight feeling of superiority which made her horrified at herself.

"Lock me up!" Pierre repeated ironically. "They're crazy. What can walls do to me. Maybe they think that's going to stop me. I sometimes wonder if there aren't two groups. The real one, the Negro—and then a bunch of fools trying to stick their noses in and making mistake after mistake."

He made his hand jump up from the arm of the chair and looked at it happily.

"I can get through walls. What did you tell them?" he asked, turning to Eve with curiosity.

"Not to lock you up."

He shrugged. "You shouldn't have said that. You made a mistake too ... unless you did it on purpose. You've got to call their bluff."

He was silent. Eve lowered her head sadly: *They grab things!* *How scornfully he said that—and he was right. Do I grab things too? It doesn't do any good to watch myself, I think most of my movements annoy him. But he doesn't say anything.* Suddenly she felt as miserable as when she was fourteen and Mme. Darbédat told her. "You don't know what to do with your hands." She didn't dare make a move and just at that time she had an irresistible desire to change her position. Quietly she put her feet under the chair, barely touching the rug. She watched the lamp on the table—the lamp whose base Pierre had painted black—and the chess set. Pierre had left only the black pawns on the board. Sometimes he would get up, go to the table and take the pawns in his hands one by one. He spoke to them, called them Robots and they seemed to stir with a mute life under his fingers. When he set them down, Eve went and touched them in her turn (she always felt somewhat ridiculous about it). They had become little bits of dead wood again but something vague and incomprehensible stayed in them, something like understanding. *These are* his *things,* she thought. *There is nothing of mine in the room.* She had had a few pieces of furniture before; the mirror and the little inlaid dresser handed down from her grandmother and which Pierre jokingly called *"your* dresser." Pierre had carried them away with him; things showed their true face to Pierre alone. Eve could watch them for hours: they were unflaggingly stubborn and determined to deceive her, offering her nothing but their appearance—as they did to Dr. Franchot and M. Darbédat. Yet, she told herself with anguish, *I don't see them quite like my father. It isn't possible for me to see them exactly like him.*

She moved her knees a little: her legs felt as though they were crawling with ants. Her body was stiff and taut and hurt her; she felt it too alive, too demanding. *I would like to be invisible and stay here seeing him without his seeing me. He doesn't need me; I am useless in this room.* She turned her head slightly and looked at the wall above Pierre. Threats were written on the wall. Eve knew it but she could not read them. She often watched the big red roses on the wallpaper until they began to dance before her eyes. The roses flamed in shadow. Most of the time the threat was written near the ceiling, a little to the left of the bed; but sometimes it moved. *I must get up. I can't . . . I can't sit down any longer.* There were also white discs on the wall that looked like slices of onion. The discs spun and Eve's hands began to tremble: *Sometimes I think I'm going mad. But no,* she thought, *I can't go mad. I get nervous, that's all.*

Suddenly she felt Pierre's hand on hers.

"Agatha," Pierre said tenderly.

He smiled at her but he held her hand by the ends of his fingers with a sort of revulsion, as though he had picked up a crab by the back and wanted to avoid its claws.

"Agatha," he said. "I would so much like to have confidence in you."

She closed her eyes and her breast heaved. *I mustn't answer anything, if I do he'll get angry, he won't say anything more.*

Pierre had dropped her hand. "I like you, Agatha," he said. "but I can't understand you. Why do you stay in the room all the time?"

Eve did not answer.

"Tell me why."

"You know I love you," she said dryly.

"I don't believe you," Pierre said. "Why should you love me? I must frighten you: I'm haunted." He smiled but suddenly became serious. "There is a wall between you and me. I see you, I speak to you, but you're on the other side. What keeps us from loving? I think it was easier before. In Hamburg."

"Yes," Eve said sadly. Always Hamburg. He never spoke of their real past. Neither Eve nor he had ever been to Hamburg.

"We used to walk along the canal. There was a barge, remember? The barge was black; there was a dog on the deck."

He made it up as he went along; it sounded false.

"I held your hand. You had another skin. I believed all you told me. Be quiet!" he shouted.

He listened for a moment. "They're coming," he said mournfully.

Eve jumped up. "They're coming? I thought they wouldn't ever come again."

Pierre had been calmer for the past three days; the statues did not come. Pierre was terribly afraid of the statues even though he would never admit it. Eve was not afraid: but when they began to fly, buzzing, around the room, she was afraid of Pierre.

"Give me the ziuthre," Pierre said.

Eve got up and took the ziuthre: it was a collection of pieces of cardboard Pierre had glued together; he used it to conjure the statues. The ziuthre looked like a spider. On one of the cardboards Pierre had written "Power over ambush" and on the other, "Black." On a third he had drawn a laughing face with wrinkled eyes: it was Voltaire.

Pierre seized the ziuthre by one end and looked at it darkly.

"I can't use it any more," he said.

"Why?"

"They turned it upside down."

"Will you make another?"

He looked at her for a long while. "You'd like me to, wouldn't you," he said between his teeth.

Eve was angry at Pierre. *He's warned every time they come: how does he do it? He's never wrong.*

The ziuthre dangled pitifully from the ends of Pierre's fingers. *He always finds a good reason not to use it. Sunday when they came he pretended he'd lost it but I saw it behind the paste pot and he couldn't fail to see it. I wonder if he isn't the one who brings them.* One could never tell if he were completely sincere. Sometimes Eve had the impression that despite himself Pierre was surrounded by a swarm of unhealthy thoughts and visions. But at other times Pierre seemed to invent them. *He suffers. But how much does he believe in the statues and the Negro. Anyhow, I know he doesn't see the statues, he only hears them: when they pass he turns his head away; but he still says he sees them; he describes them.* She remembered the red face of Dr. Franchot: "But my dear madame, all mentally unbalanced persons are liars; you're wasting your time if you're trying to distinguish between what they really feel and what they pretend to feel." She gave a start. *What is Franchot doing here? I don't want to start thinking like him.*

Pierre had gotten up. He went to throw the ziuthre into the wastebasket: *I want to think like you,* she murmured. He walked with tiny steps, on tiptoe, pressing his elbows against his hips so as to take up the least possible space. He came back and sat down and looked at Eve with a closed expression.

"We'll have to put up black wallpaper," he said. "There isn't enough black in this room."

He was crouched in the armchair. Sadly Eve watched his meagre body, always ready to withdraw, to shrink: the arms, legs and head looked like retractable organs. The clock struck six. The piano downstairs was silent. Eve sighed: the statues would not come right away; they had to wait for them.

"Do you want me to turn on the light?"

She would rather not wait for them in darkness.

"Do as you please," Pierre said.

Eve lit the small lamp on the bureau and a red mist filled the room. Pierre was waiting too.

He did not speak but his lips were moving, making two dark stains in the red mist. Eve loved Pierre's lips. Before, they had been moving and sensual; but they had lost their sensuality. They were wide apart, trembling a little, coming together incessantly, crushing against each other only to separate again. They were the only living things in this blank face; they looked like two frightened animals. Pierre could mutter like that for hours without a sound leaving his mouth and Eve often let herself be fascinated by this tiny, obstinate movement. *I love his mouth.* He never kissed her any more; he was horrified at contacts; at night they touched him—the hands of men, hard and dry, pinched him all over; the long-nailed hands of women caressed him. Often he went to bed with his clothes on but the hands slipped under the clothes and tugged at his shirt. Once he heard laughter and puffy lips were placed on his mouth. He never kissed Eve after that night.

"Agatha," Pierre said, "don't look at my mouth."

Eve lowered her eyes.

"I am not unaware that people can learn to read lips," he went on insolently.

His hand trembled on the arm of the chair. the index finger stretched out, tapped three times on the thumb and the other fingers curled: this was a spell. *It's going to start,* she thought. She wanted to take Pierre in her arms.

Pierre began to speak at the top of his voice in a very sophisticated tone.

"Do you remember Sankt Pauli?"[4]

No answer. Perhaps it was a trap.

"I met you there," he said, satisfied. "I took you away from a Danish sailor. We almost fought but I paid for a round of drinks and he let me take you away. All that was only a joke."

He's lying, he doesn't believe a word of what he says. He knows my name isn't Agatha. I hate him when he lies. But she saw his staring eyes and her rage melted. *He isn't lying,* she thought, *he can't stand it any more. He feels them coming; he's talking to keep from hearing them.* Pierre dug both hands into the arm of the chair. His face was pale; he was smiling.

"These meetings are often strange," he said, "but I don't believe

4. The nightlife district of Hamburg.

it's by chance. I'm not asking who sent you. I know you wouldn't answer. Anyhow, you've been smart enough to bluff me."

He spoke with great difficulty, in a sharp, hurried voice. There were words he could not pronounce and which left his mouth like some soft and shapeless substance.

"You dragged me away right in the middle of the party, between the rows of black automobiles, but behind the cars there was an army with red eyes which glowed as soon as I turned my back. I think you made signs to them, all the time hanging on my arm, but I didn't see a thing. I was too absorbed by the great ceremonies of the Coronation."

He looked straight ahead, his eyes wide open. He passed his hand over his forehead very rapidly, in one spare gesture, without stopping his talking. He did not want to stop talking.

"It was the Coronation of the Republic," he said stridently, "an impressive spectacle of its kind because of all the species of animals that the colonies sent for the ceremony. You were afraid to get lost among the monkeys. I said among the monkeys," he repeated arrogantly, looking around him, "I could say *among the Negroes*! The abortions sliding under the tables, trying to pass unseen, are discovered and nailed to the spot by my Look. The password is silence. To be silent. Everything in place and attention for the entrance of the statues, that's the countersign. Tralala . . ." he shrieked and cupped his hands to his mouth. "Tralalala, tralalalala!"

He was silent and Eve knew that the statues had come into the room. He was stiff, pale and distrustful. Eve stiffened too and both waited in silence. Someone was walking in the corridor: it was Marie the housecleaner, she had undoubtedly just arrived. Eve thought, *I have to give her money for the gas*. And then the statues began to fly; they passed between Eve and Pierre.

Pierre went "Ah!" and sank down in the armchair, folding his legs beneath him. He turned his face away; sometimes he grinned, but drops of sweat pearled his forehead. Eve could stand the sight no longer, this pale cheek, this mouth deformed by a trembling grimace; she closed her eyes. Gold threads began to dance on the red background of her eyelids; she felt old and heavy. Not far from her Pierre was breathing violently. *They're flying, they're buzzing, they're bending over him*. She felt a slight tickling, a pain in the shoulder and right side. Instinctively her body bent to the left as if to avoid some disagreeable contact, as if to let a heavy, awkward object pass. Suddenly the floor creaked and she had an insane desire to open her eyes, to look to her right, sweeping the air with her hand.

She did nothing: she kept her eyes closed and a bitter joy made her tremble: *I am afraid too*, she thought. Her entire life had taken refuge in her right side. She leaned towards Pierre without opening her eyes. The slightest effort would be enough and she would enter this tragic world for the first time, *I'm afraid of the statues*, she thought. It was a violent, blind affirmation, an incantation. She wanted to believe in their presence with all her strength. She tried to make a new sense, a sense of touch out of the anguish which paralysed her right side. She *felt* their passage in her arm, in her side and shoulder.

The statues flew low and gently; they buzzed. Eve knew that they had an evil look and that eyelashes stuck out from the stone around their eyes; but she pictured them badly. She knew, too, that they were not quite alive but that slabs of flesh, warm scales appeared on their great bodies; the stone peeled from the ends of their fingers and their palms were eaten away. Eve could not *see* all that: she simply thought of enormous women sliding against her, solemn and grotesque, with a human look and compact heads of stone. *They are bending over Pierre*—Eve made such a violent effort that her hands began trembling—*they are bending over me.* A horrible cry suddenly chilled her. They had touched him. She opened her eyes: Pierre's head was in his hands, he was breathing heavily. Eve felt exhausted: *a game*, she thought with remorse; *it was only a game. I didn't sincerely believe it for an instant. And all that time he suffered as if it were real.*

Pierre relaxed and breathed freely. But his pupils were strangely dilated and he was perspiring.

"Did you see them?" he asked.

"I can't see them."

"Better for you. They'd frighten you," he said. "I am used to them."

Eve's hands were still shaking and the blood had rushed to her head. Pierre took a cigarette from his pocket and brought it up to his mouth. But he did not light it.

"I don't care whether I see them or not," he said, "but I don't want them to touch me: I'm afraid they'll give me pimples."

He thought for an instant, then asked, "Did you hear them?"

"Yes," Eve said, "it's like an airplane engine." (Pierre had told her this the previous Sunday.)

Pierre smiled with condescension. "You exaggerate," he said. But he was still pale. He looked at Eve's hands. "Your hands are trembling. That made quite an impression on you, my poor Agatha. But don't worry. They won't come back again before tomorrow." Eve could not speak. Her teeth were chattering and she was afraid Pierre would notice it. Pierre watched her for a long time.

"You're tremendously beautiful," he said, nodding his head. "It's too bad, too bad."

He put out his hand quickly and toyed with her ear. "My lovely devil-woman. You disturb me a little, you are too beautiful: that distracts me. If it weren't a question of recapitulation . . ."

He stopped and looked at Eve with surprise.

"That's not the word . . . it came . . . it came," he said, smiling vaguely. "I had another on the tip of my tongue . . . but this one . . . came in its place. I forget what I was telling you."

He thought for a moment, then shook his head.

"Come," he said, "I want to sleep." He added in a childish voice, "You know, Agatha, I'm tired. I can't collect my thoughts any more."

He threw away his cigarette and looked at the rug anxiously. Eve slipped a pillow under his head.

"You can sleep too," he told her, "they won't be back."

. . . *Recapitulation* . . .

Pierre was asleep, a candid, half-smile on his face; his head was turned to one side: one might have thought he wanted to caress his check with his shoulder. Eve was not sleepy, she was thoughtful: *Recapitulation*. Pierre had suddenly looked stupid and the word had slipped out of his mouth, long and whitish. Pierre had stared ahead of him in astonishment, as if he had seen the word and didn't recognize it; his mouth was open, soft: something seemed broken in it. He stammered. *That's the first time it ever happened to him: he noticed it, too. He said he couldn't collect his thoughts any more.* Pierre gave a voluptuous little whimper and his hand made a vague movement. Eve watched him harshly: *how is he going to wake up.* It gnawed at her. As soon as Pierre was asleep she had to think about it. She was afraid he would wake up wild-eyed and stammering. *I'm stupid*, she thought, *it can't start before a year; Franchot said so.* But the anguish did not leave her; a year: a winter, a springtime, a summer, the beginning of another autumn. One day his features would grow confused, his jaw would hang loose, he would half open his weeping eyes. Eve bent over Pierre's hand and pressed her lips against it: *I'll kill you before that.*

ALBERT CAMUS

(1913–1960)

The Renegade (Le Renégat)*

"What a jumble! What a jumble! I must tidy up my mind. Since they cut out my tongue, another tongue, it seems, has been constantly wagging somewhere in my skull, something has been talking, or someone, that suddenly falls silent and then it all begins again— oh, I hear too many things I never utter, what a jumble, and if I open my mouth it's like pebbles rattling together. Order and method, the tongue says, and then goes on talking of other matters

* 1957. Copyright 1958 by Alfred A. Knopf, Inc. Reprinted from *Exile and the Kingdom* by Albert Camus, translated by Justin O'Brien, by permission of Alfred A. Knopf, Inc.

simultaneously—yes, I always longed for order. At least one thing
is certain, I am waiting for the missionary who is to come and take
my place. Here I am on the trail, an hour away from Taghâsa,
hidden in a pile of rocks, sitting on my old rifle. Day is breaking over
the desert, it's still very cold, soon it will be too hot, this country
drives men mad and I've been here I don't know how many years.
. . . No, just a little longer. The missionary is to come this morning,
or this evening. I've heard he'll come with a guide, perhaps they'll
have but one camel between them. I'll wait. I am waiting, it's only
the cold making me shiver. Just be patient a little longer, lousy
slave!

But I have been patient for so long. When I was home on that
high plateau of the Massif Central,[1] my coarse father, my boorish
mother, the wine, the pork soup every day, the wine above all, sour
and cold, and the long winter, the frigid wind, the snowdrifts, the
revolting bracken—oh, I wanted to get away, leave them all at once
and begin to live at last, in the sunlight, with fresh water. I believed
the priest, he spoke to me of the seminary, he tutored me daily, he
had plenty of time in that Protestant region, where he used to hug
the walls as he crossed the village. He told me of the future and of
the sun, Catholicism is the sun, he used to say, and he would get
me to read, he beat Latin into my hard head ('The kid's bright
but he's pig-headed'), my head was so hard that, despite all my
falls, it has never once bled in my life: 'Bull-headed,' my pig of a
father used to say. At the seminary they were proud as punch, a
recruit from the Protestant region was a victory, they greeted me
like the sun at Austerlitz.[2] The sun was pale and feeble, to be sure,
because of the alcohol, they have drunk sour wine and the children's
teeth are set on edge, *gra gra*,[3] one really ought to kill one's father,
but after all there's no danger that *he*'ll hurl himself into missionary
work since he's now long dead, the tart wine eventually cut through
his stomach, so there's nothing left but to kill the missionary.

I have something to settle with him and with his teachers, with
my teachers who deceived me, with the whole of lousy Europe,
everybody deceived me. Missionary work, that's all they could say,
go out to the savages and tell them: 'Here is my Lord, just look at
him, he never strikes or kills, he issues his orders in a low voice, he
turns the other cheek, he's the greatest of masters, choose him,
just see how much better he's made me, offend me and you will
see.' Yes, I believed, *gra gra*, and I felt better, I had put on weight,
I was almost handsome, I wanted to be offended. When we would
walk out in tight black rows, in summer, under Grenoble's hot sun
and would meet girls in cotton dresses, I didn't look away, I despised them, I waited for them to offend me, and sometimes they
would laugh. At such times I would think: 'Let them strike me

---

1. the mountainous region that covers
one fifth of the area of France.
2. Here,

the Austrians and Russians.
3. an inarticulate sound.

and spit in my face,' but their laughter, to tell the truth, came to the same thing, bristling with teeth and quips that tore me to shreds, the offense and the suffering were sweet to me! My confessor couldn't understand when I used to heap accusations on myself: 'No, no, there's good in you!' Good! There was nothing but sour wine in me, and that was all for the best, how can a man become better if he's not bad, I had grasped that in everything they taught me. That's the only thing I did grasp, a single idea, and, pig-headed bright boy, I carried it to its logical conclusion, I went out of my way for punishments, I groused at the normal, in short I too wanted to be an example in order to be noticed and so that after noticing me people would give credit to what had made me better, through me praise my Lord.

Fierce sun! It's rising, the desert is changing, it has lost its mountain-cyclamen color, O my mountain, and the snow, the soft enveloping snow, no, it's a rather grayish yellow, the ugly moment before the great resplendence. Nothing, still nothing from here to the horizon over yonder where the plateau disappears in a circle of still soft colors. Behind me, the trail climbs to the dune hiding Taghâsa, whose iron name has been beating in my head for so many years. The first to mention it to me was the half-blind old priest who had retired to our monastery, but why do I say the first, he was the only one, and it wasn't the city of salt, the white walls under the blinding sun, that struck me in his account but the cruelty of the savage inhabitants and the town closed to all outsiders, only one of those who had tried to get in, one alone, to his knowledge, had lived to relate what he had seen. They had whipped him and driven him out into the desert after having put salt on his wounds and in his mouth, he had met nomads who for once were compassionate, a stroke of luck, and since then I had been dreaming about his tale, about the fire of the salt and the sky, about the House of the Fetish and his slaves, could anything more barbarous, more exciting be imagined, yes, that was my mission and I had to go and reveal to them my Lord.

They all expatiated on the subject at the seminary to discourage me, pointing out the necessity of waiting, that it was not missionary country, that I wasn't ready yet, I had to prepare myself specially, know who I was, and even then I had to go through tests, then they would see! But go on waiting, ah, no!—yes, if they insisted, for the special preparation and the tryouts because they took place at Algiers and brought me closer, but for all the rest I shook my pig-head and repeated the same thing, to get among the most barbarous and live as they did, to show them at home, and even in the House of the Fetish, through example, that my Lord's truth would prevail. They would offend me, of course, but I was not afraid of offenses, they were essential to the demonstration, and as a result of the way I endured them I'd get the upper hand of those savages like a strong sun. Strong, yes, that was the word I constantly had on the tip of my tongue, I dreamed of absolute power, the kind that makes people kneel down, that forces the adversary to capitulate, converts him in short, and the blinder, the crueler he is, the more he's sure of himself, mired in his own conviction, the more his consent establishes the royalty of whoever brought about his collapse. Converting good folk who had strayed somewhat was the shabby ideal of our priests, I despised them for daring so little when they could do so much, they lacked faith and I had it, I wanted to be acknowledged by the torturers themselves, to fling them on their knees and make them say: 'O Lord, here is thy victory,' to rule in short by the sheer force of words over an army of the wicked. Oh, I was sure of reasoning logically on that subject, never quite sure of myself otherwise, but once I get an idea I don't let go of it, that's my strong point, yes the strong point of the fellow they all pitied!

The sun has risen higher, my forehead is beginning to burn. Around me the stones are beginning to crack open with a dull sound, the only cool thing is the rifle's barrel, cool as the fields, as the evening rain long ago when the soup was simmering, they would wait for me, my father and mother who would occasionally smile at me, perhaps I loved them. But that's all in the past, a film of heat is beginning to rise from the trail, come on, missionary, I'm waiting for you, now I know how to answer the message, my new masters taught me, and I know they are right, you have to settle accounts with that question of love. When I fled the seminary in Algiers I had a different idea of the savages and only one detail of my imaginings was true, they are cruel. I had robbed the treasurer's office, cast off my habit, crossed the Atlas,[4] the upper plateaus and the desert, the bus-driver of the Trans-Sahara line made fun of me: 'Don't go there,' he too, what had got into them all, and the gusts of sand for hundreds of wind-blown kilometers, progressing and backing in the face of the wind, then the mountains again made up of black peaks and ridges sharp as steel, and after them it took a guide to go out on the endless sea of brown pebbles, screaming with heat, burning with the fires of a thousand mirrors, to the spot on the confines of the white country and the land of the blacks where stands the city of salt. And the money the guide stole from me, ever naïve I had shown it to him, but he left me on the trail—just about here, it so happens —after having struck me: 'Dog, there's the way, the honor's all mine, go ahead, go on, they'll show you,' and they did show me, oh yes, they're like the sun that never stops, except at night, beating sharply and proudly, that is beating me hard at this moment, too hard, with a multitude of lances burst from the ground, oh shelter, yes shelter, under the big rock, before everything gets muddled.

The shade here is good. How can anyone live in the city of salt, in the hollow of that basin full of dazzling heat? On each of the sharp right-angle walls cut out with a pickax and coarsely planed,

---

4. a range of mountains in Morocco, Algeria, and Tunisia.

the gashes left by the pickax bristle with blinding scales, pale scattered sand yellows them somewhat except when the wind dusts the upright walls and terraces, then everything shines with dazzling whiteness under a sky likewise dusted even to its blue rind. I was going blind during those days when the stationary fire would crackle for hours on the surface of the white terraces that all seemed to meet as if, in the remote past, they had all together tackled a mountain of salt, flattened it first, and then had hollowed out streets, the insides of houses and windows directly in the mass, or as if—yes, this is more like it, they had cut out their white, burning hell with a powerful jet of boiling water just to show that they could live where no one ever could, thirty days' travel from any living thing, in this hollow in the middle of the desert where the heat of day prevents any contact among creatures, separates them by a portcullis of invisible flames and of searing crystals, where without transition the cold of night congeals them individually in their rock-salt shells, nocturnal dwellers in a dried-up icefloe, black Eskimos suddenly shivering in their cubical igloos. Black because they wear long black garments, and the salt that collects even under their nails, that they continue tasting bitterly and swallowing during the sleep of those polar nights, the salt they drink in the water from the only spring in the hollow of a dazzling groove, often spots their dark garments with something like the trail of snails after a rain.

Rain, O Lord, just one real rain, long and hard, rain from your heaven! Then at last the hideous city, gradually eaten away, would slowly and irresistibly cave in and, utterly melted in a slimy torrent, would carry off its savage inhabitants toward the sands. Just one rain, Lord! But what do I mean, what Lord, they are the lords and masters! They rule over their sterile homes, over their black slaves that they work to death in the mines and each slab of salt that is cut out is worth a man in the region to the south, they pass by, silent, wearing their mourning veils in the mineral whiteness of the streets, and at night, when the whole town looks like a milky phantom, they stoop down and enter the shade of their homes, where the salt walls shine dimly. They sleep with a weightless sleep and, as soon as they wake, they give orders, they strike, they say they are a united people, that their god is the true god, and that one must obey. They are my masters, they are ignorant of pity and, like masters, they want to be alone, to progress alone, to rule alone, because they alone had the daring to build in the salt and the sands a cold torrid city. And I . . .

What a jumble when the heat rises, I'm sweating, they never do, now the shade itself is heating up, I feel the sun on the stone above me, it's striking, striking like a hammer on all the stones and it's the music, the vast music of noon, air and stones vibrating over hundreds of kilometers, *gra*, I hear the silence as I did once before. Yes, it was the same silence, years ago, that greeted me when the guards led me to them, in the sunlight, in the center of the square, whence the concentric terraces rose gradually toward the lid of hard blue sky sitting on the edge of the basin. There I was, thrown on my knees in the hollow of that white shield, my eyes corroded by the swords of salt and fire issuing from all the walls, pale with fatigue, my ear bleeding from the blow given by my guide, and they, tall and black, looked at me without saying a word. The day was at its midcourse. Under the blows of the iron sun the sky resounded at length, a sheet of white-hot tin, it was the same silence, and they stared at me, time passed, they kept on staring at me, and I couldn't face their stares, I panted more and more violently, eventually I wept, and suddenly they turned their backs on me in silence and all together went off in the same direction. On my knees, all I could see, in the red-and-black sandals, was their feet sparkling with salt as they raised the long black gowns, the tip rising somewhat, the heel striking the ground lightly, and when the square was empty I was dragged to the House of the Fetish.

Squatting, as I am today in the shelter of the rock and the fire above my head pierces the rock's thickness, I spent several days within the dark of the House of the Fetish, somewhat higher than the others, surrounded by a wall of salt, but without windows, full of a sparkling night. Several days, and I was given a basin of brackish water and some grain that was thrown before me the way chickens are fed, I picked it up. By day the door remained closed and yet the darkness became less oppressive, as if the irresistible sun managed to flow through the masses of salt. No lamp, but by feeling my way along the walls I touched garlands of dried palms decorating the walls and, at the end, a small door, coarsely fitted, of which I could make out the bolt with my fingertips. Several days, long after—I couldn't count the days or the hours, but my handful of grain had been thrown me some ten times and I had dug out a hole for my excrements that I covered up in vain, the stench of an animal den hung on anyway—long after, yes, the door opened wide and they came in.

One of them came toward me where I was squatting in a corner. I felt the burning salt against my cheek, I smelled the dusty scent of the palms, I watched him approach. He stopped a yard away from me, he stared at me in silence, a signal, and I stood up, he stared at me with his metallic eyes that shone without expression in his brown horse-face, then he raised his hand. Still impassive, he seized me by the lower lip, which he twisted slowly until he tore my flesh and, without letting go, made me turn around and back up to the center of the room, he pulled on my lip to make me fall on my knees there, mad with pain and my mouth bleeding, then he turned away to join the others standing against the walls. They watched me moaning in the unbearable heat of the unbroken daylight that came in the wide-open door, and in that light suddenly appeared the Sorcerer with his raffia hair, his chest covered with a breastplate of pearls, his legs bare under a straw skirt, wearing a mask of reeds and wire with two square openings for the eyes. He was followed by musicians and women wearing heavy motley gowns that revealed nothing of their bodies. They danced in front of the door at the end, but a coarse, scarcely rhythmical dance, they just barely moved, and finally the Sorcerer opened the little door behind me, the masters did not stir, they were watching me, I turned around and saw the Fetish, his double ax-head, his iron nose twisted like a snake.

I was carried before him, to the foot of the pedestal, I was made to drink a black, bitter, bitter water, and at once my head began to burn, I was laughing, that's the offense, I have been offended. They undressed me, shaved my head and body, washed me in oil, beat my face with cords dipped in water and salt, and I laughed and turned my head away, but each time two women would take me by the ears and offer my face to the Sorcerer's blows while I could see only his square eyes, I was still laughing, covered with blood. They stopped, no one spoke but me, the jumble was beginning in my head, then they lifted me up and forced me to raise my eyes toward the Fetish, I had ceased laughing. I knew that I was now consecrated to him to serve him, adore him, no, I was not laughing any more, fear and pain stifled me. And there, in that white house, between those walls that the sun was assiduously burning on the outside, my face taut, my memory exhausted, yes, I tried to pray to the Fetish, he was all there was and even his horrible face was less horrible than the rest of the world. Then it was that my ankles were tied with a cord that permitted just one step, they danced again, but this time in front of the Fetish, the masters went out one by one.

The door once closed behind them, the music again, and the Sorcerer lighted a bark fire around which he pranced, his long silhouette broke on the angles of the white walls, fluttered on the flat surfaces, filled the room with dancing shadows. He traced a rectangle in a corner to which the women dragged me, I felt their dry and gentle hands, they set before me a bowl of water and a little pile of grain and pointed to the Fetish, I grasped that I was to keep my eyes fixed on him. Then the Sorcerer called them one after the other over to the fire, he beat some of them who moaned and who then went and prostrated themselves before the Fetish my god, while the Sorcerer kept on dancing and he made them all leave the room until only one was left, quite young, squatting near the musicians and not yet beaten. He held her by a shock of hair which he kept twisting around his wrist, she dropped backward with eyes popping until she finally fell on her back. Dropping her, the Sorcerer screamed, the musicians turned to the wall, while behind the square-eyed mask the scream rose to an impossible pitch, and the woman rolled on the ground in a sort of fit and, at last on all fours, her head hidden in her locked arms, she too screamed, but with a hollow, muffled sound, and in this position, without ceasing to scream and to look at the Fetish, the Sorcerer took her nimbly and nastily, without the woman's face being visible, for it was covered with the heavy folds of her garment. And, wild as a result of the solitude, *I* screamed too, yes, howled with fright toward the Fetish until a kick hurled me against the wall, biting the salt as I am biting this rock today with my tongueless mouth, while waiting for the man I must kill.

Now the sun has gone a little beyond the middle of the sky. Through the breaks in the rock I can see the hole it makes in the white-hot metal of the sky, a mouth voluble as mine, constantly vomiting rivers of flame over the colorless desert. On the trail in front of me, nothing, no cloud of dust on the horizon, behind me they must be looking for me, no, not yet, it's only in the late afternoon that they opened the door and I could go out a little, after having spent the day cleaning the House of the Fetish, set out fresh offerings, and in the evening the ceremony would begin, in which I was sometimes beaten, at others not, but always I served the Fetish, the Fetish whose image is engraved in iron in my memory and now in my hope also. Never had a god so possessed or enslaved me, my whole life day and night was devoted to him, and pain and the absence of pain, wasn't that joy, were due him and even, yes, desire, as a result of being present, almost every day, at that impersonal and nasty act which I heard without seeing it inasmuch as I now had to face the wall or else be beaten. But, my face up against the salt, obsessed by the bestial shadows moving on the wall, I listened to the long scream, my throat was dry, a burning sexless desire squeezed my temples and my belly as in a vise. Thus the days followed one another, I barely distinguished them as if they had liquefied in the torrid heat and the treacherous reverberation from the walls of salt, time had become merely a vague lapping of waves in which there would burst out, at regular intervals, screams of pain or possession, a long ageless day in which the Fetish ruled as this fierce sun does over my house of rocks, and now, as I did then, I weep with unhappiness and longing, a wicked hope consumes me, I want to betray, I lick the barrel of my gun and its soul inside, its soul, only guns have souls—oh, yes! the day they cut out my tongue, I learned to adore the immortal soul of hatred!

What a jumble, what a rage, *gra gra*, drunk with heat and wrath, lying prostrate on my gun. Who's panting here? I can't endure this endless heat, this waiting, I must kill him. Not a bird, not a blade of grass, stone, an arid desire, their screams, this tongue within me talking, and since they mutilated me, the long, flat, deserted suffering deprived even of the water of night, the night of which I would dream, when locked in with the god, in my den of salt. Night alone with its cool stars and dark fountains could save me, carry me off at last from the wicked gods of mankind, but ever locked up I could not contemplate it. If the newcomer tarries more, I shall see it at least rise from the desert and sweep over the sky, a cold golden vine that will hang from the dark zenith and from which I can drink at length, moisten this black dried hole that no muscle of live flexible flesh revives now, forget at last that day when madness took away my tongue.

How hot it was, really hot, the salt was melting or so it seemed to me, the air was corroding my eyes, and the Sorcerer came in without his mask. Almost naked under grayish tatters, a new woman followed him and her face, covered with a tattoo reproducing the mask of the Fetish, expressed only an idol's ugly stupor. The only thing alive about her was her thin flat body that flopped at the foot of the god when the Sorcerer opened the door of the niche. Then he went out without looking at me, the heat rose, I didn't stir, the Fetish looked at me over that motionless body whose muscles stirred gently and the woman's idol-face didn't change when I approached. Only her eyes enlarged as she stared at me, my feet touched hers, the heat then began to shriek, and the idol, without a word, still staring at me with her dilated eyes, gradually slipped onto her back, slowly drew her legs up and raised them as she gently spread her knees. But, immediately afterward, *gra*, the Sorcerer was lying in wait for me, they all entered and tore me from the woman, beat me dreadfully on the sinful place, what sin, I'm laughing, where is it and where is virtue, they clapped me against a wall, a hand of steel gripped my jaws, another opened my mouth, pulled on my tongue until it bled, was it I screaming with that bestial scream, a cool cutting caress, yes cool at last, went over my tongue. When I came to, I was alone in the night, glued to the wall, covered with hardened blood, a gag of strange-smelling dry grasses filled my mouth, it had stopped bleeding, but it was vacant and in that absence the only living thing was a tormenting pain. I wanted to rise, I fell back, happy, desperately happy to die at last, death too is cool and its shadow hides no god.

I did not die, a new feeling of hatred stood up one day, at the same time I did, walked toward the door of the niche, opened it, closed it behind me, I hated my people, the Fetish was there and from the depth of the hole in which I was I did more than pray to him, I believed in him and denied all I had believed up to then. Hail! he was strength and power, he could be destroyed but not converted, he stared over my head with his empty, rusty eyes. Hail! he was the master, the only lord, whose indisputable attribute was malice, there are no good masters. For the first time, as a result of offenses, my whole body crying out a single pain, I surrendered to him and approved his maleficent order, I adored in him the evil principle of the world. A prisoner of his kingdom——the sterile city carved out of a mountain of salt, divorced from nature, deprived of those rare and fleeting flowerings of the desert, preserved from those strokes of chance or marks of affection such as an unexpected cloud or a brief violent downpour that are familiar even to the sun or the sands, the city of order in short, right angles, square rooms, rigid men——I freely became its tortured, hate-filled citizen, I repudiated the long history that had been taught me. I had been misled, solely the reign of malice was devoid of defects, I had been misled, truth is square, heavy, thick, it does not admit distinctions, gold is an idle dream, an intention constantly postponed and pursued with exhausting effort, a limit never reached, its reign is impossible. Only evil can reach its limits and reign absolutely, it must be served to establish its visible kingdom, then we shall see, but what does 'then' mean, only evil is present, down with Europe, reason, honor, and the cross. Yes, I was to be converted to the religion of my masters, yes indeed, I was a slave, but if I too become vicious I cease to be a slave, despite my shackled feet and my mute mouth. Oh, this heat is driving me crazy, the desert cries out everywhere under the unbearable light, and he, the Lord of kindness, whose very name revolts me, I disown him, for I know him now. He dreamed and wanted to lie, his tongue was cut out so that his word would no longer be able to deceive the world, he was pierced with nails even in his head, his poor head, like mine now, what a jumble, how weak I am, and the earth didn't tremble, I am sure, it was not a righteous man they had killed, I refuse to believe it, there are no righteous men but only evil masters who bring about the reign of relentless truth. Yes, the Fetish alone has power, he is the sole god of this world, hatred is his commandment, the source of all life, the cool water, cool like mint that chills the mouth and burns the stomach.

Then it was that I changed, they realized it, I would kiss their hands when I met them, I was on their side, never wearying of admiring them, I trusted them, I hoped they would mutilate my people as they had mutilated me. And when I learned that the missionary was to come, I knew what I was to do. That day like all the others, the same blinding daylight that had been going on so long! Late in the afternoon a guard was suddenly seen running along the edge of the basin, and, a few minutes later, I was dragged to the House of the Fetish and the door closed. One of them held me on the ground in the dark, under threat of his cross-shaped sword, and the silence lasted for a long time until a strange sound filled the ordinarily peaceful town, voices that it took me some time to recognize because they were speaking my language, but as soon as they rang out the point of the sword was lowered toward my eyes, my guard stared at me in silence. Then two voices came closer and I can still hear them, one asking why that house was guarded and whether they should break in the door, Lieutenant, the other said: 'No' sharply, then added, after a moment, that an agreement had been reached, that the town accepted a garrison of twenty men on condition that they would camp outside the walls and respect the customs. The private laughed, 'They're knuckling under,' but the officer didn't know, for the first time in any case they were willing to receive someone to take care of the children and that would be the chaplain, later on they would see about the territory. The other said they would cut off the chaplain's you know what if the soldiers were not there. 'Oh, no!' the officer answered. 'In fact, Father Beffort will come before the garrison; he'll be here in two days.' That was all I heard, motionless, lying under the sword, I was in pain, a wheel of needles and knives was whirling in me. They were crazy, they were crazy, they were allowing a hand to be laid on the city, on their invincible power, on the true god, and the fellow who was to come would not have his tongue cut out, he would show off his insolent goodness without paying for it, without enduring any offense. The reign of evil would be postponed, there would be doubt again, again time would be wasted dreaming of the impossible good, wearing oneself out in fruitless efforts instead of hastening the realization of the only possible kingdom and I looked at the sword threatening me, O sole power to rule over the world! O power, and the city gradually emptied of its sounds, the door finally opened, I remained alone, burned and bitter, with the Fetish, and I swore to him to save my new faith, my true masters, my despotic God, to betray well, whatever it might cost me.

Gra, the heat is abating a little, the stone has ceased to vibrate, I can go out of my hole, watch the desert gradually take on yellow and ocher tints that will soon be mauve. Last night I waited until they were asleep, I had blocked the lock on the door, I went out with the same step as usual, measured by the cord, I knew the streets, I knew where to get the old rifle, what gate wasn't guarded, and I reached here just as the night was beginning to fade around a handful of stars while the desert was getting a little darker. And now it seems days and days that I have been crouching in these rocks. Soon, soon, I hope he comes soon! In a moment they'll begin to look for me, they'll speed over the trails in all directions, they won't know that I left for them and to serve them better, my legs are weak, drunk with hunger and hate. Oh! over there, *gra*, at the end of the trail, two camels are growing bigger, ambling along, already multiplied by short shadows, they are running with that lively and dreamy gait they always have. Here they are, here at last!

Quick, the rifle, and I load it quickly. O Fetish, my god over yonder, may your power be preserved, may the offense be multiplied, may hate rule pitilessly over a world of the damned, may the wicked forever be masters, may the kingdom come, where in a single city of salt and iron black tyrants will enslave and possess without pity! And now, *gra gra*, fire on pity, fire on impotence and its charity, fire on all that postpones the coming of evil, fire twice, and there they are toppling over, falling, and the camels flee toward the horizon, where a geyser of black birds has just risen in the unchanged sky. I laugh, I laugh, the fellow is writhing in his detested habit, he is raising his head a little, he sees me—me his all-powerful shackled master, why does he smile at me, I'll crush that smile! How pleasant is the sound of a rifle butt on the face of goodness, today, today at last, all is consummated and everywhere in the desert, even hours away from here, jackals sniff the nonexistent wind, then set out in a patient trot toward the feast of carrion awaiting them. Victory! I raise my arms to a heaven moved to pity, a lavender shadow is just barely suggested on the opposite side, O nights of Europe, home, childhood, why must I weep in the moment of triumph?

He stirred, no the sound comes from somewhere else, and from the other direction here they come rushing like a flight of of dark birds, my masters, who fall upon me, seize me, ah yes! strike, they fear their city sacked and howling, they fear the avenging soldiers I called forth, and this is only right, upon the sacred city. Defend yourselves now, strike! strike me first, you possess the truth! O my masters, they will then conquer the soldiers, they'll conquer the word and love, they'll spread over the deserts, cross the seas, fill the light of Europe with their black veils—strike the belly, yes, strike the eyes —sow their salt on the continent, all vegetation, all youth will die out, and dumb crowds with shackled feet will plod beside me in the world-wide desert under the cruel sun of the true faith, I'll not be alone. Ah! the pain, the pain they cause me, their rage is good and on this cross-shaped war-saddle where they are now quartering me, pity! I'm laughing, I love the blow that nails me down crucified.

* * *

How silent the desert is! Already night and I am alone, I'm thirsty. Still waiting, where is the city, those sounds in the distance, and the soldiers perhaps the victors, no, it can't be, even if the soldiers are victorious, they're not wicked enough, they won't be able to rule, they'll still say one must become better, and still millions of men between evil and good, torn, bewildered, O Fetish, why hast thou forsaken me? All is over, I'm thirsty, my body is burning, a darker night fills my eyes.

This long, this long dream, I'm awaking, no, I'm going to die, dawn is breaking, the first light, daylight for the living, and for me the inexorable sun, the flies. Who is speaking, no one, the sky is not opening up, no, no, God doesn't speak in the desert, yet whence comes that voice saying: 'If you consent to die for hate and power, who will forgive us?' Is it another tongue in me or still that other fellow refusing to die, at my feet, and repeating: 'Courage! courage! courage!'? Ah! supposing I were wrong again! Once fraternal men, sole recourse, O solitude, forsake me not! Here, here who are you, torn, with bleeding mouth, is it you, Sorcerer, the soldiers defeated you, the salt is burning over there, it's you my beloved master! Cast off that hate-ridden face, be good now, we were mistaken, we'll begin all over again, we'll rebuild the city of mercy, I want to go back home. Yes, help me, that's right, give me your hand. . . .'

A handful of salt fills the mouth of the garrulous slave.

ALEXANDER SOLZHENITSYN

(1918–)

Matryona's House (Matrionin Dvor) *

Some one hundred and eighty-four kilometers from Moscow, and a good half year after the incident, all trains slowed down their march almost as if groping. The passengers clung to the windows, went out into the vestibule. Were they repairing the tracks or what? Was the train off schedule?

No. Having gone beyond a crossing, the train picked up speed again and the passengers settled back.

Only the engineers knew and understood what it was all about. And so did I.

I

During the summer of the year 1953, I came back at random from the hot, dusty desertlands—simply to Russia. No one was waiting for me or had invited me anywhere, because I had been detained from returning for a little stretch of ten years. I simply wanted to get back into the heart of the country—out of the heat, into woodlands with rustling leaves. I wanted to cut myself loose and get lost in the innermost heart of Russia—if there were any such thing—and live there.

For a year afterward I might perhaps get a job on this side of the Ural mountains merely pushing a wheelbarrow. Already after considerable construction work had been completed, they had turned me down as an electrician. But I really had a longing to be a teacher. Well-informed people told me that I had wasted my money on the ticket and had stopped there in vain.

But some things were changing already. When I went up the stairway of the District Board of Education and asked where the cadre section was, I noted with astonishment that here the party officials were no longer sitting behind dark leather-upholstered doors, but behind glassy partitions, as in a pharmacy. I went hesitatingly up to one of the little windows, greeted the person on the other side, and inquired, "Tell me, don't you need mathematics teachers somewhere farther along the railroad line? I want to settle there permanently."

They probed through every letter of my personal documents, went from room to room, and called somewhere. For them this was a rare switch—someone asking to get out of the city and into the boondocks. Then suddenly they found a spot for me in Vysokoe

* Reprinted from "We Never Make Mistakes," second edition, by Alexander Solzhenitsyn, translated by Paul W. Blackstock, by permission of the University of South Carolina Press. Copyright 1971 by the University of South Carolina Press.

Pole [High Fields]. I felt good just hearing the name of the place.

The name did not lie. Set in hills and hollows and then more little knolls, covered with heavily tangled woods, ponds, and embankments, Vysokoe Pole was the one place I was looking for where it would not be an insult to live and to die. There I could sit on a stump in the woods and think for a long time about whatever I wanted to, without worrying about lunch or supper, if only I could remain there and listen at night to the branches rustle in the tree-tops—when the whole world was silent, and not one radio was audible anywhere. But, alas, there was no bread baked there. Nothing edible was sold. The entire village carried its food in bags from the one city in the region.

I returned to the cadre section and made another request at the little window. At first they didn't even want to talk to me. Afterward they all went from room to room, telephoned someone, scratched something with their pens, and stamped my orders: "Torf Produkt" [Peat Products].

Torf Produkt? Ah, Turgenev never knew what such an expression could include.

At the Torf Produkt station, a gray, wooden barracks aging with time, hung the stern warning: "For trains sit only on the waiting-room side"; and scratched with a nail on a board beneath: "And without tickets." But at the ticket window, displaying the same melancholy ingenuity, someone had carved out permanently with a knife: "No tickets." I was to appreciate the precise significance of those additions later. It was easy to arrive at Torf Produkt, but not to leave.

And here in this place had stood, and had remained long after the revolution, thick impenetrable forests. Later they were cut down by the peat exploiters and the neighboring kolkhoz [collective farm]. Its manager, Shahkov, razed quite a few acres of timber and then profitably sold it in the Odessa region.

In the midst of the peaty lowlands the little settlement had grown up haphazardly—monotonous barracks dating from the thirties, and little houses with carved facades and glassed-in verandas, built in the fifties. But one could see that the insides of these little houses were not cut up by partitions reaching up to the ceiling, so that I could not rent a room with four regular walls.

Above the village smoked the factory pipes. Here and there throughout the settlement the narrow-gauge had been extended, and its engines, also belching thick smoke and whistling sharply, drew trains of brown peat, peat slabs, and briquettes. I could assume without error that in the evening over the door of the club the loudspeaker would blare forth, and on the streets drunks would whoop it up a while, not without thrusting at each other with knives.

That was where my dream of a quiet little corner in Russia

brought me. But, of course, I could have stayed where I was and lived in an adobe hut, with a view of the desert, with a fresh breeze blowing at night, and the starry vault of the heavens opened wide overhead.

I couldn't sleep on the station benches and at daybreak I strolled through the village again. Now I saw the tiny little market. A solitary woman was there early selling milk. I took a bottle, stood by her, and drank it down at once.

Her speech struck me. It wasn't actually speech, but rather a pleasant singsong. Her words were the kind I had longed to hear, a longing which brought me back from Asia, "Drink! Drink to your heart's content! You dear soul, you're probably a newcomer, aren't you?"

"And where are you from?" I asked, already feeling better. I discovered that not all the inhabitants in the vicinity were peat workers, that behind the railroad was a small hill, and that behind the hill was a village. This village is called Talnovo, and has been there, surrounded by dense forests, since time immemorial, from the days of the former landed gentry. Then follows a whole region of villages —Chashlitsy, Ovintsy, Spudni, Shevertni, Shestimirovo—all deeper in the woods, all a little farther from the railroad and closer to the lakes.

These names drew me like a soothing breeze. They promised me the very core of Russia.

I asked my new acquaintance to take me to Talnovo after the market was over and try to find an *izba* [peasant's hut] where I could find quarters.

It appeared profitable to have me as a tenant. In addition to the rent, the school also promised me a truckload of peat for the winter. The woman's pleasant expression changed to one of concern. There was no place for me at her house (they, she and her husband, were taking care of her aging mother). That's why she took me over to one of her relatives and then to another. But there were no separate rooms at either house, and they were crowded and noisy.

Thus we came to a dammed stream which was drying up and had a little bridge over it. This place caught my fancy more than any other in the village. There were two or three willows, and a crooked little *izba* which leaned far over toward the ground, while ducks were swimming in the pond, and geese, which had gone up the bank, were shaking themselves off.

"Well, perhaps we should call on Matryona," said my guide, already tiring of me. "Only it isn't very clean at her place. She neglects things and is often sick."

Matryona's house was standing there not far distant with four little windows lined up in a cold, ugly wall, its roof shingled on both slopes, and with an ornamented garret window below its tower room. However, the roof was rotting out, the logs of the framework were turning gray with age and although the gate had once been stronger, its pales were thinning out.

The wicket gate was bolted, but my guide did not stop to knock. She slipped her hand under the bottom and turned the latch bolt, a simple device to keep the livestock out. There was no cover over the yard, but most of the house was under one roof. Behind the entrance door an inside stairway rose to a wide landing which was shaded by the roof high overhead. On the left more steps led up to the *gornitza*, a separate structure without any stove, and steps led down to the storage chamber. To the right was the *izba* itself, with garret and cellar.

It had been built long ago and of high quality materials for a large family, but now a solitary woman of sixty lived there.

When I entered the *izba* she was lying down on the Russian stove right there at the entrance, and was covered with nondescript dark rags of the kind which are invaluable in the life of the workingman.

The spacious *izba* and especially the best portion near the windows was strewn with stools and benches on which were earthenware pots and tubs full of rubber plants. They filled the loneliness of the proprietor with a mute but living company. They grew up untrammeled, capturing the feeble light on the north side. In the meager light, the roundish face of the landlady peering behind the stove pipe seemed sallow and sickly in tone. From her eyes which had grown bleary, one could see that illness had exhausted her.

As she talked to me, she was lying up there, face downward on the stove without a pillow, her head toward the door, while I stood beneath. She did not show any enthusiasm at getting a lodger, and complained of the black illness through the paroxysms of which she had just now passed. The illness did not strike her every month, but when it did, was so overpowering that, as she said, "For two or three days I won't be able to get up or wait on you. But I'm not particular about the *izba*, and you can live here if you want to."

And she named off for me other landladies where it would be more restful for me, and where I would be more welcome, and sent me round to them. But I had already seen that it was my destiny to lodge in this dimly lit *izba* with its lusterless mirror in which it was quite impossible to see oneself, and, hanging on the wall for decoration, two garish posters bought for a ruble each, one advertising books and the other the harvest.

Matryona made me look elsewhere in the village for quarters, and on my second visit she made long excuses, quoting one of her sayings, "If one neither cleans nor cooks, how can one please?"

Nevertheless she met me standing up, and already something like pleasure struggled to express itself in her eyes because I had returned.

We came to an understanding on the price and on the peat which the school would supply. I learned only later that year after year, for many years, Matryona Vasilyevna had not earned a ruble from any source, because they didn't pay her a pension. Occasionally her relatives helped her out a little. In the kolkhoz she used to work, not for money, but for "credits" in the dog-eared account books.

So I lodged in Matryona's house. We didn't divide off a room. Her bed was near the stove in the corner by the door. I fixed myself a primitive cot by one window, and pushed aside Matryona's beloved rubber trees to set up a small table in the light from another. There was electric lighting in the village—it had already been extended from Shatury in the twenties. At the time, the newspapers wrote about "little Ilyich [Lenin] lamps" and the peasants, their eyes goggling, called them, "The Tsar's lights!"

Perhaps to one of the more wealthy villagers, Matryona's *izba* may not have seemed habitable; nevertheless, for that fall and winter with her it was fine. It still didn't leak from the rains, and the cold winds did not blow the warmth from the stove at once, but only towards morning, especially when it blew from the other side.

Other things lived in the *izba* besides Matryona and myself, such as a cat, mice, and cockroaches.

The cat was elderly, and more important—lame. She had been picked up out of pity by Matryona and had struck roots. Although the cat walked on four legs, she limped badly, and favored one leg, since that foot or leg had been injured. When the cat jumped down from the stove, the sound of her contact with the floor was not a soft feline sound as with other cats, but a powerful, instantaneous strike with the three feet—"toop!"—such a powerful blow that, not being accustomed to it at first I would wince. She placed the three feet together under her in order to protect the fourth.

The mice were in the hut but not because the lame cat couldn't cope with them. On the contrary, she sprang at them like lightning from the corner and carried them out in her teeth. But the mice were inaccessible for the cat, because someone in better days had papered the *izba* for Matryona with a figured greenish wallpaper, and not with just one, but with five layers. When these layers stuck together the paper worked fine, but they had peeled from the walls in many places, and formed a sort of internal skin for the hut. Between the wood frame of the *izba* and the skin of the paper the mice had made themselves passages, and rustled about brazenly, as they ran through them even under the ceiling. The cat angrily followed their rustling with her eyes, but was unable to reach them.

Occasionally the cat ate the cockroaches, but they didn't agree with her. The only thing the cockroaches respected was that line of the partition separating the mouth of the Russian stove and the kitchen from the clean area of the hut. They did not creep into this area.

On the other hand, the cockroaches swarmed over the kitchen at night. Whenever I went there for a drink of water late in the evening and turned on the light, the entire floor, the big bench and even the wall were almost solid brown and astir with them. I brought home some borax from the school laboratory and by mixing it with dough, we almost got rid of them. The number of cockroaches decreased, but Matryona was afraid of poisoning the cat along with them. We stopped pouring the poison and the cockroaches multiplied again.

At night when Matryona was already asleep, but I was busy working at the table, the thin, quick pattering of mice under the wallpaper merged with and drowned out the rustle of the cockroaches behind the partition, like the distant sound of the ocean. But I grew accustomed to them. There was nothing evil about either the mice or the cockroaches, and they told no lies. Their rustling was simply for them their life.

And I also became accustomed to the advertising poster beauties which, stuck on the wall, offered me *Belinsky, Panferov,* and reams of other books—only these were silent. I got used to everything in Matryona's hut.

Matryona used to get up between four and five in the morning. Her clock was twenty-seven years old, and had been purchased at the village store. It was always fast, but Matryona was not worried as long as it did not lose time and make her late in the morning. She would turn on the little lamp behind the kitchen partition, and quietly, courteously, trying not to make any noise, heat up the Russian stove. Then she went to milk the goat (it was all the stock she had, this one, dirty-white, crinkly horned goat). She fetched the water and cooked breakfast in cast-iron pots—one for me, one for herself, and one for the goat.

She brought up potatoes from the cellar—the smallest one for the goat, little ones for herself, and egg-sized ones for me. As for large potatoes, her sandy garden plot had not been manured since the war and, although she was always planting potatoes, potatoes, and more potatoes, it never produced any big ones.

I hardly heard her bustling about in the morning. I slept long, woke up in the late winter light, stretched myself, and stuck my head out from under the blanket and sheepskin. The latter, plus my prison-camp jacket covering my legs and a sack padded with straw underneath, kept me warm even on those nights when the hard frost from the north pushed through our puny window.

When I heard her restrained clatter behind the partition, I always said in measured tones, "Good morning, Matryona Vasilyevna!"

And she always greeted me from behind the partition with the same kind words which began with a low, warm gurgle of the sort grandmothers make in fairytales: "M-m-mm . . . the same to you!"

And a little later, "Your breakfast is ready."

She never announced what was for breakfast, but that was easily figured out: boiled potatoes, or "poh-tah-to" soup (the way everyone in the village pronounced it) or fine-ground barley gruel. That year you couldn't buy any other kind of groats in Torf Produkt except barley, and you had to fight for it at that, because it was the very cheapest, was used to fatten pigs, and was bought by the sackful. Even this was not always salted, as it should have been, was often burnt and after the meal left a thin coating on the palate and gums, and caused heartburn.

But all that was not Matryona's fault. There was simply no butter in Torf Produkt, the margarine went like hot cakes, and only mixed fats were sold on the free market. Besides, the Russian stove, as I found out, was not suitable for cooking. The cooking took place in the interior hidden from the cook himself. The heat approached the cast-iron pot unevenly. I suppose the stove came down from our ancestors in the Stone Age since once it had been stoked early in the morning, all day long it kept fodder and mash warm for the livestock, and food and water warm for man. It was also warm for sleeping.

I submissively ate everything that was cooked for me, and patiently put aside anything that fell in it and didn't belong, like hair, a bit of peat, or a cockroach leg. I didn't have the heart to scold Matryona.

In any case, she herself always anticipated me by saying, "If one neither cleans nor cooks, how can one please?"

"Thanks," I said, simply.

"For what? Thanks for nothing?" she smiled, disarmingly. And with an ingenuous glance of her faded, pale blue eyes, inquired, "Well, now, what shall I fix you for dinner?"

"For dinner" meant for the evening meal. I ate twice daily, like at the front. What could I order for supper? Always the same thing —potatoes or poh-tah-to soup.

I reconciled myself with this because life had taught me not to consider food the point of daily existence. I placed a higher value on the smile in her roundish face, which I finally tried to capture with a camera, but in vain. When she saw herself in the cold eye of the camera lens, Matryona took on either a strained or an abnormally severe expression. Only once did I get a picture of her as she looked out of the little window toward the street smiling at something.

That fall many injustices were done to Matryona. Her neighbors advised her to try to get her pension. She was all alone and when she became very sick, they had dismissed her from the kolkhoz. Many injustices were heaped on Matryona's head: she was sick, but did not count as an invalid; she had worked for a quarter of a century for the kolkhoz, which, however, was not a factory so the pension was not supposed to be paid out on her account, but on account of her husband, that is, against loss of the breadwinner. But her husband had been dead for twelve years—since the beginning of the war. And now it was not easy for her to obtain certificates from the various places where he had lived, and papers showing how much he had earned. It was a lot of trouble to get these certificates stating that he used to earn at least three hundred rubles a month, testifying that she lived alone, received no help from anyone, and was born in such-and-such a year. Afterward she had to bring all that to the Social Security Office and, having made corrections, discover that it wasn't done that way. So she brought it back again, and tried to find out whether they would give her the pension.

These troubles were made even more difficult by the fact that the Talnov Social Security Office was twenty kilometers to the east, the village Soviet ten kilometers to the west, and the settlement Soviet an hour's walk to the north.

They drove her from office to office for two months—to one for a comma, to another for a period. Each trip meant a day lost. She would arrive one day at the village Soviet, only to find that the Secretary wasn't in, or simply that he was out somewhere in the village. So "come again tomorrow." Now the Secretary is in, but he doesn't have an official stamp. "Come again" a third day. "Come again" a fourth day because, by mistake, they signed the wrong form—Matryona had pinned all the papers together in a single sheaf.

"They're murdering me, Ignatich," she complained to me after such fruitless trips. "I'm worn out with it."

But her face did not remain clouded for long. I observed one thing: she had a sure means of putting herself back into a good mood—work. She immediately either grabbed a shovel and dug up potatoes or, with a sack under her arm, went out to dig peat. Or else, with a wicker basket, she went out to pick berries in the distant woods. Having bent over bushes instead of an office desk, and carrying a back-breaking load, Matryona would return to the *izba* beaming again, satisfied with everything, and with a pleased smile on her face.

Talking about the peat, she said, "Today I struck it rich, Ignatich. I found just the right spot, and now I know where to take it from. It's a pure joy!"

"But, Matryona Vasilyevna, don't you think my peat supply is enough? A whole truckload?"

"Pooh! Your peat! If we had as much as yours and as much again —then, perhaps, there would be enough! When winter strikes and the wind battles at the windows, the heat escapes as fast as you can stoke up the stove. Last summer we laid in a supply of peat by the pile. I would have brought in as much as three truckloads by now if they weren't after us. They've already started to drag one of us old women through the courts!"

Yes, that's the way it was. The frightening breath of winter was already beginning to blow. Excavators growled through the peat bogs, but did not provide peat for the inhabitants, only for the authorities—the teachers, doctors, factory workers—everything for the authorities by the truckload. Fuel was not authorized for Talnov —and no one was supposed to inquire about it. The kolkhoz chairman walked through the village, looked at you with either demanding or ingenuous eyes, and talked about whatever you wanted to except fuel, because he had already laid in a supply for himself. But winter wouldn't wait.

And so, just as they had formerly stolen wood from the land-owners, now they hauled off peat from the Trust. The old women gathered together in groups of five or ten to give each other courage. They went during the day. During the summer the peat was piled up everywhere and arranged in stacks for drying. That's the good thing about peat, once dug up it can't be hauled off immediately. They let it dry through the fall and even into winter if the road was not clear. About this time the old women took it. At one stroke they carried away in bags six peat bricks if they were still damp, ten if they were dry. One of these sacks was enough to stoke up the stove once; it had to be carried as far as three kilometers and weighed two poods. [One pood equals about 36 pounds.] There were two hundred days of winter and we had to have heat—in the morning with the Russian stove, in the evening with the tiled "Dutch" stove.

"We've sunk this low!" Matryona exclaimed angrily at some invisible person. "Since we have no more horses, unless you cart stuff home on your own back, you don't have it. My back will never heal. During the winter I pull toboggan loads by myself, during the summer bundles—and that's the God's truth!"

The women went during the day—and not just once. On good days Matryona brought back as many as six bags full. She stacked my peat in the open; hers she hid under the landing, and each evening covered the opening with boards.

"Unless the devils just happen to guess where it is," she said, wiping the sweat off her forehead, "they won't find it for the life of them!"

What could the Trust do? They couldn't free enough staff to post guards all over the peat bogs. Since they had officially reported ample production, they were probably able to write it off as a loss due to crumbling and rains. Occasionally they tried to gather a patrol and catch the women at the entrance to the village. The women threw away their sacks and scattered. At other times, when someone informed, they made a house-to-house search, drew up a report on the stolen peat, and threatened court action. For a while the women would stop bringing peat, but winter approached and drove them to it again—with sleds at night.

Generally speaking, as I got accustomed to Matryona, I observed that, quite apart from cooking and housework, she had to take care of a number of other things every day. She kept the regular order of these things in her head and, rising early in the morning, always knew what she would do. Besides the peat, she collected old stumps wrenched out of the peat bogs by the tractors, and red cowberries which she preserved for the winter in quarter-litre bottles ("Try your teeth on them, Ignatich!" she used to say as she treated me to them). Besides digging potatoes, and running about on account of the pension business, she had to get fodder from somewhere for her one and only, dirty-white goat.

"But why don't you keep a cow, Matryona Vasilyevna?"

"A-ah, Ignatich," explained Matryona, as she stood in her soiled apron at the passageway by the kitchen stove, and turned round toward my table, "the milk from the goat is enough for me. And if I were to get a cow, it would eat me out of house and home. They don't let me mow on the embankment because it belongs to the railway, nor in the woods, which are under the forest service. And since, alas, I'm no longer a member of the kolkhoz, they won't allow me there. All the grass goes to the kolkhoz until late fall, and even the women of the kolkhoz have to scrounge for it after the snow begins. What kind of grass can you find under the snow? In the old days we cut grass from the end of June to the end of July. We used to clear it away—when the meadows were as sweet as honey."

So, gathering grass for her scraggly goat was hard work for Matryona. She took a sack and a sickle, and went out in the morning to places where she remembered it grew in tufts along the roadside or on islands in the peat bogs. When she had stuffed a sack full of fresh, heavy grass, she dragged it home and spread it out in layers in the courtyard. From each sack she obtained a pitchfork full of dried fodder.

The new Chairman, recently sent out from the city, cut off the kitchen gardens of all the invalids as his first official act. Fifteen *sotok* [about .37 acre] of sand lot was left Matryona, but ten *sotok* lay idle beyond the fence. On the other hand, when there were not enough hands on the kolkhoz, when the women made really stubborn excuses to get out of work, the Chairman's wife went to see Matryona. She was a city type—determined. She wore a short, gray jacket, and a threatening look, as if she were in the military.

She entered the hut without a greeting and looked sternly at Matryona. The latter was uneasy.

"So-o-o," said the Chairman's wife, dividing the word into syllables for emphasis, "Comrade Matryona, you've got to help at the kolkhoz! You've got to go out tomorrow and haul manure!"

Matryona's countenance took on a half-apologetic smile—as if she were ashamed for the Chairman's wife because the latter would not be able to pay her for the work.

"Well, ah . . . ," she drew the words out. "After all, I'm sick, and I'm no longer officially a member of the kolkhoz." And then hastily correcting herself, she asked, "What time should I be there?"

"And bring your own pitchfork!" added the Chairman's wife as she went out, her stiff petticoat rustling.

"How about that!" Matryona exclaimed reproachfully afterward. " 'Bring your own pitchfork!' she says! There's not a shovel or a pitchfork anywhere on the kolkhoz. And I'm living without a man! Who's going to do my planting for me?"

And she pondered over it all evening, "Well, what can you say, Ignatich? After all, they've got to have help—what kind of harvest would there be without manure? And what a hell of a way to run a kolkhoz, anyhow! The women stand around the kolkhoz leaning on their shovels and wait for the factory whistle at noon. Then there's still some business to take care of. The accounts have to be settled as to who came and who didn't. I prefer to work as if there weren't any whistle, only 'oy-oy-oyinki', before you know it, it's evening, and time to fix supper!"

In the morning she went off with her pitchfork.

Not only the kolkhoz, but also a distant, favorite relative or simply a neighbor would come to Matryona in the evening and plead, "Come help me a little while tomorrow, Matryona! We'll dig up some potatoes."

And Matryona couldn't refuse. She abandoned the normal course of her chores, went out to help her neighbor, and returning, would say without envy, "Oh, Ignatich, what big potatoes she has! I dug them up freely. I didn't want to leave that piece of land! And that's the God's truth!"

They never passed over Matryona, especially when it came to plowing anybody's garden plot. The Talnov women had arranged things so that it was harder and took longer for any one of them to dig up her own garden plot with a shovel than if all six harnessed themselves to a wooden plow and tilled the six garden plots collectively. For this reason they called on Matryona for help.

"Well then," it occurred to me to ask one of them, "did you pay Matryona for it?"

For an answer I got, "Oh, she doesn't take any money for it! You have to hide it on her when she's not looking!"

Still another commotion occurred when it was Matryona's turn to feed the goatherds. One of these was healthy, but a deaf mute, and the second was an urchin with a slobbery little cigar stuck between his teeth. Her turn to feed them came around only every six weeks, but it drove Matryona to a great deal of expense. She went to the village store, bought tinned fish, and splurged on sugar and butter, which she never ate herself. It seemed that the women outdid each other trying to see who could feed the goatherds best.

"Everyone is afraid of tailors and goatherds," she explained to me. "They'll give you a bad name all over the neighborhood if something doesn't suit them."

And into this life, already crowded with anxieties, burst periods of serious illness, when Matryona would lie flat on her back for two days and nights without so much as a complaint. On such days Masha, Matryona's closest friend since her earliest childhood, often came over to take care of the goat and to fire the stove. Matryona herself never ate, nor drank, nor asked for anything. To call the doctor from the village medical center to the house would have been unheard of in Talnov. And her neighbors would have thought it inconsiderate—behaving like one of the upper classes. When they did send for the doctor on one occasion, she arrived very annoyed, and ordered Matryona, as soon as she could get up to come to the medical center. Matryona went, against her will. They put her through various examinations, sent the reports to the regional hospital—and there the matter died. Matryona, herself, was partly to blame.

But her affairs called her back to life. Soon Matryona began to get up, at first moving slowly, but later briskly again.

"You didn't get to see me in the old days, Ignatich," she said, to justify to herself her having been sick. "I could lift any old sack, even one weighing five poods! My father-in-law used to yell, 'Matryona, you'll break your back!' My brother-in-law didn't have to come help me lift logs in the wagon. We had a big, strong horse by the name of Volchek which we got from the military. It was a war horse."

"What do you mean, a war horse?"

"Because, together with the healthy horses which they took to the war, was this wounded one, which they left us. He was a high-spirited animal, and once he pulled our sled into the lake from fright. The men jumped off, but I held on the reins and stood fast, so help me! He was full of oats, that horse. Our men liked to feed horses well. A horse that is full of oats doesn't feel a heavy load."

But Matryona was by no means fearless. She was afraid of fires and of lightning, but most of all—no one knows why—of trains.

"Once I rode the train to Cherusti as it came from Nechayevka. Its bright lights blazed and the rails hummed. Ah-h, what a fever it gave me! How my legs shook!—and that's God's truth!" she said, astonished with herself, and shrugged her shoulders.

"You don't suppose you were frightened because you didn't get a ticket, Matryona Vasilyevna?"

"At the little window? They try to shove first-class tickets off on you. But the train was already moving. We dashed here and there saying, 'Please help us!' The men climbed up a ladder onto the top of the car. Then we found an open door and shoved straight ahead without tickets, and the cars were empty, all empty. You could even stretch out on the benches. Why the unfriendly parasites at the window never gave us tickets, I don't know . . ."

Matryona had new felt boots made for herself. She bought a new quilted jacket. And she had a coat made out of a railroad worker's leather overcoat, which was given her by an engineer from Cherusti, the husband of Kira, Matryona's foster daughter. A hunch-backed tailor from the village lined it with cloth batting, and Matryona got a nicer coat out of it than she had been able to sew for herself in the sixty years of her life.

In the middle of the winter Matryona sewed two hundred rubles into the lining of the coat for her burial expenses.

For a moment she was happy, "I feel a little better about things, Ignatich."

December passed, and then January—for two months her illness had not struck. In the evening Matryona often went over to Masha's house, sat for a while, and chewed sunflower seeds. Matryona never asked guests over in the evening to her own house out of respect for my work. Only once on Epiphany, when I returned from school, I found people dancing in the *izba*, and was introduced to three of Matryona's own sisters, who, since she was the oldest, called her *nyanya* or *lyolka* [nannie or nurse]. After that occasion, we rarely saw the sisters again. Perhaps they were afraid that Matryona would ask them for help.

Matryona's holiday was clouded by only one event or premonition. She had walked five *versts* [about three miles] to church for holy water, and had set her pot down among the others. When the blessing of water was over, the women rushed in to get it, pushing each other. Matryona was too late to be among the first, and came in at the end. She couldn't find her pot, and no other piece of tinware had been left in exchange for it. The pot had disappeared, as if carried away by an evil spirit.

"Ladies!" Matryona cried, as she walked among the praying women. "Did one of you take, by mistake, somebody else's holy water? In a tin pot?"

No one acknowledged her question. They say that one of the little boys filched it—there were some boys there. Matryona was sad when she returned.

However, this doesn't mean to say that Matryona was a fervent believer. Rather she was superstitious. She was always coming up with superstitions, such as: you shouldn't go into the garden plot during *Ivan Postno* [Lent], otherwise there would be no harvest in the coming year; if the snow whirled during a storm, someone had hung himself somewhere; or, if you pinched your foot in the door, there would be guests. As long as I lived in her house I never saw her pray, and not once did she even cross herself. But all important affairs began with "God bless!" and she insisted on saying "God bless you" every time I left for school. Perhaps she did pray, but gave no sign of it either because she was shy in my presence or feared it might annoy me. There were icons hanging in the hut. On weekdays they were left dark, but at times of vespers and matins, and on the morning of holidays, Matryona used to light icon lamps under them.

Her sins, however, were less than those of her lame cat—the latter throttled mice.

With the past difficulties of her life somewhat eased, Matryona began to stand and listen attentively to my radio on occasion. (I didn't waste any time in turning on the knob—the "kh-nob" as Matryona called it.)

When she heard over the radio that some new machine had been invented, Matryona grumbled from the kitchen, "Always new machines, new machines! They don't want to work with the old ones, but where will they put all of them?"

When they broadcast a report that clouds had been seeded by airplanes, Matryona shook her head over the stove, "Oy-oy-oyinki! They're going to do away with either the winter or the summer!" Once Chaliapin was singing Russian songs. Matryona stood and stood, listening, and then remarked thoughtfully, "He sings strangely, not the way we peasants do."

"But, of course he does, Matryona Vasilyevna, just listen!"

She listened a little while longer, pressed her lips together, and said, "No. That's not it. That's not our way. Besides, his voice quavers."

However, Matryona made up for it. Once they were playing a concert of Glinka's love songs. Suddenly, after the fifth song, Matryona, holding on to her apron, came out from behind the partition, deeply moved. Astonished, she whispered, "Ah, that's it, that's our way!"

II

Thus Matryona became accustomed to me, and I to her, and we got along together. She never annoyed me with questions. Either because she was naturally discreet, or because she lacked the usual curiosity of old women, she never once asked me whether I had been married. All the women of Talnov importuned her with questions trying to find out about me. She always answered them, "If you need to find out something, ask him. I know only one thing about him—he's from far away!"

And when long afterwards I told her that I had done a lot of time in prison, she merely shook her head in silence as if she had earlier suspected as much.

I saw only the present Matryona, failing in her old age, and I in turn did not disturb her past, nor did I imagine that there was much to be searched for in it. I learned that Matryona had been married even before the revolution, right in the same hut in which we were living now, and right "at the oven." (That meant that there were neither mother-in-law, nor older, unmarried sisters-in-law around, and on the first morning of their marriage, Matryona started baking.) I found out that she had had six children, all of whom died, one after another, very early, so that no two were ever alive at the same time. Later, there was a sort of foster daughter, Kira. Matryona's husband never returned from the war, but there had been no death notice. Villagers who had been in his company said that he might have been taken prisoner or killed, but they never found his body. Eight years after the war even Matryona herself decided that he was no longer alive. And it was good that she thought that way—better than if she thought he were still alive and married somewhere—say in Brazil or Australia, and the village of Talnov and the Russian language had been blotted out of his memory.

Once, returning from school, I found a guest in our *izba*. A tall, old man, his hat on his knee, was sitting by the "Dutch" stove on a stool which Matryona had brought out for him into the middle of the room. His entire face was framed with dark hair, which was only lightly touched with gray. A thick dark mustache blended into his broad beard so that his mouth was barely visible. Continuous dark sideburns, almost concealing his ears, merged into his dark, matted drooping hair. His even broader, dark eyebrows grew together like a bridge. The bald dome of his forehead blended into the hairless top of the skull. The entire appearance of the old man indicated great wisdom and dignity. He sat stiffly, his hands folded on top of his staff, which was resting plumb with the floor. He sat in an attitude of patient expectation, and it was evident that he had hardly spoken to Matryona who was busy behind the partition.

When I came in, he slowly turned his majestic head toward me and addressed me suddenly, "My dear fellow! ... I can't see you clearly. My son is a pupil of yours—Grigoriev, Antoshka."

He wouldn't have had to say anything more. Along with my impulse to help this venerable old man, I knew in advance and rejected all the useless things he was now about to say. Antoshka Grigoriev was a round-faced, high-colored stripling in the eighth grade, with a look like a cat that had finished off a canary. He came to school as if he were on a holiday, sat over on one side, and smiled lazily. Moreover, he never prepared his lessons at home. But, most importantly, the schools of our district, province, and neighboring provinces were noted for passing a high percentage of students. For this reason he was passed year after year. He clearly understood that no matter how much his teachers might threaten him, he would pass anyway at the end of the year, so there was no need to study. He simply laughed at us. He sat in the eighth grade, although he had never mastered fractions, and couldn't tell one triangle from another. For the first two quarters he had a hard struggle with failing grades, and the same fate awaited him during the third quarter.

The half-blind old man looked more like Antoshka's grandfather than his real father. He came to me humbly, his hat in his hand as they would say today, to complain. How could I tell him that the school had been deceiving him year after year? That this could go on no longer, otherwise the whose class would go to pieces, and would turn into chatterboxes? If I did so, I would be reflecting unfavorably on my work and on my own prestige as a teacher.

So I patiently explained to him that his son had been badly neglected, that he lied both at school and at home, and that he should check on the boy's grade book more often. The boy should be taken severely in hand by both of us.

"But, my dear fellow, I've already roughed him up," my guest confirmed. "I already beat him once a week, and I have a heavy hand!"

During the conversation I recalled Matryona herself had once interceded for Antoshka Grigoriev. At the time I hadn't asked whether he was a relative of hers and declined to do what she requested. Matryona stood at the kitchen door, a silent suppliant on this occasion too.

When Faddei Mironovich left, saying that he would call and check up on things again, I said, "I don't understand, Matryona Vasilyevna, how Antoshka is related to you."

"He's the son of my brother-in-law," Matryona answered stiffly, and went out to milk the goat.

When I had figured it out, I realized that this dark, persistent old man was the brother of her husband who had disappeared without a trace.

The long evening passed. Matryona didn't refer to the afternoon's conversation again. Only late in the evening when I had forgotten about the old man and was working in the quiet of the hut to the rustle of the cockroaches and the ticking of the clock, suddenly from the darkness of her corner Matryona said, "Once upon a time, Ignatich, I almost married him."

I had forgotten about Matryona herself, that she was there, and didn't hear her, but she spoke out of the darkness in agitated tones, as if the old man were still wooing her. Obviously, that was all Matryona had thought about all evening.

She got up from her wretched, raggedy bed, and slowly came toward me, as if she were following her own words. I leaned back and for the first time saw Matryona in an entirely new light. There was no overhead light in our room as it was filled with a forest of rubber trees. From a table lamp the light fell in a circle only on my notebooks. To eyes distracted by this light, all the rest of the room appeared in rose-colored semidarkness. Out of this darkness Matryona came forward. For a moment I imagined that her cheeks were not yellow as usual, but rose-colored instead.

"He proposed to me first . . . even before Yefim . . . He was his older brother . . . I was nineteen, Faddei twenty-three. They lived right here in this very house. It was their house. Their father built it."

I involuntarily looked around me. Suddenly throughout the old, gray, rotting house with its two faden-green skins under which the mice were running, oozed the cheery, resinous smell of fresh pine logs, as yet undarkened, still unplaned.

"And you . . . loved him? Well, and then what?"

"It was during that summer. We went for a walk and sat down in the grove," she said in a whisper. "There was a grove there where the stables are now. They've since cut it down. I almost got married, Ignatich, but war with the Germans was beginning, and they took Faddei off to the war."

As her words fell, there flashed before me the deep white and yellow July of the year 1914—a peaceful sky, drifting clouds and people bustling about in the ripe stubble. I pictured them beside each other—he was a black-haired Hercules with a scythe over his shoulder, and she, a blushing girl with her arms around a sheaf of wheat. And there was singing, singing under the open sky the way people no longer sing in this machine age.

"He went off to war—and fell. For three long years I kept silent and waited, but not a line, not a word from him."

Matryona's senile, roundish face, wrapped in a faded little shawl, looked at me in the soft, indirect light of the lamp. It seemed suddenly detached from her everyday, slipshod dress, and free from wrinkles, like the face of a frightened young maiden before a terrible choice.

"Yes, yes . . . I remember . . . The leaves were flying everywhere; the snow fell—and later melted. They ploughed again, they sowed again, and again they wept. Once more the leaves were flying, and again the snow fell. Then came one revolution; then another, and the world turned upside down. Their mother died, and Yefim asked me to marry him. He said, 'If you want to come to our house, then come and live with me.' Yefim was a year younger than I. We have a saying: 'The wise girl married after Michaelmas Day [in the fall] —the fool after St. Peter's Day [June 29th]!' They didn't have enough hands at their house, so I came to them. The marriage ceremony took place on St. Peter's Day, and on St. Nicholas' Day that winter, Faddei returned . . . from a Hungarian prison camp."

Matryona closed her eyes. I kept silent.

She turned toward the door, and spoke excitedly, "He was standing on the threshold. How could I shut him out? I wanted to throw myself at his feet! But that was forbidden . . . 'Well,' said he, 'if

Yefim weren't my own brother, I'd cut you both down with this axe!' "

I shuddered, I could vividly imagine her anguish and fear, as he stood there, dark, in the shadow of the door, and threatened Matryona with his axe.

But she quieted down, and leaning on the back of the chair in front of her, continued in a singsong voice, "Oy-oy-oyinki, the poor dear man! There were so many girls in the village, but he married none of them! Faddei said, 'I shall look for another Matryona to take your place!' So he married Matryona from Lipovka. They built a separate log *izba* for themselves where they are living now. You pass by their place every day as you walk to school."

Oh! So that was it! Now I realized that I had seen the second Matryona more than once. I didn't like her. She was always coming over to my own Matryona to complain that her husband beat her, that he was niggardly, and that he was working her to death. She would cry for hours, and her voice was always full of tears. But it turned out that my Matryona had nothing to regret. Faddei had always been that way to his own Matryona all his life and had always kept a heavy hand on the entire household.

Speaking of Yefim the old woman continued, "He never once beat me. He used to take after men on the street with his fists, but not once after me. What I mean is, there was one time when I had been quarreling a while with my sister-in-law, when he smashed a wooden spoon on my forehead. I jumped up from the table and shouted, 'I hope you choke to death, you drones.' I ran off in the woods and he never touched me again!"

It appears that Faddei had no reason to complain. His second Matryona had borne him six children and they all survived. Among them was my Antoshka; he was the youngest, the runt. But no children remained to Yefim and Matryona—they never lived as long as three months, and though none was sick, each died.

"I remember one little daughter, Elena, when she had only just been born. They had just washed her body when, as she was lying there, she died. That spared the washing of the dead body. Just as my wedding was on St. Peter's Day, so I buried my sixth child, Alexander, on St. Peter's Day."

So the whole village decided that Matryona was "hexed."

"A hex on me?" Matryona shook her head with conviction. "They took me to a woman who used to be a nun, for treatment. She poured something down my throat and waited for me to cough out the hex, like a frog. Well, nothing ever came out!"

Years passed, like water flowing. On the forty-first [in 1941] they didn't take Faddei for the war because of his poor sight. However, they did take Yefim away. And like the older brother in the first war, the younger one vanished in the second. And this one really didn't return. The once noisy but now deserted *izba* was rotting away and advancing in years, and growing old within it was Matryona, forgotten and abandoned.

So she asked the second Matryona—whom everybody persecuted —for her youngest daughter, Kira, for a child of her womb (or was it a spot of Faddei's blood she wanted?)

For ten years Matryona took care of Kira like one of her own children who never survived. And not too long before I came she had given her in marriage to a young railroad engineer from Cherusti. Recently she had been getting a little help from Cherusti, occasionally sugar, or when a pig was slaughtered, some of the fat. Since she was suffering from ailments and expected her death in the near future, Matryona announced her will. After her death the separate wood frame of the big room, the *gornitza*, which was connected with her *izba*, was to be given as a legacy to Kira. She said nothing at all about the *izba* itself, and her three sisters still hoped to get hold of it.

Thus, it was on that evening that Matryona completely opened up her heart to me. And it so happened, as the connections and meaning of her life had been made somewhat clear to me—during those very days—things started moving. First, Kira arrived from Cherusti, and the old man, Faddei, became worried. It seemed that in Cherusti the young couple would have to put up some kind of a dwelling in order to obtain and hold a plot of land. The *gornitza*, that is, the wood frame of Matryona's house, was just right for this purpose. There was no way to put up another, because they couldn't get hold of the wood for it anywhere. Not only Kira and her husband, but especially old Faddei, were eager to get that strip of land in Cherusti.

So Faddei became a constant visitor at our house. He came again and again, spoke to Matryona in an authoritative tone, and demanded that she give away the *gornitza*, immediately, while she was still living. On these visits he did not give the appearance of an old man, leaning on a cane, who might fall to pieces at the first shove or harsh word. Although he was slightly hunched over with backache from disease, this impressive old man, more than sixty years old, who had kept his hair lush, dark and youthful, pressed his claim hard, and with fervor.

Matryona didn't sleep for two nights. It was not easy for her to make up her mind. She didn't mind giving up the empty *gornitza*, since it wasn't being used anyway, just as she had never minded giving her care, work, and property to others. In any case the *gornizta* had been willed to Kira. But she was terrified at the idea of tearing down the roof under which she had lived for forty years. Although I was only a tenant, even I felt sick at the thought of their tearing off the boards and pulling out the logs of the house. And, for Matryona, it would mean the end of everything.

But the others insisted on it and knew that Matryona's house would have to be torn apart while she was still living.

One February morning Faddei arrived with his sons and sons-in-law, and the five of them began working with their axes, setting up a squealing and creaking as they ripped off the boards. Faddei's eyes flashed with businesslike efficiency. In spite of the fact that his back would not straighten out entirely, he climbed dexterously up under the rafters, and bustled vigorously about, shouting occasionally for helpers. As a little boy he himself had helped his father build the house. That *gornitza* belonged to him, the eldest son, and had been put up so that he might move in with his bride. Now he was fever-ishly tearing the *gornitza* apart, to carry it away from Matryona's yard. After numbering the logs and marking the ceiling boards, they dismantled the *gornitza*, including the storeroom underneath. The *izba* itself, with what was left of the landing, they boarded up with a thin, temporary wall. They left chinks in the wall, and everything indicated that they were wrecking the place, not building it, and that they did not suppose Matryona would be living there much longer.

While the men were breaking things up, the women were making home-brew for the day of loading. They made their own liquor because it would have been too expensive to pass vodka around. For the makings, Kira brought a pood of sugar from the Moscow district, while Matryona Vasilyevna, under cover of the night, carried over the sugar and the bottles for the home-brew.

The logs were carried off and stacked outside the fence, ready for the engineer to arrive with the tractor from Cherusti.

On the same day a heavy snowstorm began—a "blower" as Matryona called it. It howled and whirled for two days and nights piling huge snowdrifts on the road. Afterwards, when the road had just been treaded down, another truck would drive past. Then there was a sudden warm spell, and in one day everything thawed at once. A gray fog formed; streams broke through the snow and babbled forth; and you got stuck up to the top of your kneeboots.

For two weeks the tractors couldn't reach the disassembled *gor-nitza*. These were two weeks of perplexity for Matryona. One of the heaviest burdens she had to bear was her three sisters, who came over and with one voice called her a fool for giving the *gornitza* away; they said they never wanted to see her again, and then left.

On the same day the lame cat ran out of the courtyard and disap-peared. The first event went with the other. This also depressed Matryona.

Finally the road, which had been melting away, was hardened by frost. A sunny day came, warming the heart. Matryona had had pleasant dreams the night before. In the morning she learned that I wanted to take a photograph of someone standing beside one of the old-fashioned looms which remained in two *izbas* in the village, and which had been used to weave coarse rugs.

Bashfully, and smiling ironically, she said, "Why not wait a little, a couple of days, Ignatich, until they take away the *gornitza*, and snap the picture then? I'll put up my own loom; I've still got it, and that's the God's truth!"

Clearly, she liked to picture herself in an old-fashioned setting.

The red, frosty sun flooded everything with an almost rose-colored light. As it streamed through the frost-covered window of the enclosed passageway, which had been partly cut down, this light cast a warm glow over Matryona's face. Such people always have fine faces, in tune with their consciences.

Later, as I was returning from school, just before twilight, I saw movement around our house. A big new tractor-drawn sledge was already loaded with logs. But there was no room for a lot of the timbers, so the family of old Faddei, and others who had been invited to help, had nearly finished knocking together a second homemade sledge. All were working like mad, almost with desperation, as is so often the case with people who have caught the scent of big money, or who anticipate an orgy of food and drink. They were yelling at one another, and arguing among themselves.

The argument was about how the sleds should be pulled—separately or together. One of Faddei's sons, who was lame, and the son-in-law engineer kept harping that they shouldn't try both sleds at once, because the tractor couldn't pull them. But the tractor driver, a lusty, self-opinionated, bull-faced lout, shouted that it was obvious that he was the driver, and that he would pull both sleds together. His calculation was clear—according to the plan, the engineer would pay him for the transportation of the *gornitza*, not by the trip. Two trips in a single night were out of the question. It was twenty-five kilometers each way and one return journey. And by morning he had to be back with his tractor in the garage from which he had secretly taken it for this job on the side.

The old man, Faddei, couldn't bear not to move the whole *gornitza* in one day, and so motioned to his sons to give in. The second sled, put together in a slapdash fashion, was hooked on to the stronger one.

Matryona ran among the men, bustling about, and helping roll the logs on the sledges. I then noticed that she was wearing my quilted coat. She had already smeared the sleeves with icy mud from the logs, and I spoke to her about it with displeasure. I had a sentimental attachment to that padded coat; it had kept me warm during my troubled years.

And so for the first time I got angry at Matryona Vasilyevna.

"Oy-oy-oyinki, my poor old head!" she exclaimed, taken aback. "Why, I simply grabbed it on the run and forgot it was yours! I'm sorry, Ignatich."

And taking it off, she hung it up to dry.

The loading was finished and all who had been working, about ten men in all, thundered past my table, and dived behind the kitchen curtain. There was a muffled clinking of glasses. Occasionally a bottle tinkled. The voices grew louder, bragging and laughing. The tractor driver was especially boastful. The heavy odor of homebrew rolled toward me.

But they didn't spend much time drinking—the darkness compelled them to hurry. They began to leave. Self-confident, with a brutal face, the tractor driver left first, and then, in order to accompany the sleds to Cherusti, the engineer son-in-law, Faddei's lame son, and one of the nephews. The rest of them dispersed and went home. Faddei, brandishing his staff, hurried to catch up with someone and set him straight about something. The lame son lingered at my table for a smoke, and suddenly began to speak, telling me that he loved Aunt Matryona, that he had recently gotten married, and that his wife had just given birth to a son. Then the others called him, and he left. Through the window I heard the tractor roaring.

Last of all, Matryona darted hastily out from behind the partition. She shook her head anxiously at those who had gone. She was wearing her quilted coat, and had put on a shawl.

From the doorway she said, "Why didn't they reckon on two tractors? If one broke down, then the other could pull the load. But what will happen now—God only knows!"

And she ran off after the others.

After the drinking, the arguments, and the departure, it was especially quiet in the abandoned *izba*, which was chilled from the frequently opened door. Outside the windows it was quite dark. I also put on a quilted jacket, and sat down to check over some examination papers. The tractor could no longer be heard in the distance.

An hour passed; another, and then a third. Matryona had not returned, but then I wasn't surprised. After seeing the sledges off, she must have gone over to see her friend, Masha.

Another hour passed, and still another. It was not only dark, but a short of deep quiet prevailed. At that time I didn't grasp the reason for this stillness, or why, as it happened, during the whole evening not one train passed by on the tracks, which were about a third of a mile away from the house. My radio was silent, and I noticed how much—more than ever before—the mice were romping, how impudently and noisily they ran around under the wallpaper, squeaking and scraping.

I fell asleep and when I awoke, it was one o'clock in the morning and Matryona had not yet returned. Suddenly I heard several loud voices from the direction of the village. Although they were still distant, something told me they were coming to the house. And sure enough, soon a sharp knock sounded at the gate. A powerful, strange voice shouted for me to open up. I went out with a flashlight into the pitch darkness. The village was sound asleep. There wasn't a light visible in any window. Even the snow, which had started melting in the past week, reflected no light. I turned the lower night latch and let them in. Four men in greatcoats entered. A very unpleasant sensation that—when men burst into your house at night, noisily, and in greatcoats.

I examined them in the light, however, and recognized that two of the men in the overcoats were railroad officials.

The older, a heavy-set man with a face like that of the tractor driver, asked, "Where's the owner, the old lady?"

"I don't know."

"Did the tractor with the sledge leave from this courtyard?"

"Yes, from here."

"Were they drinking here before leaving?"

All four were looking around and screwing up their eyes in the half-light from the table lamp. I realized that either they had already arrested someone, or wanted to make an arrest.

"Why, what happened?"

"Answer our questions!"

"But . . ."

"Did they go away drunk? Were they drinking here?"

Had they killed someone? Or was it forbidden to carry away the *gornitza?* They were pressing me very hard. Only one thing was clear: Matryona might have to do time for making the home-brew. I stepped back toward the partition and thus screened off the kitchen area.

"I really didn't notice. I didn't see anything."

(I actually hadn't seen anything—I had only heard.)

And as if perplexed, I gestured with my hands, indicating the furnishings in the hut: the peaceful light of the table lamp on the books and notebooks, the crowd of startled rubber plants, the severe cot of an anchorite[1]—no trace of debauchery.

Then they themselves disappointedly observed that there hadn't been any kind of carousing going on. They turned to go out, saying among themselves that even if a drinking bout had not taken place in the *izba*, it would be a good idea to report that it had. I followed them, and tried to find out what had happened.

Only when he reached the wicket gate, one·of them growled at me, "It raised hell with all of 'em. They can't even pick up the pieces!"

Another added, "But that's a small detail. The one o'clock express nearly jumped the track—that's what happened!"

And they all left hurriedly.

Stunned, I turned back into the hut. Who were "all of 'em?" Where was Matryona? I drew aside the kitchen screen. The stench of home-brew struck me. The place was a shambles—tables and

1. hermit.

benches overturned, empty bottles lying around, one of them half-empty, glasses, half-finished herring, onions and sliced fat pork.

Everything seemed dead, except for the cockroaches crawling undisturbed on their battlefield.

They had said something about the one o'clock express. Why? Perhaps I should have showed them all that mess behind the screen. I still had my doubts about the whole business. But what kind of damned manners did they have? Not to explain anything except to officials!

Suddenly our wicket gate squeaked, and I quickly ran out toward the bridge. "Is that you, Matryona Vasilyevna?"

The door to the courtyard opened.

Wringing her hands and unsteady on her feet, Matryona's friend, Masha, entered the house.

"Matryona . . . Our Matryona, Ignatich!"

I had her sit down, and, hampered by her tears, she told the story.

At the railroad crossing there was a little hill after a steep approach. There was no barrier. The tractor had pulled the first sled across when the rope broke and the second sled, the homemade one, got stuck and began falling to pieces. (Faddei had provided inferior wood for it, for the second sled, that is.) The tractor driver and Faddei's lame son managed to pull the first sledge a little way off, and had returned to the second. They were splicing the rope when Matryona—heaven knows what brought her there—rushed in between the tractor and the sledge.

Now how did she expect to help the men? She was perpetually getting herself mixed up in men's affairs, such as the time at the lake when a horse almost knocked her down through a hole in the ice. And why did she go to the damned crossing anyhow? She had already given away the *gornitza*, and all her debts had been settled. The engineer kept looking to make sure that the train from Cherusti didn't appear suddenly. He could have seen the lights in the distance. But from the other direction, from our station, two engines coupled together came up—without lights and moving backward. Why they were running without lights nobody knows. When an engine backs up, coal dust pours into the engineer's eyes from the tender so that he can't see very well. They came flying up, and crushed to a pulp the three people who were between the tractor and the sledge. The tractor was wrecked, one sledge was split into kindling wood, the tracks were thrown off the ramp, and both engines turned over on one side.

"But why didn't they hear the engines coming?"

"Because the tractor ahead of them drowned out the noise!"

"And what about the dead bodies?"

"They won't permit anyone to touch them. They've roped off the area."

"But what was it I heard about the express? Was there one?"

"The ten o'clock express was already moving out of our station and toward the crossing. But when the engines crashed, the two engineers weren't hurt. They jumped free, ran back down the tracks waving their hands, and managed to stop the train."

The nephew was hit by a log which rolled across the tracks. He hid out at Klavka's house, so that no one would know that he too was at the crossing. Otherwise he would be dragged into court as a witness. As the Russian proverb puts it: "The one who sleeps on the stove never gets bothered—the others all get caught!"

"Kira's husband got off without a scratch. He tried to hang himself, but they pulled him out of the noose. 'Because of me,' he says, 'my aunt and brother were killed!' Then he went and had himself arrested. But now instead of going to jail, he'll go to the insane asylum. Oh, Matryona, my dear little Matryona!"

Matryona was no more. Someone close to me had been killed—and only the day before I had reproached her for wearing my quilted coat! From the book advertising poster on the wall, the reddish-yellow figure of a woman continued smiling happily.

Old Masha sat a while longer and continued to cry.

When she rose to leave she suddenly inquired, "Ignatich! You remember? Matryona had a large gray knitted shawl . . . She really intended it after her death for my daughter, Tanya, right?"

She looked at me hopefully through the half-darkness. Was it possible that I had forgotten? But no, I remembered.

"Right—she really had intended it for Tanya."

"Then look here! Maybe you won't mind if I take it with me right now? Tomorrow the whole family will come flying over, and afterward, it'll be too late for me to get it!"

Again she looked at me hopefully, pleading—this friend of Matryona's for half a century—the only one in all the village who really loved her. Surely she deserved it.

"All right—take it!" I confirmed.

She opened the small trunk, took the shawl, thrust it under her skirt, and left.

Some sort of madness had seized the mice. They were running so furiously up and down the walls that the green wallpaper seemed to move in almost visible waves over their backs.

In the morning I had to go to school. It was three a.m. There was nothing left for me to do except to bolt the door, and lie down to sleep.

Lock the door because Matryona wasn't coming back!

I left the light on and lay down. The mice were squeaking—almost groaning—and running—running all over the place. I had to rid my tired, incoherent mind of an involuntary anxiety—a feeling that Matryona had returned invisibly to say farewell to her house. And suddenly in the darkness on the path in front of the entrance,

I imagined that I saw the young, dark-haired Faddei with his axe raised, "If he weren't my own brother, I'd cut you both to pieces!"

Forty years had flown by since his threat had been made from the corner there. The threat had hung like an old broadsword—which had struck at last!

III

At daybreak the women, using a sled, brought back all that remained of Matryona, which had been covered with a dirty sack. They took off the sack in order to wash her. Everything was jumbled together. The feet, half of the trunk, and the left hand were missing.

One of the women said, "God left her little right hand so that she can cross herself where she's going!"

The whole crowd of rubber plants which Matryona had loved was taken out of the *izba*. She had loved them so much that once when she had been awakened in the night by smoke, she didn't rush to save the *izba*, but to turn the plants over on the floor so they wouldn't suffocate. The floors were swept clean. They curtained over Matryona's lusterless mirror with a wide towel of old, homemade cloth. They snatched the cheerful posters from the walls. They moved my table. On stools by the window, under the icon, they set the plain, unadorned coffin, which had been hastily knocked together.

Matryona lay in the coffin. Her lifeless, mangled body was neatly and simply covered with a clean sheet. Her head was enveloped in a white kerchief, but her face, undamaged and peaceful, seemed more alive than dead.

The villagers came to stand around for a while and have a look. The women brought their children to stare at the deceased. When anyone began to cry, the women, as if obliged to do so—even if they had come out of empty curiosity—all stood around the walls and the door and wept as if they were an accompanying chorus. But the men stood silently at attention, their caps in their hands.

It fell to the lot of the relatives to do most of the mourning. I observed in the weeping a coldly thought-out, ages-old established order. Those who were somewhat distant relatives came up to the coffin for a short while and lamented softly over it. Those who considered themselves part of the dead woman's family began weeping while still on the pathway, and having reached the coffin, bent down and wailed in the face of the deceased. There was a different, homemade melody for each mourner, and each set forth her own thoughts and feelings.

Then I realized that the mourning over the deceased was not simply mourning, but a kind of political contest in its own right. The three sisters had flown in together. They had seized Matryona's *izba*, her goat, and the stove. They had closed the trunk and locked it. They had also dug the two hundred rubles saved for burial expenses out of the lining of Matryona's coat. They tried to prove to all who came that they alone were the closest to Matryona.

Over the coffin they mourned, "Ah, *nanya, nanya!* Ah, *lyolka, lyolka!* And to think you could have lived so quietly, so peacefully! And we would always have taken such tender care of you! Oh, why did your *gornitza* lead to your destruction? The cursed *gornitza* dealt a final blow to you! Why did they break up your things? And why didn't you listen to us?"

The laments of the sisters were indictments of Matryona's husband's family. Obviously they were meant to prove that there was no need to break up Matryona's *gornitza*. While the underlying thought was: "The men have grabbed the *gornitza* and we're not about to give up the *izba* itself!"

The husband's family, Matryona's sisters-in-law (i.e., the sisters of Yefim and Faddei) and a few assorted nieces, then went up to the coffin and mourned in this fashion: "Ah, auntie, little auntie! Why didn't you guard yourself against them? And now they most likely take offense at us! To think that *you*, our dear relative, that it was all your fault! And the *gornitza* had nothing to do with it! But why did you go there, where death rubbed you out? No one called you there! And the way you died! Unthinkable! Why didn't you listen to us?" And behind all this lamentation the real reason stood out clearly: "We're not responsible for her death, and we're still going to talk about who gets the *izba!*"

By then the gross, broad-faced "second" Matryona, the substitute Matryona whom Faddei had taken only because of her name, had gotten into the contest, wailing simple-mindedly, and crying hysterically over the coffin: "Yes, you there, my darling little sister! Is it possible that you could take offense at me? There was a time when we two talked and talked together. Please forgive me, a poor, unfortunate creature! Oh-ma! You went to your dear mother, and surely you will return for me, too! Oh-ma-ah!"

With that "Oh-ma-ah" she literally exhausted all her breath, and began beating, beating her breast against the side of the coffin.

Then, since her wailing had exceeded the accepted norm, all the other women, as if they recognized that her mourning had succeeded only too well, advised in a friendly tone, "Cease! Cease!"

Matryona stopped, and afterward went up and sobbed again, even more fervently. Then an old woman from the village came out of the corner.

She placed her hand on Matryona's shoulder and said solemnly, "There are two riddles in this world: How I was born—I don't remember; how I shall die—I don't know!"

Matryona fell silent at once, as did all the others, so that there was an interlude of absolute quiet.

But this same old woman, who was much older than all the

others present, and almost a total stranger to Matryona, after a brief interlude, also wailed, "Oh, you, my poor sick one! Oh, you, my Vasilyevna! Oh, I'm growing tired of saying farewell to all of you!"

And somewhat unusually, with the plain sobbing characteristic of our own age (which has had plenty of practice at it), the ill-starred Kira wept—Kira, Matryona's adopted daughter from Cherusti, for whom they had broken up the *gornitza* and moved it away. Her wavy curls were pitifully disarrayed. Her eyes were red, as if they had been wiped with blood. She didn't notice her scarf had slipped to one side in the frosty air and her coat sleeves hung down past her arms. Beside herself, she had gone from the coffin of her foster mother in one house to the coffin of her brother in another. They also feared for her reason because her husband would have to stand trial as well.

It appeared her husband was guilty on two counts—he not only removed the *gornitza*, but he was also a railroad engineer, who knew the regulations about unguarded railroad crossings, and should have gone to the station to give advance notice about the tractor. A thousand human beings were on the Urals express that night, sleeping on upper and lower benches in the half-light shed by the train's lamps. They could have all been killed! Back of the whole affair was the greediness of a few people to get hold of a strip of land, or to spare the expense of making a second trip with the tractor. And behind all that was the *gornitza*, on which a curse had lain ever since Faddei's hands had seized and broken it up.

As for the tractor driver, he was already beyond human justice. But the railroad administration itself was also guilty because they had not guarded the busy intersection, and because the coupled engines were running without lights. That was why they tried to switch the blame on the drinking, and then to keep the case out of court.

The rails and roadbed were so badly torn up that for the three days during which the coffins rested in their respective houses, the trains did not run. They were rerouted on another branch line. All Friday, Saturday, and Sunday, from the end of the inquest to the burial, the tracks were repaired night and day. The repair crew were freezing. For warmth by day and for light at night, they built a fire out of the boards and logs which they picked up for free from the second sled, scattered near the crossing.

But the first sled, loaded and intact, stood not far from the crossing and it was precisely this which tormented the soul of the dark-bearded Faddei all day Saturday. One sledge was waiting there with its ropes ready, teasing him, and perhaps Faddei might still save the second from the fire. His daughter's mind was disturbed, and the outcome of the trial hung over his son-in-law. In his own house lay his son, killed by himself on the same street on which he had killed the woman he once loved. Faddei had come and stood by the coffin, clutching his beard, but not for long. His high forehead was clouded by painful thoughts, but the thoughts were about how to save the logs of the *gornitza* from the fire and from the crafty designs of Matryona's sisters.

As I thought about the townspeople of Talnov, I realized that Faddei was not the only one in the village with such thoughts.

As for our property—either personal, or the people's—it is strange that the language calls it "goods." And yet losing any of it would be considered disgraceful and stupid by the people!

Faddei rushed about, now in the settlement, then at the station, from authority to authority, without stopping to take a seat anywhere. Capitalizing on his back, which he couldn't straighten up, and leaning on his staff, he asked each authority to make allowance for his old age and to decide that the *gornitza* should be given back to him.

Someone handed down a decision in his favor. Faddei gathered together his surviving sons, sons-in-law, and nephews, borrowed horses from the kolkhoz, and hauled back the remains of the *gornitza* into his own yard along a winding road which passed through three villages. He completed the job during Saturday night and Sunday.

The burial took place on Sunday. The two coffins met and went down the center of the village, with the relatives quarreling over which coffin should go first. Afterward the old woman and her nephew were placed in a single, wheeled *rozvalni* [a sort of wide sledge]. Over the February snow crust, which had recently thawed, under a cloudy sky, they brought the deceased to the church graveyard, which was two villages away from us. The weather was windy, very unpleasant, and the priest with his two deacons waited in the church without going out to Talnov to meet them.

The people followed slowly to the edge of the village and sang in chorus. Afterwards they fell back.

The bustling of the old women had not quieted down even on Sunday evening. One old woman purred the psalter over the coffin. Matryona's sisters scurried around the Russian stove with the oven prongs. Out of the mouth of the stove blazed heat from the peat which had been fired up—peat which Matryona had brought in a sack from a distant bog. Using some wretched flour, they baked tasteless patties.

It was already getting on toward evening when they returned from the burial and gathered for the funeral banquet. They seized the tables, putting them in line in the place where the coffin had been that morning. First they all stood around the table and an old man, husband of the sister-in-law, read aloud the Lord's Prayer. Then they poured out for each of us just enough honey and hot water to cover the bottom of a small wooden bowl. Using spoons, we ate this slowly without anything to go with it. Afterward we ate a little something, drank vodka, and the conversation became livelier. Before eating the *kissel* [a jellylike oatmeal porridge] we all rose and sang "Eternal Memory." (They explained to me that it was obligatory to sing this song before eating the *kissel*.) There was more drinking, and the talk became even louder, but it was not about Matryona at all.

The husband of the sister-in-law boasted wildly, "Did you notice, orthodox believers, that the funeral service was conducted slowly today? That's because Father Mikhail noticed me. He knows that I know the service. Otherwise he would only have waved the incense censer, and, 'Saints defend us, homeward wend us,' that would have been the end of it!"

At last the supper ended. Again all rose and sang, "She is worthy!"

And again, with three repetitions, they sang, "Eternal Memory." But the voices wheezed, and were discordant. Their faces were drunk, and no one put much feeling into this "Eternal Memory."

Afterward, the special guests left and only the nearest relatives remained. They pulled out their cigarettes and smoked, laughing and joking.

There was some mention of Matryona's husband, who had disappeared without a trace. The sister's-in-law husband, beating his breast, assured me and the bootmaker, who was married to one of Matryona's sisters, "Yefim died, I tell you! Otherwise why couldn't he come back? Why even if I knew they would hang me when I returned to my native land, I'd come back all the same!"

The bootmaker nodded his head in agreement. He had been a deserter who had never left his native land at all. He had spent the entire war at his mother's house, hiding in the cellar.

High on the stove, getting ready to spend the night, sat that stern silent old woman, more ancient than all the ancients. She looked down from above in mute disapproval of the boisterous, unseemly conduct of the fifty- and sixty-year-old young people.

Only the unfortunate foster daughter, who had grown up within those walls, slipped behind the partition and wept.

Faddei did not attend Matryona's funeral supper because he held one of his own for his son. But during the next few days he aggressively entered the hut twice for talks with Matryona's sisters and the bootmaker-deserter.

A quarrel began over the *izba*—over whom it belonged to, to the sisters or the foster daughter. They almost took the case to the law court but came to a reconciliation, having decided that the court would give the *izba* to neither of them, but to the village Soviet. They made a deal. One of the sisters was allotted the goat, and the *izba* went to the bootmaker and his wife. In figuring Faddei's share, since, as he said, he "had raised every little log with his own hands," the *gornitza*, which had already been hauled away, went to him. They also let him have the shed where the goat lived, and the whole of the inner fence between the yard and the garden plot.

And once more, although a prey to infirmities and rheumatic pains, the grasping old man revived, and became young again for a while. Once more he gathered together his remaining sons and brothers-in-law. They dismantled the shed and the fence, and he himself hauled away the logs on little sleds, one after another, with only little Antoshka from the eighth grade to help him towards the end—only on this job he couldn't dawdle.

They boarded up Matryona's *izba* until spring, and I moved in with one of the sisters-in-law, not far away. On various occasions this sister-in-law recalled things about Matryona, and enlightened me on new facets of the dead woman's character.

"Yefim didn't really love her. He used to say, 'I like to dress up, like quality folks, but she dresses any old way, and always looks like a hick. Well,' he says, 'in that case she doesn't need anything,' and he began to squander their savings on drink. One time we drove to the city with him, looking for work. Yefim had acquired a mistress there, and he didn't feel like coming back to Matryona."

All her references to Matryona were disparaging—she was slovenly —she didn't care about material things—she was not thrifty—she didn't even keep a suckling pig. For some unknown reason, she didn't like to fatten them. Also she wasn't very smart because she helped other people without getting paid for it. (And indeed, there was cause for her to remember Matryona, because now she could no longer call on her to pull the plough in her garden plot.)

Even Matryona's warmth and simplicity, which her sister-in-law acknowledged, she spoke about with scornful pity.

And it was only thus—through these disparaging comments of her sister-in-law—that an image of Matryona emerged, one which I had never fully grasped while we were still living side by side.

And indeed! Every *izba* had its suckling pig—but Matryona's house had none. What can be simpler than to feed a greedy piglet which cares for nothing in the world except food? What could be simpler than to warm its swill three times a day, to live for it, and afterwards to cut its throat and have the fat back?

But Matryona never had it.

She never tried to acquire things for herself. She wouldn't struggle to buy things which would then mean more to her than life itself. All her life she never tried to dress smartly in the kind of clothes which embellish cripples and disguise evildoers.

She was misunderstood and abandoned by her husband, having buried six of his children. Her moral and ethical standards made her a misfit. She was considered "odd" by her sisters and her sisters-in-law—a laughingstock—because, as they said, she was so stupid as to work for others without pay. She never accumulated property against the time of her death when her only possessions were a dirty-white goat, a crippled cat, and rubber plants . . .

We all lived beside her, and never understood that she was that righteous one without whom, according to the proverb, no village can stand.

Nor any city.

Nor our whole land.

A Note on Translation

Reading literature in translation is a pleasure on which it is fruitless to frown. The purist may insist that we ought always read in the original languages, and we know ideally that he is right. But his counsel is a counsel of perfection, quite impractical even for him, since no man in one lifetime can master all the languages whose literatures he might wish to explore. Master languages as fast as we may, we shall always have to read to some extent in translation, and this means we must be alert to what we are about: if in reading a work of literature in translation we are not reading the "original," what precisely are we reading? This is a question of great complexity, to which justice cannot be done in a brief note. Nevertheless, the following sketch of some of the considerations that a mature answer would involve may be helpful to those who are coming into a self-conscious relation with literature in translation for the first time.

One of the memorable scenes of ancient literature is the meeting of Hector and Andromache in Book VI of Homer's *Iliad*. Hector, leader and mainstay of the armies defending Troy, is implored by his wife Andromache to withdraw within the city walls and carry on the defense from there, where his life will not be constantly at hazard. In Homer's text her opening words to him are these: δαιμόνιε, φθίσει σε τὸ σὸν μένος. How should they be translated into English?

Here is how they have actually been translated into English by capable translators, at various periods, in verse and prose.

1. George Chapman, 1598

O noblest in desire,
Thy mind, inflamed with others' good, will set thy self on fire.

2. John Dryden, 1693

Thy dauntless heart (which I foresee too late),
Too daring man, will urge thee to thy fate.

3. Alexander Pope, 1715

Too daring Prince! ...
For sure such courage length of life denies,
And thou must fall, thy virtue's sacrifice.

4. William Cowper, 1791

> Thy own great courage will cut short thy days,
> My noble Hector....

5. Lang, Leaf, and Myers, 1883 (prose)

> Dear my lord, this thy hardihood will undo thee....

6. A. T. Murray, 1924 (prose, Loeb Library)

> Ah, my husband, this prowess of thine will be thy doom....

7. E. V. Rieu, 1950 (prose)

> "Hector," she said, "you are possessed. This bravery of yours will be your end."

8. I. A. Richards, 1950 (prose)

> "Strange man," she said, "your courage will be your destruction."

9. Richmond Lattimore, 1951

> Dearest,
> Your own great strength will be your death....

From these strikingly different renderings of the same six words, certain facts about the nature of translation begin to emerge. We notice, for one thing, that Homer's word μένος is diversified by the translators into "mind," "dauntless heart," "such courage," "great courage," "hardihood," "prowess," "bravery," "courage," "great strength." The word has in fact all these possibilities. Used of things, it normally means "force"; of animals, "fierceness" or "brute strength" or (in the case of horses) "mettle"; of men, "passion" or "spirit" or even "purpose." Homer's application of it in the present case points our attention equally—whatever particular sense we may imagine Andromache to have uppermost—to Hector's force, strength, fierceness in battle, spirited heart and mind. But since English has no matching term of like inclusiveness, the passage as the translators give it to us reflects this lack and we find one attribute singled out to the exclusion of the rest.

Here then is the first and most crucial fact about any work of literature read in translation. It cannot escape the linguistic characteristics of the language into which it is turned: the grammatical, syntactical, lexical, and phonetic boundaries which constitute collectively the individuality or "genius" of that language. A Greek play or a Russian novel in English will be governed first of all by the resources of the English language, resources which are certain to be in every instance very different, as the efforts with μένος show, from those of the original.

Turning from μένος to δαιμόνιε in Homer's clause, we encounter a second crucial fact about translations. Nobody knows exactly what shade of meaning δαιμόνιε had for Homer. In later writers the word normally suggests divinity, something miraculous, wondrous; but in Homer it appears as a vocative of address for both chieftain and commoner, man and wife. The coloring one gives it must therefore be determined either by the way one thinks a Greek wife of Homer's era might actually address her husband (a subject on which we have no information whatever), or in the way one thinks it suitable for a hero's wife to address her husband in an epic poem, that is to say, a highly stylized and formal work. In general, the translators of our century will be seen to have eschewed formality in order to stress the intimacy, the wifeliness, and, especially in Lattimore's case, the tenderness of Andromache's appeal: (6) "Ah, my husband," (7) "Hector" (with perhaps a hint, in "you are possessed," of the alarmed distaste with which wives have so often viewed their husbands' bellicose moods), (8) "Strange man," (9) "Dearest." On the other hand, the older translators have obviously removed Andromache to a certain epic or heroic distance from her beloved, whence she sees and kindles to his selfless courage, acknowledging, even in the moment of pleading with him to be otherwise, his moral grandeur and the tragic destiny this too certainly implies: (1) "O noblest in desire, . . . inflamed by others' good"; (2) "Thy dauntless heart (which I foresee too late), / Too daring man"; (3) "Too daring Prince! . . . / And thou must fall, thy virtue's sacrifice"; (4) "My noble Hector." Even the less specific "Dear my lord" of Lang, Leaf, and Myers looks in the same direction because of its echo of the speech of countless Shakespearean men and women who have shared this powerful moral sense: "Dear my lord, make me acquainted with your cause of grief"; "Perseverance, dear my lord, keeps honor bright"; etc.

The fact about translation which emerges from all this is that just as the translated work reflects the individuality of the language it is turned into, so it reflects the individuality of the age in which it is done, and the age will permeate it everywhere like yeast in dough. We think of one kind of permeation when we think of the governing verse forms and attitudes toward verse at a given epoch. In Chapman's time, experiments seeking an "heroic" verse form for English were widespread, and accordingly he tries a "fourteener" couplet (two rhymed lines of seven stresses each) in his *Iliad* and a pentameter couplet in his *Odyssey*. When Dryden and Pope wrote, a closed pentameter couplet had become established as the heroic form *par excellence*. By Cowper's day, thanks largely to the prestige of *Paradise Lost*, the couplet had gone out of fashion for narrative poetry in favor of blank verse. Our age, inclining to prose and in verse to proselike informalities and relaxations, has predictably produced half a dozen excellent prose translations of the *Iliad*, but only one in verse, and that one in swirling loose hexameters which are much of the time closer to the verse of William Carlos Williams and some of the prose of novelists like Faulkner than to the swift firm tread of Homer's Greek. For if it is true that what we translate from a given work is what, wearing the spectacles of our time, we see in it, it is also true that we see in it what we have the power to translate.

Of course there are other effects of the translator's epoch on his translation besides those exercised by contemporary taste in verse and verse forms. Chapman writes in a great age of poetic metaphor and therefore almost instinctively translates his understanding of Homer's verb φθίσει ("to cause to wane, consume, waste, pine") into metaphorical terms of flame, presenting his Hector to us as a man of burning generosity who will be consumed by this very ardor. This is a conception rooted in large part in the psychology of the Elizabethans, who had the habit of speaking of the soul as "fire," of one of the four temperaments as "fiery," of even the more material bodily processes, like digestion, as if they were carried on by the heat of fire ("concoction," "decoction"). It is rooted too in that characteristic Renaissance élan so unforgettably expressed in characters like Tamburlaine and Dr. Faustus, the former of whom exclaims to the stars above:

> ... I, the chiefest lamp of all the earth,
> First rising in the East with mild aspect,
> But fixèd now in the meridian line,
> Will send up fire to your turning spheres,
> And cause the sun to borrow light of you....

Pope and Dryden, by contrast, write to audiences for whom strong metaphor has become suspect. They therefore reject the fire image (which we must recall is not present in the Greek) in favor of a form of speech more congenial to their age, the *sententia* or aphorism, and give it extra vitality by making it the scene of a miniature drama: in Dryden's case, the hero's dauntless heart "urges" him (in the double sense of physical as well as moral pressure) to his fate; in Pope's, the hero's courage, like a judge, "denies" continuance of life, with the consequence that he "falls"—and here Pope's second line suggests analogy to the sacrificial animal—the victim of his own essential nature, of what he is.

To pose even more graphically the pressures that a translator's period brings, consider the following lines from Hector's reply to Andromache's appeal that he withdraw, first in Chapman's Elizabethan version, then in Lattimore's twentieth-century one:

Chapman, 1598:

> The spirit I did first breathe
> Did never teach me that—much less since the contempt of death
> Was settled in me, and my mind knew what a Worthy was,
> Whose office is to lead in fight and give no danger pass
> Without improvement. In this fire must Hector's trial shine.
> Here must his country, father, friends be in him made divine.

Lattimore, 1951:

> ...the spirit would not let me, since I have learned to be valiant
> and to fight always among the foremost rank of the Trojans,
> winning for myself great glory, and for my father.

If one may exaggerate to make a necessary point, the world of Henry V and Othello suddenly gives way here to the world of Willie Loman; we are still reading the *Iliad*, but we have obviously come home.

Besides the two factors so far mentioned, language and period, as affecting the character of a translation, there is inevitably a third—the translator himself, with his particular degree of talent, his personal way of regarding the work to be translated, his own special hierarchy of values, moral, esthetic, metaphysical (which may or may not be summed up in a "world view"), his unique style or lack of it. But this influence all readers are likely to bear in mind, and it needs no laboring here. That, for example, two translators of Hamlet, one a Freudian, the other an Existentialist, will produce impressively different translations is obvious from the fact that when Freudian and Existentialist argue about the play in English they often seem to have different plays in mind.

We can now return to the question from which we started. After all allowances have been made for language, age, and individual translator, is anything of the original left? What, in short, does the reader of translations read? Let it be said at once that in utility prose —prose whose function is mainly referential—he reads everything that matters. "*Nicht Rauchen*," "*Défense de Fumer*," and "*No Smoking*," posted in a railway car, make their point, and the differences between them in sound and form have no significance for us in that context. Since the prose of a treatise and of most fiction is preponderantly referential, we rightly feel, when we have paid close attention to Cervantes or Montaigne or Machiavelli or Tolstoy in a good English translation, that we have had roughly the same experience as a native Spaniard, Frenchman, Italian, or Russian. But "roughly" is the correct word; for good prose points iconically *to* itself as well as referentially beyond itself, and everything that it points to in itself in the original (rhythms, sounds, idioms, word play, etc.) must alter radically in being translated. The best analogy is to imagine a Van Gogh painting reproduced in the medium of tempera, etching, or engraving: the "picture" remains, but the intricate interanimation of volumes with colorings with brushstrokes has disappeared.

When we move on to poetry, even in its longer narrative and dramatic forms—plays like *Oedipus*, poems like the *Iliad* or the *Divine Comedy*—our situation as English readers worsens appreciably, as the many unlike versions of Andromache's appeal to Hector make very clear. But, again, only appreciably. True, this is the point at which the fact that a translation is *always* an interpretation explodes irresistibly on our attention; but if it is a good translation, the result will be a sensitive interpretation and also a work with intrinsic interest in its own right—at very best, a true work of art, a new poem. It is only when the shorter, primarily lyrical forms of poetry are presented that the reader of translations faces insuperable disadvantage. In these forms, the referential aspect of language has a tendency to disappear into, or, more often, draw its real meaning and accreditation from, the iconic aspect. Let us look for just a moment at a brief poem by Federico García Lorca and its English translation (by Stephen Spender and J. L. Gili):

> ¡Alto pinar!
> Cuatro palomas por el aire van.
>
> Cuatro palomas
> vuelan y tornan.
> Llevan heridas
> sus cuatro sombras.
>
> ¡Bajo pinar!
> Cuatro palomas en la tierra están.

> Above the pine trees:
> Four pigeons go through the air.
>
> Four pigeons
> fly and turn round.
> They carry wounded
> their four shadows.
>
> Below the pine trees:
> Four pigeons lie on the earth.

In this translation the referential sense of the English words follows with remarkable exactness the referential sense of the Spanish words they replace. But the life of Lorca's poem does not lie in that sense. It lies in such matters as the abruptness, like an intake of breath at a sudden revelation, of the two exclamatory lines (1 and 5), which then exhale musically in images of flight and death; or as the echoings of *palomas* in *heridas* and *sombras*, bringing together (as in fact the hunter's gun has done) these unrelated nouns and the unrelated experiences they stand for in a sequence that seems, momentarily, to have all the logic of a tragic action, in which *doves* become *wounds* become *shadows*; or as the external and internal rhyming among the five verbs, as though all motion must (as in fact it must) end with *están*.

Since none of this can be brought over into another tongue (least of all Lorca's rhythms), the translator must decide between leaving his reader to wonder why Lorca is a poet to be bothered about at all, and making a new but true poem of his own, whose merit will almost certainly be in inverse ratio to its likeness to the original. Samuel Johnson made such a poem in translating Horace's famous *Diffugere nives*, and so did A. E. Housman. If we juxtapose the last two stanzas of each translation, and the corresponding Latin, we can see at a glance that each has the consistency and inner life of a genuine poem, and that neither of them (even if we consider only what is obvious to the eye, the line-lengths) is very close to Horace.

> *Cum semel occideris, et de te splendida Minos*
> *   fecerit arbitria,*
> *non, Torquate, genus, non te facundia, non te*
> *   restituet pietas.*
>
> *Infernis neque enim tenebris Diana pudicum*
> *   liberat Hippolytum*
> *nec Lethaea valet Theseus abrumpere caro*
> *   vincula Pirithoo.*

Johnson:

> Not you, Torquatus, boast of Rome,
> When Minos once has fixed your doom,
> Or eloquence, or splendid birth,
> Or virtue, shall restore to earth.
> Hippolytus, unjustly slain,
> Diana calls to life in vain;
> Nor can the might of Theseus rend
> The chains of hell that hold his friend.

Housman:

> When thou descendest once the shades among,
>   The stern assize and equal judgment o'er,
> Not thy long lineage nor thy golden tongue,
>   No, nor thy righteousness, shall friend thee more.
>
> Night holds Hippolytus the pure of stain,
>   Diana steads him nothing, he must stay;
> And Theseus leaves Pirithous in the chain
>   The love of comrades cannot take away.

The truth of the matter is that when the translator of short poems chooses to be literal, he loses most or all of the poetry; and when he chooses to make his own poetry, he loses most or all of the author. There is no way out of this dilemma, and in our own selection of short poems for this edition we have acknowledged the problem by excluding translations in favor of short poems written originally in English.[1]

We may assure ourselves, then, that the reading of literature in translation is not the disaster it has sometimes been represented. It is true that, however good the translation, we remain at a remove from the original, the remove becoming closest to impassable in the genre of the lyric poem. But with this exception, it is obvious that translation brings us closer by far to the work than we could be if we did not read it at all, or read it with a defective knowledge of the language. "To a thousand cavils," said Samuel Johnson, "one answer is sufficient; the purpose of a writer is to be read, and the criticism which would destroy the power of pleasing must be blown aside." Johnson was defending Pope's Homer for those marks of its own time and place that make it the great interpretation it is; but Johnson's exhilarating common sense applies equally to the problem we are considering here. Literature is to be read, and the criticism that would destroy the reader's power to make some form of contact with much of the world's great writing must indeed be blown aside.

MAYNARD MACK

1. So in the first two editions. In this edition we have been less exclusive for the reasons given in the Preface.

Index